Fundamentals of Organizational Behavior

Michael R. Carrell
Morehead State University

Daniel F. Jennings
Baylor University

Christina Heavrin, J.D.
Deputy Mayor
Louisville, Kentucky

Prentice Hall, Upper Saddle River, New Jersey 07458

Acquisitions Editor: David Shafer
Associate Editor: Lisamarie Brassini
Editorial Assistant: Brett Moreland
Editor-in-Chief: James Boyd
Marketing Manager: Sandra Steiner
Production Editor: Cynthia Regan
Production Coordinator: David Cotugno
Managing Editor: Carol Burgett
Manufacturing Supervisor: Arnold Vila
Senior Designer: Ann France
Design Director: Patricia Wosczyk
Interior Design: Delgado Design, Inc.
Cover Design: Patricia Wosczyk
Illustrator (Interior)/Project Management: Monotype Editorial Services
Composition: Monotype Composition Company
Cover Art: Robert Zimmerman

Copyright © 1997 by Prentice-Hall, Inc.
A Simon & Schuster Company
Upper Saddle River, New Jersey 07458

Carrell, Michael R.
    Fundamentals of organizational behavior / Michael R. Carrell,
  Daniel F. Jennings, Christina Heavrin.
        p.   cm.
    Includes bibliographical references and index.
    ISBN 0-02-319521-5
    1. Organizational behavior.   I. Jennings, Daniel F.   II. Heavrin,
  Christina.   III. Title.
  HD58.7.C349   1997
  158.7—dc20   96-30614
                                                                        CIP

Prentice-Hall International (UK) Limited, London
Prentice-Hall of Australia Pty. Limited, Sydney
Prentice-Hall Canada, Inc., Toronto
Prentice-Hall Hispanoamericana, S.A., Mexico
Prentice-Hall of India Private Limited, New Delhi
Prentice-Hall of Japan, Inc., Tokyo
Simon & Schuster Asia Pte. Ltd., Singapore
Editora Prentice-Hall do Brasil, Ltda., Rio de Janeiro

Printed in the United States of America

10   9   8   7   6   5   4   3   2   1

This work is dedicated to John Paul Nelson,
who took me under his wing when I needed it most—
as a struggling undergraduate student—
and has continued to serve as my mentor and friend.
—MC

To my family:
Kay, Courtney, Christopher, Jim, and Jackson (the Roo!)
—DJ

My work on this book is dedicated to my husband,
Congressman Mike Ward (D-Ky.), my sons Jasper
and Kevin, and my mother and father-in-law,
Lukey and Jasper Ward, for all their support and
encouragement; and to my sister, Marilyn Byrne, and
my brothers Russell, Bill, Chris, and Denis Heavrin,
for always being there when I need them.
—CH

BRIEF CONTENTS

CONTENTS

PREFACE

Today, organizations are changing and evolving at a faster pace than ever before in modern history. This rapid rate of change is caused by several factors: a new diversified work force of individuals within organizations; external challenges from the global and technological environments; new internal group processes of employees working in teams; and exciting new organizational structures and cultures which emphasize quality and innovation. What is amazing is that all of these influences are occurring at the same time, making it virtually impossible to use any of the old methods of managing organizations. Many of the traditional management theories and practices simply no longer work in today's organizations.

Managers who once found their organization's comparative advantage (whether it was in technology, location, size, computers, etc.) to be the key to success and longevity now realize that any such advantage is short-lived. Instead, the key to continued success today is the *people* within organizations and their ability to anticipate and analyze the problems and opportunities which result from rapidly changing conditions. Thus, the challenge to successfully manage people at work within rapidly changing organizations is met.

This book was written to provide substantial coverage of these fresh, proven approaches to managing people at work in the 1990s while also providing sufficient coverage of traditional organizational behavior concepts.

In addition, the new American Assembly of Collegiate Schools of Business (AACSB) standards were carefully considered in the design of the text and substantial coverage of several topics within the new standards is provided:

- *Demographic Diversity.* Chapter 9, The Diversified Work Force and Chapter 12, Culturally Diverse Groups, provide extensive coverage of this important new topic. In addition, diversity is a theme which is discussed where appropriate throughout the text.
- *Ethics.* Early in the text, Chapter 3, Ethical Behavior, a basis for understanding why ethical considerations must be an integral part of managers' decision making is explored.
- *Working in Teams.* The very structure of organizations and how they allocate work has fundamentally changed when employee teams are utilized. Chapter 11 discusses three types of employee teams: self-managed, project, and problem solving.
- *Global Environment.* The importance of recognizing the impact that the expanding international

marketplace has on organizations is discussed in Chapter 8, The Global Context of Organization, and is reinforced throughout the text.
- *Quality and Innovation.* A leadership philosophy which encourages innovation and develops processes for continuous improvement through employee empowerment and quality of life programs is emphasized in the following chapters: Chapter 14, Leadership; Chapter 17, Organizational Culture; and Chapter 19, Quality and Innovation within Organizations.

Chapter Features

Each chapter contains several features designed to enhance student learning.

1. *Opening Case.* The concepts of the chapter are illustrated by a "real world" case to provide a foundation for practical application of the chapter's material.
2. *Personal Profiles.* To expand upon the chapter opening case, successful people from a wide variety of organizations discuss key concepts and applications to help students understand and apply chapter material.
3. *"Real-Life" Examples.* Important theories, concepts, and terms are easier for the reader to understand by the extensive discussions of real-life applications by managers and organizations.
4. *OB in Practice.* Several brief articles about current organizational practices which relate chapter material to current events are presented in a "boxed" format in each chapter.
5. *Learning Objectives.* Concise behavioral learning objectives are provided at the opening of each chapter. They help students gain an overview of the chapter material and can be utilized as a checklist by the reader to determine if they sufficiently understand the concepts.
6. *Experiential Exercises.* The active learning of material can be achieved through the assignment of experiential exercises as homework or in-class activity. Two exercises per chapter reinforce the key theories and concepts and help students expand their knowledge to real-life situations.
7. *Case Studies.* Short case studies based on an actual organization help students apply chapter material to real-life situations.
8. *Review Questions.* Students can test their understanding of chapter material by answering these straightforward questions which focus on the major topics of the chapter.

9. *Discussion Questions.* These questions are designed to stimulate and enhance classroom discussion beyond the chapter material.

10. *Conclusions and Applications.* Brief summary statements are provided emphasizing the important points of the chapter and their relationship to managing people at work.

11. *Glossary.* To assist in learning, a glossary of all important terms is presented in the margin next to where each term appears in the text.

12. *Take It to the Net.* World Wide Web-based exercises that students can find at http://www.prenhall.com/carrell.

The following ancillaries are available for instructors:

- Instructor's Manual with Video Guide
- Test Item File
- Windows Custom Test
- PowerPoint Electronic Transparencies (100)
- ABC 1997 OB Video Library
- Color Overhead Transparencies (50)

Reviewers for Prentice Hall: Dennis Dossett, *University of Missouri;* Craig Tunwall, *Ithaca College;* Charles White, *Edison Community College;* and Tony Buono, *Bentley College.*

Acknowledgments

A significant portion of this book was either written or otherwise provided by a number of successful executives, owners, managers, and professionals from a variety of organizations. We are sincerely grateful to them for sharing the wisdom of their experience and expertise with our readers.

In alphabetical order they are:

John Akers, *Former President and Chief Executive Officer, IBM Corporation;* **Sheryl L. Barbich,** *Owner and Founder, Barbich Associates, Management Consulting;* **F. Lynn Blystone,** *President and Chief Executive Officer, Tri-Valley Corporation;* **David A. Bridgers, J.D.,** *General Counsel, Thornton Oil Company;* **Barbara Butterfield,** *Vice President for Faculty/Staff Services, Stanford University;* **W. Randolph Coe,** *Director, Everything's £1 Limited;* **Ronald Compton,** *Chairman of the Board, Aetna Life and Casualty Insurance Company;* **Carolyn Cooksie,** *Deputy Assistant Administrator, United States HUD;* **Ina Cooksie,** *Teacher, Jefferson County Public Schools;* **Janice Cooksie,** *Management Intern, Humana, Inc.;* **Kathy Cooksie,** *Personnel Manager, Louisville and Jefferson County, Metropolitan Sewer District;* **Donald L. Cox,** *Attorney, Partner, Lynch, Cox, Gilman & Mahan;* **Donald D. Davis,** *Senior Vice President, Employee Relations, CSX Transportation;* **Joseph Drew,** *Chief Executive Officer, Metropolitan Transportation Authority, Los Angeles, CA, Former County Administrative Officer, Kern County, CA;* **Glenn Edelen,** *President, Edelen, Edelen Realtors;* **Barbara Elliott,** *Former City Attorney, Bedford, Texas;* **Susan Falzon,** *Management Consultant, Falzon and Associates;* **Michael K. Fisher,** *President, Chavez, Fisher and Keathley, Certified Public Accountants, Inc.;* **John Alex Floyd, Jr.,** *Editor, Southern Living Magazine;* **Rhonda Fryman,** *Team Leader, Toyota Motor Manufacturing;* **Catherine D. Fyock,** *SPHR, President, Innovative Management Concept;* **Raymond Gilmartin,** *President and Chief Executive Officer, Becton Dickinson Corporation;* **Margaret Greene,** *President, South Central Bell Telephone Company;* **Melvin Greer,** *Chair of the Department of Philosophy, University of Louisville;* **Andrew Grove,** *President and Chief Executive Officer, Intel Corporation;* **Maury Hanigan,** *President, Hanigan Consulting Group;* **John Heavrin,** *Humana Corporation;* **Arnold Hiatt,** *Chairman, Stride Rite Corporation;* **James R. Houghton,** *Chairman and Chief Executive Officer, Corning, Incorporated;* **Ken Iverson,** *Chief Executive Officer, Nucor Steel Corporation;* **Dave Jensen,** *President, Search Master's International;* **Lee Kaukas,** *Former Coordinator for International Relations, International Affairs Division, Miyagi Prefectural Government, Miyagi, Japan;* **David Kearns,** *Former Chief Executive Officer, Xerox Corporation;* **Herb Kelleher,** *President and Chief Executive Officer, Southwest Airlines;* **Chris Kerbow,** *Manager, Schaumburg, Illinois, Marriott;* **Ralph Larsen,** *President and Chief Executive Officer, Johnson & Johnson Corporation;* **Edward E. Lawler, III,** *Director of the Center for Effective Organizations, University of Southern California;* **J. Ignacio Lopez de Arriortuna,** *Senior Executive, Volkswagen;* **Henri Mangeot,** *Executive Director, Louisville Labor-Management Committee;* **Everett Mann,** *Colonel, United States Army, Retired;* **Michael Milken,** *Financier, Former Executive, Drexel Burnham Lambert, Inc.;* **David A. Nadler,** *President, Delta Consulting Group;* **David A. Parker,** *President, Parker Consulting Group;* **Michael Paynter,** *Former President, Spacecards Corporation;* **Renee Rodriguez,** *Administrator of Creative Services, Sara Lee Corporation;* **Martin Rosenblum,** *Archivist, Harley-Davidson;* **Richard Rosett,** *Dean, College of Business, Director, Quality Cup Program, Rochester Institute of Technology;* **Willow Shire,** *Former Vice President, Digital Equipment;* **Jerry K. Stanners,** *President and Chief Executive Officer, Freymiller Trucking, Inc.;* **Jerre Stead,** *Executive-in-Residence, University of Iowa;* **W. Thomas Stephens,** *Chairman, President, and Chief Executive Officer, Manville Corporation;* **Jackie Strange,** *Former President, Professional Search Consultant, Inc., Vice President of Staffing/Director of Human Resources, Corporate Headquarters, Brown-Forman Corporation;* **Jennifer Synhorst,** *Team Leader, Milgard Windows;* **David L. Taylor & Ruth Karin Ramsey,** *Cummins Engine Company;* **John Wallace,** *Former Chief Executive Officer, Wallace Company;* **Mike Walsh** (Deceased), *Former President and Chief Executive Officer, Tenneco;* **Jack Welch,** *Chairman and Chief Executive Officer, General Electric Corporation;* **Kevin Winstead,** *Labor Attorney;* **Daisy Woods,** *Manager, Recruiting and Diversity Division, General Electric Appliances*

FUNDAMENTALS OF
ORGANIZATIONAL BEHAVIOR

CHAPTER 1

Introduction: What is OB?

CHAPTER OBJECTIVES

1. To understand the term *organizational behavior*.
2. To know why James Houghton, Chairman of Corning Glass, Inc., believes that today's manager must create a "new agenda" for organizations.
3. To define the Protestant Work Ethic, and its impact on traditional management theory and practice.
4. To describe the principles of the Scientific Management, Human Relations, Contingency Approach, and Human Resource approaches to managing organizations.
5. To understand how a mission statement and ethical practices can provide direction to an organization.
6. To define the four basic management functions.
7. To appreciate what a day in the life of a manager requires of a person.
8. To understand the impact of our newly diversified work force and employees working in teams.
9. To identify the concepts of organization design, organization development, and Total Quality Management.
10. To describe the terms generally utilized to present OB research information.

Corning, Incorporated

James R. Houghton is Chairman and CEO of Corning Incorporated and serves on the boards of Metropolitan Life Insurance Company and CBS, Inc. Houghton believes that for American organizations to return to the forefront of worldwide competition they must create a "new agenda." This agenda requires nothing less than the total reinvention of the organization and styles of management. Houghton further stresses, "We cannot continue to rely on a management system that was designed for an era that is past; it was effective in the industrial age but is not compatible with the demands of the information age." Houghton cites five factors critical to the new agenda of organizations if they are going to survive and prosper:[1]

Diverse labor pool. Our work force is increasingly diverse. Organizations that encourage minorities, women, and foreign nationals to contribute will have a distinct competitive advantage. Houghton also believes

"our diversity as a nation can work for us if we let it."

Empowered work force. Employees demand and can best succeed when given greater authority, ability to make their own decisions, and the opportunity to share their ideas and enthusiasm. Jobs today are more complex, and thus require a more skilled and educated work force. Empowered, employees armed with the necessary technology and information can meet the challenges of global competition but cannot work in the organizational frameworks of the past.

Information age management. Management must effectively use information to assist in the design, development, and delivery of new products and services. Access to information and teamwork in the automotive industry, for example, has cut the critical new development cycle in half while making huge jumps in quality.

- *Commitment to quality.* A basic tool organizations can utilize to achieve their "new agenda" is Total Quality Management (TQM) which goes far beyond quality control. TQM includes analyzing every aspect of the organization—changing how they work by cutting unnecessary levels of management, removing restrictive rules, and getting employees directly involved in doing what is best for the customer. TQM also requires teamwork.

- *Alliances of people.* The pace of technological change means no one person or department can do it all. Thus successful alliances are maintained with other people from different departments or functions whose combined knowledge and skills are needed and necessary. This, however, requires employees who can work independently and are delegated decision-making authority. It also requires the development of an organizational culture which provides common values, beliefs, and philosophies which then provide the overall direction for employees who are from different functions or departments.

James Houghton's call for a new agenda is being echoed by managers, CEOs, and scholars who recognize the historic changes that are taking place in how organizations work and in the work force. This change has been described in business books such as: Peters's and Waterman's *In Search of Excellence,*[2] Goldston's *The Turnaround Prescription,*[3] Kouzes's and Posner's *The Leadership Challenge,*[4] and Wellin's *Empowered Teams.*[5] The common theme to all of these works, as well as hundreds of others, is that the basic principles of how organizations should be designed, people managed, and workplace policies and procedures developed have rapidly changed. Organizational principles which for over 100 years were considered cornerstones for success since the American industrial revolution have suddenly, within a single generation of managers and employees, become obsolete. These changes, however, make today an extremely exciting time to study and practice the management of organizations.

Organizational Behavior (OB) Defined

Organizational behavior (OB) A field of study which investigates the managing of people at work within organizations.

Organizational behavior (OB) is the field of investigation into the managing of people at work within organizations.

As a field of study, it is helpful to break down OB into three levels: individuals, groups, and the organization. OB is somewhat unique within the curriculum of most business schools because for many students it is not an easily recognizable field such as accounting, finance, or marketing. That is because it is the study of the entire organization and not individual functions or disciplines. OB encompasses the study of all types of organizations including businesses, governmental units, not-for-profit organizations, hospitals, educational institutions, and professional firms. The concepts, practices, and theories of OB effectively apply to all of these types of organizations. As a field of study OB focuses on the impacts individuals, groups, and structures have on the ultimate success of the organization.

OB CONCEPTS AND PRACTICES: PAST AND PRESENT

Modern OB theories and their application in organizations have evolved over a period of approximately 100 years. Today more than ever, as James Houghton stated in the chapter opening, managers must apply new behavioral concepts and practices within organizations. However, we can better understand today's issues by realizing what was practiced in the past (see Figure 1-1), which may help us better understand how successful organizations can be managed.

FIGURE 1-1 Lessons Learned from Past OB Theories and Practices

Period	Theory	Beliefs	Limitations
Prior to 1880s	Traditional Management	Protestant Work Ethic Superiors perform all managerial duties All employees are equal in skill and ability and interchangeable	All employees do not follow the Protestant Work Ethic Employees can successfully perform some managerial duties Employees are not equal in skills and abilities
1880 to 1920	Scientific Management	"One best way" to perform each job Select employees to match the needs of the job and train them Employees are only motivated by economic gain Highly specialized jobs	Employees are not factors of production Motivation is a complex phenomenon; economic gain is only a part of a person's motivation Highly specialized jobs are boring, lead to employee problems
1920s to 1940s	Human Relations	Employees are affected by their social setting Managers must get to know employees and understand their feelings, allow them to participate	"Happy worker . . ." is an overly simplistic theory of OB Workers have individual needs and values Organizational goals, needs must be met
1950s and 1960s	Contingency Approach	There is no universal best method of managing Each situation must be analyzed and the appropriate technique selected An organization's environment is constantly changing	Provided no new managerial techniques Limited guidance in selecting successful managerial techniques
1970s and 1980s	Human Capital	Employees are valuable investments which provide long-term returns The economic and emotional needs of employees must be met Organizational and employee objectives can both be met	Did not recognize the diversifying of the work force Global issues were not addressed Jobs were only designed for individuals (not teams) Employees were given limited authority
1990s	"New Agenda"	The diversification of the labor force is changing OB practices Empowered employees and teams can be more efficient and allow right-sizing Pay-for-performance for individuals and/or teams is still important Commitment to quality throughout the organization is critical	Could become management "fads" if not truly accepted and implemented at all levels of management

Traditional Management

Early in the 1900s the American work force began to move from farms to small towns and growing cities. The strong beliefs and values of the agricultural workers were carried into their new jobs. Often referred to as the *Protestant Work Ethic* these beliefs included: (1) work itself is rewarding; (2) hard work will be recognized and rewarded by others and by God; (3) owners have been chosen by God for their efforts and wisdom and thus should be followed without question. Thus the separate roles of the owners and the workers within organizations was clear; the role of the owner/manager was to provide all direction and control; while the role of the worker was to follow those directions without questioning them. This provided a simple, universal principle of how to manage organizations: managers performed all managerial duties due to their position and superior intelligence. All workers who were generally equal in ability and motivation were given simple, routine jobs and thought of as interchangeable spokes in the wheels of the organization, because they were all equally productive and could be easily replaced with other equally productive employees.

Protestant Work Ethic
The strong beliefs and values of agricultural workers that carried into the general work force.

Scientific Management

The first major change in traditional management principles was known as *Scientific Management*—the systematic analysis of work, people, and how work can be accomplished most efficiently. Led by the research and successful applications of Frederick W. Taylor, Frank and Lillian Gilbreth, and Henry Gantt, this approach to managing organizations employed scientific data collection and analysis instead of the intuition of the owner/manager. Taylor, known as the "father of scientific management," and the others believed that managers should: (1) study how work can be most efficiently accomplished; (2) select workers according to their ability to perform a particular job; (3) and train workers to perform the job according to the "one best way." He also emphasized the study of each motion required for each task and the most efficient use of tools to make the worker more productive. Workers were viewed according to the *economic man* theory which held that people are primarily motivated by economic gain—thus workers would maximize their productivity only if they were offered financial incentives. Thus Taylor analyzed the time needed to perform tasks and then set performance standards for each job. When a worker exceeded the standard they would receive a financial incentive. This *piece-rate system* of compensation replaced systems of equal pay for everyone and replaced it with one in which one's pay varied according to his or her productivity. It can still be found in use today within some organizations.

Scientific Management
The systematic analysis of work, people, and how work can be accomplished most efficiently.

Economic man theory
People are motivated primarily by economic gain.

At first these principles of scientific management were doubted because they required managers to think and plan work rather than just tell workers to get the job done. Time spent by managers on selection, job design, and training was also generally viewed as wasted and could be better spent on other activities. However, several highly successful implementations, in particular one at Bethlehem Steel Corporation, received widespread praise in newspapers and in a series of Congressional hearings in 1914. Then the principles of scientific management spread quickly and were generally viewed as accepted principles.

The treatment of workers, as a factor of production similar to raw materials, land, and machinery eventually, however, led to problems with scientific management applications. Taylor himself once declared that "one of the very first requirements for a man who is fit to handle pig iron as a regular occupation is that he shall be so stupid and so phlegmatic that he more nearly resembles in his mental makeup the ox."[6] This attitude toward workers' mental ability led scientific managers to design jobs to be highly specialized and routine, involving no mental effort on their part. All decisions and situations requiring judgment were referred to managers. In fairness to Taylor, however, it should be pointed out that workers of his day had little or no formal education or training, thus may not have been able to contribute the high level of mental effort commonly provided by today's employees.

Human Relations

During the 1920s and 1930s managers began to question some of the principles of scientific management and began applying what today is termed a *human relations* approach. This approach to managing employees in organizations focused on workers as human beings who are affected by their social setting. The so-called "Hawthorne" studies by Mayo and Roethlisberger conducted at the Western Electric Company's Hawthorne plant were the basis of the human relations movement. These studies generally produced evidence that complex human factors—feelings, emotions, group relationships, leadership styles, and the attitude of management—could have a significant impact on the productivity of employees. The human relations movement generally emphasized: (1) managers should get to know their employees and pay attention to their individual needs; (2) they should allow participation by employees in those decisions which affect their work; and overall, (3) satisfied (or happy) workers are productive workers and thus managers should strive to keep employees happy.[7] The central difference between the human relations philosophy and that of scientific management was the recognition of the employee as an individual with human feelings and needs, rather than a factor of production. Thus employee productivity was not only affected by the design of the job and economic incentives as espoused by Taylor, but also by certain social and psychological factors.

Human relations Approach to managing employees focused on workers as human beings affected by their social setting.

The human relations approach received enthusiastic support from behavioral scientists, but over time began to receive the following criticisms:

- The "happy worker is a productive worker" is an oversimplified concept of organizational behavior. Several other factors also affect the productivity of individuals and groups within organizations and require equal or greater consideration.
- Workers are complex with different needs and values. What motivates one person may or may not motivate others, thus managers cannot assume a friendly style will keep everyone "happy and productive."
- The approach failed to recognize the need for production and quality standards and the need to achieve organizational goals as well as employee goals. The failure to relate organizational objectives to employee objectives was a major failure of the human relations approach.

Contingency Approach

The contingency approach to managing was largely developed in the post–World War II era. This approach emphasized the need for managers and decision makers to realize that previous OB theories had each advocated one universal theory to managing organizations. The contingency approach emphasized there is no one best way of managing all people in all situations. Instead, managers should carefully analyze the facts of a given situation and choose the method or tool (from their bag of tricks) which might best accomplish the objective. The keys to the success of this process were believed to be: (1) the manager is able to correctly analyze the situation; (2) the manager is well versed in various managerial techniques and thus can choose the best alternative; and (3) the technique selected can be successfully implemented considering other internal and external constraints. While the contingency approach itself did not add a new OB tool or technique, it did permanently lay to rest the idea that one universal approach to managing organizations should be applied in all situations.

Human Capital

Behavioral science research and management practices in the 1970s developed the human capital approach to managing organizations. This approach viewed employees as resources rather than factors of production or human beings who only respond on the basis of feelings and emotions. The human resource approach viewed employees as investments which, if effectively developed and utilized, will provide long-term benefits to the organization. The knowledge, abilities, and skills which employees developed over several years were viewed as valuable assets of the organization that should be valued and protected. In addition, this approach posited that management must provide an environment in which both the goals of the organization and the goals of the employees can be successfully met. The primary lessons from scientific management as well as the human relations approach were accepted. Thus effective behavioral programs and practices should be designed to also meet the economic and emotional needs of employees.

The OB "New Agenda"

Today nothing less than a revolution in the management of organizations is underway. In the chapter opening Corning's James Houghton defined the revolution as the "new agenda" for CEOs, managers, and scholars. To learn how some U.S. corporations have adjusted read "OB in Practice: The New Corporate America," from *Dinosaurs to Teams*. This revolution in behavioral practices has been caused by many factors including:

- A long-term decline in the quality of American goods and a stagnation of productivity.
- Technological change occurring at a pace unimagined only a few years ago. Just keeping up with this change has caused major problems and at the same time major opportunities for American organizations.
- The diversification of the labor force. The dramatic increase in the number of women, minorities, foreign nationals, and elderly workers has altered the needs, desires, and motivation of the American labor force.
- The globalization of the world's economy has brought increased competition to every sector of American business. The inability of American businesses to successfully compete internationally has caused the United States to suffer huge balance of trade deficits and thus a gradual decline of the American standard of living.

All of these factors are affecting organizations at the same time, thus increasing the pressure on management to develop methods of increasing productiv-

OB in Practice

The New Corporate America: From Dinosaurs to Teams

The giant bureaucratic organizations that materialized in the post–World War II era began to lose their markets and profits during the 1970s and 1980s. Today, they are changing from slow-moving organizational "dinosaurs" to fast-paced collections of small units composed of empowered employees or self-directing employee teams. U.S. corporations which have pioneered this change include Pepsico, General Electric, Saturn, Southern California Gas, Goodyear Tire & Rubber, Johnson & Johnson, Hallmark Cards, Colgate-Palmolive, and Texas Instruments. At the center of the changes made by these as well as others are OB concepts largely unknown only a few years ago:

- *Right-sizing and employee teams.* The transfer of authority from centralized offices to independent groups of employees or self-directed teams. This often includes the "right-sizing" of the corporate structure which requires eliminating layers of middle management which previously checked the work of others.
- *Boss: from bully to coach.* In this new information-based world, managers recognize that workers closest to the process understand it best. So today's boss does not look over the shoulders of people but listens to them and facilitates changes needed by employees.
- *Focus on customers.* Insular, inward-looking companies did fine in the post–World War II era when customers had few choices. But today they are doomed to fail. The success of discount chain Wal-Mart Stores, that concentrates obsessively on pleasing customers, is a textbook example of focusing on customers, while Sears and K-Mart had to rush to catch up.
- *Large organizations are nonresponsive and must be broken into manageable parts.* While the optimum size depends on the company, William G. Ouchi, a professor at UCLA's John E. Anderson Graduate School of Management, contends: "Companies should never grow beyond the limits of knowledge of a normal human being. We are seeing large-scale disaggregation of big companies into their constituent pieces."
- *Company walls must be removed to form the "boundaryless" corporation.* A revolutionary concept, this was the brainchild of GE Chairman John F. Welch. In this vision, workers spring from one project to another without regard to permanent structure. At GE, that means sonar experts from the aerospace division can jump in to advance ultrasound technology in the medical-systems business without bureaucratic restraint.

What are the effects of these historic changes on corporate bottom lines? At Frito-Lay, which has developed into a model of corporate change, after two years with teams organization safety improved 60 percent, turnover dropped from 30 percent to 5 percent, and the cost per pound, employee grievances, and customer complaints all improved substantially. Steve Smith, manufacturing manager at Frito-Lay noted: "At first, workers viewed us suspiciously when we said we were going to turn management over to them (hundreds of managers were laid off)." But today, Margie Valentino, a packaging machine operator at Frito-Lay says: "I think that people have more pride in their work now. At the end of the day we go to the computer and see how much we made or lost. If the numbers are good, we feel proud because we know we did it. If they aren't so good we get together with our team members and figure out what's wrong. Before we weren't very interested in the business, we seldom even saw the numbers."

Source: Linda Grant, "Breaking the Mold: Companies Struggle to Reinvent Themselves," *Los Angeles Times,* May 3, 1992, D1, 7.

ity and quality. They are faced with rapid technological change in how to accomplish work and must meet increased foreign competition with successfully mastered change. At the same time managers are trying to develop and train older workers and meet the demands of the new diversified work force.

What are some approaches to managing people that can successfully enable organizations to meet today's challenges? Several will be provided in the following chapters of this book. However, let us briefly preview a few successful approaches to managing organizations in our fast-changing world:

- *Right-sizing* the design of organizations, that largely means eliminating layers of middle management. As one General Motors executive noted that GM eliminated thousands of people who checked the work of others and thousands of jobs of "people who checked the checkers."[8] This reduction of management positions requires the decentralization of authority and responsibility to the employees who actually do the work and must assume new managerial duties.

- *Empowering employees* to make decisions within broad guidelines, take risks without fear of reprisal, and work without supervision. Empowered teams of employees performing several tasks are increasingly replacing old organizational structures which emphasized highly specialized, routine jobs performed by individuals.

- *Pay-for-performance.* Frederick Taylor was partially right—monetary incentives are important. However, since his piecework method simply is not appropriate for most of today's complex jobs, other plans including profit sharing and team-based incentives are more likely to be successful at developing the critical link between employees' performance, the success of the organization, and the rewards received by the employees.

- *Commitment to quality.* For many years American businesses focused on higher quantity goals and assumed quality would follow. W. Edwards Deming, the recognized father of the quality movement in Japan and the United States, has explained this lack of attention to quality by the "traditional American way" of building products and then inspecting for quality. What worked, Deming believed, was building in quality rather than inspecting for it. Deming also posited that a critical goal for American organizations was to make customers the most important people in our businesses if we are to achieve quality service.[9]

- *Diversified work force.* As James Houghton emphasized, organizations will find the labor force is increasingly more female, minority, and foreign-born. Those organizations that successfully attract and develop members of this diversified labor force will have a competitive edge over those which do not.

ORGANIZATIONS

Our study of organizational behavior includes organizations of all sizes and purposes—corporations, governmental units, schools, small businesses, hospitals, etc. A common element across all organizations is that they are formed for a similar purpose—to produce goods or services. They also all consist of certain assets: land, building and equipment, capital, materials, and people. It is the behavior of the people within organizations that forms the central focus of inquiry of the field of organizational behavior.

Mission

Organizations are usually formed and maintained to enable a number of people to work together in an effort to achieve certain purposes. In many organizations these purposes are formally expressed in a *mission* statement. The mission statement not only states the product or service goals and objectives of the organization but also the strategies, values, and commitments which provide direction and guidance to its employees, stockholders, and customers. For example, the mission statement of TRINOVA Corporation, an Ohio-based manufacturer of automotive, industrial, and aerospace motors, pumps, controls, and related devices, appears in Figure 1-2. The statement begins by describing the product line of the company. The statement then provides stockholders TRINOVA's commitment to 16 percent returns on equity, and the long-term growth objective of $10 billion. The statement also emphasizes the core values of the organization including ethical conduct, investment in technology and innovation, quality and customer orientation, and the utilization of employee teams.

Mission statement
States the products, services, and objectives of the organization as well as the strategies, values, and commitments which provide direction and guidance to its employees, stockholders, and customers.

Management Functions

Exactly how the people who work within an organization achieve the goals and objectives or mission of the organization is largely determined by management. Management refers to the persons whom the owners have chosen to run the organization—make decisions, allocate resources, and direct the activities of employees in a coordinated effort to achieve the specified goals.

One of the first individuals to study the function of managers was Henri Fayol. In 1916 Fayol, a French industrial engineer, described what he believed were the five primary managerial functions: planning, organizing, directing,

---

Our Mission

TRINOVA is a world leader in the manufacture and distribution of engineered components and systems for industry. Our mission is to create economic value for our shareholders through superior growth and profitability.

To accomplish our mission, we will develop strategies that create sustainable competitive advantage; and we will build an organization fully capable of implementing these strategies.

Our success will not be a matter of chance, but of commitment to the core values that distinguish us.

Customer Orientation. We listen to our customers and respond to their needs.

Quality. We provide quality in everything we do.

Technology. We invest in technology to enhance our productivity and effectiveness.

Innovation. We take personal initiative for constructive change.

Integrity. We conduct ourselves ethically, respect the dignity of the individual and are responsible community citizens.

Teamwork. We work as a team across functions, businesses, and cultures.

We are the force for fulfilling TRINOVA's mission and achieving its goals. By personalizing these core values and by working hard, we will win and we will all share in our success.

Source: TRINOVA 1994 Annual Report.

FIGURE 1-2
The TRINOVA Corporation Mission Statement

FIGURE 1-3

The Four Management
Functions

Planning	• Setting goals and objectives • Developing implementation strategies • Deciding timetables of future events
Organizing	• Deciding how tasks and jobs are accomplished • Grouping work and people into efficient units • Determining the structure of the organization
Leading	• Directing and motivating employees • Making decisions, resolving conflicts, providing ethical values • Communicating information to the appropriate parties
Controlling	• Comparing actual performance to planned standards • Providing budgetary oversight • Taking corrective actions when warranted

staffing, and controlling.[10] These "classical functions of management" today still identify the primary activities of most managers' jobs except that five have been combined into four functions (see Figure 1-3).

A manager's job begins with the *planning* process. It has been said that among the four functions planning is the most important one, and the one which distinguishes a manager from a supervisor. Yet many managers facing daily problems and deadlines simply do not take the time to properly plan, and thus may unfortunately find validity to the old saying:

> If you fail to plan,
> then you plan to fail. . . .

Planning process Set objectives for the task or project under consideration; develop a strategy; and set a timetable for its achievement.

In a very broad sense, planning often requires three basic steps. The first step in the planning process is setting objectives for the task or project under consideration. The second step is the development of a strategy to achieve the objectives including specific tasks and assignments for each individual or group involved in the plan. A third common step is to set a timetable for the achievement of intermediate steps, thus assuring that the overall strategy is proceeding in a timely manner. From planning a Christmas party to a new office building these three basic steps have been successfully utilized for decades.

The successful implementation of a plan also requires the organizing of the people, materials, equipment and facilities, and data information required. The first step in this process is exactly how each task or job should be accomplished. This includes "who" should perform the task; "how" it should be achieved and exactly "what" is to be accomplished. Then the individual jobs or tasks are grouped in a logical fashion to provide efficiency and a management hierarchy or who reports to whom in a chain of command. Finally, the communication of the relevant information in the form of training, supervisory, and written policies and procedures must be provided.

Leading A function that sets the plans and organization of work into motion through direction and motivation to achieve high levels of productivity.

Setting the plans and organization of work into motion requires the function of *leading*. Directing the work of others and motivating them to achieve high levels of productivity is a critical function for all managers. Often referred to as the "people skill," this is the function which many managers find demands most of their time in formal and informal meetings and in planned and unplanned one-on-one discussions. Effective leadership requires a manager to understand individual and group behaviors in order that effective motivational methods be developed. This function also requires objective decision making on a daily basis, on small and large issues alike, for a manager to maintain credibility. Negotiation and conflict resolution are also critical leadership skills. Honest disagreements among well-intentioned employees, as well as petty personal disputes, occur on a daily basis in most organizations and require managers who will face them and fairly and quickly find a resolution. In addition, the ethical values of an organization are set by its leaders—by policy and by example.

The *controlling* function primarily is one of quality assurance and requires comparing the actual performance of individuals, groups, and units against planned levels of performance. Where negative deviations occur corrective actions must be taken, such as developing new work methods, changing materials, or providing additional training or discipline to the employees involved. However, as mentioned earlier, today quality control often focuses less on inspection and more on design as taught by TQM advocates. Making sure that costs remain within budgeted levels is another aspect of the control function. More than a few managers have been chastised or even fired for "going over their budget." Overall the control function is to make sure processes go as planned by designing for quality, monitoring critical elements—time, quality, cost, output—comparing to expectations; recognizing significant deviations, and taking the necessary corrective actions.

Controlling function
Quality assurance that compares the performance of individuals, groups, and units against planned levels of performance.

A Day in the Life of a Manager

While certainly all four of the managerial functions just discussed are important, how much time do most managers actually spend on each in an average day? And what management "skills" are needed to accomplish these functions? To provide answers to these questions carefully read "A Day in the Life of a Manager" (Figure 1-4) and keep a tabulation of how many activities are primarily planning, organizing, leading, or controlling. Some, of course, may involve more than one activity. Also, note what skill the manager employs to achieve each task. Our tabulation indicates that of the 20 activities which comprised Ms. Shipley's day, three involved (primarily) planning, two organizing, twelve leading, and three controlling. The skills required most heavily were oral and written communication skills, people skills (interviewing, counseling, personal interactions), and quantitative skills (budget), and technical skills. Your tabulation may be somewhat different, if so, it is not important. It is important that you generally realize how the four managerial functions are practiced on a daily basis, and what basic skills are utilized to achieve these functions. To help you become even more familiar with how these functions are central to most managers' jobs, ask someone you know who is a manager to briefly note their activities for one day in a format similar to Figure 1-4. Then analyze the activities in a manner similar to how we analyzed Ms. Shipley's day. Finally, suggest to your instructor that your classmates do the same and share and compare your findings. This brief exercise will give you a good starting point to understand not only the primary managerial functions, but also many of the organizational behavior topics that you are about to explore in this book.

OB TOPICS

In this book we will explore organizational behavior issues which are the keys to both individuals and organizations achieving their goals and objectives. We will explore what affects the behavior of individuals, groups of people, and organizations. In this section these topics are briefly presented and the chapters in which they are thoroughly discussed referenced.

FIGURE 1-4

A Day in the Life
of a Manager

Donna Shipley is a department head for a national actuarial firm. The following is a brief summary of a normal day at work. While no two managerial jobs are exactly the same, and no two days on any one job are exactly the same, in many aspects this day is typical of that of many managers and, one can better understand the behaviors typical of a managerial position by following Ms. Shipley's day.

Tuesday, March 30, 1994

Time	Event Number	Activity
7:20 AM	1.	Breakfast meeting with Chamber of Commerce committee. Committee is planning the development of an economic development task force.
8:50 AM	2.	Unscheduled meeting with one of Ms. Shipley's employees who asks her to review a budget for a proposed new account.
9:10 AM	3.	Ms. Shipley reviews her calendar for the day and her "to do" list noting the April 1st deadline for an annual report.
9:15 AM	4.	Telephone call from regional office manager (Ms. Shipley's immediate supervisor) regarding a question about an account estimate. Writes a brief response letter.
9:30 AM	5.	Scheduled interview with an applicant for a position that reports directly to Ms. Shipley. Writes a memo noting her impressions/observations.
10:15 AM	6.	Returns three telephone calls received during the interview. One call is from an associate asking for career advice, one is from a client, one is from another manager within the firm. Answers electronic mail.
10:30 AM	7.	Chairs task force meeting of managers from various functions within the firm. The task force is charged by the regional manager to investigate a possible TQM program in the firm.
11:55 AM	8.	Telephone call from client regarding recently completed actuarial report.
12:30 PM	9.	Lunch in the cafeteria with two other department managers. The NCAA basketball tournament and possible firm layoffs are topics for discussion.
1:07 PM	10.	Telephone call from client regarding insurance question.
1:22 PM	11.	Unscheduled meeting with employee regarding budget problem within the employees' section.
1:30 PM	12.	Scheduled interview with another applicant for an open position which reports directly to Ms. Shipley. Writes a memo noting her impressions/objections.
2:20 PM	13.	Returns two client telephone calls received during the interview.
2:45 PM	14.	Unscheduled meeting with employee to discuss a personnel problem within the employee's office. Writes a memo of inquiry to the human resources department.
3:10 PM	15.	Scheduled meeting with client to review questions regarding actuarial report. Dictates a summary of the meeting for the client's file.
3:56 PM	16.	Initiates six telephone reference checks on applicants interviewed during the morning. Three people could not be reached. Writes brief notes on those discussed with references.
4:37 PM	17.	Unscheduled meeting with employee to discuss budget proposal for a new account.
4:58 PM	18.	Unscheduled meeting with secretary to sign papers, letters, review other work in progress.

Time	Event Number	Activity
5:15 PM	19.	Receives telephone call from reference for applicant interviewed in the morning. Writes brief note on the discussion.
5:40 PM	20.	Gathers materials needed (to take home) to start writing annual report due April 1st. Answers electronic mail and departs for home.
6:20 PM	21.	Arrives home.

FIGURE 1-4
Continued

Analyzing "a day in the life" of a manager can help one recognize how basic managerial functions are practiced and the skills required of a manager.

OB Study and Research

The objective study and research of human behavior in organizations is an underlying theme of this book and of critical importance to managers and OB scholars all over the globe. Before studying specific OB topics relating to the behavior of individuals, groups, and organizations, we introduce research terms and concepts which will be utilized throughout the text. *Understanding behavior in organizations* (Chapter 2) will help readers decide how much confidence to put in a particular research conclusion or news report. Also, an understanding of how OB research is conducted will enable readers to make their own informed conclusions about data and behavioral information which they encounter in organizations.

The field of OB is somewhat unique among the fields of business inquiry because it is an applied behavioral science and thus draws upon other areas of study. These other fields include economics, anthropology, psychology, sociology, political science, and social psychology (see Figure 1-5). The purpose of OB study and research is to identify, develop, and apply methods and concepts which can be successfully applied to organizations by managers, owners, and employees. This goal requires us to think critically and question methods which might be called "quick fixes," "intuition," "gut reactions," or simply "best guesses" with careful study and scientific investigation.

FIGURE 1-5
Fields of Study
Contributing to OB
Research

Field	Focus	Contributions to OB
Psychology	The study of individual human behavior	Learning theory Motivation research Industrial psychology Personality theory Training effectiveness Job design Recruitment and selection techniques Performance appraisal
Economics	The allocation of scarce resources to alternative uses	Compensation programs (pay) Incentive programs Employee perception of equity, fairness Labor relations
Sociology	The study of the interaction of individuals within groups and organizations	Group behavior Organization theory Organization culture Organization change Work force diversity Group decision making
Social Psychology	The study of the influences individuals have on each other and their environment	Organization change Communications Conflict resolution Leadership Problem solving
Anthropology	The study of the historical development of human culture	Organization culture Societal influences on organization Demographics of the labor force Global cultural differences
Political Science	The study of government and public affairs	Government influences Laws and regulations Power and conflict Conflict resolution Unions/labor relations

Human behavior, of course, is a complex phenomenon. Exactly what causes a person, group, or organization to respond in a certain way cannot easily be determined. And whether or not the same response will occur given the same stimulus is also not always known. In the natural sciences where a laboratory research experiment can be exactly duplicated, and the same independent variable causes the same reaction in a dependent variable, in behavioral research circumstances cannot be easily duplicated and organizations are our laboratories. Thus a method which is highly successful for one manager or organization may not produce the identical result in another organization. However, in similar situations, people and organizations may respond in a consistent (but not identical) fashion to the same circumstances.

For example, given proper orientation and training most employees will wear their safety goggles when performing tasks which could harm their eyes. Yet every manager knows there will always be a small percentage who will forget, not realize the situation demands goggles, or simply refuse to comply with the work rules. What type of incentive or disciplinary program will result in 100 percent employee compliance? In a given situation perhaps any one of several might work, in another only a strictly administered system of warnings and eventual termination will bring 100 percent compliance. To some extent this is the type of organizational behavior problem which makes this field of study so interesting—it is the *human element* that makes behavioral science so challenging!

The scientific method of study is concerned with the process of moving from observations and experiences drawn from actual behavior to valid descriptions or conclusions. The results from OB research can be presented in various formats which will be cited in the chapters of this book. The following is a brief description of the terms generally utilized to present research results:

- *Case study*. The results associated with research conducted within a single organization, group, or unit of a large organization. Since the findings are from a sample of one, generalizations of the findings to other organizations cannot be made without further research.
- *Survey research*. The results of written questionnaires completed by a sample of the population of individuals, groups, or organizations being studied. Data may be collected through mail responses or in person. Generalizations of the findings to the whole population or other organizations depend upon the validity of the research methodology.
- *Laboratory research*. The results of research conducted in a controlled environment to limit the influence of outside variables. OB laboratory research often involves college students as subjects—thus limiting the ability to generalize results to employees within actual organizations. Employees are less utilized as subjects because their organizations will not allow the manipulation of the variables to create the controlled environment.
- *Field research*. The results of research conducted in an organizational setting. The subjects involved in field research are individuals or groups operating in their "natural" environment. Thus the results are more easily generalized to other similar organizations in similar situations. Field research is generally preferred to other types, but limited access to field research causes OB researchers to utilize other methods.

Ethics in the Workplace

Individuals enter the workplace with various backgrounds, experiences, values, and ethical standards. The setting and maintaining of *ethical behaviors* (Chapter 3) has received increased interest in recent years. Organizations, regardless of size or function, cannot afford to alienate customers, sacrifice employees, or risk shareholder assets by unethical practices. Individuals form their value systems as a result of interaction with their family, friends, and society. They use their value systems to make ethical choices in the workplace. Ethical decision making, however, requires people to consider their responsibility to other employees, customers, shareholders, and to the public. The moral intensity of an issue (whether good or bad), the urgency of the situation, the probability of effects, and the degree of available alternatives will affect the decision-making process. Most often decisions involving ethical considerations are not black or white but gray and thus may be difficult for the decision maker. A person's ethical standards over time, however, will be judged by others. Some practical guidelines for ethical decision making are provided by attorney David Bridgers in the Profile: *Ethics in Business*. Organizations can institutionalize ethical behavior by establishing a code of ethics, communicating it, and selecting and training employees with that code in mind. The ethical standards adopted by those individuals at the top, however, often becomes the one followed by most employees.

Human element The varied response of individuals to a situation.

Case study The results associated with in-depth research conducted with a sample of a single organization.

Survey research The results of written questionnaires completed by a sample of the population of individuals, groups, or organizations being studied.

Laboratory research The results of research conducted in a controlled environment to limit the influence of outside variables.

Field research The results of research conducted with multiple subjects in an organizational setting.

Ethical behaviors The value systems of individuals to make ethical choices in the workplace requiring responsibility to other employees, customers, shareholders, and to the public.

Profile

David A. Bridgers, J.D.
General Counsel
Thornton Oil Corporation
ETHICS IN BUSINESS

After twenty years of working in business and legal environments I have come to realize that one of the most important keys to long term satisfaction and success in the workplace is conducting your business in an ethical manner. While most people agree that we should all conduct our affairs in an ethical manner, it is quite difficult to know what the correct ethical decision is when confronted with a particular set of circumstances.

Ethical principles are not situational, however, facts are situational which is what makes it difficult at times to know what the correct ethical decision is in particular circumstances. When I state that ethical principles are not situational, I mean that truth is truth, justice is always justice, and fair dealing is always fair dealing. It is these principles when applied to particular circumstances which leads to correct ethical decisions.

If a person does not accept the premise that truth, justice, and fair dealing are important, it is unlikely that they will be equipped to make proper ethical decisions when confronted with difficult ethical questions.

What is ethical should not necessarily be judged by outcomes. The decision-making process, even when the decisions being made are ethical in nature, often leads to unexpected outcomes. What is ethical must be judged at each step in the decision-making process. It is a breach of an ethical decision-making process to compromise at any step in the decision-making process by determining that an unethical decision can be justified by an expected "good" outcome. In most cases the expected "good" outcome does not occur and in all cases such unethical decisions are weak rationalizations at best and plain dishonest at worst. Always remember, "We reap what we sow."

Obviously, there are "gray areas"; complex situations make for a difficult decision-making process. Nonetheless, what is perceived under all known circumstances to be a truthful, just and fair decision, should be the basis for each decision. Ethical decisions should be judged by the intent with which the decision was made, not by the outcome of the decision.

All of the above is more easily said than done. A few tips may be helpful:

1. Make a conscious decision to conduct yourself in an ethical manner. This may seem obvious, however, if we don't set conscious guidelines for our conduct, unexpected or unethical conduct can creep up on us.

2. Follow your instincts as to what is right and what is wrong. Truth is not complex, only facts are complex. If you are committed to making ethical decisions, the proper decision will usually be apparent. (Remember, the right ethical decision will not always lead to the preferred outcome.)

3. If you make an unethical decision, forgive yourself. You are human. Use your moral lapse as an opportunity to determine what the pressures were which led you to make the unethical decision. Most important, try not to make the same mistake again.

4. Be honest with yourself. The majority of decisions involving ethical issues will only be known to you. You should take satisfaction in having a clear conscience.

5. Realize that truth is the best defense. One need not engage in unethical conduct to protect themselves. No one can take away your reputation for being a person of integrity.

Understanding the Individual

The study of how organizations operate logically begins with the people within organizations. After all, organizations as entities do not "behave" or "perform"; it is the individuals within them who give them life and are responsible for their performance.

The general external appearance and biological systems of all individuals are much the same. However, we are well aware that internal differences including *values, attitudes, personality,* and *perceptions* (Chapter 4) make each person unique. These individual differences cause people to choose a variety of behaviors or decisions even when faced with the same situations. Thus managers and coworkers are faced with the challenge of achieving organizational objectives through the efforts of diverse individuals. Experience and research indicate that much of the interpersonal conflict that occurs among individuals, including managers and employees, stems from people acting on their own interpretation of a given situation that differs from those of others. Such conflict may be minimized by individuals striving to learn and understand the views of others involved, while still focusing on the mission and objectives. Organizations such as Eastman Kodak have found that one substantial advantage of utilizing employee teams is that members learn to routinely listen and consider the inputs of all employees involved, and thus tend to have fewer conflicts and make better decisions.

Decision making is a fundamental process in organization. People make decisions based on the information they receive from individuals within the organization and from external sources. Decision making is a key organizational behavior in the quest to achieve organizational goals. Thus in Chapter 5, *decision making, job satisfaction, and work stress,* decision making is explored from a number of perspectives including types of decisions, managerial decision-making styles, the decision-making process, and behavioral factors which influence an individual's decisions. A person's satisfaction with his or her job stems from a variety of factors including pay and benefits, promotion opportunities, treatment by supervisors, and general working conditions. It is generally believed that a person's level of job satisfaction affects many of his work-related decisions including motivation to achieve higher levels of performance, decision to look for other work, and absenteeism. A significant factor in job satisfaction is the degree of work-related stress an individual encounters in his job. Work-related stress is a rising concern in many organizations and high levels of stress can result in lower quality and productivity, higher levels of absenteeism and turnover, chemical dependency, and other health problems.

What causes individuals to take actions or to achieve different levels of productivity is a key question in the study of organizational behavior. In general, it is internal *motivation* (Chapters 6 & 7) which causes people to choose certain behaviors. Exactly what motivates people? In general individuals act in pursuit of a goal or to fulfill a need. Within an organizational context the question becomes what factors are effective stimulants that will motivate a person to expend high levels of effort to achieve organizational goals. Employees expect that their attainment of organizational goals will result in their receiving rewards which in turn fulfill their personal needs. Thus the fulfillment of employees' individual goals and the attainment of the organization's goals must be related for employees to be motivated to achieve higher levels of performance. Most classical and modern theories of motivation center on these concepts of individual needs, goals, performance, and rewards. In general, a motivating job

Motivation The effective stimulant that causes individuals to take action or to achieve different levels of productivity in pursuit of a goal.

enables a person to fulfill needs through the work environment. Individuals expect to satisfy certain personal needs through good performance which is recognized and rewarded. The failure of this motivation and resulting performance to enable an individual to meet his or her personal needs often results in perceived inequity, lower productivity, and higher levels of absenteeism. In such situations (found in some organizations), the top performers will likely leave the organization hoping to find one which will enable them to fulfill their needs, while others will remain and provide minimum levels of performance since higher levels are not recognized and rewarded.

Organizations today employ a variety of proven motivational programs including award and recognition programs, individual incentives, organizational profit sharing, and perhaps the most powerful and easiest method—praise. When given by a supervisor or peer for legitimate reasons, simple praise or recognition can be an effective motivator.

The Global Workplace

Organizations must successfully adapt to both internal and external pressures. However, today external pressures are not limited to those that originate within our national borders. Instead, for example, organizations must recognize that changes in European consumer tastes, Japanese production methods, and South American agricultural methods are as likely to affect them as changes in Californian consumer preferences, Detroit production methods, or Iowa agricultural methods. Businesses which operate in the global arena (Chapter 8) increasingly recognize that they must learn, accept, and value the customs, beliefs, and values of the countries in which they intend to manufacture, sell, or trade goods or services. Managers involved in global business relations must learn to be flexible when approaching others or encountering situations or people with values and beliefs different from their own. They also must become culturally sensitive, learn to adapt to the culture of others, and not demand others to accept their culture. The global manager must also be able to change basic management practices such as job performance expectations and reward systems to fit the employees of other cultures.

The Diversified Work Force

Thousands of research studies are published each year. Few, however, have any impact beyond a few readers. In 1987, however, the Hudson Institute released a study, *21st Century,* which immediately gained the attention of corporate America and society as a whole and initiated a whole new focus or field of study in OB—the diversified work force (Chapter 9). The Hudson study contained a great deal of demographic data which was not new, but when separate work force trends were viewed as a whole a few statistics emerged which surprised thousands of managers, owners, and researchers: In the year 2,000 new entrants into the American work force will include 15 percent white males, 61 percent women (including women of color), and 24 percent men of color.[11] This dramatic change in the labor force is largely being caused by three factors: (1) a growth rate of only one percent in the existing U.S. labor force (compared to 2.9 percent in the 1970s); (2) shifting birth rates within U.S. ethnic groups; and (3) an increase of immigrants into the American work force of a magnitude not experienced since the 1890s.

Why do American business and social leaders view this shift in the work force as a major challenge? They recognize that for their organizations to suc-

OB in Practice

Women and Asians Gain Representation in Management Positions

A U.S. Census report on occupational trends noted that women made historic strides in filling management jobs during the 1980s. The number of women in executive managerial, and administrative jobs increased 95 percent (6.2 million) between 1980 and 1990 (6.2 million). The increase in the number of men in management positions was 17 percent. The 1990 statistics also indicated that women represented 42 percent of the total 14.6 million Americans in management positions and 46 percent of the overall civilian labor force, thus significantly narrowing this historic gap. The percentage of all working women in management positions in 1990 also showed a dramatic rise to 26.8 percent—up from 20.7 percent in 1980.

The census report also showed that of all ethnic groups, Asians and Pacific Islanders have the highest percentage of workers in managerial and professional positions—30 percent. The reported percentages for other ethnic groups were: White, 25.3 percent; Hispanics, 13.1 percent; Blacks, 16.5 percent; and Indians, 16.9 percent. The ethnic group making the greatest percentage gain were Blacks—a 3.5 percent gain from 1980.

Source: U.S. Census Report, 1993.

ceed in the twenty-first century they will need to hire and develop the best workers from this new work force. And, as we just discussed, motivating the new work force requires that the needs of these diverse employees be understood and met. If American business is to survive and prosper in the future it must recognize that an emerging diversified work force will have different needs and goals than the more homogeneous work force of the post–World War II period.

Diversity in the work place generally refers to groups of people who share common heritage, traits, or dimensions. These commonalities may include age, ethnicity, gender, race, physical abilities/qualities, and sexual/effectual orientation. While everyone is an individual, he or she views organizations and others through the filter of these dimensions that provide commonalities.

A major hurdle for leaders of organizations who seek to attract a productive, diversified work force is the reduction or even elimination of stereotyping of members of groups by other employees. Such negative beliefs about groups of people usually originate from outside sources and not through direct contact with members of diverse groups. The result of stereotyping is to ignore each individual's potential and thus provide artificial limits on his or her productivity. People often perform according to the expectations of others: if those expectations are artificially limited by a stereotype, then the person's performance may be artificially limited as well.

The next major step is for organizational leaders to value diversity through efforts to recruit, train, and promote members of diverse groups. This requires a realization that top managers in organizations, often white males, tend to select, reward, and promote those who "look, think, and act" like themselves. They may not place a value on the new and different points of view and ideas of other members of diverse groups who can bring fresh ideas to the organizations because they see the world through a different filter. These diverse points of view better meet the needs of the changing customer base—which is also becoming more diverse. Organizations that successfully manage a diversified work force will most likely be able to better relate to an increasingly varied customer base. In addition, organizational research has shown that groups of employees who have a broader base of experiences and viewpoints can make better decisions and develop better solutions to problems. In Figure 1-6, for example, the DuPont Company, an international chemical industry giant, describes how members of a diverse marketing team contributed to "Stainmaster Plus" carpeting.

An important step in many organizational diversity programs is awareness training. Awareness training seeks to help employees recognize the value of a diverse work force and to treat people who are different from themselves with dignity and respect. For example, at Southern California Edison, the utility giant, diversity training has become "business as usual" and a part of every employee's training program. The Edison program includes videos, lectures, and role-playing exercises. The opening session seeks to get people to discuss stereotypes openly, and then during the training helps employees realize and be commonly made aware that these stereotypes are unfairly based on their own personal beliefs or experiences with people.[12]

Figure 1-6

Diversity Teams at DuPont Company

Source: *DuPont Magazine,* September/October 1993, p. 30. Used by permission.

Power and Politics

Within the environment of an organization there exists sources of *power and politics* (Chapter 10) which greatly influence how things are accomplished. Power is derived through many sources including formal authority, expertise, personal charisma, or information. People must utilize their power to obtain organizational objectives by influencing the behavior of others. The productive use of power requires recognizing the interests and perspectives of others and respecting them. The abuse of power by an individual usually leads to their loss of that power source.

Groups and Teams

Most employees within organizations work, formally or informally, in groups. The long-term success of *employee groups or teams* (Chapter 11) is due in part to the synergy created when people work together instead of individually. Group members also develop standards of behavior and exert peer pressure on individual members to maintain expected levels of performance. The creation of formal employee self-directed and special-project teams has been called the "productivity breakthrough of the 1990s." Thus organizations are increasingly replacing their traditional supervisor/employee work units with self-managed teams. The results are generally fewer levels of management (and manager positions), team-based decision making, and greater overall quality and productivity. Implementing successful teams, however, requires management to surrender a great deal of its control and can take years to produce expected results. The automobile industry has provided several well-publicized successful team efforts including: Volvo's self-managed production team, Ford's "Team Taurus," Chrysler's LH teams, and Toyota's self-managed production teams in the company's first U.S. plant.

Another type of effective employee team is the special project team which is assigned the task of solving a particular problem or developing a new process or product. These teams involve employees from different departments or functions within an organization for a limited period of time. Once the project is complete, the team members return to their normal position—or in some cases are assigned a new project. At Federal Express, for example, employees must learn how to use 700 identification codes needed to sort packages each night in the company's Memphis, Tennessee hub. Many employees had failed the training program because they could not master the 700 codes. Therefore, an employee project team developed a new code sequence which was easier to learn and faster to use. The result was a reduction in the training time from six weeks to three weeks and an annual cost savings of $3.5 million.[13]

Women as a group face difficult challenges in their efforts to achieve success and recognition in the workplace (Chapter 12). While women currently constitute about 44 percent of the U.S. work force, they occupy less than 5 percent of the top management positions.[14] This invisible barrier to high-level positions in business, governmental units and other organizations is called the "glass ceiling." Women, as a group, also face the very real possibility of receiving lower pay as well as experiencing sexual discrimination or harassment in the workplace. In addition, women are expected to shoulder a disproportionate share of the parental and home-care responsibilities.

Organizational leadership can take down the glass ceiling through proactive mentor programs, career plans, and executive development programs that place women in traditionally nonfemale jobs and thus provide them with a broader perspective and break possible internal stereotypes (see the photo opposite).

African Americans, as a group, face workplace challenges that are similar to those faced by women—lower representation in some job categories, lower pay within the same job categories, and employment discrimination. Male African Americans face issues that are often somewhat different than those faced by the women. Female African Americans face the real possibility of "double" stereotyping or discrimination in the workplace. Since the passage of the 1964 Civil Rights Act African Americans have improved their situation by increasing their presence in America's middle class (from 13 percent in 1964 to 34 percent in 1993); however, as a group they still suffer disproportionate rates of unemployment and layoff. Many African Americans believe that racism occurs in the American workplace, and the data continue to support their beliefs. The plateau for African Americans in American organizations is even lower than that for women.

If organizations desire to attract and retain productive African Americans then they must recognize and value the diversity they bring to the workplace. Organizational leaders must first recognize the common barriers faced by working African Americans including: (1) recruitment practices that heavily utilize internal applicants and employee referrals which generally do not include many African Americans; (2) mostly staff and not line positions (that often train people for higher positions) are filled by African Americans; (3) continued stereotyping that must be addressed through awareness training programs.

Immigrants, primarily from Asia and Latin America, represent the fastest growing sector of the American work force and by the year 2,000 will outnumber African Americans. Their challenges can be broader than those faced by women and Africans because they include language, cultural, and religious differences. At the same time, however, due to a higher proportion of those with skills and college degrees, some immigrants have fared better in business and the professions. At the other end of the work force, however, unskilled immigrants often experience high unemployment or only minimum-wage jobs. Work force diversity programs usually strive to meet the needs of this growing sector of the labor force through cultural awareness training, corporate networks, and diversity recruitment efforts.

Workplace discrimination Individuals or groups are treated differently by an organization due to their age, gender, race, national origin, religion, or disability.

Today's work force also contains three other groups who bring diversity—*older workers, people with disabilities, and workers of homosexual orientation.* Members of these groups have experienced workplace discrimination and like those of other groups view the world through their own filter. Organizations have realized that the rapidly growing older work force can bring needed skills, stability, and experiences to the job. However, family obligations, health needs, and income limits are special barriers faced by many older workers that diversity programs need to recognize. People with disabilities may be limited in major activities such as walking, seeing, hearing, or speaking. However, diversity programs which match them to jobs they can perform may bring a sizeable pool of talent to their organizations. Discrimination against people due to their sexual orientation is not prohibited by federal law at the time of writing; however, a few employers have initiated diversity programs for them.

Managers spend about 80 percent of their time engaged in communication with others. Thus the study and understanding of the *communication process* (Chapter 13) is critical to understanding the behavior of individuals and groups. The three primary methods of communicating in organizations include written, verbal, and nonverbal. Nonverbal behaviors form a major part of a person's

Successfully attracting and developing members of America's diverse work force is a key to organizational survival and growth.

understanding of the message and include facial expressions, tone of voice, posture, and mannerisms. Organizational research indicates that the pattern of communication a group utilizes affects the group's performance and the satisfaction of its members. Developing effective methods of communication is an important activity but can be achieved by developing trust, being specific, supplying background information, always being open and honest, soliciting ideas from others, avoiding sarcastic remarks, and always treating others as you would want to be treated.

Leadership (Chapter 14) is perhaps the most studied aspect of organizational behavior. Research concerning effective leaders has produced models and theories that have dispelled the old notion that successful leaders are "born and not made." Instead, we know that employee leadership skills can be developed through training and experience. Successful organizational leaders may differ in their "style of leadership"; however, most do share certain characteristics: (1) they create a shared vision of future objectives, determine how they can be reached, and convince others to commit to obtaining them; (2) they lead by example and are enthusiastic in their endeavors; (3) they challenge the status quo and take risks; (4) they take time to recognize and celebrate the accomplishments of others; and (5) they delegate responsibility and authority instead of micromanaging the work of others.

Leadership inherently involves the use of power and requires the resolution of conflict among individuals or groups within the organization. *Conflict resolution* (Chapter 15) is a skill which often must be developed by leaders. The successful resolution of a conflict requires that the person not view conflict as an abnormal occurrence, but instead as a normal result of human interaction, that, if handled properly, can be a source of growth and the discovery of creative problem solutions. Conflict resolution requires, however, that the leader involved control his or her emotions, actively listen and cooperate with all parties involved, and separate the issues involved from the personalities of the individuals. Successful resolution often requires the third-party leader or arbitrator to find a "win-

win" scenario which helps both sides save face, but, at the same time, reaches a decision which is in the best interests of the organization. A number of proven resolution techniques are attempted in most conflict situations, and, with most individuals who place the organizational interests above their own, a reasonable solution can usually be found.

The Structure of Organizations

How an organization is structured can significantly affect its operations and effectiveness. Understanding both the formal and informal aspects of *organizational structure and design* (Chapter 16) is important in learning how tasks are achieved and resources utilized. In essence, organizational structure is the method by which labor is divided into specific tasks and the coordination of those tasks to achieve the goals of the organization. Characteristics of an organization's structure that may be critical to its behavior and ultimate survival include: (1) the division of labor into specific tasks and jobs; (2) the centralization (or decentralization of authority and responsibility); (3) the chain of command; (4) and the relationships between line and staff personnel.

These structural components can be utilized by one organization in a number of different ways. Exactly how the leaders of an organization decide to divide labor into separate jobs, decentralize authority, and configure the chain of command is called organizational design. Thus the design of each organization is the result of these decisions and how they change over time. A primary task for the leaders and managers of an organization is to develop an effective design. However, they also must think of the organization as a "living organism" which must strategically react according to internal and external environmental changes, and thus the design must constantly change to respond to changes in competition, technology, government, environment, and the labor force. The successful manager, in fact, designs a structure which facilitates changes in response to various forces. In deciding exactly how organizations are designed, managers are only limited by their imagination. However, most have chosen a basic design pattern which is one of the following: functional (for example, tasks grouped into areas of accounting and finance, production, engineering, and marketing); divisional (each product line, or geographic area is self-contained); strategic business unit (groups of similar products or services); matrix (a combination of vertical and horizontal grouping of functions); or network pattern (certain functions are contracted out to other firms).

Today there are no universal principles for managers to follow when determining the structure and design of an organization. Any (or combination) of the above might be the best one for a particular organization depending on its particular needs. However, today's more successful organizations are likely to have just three layers of management: top, heads of units, and everyone else. Only a few years ago the model was a hierarchy of eight to ten layers of management. Today's organizations are also more likely to have self-managed teams or empowered employees instead of the old centralized powerful manager. Focus on function is being replaced with a focus on processes and continuous improvement of the critical processes that causes the organization to be more flexible and thus able to quickly adapt to changing pressures. Networks (old term with a new meaning) within organizations are formed to enable employees to learn the "best practices" of other organizations (see the discussion of General Electric's best practices on page 28).[15]

OB in Practice

United Nations Reports Job Stress Is a Rising Global Problem

The pressures of maintaining productivity, long hours and low pay, electronic monitoring by employers, and the pace of changing technology are common causes of increased stress to millions of workers worldwide according to a United Nations Report, *Job Stress: The 20th Century Disease*. The common elements of the increased level of stress suffered by employees are: (1) increased productivity demands from employees; (2) reduced control an employee has over his or her job and daily activities; (3) electronic monitoring by supervisors through computers. Job stress is so intense in Japan that the Japanese have coined a phrase for death by overwork = *Karoshi*.

The cost of job stress to employers in the United States alone is estimated at $200 billion each year from absenteeism, compensation claims, medical insurance, and direct medical expenses for stress-related illnesses including ulcers, high blood pressure, and heart attacks.

The three important conclusions from the report relating to the job stress phenomenon were:

- The problem is a global one.
- It is not only a "white-collar" problem but occurs in all types of work.
- It is increasing in both the percentage of employees affected and the severity of their illnesses.

Source: Adapted from International Labor Organization, *Job Stress: The 20th Century Disease*, and The Associated Press, "Job Stress Rising Worldwide, U.N. Says," March 27, 1993.

Organizational Culture

All employees within an organization, through the policies, practices, and principles that serve as the foundation of the system of management, determine what is called the culture of the organization. *Organizational culture* (Chapter 17) is the set of key characteristics that describe the essence or personality of the organization. Just as each individual person has his or her own personality, each organization develops its own personality. The mission statement of an organization, such as that of TRINOVA in Figure 1-2, can provide the framework for its culture by providing the direction, values, and philosophy that guide major decision-making situations. At least four major types of organizational cultures have been identified and large organizations often have two or more of these present within subcultures. Ensuring that subcultures do not suboptimize the organization's effectiveness is a major challenge to its leadership.

The culture of an organization often has dramatic effects on the lives of its employees. Work-related stress, job burnout, and chemical dependency are common employee problems within a dysfunctional culture. A recent United Nations report indicated that job stress is growing worldwide at an alarming rate and is common to all types of work (see OB in Practice). Factors that can affect culture lead to employee problems including pressures for greater quality and quantity of productivity, layoffs and downsizing, rapid changes in technology, difficult managers, and tension among diverse groups of employees.

The culture of an organization can be enhanced through programs that make the workplace a more attractive environment. Employees place an increasingly higher value on programs such as child and elder care, flexible hours, employee empowerment, wellness activities, and limited travel and relocation policies. Some organizations today have expressed their commitment to creating an effective organizational culture in a written policy such as the one in Figure 1-7 implemented by General Electric. The GE commitment to maintain a productive environment for its 298,000 employees is the result of CEO John Welch, who says he runs GE "like a small business," and when he first took over the reins of the company Welch also stated, "We've got to take out the boss element." The *Work-Out* and *Best Practices* concepts in the GE culture statement refer to managerial techniques implemented by Welch to involve employees in the decision-making process and to spread the news about good ideas to all departments in GE. Work-Out is a forum in which employees experience a mental workout by identifying unnecessary aspects of their jobs and working out problems with other departments. Each forum includes 40 to 100 employees and takes place in a hotel. Welch likens them to a town meeting. Groups of five or six employees tackle a problem over a day or two until a solution has been found. The key to the success of the Work-Out program is that it empowers employees to make decisions and change their environment—another goal in the GE culture statement. The Best Practices program changed the control function at GE from one of checking finished products to analyzing and improving the production process to ensure quality is built into products. In a Best Practices course managers learn the "best practices" in managing from companies like American Express and L. L. Bean and the need for continuous improvement—another goal in the GE culture statement. Thus at GE creating a successful organizational culture is not simply words on paper, but programs, practices, and policies which involve all levels of management and are openly supported by top management.[16]

Quality and Change Strategies

Internal and external forces constantly force significant *changes in organizations* (Chapter 18). Significant external forces include the shifting labor force, technology, domestic and foreign competition, and the global political climate. People instinctively resist change. Their resistance may be due to any of several com-

Work-Out and Best Practices concepts Managerial techniques implemented by General Electric Co. to involve employees in the decision-making process.

FIGURE 1-7
The General Electric Policy on Organizational Culture

Culture

We are committed to creating a culture and environment within GE Appliances in which the following characteristics are evident:

- A total *external focus* in our actions and success are measured by customer/consumer satisfaction and global competitiveness.
- An *open and candid* working environment in which *teamwork* and *integrity* are highly valued.
- *Continuous improvement* in everything we do utilizing global *best practices* and *Work-Out* to facilitate change.
- A process of *employee development and empowerment* which builds *self-confidence* and enriches employee personal and job satisfaction.
- An environment which rewards *simplicity* over complexity and *action* over bureaucracy.

mon reasons including fear of the unknown, self-interest, habit, personality, and general mistrust. Organizations also instinctively resist change due to bureaucratic inertia, group norms, threatened power, and threatened resource allocations. Thus managers face difficult challenges in planning and implementing organizational change that is often critical to success and even survival. *Organizational development* (OD) is a planned organizational change in which behavioral science techniques are applied to help individuals, groups, and the structural components of the organization achieve needed transformations.

Organizational development A planned organizational change in which behavioral science techniques are applied to help achieve needed transformations.

Managers today are constantly striving to totally commit their organization and employees to the highest possible level of quality services and products. The exact meaning of quality depends on an individual's position in the organization. To achieve total quality and effect on one's job, products and services, however, each employee must have detailed specifications of the quality dimensions of their tasks and thorough knowledge of the customers' needs. *Total Quality Management* (TQM) is a managerial philosophy which develops continuous improvement for all processes, customer satisfaction, and quality output (Chapter 19). Increases in quality, productivity, and competitiveness occur as an organization's culture is changed through employee empowerment and TQM. TQM programs can be successful in both manufacturing and service organizations because they rely heavily on the effective management of human resources to change the organization's culture, structure, strategies, and reward systems. While TQM programs have been successful in many organizations, implementation problems have limited their success in some organizations.

Total Quality Management A managerial philosophy that develops continuous improvement for all processes, customer satisfaction, and quality output.

CONCLUSIONS AND APPLICATIONS

- The field of organizational behavior includes the systematic investigation into the managing of people at work within organizations. It is the study of the entire organization and the individuals and groups within them.

- Today historic changes are taking place in American organizations. New principles of managing people in organizations as well as new concepts in designing how work is accomplished are being developed. This "new agenda" for managers is driven by more diversified employees who work more effectively with greater authority and less supervision; the need for a greater commitment to quality; and the pace of technology change.

- Today's OB theories and practices have evolved from several schools of thought. Early management practices were heavily influenced by the Protestant Work Ethic and generally followed the universal principle of managers performing all administrative duties. Workers were viewed as "spokes in the wheels" and were thought to be equal in their ability and easily replaced. Scientific Management viewed workers as motivated solely by economic gain—and, therefore, should be compensated on a piece-rate basis. The Human Resource approach focused on workers as human beings who are affected by their social setting; therefore, managers should pay attention to the needs of their employees because "a happy worker is a productive worker." A later approach, the Contingency Approach to managing emphasized the need for managers to discard universal principles and instead analyze each situation individually and apply a method contingent upon the facts of the case. The Human Capital approach emphasized viewing employees as valuable investments, which, if effectively developed, would produce long-term benefits to the organization.

- The "new agenda" approach of today's manager emphasizes the need to empower employees and provide them with flexible approaches to their work, latitude in decision making, pay for performance, lean organizational management, and a strong commitment to quality.

- Managers are those individuals responsible for running the organization, making decisions, allocating resources, and directing the activities of their employees. In a typical day managers utilize their technical and quantitative skills but most often rely on their people and communication skills to perform their jobs.

- The field of OB includes the investigation of a number of issues that are critical to both individuals and organizations achieving their objectives. These topics center around understanding the individual, the diversified work force, the global workplace, employee groups, and organizational structure, design, and change.

REVIEW QUESTIONS

1. What did James R. Houghton, CEO of Corning, Incorporated mean by his call for a "new agenda" for American managers?
2. How did the Protestant Work Ethic influence traditional management beliefs?
3. Outline the primary contributions of these approaches to managing organizations: Scientific Management, Human Relations, Contingency Approach, and Human Capital.

4. What factors have caused today's managers and OB scholars to develop new approaches to managing organizations?
5. What is an organizational mission statement?
6. Define the four primary management functions.
7. What skills are most utilized by a manager?
8. Briefly describe a real-life situation in which you have witnessed each of the OB topics introduced in this chapter.

DISCUSSION QUESTIONS

1. How does the field of organizational behavior differ from other business disciplines such as accounting, finance, and marketing?
2. Today, which of the basic tenets of the Scientific Management, Human Relation, Contingency Approach, and Human Resource theories are still generally accepted as valid? Which have been discarded?
3. Are TQM and "Commitment to Quality" merely management fads or real long-term approaches to managing organizations?

4. How can an organization's leadership keep its mission statement "alive" and thus provide real direction in decision making?
5. Which of the OB topics presented in the chapter do you believe is the most important in affecting the success of most organizations today? Explain your position.
6. How does behavioral research in organizations differ from research in the natural sciences? Which would *you* rather conduct? Why?

CASE STUDY

Morro Bay Sports Wear

Alexis Rojas has just been hired to manage the Morro Bay office of Cal Sports Wear which supplies uniforms to schools, camps, and league teams. She has received three months' training from the company in all aspects of their product lines, pricing, sales, etc. The company has rented office space for one year and stocked it with samples of all product lines as well as other necessary office equipment and supplies. Rojas has also received training in record keeping and reporting.

The company had recommended that Rojas begin operation with a staff of six people. All other human resource decisions including hours, pay, benefits, job duties and responsibilities, however, are to be determined by Rojas. The company has found that with its other offices (forty-six in four western states) the managers demand total autonomy in deciding how to best manage their employees. Rojas has discussed this issue with the managers of other stores that have been operating successfully for several years. The other managers diagrammed their own organizational structures and general management philosophies, which are illustrated in Figure 1-8.

The Stockton manager has developed the current organization structure over several years. She has found that her time is best spent on the road visiting the schools and teams in her region to sign up new clients, visiting existing ones, and

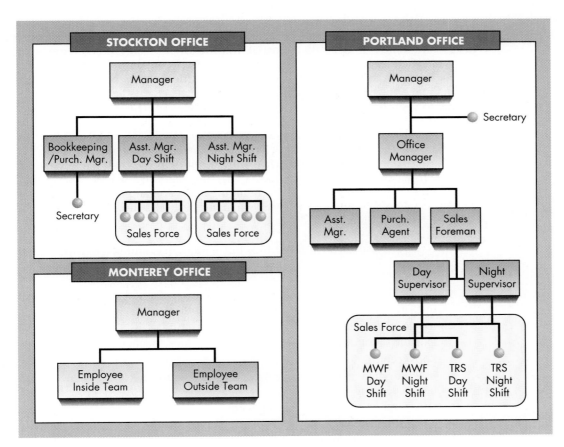

FIGURE 1-8 Possible Organizational Structures

generally performing public relations work. She has developed three good assistants—the two assistant managers who are totally in charge of their personnel, and the bookkeeper/purchasing agent. The sales force is paid minimum wage, but the average length of their employment is six months. The Stockton manager believes that the three managers are key to the success of her office. Sales personnel "simply come and go like waitresses; I've given up on trying to keep them for any length of time."

The Portland manager described his structure as one that "built itself" in response to employee demands. Over a five-year period he discovered that if he offers eight-hour shifts to employees on either Monday, Wednesday, Friday, or Tuesday, Thursday, Saturday then he can recruit and keep energetic college students who relate well to the coaches, parents, and principals and will usually work for four to five years, only leaving after graduation. Like the Stockton manager he believes his three office managers are key personnel and thus he provides them flexible hours, bonuses, and good benefits. All three have stayed with him since the office opened. He also pays his sales force about $2/hour above minimum wage but believes his total payroll cost is less than that of the Stockton office due to fewer total hours worked per shift with the flextime system he has developed.

The Monterey office has only been open for two years and the manager is still not sure if she made the right decision when she decided to form employee teams. While the store is a financial success, the monthly total payroll cost has averaged 10–20 percent above the average for all Cal Sports Wear offices due to the liberal profit-sharing plan she implemented. However, she also notes that her office has consistently ranked in the top five in terms of monthly sales growth. The two teams operate quite differently—the Inside Team is comprised of all full-time inside office personnel and the Outside Team is all part-time (mostly college students) outside personnel. The Monterey manager decided that unlike her counterparts at the other offices she wanted to delegate almost all routine functions to others, yet as a former volleyball league president, she knew that direct contact by people was a key to securing new accounts. In all other stores the office manager and/or other personnel make the outside contacts and then refer the clients to inside office personnel to take the order and follow up with the delivery. The Monterey manager, however, believed that given a liberal profit-sharing plan a larger outside sales force making repeated calls on clients could generate more sales over time. Her outside force also checks each order and delivers it to the client (outside salespeople in other offices check orders at the office and do not deliver). Each team makes all their own personnel decisions including electing their own leader, setting their own hours, and dividing up all tasks. Team members are paid minimum wage but receive a quarterly profit-sharing check which averages two months' pay. All costs, sales, et cetera of the two teams are entirely separate with each sharing a portion of the overhead.

Rojas has determined from her training, experience, and conversations with other managers that the following tasks must be accomplished in the office:

1. General management (record keeping, reporting, planning, controlling, directing, organizing work, contact with central office)
2. Inside sales (telephone and walk-in customers)
3. Outside sales (directly contacting schools, teams, leagues, etc.)
4. Bookkeeping
5. Inventory management (placing orders, follow-up, checking produced items before delivery)
6. Office maintenance and management
7. Clerical and computer
8. Purchasing (standard inventory, specialty items)

CASE STUDY QUESTIONS

1. What additional sources of information should Rojas consider investigating before deciding how to structure and manage the office?

2. If you were Rojas which of the three organizational designs (or another one) would you adapt? Why?

3. What human resource policies and practices would you recommend to Rojas?

4. Based on your answers to the first three questions, write a mission statement for Morro Bay Sports Wear office which would provide direction and indicate the organizational culture you would hope to develop.

EXPERIENTIAL EXERCISE 1

What Is Your OB IQ?

Purpose

Before you begin your journey into the field of organizational behavior perhaps you would like an idea of how much you already know about OB. Since this book will be read by people with a wide variety of OB knowledge and experience, we have pretested the following quiz on a large sample of college students entering their first OB class. Thus the scoring guide provided by your instructor should give you a general idea of how well you did compared to other OB students.

Task

Answer each of the following by circling T if the question is mostly true, is true most of the time, or is more true than false. Circle F if it is mostly false, is false most of the time, or is more false than true.

T F **1.** Organizations which have self-managed employee teams often have fewer levels of management.

T F **2.** The productivity of some people actually decreases when they join a group because they perceive their productivity is not directly measured.

T F **3.** All managers are not leaders.

T F **4.** Employer-provided group health insurance may not cover people with disabilities.

T F **5.** An employer can be held strictly liable for the sexual harassment of one of his or her supervisors.

T F **6.** About one-fourth of the new immigrants coming into the United States are college graduates.

T F **7.** The primary reason older workers are in the work force is financial.

T F **8.** The most important trait of a leader is honesty.

T F **9.** Japanese companies emphasize employee cooperation not individual performance.

T F **10.** The significant change of an organization's culture can require five to ten years.

T F **11.** About sixty-six percent of all U.S. employees report their jobs are "extremely" or "highly" stressful.

T   F   **12.** The primary reason why organizations are created is to create an economic advantage by dividing work into specialized jobs.

T   F   **13.** In most U.S. organizations, managers' spans of control (number of employees reporting to them) are increasing.

T   F   **14.** About 75 percent of U.S. employees work in service organizations (non-manufacturing).

T   F   **15.** People in organizations generally resist change.

T   F   **16.** Organizations which successfully utilize a diverse work force are more likely to attract a larger customer base.

T   F   **17.** Simple praise, when earned, can be a powerful and effective form of recognition.

T   F   **18.** Pay-for-performance compensation systems have been utilized in U.S. organizations even prior to World War I.

T   F   **19.** Changes in the American work force is changing how workers react to ethical decision-making situations.

T   F   **20.** Empowering employees to involve them in the decision-making process can lessen the need for employee discipline.

EXPERIENTIAL EXERCISE 2

Sources of OB Information

Purpose

To learn how to explore a topic on organizational behavior and to gain experience researching a topic in the library.

Task

Listed below are a number of OB topics which appear in recent academic and practitioner journals and other publications. Choose a topic of interest to you (or your instructor may assign you a topic). After your topic is determined, complete the following steps:

1. Locate at least six references which have been published within the past five years. Do not use a reference (e.g., Harvard Business Review) more than once.

2. For each reference indicate the title of the book or journal, the title of the article (if applicable), the author(s), the publisher, and the date of publication.

3. Write a one or two paragraph abstract of each reference. If the reference is a book you may write the abstract of one chapter.

OB Topics

1. Diversity (work force)
2. Child & Elderly Care Programs
3. TQM
4. Job Stress
5. Glass Ceiling
6. Sexual Harassment
7. Older Workers
8. People with Disabilities
9. Teams (of employees)
10. Toyota's U.S. Automobile Plant
11. Group Norms
12. Leadership (by attributes)
13. Mentoring
14. Management versus Leadership
15. Executive Retreats
16. Ethics in Business

17. Conflict Resolution
18. Flexible Productivity
19. Culture Shock
20. Organizational Culture
21. Employee Empowerment
22. Wellness Programs
23. Plateaued Employees
24. Job Burnout
25. Family/Work Issues
26. Mission Statements
27. Span of Control
28. Unity of Command
29. Malcolm Baldridge National Quality Award
30. Quality Circles
31. Drug Testing
32. Management by Objectives
33. Organization Development (OD)
34. Organization Design
35. Organizational Effectiveness
36. Pluralism
37. Employee Award & Recognition Programs
38. Motivation Theories
39. Part-time Workers
40. Flextime
41. Employee Involvement/Participation Programs
42. Incentive Pay Systems (Individual-based)
43. Profit-Sharing Plans
44. Generational Values
45. "Win-Win" Conflict Resolution Techniques
46. Equity Theory
47. Outward Bound
48. Job Sharing
49. Performance Appraisal
50. Vision Statements

Take It to the Net   **You can find this chapter's World Wide Web exercise at:**
http://www.prenhall.com/carrell

CHAPTER 2

Understanding Behavior in Organizations

CHAPTER OBJECTIVES

1. To understand the purpose of research.
2. To explain the research process.
3. To define research terminology in terms of certain key words.
4. To describe research designs used by researchers to test predicted relationships among variables.
5. To discuss the variety of methods used to gather information.
6. To know how research projects are evaluated.
7. To explain the four levels of analysis used in this textbook.
8. To define the notion of contingency theory and how it relates to organizational behavior.

CEO Director Edward E. Lawler, III

Edward E. Lawler joined the faculty of Yale University after receiving his Ph.D. in 1964 from the University of California at Berkeley. He moved to the University of Michigan in 1972 as Professor of Psychology and Program Director in the Survey Research Center at the Institute for Social Research. In 1978, Professor Lawler joined the faculty at the University of Southern California and in 1979 founded and became director of USC's Center for Effective Organizations (CEO).

CEO has become a well established research entity in the area of employee involvement and participative management doing important work on quality circles, self-managing teams, and union-management qual-

ity of work life efforts. At any one time CEO is likely to be doing research projects with 10–15 corporations.

The research team at CEO is composed of six full-time research scientists, in addition to Professor Lawler, and is a self-funding research unit of the School of Business Administration at USC. Such a research center as CEO produces knowledge which is drawn from organizational experience, but is looked at from a theoretical perspective and validated by empirical measures of effectiveness and impact.

By becoming involved in long-term data gathering activities with organizations, the researchers at CEO have been able to follow and measure the input of specific organizational change efforts. CEO published hundreds of articles and ten books during its first decade of operation.

Source: Edward E. Lawler, III, "Understanding Work Motivation and Organizational Effectiveness: A Career-Long Journey," Working Paper, Center for Effective Organizations, University of Southern California, 1991.

THE PURPOSE OF RESEARCH

Researchers such as Edward Lawler and research centers such as the University of Southern California's Center for Effective Organizations conduct research that pertains to the field of organizational behavior.

Importance of Research

Many times throughout this book the reader will see a term such as "research studies indicate." In fact, research findings are used as a basis for many discussions in this text. Both students and managers, however, may fail to understand the need for research and wonder why it is important to understand organizational behavior research methods. There are several good reasons for learning about behavioral science research methods. First, a knowledge about organizational behavior has become increasingly critical to a manager's performance and to his or her long-term career success.[1] An understanding of the nature of organizational behavior research allows an individual to decide how much confidence to place in a particular research conclusion after having read a research report. Also, knowing how research is conducted can help managers and students make their own observations, interpret them, and avoid making unwarranted conclusions from insufficient or biased information. Research studies also provide a framework that managers can use to diagnose problems and implement changes.[2]

Although the term research has no single, widely accepted definition, most researchers tend to define research as the process of systematically gathering and analyzing information in order to gain knowledge and understanding.[3] The Profile opposite describes how a university research professor founded his own consulting firm and is an adviser to top managers at AT&T, Corning, and Xerox.

Scientific Method

Almost all research in organizational behavior is based on the scientific method that is an objective approach toward expanding knowledge characterized by an endless cycle of theory building hypothesis formation, data collection, empirical hypothesis testing, and theoretical modification. While these terms are explained in greater detail in following sections of this chapter, Figure 2-1 represents how the scientific method is a continuous process.

THE RESEARCH PROCESS

Both organizational behavior research scholars and business practitioners engage in research activities to improve their knowledge of organizational behavior.

Profile

David A. Nadler
President of Delta Consulting Group

HOW A FORMER OB RESEARCHER ADVISES TOP MANAGERS

Earlier, as a professor in the Graduate School of Business at Columbia University, David A. Nadler published an article in the *Journal of Applied Behavioral Science* in which he developed an integrative approach to managing organizational change based on a congruence model of organizational behavior which viewed the organization as an interdependent set of elements in terms of how work, people, and formal and informal structures fit together.[4]

Later, Nadler founded a New York-based consulting firm, Delta Consulting Group, that focuses on "organizational architecture" which is a metaphor that forces managers to think more broadly about organization in terms of his congruence or "fit" model.[5] Implementation of Nadler's organizational architecture concepts leads to autonomous work teams and strategic alliances. Nadler is an adviser to top management at AT&T, Corning, and Xerox and was the hidden figure behind a major reorganization within Xerox that completely revolutionized the company and saved it by beating back the Japanese competition.[6] Nadler explains how he advised top managers as follows:

"Our approach to consulting is to form highly collaborative relationships with our clients. Part of that collaboration involves transferring our technology (concepts, methodologies, and tools) to help clients enhance their capacity to design, build, and manage effective organizations. Thus, part of our core mission involves continually refining our practical knowledge about organizations and inventing tools that enhance organizational effectiveness. Invention in our domain, however, does not occur in a laboratory, an academic office, or a library; it occurs as the direct result of working with our clients to manage large-scale organizational change. In this way, our clients have not been just customers; they have been collaborators in the development of knowledge."

However, their purpose for conducting research is usually different. For example, a practitioner may be concerned with diagnosing a particular organizational problem to help the organization become more effective, while research scholars conduct research to develop a new theory or to test an existing one. The "OB In Practice" on page 41 describes research studies involving turnover which were conducted by practitioners.

The scientific method also involves several approaches to the research process which are described as follows:

General Propositions

General propositions are statements about certain phenomena and involves both induction and deduction.

Induction begins with a set of observations or facts. A theoretical statement is then generated to explain these observations or facts. For example, a researcher counts thirty short strikes, twenty-two in large firms and eight of them in small ones. A strike is a temporary stoppage of work or a concerted withdrawal from work by a group of employees of an establishment or several establishments to express a grievance or to enforce demands affecting wages, hours, and/or working conditions.[7] These facts lead to the induction that large firms have more shorter strikes than do small firms. The theoretical statement would be "larger firms tend to have shorter strikes." In this way, the researcher moves from a set of very specific observations to a general proposition.

Induction **A theoretical statement generated to explain a set of observations or facts.**

FIGURE 2-1
The Nature of
the Scientific Method

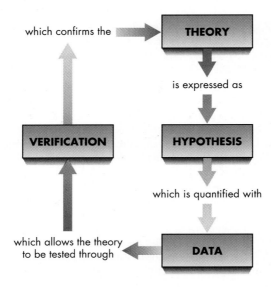

Deduction **involves the process of determining whether a particular proposition is a good representation.**

Deduction involves the process of determining whether the particular proposition is a good representation. Using our earlier proposition that larger firms tend to have shorter strikes, the researcher can test this proposition by deducing more specific statements such as "Because firms A, B, and C are smaller than firms D, E, and F, their strikes should last longer."

Verification

In the final step of the scientific method, verification, the researcher attempts to determine the truth or falsehood of a specific statement by gathering new data and checking to see if they support or refute the deduced prediction. Support for a prediction indicates that the researcher's theoretical constructions are on the right track. A failure to find support for a prediction, assuming that the researcher's research methods and deductive logic are sound, suggests that the theoretical basis for the prediction needs a revision. Back to our example of strike length and firm size, the specific statement "Because firms A, B, and C are smaller than firms D, E, and F, their strikes should last longer" can be tested with more facts—"Strike lengths for the six firms are, respectively, twenty-one, thirteen, eighteen, twelve, four and six days." In this example, the researcher's prediction regarding the relationship between strike length and firm size was supported.

Steps in the Research Process

In conducting research using the scientific method, researchers employ a number of steps as illustrated in Figure 2-2.

The beginning point in the research process is a question or problem. For example, a particular research question might be: "What is the relationship between firm size and length of strikes" or "Do large firms have shorter strikes than smaller firms?" The next step is to review the literature to determine what is known about the specific problem or question. This familiarity with existing literature provides background knowledge and insights for formulating a hypothesis to solve the problem. (In the following section, "Research Terminology," the meaning of the term "hypothesis" is defined.)

OB in Practice

Job Satisfaction Is Crucial for Professional Women

Thomas Smith, director of human relations for the Computer Science Corporation of Moorestown, New Jersey, was surprised that turnover among professional women was 50 percent more than for professional men. After polling the women who had left, Smith was shocked. "My hypothesis was that we could reduce this turnover by offering a day care center or flexible hours," stated Smith. "Instead, challenging job responsibilities, not family issues, were the decisive issues in why women left," reported Smith.

Also, Wick and Company—a consulting firm located in Wilmington, Delaware—interviewed 110 professional men and women who had left their jobs after five or more years. Wick's findings were that dissatisfied men were more likely to stay in bad jobs than dissatisfied women. Only 7 percent of the women who quit stayed home.

"It isn't what's happening at home that forces women to quit—it's what isn't happening in the office," concluded Vicki Tashjian, a Wick vice president.

Source: Adapted from Claudia Deutsch, "Why Women Walk Out on Jobs," *New York Times,* April 30,1991, Cl.

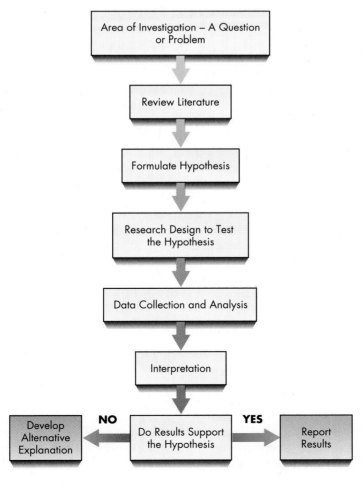

Figure 2-2
Steps Involved in the Research Process

Source: Adapted from Virginia R. Boehm, "Research in the 'Real World': A Conceptual Model," *Personal Psychology* 33, 1980, p. 496. Gregory Moorhead and Rick W. Griffin, *Organizational Behavior,* 3rd ed., Boston, Houghton Mifflin, 1992, p. 765. Robert Kreitner and Angelo Kinicki, *Organizational Behavior,* 2nd ed., Homewood, IL, Irwin, 1992, p. 763.

Following formulation of the hypothesis, the researcher designs a study to test it (the more common research designs are discussed in a following section). A part of the research design is the determination of how variables will be measured.

After a study is designed and data collected, the data are analyzed to determine whether the hypothesis is supported. When a hypothesis is not supported, researchers look for alternative explanations.

Early OB Research—The Hawthorne Studies

From 1924 until 1934, a series of investigations that systematically studied worker behavior were conducted at Western Electric's Hawthorne Plant in Chicago.[8] These studies were important because they demonstrated that certain factors, other than the job itself, can influence the behavior of workers.[9]

The purpose of the first study was to determine the impact of illumination on employee productivity. In one illumination experiment one group of female employees was selected to work under a constant intensity of light (the control group), while three other groups of females worked under varying intensities of light. Results were baffling. Productivity increased in all four groups. Also, there seemed to be no linkage between the level of lighting and performance. In fact, in one instance, the illumination of the control group was reduced to the equivalent of working by moonlight. Despite this handicap, employees maintained production levels and reported less fatigue and eyestrain than they had when working in a more illuminated situation. Apparently, something other than the level of illumination had affected the employees' reactions.

Western Electric officials called in a group of researchers from Harvard University headed by Elton Mayo to investigate a number of conditions that might affect productivity. Mayo's first experiment (known as the Relay Room Experiments) was designed to show that changes in the work setting would influence productivity. The participants were again female employees. One group of women was separated from the Relay Assembly Department and worked in a special test room. Mayo and his associates examined the impact of a variety of factors on the productivity of the work group located in the test room. For example, the factors included the introduction of rest periods, a free midmorning lunch, the length of the workday and work week, and variations in methods of payment.

Mayo hoped that his study would indicate that some conditions increased productivity while others decreased it. Surprisingly, Mayo and his research team found that productivity increased with almost every change in work conditions. Even when the employees were returned to the initial standard conditions, their productivity continued to increase.

In another experiment at the Hawthorne plant, known as the Bank Wiring Room study, male members of an existing work group were carefully observed by researchers. No attempts were made to alter the conditions under which the group worked. The observers were not allowed to become involved in conversations with the employees. The foreman of the work group supervised other employees in another room and was not always present. Also, the research observers became deliberately unobtrusive and the employees were free from constant supervision. It was noted by the researchers that the employees being studied were deliberately restricting their output by establishing an informal daily production rate of 6,600 units per person. Men who were more productive were subjected to verbal and physical abuse. In fact, all the men stopped work well before quitting time.

As a result of these studies, Mayo and his colleagues concluded that psychological aspects of the work setting contributed to productivity as well as other features. Mayo theorized that the female employees who participated in the Relay Assembly Room study reciprocated to their favorable treatment and special attention by increasing their production. In essence, because they enjoyed the attention of the researchers, their motivation and their productivity increased. This phenomenon, termed the Hawthorne Effect, often explains that the mere study of people at work can be responsible for an observed set of results.

Output was low in the Bank Wiring Room study because the men feared that an increase in production would lead to a new amount they were expected to produce and might even cost some of them their jobs. In essence, the employees had established informal rules or norms about job behavior; rules and norms that restricted production.[10]

Recently, critics have cited deficiencies in the research methods used in the Hawthorne Studies and have also offered alternative explanations of the findings. For example, these critics argue that net effects of social factors could not be correctly determined because other important elements of the work situation such as rest periods, working hours, and the tasks being performed had been modified. Furthermore, it is suggested that incentive pay rather than social factors improved productivity in the Relay Room Experiments.[11]

However, the Hawthorne Studies have exerted lasting effects on the development of organizational behavior. For example, many scholars believe that these studies indicate the importance of the social nature of employees and contradicts the rational or economic approach to employee behavior implicit in the principles of scientific management. The Hawthorne Studies played a major role in the advancement of the field of organizational behavior and are still among the most frequently cited works.[12]

In a following section, an "OB In Practice" describes a more recent organizational behavior research study that investigated the extent of managerial retaliation against whistle-blowers.

Research Publication

Researchers attempt to have their findings published in a journal. Figure 2-3 describes the major journals, listed as either academic or practitioner, devoted to topics in the field of organizational behavior. Academic journals tend to be more technical in nature, while practitioner journals are more comprehensible to practicing managers.

RESEARCH TERMINOLOGY

Organizational behavior researchers use a common set of terms to describe their activities. Business practitioners and students should be familiar with the most commonly used terms in order to fully understand the researcher's writings. Following is a discussion of the more popular terms: theory, construct, hypothesis, four types of variables (independent, dependent, intervening, and moderating), interaction effects, causality, correlation coefficient, and strategic significance.

Theory

A *theory* is a statement of interrelated principles, assumptions, constructs, and definitions that is generated by a researcher in an attempt to explain and pre-

Theory A statement of interrelated principles, assumptions, constructs, and definitions.

FIGURE 2-3
Major Journals in
Organizational Behavior

Academic Journals	Practitioner Journals
Academy of Management Journal	American Psychologist
Academy of Management Review	Business Horizons
Administrative Science Quarterly	California Management Review
American Sociological Review	Harvard Business Review
Group and Organizational Studies	HR Magazine
Journal of Applied Psychology	Human Relations
Journal of Business Research	Human Resources Management
Journal of Conflict Resolution	Human Resource Planning
Journal of Experimental Psychology	Labor Law Journal
Journal of Management	Journal of Human Resources
Journal of Occupational Behavior	Journal of Management Education
Journal of Organizational Behavior	Management Review
Management	Monthly Labor Review
Journal of Personality and Social	Organizational Dynamics
Psychology	Personnel Journal
Journal of Vocational Behavior	Sloan Management Review
Occupational Psychology	Training and Development Journal
Organizational Behavior and Human	
Decision Processes	
Personnel Psychology	
Psychological Bulletin	

Source: Adapted from Marion M. Extejt and Jonathan E. Smith, "The Behavioral Sciences and Management: An Evolution of Relevant Journals," *Journal of Management,* 1990.

dict phenomena. What motivates people in an organization is an example of a theory in organizational behavior.

Construct

Construct An abstract concept intended for theoretical use.

A *construct* is an abstract concept intended purely for theoretical use. In organizational behavior research, constructs are similar to familiar concepts, often having the same names but somewhat different definitions. For example, "need for achievement" is a construct used in personality theory and motivation and denotes a characteristic mix of behaviors that tend to cluster together within and among persons.

Hypothesis

Hypothesis A statement prescribing the potential relationship between two or more variables.

A *hypothesis* is a statement describing the potential relationship between two or more variables. In the preceding example of strike length and firm size, the statement "Because firms A, B, and C are smaller than D, E, and F, their strikes should last longer" is a hypothesis.

Variable

Variable An attribute or characteristic of an entity that has two or more different values either across entities or within the same entity over time.

A *variable* is an attribute or characteristic of an entity (person, group, firm, event, or object) that varies (has two or more different values) either across entities or within the same entity over time. If an attribute takes only one value within a population, it is a constant. For example, if a researcher is conducting research on a union with only male members, then gender is not a variable so far as the population of union members is concerned. From our previous example, in which the size of a firm affects its frequency of strikes, firm size and strike frequency are variables. Another example of a variable is that age is thought to be a cause of job satisfaction, with older employees more likely to be satisfied with

OB in Practice — Managerial Retaliation Against Whistle-Blowers

Whistle-blowing occurs when current or past organizational members "disclose illegal, immoral or illegitimate acts or omissions to parties who can take action to correct the wrongdoing."[13] For example, in 1991, an engineer employed by General Electric (GE) reported to the U.S. Government that GE had made payments of $2.75 million to an Egyptian firm as "contingency fees" on sales of a military radar system purchased by the Egyptian government. Part of the $2.75 million was used to pay transportation, lodging, meals, and other bills for Egyptian government personnel. Such payments are a violation of the False Claims Act which prohibits American firms from charging improper expenses to defense contracts. GE had billed the $2.75 million payment to the Pentagon as part of a $124.3 million radar contract. The Justice Department sought at least $9 million including treble damages for the alleged overpayments. GE argued that it should not be punished because it aggressively investigated that matter on its own. In late 1994, GE agreed to pay the U.S. Government $5.9 million to settle the lawsuit but admitted no wrongdoing. Martin Marietta, who acquired GE's aerospace business last year, agreed to pay the $5.9 settlement.[14]

An interesting question is to what extent will GE retaliate against the engineer who blew the whistle? Research conducted by Professors Marcia Miceli and Janet Near, who investigated whistle-blowers from a variety of North American organizations, reported that nearly 95 percent of identified whistle-blowers escaped retaliation altogether. Miceli and Near commented that "although the general public often believes that the incidence of retaliation is much higher—perhaps due to media coverage of dramatic cases—systematic previous studies show that between 79 percent and 84 percent of sampled federal whistle-blowers who were identified also escaped retaliation."[15]

Source: For a complete review of Miceli and Near's study, see M. P. Miceli and J. P. Near, "Relationships Among Value Congruence, Perceived Victimization, and Retaliation Against Whistle-Blowers," *Journal of Management* 20, 1995, pp. 773–794.

---

their jobs than younger employees. In this example, age and job satisfaction are variables.

Independent and Dependent Variables

An *independent variable* is one that is believed to cause changes in one or more other variables. A variable that is affected by the independent variable is a dependent variable. Using our previous examples in which the size of a firm affects its frequency of strikes and that age is a cause of job satisfaction, firm size and age are independent variables while strike frequency and job satisfaction are dependent variables. Variables that are related but about which no assumption is made as to which is the cause and which the effect, are called correlates. In certain situations, the researcher may be unsure which variable is the cause or may not care. As an example, an employee's absenteeism record may be a predictor of whether the employee is promoted to supervisor. In this case, the researcher does not need to know if high absenteeism causes a lack of promotion (management does not consider the employee to be dependable) or if the lack of promotion has led to high absenteeism (the employee is less committed to the job).[16]

Independent variable
One that causes changes in one or more variables.

Intervening Variable

An intervening variable (*w*) explains the relationship between an independent variable (*x*) and a dependent variable (*y*) by suggesting that "*x*" causes "*w*" that causes "*y*." Intervening variables explain why the independent variable affects the dependent variable and assist the researcher to understand the original relationship. For example, a researcher may determine that a relationship exists between the number of clerical employees in an office and the clerical employees' job satisfaction. The researcher needs to know why these two factors are related in order to make an effective recommendation. The linkage between the number of clerical employees and job satisfaction may be that supervisors with large numbers of clerical employees are more bureaucratic and respond slower to employees' complaints and problems. Accordingly, "bureaucratic handling" is a possible intervening variable.

Moderating Variable

A moderating variable (*m*) changes the relationship between an independent variable (*x*) and a dependent variable (*y*). In other words, the effects of "*x*" on "*y*" varies with "*m*." For example, a relationship may exist between plant size and job satisfaction only for assembly line technology and not for job-shop or continuous-flow production. "Type of technology" is a moderating variable in that only when the technology is assembly line does plant size affect job satisfaction.[17]

Interaction Effect

Interaction effect The result of two independent variables combining in a nonadditive manner to cause a dependent variable.

An *interaction effect* is the result of two independent variables combining in a non-additive manner to cause the dependent variable. For example, in a particular research setting, a researcher found that females were absent 5 percent more than males, and that younger employees were absent 10 percent more than older employees. The researcher expected that these two effects would add to a 15 percent higher absenteeism for younger females compared to older males (the effect of 5 percent of being female plus the effect of 10 percent of being younger). However, the researcher found that the difference in absenteeism between younger females and older males was actually 25 percent. The researcher concluded that there was an interaction effect between gender and age. In essence, there is something different about the category "younger females" than just age and gender. A possible difference might be in having young children at home who need extra care.[18]

Causality

Researchers seek research designs that will allow them to conclude the causality between two variables (*A* and *B*). That is, "*A*" really causes "*B*." However, the direction of causality may be actually reversed with "*B*" causing "*A*." In other cases, causation between "*A*" and "*B*" may work in both directions: each causes the other.

In order to determine whether "A" causes "B," a researcher has to meet certain criteria. Most of these criteria rely on statistical methods and are not discussed in this text.[19]

Correlation Coefficient

A correlation coefficient is a statistic that indicates the strength of a relationship between two variables and is expressed as a number that ranges from +1.0 (a perfect positive relationship) to –1.0 (a perfect negative relationship). When two variables vary directly with one another (as the value of one variable increases, the value of the other variable increases to the same relative degree), the correlation coefficient will be expressed as a positive number. A negative number indicates that the two variables vary indirectly with one another (as the value of one variable increases, the value of the other variable decreases), and the correlation coefficient will be expressed as a negative number. If two variables vary independently of each other the correlation coefficient will be zero indicating that there is no relationship between the two.[20] For example, a researcher might survey a group of employees to determine if there is a relationship between age and absenteeism. If the correlation coefficient for these data is –.50, then it would indicate that older workers are absent less often than younger ones.

Statistical Significance

Once a relationship between two variables has been detected, researchers need to know if the association is statistically significant or caused by chance or luck. A relationship is said to be statistically significant when there is a very small probability (often set at 5 percent, or one in twenty) that a relationship could be attained through chance alone. Researchers disagree over whether it is legitimate to use statistical tests of significance when the data represent a population rather than a sample.[21] In the previous section regarding the study of the relationship between age and absenteeism, if the researcher found a probability of one percent (written as .01 by researchers) then the finding that older workers are absent less often than younger ones has statistical significance.

RESEARCH DESIGNS

Researchers use a variety of procedures, called research designs, to test the predicted relationships among variables. Among the most frequently employed are case studies, field surveys, laboratory experiments, field experiments, archival research, and unobtrusive measures. Another research design, meta-analysis, is also discussed in the following section.

Case Studies

In a case study, the researcher conducts an in-depth analysis of an organization as either a participant, consultant, or as a guest. The researcher uses a variety of techniques to gather information during a case study: interviews, questionnaires, and personal observation.[22] For example, because nearly all of the research on escalating commitment has focused on individuals rather than on organizations, Professors Jerry Ross and Barry Staw conducted a case study of the Long Island Lighting Company's decision to build and operate the Shoreham Nuclear Power Plant to investigate an organizational theory of escalating commitment. Shoreham's cost estimated to be $75 million when the project was announced in 1966, rose over the next twenty-three years to over $5 billion. A negotiated agreement with New York State finally resulted in Long Island Lighting's abandoning Shoreham without its ever having begun operation.

Ross and Staw consulted "hundreds of articles" which had been published by such sources as the *New York Times, Wall Street Journal, Nation, National Review, Nature* chronicling Shoreham; examined internal documents not generally made available to the public; and interviewed participants and informed sources. From this data, Ross and Staw grouped the determinants of escalation into four broad categories: psychological, project, social, and organizational. Ross and Staw reported that: (1) when external constituencies become substantially involved, the decision to stay or withdraw can be turned into a political rather than an economic or even organizational issue; (2) the early arrival of organizational members who are not involved in plant construction (planners, operators, technical support staff) increases the likelihood of a lengthy cycle of escalation; (3) when potential losses of a project become so large that withdrawal might lead to bankruptcy—an organization becomes increasingly committed to the losing endeavor; (4) escalation problems are likely to occur when managers venture from their areas of expertise or when technological changes cause learned procedures and decision checks to no longer be applicable; (5) when external constituents are successful in preventing the closing of a losing project, the unsuccessful firm may become a permanently failing organization; (6) changes in top management can reduce psychological and social sources of commitment, thus increasing the possibility of withdrawing from a losing course of action; (7) appeals to favoring constituencies for new loans and support can change a project's economics so that withdrawal is not so costly and is more likely to be chosen as an alternative; and (8) threats to persevere in a losing course of action can influence opposing constituencies to change a project's economics, thus making it less costly and more likely for withdrawal to occur.[23]

Case studies have certain advantages. The researcher can thoroughly explore one situation in detail and obtain a considerable amount of descriptive and explanatory information. Case studies also provide insights that aid in theorizing and facilitate the discovery of unexpected relationships. Also, the results of case studies can be used to generate hypotheses for further testing in more controlled studies.

Case studies also have several disadvantages. Case study research is very time consuming and is not subject to quantitative analysis. Researchers may also delude themselves into seeing systematic causal relationships that do not exist. Also, a certain amount of selective observation and recall exists—other observers may not draw the same conclusion.

Despite these disadvantages, case studies can be a useful research design as long as the researcher understands its limitations. These limitations make case studies more useful in the exploratory stage of studying a phenomenon.

Field Surveys

Through the use of surveys, researchers can gather data about organizational behavior. A field survey is a set of questions, either oral or written, designed to collect the personal responses of people regarding a subject of interest to a researcher. The researcher uses a sample of people chosen from a larger population, analyzes the data, and attempts to make inferences about the larger population from the representative sample.[24] For example, as described in a previous "OB In Practice," in studying the extent of managerial retaliation against whistle-blowers, Professors Miceli and Near mailed a 25-page questionnaire to 3,853 Directors of Internal Auditing.[25]

Advantages of a field survey are that observations are independent of those of the researcher, easily quantifiable data are produced which facilitates statistical analysis, and formats can be standardized across studies.

The disadvantages of a field survey are that questions may be worded in such a way that they bias the respondents' answers, respondents may react to the personal attributes of the researcher and offer answers that they might not otherwise endorse, and respondents may also show certain biases. Some common biases are social desirability, the tendency to give answers that are socially desirable; answering questions in a manner that is perceived to be "logical" or "consistent" even if doing so inaccurately portrays the situation; and extremism, the tendency to either avoid or rely on extreme options when responding to a question. Field surveys, despite their disadvantages, can be used to gather large quantities of data and determine relationships among variables.

Laboratory Experiments

A laboratory experiment provides the researcher with total control over the design of the study and the selection of variables to be examined because the researcher creates an artificial setting similar to a real work situation. The term laboratory denotes only a setting that makes observation easier. The laboratory does not require elaborate apparatus nor does it have to be located on a college campus or in a psychology department. A laboratory can be located in a vacant office or in an unused classroom. All one needs for a laboratory is a setting, some subjects, and a task for the subjects. Using these minimal requirements, a researcher can study a wide range of behavior that is relevant in organizations.[26]

As an example, Professor Christopher Earley used a laboratory experiment to investigate the differences between group-focused training and individual-focused training on a person's estimate of his or her ability to perform a task. Participants included Hong Kong Chinese managers, Chinese managers from the People's Republic of China, and American managers. All participants were employed as full-time managers and were recruited as study participants from three separate management training programs hosted by universities in Southern China, Hong Kong, and the United States, respectively. The experimental task was to generate alternate daily work schedules of employees based on a three-shift workplace and thirty employees using the following rules: (1) They had to use employees' preferences and availability for shifts, (2) no employee could serve on more than a single shift on a given day, and (3) the schedules could not repeat themselves. Sets of material were prepared for the managers in their native language and they were assigned on one of three training conditions: (1) individual-focused, (2) group-focused, and (3) no training. Before assigning the managers to the three training groups, Professor Earley had determined that no significant differences existed among the participants in terms of age, education level, gender, and company size.

The results of Earley's laboratory experiment indicated that an employee's cultural orientation influences his or her training information. For a person with a group orientation, training focusing on individual-level cues and information is less effective in enhancing his or her self-effectiveness expectations than was training based on group-level information. A person with an individual orientation is best trained by targeting that employee's personal actions and potential. Also, training information provided at either a group or individual level was better than no training at all for everyone of the involved participants. Professor Earley argues that the implications of this study is that training should be in conformance with a person's cultural background as well as with individual differences.[27]

The advantages of a laboratory experiment include a high degree of control over variables, precise measurement of variables, and the elimination of confounding factors.

Disadvantages of a laboratory experiment are the lack of realism (the laboratory setting usually does not exactly duplicate a real life situation), subjects are not sufficiently involved in what happens, subjects may try to adjust their behavior to what they think the researcher's hypothesis is (this adjustment may consist of doing what looks good or acting in a manner exactly opposite of the way they think the researcher would predict), and the difficulty in generalizing findings to an organizational setting. Also, some organizational situations, such as employee terminations, cannot be simulated in a laboratory.

Field Experiments

A field experiment is a research design in which the researcher attempts to control certain variables and manipulate others to determine the effects of the manipulated variables on outcome variables.[28] For example, federal statutes recommend that four job attributes (skill, responsibility, required effort, and working conditions) be used in the evaluation of a job and the National Academy of Sciences recommends using one job evaluation method across job classifications in an organization. In a study to evaluate the validity of three job evaluation methods, researchers had departmental managers from a Midwestern city rate jobs from three classifications with which they were familiar: blue-collar, clerical, and professional-technical. Results using the three job evaluation methods were compared to the city's rank ordering of jobs determined by a job evaluation method developed by a private consultant. The findings indicated that within a classification, jobs were ordered differently depending on the method used (see Figure 2-4) and that managers assessed the worth of jobs differently with one method than with another method. The researchers suggest that the correctness of evaluations based on the four factors of skill, responsibility, required effort, and working conditions is questionable as is the use of a single method across job classifications.[29]

FIGURE 2-4
Average Rank Order
of Jobs

| | Job Evaluation Methods | | | |
Classifications	City's System	System One	System Two	System Three
Blue-collar jobs				
1st class line worker	1	1	1	1
Apprentice line worker	2	3	2	3
Operator	3	2	4	4
Assistant operator	4	4	3	2
Coal equipment operator	5	5	5	5
Clerical jobs				
Library assistant II	1	2	2	1
Library assistant I	2	4	4	3
Secretary I	3	1	1	2
Senior clerk typist	4	3	3	4
Clerk typist	5	5	5	5
Professional–technical jobs				
Detective	1	2	2	2
Police officer	2	1	1	1
Senior engineering technician	3	3	3	3
Engineering technician	4	4	4	4
Dispatcher	5	5	5	5

Source: Adapted from Judith M. Collins and Paul M. Muchinsky, "An Assessment of the Construct Validity of Three Job Evaluation Methods: A Field Experiment," *Academy of Management Journal* 36, 1993, pp. 895–904.

The advantage of a field experiment is that the organizational setting provides greater realism than a laboratory experiment. This realism allows the field experiment's results to be generalized, on a more valid basis, to other organizational situations.

Disadvantages of a field experiment are the researcher's lack of control over all potentially important variables and contamination of the results if the subjects discover their respective roles in the experiment and behave differently.

Meta-Analysis

Because most research studies focus on a single setting or single body of data to develop or test hypotheses, it is difficult to compare the findings of one study with those of another. A *meta-analysis* is a technique that converts findings from similar studies into a unified set of variables and draws out the average statistical findings for the group of studies. The result is much stronger support, or unsupport, for a particular hypothesis than could be obtained from a single research study.[30] For example, an important aspect in the study of the influence of group goals on group performance is the size of the effect of group goals on performance. In other words, what is the difference in the size of performance between groups with goals and those without goals? Researchers used a meta-analysis to examine twenty-nine studies to determine the size effect of goal setting on performance. Earlier research had not been able to determine this effect. The meta-analysis yielded twenty-six usable values for the size of the effect of group goals on performance with data for 163 groups and 1,684 individuals.

Meta-analysis A technique that converts findings from similar studies into a unified set of variables and draws out the average statistical findings for the group of studies.

The meta-analysis revealed that the mean performance level of groups that had goals was one standard deviation higher than the performance of groups that did not have goals. This size effect is considered to be large and indicates the extent to which performance is affected by groups with goals and those without goals.[31]

DATA COLLECTION METHODS

A variety of methods are used to gather information for organizational behavior research. The four techniques that are most frequently used are: direct observation, interviews, questionnaires, and unobtrusive measures.

Direct Observation

Direct observation involves watching and recording what is being observed. Observations can range from a casual, informal scrutiny of the work setting to highly structured ones in which the observer is trained to look for and record certain activities or types of events.

Interviews

In an interview, questions are presented to the respondent orally by the interviewer and can be either face-to-face or telephone interactions. Interviews are more direct than the use of questionnaires and provide greater flexibility to the researcher. For example, individuals can be more fully questioned regarding their opinions or attitudes about a particular issue, providing a richness and deeper insight than normally provided by questionnaires. Interviews require more time to administer than questionnaires and are more difficult to score. Interviews can range from open-ended types of questions (What do you like most about your job?) to highly structured, formalized questions familiar to ones used in questionnaires (How satisfied are you with your job? Are you highly satisfied, moderately satisfied, slightly satisfied, or not satisfied at all?).

Questionnaires

Questionnaires, like interviews, can be open-ended or highly structured in their format. Increasingly, more structured questionnaires are being used that contain previously developed and validated scales to measure respondents' perceptions of relevant organizational characteristics. By mailing questionnaires to potential subjects or distributing them to an assembled group, the anonymity of the respondent is guaranteed, and a vast amount of data in the form of written responses can be collected and computer processed.

Unobtrusive Measures

The three preceding methods of data collection can create the problem of reactivity, when the act of measuring something influences the response being measured.[32] Unobtrusive measures are indirect ways of collecting data in which the subjects involved are not aware of the data collection process. Unobtrusive measures can be the use of archival data regarding organizational characteristics such as turnover or absenteeism, or a form of observation in which subjects do not know that they are being observed. For example, the directors of a museum wanted to determine which of their exhibits was the most popular. To avoid the potential problems of identifying how visitors felt about the exhibits, investigators checked the frequency with which floor tiles had to be replaced around the various exhibits. This selective wear was taken as a measure of the relative popularity of the exhibits.[33]

RESEARCH EVALUATION

Collecting good data is just as important as developing a good theory. Several characteristics make some data better than others. For example, the measures of theoretical concepts must be reliable and valid. Also, another method used to evaluate research are the findings of a particular study generalizable to other individuals, groups, or situations. Finally, sometimes organizational behavior research raises ethical issues. In this section, the concepts of reliability and validity, as they apply to organizational behavior research, as well as the issue of whether findings are generalizable are discussed. Ethical issues in organizational behavior research are also examined. Figure 2-5 illustrates how the concepts of reliability, validity, generalization, and ethical issues apply to an actual research study.

Reliability and Validity of Data

Reliability refers to the consistency of the measurements in question. Measurements must be free of random errors and present a consistent and stable reflection of the concepts being investigated. For example, if your bathroom scale indicated that you weigh 165 pounds and then one hour later the same scale indicated that you weigh 140 pounds, then your scale would not be very reliable.

Validity is the degree to which a particular measure describes what it is intended to measure. As an example of whether a measure has validity, consider a research

We explain how the concepts of reliability, validity, generalization, and ethical issues are used in research by using Professor Christopher Earley's previously described study of the differences in training on a person's estimate of his or her ability to perform a task. (Earley's study is described in the section "Laboratory Experiments.")

Concept	Procedure
Reliability and Validity	To measure their self-effectiveness, participants were asked to rate their self-effectiveness for nine levels of possible performance using a scale in which 0 = "certain the performance level cannot be achieved" and 100 = "certain the performance level can be achieved." The responses to the scale were averaged for a composite self-effectiveness score and statistical tests indicated reliability and validity.
Generalization	Country of origin was used as the defining characteristic of a cultural grouping but researchers need to consider what constitutes a cultural group. Also, workers from mainland China are often assigned to their work units shortly after receiving their formal education and remain in these units for a long time. Thus, Chinese employees may have responded well to group-focused training.
Ethical Issues	Managers were asked if they were willing to participate in the exercise. After questionnaires were completed and collected, the managers were debriefed concerning the purpose of the experiment and the researcher answered any remaining questions the participants had. The relationship of the experiment to processes of work motivation and performance in organizations across various cultural settings were discussed.

FIGURE 2-5

An Illustration of the Concepts of Reliability, Validity, Generalization, and Ethical Issues

study in which the researcher is interested in employees' satisfaction with their supervisor. The researcher asks questions about pay and working conditions and averages the respondents' answers and uses the average to represent "satisfaction with the supervisor." Is this a valid measure? No, because pay and working conditions may not be related to an employee's satisfaction with his or her supervisor.

Reliability and validity are related. A measure cannot be valid if it is not reliable, but a reliable measure is not necessarily a valid one. For example, people's weight could probably be measured very reliably, but weight would have little validity as a measure of job satisfaction.

Generalization

Researchers assume that the theories examined in basic research apply universally within certain conditions.

Specific applied research studies are sometimes generalized to other circumstances, although not to the "universe" as in basic research.[34] For example, a drug treatment program tested and found to be successful in one city may be introduced in similar cities, but the results are not assumed to apply to other countries. With other research studies, little or no generalization occurs. As an example, the cause for a rash of accidents in a particular manufacturing plant is not assumed to exist in any other companies.

Research results are generalized to the extent that the researcher believes them to be applicable to situations beyond the set of conditions specifically examined in the research.[35]

Some organizational behavior research studies, however, may not be generalizable to groups of individuals other than those who participated in the original study. For example, the results of studies that use college students as subjects may not be generalizable to full-time employees in real jobs.

Ethical Issues

Organizational behavior researchers need to be aware of potential ethical problems. Three areas of concern are the individual's freedom of choice in participating in a study, the participant's right to privacy, and how the researcher conducts and reports the study results.

All prospective subjects should have the right to choose whether to participate in a study or to withdraw their participation after the study has started. The researcher should explain all procedures in advance to the participants because it is unethical to place individuals in a situation in which they could be harmed either psychologically or physically. In many governmental agencies and universities, researchers have to submit their proposals to a committee for approval before beginning a project. These committees have developed guidelines to guarantee the protection of human subjects.

Participants in a research study should not have their privacy violated without their permission. A research subject's personal opinion response, as well as other responses, should be treated confidentially. One way to avoid an invasion of privacy is to provide participants with an option to answer questions anonymously.

Considering that the threat of unethical research practices is somewhat similar to asking whether the researcher is honest with himself or herself, with those for whom the research is being conducted, and with standard research practices. It is unethical for a researcher to inaccurately report research procedures and methods used in a particular study and to falsify data.[36]

Organizational behavior research is subjected to limited scrutiny. When a researcher submits his or her research study to a journal for possible publication, expert referees review the reported procedures, methods and findings. Nothing, except ethical behavior and professionalism, prevents a researcher from falsifying a research study. No independent body examines the procedures and practices of applied research studies conducted by organizational members or outside consultants. Within an organization, the major criteria for research are cost effectiveness and relevance, and only the research budget is likely to receive any close checking.

A MODEL FOR UNDERSTANDING ORGANIZATIONAL BEHAVIOR

Organizational behavior scholars recognize that in order to fully understand why people act and think as they do in organizational settings, four levels of analysis are required.

Four Levels of Analysis

These four levels of analysis provide information about how people react as individuals (attitudes, values, and perceptions), the environment of the workplace (global contexts, cultural diversity, power and politics), the groups to which they belong (communication between them, formal and informal norms of behavior, conflicts, and leadership), to organizational processes (structure and design, culture, quality and innovation, and organizational change).

Contingency Theory and Organizational Behavior

The central thesis of contingency theory is that there are no universal principles of management that can be applied in all situations. Instead, certain contingencies or variables exist for helping managers identify and understand certain situations. What is appropriate in one situation may well be disastrous in another. For example, an organization design that is best suited for automobile production may be inappropriate for building personal computers. The contingency approach calls for managers to be flexible and to adapt to the situation at hand. Management's job is to search for important contingencies. When managers learn to identify important patterns and characteristics of their organizations, they can fit solutions to these characteristics. Important contingencies for managers include organizational design, international culture, and leadership style.[37]

As indicated in Chapter 16, the contingency approach to organization design suggests that there are several ways to design an organization. Managers at both Citicorp and Manufacturers Hanover misunderstood the nature of making loans to developing countries. Having experienced the problem of raising loan-loss reserves to cope with bad international loans, managers in the future will know how to handle this contingency in the international financial environment.[38] The aspect of contingency theory that focuses on leadership style concludes that rather than taking one basic approach to leadership in all situations, leadership style should vary according to such factors as the nature of leader-member relations, degree of task structure, the power a leader has, and the expertise and willingness of subordinates to assume responsibility. Leadership contingency theory is discussed in Chapter 14.

CONCLUSIONS AND APPLICATIONS

- An understanding of the nature of organizational behavior research allows individuals to decide how much confidence to put in a particular research conclusion after having read a research report. Also, an understanding of how research is conducted can help managers and students make their own observations, interpret them, and avoid making unwarranted conclusions from insufficient or biased information.

- Research is the process of systematically gathering and analyzing information in order to gain knowledge and understanding. Research in organizational behavior is based on the scientific method which involves induction, deduction, and verification.

- Organizational behavior researchers use a common set of terms to describe their activities. The more popular terms include: theory, construct, hypothesis, independent and dependent variables, intervening variables, moderating variables, interaction effects, causality, correlation coefficient, and statistical significance.

- To test the predicted relationships among variables, researchers use procedures called research designs. The most frequently explored research designs are: case studies, field studies, laboratory experiments, field experiments, and meta-analysis. Each specific research design has advantages and disadvantages.

- A variety of methods are used to gather information for organizational behavior research. The four most frequently used techniques include: direct observation, interviews, questionnaires, and unobtrusive measures. Research studies can be evaluated by determining whether the collected data used to measure theoretical concepts is reliable and valid. Another way in which organizational behavior research is evaluated is the extent to which the findings of a particular study are generalizable to other individuals, groups, or situations.

- Potential ethical problems are associated with organizational behavior research. Three areas of concern are: the individual's freedom of choice in participating in a study, the participant's right to privacy, and how the researcher conducts and reports the study results.

- Four levels of analysis can be used to develop an understanding of behavior in organizations: individual processes, the diversified work force, group processes, and organizational processes. An important aspect of organizational behavior is the notion of contingency theory. In essence, contingency theory states that there are no universal principles of management that can be applied in all situations. Instead, certain contingencies or variables exist for helping managers identify and understand certain situations.

REVIEW QUESTIONS

1. What is the purpose of research?
2. Explain the differences between scientific research, basic research, and applied research.
3. Describe the research process.
4. What is the difference between induction and deduction as related to the research process?
5. Discuss how the scientific method is related to organizational behavior research.
6. Describe the following: independent and dependent variables, moderating variables, interaction effects, causality, and statistical significance.

7. Discuss the advantages and disadvantages of case studies, field studies, laboratory experiments, and field experiments.
8. Describe the research design, meta-analysis.
9. Discuss the techniques used by organizational behavior researchers to collect research data.
10. What is involved in evaluating research?
11. What ethical issues are involved in organizational behavior research?
12. What is contingency theory? How is it related to organizational behavior?

DISCUSSION QUESTIONS

1. Why is theory important in research?
2. A researcher reports that the superior ratings of employee performance are reliable but not valid. Explain the meaning of the researcher's finding.
3. Discuss the trade-offs between a laboratory experiment and a field experiment.
4. In what situations is the generalizability of research findings not important?
5. State a specific hypothesis about behavior in organizations and describe how you would test this hypothesis.

6. What prevents an organizational behavior researcher from cheating or distorting research results?
7. Discuss the role of induction and deduction in the scientific method. Which of the two is more important? Why?
8. Discuss the difference between an academic journal and a practitioner journal.
9. Discuss the effects of the Hawthorne studies on the field of organizational behavior.
10. Two students in an organizational behavior (OB) class, Chris and Heather, have predicted that stu-

dents in their OB class who spend more time study-ing will receive higher grades. Chris and Heather plan to investigate their prediction. What are the independent and dependent variables in this situ-ation? What intervening and moderating variables should Chris and Heather anticipate?[39]

Case Study

Hanover Press

Hanover Press prints and binds books for a variety of publishers. Hanover uses high-quality paper and expensive book-covering materials. Each book order has unique characteristics, including a specific color and embossing pattern for the book-cover material. Hanover's manufacturing process, which is illustrated in Figure 2-6 consists of the following:

- Book-Cover Preparation Department. Based on customer specifications, each order requires the book covers to have a distinct color and embossing pattern. Book-cover material (a latex-impregnated fiber sheet) is colorized and embossed during this operation. Completed material is then transported to the Sizing Department.
- Sizing Department. Colored and embossed book-cover material is cut to required size using a high-speed machine and is then transported to the Bindery Department.
- Printing Department. Layout sheets are printed on a high-speed machine. A layout sheet contains multiple copies of each page of the book that is to be printed. Layout sheets enable the printer to arrange the maximum number of copies of one page in the book within a certain space. Completed copies are transported to the Cutting Department.

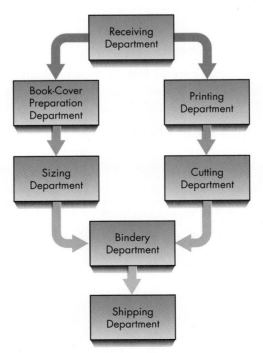

Figure 2-6
The Manufacturing Process at Hanover Press

- Cutting Department. Printed layout sheets containing multiple copies of each page are cut to the required size. (For example, one layout sheet may contain sixteen copies. Each copy may be cut to a 9 1/4 x 7-inch page.) Completed copies are transported to the Bindery Department.
- Bindery Department. Page copies of the book are arranged in order and bound with the required book-cover material. High-speed bindery machines are utilized in this department. Finished books are prepared and transported to the Shipping Department.

Serious productivity problems have developed on the day shift of the Printing Department. Plant Manager Jose Morales has asked Margaret Jackson, Hanover Press's personnel manager, to prepare a draft of a research study to determine the day shift Printing Department's productivity problem. Each department operates two shifts: A day shift (7 A.M. to 3 P.M.) and an afternoon shift (3 P.M. to 11 P.M.). Following is a copy of the proposed study received by Morales.

To: Jose Morales, Plant Manager

From: Margaret Jackson, Personnel Manager

Subject: Printing Department—Day Shift Productivity Problem

Here's my draft of the research problem.

Objective: To discover the causes of productivity differences between the day and afternoon shifts in the printing department. In particular:

1. Why is only the Printing Department affected?
2. Are there other symptoms, such as absenteeism, turnover, et cetera?
3. To what extent is waste a cause of the problem?
4. Is the cause one of differences in the source or quality of materials?
5. Is there something about the work force itself that accounts for the difference between shifts (skills, training, work attitudes, etc.)?
6. Are there differences in the way the printing machines are set up, repaired, serviced, et cetera, between the two shifts that might account for the differences?
7. Are there differences in supervision (level, style, etc.) that might account for the differences?

Please let me know if there is anything you want to add before we start gathering the data.

CASE STUDY QUESTION

1. Is Margaret Jackson's research proposal well defined? Explain.

Source: The context of Hanover Press developed by the text author, Daniel F. Jennings. Questions in Margaret Jackson's letter were adapted from John B. Kervin, *Methods for Business Research*, New York, HarperCollins, 1992, p. 48.

EXPERIENTIAL EXERCISE 1

Comparing Research Publications

In this exercise, (1) select an article from either the *Academy of Management Journal,* or *Administrative Science Quarterly,* and (2) select a second article from either the *California Management Review* or *Organizational Dynamics.*

Assignment

For each article:

1. Describe the author's major point and the research methodology used to develop this point.
2. How important is the major point you developed in question one for (a) an academic researcher, (b) a practicing manager, and (c) a student in an organizational behavior class.
3. Which article was the easiest to read? The easiest to comprehend?

EXPERIENTIAL EXERCISE 2

Developing a Research Project

For this exercise, first visit the manager of a local business and ask about an organizational problem that he or she faces. Discuss the possibilities for a research project. Is there a budget? Is there time? Is there someone who could gather the data?

Next, prepare a report for your instructor detailing the organizational problem and what data you recommend to be collected (see the Hanover Press case for an example of a proposed research project). Indicate to your instructor whether a budget exists and if someone is available to collect the data. Discuss any interest you might have in becoming involved in this research proposal.

Take It to the Net **You can find this chapter's World Wide Web exercise at:** http://www.prenhall.com/carrell

CHAPTER 3

Ethical Behavior

President Clinton, "Forty-something"

On January 20, 1993, William Jefferson Clinton was inaugurated President of the United States. At age forty-six, President Clinton is the third youngest person to occupy that office and more importantly, he is the first person from what is known as the "Baby Boomer" generation to be President of the United States. Albert Gore, Jr., age forty-four, was sworn in as Vice President of the United States on that same day. Clinton's selection of Gore as his running mate surprised many veteran political experts. Clinton and Gore, both of the same generation and both from the South, could hardly count on presenting to the electorate what has been traditionally viewed as essential to winning a "balanced" presidential ticket.

The message Clinton and Gore wanted to send to the voters, however, was that the Baby Boomer generation had come of age. The "blip" on America's population charts, which to a great extent has been driving the country's political, economic, and social agendas for the last twenty years, was ready to tackle its leadership.

In his Inaugural Address, Clinton stated his vision of America and in doing so crystallized many of the values of this Baby Boomer generation.

Today, a generation raised in the shadows of the Cold War assumes new responsibilities in a world warmed by the sunshine of freedom but threatened still by ancient hatreds and new plagues....We must do what no generation has had to do before. We must invest more in our own people, in their jobs and in their future....Let us resolve to make our government a place for what Franklin Roosevelt called "bold, persistent experimentation" a government for our tomorrows, not our yesterdays....I challenge a new generation of young Americans to a season of service—to act on your idealism by helping troubled children. . . . In serving, we recognize a simple but powerful truth: We need each other. And we must care for one another.

The values President Clinton expressed in his inaugural address—a commitment to change, a responsibility to others, and America as a bold experiment—are values commonly attributed to his generation of Americans.

In 1994, a Republican sweep of Congressional seats gave them a majority in both the U.S. House of Representatives and the U.S. Senate. The House majority resulted in the election of a Republican Speaker for the first time in forty years. At age fifty-one, Newt Gingrich joined President Clinton and Vice President Gore as another "baby boomer" coming to power.

Speaker Gingrich's election, however, was made possible by the influx of seventy-six new Republican members of the House, many in their thirties. These "baby busters," who entered the work force in the 1980's, represent a generation marked by pragmaticism, individualism, and an expectation of instant results.

It remains to be seen as these generations of Americans meet in the hallowed halls of our nation's capitol whether they can or even care to bridge the gap between them.

BUSINESS ETHICS

The values of elected leaders, as we can see from the example of President Clinton above, impacts the decisions being made, the priorities being set and the programs being implemented by government. Business is no different. The values held by the parties in the workplace will affect that organization. The philosophical study of the values and rules that humans live by is *ethics*.

In this chapter we will examine what role ethics plays in the workplace, both individual ethics and corporate ethics. In addition, we will examine the "work ethic" in place today in many businesses. These three aspects of *business ethics*—individual and corporate ethics, and the work ethic—influence how a business functions. They impact upon how a business perceives its role in society and how it fulfills that role. They give direction to employees and can decide, to a large extent, how well employees function within an organization. Business ethics, or the lack thereof, affects society at large and can have an immediate and critical impact, both good and bad, upon individuals' lives.

Business ethics Ethical behavior in the workplace that influences how a business functions, such as individual and corporate ethics.

Why the Focus on "Business Ethics" Now?

A major focus for business in the 1990s is a reassessment of the ethical behavior it requires of its work force and of itself. The causes for this focus are many. Figure 3-1 articulates some of the more common causes.

Certainly a primary cause for this renewed interest is the widely publicized breaches of ethical behavior evidenced in the 1980s by business and government leaders.

In the decade of the 1980s the American public was bombarded with reports of major white collar criminals. Ivan Boesky and Michael Milken engaged in insider trading to reap high, illegal rewards. Thousands of Savings and Loans

1. News coverage of glaring examples of unethical behavior in business and government affects employees.
2. There are more frequent opportunities for employee stealing because of a change from a manufacturing industry to a service industry.
3. The loss of "traditional" family life reduces the opportunity for parents to help children formulate ethical beliefs.
4. The service industry relies on quality customer service being provided by its employees.
5. Sophisticated employees will not accept dual standards in the workplace; one for them and one for managers.
6. A company cannot assume its employees will be loyal to it. Loyalty must be earned.
7. Developing an "ethical" framework for business is not as simple as drafting a "Code of Ethics." It will take the joint effort of employees and managers.

Source: Adapted from Alan Weiss, "Seven Reasons to Examine Workplace Ethics," *HR Magazine,* March 1991, pp. 69–74.

FIGURE 3-1

Causes for Renewed
Interest in
Business Ethics

Associations overextended their borrowing capacities and went bankrupt amid charges that S&L executives profited personally from risky loan deals. Leona Helmsley, a prominent and wealthy luxury hotel owner, went to prison for tax evasion. Members of the U.S. House of Representatives were vilified in the press and many of them lost reelection because of their in-house bank scandal where they bounced checks worth hundreds of thousands of dollars. And the U.S. Defense Department was rocked by reports of defense contractors charging exorbitant prices for nuts, bolts, and coffee machines.

Such overt unethical behavior among people in leadership positions rattled the foundations of the business and governmental communities. Confidence in the ethics of the government and business community hit rock bottom.

In a less dramatic way, unethical behavior of lower level employees in the 1980s began to have an effect on the "bottom line." As businesses downsized because of the downturn of the economy and began to compress management to reduce the layers of bureaucracy between workers and bosses, productivity of everyone on the job became critical to a business's survival. While the pilfering of goods from the workplace has long been a concern of businesses, more widespread stealing of "time" and "productivity" began to be felt in the 1980s. In order to compete in the global economy, American businesses had to be more efficient. Workers who moonlighted by running private businesses from their job site or who did not contribute a full effort at their workplace, caused a drain of resources from business. Few businesses could tolerate such losses.

Individual employee behavior became a critical business issue as more and more companies became service providers as opposed to manufacturers. The quality of the daily contact between employees and customers determined a business's ability to compete. A more sophisticated customer pool would not accept misleading information or substandard performance.

A more sophisticated work force also caused this renewed focus on ethical standards in the workplace. Managers could not say one thing and do another without creating an atmosphere in the workplace which fostered employee mistrust. If managers were going to be able to direct the work force toward a higher ethical standard, they were going to have to begin by improving their own behaviors. Management's failure to deal candidly with employees about downsizing and buy-outs caused employee mistrust and organizational disloyalty to increase. Businesses suffered from high employee turnover and the loss of skilled man-

Businesses need to remember the "customer is always right" to succeed in the highly competitive world market.

agers to competitors. Some of these desertions can be attributed to employees' observations that top-level management took care of themselves but did not take care of their employees.[1]

Certainly, for some businesses, increased criminal enforcement of illegal activity, like the new U.S. sentencing guidelines for federal criminals, caused a resurgence of interest in corporate ethics. Although many businesses might deny this, such sentencing guidelines may have caused companies to launch much needed ethical game plans within their organizations. Judge William W. Wilkins, Jr., chairman of the U.S. Sentencing Commission, predicted that a corporation with a comprehensive program for ethical behavior including a code of conduct, an ombudsman, a hotline, and mandatory training seminars for managers, would face more lenient treatment in the unfortunate event it faced criminal charges because of an employee's wrongdoing. He recognized that despite a corporation's best efforts all crimes cannot be prevented. Corporations who at least tried to prevent wrongdoing should benefit for their efforts.[2]

Historic View of Business Ethics

Interest in business ethics, however, is neither unusual nor novel. In fact, a brief look at history can reveal where some of our concepts of business ethics took shape.

Central to the development of people into societies was the interaction of human beings while providing the necessities of life: food, shelter, security. Through the march of history the progress of a people or of a nation was measured by its ability to provide for its members. The rules of behavior by individuals within any such people or nation formed the foundation for their ethical beliefs. Western ethical tradition, then, has much to do with the way we think about ethics in business even today.

ETHICS AND PROFIT   Prior to the emergence of Protestantism and capitalism in the sixteenth century in Europe, the Roman Catholic Church and the monarchy had provided the religious and economic base upon which Western societies relied. The monarchy provided for the people's physical needs through a feudal system which guaranteed a certain, albeit meager, standard of living. And the Roman Catholic Church provided a way of viewing that society as right and just. Trade, money-making and money lending were all held in the same high disregard and as largely immoral.[3]

The Protestant Reformation which coincided with the emergence of capitalism, made it possible for people to believe one could engage in trade and still be a moral person. In fact, prosperity in business was equated with goodness, for you could not succeed in such enterprises but for "God's blessing" upon you.

Settlement of the New World by those Europeans seeking religious freedom from the Catholic Church and political freedom from the monarchy, gave the United States a strong foundation in the Protestant, capitalist belief that *ethics and profits* could be linked. This expectation, therefore, is the foundation for what business ethics means in our society.

Glaring examples of when business failed to meet this expectation can be seen in the late nineteenth century era of the "Robber Barons." Jay Gould, John D. Rockefeller, J. P. Morgan, Cornelius Vanderbilt, and Edward H. Harriman built fortunes in ways many Americans felt were not only unethical, but illegal. Their activities undermined the basic capitalistic theory that competition in the marketplace will result in a fair price for a quality product. These industrialists formed monopolies that artificially reduced the price of goods until small independent businesses failed or then inflated the value of stocks so that they could profit from the stocks' sale before the prices crashed. These *"Robber Barons"* gave business a bad name and made "business ethics" sound like a joke.

Robber Barons Industrialists that formed monopolies to artificially reduce the price of goods or inflated the value of stocks to profit from their sales.

Such activities reinforced America's desire for ethical business practices. But at that juncture, the belief that business would or could control itself was replaced by a belief that ethical behavior had to be legislated. Government regulation of businesses largely began as an attempt to bring back the equation "ethics equal profitability."

PRIVATE GAIN AND THE PUBLIC GOOD   The basis for the belief that business has a responsibility to society also has its roots in the Protestant understanding of capitalism. Under the feudal system, wealth was inherited or acquired largely through conquest. Acquiring wealth through capitalism, in its purest sense, requires business to satisfy the customer's needs. Business offers to the consumer material items needed or wanted at a price the customer is able and willing to pay. Competition among businesses insured that the best offers at the lowest cost would prevail in the marketplace. Success and profit, therefore, came to those whose activities furthered the material well-being of society.[4]

Monopolies or stock manipulations can destroy that competition and leave business free to offer substandard products at higher costs. Business was seen as owing society better than that.

Adam Smith, in his book *The Wealth of Nations,* also blamed government intervention through regulating business practices for undermining the purest practice of capitalism. His perspective was that government regulation artificially favors one side or the other—business or consumer—and undermines the inherent leveler in the system, that of mutual satisfaction.[5]

It is through business supplying society what it wants that public good comes from private gain. And, as a control on business, private gain is dependent upon public good being realized.

SELF-INTEREST OR SELFISHNESS   Despite the sentiments expressed above regarding capitalism, ethics equal profits ("you can't succeed without God's blessing") and society benefits from capitalism, the morality of capitalism as an economic system has historically been questioned. Karl Marx's *Communist Manifesto* was a treatise that contended that the accumulation of wealth by the owners of businesses, the "capitalists," was at the expense of the laborers who produced the goods.[6] If selfishness is the motivation for a capitalist system, how can the *results* be moral? Or, are ethical businesses motivated by "enlightened self-interest?"

The goal of any business in a capitalistic society is to make money. This goal can be approached *selfishly* or the organization can operate from an "enlightened self-interest." Enlightened self-interest means that the organization truly appreciates all of the consequences of its corporate activities. Product, market, and personnel issues are analyzed and evaluated in light of the corporation's bottom line. Ethical concerns are included in that kind of analysis if a corporation is operating with self-interest in mind. When Johnson & Johnson voluntarily withdrew *all* Tylenol products off of the store shelves because of tampering which resulted in three deaths, its actions were hailed as heroic. With consumer confidence and admiration so high, Johnson & Johnson recovered and gained in market share when it resumed sales. Doing what is right *and therefore benefiting* is the kind of enlightened self-interest which motivates ethical business.

Business ethics is, in reality, not a new concern. However, recent well-publicized examples of wrongdoing, a change in the work force, and a need for corporate survival have led to a resurgence in interest in the ethical conduct of individuals within corporations, and in corporations themselves. The profile opposite from a Business Ethics professor crystallizes some of the more important points of this chapter.

INDIVIDUAL ETHICS

Throughout this chapter we will try to analyze what part ethics plays in the organization. We begin with the individual and will define ethics itself and suggest guidelines for individual ethical behavior. In addition, we will attempt to distinguish between ethics and values and ethical beliefs and behavior.

What Is Ethics?

Ethics The philosophical study of the values and rules that humans live by.

Ethics is the philosophical study of morality. It includes the study of the ultimate value of moral judgments, principles of conduct, and the qualities of human thought and actions known as values. There are three ethical theories which you will need to understand in order to apply the practical behaviors described later in this chapter: *ethics of purpose, ethics of principle,* and *ethics of consequence.*

Ethics of purpose demand that the means used and the ends achieved be a "good."

ETHICS OF PURPOSE   Aristotle, (384–322 B.C.) a Greek philosopher, based his explanation of ethics upon a "truth" that the inherent nature of human beings was "good."[7] In his view every endeavor of a human actor was aimed at a good. That is, no matter what the action, the goal was to achieve a "good" end. Aristotle acknowledged that a human being's ability to actually *know* what a good *end* was might be limited by his or her understanding. He also recognized that a person might "rationalize" a "bad" end as "good" in order to pursue that end. Nonetheless, Aristotle held that a human being's ultimate nature was to try to realize a truly *good* end. It is inconsistent with this essential nature of "good-

Profile

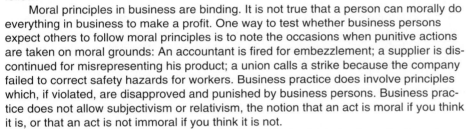

Melvin E. Greer
Professor of Philosophy, Chair of the Department of
Philosophy, University of Louisville

BUSINESS ETHICS, A CONTRADICTION IN TERMS?

Business ethics! That's a contradiction in terms!" is a typical response from my acquaintances when I tell them I teach a college course in business ethics.

When I first started the study and teaching of business ethics, comments like that struck me as amusing. Soon I decided these remarks reflect a basic, widespread misunderstanding about the nature of both business and ethics which I would like to clarify.

Business practice inherently involves many moral rules. "Do not cheat customers." "Do not treat employees inhumanely." "Do not fail to fulfill contractual obligations." In the study of business ethics, listing such moral principles that one finds in business is called *Descriptive Ethics.* Of course, such principles on such a list may be incomplete or inadequate. A search for the rules and principles that *ought to be followed* in business is called Normative Ethics, or Prescriptive Ethics. This is a rational attempt to give a complete, inclusive statement of moral rules and principles everyone is expected to follow.

Moral principles in business are binding. It is not true that a person can morally do everything in business to make a profit. One way to test whether business persons expect others to follow moral principles is to note the occasions when punitive actions are taken on moral grounds: An accountant is fired for embezzlement; a supplier is discontinued for misrepresenting his product; a union calls a strike because the company failed to correct safety hazards for workers. Business practice does involve principles which, if violated, are disapproved and punished by business persons. Business practice does not allow subjectivism or relativism, the notion that an act is moral if you think it is, or that an act is not immoral if you think it is not.

Scandals in business prove that unacceptable behavior in business is viewed as immoral. And business has produced its share of scandals. However, the horror and shock with which scandalous behavior is described indicates such actions are morally prohibited. Unfortunately, the casual reader too easily concludes that scandals in business indicate that business practice is inherently immoral. Those who use scandalous behavior as an occasion to do "business bashing" often ignore that some of the most severe critics of scandalous behavior are other business persons. Incidentally, it is easy to assume, but not to establish, that business is more prone to immorality than other areas. The briefest reflection will bring to mind scandals in the professions, religious institutions, politics, and (alas) education.

The existence of ethical standards in business does not require that everyone adopt a particular religion, metaphysics, or legal structure. Many people feel that ethics cannot be discussed outside of some such framework, usually their own. However, most of the problems of business ethics remain the same regardless of the ethical theory, religion, or legal framework in which they are considered. Business conduct usually involves transactions between people of many different religious persuasions. Hence, the ethics involved in business must be susceptible to a rational statement that thoughtful people in a wide variety of religious frameworks can understand. Also, though laws obviously embody moral principles and serve to set limits of acceptable behavior, laws cannot be viewed as the basis of ethics; otherwise, one would not be able to say that a particular law is immoral or give moral reasons for the passage of a new law.

Finally, unresolved dilemmas in business do not establish that there are no ethical standards. What the existence of unresolved problems does establish is that we do not have absolutely clear and universally accepted moral standards, nor do we have perfect ability to apply these standards to complicated issues. Unresolved dilemmas do not deny that there are many well-established moral principles; thoughtful, effective application of these principles can be made to most cases. The fact is, we must do the best we can with what we have to determine the best conduct and that is the difficult task of applied ethics.

Fortunately, most ethical disagreements in business can be resolved by brief, thoughtful consideration. And even the most difficult moral issues can be dealt with more adequately after thoughtful analysis.

---

ness" to use a "bad" means to achieve a good end result. Ethics of purpose, therefore, would demand that both the means used and the ends achieved be a "good." That good would be the realization of the inherent goodness of the human being.

Ethics of principle To apply a universal law of morality to all people and all circumstances.

ETHICS OF PRINCIPLE   Building upon Aristotle's theory, Immanuel Kant (1724–1804) a German philosopher, believed "reason" to be the building principle of human actions. He believed that each person had inherent worth—or goodness—and that clear reasoning would result in rules and principles to guide our actions toward each other. Such actions would respond to the belief that each person has worth and a duty was owed to each person to treat them as we wish to be treated ourselves. Kant moved from this point, where "I can understand how I should behave if I believe all people have value," to a rule for all people to adopt to treat everyone as valuable. Any other approach would be inconsistent and irrational. Therefore, Kant believed that reason dictates a universal law of morality applicable to all people and all circumstances. Humankind has arrived at these universally held beliefs of right and wrong through a belief in human dignity.

Ethics of consequence An action that benefits more people than it harms by requiring an estimation of the costs and benefits of alternative actions to result in the greatest happiness.

ETHICS OF CONSEQUENCE   John Stuart Mills (1806–73) an English philosopher and political economist, in his work *Utilitarianism* (1863), believed that the "result" of an action determined the morality of the action—not the purpose or the principle used. An action is "right" if it creates more happiness than unhappiness. On a pluralistic level, a "right" action benefits more people than it harms. Mills did warn that a "tyranny of the majority" had to be avoided. That, indeed, in the long term, the rights of the minority in a society had to be considered when making a moral choice because if they were harmed, the majority benefit could ultimately be threatened. Judging the morality of an act by its consequences does require an estimation of the costs and benefits of alternative actions and a clear understanding of the action which will result in the greatest happiness. Figure 3-2 briefly outlines the three areas of ethical thought.

Ethical Development

Individuals can exist in various levels of ethical development. The lowest stage is the one guided by absolutes. Laws are passed to prohibit certain behavior. If there is a law against a certain action, then the action is wrong. If there is no law on the particular action then the person has not done anything wrong. Codes of Ethics that detail every wrong action are the only effective tool for people at this level of ethical development.

The middle stage of ethical development occurs when a person recognizes that there are more wrongful actions than just those deemed illegal, but that anyone's judgment is as valid as anyone else's on what is wrong or right. A per-

Ethics of Purpose:	Aristotle:	Humans are inherently good. Therefore, humans will seek to do "good." Actions taken are good because a human is aiming toward a good end. Asks the question: "How can I reach my highest potential?"
Ethics of Principle:	Kant:	Humans are rational. Therefore, humans will see and appreciate the right way to do things. Rules can be formulated so that good results can happen. Asks the question: "How can I treat others like I wish to be treated?"
Ethics of Consequence:	Mills:	Results are what count. Therefore, the greatest happiness to the greatest number of people is a good. Each choice must be weighed to ensure the greatest good to the greatest number. Asks the question: "How can I do the greatest good or the least harm?"

Figure 3-2
Ethical Theories

son in this stage of ethical development does not accept the role of "ethical actor."

The final stage of ethical development is when a person becomes comfortable with his or her own beliefs and accepts responsibility for applying ethical standards to actions. Whether the approach involves ethics of purpose, principles, or consequences, or a combination of all three, at least a judgment based upon moral choices is undertaken.[8]

VALUES   The values upon which individuals base their ethical judgments are learned from parents, teachers, friends, siblings, and the society in which they live. All of these influences create in a person's mind the difference between right and wrong. "Right" behavior is rewarded and "wrong" behavior is punished. As children, right and wrong is taught in very simple terms: "This is clearly bad"; "that is clearly good." As we advance through the teen years, right and wrong behavior become more difficult to distinguish. There are, perhaps, things that are only wrong if carried to extreme. As adults, the line between right and wrong becomes even more difficult to find as they are called upon to make value judgments.

Even though a person's value system is formed through the unique influences on his or her life, similarities in types of value systems exist.

TYPES OF VALUES   Psychologists group categories of human values into six major types:

Theoretical. A person with a theoretical value system emphasizes the discovery of truth through reasoning.

Economics. A person with an economic value system emphasizes usefulness and practicality.

Aesthetic. A person with an aesthetic value system emphasizes form and harmony.

Social. A person with a social value system emphasizes people and love.

Political. A person with a political value system emphasizes the acquisition of power and influence.

Religious. A person with a religious value system emphasizes unity and the totality of the whole universe.

Most individuals have all of the categories of values as part of their value system but probably lean strongly toward one or another. The degree to which an individual internalizes the above listed value categories, however, may depend upon the kind of individual he or she is. Again, value systems are acquired through a person's interaction with others. This formulation may be tempered by the fact that he or she is:

Reactive. An individual who is unaware of himself as a human being, reacting only to basic physiological needs like a newborn baby, is reactive.

Tribalistic. An individual who is highly influenced by tradition and authority figures is considered tribalistic.

Egocentric. An egocentric individual is a rugged individual, responding primarily to power; he or she can be aggressive and selfish.

Manipulative. An individual who is materialistic, who seeks to achieve goals by using people, and who actively seeks status is manipulative.

Sociocentric. If an individual wants to be liked more than he or she wants to get ahead, he or she is called sociocentric.

Existential. An individual who has a high tolerance for ambiguity, a different value system, and who abhors inflexibility is called existential.

Later in the chapter we will discuss how "generational" value systems impact the workplace. A tribalistic individual, one who is highly influenced by tradition and authority figures, would probably display a political value system that emphasizes power and influence. Or a manipulative individual who is materialistic and seeks status might display an economic value system that is both practical and useful.[9]

Individual Ethical Behavior

The first place to examine business ethics is to examine the individual ethics of those in business. While companies can foster an atmosphere of ethical behavior within an organization, which we will examine later in this chapter, it is the individual who must perform and must understand how one is expected to perform. An interesting perspective of how ethical management can work in the workplace is in the "OB in Practice" opposite.

FIGURE 3-3
Spheres of Responsibility

SPHERES OF RESPONSIBILITY   Each person operates in multiple spheres of responsibility. For managers these spheres include: their private life; their roles as economic agents, company leaders, and as members of the larger society in which they operate. Figure 3-3 shows how those spheres interact.

Private Life.   The first sphere in which any manager operates is in his/her private life. Much of the morality in this sphere is intuitive, gained from a unique life experience. Values are based perhaps, on religious beliefs or ideals or examples from childhood. Basic values such as telling the truth, keeping one's word and shouldering one's share of the work are within this sphere. Individuals with

OB in Practice

The Power of Ethical Management

In a book, *The Power of Ethical Management,* Kenneth Blanchard and Norman Vincent Peale presented an alternate way for managers to view ethics in the workplace. They presented the five "P's" of ethical behavior as *purpose, pride, patience, persistence* and *perspective.*

Purpose is the objective or intention toward which you are striving. It is not the same as a goal. It is the reason underlying the goal.

Pride is the sense of satisfaction you get from your accomplishments as well as from those around you that you care about. This "p" requires self-esteem because you must like the picture you perceive as yourself.

Patience is the ability to face life with faith that things will work out, because faith in yourself means you can handle what does happen.

Persistence means not giving up. It is keeping your commitment to yourself and to others to live by your "purpose" in life.

Perspective is the last and central "p" in understanding the power of ethical management. Perspective is the ability to see *what is really important.* It means stepping back from the bustle of daily living to reflect upon the purpose of that living.

Source: Adapted from Kenneth Blanchard and Norman Vincent Peale, *The Power of Ethical Management,* New York, William Morrow and Company, Inc., 1988.

---

a strong sense of integrity and character in their private lives, carry those characteristics with them into the workplace.

Economic Agents. In the workplace, however, the individual is not only making decisions as an individual but has a role to play within the organization. In this role, the manager is responsible to the shareholders who have entrusted the work to them. As discussed earlier, the exercise of a manager's duty to increase the profit for the shareholder is consistent with ethical theories which see capitalism as promoting societal improvement.

Company Leaders. Within the corporate culture, managers play an ethical role within this sphere as company leaders. Many workplaces are minicommunities. Some employees spend more waking hours at the office than within any other social setting—family, neighborhood, or church. Managers have an obligation to exercise the power they have over their employees in a moral way. With their power comes a responsibility to respect the rights and dignity of the employees and other managers.

Societal. Having satisfied their ethical responsibilities to themselves, their shareholders, and their employees, managers must now look outside the organization and make sure they are responding to the last sphere of responsibility. This last sphere is the responsibility of managers to be aware of their impact upon the world outside of the organization. The company's interaction with government, labor unions, or consumers can affect hundreds or thousands of lives. How a manager views this corporate responsibility is of major importance.

QUESTIONS TO ASK   When faced with a moral dilemma, a manager may find that the four spheres of responsibility listed above seem to demand incompatible solutions. One approach to ethical dilemmas is to analyze the problem using the following questions addressing the ethics of purpose, principle, or consequence.[10]

Ethics of Purpose:	What can I do that is consistent with the basic values and goals of making the company all it can be?
Ethics of Principle:	Which alternative promotes the basic rights of all the parties?
Ethics of Consequences:	Which course of action will benefit the most people or harm the least?

ESTABLISH PERFORMANCE CRITERIA FOR ETHICAL DECISIONS   In order to foster the individual's commitment to ethical behavior in the workplace it is necessary to add such behavior to a manager's responsibilities and then measure the performance. Managers currently are accountable for a number of activities in the workplace: operational, functional, technical, and conceptional. At the *operational stage,* managers must be concerned with customer satisfaction, with improving the product and in conserving assets. At the *functional stage,* managers work to increase revenues, cut costs, and optimize returns. The manager must apply technology, utilize information, and involve people at the *technical stage.* And finally, at the *conceptional stage* a manager sets objectives, builds competence and gains a strategic advantage for the company.

An *ethical stage* can be added which requires managers to gain the commitment for the organization from employees, shareholders, and customers, insure cooperation among those groups, and create a community in the workplace. A key element to performance at this ethical stage would be the ability to distribute benefits and allocate harms among those parties in such a way that all consider the distribution fair, right, and just.[11] A manager, for example, may approach an upcoming budget cut by employing one of the three ethical theories explained above.

AN ISSUE-CONTINGENT MODEL   One approach to individual ethical decision making in the workplace might be found in an *issue-contingent* model. An individual's response to a moral issue can be influenced by a number of things *in addition* to his or her own value system. The nature of the moral issue, itself, will influence the actor. When Johnson & Johnson removed Tylenol from the grocery shelves, they were reacting to the very real possibility that someone else could die. This example serves well on another concern, "what is the urgency of the situation?" Johnson & Johnson could not know if they were already too late! An issue might be the probability that a particular outcome will be avoided or promoted by the decision. In the case of the poisoned Tylenol, the probability that a quick recall of the product would prevent another death was certainly high.

A person's moral decision is also influenced by his or her ability to affect the outcome of a situation. Many individuals who hold strong personal beliefs that would keep them from seeking an abortion, might not want to take a strong anti-abortion stand because of a belief that such third-party beliefs will have no influence on the outcome of another person's pregnancy. Finally, a person's decision making might be influenced by the lack of or availability of alternatives presented by the issue. One's tolerance for abortion might be influenced

The escalation of violence against doctors and workers at abortion clinics demonstrates the moral intensity of some issues.

by the availability of adoptions. Analysis of these influences can be called "moral intensity."

Moral decision making follows the following pattern: recognize the moral issue, make a moral judgment, establish a moral intent, and engage in moral behavior. Studies have found that issues of high moral intensity are more easily identified as moral issues. The high moral intensity of an issue can result in more attention being given to the moral judgment necessary to address the issue. Deciding to do something, establishing a moral intent, is also more likely if the moral intensity of the issue is high. And finally, actual moral behavior is more frequent where issues of high moral intensity are involved.[12]

How to Recognize an Unethical Company

As stated above, regardless of which approach one might want to take to behave in an ethical manner, the important thing is the effort. Ethical analysis is not a haphazard procedure but a systematic process of reasoning about an actual or potential moral issue. Individuals who wish to be a part of an ethical company have to be aware of the firm's ethical character.

Job seekers can be as aware of the ethical character of a potential employer as they can of its economic health. For example, if the firm emphasizes short-term revenues over long-term results, it may be creating an unethical atmosphere. If a firm links its ethical behavior to a code of ethics but will not address the complexity of ethical dilemmas, then the code may merely be window dressing. Vanguard organizations approach establishing a Code of Ethics as more than adopting a document. The Norton Company of Worcester, for example, created a board-level committee to monitor the ethical behavior of the organization. Ethics training programs in corporations such as Boeing, General Mills, and Johnson & Johnson demonstrate a commitment to ethics in the workplace.[13]

A firm that encourages unethical behavior or discourages ethical behavior because of the financial implications will not be where you want to work. Eth-

Figure 3-4
A Dozen Ways to Spot an
Unethical Organization

1. It emphasizes short-term profits over long-term considerations.
2. It routinely violates or ignores established professional codes of ethics.
3. It looks for simple solutions to ethical problems.
4. It is unwilling to take an ethical stand if it means a financial loss.
5. It creates an environment that encourages unethical behavior by its employees.
6. It sends ethical problems to the law department.
7. It views ethics as a public relations issue.
8. It treats its employees different than its customers.
9. It has unfair or arbitrary performance appraisal standards.
10. It lacks guidelines to use as a reference for handling ethical problems.
11. It provides no internal whistle-blowing mechanism.
12. It encourages employees to leave their personal ethics at home.

Source: Adapted from Robert Allan Cooke, "Danger Signs of Unethical Behavior: How to Determine If Your Firm Is at Ethical Risk," *Journal of Business Ethics* 10, 1991, pp. 249–253.

ical problems are not legal problems. A firm that fails to realize that distinction is at risk; as is one who only sees ethical problems as a public relations issue.

The treatment of employees can indicate the ethical nature of an organization. If employees are not treated as well as customers or if performance-appraisal standards are unfair or arbitrary, the company may be unethical. Additionally, an absence of procedures for handling ethical issues, or the lack of a whistle-blowing mechanism, or even the lack of basic communication avenues between employees and managers can indicate a firm that is ethically at risk. Finally, an organization that fails to recognize its obligations to the public as well as to its shareholders, and one that expects you to leave your private ethics at home, is an organization at risk for unethical behavior.[14] Figure 3-4 gives warning signals for an employee to recognize an unethical organization.

CORPORATE ETHICS

Just as each individual has a value system which determines ones ethical behavior, a corporation or business has a value system which will determine its ethical behavior. Individual wrongdoing in the 1980s drew attention to the lack of ethical behavior in some organizations. Numerous incidents of corporate wrongdoing, also focused attention on the lack of ethical behavior in much of the business world. The Valdez oil spill challenged corporations to take responsibility for their use, or misuse, of the earth's resources. The relocation of manufacturers from the United States to Third-World nations where the cost of labor was so low, raised issues of exploitation that were uncomfortable for many enterprises. And the scandal which erupted in 1982 when it was learned that Beechnut's "apple juice" in fact contained no apple juice but simply beet sugar, corn syrup, and artificial ingredients rightfully embarrassed Beechnut and greatly reduced its profits.[15] While some might argue that the individuals who actually made the decisions that resulted in the above unethical examples were responsible, not the corporations, it is clear that a corporation does foster a common value system within itself and often the individuals' decisions are a result of those corporate values. If unethical behavior is the result—one might look for the cause within the corporate's ethical behavior.

Ethical Development

Corporations, like individuals, can exist in various stages of ethical development. The lowest level of corporate ethical development is one in which illegal actions are the only corporate concern. As long as no law is broken, the corporation is free to act as it pleases. This can be referred to as the "do no evil" level.

The second level of corporate ethical development is one in which a Code of Ethics exists but only receives lip service from the corporation. The daily message sent and received is that the Code is there for guidance but that the corporation's bottom line can and does tolerate any number of unethical behaviors. Indeed, decisions are made in a vacuum, considering only the short-term benefits associated with the immediate action.

The third level of ethical behavior for a corporation is one in which ethical decision making is comprehensively integrated into corporate decision making. In these corporations, the rightness of a course of action must include an analysis based upon ethical concern. Using the ethical theories explained earlier in this chapter, the corporation must internalize ethical reasoning as part of its daily operations. That is, its decisions must promote the ultimate realization of the corporation as it should be (ethics of purpose); or it must adhere to basic rules of conduct founded upon the dignity of individuals (ethics of principle), or it must make decisions which do the most good and the least harm (ethics of consequences). This third level of ethical behavior can be called "being a moral actor." A corporation cannot reach this third level of ethical behavior without an understanding of why it should be a moral actor and techniques to make it happen.

Why Corporations Need to Demonstrate Ethics

A corporation exists within society and makes daily decisions that impact more on others than itself. Because of this, it must recognize all the results of its actions on others and be able to predict how such results threaten or further its existence. Becoming a "moral actor," is therefore a fundamental issue of survival for the corporation. Just as society does not exist without a value system that allows for basic social cooperation and stability, a corporation cannot exist if it fosters non-cooperation and chaos. In the "OB in Practice," "A New Order," one company tries to incorporate its ethical outlook to every aspect of its business.

Let us examine the parties at risk of corporate actions and see why a corporation must be a moral actor. Figure 3-5 gives a brief outline of these parties and how they are affected.

Shareholders and owners, as well as lenders and creditors, are the first and primary groups who can, and do, benefit from the actions of the corporation.

1. Shareholders and Owners	Understanding that self-interest demands ethical behavior.
2. Managers	Decisions based on long-term goals instead of short-term profits.
3. Employees	Loyalty to the organization fostered by an ethical workplace.
4. The Corporation	Must be a moral actor if it expects to survive.
5. Society	The beneficiary of an organization's ethical behavior.
6. Government	Passes regulations that can determine legality not unethical behavior.

Figure 3-5
Corporate Groups Affected by Ethical Decisions

A New Order

How far can an organization go in its ethical behavior and still remain viable? Traidcraft Plc., a publicly owned trading company in England, is trying to find out. Traidcraft is guided by the following unique mission statement:

> Traidcraft aims to expand and establish more just trading systems, which will express the principles of love and justice fundamental to the Christian faith. Practical service and a partnership for change will characterize the organization which puts people before profit.

Traidcraft, Plc., does not aim at maximizing returns to investors or in generating wealth for altruistic or charitable purposes. The company's mission statement represents its corporate goal of changing society by the way it does business.

Traidcraft's business is in selling craft products from Third-World countries to developed countries. Its founders wanted to address the injustices existing in the established structures and practices that resulted in enormous inequalities between those supplying the products and those buying the products. They did not want to work through a charitable organization but wanted to establish a viable business to prove that all parties to the business transaction had to be considered.

In developing its purchasing procedures, its mission statement, and its goals and objectives, Traidcraft considered all of its shareholders: the creditors, the employees, the managers, the consumers and the suppliers. The success of Traidcraft can be seen in its growth. From 1984 when its turnover was at two million pounds to 1989 when it reached 5.4 million pounds.

Traidcraft demonstrates that recognizing and addressing the needs of all stockholders in a business enterprise can spell success for an ethical business.

Source: Adapted from Richard Evans, "Business Ethics and Change in Society," *Journal of Business Ethics* 10, 1991, pp. 871–876.

After all, the primary reason for the corporation is the creation of a profit for this group. As seen in an earlier section tracing the historic role of ethical considerations in business, capitalists justify the capitalist system by grounding it in an ethical base. Deriving profit from an enterprise is dependent upon God's blessing. Only goodness can be rewarded in such a way. If a corporation acts in such a way as to threaten its continued existence and profitability, shareholders, and owners are harmed. Only by seeking to fulfill the ultimate essence of the corporation (ethics of purpose), or following well-established principles of behavior (ethics of principles), or doing the most good and the least harm (ethics of consequence) can a corporation protect the shareholders and owners' interests.

Employees are dependent upon the corporation for their continued employment and, therefore, for their financial well-being. Some writers suggest that as workers can spend up to 30 percent of their waking hours at work, the corporation may be a substitute for the family, the church, and other segments of society as the support needed to maintain a moral life.[16] The responsibility upon the corporation to foster a high ethical level of behavior for its employees stems from its need to hire employees with values. Employee disloyalty causes theft of time, productivity, and goods and leads to high rates of employee turnover.

Managers, as seen in the above section, need to act in recognition of the spheres of responsibilities that exist—self, shareholders, employees, and society. A corporation cannot expect moral actors at the management level without a corporate culture assuming itself of moral character as well. Without such guidance, managers will not be able to justify action upon the long term health of a corporation instead of simply short-term profit.

Society, representing both the consumer and the community-at-large, must also be served by the corporation, if the corporation is to survive. Sophisticated consumers will not accept shady behavior or substandard products from a corporation. An aware community places responsibility on the corporation for its actions when problems develop. In the face of litigation and/or consumer boycotts, when corporations fail to act in a morally responsible way, society demands that corporations become moral actors. Capitalism is based upon the law of supply and demand and, through competition, a business contributes to the positive furtherance of humanity. Therefore, a necessary exercise is an analysis of how society fares when a corporation acts.

The Corporation, itself, inclusive of all of its interests, will benefit from being a moral actor because "enlightened self-interest" will be substituted for selfishness. When a capitalistic organization that relies solely on satisfying interests, becomes myopic and acts only in selfishness, it becomes destructive. Beechnut learned the hard way when it decided to mislabel a product as "apple juice" when it was not. Its decision was largely based upon a short-term profit from savings it realized by buying the counterfeit product. When society learned of the deception, Beechnut's sales dropped from a 1986 level of $143 million to a 1987 level of $10.8 million—a loss of 90 percent of its business.[17]

Corporations must accept that ethical behavior is not a threat to their profits if they are to become moral actors. Recent research would indicate that, in fact, adopting ethical practices is more beneficial rather than detrimental to corporations. Cadbury-Schweppes, Atlantic Richfield, Motorola, Northern Chemical Company, and Apple Computers were profiled as "high ethics-high profit" organizations characterized by an obsession with fairness and a commitment to their social environment.[18]

In addition, corporations need to realize that a socially responsible corporation can identify opportunities for growth and minimize threats to its survival by its response to ethical issues. James Burke, CEO of Johnson & Johnson, voluntarily withdrew all bottles of Tylenol from store shelves in response to three deaths attributed to poisoned capsules. When the poison scare was over, Tylenol actually gained market share.[19]

Finally, corporations cannot become moral agents until they realize that government regulation of business alone will not result in ethical behavior. Government action through laws and regulations are after the fact enforcement of what society has determined is illegal. Immorality may still be a part of the corporate culture and yet no laws are violated.[20]

How Corporations Institutionalize Ethical Behavior

ESTABLISH THE VALUE   First and foremost in any corporation's attempt to institutionalize ethical behavior is to establish ethical considerations as a corporate value. A corporation's mission statement often details its goal of providing the highest quality product at the least cost. It recognizes its commitment to all the stockholders—owners, employees, customers, and community. In addition, it needs to add a commitment to an ethical standard. One company, Penney's, includes such a standard in its corporate policy. The question it asks itself when taking any action is: "Does it square with what is right and just?" (Ethics of Principle). The Security Pacific Corporation demonstrates a corporate credo that seeks to make the corporation reach its ultimate essence by recognizing a commitment to all of its stockholders (Ethics of Purpose). And, finally, Northrup created a list of core values that seems to rely on the end result in demonstrating an ethical goal, including ". . . to demonstrate integrity in all we do . . ." (Ethics of Consequence).[21]

COMMUNICATE THE VALUE   A corporation must communicate its commitment to ethical values to employees and external shareholders. Codes of Conduct or Ethics can be adopted. Distribution of such codes should not stop with managers; consequently, all employees should be apprised of the corporate code of behavior. Communication cannot be limited to distribution, however, because actions speak louder than words.[22] The organization is able to foster employee commitment to the corporate goal of ethical behavior in the same way that the corporation fosters employee commitment to its other goals.

An employee has a commitment to an organization in direct relationship to that employee's involvement with the organization. A corporation can influence that commitment by making sure adherence to the ethical goal is rewarded with *visibility*; being explicit in its expectations regarding ethical or unethical behavior; making clear that ethical or unethical actions result in *irreversible* results, consistent punishment, or rewards; and finally, that employees take actions of their own *volition* to act ethically or unethically and be responsible for the outcome.[23]

Visibility A corporation is explicit in its expectations regarding ethical or unethical actions.

SELECT AND TRAIN EMPLOYEES WITH ETHICAL BEHAVIOR IN MIND   Corporations can, during their recruitment process, include in their criteria the principles they look for in a manager as a moral actor. Several methods can be used to elicit this kind of information: honesty tests, background checks, along with a signed commitment by the person to the Corporate Code of Ethics. Pizza Hut, Inc.'s president Steven S. Reinemund looks for *integrity* when hiring or promoting employees for

Integrity An internal allegiance to excellence, honesty, and a sense of teamwork to achieve long-term goals and short-term profits.

Steven Reinemund, President of Pizza Hut, Inc., values integrity in his employees.

his organization. Integrity as he defines it includes an internal allegiance to excellence, honesty, a sense of teamwork, and a balanced perspective on long-term goals and short-term profits.[24]

Early in the employment process, a psychological contract is formed between the employer and employee. Psychological contracts typically cover the inducements of the employer and the contributions of the employee. The degree to which both parties satisfy the expectations established by this contract affects the success of the relationship. It is important for employers and employees to understand the ethical expectations of the psychological contract as well. If the two do not or cannot agree on this aspect, then the relationship will suffer.

Because ethical behavior cannot be reduced to simple "do's" and "don'ts," there is an ever-changing expectation on the two parties and thus there must be opportunity and structure to address an evolving set of expectations.

Training employees to make an ethical analysis as part of their decision making is critical. Training can be formal, focused on the corporation's goals and objectives and on techniques of decision making. One such technique for group decision making follows this section. Training can also be achieved through the normal socialization of a new employee. If the employer is operating within an ethical organization then the role models he or she emulates will exhibit the proper ethical behavior. The system of rewards and punishment will confirm and reinforce ethical behavior. In "OB in Practice," "The Ethics Game," one company takes ethical training to a new level.

Ethical Group Decision Making

For a corporate culture to foster ethical behavior, the culture must develop and use ethical analysis in its decision making. Few, if any, corporate decisions are made by one individual alone. Therefore, it is necessary to develop some ideas on how group decision making can include ethical reflection.

One model designed by Marvin T. Brown includes five elements to the decision-making process:

Policy Proposal. This is the "what" we want to do. The "what" should be an answer to a question which states the problem. For example, "What can we do about rising health care insurance premiums for employees?" A policy proposal might be: The company should pay the cost of a health care insurance premium as an employee benefit. As the group is presented with the problem and this suggested solution the group decision-making process begins.

Observations. The group will need to share what it knows about the problem. In this example, that would be the actual costs of health care insurance premiums and the ability of the company to pay for them. In addition the group needs to know what the employees might have to give up in exchange for the coverage. Getting your facts straight in this stage of the process is very important.

Value Judgment. Next, the group will begin to evaluate the facts and the proposal based upon its value system. Individuals in the group might not have the same values in judgment. For example, one person in the group might think health care insurance coverage should be paid for as a basic employee benefit even if it means foregoing a cost-of-living pay raise. Another might prefer the cost-of-living increase. They differ on how they value the health care coverage.

OB in Practice

The Ethics Game

Citicorp has embarked upon a unique way to communicate its corporate ethics to its 90,000 employees worldwide. In 1987, it launched as part of its employee training, "The Work Ethic"—a board and card game that presents the players ethical dilemmas they have to solve.

Although Citicorp had for many years shared its ethic policies with employees through speeches, training sessions, and distributing an ethic standards policy book, it wanted to do more. The theory behind the game is that ethical decision making is more complicated than just knowing rules and following policies. Ethical decisions involve recognizing and weighing competing interests and insights as well as differing values encountered in the workplace.

The game divides players into four levels: entry-level, supervisor, manager, or senior manager. Teams are presented with ethical dilemmas to solve and win or lose points depending upon the solutions they pick. The four levels of employment are weighted differently to emphasize that consequences from decisions made at a higher level in the organization are greater. The game presents four less than perfect solutions to each ethical dilemma. The players cannot change or adjust the problem or the solution, they just have to decide. The answer that reflects the ethical values of the Citicorp organization is given the highest number of points.

As a test or control on the organization itself, however, the game includes a right to appeal an answer. An appeals board of senior managers is made available to the training session in which the game is being used to listen to employees who disagree with the game's chosen answer. The appeals process reinforces the commitment of management to ethical decision making.

Source: Adapted from Karin Ireland, "The Ethics Game," *Personnel Journal*, March 1991, pp. 72–74.

Assumptions. To a great extent the values we have come from some basic assumptions which we count on as being true. In the above example, the one person who values the health care insurance coverage being paid by the employer might assume that the cost-of-living raise could not buy that same amount of health coverage. Whereas, the other person may assume she or he will never need the coverage because she or he has a working spouse whose company provides health benefits for the entire family.

Opposing Views. The last element in the decision-making process is expressing opposing views. This is not done as a confrontational idea, but as a way for the group to investigate and validate the four elements above. By presenting a "loyal opposition," the group process is able to uncover where a disagreement really exists. If the disagreement stems from different assumptions, the parties might find ways to reconcile the assumptions. Exploring different value judgments may not *cause* agreement but it can at least narrow the areas of disagreement.

In order to assure oneself that the elements of decision making are being adequately analyzed, the following criteria is used.

Observations. The facts we use to express our observations must be true or false. Half-truths are not enough. Intellectual honesty requires that all the facts be presented so that the group has the benefit of all the facts before proceeding.

Value Judgments. Value judgments should be humane and practical. If they are, they make sense to us and we can accept them within the context of the group discussion.

Assumptions. The criterion applied to test assumptions is: Are they responsive or irresponsive to the policy being considered, in light of the observations made and in furtherance of the value judgment of the group?

Policy Proposal. Finally, the criterion on which we judge a policy proposal is whether the proposal is right or wrong. If the observations are true, the value judgments humane and practical, and the assumptions responsive, then the policy proposal will meet the criteria.

The decision-making model is shown in Figure 3-6.

This model can be used with any of the three ethical theories explained above: ethics of purpose, ethics of principle or ethics of consequence. The value judgment which would be made in each instance would be as follows:

Ethics of purpose:	Because it promotes our highest corporate purpose
Ethics of principle:	Because it supports a universal rule, recognizing the inherent worth of people
Ethics of Consequences:	Because it does the most good for the most people

A similar approach for developing ethical analysis within the corporate decision-making process was designed for trainers to incorporate into ethics train-

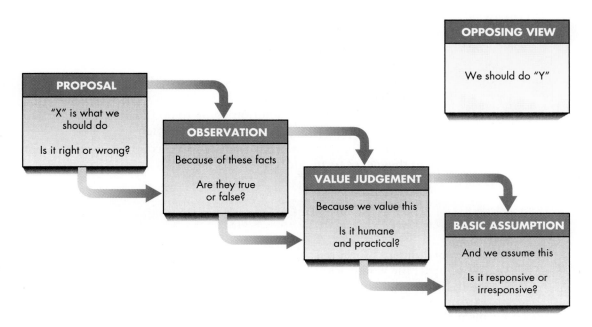

Figure 3-6 Ethical Group Decision Making

Source: Adapted from Marvin T. Brown, *Working Ethics Strategies for Decision-making and Organizational Responsibility,* San Francisco, Calif., Jossey-Bass Publishers, 1990.

FIGURE 3-7
Training Ethical
Decision Makers

Step 1	Individual solution to problem
Step 2	Group consensus, three or four people
Step 3	Large groups, consensus building
Step 4	Test solutions against ethical questions
Step 5	Test solutions against ethical theories

ing courses.[25] The participants are presented with a business dilemma and are directed through the following steps, as set out in Figure 3-7.

1. Each individual is asked to write down his or her own solution to the business dilemma. This forces an individual to examine his or her own ideas. If the individual believed that a business decision, such as, how to lay off employees, is only a financial decision, seeing it as an ethical decision is quite a challenge.

2. The participants meet in groups of three or four to share their individual answers and reach a *consensus* on a solution. Each participant, by defending his or her own original solution, is forced to test its viability. By listening to other members of the group, one is presented with alternative ways of looking at the problem.

3. All of the solutions reached by the small groups are shared with all participants and the large group is charged with, again, reaching a consensus.

4. In order to reach a consensus, each solution must be measured against the following questions:

    Will the action help more people than it will harm?

    How can those harmed recover from the harm?

    Is this a win-lose solution?

    What values does this solution honor?

    What values does this solution dishonor?

5. Having reached a consensus, the group discusses the solution in relationship to ethical theories.

    Ethics of purpose: Is the solution going to move the corporation ahead towards reaching its potential, recognizing all of the stockholders at risk?

    Ethics of consequence: Is the solution going to do the most good for the most people and the least harm to the most people?

    Ethics of principle: Is the solution one which treats others as an end and not as the means to an end?

Consensus A group of people who share their answers in order to reach a solution to a problem.

THE WORK ETHIC

A totally different aspect of ethical behavior is how the employees' value systems impact the workplace. This issue is not concerned with ethical or unethical decisions, but with behaviors that represent a particular value system. As explained earlier in the chapter, ethics is a philosophical study of rational people making choices. Values are the learned convictions against which we judge the choices made.

Our values have a lot to do with our work. They determine what work we are willing to do and for whom. These values determine the commitments we are willing to make to the organizations, our loyalties, our expectations, and what boundaries we will not cross. They might determine how well we do our job and whether we can or will be cooperative in the workplace. One's basic orientation toward work and its place in one's life is a person's *work ethic*. Just as we learn values from our families, our teachers, our friends, and the society in which we live, the way we value work is shaped during our childhood and adolescence. And while each person's life experiences are unique, the society in which we socialize creates a certain climate or context for those individual experiences.

Work ethic A value system of a work force that helps an employee decide where to work, how to approach work, and how to work together.

At the beginning of the chapter we profiled the inauguration of President Bill Clinton as a significant event affecting values in American society. Through research over the last fifty years, themes in the kinds of values Americans hold have been observed. These themes represent generational differences in values which affect the way workers relate to each other, their bosses, and the organization. These themes show a "work ethic" which differs along generational lines.

We will discuss each age group first and then examine how they act, react, and interact in the workplace.

Generational Values

ENTERING THE WORK FORCE—**1940s TO MID 1960s**   Post–World War II American workers were characterized by a desire to become part of the middle class. Many Americans from rural backgrounds were exposed to Europe, Asia, and Africa as soldiers and returned to the United States where a college education was available under the GI bill. This offered them the opportunity not to return to the farms. Women who had held jobs for the "men at war" realized that hard work and sacrifice would lead to success. Home ownership, automobiles, and keeping up with the "Jones's" motivated a whole generation of Americans who, at the end of this era, could point to a country leading the world in technology, business and industry. By this time, 70 percent of Americans were legitimately "middle class."

Referring back to our earlier section on values, Americans in this generation could be characterized as "tribalistic" and "conforming." They certainly personified the Puritan Work Ethic—hardworking, conservative, and loyal to the organization. This age group produced children in large numbers in what is now known as the "baby boom."

ENTERING THE WORK FORCE—**MID 1960s TO LATE 1970s**   The Baby Boomers began entering the work force in the mid 1960s. This period was characterized by a shift in attention from an economic agenda to a social agenda. The success of the previous era gave society the luxury of examining priorities. Economic success was assumed, so the 30 percent of the population that had not made it into the "middle class" became more visible and vocal. Self-denial, which had been so necessary for success, became passé. Personal comfort, expression, growth, and fulfillment became the dominant themes of the era. These Americans could be characterized as "sociocentric" and "existential." In their work life they were nonconforming and autonomous; loyal to themselves, not the corporation; and concerned with the quality of their life not necessarily the quality of the product produced.

By the end of this era, the bubble which started with the "flower child" burst. Baby boomers at the end of this era looked back on a country which had set a social agenda it was unable to achieve. The war on poverty, the war in Vietnam, and the war on inflation had all been lost. America's place in the world, both economically and politically was no longer number one. Childbirth during this era was down significantly and the Baby Boomers' children make up the bulk of the work force for the year 2000 and represent the smallest pool of entry-level workers in modern times.[26]

ENTERING THE WORK FORCE—**1980 TO 2000**   In the early 1980s the first of this generation, the "Baby Busters," began entering the work force. This era is marked by pragmatism. Self-denial is not necessary and self-fulfillment is passé. "To achieve" means being *better* than the next person. Competitiveness has become this generation's passion. "Just do it," is its slogan. Rejecting the "I want to have it all" notions of the baby boomers, this group is concerned that there isn't anything valuable remaining for them. Their focus is in getting theirs and getting it quickly.[27] They are impatient, wanting to reach the top immediately but resenting the work necessary. They are challenged by a search for identity and social content. As the baby boomers continue to dominate American society because of sheer numbers, the "Baby Busters" cannot find a unifying theme unless it is "why bother?" If they share a characteristic it would be "manipulative," striving to achieve goals by manipulating things and people. They are success oriented, ambitious, and loyal to their own career goals. In "OB in Practice," "Twenty-something Workers Need Special Training," a training program designed to help employers address this generation of workers is explored.

The chart in Figure 3-8 combines characteristics of these three generational groups from a number of sources.

FIGURE 3-8   Generational Characteristics

Entered the Work Force	Work Values	Personal Values	Historic Tradition Values
1940s & 1950s Puritan Work Ethic Ages 60–80 in 1990	Hard work; loyal to organization; respect authority figures; seniority should be rewarded; conformity is important; team work	Conservative; law and order oriented; ethics of principles (rules); strong family allegiance, self-sacrificing	Destiny; economic growth thru materials; individual rights oriented; conservative; self-critical realism of what needs to be done; decrease pluralism/diversity; private interest
1960s & 1970s Baby Boomers Ages 40–60 in 1990	Nonconforming; loyal to self; stress quality life; challenges authority; prefer rewards based on performance rather than seniority	Liberal; altruistic; humanistic; ethics of purpose; prefer being liked to getting ahead; self-fulfillment often meant severing the family ties; expanded definition of "family" to include society	Experimental; social fix-it; social and political innovation; increased pluralism and diversity; ideal-oriented; messianic; "what might be"; public purpose
1980s & 1990s Baby Busters Ages 20–40 in 1990	Driven to succeed; ambitious; loyal to career; pragmatic; see rewards that they should get, but recognize might not	Pseudo-conservative; competitive; ethics of consequences; manipulative; looking for a vision; returning to nuclear family	Destiny; economic growth thru materials; individual rights oriented; conservative; self-critical realism; decrease pluralism

Source: Adapted from Lawrence J. Bradford and Claire Raines, *Twenty Something: Managing and Motivating Today's New Work Force*, New York, Master Media Ltd., 1992, p. 38; and David Kolb, Irwin Ruben, and Joyce Osland, *The Organizational Behavior Reader*, 5th ed., New Jersey Prentice Hall, Inc., 1991, pp. 2–8.

OB in Practice

Twenty-something Workers Need Special Training

In a workshop designed as part of a "Managing Diversity Series," Innovative Management Concepts has included a "Bridging the Age Gap" module to address not only older workers' needs, but the needs of the "twenty-something" worker.

This training is designed to help companies compete in the "Work force 2000" competition for able workers. Companies are advised to rethink how they are attracting, retaining, and training employees.

For the teen employee, the trainer suggests that the participants revisit their first job to refresh their memories on how that job fit among the other priorities of school, dating, sports, and friendships. The training further suggests that employers can use the daily influences of a teen's life—school, parents, peers—to motivate teen employees. Honor roll programs, scholarship opportunities, or mentor programs can give teens opportunities after the employment that attracts them to a business.

For the "Twenty-something" generation, the training suggests that issues of prime importance to these workers include employee participation, training opportunities, job variety, and employee orientation. All four of these initiatives increase the possibility that the "Twenty-something" employee will make a commitment to the organization.

Source: Adapted from Catherine D. Fyock, "Bridging the Age Gap: Meeting the Challenge of Intergenerational Communications in the Workplace, Module IV of the Managing Diversity Series, Innovative Management Concepts, P.O. Box 905, Prospect, KY 40059, 1992.

Effect on the Workplace

Historians often debate whether human history is a progression or an ever-repeating cycle. Does humankind move from ignorance to knowledge, from cruelty to tolerance, from slavery to freedom, so that every day moves us toward a better human condition? Or is history a repeating story where human folly allows for the same mistakes to end in the same destruction? Where humankind's ability to understand history has no influence on our actions throughout history?

Arthur Schlesinger, Jr., in his book, *The Cycles of American History* (1986), saw American history as alternating between two traditions. One tradition was an America which saw itself as an experiment. The other saw itself *fulfilling a destiny*. In the experiment tradition, Americans see themselves as bold and innovative, striving to pull America forward. There is a public purpose, social fix-it attitude characteristic of the Baby Boomers category as shown in Figure 3-8. In the destiny tradition, Americans see themselves as fulfilling a destiny, as an example to how things should be. There is a private interest, economic growth attitude characteristic of both the "Protestant Work Ethic" and the "Baby Busters" categories as shown in Figure 3-8.

These value themes of work, personal, and historic tradition for the three major generations in the American work force influence the organizations in which they work. As stated earlier, values influence a worker's decision to join and stay with an organization. After joining an organization, values will affect how the person does the job and what effort or talents are used. Finally, because people of different generations interact in the workplace, different values can cause disruption and conflict. The profile opposite from a "Baby Buster" distills some of the competing values faced in the workplace.

CHOOSING WHERE TO WORK   Generational differences in work values impact not only where people choose to work but also how long they stay with an organization. Members of the Protestant Work Ethic generation became part of, and identified with, the organization they joined. Seniority, job security, steady wage increases, rising through the ranks resulted from and reinforced this group's loyalty to their organizations.

But as Baby Boomers came to the job scene, the quality of life-of-work became a more important reason to stay with the organization—more important even than job security or financial incentives. Workers felt that working with people who respected them and who listened to their opinions were high on the "important qualities for the job" list. Careers were important but making a difference was more important.[28]

Recent surveys of Baby Busters produce a different picture.[29] Work must be interesting, a challenge to the person's skills and abilities. Like the video games upon which they were weaned, work should be fun in a competitive sort of way. Staying in one organization is not as important as advancement.

As we will see in later chapters, part of the challenge for organizations at the turn of the century is to attract and keep good employees. Because the Baby Busters generation is a small group relative to previous work force groups (especially Baby Boomers), there will not be enough of them to go around. It will be necessary for employers to recognize this group's value system and decide how to structure the workplace so that these values are met.[30]

As the members of the Protestant Work Ethic generation retire, the Baby Boomers are transforming the traditional workplace so that individuals are able to exercise authority and take responsibility for their actions. Valuing each individual within the organization for what they can contribute has led to quality circles and other forms of participatory management.[31]

CHOOSING HOW TO WORK   In a recent survey in which 150 human resource managers across the country were asked the most important factor they considered when hiring *after* the basic skills needed to do a job, 59 percent said "work ethic."[32] The commitment a person makes to an organization is in direct relationship to how much one identifies with it. The more one shares the organization's values, the harder one works to further those values.

The members of the Protestant Work Ethic generation shared the values of economic growth and U.S. superiority in industry and technology with the organizations for which they labored. Their loyalty to those organizations demonstrated how that shared value system helped promote the work ethic.

The Baby Boomer value system has begun to transform the value systems of the organizations for which they work.

In a comparison of managers in 1981 to managers in 1991, the following trends in manager's values were noted:

- Quality and customer service, which had not even appeared in the 1981 survey, topped the 1991 survey.
- Employer's demands came second to home and personal considerations.
- A cooperative value system was necessary to improve the quality of life.[33]

Profile

John Heavrin
Humana Corporation
A TWENTY-SOMETHING PERSPECTIVE

Like many members of my "generation," I'm somewhat at a loss to define that generation or my place in it, or the extent to which I identify with it. It occurs to me that generations are defined in the past tense. I suppose that if a "baby boomer" were asked the question, "What does your generation stand for, and what has its contribution to society and this country been?" an honest answer in 1993 might differ drastically from one given in '73, or '68. My generation's values and traits are still being formed. I suspect that in the end, like the fruits of those who would distill the vast raw experience of the millions born during a particular period of years, the final call on the "baby busters" will be an endless rumination on a combination of two things. The first, the major political events, foreign and domestic, which take place during the next few decades. And the second, rationalizations and conclusions drawn by "busters" upon reaching the age at which their children began to be looked upon as a generation, a great national high school assembly, to be praised, scolded, and, above all, envied.

In a nation which values individual determination and opportunity so highly that in many ways it achieves the highest status of exaltation (inattainability), I instinctively think of myself as an exception to the values of something as collective and communal as "my generation." Moreover, I belong on the "boomer-buster" cusp. (Does this free me to proudly adopt the finer points of each and safely reject the shortcomings? Perhaps there's something to be said for this work of generations after all.) I was born in 1964, during a period of great economic prosperity in America, and even greater hope in the promise of progress on the problems of racial and economic injustice of all kinds. Yet America stood on the precipice of disillusion (nothing so horrible yet easily comprehensible as ruin).

Shortly after my birth, the Great Society began to be pursued, and many great gains were made. But the Vietnam War, the assassinations of Robert Kennedy and Martin Luther King, Jr., the Watergate scandal and the collapse of the Nixon presidency made the facts that America could be victimized by hubris, could be ugly and even stupid, and could fail, quite clear. My generation spent its childhood in prosperity, the residue of the post-war decades of dizzying economic progress. But it was not the thoughtless, unconsidered prosperity of the "baby boomers'" childhood. It is ironic that the "baby boomers" were so determined to reject the values of a society, the very prosperity and stability of which were prerequisites for such an ambitious pursuit.

My generation has not known real hardship; but nor has it known the freedom from economic concern that the "baby boomers," as a generation, took for granted. We are shaped by the same devotion to security and material well-being that all three of America's post-war generations have been. But we realize that keeping and holding that prosperity requires hard work and fiscal responsibility. We do not count on the endless prosperity of our nation to right any wrong or finance any project, because we have come to realize that it won't. The same idealistic young crusaders of the 1960s understandably free of economic concern when it came time to decide to what their lives would be devoted, in many cases became the "conservatives" of the 1980s who elected Republicans to the White House. This ushered in the great collapse of societal responsibility and the achievement of an illusion of national prosperity through the brazen use of borrowed money. We, the next generation, through no real choice of our own, are left to pick up the pieces.

So, I would say, as a "baby buster" that my view of the workplace is oddly traditional. What a "boomer" might consider to be a ruthless, manipulative concern with personal economic advancement and material improvement seems to me to be a simple, necessary reincarnation of the primary American values: you get what you earn. Perhaps our children will be anomalously free of this concern, but we are not. Our birthright can be seen in one of two ways. The social and political chaos of our youth, with economic shocks and stopgaps throughout, can lead to great cynicism on the part of "baby busters," who might then seek only to be as comfortable, fashionable, and prosperous as possible. Or, as I believe, our birthright will calmly and almost instinctively lead us to embrace the challenge to restore honor and prosperity to society and perhaps create the conditions for another idealistic stab at achieving social justice in America.

My generation is marked above all, by the notion that prosperity is not given but must be earned. It does not reject the practical fact or even the idea of government involvement when things are bad. Witness the wholesale rejection of Reaganism for Clinton and the promise of a renaissance of economic equity first, and runaway prosperity, if at all, a distant second.

I view the workplace as a competition, but not a game. A job is not the easiest thing to find, let alone keep. The determination to compete, win, and succeed economically is necessary in order to collectively restore the presumption of prosperity that America needs to underpin its efforts to achieve social justice, to "live out its creed." I think that the common view of my generation is that we are neo–Conservative, probably Republican, obsessed with material possessions, often emotionally rootless, and spiritually functionally illiterate. I don't fit that description. So much for generational identity. But the one characteristic that I certainly do have in common with others my age is the desire for a secure home and work life. I desire to succeed in work for personal reasons, but also to help the company in my case, Humana Inc., a national health insurance company, to succeed. Its success helps me to achieve personal security.

Much of the way organizations are changing, even as the kind of attention on ethical decision making seen earlier in this chapter, can be linked to the Baby Boomers who are now coming into management positions. The experimental tradition, a commitment to what can be, a push for plurality and diversity, are all indicative of that generation. Commitment to the organization comes second to commitment to those ideals.[34]

As organizations face the turn of the century and the Baby Busters generation, the degree of commitment they will get will depend upon their ability to satisfy their value systems. The organization with interesting, challenging and rewarding work, will be the organization that succeeds. Being part of a winning organization, will increase this generation's commitment to it.

WORKING TOGETHER   One's basic orientation to work and its place in life is a person's work ethic. People with different work ethics do work together and this can cause conflict.

Consider the potential conflict between the Protestant Work Ethic senior manager who expects the organization's goals and objections to be bottom-line oriented (and whose bonuses depend upon it) and the Baby Boomer middle manager pushing for a corporate commitment to environmental responsibility, even at the risk of decreasing short term profits. Add to this scene a Baby Buster new employee whose job is threatened if profits decrease even in the short term. From this scenario, one can guess that the senior manager would stay with the organization, regardless of the decision and then make the best of it. The Baby Boomer will probably move on if the organization's environmental commitment was not to his or her liking. And the Baby Buster could be on his or her way out also, looking for a spot with less risk and higher rewards.[35]

Recognizing the value systems of employees and how they impact or change the value system of the organization is as important as recognizing how the value system of the organization affects its employees.

Diversity Influencing the "Work Ethic"

In the later chapters on Cultural Diversity and the Global Workplace, the influence of multiple cultures within a workplace will be explored. Individuals from different cultures can have a different value system formed by the accident of their place of birth. Just like the age group to which one belongs, your cultural experience will influence how you perform in the workplace. Without trying to be comprehensive in this chapter or repeating material covered elsewhere, the following profiles of some of the diverse cultures you are likely to work with in U.S.-based companies might be useful to your understanding. At the risk of promoting stereotypes, some national characteristics can be identified. The emergence of Japan as a major player in the world economy, the advent of "Europe 1992," and the numbers of Hispanic immigrants being absorbed into the U.S. work force, make it necessary for U.S. businesses to understand the work ethic of workers from other cultures.

Three generations of workers meet in this organization.

JAPAN   The Japanese come from a cultural heritage which emphasizes one's place as a member of the group. Individual performance is not highlighted. Japan prides itself on providing "lifetime" employment to its citizens. In order to do this, continuous training must be made available to allow for promotion as well as for new job challenges. As a result of these two influences, the Japanese worker values "decision by consensus." He or she is not bothered by hard work but expects to have his or her talents utilized by the organization.

EUROPE   Western European countries which formed the Common Market are expanding their business relationship by launching "Europe 1992." (See Chapter 9.) "Europe 1992" will further reduce differences between the border trade of European nations. While Western Europe would certainly seem to share many of the same traditions and history with the United States, differences in work attitudes do exist. A long tradition of class differences represented by the monarchy in all of the major European cultures, even if such leadership is now gone, cannot be ignored. Class differences exist and the effect of such differences in the work place can be seen in the work ethic. Europeans work better organized in homogeneous groups. Despite their close proximity with other nations, they remain highly nationalistic. Europeans, like much of the U.S. work force, operate well individually; team work groups are not part of their tradition. But work is not the source of their identity. Their nationality is far more important to them than their occupation.

HISPANIC AMERICANS   The Hispanic culture has a strong regard for family and kinship fostered in a patriarchal society. Their work ethic is grounded in providing for their families. Although personal uniqueness is valued, the outward manifestation of achievement is not highly individualistic. Respect is a prime motivator, both respect for authority figures in management and receiving respect as an employee. The idea of a "team" management style would not be familiar nor easy for a Hispanic American. They are used to a top-down management tradition.

While certainly not exhaustive, the above examples show how culturally diverse backgrounds can impact the work ethic of an organization.

CONCLUSIONS AND APPLICATIONS

Capitalism **is an economic system in which competition between suppliers results in a quality product at an affordable cost.**

- Ethical business practices are essential to the health and viability of the organization. Organizations cannot afford to alienate customers, sacrifice employees, or risk shareholder assets by unethical practices.

- *Capitalism* is not an unethical system. It is an economic system in which competition between suppliers results in a quality product at an affordable cost. Society has benefited from the results of a capitalistic system. But abuses of capitalism undermine the ultimate good it produces.

- Three ethical theories which can be applied in the business setting are ethics of purpose, of principle, and of consequence. Ethics of purpose seeks to realize the organization's highest potential. Ethics of Principle recognizes the basic rights of all stakeholders in the performance of the organization. And ethics of consequence weighs the highest benefit to the most people in deciding organization issues.

- Individuals form their value systems as a result of interaction with their family, friends, and society. They use their value system to make ethical choices in the workplace.

- An individual in the workplace has a responsibility to self, to other employees, to the shareholders, and to the public. Ethical decision making must include consideration for all of these parties.

- The moral intensity of an issue, that is the type of good or bad involved, the urgency of the situation, the probability of effects, the degree of influence, and the availability of alternatives, will influence the decision-making process. A "high" moral intensity issue will receive more attention, be easier to identify and result in better actions.

- Employees can and should examine the ethical climate of the organization they support. Danger signals of an unethical climate need to be noted such as an overemphasis on short-term profits, a code of ethics that isn't communicated or enforced, and a callous attitude toward employees and the public.

- Corporations have value systems which are communicated to and through its shareholders, employees, managers, and the public. A corporation can institutionalize ethical behavior by establishing a code of ethics, communicating it, and training and selecting employees with that code in mind.

- Ethical group decision making can be fostered within a corporation. Policies can be tested against the facts, basic assumptions, and value judgments of the people in the organization.

- Different generations have different value systems. Different value systems affect that generation's "work ethic." The United States work force in the year 2,000 will have three generational groups working together: post–World War II workers, Baby Boomers, and Baby Busters.

- Generational values help decide where employees choose to work, how they approach the work, and how well they work together. Changes in the nature of the employer-employee relationship has come about in U.S. business, in part, because of the changing values of American workers.

REVIEW QUESTIONS

1. Why is business ethics suddenly a hot topic for discussion?
2. Why is the capitalist system consistent with ethical behavior?
3. What is the basis for ethics of purpose? for ethics of principle? ethics of consequences?
4. What are the types of values and what helps to establish different types of values with different individuals?

5. What three ways can help an individual develop an ethical decision-making process for use in the workplace?
6. How can you recognize an unethical organization?
7. Why do corporations need to be moral actors?
8. How can organizations institutionalize ethical behavior?
9. How do the three major generations in the U.S. work force differ on their work ethic?

DISCUSSION QUESTIONS

1. Discuss how President Clinton's election, his inaugural speech and decisions during his first two weeks in office are consistent with his generation's values.
2. The collapse of the U.S.S.R. and the Communist economic system it promoted has caused some to believe "good" triumphed over "evil." Discuss how evils can still exist in the "capitalist" economic system.
3. Review the value systems of the three major gener-

ational groups in the U.S. work force and compare those values to the ethics of purpose, principle, and consequences. What connections do you notice?
4. Explain how a corporation's need to be a moral actor stems from its owners, employees, managers, and public.
5. Discuss the five elements of ethical decision making in the corporate setting.

CASE STUDY

The Mid–America Manufacturers, Inc.*

Mid–America Manufacturers, Inc., is a large diversified conglomerate located in Milwaukee, Chicago, Kansas City, and Omaha. It has prided itself on being a major contributor to charities, supporting numerous patriotic causes, encouraging education by paying full tuition for its employees for any college courses students wish to take, and has been viewed as "the corporate leader."

One of Mid–America's employees, Eaton, an engineer, wished to pursue an MBA degree. At company expense, he enrolled in a course, "Ethics, Law and Management," at the local university. As the course progressed, the student learned that a major paper was required researching-discussing-analyzing an ethical dilemma. At first, Eaton could not visualize an ethical dilemma. Then Eaton wrote a paper in which he presented the following statement:

> I was at a meeting of our corporate regional engineers one week ago. Arnold Bates, senior engineer, was present. He reminded us of the agreement we had made when we were hired forbidding disclosure of any company/corporate information to any person outside the corporation, agreeing that should any such disclosure occur, it was an automatic letter of resignation,

*Printed by permission: Frank Forbes, Chairman, Department of Law and Society, College of Business, University of Nebraska, Omaha.

and an agreement to reimburse the corporation for any sums lost or amounts paid as a result of such disclosure.

In addition, Arnold pointed out that the stock option plan provided for automatic termination if such disclosure was ever made. The loss of this option would result in a new loss of $150,000 to the average engineer at the corporation. After this background and caveat, or warning, Arnold told the engineers they were to *reduce* immediately the number of tests on certain metal connectors on some military weapons being developed for the defense department. Arnold pointed out that the original bid/specifications required a test on each item, an extremely costly quality control methodology. Commencing immediately, the test would be random, one of *three*. Ten would be chosen for examination. Because of this, the engineers were to scrutinize the process more carefully than ever, report any deviation from the established standard, and stop production if necessary. Arnold stated, "our study shows that this will be as effective as per-item testing, provided each of you executes this policy properly."

That evening I was at a large company party and happened to be in an enclosed stall in the men's restroom when I overheard the comptroller and a production operations manager talking. I heard the comptroller tell the PO, "The outside auditor from New York is coming next week—we've got problems. They will be doing inventory checks in Kansas City. We need to show 300,000 MX rifles at Kansas City—since our books show 800,000 in stock nationwide. Get 200,000 down there from Omaha, then move them to Chicago. If we do that, their audit will show we have the 800,000 total. I know this isn't the usual way to deal with a budget problem, but I don't see any alternative."

I then privately, secretly checked out whether this plan was carried out, and it was. In fact, it was made much easier because one of the three principal auditors had a close personal relationship with the CEO of Mid–America Corporation and had dinner with him during the audit. At this dinner the CEO was asked, "Is everything OK with Mid–America," and was told, "We have no problems. You can take my word for that, this per item check is really a waste of your resources." The auditor had no reason to distrust his old friend, a highly respected CEO who often gave speeches on Corporate Ethics. The auditor, contrary to the guidelines for auditing, failed to check three enclosed containers, but marked the inventory sheet as "all accounted for, no exceptions." The auditors were aware that identical items were in different cities.

I think this is a true ethical dilemma—and you can quote Rawls, Kant, Betham, Mills all you want, but they don't answer my question, do I inform the Board of Directors? Any other person?

Professor Good read the draft and immediately felt very uncomfortable. Good knows this company, its products, and its importance to the community. He knows that major scandal could result in defense department retaliation—that is, contract termination, with the resulting loss of thousands of jobs including some consulting work Good has done for Mid–America. He also knows there is a real possibility that the inspections method could result in defective, dangerous products being sent to the Army, products which could even be life threatening.

Professor Good and Engineer Eaton decide to meet and discuss the problem. They invite you, their personal ethics guru, to analyze the problem and advise them of the proper course of action that should be taken.

CASE STUDY QUESTIONS

1. What advice do you provide them and why?
2. If Aristotle were asked for a rule or standard what would he say? Kant? Mills?

3. Do you see a major distinction between the legal requirements under these facts and ethical imperatives or requirements? If so, discuss them in detail.

4. Do you think laws create and/or are subsequent to ethical norms or do ethical norms lead to the creation of laws?

EXPERIENTIAL EXERCISE 1

Role Play an Ethical Decision

Purpose

To participate in a group decision-making process on an ethical issue.

Task

Step 1: Separate the class into groups and assign each a problem that is currently a hot topic in the business world. (Environmental responsibilities of organizations; employee drug testing; whistle-blowers; and the like.)

Step 2: Using the model contained in Figure 3-6, present a policy, gather facts, make a value judgment, recognize the assumptions, and express opposing views. Document all of these elements and how you used them to decide your question. Explain which ethical theory was used in making a value judgment: purpose, consequence, or principle.

EXPERIENTIAL EXERCISE 2

Organizational Ethical Audit

Purpose

To help students apply the principles outlined in Figure 3-4, "A Dozen Ways to Spot an Unethical Organization," to an actual organization.

Task

Step 1: Students, in pairs, will be asked to interview a top official in a locally operated business using the questions below.

Step 2: Students will analyze the answers and write an audit of the organization's ethics and give it a grade from A-F.

Audit questions

1. Which does your organization consider more important, long-term or short-term profits, and why?

2. Are there established professional codes of ethics applicable to your organization? If so, how do you insure such codes are incorporated into your organization?

3. When faced with an ethical problem, how does your organization approach a solution?

4. If your organization faced a financial loss as a result of the need to make an ethical decision, how would your shareholders respond?

5. How does an employee with an ethical concern normally raise that problem within the organization?

6. Does your organization equate unethical behavior with illegal behavior?

7. Has your organization ever needed to address an ethical concern through a public relations campaign? Was it successful?

8. From top management's perspective, are your customers as well as your employees of equal value to your organization? If yes, how do you demonstrate that? If no, why?

9. How do your employees view your performance appraisal system? Explain your response.

10. Do you have a Code of Ethics, or similar guidelines for your organization's ethical behavior?

11. Do employees have a protected, whistle-blowing mechanism? Why or why not?

12. Do you think your employees come to the workplace with a well established personal ethics code? Why or why not? How does that affect your organization?

Take It to the Net

You can find this chapter's World Wide Web exercise at:
http://www.prenhall.com/carrell

CHAPTER 4

Values, Attitudes, Personality, and Perception

CHAPTER OBJECTIVES

1. To understand what organizational differences are and why this concept is important.
2. To describe the nature of individual differences.
3. To discuss attitudes and attitude formation.
4. To explain factors shaping personality, personality styles, and how personality is measured.
5. To define perception, attribution theory, and learning processes.

VW Executive J. Ignacio Lopez de Arriortuna

Members of the world auto industry are asking what it is about J. Ignacio Lopez de Arriortuna that makes him so special. Lopez, a former group vice president of purchasing at General Motors, was offered one of the top three jobs at Germany's Volkswagen for a reported salary of $20 million over five years which would make him one of Europe's highest-paid executives. GM made a counteroffer in an attempt to get Mr. Lopez to change his mind: a promotion to executive vice president, more pay, and a possible commitment to build a new assembly plant in Mr. Lopez's native Basque region of Spain to test the latest Lopez theories on manufacturing. However, after accepting the Volkswagen offer, Lopez announced he had accepted GM's counteroffer but then finally decided to accept Volkswagen's offer. After leaving GM for Volkswagen, Mr. Lopez became involved in a bitter industrial espionage dispute between the two car giants. GM claims that Mr. Lopez absconded with hoards of sensitive documents when he left, while Lopez acknowledges that he may have had some sensitive documents in his possession but that they were destroyed soon after he left GM to prevent them from getting into VW's hands.[1]

Why such an interest in Mr. Lopez by two large automobile companies? In early 1992, Lopez roared out of obscurity into GM's inner circle. After sharply cutting GM's purchasing costs in Europe, Lopez landed in Detroit to work his same magic in North America. Within seven months, Lopez had cut more than $1 billion in costs and locked in another $1.5 billion in savings with new contracts.

Until recently, GM and other corporations considered purchasing to be a drab specialty. Yet, Lopez delivered significant cost reductions in a company bogged down by inertia. Analysts indicated that Lopez fostered a "cult" at GM by being different. For example, Lopez exhorted managers to switch their watches from left to right wrists to keep them uncomfortable until North American profits revived. He convened 6:30 A.M. lectures to warn about the decline of American civilization and to declare his loyalty to GM's CEO, Jack Smith. Underlings used to expense-account lunches received a copy of Lopez's forty-four-page booklet titled *Feeding the Warrior Spirit* that warned of the dangers of French fries and counseled a diet of fruits and vegetables.[2]

Because of his individualism, Lopez changed the nature of the purchasing function at GM. For example, he tore up existing contracts and demanded that GM's parts suppliers agree to double-digit price cuts. Lopez cajoled manufacturing and engineering executives to rethink ways to reduce costs and improve quality.[3]

A growing work force diversity, as discussed in Chapter 12, creates the need for managers to be aware that individual differences do exist.

What Are Individual Differences?

Each person is similar to everyone else in many ways. Our basic appearances as well as our biological systems are much the same. However, each person is also very different from everyone else. Individuals are unique in terms of their skills, abilities, personalities, perceptions, attitudes, values, and ethics.

Importance in Understanding Individual Differences

From a manager's perspective, individual differences provide both a rich texture for creating opportunities to get things done and the challenges of managing diversity. A manager's success depends on getting things done through other people. In order to achieve this success, managers need to be able to explain why employees engage in certain types of behaviors rather than others and to predict how employees will respond to various actions that the manager might take.

This chapter examines how values, attitudes, personality, and perceptions are related to individual differences.

VALUES

Milton Rokeach, a psychologist, has defined values as beliefs that guide actions and judgments across a variety of situations.[4] Rokeach's contention, which is supported by extensive research, is that different value systems contribute toward explaining individual differences in behavior. Values also affect the attitudes, perceptions, needs and motivations of individuals at work.[5] In this section we examine both the causes of values and the types of values.

Source of Values

A person's values develop from the cultural setting in which he or she lives—from parents, friends, teachers, and other external reference groups and are formed early in life. Although studies indicate that values are relatively stable and enduring, significant life events such as failing in business, surviving a serious accident, experiencing a death of a loved one, or having children can reshape an individual's value system during adult life.[6] Because individuals are exposed to different learning situations and have different experiences, their values are also different.

Types of Values

Four classification schemes have been developed to depict values. The first two that are discussed were developed by Gordon Allport and his associates and by Milton Rokeach, respectively, to describe human values in general. The third typology, developed by Geert Hofstede, described work-related values across different national cultures. The fourth classification, developed by Bruce Meglino and his associates, described the work-related values of people in the United States.

ALLPORT AND ASSOCIATES   During the early 1930s, the psychologist Gordon Allport and his associates categorized values into six types.[7]

1. *Theoretical*. An interest in the discovery of truth through reasoning and systematic thinking.
2. *Economic*. An interest in usefulness, practicality, and accumulation of wealth.
3. *Aesthetic*. An interest in beauty, form, and artistic harmony.
4. *Social*. An interest in the love of people and human relationships.
5. *Political*. An interest in gaining power and influencing other people.
6. *Religious*. An interest in the unity of experience and an understanding of the cosmos as a whole.

Using a questionnaire developed by Allport and his associates, researchers have determined that people in different occupations place different importance on the six value types. For example, one study reported that industrial scientists consider theoretical values most important and social values the least important. Purchasing executives rated economic values the highest and social values the lowest in terms of importance. Interestingly, religious values were the highest importance for ministers of churches while economic values were rated the least important.[8]

MILTON ROKEACH   Milton Rokeach classified values into two sets with eighteen items per set as illustrated in Figure 4-1. One set, *terminal values*, reflects a person's belief about "ends" to be achieved. The other set, *instrumental values*, reflects beliefs about the "means" for achieving desired ends.[9]

COGNITIVE MORAL DEVELOPMENT   Lawrence Kohlberg argued that as individuals mature, they pass through a series of six stages of moral development from middle childhood to adulthood as detailed in Figure 4-2. A person moves from stage to stage in an irreversible sequence. Fewer than 20 percent of American adults are believed to reach Stage Five.[10] Both the existence of these stages and the movement from stage to stage have been supported by a number of studies. Individuals at higher stages of moral development are less likely to cheat, more likely to engage in whistle-blowing, and more likely to make ethical decisions.[11]

Terminal values reflect a person's belief about "ends" to be achieved.

Instrumental values reflect beliefs about the means for achieving desired ends.

FIGURE 4-1

Rokeach's Terminal and Instrumental Values

Terminal Values	Instrumental Values
1. A comfortable life	1. Ambitious
2. An exciting life	2. Broadminded
3. A sense of accomplishment	3. Capable
4. A world at peace	4. Cheerful
5. A world of beauty	5. Clean
6. Equality	6. Courageous
7. Family security	7. Forgiving
8. Freedom	8. Helpful
9. Happiness	9. Honest
10. Inner harmony	10. Imaginative
11. Mature love	11. Independent
12. National security	12. Intellectual
13. Pleasure	13. Logical
14. Salvation	14. Loving
15. Self-respect	15. Obedient
16. Social recognition	16. Polite
17. True friendship	17. Responsible
18. Wisdom	18. Self-controlled

Source: Milton Rokeach, *The Nature of Human Values,* New York, The Free Press, 1973. Reprinted with the permission of The Free Press, a division of Simon & Schuster from *The Nature of Human Values* by Milton Rokeach. Copyright © 1973 by the Free Press.

FIGURE 4-2

Kohlberg's Six Stages of Moral Development

Stage	What is Considered to Be Right
1. Obedience and Punishment	Obeying rules to avoid physical punishment
2. Exchange Orientation	Obeying rules only when it is in one's immediate interest
3. Mutual Expectations	Living up to what people close to you expect
4. Societal Contribution	Obeying laws; fulfilling obligations and duties that have previously been agreed upon
5. Individual Rights	Upholding nonrelative rights and values regardless of majority opinion
6. Ethical Principles	Following self-chosen ethical principles; acting in accordance with principles when laws violate those principles

Source: Adapted from Lawrence Kohlberg, *The Philosophy of Moral Development,* vol. one, New York, Harper & Row, 1981, pp. 409–412.

Critics of Kohlberg's model that was developed from a twenty-year study of eighty-four boys argue that it does not take gender differences into account. One critic contends that women's moral development follows a different pattern: one that is based not on individual rights and rules but on responsibility and relationships.[12]

MEGLINO AND ASSOCIATES   In the early 1990s a researcher of organization sciences, Bruce Meglino, and his associates categorized four types of values with respect to people at work.[13]

1. *Achievement.* Working hard to accomplish difficult things in life.
2. *Concern for and helping others.* Having a concern for other people and an interest in helping them.
3. *Honesty.* Being truthful in dealings with others.
4. *Fairness.* Doing what is fair and being impartial in all activities.

The following "Profile" describes "new" values regarding Biotech research.

Michael Milken
Former Drexel Burnham Lambert Inc. Financier

NEW VALUES REGARDING BIOTECH RESEARCH

Three years ago, Michael R. Milken was sitting in a California prison camp. He had lost his career, more than a billion dollars in fines, and his freedom, but his Wall Street antennae and sense of irony were intact. As he watched investors pour billions into biotechnology almost indiscriminately, Milken recalls quipping to a friend: "If you can't find a Nobel laureate, just find somebody majoring in chemistry and you'll be able to get a couple hundred million dollars."

Today, however, some of those same companies seem like great investments to Milken. On the day he finished serving his prison sentence in 1993, Milken was handed a death sentence: a diagnosis of metastasized prostate cancer. He vowed to beat it, and, through radiation and medication, he is in remission and symptom-free. But the odds say he may have just a few years to live, and he is not content just hoping and praying for a break. He's determined to find a cure.

Milken, forty-eight, is not the first wealthy cancer patient to become an overnight patron of research. But it's likely that the scale of his efforts of the past twenty-two months is unprecedented. Through Cap-Cure, a prostate-cancer foundation he started, the former Drexel Burnham Lambert Inc. financier has written checks to seventy different scientists, sponsored scientific meetings, and is trying to organize a wide variety of resources for researchers, from videoconferencing to tissue banks. In September, Milken started his own biotech company, Cancer BioScience Corp., in Lexington, Massachusetts, focused on prostate-cancer treatments. And now, he says, he wants to turbocharge a wider array of cancer research in the private sector.

That has led him to biotech. Milken says he will soon begin investing a significant sum from his personal fortune in the industry and encourage other investors and large drug and chemical companies to join him. "I'm concerned about creating access to capital" for biotech, he says. Milken won't discuss his net worth, but it has been estimated at nearly half a billion, with many Wall Street sources convinced that his vast portfolio of investments from his Drexel days make his real worth several times that. His family foundation's endowment alone is $350 million.

Milken's blitzkrieg has both excited and unnerved a number of biotech companies who need money and currently don't see it coming from capital markets. With the industry in a deep slump, they're hoping Milken can reignite interest in these stocks. However, some biotech executives complain that Milken is mixing his profit and not-for-profit initiatives in ways that make them wary of getting too close. "He's trying to do what he did in junk bonds—[control] prostate-cancer research," complains one Silicon Valley venture capitalist.

Source: Adapted from Joan Hamilton, "Milken vs. Cancer," *Business Week*, January 19, 1995, pp. 36–37.

ATTITUDES

In an organizational setting, attitudes play an important part in determining performance-based behavior in such areas as organizational commitment, absenteeism, turnover, and the quantity and quality of work output. An *attitude* is a predisposition to respond to objects, people, or events in either a positive or negative way.[14] An employee who states, "I really like my job," is expressing a personal attitude about work. The following "OB in Practice" describes how young

Attitude is a predisposition to respond to objects, people, or events in either a positive or negative way.

OB in Practice

Young Women Are Insisting on Career Equality and Are Forcing the Men in Their Lives to Adjust

Young career women are not playing follow the leader any more, and that is causing difficult adjustments for their husbands and boyfriends.

Tom Abbott, Director of Public Relations for Xerox, states that the day is over of the macho man coming home and announcing: "We are moving to Detroit tomorrow. Pack up." Karen Dowd, placement director at the University of Virginia's Darden Graduate School of Business, indicates the old rules were all based on one person being the career driver. Now there are two people who feel equally powerful.

Unlike an older generation of women who broke into male bastions of management but still placed their careers behind those of their husbands, women in their twenties and early thirties are insisting on career equality. While many shy away from calling themselves feminists—largely because they don't want to be associated with militancy—they are living, breathing products of that movement. The problem is that their husbands and boyfriends, while publicly supporting them, privately still expect to be the dominant breadwinners. "Among young men, there's a lot of traditionalism floating around, at least in their dreams," observes psychologist Frank Farley of the University of Wisconsin, who is president of the American Psychological Association.

Sometimes neither partner will budge. Breaking a stalemate requires negotiating finesse that many young couples simply don't have. It's an issue psychologists and employment counselors say they address more and more with young clients.

Young couples on strikingly different career paths may face the deepest conflicts. "A woman who's a doctor married to a man with an MBA—their lives in some ways are so different professionally that they're really striking their own paths. They have to negotiate it out so the relationship feels balanced and equal," says Dr. Patricia Mendoza, director of career development counseling at the University of California, Los Angeles.

Sometimes negotiation doesn't work. A recently divorced woman in the entertainment industry says that while she accepted the social obligations associated with her ex-husband's Wall Street job, he never felt comfortable performing the duties required of a film producer's spouse. "Most of the people I worked with were guys. I think he saw me with these people being really happy, strong, and productive, and found the environment threatening," says the woman, thirty, who didn't want to be named. Says her ex-husband, "To me, the relationship was as important as my career. But she probably put greater weight on her career than on the relationship."

Daryl Mapson, a thirty-two-year-old architect, followed his wife from Cleveland to Pittsburgh when she finished engineering school and got her first job. He's comfortable with the idea of equal partnership, he says. "I think I always had a desire to marry someone that was on my same level." But his flexibility will go only so far. He's not sure, for example, that he will agree to follow his wife again if her career in mechanical engineering steered her far from Pittsburgh. "If I keep moving around, I'll never get established," he says.

Letty Cottin Pogrebin, Founding Editor of *MS.* magazine, states that women in their twenties often have not negotiated with their husbands how they will handle child care when the time comes. Eventually, the arrival of children may force many women to revert to more traditional roles. "Then it is not just a question of: I will do the bathroom and you will do the garbage," says Ms. Pogrebin. There is evidence that an increasingly large number of men have chosen to work at home and provide child care.

However, the experiences of older generations suggest that it is the woman who will make most of the career compromises.

Source: Gabriella Stern, "Young Women Insist on Career Equality, Forcing Their Men to Adjust," *The Wall Street Journal*, September 16, 1992, B1, B3. Reprinted by permission of *The Wall Street Journal*, © 1992 Dow Jones & Company, Inc. All Rights Reserved Worldwide.

women's attitudes have changed regarding career equality. In this section the sources of attitudes, cognitive dissonance, and the situational aspect of attitudes are discussed.

Sources of Attitudes

Research indicates that attitudes are based on important beliefs and values.[15] As illustrated in Figure 4-3, beliefs and values precede attitudes that influence behavior. Beliefs may change over time as relevant information is received.[16] For example, an individual's beliefs about the quality of a product may change if the product is recalled because of a particular defect.

Cognitive Dissonance

In some situations, individuals exhibit inconsistencies between their attitudes and behavior. For example, an employee may dislike the company or his or her job, yet still come to work promptly and regularly and exert a high level of effort. This inconsistency between the attitude (job dissatisfaction) and the behavior (continuing to work at the job) creates anxiety, which is known as *cognitive dissonance*.[17] Individuals may engage in dissonance reduction to reduce these inconsistencies. In the preceding example, the employee may believe that another job cannot be obtained, or that he or she will quit in the future, or rationalize that the existing job or company is not so bad after all, are instances of dissonance reduction.[18] The "Profile" on page 104 describes the attitudes of an individual towards his work.

Cognitive dissonance
The result of inconsistency between the attitude (job dissatisfaction) and the behavior (continuing to work at the job) that creates anxiety in an employee.

Situational Aspects of Attitudes

Two organizational behavior researchers, Gerald Salancik and Jeffrey Pfeffer, argue that attitudes evolve from information received from the social context.[19] As illustrated in Figure 4-4, through cues and guides, social information shapes and influences attitudes.

The "Profile" on page 105 describes how Southwest Airlines hires people with certain attitudes rather than using education or expertise as a criteria.

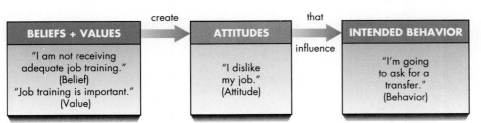

FIGURE 4-3

How Attitudes Affect Behavior

Profile

Martin Rosenblum
Archivist Harley-Davidson
ATTITUDES TOWARD WORK

The reason I get up very early and get down to the Harley-Davidson office immediately is that the company has soul. There really is a mystique involved with this motorcycle company that is rightly labeled its soul. I can't define it, but I know it's there.

Let me try to explain it. I've never been a joiner. In the Fifties, when I raced hot rods, instead of a club plaque on my rear fender, mine said LONE WOLF, NO CLUB. Before I came to Harley, I was in the music business, and I wrote poetry. I also taught English for ten years at the University of Wisconsin.

But at Harley it's different. For the first time in my life I've encountered a lifelong learning process that says that leadership involves not a dynamic personality, not a command-and-control mentality, but the ability to empower others as well as yourself. Yes, I've got tattoos. Yes, I'm a hard-core rider. But what I'm talking about goes beyond just getting a job done. It is about a very complex, difficult, personal transformation.

For me it's a real struggle because I come from a background where my father was a Swedish immigrant, a real command-and-control, you-do-this kind of environment. What I enjoy here is not bothering with your own ego, the joy of becoming an active, forward-moving individual, of being part of a team. For the first time in my life I felt humbled. I'll be honest with you, man, I've never felt humility before.

Source: Adapted from Brian Dumaine, "Why Do We Work?" *Fortune,* December 26, 1994, pp. 196–204.

FIGURE **4-4**

Situational Aspect of Attitudes

Source: Gregory Moorhead and Ricky W. Griffin, *Organizational Behavior,* 3d ed., Boston, Houghton Mifflin, 1992, p. 111. Copyright © 1992 by Houghton Mifflin Company. Reprinted with permission.

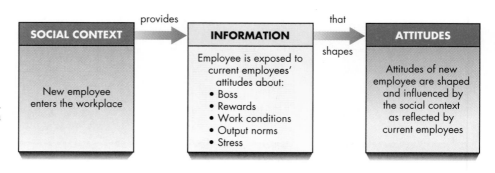

Profile

Herb Kelleher
CEO, Southwest Airlines
HIRING ATTITUDES

In 1994, despite increased competition from rival airlines, Southwest Airlines' profit for year ending 1994 was up nearly 64 percent. Also, Southwest's cost per available seat mile for 1994 was significantly lower than the rest of the other firms in the airline industry. Kelleher states that employee attitudes played a vital role in Southwest's success. Kelleher comments that from the beginning of Southwest Airlines, he has tried to instill in employees what he calls "an insouciance, an effervescence."

One result is that Southwest workers often go out of their way to amuse, surprise, or somehow entertain passengers. During delays at the gate, ticket agents will award prizes to the passenger with the largest hole in his or her sock. Flight attendants have been known to hide in the overhead luggage bins and then pop out when passengers start filing on board. Veteran Southwest fliers looking for a few yuks have learned to listen to announcements over the intercom. A recent effort: "Good morning, ladies and gentlemen. Those of you who wish to smoke will please file out to our lounge on the wing, where you can enjoy our feature film, *Gone with the Wind.*" On that same flight, an attendant later made this announcement: "Please pass all plastic cups to the center aisle so we can wash them out and use them for the next group of passengers."

Clearly, not everyone is cut out to be a Southwest employee. "What we are looking for, first and foremost, is a sense of humor," says Kelleher. "Then we are looking for people who have to excel to satisfy themselves and who work well in a collegial environment. We don't care that much about education and expertise because we can train people to do whatever they have to do. We hire attitudes."

Source: Adapted from Kenneth Labich, "Is Herb Kelleher America's Best CEO?" *Fortune*, May 2, 1994, pp. 44–52.

PERSONALITY

When people are described in terms of such traits as sociable, tense, loyal, ambitious, loud, or aggressive, they are categorized in terms of personality traits. *Personality* is the set of distinct traits and characteristics that can be used to compare and contrast individuals.[20] For example, you may have one friend who is dependable and optimistic and another who is just the opposite. In this section we examine the factors that shape an individual's personality, describe four personality theories: psychoanalytic, trait, humanistic, immaturity-maturity; six personality styles: locus of control, authoritarianism, Machiavellianism, self-esteem, Type A–Type B personality, and problem solving. This section concludes with a discussion of how personality is measured.

> **Personality is the set of distinct traits and characteristics that can be used to compare and contrast individuals.**

Factors Shaping Personality

As shown in Figure 4-5, personality is determined by the interaction of genetic and environmental factors.

An interesting question is which of these two factors (genetics or environment) influences personality the most? Research conducted on 348 pairs of twins at the University of Minnesota indicates that about half of an individual's per-

FIGURE 4-5
How Personality Is
Determined

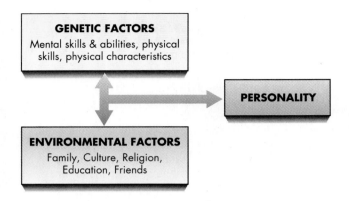

sonality is due to genetic while the other half is due to environmental factors. However, certain characteristics deviated from the 50-50 split. For example, well-being, alienation, aggression, and shunning risk were caused more by environmental factors while respect for authority, high morals, and the need for intimacy were caused more by genetic factors.[21]

Personality Theories

Four theories of personality development are:

Psychoanalytic theory **Freud, Erikson, and Piaget indicated that personality develops in stages.**

1. *Psychoanalytic Theories.* Sigmund Freud, Erik Erikson, and Jean Piaget have indicated that personalities develop in stages. Freud argued that behavior is caused by unconscious motives and that these motives are shaped by a variety of personality development stages, each having sexual undertones.[22] Erikson accepted Freud's notion of personality stages but rejected Freud's emphasis on sexual factors. Erikson focused instead on the social adaptations that people must make as they grow older.[23] Piaget also suggested stages of personality development but that the progressions between the stages were conscious activities.[24]

Trait theory **An approach to personality development which identifies a configuration of unique traits that best reflect personality.**

2. *Trait Theories.* In the trait approach to personality development, a configuration of traits are identified that best reflect personality. Gordon Allport argued that although everyone has a common set of personality traits, individuals are differentiated by a set of unique traits called personal dispositions. Allport's common traits included social, political, religious, and esthetic dispositions.[25] Raymond Cattell, a psychologist who also studied personality development from the trait approach, identified the following traits as major personality factors: reserved-outgoing, practical-imaginative, relaxed-tense, and humble-assertive.[26] Trait theories have not been successful in predicting behavior because work activities are largely ignored in trait theories.[27] Also, Allport and Odbert identified 17,953 different traits making it difficult to determine the actual importance of specific traits.[28]

Humanistic **A theory of personality development that emphasizes the growth of an individual and how others perceive all the forces that might influence that individual.**

3. *Humanistic Theories.* Humanistic theories of personality development emphasize the growth and self-actualization of the individual and how people perceive all of the forces that might influence them. Carl Rogers and Abraham Maslow are advocates of this approach.[29]

Immaturity-maturity theory **The idea that personality develops from immaturity to maturity along basic dimensions as an individual gains experience in his job.**

4. *Immaturity–Maturity Theories.* While the previous personality development theories were developed by psychologists, Chris Argyris has developed a model of personality development for the context of organizational behav-

ior.[30] Argyris indicated, as illustrated in Figure 4-6, that personality develops from immature to mature along seven basic dimensions. According to Argyris, as individuals gain experience and self-confidence in their jobs, they move from the immature end to the mature end of each dimension. This progression allows individuals to move from being passive to active and to develop long-term perspectives. Argyris argues that organizations and managers neglect the mature side of people and focus on the immature side. Thus managers tend to supervise and control more than is needed for mature individuals.[31]

Personality Styles

Organizational behavior research has focused on specific personality styles or traits that are considered to be important in understanding the complexities of individual differences. Six of these styles that are relevant to managers are discussed in this section: locus of control, authoritarianism, Machiavellianism, self-esteem, Type A–Type B personality, and problem-solving styles.

LOCUS OF CONTROL   *Locus of control* of individuals determines the degree to which they believe that their behaviors influence what happens to them. Some people, called internals, have an internal locus of control and believe that they can control what happens to them. Others, called externals, have an external locus of control and tend to think that what happens to them is determined by fate or luck.[32] Locus of control concepts have significant implications for managers. As an example, research studies indicate the following differences between individuals with an internal locus of control and those with an external locus of control.[33]

Locus of control determines the degree to which an individual believes that his or her behavior influences what happens to him or her.

- Internals have stronger expectations that effort leads to performance.
- Internals make more attempts to gain information.
- Internals perform better on learning and problem-solving tasks when performance leads to rewards.
- The relationship between job satisfaction and performance is stronger for internals.
- Internals are less alienated and less rootless.
- Internals engage in less risky behavior and have more self-control.
- Internals display a greater work motivation.

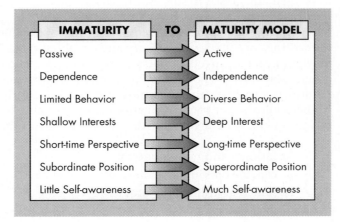

FIGURE 4-6
The Immaturity–Maturity Model

Source: Chris Argyris, *Personality and Organization: The Conflict Between the System and the Individual,* New York, Harper & Row, 1957, p. 50. Copyright 1957 by Harper & Row, Publishers, Inc. Copyright renewed 1985 by Chris Argyris. Reprinted by permission of HarperCollins Publishers, Inc.

OB in Practice

Differences in Locus of Control—Implications for Managing People

Research studies indicate that individuals with an internal locus of control attempt to exert control over the workplace by trying to influence work procedures, working conditions, relationships with peers and supervisors, and in assigning tasks. Because of this behavioral orientation, internals may resist a manager's attempts to closely supervise his or her work. To reduce any tensions, management may assign internals to a job requiring high initiative and low compliance. Externals may be assigned to highly structured jobs requiring greater compliance. Becoming directly involved in workplace decisions can also bolster the attitudes and performance of internals.

Because internals believe that their efforts lead to increased performance, internals tend to prefer and to respond more productively to incentives such as merit pay or sales commissions.

Source: Adapted from T. R. Mitchell, C. M. Smysert, and S. E. Weed, "Locus of Control: Supervision and Work Satisfaction," *Academy of Management Journal* 18, 1975, pp. 623–631. D. R. Norris and R. E. Niebuhr, "Attributional Influences on the Job Performance–Job Satisfaction Relationship," *Academy of Management Journal* 26, 1984, pp. 424–431. P. C. Nystrom, "Managers' Salaries and Their Beliefs about Reinforcement Control," *Journal of Personality and Social Psychology* 42, 1983, pp. 290–302.

- Internals are more independent and more reliant on their own judgment.
- Internals obtain higher salaries and greater salary increases.

The "OB in Practice" above describes how locus of control differences have implications for managing people.

Authoritarianism
To obey orders from someone in authority without raising objections.

AUTHORITARIANISM *Authoritarianism* is the extent to which a person believes that the power and status differences in an organization are legitimate. A person with a high authoritarianism score tends to rigidly adhere to conventional values, opposes the use of subjective feelings, and is more likely to obey orders from someone with authority without raising any serious objections, even if they recognize potential dangers. Highly authoritarian managers and supervisors tend to be rigid and closed to suggestions.[34]

Machiavellianism
Political maneuvers used to gain power and control over the behavior of others.

MACHIAVELLIANISM *Machiavellianism* is a concept that has been developed from the writings of a sixteenth-century author, Niccolo Machiavelli, that describes how political maneuvers can be used to gain power and control the behavior of others. Machiavelli's book, *The Prince,* discusses how nobility could use manipulation as a basic means of gaining and keeping control of others.[35] Research studies indicate that Machiavellianism is a personality trait that varies from person to person. An individual with a high Machiavellianism score tends to:[36]

- Be rational and nonemotional.
- Be capable of lying to achieve personal goals.
- Be skilled at influencing others.

- Put little weight on loyalty and friendships.
- Not be easily swayed by the opinions of others.

The "OB in Practice" on page 110 describes the Machiavellian traits of business students.

SELF-ESTEEM *Self-esteem* is the extent to which individuals hold positive or negative views about themselves and has become an important personality trait in recent years.[37] People with a high self-esteem believe that they possess many desirable traits and qualities and evaluate themselves favorably. On the other hand, people with a low self-esteem believe that they lack many important qualities and possess characteristics that others find unappealing and evaluate themselves unfavorably.[38]

Research indicates that feelings of either high or low self-esteem affects behavior within organizations. For example, studies indicate that individuals with a high-esteem tend to:[39]

- Have higher levels of job satisfaction and motivation than those with low self-esteem.
- Perform at higher levels in some settings and on some tasks than do those low in self-esteem.
- Be more likely to seek a higher-status job while individuals with a low self-esteem tend to be satisfied with the status quo.
- Be more successful in identifying and then obtaining appropriate jobs than do those low in self-esteem.
- Have higher levels of job performance than do people with low self-esteem.

Certainly, low self-esteem can be damaging to an individual's career. Several practical techniques, however, have been identified to counter the negative effects of a low self-esteem. These techniques include using positive feedback and training to boost both the confidence and performance of low-esteem people.[40]

TYPE A-TYPE B PERSONALITY Two cardiologists, Meyer Friedman and Ray Rosenman, concluded that their patients exhibited two very different patterns of behavior. For example, individuals with a Type A personality are more competitive, more devoted to work, more irritable and aggressive, and tend to work fast and be impatient. Individuals classified as Type B show an opposite pattern of behavior.[41] Friedman and Rosenman argued that Type As were more likely to experience coronary heart disease than Type Bs. However, recent studies indicate that Type A behavior consists of several distinct components (Friedman and Rosenman viewed Type A behavior as one-dimensional) and that the relationship between Type A behavior and the risk of coronary heart disease is not straightforward.[42]

In relating Type As and Type Bs to task performance, neither pattern appears to have an overall edge. However, Type As tend to perform better on some tasks (those involving time pressures or solitary work) than do Type Bs. Type As perform worse than Type Bs on tasks involving complex judgment, accuracy rather than speed, and working as part of a team. Type As also have poorer interpersonal relations than do Type Bs. Because they are always in a hurry, Type As tend to become angry and impatient with others, lash out at others for slight provocations, and tend to become irritable and aggressive.[43]

Self-esteem Qualities of favorable or unfavorable characteristics that an individual possesses to evaluate him or herself.

Type A-Type B personality Two very different patterns of behavior that influence health and work tasks.

OB in Practice

Machiavellian Traits of Business Students

Do you believe that business students are more Machiavellian or less Machiavellian than nonbusiness students? A study conducted by Professors Mclean and Jones of 206 undergraduates found that business students were significantly more Machiavellian than were science students but not more than art students. Marketing students were the most Machiavellian of the business students studied.

Source: Adapted from P.A. Mclean and D.G.B. Jones, "Machiavellianism and Business Education," *Psychological Reports,* 71, 1992, pp. 57–58.

Problem solving A cognitive style theory of personality developed by Jung and Myers-Briggs which conceptualized that personality is based on perception and judgment.

PROBLEM SOLVING (JUNG AND MYERS-BRIGGS)   During the 1920s, psychoanalyst Carl Jung developed a cognitive style theory of personality. Jung conceptualized that personality was based on perception and judgment. Jung proposed that two dimensions, sensation and intuition, influence a person's perception and that two dimensions, thinking and feeling, affect individual judgment. Jung believed that an individual's cognitive style of personality is determined by the pairing of a person's perception and judgment tendencies. More recently, Katherine Briggs and Isabel Briggs Myers converted Jung's theory into a test and scale now called the Myers-Briggs Type Indicator (MBTI). The test classifies people as extroverted or introverted (E or I), sensing or intuitive (S or N), thinking or feeling (T or F), and perceiving or judging (P or J). A person's answers are classified into sixteen different personality types. These sixteen types fall into one of the following four cognitive styles:[44]

- Sensation-Thinking (ST)
- Intuition-Thinking (NT)
- Sensation-Feeling (SF)
- Intuition-Feeling (NF)

Each cognitive style has unique characteristics that are described in Figure 4-7.

Research indicates there is a fit between an individual's cognitive style and the problem-solving strategy they select.[45] Organizations such as Apple, Exxon, and General Electric use the MBTI to try to fit personality styles to a particular task requirement. For example, a small firm selling electrical equipment in Mexico found that high-scoring sensation-feeling and extroverted salespeople have the best sales records in Mexico. The MBTI is used 2 million times a year to diagnose personality.[46] Figure 4-8 illustrates how the MBTI's four cognitive styles are related to specific occupations.

Measuring Personality

Hundreds of tests are available that measure a variety of personality characteristics. Two widely used tests are the Minnesota Multiphasic Personality Inventory (MMPI) and the Myers-Briggs Type Indicator (MBTI) that was discussed in the previous section. Managers tend to prefer the MBTI because the MMPI is too psychologically oriented.[47]

	ST Sensation-Thinking	NT Intuition-Thinking	SF Sensation-Feeling	NF Intuition-Feeling
Focus of Attention	Facts	Possibilities	Facts	Possibilities
Method of Handling Things	Impersonal Analysis	Impersonal Analysis	Personal Warmth	Personal Warmth
Tendency to Become	Practical and Matter-of-fact	Logical and Ingenious	Sympathetic and Friendly	Enthusiastic and Insightful
Expression of Abilities	Technical Skills with Facts and Objects	Theoretical and Technical Developments	Practical Help and Services for People	Understanding and Communicating with People

FIGURE 4-7 Different Cognitive Styles and Their Corresponding Characteristics

Source: William Taggart and Daniel Robey, "Minds and Managers: On the Dual Nature of Human Information Processing and Management," *Academy of Management Review* 6, 1981, p. 190. Used with permission.

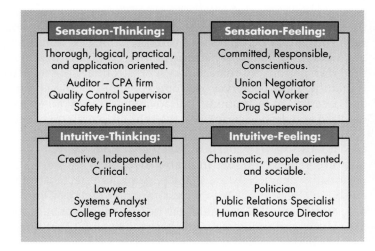

FIGURE 4-8

Four MBTI Cognitive Styles with Their Corresponding Occupations

Source: Adapted from James L. Gibson, John M. Ivancevich, and James H. Donnelly, Jr., *Organizations: Behavior, Structure, Processes* 7th ed., Homewood, IL, Irwin, 1991. Don Hellriegal, John W. Slocum, Jr., and Richard W. Woodman, *Organizational Behavior* 5th ed., St. Paul, MN, West Publishing, 1989. John R. Schermerhorn, Jr., James G. Hunt, and Richard N. Osborn, *Managing Organizational Behavior* 4th ed., New York, John Wiley & Sons, 1991.

The format of personality tests can be described in three broad categories: self-inventory, observation technique, and projective tests. Each format is described in the following section together with a discussion of the advantages and disadvantages of each.

SELF-INVENTORY The most frequently used personality test format is the self-inventory, a paper and pencil test in which people describe themselves by answering questions in the form of yes or no or agree or disagree. The advantage of *self-inventory tests* is that it is quick, efficient, and inexpensive. Large numbers of characteristics can be measured quickly with a minimum of expense. The major disadvantage is referred to as social desirability bias which is the tendency for responding individuals to describe themselves in socially flattering ways.[48] However, such a bias cannot affect ability tests. For example, an individual who wishes

Self-inventory test A paper-and-pencil personality test in which an individual answers questions in the form of yes or no or agree or disagree.

to portray him or herself as having a strong computer programming ability when this ability does not actually exist, will be unable to make a good test score on an ability test.[49]

Observation technique test The observation and then description of an individual in a particular situation, such as an employment interview or solving a work-related problem.

OBSERVATION TECHNIQUE This involves observing and then describing another person in a particular situation. Employment interviews and solving specific work situation problems are examples of the *observation technique*. In the work situation problem observation, a person is given a specific work related problem to solve. The observer then studies the person's problem-solving ability in terms of the steps taken, time required to reach a solution, and the quality of the final solution. In an employment interview, interviewers are trained to look for certain personality characteristics that indicate a good fit with the firm's culture. An advantage of the observation technique is that the interviewer can ask follow-up questions and scenarios of actual work situations can be used. A disadvantage is that the observation technique relies on a small sample of a person's behavior. Also, the observer's judgment depends on his or her own personality characteristics or abilities. Different observers may make different judgments about the same person.[50]

Projective personality test The individual perceives and interprets the test material in a manner that describes his or her own personality.

PROJECTIVE TESTS People respond to an inkblot, a picture, or a story. Only brief, general instructions are given to encourage free responses. The observer is well trained in analyzing responses. The concept of a *projective personality test* is that each individual perceives and interprets the test material in a manner that describes his or her own personality. Theoretically, the individual will project their own personality characteristics. An advantage of projective personality tests is that the trained observer overcomes the limitations of both self-inventory tests and observation techniques. A disadvantage is that projective tests are not standardized and depend heavily on the subjective opinion of the trained observer.[51]

GENERAL COMMENTS REGARDING MEASURING PERSONALITY A review of personality measurement techniques indicates there is no consensus on how to measure personality characteristics. Many personality tests lack validity, a concept discussed in Chapter 2.[52] Yet many companies such as General Motors, J.C. Penney, and American Cyanamid rely heavily on personality assessment programs to evaluate and promote employees while many other firms such as Mobil Oil use personality tests to screen applicants.[53]

PERCEPTION

Perception The process that individuals go through in order to organize and interpret their sensory impressions to give meaning to their environment.

From the perspective of individual differences, *perception* is the process that individuals go through in order to organize and interpret their sensory impressions to give meaning to their environment. However, individuals may look at the same thing but perceive it differently.[54] For example, Figures 4-9 and 4-10 illustrate an object that individuals perceive in different ways.

An illustration of perception within a work setting is that an employee may be viewed by one colleague as a hard worker who puts forth sincere effort and by another colleague as a poor worker who expends no effort at all. In the following sections, certain perceptual distortions are discussed. These distortions, which can impact on workplace affairs, include: selective perception, projection, expectancy, stereotyping, halo effects, self-fulfilling prophecy, self-serving bias, attribution theory, and learning processes.

An ambiguous picture of an inkblot: What do you see?

FIGURE 4-9
What Do You See?

SELECTIVE PERCEPTION   Because individuals cannot assimilate all they observe, they engage in *selective perception,* selecting pieces of information on the basis of their own interests, background, experience, and attitudes. The following example describes a form of selective perception. A manager is concerned primarily with an employee's final output. Because the employee is often negative during interactions with the manager, other managers conclude that the employee will probably receive a poor performance evaluation. Instead, the manager selects the employee's final performance, discarding the negative interactions or features, and evaluates the employee solely on the basis of the final results.

Individuals frequently use their own personal characteristics as benchmarks for perceiving others. If a manager wants challenge and responsibility, for example, then the manager will assume that others want the same. Individuals who assume that others are like themselves are right some of the time and wrong some of the time.

PROJECTION   Individuals often assume that others are similar to themselves. The tendency for people to attribute their own feelings or characteristics to others is called *projection*. For example, if a particular manager is status conscious or has

Selective perception
**Selecting pieces of
information on the
basis of an individual's
own interests, back-
ground, experience,
and attitudes.**

**Projection The ten-
dency for people to
attribute their own
feelings or characteris-
tics to others.**

FIGURE 4-10
What Others Have Seen

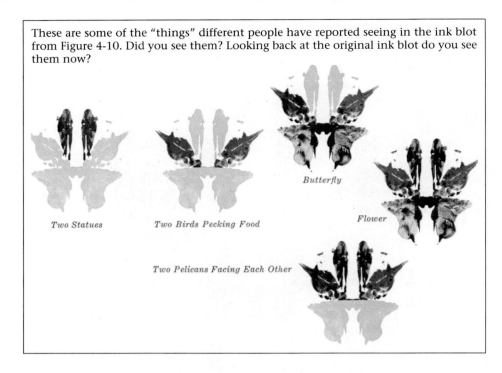

These are some of the "things" different people have reported seeing in the ink blot from Figure 4-10. Did you see them? Looking back at the original ink blot do you see them now?

Two Statues *Two Birds Pecking Food* *Butterfly* *Flower*

Two Pelicans Facing Each Other

a strong desire for power, then he or she may rationalize these traits to other managers.[55]

Expectancy An individual sees or hears what is expected rather than what actually occurs.

EXPECTANCY   *Expectancy* occurs when individuals expect to see or hear certain things. People may actually "see" what is expected rather than what is actually occurring.

Stereotyping The process of judging people by what is perceived about the group to which they belong.

STEREOTYPING   *Stereotyping* is the process of judging people on the basis of what the observer perceives about the group to which they belong. For example, a category of people is identified by their race, ethnic background, or occupation. An assumption is then made that individuals in this category have certain traits. Next, a perception is formed that everyone in this category possesses these common traits. As an illustration, suppose that a category of people, engineers, is identified by their occupation. Next, the assumption is made that engineers are creative. Finally, the perception is formed that all individuals are creative.

Halo effect This occurs when one characteristic of an individual is used to develop an overall impression.

HALO EFFECTS   A *halo effect* occurs when one characteristic of an individual is used to develop an overall impression of the individual. For example, a person may perform his or her job well but is constantly late. This tardiness may cause the individual's supervisor to devalue the employee's work efforts. Halo effects may occur from something which is either favorable or unfavorable that influences how the individual is perceived.

Self-fulfilling prophecy This occurs when an individual's expectations or beliefs determine his or her behavior and performance thus making the expectations come true.

SELF-FULFILLING PROPHECY   A *self-fulfilling prophecy* occurs when an individual's expectations or beliefs determine his or her behavior and performance, thus making his or her expectations come true. This concept was first tested in a setting involving elementary school students. A bogus test for academic potential was administered to students in grades one through six. Teachers were informed that certain students had a high potential for academic success and would be assigned to a high potential group. The teachers were also told that students with a normal potential would be assigned to a control group and that IQ tests and a reading ability test would be administered to both groups at two different time periods.

What really happened was that the people conducting the experiment never graded the bogus academic potential test and, instead, randomly assigned students to both the high potential and control groups. The IQ and reading ability tests, however, were valid tests. After the second round of valid testing, students, who had been designated as having high potential, achieved significantly higher scores in both the IQ and reading ability tests than did the students in the control group. Because of their expectations, teachers of the supposedly high potential group gave harder assignments, more feedback, and more recognition of achievement. Students in the normal potential group did not excel because their teachers did not expect outstanding results.[56]

Research studies in a variety of organizational settings indicate that when managers' expectations are raised for individuals performing a wide variety of tasks, higher levels of performance and achievement can be obtained.[57]

SELF-SERVING BIAS Individuals have a tendency to take credit and responsibility for positive outcomes of their behavior and to deny credit and responsibility for negative outcomes. This tendency is called *self-serving bias* and indicates that the same behavior will be explained differently according to events that happen after the behavior has occurred.[58] As an example, if a marketing vice president champions a product that becomes successful, he or she might attribute success to his or her understanding of the customers and the marketplace. However, if the same process is unsuccessful, the marketing vice president might attribute this to poor performance by a marketing research firm that was used.[59] The "OB in Practice" on page 116 illustrates another example of self-serving bias.

Self-serving bias A tendency to take credit and responsibility for positive outcomes of behavior and deny credit and responsibility for negative outcomes.

ATTRIBUTION THEORY *Attribution* is the process in which an observer assigns causes or motives to people's behavior.[60] This theory has important implications for managers. For example, if an employee exhibits poor performance then an interesting question is what caused this performance? One reason might be lack of effort, another might be lack of ability, while a third might be lack of support (environmental factors or situational factors such as the way the job is structured or the firm's rules and regulations). If a manager perceives the reason that an employee is not performing well is due to a lack of effort, then the manager will probably use some attempt to motivate the employee to work harder. In this scenario, the possibility of examining situational factors as a possible cause of poor performance is ignored. This oversight might sacrifice major performance gains.[61] Management scholars argue that much of the conflict that occurs between managers and their subordinates results from managers acting on their own interpretations of a given situation which may be quite different from those of their subordinates.

Attribution The process in which an observer assigns causes or motives to people's behavior.

Managers can avoid inappropriate attributions by increasing their interpersonal interactions, being able to see a situation as it is perceived by others, avoiding perceptual distortions, and placing more attention on the individual differences that exist among subordinates.[62]

LEARNING PROCESSES Individuals can learn by observing what happens to others and just by being told about something. For example, most of what we know we have learned from watching certain people: parents, teachers, bosses, television, and movie performers. Learning processes are an aspect of individual differences because people may exhibit certain behaviors based on what they have learned.

OB in Practice

Convicted Economist— an Example of Self-serving Bias?

William E. Gibson, a whiz-kid economist turned banking executive, was sentenced to thirty-three months in prison and ordered to pay $114,000 in fines for cheating American Airlines and the bank where he was the chairman out of $357,000. Gibson also had to pay $1,500 a month to "rent" his prison quarters.

Gibson received his Ph.D. in economics from the University of Chicago at age twenty-three, joined President Nixon's Council of Economic Advisors at age twenty-seven, and then began a career in banking. However, Gibson's ascension at Republic-Bank, then Texas's second largest, stalled in 1988, and he accepted an executive vice president's role at Continental Illinois in Chicago. Two years later he was asked to resign from Continental Illinois and became chairman of American Federal Savings Bank in Dallas. In less than one year, Gibson was abruptly dismissed from Federal Savings.

People who knew William Gibson commented on his intellectual prowess and his ability to charm and cajole as well as ridicule and demean. Work associates indicated that Gibson's job losses resulted from the manner in which he dealt with subordinates. Jim Westerbeck, an executive at Continental Illinois, said Gibson was known as "Teflon Bill—nothing was ever his fault. When things went wrong, he blamed coworkers and treated them cruelly. But he took credit when things went right."

Source: Adapted from Mark Wrolstad, "The Crash of Bill Gibson," *Dallas Morning News,* April 4, 1993, 1A, 14A.

When a new employee joins an existing work group, he or she already has some basis for learning how to behave as a result of education and past experiences. However, the work group provides a set of specific cues that helps the newcomer tailor her or his behavior to fit specific situations. For example, the

FIGURE 4-11
Getting Employees
to Do What They Are
Supposed to Do

Most of the time, nearly all employees do what they are supposed to do. What can supervisors do when this does not happen? Following are specific actions that supervisors can use to reduce most lapses in performance:

1. **Situation:** Employees do not receive compliments for doing their jobs. For example, employees have stated, "When I told my supervisor that the project would be finished on schedule, he said we don't give medals to people for doing what they are paid to do."

   Action: The good supervisor finds ways to encourage the right behavior. In the preceding situation, the supervisor can respond, "I noticed how hard you worked to complete that project on time; thanks." Also, do not wait for employees to finish tasks before complimenting them. When people do work that may be unsatisfying, encouraging the right behavior will lead to success.

2. **Situation:** Employees are punished for doing what they are supposed to do. For example, the employee who does difficult work is given all difficult work. The employee who comes to work early and stays late is called an "eager beaver" by his or her coworkers.

   Action: Reward employees who do difficult work well with time off before giving them additional difficult work. Eliminate sarcasm when it is directed at employees doing what they are supposed to do. Compliment employees when they put out extra effort.

Source: Adapted from Ferdinand Fournie, "Why Employees Don't Do What They're Supposed to Do," *Success,* April 1990, pp. 12–13.

group may expect its members to dress a certain way and to feel a certain way about the boss. In essence, the new employee learns how to behave in a new situation partly in response to what he or she already knows and partly in response to what others suggest and demonstrate.

Managers should be concerned about how they can teach employees to behave in ways to benefit the organization. An employee's behavior can be shaped by a manager who uses the techniques discussed in Figure 4-11. However, managers who are constantly late for work, take two hours for lunch, or help themselves to company office supplies for personal use should expect employees to receive the message they are sending and to model their behavior accordingly.[63]

CONCLUSIONS AND APPLICATIONS

- Individual differences provide managers with both a rich texture for creating opportunities to get things done and the challenges of managing diversity.

- Individual differences are the unique characteristics that differentiate people from one another, and consist of skills, abilities, personalities, perceptions, attitudes, values, and ethics.

- Values are developed from an individual's cultural setting and affect the attitudes, perceptions, needs, and motivations of people at work.

- Gordon Allport and Milton Rokeach, respectively, developed classification schemes to describe human values in general. Lawrence Kohlberg described individuals as they mature, more through a series of six moral stages while Bruce Meglino's value system described work-related values of people in the United States.

- Attitudes are based on important beliefs and values. Cognitive dissonance occurs when one's attitudes conflict with one's behavior. The situational aspect considers that attitudes evolve from information received from the social context.

- Personality is the set of distinct traits and characteristics that can be used to compare and contrast individuals. Theories explaining personality include: psychoanalytic, trait, humanistic, and immaturity-maturity theories.

- Personality traits relevant to the workplace include locus of control, authoritarianism, Machiavellianism, self-esteem, Type A–Type B personality, and problem solving.

- Personality is measured by self-inventory tests, observation techniques, or by projective tests.

- Perception is the process through which individuals organize and interpret information about their environment. Perceptual distortions include: selective perception, projection, expectancy, stereotyping, halo effects, self-fulfilling prophecy, self-serving bias, attribution theory, and learning processes.

- Attribution theory is the process in which an observer assigns causes or motives to people's behavior. Research indicates that much of the conflict that occurs between managers and their subordinates stems from managers acting on their own interpretations of a given situation that may be quite different from those of their subordinates.

- Managers can avoid inappropriate attributions by increasing their interpersonal interactions, being able to see a situation as it is perceived by others, avoiding perceptual distortions, and placing more attention on the individual differences that exist among subordinates.

REVIEW QUESTIONS

1. Why is the concept of individual differences important to managers?
2. Explain the four classification schemes used to depict values.
3. What is an attitude? How are attitudes related to values?
4. What is cognitive dissonance? How is it related to employee attitudes?
5. What is the relationship between job performance and job satisfaction?
6. Describe how personality is shaped.

7. Discuss how personality can be measured.
8. Describe the following personality styles: locus of control, Machiavellianism, Type A–Type B personality.
9. Explain the differences between selective perception and projection.
10. Describe how firms have used the MBTI to fit personality styles to a particular task environment.
11. Describe the stages of cognitive moral development. How does this concept affect ethical behavior in organizations?

DISCUSSION QUESTIONS

1. Which is more important—perception or reality? Explain.
2. Provide some examples of selective perception that can be used in accepting a new position with an organization.
3. Can you apply Argyris's immaturity-maturity model to your experiences as a student? Why or why not?
4. Prepare a brief personality profile of yourself using the following personality styles discussed in this chapter: locus of control, Machiavellianism, and Type A–Type B personality.

5. Have you experienced cognitive dissonance? Describe the situation. How did you resolve it?
6. Describe a recent instance in which you made attributions about another individual's behavior. Use attribution theory to explain those attributions.
7. Have you ever taken a personality test with respect to being hired by an organization? Were you told of the test results? Did you agree with the results?
8. Have you ever experienced a situation involving a self-fulfilling prophecy? What outcomes resulted from your experience?

CASE STUDY

Attitudes and Larry Pittman

Larry Pittman has been a production line employee for nearly eight years with American Wood Products. During Larry's employment, two strikes have occurred. The first strike lasted two days while the second lasted ten weeks. Three months ago, Larry was promoted to supervisor of the production line on which he had previously worked. Even though Larry was known as a strong union man, the supervisor's position offered nearly $14,000 more in salary per year. Larry believed the offer was too good to refuse. He was now part of management and enjoyed his position.

During the past month, two incidents have occurred that have troubled Larry. The first incident involved an argument with the union's chief steward in which the steward claimed that Larry was harassing employees for working at a slow pace. Larry denied his actions, lost his temper, and used foul language. The steward later withdrew the grievance after asking and getting Larry to apologize.

The second incident involved an employee who was repeatedly late for work. Larry documented three occurrences and, after the fourth in two weeks, sent the employee home without pay as stipulated in the labor–management agreement. Again, a grievance was filed by the union asserting that Larry was harassing the employee. During a meeting in the plant manager's office, the union produced the employee's time card indicating that the employee had clocked in on time for the day that Larry had sent the employee home. Larry insisted that the employee had been fifteen minutes late. The plant manager expressed a concern about Larry's behavior as a supervisor, stating that several other employees had confided that Larry was a nit-picker and seemed to enjoy harassing them.

Larry became angry over these situations. He believes that the union is out to get him. He likes his job as a supervisor and wonders why the employees have turned against him.

CASE STUDY QUESTIONS

1. Has Larry's attitude toward the union changed since he became a supervisor? Explain.
2. What perceptions might the employees who are union members have formed about Larry since he became a supervisor?
3. What should Larry do now?

Source: Adapted from "When the Shoe Is on the Other Foot," a critical incident appearing in Robert P. Vecchio, *Organization Behavior,* 2d ed., Chicago, Dryden, 1991.

EXPERIENTIAL EXERCISE 1

Assessing Your Machiavellian Tendencies

This exercise provides an opportunity for you to determine your own Machiavellian tendencies and to observe the Machiavellian actions of others.

Instructions

Part One: Take a few minutes to answer the following ten items. Do not tell others your Machiavellian score.

Indicate your reactions by circling one number for each statement, according to the following scale:

1 = Disagree a lot	4 = Agree a little
2 = Disagree a little	5 = Agree a lot
3 = Neutral	

1. The best way to handle people is to tell them what they want to hear.   1 2 3 4 5

2. When you ask someone to do something for you, it is best to give the real reason for wanting it rather than giving reasons that might carry more weight.   1 2 3 4 5

3. Anyone who completely trusts anyone else is asking for trouble.   1 2 3 4 5

4. It is hard to get ahead without cutting corners here and there.	1	2	3	4	5
5. It is safest to assume that all people have a vicious streak and it will come out when given a chance.	1	2	3	4	5
6. One should take action only when sure it is morally right.	1	2	3	4	5
7. Most people are basically good and kind.	1	2	3	4	5
8. There is no excuse for lying to someone else.	1	2	3	4	5
9. Most people forget the death of a parent more easily than the loss of their property.	1	2	3	4	5
10. Generally speaking, individuals will not work hard unless they're forced to do so.	1	2	3	4	5

The scale is scored as follows: First, for responses to items 2, 6, 7, and 8, reverse the score so that 5 becomes 1, 4 becomes 2, and so on. Second, add up scores on all 10 items (as adjusted). This is your total MACH score. An average score on this form is about 25. If you scored much higher than this, say 38, you would be classified as a HIGH MACH. If you scored much lower than 25, you would be classified as a LOW MACH.

Remember, this test cannot provide the final answer about your Machiavellian tendencies. Accurately assessing personality is much more difficult.

Source: Richard Christie and Florence L. Geis, eds., *Studies in Machiavellianism,* New York, Academic Press, 1970. Reprinted by permission.

Part Two: After completing the items, your instructor will *randomly* divide the class into groups of three with each group member receiving ten slips of paper. Next, read the following instructions:

Each slip of paper represents $1. Your group has a total of $30. This money is to be distributed in any way the group decides. The game is over as soon as any two members agree as to how it will be divided. Group members are free to make any arrangements they wish.

After the money has been divided, reveal your Machiavellian score to the other group members.

QUESTIONS

1. Did two people form a coalition and exclude the third participant?
2. How was the money divided in your group? Describe how the agreement was reached.
3. Did one person push for the coalition more strongly than the other two? What was his or her Machiavellian score?
4. By knowing your Machiavellian score in advance, were your actions biased in any way? Explain.
5. Obviously, the fairest distribution is $10 each. However, a selfish party could cut out the third person, and the remaining two would end up with $15 each. Suppose that one person suggests this alternative to you and that, before you decide, the left out person offers to give you $16, taking $14 as his or her share and cutting out the other person. What would you do?

Source: Adapted from Florence L. Geis and T. H. Moon, "Machiavellianism and Deception," *Journal of Personality and Social Psychology* 42, 1981, pp. 766–775. James L. Gibson, John M. Ivancevich, and James H. Donnelly, Jr., *Organizations: Behavior, Structure, Processes,* 7th ed., Homewood, IL, Irwin, 1991. Jerald Greenberg and Robert Baron, *Behavior in Organizations,* 4th ed., Boston, Allyn and Bacon, 1993.

EXPERIENTIAL EXERCISE 2

Identifying Personal Characteristics of Sensitive and Insensitive Bosses

Jim Miller, CEO of Miller Business Systems, a Texas office products distributor, has written a book, *The Corporate Coach,* that praises sensitive managers. Miller began wondering, however, about insensitive managers and now sponsors a national contest in which participants submit gruesome written descriptions of bad bosses. One such boss was described as a cross between Simon Legree and Captain Bligh, combined with the Joker.

Half of the class should describe the personal characteristics of a sensitive boss while the other half should describe the personal characteristics of an insensitive boss. Which boss, the sensitive one or the insensitive one, would you expect to have higher performing subordinates? Why?

 Take It to the Net   **You can find this chapter's World Wide Web exercise at:**
http://www.prenhall.com/carrell

CHAPTER 5

Decision Making, Job Satisfaction, and Work Stress

CHAPTER OBJECTIVES

1. To explain the decision-making process.

2. To understand the differences between the process of rational decision making and bounded rationality.

3. To understand conditions affecting decision making

4. To discuss the relationship between technological information systems and decision making.

5. To describe the major theories of job satisfaction and how to measure it.

6. To explain the major causes and consequences of job satisfaction.

7. To describe the major dimensions of job commitment.

Intel CEO Andrew Grove

In 1987, the Intel Corporation was a money-losing producer of commodity memory chips. Since then, Intel has transformed itself into the world's largest semiconductor company and the business best-positioned to profit from the enormous increase in personal computer sales. Price wars have created a mass market for personal computers, and almost all PCs employ at least one Intel chip; therefore, the company has a near monopoly on the leading-edge microprocessors that do their thinking. After investors realized that the PC sales surge was related to Intel's market dominance, Intel's stock price increased 30 percent within one month.

An important aspect of Intel's success was the willingness of CEO Andrew Grove to bet billions on research and development and on new manufacturing plants. In 1993, Intel put $2.5 billion—equal to 43 percent of 1992's revenues—into R&D and capital outlays.

Grove, who was fifty-six in 1993, fled his native Hungary in 1956 with $20 in his pocket. He earned a Ph.D. in chemical engineering at the University of California-Berkeley and helped found Intel in 1968.

According to Grove, a corporation is a living organism, and it has to continue to shed its skin. Methods have to change. Focus has to change. The sum total of those changes is transformation. The primary task of a

CEO is to recognize change and then articulate it as a strategy. Top management must reconcile action and speech. Tough decisions are required. However, in late 1994, a mathematics professor discovered a flaw in Intel's Pentium chip, the powerful new brain used in most new PCs. The Pentium's imperfection affects division problems involving numbers with many digits. For example, if 4,195, 835 is divided by 3,145,727 and then multiplied by 3,145,727, the result should be the original number 4,195,835. It does not take a computer to figure that out. But PCs with the flawed Pentium come up with a different answer: 4,195,579. At first, Intel blithely dismissed criticisms of the Pentium stating that most folks would encounter an inaccurate answer just once in 27,000 years; therefore, the errant chips would be replaced only if computer owners could demonstrate that they really needed an extra margin of accuracy. Angry users began complaining about Intel's apathy on the Internet and soon all the world knew about the flawed Pentium and Intel's response. In early December 1994, IBM contended that the Pentium's mistakes were far more frequent than Intel had acknowledged, and IBM announced it was halting shipments of all its products containing the Pentium chip. In late December 1994, Intel announced that it would replace *any* Pentium chip without question and would pay any service charges to have the chip replaced.[1]

In this chapter decision making is first examined by contrasting an idealized description of how people make decisions with a description of one that is more realistic. Later, we discuss job satisfaction and then work stress. These three topics are related. Decision making has an impact on job satisfaction while work stress is a consequence of dissatisfaction.

DECISION MAKING

Decision making is a fundamental process in organizations by which managers choose one alternative from others.

Decision making is a fundamental process in organizations by which managers choose one alternative from others. Managers make decisions based on the information they receive from the behavior of individuals or groups within the organization and also from sources external to the organization. Decision making is not always easy or pleasant, however. In organizational settings, there is a tempting tendency to postpone decisions, to wait for further developments, and to engage in additional study. When Andrew Grove, Intel's CEO, announced the decision to replace any Pentium chip without question, he stated that Intel was good in making engineering and manufacturing decisions but poor when it came to marketing decisions. Grove added that Intel's first response to the Pentium problem had appeared to be "arrogant and uncaring."[1A] H. Ross Perot, who founded Electronic Data Systems (EDS) and then sold it to General Motors, commented on the contrast between decision making at EDS and at GM shortly before leaving his position on the GM board of directors.[2]

> The first EDSer to see a snake kills it. At GM, the first thing you do is organize a committee on snakes. Then, you bring in a consultant who knows a lot about snakes. The third thing you do is to talk about it for a year.

In this section, decision making is discussed from a number of perspectives: types of decisions, managerial decision-making styles, the decision-making process, and behavioral factors influencing individual decision making. Decision making in groups is discussed in Chapter 11.

Types of Decisions

Decision making has been classified in several ways; however, the primary difference among the various systems is in terminology. A useful distinction for studying managerial decisions is the classification of decisions along a continuum ranging from routine to nonroutine. As illustrated in Figure 5-1, most decisions involve situations that contain both structured (well-defined) and unstructured (ill-defined) elements.

Decisions near the end of the continuum focus on well-structured situations and can be categorized as *programmed decisions*. Such decisions recur frequently, involve standard decision procedures, and entail a minimum of uncertainty. Common examples include payroll processing, reordering standard inventory items, paying suppliers, and so on. The decision maker can usually rely upon policies, rules, past precedents, standardized methods of processing, or computational techniques. Probably 90 percent of management decisions are largely routine, although any manager's experience is significant in determining whether a specific decision is routine.

Programmed decision A decision focused on a well-structured situation that recurs frequently and entails a minimum of uncertainty.

Decisions at the opposite—or nonroutine—end of the continuum deal with unstructured situations of a novel, nonrecurring nature and can be categorized as *nonprogrammed decisions*. Their complexity is compounded by incomplete knowledge and the absence of accepted methods of resolution. Nonroutine decisions include not only the major corporate decisions, such as merger or acquisition, but also more restricted ones, such as adoption of a new advertising theme or motivation of a particular employee. A significant characteristic of such decisions is that no alternative can be proved to be the "best" possible solution to a particular problem. A much higher degree of subjective judgment and even intuition are involved in nonroutine decisions.

Nonprogrammed decision A decision that deals with complex, unstructured situations of a novel, nonrecurring type.

One of the most important lessons a manager can learn is that virtually all important—and most minor—decisions are made under conditions of ambiguity. Ambiguous situations may be characterized by *lack of familiarity* (newness); *complexity* (interactions of events too difficult to analyze completely); or *contradictory situations* where different elements suggest different structures. Even the most sophisticated mathematical decision models, the most elaborate computer systems, and the most complete market research cannot remove the element of ambiguity from managerial decision making. At best, it can be reduced somewhat. As one source suggests, you as a manager "should take adequate precau-

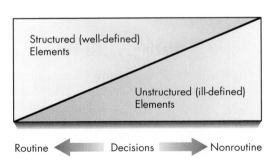

FIGURE 5-1
A Continuum of Managerial Decisions

tions by ensuring a sufficient number of alternative courses of action if your intended course turns out to be the wrong course."[3]

Managerial Decision-Making Styles

A dozen managers, each faced with the same unstructured problem, would likely use twelve widely divergent methods, or styles, to analyze the problem and formulate a solution. This variance in decision-making styles reflects the differences among managers in the way they perceive, organize, and understand their environment. These differences stem from dissimilar work backgrounds, educational experiences, social influences, value systems, and psychological attributes.

Decision-making styles have been classified in many different ways. One classification suggests the following four basic styles:[4]

- *Decisive*—refers to a manager who processes a minimum amount of information to arrive at one firm conclusion. This individual is concerned with action, results, speed, and efficiency. Long, detailed reports will be sent back, ignored, or given to someone else to summarize.
- *Flexible*—characterizes a manager who prefers concise reports containing a wide variety of briefly stated alternatives from which to choose. Rather than planning highly structured solutions, this manager prefers that solutions evolve as he or she gains acceptance from others.
- *Hierarchical*—describes a manager who carefully analyzes large amounts of information to arrive at one best solution. He or she values perfection, precision, and thoroughness. Brief or summarized reports are viewed as inadequate.
- *Integrative*—refers to a manager who uses masses of information to generate many possible solutions simultaneously (rather than sequentially as flexible managers do.) This manager constantly alters and improves his or her plans and shuns brief reports in favor of complex analyses from varying points of view.

The effectiveness of any particular decision-making style depends on the specific situation the manager is facing.

One study of managerial decision-making styles concludes that successful decision makers are inconsistent in the way they attack problems, varying their approach to fit the problem situation. One problem, for example, may require analysis at a high conceptual level, while another may require a review of operational details. In one situation, a manager may consult subordinates in solving a particular problem; the same manager may arrive at the decision alone in another situation. Unsuccessful decision makers, on the other hand, generally approach each problem in the same predictable style. Apparently, an adaptable contingency style is more effective than a single, unvarying approach to decision making.[5]

The Decision Making Process

In analyzing decision making, there is a tendency to focus upon the final moment in which the manager selects a course of action. However, decision making should not be thought of as an end but as a means for achieving organizational goals. Decisions are the mechanisms by which an attempt is made to achieve a desired state. In essence, decisions are an organizational response to problems or opportunities.

In this section, two decision-making processes are discussed: the rational approach and the behavioral approach. The rational approach is based on a classical decision theory in which the managerial world is certain, stable, and describes how managers should make decisions. The behavioral approach is developed from behavioral decision theory which argues that individuals have cognitive limitations and act only in terms of what they perceive about a particular situation.[6]

RATIONAL APPROACH   The *rational approach* to decision making involves a series of steps to maximize the attainment of goals. This approach assumes that the organization is economically based and that the decision maker recognizes all alternative courses of action, and can accurately and completely evaluate each alternative. Decision makers are viewed as attempting to make optimal decisions.[7] The steps of this approach are illustrated in Fig. 5-2 and described as follows:

Rational approach A decision based on recognizing and evaluating all alternative courses of action to attain a goal.

Goal Statement.   Adequately established goals dictate what results must be achieved. As an example, the goal of a particular organization may be to obtain a certain return on assets (ROA) or market share by the end of a specific time period.

Problem Identification.   A problem exists when there is a difference between an organization's goals and its performance. If an organization has a goal of 10 percent for ROA and an actual ROA of 6 percent, then a problem exists. In some situations a problem may actually be an opportunity. For example, some years ago, Donald Fisher, who was in the San Francisco real estate business, bought a pair of Levi cords. When he found that the pair was the wrong size, he asked his wife to exchange them for a pair in the same style but the proper size. When she could not find his size in that style, Fisher perceived an opportunity. He opened a store that carried every style and size that Levi Strauss made. The company that grew out of that single store became known as the Gap.[8]

A distinction between a problem and an opportunity is that problems present themselves while opportunities must be found. Many organizations stress searching for opportunities through strategic planning activities.[9]

Search for Alternatives.   Alternatives are developed by a search process of the organization's external and internal environments. Environmental scanning, discussed in Chapter 16, is a process of identifying opportunities and threats.[10] One theory in searching for alternatives is that managers begin their search by identifying familiar alternatives employed in previous situations. If these alternatives seem unsuitable, then less familiar possibilities are explored.[11] Nonroutine decisions, then, often require imagination and creative thinking.

Evaluation of Alternatives.   Evaluating the alternatives that are generated requires the manager to predict an uncertain future. Possible pros and cons must be considered. The manager may attempt to assign probabilities of future occurrence—based on past experience, formal forecasts, or subjective judgment—to the more pertinent factors.

At this stage, intuition may influence the decision process. Intuition "is that psychological function which transmits perceptions in an unconscious way."[12] One study reveals that senior-level managers use intuition in several different ways and in various stages of the decision-making process.[13] For instance, experienced managers can often intuitively sense when a problem exists. *Intuition*

Intuition An unconscious process in which managers integrate ideas that do not at first seem related.

FIGURE 5-2
The Rational
Decision-Making Process

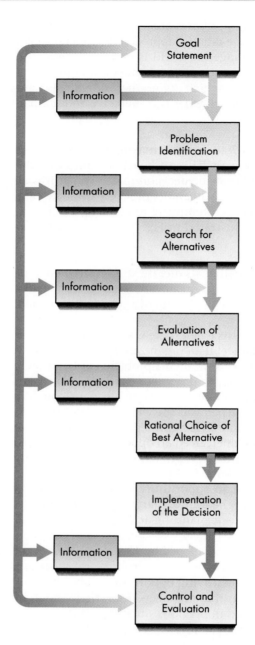

may also be used in its best-known form as an unconscious process in which managers integrate ideas that do not at first appear to be related (often termed the "aha!" experience). At the final stage of the decision process, intuition may be used by experienced managers as a check on the results of formal decision analysis models. To use intuition effectively, a manager must have extensive experience in problem analysis and decision making in his or her particular industry. Intuition is not a random guess, nor is it the opposite of rationality.

During the evaluation stage, the manager must also realize that various alternatives may have differing impacts on various parts of the organization. Special interests of specific departments and individuals tend to interfere with the process by which facts are investigated and decisions reached. A decision favorable for the firm as a whole may strengthen or weaken the positions of different departments. To protect and enhance their various positions, therefore, rival managers often compete with each other, bargain, build alliances with others, and in sometimes devious ways attempt to influence outcomes. The evaluation process, then, must include the power struggles among various factions in the organization.

The manager must also be aware that decisions at higher levels in the organization automatically trigger the need for specific operational decisions to be made at lower levels. A hospital administrator's decision to open a new intensive care unit, for example, initiates a series of decisions concerning what kinds of equipment will be needed, where it should be purchased, what types of personnel will be required, how these personnel will be organized, and so on.

Rational Choice of Best Alternative.   After all of the alternatives have been identified, then the best alternative must be selected. The selection of this best alternative is not an isolated act but is the means to an end. In the rational decision-making process, best is defined in terms of the original goal.

Implementation of the Design.   Managers use administrative and persuasive abilities and give directions to ensure that the decision is carried out.

Control and Evaluation.   As soon as the decision is implemented, a monitoring activity begins. Actual results are compared with planned results (the goal statement) and changes must be made if differences exist.

BEHAVIORAL APPROACH   Research into managerial decision making shows that managers are unable to follow the steps of the rational decision-making approach. Time pressures and the ill-defined nature of many problems make the rational approach impossible. Managers cannot evaluate every goal and alternative because they have only so much time and mental capacity. There is a limit to how rational managers can be. In essence, a manager's rationality is bounded (limited) by an incomplete understanding of the organization's goals, inadequate information, and the complexity of many problems. Thus, the circumstances of limited time, information, and resources to deal with complex problems is known as *bounded rationality*.[14]

Because neither the problem nor the alternative solutions are completely identified, the final decision usually does not yield a maximum return to the organization. Managers must instead settle for a satisfactory return. In other words, they cannot maximize; they must *satisfice,* that is, select a course of action that they believe will be satisfactory or "good enough."[15] Figure 5-3 presents a comparison between the rational decision-making process and bounded rationality. In essence, the disparity between the rational decision-making process of how managers *should* make decisions and the bounded rationality of how managers *actually* make them can be explained when the practice of management deviates from the theory of management.[16]

Bounded rationality Circumstances of limited time, information, and resources to deal with complex problems.

Satisfice Selecting a satisfactory course of action.

Conditions Affecting Decision Making

The appropriate choice to be made by decision makers depends on the amount of information available and on certain decision-making conditions. In fact, because of these different conditions, different decision makers may not select identical alternatives in the same situation. These conditions include: escalat-

FIGURE 5-3 A Comparison Between the Rational Decision-Making Process and Bounded Rationality

Decision-Making Step	Rational Decision Making	Bounded Rationality
1. Problem Identification	An important organizational problem is identified.	A visible problem reflecting the manager's interests and background is identified.
2. Search for Alternatives	A creative criteria is developed and a comprehensive list of all alternatives is developed.	A limited set of criteria is identified based on the self-interests of the decision maker. A limited number of similar alternatives is developed.
3. Evaluation of Alternatives	All alternatives are evaluated against the decision criteria. The consequences for each alternative are known.	Beginning with a favored solution, alternatives are evaluated, one at a time, against the decision criteria.
4. Choice of Best Alternative	Decision making is *maximized*. The alternative with the highest outcome in terms of the organization's goal is chosen. All alternatives are considered.	Decision making is *satisficed*. Alternatives are evaluated until a solution is found that is sufficient and satisfactory, at which time the process stops.
5. Implementation of Chosen Alternative	Because the decision maximizes the organization's single, well-defined goal, all organizational members will accept the solution.	Power and politics will influence the acceptance of, and the commitment to, the solution.
6. Evaluation	The decision's outcome is objectively evaluated against the original problem.	Objective evaluations are rare because of the evaluator's self-interests. A possible possible escalation of resources to prior commitments may occur despite previous failures or the strong evidence that additional resources are not warranted.

ing commitment, risk-certainty-uncertainty, muddling through-incremental-ism, optimizing-suboptimizing. Following is a discussion of these decision-making conditions.

ESCALATING COMMITMENT   Research indicates that organizations often continue to persist in an ineffective course of action when evidence indicates that the project is doomed to failure. Managers tend to escalate commitment to a failing decision for two reasons. The first is that managers simply do not know when to pull the plug. They tend to block out or distort negative information.[17] Continuing to invest additional money into an old car is a personal example. An organizational example involved Expo '86 held in Vancouver, British Columbia. At that time the Canadian provincial government expected the project to break even financially and that taxes would not have to be increased to pay for it. As work progressed, it became apparent that expenses were greater than projected and that the project would be in "the red." However, the organizers did not call off the event despite huge losses that would occur.[18]

A second reason for escalating commitment to a failed decision is that society values persistence and consistency. Managers that are consistent are considered better leaders than those who switch around from one course of action to another. As an example, the Washington Public Power Supply System (WPPSS) estimated that it could build three power plants for $3.1 billion. Construction was started and construction costs overruns became readily apparent. Also, managers saw evidence that expected increases in power consumption were not going to materialize. Rather than scaling back on the number of power plants to be built, WPPSS announced plans to build two additional power plants and proceeded to do so. After the five power plants were constructed, the entire project had increased from an estimated $9 billion to $24 billion; moreover, an analysis of power demand indicated that the five plants were not needed.[19]

RISK–CERTAINTY—UNCERTAINTY   The range of information that is available to decision makers can be described as a continuum ranging from complete certainty (all alternative outcomes are known) to complete uncertainty (alternative outcomes are unknown). Risk is involved at points along the continuum. In a risk situation the decision maker lacks complete information to provide certainty but has some information about possible outcomes and may be able to estimate the probabilities of occurrence of various outcomes. A decision maker who lacks sufficient information to identify outcomes at all (or to estimate probability outcomes) is facing total uncertainty.[20]

Risk-certainty/ uncertainty The range of information available to decision makers ranging from a situation where all alternatives are known to one in which there is an unknown alternative outcome.

MUDDLING THROUGH–INCREMENTALISM   Muddling through occurs when goals are made in broad terms and managers proceed to make intuitive decisions that seem to be most expedient at the time.[21] As an example, prior to its takeover by Grand Metropolitan, Pillsbury operated with broad goals such as "building the super box," a product that supposedly would provide an increased competitive advantage. Each division, however, drifted along independently pursuing their own, often conflicting, ends.[22]

Incrementalism is a different concept than muddling through. According to this view, because of a rapidly changing environment, managers often have insufficient time and information to undertake a full, formal analysis of all possible alternatives. Events are dealt with in an incremental fashion. The basic idea is that management sometimes does not know precisely its ultimate goal or its entire strategy. Bits and pieces of the strategy unfold incrementally as managers respond to a constantly changing environment. This incremental approach is necessitated by several factors, among them a lack of information about the environment, the difficulty of predicting the effects of various decisions, and the resistance that major organizational changes usually encounter. Incremental movements allow the organization to experiment with various approaches, to learn, and to build awareness and commitment among those who must implement the decision.[23] An example of incrementalism is the development of the Gillette Company's Sensor razor. Gillette's top management approved an idea to create a thinner razor that would make razor cartridges easier to clean. The technical demands for designing such a razor had several blind alleys and eventually cost Gillette $300 million. The razor, however, has been a smashing success and Gillette has recovered its investment.[24]

Incrementalism Bits and pieces of strategy are formed as managers respond to a constantly changing environment.

OPTIMIZING–SUBOPTIMIZING   An alternative that usually achieves a desired goal usually has a positive or negative impact on another goal. When two objectives cannot be fully achieved simultaneously, one is optimized and the other is suboptimized. As an example, a plant manager may optimize a short-run goal to reduce maintenance costs at the expense of a long-run goal such as product quality.

Certain behavioral factors also influence the decision-making process: values, personality, and the propensity for risk.[25] Each of these factors is discussed in this section.

VALUES   Values were discussed in Chap. 4. From the perspective of decision making, value judgments must be made for all aspects of the rational decision making approach depicted in Fig. 5-2. Values also pervade the behavioral decision making approach.[26]

PERSONALITY   Personality was also discussed in Chap. 4. Research studies have determined that a decision maker's personality traits combine with certain situational and interactional variables that influence the decision-making process.[27]

PROPENSITY FOR RISK   All organizational decisions involve some degree of risk that is based on the probability of obtaining a desired outcome. Probabilities may be objective in that they are developed from information based on concrete, verifiable data. As an example, if a large diversified firm announces an earnings decline of 40 percent because of decreased sales of its largest division that produces and distributes tobacco products, then this provides objective data for decision makers of other firms involved in producing and/or distributing tobacco products. Probabilities can also be based on personal beliefs or hunches about what will happen. An example would be an individual who places a bet on a particular football team because the team wears blue jerseys, that individual's favorite color.

Research indicates that decision makers vary greatly in their propensity for taking risks. An individual with a high aversion to risk establishes different objectives, evaluates alternatives differently, and selects different alternatives than an individual in the same situation who has a low aversion to risk.[28]

TECHNOLOGICAL INFORMATION SYSTEMS AND DECISION MAKING

Many organizations are utilizing information systems (usually computerized) to provide information in an adaptable, flexible format that facilitates different kinds of decision making.

Decision Support System (DDS)

An interactive system designed to support the decision-making activities of a particular manager. For example, a microcomputer spreadsheet program such as Lotus or Excel, using different assumptions, can generate multiple versions of a budget or project costs. The key characteristic of a DDS is to aid but not make decisions for managers.[29]

Group Decision Support System (GDSS)

An informative system that supports collective decision making when individuals work as a group on unstructured problems. GDSS assists the group in generating and evaluating ideas, as well as selecting alternatives.[30]

Expert Systems (ES)

Systems that incorporate the same decision-making logic as people. For example, American Express uses an expert system to assist in credit review and credit authorization. Because of excessive development costs, expert systems have been applied to repetitive, high-value decisions in narrowly defined areas.[31]

Future Decision Technology Systems

Much of the required support for future decision technology systems exists today in terms of both hardware and software or computer programs. The remaining task is to organize information in a form that is readily accessible and useful to the decision maker to avoid problems of redundancy, to increase accuracy and timeliness, and to provide information in an intelligible way so as to become a useful tool rather than an obstacle.[32] Decision technology systems of the future can be described as follows:[33]

MANAGEMENT INFORMATION SYSTEMS Management information systems will be used to analyze data developed as a result of actual operations in a company. Models, trends, forecasts, or other analytic tools will be applied. Reports more likely will be on demand, often in graphic form on terminals rather than via the myriad of written reports that currently are provided to managers.

DECISION SUPPORT SYSTEMS Decision support systems will allow for continuous interaction with the computer, with greater application of the decision maker's judgment and insight to formulate and structure problems as well as to tap into statistical, economic, or accounting data or models to help analyze and produce specific kinds of output needed by the decision maker.

EXPERT SYSTEMS Expert systems will provide the manager with an ability to store knowledge in a form that is readily available and can be retrieved in order to exercise judgment or use rules that have been applied previously. In this area, approaches to reasoning and judgment will become increasingly important, as well as understanding the cognitive complexity of the decision maker so as to better match the new systems to the requirements of the decision maker.

EXECUTIVE INFORMATION SYSTEMS Executive information systems provide a continuous evaluation and monitoring of the decision environment. They will be able to provide warnings, timely information, and analysis so that top-level managers who are not concerned with ongoing daily operations and the myriad details that exist in every organization can be alerted to important events and requirements for their decisions.

THE AUTOMATED OFFICE OF THE FUTURE The automated office of the future will provide all kinds of written, oral, group interaction, teleconferencing, and teleprocessing, as well as the ability to obtain information from knowledge-based systems the way we do today in databased systems. This will help support more creative thinking and application of judgment to problems confronting decision makers. As described in the "OB In Practice" on page 134, the Internet is changing how firms will conduct business.

A look far into the future indicates some startling possibilities in the application of information to support decision making. Neural networks provide a frontier that perhaps may change the way managers look at decision making and at support systems. Neural networks in a sense are crude but powerful simulations of the nervous system that try to mimic the way the brain works. Although this is not crucial, the important aspect of neural networks is that, in fact, they are a hybrid analog/digital computer with speeds about 1,000 times faster than current systems. They are able to process information one billion times faster than current conventional digital computers.

Applications include a variety of tasks from machine vision and robotics to speech recognition, tests, and handwriting recognition. They have been able to

How the Internet Is Changing the Way Firms Conduct Business

Recently the Internet was a place where millions of friends and strangers could chat and "flame" each other about every topic under the sun, from sex to Spam to Superman. People browsed through thousands of on-line libraries, played new types of games, and traded software. Now, new software and imaginative services are making the Internet one of the most exciting places ever for doing business. For example, one program called "Mosaic" is a collection of thousands of independently owned computers that work together as one in an Internet service called the World Wide Web. These computers, called Web servers, are scattered all over the world and contain every imaginable type of data. In late 1994, 21,700 commercial "domains" (the Internet equivalent of a storefront address) are officially registered on the Web, up from 9,000 in 1991. Corporations are eager to exploit the Web and the Internet so they can use it as a tool for marketing, sales, customer support, and as low-cost alternatives to fax, express mail, and other communication channels. Volvo and Alfa Romeo are using the Web to zap photos and information about new cars to virtual tire-kickers. J. P. Morgan & Co. offers clients access to its risk-management database. Hyatt Hotels Corp. promotes hotels and resorts, providing discounts for those who say they saw it on the Net. GE Plastics is leading General Electric Co.'s foray with 1,500 pages of technical data on the Web to help customers use its resins. Xerox Corp. allows customers to try out software across the Internet, and computer buyers can log into a Digital Equipment Corp., Alpha computer, to find out how quickly it can run their programs.

In Silicon Valley, a group of electronics manufacturers that includes Intel, Hewlett-Packard, IBM, and Apple Computer is building CommerceNet, an Internet marketplace for electronics goods and services. If it develops as planned, it could just about eliminate all paperwork between participating companies—everything from simple purchase orders and invoices to resumés and product specifications.

Source: Adapted from John Verity, John Carey, and Edward Baig, "The Internet: How It Will Change the Way You Do Business," *Business Week*, November 14, 1994, pp. 80–88.

---

solve very complex problems that involve patterns, such as interpretation or evaluation of military vehicles and analysis of integrated computer circuitry. In banking, neural networks have helped Chase Manhattan detect credit card fraud. Security Pacific Bank uses the system to analyze commercial and automobile loan risks. In addition to such applications, neural networks have been applied in medicine, to detect abnormal heart sounds and to interpret electrocardiograms. At Roarck University in England, an electronic nose that recognizes smells has been developed. A similar system is used in Japan to test the freshness of sushi. Ford Motor Company is developing a computer, which is actually on the automobile, that simultaneously monitors all aspects of the automotive operation—the engine, the power train, suspension, electronic steering, brakes, climate control, and so forth.

In addition to the capabilities mentioned, neural networks have been used in Japan for a variety of applications that try to simulate human behavior. They incorporate a concept of "fuzzy logic." This logic does not deal with precise values but on concepts, such as, for example, a very bright finish; however, *bright* can have a range of values, which is why this logic is called fuzzy. On the other hand, the Japanese have applied it to washing machines where the water can be determined as being dirty or not dirty—again, a fuzzy concept. We will also see a drastic change in the way computers are built and the kind of software they will use. In particular, parallel architecture that allows the program to process over a large number of electronic routes provides an ability to do things that we cannot do very efficiently with digital computers. This will enhance the processing speed but will also introduce some interesting new and yet untested capabilities. The impact on decision makers and management is yet to be determined. However, the potential of neural networks is that it tries to mimic the mind. Perhaps such a network can become humanlike and can help make more effective decisions.[34] The "OB In Practice" on page 136 describes how computer technology has the power to create jobs and to eliminate them.

INDIVIDUALS AND JOB-RELATED ATTITUDES

In Chap. 4, the concept of individual differences was examined from a number of perspectives. This section focuses on certain attitudes that individuals have about their jobs. Specifically, job satisfaction, job involvement, and organizational commitment are discussed.

Job Satisfaction

Job satisfaction—an employee's attitude about his or her job—stems from a variety of aspects of the job. As an example, pay, promotion opportunities, supervisors, and coworkers all affect employees' perceptions about their jobs. Job satisfaction also stems from factors present in the work environment: the supervisor's style, organizational policies and procedures, work-group affiliation, working conditions, and fringe benefits. However, there is evidence to suggest that job satisfaction is more intrinsic to the person than to the job. One study suggests that genetics might play a part in explaining job satisfaction. Identical twins who were reared separately achieved similar scores on certain job-satisfaction measures, such as how much feeling of accomplishment they got from their jobs.[35] An individual's needs and aspirations can also affect job satisfaction. A person finishing his or her college degree may take a particular job on a temporary basis to pay educational expenses. This person may be satisfied with the job while still in school but less satisfied with the same job on a permanent basis.

How is job satisfaction measured? This is an important question. Several measurement techniques have been developed, including interviews and critical incidents, but the most popular approach is the use of questionnaires, often called attitude or opinion surveys. One research study identifies forty-six different questionnaires, including 249 measures used to determine job satisfaction. The most commonly used instruments are the Minnesota Satisfaction Questionnaire, the Job Diagnostic Survey, the Index of Organizational Reactions, and the Job Descriptive Index (JDI).[36] Figure 5-4 illustrates twenty of the seventy-two items of the Job Descriptive Index.

There are advantages and disadvantages to these instruments. Although they can be administered easily and inexpensively to large numbers of people, scores can be easily tabulated, and norms can be used for comparisons. Job-satisfaction questionnaires measure perceptions of the workplace rather than actual on-the-job circumstances. For example, an employee may indicate low job satisfaction

Job satisfaction An employee's attitude about his or her job based on factors present in the work environment.

Computer Technology Has the Power to Create New Jobs and to Eliminate Them

Is computer technology a job creator or a job destroyer? It depends on whom you ask! In a recent survey conducted by the American Management Association, of 328 companies that cut their work forces, 14 percent reported that implementing computer technology was the reason. Furthermore, for 138 other companies that were planning layoffs, 18 percent cited computer technology.

Although many economists argue that in the end, computer technology will create more jobs than it destroys, they are not willing to bet on any numbers. However, these economists cite that in 1994, 1.5 million software engineers, systems analysts, and other computer professionals were employed in the United States, up 87 percent from 719,000 a decade ago. The Bureau of Labor Statistics projects that from 1994 to 2005, computer technology jobs will increase an additional 55 percent, compared with an overall 22 percent employment growth in that same span. Also, computer technology has spawned new products and new jobs for many fields of industry. These include on-line services and home shopping. David Mowry, a business professor at the University of California–Berkeley who studies how computer technology affects the work force, argues that computer technology will ultimately create more jobs than it destroys but that "there are losers" in the short run.

Source: Adapted from Joan Rigdon, "Give and Take—Computer Technology Creates Jobs and Eliminates Them," A Computer Technology Supplement, *The Wall Street Journal*, November 14, 1994, p. R24.

---

because he or she has to fight rush-hour traffic to get to and from work. A looming deadline may also distort an employee's responses.

Why should supervisors and managers be concerned about an employee's job satisfaction? Despite the shortcomings of job-satisfaction measurement instruments, attitude surveys can be a valuable tool for managers and supervisors. Excessive absenteeism, rapid turnover, and grievances often result when workers experience high levels of job dissatisfaction. Attitude surveys can identify major employee concerns that can be remedied. In essence, these surveys provide constructive feedback from employees to supervisors and managers. The "Profile" on page 138 describes the development of a program to improve job satisfaction of Marriott's frontline employees.

Traditionally, three views have been advanced regarding the relationship of job satisfaction to job performance: (1) job satisfaction causes job performance; (2) job performance causes job satisfaction; and (3) there is no specific relationship between job satisfaction and job performance because rewards intervene. These viewpoints are illustrated in Fig. 5-5.

Over the past seventy years, thousands of studies have been conducted that deal with job satisfaction. Certainly, managers should be concerned about the satisfaction or dissatisfaction of their employees. In this section we examine three approaches that have been used to describe job satisfaction: Herzberg's *two-factor theory*, Locke's *value theory*, and Moorhead-Griffin's *causes and consequences*.

HERZBERG'S TWO-FACTOR THEORY Frederick Herzberg asked 200 accountants and engineers to think about something that may have happened to them on their

FIGURE 5-4
Job Descriptive Index

---

20 Sample Items from the 72-Item Job Descriptive Index (JDI)

Employees are asked to respond "Y" for yes, "N" for no, or "?" for can't decide in describing whether a word or phrase reflects their attitudes about their jobs. The JDI is based on the following five dimensions of job satisfaction:

1. *Pay.* Amount of pay received and perceived equity of pay
2. *Job.* Are tasks interesting? Are opportunities provided for learning and for accepting responsibility?
3. *Promotional Opportunities.* Availability and fairness of opportunities for promotion
4. *Supervisor.* Does the supervisor demonstrate interest in and concern about employees?
5. *Coworkers.* The extent to which coworkers are friendly, competent, and supportive

A scoring procedure is used to arrive at a score for each of the five dimensions. The five scores are then totaled to provide an overall satisfaction measure.

Sample Items from the 72-Item Job Descriptive Index with "Satisfied" Responses Indicated

Work

N	Routine
Y	Creative
N	Tiring
Y	Gives sense of accomplishment

Supervision

Y	Asks my advice
Y	Praises good work
N	Doesn't supervise enough
Y	Tells me where I stand

Coworkers

Y	Stimulating
Y	Responsible
N	Talks too much
N	Gossipy

Pay

Y	Income adequate for normal expenses
N	Bad
N	Less than I deserve
N	Well paid

Promotions

Y	Good opportunity for promotion
Y	Promotion on ability
N	Dead-end job
N	Unfair promotion policy

Source: The Job Descriptive Index is copyrighted by Bowling Green State University. The complete forms, scoring key, instructions, and norms can be obtained from Dr. Patricia C. Smith, Department of Psychology, Bowling Green State University, Bowling Green, OH 43403. Reprinted with permission.

---

job that made them feel especially satisfied or dissatisfied. Herzberg found that different factors accounted for job satisfaction and dissatisfaction. As illustrated in Fig. 5-6, satisfaction stemmed from factors associated with the work itself or to outcomes directly derived from work such as promotion opportunities, opportunities for personal growth, recognition, responsibility, and achievement. Herzberg called these factors *motivators* because they were associated with high levels of job satisfaction.

Dissatisfaction was found to be associated with conditions surrounding the job: quality of supervision, pay, company policies, physical working conditions, relations with others, and job security. Herzberg called these factors *hygiene,* or *maintenance,* factors because they seemed to prevent negative reactions.[37] Thus, Herzberg's distinction between motivators and hygiene factors is referred to as Herzberg's two-factor theory of job satisfaction.

Research studies of Herzberg's theory have generated mixed results. For example, some studies supported Herzberg's finding that job satisfaction and dissatisfaction were based on different factors while other studies reported that hygiene

Profile

Chris Kerbow
Manager, Schaumburg, Illinois, Marriott

JOB SATISFACTION AT MARRIOTT

Marriott Motels annually lose about 60 percent of their frontline personnel causing the company millions of dollars to train replacements. To reduce this turnover, Marriott has begun to radically change the way it hires, trains, and deploys frontline employees. Chris Kerbow reports that when managers began examining exactly what waiters and waitresses did during the breakfast shift, for example, they discovered that servers were spending as much as 70 percent of their time not waiting on tables. Usually they were in the kitchen, picking up orders, making toast, or rummaging around in the freezer for new containers of orange juice, leaving their miffed customers to wonder why on earth it was taking so long to get another cup of coffee.

These days, servers in some Marriott hotels never enter the kitchen. The culinary staff takes care of all food preparation. When a meal is ready, the kitchen beeps the server (they all wear pagers), and a "runner" delivers the food, which the server puts on the table.

"By redesigning the job so that superior service can be delivered, we have satisfied both our employees and our customers" indicates Kerbow.

Source: Adapted from Ronald Henkoff, "Finding, Training, and Keeping The Best Service Workers," *Fortune,* October 3, 1994, pp. 110–114.

---

factors and motivators had strong effects on both job satisfaction and dissatisfaction. Herzberg's work is useful in describing the conditions of a job that people find to be satisfying and dissatisfying. His theory has stimulated considerable research and theory on job enlargement and job enrichment.[38]

LOCKE'S VALUE THEORY Locke claimed that job satisfaction occurs when the job outcomes (rewards) that an individual receives matches those outcomes that are desired. Locke's theory focuses on any outcomes that people value. In essence, Locke's theory of job satisfaction is based on the discrepancy that exists between what people have and what they want with respect to various aspects (such as pay and learning opportunities) of their job. The smaller the discrepancy, the more satisfied they are with their jobs. The larger the discrepancy, the more dissatisfied people are with their jobs.[39] Recent studies have found good support for Locke's value theory of job satisfaction.[40]

MOORHEAD AND GRIFFIN'S CAUSES AND CONSEQUENCES As depicted in Fig. 5-7, Moorhead and Griffin argue that the primary causes of job satisfaction or dissatisfaction can be grouped into three categories: Organizational Factors (pay, promotion opportunities, work itself, policies and procedures, working conditions); Group Factors (coworkers, supervisor); and Personal Factors (needs, aspirations, instrumental benefits). Moorhead and Griffin considered instrumental benefits to be the extent to which the job enables the employee to achieve other ends. The two primary consequences of job satisfaction and dissatisfaction relate to absenteeism and turnover.[41]

An interesting question is to what extent are people satisfied with their jobs? Of course, not everyone performing every type of job is equally satisfied. How-

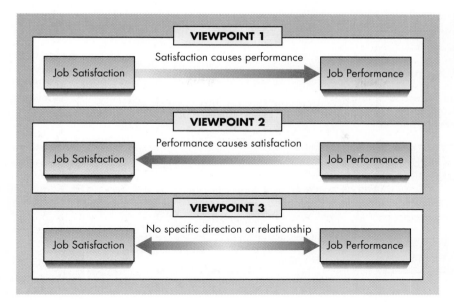

FIGURE 5-5
The Relationship Between Job Satisfaction and Job Performance

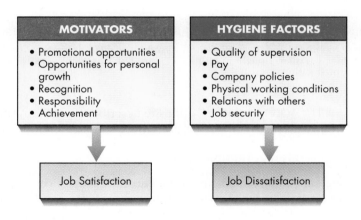

FIGURE 5-6
Herzberg's Two-Factor Theory

ever, specific patterns of job satisfaction or dissatisfaction have been clearly established for certain groups as follows:

- Managerial and professionals (white-collar personnel) tend to be more satisfied than physical laborers and factory workers (blue-collar personnel).[42]
- Older people are generally more satisfied with their jobs than younger people. Findings indicate, however, that satisfaction does not increase at an even pace. For example, people are more satisfied with their jobs in their thirties (as they become more successful), level off in their forties (as they become disenchanted), and become more satisfied again in their late fifties (they resign themselves to their lot in life).[43]
- People with more experience on their jobs are more satisfied than those who are less experienced.[44]
- Women and members of minority groups tend to be more dissatisfied with their jobs than are men and members of majority groups.[45]

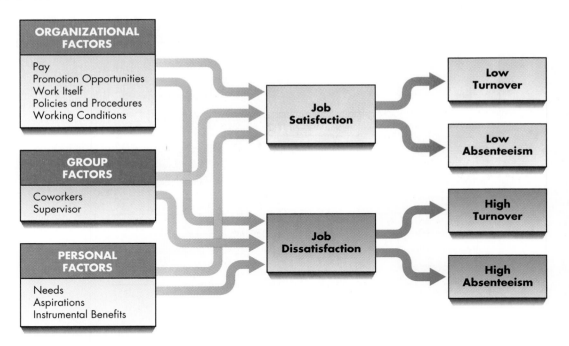

FIGURE 5-7 Causes and Consequences of Job Satisfaction and Dissatisfaction

Source: Gregory Moorhead and Ricky W. Griffin, *Organizational Behavior: Managing People and Organizations,* 3rd ed., Dallas, Houghton Mifflin, 1992, p. 113. Copyright © 1992 by Houghton Mifflin Company. Reprinted with permission.

The "OB In Practice" opposite describes the notion that the job is a social artifact that has outlived its usefulness.

Organizational Commitment

Organizational commitment is an attitude that reflects the extent to which people are involved with their organization and are unwilling to leave it. Researchers have used two theoretical perspectives to explain why people are committed to an organization: the side-bets orientation (also referred to as a continuance commitment) and the individual–organizational goal–congruence orientation (referred to also as an affective commitment).[46]

The concept behind the side-bets orientation is that an employee tends to remain in an organization because the person cannot afford to leave. For example, a person may lose their investments in time, effort, and benefits if they leave their present organization and they cannot replace these investments. The individual–organizational goal–congruence theory is based on the concept that people are willing to accept and work towards organizational goals if these goals are similar to their own personal goals. The goal–congruence theory further states that employees have a strong desire to remain in an organization because of the following three factors: (1) a belief in the goals and values of the organization, (2) a willingness to put forth effort on behalf of the organization, and (3) a desire to remain a member of the organization.[47]

Managers should be concerned about organizational commitment because committed employees tend to reduce organizational costs. Studies indicate that organizational commitment is related to lower rates of absenteeism, increased

OB in Practice — *The End of the Job?*

According to some individuals the job is a social artifact that has outlived its usefulness. This argument is that the job is an idea that emerged early in the 19th century to package the work that needed doing in the growing factories and bureaucracies of the industrializing nations. Before people had jobs, they worked just as hard but on shifting clusters of tasks, in a variety of locations, on a schedule set by the sun and the weather and the needs of the day. The modern job was a startling new idea, and to many, an unpleasant and perhaps socially dangerous one. Critics claimed it was an unnatural and even inhuman way to work. They believed most people wouldn't be able to live with its demands. It is ironic that what started as a controversial concept ended up becoming the ultimate orthodoxy, and that we're hooked on jobs.

Now the world of work is changing again: The conditions that created jobs 200 years ago—mass production and the large organization—are disappearing. Technology enables us to automate the production line where all those job holders used to do their repetitive tasks. Instead of long production runs where the same thing has to be done again and again, we are increasingly customizing production. Big firms, where most of the good jobs used to be, are unbundling activities and farming them out to little firms, which have created or taken over profitable niches. Public services are starting to be privatized, and government bureaucracy, the ultimate bastion of job security, is being thinned. With the disappearance of the conditions that created jobs, we are losing the need to package work in that way. No wonder jobs are disappearing.

To an extent that few people have recognized, our organizational world is no longer a pattern of jobs, the way a honeycomb is a pattern of those little hexagonal pockets of honey. In place of jobs, there are part-time and temporary work situations. That change is symptomatic of a deeper change that is subtler but more profound. The deeper change is this: Today's organization is rapidly being transformed from a structure built out of jobs into a field of work needing to be done.

Source: Adapted from William Bridges, "The End of the Job," *Fortune*, September 19, 1994, pp. 62–74.

---

productivity, and higher quality of work.[48] Also, committed individuals are less likely to quit and accept other jobs, which eliminates the cost of high turnover.[49]

Rewards are important to the development of organizational commitment. Although pay, fringe benefits, and the opportunity to achieve challenging goals are important, committed employees respond to interpersonal rewards: such as, status improvement and recognition, promotions, responsibility to start and finish a project or job, and relaxed supervision. In order to foster organizational commitment, managers and supervisors need to implement reward systems that focus on personal importance or self-esteem and to integrate organizational and individual goals.

WORK STRESS

Jobs create pressure. Employees are impelled, either by themselves or by their bosses, to fulfill work assignments and respond to deadlines. The effect of these tensions is stress. The evidence of *job stress* among managers, professionals, and

Job stress The effect of tensions on an employee by job pressure to fulfill job assignments and to respond to deadlines.

even blue-collar workers is widespread. Stress adversely affects their well-being, effectiveness, and health.[50]

Work-related stress is considered to be a rising concern in many organizations. The possible causes include increased domestic and foreign competition that has led to a substantial number of downsizing, layoff, and merger activities; rapidly changing technology; tension among diverse groups of employees, and increased demands for higher quality and service. Organizational managers are interested in maintaining a lower level of job stress for good reasons—high levels of stress can result in low productivity, increased absenteeism and turnover, and an assortment of other employee problems including alcoholism, drug abuse, hypertension, and a host of cardiovascular problems.

Another reason for concern over job stress is that stress-related workers' compensation claims have risen dramatically. About 14 percent of all occupational disease claims are stress related. Stress-related claims, on average, are estimated at $15,000, twice as much as those for employees with physical injuries.[51] But what exactly is job stress? Unfortunately, job stress is not easy to define or measure. Various definitions of job stress include the following:[52]

> "Stress is the force or stimulus acting upon the individual that results in a response of strain" (stimulus definition).

> "Stress is the physical or psychological response an individual makes to an environmental stressor" (response definition).

> "Stress is the consequence of the interaction between an environmental stimulus and the idiosyncratic response of the individual" (stimulus-response definition).

A comprehensive definition based on the integration of these and other definitions is:[53]

> Stress is a discrepancy between an employee's perceived state and desired state, when such a discrepancy is considered important by the employee. Stress influences two behaviors: (1) the employee's psychological and physical well-being, and (2) the employee's efforts to cope with the stress by preventing or reducing it.

Sources of Stress

As depicted in Fig. 5-8, stress is the physiological or psychological state that results from stressors. A stressor is the external agent that disturbs the individual's equilibrium. If your boss says, "I want that project completed by tomorrow," or "I want to know why," you are placed in a stressful situation. Individual differences are important determinants of the significance of particular stressors. For example, a threatening comment from a manager will be more likely to cause stress in an insecure, timid employee than in a self-confident, outgoing one.

Potential stressors are found in all aspects of work as well as in situations away from work, such as those associated with family life. The common cate-

FIGURE 5-8
A Stress Model

The loss of one's job through layoff, merger, downsizing, or firing often leads to a significant level of job stress.

gories of work-related stressors include task demands, physical demands, the physical work environment, role conflict, role ambiguity, and shift work. Following is a discussion of these stressors.

TASK DEMANDS Task demands are stressors associated with the specific job an individual performs. Some jobs, or occupations, by their nature are more stressful than others. For example, the job of a professional football coach is more stressful than that of the football team's equipment manager.

Some task demands may pose physical threats to an individual's health such as handling toxic waste or being a police officer. The lack of job security may cause dramatic increases in stress levels. Many white collar employees who had credentials, skills, and education have found their job security crumpled under the weight of numerous downsizings. The "OB In Practice" on page 144 describes how a hostile economy has cut short the careers of many of America's best and brightest. Also, many companies state that they can no longer afford to maintain their benefits program in an era of heightened global competition thereby cutting core benefits such as health insurance and pensions. These benefit reductions also increase the level of stress for affected employees.[54]

Simple, repetitive jobs that are not mentally challenging create frustration for employees. This frustration manifests itself in the form of dissatisfaction, stress, and ultimately, tardiness, absenteeism, and turnover.[55]

PHYSICAL DEMANDS Physical demands are the physical strain and exertion that a particular job involves. Strenuous labor such as loading heavy cargo can result in stress.

PHYSICAL WORK ENVIRONMENT Physical work environment plays a role in the amount of stress that an employee experiences. Working outdoors in extremely hot or cold temperatures can result in stress as can working in an improperly heated office or building. Research studies indicate that some occupations are more stressful than others. For example, such jobs as air-traffic controller, waitress/waiter, and mine employee were found to have high levels of stress while the jobs of college professor, stock handler, craft workers, and heavy equipment

OB in Practice

Stressful Times: White Collar Wasteland

Few Americans were so groomed for success as Jim Bennett of New Canaan, Connecticut. His diplomas read Princeton University and Stanford Law School. His honors include Phi Beta Kappa and his resumé boasts such gold-plated employers as General Electric. Yet when a budget cut wiped out his job as corporate counsel with Conair Corporation in February 1992, Jim Bennett was helpless as any working stiff. Since then, Bennett who was fifty-five in 1993, has not held a steady job. "Your foundation turns out to be sand," says Bennett. "There is no recovery for people like me. Life is awfully stressful."

Although the 1990–1991 recession officially ended in 1991, white-collar unemployment kept on climbing: from 2.8 million in 1991, past the 3 million mark in 1992, to 3.4 million in 1993.

Social psychologists state that many families fracture under the stress of having out-of-work husbands and fathers. Spouses become scared of their economic failure, become resentful and blame the out-of-work mate for the family's plight. Spouses also become openly hostile and rejecting. Children become insecure, needy, dependent, and eventually angry.

Yet downsizing has become an addiction as corporations strive for ever greater efficiency. Until this trend fades, even twenty-four-karat resumés like Jim Bennett's will tarnish, no matter how much polish is applied.

Source: Adapted from David Hage, Linda Grant, and Jim Impoco, "White Collar Wasteland," *U.S. News & World Report,* June 28, 1993, pp. 42–52.

---

operators had low levels of stress. Interestingly, research indicates that stress is not related to the status level of jobs in that white-collar and blue-collar employees both have high and low levels of stress as do skilled and unskilled jobs.[56] Research, however, does indicate that the repetitive and "dehumanizing" work environment created by assembly lines has been linked to high incidents of stress as well as to health related disorders.[57]

ROLE CONFLICT Role conflict occurs when two or more sets of demands are placed on an employee in such a manner that the compliance with one demand makes it difficult to comply with the other.[58] For example, a supervisor may find that upper management wants severe reprimands for employee absenteeism while the employees themselves expect consideration of their needs and personal problems. Also, a college professor may find that he or she is expected to spend considerable time in teaching and at the same time is expected to publish in highly competitive scholarly journals.

Research indicates that job satisfaction decreases as role conflict increases; moreover, role conflict is connected with heart disease, high blood pressure, elevated cholesterol, and obesity.[59]

ROLE AMBIGUITY Role ambiguity exists when there is a lack of clarity regarding the goals of one's job or the methods of performance. consider the vice president of manufacturing of a company that is performing poorly and has no clear strategy on how manufacturing relates to other departments or to overall company profitability. If this manufacturing VP is instructed to reduce costs without being told the means by which costs can be decreased then the resulting ambiguity can be devastating. Also, imagine a college professor assigning a term paper to a class without telling the students: (1) what topics to include, (2) the due date, (3) the required length, (4) how the paper will be evaluated, and (5) how much the paper will count toward the final course grade. Would this assignment create any stress for you?

SHIFT WORK   Many jobs have to be performed twenty-four hours per day and must be scheduled during evening and night shifts in addition to daytime shifts. These jobs include police officers, firefighters, medical personnel, as well as those in manufacturing and service sectors. Approximately 20 percent of the U.S. work force is involved in shift work with rotating work schedules. For example, employees may rotate from a daytime shift to the evening shift, to the night shift, and then back to the daytime shift. Research indicates that the adverse consequences of shift work is substantial. Stress symptoms associated with shift work include fatigue, difficulty sleeping, reduced social involvement, disturbances in appetite and digestion, constipation, increased sexual problems, increased accidents, and lower productivity.[60]

Extent of Work-related Stress in the United States

How common is work-related stress in the United States? Examining Fig. 5-9 indicates that over two-thirds of all workers in the United States report that their jobs are either extremely or highly stressful. In addition, one third seriously consider quitting their jobs each year due to stress. The major factors reported that cause these high stress levels are "too much work," "lack of time for self," and "little control over their jobs."[61] The "Profile" on page 146 describes how a fired executive copes with stress.

Some jobs consistently have high stress levels, such as those in Fig. 5-10, due to the nature of the work. Individuals who cannot cope with continuous stress are probably best advised to avoid those careers. The level of stress that exists in any one job or organization is not easily determined. The outcomes in high-stress situations are usually high levels of absenteeism, turnover, grievances, accidents, and chemical dependency. Accurately measuring stress levels, however, is not easy. The most common measurement techniques employ paper-and-pencil tests that ask employees about the existence of stressors in their job environment.

%	Stress Issue
66	Employees who report their jobs are extremely or highly stressful.
34	Employees who seriously thought about quitting their jobs due to stress.
25	Employees reporting stress-related illnesses.
90	Workers who think their employers should act to reduce stress.
40	Workers who feel more stress due to the recession.
$	**Stress Issue**
73,270	Average amount United States sets aside for stress-related disabilities.
1,925	Average cost of rehabilitating a stressed employee.

Source: Adapted from Jennifer J. Laabs, "Job Stress," *Personnel Journal*, April 1992, p. 43.

FIGURE 5-9

Extent of Work Related Stress in the United States

Profile   Willow Shire
Former Vice President of Digital Equipment

COPING WITH STRESS

As a vice president of loss-wracked Digital Equipment, Willow Shire's picture appeared on a cover of *Fortune* titled "Managing in the Midst of Chaos." The next day her marriage came apart, a victim of inattention. Now divorced, Shire worked between Labor Day and Thanksgiving with only one and one-half days off. Her reward came in January when Digital Equipment's marketing chief eliminated Shire's job. Forced to examine her life, Shire, forty-six, realized that her life needed repair. To give herself time to think, Shire took on just enough consulting to pay the bills and granted herself a year of contemplation. "The temptation is very great to jump into a big job, because that's what I know how to do," she says. "But I need to *not* jump into what I was doing before. I believe that if you need an answer, if you listen to yourself and just trust the process, the answer will come."

Like countless people walloped by workplace change, Shire is searching for ways to change herself.

Source: Adapted from Stratford Sherman, "Leaders Learn to Heed the Voice Within," *Fortune*, August 22, 1994, pp. 42–45.

The measurement of employee stress may enable an organization to change its work environment and thus lower the levels of stress. A good example is the Armstrong Transfer & Storage Company in Memphis, Tennessee. Armstrong suffered a serious problem with stress-related workers' compensation claims, and the company saw its claims rise from $93,000 to $272,000 in just two years. To determine the extent of workplace stress, Armstrong administered questionnaires to its 500 employees. The results showed, as an example, that employees were worried about worn-out loading equipment but failed to report it for fear that they would have to pay for it. In response to the survey results, Armstrong's management repaired or replaced broken equipment and held weekly meetings to allow employees to air their grievances. Following the stress-reduction program, accidents fell from sixty-five to ten per year, and a follow-up survey showed that perceived stress had dropped significantly.[62]

Consequences of Stress

Not all stress is bad. In fact, some stress is clearly beneficial to performance. Figure 5-11 illustrates that although an extremely high stress level contributes to a decline in performance, a moderate amount of stress has a positive effect on performance.[63]

Eustress *The positive consequences of healthy, normal stress.*

EUSTRESS   The consequences of healthy, normal stress is called *eustress* and includes increased performance, bursts of physical strength, enhanced focus in an emergency, and increased cardiovascular efficiency.

Distress *The consequences of unhealthy stress.*

DISTRESS   Unhealthy stress is called *distress* and its consequences include medical illnesses, behavioral problems, psychological disorders, decreased performance, and participation problems.[64]

Only recently have consultants and psychologists begun to study workplace tension in depth. They've discovered the most trying professions are those involving danger and extreme pressure—or those that carry responsibility without control. The symptoms of stress have been found to range from frequent illnesses to nervous tics and mental lapses. The most common tips for dealing with stress focus on relaxation. But sometimes the only answer is to fight back—or walk away.

10 Tough Jobs	Warning Signs	Ways to Cope
Inner-city high school teacher	Intestinal distress	Maintain a sense of humor
Police officer	Rapid pulse	Meditate
Miner	Frequent illness	Get a massage
Air-traffic controller	Insomnia	Exercise regularly
Medical intern	Persistent fatigue	Eat more sensibly
Stockbroker	Irritability	Limit intake of alcohol
Journalist	Nail biting	and caffeine
Customer service/ complaint depart- ment worker	Lack of concentration Increased use of alcohol and drugs	Take refuge in family and friends Delegate responsibility
Waitress	Hunger for sweets	Quit
Secretary		

Source: Annetta Miller et al., "Stress on the Job," from *Newsweek*, April 25, 1988, copyright 1988, Newsweek, Inc. All rights reserved. Reprinted by permission.

FIGURE 5-10

High-Stress Jobs, Warning Signs, and Ways to Cope

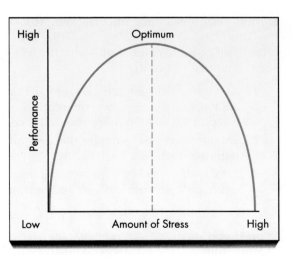

FIGURE 5-11

Relationship Between Stress and Performance

Burnout

Although stress and burnout are sometimes used interchangeably, burnout is more than stress—it occurs when a person believes he or she cannot or will not continue to do the job they have been performing.[65] The difference according to a physician who has treated both is that a person who is stressed can take an extended vacation and return rested and ready to get back to work. If that person has experienced burnout, however, within a few days after returning to work he or she feels as miserable as before the vacation. While stress usually contributes to burnout, it does not explain the whole phenomenon. *Burnout,* in essence, is the overall perception that a person is giving more than

Burnout occurs when a person believes he or she cannot or will not continue to do his or her job due to his or her overall perception that he is giving more than he is receiving.

he or she is receiving either in monetary rewards, recognition, support, or advancement. It can occur at all organizational levels, all pay levels, and in all age groups.[66]

Burnout is a general feeling of exhaustion that develops when an individual simultaneously experiences too much pressure and too few sources of satisfaction.[67] Its primary symptoms include being drained or used up and occurs among individuals who work in some capacity with people.[68] As depicted in Fig. 5-12, burnout appears to follow a stagelike process beginning with emotional exhaustion.

An example of someone who has experienced burnout is Rochelle Ruane, a human resource professional. Ms. Ruane, fresh out of college, was hired by a biotechnology company to build its human resource department from scratch. It was a job she enjoyed—"I liked the people, I liked the company. It was that wonderful start-up feeling and everybody was working together, and it was a really good atmosphere—a positive culture." The stress and eventual burnout occurred because the more Ruane did the more she was expected to contribute. "A lot of it was my own fault. . . . It's the classic situation that if the work is getting done, why should they give you any more help? . . . I did far too much and I burned out."[69]

Organizations that are interested in assisting their employees in avoiding burnout should realize that it occurs at all organizational levels and with all types of employees. An important aspect of controlling burnout is the ability to recognize the symptoms that may indicate that an individual is experiencing burnout. Figure 5-13 describes the symptoms of employee burnout.

Although it is impossible for organizations to implement a program that will prevent all possible cases of burnout, the following procedures will allow managers to reduce its occurrence.[70]

1. *Acknowledge the problem.* Recognize that burnout can occur, let employees know through policy, orientation, and training that the organization has policies to help them should it occur.

2. *Train managers* to recognize the symptoms of employee burnout and refer potential victims to counseling.

3. *Time limits* are a key to preventing burnout. Constant excessive overtime is a common cause of stress and burnout.

FIGURE 5-12

Stages of Burnout and Their Symptoms

Emotional Exhaustion	Depersonalization	Low Personal Accomplishment
Feel drained by work	Have become calloused by job	Cannot effectively deal with problems
Feel fatigued in the morning	Treat people like objects	Am not a positive influence on others
Feel burned out	Don't care what happens to people	Cannot understand others' problems or empathize with them
Frustrated	Feel others blame you for their problems	No longer feel exhilarated by job
Don't want to work with people		

Source: Adapted from S. E. Jackson, "Organizational Practices for Preventing Burnout," in A. S. Sethi and R. S. Schuler, eds., *Handbook of Stress Coping Strategies,* New York, HarperCollins, 1984, p. 92. Used with permission.

FIGURE 5-13
Symptoms of Employee Burnout

Physical

- A change in physical appearance; decline in grooming or wardrobe.
- Complaints such as headaches, backaches, or gastrointestinal problems.
- Increased absenteeism for health reasons.
- Signs and symptoms of depression, such as a change in weight, eating habits, or chronic fatigue.
- Frequent infections, especially respiratory infections.

Emotional

- Depressed appearance, such as sad expression, slumped posture or rounded shoulders.
- Appearing bored or speaking of boredom.
- Attitudes of cynicism, resentfulness, apathy or anxiety.
- Expressions of frustration and hopelessness.

Behavioral

- Decreased productivity, inability to focus on the job or complete a task.
- Tardiness.
- More frequent absenteeism.
- Withdrawal or listlessness.
- Expressions of irritability or hostility.
- Overworking.
- Abuse of drugs, alcohol, or caffeine; increased smoking.
- Excessive exercise, often to the point of injury.

Source: Hugh F. Stallworth, "Realistic Goals Help Avoid Burnout," *HRMagazine,* June 1990, p. 171. Reprinted with the permission of *HRMagazine* published by the Society For Human Resource Management, Alexandria, Va.

4. *Recognize people's contributions.* Positive feedback helps people psychologically refuel and increases their self-image.

5. *Provide outlets* for anger, frustration, helplessness, and depression. Employees must often deal with these emotions alone. By providing a person (often a boss) who can help them cope can often avoid burnout.

6. *Retraining.* Implementing a program of lateral moves for employees who feel stuck in a "dead end" position can keep a valuable employee motivated and at work.

The "Profile" on page 151 describes how a university vice president of human resources survived burnout.

Research indicates that individuals experience burnout following the aftermath of downsizing (Chap. 13 discusses downsizing). A study conducted by the Families at Work Institute, a respected research organization that consults with corporations on work and family issues, indicated that white-collar employees who remained employed after their *Fortune* 500 firms had implemented a downsizing program experienced significant burnout. As illustrated in Fig. 5-14, responding employees reported the following: 42 percent felt used up at the end of the day; 40 percent felt tired when they get up in the morning and have to face another day on the job; 30 percent felt burned out or stressed by their work; 29 percent felt frustrated by their job; and 27 percent felt emotionally drained from their work.[71] (These percentages were derived from the sum of the "often" and "very often" categories.)

Dealing with Stress

Fortunately ways exist for dealing with stress. Although research on effective ways of coping with stress is just beginning to emerge, several approaches have been identified. These actions include organizational stress management and individual stress management.[72]

FIGURE 5-14 Job Burnout and Downsizing

In the past 3 months, how often have you felt ...	Never	Rarely	Some-times	Often	Very Often	Sample Size
Emotionally drained from your work?	15%	25%	34%	14%	13%	(2,952)
Used up at the end of the workday?	8%	17%	33%	22%	20%	(2,950)
Tired when you get up in the morning and have to face another day on the job?	9%	21%	30%	21%	19%	(2,947)
Burned out or stressed by your work?	15%	27%	29%	15%	15%	(2,951)
Frustrated by your job?	13%	26%	31%	15%	14%	(2,950)

Source: Ellen Galinsky, James T. Bond, and Dana Friedman, *The Changing Workforce: Highlights of the National Study,* New York, Families and Work Institute, 1993.

ORGANIZATIONAL STRESS MANAGEMENT   Top level management can implement the following strategies to reduce the intensity and number of stressors on employees.

- *Providing emotional support.* Superiors, coworkers, and subordinates can provide emotional support to help individuals cope with stressors. Using the conflict management styles discussed in Chap. 15 builds a perception of caring, empathy, and trust that can provide emotional support within an organization.

- *Utilizing a participative process for setting objectives.* Utilizing a participative process for setting objectives reduces and resolves role conflicts and uncertainties, which are major sources of stress and burnout. Encouraging employees to participate in decisions that affect their work lives can reduce their stress levels.

- *Adapting physical environments.* Three different strategies can be utilized in adapting an organization's physical environment. The first strategy is to alter the physical relationship to reduce noise or to institute better temperature control. The second strategy is to protect employees from the environment by instituting or improving safety programs. The third strategy is to use ergonomics. Ergonomics is an applied science that involves the purposeful design of equipment and the arrangement of things to fit the requirements of the human body. Research indicates that ergonomics tends to reduce accidents, errors, stress, and mental fatigue.

- *Providing special programs.* An increasing number of organizations are providing physical-fitness facilities to improve employee morale and to reduce stress. These facilities offer exercise programs as well as aerobics, weight training, and running. Wellness programs are being implemented to help employees reduce their susceptibility to illness and the effects of stressors by changing the way they live. Wellness programs usually include courses in stress management, exercise, weight reduction, and giving up smoking. Work-scheduling techniques, such as the use of flextime, allow employees to vary their arrival and departure times within certain limits to suit individual needs and desires.

INDIVIDUAL STRESS MANAGEMENT   In addition to organizational strategies, individuals have considerable potential to reduce and control stress. Actions that can be taken to reduce stress depend on personal preferences, needs, and lifestyles and include the following.

Barbara Butterfield
Vice President for Faculty and
Staff Services, Stanford University
SURVIVING BURNOUT

I have been burned out twice—specifically when I was less mature in my career and when there was lots going on.

What have I done to prevent burnout? When I had these two flame-outs (a short-term downer in which I've experienced absolute exhaustion), they lasted about three days. The first day or two, I simply rested, because for me it's almost like the flu, and I said, okay, I've got to get my physical self back in shape first—which does something to get my mental self back in shape. Then I'd do something physical, such as tennis or taking long walks, or just go hiking in the woods. I also touch base with people I care about by phone—to rebuild my contacts. It's also been helpful to have colleagues (not necessarily in HR, but usually in the same workplace) who are close enough to talk with, or who will step in for you for a day or two, and for whom you can return the favor. They should be people with whom you can talk and who will help you put things back in perspective. A lot of folks won't do that. They think they have to pound right through it. I think that's damaging. It's hard to learn when you're first in an executive leadership position because you take all the load on yourself, and you think that if you can't do it all yourself, then something's wrong with you. Instead, what you could do is share the load and support each other. Everybody goes through it. If someone says they haven't, they aren't telling the truth. There are more ways to be tired than by being virally or bacterially ill. Will you take the time out? Will you be as good to yourself as if you just had the twenty-four-hour flu? My work is recreation to me. It's like the toughest tennis game you ever played. For me, it's a lot of fun, a lot of stimulation. Layoffs and big problems actually get me going. I want my work to be like play. That's probably why I don't burn out very often.

Source: Jennifer T. Laabs, "Surviving HR Burnout," *Personnel Journal,* April 1992, p. 85. Used by permission.

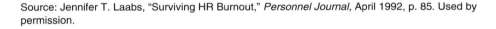

- Proper Nutrition. Proper nutrition includes planning a balanced diet, eating regular meals, maintaining a recommended weight, not smoking, and using alcohol and caffeine moderately.

- Exercise Habits. Physical exercise is one of the least expensive strategies for reducing stress. Research indicates that a sound program of physical fitness can improve mental health as well as physical well-being.

- Meditation. Meditation can reduce anxiety and improve work performance and job satisfaction. Regular relaxation techniques include transcendental meditation, prayer, and healing visualization.

- Self-Awareness. Individuals can manage stress by modifying their behaviors. Setting reasonable objectives, improving time management, and simply reducing the total number of tasks can all help individuals reduce or avoid negative stress. Also, stressors resulting from conflict incidents can be reduced by making more use of the collaborative and compromise conflict-management styles and less use of the forcing and avoidance styles.

- Withdrawal. Withdrawal in the form of being absent or changing jobs or careers is perhaps the simplest way of coping with stressors. Transferring to another department or looking for another job can be a realistic coping strategy. However, withdrawal can also be an unhealthy means of attempting to escape reality.

CONCLUSIONS AND APPLICATIONS

- Decision making is a fundamental process in organizations by which managers choose one alternative from others. Managers make decisions based on the information they receive from the behavior of individuals or groups within the organization and also from sources external to the organization.

- Managers use different decision-making styles to analyze problems and formulate decisions. This difference reflects the way managers perceive, organize, and understand their environments and stems from dissimilar work backgrounds, educational experiences, social influences, value systems, and psychological attributes.

- The decision making process has been described by two approaches: the rational and the behavioral. The rational approach is based on classical decision theory in which the managerial world is certain, stable, and describes how managers should make decisions. The behavioral approach argues that a manager's rationality is bounded (limited) by an incomplete understanding of the organization's goals, inadequate information, and the complexity of many problems. Because neither the problem nor the alternative solutions are completely known, managers satisfice (select a satisfactory course of action) by maximizing.

- The rational approach describes decision making as a multiphased process in which the actual choice is only one phase. The phases of the rational approach are goal statements, problem identification, search for alternatives, evaluation of alternatives, rational choice of best alternative, implementation of the decision, and control-evaluation.

- Alternatives selected by decision makers depend on the amount of information available and on certain decision-making conditions such as escalating commitment, risk-certainty–uncertainty, muddling through–incrementalism, and optimizing–suboptimizing. Because of these different conditions, different decision makers may not select identical alternatives in the same situation.

- Technological information systems provide assistance to managerial decision making through decision support systems, group decision support systems, and expert systems.

- Stress occurs when a person responds to physiological or psychological demands. The sources of work stress include task demands, physical demands, physical work environment, role conflict, role ambiguity, and shift work.

- Not all stress is bad. Normal stress has healthy benefits and increases performance. Distress causes both individual and organizational problems that are costly.

- Upper management can reduce the intensity of stress by providing emotional support, utilizing a participative process for setting objectives, adapting the organization's physical environment, and providing special programs such as aerobics, fitness, and employee wellness.

- Individuals can reduce the intensity of stress through proper nutrition, exercise, meditation, self-awareness, and withdrawing from stressful situations.

REVIEW QUESTIONS

1. Discuss the seven phases of the rational decision-making approach. Which phase is the most important?
2. Explain how escalating commitment is related to decision making.
3. What is bounded rationality? Satisficing? How are these terms related to decision making?
4. Describe the differences between the rational decision making approach and the behavioral approach.
5. Discuss how behavioral factors can influence decision making.
6. What techniques can be used to improve decision making?
7. How is job satisfaction measured?
8. What is stress? Eustress? Distress? How are these terms related to performance?
9. Explain the common categories of work related stressors.
10. Describe both organizational stress management techniques and individual stress management techniques.

DISCUSSION QUESTIONS

1. Figure 5-8 indicated that most people are satisfied with their jobs. Why? How might you determine whether such satisfaction is real or only apparent?
2. When you make decisions do you tend to use the rational decision-making process or bounded rationality? What factors have determined which approach you use?
3. Give a recent example of a decision in which you satisficed. What were the contributing factors?
4. Describe a recent time when stress had both good and bad consequences for you.
5. Do you know of anyone that is experiencing burnout? How would you advise that person to recover from it?
6. Have you ever used any of the stress reduction methods described in this text? Do you use others?

CASE STUDY

Shipwreck Survival

You are the first mate of the Anna Dawson, a cruise ship traveling from Seattle, Washington, to Prudhoe Bay, Alaska. It is August and during the night while in the Gulf of Alaska, a severe windstorm develops. During the storm the Anna Dawson sank and you are among thirty survivors crowded into a lifeboat designed for no more than twenty-four adults. In the lifeboat with you are:

- three other members of the Anna Dawson's crew
- two married couples
- three children whose parents went down with the ship
- three elderly men and women
- six other women
- seven other men, three of whom were severely injured during the wreck

Many of the thirty are seasick and most are terrified. The night is dark and the weather continues to worsen. The lifeboat is taking water at the gunwales and if the sea gets any rougher, the boat is sure to swamp and sink.

It looks as if the only hope for any to survive is for five or six persons to get out of the boat, leaving the rest to bail and row hoping that dawn will bring a slackening wind and chance of rescue.

Because you are an experienced seaman and the senior surviving officer of the Anna Dawson, you are looked to for leadership. After deciding that the lifeboat *must lighten* its human load, you ask for volunteers to jump overboard and take their chances in the swirling waves. No one responds, although everyone senses the danger to the overcrowded boat. You are not surprised by their lack of response and quickly decide that you must decide who shall be the unlucky six.

Voting or a contest which might work well in another situation is discarded because you believe that it is unworkable here. The method of drawing straws is also determined not to be feasible. You think of different selection processes such as designating every fifth person as an unlucky one. You also consider throwing out the last six people who got into the boat, whoever they turn out to be (you are not among them). The thought crosses your mind to calculate the utilities of all possible combinations of twenty-four survivors and to throw overboard the six with the lowest utility. However, this seems to be too complicated, time consuming, and conjectural under the circumstances.

Another thought occurs to you: The crew of the Anna Dawson has a duty to provide the passengers with a safe voyage, so the four of you should be among the six to abandon the boat. You are tempted to dismiss ethical considerations and simply have the able-bodied men grab the weakest and throw them overboard as quickly as possible. Should children or the elderly be allowed to remain?

You only have a few minutes to weigh these alternative methods of decision making judging by the fury of the wind and waves before panic or disaster overtakes all of you.

CASE STUDY QUESTIONS

1. What decision would you choose?
2. Who goes overboard and who stays?

Source: Adapted from Arthur G. Bedeian, *Management*, 3rd ed., Chicago, Dryden Press, 1933, pp. 231–232.

EXPERIENTIAL EXERCISE 1

Decision Making

Instructions

Apply the seven-step decision model illustrated in Fig. 5-2 to any recent decision you have made.

Questions

1. Explain how each step was (or was not) followed.
2. Was this an appropriate model to use in describing your decision-making steps? Explain.
3. What is the next major decision you will make in which the model could be effectively utilized? Explain how each step could be followed.

Experiential Exercise 2

Are You Burned Out?

Purpose

Everyone at one time or another feels they are burned out on the job, or with life in general. Sometimes a variation, such as a new car, hobby, promotion, or even serious illness will revitalize a person and lessen the feelings of burnout.

This exercise can give you an objective appraisal of your degree of burnout, *if* you answer it honestly. There are no right or wrong answers and only you know if your answers are accurate. Once you determine your burnout score, then you should consult the general discussion of what different scores may indicate and decide if any behavioral change is needed in your life. But don't make any major decisions based solely on this test—talk with family, friends, coworkers, even a counselor first. Wait a week and take the test again if you contemplate any substantial action.

Task

You can compute your burnout score by completing the following questionnaire. You can use it for diagnosing how you feel about your work or for diagnosing how you feel about your life just today or in general.

Compute your burnout score by completing this questionnaire.

How often do you have any of the following experiences?
Please use the scale:

1	2	3	4	5	6	7
Never	Once in a great while	Rarely	Sometimes	Often	Usually	Always

_____ **1.** Being tired.

_____ **2.** Feeling depressed.

_____ **3.** Having a good day.

_____ **4.** Being physically exhausted.

_____ **5.** Being emotionally exhausted.

_____ **6.** Being happy.

_____ **7.** Being "wiped out"

_____ **8.** "Can't take it anymore."

_____ **9.** Being unhappy.

_____ **10.** Feeling run-down.

_____ **11.** Feeling trapped.

_____ **12.** Feeling worthless.

_____ **13.** Being weary.

_____ **14.** Being troubled.

_____ **15.** Feeling disillusioned and resentful.

_____ **16.** Being weak and susceptible to illness.

_____ **17.** Feeling hopeless.

_____ **18.** Feeling rejected.

_____ **19.** Feeling optimistic.

_____ **20.** Feeling energetic.

_____ **21.** Feeling anxious.

Computation of score:
Add the values you wrote next to the following items:
1, 2, 4, 5, 7, 8, 9, 10, 11, 12, 13, 14, 15, 16, 17, 18, 21 (A) _____ .

Add the values you wrote next to the following items:
3, 6, 19, 20 (B) _____ , subtract B from 32 (C) _____ .

Add A and C (D) _____ .

Divide D by 21 _____ . This is your burnout score.

What the score means:
Of the thousands who responded to this self-diagnosis instrument, none scored either 1 or 7. The reason is obvious. It is unlikely that anyone would be in a state of eternal euphoria implied by the score 1, and it is unlikely that someone who scored 7 would be able to cope with the world well enough to participate in a burnout workshop or a research project.

If your score is between 2 and 3 you are doing well. The only suggestion we make is that you go over your score sheet to be sure you have been honest in your responses. If your score is between 3 and 4, it would be wise for you to examine your work life and evaluate your priorities and consider possible changes. If your score is higher than 4, you are experiencing burnout to the extent that it is mandatory that you do something about it. A score of higher than 5 indicates an acute state and a need for immediate help.

Source: Ayala Pines, Ph.D. and Elliot Aronson, Ph.D., "Why Managers Burn Out," *Sales & Marketing Management,* vol. 4, February 1989, p. 38.

Take It to the Net **You can find this chapter's World Wide Web exercise at:** http://www.prenhall.com/carrell

CHAPTER 6

Motivation: The Classical Theories

CHAPTER OBJECTIVES

1. To understand the relationships between employee levels of motivation, performance, and rewards and organizational success.

2. To learn why Napoleon Hill views motivation as a two-sided coin.

3. To identify the five levels of the Maslow Hierarchy of Needs.

4. To understand Herzberg's Motivation-Hygiene Theory.

5. To appreciate the importance of goal setting in individual behavior.

6. To explain how Expectancy Theory can be expressed as: Motivation = $E \times I \times V$.

7. To describe how the principles of equity theory affect the motivation of employees within organizations.

8. To explain the interclass pay equity motivational process.

9. To describe how expectancy theory can be applied to employee training.

10. To explain a model that would integrate the principles of the major motivation theories.

Century 21 Agent Glenn Edelen

Glenn Edelen is a real estate agent with Century 21. Today is a typical workday for Glenn. He will show eight homes to three different clients, engage in twenty-one telephone conversations, and meet two people considering looking for a new home "if they can afford what they want." Glenn works long hours, most weekends, and has an outstanding sales record. This is a very competitive market which witnesses many new agents coming and going each attracted by the possibility of huge commissions, the excitement of the real estate business, and encouraged by friends who tell them "you can make a lot of money in a few hours a week and you really know the neighborhoods." Then the reality of long hours, hard work, and countless dead-end efforts sets in and many of the excited new agents become statistics in a high-turnover business.

Glenn, however, has twenty years in the business. He has a wife, Leah, and four young sons to support: Bruce,

Jeff, Nick, and Andrew. It is a tough business to depend on to support a family because so many outside factors affect the market. Thus Glenn from time to time has thought about changing to a steady paycheck career, but finds he really enjoys what he does—in spite of the long hours, weekends in open houses, and slow markets, as in 1981 when interest rates were 16 percent and he sold only one-tenth of the number of houses that he sold in 1991!

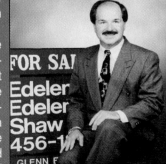

Today may be one that produces a high-commission sale, or it may only produce more hours of hard work without success. Glenn knows that to some extent luck has a hand in determining what kind of day he has. However, Glenn has enough experience to know that his extra efforts, persistence in tracking

down leads, ingenuity in putting together the right deal, and his maintaining a warm, friendly, customer-oriented personality are the keys to success. Each morning as he looks in the mirror he says, "It won't happen if *I* don't *make* it happen!" How does he make it happen? According to Glenn:

I have been excited about this business for many years. My motivation is the responsibility that is placed on us Realtors. You get to wear a lot of hats in this business, for example: Appraiser, Financial Advisor, Counselor, etc.; therefore, it makes for an interesting profession. Doing the job I do is a tremendous responsibility. My clients depend on my expertise to guide them through to a financial investment that could set their financial foundation for life; this, in itself, highly motivates me.

We all struggle with motivation at times. But it is a scientific fact that we all have unlimited energy, unused effort, and endless potential. How can we tap this?

Author Napoleon Hill describes *motivation* as a coin with two sides. One side is a desire. The other side: goals.

Why set goals? Most people don't. It's estimated that fewer than 3 percent of people have goals or focus for their life. But setting goals is important because:

- Goals give purpose and direction to your life, your career, and your day.
- Goals are the best reasons for not procrastinating.
- Goals focus energies in a specific direction.
- Goals build enthusiasm. Emerson said that nothing great has ever been achieved without enthusiasm.
- Goals make our wishes specific. If you ask people for specific accomplishments within a specific time, that's how it will get done.
- Goals save time. You spend time on what is truly important to you.
- Goals set standards for measuring your effectiveness. How do you know if

you've been successful if you have not been striving for something specific?
- Goals give a foundation for new targets when they're reached.

To make sure that you have the best chance of achieving your goals, consider these points:

- Set goals consistent with your purpose in life. If you haven't thought about your purpose in life, then it's time to consider why you are here.
- Set goals that you can get excited about. In a work environment, they may actually be someone else's goals, but at least look for some quality that is meaningful to you.
- Set goals that will meet your needs as a total person. Consider all aspects of your life: your personal needs, family, community responsibilities, financial and spiritual values.
- Write your goals down. Writing crystallizes thought and increases the probability that you will do something with them.
- Formulate a plan to achieve your goals. This means deciding the action you will take and when you will take it.
- Set realistic deadlines. Establish twelve-month, six-month, and three-month goals.

Once a goal is established, test it against the following guidelines:

- Is it conceivable? Can you see yourself accomplishing it? If you can't visualize it, chances are it won't happen.
- Is it believable? Can you dedicate yourself to it? Is your belief strong enough that you can deal with the challenges along the way?
- Is it achievable? Do you have the strength and talents to accomplish it?
- Is it controllable? Do you have the power to make it happen?
- Is it measurable? Do you have starting and ending times?
- Is it specific? Do you have numbers and an idea of what's needed?

Glenn is like everyone else who goes to work each day. To a great extent his level of success on the job

Motivation Author Napoleon Hill describes as a coin with two sides; one side is desire and the other side is goals.

depends on his level of motivation. In this chapter we will explore what factors may influence that motivation and how those factors can be changed to positively affect his motivation and therefore his performance.

What is Motivation?

Everyone is motivated every day by something that rouses the mind or emotions to take action in pursuit of a goal or to fulfill a need. In an organizational context the key question is what factors are important stimulants that will effectively motivate a person to extend high levels of effort to achieve organizational goals. Employees, of course, expect that the attainment of organizational goals will correlate with the rewards they receive from the organization, and these rewards enable them to fulfill their own personal goals. Thus a "circular" process develops (Fig. 6-1) in which higher levels of employee motivation lead to greater quality and quantity of work, which thus leads to higher organizational productivity and profits that enable the organization to provide the employee greater rewards and recognition.

The key elements required to make this intuitive model operational are: (1) the right rewards and recognition which will motivate employees; (2) employees' perceptions that greater quality and quantity of work will affect the productivity of the organization; and (3) the organization's ability to effectively link greater employee rewards to higher levels of productivity. If any of these elements is missing, then employees may not be as highly motivated in the workplace. For example, an employee may not believe that his or her own level of effort will affect the productivity of the organization, or perhaps all employees will receive the same rewards regardless of their level of work.

CONTENT THEORIES OF MOTIVATION

A few theories of what motivates people have been so intuitively appealing to managers and students of organizational behavior that they have become "classics." Their popularity largely stems from ease of understanding and general acceptance in the early years of the study of motivation rather than a firm

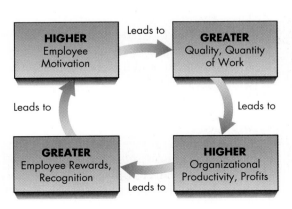

FIGURE 6-1

A Circular Model of Employee Motivation and Organizational Success

Profile | **Dave Jensen**
Search Master's International
Sedona, Arizona

MASLOW'S THEORIES—REGAINING RELEVANCE IN THE 90S

The concepts of Maslow's Hierarchy have "guided the direction I've headed in business." Understanding yourself and how you fit in with your work, your environment and your company have a great value in the business world. And those concepts are the center of Maslow's theory. Many other managers agree that the 1950s Hierarchy of Needs has regained relevance in the 1990s. In fact, the business programs which center on process improvements, customer-first practices, value, and quality—all of which require greater initiative and ability by employees—are consistent with Maslow.

The best boss I ever had introduced me to Maslow. One day while we were discussing business, he explained his management philosophy. He had a list of the personality traits of a self-actualized person—someone who is lower (on the Hierarchy) needs are fulfilled and thus is motivated primarily by a wish for fulfillment, and for making a contribution. The personality traits include awareness, independence, realism, altruism and spontaneity. The self-actualized person (or one seeking the highest level) has these traits which make him or her a great leader.

Applying Maslow to hiring people is accomplished by asking questions which enable the interviewer to estimate which level a person is on. The ideal hire is primarily motivated by self-esteem—they are usually committed to going above norms. To realize self-esteem, they need to perform to the limits of their abilities. Successful hires can also be managers who are between the social and esteem levels. The need to achieve status and gain recognition are their motivators.

I can't be portrayed as a person who has reached the plateau of self-actualization, but I'm still struggling to achieve it.

Source: Adapted from Mark Henricks, "Motivating Force," *Entrepreneur,* December 1995, pp. 68–72. Used by permission.

---

foundation of research data. No book on organizational behavior would be complete without a discussion of these classics. They have provided a foundation upon which many other theories have built their conclusions and they have substantially influenced thousands of managers who accept their basic principles.

Content theories
Theories of motivation that explain behavior in terms of what workplace factors motivate people.

These theories are often referred to as *content theories,* because they explain behavior in terms of what workplace factors motivate people. They center on internal human needs or motives that are met by factors such as pay, benefits, social environment, and interesting work. The major content theories include: (1) Maslow's Needs Hierarchy; (2) Alderfer's ERG Theory; (3) McClelland's Three Needs Theory; and (4) Herzberg's Motivation–Hygiene Theory. At the end of this section we also discuss McGregor's theory which is based on how managers interact with their employees.

Process theories **How individuals interact with their work environment and how it affects their behavior.**

In the next section we will discuss the *process theories* of motivation. These theories focus on how individuals interact with their work environment as it affects their behavior. In other words, the process theories focus on the mental processes that individuals utilize which affect their motivation and behavior.

Maslow's Hierarchy of Needs

Perhaps the most intuitively appealing theory for HR professionals today is Abraham *Maslow's Hierarchy of Needs*. According to Maslow, when a need occurs, motivational tension develops and is directed toward satisfaction of the felt need. The intensity of the effort is a function of how strong the need is.[1]

The Hierarchy comprises five levels of needs (see Fig. 6-2). *Physiological needs* are the primary needs for food, shelter, and clothing that can be directly satisfied by compensation; employees who are adequately paid can provide for their basic needs.

Once the physiological needs have been satisfied, the safety or *security needs* become a motivational factor. Many employees' most important security need is job security. There are other security factors as well that include increases in salary and benefits.

On the third level are *social needs.* At this level, employees desire social relationships inside and outside the organization. Peer-group acceptance within the work force is often an important psychological need for employees. Some people believe that the key to enable a person to meet his or her social needs is for an organization to provide a friendly working environment. For example, CEO Joe Drew in his Profile, "A Commitment to Friendliness," explains why he believes that it is essential for organizations to select applicants who possess

Maslow's Hierarchy of Needs Individuals have five levels of needs in which motivational tension develops and is directed towards satisfying the next level of unmet need.

Physiological needs Primary needs for food, shelter, and clothing.

Security needs Employees satisfy these needs through job security including salary and benefits.

Social needs Desire for social relationships inside and outside the organization—peer acceptance.

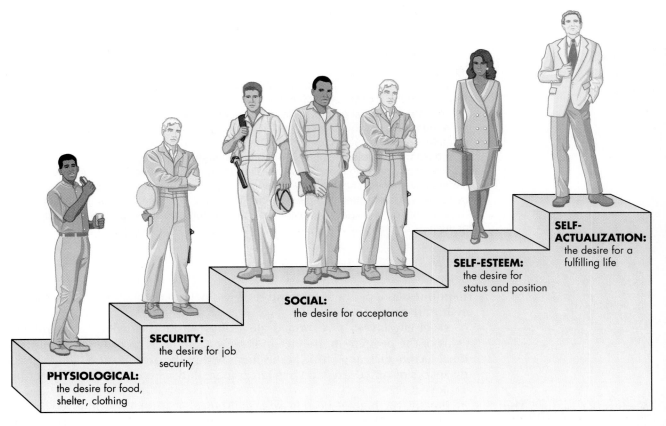

PHYSIOLOGICAL: the desire for food, shelter, clothing

SECURITY: the desire for job security

SOCIAL: the desire for acceptance

SELF-ESTEEM: the desire for status and position

SELF-ACTUALIZATION: the desire for a fulfilling life

Figure 6-2 Maslow's Hierarchy of Needs

Profile

Joseph E. Drew
County Administrative Officer
Kern County, California

A COMMITMENT TO FRIENDLINESS

What makes a job worth having: an organization worth working for? Why are some organizations able to retain good people and others struggle with constant turnover? The quick answer for many is "pay and benefits." If that were the case, all a company would have to do would be to spend money to be the best, and we know of too many examples where this has been tried and failed. The answer is found in the *quality of the social environment*. It requires that an organization has a culture that cares about and nurtures the relationships among its employees; where employees actively work at being friendly with one another and their customers. This doesn't mean that the organization must coddle mediocrity. It means each person must be committed to the organization and to each other.

Sound difficult? The fact is, any group of employees will always do more and work harder for a friend than an acquaintance. We will come early, stay late, miss lunch, or take the work home. Think about the person you have worked with for whom you have the least respect. What was the difference? In my experience, seldom is the difference associated with differences in technical ability. Most often, *personal qualities* are identified as the principal difference, with the quality of the personal relationship at the top of the list. Simply translated, what makes the important difference is how we are treated by our supervisor, our coworker. This is not surprising.

In order to make friends, we must be friendly. This is a primary requirement; there is no substitute. For people to spend nine or more hours together daily, five days a week, and achieve maximum productivity, there must be an atmosphere of friendliness and teamwork.

How does the organization bring this about? The organization must establish *friendliness as a desired personal trait in its selection process*. This is legal, and in my opinion, this is essential. The organization must actively employ team-building strategies to meld the friendly workforce together.

In the hundreds of employment selection interviews I have participated in during the last decade, I have included specific questions about a person's friendliness. For example, how would you answer the following: "What specific things do you routinely do to build friendly relationships with your coworkers?"

I want to work with friendly people. The alternative is not acceptable for me. In my leadership capacity, I have a duty to develop a work force that has *a commitment to friendliness*; a commitment to the well-being of the working team, the organization. Think about your own daily behavior. Do you routinely do the things necessary to build friendships among your superiors, your subordinates? Would I hire you?

---

friendliness as a personal trait and thus will help maintain a productive social environment.

Once employees have formed friendships within the organization and feel a part of the peer group, the need for self-esteem takes precedence. Organizational factors such as job title, status items within the organization such as parking spaces or office size, and level of responsibility become important to the employee.

Finally, the highest need is *self-actualization*. At this level, employees seek a fulfilling, useful life in the organization and in society. Employees will seek challenging and creative jobs to realize self-actualization. Maslow contends that individuals will climb the ladder of need fulfillment until they have become self-

Self-actualization **The desire for a fulfilling, useful life in the organization and in society.**

actualized. If any need is not fulfilled, the individual will continually strive to fill that need: that is, the need becomes a motivational factor. At any level, needs may be fulfilled outside the organization as well as within the organization.

The most important behavioral aspects of Maslow's Hierarchy are: (1) there are several aspects of the workplace that motivate people other than money (to provide for physiological needs); (2) since people can be at any of the levels of hierarchy, what substantially motivates one person may provide only minimum motivation to another—thus managers must be aware of the needs of each individual; and (3) what motivates a person may change over time, thus the assessment of a person's needs must be continuous. The various rewards, practices, and programs that the organization can provide to satisfy the needs of individuals are substantial—a partial list is provided in Fig. 6-3.

Physiological (Basic) Needs

  1. Furnish pleasant and comfortable environment.
  2. Provide for ample leisure.
  3. Provide for "comfortable" salary.

Security Needs

  1. Adhere to protective rules and regulations.
  2. Minimize layoffs and downsizing.
  3. Provide strong directive leadership and follow chain of command policy.
  4. Provide well-defined job descriptions.
  5. Minimize negative stroking and threatening behavior.
  6. Provide information about firm's financial status and projections.
  7. Provide "just" compensation and supportive fringe benefits.

Social Needs

  1. Encourage the team concept.
  2. Systematically use job satisfaction surveys.
  3. Use task groups to execute projects.
  4. Provide for firm and/or office business and social meetings.
  5. Provide close personal leadership.
  6. Encourage professional group participation.
  7. Encourage community group participation.
  8. Compensate on basis of total team performance.

Self-Esteem Needs

  1. Include employees in goal-setting and decision-making processes.
  2. Provide opportunity to display skills and talents.
  3. Provide recognition of advancement—for example, publicize promotions.
  4. Provide recognition symbols—for example, name on stationery.
  5. Assign associates and support staff for coaching and development.
  6. Use positive reinforcement program.
  7. Pay attention to office size, office location, parking spaces, et cetera.
  8. Institute a mentor system.
  9. Compensate as recognition of growth.

Self-Actualization Needs

  1. Provide for participation in goal-setting and decision-making processes.
  2. Provide opportunity and support for career-development plan.
  3. Provide staff job rotation to broaden experience and exposure.
  4. Offer optimum innovative and risk-taking opportunities.
  5. Encourage direct-access communication to clients, customers, suppliers, and vendors.
  6. Provide challenging internal and external professional development opportunities.
  7. Provide supportive leadership that encourages a high degree of self-control.
  8. Compensate as reward for exceptional performance.

FIGURE 6-3

Organizational Rewards, Practices, and Programs That May Satisfy the Levels of Maslow's Hierarchy of Needs

Source: Adapted from Norbert F. Elbert and Richard Discenza, *Contemporary Supervision,* New York: McGraw-Hill, Inc., 1985, pp. 81–82.

ERG Theory

Alderfer's ERG Theory
There are three groups
of needs: existence (E),
relatedness (R), and
growth (G).

Clayton *Alderfer's ERG Theory* is closely related to Maslow's Hierarchy of Needs. The theory posits three groups of needs—existence (E), relatedness (R), and growth (G). Existence needs are centered on providing the primary living requirements—similar to Maslow's psychological and security needs. The relatedness needs are centered on developing interpersonal relationships with others—similar to Maslow's social and esteem needs. The growth need is the internal desire for personal development and fulfillment—similar to Maslow's self-actualization.[2]

ERG Theory differs from Maslow in respect to how individuals fulfill their needs. While Maslow argues that one must progress "up" the hierarchy, focusing on the next unmet need, Alderfer argues that when one need is unmet or frustrated, the person may demand more of other needs. For example, if a person finds little self-actualization from a boring job, he or she may demand higher pay or more job security. Or, a person may choose to stay on a low-paying repetitious job because his or her best friends work at the same place. ERG Theory, therefore, contends that all needs are present or active in people at all times. This premise is in contrast to Maslow's belief that a person concentrates only on one need—the next unfulfilled one.

ERG Theory generally adds three often-accepted aspects to the theory of human needs: (1) More than one need may be operational at any one time; (2) if a higher-level need cannot be satisfied, the individual may become frustrated and thus the desire to satisfy a lower need increases and may substitute for the higher-level need; and finally (3) Maslow's five need categories may be collapsed into three. Research and general acceptance of these points have led to the adoption of the ERG Theory[3] as a more realistic approach to understanding human needs and as an amendment to Maslow's hierarchy.

Three Needs Theory

Three Needs Theory
Based on the
responses of individu-
als (managers), looking
at pictures which
explain their organiza-
tional needs such
as the need for
achievement, the need
for power, and the
need for affiliation.

David McClelland and others have posited a human motivation theory (or Achievement Motivation Theory) based on work with the well-known Thematic Apperception Test (TAT). The theory is called the *Three Needs Theory* and is based on the responses of individuals who look at a picture and then write about what they see in the picture. How people choose to describe the picture explains their own organizational needs that are:[4]

1. *Need for achievement*—the desire to be successful, to excel.
2. *Need for power*—the desire to affect the behavior of others.
3. *Need for affiliation*—the desire to maintain close personal relationships.

For example, three managers might be asked to view a photograph of three people in a work setting who appear to be discussing a problem. The first manager describes the photo as one of three employees working to solve an immediate problem (achievement); the second manager describes the photo as a supervisor explaining to two employees what action they need to take to solve the problem (power); the third manager describes the photo as three colleagues engaged in a casual conversation on a break (affiliation). McClelland would propose that all people have the three needs; however, one need may be dominant in a person and thus lead that person to perceive a work situation (or describe a picture of it) in terms of fulfilling that dominant need. Managers may then see the need to strengthen a person's need for achievement if it is not stronger than the other two. McClelland believed that the need to achieve often should be strengthened in people. First, of course, it needs to be measured, which is the purpose of the TAT. The TAT utilizes pictures of different situations that a person then describes in his or her own words—similar to the example mentioned above. An analysis of the description determines the person's need for achievement.

McClelland proposed that the TAT accurately measures a person's needs because when an individual "makes up a story about an otherwise meaningless picture, you project a lot more of yourself than you realize. You provide an unfiltered specimen of your normal walking thoughts." For example, a woman described a standard TAT picture of a young man and an older man in a serious conversation as "a guy who got into trouble for wasting a lot of money." When asked what personal concerns she had, a smile came across her face and she responded, "I spend all my time worrying about wasting money!"[5]

Successful business people score high on the TAT used for achievement. They often display three major traits: (1) they like to set goals for themselves to direct their behavior; (2) they set goals which are reasonably achievable—to increase the probability of attainment; and (3) they desire feedback to let them know if they are on the right track.[6]

The Three Needs Theory has led to a body of research that links job performance to the need for achievement. First, people with a high need for achievement require:

- *Feedback*. While all employees want to know how they are performing, high achievers require feedback more often and will be motivated more when it is regularly provided.
- *Higher Performance*. High achievers will usually achieve higher levels of performance because they utilize feedback received to shape their future performance.
- *Accept Responsibility*. Generally high achievers accept increased levels of responsibility and will work towards specific, attainable organizational goals.

For an exercise similar to the Thematic Apperception Test (TAT), describe what these employees appear to be doing.

Herzberg's Motivation–Hygiene Theory

Frederick Herzberg conducted an investigation into the attributes of jobs that people believed to be desirable or undesirable. His work was the first to focus on factors such as recognition, the work itself, and the sense of achievement one receives from the work. Herzberg concluded from his research that some job attributes are *maintenance or hygiene factors* (see Fig. 6-4) and cause employee dissatisfaction if not present at an acceptable level. *Maintenance factors* include such things as pay, supervision, working conditions, and work rules and policies. Herzberg also posited that the mere presence of maintenance factors will not motivate employees. Instead, motivational factors, which are centered on the job itself provide motivation. The motivating factors include: recognition, achievement, responsibility, and opportunity for advancement.[7] These factors are basically the self-actualization needs found at the top of Maslow's hierarchy.

Herzberg's theory has received a great deal of discussion over the years, both pro and con. Perhaps the greatest contribution by Herzberg was the attention his work focused on how jobs are designed. Employers like Maytag Co. have designed jobs in which the work itself is more challenging and rewarding while at the same time giving people increased autonomy to perform their job.

Another contribution of the Motivation–Hygiene Theory is the finding that the opposite of satisfaction is not necessarily dissatisfaction. Instead, the absence of job dissatisfiers (*hygiene factors*) such as poor working conditions, an irrational supervisor, or unfair policies does not guarantee a person will be satisfied with his or her position. In fact, the result may simply be he or she is not dissatisfied with these factors, but at the same time, is not motivated by his or her job. Accord-

Maintenance factors
Factors such as pay, supervision, working conditions, and work rules and policies.

Hygiene factors
Factors such as pay, working conditions, and supervision which, if perceived to be adequate, do not cause dissatisfaction. Their presence, however, is not motivational.

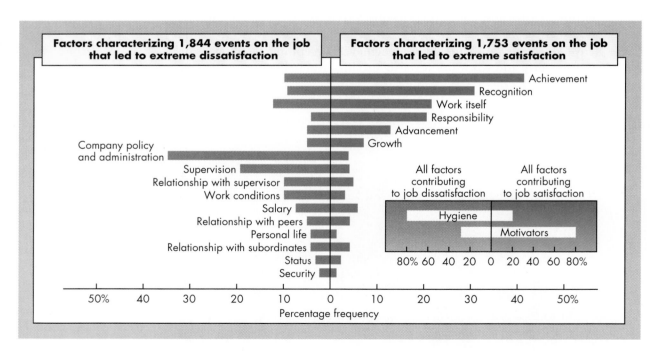

FIGURE 6-4 Comparison of Satisfiers and Dissatisfiers

Source: Reprinted by permission of *Harvard Business Review*. An exhibit from "One More Time: How Do You Motivate Employees?" by Frederick Herzberg, September/October 1987. Copyright ©1987 by the President and Fellows of Harvard College; all rights reserved.

ing to the theory only the presence of the motivating factors, in addition to the absence of dissatisfiers, will motivate a person to higher levels of performance.

Herzberg's Theory has received some research support[8] but has also received some criticism. The emphasis Herzberg placed on job design factors has provided an important influence in the movement to design more "motivating" and less highly-specialized, boring jobs. In addition recent global research on the motivation–hygiene theory indicates that employees of other cultures have similar views towards motivation and hygiene as their counterparts in the United States. For example, in the United States about 80 percent of the factors that workers indicate lead to job satisfaction, Herzberg classifies as "motivators." Workers in other countries reported similar results: Japan 82 percent, Italy 60 percent, Finland 90 percent, and Hungary 78 percent. U.S. workers indicate about 75 percent of the variables that cause dissatisfaction are hygiene factors, with similar results in Japan (65 percent), Italy (70 percent), Finland (80 percent), and Hungary (78 percent).[9] It is important to note that other motivation theories have not received such strong global support.

Theory X, Theory Y, and Theory Z

Douglas McGregor presented another classical theory of motivation. Unlike the content theories just presented, his Theory X and Theory Y was based on observations of how managers interact with their employees. He concluded that some managers choose a theory X approach to supervising others if they believe that:[10]

Employees have responded to more motivating jobs with greater quality and creativity.

- The average human being has an inherent dislike of work and will avoid it if possible.
- Because of this characteristic dislike of work, most people must be coerced, controlled, directed, and threatened with punishment to get them to put forth adequate effort toward the achievement of organizational objectives.
- The average human being prefers to be directed and wishes to avoid responsibility.
- Workers value job security above all else and have little ambition.

Thus, according to McGregor, the theory X manager designs jobs which are simple to learn, are highly specialized, and give them constant close supervision to ensure high levels of productivity.

Other managers choose a theory Y approach to supervision because they believe:[11]

- The expenditure of physical and mental effort in work is as natural as play or rest. Depending upon controllable conditions, work may be a source of satisfaction (and will be voluntarily performed) or a source of punishment (and will be avoided if possible).
- External control and the threat of punishment are not the only means for bringing about effort toward achieving organizational objectives. Individuals will exercise self-direction and self-control in the service of objectives to which they are committed.
- Commitment to objectives is a function of the rewards associated with their achievement. The most significant of such rewards (e.g., the satisfaction of ego and self-actualization needs) can be direct products of the effort directed towards achieving organizational objectives.
- The average human being learns, under proper conditions, not only to accept but also to seek responsibility.

- The capacity to exercise a relatively high degree of imagination, ingenuity, and creativity in the solution of organizational problems is widely, not narrowly, distributed in the population.
- Under the conditions of modern organizational life, the intellectual potentialities of the average human beings are only partially used.

Thus theory Y managers will likely design jobs that are more motivating, require mental effort, and are without constant supervision. McGregor believed that managers should adopt the theory Y approach if they want to maximize employee motivation and productivity. This approach emphasizes the need for employees to achieve personal satisfaction from the work they perform and the work place.

Theory Z, a third relationship alternative, has been proposed by William Ouchi. This theory emphasizes that employees should have direct input into the design of their work and the improvement of efficiency through quality circles, a method of participative management. If employees are given the opportunity by management, they can work together (in quality circles) to identify and analyze work-related activities and problems and develop effective solutions.[12] This concept will be explored in greater detail later in the next chapter.

McGregor's motivational theory, like that of Maslow and Herzberg, was largely founded on personal observations and beliefs. And like the others it contained some concepts which influenced a number of managers and scholars. Few people today if asked would identify themselves as a theory X person. Instead most would agree with the beliefs of McGregor's theory Y managers (see the Randolph Coe Profile, "The Laws of the Jungle"). They also would agree with Herzberg that motivational factors should be present in the workplace as well as with Maslow that a person strives to fulfill all levels of needs. The practical applications of these theories are presented in the next chapter in the discussion of effective recognition/reward programs, profit sharing, employee participation in decision making, flextime, quality circle programs, et cetera, as well as in the chapters on teamwork, organizational culture, and quality management.

PROCESS THEORIES OF MOTIVATION

The previously discussed content theories of motivation have provided ideas and concepts to thousands of managers, owners, and people from all walks of life. They were largely accepted on faith and not documented research but have become accepted as "classics." They also laid the groundwork for hundreds—maybe thousands—of "new" or "modern" theories of motivation, which generally have received documented research support, have withstood the test of time, and will be presented in this section. The *process theories* discussed in this section focus on the thought or cognitive processes that individuals utilize that influence their behavior. In general, while the content theories are somewhat static and descriptive of needs, process theories present the dynamic thought processes individuals experience as they evaluate their interactions with their work environment.

Process theories focus on the thought or cognitive processes that individuals utilize and influence their behavior.

Goal Setting

Goal-setting theory is based on a simple observation of human behavior: People act in a purposeful manner. Human beings possess a high capacity to reason

Profile

W. Randolph Coe
Director, Peterborough, England, and Louisville, Kentucky

THE LAWS OF THE JUNGLE

Everything's £1 Limited is a registered company in the United Kingdom. It was launched in 1992 to help satisfy the British consumer demand for retail products sold at the £1.00 price point. It is privately owned by an American holding company, with a British venture capital firm having a minority shareholding. The United Kingdom market was selected as it is a relatively stable economy with socio-economic and retailing patterns that are similar to those found in the United States.

The senior management of Everything's £1 is led by three Americans and one Englishman. All head office, branch, and warehousing personnel are British. The head office is located in Peterborough, England. The American holding company has its offices in Louisville, Kentucky.

Obtaining and retaining quality associates at all levels has been a primary goal of the senior management. The company's senior managers have other start-up business experience in the United States, Russia, Latvia, Belgium, Australia, and Spain. We are well aware of the critical need to recruit, train, motivate, reward, and retain what is the real lifeblood of any business, its personnel.

Management opportunities in an international enterprise are very similar to those found in companies limited to the United States in scope. Whether a company has branches or divisions either one hour or eight hours away from the head office, the problems encountered and opportunities to develop the business are essentially the same.

The principal role for management is to provide quality leadership. Strategic and local goals must be set and met. Communication with associates must be two-way and effective. Their motivation must be an ongoing effort by managers to help assure that they achieve the success you have set out for them. A very clear understanding must be mutually agreed upon as to how their success will be measured.

Our philosophy of employee motivation is to enable and empower associates to achieve the results the company needs in order for it to succeed and thrive. We practice the idea that "we are one." Associates are helped to understand that they are an important part of the "one." To that end we maintain a workplace environment in which every associate is treated with respect. Compensation is good. For key positions our compensation packages are above the market, helping assure we have the best available personnel. In the unfortunate instance that an associate cannot or will not succeed, then separation from the company is swift.

Our experience has lead us to reach certain conclusions regarding how budding entrepreneurs can effectively manage and motivate employees. We do not pretend to have all the answers or that these conclusions will be 100 percent effective in all circumstances. However, they seem to achieve the results we desire. We refer to them as "The Laws of the Jungle."

The Laws of the Jungle

1. *Accept challenge and risk.* The greater the risk, often the greater the reward. Never quit. Your next effort may lead to the success you desire.

2. *Lead by example.* Your associates are always watching your actions. Behave as if your every action will be shown to your loved ones on the evening television program. It keeps you humble and focused.

3. Develop and maintain a *"we are one" culture* within your company. You live or die based in large part on what your associates do or do not do. You cannot be everywhere and do everything. Do not just say it or print it in a nice company brochure. Live it.

4. The *Theory of X* in management may be necessary with a few employees, but it is absolute rubbish with management level personnel. Around the world, good managers have become too well educated to work effectively in a Theory X environment.

5. Prepare yourself and your associates academically and through life experience to overcome any foreseeable challenge and those that are unexpected. You must *continue to grow intellectually and professionally* to compete in tomorrow's marketplace. Training must be ongoing. Encourage your associates to improve themselves. You may lose some of them to other companies. You will still have benefited.

6. Hire people of whom you can be proud. If someone's *ethics* or practices are not above reproach then they will eventually hurt the business as well as reflect badly on you. There are plenty of quality people in this world whom you can hire.

7. You will not have the time to check up on every management decision of your associates. *Hire the best* and save yourself a lot of headaches. Get rid of failures quickly.

8. *Communicate often.* Most employees want the business to succeed. They will help you if you let them. Listen to them. They often know more about an issue than you. Enable and empower them as well as hold them accountable.

9. Because there are always some associates who do not or will not cooperate, you must not only expect them to follow company policies and procedures, you must inspect. *You must inspect,* even your top managers.

10. *Share the financial success* of the company with your associates. Short-term personal avarice usually means longer-term loss of personal profit. Your associates will build your equity value for your eventual exit from the company. If fairly rewarded, that value will be much greater than if you "hired cheap and paid cheap."

---

and to utilize that capacity in choosing how they behave. They have the ability to conceptualize long-range goals: such as, being paid at the end of the month, being promoted at some time in the future, et cetera, and they will choose a means to attain these goals.[13]

Thus, setting goals is a method of employee motivation that focuses on the chosen outcomes of behavior. Goal-setting is one of the few motivational theories that has received widespread, strong support from academic research and managers, and thus continues to be applied in various forms. In fact, goal-setting is applied to individuals, groups, and entire organizations as a means of motivating those involved to achieving certain objectives. Why is goal-setting often a successful motivational technique? The setting of goals provides several distinct advantages:[14]

- *Direct behavior.* Goals focus effort and attention into a specific direction and thus provide important guideposts in day-to-day decision making at all levels of the organization.

- *Provide challenges.* Goals help keep individuals motivated by giving them standards against which their performance will be evaluated. Most people react favorably when given purposeful challenges in the workplace. In fact, they may prefer having new goals to achieve instead of the old adages of "keep up the good work," or "do things like we've always done them. . . . "

- *Resource allocation.* In many situations the allocation of resources (people, time, equipment, money) is a critical decision-making process. Goals serve to provide legitimate reasons for resource allocation decisions. This can be especially important when the decision is to shift resources from one task or profit center to another.
- *Provide structure.* Goals may shape part of the formal or informal organization structure. They provide rationale for setting communication patterns, the allocation of authority and responsibility and the organizational hierarchy.

Research indicates that several factors are critical in the goal-setting process leading to increased performance. As depicted in Fig. 6-5, higher levels of performance and goal attainment is more likely to occur when:[15]

- *Goals are specific.* The utilization of measurable specific goals generally leads to greater performance. For example, an employee given the goal of reducing energy costs by 10 percent over the period of a year will likely achieve greater savings than if given the goal of reducing energy costs as much as reasonably possible.
- *Difficult, but attainable.* Individuals will generally achieve higher levels of performance when they perceive a goal to be difficult but still attainable. Within limits the more difficult the goal is perceived to be, the greater the level of performance.[16] However, if the goal is perceived to be so difficult that it can not be reached, the individual tends not to strive seriously for the goal, and performance is lowered. In addition, if a goal is perceived to be easily attained, it is believed that no additional effort is needed, and thus performance is not increased.[17]
- *Participation.* Individuals' determination and effort to reach a goal is likely to be greater if they have participated in the setting of the goal. The active involvement in goal determination increases one's sense of ownership, understanding, and acceptance of the goal, and one's desire to see it obtained. When one is simply assigned a goal, his or her desire to reach it may not be as great.

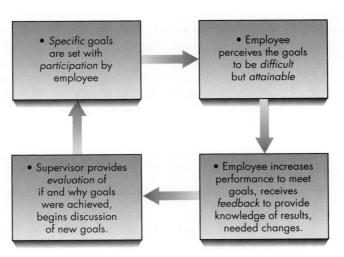

Figure 6-5
The Goal-Setting Process

- *Feedback.* Higher performance is more likely if individuals are given feedback or direction while they are striving to achieve a goal. Feedback should provide useful information as to whether or not ongoing levels of performance are likely to reach that goal.[18] For example, the employee striving to reduce energy costs by 10 percent might implement several energy-reduction techniques during the year, starting with the least expensive. If feedback is provided after each technique has had a reasonable trial period, then the employee can determine the degree to which each reduction has helped reach the goal, and if additional measures are needed.
- *Evaluation.* If individuals expect their performance to be evaluated at some point in the future, then their performance will likely be greater. Conversely, if employees perceive that goals are only set, and their future performance evaluation will not include if and why the goals were achieved, their performance is likely to be lower.

Basically, goal-setting strategies involve a systematic process whereby the manager and subordinate discuss and agree upon a set of jointly determined goals. With proper preparation, each party should be able to present a case for or against each goal. If the process is functioning effectively, the final result will be a set of goals that is in keeping with the overall goals of the organization. Moreover, the manager will have something concrete upon which to gauge the subordinate's performance. Feedback on progress is periodically supplied, enabling the worker to make necessary corrections. Above all, the link between performance, evaluation, and rewards is made explicitly clear to the subordinate, with emphasis on *what* was achieved and *how* it was accomplished.

MBO process
Management utilizes goal-setting to achieve objectives.

In practice, goal-setting theory is utilized in management by objective *(MBO) programs* (see Chap. 7: Motivation: Effective Applications). As an example, if Roberto Cosenza, manager of a video store in Orange County, California, is told in his annual review that he should "Cut down on the number of employee hours," how will he react? This vague reference to a perceived problem may cause Roberto to lay off several employees and negatively affect service. He may worry about the suggestion until it's forgotten or choose any one of several feasible actions. The problem is, of course, his supervisor did not give him a specific measurable goal, require a plan of action by Roberto, or provide feedback in the future months to see if the plan is working. Also, Roberto is not sure how achieving the goal (or failure to do so) will directly affect him. In an MBO process, the supervisor and Roberto would jointly discuss and agree upon a goal: such as, "A 20 percent reduction of total employee hours per month should be achieved by reducing the number of 10:00 A.M.–5:00 P.M. personnel by 33 percent under a flextime program. The program, with monthly reports, is to be developed by Roberto and approved before implementation. The goal represents one of three which will determine Roberto's midyear bonus."

At the start of this chapter Glenn Edelen, a highly successful real estate agent, discussed how he views goal setting as a critical key to the motivation process. Glenn also offers the following suggestions on how one can actually *reach* his or her own goals:

- Keep a project list and a daily "to do" list. Set priorities and don't overload the lists.
- Realize that activities expand to fill the time allotted. Make sure you allot only as much time as necessary to complete an activity.

- Learn to say "no" nicely without feeling guilty. You can't be everything to everybody.
- Learn to make your own decisions and don't look for approval.
- Work on your self-image daily.
- Surround yourself with people who support your goals. Negative people drain your energy and enthusiasm.
- Take care of your body.
- Manage your family time and keep a good balance.
- Make sure to reward yourself as you achieve portions of your goal. You don't have to wait.
- Take positive action. A positive attitude is not enough.

The hardest part is deciding your goals. Once you decide, the rest is simple. But there is a difference between "simple" and "easy." Establishing what you want, developing a plan, and making it happen is never easy. I firmly believe that if you work hard and do the best you can, the rewards will happen for you.

Reinforcement Theory

The concept of positive reinforcement is central to many motivation theories. It is the practice of giving valued rewards to someone who has just engaged in a desired behavior. The technique is based on the *law of effect,* which means that behavior that leads to a pleasant response is more likely to be repeated, whereas behavior that results in an unpleasant response is less likely to be repeated.[19] Reinforcement theory is a primary reason managers choose to utilize merit increases. In order for reinforcement to continue to affect employees' future behavior, a manager must make certain that rewards are meaningful and desired by each employee.[20] As Maslow's Hierarchy points out, employee needs are different; therefore the reward, whether it be recognition, pay, or changing job requirements must be tailored to fit the employee. In addition, the organization must provide a process that makes it clear that rewards are contingent upon certain behavior. While reinforcement theory makes a contribution to the study of motivation, few people would argue that it alone explains people's behavior. Reinforcement as an important element in the learning process was discussed in detail in an earlier chapter.

In practice, negative reinforcement may be more commonly utilized—an employee receives a written disciplinary notice that another unexcused absence will result in termination. Many motivation theories and practices include the basic premise of positive reinforcement in a more general context rather than a direct cause-and-effect relationship. When people receive praise, recognition, or other rewards for a particular action they will generally work to achieve similar results. Other important factors that affect a person's behavior such as his or her like or dislike of the work itself, ability, expectations, opportunities to affect productivity, et cetera, are not addressed by reinforcement theory.

Some goal-setting theorists might note that reinforcement theory and goal-setting are very different approaches to explaining motivation. Goal-setting is based on the belief that individuals internally direct their own behavior in order to achieve certain objectives. Reinforcement theory argues that people do not direct their behavior, but instead, it is shaped by external reinforcers administered by others. Which do you believe?

Expectancy Theory

Expectancy theory
A person's effort depends on the values given to the anticipated outcome of the effort and the perceived probability that the desired outcome will be obtained.

Another widely accepted theory of motivation is *expectancy theory*. The theory states that a person's effort in a situation depends on the value given to the anticipated outcome of the effort, and the perceived probability that the desired outcome will be obtained.[21] The theory also states that motivation (M) is a function of the expectancy (E) or probability that one's effort will achieve a certain level of performance, and that level of performance will be instrumental (I) in their receiving rewards or outcomes for which they place a certain value or valence (V). These critical factors can be expressed in a single equation:

$$M = E \times I \times V$$

As a further explanation the three key factors in the theory are:

1. *Expectancy.* The mental probability that a certain level of effort will enable a person to achieve a certain level of performance.
2. *Instrumentality.* The mental probability that a certain level of performance will be recognized and lead to certain organizational rewards.
3. *Valence.* The value a person gives to the reward or outcome received as a result of his or her performance. A distinction between intrinsic and extrinsic valence in motivation has been identified in organizational research. Intrinsic valence refers to outcomes that are internal to individuals: such as, job satisfaction, sense of enjoyment, or self-esteem. Extrinsic valence refers to outcomes that are external to individuals: such as,

FIGURE 6-6
Expectancy Theory

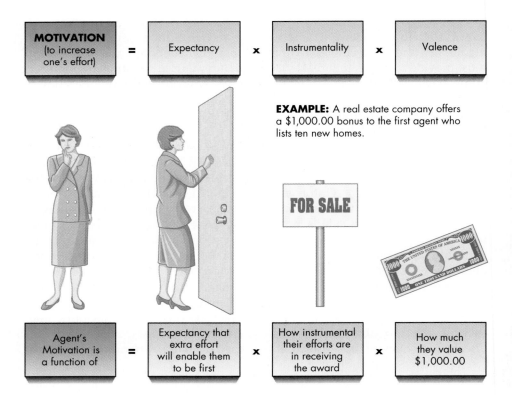

pay, promotion, or job perks. Research results indicate both intrinsic and extrinsic valences impact motivation and behavior.[22]

As an example assume a real estate company offers a $1,000.00 bonus to the first agent who lists ten new homes. Each agent's motivation to list new homes (according to expectancy theory) will depend upon his or her expectancy that an effort to list new homes will be successful. Also, that if successful, he or she will receive the reward. In this case the probability depends on the agent's perceived chance to be first, and how great a value he or she placed on the $1,000.00 bonus. To increase the motivation of their agents the firm could, for example, increase the valence by raising the bonus amount; increase the instrumentality by increasing the number of agents who could receive the bonus: for example, the first five agents to list ten new homes; and/or increase the expectancy by giving the agents a list of new leads or other methods of finding new prospects.

What practical lessons can be learned from expectancy theory? If one believed in the theory and wanted to apply it, then the organization would need to consider the following in a given situation:

1. *Reward.* The reward or outcome to be offered as a means of motivating a person should have a high value (valence) to that individual. Different people, of course, have different needs, making this a difficult assessment.
2. *Effort-performance link.* The individual must perceive that extra effort on his or her part will lead to a successful performance. Thus, exactly how he or she should expend their extra effort must be clear.
3. *Performance-reward link.* The person must perceive that the greater performance will cause them to receive the desired reward.

To summarize in a common organizational behavior context: The employee should be given a valuable incentive and instructed as to what specific performance will be rewarded with the incentive.

How valuable is expectancy theory to organizational behavior? It should not be considered a universal model of motivation which can be utilized to motivate all people to achieve higher levels of performance in all situations. However, the basic three key elements of the model are important to a highly motivated work force. First, employees should perceive that they can receive valued rewards such as promotions, bonuses, perks, et cetera, from the organization. Second, they should, in general, expect that higher sustained levels of effort will result in higher levels of performance. And third, higher levels of performance will be recognized by the organization and given greater rewards.

One area in which the application of expectancy theory has provided important research is training. Almost all employees receive training during their careers, often at several different junctures. Training often represents an expensive investment by organizations and one critical to their long-term success and survival. Employees' motivation to learn in training programs is a critical factor in their success.[23] Research has shown that employees' lack-of-training motivation is largely due to their perception that training has little utility; therefore, it will not improve their job performance or enhance their career opportunities. Expectancy theory suggests that trainees are unlikely to be motivated to learn unless they perceive the training to result in either improved job performance or career advancement. Research of organizational training programs has supported the predictions of expectancy theory and has provided three important implications for training programs:[24]

- Employees' motivation to learn will be significantly higher when they perceive the training will improve their job performance or enhance their opportunity for career advancement. Often they do not enter training programs with such beliefs, and thus for the training to succeed, they must be convinced of this benefit prior to the program.
- Employees' motivation to learn is significantly higher when they are directly involved in the decision to train and to plan the program.
- Employees' motivation to learn is significantly higher when they believe their supervisors will support the transfer of the training to the workplace. Thus supervisors must be convinced to be receptive to employees utilizing new ideas and skills learned through training in the workplace.

Equity Theory

Jan Lopez is a teller for a regional bank. She has twelve years of experience and is second in seniority only to the head teller. Jan has received a high performance review every year, likes all of her colleagues, and her supervisor. She is generally very happy with her work environment. Last week, however, by accident, Jan found out that Cora Tillett, the teller next to her, makes the same salary as Jan. While Jan considers Cora a good worker she has eight years more experience than Cora, and Jan knows that Cora has received three or four disciplinary actions due to excessive tardiness. Jan simply feels that for the two of them to be paid the same salary is unfair, but she doesn't want to "rock the boat" and complain. Today she is, however, taking a half-day off to interview with another bank for a similar position. Jan's situation is quite common in organizations—employees comparing their work and rewards to those of others—and then deciding if the employer is treating them fairly; that is what equity theory explores.

Equity theory is based on one of the cornerstones of Western culture—fairness. Political and religious groups, unions, as well as minority and women's groups have worked hard to achieve equity or fairness in the workplace. J. Stacy Adams and others have proposed that this concept carries over to the U.S. workplace. Adams proposes that workers expect an "equity norm," that is, they review the effort and performance (inputs) they give to the organization and the rewards (outcomes) they receive from the organization.[25] This outcomes/inputs ratio is then compared to the same perceived outcomes/inputs ratio of their peers or referents in the organization. The comparisons generally result in one of three possible situations (see Fig. 6-7): (1) the ratios are equal and the person feels fairly or equitably treated in comparison to others within the organization; (2) the ratio is more favorable to others—thus the person feels inequitably treated by

FIGURE 6-7
Equity Comparisons

Individual		Peers	Perception	Likely Action
1. $\frac{O}{I}$	$=$	$\frac{O}{I}$	Equity	Feeling of satisfaction, fair treatment
2. $\frac{O}{I}$	$<$	$\frac{O}{I}$	Inequity (under-rewarded)	Feeling of being unfairly treated, and some action is required to resolve the inequity
3. $\frac{O}{I}$	$>$	$\frac{O}{I}$	Inequity (over-rewarded)	Feeling of being more favorably treated, but often take no action to resolve the inequity the inequity

the organization; or (3) the ratio is more favorable to the individual—therefore, they feel more favorably treated than others. Most employees prefer the first situation; they want to feel fairly treated in comparison to others. The third situation causes some stress, but since the individual perceives they are more favorably treated than others, they do not seek a resolution of the inequity.

In the second situation, however, when a person perceives a negative inequity, it causes internal tension, and they will take some action to resolve the inequity. People will most likely choose one or more of the following actions to resolve perceived negative inequity:[26]

1. Reduce their input (performance).
2. Try to increase outcomes (ask for a raise, promotion, etc.).
3. Quit or transfer.
4. Change the perceived outcomes and/or inputs of the referent person (that job is not really better than mine or he or she really does work harder).
5. Change referent person (Bill's job is more like mine, and I get paid more than he).

There is strong research evidence to support the equity theory belief that, in fact, employees who perceive negative inequitable treatment will adopt one or more of the above actions. All of these actions, of course, are costly to the organization. Employees who perceive unequitable treatment are most likely to lower their efforts, increase their absenteeism, lower their cooperation and morale, even spread their unhappiness to others, or perhaps leave the organization. All of these actions are costly to an organization.[27]

Research has also determined that lower-echelon employees make equity comparisons between themselves and upper-echelon employees. This "interclass pay equity" perception is based upon the differences in pay and inputs between lower-echelon employees and upper-echelon employees. While lower-echelon employees realize that upper-echelon managers and executives generally contribute more to the ultimate success of the organization, if the perceived differences in these inputs do not justify the pay differential, then feelings of inequity are present.

When this interclass equity comparison leads to perceptions of inequity by lower-echelon employees, they are most likely to alleviate this tension through three aspects of their motivation: (1) commitment to top-management goals; (2) effort; and (3) cooperation. These motivational influences can ultimately affect the quality of the organization's products (see Fig. 6-8). Thus when lower-

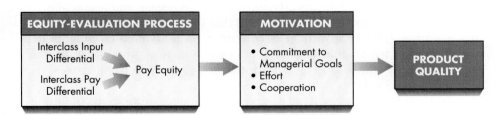

FIGURE 6-8 The Relationship between Interclass Pay Equity, Motivation, and Quality

Source: Adapted from Douglas M. Cowherd and David I. Levine, "Product Quality and Pay Equity between Lower-level Employees and Top Management: An Investigation of Distributive Justice Theory," *Administrative Science Quarterly,* vol. 37, 1992, p. 309. Used by permission.

echelon employees perceive that the differences in pay and input between themselves and upper-echelon executives are not equitable, they reduce the perceived inequity by reducing their effort, cooperation, and commitment to managerial goals, which in turn lowers product quality. Research indicates that perceived interclass pay inequity is not only a problem today, but is a problem that is likely to increase if the trends of participative management and self-managed teams continue to increase the "input" expected of lower-echelon workers while the pay gaps between them and executive-echelon personnel continues to widen.[28]

Interclass pay comparisons have occurred in many organizations. In 1991, for example, the University of California at Berkeley announced that it was eliminating merit pay increases for the second consecutive year. In the same week the university's president received a $62,000 bonus as a reward for five years of service. A faculty member posted an article reporting the president's bonus with this caption: "While Rome burns." In another example, Apple Computer's CEO John Sculley received a record-high compensation package at the same time employees received a reduction in their profit-sharing formula. One Apple worker compared employee morale to what it must have been like during the French Revolution: "Everyone wants to overthrow the royalty."[29] Perhaps the most well-known example of an interclass pay struggle occurred in 1982 when General Motors negotiated wage concessions from the United Automobile Workers union due to severe company losses, and within days announced that executives would receive large bonuses. The employee outrage caused the cancellation of the bonuses but the bitterness between management and labor remained for several years.[30]

What can organizations do to avoid unnecessary costs due to perceived inequity? Obviously, the simple answer is to treat everyone fairly. However, that is not always easy, and even the "fairest" workplaces may have pockets of unfair treatment. Thus, organizations should routinely measure employee perceptions of fairness or job satisfaction to determine if problems exist.

Measuring employee feelings about equitable treatment can be complex. Because the probability of receiving honest answers through interviews and group discussions is low, the only practical alternative may be to use anonymous written surveys. One advantage of using written questionnaires is that the possible sources of perceived inequity can often be identified. Identification can be accomplished by comparing the results of questions among departments, jobs, and supervisors. Seven areas of potential equitable or inequitable treatment are identified in one survey instrument, the Organization Fairness Questionnaire (Figure 6-9).

Generally, employers should measure employee perceptions of fairness on a routine basis. If the organization waits until a crisis occurs, employees may feel that they are being patronized and suspect that the organization does not really care how they feel. An advantage of conducting a study on an annual basis is that organizations can analyze changes in employee perceptions over time and possibly identify reactions to organizational changes such as pay increases, new policies such as flextime, new work rules, et cetera.

After reviewing the results of a survey of employee perceptions of fairness, management may consider introducing certain changes in the organization. Changes that may reduce perceptions of inequity include the following:[31]

- Reclassify jobs that appear to be inequitably paid (establish internal pay equity).
- Base promotions on more objective measures of performance.

Pay Rules (nine questions). Perceptions of the fairness of one's pay relative to one's coworkers and the fairness of the rules for granting pay increases and promotions. Sample Statement: "The rules for giving pay raises are not fair to some employees."

Pay Administration (five questions). Perceptions of the fairness of the supervisor in administering the rules for pay raises and promotions. Sample Statement: "My supervisor rates people unfairly in considering people for promotion."

Work Pace (eight questions). Perceptions of the fairness of the supervisor in maintaining a fair pace of work activity. Sample Statement: "My supervisor sees to it that all of us meet work standards."

Pay Level (five questions). Perceptions of the fairness of one's pay relative to others' pay outside of the employing organization. Sample Statement: "Other companies in this area pay people doing my kind of job less than I am getting paid."

Rule Administration (four questions). Perceptions of the fairness of supervisors in maintaining acceptable forms of general behavior in the workplace. Sample Statement: "My supervisor allows workers to tease other employees, be late to their workstations, and to act improperly in other ways."

Distribution of Jobs (six questions). Perceptions of the fairness of supervisors in distributing tasks to subordinates. Sample Statement: "My supervisor sees that everybody in my department does a share of the more unpleasant jobs."

Latitude (six questions). Perceptions of the fairness of supervisors in permitting subordinates latitude for planning and personal decision making on the job. Sample Statement: "In working with me, my supervisor is fair in letting me decide how to do my work."

Source: *Organization Fairness Questionnaire,* © by John E. Dittrich, Ph.D., 1977. Used by permission.

FIGURE 6-9

Seven Dimensions of Equity Measured in the Organizational Fairness Questionnaire

- Train supervisors to distribute work load more fairly.
- Conduct wage surveys of the local labor market to determine compatibility with local firms (establish external pay equity).
- Review "interclass" pay differences and make sure they are justified.
- Allow employees more latitude in planning and controlling their work.
- Ensure that policies, procedures, rules, and regulations are uniformly administered and enforced.

In practice perhaps the most important factor which affects employee perception of equity is pay. It is simply easy for employees to compare salaries or wages of different jobs due to their numeric quality.

To achieve equity among jobs, human resource professionals usually create a systematic relationship among the pay scales for the jobs within an organization. This process is called job evaluation.

Job evaluation is the systematic determination of the relative worth of jobs within the organization that results in an organization's pay system. Primarily, jobs are compared on the basis of: (1) the skills required to complete the job; (2) the effort required to perform the job; (3) the responsibility of the job holder; and (4) the working conditions on the job. The primary purpose of job evaluation is to develop a system of compensation that employees will perceive to be equitable. Thus, job evaluation strives to obtain both *internal* consistency among jobs, and *external* consistency with other organizations in the local labor market. Wage surveys are often utilized to obtain comparative wage and salary information from other employees.

Job evaluation
The systematic determination of the relative worth of jobs that results in an organization's pay system.

No compensation program will keep all employees satisfied all the time. If management is able to minimize turnover and lost production due to percep-

OB in Practice

Eric Dickerson: A Case of Inequity

Of all the motivation theories, equity theory is the one people can most readily identify with in their own lives and recognize in other, publicized situations. One of the most widely publicized fields in which cases of perceived "inequitable treatment" occurs is professional sports and the negotiating of athletes' contracts. While employee salaries and their negotiations are private matters in most organizations, in the sports world not only are salaries and contracts publicized, but so are the "inputs" of the players; that is, their performance statistics such as batting averages, won-loss records, average points and rebounds per game, pass completions, and rushing yardage.

One well-publicized case of perceived inequity in professional sports was Eric Dickerson, running back for the Los Angeles Rams of the National Football League (NFL). After his first four seasons with the Rams, Dickerson's contract was up for renegotiation. He had clearly become one of the NFL's premier running backs with season yardage totals of 1,808, 2,105 (NFL record), 1,234, and 1,821. In the last year of his old contract Dickerson was paid $682,000. A lot of money, but less than forty other NFL players. He was the eighth highest paid player on the Rams. Dickerson demanded a contract similar to other franchise players, his choice of equity theory "other" comparison. These other players included John Elway, quarterback of the Denver Broncos ($12 million for 6 years); Dan Marino of the Miami Dolphins ($1.5 million/year); and Brian Bosworth of the Seattle Seahawks ($11 million for 10 years). Dickerson felt a negative inequity and let his perceptions known to the Rams—"What I make in salary, they pay in taxes."

Thus as equity theory suggests, Dickerson asked to increase his salary or "outcomes" to reduce his perceived inequity. The Rams only offered a new contract similar to his old one. Dickerson then followed another option suggested by equity theory, a reduction of his "inputs." This he expressed by suggestions that he couldn't run as well as before because of the contract dispute—"the dispute . . . had taken such a toll on him that he might not be able to give it his all on the field." The Rams made a final offer of $975,000, which Dickerson refused. Then Dickerson chose another equity theory option to reduce perceived inequity, leaving the organization—he asked to be traded. He was traded to the Indianapolis Colts where he was given a $5.3 million, 4-year contract, and equity. Dickerson did not, however, pursue other equity theory options of psychologically distorting the comparison outcomes or changing referent "others," perhaps because his rushing statistics were clearly those of a "franchise" player. (See Fig. 6-10.)

FIGURE 6-10

Dickerson's Actions and Equity Theory

Source: Adapted from Sharon Clinebell and John Clinebell, "Equity Theory In Action: Examples from the World of Sports," *Journal of Management Education,* vol. 16, no. 2, May 1992, pp. 181–189.

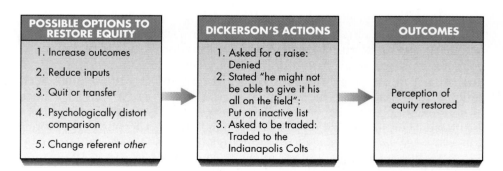

POSSIBLE OPTIONS TO RESTORE EQUITY	DICKERSON'S ACTIONS	OUTCOMES
1. Increase outcomes 2. Reduce inputs 3. Quit or transfer 4. Psychologically distort comparison 5. Change referent *other*	1. Asked for a raise: Denied 2. Stated "he might not be able to give it his all on the field": Put on inactive list 3. Asked to be traded: Traded to the Indianapolis Colts	Perception of equity restored

tions of inequitable compensation, then the goal of retaining good employees has been achieved. Not only must an organization have a very fair and equitable system, but this system must be explained to and accepted by its employees. Administrators must tell employees the various wage rates paid to the different positions and how those wage levels are determined. To achieve this perception of equity managers may involve employees in job classification and compensation committees that develop the pay system. The most equitable and fair compensation system is useless unless employees perceive it to be equitable.

INTEGRATING THE MOTIVATION THEORIES

Making practical sense out of the modern theories of motivation is certainly not easy. Billions of dollars have been spent by businesses, government, and research centers trying to discover a "magic pill" or "foolproof theory" of motivation. The only sure conclusion of this timeless endeavor has been the realization that there is no magic pill, sure-fire motivational technique, and no one theory that explains the performance of all employees. However, Everett Mann in his Profile "Motivation: What Really Works" explains how motivation theories helped him in his more than thirty years of management in both the private and public sectors.

An effective integration of the principles posited by the major motivation theories, practice, and research has been provided by Edwin Locke (see Fig. 6-11). The motivation sequence includes six steps:[32]

1. *Needs.* The needs related to human survival and well-being are the source of human behavior. The motivation process begins with perceived needs—which lead to actions that will fulfill those needs. Fulfillment however, is only temporary, needs are never permanently satisfied—thus people are constantly motivated to fulfill some need. Their actions, however, may or may not lead to need satisfaction.

2. *Values.* The discomfort of unfulfilled needs does not always motivate a person to action. Values—what people consciously desire (needs may be unconscious), cause people to act. Thus values are the link between needs

THE MOTIVATION SEQUENCE

NEEDS	VALUES	GOALS	PERFORMANCE	REWARDS	SATISFACTION
Physiological Security Social Esteem Self-Actualization	Money Achievement Power Affiliation	Promotion Bonus Performance- Appraisal	Short-Term Achievements Long-Term Achievements	Pay Increases Promotion Perks Benefits Rewarding Work	Perception of Need Fulfillment and Equity

Sequence Initiates New Needs

FIGURE 6-11 An Integration of Motivation Theories

Source: Adapted from Edwin A. Locke, "The Motivation Sequence, the Motivation Hub, and the Motivation Core," *Organizational Behavior and Human Decision Processes,* vol. 50, 1991, pp. 288–299.

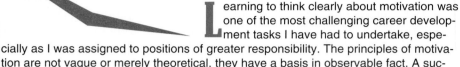

Profile

Everett Mann
Colonel, U.S. Army, Ret.
MOTIVATION: WHAT REALLY WORKS

Learning to think clearly about motivation was one of the most challenging career development tasks I have had to undertake, especially as I was assigned to positions of greater responsibility. The principles of motivation are not vague or merely theoretical, they have a basis in observable fact. A successful organizational leader must know them and know how to use them. However, motivational principles are a lot easier to describe than they are to put into practice. I found it was a good idea from time to time to consciously examine and adjust my thinking about my own motivation and my experiences as a motivator of others. What I came to discover is that one must think in terms of both internal and external factors in employing motivational techniques, and that there is a sequence of essential elements to the motivational technique.

Most reliable theories of motivation contain the concept of a hierarchy: that is a chain of needs that are 1) essentially internal characteristics of the individual, and 2) linked so that the satisfaction of the primary needs are prerequisite for the higher order needs to act as motivators. At one end is behavior that reflects a "safety first" approach that avoids risk (and also enjoyment and creativity) on the job. This is characteristic of individuals who experience a perception of deficit with respect to basic emotional and material needs, and they are more strongly motivated in terms of making a living, paying the bills, and holding onto a job.

At the other end of the hierarchy are individuals who perceive more satisfaction and fulfillment in their basic needs and are therefore more apt to be motivated by "self-actualization," and are sometimes described as "self-motivated" people. If they are given interesting work and responsibility, they perform well because they find pleasure and satisfaction in the work itself. They tend to do better when they are included in decision making; they tend to be interested in organizational goals and achievements; and they require less supervision. This is the internal state to which you seek to direct and sustain your employees, but doing it is no simple undertaking.

How to foster "self-actualizing" behavior in the workplace has been a subject of much study. Actually, the first steps are in the recruitment and selection phases of hiring. You have to start with the right people. While according to theory, almost anyone's critical need level may be raised, the tendency toward self-actualization may be thought of as virtually a personality trait. In interviews as well as through standardized testing, degrees of the tendency toward self-actualizing behavior can be observed and even measured. Moreover, experienced supervisors and personnel managers can usually spot the potential self-starter. However, the capacity for self-actualization by itself is not enough to guarantee self-motivated employees. And, it is probably safe to assume that almost all employees have enough of that capacity to react appropriately to external motivating factors.

Directing employees toward desired behaviors through self-actualization requires an appropriate and stable system of external factors, the core of which is reinforcement.

The reinforcement principle sounds deceptively simple on its face. One provides positive reinforcement to desirable behaviors. In practice, reinforcement of self-motivated behavior is not difficult. Self-motivated people generally seek and value recognition of their achievements. Poorly motivated people may have less in the way of achievement to recognize, and getting them started in a reinforcement loop may not be so easy. There are two principles that must be employed in tandem to start increasing motivation levels for such folks: incentives and goal-path information.

Reinforcement at all levels of motivation can be applied through an incentive system which is based on the expectancy principle. The first step is to communicate clearly what rewards will result from what behaviors. Employees must understand that the available rewards—recognition (employee of the month), bonuses, raises, promotions—are surely tied to defined achievement. To make this system work, a manager must then employ the "path-goal" principle. Once an individual understands about the results of his or her actions and the values of the results, she or he must clearly see how the achievement may be accomplished; that is, the path to the goal. This last link, showing the employee how to achieve the goals set out in the operational detail necessary, is a vital element. And you must not forget the iron law of reinforcement theory: certainty. When behaviors occur, the appropriate reinforcement must be applied, and when achievement occurs, the promised results must be forthcoming.

There are other external factors that are essential to effective motivation that may at first seem more mundane, but they cannot be neglected. Good supervision, relationships with supervisors and peers, salary, work conditions, organizational status, and basic security are not only among job motivators but have been found to be essential to prevent dissatisfaction that can negate all other efforts at motivation.

How do you know when this "motivation chain" is working? Motivation may be an invisible, internal drive, but its effects are unmistakable. When you observe the behavior of well-motivated employees, what you won't see is absenteeism, tardiness, late and incomplete work assignments, frequent mistakes, or half-hearted participation. What you will see are questions and suggestions about projects, participation in work-related social activities, a desire to participate in decisions about work and working conditions, and a sense of pride for accomplishments.

As you are assigned to positions of greater responsibility, your own source of job satisfaction must be tied to the work of others. You must think about being a motivator of others. Whereas before, you may have taken your greatest pride in your personal projects and contributions to work products, now your satisfaction must become more self-actualizing and long range. It is now your staff's accomplishments that will reflect the most important kind of credit on you and that should be your primary concern.

---

and actions. They are those things that the workplace can provide (money, status, social, etc.) that a person values because they meet certain human needs. Values motivate one to act; for example, the value of money may cause a person to act. The money received may be used to fill one or more needs. The value of need achievement, for example, may cause a person with high-need achievement to work harder to accomplish a task.

3. *Goals.* Goals are applications of values to specific situations. They move a person's values from the general to the specific. An ambitious employee, as an example, might set high, specific work-related goals, but does not work hard to learn the game of bridge because it is a leisure activity. As expectancy theory posits, a person's perceived belief that certain behaviors will lead to certain levels of performance and rewards, is an important motivational influence.

4. *Performance.* A person's performance is a series of actions chosen to achieve valued goals that will meet certain needs.

5. *Rewards.* People expect to experience rewards or punishment as a result of their performance. Reinforcement theory and behavior modification argue that actions that lead to positive rewards are more likely to be repeated. Equity theory focuses on the perceived equity of the rewards/performance ratio as compared to one's peers.

6. *Satisfaction.* Generally, satisfying jobs enable a person to fulfill needs through the work environment. A person expects to be able to satisfy certain needs by good performance that is recognized and rewarded. The

failure of this motivation cycle to enable him or her to meet perceived needs, or result in perceived inequity, will lead to lower levels of performance, absenteeism, or to leaving the organization.

CONCLUSIONS AND APPLICATIONS

- People are motivated to take actions that will fulfill a need or achieve a goal. Employees expect to receive recognition and rewards as a result of greater job performance. Thus they are then motivated to continue to produce higher levels of quality and quantity of work.

- Maslow's Hierarchy of Needs includes five levels of human needs. People are motivated to satisfy their current needs. Since peoples' needs differ, managers must be aware of the individual needs of each employee. Herzberg has concluded that while job factors concerning the work itself are sources of motivation, other factors only cause dissatisfaction if not present.

- McGregor concluded that Theory X managers assume employees dislike and avoid work and have little ambition. Theory Y managers believe employees see work as natural and will exercise self-direction if given the opportunity.

- Goal-setting involves a systematic process in which a supervisor and subordinate agree upon goals against which the subordinate will be evaluated. Employees' performance can often be increased if specific, measurable goals are set; if they perceive the goals to be difficult but achievable; and if they are given helpful feedback as to their progress towards meeting the goals.

- According to expectancy theory, an individual's motivation is a function of the expectancy (or probability) that their efforts will achieve a level of performance which will be instrumental in their receiving desired rewards.

- Equity theory is based on a basic belief of the Western culture—fairness. Employees expect to find equity in the workplace in many areas including pay, treatment of supervisors, fairness in the administration of rules, and work levels. If employees perceive inequitable treatment they will usually act to reduce the inequity by lowering their performance, leaving the organization, trying to increase their rewards, or changing their perceptions. Lower-echelon employees make equity comparisons between themselves and top management. If perceived differences between inputs and outcomes exist, lower-echelon employees are likely to alleviate this tension by lowering their commitment, effort, and cooperation.

REVIEW QUESTIONS

1. Define "motivation" as it applies to people at work.
2. How can an organization ensure that highly productive employees will be motivated to continue their higher levels of performance?
3. What are the primary contributions of the needs and goal setting theories?
4. Explain how Expectancy Theory and Equity Theory describe the "process" of how employees are moti-

vated in the workplace. Are these theories incompatible? Why or why not?
5. How does Herzberg characterize the difference between motivation factors and hygiene factors? Do you agree that all job factors are one or the other?
6. Think of a manager you know personally who might be described as a theory X manager. Describe several of his or her behaviors that would qualify

him or her as a theory X manager. Do the same with two other managers—one theory Y and one theory Z.

7. What are the critical elements of a successful goal-setting program?

8. Describe an actual example of reinforcement theory in practice (in a situation not involving pay).

9. The expectancy theory "equation" is: $M \times I \times V$. Explain each factor and its importance to motivation.

10. Which individuals are the employees most likely to choose as peers when they make equity comparisons? Why? Should they be encouraged to consider others?

DISCUSSION QUESTIONS

1. What unmet need is most important to you at this moment in your life? Which level of Maslow's Hierarchy best describes your need?

2. Can the "classical" motivation theories help today's managers understand employee motivation?

3. In practice do you believe that employees who have perceived "inequitable" treatment by the organization responded in one of the ways suggested by equity theory? Cite three actual examples you have witnessed.

4. Which of the motivation theories described in this chapter do you think Glenn Edelen believes would be the most useful to affect the motivation of his agents? Which could you best apply to your own life? Why?

5. What are the most common reasons that within actual organizations the circular model of employee motivation and organizational success does not operate smoothly?

6. List what you believe are six "hygiene" factors and six "motivation" factors from your own work experience. Would you agree that the absence of one of the hygiene factors would cause dissatisfaction instead of a lower level of motivation? Why?

7. What practical lessons might a manager learn from expectancy theory?

8. If employees usually act to reduce perceptions of inequity when they believe they have been under-rewarded, do they also act to reduce perceptions of inequity when they believe they have been over-rewarded? Why or why not?

CASE STUDY

Motivating Sales Representatives

Bob Myers is the owner of a successful Pontiac/Oldsmobile/ Volvo dealership—Myers of St. Matthews. For forty-four years Myers has worked long hours, six days a week to build a financially strong business with a well-deserved reputation for honesty, service, and friendliness. In fact, his nickname is "friendly Bob." He started the business after a knee injury ended his professional basketball career during his rookie season. The president of his college alumni association called Bob and offered him the first Pontiac dealership in St. Matthews. With a degree in business administration and four years' experience selling cars part-time Bob saw the offer as a great opportunity. Hard work and fair, friendly service, according to Myers, enabled the dealership to survive three recessions and two oil embargos, not to mention competition from three Japanese dealerships within two miles.

Over the last year Myers has increasingly been troubled by the higher turnover and what he believes to be poor motivation displayed by recently hired employees. Myers decided to discuss his concerns with his son, Frank, the sales manager who he expects to run the business when he retires in a few years:

BOB: This Christmas season I was struck by how hard it was to get sales representatives to work over three days a week. And sales were great! They had the opportunity to make some big commissions, but instead many chose to take vacation time.

FRANK: Well, Dad, this time of year they want to spend more time with their families. Most of them are parents and want to be home with the kids, some are single parents.

BOB: I don't blame them for that, and I'm not complaining that you did not have enough agents on the floor every day. I'm just surprised they aren't motivated to make more money—don't they need it?

FRANK: Sure they do . . .

BOB: Well, then what's the problem? The senior ones were here—Lyle, Jerry, Peggy, Richard, Pete. . . .

FRANK: No Dad, Jerry retired to Florida.

BOB: Oh, yeah, but, my concern, Frank, is that over the years a large portion of our sales and service has been due to customers getting to know our sales personnel and believing they were fairly treated. We have many third-generation buyers. . . .

FRANK: I know, I know, just yesterday a couple called from Nebraska asking for Richard. They are coming to town for a wedding and want to buy a Volvo 850 while they are here because they bought a 740 from us!

BOB: Exactly! And if we don't hire and keep more people like Richard *you* might not make it through the next recession.

FRANK: I see your point; we really have not hired any "Richards" in the last few years.

BOB: Well, didn't you have a class at the university that dealt with motivating employees?

FRANK: Yes, I did take several management classes.

BOB: Then get out your textbooks and find some answers.

FRANK: O.K.—I'll get back to you Monday.

CASE STUDY QUESTIONS

1. Considering that the dealership is quite successful and Frank scheduled enough agents, do they really have a motivation problem?

2. What societal factors might be causing the changes in motivation that are worrying Bob and Frank?

3. Which of the motivation theories presented in this chapter would you recommend Frank carefully consider for possible solutions? Explain in detail.

EXPERIENTIAL EXERCISE 1

Applying Maslow's Need Hierarchy

Purpose

To apply the principles of Maslow's Hierarchy of Needs to your life and work environment.

Introduction

This exercise has three parts: first you will complete a twenty-item questionnaire, then you will estimate your personal motivation profile and that of the class as a whole, and finally you will discuss what actions management could take to motivate people at each need level.

Part I: The Motivation Profile

Directions:

The following statements have seven possible responses.

Strongly Agree	Agree	Slightly Agree	Don't Know	Slightly Disagree	Disagree	Strongly Disagree
+3	+2	+1	0	−1	−2	−3

Please mark one of the seven responses by circling the number that corresponds to the response that fits your opinion. For example: if you "Strongly Agree," circle the number "+3."

Complete every item. You have about 10 minutes to do so.

1. Special wage increases should be given to employees who do their jobs well. +3 +2 +1 0 −1 −2 −3

2. Better job descriptions would be helpful so that employees will know exactly what is expected of them. +3 +2 +1 0 −1 −2 −3

3. Employees need to be reminded that their jobs are dependent on the company's ability to compete effectively. +3 +2 +1 0 −1 −2 −3

4. A supervisor should give a good deal of attention to the physical working conditions of his or her employees. +3 +2 +1 0 −1 −2 −3

5. The supervisor ought to work hard to develop a friendly working atmosphere among his or her people. +3 +2 +1 0 −1 −2 −3

6. Individual recognition for above-standard performance means a lot to employees. +3 +2 +1 0 −1 −2 −3

7. Indifferent supervision can often bruise feelings. +3 +2 +1 0 −1 −2 −3

8. Employees want to feel that their real skills and capacities are put to use on their jobs. +3 +2 +1 0 −1 −2 −3

9. The company retirement benefits and stock programs are important factors in keeping employees on their jobs. +3 +2 +1 0 −1 −2 −3

10. Almost every job can be made more stimulating and challenging. +3 +2 +1 0 −1 −2 −3

11. Many employees want to give their best in everything they do. +3 +2 +1 0 −1 −2 −3

12. Management could show more interest in the employees by sponsoring social events after-hours. +3 +2 +1 0 −1 −2 −3

13. Pride in one's work is actually an important reward. +3 +2 +1 0 −1 −2 −3

14. Employees want to be able to think of themselves as "the best" at their own jobs. +3 +2 +1 0 −1 −2 −3

15. The quality of the relationships in the informal work group is quite important. +3 +2 +1 0 −1 −2 −3

16. Individual incentive bonuses would improve the performance of employees. +3 +2 +1 0 −1 −2 −3

17. Visibility with upper management is important to employees. +3 +2 +1 0 −1 −2 −3

18. Employees generally like to schedule their own work and to make job-related decisions with a minimum of supervision. +3 +2 +1 0 −1 −2 −3

19. Job security is important to employees. +3 +2 +1 0 −1 −2 −3

20. Having good equipment to work with is important to employees. +3 +2 +1 0 −1 −2 −3

Source: Reproduced from *The 1973 Annual Handbook for Group Facilitators*, by J. E. Jones and J. W. Pfeiffer (eds.). Copyright © 1973 by Pfeiffer & Company, San Diego, CA.

Part II: The Class Profile

Scoring:

1. Transfer the numbers you circled in Part I to the appropriate places in the following chart:

Statement no.	Score	Statement no.	Score	Statement no.	Score	Statement no.	Score	Statement no.	Score
10	___	2	___	6	___	1	___	5	___
11	___	3	___	8	___	4	___	7	___
13	___	9	___	14	___	16	___	12	___
18	___	19	___	17	___	20	___	15	___
Total	___	Total	___	Total	___	Total	___	Total	___
(Self-Actualization Needs)		(Security Needs)		(Esteem Needs)		(Physiological Needs)		(Social Needs)	

2. Record your total scores in the chart below by marking an "X" in each row next to the number of your total score for that area of needs motivation.

	−12	−10	−8	−6	−4	−2	0	+2	+4	+6	+8	+10	+12
Self-actualization													
Esteem													
Social													
Security													
Physiological													

Low use   Neutral   High use

Once you have completed this chart, you can see the relative strength of your use of each of these areas of needs motivation.

There is, of course, no "right" answer. What is right for you is what matches your actual needs, and that, of course, is specific to each situation and each individual. In general, however, the experts tell us that today's employees are best motivated by efforts in the areas of Belonging, Esteem, and Self-Actualization.

3. The instructor will assist the class in calculating a class profile. It is established by taking a poll of the class members in terms of each individual's strongest motivational factor (the factor with the highest score).

A. Strongest Motivator	*percent**	*rank*	*B. Weakest Motivator*	*percent**	*rank*
Self-actualization	____	____	Self-actualization	____	____
Esteem	____	____	Esteem	____	____
Social	____	____	Social	____	____
Security	____	____	Security	____	____
Basic (Physiological)	____	____	Basic (Physiological)	____	____

*Percent is determined by number of students giving that factor the highest score for A (lowest score for B), divided by the number of students in the class.

Part III. Management Actions

1. Discuss what actions management can take to motivate employees who are behaving at each of the five levels of Maslow's Need Hierarchy. Write a response for each need level.
   a. Basic needs (Phys.)   d. Esteem needs
   b. Security needs   e. Self-actualization needs
   c. Social needs

2. How useful is Maslow's theory for managing the modern worker of today? Discuss this within your group and write the group response.

3. Which of the five needs is the strongest motivator for you? _____ The second strongest? _____ Based on this information, briefly describe the type of job that would best satisfy these needs for you.

4. The instructor will lead a discussion based on the information generated in question 3.

Source: Reprinted by permission. Lane Kelley and Arthur Whatley, *Personnel Management in Action: Skill Building Exercises,* 4th ed., West Publishing Co., 1987, pp. 6–11. Copyright © 1987 by West Publishing Company. All rights reserved.

EXPERIENTIAL EXERCISE 2

Equitable Pay Ranges

The concept of equity has been one of the critical elements of organizational compensation systems. To guarantee a degree of external equity, human resource departments often conduct wage and salary surveys of similar employers within their region. Once the survey information is obtained human resource professionals must determine salary ranges that correspond with the general compensation objectives of the organization and provide pay levels that applicants and employees will generally be perceived as equitable.

Purpose

To gain experience in obtaining wage survey information and developing equitable salary ranges.

Task

Step 1: Contact the Human Resource Department of five banks within the same geographic region. Explain the exercise and request the salaries included in the following table. Your instructor may choose another type of organization with different job titles, if so amend the table accordingly.

Job Title	Organization	Normal Starting Salary	Range		
			Minimum	Median	Maximum
1. Teller (full time)	1	____	____	____	____
	2	____	____	____	____
	3	____	____	____	____
	4	____	____	____	____
	5	____	____	____	____
	Average				
2. Branch manager	1	____	____	____	____
	2	____	____	____	____
	3	____	____	____	____
	4	____	____	____	____
	5	____	____	____	____
	Average				
3. Commercial loan officer	1	____	____	____	____
	2	____	____	____	____
	3	____	____	____	____
	4	____	____	____	____
	5	____	____	____	____
	Average				
4. Bookkeeper	1	____	____	____	____
	2	____	____	____	____
	3	____	____	____	____
	4	____	____	____	____
	5	____	____	____	____
	Average				
5. Vice president	1	____	____	____	____
	2	____	____	____	____
	3	____	____	____	____
	4	____	____	____	____
	5	____	____	____	____
	Average				

Step 2: Answer the following questions based on the wage survey information.

1. Do you believe all the organizations are generally paying "equitable" salaries? Explain your answer.

2. Did one or more of the five jobs have greater variance in salary than the other? If so, why might that be expected?

3. If you were starting a competing organization within the region and wanted to provide "equitable" salaries what starting, minimum and maximum salaries would you recommend?

4. Salaries represent only a portion of the total compensation package. Expand your answer to question three to include the types of benefits you believe would be important to include in an "equitable" total compensation package.

Take It to the Net **You can find this chapter's World Wide Web exercise at:** http://www.prenhall.com/carrell

CHAPTER 7

Motivation: Effective Applications

CHAPTER OBJECTIVES

1. To appreciate the impact a well-deserved word of praise may have on an employee.
2. To understand the need for effective award and recognition programs in organizations.
3. To recognize that employee suggestion systems are still effective, widely utilized methods of employee involvement and motivation.
4. To know the common methods of evaluating behavior.
5. To understand how the design of a job affects a person's ability to perform the job successfully and his or her motivation to achieve higher levels of performance.
6. To identify the major forms of alternative work schedules and their potential advantages and disadvantages.
7. To cite characteristics typically found in an employee involvement program.
8. To recognize the motivational value of pay for performance compensation systems.
9. To understand why employee-owned organizations have been found to be more successful than other organizations.
10. To know the Taco Bell Philosophy that centers on a "value strategy" and requires employees who are self-motivated, value teamwork, and have positive attitudes toward responsibility.

The Taco Bell Philosophy

The Taco Bell employee philosophy called *"Value Strategy,"* designs jobs to enable more employees to directly serve customers, provides them more freedom to act, and motivates them with the opportunity to receive a share of the resulting greater productivity and profits.

"Value Strategy"

During the last three years of the 1980s the "fast-food" restaurant market experienced a decline in sales. Yet Taco Bell sales grew by 60 percent and profits by over 25 percent (compared to a 6 percent growth rate at McDonalds). Taco Bell's success might, at first blush, be attributed to its switch to a low price menu and glitzy advertising. A more careful analysis would reveal that the real key was

management's change in operating approach that was implemented by a redirected work force. Management had determined through research that customers valued only three things: (1) food values; 2) service; and (3) physical appearance. Yet the "old" industrial service model (perfected by McDonalds) focused on manufacturing menu items while the "new" concentrates on assembling orders for customers. Thus the back room of the average McDonalds has become more complex as new menu items such as pizza and muffins complicate the store's manufacturing operation. Taco Bell, however, changed to a limited range of items prepared through automation

Value strategy A philosophy of Taco Bell to design jobs that will enable more employees to directly serve customers by providing them with more freedom to act and motivating them by receiving a share of the profits.

and assembled to meet customer needs. This enabled Taco Bell to reverse its ratio of front-room personnel to back-room personnel and thus focus more people on serving customers.[1]

Taco Bell's new "value strategy" required a 180-degree turnaround in the thinking and performance by all employees and management had to change its emphasis from direction and control to coaching and support. All human resource practices including job descriptions and compensation systems were changed to reflect the new emphasis. And management believed of critical importance was the change to a new selection process that was designed to test prospective employees' values and attitudes toward responsibility, teamwork, and self-motivation. These were determined to be keys to successful service organizations.

The selection process included detailed preliminary interviewing between managers and candidates. The total refocusing in the design of jobs, employee values, and compensation resulted in substantially higher employee morale. They reported they felt more motivated and empowered to make decisions; they had more freedom to act independently; and they had the authority they needed to act. Moreover, they were accountable for their decisions.

The change also dramatically affected the paychecks of workers that rose to a level significantly above the industry average and is causing competitors to reconsider the long-standing practice of a minimum wage and high turnover work force. Store managers' average compensation is up to 225 percent of the industry average due to a new profit-sharing program. Altogether, Taco Bell rejected the traditional service-industry model of employee management and developed its new "value-added" strategy. This focused on giving customers what they value by designing a new management model that will select and reward employees who value teamwork, increased responsibility, and authority, and who will be motivated to earn more pay. This shift in strategy has worked remarkably well at Taco Bell. In general, it represents a shift towards a philosophy of valuing customer and service-oriented employees who are given greater authority and responsibility, who work in a team, and who earn greater compensation through higher productivity.[2] This model appears to be working well, because it provides better service to customers and meets the workplace demands of employees who desire greater autonomy and decision making on the job.

The Taco Bell case illustrates how human resource management practices are critical to the behavior of an organization. Without a doubt the most valuable asset of any organization is a highly motivated work force. Thus the processes of rewarding and appraising employees are critical behavior policies that will be discussed in this chapter.

Effective Motivational Programs

Perhaps the most important concept to remember from the motivation theories discussed in the last chapter is that motivation is *internal*! Thus managers and supervisors must know and understand the internal motivation that drives each person. If the work environment enables a person to meet their personal needs through the process described in Fig. 4-8, then they will be motivated to achieve

Factor Increase	Believe Importance Is High Now	Believe Importance Will Increase
Performance-based Compensation System	52%	70%
Interesting/Challenging Work	60%	60%
Alternate Work Schedules	45%	62%
Employee Participation	25%	50%

Source: Adapted from *The Conference Board,* 845 Third Avenue, reported in *Personnel Journal Supplement,* June 1992, p. 4.

FIGURE 7-1

The Factors Managers Believe Are Important to Motivate Employees

high levels of performance in their job. So, what can the organization do to ensure that the process works? The Taco Bell case illustrates several key factors to achieve a highly motivated work force: (1) a management philosophy that is not based on control and discipline but instead on coaching and recognition; (2) designing jobs to provide for employee involvement and freedom to act; (3) providing schedules to meet employee family and work needs; and (4) providing an incentive system that gives employees a financial stake in the success of the organization. This chapter discusses effective policies and programs that have been successfully tested and utilized by organizations. They are grouped into four areas: (1) award/recognition programs; (2) job design; (3) employee participation; and (4) pay for performance.

Of all the various factors to be discussed in this chapter—challenging work, recognition, alternate work schedules, employee participation, and pay for performance—which are the most important in affecting employee motivation? According to a survey of the nation's top employers (see Fig. 7-1), the most important factors are: (1) the design of interesting/challenging jobs; (2) pay-for-performance plans; (3) alternate work schedules; and (4) employee involvement programs. Perhaps even more important is the response by employers that these factors will become more important in the future. Thus effective employee motivation policies/programs must ensure that all of these employee needs are met in the workplace.

AWARD AND RECOGNITION PROGRAMS

Recognizing the contributions of people is a simple, inexpensive, very effective source of motivation. The returns include increased morale, loyalty, creativity, and productivity. Organizations are increasingly using more award and recognition programs. A survey of employers revealed:[3]

- 94 percent of all employers utilize at least one program. Recognition programs and monetary rewards are the most common programs.
- Program levels: 64 percent report programs for individuals, 25 percent for business unit, 24 percent for teams, 21 percent for departments (most have multiple programs).
- Program effects include increased job satisfaction, morale, performance, and employee retention.

Why don't more organizations and individual managers offer recognition for good work? Possible reasons include: (1) they believe that giving a person a paycheck should be enough recognition; (2) awards and recognition are contrived, hokey, or trivial; (3) they fear that giving recognition to one person or team may alienate others; (4) they are not comfortable giving out praise or recognitions. None of these reasons, while they may be perceived as valid by some managers, justify the lack of adequate award and recognition practices. Everyone in the workplace needs attention, and there are many effective methods of providing this type of motivation.[4]

Praise

Perhaps the most powerful and easiest recognition is praise given by a supervisor, manager, or peer. Praise, given for legitimate reasons, makes both the giver and receiver feel good, reinforces correct actions, and very likely leads to further positive actions. And praise requires no structured program or expensive reward. A person has at least three types of situations that may be deserving of praise:[5]

- *Unconditional praise.* Given for what a person is—honest, sincere, hard working, etc., rather than for a specific action. Example: "Your response to that customer was very honest; you could have put the blame on someone else, but you admitted your error. Everyone makes mistakes—I like people who are honest about their errors."
- *Developmental praise.* Given for making progress toward a specific goal. Example: "You've finished all the budget tables two weeks early! Thanks, that will make it much easier for me to finish the report on time."
- *Respect praise.* Given for a specific skill or action. Example: "That Christmas display is really creative—I can't remember a better one in the twenty-five seasons we've been in business—and *I* did the displays for ten years!"

Praise may be the most effective and easiest recognition one can receive. It should only be given if earned in one of the above situations. If given to the wrong people—the boss's pet, the self-servers, reluctantly, or without cause, then it loses its value. How often should it be given? Ask any group of employees how many of them receive praise too often—but don't be surprised if no one raises a hand! Seldom do people believe they receive praise too often; unfortunately, most believe they receive it too seldom.[6] For some people (see the personal Profile on Mike Fisher, CPA) frequent praise may be a key motivational factor.

Recognition Awards

A plaque with the name and picture of Lynne Stone hangs just inside the front door of the Bistro Bar & Grill, a trendy neighborhood restaurant. You can't help but notice it when you first walk in the door. Many regular customers have complimented Lynne on the award. She received it along with two theatre tickets at the monthly meeting of the restaurant's employees. Her name was submitted by a coworker to the employee committee that makes the selection. Do such programs really motivate people? Managers and employees alike in all types of organizations believe they are effective motivators and accomplish several goals:[7]

- Express appreciation for employee contributions.
- Reinforce behaviors and performance that employers value.

The "J. Willard Marriott Medallion" is given to outstanding employees in recognition of their service.

- Publicize individual and team accomplishments to peers, customers, and affiliates.
- Provide reason to celebrate individual, team, and organizational successes with all employees.

A typical successful recognition program is the one at Marriott Corp. that honors several employees each year with its "J. Willard Marriott Award of Excellence," an engraved medallion expressing the basic values of the company: "Dedication, Achievement, Character, Ideals, Effort, Perseverance." Selection is based on the nominator's comments and length of service. Award winners are chosen from a variety of job categories. Winners and guests are flown to Washington, D.C. for the awards banquet.[8]

Nonmonetary recognition does not need to be an organizational program to be effective with employees. It can be as simple as the "At-A-Bee" program (see Fig. 7-2) created by T. R. Carter, Training Supervisor at Shell Western E&P, Inc. Carter wanted to give his employees special recognition for a job well done, but recognized that he had no monetary rewards to give them. So he started giving employees "At-A-Bee" stickers for outstanding performance as well as a written note of their action. As employees began noticing the stickers in other employee offices, the competition for them, as well as pride for ones received, increased!

Figure 7-2 "At-A-Bee" Recognition Stickers at Shell Western
T. R. Carter of Shell E&P, Inc. gives employees "At-A-Bee" stickers as recognition of a "job well done." Employees often proudly display the stickers in their offices.

Profile

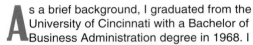

Michael K. Fisher
*President, Chavez, Fisher &
Keathley, Certified Public
Accountants, Inc.*

PIRFECT, PURFECT, PERFECT: WORKING WITH PERFECTIONISTS

As a brief background, I graduated from the University of Cincinnati with a Bachelor of Business Administration degree in 1968. I then spent twenty-two years with Peat Marwick and Price Waterhouse accounting firms, the last ten as a full partner. In 1990 I teamed up with two other accountants and formed our own firm—Chavez, Fisher & Keathley, Certified Public Accountants, Inc. My civic involvements include the Boy Scouts, United Way, Junior Achievement, and Historic Restoration. On weekends my wife Donna and I enjoy playing golf and tennis.

The accounting business is an "interesting" profession. Accountants buy hours at wholesale and sell at retail. Sounds cold, calculating, and unprofessional, doesn't it? But it's the same for many professions—legal, medical, architectural, advertising, and even education where tuition is charged.

The professional's product is the collectible time charged by the partners and staff. Therefore, it follows that the better the group, the more you can charge (as long as your clients are convinced of the value).

This concept makes one thing quite obvious. A professional organization must hire the best and brightest employees they can find and afford. And then, they must charge a fair and equitable fee for that time.

My experience is that once you understand the economics of a professional business, you must then find those people who will generate hours of high quality performance that clients lust to know and love.

So you march off to campus looking for that student with a high G.P.A., held an office in his or her fraternity or sorority, involved in student government, held down a part-time job, participated in a competitive sport, and could chew gum and whistle the school fight song at the same time. Does this describe someone you know, like yourself? If you're lucky enough to hire them then you must manage them.

On a number of occasions, I have found several who met most of the above criteria. The only problem was that these people who could walk, talk, chew gum, and whistle often were perfectionists (some on the obsessive side). Pointing out their smallest mistake could be perceived as a personal attack.

Although I am no psychiatrist, I have found that, in more than one instance, this behavior was due to parents being overly critical of their child's performance. (No matter how well they did, it wasn't quite good enough!) The child, now your employee, carries this burden of perfection right to your office door.

Please do not misunderstand me. I am not critical of perfection. It is a worthwhile lifetime goal. The problem is that some perfectionists believe it is a state of being versus a destination.

Looking for signs of a perfectionist is not an easy task, but I have observed the following:

- Pointing out technical errors was usually not a problem, whereas pointing out errors of oversight within their current capabilities would create immediate stress.

- As they developed in their field, they became rather territorial and sometimes found it hard to delegate.

- When asked if they had time for a project, they would normally answer "yes" because they did not want to be perceived as not being able to handle the load. As a result, the projects mounted up, overtime increased, and efficiency sometimes declined.

- On occasion, perfectionism exhibited itself in the form of compulsive behavior: an extremely clean desk, excessively fastidious personal dress code, or they could always straighten their tie or check their hair in the reflection from the hood of their car.

Do any of these points remind you of someone you know?

Once you come to the conclusion that an employee is one of those rare breeds, you have to deal with the situation. One thing that seems to help is a heart-to-heart talk, asking them if they perceive themselves as perfectionists and why. Ask them about their reactions to your constructive criticisms. Let them know how good they really are and that their worst critic is in the mirror. Explain that constructive criticisms are only constructive criticisms and part of their growth. And finally, let them know that there are no perfect people and you understand that "truth."

So, how does one motivate perfectionists? The primary point to remember when working with a perfectionist is that they are valuable assets to your business. They can easily be motivated, *but* their needs are unique; they require *frequent nurturing, praise* (a great deal of praise may be required), and *challenges.* It's like caring for your next Kentucky Derby contenders—those thoroughbreds who are high spirited, intense, and willing to run as fast as you let them.

Keys to Effective Programs

Award and recognition programs may be easy to initiate, but to be effective over several years they need constant effort. (See Fig. 7-3.) To continue to impact motivation they should:[9]

- *Tie rewards to needs.* Because each employee's needs are different, effective reward systems must be flexible. Examples of different awards appear in Fig. 7-3.

- *Ensure the reward's fairness.* Every employee must understand the conditions under which awards are given. If possible peers should nominate and select winners.

- *Make sure timing is proper.* Schedule presentations of rewards so employees receive them shortly after the achievement being recognized.

- Have the president or manager perform the recipient's job for a day.
- Provide a day off with pay.
- Provide tickets to sports, music, cultural events, or a cruise.
- Establish and name an award after an exceptional employee.
- Take out an advertisement in the local newspaper thanking your employees for their contributions.
- Provide a donation in an employee's name to the charity of his or her choice.
- Let recipients visit customers.
- Have an Oscar-like awards banquet with trophies and plaques.
- Provide a monetary bonus together with the recognition.

Source: Catherine M. Meek, "Everyone Needs Attention," *Small Business Reports,* December 1991, p. 13.

FIGURE 7-3
"For a Job Well Done."

- *Talk up the value of rewards.* If managers show enthusiasm for a reward at the time its presented, it adds to its perceived value.
- *Don't camouflage rewards.* Rewards must stand out and be highlighted; don't squeeze praise between a dozen other topics of conversation.
- *Present rewards in a public forum.* Rewards are not meant to be presented in the privacy of an employee's office. If possible present awards at a celebration event for all employees.
- *Don't oversell rewards.* Promote rewards, but don't oversell them. Constant talk about how great a reward is can start to make it sound ridiculous.

Suggestion Systems

Suggestion systems
Based on the belief that the people who actually perform the work are in the best position to recommend improvements, and they increase commitment and loyalty to the organization.

Suggestion systems are one of the most commonly utilized methods of successful employee involvement. They date back to 1880 when the Yale and Towne Manufacturing Company first implemented a suggestion system and others adopted similar plans. The Eastman Kodak Company, for example, began its system in 1898, ninety years later their suggestion system saved almost 12.5 million dollars in a single year. Few organizational practices have remained in widespread use as long as *suggestion systems.* The reasons for the success of the suggestion system are many. First, they are based on the belief that the people who actually perform the work are in the best position to recommend improvements. Second, they increase employees' commitment and loyalty to the organization as their affiliation with it increases. Third, they provide employees a direct means of increasing their involvement in the organization. Fourth, they work! That is, that they produce ideas that reduce costs, improve service, increase safety, and provide rewards to those directly responsible.[10]

Most suggestion systems contain similar characteristics and the following steps:[11]

Step 1: The organization places suggestion boxes that contain suggestion forms at convenient locations. Today, the forms may also be made available by electronic mail.

Step 2: An employee writes a suggestion on a form and deposits it in the box, submits it to his or her supervisor or human resource person.

Step 3: The suggestion director investigates and evaluates the idea after involving others who might be affected. Potential cost savings or other advantages are estimated.

Step 4: The director presents the suggestion to a committee that votes on the idea.

Step 5: The employee is notified of the outcome. Specific reasons are given if the suggestion is rejected. If it is accepted, a cash award is paid, often a fixed percentage of the first year's savings or a flat amount for the owner's ideas.

The monetary award historically has been credited as the incentive to generate employee interest in participating in the suggestion system process. The most often cited monetary award was given in 1928 by A. P. Giannini, founder of Bank of America, to his chauffeur. The chauffeur suggested the bank issue customers some sort of currency they could use while they traveled to reduce the need to carry currency that could be lost or stolen. Giannini gave him a $1 reward for the idea that led to the first traveler's checks. In 1991, by comparison, U.S. employers paid suggesters $164 million in incentives for suggestions that saved them over

1. Enlist the support of top management.
2. Determine the objectives top management hopes to achieve through the program.
3. Provide an environment in which managers and supervisors are receptive to ideas from others.
4. Designate an individual to administer the program—not to accept or reject suggestions but to act as a liaison between employees and management.
5. Determine an awards schedule and be prepared to follow through with it.
6. Inform employees about the plan with a written announcement explaining how the system works, how they can turn in suggestions, and how they will benefit from the program.
7. Publicize the program on a regular basis.
8. Respond promptly to each suggestion, whether it is adopted or not.
9. Keep complete and accurate records of all transactions relating to the suggesting system.
10. Have a company officer make the presentation of major awards whenever possible.

Source: Employee Involvement Association, formerly National Association of Suggestion Systems, McLean, VA.

FIGURE 7-4

Ten Tips for Successful Suggestion Systems

$2 billion.[12] Today, the national Employee Involvement Association (EIA) estimates that 65 percent of all suggestion systems continue to offer monetary awards to suggesters. The other 35 percent provide special recognition or company stock, and the trend by employers is to move away from monetary awards. This change is primarily due to the belief that the key motivation for employees is the recognition received and desire to increase their involvement in the workplace.[13]

A successful suggestion system begins with total support of top management that provides one individual to administer the program and, in addition, meets all of the ten tips that the Employee Involvement Association has developed after reviewing many programs (see Fig. 7-4). Systems can, however, experience problems. The most common problem results when employees become cynical because good ideas are not accepted or never even investigated. Another common problem is of employees being unaware a program exists due to poor publicity of the system. A third common problem of systems occur when they become overly bureaucratic by requiring excessive paperwork, lengthy investigation, and long delays in implementation. In recent years, a fourth problem has evolved due to the increased use of employee teams. Unless a suggestion system is altered to provide for team-based suggestions, the number of individual suggestions may substantially decrease.[14] At Hallmark, for example, the annual number of employee suggestions decreased from over five hundred to less than one hundred as the company converted to teams over a four-year period.[15]

All of these problems can be resolved. One key attribute of a good system is its flexibility. Suggestion systems have been able to continue to have an impact on organizational goals and those of employees for over one hundred years and often change in design, such as the ones cited in "OB in Practice" on page 204.

EVALUATING PERFORMANCE

The process of evaluating employees' behavior in the workplace is called performance appraisal, performance review, or employee evaluation. It is a critical process in developing and maintaining a motivated work force. Appraisal methods, both formal and informal, are the most common organizational source of recognition

OB in Practice — Suggestions and Award Programs That Work

United Electric Controls Co. For over twenty years United Electric had an employee suggestion box—it sat empty. Employees could earn up to $1,500 per suggestion, so what was the problem? The evaluation process was lengthy and difficult. A new suggestion program called Valued Ideas Program enabled employees to write a suggestion on a one-page form, the affected supervisor or a committee (for more complex ideas) evaluates the idea, and decides whether or not to implement it immediately. The key to the new program's success was to move away from the old cost-savings concept to one of employee involvement and recognition. Implemented suggestions give the employee recognition and $100 without a cost-savings analysis. Each person who makes a suggestion also receives a chance at monthly and annual drawings for special prizes.

- *GTE Data Services.* "The Spirit of the Best" is the theme of the four-day employee recognition event held to honor one hundred GTE employees for their outstanding achievements. Each winner receives $500, a plaque, and his or her picture and story in the company magazine, *Quest.* Employees are nominated by a peer or supervisor for their customer satisfaction or business performance.

- *Temps & Co.* Steven Ethridge, president of Temps & Co. startled his staff when he opened a meeting by confessing to a stupid mistake he had made. Then he put $250 on the table and offered it to anyone who could top his story! In an unusual "recognition" program, Ethridge still offers $100 at the start of his management meetings. He finds that by discussing their errors they are able to devise strategies to keep them from recurring. Ethridge believes that he has created a climate where people are not afraid to discuss their mistakes—and thus the company in many cases can identify methods of correction. People also feel they are able to take risks—which Ethridge feels is critical to success in their business. While other recognition programs only note successes, Ethridge believes it's also important to reward those who take reasonable risk—and learn from their mistakes.

Source: Adapted from Dawn Gunsch, "Award Programs at Work," *Personnel Journal*, September 1991, pp. 85–89.

---

for good performance and the basis for many important rewards. Employees expect and need to receive feedback on how their performance is perceived by others, especially those in positions of authority. The feedback they receive during the appraisal process often provides the "output" portion of their equity comparisons as discussed in the last chapter, and thus may significantly affect their future motivation, performance, and even tenure with the organization.

Performance appraisals are conducted to achieve two broad objectives—evaluative and developmental. Evaluative refers to uses which evaluate the employee's performance for decision-making purposes: such as, merit increases, bonuses, promotions, and termination/layoff. Developmental uses include improving future performance through feedback of strengths and weaknesses, identifying training needs, career counseling, and providing direction or goals for the future. As Fig. 7-5 illustrates, evaluative uses of performance appraisals in the areas of

Performance appraisal
A critical process in developing and maintaining a motivated work force by giving feedback to employees on their performance and determining their rewards.

Rank	Function of Appraisal	Percentage
1.	Merit increases	91
2.	Performance results/feedback/job counseling	90
3.	Promotion	82
4.	Termination or layoff	64
5.	Performance potential	62
6.	Succession planning	57
7.	Career planning	52
8.	Transfer	50
9.	Manpower planning	38
10.	Bonuses	32
11.	Development and evaluation of training programs	29
12.	Internal communication	25
13.	Criteria for selection procedure validation	16
14.	Expense control	7

Source: Charles J. Fombrun and Robert L. Laud, "Strategic Issues in Performance Appraisal Theory and Practice," *Personnel* 601, no. 6, November–December 1983, pp. 23–31. Used by permission of the American Management Association.

FIGURE 7-5
Ranked Uses of
Performance Appraisal

compensation (merit increases and bonuses) and staffing decisions (promotion, termination or layoff, succession planning, transfer, personnel planning) are the most common (seven of the top ten) uses.

While there are many different effective and legal methods of performance appraisal, most are some variation on combinations of the most popular methods—rating scales, management-by-objectives (MBO), and peer or team evaluations.

Rating Scales

The oldest and still most commonly utilized appraisal method for nonmanagerial employees is the rating scale. A typical scale identifies critical job factors (such as position responsibilities, cooperation, hustle, etc. in the Marley Co. example in Fig. 7-6), and they require the supervisor to evaluate or rate the employee's performance on each attribute. The example in Fig. 7-6 uses a five-point rating scale—one being lowest and five being highest—however, three-point and even seven-point scales are not uncommon.

In general, rating scales are quick, easy, and less difficult for supervisors to use than many other methods of performance appraisal. Also, decision makers find rating scales to be good for most evaluative purposes, because they provide a mathematical evaluation of the employee's performance, which can be used to justify merit increases or promotion decisions. For example, if the rating scale contains twenty attributes with a five-point scale for each attribute, employees can receive one hundred points if they perform perfectly. Any percentage of that total can be directly related to a merit increase or promotion probability.

Rating scales are subject to several potential liabilities. Supervisors can easily rate everyone very high (leniency error) or average (central tendency error) on most items. Many rating scales also have the disadvantage of not being related to a specific job. The attributes of the scale are so broad that they may apply to all jobs in the organization and are not developed to apply to any particular job. Rating scales also allow supervisory bias and the halo effect (rating a person high on all attributes based on only one strength) to enter the appraisal process. To

FIGURE 7-6 Graphic Rating Scale with Self and Supervisor Ratings

Job and Behavioral Summary
Factors Important to MARLEY® Mission and Personal Development

Both [E] employee and [S] supervisor shall answer separately, and record together answers on supervisor's form. Openly discuss variations.

Name: _Pat Dugan_   Date: _5-7-94_

Current Job: _Training Specialist_   Dept.: _HR_

Job Factors

Mark X at level of current belief — 1 2 3 4 5 (high)

Job Factors	E/S	1	2	3	4	5	Comments
1. Aim of process is clearly understood	E				✓		
	S				X		
2. Role in process is clearly understood	E				✓		
	S				X		
3. Information input to job is good	E			✓			Expects too much information
	S				X		
4. Training for job is sufficient	E		✓				Pat has just entered T&D program
	S				X		
5. Equipment, materials, etc provided are sufficient	E	✓					Budget limits purchases/need supplies
	S			X			
6. Management support is sufficient to accomplish goal(s)	E				✓		
	S				X		
7. Expectations of position are realistic	E			✓			Underestimates potential impact
	S				X		
8. Team participation is encouraged	E			✓			
	S			X			
9. Recognition/reward is a positive factor	E				✓		
	S				X		
10. Impact of job on overall system is clear	E			✓			Success of orientation program mixed
	S				X		

Behavioral Factors

Mark X at level of current belief — 1 2 3 4 5 (high)

Behavioral Factors	E/S	1	2	3	4	5	Comments
1. Education/experience	E					✓	Pat's MBA helps
	S					X	
2. Attendance & punctuality	E			✓			We have discussed goals & timetables
	S			X			
3. Exhibits safe practices in work performance	E					✓	
	S					X	
4. Personal effort and enthusiasm	E					✓	very enthusiastic!
	S					X	
5. Attitude toward mission/vision	E				✓		Always displays enthusiasm!
	S					X	
6. Interest in understanding and delighting customer	E					✓	
	S					X	
7. Promotes teamwork in word & action	E					✓	
	S					X	
8. Does job right the first time	E					✓	Occasionally needs to clean up stats
	S				X		
9. Communication skills	E					✓	
	S					X	
10. Personal initiative	E					✓	
	S				X		
11. Demonstrates tact and diplomacy	E				✓		
	S					X	

Include a copy of this page in my personnel file   ☑ yes   ☐ no

I have discussed job factors and behavior with my supervisor:

☑ I agree   ☐ I disagree   ☑ Comments are attached

Employee signature: _Pat Dugan_   Date: _5-7-94_

Supervisor signature: _Mel Fitzpatrick_   Date: _5-7-94_

Used by permission from the Marley Cooling Tower Co.

minimize these problems, supervisors should be required to give specific examples of the employee's behavior for each rating (under "Comments" on the Marley Co. form) and also be required to discuss the appraisal with the employee who is then given space on the form to give reasons why he or she disagrees with a rating. In addition, whenever possible, separate rating scales for each job should be developed to ensure that the attributes evaluated are job-specific.

Management by Objectives (MBO)

Another popular method of performance appraisal is *management by objectives* (MBO) that is also given other labels such as management by results (MBR). MBO is largely based on the goal-setting theory of motivation discussed in the last chapter and is most widely utilized with supervisory, managerial, and professional employees. The heart of an MBO process is the development of goals or objectives for each individual. These goals are *mutually* set by the employee and supervisor together before the appraisal period and then reviewed after the period. The active participation by the employee is setting his or her own goals *before* the performance period that can have a dramatic effect on his or her behavior during the period of time. This prior setting of goals is quite different from the rating scale method which may only review performance *after* the work period, and thus the employee is not focusing on achieving the goals during the actual work period. The *participation* by the employee in setting the goals is a key element of the MBO process, because it increases the commitment of the employee to meet the goals.

> **Management by Objectives (MBO)** **Based on the goal-setting theory of motivation. Goals or objectives for each individual are mutually set by both employee and supervisor before the evaluation period and then reviewed afterwards.**

The ability to utilize specific, *measurable* goals as opposed to broad, subjective objectives is another advantage of the MBO process. The goals in MBO programs are measurable, specific goals compared to the broad job attributes used in the rating scale in Fig. 7-6. The goals in the MBO process may include stating how they should be accomplished thus providing a specific plan of action for the employee. Most MBO programs include periodic reviews of each employee's progress toward his or her objectives. The periodic review (usually monthly or quarterly) allows for needed adjustment of objectives due to outside factors that could not have been predicted when the goals were originally set. Once the entire review period is over, the supervisor and employee together review if and how each goal was achieved; that is, to what extent was the goal met, and to what extent was the achievement due to the employee's efforts. Then the process begins again with new objectives being set for the next year.

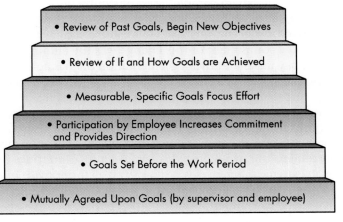

• Review of Past Goals, Begin New Objectives

• Review of If and How Goals are Achieved

• Measurable, Specific Goals Focus Effort

• Participation by Employee Increases Commitment and Provides Direction

• Goals Set Before the Work Period

• Mutually Agreed Upon Goals (by supervisor and employee)

Figure 7-7
Advantages to the MBO Process

MBO has become widely utilized for managerial, professional, and technical positions but only receives limited use for nonmanagerial positions. Its limited use for some positions, however, is often not due to any aspect of the MBO process itself but due to the desires of managers. The primary disadvantage of MBO is the time and effort the process requires of both the supervisor and the employee. Research by organizations utilizing an MBO system has provided guidelines for successful implementation of a program:[16]

- Goals should be mutually accepted by supervisor and employee; unrealistic objectives can cause the employee to discount the integrity of the process.
- Only three to five measurable objectives should be established for one period; a larger number makes it difficult for the employee to focus their action towards achieving the objectives.
- Target dates for the completion of objectives should be set whenever possible.
- Objectives should be given a ranking or weights (such as: 50 percent, 20 percent, 20 percent, 10 percent for four objectives) and a plan of action which generally details how they should be achieved.

Team Evaluations

The increased utilization of autonomous work groups or self-managing employee teams has also increased the use of appraisal by peers and reverse appraisals (see "OB in Practice" on page 211). Since the typical work group sets its own performance standards, hires new members, and assigns tasks, it is a logical extension of the team's decision-making role for peers to review each other's performance.

An excellent example of how a successful organization can change employee behavior by creating self-managing work teams is Johnsonville Foods, Inc., of Sheboygan, Wisconsin. In 1980 the company was in good shape: 20 percent annual growth rate, above-average industry profits, and a high quality (as perceived by customers) product. Yet the chief executive officer, Ralph Stoyer, perceived a major problem—"Our people didn't seem to care. Everyday I came to work and saw people so bored by their jobs that they made thoughtless, dumb mistakes—No one was deliberately wasting money, time and materials; it was just people took no responsibility for their work." So Stoyer changed the organization from one of "authoritarian control" to one of independent teams of workers who were given complete responsibility and authority for their own work. The long-term results included a reduction of product rejects from 5 percent to less than 0.5percent, increased sales, and a substantial increase in profits.[17]

A key component of this change was the elimination of annual across-the-board pay raises and the implementation of an employee-designed performance appraisal system that linked profit-sharing checks to the appraisal. The process has four steps: (1) each team member evaluates his or her own performance in three areas—performance, teamwork, and personal development—every six months using the form in Fig. 7-8; (2) each team's coach completes an identical form and then the two sit down and review evaluations together; in cases of disagreement the two scores are averaged and arbitration (by an employee group) of all extreme differences is provided; (3) all forms (with individual names deleted) are then given to a profit-sharing team of employees that places each in one of five categories: superior (about 5 percent), above average (20 percent), average

(50 percent), fair (20 percent), and poor (5 percent); (4) the total profit pool is then divided into shares with each member of the superior group receiving the most shares, etc. Overall employee satisfaction with the team appraisal process has been very high, probably because a team of employees created it, adminis-

---

**JOHNSONVILLE FOODS, INC.
COMPANY PERFORMANCE-SHARE
EVALUATION FORM**

Please check one: _____ Self _____ Coach

I. PERFORMANCE

A. Customer Satisfaction
How do I rate the quality of the work I do? Do I contribute my best to producing a product to be proud of—one that I would purchase or encourage someone else to purchase?   Score _____

B. Cost-Effectiveness
To what extent do I perform my job in a cost-effective manner? Do I strive to work smarter? To work more productively with fewer errors? To complete my job functions in a timely manner, eliminating overtime when possible? To reduce waste where possible in all departments?   Score _____

C. Attitude
To what extent do I have a positive attitude toward my personal, department, and company goals as expressed by my actions, feelings, and thoughts? Do I like to come to work? Am I thoughtful and considerate toward fellow members? Do I work to promote better attitudes? Do I demonstrate company loyalty?   Score _____

D. Responsibility
To what extent do I take responsibility for my own job? Do I accept a challenge? Do I willingly take on or look for additional responsibilities? Do I work independently of supervision?   Score _____

E. Ideas
To what extent have I offered ideas and suggestions for improvement? Do I suggest better ways of doing things instead of just complaining?   Score _____

F. Problem Solver/Preventer
To what extent have I contributed to solving or preventing problems? Do I anticipate problem situations and try to avoid them? Do I push–pull when necessary? Do I keep an open line of communication?   Score _____

G. Safety
To what extent do my actions show my concern for safety for myself and others? Do I alert coworkers to unsafe procedures? Do I alert my coach to unsafe conditions in my department?   Score _____

H. Quality Image
To what extent have I displayed a high-quality image in my appearance, language, personal hygiene, and working environment?   Score _____

II. TEAMWORK

A. Contribution to Groups
How would I rate my contribution to my department's performance? Am I aware of department goals? Do I contribute to a team? Do I communicate with team members?   Score _____

B. Communication
To what extent do I keep others informed to prevent problems from occurring? Do I work to promote communication between plants and departments? Do I relay information to the next shift? Do I speak up at meetings and let my opinions and feelings be known?   Score _____

Continued

FIGURE 7-8
Performance Appraisal Form Completed by Team Members at Johnsonville Foods, Inc.

FIGURE 7-8 *Continued*

C. Willingness to Work Together

To what extent am I willing to share the responsibility of getting the work done? Do I voluntarily assist others to obtain results? Do I demonstrate a desire to accomplish department goals? Do I complete paperwork accurately and thoroughly and work toward a smooth flow of information throughout the company? Am I willing to share in any overtime?   Score _____

D. Attendance and Timeliness

Do I contribute to the team by being present and on time for work (including after breaks and lunch)? Do I realize the inconvenience and hardship caused by my absence or tardiness?   Score _____

III. PERSONAL DEVELOPMENT

A. To what extent am I actively involved in lifelong learning? Taking classes is not the only way to learn. Other ways include use of our resource center or libraries for reading books, articles, etc.   Score _____

B. Do I improve my job performance by applying what I have learned?   Score _____

C. Do I ask questions pertaining to my job and other jobs too? Score _____

D. Do I try to better myself not only through work but in all aspects of my life?   Score _____

E. Do I seek information about our industry?   Score _____

TOTAL POINTS: _____

Scores range from 1 to 9 points, with 9 the highest and 5 the average.

Source: Reprinted by permission of *Harvard Business Review*. An exhibit from "How I Learned to Let My Workers Lead," By Ralph Stayer, November–December 1990, pp. 66–83. Copyright © 1990 by the President and Fellows of Harvard College; all rights reserved.

ters it, and revises it.[18] Advantages of this team appraisal process include that (1) it requires a self-analysis that will be reviewed with the team coach and, if necessary, an arbitration group of employees. Self-analysis removes many of the subjective and primitive aspects of other appraisal methods and forces the employee to seriously review his or her strengths and weaknesses. (2) Equity across all employees is achieved by having a team compare all appraisals, without employee names, and placing them into one of five levels of overall performance. (3) Pay is directly linked to performance by the available profits being divided according to category of performance. (4) In the end the important appraisal process is administered by a team of volunteer employees, thus this key managerial task is performed by the employees. This may be best accomplished by the process outlined in Fig. 7-9.

JOB DESIGN

A critical factor which affects the motivation of every employee is the actual work he or she performs. *Job design* refers to the process of determining exactly what an employee does on the job—the tasks, duties, responsibilities, decision making, level of authority, etc. The design of the job also determines the working relationships with other employees, supervisors, customers, etc.

These factors can be grouped into three important areas: job content, job function, and relationships. The content of a job encompasses the variety of tasks performed, the autonomy of the job holder, the routineness of tasks per-

Job design The process of determining what an employee does on a job: the tasks, duties, responsibilities, decision making, and level of authority.

OB in Practice

Reverse Appraisal at Chrysler Corporation

A corporate-wide attitude survey at Chrysler revealed serious employee concerns about upward communication. Why the concerns? According to Debra Dubow at Chrysler, "Sometimes the boss and manager have similar personalities, and the boss thinks highly of the manager, having no awareness at all of how the manager relates to his or her people." A task force then recommended a reverse-appraisal process that would give employees the opportunity to evaluate their superior. Over 1,800 managers then volunteered to take part in a pilot program. A team from the volunteers developed an appraisal instrument that required employees to respond to questions by selecting *almost always, frequently, occasionally, seldom, or almost never.* Examples of questions used by Chrysler in each category include:

- *Teamwork:* "My supervisor promotes cooperation and teamwork within our work group"
- *Communication:* "My supervisor learns current business information and communicates it to our work group"
- *Quality:* "My supervisor demonstrates meaningful commitment to our quality efforts"
- *Leadership:* "My supervisor demonstrates consistency through both words and actions"
- *Planning:* "My supervisor provides reasonable schedules so that my commitments can be met"
- *Development of the work force:* "My supervisor delegates responsibilities and gives me the authority to carry out my job"

The anonymous results of each group was then given to the managers in the pilot program. Each manager then met with his or her employees as a group to discuss and clarify the results in a nonjudgmental fashion. After two years of experience Dubow drew some conclusions about the success of the program. First, the higher the level of management, the higher the overall scores—possibly due to greater expertise at the higher levels, more honestly at lower levels, different interpretations, or less understanding of what is expected of their boss at lower levels. Second, follow-up training to help managers improve their supervisory and interpersonal skills was one obvious result. Third, a manager's willingness to be open to his or her employees' feedback depended on how open his or her own boss was in the process. Fourth, the results might best be included in the developmental section of each manager's regular performance appraisal.

Source: Joyce E. Santora, "Rating the Boss at Chrysler," *Personnel Journal,* May 1992, pp. 38–45. Used by permission.

---

formed, the difficulty level of the tasks performed, and the identity of the job holder. Also, the extent of the whole job performance by the person involved is specified. The functions of a job encompass the work methods utilized as well as the coordination of the work, responsibility, information flow, and authority of the job. The relationships of a job encompass the work activities shared by the job holder and other individuals in the organization.

Figure 7-10 shows how job design is of importance to both the worker and the organization. The design determines the varied content, functions, and

FIGURE 7-9
Initiate-Listen-Focus-
Probe-Plan Technique

The Initiate-Listen-Focus-Probe-Plan technique provides a powerful tool to avoid making employees defensive during performance appraisals. Try the following exercise with one of your employees or co-workers. This is not a performance appraisal interview; it's just a job-related discussion. Begin with a general question about performance.

Initiate: "How would you rate your performance during the last six months?" or "How do you feel about your performance during the last quarter?"

Listen: If you get a general response like "fine" or "pretty good" or "8 on a 10-point scale," follow up with a more focused question: "What in particular comes to mind?" or "What have you been particularly pleased with?" Your objective is to discuss a positive topic raised by the other person.

Focus: "You mentioned that you were particularly satisfied with . . . Let's talk further about that aspect of your job."

"How" probe: "How did you approach it?" or "What method did you use?"

"Why" probe: "Why did you happen to choose that approach?" or "What was your rationale for that method?"

"Results" probe: "How has it worked out for you?" or "What results have you achieved?"

Plan: "Knowing what you know now, what would you have done differently?" or "What changes would you make if you worked on this again?"

In hundreds of training courses, about 80 percent of people questioned in this way have made specific suggestions to improve their performance in a part of their job that they feel they have done well.

Source: James G. Goodale, "Seven Ways to Improve Performance Appraisals," *HRMagazine,* May 1993, pp. 77–80. Reprinted with the permission of *HRMagazine,* published by the Society for Human Resource Management, Alexandria, VA.

responsibilities that influence the person's ability and motivation, which, in turn, affect his or her performance and job satisfaction. A worker's favorable reaction to job design means greater accomplishment, greater job satisfaction, less absenteeism, fewer grievances, and less turnover.

FIGURE 7-10
Job Design Dimensions

Source: *Organizational Behavior and Performance,* 5th ed., by Andrew D. Szilagyi, Jr. and Marc J. Wallace, Jr. Copyright © 1990, 1987, 1983, 1980, 1977 Scott, Foresman and Company. Reprinted by permission of HarperCollins Publishers, Inc.

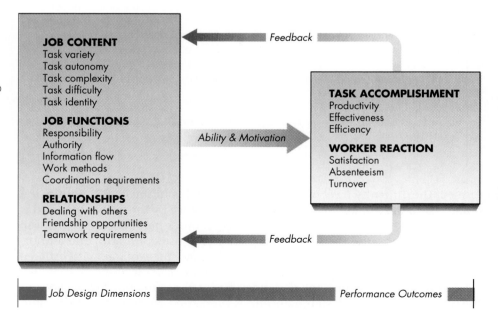

JOB CONTENT
Task variety
Task autonomy
Task complexity
Task difficulty
Task identity

JOB FUNCTIONS
Responsibility
Authority
Information flow
Work methods
Coordination requirements

RELATIONSHIPS
Dealing with others
Friendship opportunities
Teamwork requirements

Feedback

Ability & Motivation

TASK ACCOMPLISHMENT
Productivity
Effectiveness
Efficiency

WORKER REACTION
Satisfaction
Absenteeism
Turnover

Feedback

Job Design Dimensions   Performance Outcomes

How should jobs be designed? This topic has been discussed widely since the Industrial Revolution. Traditional approaches to job design have been seriously questioned in recent years. Henry Ford described his assembly line as "a haven for those who haven't got the brains to do anything else." Ford's assembly line is an excellent example of the job-design method known as job specialization.

Highly specialized jobs are characterized as having a few simple tasks that are repeated, require little decision making or mental input, and are given little responsibility or authority. Jobs designed to be highly specialized offer several potential advantages to the organization:

- Unskilled, low-paid labor can be hired.
- Less training time is required.
- Fewer skill errors occur on simple, routine tasks.
- Fewer mental mistakes occur because the employee makes few decisions.

Jobs designed to be highly specialized, however, especially with today's educated work force, may generate employee motivational problems:[19]

Boredom.   People perform only a few tasks, which must be repeated many times a day. This quickly leads to boredom. There is little challenge to learn anything new or to improve the job.

Mechanical pacing.   People are restricted by an assembly line, which makes them maintain a certain regular pace of work, which is determined by others.

No end product.   People find that they are not producing any identifiable end product; consequently, they have little pride in and enthusiasm for their work.

Little social interaction.   People complain that because the routine tasks require constant attention, there is little chance to interact on a casual basis with other employees. This makes it difficult for employees to develop significant social bonds at work.

No input.   People complain that they have little chance to choose the methods by which they perform their jobs.

No autonomy.   People are often given little or no autonomy in their work, no authority to make even obvious, simple decisions.

Jobs can be, in general, designed to overcome these motivational problems if they provide the person with more complex, interesting, and challenging work. This often requires hiring people with greater skills and/or providing additional training. The outcome may be jobs which motivate people to higher levels of performance (in comparison to specialized jobs), fewer absences, and less employee turnover. Thus one major approach to designing jobs—job specialization, largely increases the relative ability of workers to perform the job successfully by simplifying the task, duties, and responsibilities. The other major approach to designing complex jobs largely increases the motivation of the person by offering more interesting, rewarding work. Figure 7-11 summarizes these approaches. Even automobile assembly jobs (See "Profile" on Rhonda Fryman) can be designed to provide interesting, challenging work with a high degree of autonomy—and thus employee motivation and productivity.

Profile

Rhonda Fryman
Team Leader, Toyota Motor
Manufacturing, Georgetown,
Kentucky

A DAY ON THE LINE

What is it *really* like to work on the assembly line at one of the most successful automobile assembly plants? Most workers, or team members, as Toyota refers to them, respond that it's a great place to work. Yes, the pay and benefits are very good—they average $19/hour ($40,000/year) plus $7/hr.

in benefits not including overtime or employer-provided child-care and fitness centers.

However, workers claim there's much more to explain their high levels of motivation and productivity—the Toyota philosophy of striving to create a warm, caring atmosphere with a high degree of respect for workers and customers.

To see how this works, a *Lexington Herald-Leader* reporter spent a day with Rhonda Fryman, a Toyota team leader. She is twenty-nine years old, married, and has a four-year-old son. The following was a typical day for Fryman:

5:40 A.M. Fryman is among several thousand Toyota workers who commute several miles to the plant each day. She lives seventeen miles away in Connersville, Kentucky, on a 206-acre family farm.

6:00 A.M. Fryman starts one-half hour before most workers because she is a team leader. Her job is to work with and supervise four team members who operate two press machines in the metal-stamping department. At least half her shift is spent operating the machines on the line, but she must also keep a watch to maintain a sufficient level of "just-in-time" inventory, which is about a 12-hour supply. In her first three hours, Fryman attended a group leader meeting, filled in on the line, and took inventory.

At the start, middle, and end of each press run, Fryman inspects two parts. If one indicates a flaw, the line is stopped to fix the problem.

9:15 A.M. Another team leader finds a bump on the outside of a door probably caused by a speck of dirt on the sheet metal. Fryman stops the line and helps him sand down the bump. She adds her initials to the door indicating she assisted on the repairs. This attention to detail illustrates Toyota's dedication to quality.

1:15 P.M. The most important daily decision for Fryman—to determine if her team needs to work overtime when the shift ends in two hours. She knows her team hates working overtime, yet an adequate stock must be maintained. She inspects her team's inventory and decides no overtime today.

Fryman attends a training class on the "just-in-time" inventory system, and problem solving. She previously served on the Avalon Project Team, quite an honor.

2:00 P.M.   15-minute break.

3:15 P.M.   End of the day. "I never have the same day twice," says Fryman, "it's not boring!"

Source: Adapted from Ameet Sachdev, "A Day on the Line," *The Lexington Herald-Leader*, Dec. 10, 1995, A13.

To be successful, employees must have a certain degree of both ability and motivation to perform the job. Therefore, choosing the best mix of the specialization approach and the motivation approach becomes the difficult but important task for the job designer. Highly specialized jobs generally enable the organization to easily hire workers and train them to learn the job quickly and successfully. However, the employees often then become bored with the job, find they do not meet their expectations, productivity suffers, and often they eventually leave. The turnover cost is of course high and becomes a significant job design consideration. Other techniques, however, have been successful in dealing with the problems associated with highly specialized jobs—they include job rotation, job enlargement, and job enrichment. All have been successfully utilized in various organizations as methods of overcoming job boredom.

Job Rotation

One technique designed to enhance employee motivation is *job rotation,* the periodical assigning of employees to alternative jobs or tasks. For example, an employee may spend two weeks attaching bumpers to vehicles and the following two weeks making final checks of the chassis. During the next month, the same employee may be assigned to two different jobs. Therefore, the employee would be rotated among four jobs. The advantage of job rotation is that employees do not have the same routine job day after day.

Job rotation The periodic assigning of employees to alternative jobs or tasks.

Because job rotation does not change the basic design of specialized jobs, it may be criticized as nothing more than having an employee perform several boring and monotonous jobs rather than performing one. Some employees dislike job rotation more than being assigned to one repetitive job, because when they are assigned to one job, they know what work to expect each day and see the same people. Workers quickly realize that job rotation does not greatly increase their interest in their work.

Why then is job rotation still common practice? Although it may not provide employee motivation, it does give managers a means of coping with fre-

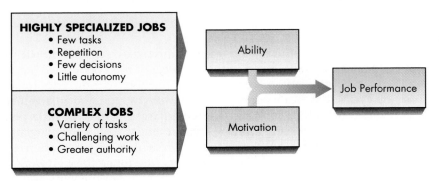

FIGURE 7-11
Job Design Consideration

OB in Practice

Job Rotation Reduces Employees' Trauma at TV Plant

Assembly line work and other types of work that require repetitive physical motions are often the cause of *cumulative trauma disorder (CTD)*. Employers in several industries have searched for methods—often very expensive—to reduce their incidence of CTD related accidents and injuries.

At the world's largest color television assembly plant in Bloomington, Indiana, Thompson Electronics was able to significantly reduce CTDs and their related workers' compensation claims. Thompson had experienced a 44 percent increase in CTDs (carpel tunnel, tendinitis, etc.) within a short period of time at the plant that produces KCA, GE, and ProScan color televisions. A team of safety, human resource, and engineering personnel developed a solution plan of four factors.

1. Identification of jobs which had high rates of CTDs.
2. Training all employees in proper lighting and holding methods of air guns, screwdrivers, etc.
3. Installing lighter air guns and lifting aids.
4. Requiring mandatory job rotation among jobs at risk.

While all four points were important, clearly the key change was the job rotation program. Voluntary job rotation had been tried without success in the past. The union's resistance and the thirty-one job classifications killed the voluntary program. However, by reducing the number of classifications to six, and changing certain work rules, the mandatory job rotation system reduced CTDs by 46 percent within a year, and by nearly 75 percent within two years. Eventually, most employees reportedly preferred rotation for safety reasons—and as a means of breaking up their day. The union eventually dropped an initial grievance as the program won employee approval.

Source: Adapted from Lance Hazzard, Joe Mautz, and Denver Wrightman, "Job Rotation Cuts Cumulative Trauma Cases," *Personnel Journal*, February 1992, pp. 29–32.

quent absenteeism, turnover, and injuries and accidents that result from repetitive tasks (see "OB in Practice"). Thus, when absenteeism or turnover occurs in the work force, managers can quickly fill the vacated position because each employee can perform several jobs.

Job rotation is also effectively used as a training technique for the new, inexperienced employees. At higher organizational levels, rotation also helps develop managerial generalists because it exposes them to several different operations.

Job Enlargement

Job enlargement A method of increasing the number of tasks performed on a job.

A second potential method of increasing employees' satisfaction with routine jobs is *job enlargement*, or increasing the number of tasks performed (i.e., increasing the scope of the job). Job enlargement, like job rotation, tries to eliminate short job cycles that create boredom. Unlike job rotation, job enlargement actually increases the job cycle. When a job is enlarged, either the tasks performed are enlarged or several short tasks are given to one worker. Job enlargement programs change many methods of operation, in contrast to job rotation, in which the same work procedures are used by workers who rotate through work stations. Although job enlargement actually changes the pace of the work and the operation by reallocating tasks and responsibilities, it does not increase the depth (decision-making and employee autonomy) of a job.

The focus of designing work for job enlargement is the exact opposite of that for job specialization. Instead of designing jobs to be divided up into the fewest number of tasks per employee, a job is designed to have many tasks for the employee to perform. An enlarged job requires a longer training period, because there are more tasks to be learned. Worker motivation should increase, because boredom is reduced as the job scope is expanded. However, job-enlargement programs are successful only if workers are more satisfied with jobs that have increased scope; such workers are less prone to resort to absenteeism grievances, slowdowns, and other means of displaying job dissatisfaction.

A job-enlargement program at the Maytag Company is a good example of this approach. Maytag undertook fifteen job-enlargement projects during a three-year period. At the conclusion, Maytag managers observed the following:[20]

- Quality of production was improved.
- Production costs were lower.
- Employees reported higher job satisfaction. They especially preferred the slower work pace that resulted from an enlarged job that did not have a repetitious cycle and that required a greater variety of skills.
- Greater efficiency arose because of reduced materials handling and a stability of production standards being met.

Although job enlargement is still considered a valid means of addressing specialization problems, it has been augmented by a more sophisticated technique known as job enrichment. Most modern redesign projects involve job enrichment rather than job enlargement, although the two techniques have distinctly different applications.

Job Enrichment

In *job enrichment* programs, the worker decides how the job is performed, planned, and controlled and makes decisions concerning the entire process. The overall purpose is to improve a job by making it more challenging and rewarding.

Job enrichment To improve a job by making it more challenging and rewarding.

Job enrichment goes further than job enlargement by grouping a set of tasks of sufficient complexity to require choices (discretion) and by bringing together the various operations and know-how to get the job done. It is usually quite comprehensive. When one job is enriched, typically the functions of supervisors and other employees are altered. For example, instead of simply feeding material into a machine, the worker with an enriched job might perform machine "set-up," feed the machinery, inspect the output, adjust or perhaps even repair the machine. Not only are more tasks added, thus increasing variety, but the worker can see the process through from start to finish, a process called task identity. Prior to the change, the worker probably had a hard time believing the quality of workmanship really mattered; now the worker can take responsibility for a significant portion of the overall product. And by inspecting the completed product, the worker receives timely feedback on whether it was made properly or not.[21]

Clearly, this type of program requires a great deal of commitment and planning by top-level management, retraining of employees, and substantial changes in leadership styles from supervisors and managers. The last change is particularly difficult for those managers who are accustomed to tight controls. Convincing these types of leaders to change their styles is perhaps the most critical step when implementing job-enrichment programs.

Job-enrichment programs can also be used successfully in service organizations. The First National Bank of Chicago, for example, redesigned the "paperwork assembly line" in a credit department. The one hundred ten-member department had been designed with highly specialized jobs. Tasks were fragmented for 80 percent of the employees; one person, for example, had only one task, feeding tape into a Telex machine. Over a six-month period, the employees and outside consultants totally redesigned all jobs by consolidating tasks to be performed by broadly trained workers. The employees then received training to upgrade their skills and were assigned to new, enriched jobs with 20 percent higher salaries. The result? The first year with the redesigned jobs produced:[22]

- Substantial increases in profits for the department ($2 million) and total volume sales.
- Higher job satisfaction and salaries for employees.
- Improved customer relations due to shorter credit application approval time.

ALTERNATIVE WORK SCHEDULES

In the traditional American family of the 1950s the father worked nine to five five days a week and the mother stayed at home and raised 2.5 children. Today the traditional American family accounts for less than 7 percent of all U.S. families. Single working parents, both parents working, one or both working a second job to maintain a standard of living are more common home environments. Additional demands on employees' time include day-care, after-school events, care for grandparents, exercise routines, hobbies, etc. Recognizing the employee as a twenty-four-hour human being who has other important, long-term commitments is a reality for today's employers. A basic question that has therefore arisen is—are traditional work schedules counterproductive to the needs of employees who must balance complex work and family demands?[23]

Alternative work schedule A different work schedule to enable an employee to meet his family and work demands.

Another significant question is will different work schedules affect employees' motivational level—and can job boredom be reduced by a different work schedule? The answers to these questions has been "yes" for many employers who have found that an *alternative work schedule* can enable employees to more easily meet family and work demands, decrease stress, and increase their workplace motivation.

The traditional five, eight-hour days per week work schedule was largely due to the 1938 Fair Labor Standards Act. The Act requires overtime pay for hours worked over forty per week at a rate of one and one-half of the normal rate of pay. Thus employers quickly adopted the forty-hour workweek as a standard. In recent years, however, employers and employees alike have found that in many work environments alternating work schedules can be more beneficial to both the employer and employee. Figure 7-12 outlines the primary work scheduling alternatives.

Compressed Workweeks

Compressed workweeks are schedules with fewer than the traditional five workdays a week for forty hours, or 5/40. The hours worked per day are increased so

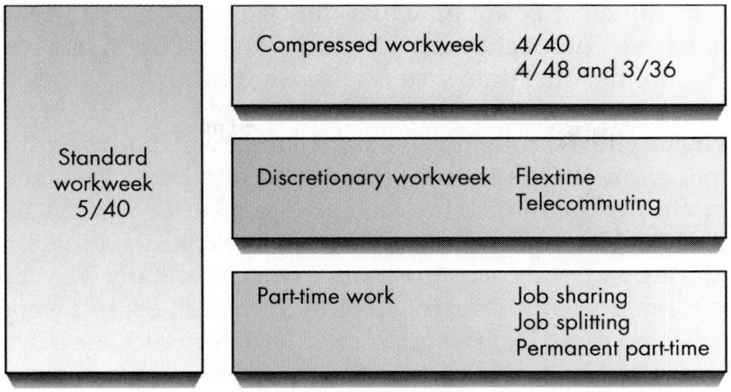

FIGURE 7-12
Alternative Work
Schedules

Source: Adapted from Michael R. Carrell, Norbert F. Elbert, and Robert D. Hatfield, *Human Resource Management,* 5th ed., Englewood Cliffs, NJ, Prentice Hall, 1995.

that the hours worked per week still total forty. The most common *compressed workweek* is the four-day workweek. Managers of manufacturing organizations report substantial savings from compressed workweeks because of reduced start-up time and increased energy conservation. Savings typically are also gained from an increase in employee morale and productivity.

The typical four-day workweek consists of four ten-hour days, or 4/40. Sixty percent of all compressed workweeks fall into the 4/40 category. In practice, some of the forty-hour workweeks have actually become four nine-hour work periods as employees trade coffee breaks and clean-up time for extra hours off. With this schedule, managers believe that they are often getting as much work accomplished in four nine-hour days as they might in a 5/40 workweek, because they save start-up time as well as maintenance, which is often scheduled for the fifth day of work.[24]

An alternative to the 4/40 compressed workweek is a week that rotates four-day and three-day shifts. In this arrangement, employees who work four twelve-hour days are off for three days. Then they work three twelve-hour days, followed by four days off. Thus, employees work forty-eight hours one week and thirty-six hours the next, or 4/48 and 3/36. For forty-eight hour weeks they automatically receive eight hours of overtime pay. This system requires two crews of employees for each shift. One crew works from 9 P.M. to 9 A.M. as the night shift, while the other crew works from 9 A.M. to 9 P.M. as the day shift. In total then, four shifts of employees work twelve-hour days with three-day workweeks alternating with four-day workweeks throughout the year.[25]

Discretionary Workweeks

A second type of alternative work schedule is the discretionary workweek, which offers employees greater freedom in choosing their daily work schedules. Retail stores, service organizations, and some manufacturers have successfully implemented various types of flexible schedules.

FLEXTIME   A system of flextime provides a true alternative work schedule for employees, who may follow different schedules of work each day of the workweek. *Flextime* has been particularly beneficial to service organizations, such as, retail outlets, banks, savings and loan associations, and insurance companies.

Virtually all studies show companies reporting more advantages than disadvantages to flexible work schedules, regardless of size or type. Savings in employee turnover, absenteeism, and tardiness are reported so often and over

Compressed workweek The hours worked per day are increased so the weekly hours still total forty. Most common is the four-day workweek.

Flextime An alternative work schedule that allows for employees to choose their schedule of work each day of the workweek, within limits.

such long periods of time that these advantages must be considered valid attributes of flexible schedules.

In most flextime systems there are two requirements: (1) a core time when the employee must work, and (2) a total number of hours per day. For service organizations, core time is a time during which most customers arrive; for example, from 10:30 A.M. to 1:00 P.M. for a retail outlet where most customers come in during their lunch breaks or five-to-nine for suburban shopping locations. As Fig. 7-13 indicates, the employer also establishes the total hours of operation during which the employee must work. Normally, the employee must work the core hours within the total eight hours worked. If the core time is not worked, the employee does not get credit for the workday; usually an employee does not arrive for work at all if the core time cannot be worked. The organization may alternate core times for different days of the week if this is necessary to meet customers' demands.

Most employees in the United States and elsewhere favor flextime operations. Employees particularly like the control flextime gives them over their personal lives. They can better schedule leisure activities, family responsibilities, and take care of personal business without asking for permission or inventing excuses.

Other flextime advantages for employees include reduced commuting time and faster shopping during slack times. Parents enjoy the advantages flextime gives them, because they are often responsible for school-age children.

Organizations that have experimented with flextime report many advantages to the system: improved employee morale, increased productivity, and decreased absenteeism and turnover. Tardiness is practically eliminated since employees can start their total workday later and still work the same hours. Flextime also reduces timekeeping by supervisors. Employers report that employees usually arrive ready to begin working since personal needs can be taken care of before work. Another advantage is the reduction of overtime costs. By setting

FIGURE 7-13

Flextime Programs

Source: Adapted from Michael R. Carrell, Norbert F. Elbert, and Robert D. Hatfield, *Human Resource Management*, 5th ed., Englewood Cliffs, NJ, Prentice Hall, 1995.

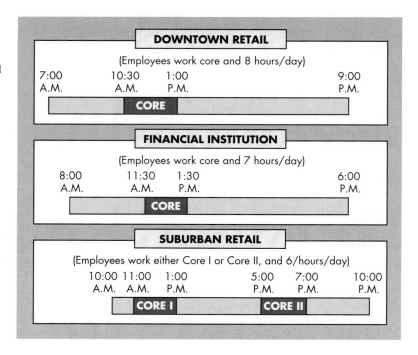

core hours during the busiest periods of the day, managers avoid scheduling overtime or hiring part-time employees for busy periods. Often retail and service organizations must overstaff to be sure that an adequate number of employees is available during a rush period. Overstaffing is less necessary in flextime.

Flextime may be a key factor for employers who successfully attract and retain employees of diverse ethnic backgrounds. Arnold Manseth, director of employee relations at the Pacific Northwest Bell Telephone Company, believes that trust between employer and employees is all that is required to implement flexible work hours. Manseth claims, "Today's employees are no longer content to follow their fathers' footsteps and put the job above everything else. Instead, they must balance the job with other aspects of life and are asking the employer for assistance. For those (employers) who do, they'll find the quality of work will not drop. A happy employee is a productive one.[26]

Creating a flexible work force may also enable employers to hire and retain older employees. Flextime is often attractive to older workers who view it as a great opportunity to ease their work demands.

Other discretionary workweeks, staggered start or variable hours are sometimes called flextime systems; however, they do not offer employees the degree of daily choice that is characteristic of true flextime systems. Instead staggered start allows employees to choose one of several starting times and then work their full number of hours. Management usually limits the number of employees per starting time and requires them to maintain the same schedule. While these reduced flexibility systems do not offer all the freedom and advantages of a flextime system, they do offer advantages in comparison to a fixed, uniform work schedule.

TELECOMMUTING   New technological opportunities such as electronic mail and bulk-data transmission have created a new discretionary schedule alternative, telecommuting. *Telecommuting* allows employees to complete some or all of their work at home, and usually, therefore, gives them complete discretion in setting their hours of work. For example, computerized clerical work and computer programming can be accomplished at home, because the job does not require constant supervision or contact with customers or coworkers. About 30,000 employees are working at home.[27] Estimates of the number of Americans who will use home offices by the year 2000 range as high as 22 percent of all jobs; the most common types of jobs will be computer data-entry tasks. IBM alone has over 2000 employees with terminals at home.[28] Now, fiber-optic and fax technology are making telecommuting attractive to even more employers and employees.

Telecommuting allows employees to complete all or some of their work at home.

There are many potential benefits to telecommuting. Total labor costs may decline because employees work without direct supervision. Less office space is required, and employer utility costs are likely to be lower. Employees enjoy flexibility in their work schedule, cost savings because of lunch at home and no commuting, and the opportunity to stay with their families.

But there may be disadvantages to telecommuting. Employees miss the social contacts at work that are important for personal and professional needs. Also, they are not privy to the office grapevine or networking opportunities.

Telecommuting projects have produced an unexpected benefit in some cases—substantial productivity increases. Control Data conducted a program that resulted in productivity increases for individual employees of between 20 and 35 percent. New York Telephone reported increases of between 15 and 85 percent. The J.C. Penney telecommuting catalog-order program experienced not one paid sick day in its first two years.[29]

Part-time Work

Part-time work has become a very popular work schedule alternative. The influx of women and older workers into the job market has increased the supply of workers seeking part-time work. Managers have realized the potential benefits—higher enthusiasm and lack of boredom—which may result from employees spending few hours per week in highly specialized routine jobs. At least three types of part-time schedules—job sharing, job splitting, and permanent part-time positions—have emerged in recent years.

Job sharing refers to dividing full-time jobs into two part-time related positions.

JOB SHARING   Job sharing has evolved as one method of career part-time employment. *Job sharing* generally refers to dividing full-time jobs into two or more part-time positions, often without particular regard for how the full-time job is divided. The term generally means that two employees hold the same position together, whether as a team jointly responsible for the position or as individuals responsible for only half of the position.

Job sharing as an alternative scheduling technique provides several possible advantages: increased productivity from better-rested people, a greater pool of qualified applicants, and the potential of reduced costs. The most common result is an influx of new energy and enthusiasm brought to the job by a second person. The employer may benefit from more than twice the talent from having two workers perform the same job. When job sharing was studied in the mass assembly department of a southeastern manufacturing firm, workers found four hours to be far less tiring than eight and so were able to work at a faster pace. Also, fatigue-caused errors were reduced.

In another example a Wisconsin state telecommunications department head stated that the primary advantage of job sharing is that employees working a few days a week or four hours a day are more satisfied with their jobs than full-time workers.

Job sharing may have disadvantages. Communication problems may increase between job sharing partners and between them and other members of the work force. Job sharing may make it more difficult to assign responsibility to a particular individual. Perhaps the greatest obstacle to job sharing is that it is often not positively viewed by managers. Generally, they feel that job shares do not take the shared job seriously enough or lack the commitment to a job that a full-time employee would have.

Steelcase, Inc., in Grand Rapids, Michigan, one of the nation's largest manufacturers of office furniture, has had a job sharing program for many years. After several years, Steelcase concluded that job sharing lowers absenteeism and turnover by retaining employees who want part-time work. Also of importance, sharing can provide a resource for covering peak periods and offers a new option to older employees.

Job splitting The tasks of a full-time job are divided into two entirely independent part-time positions.

JOB SPLITTING   A second method of scheduling part-time work is *job splitting,* in which the tasks of a full-time job are divided into two entirely independent part-time positions. The employees do not perform the same duties, as they do under job sharing. Managers find that job splitting has most of the advantages of job sharing since employees are still working part-time. Job splitting may be referred to as job sharing since the latter term has wider usage and often includes situations where two or more employees work one full-time job.

Permanent part-time work Employees perform permanent part-time work during peak demand hours.

PERMANENT PART-TIME WORK   The most common method of scheduling part-time work is designing *permanent part-time work*. Retail and service organizations have found that permanent part-time positions may result in several advantages. Permanent part-time employees may be hired at lower salaries and yet may not have the morale problems of full-time employees. Further, employees performing permanent part-time work during peak demand hours are beneficial to organizations in a number of ways. Organizations catering to the general public find permanent part-time work schedules more beneficial than full-time schedules since fewer slack times are worked. Employers may find that they need both types of schedules because technical or administrative positions cannot be adequately performed by part-time employees. Frequently, permanent part-time positions are restricted to entry-level positions such as clerks, clerical operatives, and sales representatives.

Effects of Alternative Work Schedules

The alternatives just discussed are the most common forms of alternative work schedules. Many varieties of these popular forms as well as entirely new alternatives are being developed each year. The three major work scheduling alternatives—compressed workweek, discretionary workweek, and part-time work—have been very successful and continue to spawn other forms. The advantages of alternative work schedules generally provide (Fig. 7-14) a substantial gain in employees' satisfaction with their jobs and work environment. However, there have also been disadvantages associated with alternative work schedules:

- *Employee Resistance.* Employees often resist change of any type. Uncertain of what the new system will bring, and at least partially satisfied with the current system, employees may resist changes in their basic work environment even when they are dissatisfied. When asked for their input about a possible change in work schedule, employees are concerned about the new schedule's effect on: (1) their personal life, including their fam-

	Four-day Workweek	Flextime	Permanent Part-time
Employee Advantages			
Reduced commuting time	U	A	U
Less boredom on specialized jobs		P	U
Greater latitude in setting hours		A	P
Ease in completing personal business	A	A	A
Organization Advantages			
Decreased benefit costs			U
Increased energy conservation	U		
Less start-up time	U		
Decreased tardiness		A	U
Decreased wages		U	U
Disadvantages			
Fatigue	U		
Communication problems		P	P
Interrelated work problems		A	P
Poorer customer relations		P	P

(P = possibly, U = usually, A = always)

Source: Michael R. Carrell, Norbert F. Elbert, and Robert D. Hatfield, *Human Resource Management,* 5th ed., Englewood Cliffs, NJ, Prentice Hall, 1995.

FIGURE 7-14
Common Effects of Alternative Work Schedules

ily; (2) organizational environment—particularly social interactions; and (3) customer service.[30]

- *Communication Problems.* A common disadvantage encountered by employers using alternative work schedules is communication problems. Inconsistent work hours change common communication patterns; at times some employees may be inaccessible for group meetings or to provide needed assistance to others. This problem may be minimized by careful planning and correct implementation of the work schedule core hours.

- *Fatigue.* A complaint of some employees about compressed workweek schedules has been fatigue. Compressed workweek schemes involve longer days and mental and physical fatigue can become a serious problem to the point that some compressed work weeks have been discarded after a trial period.

- *Interdependence of jobs.* Serious problems with flextime or part-time alternative work schedules are sometimes created by the interdependence of jobs. In fact, highly interdependent jobs such as assembly line operations probably make these scheduling procedures simply impractical. Flextime and other discretionary workweek programs have been utilized primarily by service or small manufacturing organizations that do not have highly interdependent jobs.

EMPLOYEE INVOLVEMENT

The workers of past generations generally accepted their limited roles in the decision making, problem solving, and planning of their work and its products or services. However, today's educated, diverse, and independent workers expect and are motivated by their greater involvement in the planning, decision-making, and problem-solving aspects of their jobs. This substantial movement toward greater employee involvement (EI) or sometimes called participative management takes many forms and exists in virtually any type of organization. In general, EI programs decrease the authority and decision-making of top managers and supervisors and increase the involvement of those employees who directly perform the work—or delegate the authority to them completely. It is McGregor's Theory Y and Ouchi's Theory Z in practice.

EI Programs

Employee involvement (EI) programs enable workers to achieve desired involvement in the workplace and at the same time benefit the organization by increasing his or her commitment to organizational goals.

Employee involvement programs enable workers to achieve desired empowerment in the workplace, and at the same time benefit the organization by increasing employees' commitment to organizational goals, decreasing the number of middle-management positions, and increasing creativity. According to a survey conducted by *Industry Week* companies which have EI programs report:[31]

	(Percent of those responding)
• Increased employee motivation	(92%)
• Improved quality	(76%)
• Increased productivity	(73%)
• Increased profits	(59%)

The key differences in organizations that have authoritarian management styles and those with employee involvement are outlined in Fig. 7-15. Essen-

Authoritarian	**Participative**
Decisions handed down	Shared decision making based on equity, consensus
Top-down communication on a need-to-know basis	Open, two-way communication
Centralized, strict procedures; tight control of decision making	Shared power and trust in employee decision making
Individual input stifled	Individual input encouraged
Authority/hierarchy clearly distinguished	Egalitarian philosophy with leaders/facilitators, not supervisors
Values individualism, independent units	Values teamwork, common goals

Source: Matthew P. Conring, "Communication Makes Employee Involvement Work," *Public Relations Journal,* November 1991, p. 40. Used by permission.

FIGURE 7-15

Characteristics Typical of Management Styles

tially, the authoritarian style is characterized by centralized control of employee behavior, decision making only by supervisors and managers, and success measured in terms of individuals and departmental units. The participative style is characterized by shared decision making and authority, two-way communication, and common, organizational goals. The key to an effective EI program is top management commitment—and the willingness to relinquish the centralized authority and responsibility that has often been their basis of power for decades. Often CEOs or top managers approach EI with hesitation—"We're not running a social experiment," said Doug Anderson, Vice President of Deere-Hitachi in Kernsville, North Carolina. However, "The result (of an EI program) was a safe work environment that has better efficiency and productivity with less effort!"[32] Other examples of successful EI programs include:

- *Ford Motor Co.* The automobile giant was the pioneer in EI programs. When the program first began, many union leaders and employees were against it, because they believed that in the long run it would diminish the role of the United Automotive Workers Union (UAW). The Employee Involvement program at Ford, however, has been a success and is now widely supported. The reasons for the change in attitudes toward the program can be found in the words of a veteran UAW member, "In my new department there was a strong EI group. People met for an hour on Wednesday afternoons after work in the conference room, and we got paid for it. We talked about all kinds of problems—anything from oil coming out of hoists to bolts not going in, case nuts coming off, bad clips, bad metal. We discussed how the company could improve quality and improve our jobs. In the past nobody was taking care of these problems. It was dog-eat-dog. You came in, you hated your foreman, and your foreman hated you, you did your job, and you hoped they didn't mess with you. . . . Those days are gone, and EI helped get rid of them. You don't see people these days deliberately trying to make life miserable for their foreman. When I'm running EI meetings, I make sure we stay away from contractual issues. EI is not supposed to touch anything that's in the contract . . . EI is supposed to deal with quality issues—bad parts, bad stock, and other things that get swept under the rug in the rush to keep up production. We're seeing a log of improvement in the plants today because of EI and because of profit sharing."[33]

- *Aluminum Company of America.* The Pittsburgh, Pennsylvania company instituted an EI program as a cornerstone of its "Quality Through Excellence" philosophy.
- *Harley-Davidson.* The motorcycle manufacturer started writing a vision statement that centered on EI. Management and union representatives then took eight months to hammer out the details of the EI program.[34]

So why don't all organizations implement employee involvement? Some research on over 1,000 programs suggest: (1) American culture is based on individualism—not shared authority; (2) large companies have difficulty with EI programs—they may improve one department by wrecking another; (3) unions often can successfully resist their implementation; (4) EI programs may not be given enough clout to address serious issues, thereby, employees see them as shams; and (5) recession-forced layoffs undermine EI programs' employee confidence.[35] At least four common problems in EI program implementation and potential methods of their resolution are identified in Fig. 7-16.

Employee Ownership

Employee ownership can be viewed, perhaps, as the ultimate type of employee incentive. The concept of the employee-owned organization certainly is not new in the United States. Peter Kiewit Sons', Inc., for example, has been employee-owned for over one hundred years (see "OB in Practice" on page 229). In recent years, however, the number of U.S. employee-owned firms has grown substantially from 300 in 1974 to over 8,500 by 1990. Also, the number of employees with an ownership stake in their organizations grew from 250,000 to over 18 million during the same period.[36]

Employee ownership may be defined as a plan in which most of an organization's employees own at least some stock in the company.[37] The most common form of employee ownership in the United States is the Employee Stock Ownership Plan (ESOP) that is a legal entity established by the Employee Retirement Income Security Act (ERISA) of 1974 in which the owners of a public or private firm can share ownership with employees. The 1986 Tax Reform Act provided ESOP's increased tax incentive.

An ESOP essentially is a deferred employee benefit plan. It operates somewhat similar to a pension fund. Employees contribute a portion of their income, which may or may not be matched by the organization, to a trust fund. The trust acquires the stock of the organization. In most privately owned firms employees do not receive the voting rights to their shares; because the shares are held in the trust, and the trustees of the ESOP vote the shares. In most publicly held firms the trust transfers the stock ownership to the employees who have the same voting right as any other stockholder.

The rapid increase in employee ownership plans may be credited to three influences: (1) the federal legislation that created ESOPs and provides their tax advantages (employer contributions are tax deductible); (2) increased employee interest in the management of their organizations; and (3) the belief by proponents that employee ownership increases employee motivation and productivity, and, therefore, the success of the organization. Research studies have consistently found that employee-owned firms are more profitable, experience higher rates of productivity, and achieve greater employment growth. These impressive gains only occur consistently when employee ownership is combined with greater employee participation in the management of the organization.[38] Thus the exact

1. *When employee involvement groups brainstorm, they often go off on tangents.*

   Stay focused on one problem. "In our company, every division comes up with a mission statement," says a manager at a Midwest pharmaceutical firm. Next, each division comes up with a list of fundamental objectives that, in turn, spawns a list of projects.

   At this point, the employee involvement group can wrestle with a specific project. "The group begins by drafting a statement that defines the problem, and then writes a very detailed proposal for solving it, with action items. That's how we stay focused so that the team doesn't go off chasing rainbows," explains the manager.

2. *Senior management talks a lot about participative management, but employees don't get the feeling that they're sincere.*

   "People at the top have to establish a culture based on honesty," explains John Simmons. He suggests that senior management hold a closed door meeting to talk about "what the implementation of those values means. At the end of a half-day discussion, you'll be able to clear out a lot of the garbage and reduce the noise in the system. As a result, employees will get the real message instead of a mixed message," he says. "Alignment begins to occur between what top managers say and what they do. Then, middle and lower level managers and employees understand that the people at the top are serious about new ways of problem solving."

3. *Employees complain that managers don't take their suggestions seriously. They claim that management still makes all the decisions.*

   Managers who solicit employee opinions on how to solve a problem need to explain at the outset how the final decision will be made. According to Simmons, there are three options: You can ask for input but make the final decision yourself; you can follow the group's consensus; or you can ask for the group's recommendation and participate in the discussion, but reserve the right to veto the decision if you think that is appropriate. The point is, as long as you clearly define how the problem will be solved, employees will feel that their advice has been recognized. Problems arise when employees feel that you have misled them.

   Many good participative managers have found that the easiest way to solve problems is to seek advice, and make the final decision alone. "There are some cases where you have to make the decision and live with the consequences," says Mike Carioscio, director of corporate automation at Kemper Financial Corp.'s Chicago office. "It's tough to get a consensus," continues Carioscio. "You can't split a nickel three ways."

4. *Employees complain that they come up with ideas, but management still reaps the rewards.*

   There's really only one way around this. You must reward teams or departments for good performance, rather than rewarding individuals. "If you're still rewarding people individually, of course, it's not working," says consultant Douglass Lind. Nobody works in a vacuum. By eliminating individual awards, you eliminate the risk of rewarding only the team leader.

Source: Donna Brown, "Why Participative Management Won't Work Here," *Management Review*, June 1992, pp. 43–44. Reprinted by permission of the publisher, American Management Association, New York. © 1992. All rights reserved.

FIGURE 7-16
Common EI Problems—
and Solutions

motivational and behavioral processes of employee ownership that affects the outcomes of the entire organization are not understood, but have been the topic of a great deal of research. This research has largely focused on three distinct models which link employee ownership to organizational success (see Fig. 7-17).

The Intrinsic Satisfaction model suggests that ownership alone is enough to increase employee satisfaction, motivation, and productivity. Simply knowing that they own a part of the organization is enough to affect employees' perceptions and behaviors to a significant extent. The Instrumental Satisfaction model suggests that ownership increases employees' influence in company decision making and their perceived control over their own work. These factors then increase employees' satisfaction, motivation, and productivity. Thus, the mere fact of ownership is not important but, instead, the increased perceived influ-

Model	Concept	Research Results	
	Intrinsic satisfaction	Mere ownership affects satisfaction, motivation, productivity	Not supportive
Employee ownership	Instrumental satisfaction	Ownership increases employees' organizational influence and control over their work, which then affect satisfaction, motivation, productivity	Supportive
	Extrinsic satisfaction	Ownership is viewed as a financial investment, which if rewarding affects satisfaction, motivation, productivity	Supportive

Source: Adapted from K. Klein, "Employee Stock Ownership and Employee Attitudes: A Test of Three Models," *Journal of Applied Psychology*, vol. 72, 1987, pp. 319–332. Copyright 1987 by the American Psychological Association. Adapted with permission.

ence and control. The Extrinsic Satisfaction model suggests that employees view ownership as a financial investment. If that investment is perceived to be rewarding, then employees increase their satisfaction, motivation, and productivity.[39] Research has generally supported the Instrumental and Extrinsic models, but not the Intrinsic model.[40]

Thus, employee ownership, when it increases employees' perceived organizational influence and control over their work, and is believed to be financially rewarding does generally increase employee motivation and performance, while at the same time, affects the bottom-line success of an organization. However, ownership plans, per se, will not increase these organizational outcomes unless the perceptions of control, influence, and financial rewards are present. Employees apparently expect that when they become owners through an ESOP or other method, they will realize greater influence on their daily work situation and realize financial rewards. Organizations considering the implementation of such a plan might adopt a worker involvement program to ensure that employees, as new owners, will have greater influence and involvement in the organization.[41]

Incentive Plans

The desire to relate a person's pay to his or her performance or direct contribution to the goals of an organization has received increased support in recent years. According to Equity Theory and Expectancy Theory as discussed in the previous chapter there is little doubt that employees will be more motivated by a compensation system that focuses on their contributions to the goals of the organization.[42] Most owners and managers would quickly agree, and a survey of over 4,700 organizations reported that after changing from a time-based (pay only according to hours worked) pay system to a *performance-based pay system*, organizations reported average productivity increases ranging from 29 to 63 percent.[43]

Performance-based pay system A compensation system that links an employee's performance to his or her rewards.

Employers generally prefer some type of performance-based pay system to a time-based pay system for several reasons: (1) Employees realize the link between their performance, the productivity of the organization, and their pay—thus giving them a direct incentive to help achieve organizational goals; (2) increased incentive payments are only made if the individual or organization as a whole is more productive and thus usually in a better financial position; (3)

| OB in Practice | Peter Kiewit Sons' Inc.: Successful and Employee Owned |

Peter Kiewit Sons' Incorporated is one of the largest, oldest, wealthiest, and most successful general contractors in the United States. It is also 100 percent employee-owned. Kiewit built more miles of the U.S. Interstate highway system than any other contractor. It also operates the Gilbert companies that builds projects ranging from $40,000 paving jobs to the $200 million outfall tunnel project on Deer Island in Boston Harbor, as well as $300 million in California wastewater treatment plants.

Kiewit's success is credited to three factors: (1) strong, stable leadership; (2) Midwestern roots, ethics, and values; (3) and its employee ownership incentive program. The stock plan is considered a great value by Kiewit's competitors. "People like to be employed by Kiewit," says Terry Farley, President of Bechtel Construction Co. "That's (the stock ownership plan) the way they get their people to have the Kiewit logo emblazoned on their underwear." But all Kiewit employees are not offered stock. Each year two top Kiewit executives review the annual performance appraisal of each of the 2,600 salaried employees. Then the company offers stock to those who have been employed by Kiewit for several years and "who contribute to the bottom line of the company." Being a Kiewit stockholder has been quite lucrative, a fact that contributes to the firm's extremely low turnover.

Source: Adapted from Judy Schriener, "No Grand Plan But Plenty of Cash," *ENR*, March 22, 1993, pp. 24–30.

---

unlike cost-of-living adjustments, increases are not tied to inflation that may not be related to the organization's financial position; and (4) employees develop an increased interest in the organization and thus strive to decrease waste and increase efficiency in areas other than their own jobs.

IBM, for example, was able to increase labor productivity in typewriter manufacturing by nearly 200 percent over a ten-year period. The reason cited was the use of two policies: (1) pay for productivity, only for productivity, and (2) promote for productivity, only productivity.[44]

Performance-based systems are certainly not new. At Anderson Corporation of Bayport, Minnesota, the nation's largest manufacturer of windows, profit-sharing bonuses have been a tradition since 1914. In one year the 3,500 workers who produce high-quality, customized products received $72 million in their bonus checks—the equivalent of almost nine months' pay! The Anderson program contains three basic points: (1) Produce the best-quality products; (2) hire the best people; and (3) pay the top wages in the industry.[45]

Performance-based systems can be divided into two categories: *individual-based incentive systems,* which provide a pay incentive to each worker based on their level of productivity, and *organization-wide incentive systems,* which base their rewards on total organizational performance, usually profits.

INDIVIDUAL INCENTIVE PLANS   Many individual incentive systems are piece-rate or related plans. Such plans include a guaranteed base rate of pay for individuals who fail to achieve a standard level of production. The guaranteed rate is usually a minimum hourly rate of pay. Employees then receive a bonus for each piece or unit produced or sold above the standard. Thus a portion of their pay is directly related to their performance.

Piece-rate systems often have the advantages of being easily understood, simple to calculate, and motivational. However, many jobs do not easily lend themselves to such a pay system, because the output of the employee cannot be directly measured in units. In addition, most employees' performance is affected by the output of others. Thus their productivity is not directly proportional to *only* their input. Finally, employers and employees can seldom agree on what is a fair production standard.

COMMISSIONS   A common incentive system used in sales positions is the commission. Employees receive a percentage of their sales (measured in units or dollars). Employees who are paid on commission generally receive either (1) straight commission, which means their total pay is determined by the commission formula, or (2) salary-plus-commission, which combines a monthly salary base with a commission incentive. The salary-plus-commission method has the advantage of providing a minimum income level that employees can depend upon to pay their monthly expenses. This minimum provides stability against factors beyond the control of the employee that can affect sales, such as seasonal swings, increased competition, and inventory shortages.

How much of a salary-plus-commission total income should be commission? There is no easy or correct answer to this difficult question. In general, the commission portion is usually 20 to 40 percent of the total. However 100 percent commission jobs are not uncommon. The higher the percentage that is commission, one might argue, the more motivating to the employee. However, one problem with any commission system is determining what is a fair percentage of each sale. If the percentage is too low, employees may not find it motivating and simply rely on their salary; if it is too high the company may find it has created some millionaire sales representatives. In one case, new management of a regional television station substantially increased the commission percentage paid to its sales executives and in one case the sales representative consistently received higher paychecks than his supervisor—prompting the supervisor to demand a raise!

ORGANIZATIONAL INCENTIVE PLANS   The problems associated with individual incentive systems and the increased designing of more technical and interdependent jobs has led to increased use of organizational incentive plans. Employers want employees to realize the link between a portion of their compensation and the performance of their group or the entire organization (see "OB in Practice" on page 232).

Profit-sharing plans are the most common type of organizational incentive plan. In these plans employees each receive a share of the company's profits reported for a certain period of time—usually a year. Employees are paid hourly wages or an annual salary as their base pay but realize that they may receive a substantial bonus if the employer records higher profits—thus they are not only motivated to work harder (and smarter) themselves but may very well encourage others to be more productive as well.

Viking Freight System Inc. is an excellent example of how a successful incentive pay system can affect (in this case possibly save) a company. In the mid-1980s the federal deregulation of the trucking industry left many firms, including Viking, in a perilous situation. The top management realized that "business as usual" would no longer allow the company to survive and instead developed the highly successful Viking Performance Earnings Plan (VPEP). The plan was based on the principle that all employees should be rewarded for their direct

FIGURE 7-18

Seven Keys to the Viking
Freight Incentive Pay
Program

1. Include all employees in the plan to generate companywide cooperation and support.
2. Develop objectives that reflect the company's critical performance areas, are controllable by employees, and are easily measurable.
3. Tie the incentive program to the company's bottom line, so that payments won't be made unless the company is profitable.
4. Communicate, communicate, communicate!
5. Keep payments separate from base wages for greater visibility.
6. Listen to employees to bring about effective and rewarding change.
7. Review the program regularly and revise as necessary to ensure that it continues to meet company objectives.

Source: Terry Stambaugh, "An Incentive Pay Success Story," *Personnel Journal,* April 1992, p. 50. Used by permission.

contribution to the achievement of corporative objectives. The plan divided employees into distinctive groups (truck drivers, terminal operators, claims administrators, salespeople, and maintenance personnel) that shared common goals. Each group was then given specific, measurable performance objectives. Terminal managers, for instance, could increase their pay as much as 20 percent if they met performance objectives. The objectives for the freight terminals, for example, were:[46]

An incentive pay program at Viking Freight Systems, Inc. increased productivity 103 percent in only its third year.

1. Revenue attainment. Each terminal must generate a specified amount of revenue to earn payments.
2. Percent of performance. Actual performance must meet or exceed engineered standards.
3. On-time service. At least 98 percent of a terminal's shipments must be delivered on time.
4. Claims ratio. The cost of lost and damaged freight must be kept below a certain percentage of revenues.

The VPEP program at Viking enabled the company to achieve higher profits, continued growth, and greater productivity during a turbulent period in the industry which saw many of its competitors fail. The team that developed the Viking program created what they believed were the keys to a successful program that appear in Fig. 7-18.

One example of a highly successful profit-sharing plan is that at Ford Motor Company. In 1989, for example, the average Ford worker received a profit-sharing check of $2,800. Peter Pestillo, Ford's personnel chief and chief labor negotiator, noted, "We think it's money well spent. They get more, and they get more done. We think we get a payback in the cooperation and enthusiasm of the people." The 1984 Ford–United Auto Workers' master agreement was the first to contain a profit-sharing provision pushed by management as a means of avoiding the UAW proposed 3 percent annual raises.[47]

CONCLUSIONS AND APPLICATIONS

- Award and recognition programs are utilized by virtually all employers. They can sincerely express appreciation for a job well done, reinforce successful performance, publicize accomplishments, and provide role mod-

OB in Practice

Camberley Hotel Company Incentives

Some service industry employers believe that employee incentive plans only work in the manufacturing sector. Others see linking employee compensation to total company performance as "revolutionary." That is not the case at the Camberley Hotel Company where 40 percent of total annual compensation is due to the incentive performance.

All of the Camberley employees can earn incentives. A housekeeper, for example, has a vested interest in controlling energy costs, because a monthly energy conservation incentive is a split 50-50 share with the house on amounts below the budgeted costs for energy consumption per occupied room.

For example, at The Brown Hotel in Louisville, Kentucky, fifty-seven room attendants have earned up to $16.50 extra per month on average since the incentive began. How do they do this? One way is by quickly checking all guest rooms before cleaning begins to see that the lights are off and the thermostats are regulated.

Last year, at The Crowne Plaza in Tampa, Florida, their kitchen staff averaged $58 in monthly incentives by focusing on labor and food costs. In fact, at four Camberley hotels, cost incentives in the food area alone brought costs down 5 percent from the previous year and added $82,000 to the net operating profit.

For instance, in February of 1993, The Brown showed these results from the incentive program: The chef, whose incentive is 20 percent on food revenues and 40 percent each on labor and food costs, achieved 35 percent of his 100 percent potential because his labor costs were under budget. So he pocketed an extra $306.

The housekeeping supervisor received $258 in incentives because she achieved 45 percent, or all but 5 percent of a 50 percent potential on labor costs; and 30 percent of 100 percent of her potential on energy costs. (Among the room expense considerations are guest room amenities, linens, cleaning and paper suppliers, printing and stationery, and uniforms.)

Overall, The Brown was $3,647 under budget in salaries and wages in one month. These examples, multiplied department by department, mean increased profitability for Camberley. While there's no specific savings, the incentives as much as anything are responsible for a 40 percent increase in Camberley's net operating income since the incentive program was initiated.

Source: *Financial Executive*, May/June 1993. Used by permission.

---

els to other employees. Praise is a powerful means of recognition and can not be given too often in deserving situations.

- Interesting and challenging work is a critical component of a person's motivation. Designing jobs that people find motivating is often difficult with highly specialized work environments. Job rotation, enlargement, and enrichment programs can help alleviate the problems associated with boring, repetitive jobs.

- Alternative work schedules can affect employees' motivation level by enabling them to more easily meet family and work demands. Both organizations and employees have experienced significant positive effects of alternative work schedules. However, some problems have occurred, suggesting that communications, fatigue, and the interdependence of jobs be considered before a new program is implemented.

- Employee suggestion systems date back to 1880, yet they still save organizations millions of dollars per year today because they are easy to implement, they increase employee commitment, and they work!

- Performance appraisals are primarily used to (1) evaluate past performance to decide bonuses, merit increases, promotions, etc., and (2) develop future performance through effective feedback. Rating scales, MBO, and team appraisals are common evaluation methods. Each method has distinct advantages and uses.

- Today's work force members are motivated by employee involvement (EI) programs which provide them greater input in the planning, decision-making, and problem-solving aspects of their jobs. Employers with EI programs also report increased productivity, profits, and improved quality. Organizations with an EI style of operation can be characterized quite differently from traditional, centralized organizations.

- Performance-based pay systems relate at least a portion of an employee's pay to their individual level of productivity or the performance of the entire organization. Profit-sharing plans have increased in use due to their perceived ability to increase employee commitment and productivity.

- Employee ownership has increased rapidly in the United States in recent years. The increased popularity of ESOPs is probably due to federal legislation, increased employee interest in the management of organizations, and the fact that employee-owned firms are more successful. Research indicates that the increased success is due to employees' perceived increase in influence in organizational decision making, control over their own work, and financial well-being. These factors lead to greater employee satisfaction, motivation, and productivity, which in turn increases organizational outcomes.

REVIEW QUESTIONS

1. What are the keys to implementing and maintaining a successful employee suggestion system?
2. What are the key components to the Taco Bell "Value Strategy"?
3. What are the primary purposes of the performance appraisal? List the advantages of rating scales, MBO, and team appraisals.
4. What are the potential benefits of award and recognition programs? Describe the key elements of effective programs.
5. What are the advantages and disadvantages to jobs that are designed to be highly specialized?
6. How can flextime provide real savings to an organization while also benefitting its employees? When might a flextime program not be practical?
7. In what ways are employee involvement (EI) organizations different from the traditional, centralized organization?
8. What are the common types of "pay for performance" plans? Why are they increasingly popular with employers?
9. How can a manager use praise to affect employees' motivation?
10. Why have employee-owned organizations achieved greater success than other organizations?

DISCUSSION QUESTIONS

1. Discuss how an organization you are familiar with might benefit from the "Taco Bell Philosophy."
2. Can the old suggestion box be made effective in an organization that has successfully organized around

self-directed employee teams that simply implemented their own suggestions without a formal process?

3. If simple, well-deserved praise is such an easy, inexpensive, and effective form of recognition, why don't people give it more often?

4. Think of a job that you have performed that generally was not one you found to be highly motivational. Describe how job rotation, enlargement, or enrichment might have helped make the job more interesting and challenging as well as benefit the organization.

5. Why do workers in the 1990s desire more employee

participation in the management of the organization than their grandfathers of the 1950s?

6. Suggest forms of simple, inexpensive recognition similar to the "At-A-Bee" stickers in Fig. 7-2.

7. Which of the following general programs do you believe would be the *most* effective in increasing the motivation level of employees: (1) profit sharing, (2) job enrichment, (3) flexible work scheduling, (4) suggestion system. Explain your answer.

8. How might the advantages of employee ownership be realized in organizations that are not owned by stockholders, such as small businesses, nonprofit, and family-owned firms?

CASE STUDY

Central States Windows

Carole Willen is the Marketing Director of Central States Windows, a new window manufacturing and sales company in Fargo, North Dakota. The company was started three months ago by Kim Lee who was production manager of a similar company in Lansing, Michigan. Lee was not familiar with the marketing department in Lansing except he knew that all salespeople were paid a straight salary and their job primarily consisted of contacting large outlet stores which carried their windows.

The windows in the North Dakota plant will be "high end" (expensive) custom-made and the most energy efficient ones on the market thanks to a new patented triple glaze sealant process. However, the product is still an unknown entity in the conservative Midlands.

Lee has instructed Willen, who has twenty years experience in appliance sales, to set up two sales forces—inside salespeople who will work with builders, building owners, etc., directly, and outside salespeople who will go on the road to work with builders and contractors within their state. The company plans to sell in six states that currently do not have a similar plant that can deliver custom windows quickly. Each outside sales representative will be given a separate state but the inside salespeople can call anyone within five hundred miles. Lee believes in "pay-for-performance" and thinks that a fair but motivating commission system should help the new company achieve far higher sales than the Lansing firm's method of straight salary. However, Lee also realizes that Central States is a new company, thus sales may be slow for several months; and unless the staff is making a reasonable income, they are likely to leave, especially the best ones. He is also aware that turnover can be very costly in this business, because it takes time for sales representatives to build trust with their clients, and often a firm's reputation depends on its representation.

CASE STUDY QUESTIONS

1. How should Willen structure the relationship between the inside and outside sales forces?

2. From library-based research and other sources how large would you estimate the market to be in each of the six states—North Dakota, South Dakota, Nebraska, Kansas, Missouri, Iowa?

3. If you were Willen would you recommend a salary-plus-commission pay system or straight commission?

4. Who might Willen contact for information before answering question three?

EXPERIENTIAL EXERCISE 1

Develop a Rating Scale

Purpose

To gain experience in developing a performance appraisal rating scale using easily recognized attributes of job performance.

Task

Step 1: Select the ten most important behaviors of a college professor. Then write a brief description of each point on a rating scale, for example:

Behavior	**Points**		
	1 *Poor*	3 *Average*	5 *Excellent*
Test Material Covered in Class	Many questions were on topics not covered in class at all.	Most questions were generally related to class discussions.	Each question area was discussed in class.

Step 2: Choose (individually or in groups according to instructions) a professor other than the one for this class and evaluate him or her on your scale. Write a sentence explaining each rating.

College Professor Rating Scale

1. _____   *Poor*   *Average*   *Excellent*

Explanation: _____

_____

2. _____   *Poor*   *Average*   *Excellent*

Explanation: _____

_____

3. _____   *Poor*   *Average*   *Excellent*

Explanation: _____

_____

4. _____   *Poor*   *Average*   *Excellent*

Explanation: _____

_____

5. _____   *Poor*   *Average*   *Excellent*

Explanation: _____

_____

6. _____   *Poor*   *Average*   *Excellent*

Explanation: _____

_____

7. _____   *Poor*   *Average*   *Excellent*

Explanation: _____

_____

8. _____   *Poor*   *Average*   *Excellent*

Explanation: _____

_____

9. _____   *Poor*   *Average*   *Excellent*

Explanation: _____

_____

10. _____   *Poor*   *Average*   *Excellent*

Explanation: _____

_____

EXPERIENTIAL EXERCISE 2

How Should These Employees Be Paid?

Purpose

To examine the various ways of compensating people using incentive plans.

Introduction

While a majority of employees are paid a salary for the period of time worked, there is an increasing trend toward *pay for performance,* whereby employees, in addition to their normal salary, are paid an incentive for high performance. The increasing use of incentive systems is primarily the result of organizational efforts to increase profits and competitiveness through increased employee productivity. Studies show that incentive plans, if well constructed and implemented, can have a dramatic effect on employee productivity. Keep in mind that incentive plans can be individual-based or organizational-based.

An incentive pay system is impractical to administer unless certain key conditions can be met. Those conditions include the following:

1. The output must be measurable and suitable for standardization.
2. There must be a consistent relationship between the employee's skill and effort and the employee's output.
3. The output can be measured and credited to the proper individual or group.
4. The incentive system should lead to an increase in productivity.
5. The employees, the union (if one exists), and management must all support the incentive system.

Task

Listed below are several jobs. For each job, complete the questions in the figure provided. Some jobs may be appropriate for individual or group incentive compensation systems, while others are more appropriate for a wage or salary system. Your task is to choose the pay system that would have the greatest motivational effect on the employee.

Valerie McCloud—Forklift Driver

Valerie McCloud drives a forklift for a small metals manufacturer. She picks up parts that have been boxed and loaded onto pallets and delivers them to the warehouse for shipping. She occasionally also performs odd jobs throughout the day at the request of her supervisor. McCloud is a member of the Teamsters' Union.

Jill Peters—Seamstress

Jill Peters works as a seamstress for a large textile firm in South Carolina. She works independently using an industrial sewing machine. All day, she sews sleeves and pockets to men's shirts. Her output is tallied twice a day by her supervisor.

William Grant—Assembly-Line Worker

William Grant is an assembly-line worker for a large home appliance manufacturer. He attaches parts to washing machines as they reach his position on the line. Twenty-seven employees work on this particular assembly line in the plant. Daily output for the group is recorded by the employees' supervisor.

Claire Walker—Computer Account Clerk

Claire Walker is a data entry operator for a large state government agency. Her work varies from day to day, although much of it is very similar in nature. Her supervisor receives a weekly computer printout that details each person's production rate and quality index.

Rick Fernstein—Accounting Instructor

Rick Fernstein is an assistant professor for a large urban university. He is responsible for activities involving teaching, research, and community service. Annually, he prepares the performance report covering all activities for the year. This report includes summaries of student course evaluations, publications, committee work, and other school-related activities. Fernstein's department head closely reviews the report and assigns an overall performance evaluation of "excellent," "good," "satisfactory," "below satisfactory," or "unacceptable."

Dennis Cuestick—Automobile Salesman

Dennis Cuestick is an automobile salesman for a Ford dealer in a midwestern town. Six days a week he "works the floor." The company's sales personnel have an informal system for taking turns when customers enter the showroom or call to make inquiries about a car. Sales are recorded daily by the sales manager.

Paul McCleskey—Route Salesman

Paul McCleskey is a route salesman for a large cola manufacturer. His route covers a large rural area in central Georgia and consists primarily of servicing small mom-and-pop grocery stores, lounges, and restaurants. At the end of each day, McCleskey turns in a report to his supervisor detailing his sales activity for each account.

Charley Bedeman—Farm Laborer

Charley Bedeman is a farm laborer for the Jiffy Orange Juice Company in Orlando, Florida. He rises daily at 6:00 A.M. and is in the groves picking oranges by 7:00 A.M. Using a centuries-old technology, he carefully places each piece of ripe fruit in his deep "picking bag" slung over his shoulder. He dumps a full bag into a box and starts all over until quitting time at 5:00 P.M.

Kathy Miller—Secretary

Kathy Miller is a secretary to the dean of the Arts and Sciences School at a small, private liberal arts college. She types correspondence and reports, keeps the budget, files, maintains the dean's schedule, and so on. Miller's work is evaluated by the dean annually, using a performance-evaluation form that includes quantity of work, quality of work, dependability, judgment, communication skills, ability to get along with others, and loyalty. For each of these traits, she is assigned a rating of "very good," "above average," "average," "below average," or "unsatisfactory." One of these ratings is also given to Miller to designate her overall performance for the year.

Christy Song—Attorney

Christy Song, a recent graduate of a prestigious eastern law school, works for a reputable Washington law firm specializing in corporate law. Song is assigned to the division that handles patent and trademark violations. She works directly with clients, researches cases, writes briefs, and represents clients in court. Her performance is reviewed informally about every six months. No special forms are used to conduct these evaluations.

Instructions: Place an "X" in the box (A–E) that you believe would be the best pay plan.

	COMPENSATION PLAN					INCENTIVE PLAN	
	(A) Hourly only	(B) Hourly plus incentive	(C) Salary only	(D) Salary plus incentive	(E) Incentive only	If you checked B, D, or E, indicate the appropriate *form* of incentive: individual-based or organization-based	If you have recommended some form of incentive, indicate the type of output (net sales, per item manufactured) for an individual-based plan or define the distribution of an organization-based plan (each employee with 3 months or more service receives an equal dollar share of 50% of net profits).
Valerie McCloud							
Jill Peters							
William Grant							
Claire Walker							
Rick Fernstein							
Dennis Cuestick							
Paul McCleskey							
Charley Bedeman							
Kathy Miller							
Christy Song							

Source: Adapted from Michael R. Carrell, Norbert Elbert, and Robert D. Hatfield, *Human Resource Management*, 5th ed., Englewood Cliffs, NJ, Prentice Hall, 1995.

  Take It to the Net **You can find this chapter's World Wide Web exercise at:** http://www.prenhall.com/carrell

CHAPTER 8

The Global Context of Organization

CHAPTER OBJECTIVES

1. To understand what U.S. companies must do to compete in a global marketplace.

2. To outline the kinds of changes at play in the world economy which will change the way U.S. companies do business.

3. To examine new competitive standards and how to achieve them.

4. To learn the most important influences on a multicultural corporation.

5. To recognize the major characteristics of diverse cultures and how those characteristics affect operations.

6. To compare the five dimensions of culture that impact management styles in diverse cultures.

7. To explore aspects of culture that impact how people relate to each other and to the workplace.

8. To learn what it means to be a global manager.

9. To understand culture shock and how corporations prepare their employees to survive it.

10. To review the relationship U.S. businesses have with other economic superpowers—Japan and Europe.

KFC Inc. International

Kentucky Fried Chicken! What could be more American than that? Well, don't look now but you're standing on a street corner in Tokyo, Japan, looking at a building with a slightly oriental frontage. But inside the Japanese offer you "chicken done right" the Col. Sanders way.

KFC, International, with outlets in sixty-three countries and territories is a perfect example of an American company competing in the global marketplace. Some business analysts point to the product of KFC, chicken, as the first and primary reason for its success. Chicken is almost universally accepted as a source of protein. And, except in vegetarian cultures, chicken is seldom forbidden by a culture or a religion as some meats are.

The road to success in different cultures was certainly bumpy for KFC. In Japan, for example, the first store it opened in 1970 could have been its last but for the leadership of its Japanese partner, Shin Ohkawara. KFC's state-side standard was to locate its restaurants in a suburban area where land was cheaper and where plenty of road traffic could be expected. Unfortunately, such a location did not work in Japan. Mr. Ohkawara convinced KFC to move the store to an urban location with plenty of foot-traffic. While the initial investment in the location was expensive, the investment paid off.

Don't look for the familiar red and white bucket when "ordering out" at KFC in Japan. Japanese consumers prefer single layer packing to minimize grease saturation. With over 7000 outlets, KFC has made its mark in the global fast-food market.

Source: Adapted from Alan I. Kirschenbaum, "The Original Recipe for International Success," *The Lane Report,* Lexington, Kentucky, May 1, 1992.

THE WORLD ECONOMIC STAGE

It is said that the only *constant* is *change*. Nowhere is the truth of that statement more evident than in the recent events surrounding the end of the Cold War. For the nearly fifty years since the end of World War II, global politics has revolved around the superpowers, the United States and the Soviet Union, and the ever present threat of a third world war.

The influence of that political agenda on the world economy cannot be overemphasized. The United States dominated the world economy and focused much of its energies toward perfecting its defense systems. Significant American technology emerged from the nation's investment in the weapons industry. Now that the Iron Curtain has come down, we can see the devastating results of the USSR's commitment to that same weapon's industry. The drain of resources from its people to the creation of a nuclear arsenal has left Russia, at best, a third world economy.[1]

As the United States focused its energy on preserving world order, Japan and the European community worked first, to recover from World War II, then to compete as players in the worldwide market. Their success is touted by some economists as the second most dramatic change to the world's economic picture. The United States no longer dominates the world economy—it shares the stage with Europe and Japan.[2] With the threat of war by the U.S.S.R. largely eliminated, Europe and Japan no longer need to acquiesce to the wishes of the United States as it relates to economic issues in return for protection from war.[3] The emergence of three roughly equal *economic superpowers*—United States, Japan and Europe—has a significant impact upon how U.S. companies do business. U.S. companies have been integrating more and more into the world economy. U.S. companies formed some 2,000 international alliances in Europe during the 1980's alone.[4] This move *outward* will continue. Peter Drucker, a noted corporate economist, recently predicted that U.S. companies will continue to integrate themselves into the world economy by forming "alliances" with international companies.[5]

In addition, with the end of the Cold War, the economy rather than defense issues, has taken center stage in the world's attention. While previously "economic summits" played second fiddle to "peace summits," now the survival of a nation's economy depends upon international cooperation and understandings. The threat of "economic wars" is ever present. The need for the United States to compete in the world economy is, quite simply, a matter of survival.

In this chapter we will examine how participating in the global economy affects how U.S. businesses operate and what U.S. managers need to know to become global managers.

U.S. companies are competing in the worldwide economy in a number of ways. Companies that have established offices or subsidiary companies abroad are the most noticeably *global*. They might be called *multinationals* or *transnationals*. These names indicate that the organization's activities are in more than one nation and culture. Partnerships, joint business ventures, and licensing arrangements between U.S. companies and other national or international companies are also common ways U.S. companies operate in the world economy.

U.S. companies also are in the world economy by competing in the United States with "foreign" businesses locating here. The revolution in the U.S. auto industry caused by the growing number of Japanese auto companies locating in

Toyota's Camry plant in Simpsonville, Kentucky continues to expand. In January 1995, it had 6,500 employees.

California, Indiana, Tennessee, and Kentucky, cannot be ignored. Later in this chapter we will touch on some of the issues Japanese companies have raised through their business practices. Finally, U.S. companies compete in the world wide economy through the competition for a quality labor base.

Workers are no longer limited to their immediate surroundings. Travel and communication has increased so rapidly that there are no untappable labor pools. U.S. companies will need to have a large immigrant labor influx if it is to have a large enough worker base. With a more culturally diverse work force, U.S. managers will need to prepare to compete in the global economy in their own backyard.

THE NATURE OF INTERNATIONAL ECONOMIC RELATIONSHIPS

Later in this chapter we will discuss how managers can cope in a "foreign" culture and become global managers. Whether that culture is the corporate culture of the future, the culture of a business located in the United States with a diverse work force and/or clientele, or a business located outside of the United States, the challenge is the same. In this section we will discuss the different ways companies interact in the international marketplace: why they exist, how they operate, and how they are organized.

Global Competition

Global competition The ability of the United States to compete in the global marketplace.

The United States must be able to compete in the global marketplace because of the changes in the way the world does business. Specifically these changes were caused by the creation of worldwide consumer demands and quality standards; by changes in the doctrine of 'comparative advantage'; and by a revolution in how manufacturing is done.[6]

Worldwide consumer market Everyone in the world is a potential customer.

What's in a Name? Everyone in the world is a potential consumer. Ad agencies and marketing research groups spend millions of dollars each year to discover what sells. The United States has long been a country of "name brands." Now, we can point to a *worldwide consumer market* that demands the elegance of a Gucci shoe, the consistency of a McDonald's hamburger, and the practicality of disposable diapers from Proctor and Gamble. This name brand market grew up in the world's richest countries and has spread to every corner of the globe. A worldwide standard of performance associated with a name brand is created by active marketing such as the syringe manufacturer in the example below in the "OB in Practice." In addition, the product presented in the marketplace as the *best* has had to perform that way in order to maintain the demand. In order to create *the best,* a company must be big enough, and profitable enough to invest in the research and development necessary to make and keep its product the best. Unless companies are in the worldwide marketplace, they do not have enough capital to keep up with their competitors. In addition to the need for capital, businesses must go international to take advantage of the rapid development of technology. Companies have to form alliances to secure access to new technologies and to share in the risk of capital investments.[7]

Comparative advantage Economists explained the international competition of nations in trade through the doctrine that they should concentrate their efforts in areas where they had a competitive advantage.

CHANGES IN "COMPARATIVE ADVANTAGE"   In the past, economists explained the international competition of nations in trade through the doctrine of *comparative advantage*. The doctrine is simple enough: nations concentrated their efforts in the area where they had a competitive advantage. In Florida, for example, farmers grew grapefruit and oranges because of the soil and weather. In Iowa they grew corn. Michigan produced cars and trucks because of the nearby steel industry and energy resources. In South Carolina, the garment industry took hold.

Before the availability of labor, energy, and raw materials became global, this doctrine worked well and defined "free trade" among nations. Now, few resources are so static as to preclude their availability elsewhere. Labor is mobile; energy is plentiful; and raw materials are transportable. Companies must seek their competitive advantage separate from their nation's historic competitive advantage. To "capture the market" companies must not only create the best so that consumers demand their products, they must produce them at the price consumers can pay. To drive down the price and maintain the quality, products must be produced in bulk with savings realized by the *economics of scale*; that is, companies must be able to provide enough of a product so that the price per individual item is reduced.

Economies of scale For savings, products must be produced in bulk to provide enough of a product so that the price per individual item is reduced.

Quality control Organizing workers into teams, manufacturers include all employees in ensuring the high quality of their products.

MANUFACTURING REVOLUTION   From Henry Ford's creation of the assembly line in 1915 to the industrial union *Master Agreements* of the 1950's, manufacturing in the United States defined efficiency. "Planned Obsolescence" of manufactured products insured a continuous market. Uniformity of costs in major U.S. companies were arrived at through nationwide union agreements controlling wages and domestic suppliers controlling availability of raw materials. Competition was not an "all or nothing" situation. "Market shares" were traded among the big players depending upon who could offer the latest *new* and *improved* model.

External competition developed in the 1970's when Japanese-made products exceeded U.S.-made products in quality at reduced prices.[8] The Japanese had discovered *quality control* and converted their straight-line assembly plants into team assembly plants. The workers in the teams worked on and saw the finished product instead of seeing only their discrete part of a long assembly process.

OB in Practice

Capturing the "Syringe" Market

Becton-Dickinson is not a household name to most U.S. consumers. But in the worldwide market for hospital supplies it has become a "hospital-hold" name in supplying plastic syringes to countries all over the world. Becton-Dickinson is a case study in how to enter into and control a worldwide market. By utilizing opportunity and technology to its advantage, it has taken the leading share of this new global market for plastic syringes.

The opportunity began because doctors set the standards for acceptable medical instruments. For years, other countries have sent their doctors to the United States for training. As these doctors returned to their countries, they created a demand around the world for medical implements, with a uniform quality standard such as those they had used in the United States.

In the 1960s the technology developed to substitute disposable plastic syringes for the reusable glass ones. Plastic syringes are lighter and less breakable, therefore, they are much easier to ship. And, if manufactured in bulk, are much cheaper.

Becton-Dickinson could use this emerging global quality standard and the new technology, which made it cost-effective to produce on a worldwide scale, to enter the world marketplace. It jumped at the opportunity. By creating manufacturing, shipping, and distribution centers all around the world, it marketed the "plastic syringe" with missionary zeal. It took advantage of its multinational locations to shift production from one country to another to adjust for the most favorable export conditions.

Its vision, energy, and flexibility have taken Becton-Dickinson from a middle-size New Jersey company to a worldwide manufacturer of hospital supplies.

Source: Adapted from: Charles R. Morris, *The Coming Global Boom,* New York, Bantam Books, 1991, pp. 11–12.

It became clear to the worker how important his or her "part" was to the whole. Quality control became the responsibility of each worker.

The Japanese manufacturers had also learned the value of automation in quality control. Automation did not give Japan a competitive advantage because it reduced labor costs, but because it increased both the quality and efficiency of the manufacturing process. Workers on the assembly line might allow an irregular or damaged piece of goods to get by them—an automated system did not. In addition, an automated system coupled with a "just-in-time" inventory system forces the reduction of inefficiencies because in order for it to work, it must run perfectly.

In response to the loss of the United States's superiority in the worldwide consumer market, U.S. companies tried a number of avenues. First, they pushed for protection from the importation of foreign manufactured products. The success of such embargoes was short-lived. External competitors simply circumvented the bans or imported the discrete pieces of a product and assembled it on U.S. soil. Second, U.S. companies tried to beat the price of competitor goods by cutting costs to the bone. They closed inefficient plants and laid off workers. They moved operations to the very countries their competitors came from and set up "cheaper" plants. But they still couldn't beat the price of their foreign competitors. Third, U.S. companies embarked in the 1960s and 1970s on transforming themselves into financial holding companies—buying and selling corporate assets, engaging in unfriendly takeovers, and leveraged buyouts. Such transactions changed the bottom line numbers for a given year, but did nothing to restore the health of the operation.[9]

In the 1990s American industry began to recover its ability to compete effectively in a global economy through the utilization of new technology, right-sizing, employee empowerment, self-managed teams, TQM, and other methods.

U.S. retailers, taking advantage of the global marketplace, boasted of aggressive expansion into Europe, Mexico, Asia, and Africa. In 1995, fifty U.S. retailers were up and running in Europe where three years before only fourteen had been. Wal-Mart was operating sixty-seven discount stores in Mexico and preparing to expand into China.[10]

How International Companies Operate

Competitive standards
In the global market, the U.S.-based companies use the standards of productivity, quality, variety, customization, timeliness, and convenience as methods of operation.

Globally, competitive United States-based companies have substantially changed their traditional structure and methods of operation. The *competitive standards* at play in the global market are productivity, quality, variety, customization, timeliness and convenience. Linking all of these standards is the need to be flexible.[11]

FLEXIBLE PRODUCTIVITY IN MANUFACTURING   Flexible productivity in manufacturing is seen as necessary to meet global competition. As manufacturers regroup, retrain, and retool to manufacture in a more efficient and effective way, it takes something more to pull away from the pack. Being able to produce unique products for different demands at the same manufacturing plant gives companies that competitive edge. Using automation, robots, and computerization, an assembly operation can change and adapt products for isolated, consumer markets with ease and at low cost. U.S. manufacturing had been designed to produce homogeneous products to satisfy an upwardly mobile American population. The use of automating and unskilled work was productive for that type of product. But to produce many, unique products of high quality for a worldwide market of eager consumers willing to pay for customized goods demands flexible and skilled employees. New technology is being used to tailor products to unique needs.

FLEXIBLE PRODUCTIVITY IN SERVICES   Flexibility is not limited to the manufacturing of goods. Leading-edge companies are relying upon customized *knowledge* and *service* as well as customized products for sale in the marketplace. Such businesses are peopled by problem solvers, problem identifiers, and strategic brokers. *Problem solvers* are able to constantly change and adapt a product to the customer's needs; *problem identifiers* are able to identify customers' needs and show how the customized goods fill those needs; and the *strategic brokers* are the parties who put the problem solvers and problems identifiers together.[12]

Such businesses naturally shed the pyramid bureaucracy of the past to enable these three groups to properly interrelate. In addition, a network that includes suppliers, customers, regulators, and financiers is established to enable them to beat their competition. In an "out of the box thinking" exercise, fifteen executives from leading U.S. companies designed just such a theoretical network and demonstrated that such an operation could produce a custom-made, defect-free automobile in three days.[13] The valuable asset of these enterprises is its employees. Workers for these businesses can no longer be interchangeable. The days of "cheap labor" are over. Education, experience, and inventiveness are required. Competition for good employees is fierce.

William B. Johnston, author of *Workforce 2000,* studied world work force trends and concluded that companies prepared to operate globally and compete for human resources on a worldwide basis can develop a competitive advantage.

The willingness to tap worldwide labor sources means that changes have to be made. Mr. Johnston suggests that the flow of skilled and unskilled labor from the developing world to the well-paid jobs in cities of the industrial world causes nations to reconsider their immigration policies. It may become cost-effective for U.S. companies to locate in countries economically underdeveloped but with a well-educated work force, like Cuba, Poland, and Hungary. And it may lead to standardized labor practices.[14] Figure 8-1 gives a very brief overview of work force growth in a number of countries.

FLEXIBLE PRODUCTIVITY IN IDEAS   The third and final area of flexibility which some U.S. companies have adopted from international companies is to be alert to new opportunities and make change happen. As you will study in a later chapter on conflict resolution, leading edge companies use conflict productively. Conflict caused by internal and external competition is directed toward innovative solutions. Companies that have been bested by their competitors have learned to change the rules. When 3M introduced the photocopier, they thought they stood alone and apart from their competitors. But three years later Xerox had left them behind by supplying the photocopier market with rentals instead of sales. At that time, it was a quite a revolutionary thought. Hitachi overtook Caterpillar in the marketing of heavy machinery by leasing the heavy equipment through Hertz Rent-a-Car locations. And, of course, the Japanese-devised Toyota Production System is pointed to as the most significant factor for quality improvement in Japanese products since World War II.[15]

Flexibility in organizations enables them to compete in timeliness. There is a rush to develop new products and then a rush to produce them and put them in the consumer's hand. There continues to be a need to improve the product before your competitor does and then to use what you've learned to develop the next new product.[16]

Figure 8-2 outlines three important steps to globalizing a business.

Flexibility The necessity for a manufacturing organization to participate in global competition, especially in productivity, service, and ideas.

Country Region	Labor Force 1970	Labor Force 1985	Labor Force 2000	Labor Force Annual Growth Rate 1985–2000
United States	84.9	122.1	141.1	1.0
Japan	51.5	59.6	64.3	0.5
Germany	35.5	38.9	37.2	–0.3
France	21.4	23.9	25.8	0.5
Canada	8.5	12.7	14.6	0.9
China	428.3	617.9	761.2	1.4
Indonesia	45.6	63.4	87.7	2.2
Mexico	14.5	26.1	40.6	3.0
Turkey	16.1	21.4	28.8	2.0
Philippines	13.7	19.9	28.6	2.4

FIGURE 8-1
World Work Force
Growth in Millions

Source: Adapted from William B. Johnston, "Global Work Force 2000: The New World Labor Market," *Harvard Business Review,* March–April 1991, p. 17.

FIGURE 8-2

Three Steps to Globalize Your Business

1. Rethink business strategies
   - Who are your customers and what are they looking for from you?
   - Who are your competitors and what is giving them their edge?
   - Who are your employees and leaders and what characteristics do they need?
2. Rethink work processes
   - What drives your processes and information flow?
   - What changes are necessary to meet changing expectations?
3. Rethink training
   - How can employee training equip the organization with global skills, knowledge, perspective, and attitudes?
   - How will new training functions affect employee selection development?

Source: Adapted from Bren White, "The Globalization Factor," *Training and Development,* September 1991, pp. 12–13. Copyright September, 1991, *Training and Development,* American Society for Training and Development. Reprinted with permission. All rights reserved.

How International Business Is Organized

A multinational or transnational corporation operates in one or more countries in addition to the country of its origin—its home country. The extent to which having multiple operations in different nations affects its identity depends upon such things as how much of its operation is here or there; who owns and controls the operation; how it is "legally" organized; and who are its employees and managers.

GEOGRAPHY AND SCOPE   Multinational Corporations (MNC), transnational organizations, or global enterprises are all terms used to describe businesses that operate in the international arena. These are businesses that do more than just buy or sell abroad. Some significant portion of their operation is carried on across national borders.

This IBM plant, located in Mexico, is an integral part of the U.S.-based company.

Every business is housed at some specific location or locations within the boundaries of a nation. Typically an organization identifies itself by that nation—a U.S. business, a German company, or a Japanese corporation. Multinational corporations are said to be "stateless." For an MNC to be stateless either the country in which it operates in has no influence on its operation, or *each* country it operates in has an *equal* influence on its operation. As an example, a study disputes the likelihood that each country it operates in has an equal influence on it. The study compares a company's assets and the number of employees in its *home country* with assets and employees *outside* of its home country. The chart in Fig. 8-3 demonstrated that more than 50 percent of a company's assets and employees usually reside in one's home country.

As likely as not, "outside of home country operations" will be distributed through many different countries; therefore the home country is still a *major influence* on the company's business.

OWNERSHIP AND CONTROL   Most multinational corporation operate as parent companies, located in the home country, with subsidiaries in one or more foreign countries. Under this structure the influence of the home country on the MNC is significant, because it is most likely that the controlling shareholders of the parent corporation are citizens of the home country. Certainly with 100 percent of the ownership of the subsidiaries by the parent company, the home country exerts a significant influence on subsidiaries.

Ownership of the subsidiaries by the parent company means that all profits of the subsidiaries belong to the parent company. The parent company would trade and deal in its home currency, which would probably influence the MNC to keep investment in its home nation. Because subsidiaries are wholly owned by the parent corporation, the people of the foreign country in which it is located could not have any ownership interest in that company. Their control would be limited to what they might exert as employees.

EMPLOYEES   For most MNCs, the majority of its work force are citizens of its home country rather than of any other *one* country. Collectively, employees of its foreign operations may represent more than the home country employees, but no other *one* nationality will exceed its home base employees. Typically, the top management of an MNC's subsidiaries are home country nationals or host country nationals who, by working for the parent corporation in the home country, have proven to be compatible.

The options for an MNC to choose its personnel in the global marketplace must be carefully considered. Typically, an MNC will use one of two approaches in staffing a "host" country office. Either a manager from the home country who has international experience will be detailed to the host country; or a host coun-

Company	Percent of Assets *outside* home country	Percent of Employees *outside* home country
IBM (1989)	46	44
General Motors (1989)	24	31
Dupont (1989)	35	24
General Electric (1989)	9	17

Source: Copyright 1992 by The Regents of the University of California. Reprinted from the *California Management Review*, vol. 34, no. 2. By permission of The Regents.

FIGURE 8-3

Examples of Multinational's International Presence

try manager who has trained and worked within the MNC's home country will be promoted to the host country slot.

In either case problems can develop. For the home country managers, the out-of-country assignment is probably a step on a career ladder and will be of brief duration. However, the home country manager could fail to ever get command of the needs of that host country office before moving on. The host country manager might perform better being familiar with the needs of the host country operation, but may never fully accept or be accepted by the MNC. Typically, such host country managers *are not* candidates for promotion to the top slots of the MNC. With that kind of segregation, few MNCs can boast of a truly "global work force."[17]

LEGAL SITE   A company is chartered or formed under a nation's laws. There are no "international" charters. Therefore, from a purely legal perspective, an MNC has to have a home country. The home country of an MNC may raise questions about such things as which tax and environmental laws apply to the subsidiaries. Issues of security and diplomatic allegiance might also be raised.

To the degree that the various components above exist within an MNC, its corporate culture will be influenced by the national culture of its home country. However, albeit to a lesser extent, its subsidiaries will also exert an influence on its corporate culture. Understanding the varieties of national cultures may enable a global manager to better prepare his or her company for the international arena.

UNDERSTANDING CULTURES

Corporate culture A system of shared beliefs, values, and behaviors that develop within a corporation.

In a later chapter we will study the *corporate culture* as the system of shared beliefs, values, and behaviors that develop within a corporation. The corporate culture affects how an organization copes with change and competition, whether it is in the terms of technology or its people. The corporate culture is, by necessity, influenced by the personal culture or cultures of its employees, its customers, its suppliers, and its regulators. An individual is raised in a society with a style of living developed and transmitted by people of the past. Ideas, habits, attitudes, customs, and traditions have become acceptable and standardized for a particular group as their way of coping with their environment and its changing conditions. Whether a U.S. company trades, hires, or relocates across borders, it must be able to interact with people from different cultures. Following are some ways managers can learn to appreciate other cultures.

Characteristics of Culture

People create a culture as a way of adapting to their physical environment. Customs, practices, beliefs, and traditions for development and survival are passed along from generation to generation. We are conditioned to accept what has been passed down as a fundamental truth whose source can no longer be identified. Culture helps us make sense out of our surroundings and by providing ready-made solutions to problems, establishing patterns of relations, and preserving group consensus, facilitates day-to-day living.

The following ten characteristics of cultures can help managers study their own and other cultures.

- *Sense of Self and Space.* Each culture provides an individual with a sense of comfort within one's self. Cultures can provide that self-identity and appreciation in different ways manifested from extreme independence to extreme interdependence. The use of "one's space" and how people deal with interference of that space is also a characteristic of culture.

- *Communication and Language.* Verbal and nonverbal communication distinguishes one culture from another. A multitude of languages, dialects, and colloquialisms combine with body language and gestures to make communication very unique within cultures and subcultures.

- *Dress and Appearance.* This includes clothes, body adornments or decorations, hair, uniforms, and the like that predominate in a culture.

- *Food and Feeding Habits.* The manner, timing, and frequency of how food is selected, prepared, and eaten certainly differs from culture to culture.

- *Time and Time Consciousness.* How a culture views time can have a significant impact on how the culture functions. In cultures that view time as a cycle, constantly reoccurring, time is of little consequence. But in cultures that view time as lineal, it is very valuable because time, once lost, is never regained.

- *Relationships.* Cultures can organize its relationships between its members by age, sex, status, or degree of kinship. The family unit is the most common basic relationship within a culture, but within each culture the family has unique properties.

- *Values and Norms.* The needs of a culture will dictate its values and norms. A culture concerned with physical survival will value the gathering of food and the creation of shelter. A culture that has control of its physical environment may value the quality of life and meaningfulness of its existence.

- *Beliefs and Attitudes.* All cultures concern themselves with some beliefs or attitudes about the existence of some "supernatural" influence. Religions and religious practices play an important role and influence in the cultural development of a people. Attitudes toward women within a culture, for example, often flow from religious beliefs.

- *Mental Process and Learning.* Each culture has a reasoning process and an accepted system for learning. One might emphasize abstract thinking and another rote memory.

- *Work Habits and Practices.* How a people view work, its divisions, its rewards, and the types of work it values is an important characteristic of its culture.

The "OB in Practice," Negotiating in the Global Workplace, gives the student a practical look at how cultural differences can affect the workplace.

Cultural Systems

Anthropologists offer a systems approach to understanding the differences between cultures. The systems outlined below refer to the ordered assemblage of related parts that form a unitary whole. Again, a global manager can learn to distinguish and appreciate diverse cultures by reviewing them in these systems.

OB in Practice

Negotiating in the Global Workplace

It is increasingly clear that understanding cultural diversity is becoming as important as technical competency, good management and sufficient capitalization in insuring the success of an organization. Because *negotiating* is a key part of everyday business transactions, recognizing the differences in cultures as to negotiations is critical.

Besides language differences which might impede negotiations, you should be aware of other *communication* differences between diverse cultures. One's attitude toward *time* is an example. For U.S. citizens operating abroad, being "on time" means one is there to do business and must be respectful of the other party. However, a person from another culture who is *not* on time is not necessarily disrespectful. They may just view time differently. For example, in African cultures, time is not seen as rigid. They value the flexibility of time and view people in a hurry with suspicion.

Some cultures shun confrontation, and so individuals may seem to agree with you on an item under negotiation in order to avoid overt confrontation. And yet, agreement has actually not been reached.

U.S. business people tend to behave informally in business sessions using first names and ignoring titles. Many cultures prefer formality during business negotiations and find the U.S. approach disrespectful.

Even a "contract" can be viewed differently by people from two different cultures. In the United States a contract is the end result of negotiations and contains all of the details of the relationship between the parties. In some cultures the contract is just symbolic of the *start* of a relationship. The business relationship is ever-changing according to need.

In the U.S. culture, a lone negotiator can "do it all," but many cultures separate the roles within a negotiation: one person to talk, one to record, and one to think up questions or answers. The approach that a U.S. negotiator will often take is to break the discussion down into discrete parts and trade items. Each piece can be decided and then put aside. Many other cultures, however, see the negotiations as a singular item, so that no piece is decided until *all* the pieces are decided.

Finally, U.S. negotiators have to be aware of where the decision-making power resides in the other party. Some cultures have a very rigid vertical hierarchy and no one but the person at the top can decide. Negotiations that seem to have concluded may well be reactivated when the top fails to agree to what their negotiators said.

Source: Adapted from Michael Kublin and Robert Brady, "International Business Negotiating," *Nebraska Business Development Center Report*, no. 145, December 1991, pp. 1–4.

KINSHIP SYSTEM   Cultures are analyzed, compared and contrasted by the way people relate to one another. How a family is defined and how children are born, trained, and socialized are examples. Differences in the familiar relationships between cultures can impact the way jobs are acquired or managed.

EDUCATIONAL SYSTEM   A culture provides its young or new members with information, skill, knowledge, and values through formal and informal education. The ability to train employees may depend upon how that training coincides with the educational culture of the employees.

ECONOMIC SYSTEMS   For the current generation of Americans, separating cultures by their economic systems was certainly the most understandable. Cultures were either capitalistic or socialistic. With the collapse of the Communist world, the economic systems within cultures will have to be reexamined. How each culture produces and distributes its goods and services within and outside of its own sphere has a tremendous impact upon the shape of multinational companies.

POLITICAL SYSTEM   Democracy, communism, dictatorships, oligarchy, and monarchies all still exist in various forms, pure or diluted, throughout the world. Operating within these diverse systems is one major challenge of the multinational corporation.

RELIGIOUS SYSTEM   The spiritual side of a culture provides the meaning and the motivation of a people beyond its material concerns. Numerous wars have been waged over differences between the religions of two cultures. And certainly of all interactions between cultures, attempts to change the religious beliefs of a culture stands out as the most destructive.

Five Dimensions of Culture

The third way cultures can be dissected to assist global managers in their understanding is to identify the *five dimensions of culture* which impact management styles. These five dimensions were formulated by Dr. Geert Hofstede and Michael Harris Bond from studies they conducted.[18] The dimensions are power distance, uncertainty avoidance, individualism–collectivism, masculinity–femininity, and Confucian dynamism.

Dimensions of culture
Power distance, uncertainty avoidance, individualism–collectivism, masculinity–femininity, and Confucian dynamism.

POWER DISTANCE   The first dimension of a culture, *power distance*, indicates to what extent a society accepts that there is an unequal distribution of power within its society.

Power distance
Indicates to what extent a society accepts that there is an unequal distribution of power within its society.

If a culture has a *small power distance,* then it believes the inequity in society should be eliminated. Both superiors and subordinates see each other as people and accept the hierarchy only as a necessary convenience. A redistribution of power among the various parties is possible and to a certain extent nonthreatening. Redistribution of power is a way to change society.

If a culture has a *large power distance,* then the inequality experienced in that culture, the ordering of people into a high or low place is correct and should be protected. Superiors and subordinates are not the same kind of people. The hierarchy exists because of the inequality and needs to be preserved to protect the social system. Change to the system only comes through a dethroning of those in power and is, therefore, threatening to the culture.

UNCERTAINTY AVOIDANCE   This dimension of culture, *uncertainty avoidance*, indicates to what extent a society feels threatened by uncertainty.

Uncertainty avoidance
To what extent a society feels threatened by uncertainty.

If a country has *weak uncertainty avoidance,* it accepts that uncertainty is inherent in life. There is less stress; aggressive behavior is frowned upon; tolerance of differences is higher and dissent is allowed. Time is free and rules should be scarce.

A *strong uncertainty avoidance* culture views uncertainty as a threat and its anxiety is high. Time is money; aggressive behavior is accepted and hard work the norm. Consensus is very important and rules are there to be followed and enforced.

Individualism—collectivism Compares a loosely knit social framework in which people care for themselves and their immediate family with a tight social framework.

INDIVIDUALISM–COLLECTIVISM   This dimension, *Individualism v. Collectivism,* compares a loosely knit social framework in which people care for themselves and their immediate family with a tight social framework in which *in-groups* look after each other and expect absolute loyalty.

In an *individualist* culture, the "I" is predominant. Identity is based on the individual. Involvement with organizations is calculative, that is, only done for a purpose. Leadership, individual performance, and initiative are valued.

In a *collectivist* culture, "we" consciousness is paramount. Identity is based in the social system. Involvement with organizations is moral; membership an ideal. Order, duty, and security are valued and are provided by the group.

Masculinity—Femininity Attributes that are measured in the dimensions of culture. If masculine culture: men are assertive, women nurturing; if feminine culture: sex roles are more fluid and equality of the races is normal.

MASCULINITY–FEMININITY   So called "masculine" and "feminine" attributes are measured in this dimension of cultures.

In a *masculine* culture, men are assertive and women nurturing; sex roles are clearly delineated and men dominate the society. One lives to work; money and things are important; and big and fast are beautiful. Ambition and performance counts; machismo is appreciated.

In a *feminine* culture sex roles are more fluid and equality of the races is normal. While you need to work to live, the quality of life is important as are people and the environment. Service and cooperation counts; sympathy for the unfortunate is appreciated.

Confucian Dynamism Identifies the value a society places on persistence, ordered relationships, thrift, a sense of shame or guilt, and status, as well as a respect for tradition and personal stability.

CONFUCIAN DYNAMISM   This dimension of culture identifies the value a society places on persistence, ordering relationships, thrift, a sense of shame or guilt, and status as well as saving face, respecting tradition, and personal stability. In a culture that is high in Confucian dynamism, these values are held in high esteem. In a culture low in Confucian dynamism, those values are not of primary concern.

The practical application of an understanding of the cultural dimensions above might be demonstrated by reviewing employee performance review systems in the different cultural settings.

In an individualistic society like the United States, the performance appraisal is critical to the employer–employee relationship. Evaluating exactly how well or how poorly an individual is performing is necessary.

In a collectivistic culture, such an individual evaluation might be meaningless. As a group member, the employee never stands alone or apart from the group. It might be impossible to evaluate an individual on his or her solitary performance.

In a masculine culture the end might justify the means, so a performance appraisal may be nothing more than a recitation of end results. Whereas in a feminine culture, the performance of an employee might be judged on how he or she interacted with coworkers; and how he or she improved the work environment while meeting work objectives.

One can imagine that in a culture with a small power distance, the appraisal process is oriented toward a dialogue between the superior and subordinate, not quite as equals, but darn close. While in a high power distance culture, the evaluation process itself, might not even exist. Power inequality would make feedback from an inferior an anomaly.

Finally, imagine the reaction to a performance appraisal in a strong uncertainty avoidance culture where anxiety manifests itself in stress, aggressiveness, and rigid rules. Certainly the appraisal process is seen as a threat to one's job and security. A superior would have to approach the subordinate prepared to *defend* the appraisal. Whereas, in a weak uncertainty avoidance culture, a much more *laissez-faire* attitude toward evaluations might be exhibited. Criticism might be seen as constructive and useful, and not necessarily threatening.[19]

Figure 8-4 lists examples of how nations fall into the five dimensions outlined above.

Aspects of Culture

Let us explore the various aspects of culture as each impacts the business culture.

FIGURE 8-4

Nations Exhibiting Extremes in Cultural Dimensions

Small Power Distance	Large Power Distance
Austria	Philippines
Denmark	Mexico
Israel	Venezuela
New Zealand	Yugoslavia
Ireland	India
Sweden	Singapore

*United States is 15th among 40 so tends to small power distance.

Weak Uncertainty Avoidance	High Uncertainty Avoidance
Singapore	Greece
Denmark	Portugal
Sweden	Japan
Hong Kong	Belgium
Ireland	Peru
Great Britain	Yugoslavia

*United States is 9th out of 40 so tends to weak uncertainty avoidance.

Individualistic	Collectivist
United States	Pakistan
Australia	Colombia
Great Britain	Venezuela
Netherlands	Taiwan
Canada	Peru
New Zealand	Singapore

*United States is 1st out of 40 so is highly individualistic.

Masculine	Feminine
Japan	Sweden
Austria	Norway
Venezuela	Denmark
Italy	Netherlands
Mexico	Yugoslavia
Ireland	Chile
Switzerland	Finland

*United States is 28th out of 40 so tends to be masculine.

High Confucian Dynamism	Low Confucian Dynamism
Hong Kong	Canada
Singapore	United Kingdom
Japan	United States
South Korea	Pakistan
Taiwan	Philippines

*United States is grouped with other 'Nordic' countries with low Confucian dynamism.

Source: Adapted from Geert Hofstede, *Culture's Consequences: International Differences in Work-Related Values,* Beverly Hills, California: Sage, 1984, and Geert Hofstede and Michael H. Bond, "The Confucius Connection: From Cultural Roots to Economic Growth," *Organizational Dynamics,* vol. 16, 1988, and Geert Hofstede, "Motivation, Leadership and Organizations: Do American Theories Apply Abroad?" *Organizational Dynamics,* Summer 1980.

Communication
A process of interaction.

COMMUNICATION   Communication is a process of interaction, it involves a sender, a receiver, and a message. Every individual approaches his or her role as sender or receiver from a unique field of experience. Included in all of the things of your makeup is your culture. Therefore, culture plays a significant part in any communication.

Communication cannot be avoided. We communicate by our activity or inactivity. We send some kind of message in every human contact. Communication does not mean comprehension. Understanding is dependant upon the sender and the receiver interpreting the symbols used—be they words or actions—in the same way. Communication happens and cannot be undone or withdrawn. It can, however, be explained, clarified, or excused. Communication in the global context can be anything but simple. The young American in the following "Profile" has some very practical communication advice for someone hoping to do business in Japan.

Language is one of the features of human beings which sets us apart from animals. By language we not only convey information about past, present, and future, but we also define our social life. We developed language as a primary way of communicating our culture to future generations. As language reflects reality as we perceive it, differences between cultures will be reflected in differences in their languages. Learning a new language may open one's eyes to the culture of those who use that language.

The global manager needs to communicate with employees, suppliers, customers, and governments. He or she can use interpreters, rely on bilingual managers or learn the language. Learning the language is, obviously, the best approach and indicates to the persons whose language you learned their importance to you.[20]

Nonverbal communication may be an even more difficult area for a global manager. Nonverbal communication includes sign language, such as a gesture for a waiter's attention, and action language—movements that accompany normal activities, such as making or not making eye contact when conversing. In some cultures, people stand very close to each other when talking. In the United States, people like a "comfort zone" around them and are uncomfortable when someone comes in too close. Insensitive Americans have been known to back up continually during social events in a foreign country, just to be followed by the person who could not understand the distancing.[21]

Cultural differences in both areas of communication need to be understood.

EDUCATION   For the global manager, the differences between educational systems among world cultures is critical. Education, values, and religion are three aspects of culture that give individuals their basic motivation for actions.

Education includes the socialization of a child who, at birth, can only be egocentric, recognizing only his or her own needs. As a child is socialized, he or she learns of others' needs and recognizes that rules exist within a society to balance competing needs.

The way one's culture approaches the education of its youth has significant impact upon the way workers can be trained or educated in the workplace. In a survey of over 11,000 managers around the world conducted by Harvard Business School in 1991, 77 percent believed their businesses should be actively involved in their country's education system. They believed that the quality of education in their country suffered if the business community was not involved.[22] Global managers need to take into account the cultural education of its employees when designing training programs. A corporation may have to decide whether

Profile

Lee Kaukas
Coordinator For International Relations
International Affairs Division
Miyagi Prefectural Government
Miyagi, Japan

DOING BUSINESS IN JAPAN

In building any business relationship, one must do her homework before meeting with the prospective client, coworker, or employer. This also holds true for Americans forming business relations with the Japanese. To successfully deal with the Japanese in business, there is no formula for Americans to follow, but there are many things for us to learn about and consider. By looking at a few basic do's and don'ts, you will have a better idea of how to understand what's going on around you (even if you don't speak Japanese), and you will have begun your homework for a business challenge that, with the shrinking of our world through the expansion of economic ties, is coming closer and closer to home.

Do's

1. Do go into the beginning of the relationship expecting it to take a long time for anything to actually get done. The Japanese are infamous for the layers of red tape they use to make mailing even a form letter a week-long process. If you realize that the process will be long, you put the Japanese at ease, and you make the process easier on yourself.

2. Do be sensitive to mixed signals from your Japanese counterparts. If they seem to be smiling and nodding politely while being very wary of committing to anything, pay attention.

3. Do have your own goals and motivations clearly defined. By doing so, you eliminate confusion.

4. Do find out what the people with whom you are speaking can really do to form a relationship between your business and theirs. The people you see most often probably have little actual clout. The higher-ups will probably really be making decisions, based in part upon the information they receive from the people you see.

5. Do be open to being socially entertained after business hours. The Japanese love to take guests out on the town, and they find this time in a relaxed environment essential to making business deals. You do not have to drink a lot at these gatherings, just being there and taking part is enough.

Don'ts

1. Don't ask questions too directly. Of course, you want to figure out what the company you are dealing with does and their attitudes and ideas about a variety of issues, but bombarding them with too many questions too soon will not help you. This does not mean that you should not ask any questions, but take it slow.

2. Don't be negative. Do be positive. Even though the Japanese act like they haven't taken great pains to plan your visit, they have. Show them how much you appreciate it by telling them so.

3. Don't be too worried about making social faux pas while in Japan. The Japanese are very understanding about foreigners not being comfortable or familiar with their customs. They will tell you what's appropriate for you to do. Pay attention to what they are doing, and you won't have problems.

4. Don't forget to take gifts to the Japanese. Even though you shouldn't worry too much about making social faux pas, this will be a kind gesture that the Japanese appreciate. These gifts need not be anything big; small token gifts, like buttons or pens from your company, are fine.

5. Don't wear clothing that is not "bow-able." Scoop-necked blouses will be problematic when you are trying to politely bow to the president of the Japanese company with which you're trying to form an alliance. Consider this when you dress.

---

it is training the employees in a technical skill only, or if it wants to train them in the corporation's culture as well. The manager may find that training cannot be done in a traditional textbook—classroom format—but must be a demonstration, show-and-tell format, because of the language differences confronting him or her.

The training system, as for other performance systems, must have a reward system that reflects the values of the employees' culture. Team rewards or recognition may be preferable to individual spotlights.

VALUES   Another aspect of culture is the value system that is in place within a culture. Answers to the following questions can give you an example of a culture's values.

1. How does this culture view the innate nature of human beings? Good, evil, or a mixture?
2. How does this culture interact with nature? As master, as subject, or in harmony?
3. What time orientation does this culture have? To the past, the present, or future?
4. What orientation to activity does this culture have? To doing, being, or controlling?
5. What are the social relationships within this culture? Individualistic, group-oriented, or hierarchical?
6. How does this culture view space? As private, as public, or as a combination of the two?

Using the outline as summarized in Fig. 8-5, you can see how a culture's value system impacts a manager's job. Certainly, how one views the *nature* of a human being will determine the degree of trust one gives him or her, or the nature and extent of discipline in the workplace. If a culture believes the nature of human beings is basically *good,* managers would tend to delegate responsibilities and rely upon workers' honesty in dealing with workplace thefts, for example. However, a culture that understands human nature as a struggle to overcome evil impulses, the manager may impose rigid systems to ensure honesty on the job.

One's understanding of humanity's relationship to nature may determine the environmental orientation of the workplace. In the U.S. culture, man has been seen as the master of nature. Subjecting nature to our needs, rather than modifying our needs to preserve nature, has been part of our value system. Other cultures that view harmony with nature as a value may tend to produce managers with more environmentally sound programs. Goal-setting, planning, and benchmarks for success may be difficult for someone whose culture is more past than future oriented. A manager in a culture that is more past oriented, revering, for example, glories of its past, may find it difficult to embark upon a new way of functioning.

	A	B	C
Nature of humans	Good	Good/Evil	Evil
Man to nature	Subject	Harmony	Master
Man to time	Past	Present	Future
Activity	Do	Control	Be
Man to man	Individualistic	Hierarchical	Group
Man to space	Private	Public/Private	Public

Source: Adapted from Philip R. Harris and Robert T. Moran, *Managing Cultural Differences*, Houston, Gulf Publishing Co., 1991, pp. 264–272. Copyright © 1991 by Gulf Publishing Company, Houston, Texas. Used with permission. All rights reserved.

FIGURE 8-5
Cultural Values

In a culture that promotes action ("Just do it!") motivating employees is not difficult. Motivating workers in a culture that values "being" might be a challenge. Self-starters in some cultures are a manager's delight. But in another culture the tendency to take control and get the job done may offend the manager's need to control the activity. Training workers from a highly individualist culture to group-think and group-act might be impossible. The "rugged individualist" is certainly an American ideal that is severely challenged by group decision making. But in cultures where a person identifies oneself through membership in a group, this management technique should flourish. Finally, organizing an international work force into the proper mix of open and private work space will challenge the most skilled global manager. For cultures that value individual privacy, open work areas create conflict. And a manager who tries to isolate individuals with a strong value of belonging to a group will affect productivity.

RELIGION   To understand the motivations of employees of a foreign culture, a global manager has to understand their religion. Whether one calls it the will of Allah, fate, God's will, or witchcraft, religion gives meaning to the unanswerable problems of mankind: suffering, injustice, ignorance. Religious beliefs can motivate a person's actions either by giving a reason for a good act or a reason to avoid a bad act, and can be the basis for acceptance of an inequitable social system. Following is a look at some of the major world's religions.

Nonliterate religions include a variety of beliefs such as Animism, tribal religion, or folk religion that are passed through an oral tradition. These religions share a belief that the transcendental power ruling the universe resides in natural phenomena or in identifiable spirits such as Mana or Wakanda. Most include ancestor worship and a reverence for nature.

Hinduism began in India where invaders from Persia met the indigenous population of southern India. As it migrated out of Africa to the Caribbean and to various southeast Asian countries, it changed to reflect the social practices of those nations. Therefore, the Hindu religion does not have one creed but many with some resemblance. For example, a basic notion of Hinduism is that all units of creation are different and unequal, and all groups within the units are ranked according to purity and power. This notion is seen most clearly in the "caste system" observed in India. The caste system is the basis for a division of labor in India where individual are born to be either landowners, priests, or servants. Hindu beliefs also include the notion of reincarnation, that is, actions in this life affect your future lives.

Buddhism was also started in India and migrated south and southeast to East Asia where it is the dominant religion. Buddhism was, in part, a reaction to Hinduism. The inspiration for Buddhism comes from a historic figure, Siddhartha

Guatama, who around 500 B.C. created a contemplative ethical system for people to follow. The four truths of Buddhism are that all existence is suffering; that desires cause suffering; that suffering ceases when desires cease; that the following beliefs will lead to an end of desires—accepting the four truths, having thoughts free from lust, ill-will or cruelty, abstaining from lying, killing, stealing, or sexual misconduct, avoiding violence and evil, promoting good, and engaging in meditation. The practice of Buddhism is less a religious practice (except for monks who dedicate their lives to reaching the *nibbana* or *nirvana*) than an ethical pattern of behavior. It has merged with the national cultures it encountered and has changed to accommodate certain realities. In Japan, for example, the Zen religion is an outgrowth of Buddhism but it emphasizes contemplative *action* not the contemplative *life.*

The *Islam religion* is dominant in the Middle East and northern Africa. Muslims accept and submit to the Will of Allah. Mohammed was a prophet of Allah who enlightened the people regarding Islam. There are five duties for a muslim—accept Allah as the only God and Mohammed as his prophet; observe the periods of prayer each day; give alms; fast during Ramadon (30 days on the Muslim Calendar), and make a pilgrimage to Mecca. The Quran, or their holy book, and the law of Islam guide the daily life of Muslims. Theirs is not a religion practiced one day a week, it is a way of life. There is a traditional group within the Islamic world—the Shiites—who are fundamentalists and who reject any non-Muslim ways. The more progressive arm of Islamic religion are the Sunnis.

Christianity is the belief in God as Jesus Christ preached it, and through His intervention, people can gain salvation. While there is division in the Christian world between the Roman Catholic Church and protestant churches about their beliefs in the sacraments, the role of Mary, Jesus' mother, and the way to salvation, probably the most critical difference is in the religions' hierarchy. The Roman Catholic Church has a global hierarchy with the Pope as the one and only leader of the church. Different protestant sects organize themselves separately and range from a church with an Archbishop as head to a church with no ministers, only elders. As discussed briefly in Chap. 3, the evolution of Protestant religious beliefs coincided with the rise of capitalism as an economic system. Justification for the accumulation of wealth became a religious tenet.

These very brief sketches of the five major world religions can alert a global manager to the differences which he or she might face in a different culture. The major religious events—the holy days or seasons of each religion—obviously differ and will impact production or consumption patterns. Specific taboos of food or drink might affect a business in certain countries. Alcohol, for example, is banned in some Islamic nations. A global manager must be aware of social unrest as a result of religious wars in some foreign countries and plan accordingly.[23]

Figure 8-6 gives some interesting statistics on the world's major religions.

SOCIAL ORGANIZATIONS   Each culture organizes itself so that individuals know how to relate to nature and to one another; they know their place or role; and they know what is and what is not acceptable behavior. The technological and communications systems in place impact upon a nation's culture. The goals for a society are to have a technological system that is environmentally feasible. It should produce a livelihood for its members without depleting its natural resources. It should be stable so it can absorb natural disasters such as droughts or storms. And it should be resilient, open to change if necessary.

Christian	32.9%
Hindu	13.2%
Islam	17.1%
Buddhism	6.2%
Nonreligious and Atheists	20.9%
All others	9.7%

FIGURE 8-6
Adherents of Major Religions as Percentage of World Populations

The challenge for the MNC and its global managers is to adapt its technology to the culture it must operate within. And it must address the social and environmental impacts of any transferred technology.

Social relationships in host nations affect the operations of MNC. A global manager needs to study and appreciate those relationships. How people organize themselves into families is a primary area of study. Extended families and strong family identification systems can promote family-owned businesses and/or closed employment opportunities. A hierarchy of classes within a society can have a direct impact upon how a business operates. An upper, middle, and lower class may or may not provide either employees or customers for a particular business. The ability or inability of persons to move up within the society's classes impacts on how well a company might function. The existence or nonexistence of labor organizations or professional groups can tell one a lot about the culture of the country. These organizations might exemplify the difference between an individualistic or collectivist orientation.

Finally, the *political system* or environment of a host country has to be acknowledged by a global manager. The practical aspects of security, adherence to laws, the rights and responsibilities to a political system imposed upon individuals are critical to an MNC's operations.

HOW TO BE A GLOBAL MANAGER

The Role of Global Manager

In a recent survey conducted by Harvard Business School answered by over 11,000 managers around the world, the findings confirmed that changes were indeed occurring everywhere—but the idea of a global corporate culture was more dream than reality. The study noted that despite increased cross-cultural business, cultural affinity was noted among managers from countries that shared a cultural heritage regardless of geographic proximity or current trade relationships. Managers from the English-speaking countries of Australia, Canada, Great Britain, New Zealand, and the United States have deep similarities. For example, they were considered the least cosmopolitan. Managers from Spain and Italy shared more with managers from Argentina, Brazil, Mexico, and Venezuela than Europe as they participated in more privately held companies and relied on governmental trade policies for industry protection. And managers from Austria, Belgium, Finland, France, Germany, the Netherlands, and Sweden boasted of being the most cosmopolitan and yet the most pessimistic about the future.[24]

The role of global manager is to make use of the understandings, observations, and learning about other cultures to perform differently than managers previously.

A global manager is *cosmopolitan* not ethnocentric; is open and flexible when approaching others; and is not threatened by situations or people quite different from those of one's own background. A global manager recognizes the need for *communication* and will learn to appreciate different verbal and nonverbal communication of others. Because a global manager is *culturally sensitive,* he or she uses the understanding of another's culture to establish effective relationships and guards against culture shock by *adapting to different cultures.*

The global manager must be willing and able to *adapt management practices* within the MNC culture to recognize cultural differences of its employees, and because he or she appreciates how cultural differences affect job performance, the global manager must know how to *motivate and reward* as well as discipline employees. Taking the best from all the cultural influences around him or her, a global manager *blends* differences and emphasizes simulation to create a work culture that values the employees of the corporation as *they are* and as *they can make* the corporation become.

To be *cosmopolitan,* a manager must be able to appreciate other cultures. This appreciation should be felt by people in another culture in the manner a manager displays *respect* for them. A cosmopolitan manager tolerates ambiguity and unpredictable situations without displaying irritation or discomfort. The manager relates to people in a nonjudgmental way, again accepting the differences in cultures as just differences, not "right" or "wrong." Finally, a cosmopolitan manager needs to be persistent. Tasks cannot always be accomplished as timely or in the same manner as one does in his or her own culture.

A cosmopolitan manager recognizes the *organization culture* of his or her global business as being unique to the organization and the national culture in which it resides. The ten aspects of a corporate culture, just as with a national culture, are: mission, scope, attitudes, values, language, training processes, reward system, rituals, relationships, and reputation. Regardless of the company's home office, its business within a different national culture will reflect that nation's culture. A cosmopolitan manager has to, again, respect those differences and put them to work for the organization.[25]

A unique approach to training global managers has emerged from Global Leadership Programme Consortium. This consortium is made up of 13 U.S. corporations, 12 Japanese corporations, and nine corporations from Western Europe that are selected to represent the "best practice" in multinationals based in Northern America, Japan, and Europe.[26] Following the "outward bound" school of management team training, executives from these corporations participate in a five-week program which includes 'survival' exercises, seminars, and international travel to analyze business opportunities in four or five different countries.

Participants learn to change the way they attack problems—recognizing, for example, that everyone does not view *time* the same way. "Global speed" is not "American speed." Misunderstandings became opportunities to learn how others approach a problem. These executives learned what it was like "to learn" when starting from a different point of view.[27]

A different approach to cross cultural training can be seen in the way United Airlines has addressed its need to think "globally." Once it began to operate internationally, United needed to instill awareness among its employees of the cultural diversity of its customers. More importantly, it sought to make each of its

28,000 employees commit to provide "world class service" to its worldwide clientele. For on-ground personnel, training sessions cover technical concerns such as visas, vaccinations, and customs laws, as well as United's routes, levels of service, and frequent-flyer rules. Cultural differences are viewed as they relate to customer service, although care is taken to avoid stereotypes.

Training for flight attendants is longer and more intense because the in-flight contact with international customers is, of course, more extensive than for on-ground personnel. In addition to cross-cultural awareness, the training focuses on service skills, again, to present world-class employees to its international clientele.[28]

Finally, examine what one university is doing about global training. Since 1947, the American Graduate School of International Management has prepared students to work in the international arena. A school of approximately 1,300 students, Thunderbird (as it is called) boasts that more than 25 percent of its faculty are *not* U.S. citizens and its student body is made up of young people from over 106 countries.

Students spend twelve to eighteen months of class time focusing on business training, proficiency in foreign language, and an international studies core curriculum to earn a Master's of International Management. The emphasis of their studies is on flexibility and the human factors critical to success in another culture. The school produces managers who welcome diverse challenges rather than treating challenges as a necessary evil.[29]

Recruiters view an international MBA as a plus when filling positions for executives who will implement a global strategy. Jerome Chuzen of Liz Claiborne, Inc., and Colleen Hulce of Korn/Ferry International both responded to a *World Trade* magazine survey by calling such training a must.[30]

Airlines with international routes have to prepare their employees for cross-cultural exchanges.

Culture Shock

A global manager must be prepared for culture shock. Cultural shock, popularly known as *culture shock,* is a very real psychological disorientation caused by the anxiety that results from losing the familiar signs or symbols of our normal daily lives. We depend upon certain cues—words, gestures, customs, norms—to orient ourselves to what is happening around us. We are not consciously aware of all these cues, perhaps, until they are gone. When someone is put into a new and different cultural setting, culture shock can result.

Culture shock follows a predictable pattern. Initially, one might be excited and optimistic about the new surroundings because of the novelty of it all. Tourists are usually excited about the cultural differences they encounter on their travels. However, after a while, the novelty wears off, and one begins to struggle with living in the new and strange environment. Frustration and confusion at this stage is more notable and one's mood, if suffering from culture shock, is at its lowest point at this phase. Finally, if one is going to adapt, he or she begins adapting. One is able to sort properly the new and different cues that are part of this new culture, giving attention to those that are important and ignoring the others. This progression from euphoria, depression, and frustration, and finally adjustment takes four to six months in most people.

The global manager who has gone through culture shock and becomes acculturated might experience "reentry shock" when returning to his or her home country. Having viewed the home country from afar, coming back into the home culture might be uncomfortable. The global manager might find colleagues at home narrow or closeminded about other cultures. The global manager's more

Culture shock A psychological disorientation caused by the anxiety resulting from losing the familiar signs or symbols of our normal daily lives.

accepting attitude toward cultural differences might really separate him or her from those colleagues and make the workplace uncomfortable.

The loss of some of the perks of expatriate living, like housing allowances and servants, will probably cause the global manager some adjustment period. Probably, the global manager exercised, out of necessity, considerable independent authority for the corporation due to the location of the overseas assignment. The loss of that independence and responsibility can be very difficult to overcome upon reentry.

Corporate Responsibility

A corporation can maximize its success in its foreign operations by carefully selecting and training its candidates for foreign assignments and by devising reentry programs. The need to prepare employees for overseas assignments can be demonstrated by the enormous expatriate failure rate many U.S. companies experience. The Business Council for International Understanding (BCIU) estimates the failure rate for U.S. citizens living and doing business in London is 18 percent, in Tokyo 36 percent, and in Saudi Arabia 68 percent. While some companies just compensate by hiring, training and sending more employees, the BUIC warns such an approach can be very expensive. Their suggestion is to prepare employees before dispatching them.[31]

In selecting candidates for foreign assignment, organizations should look for individuals who have well-integrated personalities. That is, they must be flexible, personally stable, socially mature, and professionally inventive.

Some issues to be examined when selecting a candidate for overseas assignments might be:

- to what degree does the candidate believe his or her own value system to be appropriate for anywhere in the world;
- to what degree has the candidate already experienced a different culture—travel, work, or study;
- to what degree is the candidate able to change his or her own behavior because of new experiences;
- to what degree is the candidate familiar with any different cultures and the specific culture where they may be assigned;
- to what degree is the candidate aware of the patterns of cultural differences and human behavior and understands verbal and nonverbal human behavior.[32]

Once a person is selected to go to a foreign assignment, the corporation should do some specific training to assist his or her successful acculturation. Among other things, global managers should be given extensive culture awareness training, in general, and specifically regarding the proposed location. Training should include language study, if necessary, and if possible, contacts with natives of the target country while still in one's home country.[33]

The corporation should make sure that the physical needs of the global manager regarding the move and the relocation are all planned. If possible, the global manager should be allowed to take a trip to the assignment area to get his or her bearing before the actual move. After arriving in the host country, more orientation and briefing about the country's culture and the corporation's culture at this location should take place. In "OB in Practice" guidelines utilized to prepare global managers by numerous multinational corporations are outlined.

OB in Practice

Employee Orientation for Overseas Assignments

In *Managing Cultural Differences,* author Philip R. Harris and Robert T. Moran have surveyed numerous multinational corporations who prepare their managers for overseas assignments. They have summarized the portions of these companies' programs as to the orientation of the employees as follows:

Phase One—General culture/area orientation

1. Become culturally aware of the factors that make a culture unique, and the characteristics of the home culture that influence employee behavior abroad.

2. Seek local cross-cultural experience and engage in intercultural communication with microcultures within the homeland, so as to sensitize self to cultural differences and how to cope with them.

3. Encourage spouses to develop programs and experiments that foster more cosmopolitan attitudes in the family, and counteract ethnocentrism.

4. Read, understand, and practice the corporate policies on equal employment opportunity and affirmative action.

Phase Two—Language orientation

1. Undertake sixty to eighty hours of formal training in the language of the host country to which assigned.

2. Supplement classroom experience with 132 to 180 hours of self-instruction in the language—listen to audio cassettes or records in the foreign tongue, read newspapers, magazines, or books in the new language, speak to others who have this language skill, and listen to music in the language.

3. Build a 500 word survival vocabulary.

4. Develop specialized vocabularies—on the job, with the maid, in the marketplace, etc.

5. Seek further education in the language before departure, but most certainly, upon arrival in the country of assignment.

6. Practice the language at every opportunity, especially with family members.

7. Use audio or videocassettes before departure and abroad to increase proficiency in the target language.

Phase Three—Culture specific orientation: training and learning

1. Learn about the specific culture of the country to which you are assigned, preferable during the six months prior to departure. Gather data about the size of the country and its population (demographic facts), the customs, mores, values, taboos, history, social systems, and communication patterns. Learn what is necessary regarding the host culture's family, educational, political, and social system; history and laws; regulations and taxes; food and housing; recreational and travel prospects. Understand and prepare for "culture shock."

2. Check out specific company policies for the assigned country relative to allowances for transportation, housing, education, expense accounts, and provisions for salaries, taxes, and other fringe benefits including medical service and emergency leave.

3. Find out and obtain necessary transfer documents (passports, visas, etc.), and learn customs policies and regulations, as well as currency restrictions, for entry and exit of both assigned country and the native land.

4. Interview fellow employees who have returned from the host country. Get practical information about banking, shopping, currency, climate, mail, and law enforcement.

5. Read travel books and other information about the country and culture, especially that provided by the sponsoring organization.

Phase Four—Job orientation: information gathering

1. Obtain information about the overseas job environment and organization; the clients and contractors; key personnel; the work schedule and hours; hiring status and contract monitoring; job drawings; specifics or other papers; purchasing and field procurement; project procedures and progress reports; quality control and job-site security; and labor relations, especially with third-world nationals and host country nationals.

2. Learn of the local population's attitude toward the project to which you are assigned, especially the government officials. Know what customs and restrictions to observe relative to the job.

3. Arrange for necessary technical training to assure high performance abroad.

Source: From *Managing Cultural Differences* by Philip R. Harris and Robert T. Moran. Copyright © 1991 by Gulf Publishing Company, Houston, TX. Used with permission. All rights reserved.

At this point, the novelty of the new location wears off and to a lesser or greater degree culture shock sets in. The corporation at this stage needs to monitor its global manager and continue to give support as he or she faces the frustrations that are predictable. As the successful global manager passes through that phase, he or she adapts to the second culture, develops friends, and works well for the corporation. A check list used by one company to make sure its managers receive appropriate global training is contained in Fig. 8-7.

The corporation can also take steps to help its global manager reenter his or her home country and domestic organization. For some global managers the experiences outside of their own culture has caused them to question their own values, attitudes, and priorities. When they return, their new ideas and attitudes may make it difficult for them to return to the same job they previously held. The corporation can help their returning employees by recognizing the reentry problems they face. First, the corporation should help the global manager as he or she prepares to depart the foreign location. Travel and transition assistance should be made available. Second, the corporation should recognize the changed

FIGURE 8-7

HR Checklist for Training Overseas Managers

1. Developing an overseas compensation and benefits plan, taking into account cost-of-living differences and any special needs.
2. Giving tax advice and financial counseling.
3. Supervising the sometimes extensive paperwork involved.
4. Assisting with housing and selection of good schools.
5. Helping the employee set up banking accounts and make cash transfers.
6. Transferring medical, dental, and school records, and assisting with inoculations.
7. Helping with absentee ballots and international driving license.
8. Providing language training, often through "immersion" courses.
9. Assisting with moves of household furniture and goods abroad.
10. Helping the training spouse get work permits and jobs abroad, if possible.

Source: Ellen Brandt, "Global HR," *Personnel Journal*, March 1991, pp. 38–44.

and enhanced talent and aspirations of the returning employee and give him or her the opportunity to use these talents *within* the organization. Finally, if necessary, counseling can be offered to the employee and his or her family if the reentry shock is significant and disruptive of his or her personal happiness.[34]

Relating to Economic Superpowers

As stated earlier in this chapter, economists see a new world order following the collapse of the Soviet Union. This new world order is economic and dominated by three superpowers: the United States, Japan, and the European Community. We will examine a couple of the current issues facing the United States as it competes in the global workplace with Japan and Europe.

JAPAN   The United States has for the past decade been obsessed with the rise of Japan as an economic power. Comparisons of how Japan and U.S. companies operate are plentiful. Hideo Ishihara, deputy President of the Industrial Bank of Japan, Ltd., in a speech at Duke University in the fall of 1991, contrasted Japanese and U.S. business structure and practices by describing Japan's as functioning on the "logic of community" and the United States as functioning on the "logic of the market."[35]

In Japan, corporate cultures emphasize long-term objectives over short-term profits, and employee cooperation over individual performance. Both of these traits are a reflection of the Japanese culture.

In the human resources area, four elements contribute to the cooperative atmosphere found in Japanese companies: lifetime employment, seniority systems, companywide unions and a "bottom-up" decision-making system.

About 80 percent of Japanese employees are hired by a company fresh out of school, universities or high schools. These employees expect to remain with the same company through their retirement. Frequent job reassignments within the company keep employees from falling into inertia while enjoying such *lifetime employment*. Most promotions are made on the basis of *seniority*. And, while a strict seniority system may result in a more able but newer employee being supervised by a less able employee, the benefit to the corporation is that all of the employees have an expectation of rising through the system.

In addition, the subjective nature of promotion based upon a merit system would not work well in the Japanese culture. Self-promotion and taking individual credit for success are not cultural traits.

Unions in Japan are primarily companywide unions. While such company-housed unions might join in associations with unions from other companies, the associations are not the major players. Negotiations are carried on within each company and the union is very much in partnership with the company.

Finally, Japanese companies are characterized by their management styles. As discussed earlier, Japanese companies use a team approach to utilize all of their human resources to produce quality products. Rather than a "top-down" principle, they work on a *"bottom up"* principle. The principle of quality control at the lowest level was taught to the post-war Japanese by an American, Dr. W. Edwards Deming. Deming's principles are discussed more fully in chapter 19.

Japanese business emphasizes long term performance over short-term profits. Part of this strategy can be attributed to the origin of its major players. Six Japanese corporations have accounted for about one-fourth of Japan's gross national product since World War II. Of those six, three are essentially descendants of family-owned industrial groups dismantled by U.S. forces after World

War II.[36] Japanese industrialists believe their roles within Japanese culture is to make their companies grow, to create employment, and to be an integral part of their nation's building.[37]

The intertwining of Japanese companies in *vertical* and *horizontal* groupings is also pointed to as a reason for Japan's incredible share in the world's economic pie.

Vertical grouping **Refers to the pyramid-type relationship between a manufacturer and its suppliers.**

Vertical grouping refers to the pyramid-type relationship between a manufacturer and its suppliers. Take, for example, an automobile company that relies on hundreds of suppliers for the components it needs to produce an automobile. The Japanese auto company forms intimate and stable relationships with its suppliers. Such relationships enable the manufacturers to take advantage of the "problems solvers" within those suppliers' companies. Innovative "just-in-time" management styles also become possible. These formal alliances among Japanese companies consisting of supplies–manufacturers–customers are called *Keiretsu*. Even Japanese companies operating in the United States will use a keiretsu supply company, before using an American supplier.[38]

Keiretsu The formal alliance among Japanese companies consisting of suppliers-manufacturers-customers.

Horizontal grouping **Business alliances formed by large corporations who meet regularly to compare notes.**

The *horizontal grouping* of Japanese companies refers to the business alliances formed by large corporations who meet regularly to compare notes. These alliances are characterized by close cooperative relationships, joint development of new businesses, and interdependent business decisions. In many instances, these companies have mutual or cross-holding interests in each other's company. Well established companies like Mitsubishi, Mitsui, Toyota, and Fujitsu participate in such alliances, also known as *Keiretsu*.

Joint decision making by these types of alliances and the Japanese government stabilized Japanese companies and provided the long-term growth that has placed Japan in a leadership position in the world's economy.[39]

Europe 1992 The European Single Act, lifted border restrictions regarding goods, services, labor, and capital between twelve Western European countries and established uniform standards affecting trade.

"EUROPE 1992"   The European Single Act, as of the end of 1992, lifted border restrictions regarding goods, services, labor, and capital between twelve Western European countries and established uniform standards affecting trade.

This agreement created four steps of economic and political integration of the European community. The first step, that farthest away from a unified European community, includes the emerging democracies of Eastern Europe: Hungary, Poland, and the former Czechoslovakia. The relationships in this step are built around various types of trade and financial cooperation. However, these relationships are new and largely undefined.

The next step includes the countries of the EFTA (European Free Trade Association): Norway, Sweden, Finland, Switzerland, Iceland, and Austria. These mainly Eastern European countries never joined the common market but may need to if they are going to remain competitive. Their participation is likely to increase as *Europe 1992* proves successful.

The third step includes the six countries that are full members of the European community but are not the initiators of the *Europe 1992*: Spain, United Kingdom, Portugal, Greece, Denmark, and Ireland. These countries have participated in past economic European unions, but not necessarily as the major players.

Finally, the last step, and the one the other countries are heading for, includes the six countries credited with establishing the European Community: Belgium, France, Germany, Italy, Luxembourg, and The Netherlands. Figure 8-8 lists the steps and the countries represented by each.[40]

The ability of the European nations to overcome cultural and historical differences and cooperate in the global marketplace remains to be seen.[41] The impli-

Japan prides itself on having the most efficient manufacturing plants in the world.

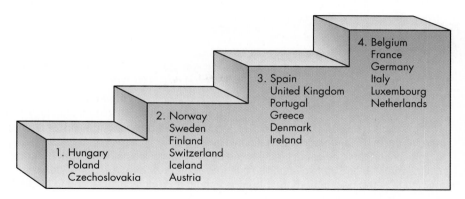

FIGURE 8-8
Levels of Participation
in *Europe 1992*

cation for U.S. companies if *Europe 1992* is a success is one of opportunity and threat. U.S. companies need to take advantage of the new markets and growth opportunities in Europe or risk losing its competitiveness in the global economy.

With uniform quality requirements, U.S.A.-made products will have a wider European market but U.S. manufacturers will still have to supply culturally specific goods. Marketing to a Euro-market will be easier, as will shipping and distribution. Uniform regulations will result in more uniform pricing. Operating throughout the European community will challenge U.S. companies to achieve the acculturation they need, not only abroad, but within their U.S. operations.

Despite the historic linkages with Europe, U.S. companies are still challenged in doing business with some European Companies. The gentleman in the following profile explains his experience as a U.S. manager of a French company located in the United States.

NAFTA AND GATT   One U.S. response to the consolidation of Europe's markets has been an increased effort to create a free-trade zone throughout North America. The U.S.–Canada Free Trade Agreement signed in 1988 and the beginning of a U.S.–Mexico Pact in 1991, signaled the commitment of North American countries to remove artificial impediments to trade and investment on the continent.[42]

In 1993, Canada, Mexico, and the United States completed their goal by the passage of the North American Free Trade Agreement (NAFTA). NAFTA created a free-trade zone for the flow of goods, services, and investments across the three nations' boundaries. The consideration of the trade agreement by the U.S. Congress generated opposition and predictions of a *negative* impact on the U.S. work force. Unions were particularly concerned that reducing trade restrictions would cause U.S. companies to relocate to Mexico for cheaper labor costs.

Initial reports about three months after the agreement took effect demonstrated a record increase in trade levels between the United States and Mexico. Mexican exports increased more than U.S. exports, but there was more Mexican investment in the United States recorded than the other way around.[43]

As the first year under NAFTA approached, exports to Mexico from the United States surged 22 percent over the previous year and exports from Mexico to the United States 23 percent. Ford Motor Company expected to export 18,000 autos in 1994 as compared to 1,300 in 1993.[44]

The next initiative in the U.S. effort to ensure its competitiveness in the world marketplace was the approval of the General Agreement on Tariffs and

Profile

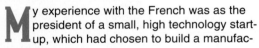

Michael Paynter
Former President
Spacecards Corporation

BUSINESS CULTURE EXCHANGE: FRENCH/AMERICAN

My experience with the French was as the president of a small, high technology start-up, which had chosen to build a manufacturing facility in the Jefferson International Riverport.

In accepting this position, I felt excited by the possibilities of working with a true multinational in blending two separate cultures into a new one. It was my idealistic dream to take the best of both the American and the French cultures and to blend them into a new hybrid embodying the strengths of both.

As the president, it was my responsibility to negotiate a construction contract for a 21,000 square foot manufacturing facility, work with the State, County, and the City, on a $1.5 million economic development bond issue, hire a staff, develop a marketing strategy, establish all of the appropriate business licenses needed, oversee construction, equip the plant, establish a network of material suppliers, and so on and so forth.

From my experience I will make several broad generalizations about French attitudes. First, punctuality is a very loosely defined concept. Once, when a very important meeting had been set with local bankers, our delegation arrived almost twenty minutes past the appointed hour. As we approached the bank, the lead of our group glanced at a nearby clock and declared in broken English, "good, we're on time." In my association with them, we never arrived at the appointed time for a meeting despite my efforts.

The French also have a very "proud" nature in terms of their designs and approaches to problem solving. Unfortunately for me, I did not understand what this attitude really meant until I was told that most French engineers "knew" that their designs were superior to others from around the world.

The French also are much more aware of and concerned with "aesthetics" of their products and surroundings versus the utilitarian attitudes of most Americans. In other words, my experience with the French left me with the feeling that they stressed "form over substance."

The decision to open the facility in the United States reflects another interesting attitude of the French. Given their attitudes about their engineering prowess, they are amazed that Americans will buy any electronic device that says "Made In Japan" or "Made in the Republic of Korea or China" but do not give their products the same respect and consideration.

In order to develop a successful business venture with a product they viewed as significant, a decision was made to include "Made In America" as part of the total package.

Another surprise for the French was the lack of "social support" on the part of the federal government here in the United States. Family leave, national health care, and other issues just beginning to gain discussion status here have long been a part of the socialistic society of France.

My most striking conclusion is that the French business persons that I dealt with did not have a very high regard for American professionals such as bankers, lawyers, and certified public accountants. In the United States, these professionals are an integral part of the business planning and execution process; however, the French that I dealt with reflected an attitude similar to that of the French judicial system. Whereas persons charged are considered guilty until proven innocent, these professions are utilized to rescue the business from trouble rather than pro-actively prevent firms from becoming embroiled in problems.

One of the most striking differences between the two cultures was the misconception that the French have of local U.S. politicians and the power and influence they wield on the business community, primarily financial institutions. During the course of negotiations on a revenue bond issue to be used for construction and plant equipment, the French called upon the mayor of the city when they were given terms by a bank that they did not find to their liking.

In their minds, the mayor held substantial power over not only political but also social and economic institutions. They continually attempted to manipulate all aspects of their move into the area by evoking the name of the mayor.

One of the most enjoyable aspects of working with the French is the reverence and ceremony placed around dining. No business of any importance was ever conducted without lengthy lunches, almost four hours on one occasion, with the appropriate mix of French pates, cheeses, and wines. Dinner was always after nine or ten P.M. and coffee, not the weak watery American brand, but coffee that would make U.S. espresso fall into the "lite" category was always the topper.

The most frustrating issue that I dealt with was that of effective time management. I consistently found that the French spent hours debating and discussing issues that most U.S. business persons would have dealt with in much less time. It was not so much the point as it was the battle. It seemed that there was constant positioning on even the most minute point.

I once jokingly told several of the Americans that I had brought onto my staff that I believed that the French felt obligated to fill every possible hour of the day with activity, no matter how mundane or unimportant.

While the experience did not end in the "new hybrid culture" I had hoped for, I carry with me many fond memories of the people of France, their hospitality, and their intense passion for life.

Trade (GATT) in December 1994. This rewrite of an existing agreement on global trading rules set a minimum standard of tariff reduction by an average of 38 percent worldwide and put into place protection of intellectual property rights. The 124-nation agreement was praised by supporters as providing a boost to the U.S. economy and by opponents as a threat to U.S. sovereignty.[45]

CONCLUSIONS AND APPLICATIONS

- The creation of worldwide consumer demands and quality standards, the elimination of comparative advantages in the mobility of resources and labor, and changes in the way manufacturing is done have all made it necessary for U.S. companies to reassess how they do business in the global marketplace.

- The competitive standard at play in the global marketplace are productivity, quality, variety, customization, timeliness, and convenience. U.S. businesses must find the flexibility in production and management to be competitors.

- Flexible management will involve consumers, suppliers, and manufacturers acting as a team so that unique products can be created in a timely and cost effective way. Problem identifiers, problem solvers, and strategic brokers are the employees of the future.

- Multinational Corporations cross country boundary lines in their operations, but they are still bound to their country of origin by virtue of their ownership, their employees, and their legal creation by their home country.

- National cultures develop as the way a particular group of people adapt to their physical environment. Their language, appearance, social relationships, and work/living habits are easy to identify. Their sense of self, of time, their attitudes and beliefs, their values, and their way of reasoning are more difficult to learn. All of these characteristics must be looked at when studying diverse cultures.

- Cultures can be studied by examining how kinship is handled within a culture: what educational system exists, or what economic or political system is in place in that culture. For some cultures, the religious beliefs they hold define and explain their cultures.

- The five dimensions of culture that can affect the management styles that can be used effectively in that culture are: power distance, uncertainty avoidance, individual–collectivism, masculine–feminine, and Confucian dynamism. How a culture views the allocation of power, the threat of uncertainty, the value of individual or collective achievement, the role of ambition, and the value of "saving face" tells a manager how employees in that culture might be motivated.

- Communication is a key aspect of cultures, both verbal and nonverbal communication. The failure to recognize how people from different cultures communicate can lead to unnecessary misunderstandings.

- Global managers are open and flexible when approaching a different culture. They are willing and able to adapt management styles to meet the needs of a different corporate reality. Global managers can learn to appreciate diverse cultures through formal education programs or through corporation sponsored cross-cultural training.

- Culture shock is a real psychological disorientation experienced by people who have lost the familiar signs or symbols of their own culture and are expected to process new and unknown signs and symbols of a different culture. Culture shock experienced by employees relocating overseas can be reduced if their employer makes an effort. Selecting the right person for a cross-cultural experience, as well as offering a comprehensive cross-cultural orientation for the employee and the employee's family can go a long way in reducing the expense and inconvenience of a failed expatriate experience.

- The Japanese way of doing business that links suppliers, manufacturers, and consumers into a vertical relationship and Japanese supercompanies into a horizontal relationship, furthers their national objectives of creating employment and rebuilding their nation.

- The formation of a truly united economic Europe under *Europe 1992* will present the United States with both opportunity and a threat. The opportunity exists if U.S. companies can master the flexibility necessary to supply culturally specific goods to the European market in a timely and cost-effective manner. The threat exists if the United States fails to do so and must concede the European market to Europe and Japan.

REVIEW QUESTIONS

1. Explain how worldwide consumer demands develop.
2. Why is the doctrine of comparative advantage outdated?
3. What is the revolution in manufacturing all about?
4. List ways U.S. companies tried to compete with foreign companies doing business in the United States. Why didn't these measures succeed?

5. Can a multinational corporation be "stateless"? Why or why not?
6. What are the ten characteristics of cultures and how can they affect the cultural systems in place within a culture?
7. Explain the five dimensions of culture and apply the extremes of both to a workplace example.

8. List the qualities necessary to be a global manager and explain how each is utilized.
9. What is culture shock? How can someone lessen the chance of suffering from culture shock?
10. Explain the way Japanese companies interact in *keiretsu*.
11. What is *Europe 1992* and what will it accomplish?

DISCUSSION QUESTIONS

1. The corporation of the future will rely on employees who are flexible, innovative and smart. Discuss how U.S. companies can find and/or develop such employees.
2. Present both sides of the argument that "multinationals" can claim no "home country."
3. Review the cultural values of Japan, Germany, and the United States as seen in the dimensions in Fig.

8-4. Using those values, explain why the Japanese *keiretsu* will or will not work in Germany and the United States.
4. Discuss the cultural shock some U.S. citizens experience upon reentry into the United States. How might that be avoided?
5. How are NAFTA and GATT affecting the U.S. economy and its role in the global marketplace?

CASE STUDY

Mid-American Multinational

Mid-American Multinational is a Japanese company that located its airplane assembly plant in Charity, Arkansas. When it opened its plant it went through a very special employee selection program. Applicants who passed written, medical, and drug tests were also screened for their ability to *learn and teach* new skills. After being hired they spent weeks in training to learn not only their own job, but some of the other jobs at the plant.

Mid-American MNC, however, still found that its American employees would stop work on the line immediately when their shift was over. Management decided it had to change the way its American employees worked for the company if it was going to be successful.

Mid-American MNC accomplished this by the following:

1. It instituted a no-lay off policy at the plant. If there are business slowdowns, new jobs are created so that no employee is let go.
2. The assembly line was slowed down and each employee was trained and assigned an average of ten operations before the product was moved on.
3. A "hot line" was installed so employees could ask any questions they might have of management. Even anonymous questions were answered in the plant's newsletter.
4. Monthly meetings with management insured that all employees knew the current status of sales and production and any other matters of concern. Employees who were being promoted were recognized at these meetings.
5. Roundtable meetings with top management and twenty employees selected at random were conducted periodically to discuss ways to make the workplace as pleasant as possible.

6. Mid-America's MNC Japanese CEO for the plant in Charity knew several hundred of the employees by their first names. He mixed with the employees, talked, and joked with them.

Mid-American MNC's employees in Charity, Arkansas, no longer leave the line when the shift bell rings; they finish the task they started. Turnovers at the plant are rare and only because of a change in marital status or because a spouse has been transferred to another city. The quality of the plant's airplanes are unequaled. Profits are up and there's talk of a plant expansion and upgrade to better current production numbers.

CASE STUDY QUESTIONS

1. How has this Japanese company adapted its business practices to its U.S. location? Why were these adaptations so successful?
2. When the Japanese CEO returns to live and work in Japan, what do you think he might be able to use from U.S. business practices to his company's advantage?
3. The employees of Mid-American MNC in Charity, Arkansas, rejected a bid for union representation. Do you think they made the right decision? Why or why not?

EXPERIENTIAL EXERCISE 1

Contrasting Cultures

Purpose

To learn to appreciate other cultures by observing how they differ from your own.

Step 1: Fill out the following questionnaire regarding your *own* culture or, if appropriate, subculture. If there is sufficient diversity in the class, divide into pairs and compare/contrast the aspects of your cultures. If there is insufficient diversity, invite students from other classes to join you for this exercise. Each student should be paired with someone from a different culture. Rejoin the class and share observations.

Your Culture

1. Communication style (nonverbal and verbal, as well as the language of business):

   _____

   _____

   _____

2. Food and diet: _____

   _____

   _____

3. Clothing (especially business dress): _____

   _____

   _____

4. Time sense: _____

_____

_____

5. Values and business ethics: _____

_____

_____

6. Work habits and practices: _____

_____

_____

7. Attitudes/practices with "minority" workers: _____

_____

_____

8. Family and marriage: _____

_____

_____

9. Other customs, traditions and beliefs: _____

_____

_____

10. What problems or challenges do you see in this business relationship because of some of the differences which you have noted above? _____

_____

_____

Experiential exercise 2

Your Foreign Assignment

Purpose

To prepare you for an overseas foreign assignment.

Step 1: The instructor will assign each student a different country assignment. You will be relocating to that country. Using only the information in this chapter and from your current knowledge about that country you will be going to, answer the fifty questions below.

Step 2: After answering the questions from your own current understandings, research your assigned country either through personal interviews or library references. Re-answer the questions.

Evaluate how "close" your answers were before you did your research.

1. There are many prominent contemporary and historical people of whom a country is proud. Name one of each:

	Contemporary	Historical
Leadership/Celebrities	_____	_____
A Politician	_____	_____
A Poet	_____	_____
A Philosopher/Intellectual	_____	_____
A Musician	_____	_____
A Writer	_____	_____
An Actor/Actress	_____	_____
A Radio/TV Broadcaster	_____	_____
An Inventor	_____	_____
A Religious Leader	_____	_____
An Artist	_____	_____
A Sports Figure/Athlete	_____	_____
A Business/Corporate Leader	_____	_____

2. Identify current, prominent political leaders and their titles.
3. Describe the political process or system of government.
4. Are women allowed to vote and hold public office?
5. Name the principal city and main industry.
6. What nonverbal behavior patterns that you use may be interpreted as "offensive" in this country?
7. What is the appropriate speaking distance between persons who are getting to know each other in a social context? In a business context?
8. How do people greet each other? Greet foreigners?
9. How do people say "good-bye"?
10. Is gift-giving a custom?
11. What are the people's work practices?
12. What is the state religion? Are other religions tolerated?
13. How does religion influence the people?
14. What are the religious holidays?
15. What are some differences between your religious beliefs and the beliefs of the religion(s) of the country?
16. What are the class or caste divisions?
17. Do people generally employ servants?
18. Is discrimination recognizable in the social structure?
19. Does dress reflect social or economic status?
20. What are the major occupations of people?
21. What are the patterns of social roles and relationships? (What qualities constitute a good husband? Wife? Daughter? Son? Grandparent? Businessman? Businesswoman? Foreign Businessman? Foreign Businesswoman? Guest? Neighbor?)
22. Is the "group" more important than any "individual" member of that group?
23. Whom do people go to for advice regarding their different problems?
24. Is education free? Compulsory? How many years of attendance is required?
25. Compare their educational system to yours.
26. Are female and male children equally desired?

27. Do members of both sexes share equally? Are they delegated similar responsibilities?

28. Are there differences between male and female roles in business? Do women have positions in all areas of responsibility?

29. What are the most important elements of success? salary? title? power?

30. Is there a strong "task orientation"? Is work more important than relationships?

31. What are some of the dominant business values?

32. What determines whether you will succeed or fail in business?

33. What are the "time" customs for appointments? Late or early?

34. In what situations do you behave formally or informally?

35. How do you expose an error to a colleague?

36. How is a reward given? Is an increase in pay an incentive to work harder?

37. How are people motivated in the host culture?

38. What ways might persuade effectively in this culture?

39. What kinds of food are eaten?

40. Are you expected to eat all foods?

41. Will you be expected to drink the local beverage?

42. What are their dining practices?

43. What rules govern dining at a restaurant?

44. What is the government's attitude toward the media? Is freedom of public expression carefully controlled?

45. What medical facilities are available? What is their state in terms of modern medical practice?

46. What preventive measures are necessary to maintain good health?

47. What kind of humor is understood and appreciated?

48. What is the relationship between this country and the United States?

49. Are Americans liked?

50. Do you think you will experience "culture shock"?

Take It to the Net

You can find this chapter's World Wide Web exercise at:
http://www.prenhall.com/carrell

CHAPTER 9

The Diversified Work Force

CHAPTER OBJECTIVES

1. To understand why a diverse work force presents a challenge to the organization.

2. To explore what "diversity" in the workplace means and why it exists.

3. To outline the differences between valuing diversity, equal employment opportunity, and affirmative action.

4. To learn some practical approaches to recruiting a diverse work force.

5. To discover the advantages available to companies that value diversity.

6. To understand the basic components necessary to change the nature of a corporation from one that ignores diversity to one that values diversity.

7. To become familiar with typical exercises in diversity-training workshops.

8. To understand how basic workplace communication can be a major obstacle to valuing diversity.

9. To review some cross-cultural differences in an effort to better understand other cultures in the work force.

Diversity Trainer

Daisy Wood enjoys her work. Her voice, her eyes, and her hands capture your attention, and what she says can surprise and amaze any group of business professionals. Ms. Wood tells the future! No, she is not a fortune-teller; she's a human resource professional and a talented, knowledgeable cultural diversity trainer. Recently promoted to manager of the Recruiting and Diversity Division of GE Appliances, a General Electric Company, Ms. Wood is responsible for all recruitment for the over 25,000 GE appliance employees as well as its diversity program. The future she foretells is about the American workplace in the next century.

Ms. Wood first approaches a group who wants to "manage diversity" by challenging them to imagine. Imagine a culture of the future where twenty-nine body parts can be replaced in the human body, where national leaders will need to be fluent in four languages, and where one million of the people in the United States. will be over one hundred dred years old!

The audience she is addressing is going to be asked to open their minds to such possibilities and to realize that if they and their organization are to survive in such a world *all* of their employees and all of their talents must be harnessed.

As Ms. Wood leads the group through various "awareness raising" exercises, the force of her conviction that we must value all people within an organization spills over onto the participants. It is not of question of "why?" anymore, but of "*how*?"

Since January 1990, Daisy Wood has been responsible for developing, communicating, and monitoring a companywide minority/female recruiting and development plan for the General Electric Company. In other words, she is supposed to ensure that the "GE is

Me" slogan in fact reflects the cultural diversity of the world GE serves. To hear her tell it, it is a labor of love. "Yes, I like it because it's the kind of work that makes a difference both individually and collectively. I'm helping individuals reach their potential, and I can enjoy the euphoria the group feels when they realize the advantages to treating the business environment like a salad, instead of a melting pot."

Ms. Wood's expertise comes from over twenty-eight years of experience in personnel issues that were not minority or women-oriented. She was with Exxon Corporation for twenty-two years developing a number of employee training and development programs. It was only in her last four years with Exxon that she focused on the "Year 2000 Project" that involved defining and planning for the influx of women and people of color into the work force.

A product herself of Affirmative Action goals in the early 1960s, Ms. Wood knows the need to move past equal employment opportunity and affirmative action to a society that values and uses the diversity around us. "Eventually, I would like to drop 'diversity' from my title. Recruiting new employees and bringing them into the company fully aware of GE's diversity culture will totally change the workplace. Diversity will be a way of life, not a goal."

The Nineties and a New Century

It's the '90s and the United States is facing an enormous challenge. The demographics of its work force has changed dramatically, and the turn of the century heralds a revolution in the way work will be done in America.

Sound familiar? With the recent advent of "Cultural diversity" as a management concept, it should. But the '90s referred to above are not the 1990s, they're the 1890s. Before the turn of this century, America faced the challenge of converting from an agrarian to an industrial nation, and of accepting and accommodating over twenty-six million immigrants who had come to this country during the half-century after the Civil War.[1] At first these immigrants were primarily western European—Irish, Scandinavian, English, and German. Soon, however, word spread of the opportunities for work and religious freedom, and masses of immigrants came from Italy, Poland, Austria, Hungary, and Russia. From all of these countries groups migrated to escape direct and persistent discrimination in their native lands.[2] This second wave of immigrant workers from southern and eastern Europe also came about because of America's need for cheap, plentiful labor to fill the factories and mines that multiplied during the Industrial Revolution.

Business in the 1890s had to create working environments that would enable people with limited experience and limited knowledge of English to function. Frederick Taylor, author of *Principles of Scientific Management,* and Henry Ford, whose success with the assembly line is legendary, are credited with establishing the work principles in organizations still largely in use today. These work principles:

Fractionalization of work Workers are taught discrete, repetitive tasks regardless of language barriers or educational achievement.

the fractionalization of work, where workers could be taught discrete, repetitive tasks regardless of language barriers or educational achievement;

the "one best way" theory, where the most efficient way to perform a job is determined by clipboard and stop watch;

dividing the work force, by clearly separating those who are hired to "think" (manage, direct, plan) and those hired to "do" (produce, perform);

protecting the process from the worker, with a system of control and compliance;

created the "top-down" management organization typical of U.S. corporations. And certainly, the growth of the labor union movement has its origins in the industrialized society of early twentieth century America.

Through World War I, the Depression, and World War II, America's production continued and after World War II flourished. Unlike Europe and Japan, the United States emerged from the Second World War with its industrial base intact. Our production system was geared to turn out standard, assembly-line products in high volume. It was a seller's market for the United States. There were plenty of customers, domestically or internationally, ready to absorb our goods.

But while we continued to organize and produce in the same way for most of the twentieth century, other countries were rebuilding using the technology of the twenty-first century in that rebirth. Their post–war recovery was slow, and out of necessity, designed to supplant the United States as the main producer of goods worldwide. This build-up of industry in sync with the latest technology during the last quarter of this century, placed the United States in a competitive disadvantage. The combination of facing this global competition and utilizing new technology has made U.S. companies reassess its most important asset—its work force.

In this chapter, we will examine the American work force as a diverse work force, how the diversity came about, and why managing it is seen as the challenge of the 1990s. We will explore approaches to that management and review real-life programs by companies on the leading edge of "diversity" training.

In subsequent chapters, those issues unique to the groups providing diversity to the work force will be discussed in detail.

THE DIVERSITY ISSUE

Workforce 2000

In 1987, the Hudson Institute, funded by the U.S. Department of Labor, released the study, *Workforce 2000: Work and Workers for the 21st Century.* The predictions of that study grabbed the attention of corporate America. While probably not the first indication of a changing American work force, the study certainly brought the future of America's work force changes into clear and dramatic focus.

The study predicted that the homogeneous work force, long composed of and lead by, white males, born in America would soon begin to change. New entrants into the labor force by the year 2000 would only be 15 percent native white males. Women, (white and women of color) would make up 61 percent of new workers; and people of color (including women of color) would provide 29 percent of the *new* century's beginning work force. Coupled with the changing faces of the work force will be a reduction of the numbers of new entrants as well. In the 1970s, when "baby boomers" were still joining the employment lines, the labor force grew by 2.9 percent a year. A growth of only 1 percent a year has occurred in the 1990s.[3] A new wave of immigrants into the American work force will be the solution to the shrinking labor pool just as it had been in the late 1890s.

The changing "face" of the American workplace is typified by LOTUS.

To meet the challenge of the twenty-first century, American businesses must have access to the best and the brightest employees. The work force must be willing and able to provide the skills and commitment necessary to compete in the world economy. They must be trained in new technologies, sometimes two or three times during their work careers just to stay even.

Leaders must emerge from the work force to motivate and direct the work place. These leaders must be able to understand the needs of the organization and its employees and see that both are reached. Figure 9-1 gives examples of just some of the changes that can be expected in the workplace by the year 2000.

If American business is to succeed, it must recognize the emergence of the diversified work force and find the ways and means to harness the energies, talents, and differences for tomorrow's challenges. Subsequently, we will look at specific issues affecting the diverse groups, but here, in brief are the major groups that provide "diversity" in the work force.

RACIAL AND ETHNIC GROUPS   Currently, racial and ethnic groups—people of color—make up one-forth of America's population. If current trends in immigration and birth rates continue by the year 2050, these groups will outnumber whites in the general population. More specifically, African-Americans now comprise 11 percent of the labor force and are projected to reach 12 percent by 2000. Hispanics are seven percent of the work force today and will be 10 percent by the year 2000, if they contribute the projected 23 percent of new work force entrants by that date. Three percent of the work force is now filled by Asian Americans, Pacific Islanders, and native Americans. By 2000 these groups will represent four percent of the work force.

Immigrants who contribute to this increase of people of color are underrepresented in the growth occupations that require technical skills and education. They are overrepresented in slow-growing or declining occupations such as farm and factory work.

Technological	By the year 2015, one million Americans will be over the age of one hundred years.
Productivity	Twenty-eight million American workers will work out of their homes.
Globalization	Successful executives will have to have a working knowledge of four languages.
Organization	Management layers will compress from an average of twelve to an average of six.
Competition	Workers will shift careers more frequently, some as often as every five years.
People	Companies will discover that its people are their biggest asset and diverse individuals will be able to make professional contributions to the workplace.

FIGURE 9-1

Changes in the Year 2000 and Beyond

WOMEN   Females are expected to provide almost two-thirds of the fifteen-million new entrants into the job market by the year 2000. The availability of women will offset the decline in younger workers. But female workers are still not utilized by corporations in top management positions. Women also concentrate in occupations that have been seen as "female" occupations and that pay less than traditionally "male" occupations.

OLDER WORKERS   Of the twenty-six-million people in the United States who are sixty-five years or older, four million are still in the work force. In the year 2000, the average age of America's worker will be thirty-nine, up from today's average of thirty-six years.[4]

AMERICANS WITH DISABILITIES   Depending upon the definition used, the U.S. Department of Health and Human Services has estimated that the number of Americans with one or more disabilities could be as high as forty-three million. Approximately twenty-one million of them are able to work. But fewer than six million have jobs. That leaves fifteen million, or nearly 72 percent, unemployed.[5]

SEXUAL/AFFECTIONAL ORIENTATION   The famous Kinsey report on the sexual attitudes of men and women in America estimated that at least 10 percent of the population is gay. If that is a correct assumption then 10 percent of the men and women in the work force are gay and constitute a greater percentage of the work force than some other minorities.[6]

The changing demographic structure of the U.S. work force mirrors the diversity of the U.S. population as a whole. This diverse customer base and the increased importance of globalization on U.S. industry will challenge organizations to appeal to a diversified marketplace. The challenge of managing a diverse work force will not be for organizational peace alone, but necessary for organizational survival.

The technological revolution that replaces unskilled laborers with machines is changing the way companies work in America. More skilled workers demand a more receptive environment. Companies who want to succeed in the twenty-first century are going to have to form pluralistic organizations.[7]

What is Diversity?

Every individual is unique. At the same time we share biological and environmental characteristics with any number of others. "*Diversity*" in the workplace

Bill Heavrin, as Chair of the Commonwealth of Kentucky's Task Force on ADA compliance, advocates for people with disabilities.

Diversity in the workplace The recognition of groups of people who share biological and environmental traits.

FIGURE 9-2

Primary and Secondary Dimensions of Diversity

Source: Marilyn Loden and Judy B. Rosener, *Workforce America! Managing Employee Diversity as a Vital Resource,* Homewood, Illinois, Business One Irwin, 1991, p. 20.

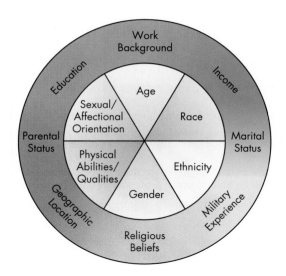

Dimensions of people
The properties and characteristics that constitute a whole people that both unites and divides us.

is most commonly used to describe the recognition of the groups of people who share such common traits. *Dimensions*—the properties and characteristics that constitute a whole person—both unite and divide us.

Primary dimensions are those human differences that are inborn and that exert a major impact upon us. Age, ethnicity, gender, race, physical abilities/qualities, and sexual/affectual orientation are primary dimensions at the core of individual identities. All of us view and experience the world through the filter of these dimensions.

Secondary dimensions are more mutable and can be changed, discarded, or modified throughout our lives. Secondary dimensions add depth and individuality to our lives. Such things as education, geographic location, income, marital status, military experience, religion, work experience, and parental status are examples of secondary dimensions. One can see the primary and secondary dimensions as a circle as shown in Fig. 9-2, with the primary dimensions residing within the center and the secondary dimensions on the outside ring of the circle.

People are grouped and identified most often and certainly in any initial encounter, by the primary dimensions that are most readily observed: age, gender, race, and physical abilities/qualities. Many of us live in homogeneous communities, or at least in communities far less diverse than our society as a whole. Therefore, our entry into the workplace may be our first encounter with a diverse population. As seen in the "OB in Practice" above, even "ugly" people are claiming rights in the workplace.

In a recent random survey of U.S. business organizations of all types and sizes, employers were asked about diversity issues. To the question, "What is meant by 'diversity' to decision makers in your organization?" from the 481 samples received, the characteristics of diversity were ranked as seen in Fig. 9-3.

Some employers volunteered the additional characteristics of language, education and sexual preference as also constituting diversity.

With the noticeable exception of "physical abilities/qualities," the survey confirms the recognition in the workplace of those *primary* dimensions of diversity that make up the core of an individual's identity.

In the past, the group that dominated the workplace—able-bodied, white males, between the ages of thirty to fifty years—set the standard for the most

OB in Practice

"Ugly People" Gain Protection

An antidiscrimination law passed in Santa Cruz, California, expanded the protections typically reserved for women and minorities to a new class of people. By forbidding jobs and housing discrimination against people on the basis of their weight, height, or physical characteristics, Santa Cruz became the first American city to actually grant legally enforceable protection to ugly people.

The law was in response to a newspaper story about a three hundred pound woman who was refused a job in a health foods store because she could not navigate narrow aisles to restock the shelves. The City Councilman who sponsored the law believed that women were often the target of unfair job discrimination because of their weight or looks.

Source: Adapted from Richard C. Paddock, "Santa Cruz Grants Anti-Bias Protection to the Ugly," *Los Angeles Times,* vol. CXI, no. 174.

---

acceptable employees. That standard resulted in an effort to exclude anyone who was different from meaningful participation in the organization.

In this chapter, we will explore in more detail the nature of prejudice and discrimination that excluded certain people from participation in the workplace. In later chapters we will look in detail at the federal legislation passed to relieve people of color, women, aged, and handicapped from discrimination. In this chapter, we will briefly review the 1964 Civil Rights Act and the resulting Equal Employment Opportunity and Affirmative Action programs as they relate to diversity in the workplace.

Stereotypes and Prejudices

A stereotype is a fixed and distorted generalization about members of a group. Stereotyping that stems from the primary dimensions of diversity—race, gender, age, physical abilities/qualities or sexual orientation—attributes incomplete, exaggerated, or distorted qualities to members of these groups.

As human beings, we process information by use of learned knowledge. A child whose fingers are burned when touching a stove learns not to touch the

Rank	Characteristic	Yes %	No #	Uncertain %
1.	Race	94.1	4.2	1.7
2.	Culture	86.3	8.4	5.3
3.	Gender	84.5	11.6	3.9
4.	Natural Origin	83.6	11.4	5.0
5.	Age	70.6	24.7	4.7
6.	Religion	57.5	34.6	7.9
7.	Regional Origin	36.9	48.4	14.7

Source: Michael R. Carrell and Everett E. Mann, "Defining Workplace Diversity Programs and Practices in Organizations," *The Labor Law Journal,* vol. 44, no. 12, December 1993, pp. 755–64. Reproduced with permission from *The Labor Law Journal,* published and copyrighted by CCH Incorporated, 2700 Lake Cook Road, Riverwoods, Illinois 60015.

FIGURE 9-3
Characteristics of Diversity

stove again. Such generalizations about the world around us are arrived at through logic, experience and available facts.

Stereotyping is not generalization. A stereotype usually comes through outside sources, not individual experiences. A belief is formed early in life by contact with our parents, teachers, neighbors, and contemporaries. A statement might be made that: "A woman's place is in the *home.*" In and of itself such a statement may be nonthreatening to a woman's right to equal employment. Nonetheless, it becomes a stereotype when exaggerated beliefs about a woman's ability to function in the workplace are told and retold and begin to be believed. A *stereotype* requires that the exaggerated beliefs about a group be sustained by selective perception and/or selective forgetting of facts and experiences inconsistent with the particular stereotype. All the years of experience each of us have had with women teachers, for example, are suddenly forgotten when one questions a woman's ability to succeed.

Stereotype An exaggerated belief about a group sustained by selective perception or forgetting of facts and experiences inconsistent with the particular stereotype.

The impact of stereotyping is to negate each person's individuality and limit their potential. To a great extent, people perform according to the expectations placed upon them. If the stereotype is that the person is not competent, then he or she might not perform competently.

Clinging to negative stereotypes about people different from ourselves results in prejudice. *Prejudice* is processing our stereotypes in such a way as to reinforce our own superiority over the members of that group.

Prejudice The processing of our stereotypes so as to reinforce our own superiority over members of that group.

Stereotyping and prejudice against diverse groups has been institutionalized in the workplace. It becomes, therefore, a function of the organization to recognize and eradicate both the stereotyping and the prejudice.

RESPONSE TO DIVERSITY

Equal Employment Opportunity and Affirmative Action

It became apparent during the Civil Rights movement of the 1960s that prejudice against African-Americans would not go away easily. In every area of society—educational, religious, and political institutions—the challenge was there to change the way white Americans thought and felt about black Americans. More importantly, it was a matter of urgency that white Americans changed the way they treated Black Americans.

Changing hearts and minds would take generations. Changing behavior became a matter of legislating rights and responsibilities.

Opening American institutions to African-Americans also opened such institutions to other people with differences.

In 1964, the federal government enacted the Civil Rights Act that made it "unlawful" to discriminate against an individual with respect to basic employment practices because of race, color, religion, sex, or national origin. In 1972, the Act was amended by the Equal Employment Opportunity Act which enabled the EEO Commission to enforce the Civil Rights Act in federal court when voluntary compliance failed. Affirmative Action grew out of these nondiscrimination, equal opportunity pieces of legislation. The federal government created the concept when President Lyndon Johnson, in 1965, issued Executive Order 11246 to require federal contractors to analyze their work forces and set goals and time tables to increase by positive action, their numbers of minority or women employees.

As opportunities in the workplace developed for those who were "different," people of color, women, and immigrants, the dominate group in the workplace—white males born in the United States—needed to respond. Because these hiring initiatives were "mandated" by government, the typical response was grudging compliance.[8] Six misconceptions about diversity developed within organizations.

- Being "different" meant being less able; as it took legislation to get those who were different into the workplace.
- Bringing diverse people into the workplace threatened the organization, because employees would no longer share a common heritage or have common goals.
- Sensitivity of members of diverse groups to an organizational culture that is sexist or racist is "oversensitivity" and disruptive of the workplace for no *good* reason.
- Members of diverse groups want to be just like members of the dominant group. Success depends upon emulating their attitudes, style, and behaviors.
- Equal treatment, which is required under the law, means the *same* treatment.
- Diverse people entering the organization must do the changing and adapting; the organization cannot, or will not, change.

The response in the workplace to the influx of people who are different was, in a word, assimilation.

Assimilation

Assimilation is the process of integrating members of diverse groups into the organization by changing them to *look, act,* and *feel* like the dominant group in the work force—basically, white males. How an organization goes about assimilating diverse employees into their work force might differ but some practices include:

Assimilation The process of integrating members of diverse groups into an organization by changing them to look, act, and feel like the dominant group in the work force.

1. Performance appraisals based upon the "white, male" standard, thereby forcing a diverse person to conform
2. Credibility and competency must be reearned at every level
3. Informal communication networks and decision making is closed except to those who are "like" those in positions of authority
4. Discouraging diverse groups from maintaining a support group as antiorganizational

Assimilation assumed that the dominant group's performance and style was superior to someone who was not in the dominant group. This devalued diversity in the organization and reinforced the value of homogeneity. "The problem with measuring everyone against that white male standard," says Gerald Adolph, a management consultant and principal at Booz, Allen, and Hamilton, "is that you set up a sizable portion of your work force for failure."[9]

Organizations may contend that assimilation is a proper response to diversity. Some companies believe they have been successful because the homogeneous ideal—a Lee Iacocca or a Ross Perot—made them succeed by their tough-no-compromise, macho approach to management. They believe that if diverse employees conform to those traits, they too will be successful.

But for companies that value diversity, assimilation is not the ideal. The basis for assimilation is bias. Pressuring diverse employees to conform lessens them as individuals. While in the process of trying to gain acceptance with the dominant group, they may lose touch with their own cultural background. An example is a woman manager who has been told to be more assertive and then later accused of being pushy and unfeminine.

When diversity is not valued, the diverse employee's accomplishments may not be noted, although mistakes may be magnified. African-American managers often complain that they are expected to prove themselves before getting a promotion while white managers are promoted on their potential.[10] There are few role models for diverse employees, and, to a great extent, those diverse employees who have taken positions of authority within an organization do not share the clout of white, male authority figures. Women and minority managers find themselves frozen in middle management positions or advancing only in "staff" type positions.[11]

Finally, the energy and effort used by diverse employees to assimilate drains them of enthusiasm for the goals of the organization. More and more diverse people are leaving the struggle to succeed within corporations and embarking on their own businesses. Between the years 1974 to 1984, women started their own businesses at six times the rate of men. Companies, like Corning Glass Works, in an effort to stem the flow of women and minorities, had to devise specific programs to retain a diverse work force.[12]

Pushing assimilation does not benefit the dominant workforce group either. It reinforces the bias that spawns this approach. It perpetuates stereotyping and prejudice in the workplace. Companies whose work force cannot adapt to the new century will not survive. And if the organization fails, the current "dominant" group will find itself jobless along with fellow diverse employees. With the breakup of AT&T in 1984, the downsizing of more than 100,000 employees caused some white men to rethink their biases. They became pragmatic when they realized it was going to take everyone, people of color and women, to keep the corporation functional.[13]

Valuing Diversity: "Diversity versus EEO"

The first step in getting a company to value diversity is to acknowledge the fundamental difference between valuing diversity and equal employment opportunities and/or affirmative action. As stated earlier, *equal employment opportunity* is a legalistic approach to workplace discrimination. It is against the law to deny a person a job or a job advantage because of race, gender, age, etc. *Affirmative Action* is a response to underutilization of protected groups in various job categories in which a business attempts to attract and advance people from such groups. Their failure to do so in the past was the result of discrimination. Valuing diversity moves past both of these concepts and results in management designed to reap the benefits that a diverse work force offers.[14]

Unfortunately, for many companies managing diversity is still seen as part of its Affirmative Action/EEO policies. In the survey referred to in Fig. 9-3, employers were asked if they believed "work force diversity" to be substantially different from equal employment opportunities and Affirmative Action. The results from the 481 businesses that responded were disturbing. Only 41.6 percent thought diversity was different from EEO and AA; 40.8 percent did not think

Equal Employment Opportunity A legalistic approach to workplace discrimination. It is against the law to deny a person a job because of race, gender, or age.

Affirmative action protects groups in various job categories from being discriminated against so that a business will attract and advance people from all groups without discrimination.

OB in Practice

Valuing Diversity Is More Than Equal Employment at Kinney Shoes

John Kozlowski, senior vice president of human resources of Kinney Shoes believes that serving a diverse customer base requires a diverse work force. He also believes that compliance with equal opportunity employment laws is not enough. "When we say equal employment opportunity is a good business practice, but all we do is compliance, we demean it," Kozlowski says.

In a proactive approach to diversity, Kozlowski created Kinney's Office of Fair Employment Practice that is not part of its human resource EEO/AA compliance arm. Through education of their managers, Kinney is trying to instill within the corporate culture the best hiring and management practices, so that the *best* candidates for hiring or promoting are identified regardless of race, culture, or gender.

The program used by Kinney includes an eight-hour "Valuing Diversity" seminar for executives and store managers that focuses on managing persons from different cultural backgrounds. Through a number of problem-solving situations, the training teaches the managers how different persons react to the same workplace situation. One example is to show how a native American is embarrassed by public praise from a supervisor, while a white American is honored.

Kinney Shoes, a wholly owned subsidiary of Woolworth Corporation, recognizes that its customer base, as well as its work force pool, will be made up of a greater number of women and minorities by the year 2000. Kozlowski sums it up, "If you're going to be in a business that serves this mix of people, you had better have a mix of people who understand them. Today's retail environment needs a diverse work force to service a diverse customer base."

Kinney Shoes boasts of a diverse customer base serviced by a diverse work force.

Source: Adapted from Joyce E. Santora, "Kinney Shoe Steps Into Diversity," *Personnel Journal,* September 1991, pp. 72–77.

they were substantially different at all; while 13.2 percent were uncertain as to their relationship.

As you continue studying this and subsequent chapters you will begin to see the differences in equal employment opportunity/Affirmative Action and valuing diversity. EEO and Affirmative Action are government initiated, legally driven efforts to change—from a quantitative standpoint—the makeup of a company's work force. From their inception, the emphasis was on numbers and assimilation.

Valuing diversity is a company specific, necessity driven effort to change—from a qualitative standpoint—the utilization of the company's work force. From its inception, the emphasis is on performance by individuals, as individuals. In an organization that values diversity, managing diversity becomes the substitute for assimilation.

Recruiting a Diverse Work Force

The transition from managing a diverse work force as an equal employment/affirmative action problem to an opportunity for an organization's success is difficult. It is interesting that almost 70 percent of the employers who responded to the random survey referred to in Fig 9-3, had a "recruitment" program that considered the concept of diversity, but only 16.6 percent had a program or policy regarding "career management" that included diversity.

The recognition that "recruitment" had to address diversity is more a function of facing reality than of a proactive attempt to value diversity. Recruiters are finding that the shortages projected for the year 2000 may already be upon us.

In a follow-up to the *Workforce 2000* study, the Hudson Institute surveyed 645 companies around the United States and found that over 50 percent of the companies are having difficulty in hiring secretaries and clerical workers that make up 15 percent of the work force, and an equal number are having trouble hiring professionals.[15]

Business must improve the way it recruits workers from diverse backgrounds if it expects to compete in the dwindling employee pool. In later chapters we will explore some of the internal changes companies are making in such things as benefit programs and career development to attract and retain diverse employees. This section will deal with the approach companies are taking to attract job applicants from diverse backgrounds.

Companies that value diversity want the very best applicant regardless of their race, gender, age, physical abilities, or ethnic backgrounds. To start the recruitment process they must recognize and acknowledge that diverse workers exist and need to be approached. Depending upon what the company believes its opportunities are to attract applicants among the diverse groups, it may target one market.

The City of Santa Ana, California wanted to increase its Hispanic employee population because 65.2 percent of its population was Hispanic. To do this each department established its own outreach plan. The outreach plan went beyond nondiscrimination to active recruitment. Each department was held accountable for the success or failure of its outreach plan.[16]

Many companies agree that in order to attract a diverse work force, you had better be able to demonstrate the job opportunities available to a diverse employee within the organization. Vons, a supermarket firm, is presided over by a Hispanic, Bill Davila. His success is touted by recruiters when trying to attract Hispanics to the food industry.[17]

Appropriate recruitment material should be prepared and presented. One company that was trying to increase its African-American labor pool got little from its advertising campaign that featured a white actor. When it changed to a black actor, applicants doubled.[18]

To recruit older workers, experts suggest becoming familiar with magazines that are focused on the "mature market" *Modern Maturity, 50 plus* and *Renaissance*.[19] One company, GB Tech, Inc., a Houston-based information-systems company, recruited retired high-technology workers to act as consultants for its bid proposals to NASA. The Company believed the experienced retirees would give this relatively *new* company credibility.[20] Other major media sources for various groups follow in Fig. 9-4. With the competition for skilled workers with diverse backgrounds increasing, organizations have to aggressively pursue talent in targeted media markets. In Jackie Strange's Profile, she warns employers how not to recruit women and people of color.

Unions and Diversity

Unions have been seen by many as the last refuge of white, male, native-born American workers. While perhaps still predominately that, women and people of color are joining unions in increasing numbers. African-Americans are more unionized (15 percent of organized labor) than the work force as a whole (11

FIGURE 9-4
Market Profile

Black Recruitment Market

MAJOR MEDIA SOURCES

Title	Frequency	Circulation
Black Careers	6x/year	400,000
Black Enterprise	Monthly	270,000
Black Collegian	4x/year	112,000
Dawn Magazine	10x/year	491,500
National Black Monitor (newspaper supplement)	Monthly	1.15 million
Dollars & Sense	7x/year	285,750

Asian Recruitment Market

MAJOR MEDIA SOURCES

The dizzying variety of languages makes newspapers the most cost-effective way to target Asian groups. However, researching the appropriate newspapers can be tricky. In California alone, for example, there's one newspaper that targets all U.S. Asians, three that target Japanese, four that target Chinese, and one that targets each: Filipino, Korean, Asian, Indian, and Vietnamese Americans. Standard Rate and Data Service can help you locate these publications.

Hispanic Recruitment Market

MAJOR MEDIA SOURCES

Title	Frequency	Circulation
Hispanic Magazine	11x/year	150,000
Hispanic Business Monthly	Monthly	140,000
Hispanic USA Magazine	Monthly	118,400
Vista (newspaper insert)	Weekly	1 million

HispanData has a database of more than 3,000 resumes in a variety of fields (805/682-5842).

Source: "Market Profile: Minority Recruitment,"*Personnel Journal*, December 1991, supplement.

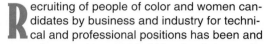

Profile
Jackie Strange
President, Professional Search Consultant

HOW NOT TO RECRUIT A DIVERSE WORK FORCE

Recruiting of people of color and women candidates by business and industry for technical and professional positions has been and continues to be a difficult arena. The corporate consciousness in hiring tends to gravitate toward those potential employees who "fit the corporate culture." That is, the candidate who possesses the personalty type, leadership style, professional image, and cultural values that match those of the corporation as a whole. However, for the majority of recruiting industries, the "corporate culture" is predominantly defined by Anglo-Saxon males. Therefore, problems arise in attracting women and people of color to these corporations as well as to effectively evaluating potential employee pools.

Attracting people of color and female candidates to an employer overtly desiring to recruit from one of these groups can be both delicate and competitive. These candidates may resist such recruiting for a variety of reasons, including tokenism. People of color and women candidates, specifically those with long-term career goals, often want to be considered on their merits and not because they are a member of a protected class. These candidates will also scrutinize the minority hiring and promotion records of these companies. Often the recruiting corporation is placed in the position of bidding against competitors in order to obtain a quality person of color or woman employee. This situation can force a company to make concessions to a person of color or woman recruit regarding salary and/or benefits—concessions that are not congruent with the corporation's established personnel policies. This, in turn, can cause internal problems among similarly situated employees already with the corporation. Ironically, it is corporate attitudes and cultural benchmarks that have ultimately caused this problem.

Examination of top management at the vast majority of corporations reveals almost a complete lack of people of color and women involvement. Although some people of color have gradually and recently attained representation in the middle management ranks, they continue to encounter serious resistance in obtaining the true decision-making or power positions. In addition to encountering this *glass ceiling,* women and people of color are also prevented from obtaining the types of business experience that corporations later find themselves in a position to need to recruit from top management. For example, women and people of color tend to be found in staff or support functions and not in the more powerful line or profit center positions. Thus, a company seeking an experienced plant manager will find the pool of potential women and people of color applicants extremely small. Why, then, do companies follow a course of management development that will ultimately force them to recruit in such a competitive mode? The answer lies in the social or cultural mores or traditions of the corporation.

Corporate decisions to promote involve consideration of not only performance and ability, but also personality characteristics such as management style, executive presence, and professional image. Unfortunately, when comparisons are made between white males and people of color or women promotional candidates, the people of color or women candidates are eliminated on personality. They do not meet the criteria of their predominately white, male managers. For example, women and Afro-Americans tend to reflect a more cooperative leadership approach that is a general result of their overall cultural experiences. This cooperativeness, however, is often viewed as a weakness by the homogeneous top management group. In addition, the top management group often has strict standards regarding professional *image,* a standard difficult for some people of color and women to achieve. This kind of decision making effectively eliminates significant social and ethnic diversity so desperately needed in the competitive business climate of the 1990s.

percent of the population).[21] And while less than 12 percent of the women in the work force are unionized, movements like the Coalition of Labor Union Women (CLUW) hope to expand upon that base.[22]

Unions have discriminated against women and people of color in the past. One study of public sector union discrimination outlined the possible reasons for such discrimination.

MONOPOLY POWER   Under monopoly power, a group is able to exclude people from an activity or occupation to keep the labor force inelastic and in demand, thereby raising their value. At the beginning of this century this power was used to exclude women and people of color from membership in unions. As the Labor Movement grew and gained strength, unions were able to control the flow of work to their members. In the public sector, police and fire fighting unions excluded women and people of color through stringent agility exams and discriminatory hiring practices. Seniority provisions that are strongly supported by unions have a disproportionate negative effect on women and people of color who have come lately into the work force.

PERSONAL PREJUDICE   Unions may discriminate simply because individual union members have personal prejudices that cause them to prefer homogeneity to a more diverse workplace.

ROLE PREJUDICE   Role prejudice is stereotyping people into one role or uniting them to certain skills because of their race or gender. The most common role prejudice is sex discrimination that denies a woman an equal chance to succeed at a job because it is not seen as a woman's role. In the public sector, again, the police and fire fighters' union are the most visible unions displaying role prejudices against women.

CLASS CONFLICT   Discrimination based on class conflict occurs if it is advantageous for unions to keep a class of workers out of the work force. In this area, craft and noncraft unions have separated and are reacting differently. Craft unions are unions of "skilled" laborers, police and fire fighters, mechanics, carpenters, electricians, and other specialists. The ability of women and people of color to compete with union members for the available jobs in these craft areas is limited, because they lack the necessary training. Noncraft or industrial unions are nonskilled, assembly line workers, whose positions can be filled by women and people of color fairly easily. When women and people of color present noncraft unions with competition, these unions must try and keep them from getting the increasingly scarce jobs.[23] Or, they can accept them into the union and continue to influence the workplace with a unionized work force.

Just as unions are being forced to examine how they will function in a decreasingly industrial society, so will they have to address the increasing diverse work force. A model that they may want to follow can be found in the aerospace industry. A partnership of private companies, people with disabilities, medical professionals, and the International Association of Machinists and Aerospace Workers, has been formed to increase the job opportunities for people with disabilities in that industry. Through their cooperative efforts, people with disabilities are assessed and matched to appropriate jobs; they are trained on the job; when necessary, the job or environment is changed to meet their needs; and there is support and follow up while on the job. Since 1981, this program has placed 5,395 individuals into the aerospace industry.

All of the members of the partnership benefit. The person with a disability gets a satisfying, well-paying job; the employer has a motivated, well-trained employee; the union opens up a whole new group of people as potential union workers.[24]

A union can become a partner in a company's efforts to diversify the work force. Most diversity programs are still focused on a management level as you will see later in this chapter. But if a corporate culture changes to value diversity, union jobs and the place of unions in the work force must also change.

CHANGING THE WAY A CORPORATION VALUES DIVERSITY

Motivation

An organization must be clear about its motivation in managing diversity. Being in compliance with equal opportunity laws is not enough. The organization must recognize the business necessity involved in *having* a diverse work force and in tapping the human potential of that work force.

Typically, such motivation is articulated as part of an organization's mission statement or strategic plan. The following is a vision statement of U.S. West, a corporate leader in diversifying its work force:

> **Our culture will be devoid of racism, sexism and all other forms of discrimination: Equal opportunity will maximize the contributions of all individuals to the profitability of the business.**

A corporation is advised to reread its mission statement. Does it really say where the corporation is and where it wants to be? Are its goals clear and will it mean the organization will be able to do business in the twenty-first century?

There are benefits involved in managing diversity and costs for not doing so. Organizations that refuse to change will be faced with higher employee turnover and higher recruitment and training costs. Employee conflicts that may result in sabotage or high absenteeism can be expected. Misunderstandings can lead to expensive discrimination litigation.[25]

Benefits to an organization that values diversity can be quantified.

- *"Bottom line."* Companies who had experienced high absenteeism and job turnover rates from its diverse employee populations found that frustration over career growth and cultural conflict with the dominant, white male culture was most often the cause of employee unrest. As these populations grow within the work force, companies that satisfy their diverse needs will have a competitive advantage. Success for such accommodation can be seen in a study of one company that instituted four benefit-liberalization changes associated with pregnant workers. The higher the company's score for accommodation, the lower the number of sick days taken by the pregnant workers. Instituting company-sponsored day care centers reduced absenteeism in two companies dramatically, and flextime work scheduling also reduced absenteeism and increased worker performance.[26]

- *Getting the best person for the job.* For companies it will be a question of human resources and the ability to attract the very best of those available from a predominately female, nonwhite work force. Companies are already having difficulty in recruitment. A survey of 645 human resource professionals conducted as a follow-up to the "Workforce 2000" report found that 55 percent of the respondents cited problems in hiring entry level secretaries and 53 percent had difficulties in hiring entry level professionals.[27]

CSX Transportation has had a commitment to recruiting and training women and people of color for a number of years. However, the steady downturn in the rail transport business over the last eight years has limited CSX's ability to realize some of its goals. In the "Profile" from Don Davis, CSX's senior vice president, employee relations, he tells of some of their efforts and problems.

- *Value the 'diverse' customer.* The diversity in the work force mirrors the diversity in the consumer market. The organizations who know how to manage a diverse work force will be able to sell itself to a diverse customer base. Low profitability in inner-city markets gave Avon Corporation the motivation to "buy into diversity." Those markets are, now, among their most profitable.[28] U.S. West realized its English-speaking employees were not communicating with a large portion of its customer base in the southwest part of the United States., Spanish speaking Hispanics. Because of its ground breaking approach to diversity, it now boasts that people of color constitute 13 percent of its managers.[29] U.S. companies cannot ignore the need to compete in a global market. With the diversity of its own population to rely upon, companies in the United States should have a competitive edge if they manage that diversity.

- *Innovation means profits.* For companies to compete in the next century, they will have to be creative, innovative, and flexible. Studies have shown that heterogeneous groups show more creativity and better problem solving than homogeneous groups. The broader, richer base of experience provided by people of diverse backgrounds improved problem solving and decision making. While complete diversity might be disruptive, and complete homogeneity may be nonstimulating, cohesive groups of diverse people provide an increased number of alternative ideas that are then subjected to a high level of critical analysis, resulting in a much better product.[30] As organizations become more flexible in their basic employment practices in order to respond to the changing work force, they become more flexible in their practices. This flexibility can be seen in a company like Levi Strauss. Levi Strauss & Co., a San Francisco-based apparel manufacturer, developed a mission statement that had as its goal to create a company that supported employees balancing their work and personal lives. In reaching this goal, it experimented in telecommuting, in flexible work schedules, in job sharing, and in part-time work, programs unheard of in the garment industry.[31]

Taylor H. Cox and Stacy Blake have distilled the above "competitive advantage" factors into Fig. 9-5.

Leadership

An essential element to the successful cultural change of an organization is a commitment of its leadership to change. Experts in the field agree that while

Donald D. Davis
Senior Vice President, Employee
Relations, CSX Transportation

"DOWNSIZING" LIMITS EFFORTS TO DIVERSIFY THE WORK FORCE

CSX clearly understands the need to provide a positive work environment for all of our employees, but particularly our female and minority employees. The "Glass Ceiling" issues are real and disturbing and we realize must be overcome if we are to attract our fair share of a growing body of female graduates. Furthermore, the limitations on personal growth that result from "Glass Ceiling" problems make it impossible for employees to develop and perform to the maximum of their capability.

To combat these problems, CSX has implemented two activities: a mentoring program and an identification of high potential female employees. These programs are discussed below.

Mentoring

A program has been implemented to provide female and minority employees with a "mentoring" relationship with a coexecutive. All participants go through a training experience to prepare them for the mentor relationship. They understand what are and are not legitimate expectations of the program; what are the responsibilities of the participants; and how the program will operate.

The fundamental objectives of the program are:

- To help participants better understand the company and the criteria for success.
- Provide participants with someone in whom they can confide and from whom they can seek counsel and advise.
- Assist the employees in thinking through their career goals, and what they must do to prepare themselves to accomplish these goals.

While the formal program lasts approximately one year, mentoring relationships go on indefinitely.

High Potential Identification

As part of our Succession Planning activity, we identify high potential employees we believe have the capability of ultimately moving into senior management positions. In this program, we put particular emphasis on the identification and development of female and minority employees. Once we identify these employees, we work with them to determine career interests, personal strengths, skills and qualifications. We then design approximately thirty-six-month development plans that support their career preferences and provide the desired training and business experience consistent with their background and prior work experience.

Each year we update this plan, evaluate current performance, and determine what, if anything else, should be done to facilitate the development of these employees. We are careful in selecting the supervisors who are assigned to high potential employees. We want them to be supportive supervisors who are interested in nurturing and developing these future executives.

While these programs have helped us to attack the "Glass Ceiling" and related types of problems, our success has been limited by problems in the basic business. Downsizing requirements have forced us to annually reduce headcount. Not only do these manpower reductions limit hiring (and thus the opportunity to attract new female employees), the reductions also restrict promotions and even developmental assignments. Furthermore, they absorb the energy of managers and jeopardize the advantages and potential of these developmental programs. As a result, "Glass Ceiling" issues are still *with* us and continue to need attention.

		FIGURE 9-5

1. Cost argument	As organizations become more diverse, the cost of a poor job in integrating workers will increase. Those who handle this well, will thus create cost advantages over those who don't.
2. Resource	Companies develop reputations on favorability as prospective employers for women and ethnic minorities. Those with the reputation for managing diversity will win the competition for the best personnel. As the labor pool shrinks and changes composition, this edge will become increasingly important.
3. Marketing argument	For multinational organizations, the insight and cultural sensitivity that members with roots in other countries bring to the marketing effort should improve these efforts in important ways. The same rationale applies to marketing in subpopulations within domestic operations.
4. Creativity argument	Diversity of perspectives and less emphasis on conformity to norms of the past (which characterize the modern approach to management of diversity) should improve the level of creativity.
5. Problem solving	Heterogeneity in decision and problem-solving groups potentially produces better decisions through a wider range of perspectives and more thorough critical analysis of issues.
6. System flexibility argument	An implication of the multicultural model for managing diversity is that the system will become less determinant, less standardized, and, therefore more fluid. The increased fluidity should create greater flexibility to react to environmental changes (i.e., reactions should be faster and at less cost).

FIGURE 9-5

Managing Cultural Diversity Can Provide Competitive Advantage

Reprinted with permission: Taylor H. Cox and Stacy Blake, "Managing Cultural Diversity: Implications for Organizational Competitiveness," *Academy of Management Executive,* vol. 5, no. 3, August 1991, p. 47.

every level of the organization must change, without top management's support and real commitment to cultural diversity, the change won't happen.[32] The recent survey of U.S. businesses conducted by Michael R. Carrell and Everett E. Mann in which 481 companies responded shows a lack of top corporate involvement in the diversity issue. When asked who within the organization initiated diversity policy programs or activities, the Human Relations/Personnel Departments were the overwhelming favorite. Figure 9-6 shows the complete results.

FIGURE 9-6

Initiator of Diversity Policies

In your organization, who has initiated diversity policies, programs, or activities?

Rank	Entity	Percent
1.	Human Resources/Personnel Department	63.9
2.	Chief Executive Officer	33.4
3.	EEO/AA Department	25.5
4.	Other*	17.3
5.	Board of Directors	7.3

*Other: Typical responses to open-ended item included line department heads; employee associations; a labor union; ad hoc task forces and special committees; deans, faculty, and student organizations; an employee assistance program; and mid-level managers.

Source: Michael R. Carrell and Everett E. Mann, "Defining Workforce Diversity Programs and Practices in Organizations," *The Labor Law Journal,* vol. 44, no. 12, December 1993, pp. 755–64. Reproduced with permission from *The Labor Law Journal,* published and copyrighted by CCH Incorporated, 2700 Lake Cook Road, Riverwoods, Illinois 60015.

When an organization pursues the educational component of value diversity, senior management should be the first group involved. Employees receive a powerful message when they learn that senior managers think this is important enough for them to spend two days learning about it.[33]

Personal commitment to learning about diversity is not enough however. Senior staff have to be willing to change certain employee systems that have discouraged diversity. Performance appraisal systems based on meeting the "white male" expectation will need to be revised. Employee benefits systems that were designed for single wage earner families cannot continue unaltered if companies are going to be able to attract diverse employees.

Top management's commitment to organizational change must be for the long haul. The resources in time and money must be there for the many years it will take to change the organizational culture.

And, to the extent that top management is made up of white males, the commitment to participation in this cultural change marks the realization of top management that change is not only necessary, but valuable to the organization.

Managers

Managers will be the key to creating pluralistic organizations. It will be their job to recognize the diversity that exists in the American workplace: to value it and to build the relationships necessary to make it work. New skills will have to be cultivated so that managers communicate effectively with workers from different cultural backgrounds; so that they can motivate their workers and evaluate their performances objectively.[34]

Managers, like other people, come to an understanding of those "different" from themselves early in life. If they are to manage those with diverse cultural backgrounds, they must first become aware of their own prejudices and be able to relate to such issues as stereotyping and cross-cultural insensitivity. Training can be approached in two ways. If the goal is to foster an attitude change within the organization, awareness training and patience might be the proper approach.

Some organizations, like Digital Equipment Corporation, deliberately foster a consciousness-raising approach to diversity. In the 1970s, Digital noticed that its managers were afraid to discuss issues of race and sex. Digital began to encourage small, core groups to meet to discuss the effects of affirmative action on them and on the organization. The initial focus on minorities and women soon changed to a focus on any number of differences in the work force. This resulted in core groups that led to a grass roots effort to value diversity within the organization.[35]

If the goal is to effect a behavioral change within the organization, then the training will focus on changing concrete managerial practices. The training may include an exercise designed to make managers aware of their own biases, but follow-up will include subordinate feedback, performance appraisals, and an award system. Honeywell Corporation used this approach when it decided to work on the diversity issue. It had found that awareness training was not enough. Managers could not successfully manage a "diverse work force" until they were taught to simply manage well.[36] Three pilot programs were designed with diversity in mind to work on managers' people-management skills. The pilot program uses an instrument called the *management practices index* to provide upward feedback from subordinates to managers on their management styles.[37]

Management practices index An instrument that provides upward feedback from subordinates to managers on their management styles.

Whether the goal is a long term attitude change or a short-term behavior change, both start with the need to understand prejudices and the role stereotypes play in the workplace.

Employee Support

As awareness grows, some employees will want to help the process. There are two basic types of employee organizations supporting a diversity program: special focus groups and a diversity task force.

A special focus group is a group made up of employees of similar core identities—women, people of color, and physically disabled. Such groups enable the employees to identify their problems and special needs and bring them to a manager's attention.

Diversity task forces are made up of individuals representing a cross section of the work force—age, gender, race, functional disciplines, and organizational levels. Such groups are often used to direct a diversity program, and they are a focal point for feedback and evaluation of the success of an organization's diversity program.

Diversifying Work Groups and Decision-Making Groups

Companies that value diversity demonstrate their commitment by ensuring full participation of the diverse population within the managing ranks of the organization. Most diversity programs support training and educational opportunities for their employees as well as supplying mentors and support programs to ensure appropriate preparation for advancement.

Rewarding Diversity Achievements

Concrete, behavior changes that increase the value of diversity to the organization should be rewarded. Some organizations believe that managing diversity is just "good management." Managers adjust their management practices to match the needs of the people they manage. Diversity awareness training enables them to better identify those needs.

Rewards, then, are a result of performance. Managers might be assessed based on the profile of employees they have hired or promoted. Salary incentives, bonuses, and special recognition may be given to managers who have advanced workers from a variety of backgrounds.

Rewards are a result of performance—given to employees for work well done.

Enhance Benefits Plans

Employee benefit plans need to be seen as an extension of efforts to value diversity. Many of the benefits in companies stemmed from the needs of a one-wage earner family—husband working with the wife staying in the home with young children. Once a company audits its work force, it may well have to institute new employee policies. A company with a large number of single parents could look at flextime alternatives or an on-site day care. Most two wage earner families would like flexibility in health care coverage, leave time, and retirement benefits.

A survey conducted among over four hundred Human Resource managers from all types and sizes of organizations, shows the varied programs organizations might have to manage diversity. Educational and career support were the most used programs, while a vast majority of the respondents agreed that awareness training had to increase. Figure 9-7 gives a complete listing of various approaches uncovered in the survey.

FIGURE 9-7 Managing Diversity Policies

Policy/Program	Policy Exists, %	Need Policy/ *Need To Do More, %
Building a Valuing-Diversity Culture		
• Discussion groups to promote tolerance and understanding	49.9	75.1*
• Diversity training for supervisors	38.0	74.5
• Efforts to change corporate culture to value differences	37.0	61.4
• Team building for diverse groups that must work together	35.3	68.8
• Diversity task force to recommend policy changes where needed	34.6	44.9
• Holding managers accountable for increasing diversity in the managerial ranks	32.7	65.5
• Awareness training to reduce prejudice	11.6	26.2
Educational Initiatives		
• Incentives for younger workers to complete their education	65.5	72.7
• Basic education classes (reading, (reading, math)	29.8	57.1
• Classes in English for non–English speaking employees	21.4	64.8
Career Support		
• Minority internships	58.5	62.2
• Networking among minority groups	41.7	70.3
• Programs to steer women and minorities into "pivotal" jobs—key positions critical to rapid advancement	25.7	61.8
• Specific goals to diversify middle and upper management	27.7	57.1
Accommodating Special Needs		
• Scheduled days off to accommodate religious preferences	58.2	40.5
• Policies to hire retirees for temporary assignments	45.1	51.6
• Day-care arrangements or benefits	24.5	48.8
• Work-at-home arrangements	19.5	32.7
• Job redesign to accommodate disabled employees	17.3	49.4
• Translation of written materials (manuals, newsletters) into several languages.	12.6	21.0

Source: Benson Rose and Kay Lovelace, "Piecing Together the Diversity Puzzle," *HRMagazine,* June 1991. Reprinted with the permission of *HRMagazine,* published by the Society for Human Resource Management, Alexandria, Virginia.

AWARENESS TRAINING

Education begins the process of cultural change within an organization that has the motivation and the requisite leadership to change. As stated earlier, the first group to undergo this training should be top management. General manager and employee training, primarily about stereotyping and the dimensions of diversity, should follow in fairly quick order. Education in "managing diversity as a resource" is on-going and will be fairly unique to each company's needs.

Facing Stereotypes and Prejudices

As stated above, a stereotype is a fixed and distorted generalization about members of a group. Prejudice is processing our stereotypes in such a way as to reinforce our own superiority over the members of that group.

Stereotyping and prejudice against diverse groups have been institutionalized in the workplace. It becomes, therefore, a function of the organization to recognize and eradicate both the stereotyping and the prejudice.

Awareness training seeks to get employees to recognize the worth and dignity of everyone in the workplace and to treat them with respect. It also seeks to diminish the negative impact of individual prejudices by getting each person to *accept responsibility for the problem.* Role playing and/or listing commonly held stereotypes are two ways trainers get employees to see themselves through their fellow worker's eyes. Unlearning biases is a long-term process. Individuals must be willing to reevaluate and reprogram a lot of deeply held beliefs. Awareness is the first step.

Training Exercises

Diversity training takes various forms. It might involve "encounter" type retreats or quiet consciousness-raising sessions. Following are some exercises which might be used in diversity training:

1. *Values clarification.* A checklist of values—like punctuality, honesty, acceptance, and financial success—are prioritized by each individual as to his or her own preference and how he or she believes his or her organization prioritizes the values. The group then discusses the differences and similarities in the priorities.

2. *Perceptual differences.* The participants are asked to give a precise percentage definition to such terms as "always," "frequently," and "almost always." The exercise uncovers the imprecise communication that might exist in the workplace.

3. *Problem-solving case studies.* The participants are given a partial description of a job applicant and are told to come up with a complete profile. Depending upon the limited facts, the profile may uncover any number of biases when the group completes the picture. For example, one group was told to profile a woman who was returning to the work force and was responsible for two children. The group profiled her as a recently divorced woman who had stopped working to raise her children. The group leader pointed out that she could, in fact, have been out of the work force completing her education and not be without a husband.

4. *Exploring cultural assumptions.* The participants can openly explore assumptions one group may make about another. For example, at one such aware-

Mayor Jerry Abramson led the Diversity Training exercise for his top administrators before launching in-house sessions.

ness session, there was a lively discussion on whether or not it was ever acceptable for women, or men for that matter, to cry in the workplace.

5. *Personalize the experience.* The awareness trainer may try to make everyone aware of his or her own uniqueness and the possibility that they can be different. One trainer had the group recount the first time they became aware that there were people different from themselves—in color, in gender, perhaps in religion, or by their wealth or lack of wealth. By doing this, even white males can experience the "differences" that surround them.

Communication

At a recent Labor-Management Legal Seminar attended by an equal number of male and female professionals, a luncheon speaker warned the audience of the impact of diversity in the work force by saying, "I'm sorry to say but by the year 2000, the work force will be made up of nearly 50 percent women." There were audible objections by a number of the women present and embarrassed looks by the men. The speaker seemed totally unaware of the impact of his statement on the audience.

This incident points to the powerful role language plays in reinforcing stereotypes and in dividing workers in the work force. While the real message of the speaker referred to above was that U.S. companies were not prepared for "Workforce 2000" and had better get prepared, the message received was that a work force made up of more than 50 percent women was something to be *sorry* about.

Language sensitivity and guidelines for appropriate language help managers value a diverse work force. Some rules would seem to be so obvious as to not need repeating, but unfortunately they do.

- Don't tell jokes directed at a group of people stereotyped because of their primary or secondary dimensions.
- Use metaphors and analogies from diverse sources and diverse disciplines, like the arts or sciences, as well as sports.
- Avoid terms that devalue people—"crippled, boy, girl"; or that spotlight differences—"black doctor, old supervisor."
- Be aware of and sensitive to the preferences of members of diverse groups as to titles or terminology. "People of color" seems to be the most acceptable reference for those who have been called minorities. And "physically disabled" is the current term used most often to refer to differently abled people.

Figure 9-8 contains a list of "correct" words used to communicate in a diverse environment.

In addition to sensitivity to the words being used, managers will need to discern other differences in communication styles. For example, Fig. 9-9 shows eleven elements of personnel communication styles, each of which has a range of responses. An individual who associates a particular response with a stereotype will react to the style of the person rather than to the actual message.

In diversity training, managers learn how to identify their own personal communication style and to recognize how they, therefore, value that style over other styles. Managers will then have to distinguish between the style they are comfortable with and value highly, and any other style that produces the results hoped for in the workplace.

When Referring to	Use	Instead of
Women	Women	Girls, ladies, gals, females
Black people	African-Americans, Caribbean-Americans, Black people, people of color.	Negroes, minorities
Asian people	Asian-Americans, Japanese, Koreans, Pakistanis, etc. Differentiate between foreign nationals and American born. People of color.	Minorities
Pacific Islanders	Pacific Islanders, Polynesians, Maoris, etc. Use island name, for example, Cook Islanders, Hawaiians. People of color.	Asians, minorities
American Indians	American Indians, Native Americans, Name of tribe, for example, Navajo, Iroquois. People of color.	Minorities
People of Hispano—Latin-American origin	Latinas/Latinos, Chicanas/Chicanos Use country of national origin, for example, Cubanos, Puerto Ricans, Chileans. People of color, Hispanics.	Minorities Spanish-surnamed
Gay men and lesbians	Gay men, lesbians	Homosexuals
Differently abled people	Differently abled, developmentally disabled, physically disabled, physically challenged.	Handicapped, crippled
White people	European-Americans. Use country of national origin, for example, Irish-Americans, Polish-Americans. White people.	Anglos, WASPS
Older/Younger adults	Older adults, elderly, younger people, younger adults.	Geriatrics, kids, yuppies

Source: Marilyn Loden and Judy B. Rosener. *Workforce America! Managing Employee Diversity as a Vital Resource*, Homewood, Illinois, Business One Irwin, 1991, pp. 85–86.

FIGURE 9-8
Appropriate Diversity Terms

Cultural Differences

Valuing diversity means finding and using the talents, skills, abilities, and uniqueness of each individual in the workplace. And while it is important to discover and eliminate negative stereotypes, it is equally important to recognize the *cultural differences* that diverse people bring with them into the workplace.

Cultural differences The talents, skills, abilities, and uniqueness of each individual that are brought to the workplace.

Cultural differences based on life experiences of a group of people over an extended period of time do exist. Valuing diversity means being able to react to such differences in the workplace.

One cultural anthropologist has studied cultures around the world and has developed a concept that may be useful in communicating with people from diverse backgrounds. Edward T. Hall evaluated the communication style of people of different cultures and placed them on a continuum of high-to-low context. High context cultures place value on body language and other cues in the environment in addition to the spoken word. High-context culture also uses communication for interaction as well as information exchange as a way to establish and maintain a relationship. Low-context cultures rely heavily upon the spoken word. External surrounding factors are screened out and objective facts are relied upon for the information gathered.

FIGURE 9-9

Elements of Personal
Communication

Mode of Interaction:

Initiating---------------------------------------**versus**------------------------------------**Listening**
    The degree to which one initiates discussion or listens and responds as a primary
    mode of interaction.

Reference Point:

Individual--------------------------------------**versus**------------------------------------**Group**
    The degree of emphasis placed on personal involvement and achievement versus
    group involvement and achievements in communications.

Authority Base:

Facts---**versus**------------------------------------**Intuition**
    The degree to which one relies on factual data versus intuitive judgments as the
    basis for reasoning and persuading.

Degree of Self-Disclosure:

Impersonal-------------------------------------**versus**------------------------------------**Personal**
    The emphasis placed on tasks versus sharing personal data in building new
    relationships and communicating with others.

Mode of Expression:

Rational---------------------------------------**versus**------------------------------------**Emotional**
    The degree of reliance on rational descriptions and facts only versus emotional
    reactions and embellishment.

Method of Support:

Challenge-------------------------------------**versus**------------------------------------**Agreement**
    The degree of challenge versus praise and agreement used to support others' ideas,
    views, and so on.

Method of Disagreement:

Confrontation---------------------------------**versus**------------------------------------**Compliance**
    The degree of confrontational versus compliant behavior exhibited in conflict
    situations.

Vocal Characteristics:

Low--**versus**------------------------------------**High**
    The vocal pitch, accent, and volume displayed in verbal communications.

Method of Assertion:

Direct--**versus**------------------------------------**Indirect**
    The degree of reliance on direct statements describing one's position or point of
    view versus indirect references, use of questions, and so on.

Physical Proximity:

Distant---------------------------------------**versus**------------------------------------**Close**
    The degree of physical distance versus closeness maintained and preferred in
    interactions with others.

Reliance on Protocol:

High---**versus**------------------------------------**Low**
    The degree of emphasis placed on formality and tradition versus spontaneous
    behavior in communications with others.

Source: Marilyn Loden and Judy B. Rosener, *Workforce America! Managing Employee Diversity
as a Vital Resource,* Homewood, Illinois, Business One Irwin, 1991, pp. 88–90.

       Individuals from a high-context culture place a great value on being a mem-
ber of a group, starting with the family. Achieving harmony within the group
often requires considering the good of the whole, as opposed to one's own
advancement. The low-context culture values and rewards individual achievement, initiative, and independence. Mr. Hall warns that not everyone within a
cultural group will display the extremes of the high and low culture, but there
are definite patterns. Figure 9-10 shows his findings.[38]

Culture may be placed on a continuum of low-to-high context, based on the relative importance of nonverbal communication. High-context cultures place more value on body language and other cues.				

Figure 9-10
Diversity in Context

Low	**Medium-low**		**Medium**	**High**
Northern European	Anglo American	Anglo American	Southern Europe	Asian
Swiss	Male	Female	Middle Eastern	Hispanic
				American Indian
				African-American

Source: Jim Kennedy and Anna Everest, "Put Diversity in Context," *Personnel Journal*, September 1991, p. 52.

As we have seen from other readings, the growth in the labor market will be in the area of these high-context cultures—Asian, Hispanic, American Indian, and African-American. Much of the advice given to black managers discussed in a later chapter in the book is how someone from a high-context culture copes within a low-context environment. That focus is on channeling into words the nonverbal information a black manager receives so that he or she can make sure a white supervisor or subordinate can "get it."

In an organization that values diversity, however, the organizational culture will try to adapt to the employees, not require the employees to adapt to it. The "OB in Practice," Eye Contact, explores how something as simple as eye contact varies in different cultures.

Attributes of Ethnic Groups

While it may be possible to outline basic cultural attributes of the many groups that make up our diverse work force, it is impossible to list them all or to be totally accurate. The effect of time and place on people of color, for example, who have lived in America can be significant. It will be more helpful for a manager who wishes to value diversity to learn the items to study within a culture to identify cultural differences. Following are categories one might use to study the culture of others.[39]

1. Sense of self and space
2. Communication and language
3. Dress and appearance
4. Food and feeding habits
5. Time and time consequences
6. Relationships
7. Values and norms
8. Beliefs and attitudes
9. Mental process and learning
10. Work habits and practices

Let's look at how the culture of people of color in America, as an example, might differ in some of these areas from the dominant white culture in the workplace.

Eye Contact

In Japan children are taught to lower their eyes when talking to a superior as a gesture of respect. Americans associate someone who cannot look you in the eyes as untrustworthy or insecure. Some African and Latin American cultures consider staring rude, but only if the individual staring is of a lower social status than the individual being stared at. An English person is taught to listen attentively and blink his or her eyes to let the speaker know he or she has been understood. Americans signal interest and understanding by nodding their heads. While a person from India will shake his or her head left to right to signal comprehension.

A widening of the eyes in an American is often a sign that the person is surprised or alarmed. But a Chinese may be signaling politely suppressed anger.

Initial contact with a person of a different culture can often happen in the blink of an eye. It is important to understand what that blink might mean.

Source: Philip R. Harris and Robert T. Moran, *Managing Cultural Differences,* 3d ed., Houston, Texas, Gulf Publishing Company, 1991, p. 44; Jim Kennedy and Anna Everest, "Put Diversity in Context," *Personnel Journal,* September 1991.

- *Sense of self and space.* As stated above, the white American dominant culture values individual achievement and reward. In many other cultures the sense of belonging to a group defines the individual as a part of the whole. Teamwork and conformity may take precedence over putting oneself forward. Dr. Dickens in his work, *The Black Manager,* attributes the reluctance of African-Americans to step forward as a defense mechanism bred into them by their history of oppression in the United States

- *Communication and language.* Again, the use of words and the circumstances surrounding the words can be vastly different in different cultures. Asian-Americans tend to speak in soft tones and in a nonaggressive manner. For white Americans, this may be interpreted as a lack of conviction in their own talents or of the necessary talent to be a manager.

- *Relationships.* The importance of the extended family in the Hispanic culture can have an effect on the performance of the employee in the workplace. The need to attend a relative's funeral, even distant cousins and uncles, might be difficult for a member of the white American culture to understand.[40]

- *Values and Norms.* Even within the dominant white culture of the American workplace, there may be subgroups, such as the older generation of Americans raised during the depression and the "baby boomers" raised in affluence. Work values of these two groups are compared in Chapter 3 in detail. In summary, baby boomers lack the loyalty some older workers feel for their employers.

- *Beliefs and attitudes.* Certainly in the African-American culture the history of slavery and oppression has formulated basic beliefs and attitudes. The need for white Americans to understand this, face it, and find ways to work together in spite of it, is self-evident.

- *Work habits and practices.* In high-context cultures, such as Asian-American or Hispanic, it might be uncomfortable to be singled out for praise for a job well done. For the Hispanic worker, a better reward for a job well done might be time off with his or her family.[41]

CONCLUSIONS AND APPLICATIONS

- By the year 2000, the American work force will no longer be dominated by white, American-born, male workers. The work force of the future will be predominately "diverse," that is, females, people of color, and non-American born workers. For American companies to succeed, they must be able to attract, train and motivate this diverse work force.

- Prejudices against people of diverse cultures, races, age, disabilities, and gender stem from stereotypes most of us learn as children. Understanding that the negative traits we attribute to a whole group of people devalues the individual and that any one of us can be the target of such unfair and unwarranted prejudice, enables us to *unlearn* those attitudes.

- The legalistic approach to eliminating discrimination in the workplace was to mandate "equal employment" and to promote "affirmative action." Both approaches sought to assimilate people of color, women, and people with disabilities into the work force so that no one would notice a difference. Valuing diversity is not about assimilation. The diversity of the work force should be recognized and used so that the talents and values of everyone enriches and changes the workplace.

- The recruitment process that companies utilize must be designed to attract the best and the brightest of the "new" work force. Traditional methods of in-house and word-of-mouth recruitment cannot bring in diverse workers. The existing work force, especially at the upper management levels, is still too homogeneous. Active recruitment in colleges and universities of nontraditional workers and targeted advertising and outreach in diverse publication and minority neighborhoods have all been used by companies hoping to project a "valuing diversity" image.

- Companies are motivated to recruit, train, retain, and promote a diverse work force because of the tangible benefits they gain. Competing in a global economy and faced with an ever increasing diverse society, valuing diversity is not a "do-gooder" objective but a corporate necessity. The competition for quality employees in the future means that the company that can get and keep a quality work force *now* will be ahead of its competitors.

- A change in the corporate culture from one that ignores diversity to one that values diversity demands leadership from the very top of the corporation. Without that, change cannot happen. Employee support, diversity training, and cross-cultural communication are also necessary elements to a corporate change.

- Diversity training enables employees to face their own prejudices and stereotypes and to learn how to change them. Open discussions about individual values and how one arrives at them, problem-solving cases that expose unrecognized prejudices, and similar exercises break down the divisions and let employees see value in another person's talents.

- Sensitivity to the ways people communicate, both verbal and nonverbal communication, can enhance the diversity of the workplace. Reward systems may differ in order to motivate each individual according to his or her needs, and can be designed to be dependent upon what's important to the worker. Promotional systems can be sensitive to the different ways people lead, recognizing that not everyone leads in the same way. Effective leadership, however, produces results and the results can be the measure of success not the conformity of the leadership style.

REVIEW QUESTIONS

1. Why has the diversity of the work force become a crisis as well as an opportunity to American business?
2. Describe the primary and secondary dimensions of diversity. Why does discrimination come about against people because of these dimensions?
3. Discuss the origins of equal employment opportunity and affirmative action programs. Compare and contrast EEO/AA and valuing diversity.
4. How does a company recruit a diverse work force?

5. Outline the major motivational factors an American company has to value a diverse work force.
6. Why is support at the very top of a corporation necessary to change the corporate culture?
7. What are some of the typical components to a "diversity" program?
8. What is the method and objective of diversity awareness training?
9. List some do's and don'ts for effective cross-cultural communication.

DISCUSSION QUESTIONS

1. Many companies have recognized the need to diversify their work force because of demographic changes. Do you think American businesses are ahead or behind other major institutions in the United States, such as government or churches, on valuing diversity?
2. Assimilation of diverse people into the corporate culture is no longer a goal of "enlightened" businesses. Which do you think is better in the workplace, assimilation or diversity, and why?
3. Many companies leave the issue of "diversity" of the work force to the Human Resources or Personnel

Department to handle. Discuss why this approach is not going to be successful.
4. Discuss how employee support groups can help change the corporate culture.
5. "What's in a name?" When are labels we use to describe others an obstacle to communication in the workplace?
6. Give examples of when an individual from a "high context" culture can be misunderstood in the workplace.

CASE STUDY

The Disappearing Worker

Texas Sounds manufactures automotive radio/tape deck components. It has relocated from Detroit where its work force of around 950 people had been unionized and consisted predominately of white, male native-born Americans. Its facility in Detroit had become obsolete and noncompetitive. In order to supply parts to a new Japanese–American automobile manufacturer, it has relocated to a state-of-the-art facility in south Texas that was partially financed through a state economics development program. Texas, as a "right-to-work" state has few Unions. Although Texas Sound's employees were offered jobs at the new facility, very few outside of management made the move.

Government assisted Texas Sound to make the move by agreeing to prepare local workers for the company's needs.

Technical training programs began a year or so before the company relocated, and the work force Texas Sound found upon its move was prepared for the jobs offered. The management employees who relocated with the company did not receive any additional training nor did any management policies change.

With all of the government involvement, the diversity of the work force would have been assured even if the demographics of the area had not dictated a high percentage of Hispanic and female employees.

Texas Sound began production with high hopes and even higher expectations that its new modernized plant and superiorly trained work force would ensure that it could supply its customers with quality products at competitive prices. However, from the beginning the company was plagued with a high rate of turnover among the newly trained work force. Departing employees, mostly women and Hispanics, found the transplanted managers too difficult. They were very rigid when it came to work rules. Seldom, if ever, did they praise or encourage the workers. Many of the workers had been led to believe during their training that they would have opportunities to vary their work experience in the new plant; but most managers placed the workers at one location and refused to discuss changes. The managers' experiences with a unionized work force and rigid contract terms carried over into this workplace.

Within a year the following conversation between the company's president and the director of personnel was recorded:

Director of Personnel: The turnover rate for our production employees this year has been overwhelming. I cannot train new employees fast enough to replace them. We've got to do something fast. The overtime costs alone are causing every department major budget problems. None of our projections for employee costs are coming out close.

President: Certainly we anticipated a shake-down time during this first year. I'm disappointed that we've lost so many new employees but I would expect this next year to be different.

Director of Personnel: I don't think so. Even our recruitment of new employees seems to be in trouble. Disgruntled employees have spread the word that we're not the company to work for in the community. I think some of our managers have displayed less than respectful attitudes toward some of our Hispanic employees. There's no overt discrimination, but there's certainly an undercurrent that I don't like.

President: I don't understand. This community has a high unemployment rate, are you telling me we can't find people willing to work for us? I don't believe it.

Director of Personnel: There is high unemployment, but the better trained applicant is going elsewhere. That year of government sponsored training before we got here prepared our first wave of employees. From now on we have to train them if we can't retain our employees. I just don't think we've got the money to continually train a turnover work force.

President: OK. What are you going to do about it?

CASE STUDY QUESTIONS

1. If you were the Director of Personnel, how would you convince the company President that the problem could not be solved by the Personnel Department alone?

2. Could Texas Sound have avoided this crisis? How?

3. Design a step-by-step diversity program for Texas Sound that could help retain the trained work force.

EXPERIENTIAL EXERCISE 1

Exploring Biases

Purpose

To give students an opportunity to recognize their own cultural biases.

Task

Step 1: Divide the class into groups and give each group the descriptions listed below. Each group should make certain assumptions and complete the sketches in order to answer the questions. Each group should report back their assumptions and solutions.

Step 2: The professor will share the author's answers with the class. Discuss the differences between each group's conclusions and the ones provided by the professor. Can you determine the basis for each group's assumptions?

1. A young, attractive woman is hoping to get a job in the federal government as an FBI agent but has run into a problem involving discrimination. What do you think the problem is and how might the problem be resolved?

2. A young man is stopped for a traffic violation and, instead of just receiving a ticket is taken into custody by a white police officer. What are the circumstances of the arrest?

3. An immigrant studies for eight years after coming to the U.S. but can only find work in a fast food restaurant for minimum wage. Explain the reason why and how the immigrant might overcome this problem.

4. A male professor at a co-educational college asks that a class on psychology which focuses on the behavior of male sex offenders be limited to ten students. A number of female students who were not admitted into the class confronted him claiming discrimination. What reasons could the professor have for refusing their admission into the class?

EXPERIENTIAL EXERCISE 2

Diversity Awareness

Purpose

To sample the kinds of diversity training actually being used in the work force.

Task

Step 1: Divide the class into pairs and assign each pair an organization to approach regarding their "diversity" training. Organizations should include large and small companies, locally owned, and subsidiaries of larger companies, government, the university, and franchised operations.

Step 2: Each pair should do a synopsis of the diversity training programs, if any, going on at their assigned organization. Report back to the class.

Step 3: If available, each pair should bring back a "diversity awareness" training exercise for the class to try and to grade.

 Take It to the Net **You can find this chapter's World Wide Web exercise at:** http://www.prenhall.com/carrell

CHAPTER 10

Power and Politics within Organizations

The Prince

"In examining the nature of the different principalities, it is proper to consider another point; namely, whether a prince is sufficiently powerful to be able, in case of need, to sustain himself, or whether he is obliged always to depend upon others for his defense. And to explain this point the better, I say that, in my judgment, those are able to maintain themselves who, from an abundance of men and money, can put a well-appointed army into the field, and meet any one in open battle that may attempt to attack them. And I esteem those as having the constant need of support of others who cannot meet their enemies in the field, but are under the necessity of taking refuge behind walls and keeping within them. Of the first case I have already treated, and shall speak of it again hereafter as occasion may require. Of the second case I cannot say otherwise than that it behooves such princes to fortify the cities where they have their seat of government, and to provide them well with all necessary supplies, without paying much attention to the country. For any prince that has thoroughly fortified the city in which he resides, and has in other respects placed himself on a good footing with his subjects, as has been explained above, will not be readily attacked. For men will ever be indisposed to engage in enterprises that present manifest difficulties; and it cannot be regarded as an easy undertaking to attack a prince in a city which he has thoroughly fortified, and who is not hated by his people."

"A prince, then, who has a well-fortified city, and has not made himself odious to his people, cannot be readily attacked; and if any one be nevertheless rash enough to make the attempt, he would have to abandon it ignominiously, for the things of this world are so uncertain that it seems almost impossible that any one should be able to remain a whole year with his army inactive, carrying on the siege.

"And if any one were to argue that, if the people who have possessions outside of the city were to see them ravaged and destroyed by the enemy, they would lose their patience, and that their selfish desire to protect their property would cause them to forget their attachment to the prince, I would meet this objection by saying, that a powerful and valiant prince will easily overcome this difficulty by encouraging his subjects with the hope that the evil will not endure long, or by alarming them with fears of the enemy's cruelty, or by assuring himself adroitly of those who have been too forward in expressing their discontent.

"It is moreover reasonable to suppose that the enemy will ravage and destroy the country immediately upon his arrival before the city, and while its inhabitants are still full of courage and eager for defense. The prince, therefore, has the less ground for apprehension, because, by the time that the ardor of his people has cooled somewhat, the damage has already been done, and the evil is past remedy. And then the people will be the more ready to stand by their prince, for they will regard him as under obligations to them, their houses having been burned and their property ravaged in his defense. For it is the nature of mankind to become as much attached to others by the benefits which they bestow on them, as by those which they receive.

"All things considered, then, it will not be difficult for a prudent prince to keep up the courage of his citizens in time of siege, both in the beginning as well as afterward, provided there be no lack of provisions or means of defense."

Source: Niccolo Machiavelli, *The Prince*, Clinton, Mass., Colonial Press, Inc., 1965, pp. 54–56. Reprinted with permission.

POWER AND POLITICS

The Prince, written in 1513 by Niccolo Machiavelli, has been cited for centuries as a treatise on how to obtain *power* and how to preserve *power* after it is obtained. Seemingly, the theme of Machiavelli's work was "seeking power for power's sake." But as the excerpt from his work reveals, the acquisition of power by a Prince in Italy in the sixteenth century was, very simply, a matter of self-preservation. He accumulated resources for the purpose of being able to use those resources in defense of his city. Those "resources" such as troops, provisions, and the support of citizens gave the Prince *power* to resist attack. The ways he accumulated those resources and used them is called *politics*. As we examine power and politics within an organization, it is necessary for students to reevaluate the bias and prejudices they might have about power and politics.

In this chapter we will examine the nature of power, its sources, and how power is developed within organizations. Organizational politics is often the term used to describe the use of power to influence decisions within the organization. We will look at how power is used productively and how power is used to manage effectively. Finally, we will discuss empowering employees as an alternative to the traditional understanding of power within organizations.

POWER

Attitudes toward power are strongly held. "Power corrupts, and absolute power corrupts absolutely," is not only a famous quote but a frightening reality.[1] People are acutely aware that the exercise of unbridled political power has subjected millions of people to the abuses of dictatorships. The "Great Powers" of the Cold War engaged in a constant power struggle that threatened the very lives of those they were trying to protect. In this struggle a *balance of power* meant the demonstrated ability of either side to annihilate the other and to destroy civilization in the process. It is no wonder that "power" is not a favored concept.

More immediate to members of any organization is the existence of power within that organization. Webster's Dictionary defines *power* as the *possession of control,* authority, or influence over others, and the ability to act or produce an effect. In the workplace, power is seen as the *ability to get things done by exerting influence over others.* And while titles and authorities may differ, people within an organization can almost always identify those with the power.[2]

Power The possession of control, authority, or influence over others and the ability to act or produce an effect. The ability to get things done in the workplace by exerting influence over others.

Why Fear Power?

Everyone exists within an organization for a reason. Each worker across the organizational structure from CEO, managers, foremen, laborers, clerical, to cleaning staff have a job to perform and something to contribute to the organization. In filling a "need" each individual within an organization has some power; possesses some *ability to get things done.* Some level of power is, therefore, a normal attribute for everyone within an organization.

An organization exists to fulfill a purpose. It manufactures and sells products; it provides an education for students; or it administers health care to patients. Regardless of its reason for being, it relies upon its members to fulfill that purpose, to use the individual talents toward that end. Without the use of each individual's ability to get things done, power, the organization does not

Without these individuals cooperating in the workplace, this hotel would not be able to serve the public.

function. Moreover, the decisions involved in *what* the goals of the organization will be and *how* to achieve those goals come from individuals within the organization. Who makes those decisions and how and why those decisions are made involves the exercise of power. If the exercise of power is so necessary, why do we resist, at least in theory, the exercise of power within organizations?

The first and most obvious reason is the experiences people have had with the *misuse* of power. When everyone within an organization has an assigned sphere of influence and acts only within that sphere, observers would not generally regard their actions as exercises of power. It is the exception rather than the rule which causes one to note a "power play." So most people will observe the exercise of power when someone steps out of their assigned role and influences the organization. It would not be noticed, however, if a supervisor decided not to call the boss at home to report a mechanical problem at the plant. But the same decision by the boss's secretary could raise eyebrows. Most people also notice the exercise of power when harm results from that exercise. As discussed in an earlier chapter, in evaluating the *ethics* of a course of action, both the *means* and the *end* need to be included. Even the exercise of power as a means to a *good* end requires accountability. When the use of power is not held to that standard, abuses result.

Another reason workers resist the use of power within organizations is a lack of appreciation for the interdependency of most jobs. The culture in the United States values rugged individualists. Our education system has prized *individual* learning and achievement. We would like to believe that one can succeed through individual effort. Power is based upon need. If you *need* something from someone, they have power over you. Within an "individualistic" society, such dependence is resisted.

Finally, the exercise of power is resisted because we would like to believe there is one right way of doing something; there is one right answer to every question. If this is true then simply exposing the *right* answer, the *right* solution to a problem eliminates the need for anyone exerting influence in reaching a decision or in providing a solution. In reality, there may be a number of good decisions or solutions to a problem. The evaluation of which decision or solution is absolutely the best may not be possible until long after the fact. An organization almost always needs to act without knowing whether the decision or solution selected is good, bad, or indifferent.

Dependency

In social science and organizational behavior research, there are any number of descriptive classifications of power. These can describe *power* from the standpoint of power bases with power sources. The work most commonly referred to in organization behavior studies was done by John R.P. French and Bertran Raven in 1956 who described the following five bases of social power:

> *reward power,* controlling resources that could reward
> *coercive power,* controlling resources that could punish
> *expert power,* controlling necessary knowledge or information
> *reference power,* being attractive to others so they seek you out
> *legitimate power,* authority vested in you by your position.[3]

The bases of power have similarly been classified as: threats and promises, persuasion, reinforcement control, and information control.[4] And still another

Expertise in medicine gives this doctor power within the organization.

study described these five types of power: exploitative, manipulative, competitive, nutrient, and integrative.[5] A more lengthy list was supplied in 1984 as: special skills and abilities, expertise about the task, personal attractiveness, control over rewards and/or punishments, formal position, loyal allies, persuasive skills, and control over critical group possessions.[6] In a later chapter on conflict resolution, the bases of power are described as expertise, resource control, interpersonal linkages, and communication skills.

All of the descriptive discussions are helpful in classifying power. But in deciding how best to discuss power within a complex organization, one must answer the question—why do others respond to the exercise of power? The answer is, quite simply, they must. The first issue to understand when discussing power is *dependency*. One person or entity has what others need or want. Their dependency is such that they are willing to respond to the exercise of power by another.

Dependency One person or entity has what others need or want; therefore, they are willing to respond to the exercise of power by another.

As the excerpt from *The Prince* at the beginning of the chapter demonstrates, the Prince offered a well-fortified city to his subjects in order to get their allegiance. The citizens needed his leadership in order to survive and were, therefore, willing to support him against an invading Prince. At the same time, the Prince needed the support of his citizens in order to fortify the city against attack. Both parties had needs the other could fill. Both, therefore, had power over the other.

Within a typical organization, power is found with those who have *formal authority* or *the personal attributes* to influence others and with those who control the organization's *resources* or *information*. A base of power can also be found in empowered employees. Within these bases of power, there are a number of sources of power.

Bases and Sources of Power

FORMAL AUTHORITY AND PERSONAL ATTRIBUTES AS A BASE OF POWER   One who has power by virtue of the position he or she holds within the organization or

Lee Iacocca derived enough power from his position as CEO of Chrysler to survive major economic downturns.

Formal authority One who has power by virtue of the position he or she holds within an organization or through his or her own personal attributes.

through his or her own personal attributes is said to have a base of power through *formal authority.*

The first *source* of one's power through this power base is by having a *position* within the organization that is recognized as having power, being the "boss." This source works and is dependent upon those in the organization accepting the position. In other words, following the directive of the person "in power." This particular source of power needs to be understood when the formal authority is being exercised in the absence of rewards or punishments (although the possibility of rewards and punishments may be in the background).

A study done by Stanley Milgram at Yale University has been widely discussed as proving that individuals will "follow orders" given by someone in a "position of authority" even when the reward or punishment was negligible. The Milgram experiment paired "teachers" who believed they were helping to explore the effect of punishment on learning with "learners" who were acting their parts. The subject was told to ask the learner who they could not see, only hear, a question, and when the learner gave the wrong answer to administer a mild electric shock. As the questioning continued, the learner gave more wrong answers, and the "teacher" continued to increase the level of the electrical shock. If the "teacher" objected or asked the person in charge what to do, the person— who was seen as being in authority—would tell them to continue. Despite the very good acting of the "learners" whose screams indicated considerable pain, a surprising number of the "teachers" continued the experiment. Milgram's study was, in part, designed to answer the question posed by World War II as why German citizens followed Hitler's orders.

The tendency to obey those in authority can be explained in three ways. First, most activities involve interdependent action, that is, two or more people working together. It is usual for someone to take the lead to accomplish the purpose of the act. One defers to authority, then, to succeed. Second, most people's experiences are that someone who has reached a position of authority through merit, is, therefore, a person who knows what he or she is talking about, and should be obeyed for the good of the organization. Third, deferring to authority becomes institutionalized and is, therefore, automatic. Very little decision making is done when one reacts to the organizational culture consistent with others in the organization.

Another source of power through formal authority is one's personal attributes. *Charisma* is often discussed as a leadership quality. It is also a source of power. Again, this involves influencing others without the granting or withholding of resources or the control or manipulation of information. Charisma may involve people acceding to your influence either as a way to get close to you or through persuasion on your part.

Finally, a source of power through authority is one's *performance* or *expertise.* If someone has a reputation for having gotten things done, one is more likely to have considerable power to influence the actions of others. Proven performance gives one power to direct the activities of others the next time. Akin to this concept of performance is the idea of opportunity through expertise. Doctors and lawyers are examples of people who have considerable power by virtue of their expertise, and their power is not always limited to influence in their field. Many civic or political organizations allow doctors and lawyers considerable deference, even though the issue may not involve their "professional" expertise at all.

Figure 10-1 depicts these bases and sources of power discussed here in abbreviated form.

FIGURE 10-1

Bases and Sources of
Power

Bases	Sources	Explanation
Authority	Position	Being the boss; why it works
	Charisma	Reputation and leadership
	Expertise	Knowledge and performance
Resources	Reward and punishment	Control and allocate resources
		Create resources
		Create allies
Information	Communications and control of information	Physical location
		Strategic location
Empowered employees	Delegation results	Increased time and effectiveness
		Setting and supporting standards of excellence

RESOURCES AS A BASE OF POWER   Control over resources, being able to reward or punish by giving or taking those resources, is perhaps the easiest base of power for one to understand. After all, as one author stated his understanding of the ". . . New Golden Rule: the person with the gold makes the rule."[7]

The first source of this power base is the right or ability to *give* as a reward or *take* as a punishment some of the organization's resources. Such basics as control over hiring and firing, pay raises, or promotions are all sources of power. But it is also a considerable source of power to make job assignments, to determine when or if someone is given a job that will put him or her in touch with individuals in the organization who wield power. Some people control office assignments and use this control as a source of power within an organization.

A second *source* of *resource power* may also be found in the allies one has within an organization. One need not rely on sole control over a resource, if, by forming alliances, he or she can exercise control through another. For example, the *control* over office assignments may lie with a manager whose job is to take care of the physical facilities of the organization. Cultivating a good working relationship with that manager may mean that your request for control over a particular office assignment may be honored. Even though you don't control the asset directly, you can influence the decision through control of an ally.

The amount of power someone has through control of a resource depends upon the value of the particular resource to others in the organization. At one time, Robert Moses, the legendary "Parks Commissioner" in New York City, controlled public funds for the building of parks, roads, bridges, and tunnels. Governors of New York and Mayors of New York City valued these public works projects so highly that Robert Moses was able to dictate public policy despite his not being an elected official.[8]

The *third* source of resource power is, therefore, making the resource one controls *more* valuable to the organization. In Robert Moses's case, he controlled "discretionary" public spending during the Great Depression. By superior performance, he made sure his office was a very valuable asset to New York.

INFORMATION AS A BASE OF POWER   Control over information and being in a position to create or communicate that information, is a common *base* of power. This information base is not dependent upon any expertise except in the communication or noncommunication of information.

The first *source* of one's power within this power base is one's physical position within a communications network. One can be *physically* located near cen-

Resource power A base of power achieved through granting rewards or punishments; having allies; controlling resources within an organization.

Informational power Having control over information.

Charisma is sometimes seen in politicians like President John F. Kennedy, who many say invented the concept for the modern-day United States.

ters of power and, therefore, have power. For example, an executive secretary to a CEO may control what information reaches him or her. Obviously, the value given to the executive secretary's control depends upon the relationship of the CEO to the executive secretary. Being close to a person in power has traditionally been a source of power. No example of this is more glaring than the power of America's First Ladies. Eleanor Roosevelt, Lady Bird Johnson, and Nancy Reagan all held positions of influence in their role as First Lady. The "OB in Practice" opposite explores how Hillary Rodham Clinton may be redefining that role.

The second source is one's *strategic* position within a communication network. A midlevel manager may have access to certain critical data which can give that manager certain influence and power within the organization.

In addition to being centrally located within an organization in order to control the flow of information, one has power if one controls the *relative importance* of the information available. Being able to show that certain information is critical to the organization can make one powerful. For example, as computer technology becomes more and more critical in most organizations, a lawyer who is also a computer whiz can become more important to the legal department by his ability to show the department how computers can be used rather than his legal ability.

A third example of a source of power through information is the *withholding* of information. Not sharing information can be a source of power if the parties who need it cannot get the information elsewhere or if withholding the information is seen as justified. In the "OB in Practice" concerning the Federal Reserve System on page 322, the reliance on the confidentiality of the System's deliberations has given it considerable power. Parties in positions where expertise is involved can also *withhold* the information by clinging to technical language or jargon when sharing the information and insuring that no one will understand it.[9]

"Empowered" Employees as a Base of Power   It is important to examine the impact the current trend toward "empowerment" has on the traditional bases and sources of power within an organization and upon organizational politics.

As these employees learn to work together in a seminar activity, they begin to see the advantages to "teamwork" in their daily tasks.

OB in Practice

A Powerful First Lady

As the Clinton administration settled into power, a new kind of First Lady appeared. America has never doubted the influence a wife had on her husband's presidency. From Martha Washington, Edith Wilson, Jacqueline Kennedy, to Nancy Reagan, First Ladies have had the power of their relationship to the President to influence many things. But their power of influence was downplayed or denied altogether because acknowledging it might lessen the President's power.

Hillary Rodham Clinton certainly has power that stems from her relationship to President Bill Clinton. But, in addition, her power also comes from her considerable expertise and experience as an attorney, and as the major author of the Arkansas educational reform package. Moreover, as seen in her first few weeks in Washington, Hillary Clinton displayed considerable talent in the communication skills necessary to wield power successfully. After being charged by the President to head his Administration's Task Force on Health Care Reform, she visited influential members of Congress from both parties. Democratic and Republican leaders came away impressed by her savvy and her promise to work closely with them.

The Clintons have not downplayed or denied the power Hillary Clinton will have in the new Administration. Instead, they have offered it to Americans as a new model, and perhaps a truer model, of how the Presidency does or should work. Time will tell how we will react.

Source: Adapted from Howard Fineman and Mark Miller, "Hillary's Role," *Newsweek,* vol. 1, CXII, no. 7, New York, Newsweek Inc., February 15, 1993, pp. 18–25.

Empowerment, as it is discussed in various places throughout this text, is allowing employees who previously had little or no independence to act with more autonomy. In other words, through management changes, employees who typically had little influence on the organization have been given permission to exert some influence on the organization.

Empowerment
Allowing employees to act with more autonomy.

In many instances, this trend toward "empowerment" can be seen in organizations that, by necessity, have downsized and by eliminating layers of management have fewer managers responsible for more employees. In order to function, those managers have had to reexamine their styles of directing their work force.[10]

Empowerment can also be seen in organizations that have embraced "total quality management" and "work teams" concepts as necessary for successful competition in the global marketplace.[11] Whether it is an individual manager or an organization that decides to empower employees, dependency is still the key. There is recognition that those in charge are dependent upon the work of the employees. Better performance by the employees will mean more benefits to the manager or organization.

Ideally, empowered employees then represent an additional base of power. The first source of this base of power is through *delegation.* A manager who tells his or her employees what their responsibilities are and who gives them the requisite authority to perform those responsibilities multiplies his or her effectiveness. That manager then has the time and energy to do more, to excel, to become essential to the organization. Delegation requires that a manager trust the employ-

OB in Practice

The Federal Reserve System: An Abuse of Power?

William Greider, columnist and author of *Secrets of the Temple* and *Who Will Tell the People,* both books about power and its use, testified before a Congressional Committee about the Federal Reserve and its conduct. Citing its veil of secrecy, he charged that by making its deliberations on federal monetary policies behind closed doors, and by ensuring that what information is released is basically unintelligible, this Agency, run by nonelected directors, is wielding incredible power—power based upon having developed a unique expertise and refusing to allow such expertise to be analyzed by others. While Greider did not attribute bad motives to the Governors of the Federal Reserve System, his testimony raised valid and disturbing questions about how power has been acquired by this Agency, power that some say equals or exceeds that of the U.S. Congress or the U.S. Presidency, itself. Greider suggested to the Congressional Committee that the doors of the Federal Reserve System be opened to public scrutiny, a move he predicted the Federal Reserve would oppose. "As a political institution, it has skillfully mobilized its constituencies over the last eighty years to oppose any intrusion on its mystique," he said.

As predicted, Alan Greenspan, Chairman of the Federal Reserve System appeared before the Congressional Committee and argued that public exposure of Federal Reserve policy discussions would jeopardize those policies.

Source: Adapted from William Greider, "Why Alan Greenspan Should Show You His Hand," *The Washington Monthly,* no. 12, December 1993, pp. 36–44.

---

ees to perform. Empowering employees through delegation also requires that managers free employees from the fear of failure that is present when power only resides above them. Accepting the responsibilities of a job empowers the employee to succeed and fail with predictable, fair consequences.

The second source of power by empowering employees is *results*. By setting standards for employees, giving them the training, information, and support to meet those standards and then the recognition and respect they have earned by meeting those standards, the *results* convey power. The organization is rewarded by higher profits, happier employees, better innovations, etc. Figure 10-2 summarizes these principles for empowering employees.

Jack Welch, CEO of the General Electric Company, is credited with creating a companywide empowerment program known as a "workout." Ideally, the GE

FIGURE 10-2

Ten Principles for Empowering People

1. Tell people what their responsibilities are.
2. Give them authority equal to the responsibilities assigned to them.
3. Set standards of excellence.
4. Provide them with training that will enable them to meet the standards.
5. Give them knowledge and information.
6. Provide them with feedback on their performance.
7. Recognize them for their achievements.
8. Trust them.
9. Give them permission to fail.
10. Treat them with dignity and respect.

Source: Diane Tracey, *10 Steps to Empowerment,* New York, William Morrow, 1990, p. 163. Copyright © 1990 by Diane Tracey. By permission of William Morrow & Co., Inc.

work force was to be organized into flexible, natural teams that met frequently and discussed how to improve the work process. GE was transformed by this empowerment from a "lumbering behemoth to a lean-and-mean global leader" since Welch took over in 1981. A key issue that made workout a success was the necessity that management responded immediately to suggestions of the work-out groups.[12]

The "Profile" on page 324 is an example of how empowering employees can convey power.

Not all empowerment efforts are as successful as those discussed above. The *Harvard Business Review* presented a case study of a fictional company that could not pull it off. The reason was, primarily, the lack of buy-in on management's part to actually listen to the employees' suggestions.[13]

HOW TO DEVELOP POWER

Critical to understanding the use of power within an organization is under-standing how power is developed. How does one get control over resources or information; how does one get into a position of authority? In describing the *sources* of power above, there is some insight as to how power is developed. Note that power is a dynamic concept, in that it is not something that exists like an object. "I hold the power in my hand." It only exists as an activity. "I hold the power in my hand to start World War II."

By the Situation

Practically speaking, as one undertakes any activity or job within the organiza-tion, she has the possibility of developing *situational power*. One can find or put oneself in a *situation* to gain power.

Power can be developed in what is commonly called *"line positions,"* that is, positions within the organization where the product of the organization is pro-duced. In manufacturing operations, the production positions are more power-ful because the money being produced depends upon the creation of the prod-uct. In a service organization, like a hospital, the positions giving direct services to customers like nurses, administrators, and orderlies, are more important, per-haps, than the services of a physician, because the quality of the care they give may determine which hospital consumers and their physicians use.

However, performing the activities assigned will not produce power if some other factors are absent. First, the performance required must be *extraordinary*: such as, initiating new or innovative solutions to organizational problems or taking risks and succeeding in pushing the organization's objectives forward. Second, the performance must be *visible;* those higher up in the organization must be impressed by the success of the activity. Finally, the activity must be *relevant* to the organization: the goals of the organization must be enhanced by the activity.

Take, for example, the story of Wendy Strothman, President of Boston's Bea-con Press. Beacon Press hired Ms. Strothman from University of Chicago Press in 1983 in a desperate attempt to survive. Once a small but successful publisher of unique nonfiction works, Beacon had tried to gain commercial success through how-to and self-help books and failed.

Ms. Strothman recognized that Beacon had a role to play that was unique in the publishing world. "Our mission," she said, "is to publish books that change

Situational power An individual is able to put himself or herself in a situation to gain power, such as a line position, a position within an organization where the product is produced.

Profile — David L. Taylor & Ruth Karin Ramsey
Cummins Engine Company
EMPOWERING EMPLOYEES TO "JUST DO IT"

Many companies are continually trying to improve work processes and reduce operating costs to remain competitive. Along with being continuous, the best improvement efforts are low-cost and immediate.

At Cummins Engine Company's Jamestown Plant in Lakewood, New York, we've developed a training program that combines Japanese *kaizen* methodology with a belief that employees should be empowered to improve processes and eliminate waste immediately. The five-day training program, called JDIT-Kaizen, emphasizes immediate change. JDIT stands for "Just do it."

Kaizen is a Japanese philosophy of continuous improvement that promotes using the creative talents and collective energies of people at all levels of the organization to achieve gradual, unending improvements and higher standards of excellence. Kaizen encompasses a process-oriented way of thinking and a belief that people make a difference.

To begin developing a kaizen program, we formed a program-design group whose goal was to apply the kaizen concepts suggested by Masaaki Imai and to improve work processes. Simply reproducing someone else's program would not do, no matter how successful the original one was.

After using kaizen tools to brainstorm improvements, the plant's program-design group decided that several factors deserved consideration.

The initial program design would need to include a process for applying the JDIT-Kaizen concepts to real tasks.

Second, more than fifteen years of experience with participative work systems in the plan had shown that employee involvement was critically important for gaining long-term commitment. To make the program successful, we knew we had to involve people from the work areas that would be directly affected by the improvement decisions.

Third, the design team decided that cross-functional kaizen teams of technical and nontechnical people should coordinate the JDIT-Kaizen work. This would require commitment from the top levels of the organization to eliminate barriers and provide resources to the kaizen teams. Empowering people to make immediate improvements would also require management support and cooperation because production could be temporarily interrupted.

Fourth, the training program would need to allow adequate time for participants to acquire kaizen concept knowledge and to apply it directly to actual work.

Finally, the results of the kaizen activities and employee involvement would require some form of recognition. Although innovation and continuous improvement, no matter how small, were the desired outcomes, participants' energy and enthusiasm were important, too, and deserved recognition.

Ten Rules for "Just Do It" Kaizen

- Discard conventional, fixed ideas about doing work.
- Think of how to do it rather than why it cannot be done.
- Start by questioning current practices.
- Begin to make improvements immediately, even if only 50 percent of them can be completed.
- Correct mistakes immediately.
- Do not spend money on JDIT.
- Gain wisdom from facing hardship.
- Ask "why" five times and seek root causes.

- Seek the wisdom of ten, not the wisdom of one.
- Remember that JDIT ideas are infinite.

The Benefits

So far, 223 plant employees have completed the JDIT-Kaizen training program, resulting in sixty-one documented process improvements. Tangible results include higher quality, lower cost, reduced cycle times, improved safety, less inventory, and more efficient use of personnel.

Source: David L. Taylor and Ruth Karin Ramsey, "Empowering Employees to 'Just Do It,'" copyright May 1993, *Training & Development,* American Society for Training and Development. Reprinted with permission. All rights reserved.

---

people's minds, make people's lives better, or recognize the inherent worth and dignity of individual human beings." With that goal in mind, Ms. Strothman also set about making Beacon a commercial success. She combined a commitment to literary freedom with a willingness to listen to the public thereby providing works that gave readers an opportunity to learn. The commercial successes of Beacon under her leadership resulted in her being named "Woman of the Year" at the 1993 New York's Book Publishers World Convention.[14]

An additional way to foster power through one's situation is by recognizing the value of a *subunit* to the organization and using that to one's advantage. A powerful subunit is one that displays unity and cooperation; solves critical problems to the organization; is irreplaceable; or is pervasive in its activities or involvement.[15] By promoting such a subunit, individuals within the subunit gain power.

A unified subgroup operates from *consensus* and, therefore, has more predictable and efficient *results.* Such results convert to a high *favorable profile* within the organization. That profile attracts and retains talented people in the subunit, thereby increasing the subunit's results, etc. This cycle of consensus—results—and positive profile as depicted in Fig. 10-3, can be achieved by selecting people for the unit of similar backgrounds or perspectives, or by using consensus-building techniques.

A subunit can be powerful if it handles problems *critical* to the organization. At any given time, the subunit responding to a critical problem might be different. While the subunit is in the midst of its critical activities, the individuals within the unit have considerable influence with the organization. An example of this can be found in the "Profile" by Donald L. Cox.

A subunit has more power within an organization if it is *irreplaceable,* that is, if it controls a resource for which there is no alternative. As every worker strug-

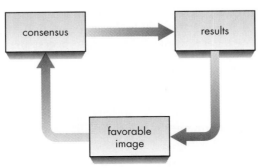

FIGURE 10-3
Subunit Performance

Profile

Donald L. Cox
SUBUNIT POWER DURING CRISIS

In 1988, the Louisville/Jefferson County Regional Airport Authority undertook a $300 million airport expansion within the City. In order to redesign and build the expanded airport, over 1,800 homes and businesses had to be acquired and demolished in neighborhoods surrounding the existing facility. Funding for the expansion came from federal, state and local government resources, as well as private companies that used the airport. The Airport Authority and its consultants enlisted the help of all the funding sources to create a management team to guide the policymakers in completing the seemingly overwhelming task. Subunits of the management team directed the financial, environmental, regulatory, public relations, land use, and legal aspects of the projects. At the inception of the project, the public relations unit wielded considerable power as public support for the project was rightfully considered critical to its success.

Even though litigation began almost as soon as the project was launched, the legal unit had little influence on the project until the court ruled that the entities did not have the legal authority upon which they had based some of their actions. Suddenly, the legal team became the critical subunit.

All the activities of the remaining subunits: land use, financial, environmental, and public relations became dependent upon the progress, or lack of progress, by the legal team. Bi-weekly strategy meetings became common. Legal review of every activity undertaken by *any* member of the management team became the norm. It became apparent that the legal subunit was wielding considerable influence when its members outnumbered everyone else at the monthly management team meeting. Its charge, to resolve the legal quagmire surrounding the project, gave it considerable and some felt unbalanced influence on the project as a whole.

When the case settled, at a cost of over $6 million, the reliance on the legal subgroup diminished. Meetings of the subunits became less frequent and the attendance at policy meetings by members of the legal team stopped altogether.

gles to become computer literate, the technology revolution has created very powerful subunits within organizations that control computer technology. Many times using computer jargon or language keeps the subunit in exclusive control of the expert information it has.

Finally, the *pervasiveness* of the involvement or activity of a subunit can give it increased power. Many in-house legal staffs increase their value to their organizations by proactive involvement into all aspects of the organization. By engaging in a legal analysis of another department's goals and objectives at the start of a process, it wields influence on how such activity is undertaken and makes the legal unit necessary to the successful completion of the projection.[16]

By the Person

Being in a situation that enables one to acquire power is not enough. A person must have the *desire* and ability to acquire and use power. Some personal attributes that have been observed in people willing to acquire and use power include the following.

ENERGY, ENDURANCE AND PHYSICAL STAMINA   Managers who work productively for sixty to sixty-five hours a week succeed over their competition by outlasting them and by outproducing them. Such a manager becomes a role model that others emulate.

FOCUS   Managers succeed if they not only see and appreciate the big picture but can attend to details and move the organization toward a desired goal.

SENSITIVITY   A manager cannot gain or use power if she or he is unable to influence the behavior of others in some way. Being able to understand others' perspectives is important to motivating them.

FLEXIBILITY   While having convictions is, of course, a laudable attribute, being intransient in your opinions demonstrates an inability to listen to others and to continue learning. As discussed earlier, there are few "right" or "wrong" answers within an organization's daily activities—just opportunities to influence its operations.

TOLERATE CONFLICT   Power acquired, retained, and used involves the probability of conflict. One who shrinks from conflict cannot exercise influence.

SHARE LIMELIGHT   Effective managers or people of influence know how and when to submerge their own ego and make sure others participate in the exercise of power. In 1994, the Walt Disney Co., led by CEO and Chairman of the Board, Michael Eisner, suffered a terrible loss when Disney's President Frank Wells died in a helicopter crash. And, although he had successfully operated the Walt Disney Studios for ten years, Jeffrey Katzenberg also left Disney when Eisner failed to name him as Wells's successor. As *Fortune Magazine* reported, ". . . the Eisner-Katzenberg spat shows how essential—and how difficult it can be for executives to reward talent, share power, and develop a clear plan for succession."[17]

The "OB in Practice" on page 328 profiles one CEO who agreed to take on a challenge and, by succeeding, created not only the power but a mystique of power.

By the Location

A study done in 1984 in a newspaper publishing company identified one's position within an organization as the critical factor in gaining power. That study identified three networks in which a party could be exercising influence depending upon their position within that network. In the *workflow network* power can be found in the position holder whose task is *critical* to the continuation of the flow of work. That position holder's influence is decreased or increased by dependence or independence on others to keep the work flowing. And the position holder's influence is greatly increased if they hold a position that encounters uncertainty and can handle such uncertainty on his or her own.

In examining the *communication network,* being central within the department in which one works is as important as being central to the whole organization, the degree to which one is the *sole* central source of information within one's subunit had a very positive effect on the influence one was able to wield.

Finally, the *friendship network,* referring to the informal flow and exchange of work/information within an organization, was not found to be a significant source of power when the overlap with the communications network was eliminated.[18]

OB in Practice

The Softer Side of Sears

The 1993 advertising campaign for the Sears Department Store chain emphasized its serous commitment to women's fashions in contrast to its "hard goods" reputation. The corporation's CEO, Arthur Martinez, however, displayed anything *but* a "soft side" when he took over the helm of the troubled Sears Company in 1992. Martinez diagnosed the problem of the department store chain as being stuck in the past. The Sears catalog, which was as sacred a "sacred cow" as something like that could be, no longer made money for the company. Because of its bureaucracy, there was too little accountability at individual stores for profitability and, therefore, very little creativity.

Martinez recommended to the Sears Board of Directors that 50,000 employees be dismissed, that 113 stores be closed, and that the catalog be discontinued. He changed the emphasis of the store's merchandizing from men to women. In Herculean-like manner, these dramatic changes turned Sears from its $8 million loss in 1992 to profits of $441 million by September of 1993.

Along the way, Martinez displayed characteristics typical of people who can acquire and use power. He was viewed by his employees as a workaholic who demanded the same kind of commitment from them. He devised and executed the master plan for revitalizing Sears almost with blinders on, focused totally on that goal. He found kindred spirits among the younger, talented executives and enlisted their help and enthusiasm in pushing his master plan forward. Finally, as his success is touted, Martinez includes the Company's Chairman of the Board, Board of Directors and talented executives as part of that success.

Sears' "softer side" campaign turned the corporation around in the early 1990s.

Adapted from: John McCormick, "The Savior at Sears," *Newsweek,* November 1, 1993, pp. 42–47.

ORGANIZATIONAL POLITICS

The acquisition and use of power within an organization, just as within society at large, is called politics. The term "office politics" can be as negative a term as "power," unless it is understood as a dynamic process for furthering the objectives of the organization. The use of power within an organization needs to survive the ethical test discussed in a previous chapter; that is, both the "ends" and the "means" must be pursued ethically.

Organizational politics
The ethical acquisition and use of power within an organization to further the objectives of an organization through the dynamic process of office politics.

When Is Power Used?

The exercise of power occurs within an organization when certain factors exist. In studies conducted in the early 1980s, one of the actual decisions made and one of the perceptions of managers on the decision-making process was that workers were acutely aware of the existence of office politics. The response of the workers are summarized in Fig. 10.4.

Not surprising, certainly, was the perception that politics played more of a role within the organization at the *top of the organization*.[19] It is at the higher levels within an organization that decisions are made. Policy decisions on the goals and objectives of an organization require interaction between the policy makers.

A necessary element for the use of power and, therefore, office politics, is *interdependence*. If the parties are dependent upon each other, then they have the incentive to work together, coordinate their activities and, in fact, forge common goals. There is more interdependence higher up in the organization, because, again, the discreet tasks are delegated to functional levels below. The direction of the organization is, by and large, decided at the top levels. Interdependence is more prevalent in staff positions than in line positions as well. Line positions tend to control resources by virtue of their function. Staff positions need to acquire power through the various methods discussed above.

Office politics increases when there is a *scarcity of resources* as opposed to an abundance of resources. During cutbacks, layoffs, and reductions in force, the exercise of power becomes critical. Even in good times, the competition for scarce resources can lead to high interdependence and more office politics.[20]

Process	Always or Frequently %
Promotions and transfers	59.5
Hiring	22.5
Pay	33.1
Budget allocation	37.6
Facilities, equipment allocation	49.2
Delegation of authority	58.7
Interdepartmental coordination	68.4
Personnel policies	28.0
Disciplinary penalties	21.5
Work appraisals	42.4
Grievances and complaints	31.6

Source: Jeffrey Gandy and Victor V. Murray, "The Experience of Workplace Politics," *Academy of Management Journal*, no. 2, June 1980, p. 242. Used with permission.

FIGURE 10-4

Perceived Politicalization of Organizational Processes

Even with interdependence and scarce resources, a *difference of opinion* needs to exist for the exercise of power to become necessary. If the decision makers agree, there is no need for a power play.

One way to avoid conflict is to have the group reach consensus on the goal that is being sought. While this is laudable, it isn't always possible to agree on the goal or on the methods to reach the goal. In large, complex organizations, greater task division within specialties will work against consensus. An engineering solution to a corporate challenge may not satisfy the accountants, and vice versa. Occasionally, an external threat can be the catalyst for group consensus.

Finally, the exercise of power within an organization increases in direct proportion to the *importance of the issue* to the organization. If the issue is important enough to the parties, they are willing to exercise power to resolve the issue. Occasionally, the use of power on unimportant issues can backfire.

Recognizing Organizational Politics

Understanding how power is used within an organization means first recognizing the power distribution within the organization. That means recognizing the players and assessing their relative strengths as well as their interdependence. Then one must learn to identify the use of power.

THE PLAYERS   In identifying both individuals with power and political subunits with power within an organization any one of the following may indicate the *makeup* and *importance* of a person or subunit:

   a. location of office
   b. tenure of person or employees
   c. department assignment
   d. staff or line position
   e. rank (officers, managers or rank and file)
   f. gender or ethnic characteristics
   g. academic background or training

A more unified subunit has a potential for more power. Therefore, look to the most inclusive and homogeneous groups within an organization first to determine powerful subunits.

Another indicator of personal or subunit political power is a look at previous decisions within an organization and how these decisions were made.

REPUTATION   A newcomer to an organization may quickly assess the power of different persons or subunits by asking. Within an organization a person or unit that can get things done will have a reputation for getting things done. If it is acceptable within the organization's culture to discuss such effectiveness, reputation will indicate power.[21]

REPRESENTATION   An observer may be able to assess a person or a subunit's power by the breadth or depth of its representation throughout the organization. When President Bill Clinton, an attorney, took office, the predominance of attorneys throughout his top level appointments was noted as a contrast to the business people they replaced.

CONSEQUENCES   Observing the consequences of previous power struggles may indicate where the power exists. If such information is available, salary differentials across department lines within an organization may indicate the relative political power of a person or a department. Budget allocations may indicate political power, especially in the distribution of discretionary funds. Within most organizations annual budgets tend to maintain a constant funding for a continuation of the operation at an acceptable level. Decisions in new initiatives, and, therefore, the expenditure of "discretionary" dollars, can give a clear indication of the relative political power of a person or subunit.

SYMBOLS   A newcomer may be able to ascertain the relative power of a person or subunit by the symbols of power. For example, in many organizations the highest floors are reserved for top management. Corner offices with windows are reserved for "partners." When reorganization within an organization causes relocation, the persons or units moved closest to the center of corporate decision making have, at least, a symbol of power.

CULTURAL DIFFERENCES   All of the indicators above have to be used in context if one is to be able to assess the relative influence of various persons or subunits. As U.S. organizations move toward changes in *how* they conduct business, many of the old symbols have changed meanings. In their new corporate headquarters, for example, Providian, an insurance holding company, built fewer individual offices and placed them in the center of the building. Only the open spaces occupied by lower-level workers have windows, a privilege previously enjoyed by top management.

DEPENDENCE   Recognizing the interdependence of persons and subunits will indicate how power is used within an organization. As discussed earlier, one way power is acquired is through alliances. The need to develop consensus within an organization means recognizing how various people and groups depend on one another. Looking for supporters as well as opponents to an idea or goal may tell one more about power within an organization than the subject matter at issue. When Lee Iacocca left Chrysler, in 1992, he was replaced as Chairman and Chief Executive by Robert J. Eaton, an executive from General Motors. Most observers expected Chrysler President Robert A Lutz and then key executives to leave or be replaced by Eaton's people. Eaton, however, arrived alone and not only promoted from within but left Lutz as President, giving him responsibility for day-to-day auto operations. The approach worked. Chrysler's performance rose steadily in the first two years of Eaton's chairmanship, resulting in a $3.7 billion profit in 1994.[22]

The Techniques

The use of power to influence decisions can be identified by certain strategies and techniques often employed by parties in the workplace.[23] Figure 10-5 lists some typical tactics and a percentage of respondents who identified the tactics from among senior staff and supervisory personnel who participated in the survey.

Following is a brief discussion of these and similar tactics used in the workplace.

INDIVIDUAL INFLUENCES   Nice, attractive, *pleasant* people tend to have more influence. This is true even of executives. The need to form and maintain allies

FIGURE 10-5

Managerial Perception of
Organizational Politics,
Tactics

Percent of Respondents that Mentioned Tactics	
Tactic	*Percent*
Attacking or blaming others	54.0
Use of information	54.0
Image building and impression management	52.9
Support building for ideas	36.8
Praising others, ingratiation	25.3
Power coalitions, strong allies	25.3
Associating with the influential	24.1
Creating obligations and reciprocity	12.6

Source: Copyright 1992 by The Regents of the University of California. Reprinted from the
California Management Review, vol. 22, no. 1. By permission of The Regents.

no matter where one is in the organizational chart belies the long-term success of an unpleasant, autocratic leader. The old saying, "Watch how you treat people on the way up, you may meet them again on the way down," is a wise saying.

Being pleasant, flattering, and helpful need not be insincere. In all likelihood, if it *is* insincere it will not produce the desired results. In having power through personal attributes, being articulate and sensitive were the two top-rated attributes.[24]

Personal attributes such as being socially adept, competent and self-confident help create a *positive image*. Being cooperative and generous can gain one allies, a source of power discussed earlier.

Unfortunately, negative attributes can also be used in organizational politics and often are. Blaming or attacking others or being devious are ways individuals wield influence in the workplace.

Some people use the control or lack of control over *emotions* to influence a decision. Business settings seldom lend themselves to "emotional outbursts" but control over one's emotions often has an influence on the outcome. Waitresses make most of their income from tips. Studies contrasting the tips given a patient, smiling waitress, and a nonsmiling waitress confirms the effect.

USE OF INFORMATION   The technique often used to make sure an issue is dealt with the way one who is wielding power wishes is *framing*. If someone, for example, wants to pursue an expensive product change, the change is compared and *contrasted* with another option that costs more. The more expensive and, therefore, least desirable option is presented first. In comparison, the option one wants pursued will appear more favorable to the organization.

An issue can be framed as a "continuation" of previous decisions that will, of course, give it more weight. Recognizing that previous decisions have created a *commitment* of the organization toward a particular end, if a change can be framed as a natural outgrowth of that course, parties are more likely to embrace the change.

The scarcity of an item may determine its value. In framing an issue to one's advantage, if an aspect of *scarcity* can be included, it influences the decision. Scarcity can be real or perceived. Job seekers are often advised to present themselves at interviews as having other job opportunities and knowing other employers who may want them, increase their value in the marketplace.

The *order* of presenting things for consideration is a way to influence a decision. There are three approaches to presenting items in order. First, one presents a proposal *after* another's proposal *if* it will make the proposal benefit from the comparison; being cheaper, safer, more likely to succeed, et cetera.

Or, if one is advocating two things, place the weaker first. Win or lose on that proposal, the second, stronger proposal will have a better chance of being adopted. If the first, weaker proposal was acceptable, why wouldn't a second, stronger proposal? Or, if one loses the first time, there will be a tendency to accept the second.

Third, if one is committed to only one proposal, it might be advisable to limit discussion to that one item. If *only* one item can be discussed, it is more likely to be adopted than not, since people prefer action to inaction.

Finally, in framing an issue, the ability *both* to *ask* and *answer* the *question* influences the decision. If one is in a position to "frame the question," the answer can only lead to the outcome sought. For example, when Johnson & Johnson's CEO, James Burke, was faced with the tampering of Tylenol® capsules that resulted in three deaths, he voluntarily withdrew *all* bottles of Tylenol® from the market until the source of the poisoning could be determined.[25] One can imagine that this solution came as a result of a carefully crafted question along the lines of "how can we guarantee no more deaths?" Compare that question and solution to the one taken by Beech-nut® when its apple juice was found to have no actual apple juice in it. Beech-nut® hid the finding and continued to sell the juice in the United States and then abroad; resulting in prison sentences for Beech-nut® executives and a huge loss of profits.[26] The question framed for Beech-nut's decision makers could not have been "How can we guarantee a pure product for consumers?" and result in that solution.

Analysis of information is a useful technique for influencing decisions. Basing one's decision on facts and figures insulates him or her from criticisms of being capricious or unprofessional. It can also cut down on power plays within an organization. Therefore, to influence a decision, one can provide analysis and information to support that decision. Oftentimes an "outside expert" is used to lend credibility to the recommendation. Care must be taken, however, when basing decisions on facts and figures, that the context of those facts and figures are also understood. By relying on facts and figures alone, Beech-nut decided *not* to pull their apple juice from the market. Their decision reflected a lack of common sense or judgment as to the public's reaction to their deceptive practice.

Selecting the correct argument and therefore the appropriate information is another technique when using the power source of knowledge. If one is presenting options to a decision maker with a technical background in engineering, he or she would frame the argument and statistics differently than to a person with a legal background. Information that could be used that is not helpful should not be presented.

TIMING In some circumstances, getting *out first* means setting the agenda. When one sets the agenda, his other solution is more likely to meet the needs of that agenda than someone else's. Although there is risk in getting out ahead of others, sometimes the element of surprise can give one an advantage.

The best way to stop something from happening when you don't have enough power to do so directly is to *delay* its happening. Calling for further study or consideration can almost always delay a decision, especially if the solution being pushed is a departure from the organization's previous activities. Delay can cause those pushing a solution to lose the momentum necessary to carry it off. Delay may result in proponents of the idea being gone when a decision is finally made. And, if working under a deadline, delay may result in missing the deadline.

In contrast, *deadlines* can be used to push a decision toward the desired conclusion. An advocate who has momentum on his or her side can use the pressure of meeting a deadline to get a positive decision. Congress manages to complete its determinations on controversial subjects often on the eve of adjournment after having delayed for months. The need to pass something before adjournment provides significant incentive for compromise.

"Politics" is described as an art and a science. Office politics is no different. There are *propitious moments* to pitch an idea or solution to an organization's problem, and recognizing that moment is more akin to being an artist than a scientist. Obviously, a well-defined goal or objective, a clear threat or opportunity will have focused the organization so that a proffered solution gets a favorable review.

STRUCTURE CHANGES   Another technique used to exercise influence within an organization is to substantively or symbolically change the power structure.

One way to decrease the effectiveness of a powerful subunit is to break it up. In one corporate setting a corporate counsel and the in-house legal staff wielded a great deal of influence while being centrally located in the corporate headquarters. When a reorganization caused the lawyers to be dispersed throughout the organization, in distant plants and subsidiary locations, the influence diminished greatly.

Another change that can be used to redistribute power within an organization is to increase one's control over resources by pulling subunits together. A larger domain in which to exercise power, also means an increase of power within the organization.

A "camel" has been described as a "horse" designed by committee. Task forces and committees can be bases for influencing decisions. It is not unusual for someone to use a committee he created to shepherd a project forward simply to legitimize the decisions already made elsewhere.

Some nonsubstantive changes can have a profound effect upon an organization's decisions. Language and emotions can sway decisions when used effectively. President Reagan's administration never used the term "tax increases" although his "tax reform" efforts resulted in more tax revenues for the federal government. Title changes, even when not accompanied by a pay increase or an increase in responsibilities, can be an effective reward because of its symbolism within an organization.

Ceremonies, ranging from regular staff meetings, annual board meetings, to corporate appreciation dinners give opportunities for political influence. How individuals are seated, who is invited, who controls the agenda are all messages about influence.

The physical environment as an indicator has been discussed in detail earlier in this chapter.

Productive Use of Power

Using power and productively using power are critically different concepts. Using any or all of the techniques above to acquire and wield power will not necessarily result in a better organization. Organizational politics can be harmful to the organization if it monopolizes the energies of the parties; if it results in rewards not based on merit; if it allows for unwise allocation of resources or relies on hasty decisions. The belief that office politics has a negative effect on organizational politics is reflected in the opinions one surveyor found when ques-

Statement	Strong or Moderate Agreement %
a. The existence of workplace politics is common to most organizations	93.2
b. Successful executives must be good politicians	89.0
c. The higher you go in organizations, the more political the climate becomes	76.2
d. Only organizationally weak people play politics	68.5
e. Organizations free of politics are happier than those where there is a lot of politics	59.1
f. You have to be political to get ahead in organizations	69.8
g. Politics in organizations are detrimental to efficiency	55.1
h. Top management should try to get rid of politics within the organization	48.6
i. Politics help organizations function effectively	42.1
j. Powerful executives don't act politically	15.7

Source: Jeffrey Gandy and Victor V. Murray, "The Experience of Workplace Politics," *Academy of Management Journal*, no. 2, June 1980, p. 244. Used with permission.

FIGURE 10-6
Responses to Statements about Workplace Politics

tioning employees about their perceptions of workplace politics. Their agreement or disagreement with statements about workplace politics, as shown in Fig. 10.6, reflects that close to three-fourths of the responders thought organizational politics harmful.[27]

The harmful effects of organizational politics can be minimized by insuring an even distribution of resources; agreeing upon clear, achievable goals for the organization; and avoiding conflicts that are "personal" as opposed to "programmatic" in nature.

To manage with power is to incorporate the skills necessary to acquire power with the self-control to use that power productively.

Recognize varying interests. The first step is to figure out the various interest groups within an organization and their relative importance in the organization's politics.

Understand others' perspectives. Ascertaining a perspective held by various subunits in an organization is not enough. One must understand the basis for this perspective if such interests can be met.

Accept the need for power. There is going to be influence used in the workplace. Power is the ability to get things done. Without power one will not be able to manage effectively.

Understand power strategies and tactics. By understanding the dynamics involved in acquiring and using power one is better able to utilize an appropriate technique when necessary and more able to understand the exercise of power by others in the organization.

Recognize how power is lost. One cannot manage with power unless they realize how power can be lost. A reorganization can strip someone of power—sometimes purposefully and sometimes as a result of one's inability to change with a changing organization. If political power comes with a position and no effort is made to shore up that power through control over resources or knowledge, such power can be easily lost. Lack of patience, pride, or excessive privilege can lead to a loss of power. Even as Machiavelli pointed out in his classic, *The Prince,* the "goodwill" of the governed is necessary for holding power. If the members of the organization do not accept the influence of the person who is thought to have power, then obviously he or she doesn't have power.

CONCLUSIONS AND APPLICATIONS

- Power in the workplace means the ability to get things done. As such it is a necessary element to the success of the organization.
- Power exists because of dependency. Within the workplace formal authority, personal attributes, control over resources and/or information are the bases of power.
- One has power through formal authority or personal attributes because of the position one holds, his or her charisma or expertise.
- One has power through control over resources when he or she can reward or punish by the granting or withholding of such things as pay, promotions, offices, et cetera. One may control resources oneself or through allies. The more important the resource, the more power one has.
- One has power through control of information by being centrally located in either a physical or strategic way to pass on or withhold information. If one can increase or decrease the importance of the information to the organization then one wields considerable power.
- Power can be developed by using one's situation to become critical to the success of the organization. "Line positions" are potentially more powerful than staff positions. Being in a powerful subunit gives one more power in an organization.
- A person must be willing to obtain and wield power. Some personal attributes that are necessary are energy, focus, sensitivity, flexibility, and the ability to tolerate conflict.
- Organizational politics occur when there is considerable interdependence so that no one is a lone actor; when there is a scarcity of resources at stake; and when a difference of opinion exists as to where the organization is heading and when the issue is of importance to the organization.
- One can determine the *players* involved in organizational politics by reputation, by observing their representation within the organization, by the consequences of past actions, and by the dependent relationships that exist within the organization.
- Techniques often used to exert power and influence within an organization include: framing an issue; using individual influences; control of the timing of an activity; using information and analysis; and making structural changes.
- Productive use of power means recognizing varying interests and perspectives and respecting them; understanding the use of power as a positive objective; and knowing how the abuse of power leads to the loss of power.

REVIEW QUESTIONS

1. Explain the reasons why people fear the use of power within an organization.
2. What are the bases of power within an organization?
3. What are the sources of each power base?
4. How can one develop power within an organization?
5. How does one person or subunit become more powerful than another within an organization?
6. When is power used within an organization?
7. How can one distinguish who the players are in organizational politics?
8. What techniques are applied by people using power within an organization?
9. How can political power within an organization be used productively?

DISCUSSION QUESTIONS

1. Compare and contrast the elements of power discussed in the excerpt from *The Prince* with the bases of power discussed in the chapter.
2. Give examples of the misuse of power within an organization and point out how such misuse could be remedied.
3. Discuss why power is based upon *mutual* dependency.
4. Explain why *charisma* is a source of power by giving examples in your own life.
5. Can you distinguish between those actions directed at gaining "power" and those actions directed at doing your job? Why or why not?
6. What are some questions you could ask of a fellow worker when you first join an organization to determine where the power lies?
7. In framing an issue what are some important points to remember? Is it dishonest to "frame" an issue with a particular result in mind?
8. Why is it important to understand how power is lost?

CASE STUDY

Flight Attendants Strike at American Airlines, 1993

The effectiveness of workers' strikes has decreased remarkably in the United States as membership in unions declined; as technology allowed for the replacement of workers by machines; and as unemployment increased. Employers facing a strike could often continue in operation with supervisors replacing laborers or by hiring replacement workers who were willing to cross picket lines. In November, 1993, however, flight attendants at American Airlines were able to call a strike and cause the company to resume contract negotiations toward a more favorable contract by correctly assessing and using their power.

Recognizing their airline's busiest season, the flight attendants called for a strike the week before Thanksgiving. Because federal safety laws required a certain number of flight attendants on each flight, the skeletal staffing the company could put together caused cancellations of numerous flights during its most busy and profitable season.

In order to prevent the airline from hiring replacement flight attendants, the union called for a strike of only ten days duration, designing it to affect the Thanksgiving holiday but limiting it so replacement workers would have no reason to take their jobs.

Despite the fact that the Airline Pilot's Union did not go on strike with the attendants, some pilots walked the picket line.

The strike strategy was so effective that President Bill Clinton intervened and made sure that the airline's management resumed negotiations with the Flight Attendants Union before the holidays began, thereby restoring the regular flight schedule.

CASE STUDY QUESTIONS

1. List the players and the power they had to use in this case study through an explanation of the dependencies involved.
2. Discuss how this situation would have been different if federal law did *not* require a certain number of flight attendants per flight. How could the Flight Attendants Union have changed the strategy to address this changed fact and still have had a successful strike?
3. Assume President Clinton had not met with airline's management. Do you think that the result of the strike would have been the same? Why?

EXPERIENTIAL EXERCISE 1

In the News

Purpose

To identify the parties and their relative power in resolving a conflict.

Task

Pick a local controversial issue either at your school or in your community. Outline the issues involved, the parties and their positions. Identify the basis of power each person or group brings to the issue by determining the dependencies. If the controversy has not yet been resolved, predict the outcome and tell why. If it has been resolved, explain how the players used their power to affect the outcome.

Issue	Parties	Positions	Power Basis	Outcome
	1			
	2			
	3 (etc.)			

EXPERIENTIAL EXERCISE 2

Power Plays

Purpose

To understand how power is acquired by role playing.

Task

Your professor probably utilizes a combination of test scores, class participation, and research papers and assigned written work as a way of determining grades for this course. Assume your professor is *willing* to alter that system; the class determines *by consensus* it wants to be graded for this semester's work. Your task is to reach consensus.

Step 1:   Brainstorm as a group, to list all the possible measures which could be used to grade the course.

Step 2:   Identify a champion for each measure. That champion will be advocating just *one* measure: test scores or research papers, et cetera.

Step 3:   The champions will have three weeks to gain support for their measure among the class outside the classroom.

Step 4:   After the three weeks a decision by the class will be made regarding the system of grading.

Step 5:   After the class decision is made, break the class into groups and discuss and record, using your understanding of power and politics, *why* the class decided the way it did.

Take It
to the Net   **You can find this chapter's World Wide Web exercise at:**
             http://www.prenhall.com/carrell

Chapter 11

Autonomous Work Groups: Employee Teams

Ken Iverson and Nucor Steel

F. Kenneth Iverson is the Chief Executive Officer (CEO) of Nucor Corporation. Nucor is America's seventh largest steel company, and the only one to consistently make a profit during the past twenty years. Nucor has paid an increased dividend each year and has operated profitably in each quarter of every year since 1968 in an industry that has lost money in over half of those years. In addition, Nucor, by policy, has not laid off one worker while the steel industry has laid off over 300,000 workers and shut down numerous plants. Wall Street, it has been said, is "in love with Nucor Corp. and its maverick CEO Iverson." Former U.S. Secretary of Labor Ann McLaughlin said, "Every manager who wonders what it will take to compete in the twenty-first century needs to know the Nucor story."[1]

How has Nucor succeeded in the steel industry while the other U.S. firms have struggled? Ken Iverson proudly but without hesitation cites five reasons:[2]

1. *Employee teams.* All tasks in Nucor's mills are performed by employee teams. Each team is in charge of complete tasks and receives a production bonus when their work standard is exceeded. There is no maximum or "cap" on the bonuses, and they are received the week after they are earned. Team bonuses (each member receives an equal share if they worked each day) *average* 120 percent to 160 percent of the worker's base pay!

2. *Four levels of management.* Iverson believes those closest to the work should make the decisions whenever possible. Thus, the fewer the levels of management, the greater the autonomy given to the team—there is no "hierarchy of middle managers" creating roadblocks to team success. Also, the limited number of management layers allows communications to reach the workers with a minimum of distortion.

3. *Limited staff.* Iverson also believes that staff tend to "get in the way" of effective work teams—so Nucor operates six steel mills, six joist plants, and two products divisions with only a *twenty-two* person staff! The staff are all located at the corporate headquarters in Charlotte, North Carolina.

4. *No layoff policy.* For well over twenty years Nucor has maintained a "no layoff" policy in an industry that has laid off over 350,000 U.S. workers. During lean times Nucor, instead of layoffs, utilizes a "share the pain" policy. This plan reduces the number of days per week the team works according to sales. Some teams have experienced as much as a 60 percent reduction in hours worked—but not one person was laid off. During lean times everyone at Nucor shares the pain; all of the management team, including Iverson experience a loss of income. This sharing policy also extends to benefits. There are no management privileges at Nucor— no reserved parking spaces, company cars, executive dining rooms, et cetera.

5. *Technology.* Iverson believes in investing in state-of-the-art technology. Nucor utilizes continuous casting steelmaking. This method is highly efficient, because the molten steel is directly converted into solid shapes for finishing— thereby eliminating costly intermediate steps common to the old steel furnaces.

These five management principles have enabled Nucor employee teams to average 1200 tons of steel per employee each year compared to 420 tons for the rest of the industry. The average cost of Nucor steel is $60 a ton compared to $140 a ton for the industry. All Nucor mills and plants are located in rural areas and are nonunion; yet Nucor steelmakers consistently average higher annual incomes than unionized workers due to their high levels of productivity and the bonus plan.

The five Nucor principles together build an environment that supports autonomous teams of employees by allowing them to strive for maximum productivity that maximizes their bonus; by working with state-of-the-art technology that increases the productivity of their labor; and by minimizing interference from management or staff. In addition, the teams have a great deal of job security due to the no-layoff policy and thus are able to concentrate on their work more easily than their counterparts in the steel industry.

EMPLOYEE GROUPS

Much of the activity within organizations occurs within groups—from informal groups of employees whose strong friendships affect their working relationships with each other and others within the organization, to formal autonomous work groups such as those at Nucor Corporation. Group activities can be critical to the success of the organization. The utilization of groups in task forces, committees, project teams, problem-solving teams, or self-managed teams is common in organizations.

Characteristics of Groups

One reason for the frequent utilization of groups is *synergy*—the production of the whole (group) is greater than the sum of the parts (individuals). When people work together—on a one time basis or daily in a work team, they exchange ideas, learn from each other, and motivate each other to achieve more than they typically achieve when working in isolation. The heart of this interaction is the social interaction of the group—employees build strong friendships with each other, in fact, often their best friends are their coworkers. Thus, when a group develops a successful working interaction, synergy occurs and it can achieve more as a group than the members could by working individually. This enhanced productivity occurs in three primary areas:[3]

Synergy The production of the whole (group) is greater than the sum of the parts (individuals).

1. *Decision making.* Without a designated leader, who is looked to for most decisions, groups make better decisions than the members would if acting alone.
2. *Problem solving.* Through the exchange of ideas and sharing of information, groups usually solve common problems better than individuals.
3. *Creativity.* With member support for risky decisions, groups are more willing to make innovative or creative changes in their tasks.

When NBC replaced *Today* show newscaster, Jane Pauley, with Deborah Norville, the top-rated show began a ratings plunge. The reason, according to management consultant Michele Jackman, is that NBC overlooked an irreplaceable ingredient of the four-person team—the team's synergy. The old team was a finely tuned group in which members complemented each other—and the whole was greater than the sum of the four talents. The new team may have added a talent, but it never developed the chemistry or synergy that made the old one a top rated group.[4] When NBC replaced Jane Pauley with Deborah Norville, the synergy of the team declined and so did the ratings.

A common characteristic of groups is the development of *norms*. Work-group norms are the standards of behavior or performance that the members of a group expect from each other. Peer pressure on a person to perform according to what

Norms are common characteristics of groups; work-group norms are the standards of behavior or performance that the members of a group expect from each other.

NBC replaced Jane Pauley with Deborah Norville and the top-rated show started a ratings dive. The new team lacked the chemistry of the old one.

other group members expect can be a very powerful influence on one's behavior—often even more powerful than the expectations of a supervisor. Nonconformity with the groups' norm can threaten the very existence of the group, as well as potential recognition, advancement, and rewards.

Group norms, however, can expect low performance as well as superior performance. For example, a group of union workers may have negotiated easy daily performance standards and bonuses for work above those standards. A new group member who works very hard and regularly achieves 200 percent of the standard may be called a "rate buster" by his or her coworkers within the group. They fear, of course, that management may decide to permanently raise the standard production rate or standard if an employee (especially an inexperienced one) can regularly achieve 200 percent of the standard. Thus, an accepted group norm may cause an individual to perform at a lower level than if he or she worked independently.

Another characteristic of a group norm is called *social loafing*. The average productivity of some people may be lower when they work in a group than individually, because they perceive that their individual productivity is not directly measurable or observed by others.

Research on the problem of social loafing in organizations suggests that both extrinsic and intrinsic task-related factors influence social loafing in organizational work groups. Findings indicate that:[5]

- Workers are more likely to engage in social loafing when they believe their behavior is not being monitored. Thus they believe that the relationship between their individual effort and extrinsic rewards or sanctions is weak. This is more likely to occur when individual contributions to group performance is not identifiable.
- Workers are less likely to engage in social loafing when they have high levels of intrinsic involvement (belief that the work is significant and meaningful).
- The greatest reduction in social loafing is likely to occur when individuals are held directly accountable for their own contributions, either by supervisors, team members, or other methods.

When social loafing is experienced possible solutions include (1) enriching or redesigning the job to provide more interesting, challenging work; (2) communicating to individuals the importance of their efforts to the success of the group; (3) utilizing peer evaluations and group productivity bonuses like those at Nucor Corporation. However, it should be recognized that some jobs are boring, dull, and thus provide little intrinsic motivation. Also these jobs can not be redesigned, and social loafing is likely to occur. To reduce its occurrence supervisors often need to maintain a strong presence, keep only small groups, and make individual group members accountable for specific tasks where possible.[6]

Why People Join Groups

A critical factor in the development and continuation of successful work groups is the group's ability to satisfy the needs of its own members. This leads one to ask—Why do people join groups?

Groups, formal and informal, can offer the individual employee a means of fulfilling social, security, esteem, and even self-actualization needs—all the levels of Maslow's Hierarchy of Needs. Often when an employee fulfills these needs through the workplace, it is not the organization, but their formal or informal work group that, in reality, provides the mechanism to fulfill his or her needs. The organization, in fact, may only be a large impersonal institution that provides no basis of interaction for the individual employees. Thus people usually join a group or choose to work effectively within a group to which they have been assigned to meet one or more of their needs.

SECURITY   Most people feel relieved and motivated when they hear that others have the same problems, concerns, and desires. Alone they may feel powerless to act—fearing their thoughts are out of line, or worse, fearing reprisals from their superiors for bringing up the situation. Once they realize their concerns or problems are commonly shared by others, people often feel reinforced, and may act on their concerns. "Strength in numbers" is a popular union slogan. In fact, labor unions largely developed because their members perceived that collectively they could achieve goals that could not be achieved alone.[7]

SOCIAL   Take a piece of paper and write down the names of your ten best friends (nonfamily). Now look at the list and circle the names of those who are people that you work (or have worked) with. If you are like most people, a substantial portion of your friends are people you know from your work environment. Or, ask someone who recently retired what they miss about their work life. Is it the work itself, the affiliation with the employer, or their workplace friends?

Most will cite their friends as what they miss the most. Human beings are social animals, and if we spend eight hours a day with a group of people, it is only natural that some members of that group become our closest friends.

SELF-ESTEEM   "I worked for DuPont for thirty-two years. The most exciting years were when I was a member of the team that developed Dacron." The DuPont retiree, in that brief quote, is conveying what occurs to many people. Their self-esteem is partly due to their affiliation with a group or team that has reached a high level of achievement. Certainly, the members of each year's state high school championship will long be referred to as "one of the champs." In a similar fashion each member of Ford Motor Company's "Team Taurus" will continue to be identified within Ford, the automotive industry, and the entire world of auto enthusiasts as someone who changed automotive history by developing the car that saved Ford Motor Company and convinced U.S. auto executives that the "team" concept could work in this country.[8]

Certainly the same self-esteem can be found in groups or teams within small employers. Pat Biedar, President of Priority Manufacturing, a precision sheetmetal company in Dale, Illinois, credits the creation of work teams with saving her company. She inherited the business upon the death of her husband. At first she turned over the twenty-two employee company to one manager. Then she intuitively realized that was a mistake because "If I worked in a company and was part of a team, I'd love it. It would make me feel more involved. It would make me feel better about myself. It would give me enthusiasm." Thus Priority was changed from the centralized, top-down management to one of independent employee teams, and the change initiated a period of substantial growth.[9]

SELF-ACTUALIZATION   People who are lucky enough to achieve self-actualization, that is, believe they have utilized their abilities to the fullest extent, seldom take the credit for their success. Instead they will cite "those who helped me . . ." just as a football quarterback will credit the linemen, ends, and other members of the team who made it possible for him to set records.

GROUP DECISION MAKING

Many decision making tasks are performed by interactive groups—groups whose members work together in unstructured, face-to-face interactions. For example, employees in an automobile firm's TQM group who are solving a production problem may meet as an interactive group.[10] A management team discussing the merits of a cost reduction program may meet as an interactive team. Also, decision-making groups such as committees, teams, and task forces have the responsibility for making decisions. In fact, in today's business environment, decision-making groups are a well-established aspect of modern organizational life. Because of this, it is important to consider the advantages and disadvantages of using groups to make organizational decisions.

POTENTIAL ADVANTAGES AND DISADVANTAGES   The potential advantages associated with group decision making include: (1) A greater understanding of the decision because group members participate in the various stages of the decision-making process; (2) Groups have more knowledge and information through the pooling of member resources; (3) Groups generate more ideas than individuals and are able to evaluate ideas better than individuals; and (4) Increased commitment to, and acceptance of, the decision because group members had a voice in it. The disadvantages of group decision making include: (1) The amount of time required to reach a decision because groups work slower than do individuals in making a decision; (2) The group may be dominated by a strong individual or clique who may ramrod decisions; (3) Pressure on members to conform or to "fit in" with the group often develops; and (4) On poorly structured, creative tasks, individuals may perform better than groups.

After considering these advantages and disadvantages when should decisions be made by groups and when should they be made by individuals? Research comparing the performance of groups and individuals on a complex learning task has shown that groups as a whole performed better than either the average individual or even the best individual member of the group.[11] Such findings support the idea that the benefits of working in groups goes beyond the simple combination of individual skills.[12] When performing complex problems, groups are superior to individuals if certain conditions prevail (group members have heterogeneous, complementary skills, ideas can be freely shared, and good ideas are accepted). However, when performing simple problems, groups will perform only as well as the best individual in the group, and then only if that person has the correct answer and the response is accepted by the group.[13] Research also indicates that individuals are more productive in solving creative problems than are groups.[14] Research findings also suggest that creativity may be inhibited when individuals are in groups and that groups may slow down the process of bringing creative ideas to fruition.[15]

After having discussed the effectiveness of decision-making groups, an important question is what are some of the factors that may potentially limit the functioning of group decision making? In the following sections we examine two factors that are obstacles to quality group decisions: groupthink and group polarization.

Groupthink

Irving Janis and others have identified an aspect of groups that may affect their ability to objectively discuss issues, evaluate alternative courses of action, and make sound decisions. This characteristic is called *groupthink*. Groupthink can

Groupthink A mode of thinking that people engage in when they are involved in a cohesive group, when the members' desire for unanimity overrides their personal motivation to realistically appraise alternative courses of action.

be defined as "a mode of thinking that people engage in when they are deeply involved in a cohesive group, when the members' desire for unanimity overrides their personal motivation to realistically appraise alternative courses of action."[16]

Public policy fiascos that some theorists believe were caused by the groupthink phenomenon include: The decision of the National Aeronautics and Space Administration (NASA) to launch the space shuttle *Challenger* despite warnings about the potential for the O-ring to fail in colder temperatures. The NASA group was deeply concerned about the lack of public and congressional support the program might have suffered if the launch was delayed further. There were the decisions by members of the Reagan administration to exchange arms for hostages with Iran and to continue commitment to the Nicaraguan contras despite official U.S. policy against such actions. President Reagan's national security advisor Robert McFarland testified the mistake occurred because he didn't "have the guts to stand up and tell the President that . . . ,"[17] which is exactly what groupthink can cause—reluctance of individual group members to object to group decisions they believe are wrong and instead go along with the majority. Other historical examples of groupthink include: The Kennedy administration's decision to invade Cuba at the Bay of Pigs without allowing the military to conduct a full operation; the Nixon administration's decision to coverup the Watergate breakin; and the Johnson administration's decision to escalate the Vietnam war.[18]

Certainly everyone has experienced, to some extent, groupthink—being convinced by high school friends to try alcohol or smoking, going along with coworkers who pass around a petition demanding changes, or agreeing to go with friends who want a new thrill—like skydiving.

When will the groupthink phenomenon occur? Some possible warnings that a group may be experiencing groupthink are presented in Fig. 11-1. Guidelines for preventing the problem are presented in Figure 11-2.

1. Illusion of invulnerability	Group members ignore obvious danger signals, are overoptimistic, and take extreme risks.	
2. Collective rationalization	Group members ignore or discredit warning signals that are contrary to group thinking.	
3. Unquestioned morality	Group members believe that the group's position is moral and ethical, while all others are inherently evil.	
4. Negative stereotyping	Group members cast outsiders in negative terms, making it easier to ignore them because their opposition is expected.	
5. Pressure to conform	Group members are discouraged from expressing dissenting opinions. Members that do may be ostracized or expelled.	
6. Self-censorship	Group members withhold counterarguments or dissenting ideas keeping these to themselves.	
7. Illusion of unanimity	Group members share the false belief that everyone in the group agrees with their judgments.	
8. Mind guards	Group members protect the group from negative, threatening information.	

FIGURE 11-1
Warning Symptoms of Groupthink

Source: Adapted from Irving L. Janis, *Groupthink: Psychological Studies of Policy Decisions and Fiascoes*, 2d ed., Boston, Houghton Mifflin, 1982. Copyright © 1982 by Houghton Mifflin Company. Adapted with permission.

- Group leader should not state his or her position on an issue prior to the group's decision.
- Group members should each assume the role of critical evaluator—actively voicing objections or doubts.
- Have several groups that simultaneously work on the decision.
- Use outside experts to evaluate the group's process.
- Consistently appoint a devil's advocate to question the group's decision.
- Carefully evaluate the competition.
- After a consensus is reached, rethink the alternatives.

Source: Adapted from Irving L. Janis, *Groupthink: Psychological Studies of Policy Decisions and Fiascoes,* 2d ed., Boston, Houghton Mifflin, 1982. Copyright © 1982 by Houghton Mifflin Company. Adapted with permission.

Group Polarization

As a graduate student at MIT, James Stoner noticed that individuals tended to make less risky decisions while groups favored riskier actions. However, when the individuals were placed in a group setting, they shifted to a riskier position. The situation in which a group endorses a riskier position than would its individual members is called the "risky shift." Other studies have shown that, on occasion, groups have chosen a more cautious action than individuals. Such a move is known as "cautious shift."[19]

Researchers quickly become interested in these shifts, and study how groups behave when faced with a decision-involving risk. The studies involved premeeting with group members on an individual basis in which their preference for risk was determined. Following the premeeting, group discussions were conducted. The studies reported that if the premeeting inclination is toward caution, then the group's decision tends to go towards the extreme of the cautious direction. If the premeeting inclination is toward risk, the group's decision tends to be toward the risky extreme. The tendency of groups to move toward extremes is known as *group polarization.*[20] Several reasons have been advanced in attempts to explain the causes for group polarization. One explanation, the social comparison view, suggests that individuals prior to group discussions believe they hold better views than other members. During group discussions, these members see that their views are close to the average of the others, so they shift to more extreme positions.[21] Another explanation, the shared persuasive argument view, is that during group discussions members may be exposed to arguments they had not previously considered. After hearing these arguments, individuals who were initially against an issue become more radically opposed to it while individuals who were in favor of the issue become more strongly supportive following discussion.[22]

Managers should be aware that groups may make increasingly extreme decisions and that these decisions are generally low in quality. If individuals are leaning toward a dangerous decision, then they may tend to support it more strongly following discussion.

Techniques for Improving Group Decisions

Several techniques, which are discussed in this section, have been developed to improve group decision making. These include the structuring of group discussions in certain ways, as well as improving the skill of group members. The techniques include brainstorming, nominal group technique, delphi technique, and electronic brainstorming. (See Fig. 11-3.)

FIGURE 11-3   Four Group Decision-making Techniques in Action

Brainstorming The use of a diverse group of knowledgeable people to generate ideas.

BRAINSTORMING   A primary reason to utilize groups is the generation of new ideas for analyzing problems. The use of a diverse group of knowledgeable people to generate ideas is called *brainstorming*. This practice has received managerial and research support for many years. It has the advantage of being easy to understand and requires little or no training and few rules need to be followed. Generally brainstorming sessions, to be successful:

1. Include three to twelve people knowledgeable about the issue.
2. A group leader introduces a problem or situation that requires innovative ideas or concepts. Members are encouraged to "expand the boundaries," "break the mold," and disregard costs, time, and resource constraints.
3. Group members are asked to throw out any idea that occurs to them. One rule is that no one is allowed to criticize or evaluate any idea; instead, the primary advantage of the process is to build upon the thoughts of others and try to generate as many ideas as possible.
4. The group leader records all ideas generated that will receive discussion and analysis at a later time. The objective of the process is to generate as many new ideas as possible.

Research on brainstorming has concluded that it can be an effective technique to generate new ideas or identify potential solutions to problems.[23] However, the productivity of brainstorming groups declines as the groups exceed a certain size of approximately twelve members. Another problem with brainstorming groups is that some members may feel apprehensive about vocalizing their ideas if they feel their ideas may be ridiculed or rejected, or if they are intimidated by higher-status members in a group. Another problem with the brainstorming technique is called production blocking, which occurs when an individual cannot express their ideas because another person is talking. If the group contains even one or two domineering people, the synergistic effect brainstorming should produce can be lost due to production blocking.

Nominal group technique In making decisions, group members act independently and are given anonymity.

NOMINAL GROUP TECHNIQUE   A group method that research has shown to be generally superior to brainstorming is the *nominal group technique*. This process is similar to brainstorming except group members act independently and are given anonymity. The process generally is as follows:[24]

1. Three or more knowledgeable people meet, but without discussion, and each writes down his or her suggestions or ideas.
2. The group leader asks each member, in turn, to contribute his or her ideas that are displayed on a flipchart, blackboard, et cetera. The ideas are not explained or evaluated until all are presented.
3. The group members explain and discuss each idea without criticism or evaluation.
4. A final comparison is made by each group member rank-ordering the ideas independently. An aggregate ranking then determines the final comparison.

The nominal group process, compared to brainstorming, has the advantages of minimizing production blocking since members are independently generating ideas and each is given a chance to contribute and explain his or her suggestion. In addition, by providing anonymity to the listing of ideas, members are less inhibited by higher-status members. The primary advantage of the nominal group process is the elimination (or minimization depending on the skills of the group leader) of the arguments and hostilities that can occur during group meetings. The process also produces a final rank-ordered comparison of the ideas, which is usually not the goal of a pure brainstorming session.

Another advantage of the technique is that a group decision can be developed in only a few hours. This technique can also be used in situations in which participants fear criticism from others. A disadvantage of the technique is its highly structured format. Usually, only one narrowly defined problem can be considered at a time.[25]

DELPHI TECHNIQUE   A third approach is the *Delphi technique* that was first developed by the Rand Corporation. The unique feature of this method is that the group members are never brought together in one location. Instead questionnaires are utilized to communicate with the group members. Today, with electronic mail and FAX machines, this method no longer has the disadvantage of being more time-consuming than the others. At the same time individuals who are located in several locations or whose schedules are conflicting can participate in a successful group-decision process. The steps, in general, are as follows:

Delphi technique The use of a questionnaire developed by the group leader that states the problem and requests solutions or ideas, which are submitted anonymously.

1. The group leader develops and distributes questionnaires that state the problem and requests solutions or ideas.
2. Potential solutions or ideas are submitted anonymously by group members.
3. The group leader summarizes the input from the members in a new questionnaire that is distributed to the group members.
4. Members respond to the initial set of ideas or solutions presented in the second questionnaire. If no decision is reached, the group leader can repeat the process.

ELECTRONIC BRAINSTORMING   An emerging new method of group decision making is *electronic brainstorming*. In an electronic brainstorming (EB) session, group members utilize computer technology in the generation of ideas and solutions.

Electronic brainstorming Group members utilize computer technology in the generation of ideas and solutions.

Members simultaneously type their suggestions into a computer that then distributes them to the computer screens of all group members at the appropriate time. This process combines the main advantage of traditional brainstorming—the synergy created by simultaneous sharing of ideas with advantages of the nominal group process—being able to generate ideas without inhibitions or production blocking. The process, which may vary, may go as follows:[26]

1. The group leader explains the rules of brainstorming and how EB functions to the members who are seated around a U-shaped table. Each member has a computer monitor and keyboard. The group may use one or two practice problems to become comfortable with the technology.
2. The group leader types in the problem that is displayed on each member's screen.
3. Group members then simultaneously type in their ideas that are displayed on all screens.
4. The group leader records all ideas. In a process similar to nominal group technique, the members may be asked to rate or rank the order of the ideas to produce an aggregate evaluation.

Research results on EB have produced significant implications and suggest that the method may provide several advantages:[27]

- Participants feel satisfied with the process and believe they can express their ideas quickly.
- The anonymity provided reduces the inhibitory effects of traditional brainstorming. Lower-status members are less apprehensive about presenting their ideas.
- Increasing group size does not constrain the generation of ideas that can occur with larger groups in non-EB settings.
- Production-blocking does not occur since all members can contribute ideas simultaneously. The process also prevents one or two members from dominating the process.
- Group members can be at separate locations (similar to the Delphi technique) and still generate ideas interactively.

The possible disadvantage of EB is that all group members must have access to computer equipment and be willing to participate in a technology-based process. However, with the rapidly increased utilization of computer technology and computer conferencing, this may be a disadvantage to a smaller number of groups.

EMPLOYEE TEAMS

In most organizations today formal groups may consist of employees who are responsible for an identifiable work process, a specific project, or a problem that needs solving, often called "teams" or "autonomous work groups." These teams or work groups have been called the productivity breakthrough of the 1990s—even though some of the first ones have been in existence for over twenty years like those at General Foods in Topeka, Kansas. In fact, it was in 1971 when five General Foods executives and a Harvard business professor inaugurated a new dog food production facility in Topeka, Kansas. Often referred to as the "Topeka System" in the early years, the managers decided it was time to shake up the system and design an organization that would eliminate the "blue collar blues" of boredom and alienation so common in manufacturing plants. They ignored the basic principles that fueled the Industrial Revolution by organizing work through a system of autonomous work teams, and in the process avoided highly specialized jobs and centralized management control. Team members were trained in a dozen or more skills, and the group was given the authority and responsibility previously handled by supervisors. Then, the management hierarchy was flattened to only three levels. For over twenty years the Topeka System has worked; The plant continues to be highly efficient. There are problems though, such as no opportunity for promotion, but the team members still rate Topeka as a great place to work![28]

Why haven't more organizations developed work teams, and why did so many that have them wait until the 1980s or 1990s? A survey of over 500 organizations that successfully organize work around employee teams found, and most experts agree, that the reason is Frederick Taylor. Taylor around the turn of the century recommended "Scientific Management" principles that centered on designing jobs that contained a few simple repetitive tasks provided under close supervision. All decisions would be made by top management, which was in the best position to judge what was best for the organization. Taylor's principles were widely adopted by industrial America. Workers who in large numbers had previously worked on the farm or in small craft shops were hired by large manufacturing firms where they had little sense of ownership, participation, or control. Taylor's principles were expanded by owners and managers and through centralized management, a large scale, high volume facility with highly specialized jobs became the norm.[29] These organizations in many cases were highly successful, but many over time suffered from poor quality, high absenteeism and turnover, high rates of accidents and injuries, and little innovation or creativity.

American management in the 1960s did, however, begin to question some of the principles of scientific management and began moving toward greater employee participation and an enhanced "quality of worklife." In the 1970s quality circles involving groups of employees working together to analyze and solve specific problems, greatly enhanced the idea of teams of employees working together, without management control, to increase productivity. While the Topeka System began in 1971, only a few pioneering American firms extensively utilized employee teams until the 1980s when the number grew rapidly.[30] The value of successful teamwork in today's organizations is seen as critical to an organization's prosperity and survival by one CEO of twenty-seven years—see "Profile" on F. Lynn Blystone.

Formal employee teams can generally be divided into three categories: special project teams, problem-solving teams, and self-managed teams. *Self-managed teams* are characterized as permanent groups of employees who perform all tasks required of one general activity and perform the supervisory duties related to their work. The Nucor Corporation and Topeka System (General Foods) teams discussed earlier would fall in this general category. Special project teams are usually formed by combining people from different functions to design, develop, and produce new products or services. Problem-solving teams usually meet on a regular basis to analyze, recommend, and implement solutions to selected problems.

Self-managed teams Permanent groups of employees who perform all tasks of one general activity and perform the supervisory duties related to their work.

Project Teams

In the 1980s a handful of U.S. companies began using a new approach to new product development—the project team. *Project teams* most often consist of ten to fifteen people from different functions such as research and development, engineering, manufacturing, and marketing brought together to design and develop a new product quickly and successfully. How do these groups manage to produce results within time constraints? Research indicates that a key factor in the success of these groups is their ability to pace themselves through creative work. In general, successful groups do not use several points to mark their progress against the deadline, but instead utilize the midpoint to judge their efforts. They often experience a deliberate, abrupt shift at the midpoint towards their deadline by either (1) declaring the work up to then, complete, and start the next phase, or (2) dropping their approach up to that point and adapt a new one. All teams or groups use some form of pacing to complete special projects, and most use the midpoint as the critical point to assess their progress, agree upon completed work, and move on to final phases of their efforts.[31] The project team is viewed as an autonomous group operating independently within the organization. Some of the early project teams' successes include the IBM Personal Computer, 3M's Post-It, and Jell-O's Pudding Snacks.[32] (See Fig. 11-4.)

Project teams consist of ten to fifteen people from different functions, such as research and development, engineering, manufacturing, and marketing brought together to design and develop a new product quickly and successfully.

Profile

F. Lynn Blystone
President & Chief Executive Officer
Tri-Valley Corporation
Bakersfield, California

TEAMWORK IN BUSINESS

Today the constituencies involved in business are many and growing. They include all levels of government and a myriad of special interests as well as those specific to one's industry and company such as vendors, owners, and employees. Thus, to the extent one thinks of only the employed staff as "the team," one risks creating a host of nonteam relationships that can actively overwhelm, if adversarial, or apathetically fail to provide critical support.

I have spent twenty-seven years as a chief executive officer of a variety of organizations. These include a nonprofit youth organization as well as for profit firms engaged in venture capital, insurance, Learjet charter service, commercial construction, municipal finance and extractive industries. I have worked through 21 percent prime rate, stock market crash, and massive withdrawal of investment support from my segments of business.

Since 1981, I have been CEO of a full-reporting publicly traded company engaged in petroleum and mineral exploration, production, and derivative technologies. During that time, 70 percent of my industry has disappeared and downsizing and flight of capital continues. Still, we have managed to gain 146 places on the *Oil & Gas Journal* annual list of U.S. petroleum companies and become a major producer of natural gas in California.

I can tell you that, very often, broadly based teamwork and its associated goodwill surpassed all our balance sheet resources in assisting our survival and prosperity.

Business teamwork is a method of stimulating a common orientation of workday effort among all parties involved. It usually proceeds in ever-widening relationships from the employed staff. It will not long endure with negative factors of greed, duplicity, ruthless ambition, or excessive privilege.

It can be fostered and sustained through attitudes of service, fairness, openness, accuracy, and timely performance. It can be extended by appropriately advising parties of their inclusion in the teamwork process.

It helps to declare a mission with goals and objectives. Written plans tend to refine and define both. People are more likely to support, or at least not oppose, objectives and means in which they have had a voice in determining. Sometimes disagreements cannot be bridged and sometimes a CEO must persevere even without majority support. The temporary disunity that may result when a CEO must make an unpopular decision will generally be short-lived if the reasons for the action are understood as ultimately beneficial to the overall team.

While certain entrepreneurial enterprises seem to flourish in a laissez-faire environment, teamwork is more likely to sustain with fair discipline. However, a blizzard of procedures can obscure central goals that can be commonly held, and teamwork will evaporate to be replaced by turf wars and insular, noncooperative attitudes.

Thus, goals that can be commonly held, procedures that are perceived as fair, communication/involvement to accommodate changes in conditions and competent performance can build and maintain teamwork. In a time of economic and political uncertainty, it will carry the day against adversity and competitors focused on internal turf wars no matter how well capitalized they are.

The factors that have caused a growing number of companies to turn to project teams include: (1) rising global competition has greatly increased the need to reduce the time required to successfully put a new product on the market; (2) employees today expect and are able to provide greater meaningful input into the development of new products, (3) the past successes of project teams as well

FIGURE 11-4
What's a Team?

There are several types of teams. Here are three of the most common:

Problem-Solving	**Special Project**	**Self-Managed**
Usually five to twelve volunteers who meet a few hours a week to discuss ways of improving quality, efficiency, and work environment.	Usually ten to fifteen people from different functional areas. May design and introduce work reforms or new technology, or meet with suppliers and customers. In union shops, labor and management collaborate at all levels.	From five to fifteen workers who learn all production tasks and rotate from job to job. Teams do managerial duties such as schedule work and order materials.

Source: Aaron Bernstein, "Putting a Damper on That Old Team Spirit," *Business Week*, May 4, 1992, p. 60.

as other employee teams has convinced more managers to relinquish their authority to project teams; and (4) the synergy factor discussed earlier is believed to be a significant force that drives team members to be more creative, work harder, and achieve greater productivity than they would if they were given only a limited view of the project.

Studies of successful project teams indicate they may differ from the traditional functional organizational structure in one of three common formats. As Fig. 11-5 illustrates, the traditional functional organization groups jobs into disciplines (such as engineering, manufacturing, marketing) under one general manager. When a new project idea is introduced by the general manager, the function managers meet to coordinate ideas and processes. The actual work on the project then passes sequentially from one function to the next. The advantage of this process is the utilization of job specialists. The primary disadvantage of the traditional process is that people are evaluated independent of the overall success of the project. Thus no one involved in the details of the project is responsible for the final results!

Three types of project team structures also appear in Fig. 11-5. The "lightweight" structure is similar to the traditional structure in that the team members remain in their functional areas, but each functional group of employees working on the project designates a "liaison" person to represent it on a project committee. These liaisons work with a "lightweight project manager" who coordinates the activities of the project. In this structure the project manager is a "lightweight" because they are usually a junior-level person with little decision-making authority, and most importantly, the resources and functional employees are still controlled by the functional manager. The primary advantage of the lightweight structure over the traditional structure is improved communications, and at least one person (the lightweight project manager) is striving to keep the project on track. Another advantage is the minimal disruption to the organization's normal operations.

Unfortunately, however, this structure does not guarantee the speed or success of a new project to the extent the last two structures provide. In the "heavyweight" project team structure the project manager is usually a senior manager who outranks the functional managers, has direct authority and responsibility for all people working on the project (see Fig. 11-5), and has control of the project from concept to market. The employees in the functional areas remain

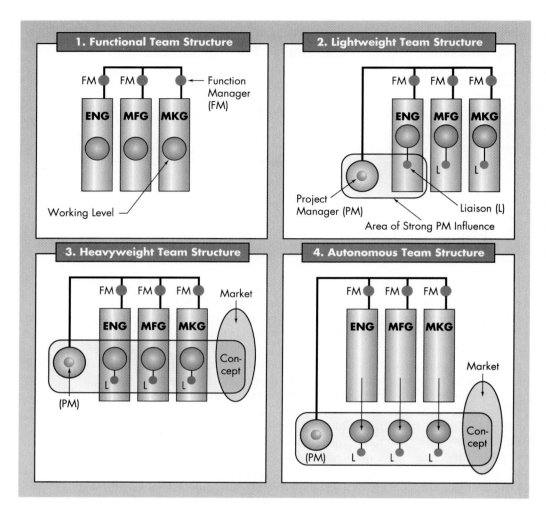

FIGURE 11-5 Traditional Functional and Project Team Structures

Source: Reprinted from Kun B. Clark and Steven C. Wheelwright, "Organizing and Leading 'Heavyweight' Development Teams," *California Management Review*, vol. 34, no. 3, Spring 1992, pp. 9–28. Copyright © 1992 by the Regents of the University of California. By permission of The Regents.

assigned to those areas and report to their functional manager once the project is complete. Due to the greater control of resources and all employees involved in the project, the heavyweight structure is more likely to be successful—but also is more disruptive to the functional team structure. The autonomous team structure formally assigns, and often physically locates, the employees involved in the project to the project manager, who is the sole evaluator of their performance. In the other three structures this is shared with the function manager. In this structure the project team is totally responsible for the success or failure of the project—the functional managers are not held accountable for the project at all.

The primary advantage of the autonomous project team structure is that its total control of resources allows it to focus on the rapid completion of the project. Cross-functional integration can be maximized because the team can attract and select team members with the needed talents and commitment.[33] Like the heavyweight structure, in the autonomous structure all employees involved in the project work for the project manager from the concept stage to market. The disadvantage, of course, is the entire separation of the employees involved from their functional areas.

The increased utilization of project teams has generally involved the heavyweight or autonomous team structure. The very nature of these teams makes them highly focused on their mission, independent from other organizational procedure or process constraint policies or politics, and usually quite broadbased in skills and abilities. A major challenge to the organization is to keep project teams from significantly disrupting the ongoing activities of the rest of the organization.

The five keys to selecting and developing successful special project teams, according to Ken Murphy of Union Carbide Chemicals and Plastics Company Inc., Danbury, Connecticut, are:[34]

- *Priority.* The organization must be willing to specify the project as a top priority and give the team the needed resources and total control of the project. If the team cannot secure the needed resources or depart from past practices and procedures, it will probably not succeed.
- *Recruiting team members.* Joining a project team is a high risk for employees who may see career doors closed if the project fails. Successful teams often recruit management superstars accustomed to taking risks and "rock solid" middle managers thrilled at the chance for a new challenge. The key ingredient for all of the team players is that they can work together with people from other disciplines and focus entirely on one objective.
- *Team management.* Successful project teams generally work together within the space in the company, not isolation, report only to top management, make all decisions on the project, and receive significant bonus incentives if the team meets or exceeds goals.
- *Team leader, members.* The team leader largely keeps the team focused on the goal and secures the resources the members request. Members should assume equality during the project regardless of differences in salary, status, or job function.
- *Managing expectations.* Success or failure may largely be due to the expectations the team sets for itself and communicates with others. Underpromising and overdelivering is often a successful team strategy!

Companies that successfully utilized project teams include:

- *NCR.* In 1990, NCR decided it had to have a new vertical floorstand computer with several new features if NCR was to remain competitive. Management decided the traditional functional approach would not work and instead appointed a new project team. The result was the NCR System 3000 floorstand computer that required fewer assembly operations, contained fewer parts, and cost less than its predecessor! And, the project was completed in seven months.[35]
- *AT&T.* John Hanley, AT&T's vice president of Product Development needed a new cordless phone in half the time taken to design similar products in the past. Hanley created project teams that had the authority to make every decision—cost, physical appearance, how it would operate, etc. Specific requirements regarding quality of the phone, however, were set by management. The new phone was on the market in under a year (compared to two years for similar new phones) and all quality, design, and operational requirements were met.[36]

OB in Practice

Project Teams at Freudenberg-NOK

Freudenberg-NOK is a partnership between a German manufacturing company, Freudenberg & Company, and a Japanese manufacturing company, NOK Corporation. It operates fourteen manufacturing facilities in North America. One plant in Cleveland, Georgia began operation in 1989 and soon began to draw a great deal of attention outside of the company and the entire industry. Why? It was operating at a level *60 percent* higher than the average American competition. Top management at Freudenberg-NOK quickly realized that "something good was going on here" and wanted to replicate it.

The key to the success of the plant, according to its chief administrator, Gary Johnson, was utilizing cellular manufacturing with a team-centered organization, which utilized a kaizen (continuous improvement) program.

The kaizen programs at Freudenberg-NOK are typically four days in duration. It starts with one-half day's training on the tools of the Toyota Production System. Then teams are given quantifiable goals and 3.5 days to work toward the accomplishment of these goals. At the end of this time they will present a report—text and physical examples—to management (certainly including managers up to the plant manager and possibly including president and CEO Joe Day—who had participated in a kaizen) on what they've accomplished.

The Toyota Production System was developed after World War II by Taiichi Ohno, who was Toyota's vice president of Operations. Dr. Ohno personally trained a small cadre of Toyota people in the system, who then went out and evangelized. A few of those people retired from Toyota and subsequently formed a consulting group called Shingijutsu. In 1991, Anand Sharma formed TBM Consulting. He had been a vice president at Union Switch & Signal, an American Standard Company, who had been responsible for implementing JIT manufacturing practices at the company's worldwide facilities, the organization that brought him into contact with the people of Shingijutsu. TBM Consulting and Shingijutsu then established a strategic alliance, so that in some cases people from both firms worked on projects. This was the case at Freudenberg-NOK.

Kaizen project teams are running with regularity at all Freudenberg-NOK plants. The consequences of these events make it clear why they are being performed:

- Leadtime: 48 percent improvement
- Productivity: 58 percent improvement
- Work-in-Process: 78 percent improvement
- Floor space: 30 percent improvement
- Distance traveled: 71 percent improvement
- Cycle time: 81 percent improvement
- Scrap: 17 percent improvement

In the spring of 1992, Kaizen teams began operating at the Legonier, Indiana plant. Within two years the plant's productivity had doubled.

Source: Gary S. Vasilash, "Walking the Talk of Kaizen at Freudenberg-NOK," *Production*, December 1993, pp. 66–71.

- *Motorola.* The Motorola Communications Section was given the task of developing a belt-worn pager to be added to its highly successful line of Bravo pagers. A project team was formed with representatives from engineering, robotics, process engineering, procurement, product design, accounting, and human resources. In less than eighteen months production of the new pager was begun (less than half the normal time required), cost objectives with substantially higher, profit margins were met, and the product exceeded reliability standards.[37]

Problem-solving Teams

Special project teams and self-managed teams are the most common and, perhaps, best publicized types of employee teams. *Problem-solving teams* have increased in popularity and are used to a lesser extent, but can be highly successful. Many problem-solving teams have their roots in quality circles (see Chapter 19) and may be characterized as mature, fully empowered, quality circles. The creation of permanent problem-solving teams should not be surprising—a 1991 American Society for Training and Development survey of organizations with employee teams found the most common objective of all teams is problem solving (72 percent of those responding listed this as an objective), team building was second (61 percent), and improving quality was third (58 percent).[38] Thus many organizations with positive experiences with quality circles and problem solving as an ongoing concern, allowed the evolution of quality circles or similar groups into permanent problem-solving teams.

An excellent example is the Wallace Company Inc., a Houston, Texas-based pipe distribution company. While the oil industry was suffering one of its worst slumps during the mid-1980s, Wallace was able to increase sales per employee for six straight years and increase its critical quality measure—on-time delivery to 92 percent from 75 percent. When the slump began, however, Wallace was forced to close three offices and lay off employees. The company then made a switch in focus of operations from sales to repair and maintenance. At the time of the change CEO John W. Wallace hired a consulting firm to perform a needs assessment. The results told him that fear was prevalent and the employees were afraid to discuss ideas on problems with management. That led Wallace to change the management style of the company as well. The firm's quality circles that had started a few years earlier had a record of success but limited scope of authority. Wallace led the development of the circles into a fully empowered Quality Improvement Process network of teams. Eventually, the QIP teams were responsible for "more than 80 percent of the day-to-day decisions at Wallace."[39]

Most employees at Wallace belong to more than one team. They primarily belong to a natural work team, but also belong to other teams appointed to solve a specific problem. The Director of Education and Training assigns team members, helps develop a mission statement, and follows the team's progress. Teams are even utilized to develop marketing plans for new accounts. Within two years after the QIP teams were started, not only did on-time deliveries rise by 17 percent but absenteeism and turnover declined by over half. One specific example of a team's success was the change in the safety program from a "policing type-turn in offenders" to empowering any associate (employee) to stop any operation when a safety problem exists. The new safety program saved Wallace over $500,000 in insurance-related expenses in its first year of operation.[40]

In 1990, The Wallace Company Inc. became only the second smallest company (280 employees) to win the highly acclaimed Malcolm Baldrige National Quality Award.

Problem-solving teams
Through the exchange of ideas and sharing of information, groups of employees analyze and solve assigned problems.

Problem-Solving Teams at Reynolds and Reynolds

A problem-solving team at Reynolds and Reynolds, a computer repair operation in Dayton, Ohio increased productivity by 35 percent in less than one year at almost no cost. The plant manager, Randall Selleck, started the change by asking for volunteers to join an employee team that would work on solving problems. Only eleven people responded and only five joined the first team! Others soon followed. The team, however, responded quickly by funneling ideas to management and cross-training technicians. The team named itself ACT, Accomplishing Communications Team, and set improving communications as its primary goal. No supervisors or managers were allowed in the meetings. Among the changes implemented were:

- A weekly schedule developed by repair and distribution workers that specified priorities.
- Cross-training repair technicians to enable them to perform all repairs necessary on each computer instead of, for example, only repairing monitors.
- Development of an on-line computer network that listed all parts on back order.
- Placing a static seal on the inner bag and a label on the outer carton of finished computers. Thus, if a part was returned, the seal would indicate if it had been opened.

The ideas were not farfetched or expensive. Gordon Petrik, a supervisor, commented: "Letting go wasn't too hard. By doing so, we were also asking the workers to take ownership of problems." The results included a remarkable increase in the number of units repaired—from 4,800 a month to 6,500 a month in less than a year with no new positions and only one new piece of equipment—a conveyor belt. The average cost of a repair at Reynolds is $35—compared to $185 on the outside that saves the parent company about $8 million each year. Improvements in quality included:

- Reducing back orders from 5 percent to 1.3 percent.
- Reducing average repair time from two weeks to twenty-four hours.
- Cutting the time required to box repaired units from thirty days to one-half day.
- Eliminating the need to recheck returned parts (10 percent of total work previously) by sealing them in plastic bags.

Source: Adapted from Cox News Service, *Omaha World-Herald,* November 15, 1992, p. 56.

Self-managed Teams

Self-managed employee teams (also called autonomous work groups or self-directed teams) have emerged as a new way of life in many American organizations. They have even been called "the new American industrial weapon" in cover stories in *Business Week, Fortune,* and other business publications.[41]

Exactly what are self-directed or self-managed teams? While no universal definition exists, one that is quite good follows:[42]

A *self-managed team* is a small group of employees responsible for an entire work process or segment. Team members work together to improve their operation or product, plan their work, resolve day-to-day problems, and manage themselves.

Thus self-directed teams are groups of employees who normally work together on an ongoing day-to-day basis. They are not groups formed to design and develop special projects or new products, or to analyze and solve problems as discussed previously in the prior two sections. Their members have not been selected from functional areas to work together as a team. Instead, these teams are permanent components within the organization that "get the work out" on a daily basis. The key difference is that their work is assigned to a team; in traditional organizations, it would be assigned to a department with a supervisor or head who then assigned portions of the work to individuals within the department.

The characteristics of self-managed teams include:[43]

- They plan, control, and make decisions about their work; they self-manage!
- They set their own productivity goals and inspect their own work, within limits.
- They set their own work schedules.
- Members select, appraise, and discipline each other.
- They are responsible for the quality of their work.

Organizations that have chosen to organize work to be performed by self-managed teams are quite different than traditional organizations with highly specialized jobs. They often have far fewer levels of management. For example, in the chapter opening discussion of the Nucor Corporation, we note it has only four levels of management compared to an average of ten in the steel industry. The teams perform many of the functions normally performed by the additional layers of management—assign work, check to see that it is done properly, discipline people when necessary, hire employees, appraise performance, et cetera. The supervisor's role largely vanishes, because the team members supervise themselves. And thus, of course, their vanished supervisors don't need another layer of management to supervise them. A large amount of savings often occurs from the reduction in the number of supervisors and managers that are eliminated by self-managed teams.[44] Another difference is that all members of the teams must learn all the tasks and jobs, not just a single job as they would in a traditional organization.

The key differences between traditionally designed organizations and self-directed team organizations are summarized in Fig. 11-6.

The successful creation and utilization of self-directed teams has been reported by a large number of U.S. companies including Ford Motor Company,

Element	Traditional Organizations	Self-Directed Teams
Organizational structure	Layered/individual	Flat/team
Job design	Narrow single-task	Whole process/multiple-task
Management role	Direct/control	Coach/facilitate
Leadership	Top-down	Shared with team
Information flow	Controlled/limited	Open/shared
Rewards	Individual/seniority	Team-based/skills-based
Job Process	Managers plan, control, improve	Teams plan, control, improve

Source: Richard S. Wellins, William C. Byham, Jeanne M. Wilson, *Empowered Teams,* San Francisco, Jossey-Bass, 1991, p. 6. Copyright © 1991 by Jossey-Bass Inc., Publishers. Used by permission.

Figure 11-6

Key Differences between Self-directed Team Organizations and Traditional Organizations

Procter and Gamble, Digital Equipment, IDS, Honeywell, Cummins Engine, General Electric, Boeing, and LTV Steel. In general, these companies all report many positive benefits from their experience with self-directed teams including higher productivity, improved quality (usually the major goal), improved employee morale, better attendance, and lower turnover.[45] A survey of top managers of these and other companies that are using self-directed teams asked why other organizations should consider developing teams, the major reasons cited were:[46]

- *Improved Quality, Productivity, Service.* To stay competitive most organizations must continually improve quality, service, costs, and speed. This requires the day-to-day attention of all employees. The Japanese call it *kaizen*—continuous improvement. The sense of ownership that members of a team develop makes continuous improvement possible.
- *Greater Flexibility.* Organizations must be able to constantly respond to changing customer needs. Work teams communicate better, identify new opportunities faster, and implement needed changes more quickly, because they do not need to wait for approval from a traditional hierarchy. The team members are more proactive and alert to customer needs, because they realize they can make the difference between success and failure.
- *Reduced Operating Costs.* Self-directed teams enable organizations to reduce costs by eliminating layers of middle management. The teams make the decisions, plan the work, and solve problems, et cetera, that are "passed up the organization" in traditional companies.
- *Faster Response to Technological Change.* New technologies demand greater skills, communication among workers, and greater coordination among work activities, thus workers who previously worked alone must work more closely together. Teams provide a natural environment for such coordination.
- *Fewer Job Classifications.* Increased technology demands multiskilled employees with greater flexibility to perform many related job functions. Traditional organizations often have many job classifications each with one or two employees. Self-directed teams train their members to perform all tasks—thus each work team has only one job classification. In addition, the reduced number of management layers, as previously discussed, also reduces the number of classifications. The Toyota plant in Georgetown, Kentucky, for example, has only three job classifications, compared to an average of one hundred fifty in most U.S. plants.
- *Ability to Attract and Retain Good People.* Employees in today's work force want greater autonomy, challenge, and responsibility in their jobs. Teams offer the type of jobs desired by the most creative and talented members of the work force. The two help wanted ads in Fig. 11-7 both appeared in the same newspaper from two different automotive companies seeking maintenance personnel. One firm operates in a traditional manner, the other with self-directed teams—which would you rather work for?

Productivity of Work Teams

Creating self-directed work teams requires a substantial change in the design of the work process, employee roles, and an acceptance of less authority and responsibility by management. Teams can take up to two years to become fully pro-

OUR TEAM NEEDS ONE GOOD MULTISKILLED MAINTENANCE ASSOCIATE

Our team is down one good player. Join our group of multiskilled Maintenance Associates who work together to support our assembly teams at American Automotive Manufacturing.

We are looking for a versatile person with skills in one or more of the following: ability to set up and operate various welding machinery, knowledge in electric arc and M.I.G. welding, willingness to work on detailed projects for extended time periods, and general overall knowledge of the automobile manufacturing process. Willingness to learn all maintenance skills a must. You must be a real team player, have excellent interpersonal skills, and be motivated to work in a highly participative environment.

Send qualifications to:

AAM

American Automotive Manufacturing
P.O. Box 616
Ft. Wayne, Indiana 48606
Include phone number. We respond
to all applicants.

MAINTENANCE TECHNICIAN/WELDER

Leading automotive manufacturer looking for Maintenance Technician/Welder. Position requires the ability to set up and operate various welding machinery and a general knowledge of the automobile production process. Vocational school graduates or 3–5 years of on-the-job experience required. Competitive salary, full benefits, and tuition reimbursement offered.

Interviews Monday, May 6, at the Holiday Inn South, 3000 Semple Road, 9:00 a.m. to 7:00 p.m. Please bring pay stub as proof of last employment.

National Motors Corporation
5169 Blane Hill Center
Springfield, Illinois 62707

FIGURE 11-7 Two Employment Advertisements for Maintenance Positions: One from an Automotive Work Team, One from a Traditional Employer

Source: Richard S. Wellins, William C. Byham, Jeanne M. Wilson, *Empowered Teams,* San Francisco, Jossey-Bass, 1991, p. 20. Copyright © 1991 by Jossey-Bass Inc., Publishers. Used by permission.

ductive, and the experience of most organizations is that employee turnover will increase and productivity decrease during the period of adaptation. So why then are many employers paying the costs of an organization built on employee teams? Because in the long-run, work teams result in greater quality and productivity. A survey by the American Society of Training and Development of companies that use self-directed teams indicated the following factors had "improved" or "significantly improved":[47]

- Productivity (77 percent of the firms)
- Quality (72 percent)
- Job Satisfaction (65 percent)
- Customer Service (57 percent)
- Waste Reduction (55 percent)

The one factor reported that most likely affects all the others is job satisfaction or employee morale. The employees at Northern Telecom's Morrisville, North Carolina operation are probably typical of the attitudes reported by work team members:[48]

"I now look forward to coming to work. I don't *have* to go to work. I *get* to go to work."

Al Reynolds

"I enjoy what I do. I enjoy the challenge. Every day I'm learning something new."

Amanda Dunston

Certainly every manager, supervisor, or owner would hope that each of their employees would express themselves like Reynolds and Dunston. Employees with such high levels of motivation are naturally going to increase productivity, quality, and customer service. Debra Boggan, Northern Telecom's plant manager explains: "The status quo wasn't going to cut it . . . In the 1990s the companies that will succeed are the ones that put innovation and team spirit back into the workplace." Northern Telecom experienced a 63 percent increase in revenues, productivity per employee increased by 60 percent, earnings increased by 46 percent, and with 40 percent *fewer* quality inspectors, quality increased 50 percent![49]

Other firms' experiences with self-managed teams have reported similar positive results:[50]

- *Westinghouse Furniture Systems* increased productivity by 74 percent in three years.
- *Federal Express Corporation* reduced service errors (from an industry-leading low) by 13 percent.
- *Carrier,* the heating/air division of United Technologies Corp., reduced average turnaround (completion) time.
- *General Electric*'s Salisbury, North Carolina plant increased productivity by 250 percent compared to other GE plants producing the same products.
- *Corning Glass* decreased defect rates from 1,800 parts per million to nine parts per million at its work team ceramics plant.
- *General Mills*'s food processing plants that use teams average 40 percent higher productivity than the traditional plants.

Jack Bergman, a thirty-eight-year General Electric employee explained the remarkable 250 percent above-average production level in the Salisbury plant: "Team direction is one of the best techniques for realizing a payback in quality and customer service. It's the ultimate productivity tool." GE has continued to expand the team concept following the success of the Salisbury plant. Rob Birch, Vice President of Operations, Steelcase, Ltd., agrees with Bergman. At Steelcase he led the effort to establish the first work teams because, "We recognized that our people were underutilized. They weren't being challenged." Birch saw the expansion of teams at Steelcase reach over 80 percent of the work force.

Potential Work Team Problems

Why aren't all employers changing to self-directed work teams? According to Anna Ver Steeg of Northern Telecom, it's because it is a difficult, time-consuming process. In addition, research and case studies of organizations that try to change to work teams conclude that there are some initial, potential problems:

- *Supervisor Turnover.* Significant change is always difficult for employees to accept. The members of the management team most affected by a change to work teams are the first-line supervisors who see their jobs change from managers to coaches and realize a substantial loss in their authority. The transition from supervisor to team member is not an easy one but can be accomplished if one has the view of Jennifer Synhorst (see "Profile," Supervisor to Team Leader). Northern Telecom and Steelcase both reported a loss of over 25 percent of their first line supervisors after changing to work teams.[52]

- *Social Loafing.* Since the focus of productivity shifts from the individual to the group, it is possible for one or more members to decrease their output, because they feel the reduction cannot be detected. Research indicates that, in fact, social loafing is more likely to occur when people work in groups and perceive they have a low visibility. The problem, however, is moderated when employees have a high level of involvement in their work. If self-directed teams achieve the high level of job satisfaction often reported, social loafing should be minimized if not eliminated due to members' intrinsic involvement in their work.[53]

- *Higher Absenteeism and Turnover.* The transition from a traditional organization to work teams often requires up to two years. During this time higher than normal levels of team member absences and turnover have been reported. The longer hours and greater training required may be significant causes of these problems.[54]

Even when teams have been established and are operating beyond the experimental stage, a number of factors can limit the maximum productivity of teams. Regardless of an organization's efforts to successfully develop work teams, research on over 500 organizations with operational teams found two major factors that can limit their success—individual factors and organizational factors:[55]

Individual Factors:

- An unwillingness of team members to set aside position and power
- Diverse levels of ability, knowledge, and skill among group members, placing more burden on some members than on others
- Challenges to and conflicts arising from individual members' personal beliefs

Organizational Factors:

- Rewards and compensation that focus on individual performance only
- Performance appraisals that ignore the employee's team performance
- Unavailability of pertinent information
- Lack of commitment of top management
- Internal competition that limits effectiveness

While the keys to avoiding the above factors are obvious—careful selection and training of team members, team-based appraisal, and incentive systems (discussed in the following sections)—it cannot always be assumed that one or more of these negative factors will not cause the eventual failure of a work team. The lack of true commitment by top management to a long-run change in a culture of centralized decision making to one of self-directed teams, or the continued resistance of a senior, powerful employee can become substantial obstacles. Management must realize, as other organizations have reported, that the change to work teams usually does not occur quickly (at least two years) or easily (productivity may actually drop in the beginning). In addition, individual employees who continue to openly sabotage a work team must be effectively dealt with, including transfer or termination as disciplinary actions. It should be remembered, however, that such negative individual or organizational factors occur infrequently especially if the formation of the team is voluntary.

IMPLEMENTING WORK TEAMS

Establishing productive, creative, efficient, comfortable work teams can take several years. Most organizations report that eighteen months to two years is the minimum amount of time needed if no major problems occur. Allowing teams to form voluntarily can remove a great deal of anxiety and fear that will likely be encountered if employees are forced to change to teams. Milgard Windows, Inc. (see "Profile" of Jennifer Synhorst), for example, decided that work teams should be tried, but allowed all offices and employees to form teams voluntarily. At first employees were hesitant, but after a few successes, many employees chose to form teams. So what are the keys to the successful development of self-managed teams? Phil Weis, manager of Dana Computer Services, Toledo, Ohio, has successfully implemented work teams at Dana, offers the following keys:[56]

- Management must be willing and able to share authority and let team members make decisions that will affect their work.
- Teams must be given the freedom to take risks without reprisals.
- Management and team members must be patient. Working as part of a team takes a great deal of time, training, and effort for most people who have little or no similar work experiences.
- Expect the team approach to be traumatic to some individuals, and they will leave the organization. Others will wait for it to fail or be replaced by the next "trend" in management.
- Creative, flexible people who didn't like the traditional organization will embrace the team approach immediately and lead the change.

Self-directed teams at Dana Computer Services have become the center of its operation as expressed in its mission statement in Figure 11-8.

The primary reason work teams require several months to "jell" is that they progress through a series of developmental stages typical of small group behavior. This series was first identified by Bruce Tackman and is popularly known as "forming, storming, norming, and performing" (see Fig. 11-9).[57]

In the first stage of development, *forming,* a group will primarily concern itself with orientation to the tasks, work rules and interpersonal relationships. Working relationships are still based on individuals, not the group.

Informal leaders and norms of behavior eventually evolve as the group completes its formation. The second stage, *storming,* is characterized by individuals

Figure 11-8
The Mission Statement of Dana Computer Services, Dana Corporation, Toledo, Ohio

We are a group of focused teams, passionate about helping our customers reach beyond their expectations, demonstrated by engaged, creative people in an atmosphere of trust, pride, support and fun.

Mission Statement
Dana Computer Services

Source: Phil Weis, "Achieving Zero-Defect Service Through Self-Directed Teams," *Journal of Systems Management,* vol. 43, January 1992, pp. 26–36.

Profile

Jennifer Synhorst
Team Leader
Inside Sales Team
Milgard Windows
Sacramento, California

SUPERVISOR TO TEAM LEADER

Milgard Windows, Inc., is a leading West Coast prime window manufacturer. The firm started in 1965 in Tacoma, Washington, and today employs over 500 people in seven plants in California, Washington, Oregon, and Nevada.

In 1990, management, after much discussion, formally started utilizing work teams. All branches of Milgard were allowed to voluntarily develop the teams that are empowered to choose their own leaders, design and assign work functions, and implement new ideas. Teams usually contain five to fifteen people and have been formed in four major areas—manufacturing, office, inside sales, and outside sales.

As supervisor of the inside sales department at our Sacramento office, I strongly supported changing to a work team—even though it meant a loss of authority for me. I believe it was a "natural change" to empower my people by spreading out the authority, responsibility, and rewards. I first discussed the team concept with my employees. They liked the idea, and after receiving permission from management, we became the inside sales team.

The team is compensated in three ways: a base monthly salary, a monthly commission based on their individual contribution to total sales volume for the previous month, and a yearly performance incentive based on completion of team goals for the year. Since all decisions and work assignments are shared as a team, the team is allocated an equal share of the yearly performance incentive when it is distributed. Previously, the yearly performance incentive was given exclusively to the inside sales supervisor.

Our team meets for dinner monthly (off the clock) to cement our social and working relationships. Leaders from all the teams meet weekly to gain a broader insight into the other departments and provide the necessary communications. Our team rotates the task of attending these meetings to ensure that everyone share in the responsibility and build their own level of involvement. The results of changing to a team have generally been very positive and include:

- Members assume a much greater interest in the department as a whole, not just their individual jobs.
- Performance goals are higher and more realistic because members want the team to be the best it can, and because the goals are openly discussed with management.
- Members genuinely like the greater responsibility and authority and broader task assignments, thus morale is higher.
- Absenteeism is lower, because members readily note each other's absence.
- Members consult each other for help, rather than a supervisor.
- New members are selected by the team, thus each member takes a greater interest in their orientation and training.

The change has brought some problems, however:

- As the former supervisor, I feel a personal loss of authority. I'm also no longer the only person people approach to solve problems, and I miss that.
- The team members do not want to perform appraisals of each other, thus we have developed written anonymous reviews, which may not be as effective as face-to-face appraisals.
- The additional cross-training required for each member to learn all tasks required a great deal of time.

Overall, there is no question that the change to a work team was very positive both for Milgard and for our members. In an organization such as Milgard in which flattening out the management structure has led to fewer advancement possibilities, the team concept may be the best method of challenging people and providing them the recognition they deserve. The company still looks at the bottom line to determine our productivity, and our team is constantly improving our bottom line.

In order to survive and prosper today, companies need to be continuously improving. The individual, in order to survive, must remain flexible. I look at this move to team empowerment, and the other ideas Milgard has implemented over the past few years as crucial to Milgard's continued profitability and, therefore, my own job security.

---

resisting outside influences especially when tasks are of a personal nature. The third stage, *norming,* occurs when the group begins to develop a cohesive nature, thus overcoming the storming stage when people are mostly concerned with their own tasks and behaviors. At this stage the group begins to think "we feel" instead of "I feel" and group values and norms are developed. In the last stage, *performing,* the members become flexible in their roles and channel their efforts and ideas into the group's functions.

Thus synergy within the group occurs at this stage as the group's members focus on the tasks at hand and channel their individual efforts into roles that will maximize the productivity of the group, and not their individual outcomes.[58] Once established, research indicates that groups will change their strategy and membership according to the economic environment of the organization. Groups alter their strategy (members' desire for conformity or innovation) during periods of growth and decline rather than periods of economic stability. Changes in group membership, however, are more likely to occur during periods of decline, with few changes during periods of stability or growth. While organizations may add personnel during periods of growth, existing groups remain focused on objectives.[59]

Team Training

The skills needed by members of self-directed work teams are usually far more extensive than those required of employees performing the same jobs in traditional organizations for four reasons:[60]

1. Each team member is expected to learn all the jobs on the team—often four to six more jobs than they would normally be expected to learn. Self-directed teams often use job rotation or multiskilling to provide this training.

2. Team members are expected to learn "team jobs" performed by staff or other people outside the unit in traditional organizations. In one printing company, for example, press operators were required to learn maintenance and repair operations, processing medical claims, and running software programs.

3. Managerial and supervisory duties assumed by work teams must be acquired. Thus most team members receive training in budgeting, human resource management techniques, problem-solving skills, and communication skills.

4. Teamwork concepts and skills must also be learned by members of newly-created teams. They need to become attuned to the concepts of self-

FIGURE 11-9
The Four Phases of Small Group Development
Source: Adapted from Bruce W. Tackman, "Developmental Sequence in Small Groups," *Psychological Bulletin* 63, no. 6, 1965, pp. 384–99.

direction and empowerment. In addition, they need to learn how the team can acquire maximum value from each member's individual skills and values.

A survey of managers in organizations were asked what factors most influenced the success of their employee teams. The most common response was training. The specific areas in which new team members receive training, according to the same managers is reported in Fig. 11-10. These areas do not include the job training and support functions discussed in reasons one and two, above, but instead refer to the skills needed to meet reasons three and four—the managerial and teamwork skills in which most new team members have had little prior experience or training. A typical example is Corning Glass where new team members spend up to 20 percent of their time in training until the team reaches the fourth development stage—performing.[61]

Team Incentives

Incentive plans designed to motivate and reward people for their performance and contribution to organizational goals are a cornerstone of compensating systems. Whether the plan is a traditional piecework plan, sales commission, or some other type, it focuses on one thing—the performance of the individual. So what happens when the individual is a member of a self-managed team? Then the performance of the team, as a group, often becomes the basis of the incentive rather than the individual's performance.

Types of Training	Percent
Group Problem Solving	83
Running Effective Meetings	65
Communication Skills	62
Resolving Conflict	61
Roles and Responsibilities of Teams	58
Quality Tools and Concepts	56
Evaluating Performance	39
Work Flow and Process Analysis	36
Selecting Team Members	35
Presentation Skills	35
Influencing Others	29
Budgeting	14

Source: Richard S. Wellins, William C. Byham, Jeanne M. Wilson, *Empowered Teams,* San Francisco, Jossey-Bass, 1991, p. 166. Copyright © 1991 by Jossey-Bass Inc., Publishers. Used by permission.

FIGURE 11-10
Types of Training Received by New Team Members

OB in Practice — Outdoor Team Training

Some employers, a small but growing number, are utilizing a method of team building that goes far beyond the typical classroom lectures, exercises, cases, etc.—outdoor physical challenges. These team-building programs are usually one of two kinds: wilderness and outdoor-based.

Wilderness programs typically include a facilitator who creates challenges or "initiatives" for the participant to solve. Outward Bound of Santa Monica, California, is the oldest (est. 1942) outdoor training program in the United States. Its program requires four to nine days because "team-building can't be learned in a day." Activities include whitewater rafting, mountain climbing, hiking through the desert, as well as outdoor living. Group dynamics are a critical factor of the course.

Outdoor-based programs provide training at one specific cite—such as a conference center and include indoor activities. Events include rope climbs, "trust falls" (one person falls backward into the arms of others), scaling walls, et cetera.

Does It Really Work?

Yes: Centel Corporation, a Chicago telephone and cellular service company, has been sending employees through Outward Bound since 1988—over 400 people thus far. Susan Thieme, the Centel coordinator sees several benefits from the training: "When you're service-oriented, team training is an important aspect of your company. People come back enthused and say they have increased confidence . . . We feel the things people learn about themselves do carry over to the work site."

Barry Marshall of TCI West, Inc., in Bellevue, Washington, chose Outward Bound because he saw it as: "Something that would put all participants on equal footing and break down the barriers of communications." Some of the lessons learned according to TCI's Sally Howe, include trust—members learn to trust each other to accomplish goals; rude awakenings—you can't always be the leader and sometimes you're the person slowing down the pack; and that relying on others isn't a weakness—it's teamwork.

No: Barbara Vucich, director of marketing at TCI West was not convinced of the value of the Outward Bound training. She did not find the team-building to be worthwhile: "There's a vaiuable lesson to be learned in being able to ask for help and graciously accept it, but the reality is I don't have a 40-pound pack on my back at the office . . . Do I think that everything we did translates to the office environment as well as other (training) activities would? Probably not!"

Nelson Farris, internal relations manager for Nike, the "Just Do It" company, was skeptical but participated in an outdoor training program to assess its value. He thought the training had some value, but could not convince top management that swinging from ropes and rafting down the Colorado River would develop better employees.

Critical issues for employers considering outdoor training include: (1) *Mandatory v. voluntary attendance.* If employees are forced to go, those of lesser outdoor interests and physical abilities may resent it and fear looking foolish; if it's voluntary and only three-quarters go, how can team-building occur? Employees with physical concerns should be exempt—and pose a similar problem. (2) *Insurance.* Typical group health insurance policies do not cover outdoor training programs—thus, either the training firm must provide the insurance or purchase special insurance. (3) *Safety.* The potential for injury exists regardless of the precautions taken. The very nature of the programs creates risks. The safety record of a training program should be thoroughly checked. (4) *Personal beliefs.* Some training programs include discussions of personal values and belief systems. In some cases employees have objected to such discussions on the basis that they were an affront to their personal or religious beliefs. Employers may want to avoid such discussions, or warn employees in advance and allow them to abstain from such discussions.

Outdoor training may be used as a method of team-building.

Source: Adapted from Jennifer J. Laabs, "Team Training Goes Outdoors," *Personnel Journal*, June 1991, pp. 56–63.

Team incentives fall somewhere between individual and whole organizational plans such as profit sharing or gain sharing. These goals and incentives may be only part of a total incentive plan that includes: (1) a base hourly wage or monthly salary, (2) incentives based on team performance, (3) and incentives based on an individual's contribution to team objectives. Such a plan is utilized by Milgard Windows, Inc. (see "Profile" of Jennifer Synhorst). Teams may be given goals that the team as a whole should accomplish. Team incentive plans compared to individual or organizational plans offer several advantages to self-managed teams.[62] First, the contributions members make to the teams' productivity are given value—thus reinforcing the organization's emphasis on work teams. Second, the individual member's performance is still valued and considered, usually in a team appraisal process as discussed above. Third, the cohesiveness of the team is increased; because the members realize that if the team is successful, they will realize greater individual rewards. And fourth, members often strive harder to achieve team goals, because they are helping their coworkers succeed as well as themselves (or they may view themselves as having let down their coworkers). This additional motivation may also be realized because it helps members meet their "social" need as described in Maslow's hierarchy. This need obviously cannot be met by individual incentive plans that, in fact, may place coworkers in competitive roles instead of cohesive roles. A fifth potential advantage of team incentives, compared to organizational incentive plans, is that team members perceive a more direct link between their performance and the incentives received.

Effective team incentives can be found in virtually all industries, for example:[63]

- A bank implemented a team incentive plan to replace an individual-based plan, because customers reported they were "oversold" products. The team plan rewarded customer overall satisfaction with the branch.

- A biotechnology company implemented a team incentive plan to speed up the development of new products. Previously, researchers, technical writers, and marketing people were only concerned with their own functional area, and new products were slowly developed. The teams included members from all areas, and incentives were given when new products won FDA approval.

- An insurance company encountered friction between the allegations that the data processing people were slow in their work, while on the other hand, the data processing people complained about unreasonable and changing priorities. Once teams were formed with members from both departments and rewarded according to customer needs, the members devised methods to increase quality and lower turnover time.

AUTOMOBILE INDUSTRY TEAMS

The automobile industry has utilized more work teams in recent years, both project teams and self-managed teams, than any other major industry. The glamour and size of the industry has caused a great deal of attention to be placed on the industry's experimentation with teams. Not long ago, in the early 1970s the U.S. automobile companies ignored teams and instead invested heavily in robotics as a means of maintaining their competitiveness. While robots certainly provided them some cost savings and consistency in quality, most industry officials today agree—by their actions, not their words—that changing to teamwork has been a critical strategy for success.

The teamwork concept in automobile design and manufacturing was initially developed in Japan and Sweden. With automotive teams, the product engineers, manufacturing engineers, production workers, financial administrators, suppliers, and marketing personnel all work simultaneously and make decisions by consensus. The traditional "chimney system" utilized by the big three U.S. automakers was a compartmentalized process in which people from different disciplines worked in sequence—one "on top of the other, like a chimney," they rarely communicated with each other and decisions were imposed by high-level management.[64]

Volvo Work Groups

Since Henry Ford designed his first automotive assembly line, most automobile plants around the world were designed with one common principle—the machine-paced moving assembly line. The moving assembly line, by its very existence, required most jobs in an automotive plant to be designed with highly repetitive tasks. The line transports the car past a series of work stations where workers complete a small portion of the overall assembly required. The resentment against the machine pacing of the work, the repetition, and, above all, the boredom, has been confirmed by hundreds of thousands of workers and research studies. Many people immediately think of the automobile industry line when the subject of boring specialized jobs comes up—even though they have never seen an automobile assembly plant! Volvo, like all other auto producers, believed that the specialized jobs caused high levels of absenteeism and turnover, as well as lower product quality. Volvo also believed the specialized jobs were incompatible with the generally higher level of education in Sweden. Thus management sought a bold, innovative change in plant and job design for a newly planned facility. Volvo decided to build such a plant in Kalmar, Sweden, and made automotive history! The new plant's design was founded in a new concept, according to Volvo President Pehr G. Gyllenhammar:[65]

> The objective of Kalmar will be to arrange auto production in such a way that each employee will be able to find meaning and satisfaction in his work. That will be a factory which, without any sacrifice of efficiency or the company's financial objectives, will give employees opportunities to work in groups, to communicate freely among themselves, to switch from one job assignment to another, to vary their work pace, to identify with the product, to be conscious of a responsibility for quality, and to influence their own working environment.

The new Kalmar plant opened in 1974 and was considered. . . a breakthrough in auto manufacturing. The plant was, not just in theory but in reality, designed around the concept of the "assembly team." The teams of fifteen to twenty people each had total autonomy over their work. Each team had its own materials inventory. The teams traveled and worked on metal transport carriers that were guided along magnetic tracks embedded in the floor. The carriers were constructed to allow workers to easily rotate car bodies ninety degrees to make all working positions comfortable. Workers could assemble, for example, the exhaust system while standing next to a rotated car on its side.

The overall success of Kalmar's work teams convinced Volvo to utilize teams in its next new plant in Uddevalla, which opened in 1989. However, there were modifications in the work team process. The Uddevalla plant employed teams of seven to ten hourly workers. Each team worked in one area and assembled four cars per shift. Since members were trained to handle all assembly jobs, they worked an average of three hours before repeating the same task. Uddevalla thus avoided the classic problems associated with work cycles of only one or two minutes on conventional assembly lines, where the mind-numbing routine leads to boredom, inattention, poor quality, and high absenteeism.

Roger Holtback, President of Volvo Car Corp., insists that Uddevalla is an effort to make workers happy. Uddevalla already produces cars with fewer hours of labor and better quality than the three other Swedish plants (including Kalmar). But Volvo has had a problem that haunts all Swedish manufacturers: The country's highly educated, well-trained labor force doesn't like to work in factories. Volvo's other Swedish plants suffer absenteeism of 20 percent, and almost one-third of its workers quit yearly. More pay does not motivate Swedes; taxes take up to 70 percent of any overtime pay. With unemployment at 1.6 percent there is no lack of jobs. Says one union official: "The main problem simply will be to keep a work force."[66]

Uddevalla utilizes work teams to an even greater extent than Kalmar. It is divided into six assembly plants, each of which has eight teams. The teams also have more autonomy, manage themselves, handle scheduling, quality control, hiring, and other duties normally performed by supervisors. There are no first-line foremen and only two levels of managers. Each team has a spokesperson/ombudsman, who reports to one of six plant managers, who in turn report to the president of the entire complex.

Morale seems high at Uddevalla. Absenteeism is only 8 percent. The plant is well lighted, and noise is subdued. Volvo gives its workers sixteen weeks training before they are allowed near a car, and on-the-job orientation lasts sixteen

Volvo Car, Inc. has been a global pioneer in using employee teams to assemble automobiles instead of a continuous line.

months more. Inside Uddevalla one can't help but notice the car bodies that glide noiselessly on magnetic tracks to the assembly points, where Volvo-designed machines lift and tilt the body to any angle. More than 80 percent of the assembly can be done from a comfortable working position with no bending or stretching. Teams determine how long they'll work on a car and take responsibility for fixing defects. One Volvo employee boasted, "This isn't just new production technology. It is the death of the assembly line. We've brought back craftsmanship to automaking."[67]

Team Taurus

In the 1980s "Team Taurus" became the most famous project team in U.S. manufacturing history. The members of the Ford Taurus project design team, Team Taurus, organized in 1980. That year Ford suffered a $1.5 billion loss—the largest in company history at that time. The losses continued for the next three years and totaled over $3 billion. 1980 was also a Ford milestone because Philip Caldwell was the first non-Ford family member to be elected chairman of the board. This came only two years after Henry Ford II had fired Lee Iacocca, who had been president since 1970 and had been considered to be the father of the Mustang—Ford's most successful new car. He had been the logical choice to succeed Henry Ford II as chairman of the board. Therefore, in 1980, Ford was experiencing record losses, had lost its popular president, Lee Iacocca, and for the first time in its history had someone other than a Ford at the helm. And, 1980 was the year Ford's top management realized the company was at a crossroad and gambled $3.35 billion on a new car. Taurus had a new concept—a project team. If the Taurus had failed it could have easily been the end of the Ford Motor Company.

Ford management chose the project team to design a totally new midsize (believed to be the market of the future) car. The key to the team concept was the idea of concurrent rather than sequential car design and development. Team Taurus was led by Lew Veraldi who is credited with the determination of using a project team to create the Taurus instead of "the chimney method" in which "everything was done in segments": The designers turned the work over to the engineers, who turned it over to manufacturing, who gave the product to marketing to sell and to the dealers to service. Routine problems like "I can't assemble or service it this way" were ignored. The various disciplines didn't care about what they passed on to the next group. It was called "tossing the baton over the wall"; I'll work on it and toss it over to you to do your part; nobody ever talked to each other.[68]

Team Taurus, however, included over 150 vice presidents, directors, managers, and others from all areas of the company including engineering, manufacturing, service, legal, and marketing. The team included people who were in the mainstream of the company but were not removed from their regular work. All disciplines were included in Team Taurus from the very beginning. Input was not only sought from team members but from other parties including ergonomics experts, UAW leaders, consumers, and insurance experts. For example, the insurance experts were asked how the car could be designed to ensure better accident coverage. Their ideas were largely followed, and Allstate and State Farm offered substantial discounts to Taurus owners. Altogether 1,401 ideas were submitted to the team from internal and external sources, and 68 percent were included in the Taurus! Some of the suggestions that originated from Ford's Atlanta plant workers (where the Taurus was first built) included:[69]

- Changes were made in the utilization of nuts, bolts, and tools. Formerly, nuts and bolts came in many sizes, which made it more time-consuming and tedious to fasten interior moldings. Workers had to keep changing the heads on their screw-torquing power tools. Today, however, a single, standard size is used. The same change was made with the nuts and bolts that were fastened underneath the car.

- The number of body side panels was reduced from twelve pieces to two pieces, which greatly reduced the likelihood of outside noise and water leaks from door openings.

- The interior plastic trim pieces were enlarged, which made them easier to install. Not only did this result in a better fit, but the appearance also was improved.

- Door trimming is now installed as an off-line assembly operation, before the doors are put on the car. Previously, after doors were affixed to the body of the car, workers would install the trim to each door. Workers had to climb into the car and crawl on their hands and knees to make the installations.

Team Taurus was able to incorporate these and most of the 1,401 ideas into the Taurus, because all disciplines were included in the process from the beginning, and decisions were made with all members involved—thus, the project was developed simultaneously rather than sequentially. Even the market research people were included from the start. In the past they were given a new car and told to develop a sales campaign. The marketing people used focus groups in which people were asked to inspect preproduction models. Several useful ideas came from the focus groups, including one from a Florida woman who said she could not find the hood release and asked, "Why don't you make it yellow?" The Taurus was given a yellow hood release. Team Taurus has been credited with producing one of the most successful new cars in automotive history and forever changing the chimney or sequential project design process to the project team concept. Some particularly noteworthy accomplishments of the team include:[70]

- The Taurus was completed at a cost of under $3 million or over one-quarter million under budget, an incredible feat in the automotive industry.

- The average Ford plant requires ten to fifteen cars per 100 assembled to be taken off the assembly line for repair. The Taurus has averaged less than 1 car per 100.

- Former Ford President Dan Peterson noted that while robots were designed and utilized in the Taurus assembly plants: "Eighty-five percent of the (production) gains are attributed to managing smarter and only 15 percent to new technology."

- The Taurus was the 1986 *Motor Trend* Car of the Year in its first year of production. In 1987 it was the number one selling car in the United States and remained first or second in sales for six years.

- Ford chose the project-team approach for its next new car development —the mid-1990s Mustang. Team Mustang was given even greater design authority than Team Taurus and is called the "dedicated team" approach.

Toyota

Toyota, Japan's largest automobile producer, built its first U.S. automobile assembly plant in Georgetown, Kentucky. The stereotype "nuts and bolts" production worker would not meet Toyota's selection standards. Instead, Toyota wanted workers who could: (1) demonstrate initiative and learn new tasks quickly; (2) take an active role in decision making and problem solving; (3) be flexible, adaptive, and energetic; and, most of all, (4) work well in a team-oriented environment. This would enable Toyota to develop "Kaizen," the gradual, ongoing improvement by every member of the work force. The selection system developed entirely for this one plant focused on potential rather than education and experience. The selection process followed eight phases, with each phase reducing the number of applicants:[71]

1. *Advertising.* Jobs were advertised in twenty-eight Kentucky employment offices. Only three job categories were listed—team member, team leader, and group leader—and all production and skilled jobs were one of the three categories.
2. *Application and Orientation.* Applicants completed state and Toyota employment forms and viewed a video that explained Toyota's management philosophy and selection process.
3. *Technical Skills.* Applicants completed written tests, including the General Aptitude Test Battery (GATB), a validated test of cognitive ability and psychomotory skills. Candidates also completed the Job Fit Inventory, a test of people's motivation to work in a highly participatory/team environment.
4. *Interpersonal Assessment Center (IAC).* Candidates participated in four simulations (eight hours) designed to assess teamwork skills, communication skills, decision-making skills, and manufacturing assembly ability.
5. *Leadership Assessment Center (LAC).* Remaining candidates completed three exercise simulations designed to measure: (a) ability to delegate responsibility; (b) ability to write letters and study reports; (c) training and counseling ability; and (d) ability to schedule work.
6. *Technical Performance Assessment.* Maintenance applicants took hands-on tests in technical areas.
7. *The Toyota Assessment.* Remaining candidates were interviewed by a team of Toyota human resource department and line management. Hiring recommendations were made by the team based on the interview and performance in other phases.
8. *Health Assessment.* Recommended applicants were given drug and alcohol tests and a physical exam.

Toyota opened the Camry assembly plant in 1989 utilizing self-managed work teams. Within three years the highly successful plant added a second shift—of self-managed teams.

Chrysler

After noting the success of Team Taurus as a project design team and the successful self-managed assembly teams in Sweden and Japan, Chrysler utilized teams in both the design and assembly process with its LH automobiles. Chrysler dubbed the LH team a "platform team" and included engineers, manufacturing engineers, purchasing agents, assembly workers, and suppliers. Similar in concept to Team Taurus, the LH platform team made decisions together—instead of in the traditional compartmentalized "chimney" that had prevailed previously at Chrysler. Glenn Gardner, General Manager of the LH team, described the change as "a culture shock—people lose their identity. They have to establish a new identity, a different esprit de corps."

The LH cars were the first Chrysler products to be developed from start to finish with the team approach. The LH project teams consisted of 850 members. Individualism had been drummed into the members and led to a rough start. To combat the tendency to blame others, the team managers decided that anyone who pointed a finger of blame at another team member would be brought in front of the team and embarrassed. Trust-building and consensus-building training was provided all team members to help build a team environment. After three years, the LH team completed the development of the radically new and highly successful LH cars—Dodge Intrepid, Chrysler Concorde, and Eagle Vision—nearly one year faster than any other new Chrysler automobile.

Team members strongly embraced their new team concept. "I worked here for twenty-five years and I never knew how everything came together—I feel like I changed companies without changing companies," noted hourly worker Ivan Mijatorie.[72]

General Motors's Gardner became convinced that the team concept was critical to success after working with a Mitsubishi team on the joint Chrysler–Mitsubishi Diamond Star product department. Many skeptics at Chrysler remained, however, until the LH prototype was built an incredible ninety-seven weeks before production. This early milestone enabled teams of production workers to scrutinize the LH car and detect aspects that would not work at assembly line speed. Needed changes could then be made in days, and production line problems were avoided. Overall, the LH team clearly produced benefits for Chrysler:[73]

- The LH car was developed in three and one-half years—a full year less than any other new Chrysler product.
- The LH team utilized 40 percent fewer engineers than the traditional "chimney" product program.
- The LH was developed for about $1 billion—far less than Ford's $3 billion Taurus/Sable or GM's $3.5 billion Saturn.
- Each LH car requires about twenty-four production hours—the lowest of any Chrysler plant.

CONCLUSIONS AND APPLICATIONS

- Much of the productivity within organizations occurs within groups (formal or informal) of employees. Groups are often successful in part due to the synergy created when people work together instead of individually. Members of groups develop standards of behaviors (norms) that create peer pressure for individual members to maintain an expected level of performance.
- People seek to join groups, because it enables them to fulfill basic social, security, esteem, and self-actualization needs. Fulfilling these needs through the workplace generally increases employees' morale and loyalty to the organization.
- Employee teams have been called the "productivity breakthrough of the 1990s." Formal employee teams are generally utilized for one or more of

three general purposes: special project teams assigned to develop new products or services; problem-solving teams and self-managed teams that work together on an ongoing day-to-day basis and replace the traditional supervisor-employees work unit.

- Several factors have caused a growing number of organizations to develop project teams, competition has increased the need to reduce the time required for new product development; employees today expect and are able to provide the required knowledge and experience; managers are more willing to relinquish their authority to teams; and the synergy of the team can create a better overall result.

- Organizations that organize work through self-managed teams are often characterized as having fewer levels of management, an open, shared leadership style, and team-based (versus individual-based) planning, controlling, and decision making of the job process. Self-managed teams have generally resulted in higher productivity, product or service quality, and employee morale. They do require that management relinquish a sizable portion of its authority, and that team members learn more tasks and assume new management skills.

- Implementing self-managed work teams can take years and may require a substantial shift in management philosophy. New teams usually go through four phases of development: forming, storming, norming, and performing. The group synergy and maximum productivity is usually not achieved unless it achieves the final stage.

- Teams are likely to be most productive and successful if they assume the function of performance appraisal. Team members each provide input on each appraisal of each peer and may utilize self-appraisal and a review committee. Incentive plans based on the team's performance compared to predetermined objectives often replace individual-based incentive plans in self-managed teams. The individual's contribution to the team's performance, however, is still evaluated in the peer appraisal process.

- The automobile industry has successfully utilized both project-development teams and self-managed teams. Volvo, in Sweden, was the international pioneer of self-managed production teams. Volvo teams of workers are given total autonomy over their work and have increased production and quality while lowering costs. Ford Motor Company's project team, "Team Taurus," sent shock waves through the U.S. auto industry by developing a highly successful, entirely new product in record time. This three-year development process replaced the traditional sequential design process and was followed by Chrysler's LH team and Ford's "Team Mustang." Toyota opened its first U.S. plant in Kentucky with self-managed work teams in 1989. The plant has been highly successful to the point of exporting Camrys to Japan.

REVIEW QUESTIONS

1. What can cause the combined productivity of individuals to increase when they are formed into a group?
2. Why do people usually want to join formal or informal work groups?
3. Describe the membership and primary purposes of special-project, problem-solving, and self-managed teams.
4. What are the organizational characteristics of a self-managed work team? What problems might be anticipated by a firm considering changing from individual-based job design to one with self-managed teams?
5. Define the term "social loafing." How can it be minimized within self-managed teams?

6. What training do members of self-directed teams require that are not usually needed in traditional organizations?
7. What potential advantages do incentive plans offer based on the performance of work teams (instead of the performance of individual members)?
8. Describe how the automotive industry has successfully utilized special project and self-managed work teams.
9. What problems might be anticipated by an organization planning to change to self-managed work teams?
10. How did the Toyota selection process differ from traditional ones, when it searched for employees for the Georgetown, Kentucky plant?

DISCUSSION QUESTIONS

1. Nucor Corporation has been remarkably successful for many years in the steel industry while other producers have lost millions of dollars, laid off thousands of workers, and in some cases gone out of business. Of the "five reasons" for Nucor's success cited by CEO Iverson, how important is the utilization of employee teams? Why? Why haven't all other steel producers developed similar teams?
2. Why are Frederick Taylor's scientific management principles less useful today than in the 1920s? How do they conflict with the formation of self-managed work teams?
3. If you were organizing a special-project team within an organization, what factors would you consider before choosing a traditional, lightweight, heavyweight, or autonomous team structure? What are the "keys" to selecting and developing successful special project teams?
4. Why should any organization consider changing to self-managed teams? Should the total work process

be designed into work groups, such as Nucor and Toyota, or should groups be given the choice of forming self-managed teams following the example of G.E. and Milgard?
5. Do you think outdoor team training is a passing fad or can it really provide effective team building? What issues should management consider before scheduling an outdoor team training program?
6. How should the work of members of self-managed teams be appraised? Should productivity bonuses or incentives be given to teams as a whole or to individual members? Why?
7. "Team Taurus" replaced the traditional "chimney system" in the design and development of the Taurus/Sable. Since no new technology or expertise was utilized, why did this simple change in project structure receive such acclaim?
8. How did the Volvo "assembly teams" differ from Henry Ford's "assembly line"? Was the change a positive one?

CASE STUDY

American Security Systems

American Security Systems is a leading midwestern home and office security systems company. The company was started in 1968 by John and Pam Ryan, a husband and wife team that has developed the business into a 400 employee business in four states: Iowa, Nebraska, Kansas, and Missouri. The firm's motto "Your Safety Is Our First Priority" has guided a customer-oriented philosophy that the own-

FIGURE 11-11
The American Security
Systems' Organization
Chart

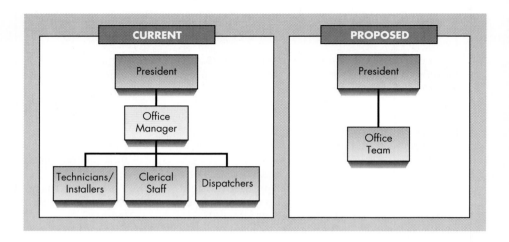

ers credit to their success. All products and services are given unconditional lifetime guarantees, and service runs are made within an hour, 365 days a year. In addition, a lean management team, generous pay and benefits, flexible hours, and a generous profit-sharing plan have helped build a loyal, hard-working group of employees.

Pam Ryan returned from this year's national association meeting convinced that they should offer the employees the opportunity to form self-managed work teams. She has discussed this concept with owners of other businesses that have teams, and after six months of planning has decided to allow the employees in each of the ten branch offices to volunteer to form teams. The teams would be empowered to choose their own leaders, design jobs and assign hours, implement new ideas, and select and appraise their own members. The current manager of each office must, however, support the change. Teams would be evaluated by the home office every six months on three standards—profitability, number of new clients, customer satisfaction index (computed by the home office). If an office had generated a profit and had met agreed upon goals for new clients and customer satisfaction, then the team would be given a profit bonus (in addition to a monthly salary) that it could divide according to its own formula. Last year, under the current profit-sharing plan, employees' annual bonuses averaged 33 percent of their annual salaries. The change in the organizational chart would appear as follows in Figure 11-11.

The Des Moines, Iowa, office is considering President Ryan's offer. Four other offices have made the change within the last year. The Des Moines office has been the most profitable office for the last three consecutive years. Employees are very happy working together, with the status quo, and with the office manager, Gary Shipley. In fact, no employee has left the office for seven years. After three days of discussion, no decision has been made. The last discussion left the decision up to Shipley; everyone trusts him to make the right one.

CASE STUDY QUESTIONS

1. If you were Shipley, what information would you want before you made a recommendation?
2. What are the potential advantages of the office changing to a self-managed team? Disadvantages?
3. If you were Shipley, what would you recommend? Why?
4. Would your answer to question three be different if the Des Moines office had been the least profitable and experienced high turnover and low morale? Why?

EXPERIENTIAL EXERCISE 1

Team Building

Purpose

This exercise is designed to give you experience in the common organizational task of team building. In this case you and several fellow students will become a "project team" and are asked to conceptualize, design, and build a new project under a tight deadline. Your team will be empowered to choose any form of leadership you find useful, assign tasks, and make all necessary decisions related to the project. The organization is not interested in how you choose to accomplish your task, only the bottom line—building the most competitive product. Your direct competition will be the other teams of students in the class. As a suggestion, your team may want to: (1) brainstorm and create a vision, (2) develop a plan of action, and (3) assign duties.

Task

The instructor will divide the class into five-member teams. Ideally, no team should contain more than one student from the same field—accounting, marketing, engineering, history, et cetera. Each team will then be given a box of building units (blocks, cubes, etc.). The boxes and units are identical. Each team will be given fifteen minutes to plan their project before anyone can start. The task for each team is to build the tallest structure possible in ten minutes. The structure must stand entirely on its own (no foreign substance, only the units). Any shape or design is permissible.

    The team with the highest structure (measured in inches from the desk or table) is the winner and is chosen as the "Best Project Team" by the organization.

    Hint: Successful and rapid adaptation in response to a fast-changing environment is critical.

EXPERIENTIAL EXERCISE 2

How Does Your Group Make Decisions?

Purpose

How a group or team makes decisions is an important characteristic of the group. Managers or supervisors when asked may respond: "This is a consensus-building group!" while the members may or may not agree. This exercise is designed to provide a quick, objective assessment of the decision-making style of a group or team as reported by its members.

Task

Each member of a team or group should think independently about how the group makes decisions on a day-to-day basis. Then each member should read each of the following fifteen statements and circle the number of the five that are most typical of how decisions are made. When you have selected five, refer to the Decision-Making Interpretation chart below.

    The individual members may choose to then discuss what each perceives to be decision-making style, and whether or not change is desired.

1. When decision making is necessary, a few of us usually get together and take care of it.
2. The senior person usually decides, and that is it.
3. People really get a chance to express their views.
4. Typically, everyone agrees somewhat with the decisions made.
5. We frequently decide on the basis of "majority rules."
6. One person is in charge and effectually makes decisions.
7. Everyone often freely agrees with decisions and supports them wholeheartedly.
8. There is a small clique that runs things around here.
9. Decisions are made when people decide on a particular course of action.
10. We would not make a decision until everyone is completely in agreement.
11. People are free to air their views, but the boss decides.
12. A few people usually dominate the group.
13. Decisions are not made unless everyone can accept proposals to some extent.
14. A numerical majority is required before decisions are made.
15. Each member actively supports decisions.

Decision-Making Interpretation Chart

After you have marked five statements, circle the statement numbers in the first column shown below, then total each row. The highest scores represent the typical decision-making styles of your group.

Statement Numbers	Totals	Style
2 - 6 - 11		Individual dominance
1 - 8 - 12		Minority influence
5 - 9 - 14		Majority democracy
3 - 4 - 13		Consensus
7 - 10 - 15		Unanimous view

Source: Adapted from Glenn H. Varney, *Building Productive Teams,* San Francisco, Jossey-Bass, 1989, p. 86.

Take It to the Net   **You can find this chapter's World Wide Web exercise at:**
http://www.prenhall.com/carrell

CHAPTER 12

Culturally Diverse Groups

CHAPTER OBJECTIVES

1. To understand why in some organizations a "Glass Ceiling" exists for women and people of color.

2. To examine the perceived differences in male or female leadership styles and of whites or people of color in the workplace.

3. To understand issues peculiar to women such as "Mommy Track," comparable worth, and sexual harassment.

4. To examine changes in basic benefits and work rules that may be needed to accommodate a changing work force.

5. To distinguish the unique organizational behavior issues facing women of color.

6. To review the influx of immigrants into the American work force and look at their effect on the workplace.

7. To understand why older workers can contribute to organizations more than many employers have realized.

8. To recognize who are people with disabilities and their value in the workplace.

9. To introduce the student to those who have been discriminated against because of their sexual orientation/affection as part of the diversity culture.

argaret Greene, President
South Central Bell Telephone Co.

Meet Margaret Greene. In 1991, at age thirty-nine, she became the first and only woman to head up a state operation for South Central Bell Telephone Company. As president of its Kentucky operations, she presides over a company with 3,900 employees and annual revenues of $700 million. Ms. Greene's entrance into the Bell-South Company was as an attorney in the Birmingham, Alabama, headquarters of South Central Bell. Birmingham houses both the corporate headquarters and the headquarters for their Alabama Division. Ms. Greene served as an attorney with both the Alabama Division and the headquarters of South Central Bell during her eight years with the company before being named president of the Kentucky division.

Ms. Greene credits Roger Flynt, Senior Vice President of BellSouth Telecommunications and Will Booker,

former general counsel for South Central Bell, with giving her the opportunity to move ahead in the BellSouth Company. Booker hired her and became her mentor. He supervised her in several assignments in the legal department and was impressed by Greene's job performance. "I have never seen her in a job that she hasn't done exceptionally well." With mentors in senior management and a proven track record, Greene was poised for advancement. But even Greene was surprised  that she was transferred from a legal division and put in charge of operations. That, and her relatively short time with the company (eight years) could have been seen as a distinct disadvantage to her promotion. Greene wanted to take the leap from legal to operations, because it allowed her to expand her work responsibility into the political arena and into the community, both of which she enjoyed.

Carl Bailey, cochairman of Bell-South Telecommunications and Greene's boss cites Greene's human relations skills as one reason for her appointment. Rick Wallace, president of the Communication Workers of America Local, which represents the 1,460 union employees in South Central Bell's Kentucky Division agrees. "She has the ability to go to the regular employees and talk right to them," he says. This skill is a critical need for the Kentucky Division because corporate reorganization has reduced employment in the state by more than half over the past twelve years.

Bailey also believes Greene was the right person for the job because of her common sense and because she was tough-minded and could make the hard decisions. In describing her own management style, Greene admits, "I'm not shy. I'm not hesitant to make a decision. But I'm trained as a lawyer, so I'm a good listener and a good fact-finder."

Greene's move to the next rung of the corporate ladder was not without sacrifice. Married to attorney Scotty Greene and mother of two young children, Luke and Riley, the promotion involved the whole family. Scotty Greene gave up his law practice in Birmingham and a lifelong involvement in Alabama's Democratic party to relocate, gain admission to the Kentucky Bar, and build a private law practice with a Louisville firm. The occasions for husbands to make sacrifices to further their wives' careers are still rare enough that when one does, it can demonstrate the woman's commitment to her corporation. For Margaret Greene, however, that commitment isn't more important than her family, which she says is her number one priority.

Greene looks forward to mastering the job as president of South Central Bell's Kentucky Division and advises that women should avoid placing limits on themselves. "I have never accepted it when someone says, 'Oh, a woman can't do that job,' There's no job a woman can't do. I have never been the kind of person who has a five-year plan or a ten-year plan. I just do the job and remain open to opportunities. Young women entering the work force need to try as many different avenues to top management as they can. I think the opportunities are there. I know they are for me."

Parts of this profile were adapted from Roger Harris, "Greene Traveled a Long Distance for Her Calling," *Business First,* October 14, 1991, p. 22; and Ric Manning, "Executive Answers Bell Call for Change," *Louisville Courier Journal,* August 18, 1991, p. E–1.

In earlier chapters we discussed both the global nature of corporations and the increase of a diverse work force in U.S. companies. As companies compete for the *best* workers, it is important that they recognize some diverse issues that arise in the workplace such as: prejudice against immigrants and people of color; lack of respect for women or older workers; an inability to recognize the value of people with disabilities; and intolerance of people whose sexual orientation sets them apart from mainstream America. These issues will hamper the workplace of the 21st century.

In this chapter we will examine how people of color and women have been denied advancement to top management positions because of an invisible but very real barrier in many organizations. Issues relevant to women, such as receiving equal pay and time off to raise children and the obstacles in the workplace for people who are "different" will be discussed. We will look at organizations who see older workers and workers with disabilities as resources rather than as liabilities. Throughout the chapter, students will be challenged to explore their own reactions to diverse groups and to see how accommodation benefits both the individual and the organization.

AFRICAN-AMERICANS

The Original Minority

The Civil Rights Movement of the late 1950s and early 1960s came about through the leadership of Dr. Martin Luther King, Jr. African-Americans demanded the end to racial segregation and discrimination in government, in public accommodations, in jobs, in housing, in education, and in voting. The Civil Rights Act of 1964 put into law those changes being demanded. No longer would it be legal to deny a job to an African-American just because he or she was not white. No longer would he or she be denied the vote, be turned away from a lunch counter, or be denied admission to public colleges just because of race.

The creation of the Equal Employment Opportunity Commission gave African-Americans an agency of the federal government whose goal was to ensure the end to illegal discrimination. And the creation of Affirmative Action Plans to undo the results of past discrimination gave African-Americans access to jobs previously denied to them.

While today the protections of the Civil Rights Act are sought by many others who come under the religion, sex, age, or national origin language of the Act, no one can dispute that African-Americans were the focus of and the catalyst for the original legislation.

Now African-Americans are just one group representing the diversity in the work force. As we look to the year 2000, women will make up more than 47 percent of the labor force. Hispanic workers will make up 10 percent, just 2 percent below the projected 12 percent African-American workers in the labor pool. How have African-Americans fared as a result of the Civil Rights Movement and what can they expect in this new age of cultural diversity?

For many African-Americans the past twenty-five years have resulted in progress. In the 1960s, only 13 percent of African-Americans were part of the American middle class. By 1988, 33 percent of African-American families were considered part of the middle class with incomes solidly between the $25,000 to $50,000 range. The most remarkable feature of this achievement is that most of the individuals who make up these statistics, are "first generation" members of the middle-class, as demonstrated in the "OB In Practice," A Woman of Color in the Corporate Environment. Their parents were domestics, farm hands, and unskilled laborers. As opportunities for education and upwardly mobile jobs opened up, these children were pushed toward a better future.

To a great extent African-Americans believe they can achieve that better future. A Louis Harris & Associates, Inc. poll, conducted in 1988, showed that 50 percent of the 531 African-Americans polled believed that African-Americans had the same opportunity as whites to live a middle class life. In that same poll 56 percent of the African-Americans polled believed that pressure from Civil

OB in Practice

A Woman of Color in the Corporate Environment

Michele J. Hooper, named as one of twenty-one women of power and influence in corporate America by *Black Enterprise* magazine and featured in a *Business Week* article on corporate women, exemplifies the emergence of the new black middle class. Ms. Hooper is the daughter of a Pennsylvania coal miner. One of eleven children, she was the first member of her family to get a college degree. With an undergraduate degree in economics and a masters degree in business and administration, she was amply prepared to head Baxter International Incorporated's Canadian division. Baxter is a major health care products company. Hooper was named its president of a new alternate-site international unit. Her ability to take on risky assignments successfully prepares her for more senior management positions. In her own words, Ms. Hooper sees valuing diversity as a corporate necessity.

"Women and people of color are going to be the future leaders as we go into the next century. Together I think we can begin to replace that old order with one that embraces differences, embraces the ability to all people to contribute to the organization regardless of color, gender, background, or anything else. After all, that's my story. I'm proof that it can happen."

Source: Adapted from Julia Flynn, "Mapping Out Home Care," *Business Week,* June 8, 1992, and Bill Deener, "Executive Sees 'New Order' for Women in Workplace," *The Dallas Morning News,* April 15, 1992, p. 2–D.

Rights organizations and individual initiatives by African-Americans caused the progress African-Americans had made for the past thirty years.[1]

Appreciation for some of the current success of African-Americans does not dispel concerns, however. When segregation was fairly universal, the African-American middle class was made up of teachers, clergy, and small tradesmen who served their fellow African-Americans. Today's African-American middle class is tightly linked to the larger American economy. During difficult economic

Preserving and expanding the African-American middle class is the major diversity issue for many organizations.

times, African-Americans are more vulnerable to layoff. Often hired in staff areas like personnel or urban affairs, African-Americans fall disproportionately into the ranks of the unemployed. And a study done of cutbacks in the Federal Government during the early 1980s found that African-American workers were laid off twice as often as whites. In the Harris Poll referenced above, 33 percent of the African-Americans polled believed that African-Americans were more vulnerable to job loss during a changing economy.

Joining the ranks of the middle class will not achieve for African-Americans all they want to achieve. The progression within the workplace to supervisory and top management positions has not been good. The "Glass Ceiling" stops African-Americans as often, if not more often, than women. A 1989 EEOC report showed that while 12.7 percent of the work force was African-American, only 5 percent were managers and only 0.6 percent were senior managers.[2] A closer look at the impact of the Glass Ceiling on people of color follows in this chapter, and Fig. 12-1 shows the small progression of African-Americans into the ranks of upper middle class.

Even for the African-Americans who are succeeding, all is not well. African-Americans still encounter racism in the workplace. White subordinates who resist direction from an African-American supervisor, or an African-American who is passed over for promotion, still find the source of these actions are often prejudice. In a career survey conducted by *Black Enterprise Magazine* in 1989, 48 percent of the respondents believed they had little opportunity for advancement, 60 percent believed they were underpaid, and most felt they were the victims of discrimination in the workplace.[3]

In a series of interviews conducted in 1993 by *Newsweek Magazine,* middle and upper class Africa-Americans discussed their frustrations and the obstacles

FIGURE 12-1
African-Americans in Upper Middle Class

Education		Whites, %	African-Americans, %
Percentage of racial group with four years of college			
1940		5	1
1971		12	5
1991		22	12
Occupations			
Percentage of racial group in certain jobs (1992)			
Manager/Professional		28	17
Technical/Sales/Admin.		32	28
Service		12	24
Construction		12	8
Laborers		14	22
Income			
Percentage of racial group income			
1982	$50,000-$75,000	19	9
1992	$50,000-$75,000	21	11
1982	$75,000-$100,000	7	2
1992	$75,000-$100,000	8	3
1982	$100,000+	5	1
1992	$100,000+	7	2

Source: Mark Whitaker, "White & Black Lies," *Newsweek,* Nov. 15, 1993, p. 54, © 1993, Newsweek, Inc. All rights reserved. Reprinted by permission.

they still face in the workplace because of their race. The main complaints were summarized as follows:

1. Not being seen as "fitting in"
2. Lack of respect
3. Low expectations from them
4. Shattered hopes
5. Being seen as an "exception"
6. Fatigue from "coping"
7. Being pigeonholed
8. Having identity problems
9. Self-censorship and silence
10. Tired of being lied to and about
11. Being blamed for sins of others
12. Being excluded from the "club"[4]

The dichotomy facing African-Americans as they strive for success in the workplace is that assimilation will mean loss of identity. The corporate culture is not changing as quickly as it will need to if it is to *value the diversity* offered by African-Americans rather than fold them into their current culture.

The response for some African-American professionals to prejudice, lack of opportunity, and resistance to assimilation is to leave their companies to create their own enterprises or to join African-American businesses. *Black Enterprise* magazine reports that African-American owned businesses are actively recruiting African-American managers and college graduates, with great success.[5]

If companies are going to attract and keep qualified African-Americans, they must deal with the glass ceiling facing them and the corporate culture that does not value them.

The Glass Ceiling for African-Americans

As a result of equal opportunity laws and affirmative action programs, African-Americans are making it into the work force in greater numbers. However, their advancement through the workplace hierarchy into top management has not been as successful.

IDENTIFYING THE PROBLEM   The U.S. Department of Labor conducted a study between 1988 and 1990 of ninety-four "Fortune 1000" sized companies. The study showed that while African-Americans represented 15.5 percent of the total work force of the companies, only 6 percent were in any level of management, and only 2.6 percent were managers at the executive level.[6]

In a follow-up to this study, the U.S. Department of Labor undertook a pilot project to try to identify systemic barriers to the career advancement of African-Americans and women. The pilot project was also undertaken to launch initiatives to eliminate these barriers.[7] In this section we will focus on their findings particularly as to African-Americans.

The pilot project selected for review nine "Fortune 500" companies that had federal contracts. While each company had a unique culture and experienced different problems regarding African-Americans, there were five common findings.

1. If Not a Glass Ceiling, a Plateau. Initially, the Department had intended to study the very highest level of the corporate structure to determine

how advancement had been made by the few African-Americans at that level. Unfortunately, the sample was so small that the focus had to be put back to the midmanagement level. Even at that level, it was noted that when a certain plateau was met by women and African-Americans, there was little advancement past the plateau. The plateau for African-Americans was *lower* than that for women.

2. Equal Opportunity Principles Not Embraced by Corporation. Almost none of the corporations in the study viewed the development of management staff in conjunction with equal opportunity policies. Internal and external training and development opportunities, corporate outreach through civil involvement, or special projects or assignments were not monitored to ensure *all* qualified employees were given equal access.

3. Compensation and Appraisal Systems Not Monitored. Not one of the companies surveyed reviewed their *total* compensation packages to ensure nondiscrimination in those packages. The companies were not monitoring performance appraisal programs to make sure there was no discrimination in their application. Because pay increases and advancement to higher paying positions are dependent upon good performance appraisals, the employer must ensure equity in that system.[8]

4. African-Americans are Placed in Staff Positions More Often Than in Line Positions. Staff positions, such as human resources, research, administration, and public relations are less likely to lead to top management positions. Line functions, such as sales or production, affect the corporation's bottom line and experience in these areas are critical for promotion.

   The survey by the Labor Department found that few African-Americans were placed in feeder positions for line function manager promotions.

5. Inadequate Record Keeping. Another common trait among the companies surveyed was the lack of records in regards to their EEO/Affirmative Action responsibilities.

   The Department of Labor attributed this lack of documentation to an overall lack of awareness that the EEO/Affirmative Action principles applied *across the board* to *all* employment practices, not just hiring of entry level employees.

Just as the companies exhibited common traits, the survey found common barriers to the career advancement of African-Americans in each of the companies.

RECRUITMENT PRACTICES   A majority of the firms in the study filled top management positions from within, and as African-Americans are just beginning to fill the lower management slots, it will take time for internal promotions to increase their participation at top levels.

In addition, certain recruitment practices of these companies increase artificial barriers to African-American promotions.

(a) When top management positions are being filled from within, top management officials identify, recruit, or promote others outside of the formal recruitment process. The subject may be discussed and decided at social gatherings or on the golf course. The result of this is that qualified African-Americans might not even be considered.

(b) Occasionally, management employees are encouraged to refer people for employment or promotion. If the number of African-Americans in management is already low, the field for African-American referrals remains low.

(c) Search firms often do the outside recruitment for companies seeking to fill top management positions. Without specific direction, search firms will not actively recruit African-Americans for top level positions.

LACK OF OPPORTUNITY   Key employees were identified and were developed for promotion. Their assignments were rotated to make sure they had line function experience; were offered external development opportunities, both for training and exposure; and they received special project assignments, so that they became highly visible to the company's top management.

In some of the companies surveyed, the selection of "key employees" was left to the executive who would be grooming his or her own successor. The predominance of white males in these positions made the selection of white males as successors more likely than not. The system created *mentors* for the white male employees who would then very likely succeed in advancement.

UNDERSTANDING THE EEO RESPONSIBILITY   Another barrier to the advancement of African-Americans within the companies surveyed was a misunderstanding of the EEO's responsibility. Most companies did not consider their own EEO guidelines and policies when filling top corporate positions. There was no role for their EEO officer, for example, in their recruitment of these top positions. Training and awareness programs required for managers of entry level positions, were not required for upper management.

Women of Color

Women of Color
African-American, Hispanic, Asian-American, and native American women are discriminated against in the workplace with the double burden of racism and sexism.

African-American women, Hispanic women, Asian-American women and native American women—*women of color*—must overcome the double burden of racism and sexism in the workplace. The glass ceiling, sexual harassment, unequal pay, and racial prejudice have all played a part in the work lives of women of color. Either counted as a "woman" for purposes of affirmative action or as a "person of color," women of color have been lost as a distinct disadvantaged group. One company, U.S. WEST, looked at its promotion of women of color and came up with disturbing statistics. One in 21 white males, one in 42 men of color, and one out of 136 white women had the opportunity to reach midlevel management and above compared to one in 298 women of color. While there is little study done on women of color as a distinct group, one such study of black women in higher education was undertaken to demonstrate that minority groups are not sexually monolithic. The study's findings and conclusions, though based on campus life, are not too dissimilar to the experiences of women of color in the workplace:

- Women of color found that there was less expected of women in the white, traditional male-oriented educational community, and even less expected of women of color. In the classroom, teachers expected white males to demonstrate the intellectual competence and leadership abilities normally attributed to white males. A competent woman of color is a surprise and is treated as an exception not the rule.[9]

- Just as women have discovered in their climb up the corporate ladder, women of color in the education setting can be accused of "sullenness" if silent in the classroom, or if willing to speak up, challenging and disrespectful.

- Women of color on college campuses face many of the same barriers to success that women of color face in the workplace. Women of color in higher education are steered toward traditional "helping" fields—education, social work, nursing and not business, engineering, or mathematics. At the workplace, women of color fill staff level positions—personnel, customer service areas—that do not necessarily position them for promotion.

- Women of color in higher education lack role models on the faculty just as they lack role models in top management in the workplace.

- Women of color on college campuses are isolated by being a small minority of the school enrollment. Just as in the workplace, women of color in higher education need to seek out a support group and establish a network of other women of color who share the same problems.

- As women of color advance through the academic system and gain admission into graduate schools, they fight the same stigma as women of color promoted in the workplace. Viewed as the "affirmative action candidate," they are forced to prove their competence over and over again.

- Women of color in colleges and universities find themselves pushed into the role of spokesperson for their race. If the classroom topic is about a "Black" issue, teachers assume an African-American woman can speak on it with authority. Such stereotyping in the workplace leads supervisors to impose on women of color to handle workplace issues of race, whether they have the expertise or not.

- Women of color have traditionally balanced the roles of provider and nurturer. The racism that limited the job opportunities of people of color to lower paid and less stable positions required women of color to contribute to a family's income. While a two-income family became a necessity in white America relatively recently, black Americans always needed such an arrangement. The cost of the dual burden on women of color in both the academic and workplace setting is similar. The traditional white, male-oriented organization promotes people who put the organization above family or personal concerns. Women of color, like white women, if functioning in an unchanged corporate/academic culture, must give up some of their family and personal objectives to succeed.

The Profile from four professional women of color, who happen to be sisters, gives insight into the struggle they have had through the workplace.

U.S. WEST, a consistent leader in diversifying its work force, reacted to the lack of promotion opportunities within its organization for women of color by its Women of Color Project. This project identified fifty women of color capable of filling leadership positions and provided them with the training and development necessary to succeed. The project began with a four-week workshop which featured the following:

1. An orientation that included the women's spouses. The company wanted the women to have the support at home as well as at work that would be necessary for the women to advance.

2. An "Efficiency Workshop." Women are taught as children to be helpless. Unless that learned behavior is understood, women cannot unlearn it.

Profile

African-American Women: Keys to Success

Ina Cooksie, Teacher, Jefferson County Public Schools
Kathy Cooksie, Personnel Manager, Louisville and Jefferson
 County Metropolitan Sewer District
Carolyn Cooksie, Deputy Assistant Administrator, U.S. HUD
Janice Cooksie, Management Intern, Humana, Inc.

Quite often, you may find others who will try to determine your capabilities and worth based upon your skin color, your sex, or your family background. We are the first generation of our family to ever go to college. If we allowed circumstances to limit us to our parents' educational level, we wouldn't be where we are today. Our mother has a high school diploma and wanted to become a nurse but could never afford to go to nursing school. Our father didn't even get past the eighth grade. This is nothing we're ashamed of; in fact, we're proud of our parents for striving to provide more for us than they ever had for themselves.

The first and most important bit of advice that we can give to any woman of color is that she should strive for educational attainment. This is the key that unlocks many doors. You need to reflect upon what it is that you want out of life and to prepare yourself, through education, to be the best that you can be. No one can take that knowledge from you. You must recognize the power of knowledge and learn its use.

It is also important for you as a student to always take courses that prepare you for subsequent levels of education or any other vocation which might be your goal. You must set goals so that there will be something definite to strive for, and you should seek career counseling. Take time to talk with someone who is already doing what you wish to do. This will give you valuable insight.

While grades are important in that they are used as a measure, you should not let a low grade discourage you. Be encouraged to do better. It takes someone who is willing to keep going despite difficult times, never giving up on themselves, always believing the "I can make it," in order to achieve. Overcoming obstacles is simply a matter of hard work and a positive attitude. Giving up is the worst thing to do.

Once you have entered the workplace, you must recognize the realities to overcome road blocks. Women of color are faced with a double bias in the job market: being black and being female. When a woman, particularly a woman of color, gets a job she must work twice as hard to prove herself capable. This is true despite your education. Women, particularly black women, have to perform 200 percent in their careers to break even with their male counterparts. Have confidence in your abilities as you have prepared yourself through education. Continue to develop yourself. Don't stop the educational process just because you have your degree.

Another important tool is to develop composure. Don't wear your heart on your sleeve. College cannot always prepare you for the politics in most organizations. Be extremely cautious and on your toes. Don't forget who you are. We, as black females, cannot always get away with what some others may do. There are those who will try to test your abilities or intimidate you. The most important thing here is to "never let them see you sweat." Even if you don't have all the answers, be willing to seek them out and don't be ashamed to say, "I don't know, but I can find out." Keeping your composure says to coworkers, "This person is level-headed." This doesn't mean that you should never fight for what you believe in—rather, do it in a composed manner that garners respect. Be diplomatic but strong in your convictions.

This leads to another key component of success; you should always strive for excellence and use your knowledge tactically. Know what you're talking about when you address issues. Know which battles to fight because too many little battles may hurt you when it comes to winning the war. Be flexible in your career, since this allows many doors of advancement to open up to you. And never, never burn your bridges!

Fundamental to all that is said is to "know thyself." Study and learn our true history. African-Americans have a substantive and valuable history that reaches back into antiquity. Knowing our past helps us to fashion our future. It will give you a firm foundation from which to launch your career and allow you to advance with confidence.

Last but not least, our strength is deeply rooted in our spirituality. A strong belief in God and the strength you draw from Church will enable you to persevere and excel.

---

3. A "Discovery Exercise." Women were put through role playing exercises where they became officers of the corporation and were expected to delegate, prioritize, communicate, lead and make decisions.

Additionally, the program exposed the women of color to company officers through social events and more formal mentoring assignments. The women of color in the project participated in an Outward Bound week where they experienced team building and examined their own leadership abilities. Finally, the participants went through a "Corporate Savvy" workshop where the idea of corporate politics was explored.

While U.S. WEST did not guarantee promotions to the participants of this 1988 Women of Color Project, a year later it reported that 46 percent of that initial group had been promoted at least once and 8 percent had been promoted twice. More significant, perhaps, is that virtually all of the participants (96 percent) have moved to other departments, thereby gaining the experience necessary for future progress.[10]

WOMEN

The Majority Minority

In the opening profile of this chapter, you met Margaret Greene, President of South Central Bell Telephone Co. The scrutiny Margaret Greene will undergo as the first woman President in the BellSouth family will not be the same as any forty-year-old, white male executive thrust into the same role. Although women make up 44 percent of the U.S. labor force now, and are projected by the year 2000 to make up 47 percent of the work force, women in top management positions continue to be rare.[11] Women confront not only a glass ceiling on their way through corporate America but also the possibility of sexual discrimination and sexual harassment. Although by the year 2000, 80 percent of women of working age will be in the work force, society's demands on women to not only work outside of the home but to shoulder the major part of the work burden in the home, will necessitate a major reevaluation of how women work.

The Ways Women Lead

As corporations attempt to monitor and perhaps remove the barriers for women to advance in the workplace, the debate over cause and effect continues. While the Center for Creative Leadership found that women and men had remarkably similar characteristics, abilities, and motives when competing in the marketplace,[12] subsequent studies cite differences in style as being a cause critical to the glass ceiling effect.

With the publication of a controversial study in 1990, Judy B. Rosener proposed that women, in fact, manage through a leadership style decidedly different from men.[13]

Ms. Rosener's study was based upon a survey of 456 male and female leaders in a variety of organizations nationwide. It concluded that women lead by using an "interactive" leadership style that encourages participation and builds self-worth. And that men used a "command and control" style, viewing job performance as a series of transactions with subordinates for which rewards were given for good performance. Figure 12-2 gives a shorthand version of these two styles of leadership.

As Ms. Rosener points out, "No matter how hard they try, women cannot be men, thus as long as sameness is valued, women will continue to be disadvantaged merely because they are women . . . the point being is that there is more than one effective way to lead . . . "[14] If there is a difference in leadership style, then it follows that one reason that the glass ceiling may exist is that the decision makers are using criteria for managers based upon a "male" leadership model. When surveying managers, one trainer sought to elicit the eight characteristics the respondents believed managers had to have for effective leadership. When the responses from males and females were separated, the trainer found that included in the males' lists among the top five were aggressiveness, confidence, and objectivity. But the women's responses listed appreciation, recognizing strengths, fairness, and accessibility as the most important characteristics of a leader.[15] Women managers are obviously acting upon these beliefs as they function in the workplace. Male superiors, however, continue to judge leadership on the male model.

As the differences in leadership style hamper women's advances, so do the perceptions of that style. While confidence is a quality most people would want to see in a leader, a woman's style of encouraging subordinate's participation in decision making might be perceived as a weakness or a lack of confidence.

FIGURE 12-2

Differences in Leadership Styles between Men and Women

	Male Model	Female Model
Operating style	Competitive	Cooperative
Organizational structure	Vertical & hierarchical	Horizontal & equalitarian
Object	Winning	Quality output
Problem solving	Rational & objective	Intuitive & subjective
Key characteristics	High control	Low control
	Strategic	Empathetic
	Unemotional	Collaborative
	Analytical	High performance

Adapted from Marilyn Loden, *Feminine Leadership or How to Succeed in Business Without Being One of the Boys*, New York, Times Books, 1985.

Assertiveness in a male might be shown through his control of others, while a woman may not assert herself in that manner. In fact, if a woman acts too aggressive, she is penalized for being nonfeminine.

A study of 24 corporate women who had failed to make it to the top of their organizations found that what holds women back, at least in part, is the way they and their male peers perceive their ability to wield power.[16] It was the *perception* of what women can and can't do that limited them, not the reality of what they can and can't do. When measured against a male-dominated past, women fell short of reaching the necessary criteria.

And, while the Center for Creative Leadership rejected the basic differences between male and female leaders, it acknowledged that while men and women shared the same lessons for success, the opportunities for women to learn those lessons were much more limited.

Using the differences in style as a plus instead of a disadvantage, some employers contend that "female" leadership traits are helpful in solving three corporate problem areas: providing better customer service; meeting the demand for higher quality; and filling the need for leadership itself within the company.[17] In the health industry, for example, proponents of the interactive leadership style believe that style will become increasingly more important for that industry if quality demands are to be met.[18]

Mommy Track

Demographics for America's work force in the coming decade points to an increasing female work force. Just as many of the current workplace policies and programs reflected the needs of the "breadwinner" of the past, the workplace will change to reflect the changing needs of its female workers.

A controversial article published in 1989 by Felice N. Schwartz, entitled *Management, Women, and the New Facts of Life,*[19] and dubbed the "Mommy Track" by the news media, proposed a separate professional career path for women with children. Ms. Schwartz contends that such a corporate policy would ensure the return of women to their company after their children are born, thereby reversing the present trend that has women in managerial positions with a turnover rate one and one-half times greater than for men.

The "Mommy Track" A proposal for a separate career path for women with children to ensure their return to their company after their children are born.

Women obviously felt threatened by the suggestion that women returning to the job be segregated and in some ways limited by their status as mothers. No one suggested that fathers be placed on a separate career tract by virtue of their fatherhood.

Schwartz defended her concept by stating, "My theory is that women have entered a world created by men for men and that world has to accommodate to women. . . . If women have to live by men's rules and in men's environment, they're not going to succeed. Things aren't going to change unless we really face up to what the problems are that women are coming smack up against in the corporate and professional world."[20]

Ms. Schwartz's theory is that unless women with children are treated differently by corporations, then such women will suffer in the job market. This theory is supported by a couple of studies. Approximately 200 women with MBA's were studied by Professor Joy Schneer of Rider University and Professor Frieda Reitman at Pace University's Lubin School of Business in Pleasantville, New York. One hundred twenty-eight had no gap in their employment while sixty-three had an average break of 8.8 months. The results of the study were that women who interrupted their career earned 17 percent less in 1993 than their counterparts who had not taken time off. Also, while 60 percent of the women who didn't take time off had reached upper-middle management, only 44 percent of the "mommy trackers" had.[21]

Another side to this same problem has been demonstrated by a study presented in August of 1994, at the annual meeting of the Academy of Management. Linda Stroh of Loyola University of Chicago surveyed 348 male managers at twenty Fortune 500 companies and found that the men with stay-at-home wives earned 20 percent higher wages than men with working wives. This "phenomenon," which has been researched and reported in at least three additional studies, represents the pressures placed on individuals, male and female, who put work above family.[22]

As controversial as the notion is, corporate America must at least explore options if they are to attract and retain the most talented men and women in the work force.

Balancing Work and Family

Regardless of how the return to work of executive women is handled in the future, corporations have to deal with the competing interests most working women feel when torn between home and the workplace. Over 70 percent of the women who work are either married, widowed, divorced, or separated. Almost half of the women in the United States with children under three years of age are employed. A study done in 1983 reported that less than 38 percent of husbands helped their working wives at home. Women work an average of 13.4 hours more per week than their husbands as they put in a "second shift" at home. Even women managers who delegate the actual physical labor continued to administrate and coordinate the household.[23]

Companies have found that allowing employees to balance the demands of work and home is good business. It makes it possible for employees, male and female, to stay with the company as demands on them from the outside increase and/or decrease.

One hot topic among benefit administrators is the company's maternity leave policy. In an analysis of 9,000 women done by the Census Bureau, 71 percent of the women with maternity benefits returned to their job within six months of the child's birth, while only 43 percent of women without benefits returned.[24]

The Pregnancy Act of 1978 requires employers to provide the same leave for pregnancy-related disabilities, as they do for other disabilities. By liberalizing their disability policy to accommodate new parents and addressing family concerns, many employers are reaping the benefits of lower employee turnover. *Fel-Pro,* a Skokie, Illinois manufacturing company is one such company. Its family-friendly programs include:

- a subsidized, on-site day care center
- an emergency caregiver program
- a summer day camp for older children
- a scholarship fund for children of employees
- both on- and off-site recreation opportunities
- an information and referral service for elder care

DuPont became a pioneer in the area of family issues with a set of policies and programs designed to change its corporate culture to meet the changing needs of its work force.

- As early as 1985, DuPont responded to a work-family survey of its employees by creating a child care resource and referral agency. This agency was the first such agency in the state of Delaware and was created as a non-profit organization to serve the wider community, not just DuPont employees. In 1988, the agency expanded its services to elder care and became a nationwide service.

- DuPont's "maternity leave" policy was changed, updated, and expanded to become a family leave policy, equally available to men and women. The leave issues were also expanded to include, in addition to the birth of a child, adoption, or serious illness of a child, parent, or spouse.

- In the area of education, DuPont initiated "School Match," a program that helps employees assess a school system in relation to the needs of their children.

- While DuPont did not provide on-site day care centers, it did invest more than $1.5 million in day care centers near its major locations and fostered an incentive grant program for day care providers to become professionally accredited.

- DuPont's two studies of work–family issues, in 1985 and 1988, indicated that one of the most important changes to make was to establish a permanent committee of employees to do ongoing study on work–family issues. Anything short of that would not keep up with the work force changes.

- DuPont is preparing to address the issue of flexible work options—part-time work with benefits, adjustable work hours, flextime schedules, longer personal leaves, sabbaticals, job sharing, and shared retirement. More and more of DuPont's male employees are requesting flexibility in work hours that had been the exclusive desire of female employees.[25]

Johnson & Johnson, a New Jersey-based company amended its corporate credo to include the statement: "We must be mindful of ways to help our employees fulfill their family responsibilities." It released this statement when announcing a dozen work/family initiatives adopted to keep Johnson & Johnson competitive.[26]

Levi Strauss and Company, a San Francisco-based company is considered a leader in quality-of-life issues, also. Its innovations are geared to changing its corporate culture leading to success with such things as:

- Developing a mission statement that says the company wants to create an environment that is supportive of employees balancing their work and personal lives. The company does not limit its concern to traditional areas such as child care or leave programs, but looks at any policy of the company that puts pressure on its employees.

- Conducting a training program for managers to learn how to manage in a flexible workplace.

- Instituting flexible work schedule programs including telecommuting— where employees use computers at home to do their work and flextime, where sewing machine operators can report for work late or leave work four hours early as long as the core time, 10:00 A.M. to 2:00 P.M., is covered.

- Changing the old vacation policy, sick policy and floating holiday policy to a TOPP (Time Off With Pay Policy) which is a bank of days the employees can use at their discretion.[27]

The "OB in Practice" opposite, Why Should You Promote a Pregnant Woman?, challenges employers on this issue.

In a recent survey of 398 health professionals with children aged sixteen years or younger, researchers found that the presence of family–supportive work policies and practices produced significant benefits in terms of employee attitudes and well-being. The major policies concerned company-provided child care services or referrals and flexible work schedules; and the practices involved family–supportive supervisors. The most significant factor was the perception by the employee of an ability to control a work schedule in order to address work-family conflicts. This sense of control reduced stress-related illnesses and absences.[28]

The Glass Ceiling for Women

As discussed earlier, anti-discrimination laws gave women and people of color more access to the work place. Nevertheless, with almost thirty years of legal protection behind them, women and people of color hold less than 5 percent of the managerial positions in the country's 1,000 largest corporations.[29] Why have managerial positions been out of reach for women and people of color?

In a three-year study of top female executives in Fortune 100 sized companies, the Center for Creative Leadership explored the existence of a barrier to women's advancement within corporate America.[30] The results of the survey were published in 1987 and confirmed that not only a "glass ceiling" but a "wall" existed through which women were not allowed to pass. Seventy-six women were surveyed in the center's study, all of whom held jobs in or near the general management level in a mix of twenty-five service and manufacturing companies. In addition, twenty-two executives responsible for identifying and selecting executives were surveyed as to how they viewed women in the corporate structure.

Glass Ceiling Exists for women and people of color, and stops them from advancing in their field or getting the jobs that they are qualified for.

A major premise of the study was that women executives as compared to men executives begin with two additional strikes against them when undertaking an executive role. Besides the inevitable stress every executive faces in order to handle the responsibilities of the job, women have the additional stress of being in the limelight as a "female executive." As "tokens" to a large extent, women executives find themselves being both "representatives" and "exceptions." Perhaps representing women when they fail and being an exception when they succeed.[31]

In addition to the pressure of being a token, women face the continued pressure that they play the major role in maintaining the home front. Accepting more responsibility in the corporate world has not lessened most women's responsibilities to spouse and children.[32] A University of California at Berkeley study found that four out of five men do not share the daily chores at home with their wives. A *Savvy Woman* survey revealed that women who work outside the home have 25 percent less leisure time than men who work outside the home because of household responsibilities.[33]

What does it take for a woman to succeed in the workplace? And why will someone fail? In their study of female executives, the Center for Creative Leadership found several success factors common to successful female executives.

1. *Help from above.* Successful women have mentors among the top levels of their companies. For the exceptional women, these mentors were willing to risk pushing them forward and upward within the corporation.[34]

OB in Practice

Why Should You Promote a Pregnant Woman?

With more women in the work force, children have an impact on business. The cost of being inflexible when it comes to family issues is a high rate of turnover, losses in productivity, and the loss of women and men with good potential from consideration for top corporate positions.

A corporate manager in a corporation that values diversity has two things to consider when evaluating its company's attitude toward pregnant women.

Many companies don't want to hire or promote a pregnant woman because so many women quit their jobs after their baby is born. Companies have to analyze how they treat a pregnant worker. Are women quitting because they have a great desire to stay home, or are they just rejecting the work environment? Has the employer been supportive during the pregnancy and the leave? Is the woman welcomed back or has her job been changed?

Many companies don't want to experiment with flexible work arrangements to accommodate women with children. In some industries, like the health industry, flexible work schedules to accommodate nurses is not an option—it is a necessity. The workplace of the future will not have workers unless such flexibility becomes standard operating procedure.

Source: Adapted from Felice N. Schwartz, "Why on Earth Should I Promote a Pregnant Woman," *Executive Female*, July/August 1992, pp. 38–41.

Susan J. Davidson credits her success at Chase Manhattan Bank, where she serves as Vice President for Human Resources, to a mentor/sponsor she had: ". . . he was in a position of significant authority, and he believed I had a lot of potential, so he did promote and sponsor me."[35]

Chubb and Son, Inc., a New Jersey financial services company, doesn't leave mentoring to chance. In 1990, it instituted a formalized mentoring program that matched senior management with high potential employees. Through this mentoring program, minority and women employees gained experience and insight by being assigned special projects at the direction of their mentor.[36]

2. *Track record of Achievements.* A successful woman must demonstrate competence and the ability to get the job done.

Judy Zaleski, Vice President of Merrill Lynch in Winter Park, Florida, was singled out by a supervisor for management training, because she proved herself during her ten years with the company. "He felt that because of my success in acquiring clients nationally and managing their assets that I would be a good candidate."[37] Charlotte Beers became chairwoman and chief executive officer of Ogilvy and Mather Worldwide, a powerful Madison Avenue advertising agency, after piloting Tatham RSCG, a midsize Chicago ad agency for ten years. Her success at the Chicago firm proved her worthy of the New York position.[38]

3. *Desire to achieve.* Commitment to the organization outweighed any commitment to self or family for these successful women. Demonstrating to superiors that work is a priority, no matter what is going on in one's personal life, is a necessity for a woman who wants to succeed.[39]

4. *Ability to manage subordinates.* Motivating subordinates and demanding performance from them as well as being loyal to them was typical of a successful woman executive. Judy Zaleski, the Merrill Lynch vice president, whose ability to successfully manage twenty-three financial consultants and eleven office employees was due to her employer's policy toward occupational enhancement.[40]

5. *Willingness to take career risks.* A typical trait in the successful executive woman was her willingness, in fact, her insistence on moving into nontraditional, line authority jobs. By learning the nuts and bolts of the organization these women were more prepared to step into leadership roles.

   Prudential Insurance Company of America, a New Jersey-based company, has a strong commitment to developing women and minorities through its executive development process. In a series of meetings involving the members of the Board of Directors and senior management, the capabilities of top and middle management staff are discussed. The group develops rotations of job assignments, training programs, and task-force assignments and makes sure that high-potential women are given the experience necessary to succeed. Today, 42 percent of Prudential's managers and 12 percent of its company officers are women.[41]

6. *Ability to be tough, decisive and demanding.* Success was linked to willingness to demand results from subordinates, resources from bosses, and unpopular stances with colleagues. At the same time, a woman executive had to walk a fine line between being tough and being masculine.

   Linda Wachner, Chief Executive Officer of Warnaco, Inc., a lingerie manufacturer with $563 million in sales annually, has a reputation as a tough boss. "Quite frankly, a lot of people complained that Linda was very, very, difficult to work for," according to Joel Orenstein, a former employee. Ms. Wachner doesn't attribute such criticisms to her being a woman but simply to people who are jealous of her success. "Do I think there are jealousies out there in the world . . . Sure . . . But it's not against women. If I thought that way, it would slow me down."[42]

Women who couldn't make that break through the glass ceiling also shared common attributes described below as failure factors.

1. *Inability to adapt.* The study identified women who lacked the ability or desire to make the changes necessary to conform to what the organization needed or demanded of them. Judith Call, President and CEO of Holy Redeemer Health System, Inc., Pennsylvania, chooses to remain single in order to have the mobility necessary to climb the corporate ladder in the health care field. "I did make an early decision that career was important to me, and that I needed to be flexible and able to move."[43]

2. *Wanting too much (for self or other women).* Derailed women were seen as those who weren't team players, who were mainly interested in their own advancement—not the company's well-being. In a recent study of gender differences in the work place, 56 percent of the women surveyed thought "being a team player" was not a prerequisite to a promotion to manager while 67 percent of the men did.[44]

3. *Performance problems.* Women executives who were not consistently outstanding were considered weak performers.

4. *Not being able to manage subordinates.* The opposite of the success factor, women executives derailed when they couldn't get performance from their subordinates.

5. *Poor image and business relationships.* Often executive women fall subject to criticism because of the competing demands placed on them in the workplace:

> Take risks—but be constantly outstanding
> Be tough—but not macho
> Be ambitious—but don't expect equal treatment
> Be responsible—but follow other's advice.[45]

6. *Inability to see the big picture.* Women executives often operate in staff positions or in typical "women slots": personnel, affirmative action, and equal employment opportunity roles, and public relations. The lack of exposure to the broader, corporate mission dooms them to limited vision.[46] The former CEO, David Maxwell, of Fannie Mae, a government sponsored loan agency, provided promotion and recognition for qualified women by placing them in highly visible jobs. This proactive support resulted in an increase of women in management from the 4 percent in 1981 to 32 percent in 1991.[47]

The significance of the success and failure factors for executive women lies not in their substance—because these were the same factors for success and failure cited in the records of male executives. Their significance attested to the fact that these factors were applied unequally to female executives. Women who failed were cited as having, on an average, four of the derailment factors to the men's 3.5; and in the success rate women had an average of 10.4 success factors to the 5.7 average of successful men. Women had to be better, not the same as men to succeed! As one executive woman put it, "an average woman is not tolerated, you have to be exceptional."[48]

As women begin to break through the glass ceiling and claim management positions, many find that senior management positions are still closed to them.

Women are reaching general management levels by following the success factors listed above and by three extra boosts. A woman comes to the attention of top management by exhibiting a credibility either inside or outside of the workplace through a successful project or perhaps by having a prestigious degree from an Ivy League school. Once in such a position, another executive is willing to advocate for the woman executive's rise through the corporation. And finally, most women cited some old fashioned luck of being in the right place, at the right time, to enjoy the success offered.

The Center for Creative Leadership study demonstrated that one reason women break through the glass ceiling only to hit the wall of senior management is that women are perceived as "different" with a "feminine style" and that difference, at the very top level of the organization, is not appreciated for what it brings to the organization, but simply for what it is not.[49]

The attitude of top management causes a drain of talent as women either settle for not reaching the top or leave to pursue their own business. The Bureau of Labor Statistics reported in 1985 that there were 2.8 million self-employed women, a 43 percent leap from 1975. Women who are tired of being better at every job just to stay even with male peers, are dropping out of the corporate rat race.

There is evidence, however, that things are changing. Employers regard "Workforce 2000" as a challenge to prepare for a changing work force. They know that they must change how they treat their employees today to be able to attract the most talented and capable of that future work.[50]

Companies, like South Central Bell, are finding ways to help eliminate the glass ceiling and the wall within their companies. Borrowing from many of the success factors listed above, companies are making it corporate policy to prepare women (and minorities) for senior management. Employers have successfully institutionalized the success factors discussed above, giving women new opportunities to succeed. For example:

- *Tenneco* CEO, James L. Ketelson established a Women's Advisory Council of women executives and managers to identify problems that hinder the development of women.[51] More importantly, Tenneco linked bonuses of its executives to their success in developing women (and minority) managers. Women are targeted for line positions and informal mentoring is assured.

- *Prudential Insurance Company of America* also ties compensation directly to managers' performance in promoting women. Prudential's success stems, also, from a strong message from the top that executive development of women and minorities is a corporate goal.

- *Fannie Mae* relied partly on appointing women to very visible positions as a signal that women could and would be cultivated for management positions. Sponsoring employees in MBA programs and executive development programs added to its commitment.

- *Chubb and Son, Inc.* focused on mentoring to increase access of high-potential employees to senior management. The mentoring program is composed of both women and men but at an 8–2 ratio. The company encourages special projects and shifts of assignments into line positions for women to gain critical experience necessary for advancement.[52]

In the "Profile" opposite, Barbara Elliott, a city attorney, gives women some helpful suggestions on getting through the glass ceiling.

Sexual Harassment

Many women face the frustration of not succeeding within the corporate because they are a woman. More, however, face actual discrimination in the workplace in the form of sexual harassment. Sexual harassment is against the law.

It took years for the theory of "sexual harassment" to be recognized by the courts as a form of discrimination. While it may seem self-evident that harassment on *the basis of sex* would violate the law, courts initially labeled supervisory sexual advances as simply "satisfying a personal urge."[53] However, when a Justice Department employee claimed she was fired when she refused the sexual advances of her supervisor, the courts took notice of the violation.[54]

Based on the Civil Rights Act, the EEOC developed guidelines that declared *sexual harassment* a form of illegal sex discrimination. Sexual harassment constitutes a form of behavior directed towards an employee specifically because of his or her sex. (Most incidence of sexual harassment are directed towards women, but research shows that male employees are also sexually harassed on the job, though such incidences are few compared to the problems reported by women.) The EEOC also issued a guideline that set forth a working definition of sexual harassment:

Sexual Harassment Constitutes a form of behavior directed towards an employee specifically because of his or her sex—illegal sex discrimination.

Profile

Barbara Elliott
City Attorney
Bedford, Texas

HOW TO BREAK THROUGH THE GLASS CEILING

Although many women have advanced into middle management positions there is still a discrepancy in the number of women reaching top management positions as compared to the number of men. Women have historically assigned "luck" a greater portion of the responsibility for their advancement than do men. However, being in the right place at the right time is not just a matter of luck.

Successful women prepare themselves to take advantage of opportunities that become available by taking positive steps to develop their leadership abilities and to have others recognize their ability to manage.

Here are some techniques for capitalizing on leadership opportunities and making sure that getting to the right place is more than just luck.

1. Be prepared with thorough, but concise papers or presentations. People are more willing to listen to your ideas, even if they are pressed for time or maybe not even really interested, if they know you will value their time by being as expeditious as possible.

2. Become a good listener. Recognize when someone needs you as a sounding board. Good listeners often pick up valuable information in this fashion.

3. Participate in activities or organizations, both inside and outside of the work environment, where leadership skills can be practiced and honed as well as be appreciated and recognized by others.

4. Only "fight" a major battle where cooperation or persuasion is not practical or will not work. "Consensus building" provides a smoother path toward a goal and gets others to support and work with you in accomplishing a goal.

5. Do not hesitate to speak up with different ideas or innovations if you can support them with adequate information.

6. "Raise the consciousness" of those around you to make them aware of policies or practices that serve to limit opportunity. Many well-meaning people fail to see how their actions can promote the existence of a glass ceiling.

7. Take on new responsibilities and difficult tasks. Show a willingness to get the job done.

8. Seek input and advice from others who have been successful in your profession or business, or in obtaining goals that are similar to yours.

9. Be comfortable with yourself and the way in which you work to achieve a goal. Do not sacrifice your innate sense of what is the correct way for you to succeed.

Unwelcome sexual advances, requests for sexual favors, and other verbal or physical conduct of a sexual nature constitute sexual harassment when (1) submission to such conduct is made either explicitly or implicitly a term or condition of an individual's employment, (2) submission to or rejection of such conduct by an individual is used as a basis for employment decisions affecting such individual, or (3) such conduct has the purpose or effect of unreasonably interfering with an individual's work performance or creating an intimidating, hostile, or offensive working environment.[55]

Points (1) and (2) of the EEOC guideline above describe the type of harassment known as *quid pro quo*: sex in exchange for favors, such as a job, promotion or pay raise, and/or to avoid adverse actions, such as being fired. Point (3) of the guideline describes a type of harassment that results in a "hostile work environment," that is, a workplace where sexual remarks, pitching, horseplay, or the like is allowed to occur.

UNWELCOME SEXUAL ADVANCES   It is critical to understand what "unwelcome" means in the EEO guideline above. A person may have acquiesced in some type of conduct, but the conduct can still be unwelcome. Acquiescence to the conduct may have happened because the person feared loss of his or her job or some other job retaliation. If the conduct was unsolicited, if the victim viewed the conduct as undesirable or offensive and did nothing to initiate it even if it was agreed to, it could still be *unwelcome.*

SEXUAL NATURE   For harassment to be based on sex, as that term is used in the Civil Rights Act, there must be something of a sexual nature in the conduct. Usually, that test is met when a person is propositioned, comments or jokes are made about the person's anatomy, or pictures of people nude and/or in sexually suggestive poses are displayed. Conduct of a sexual nature can also be found when a "but for" situation arises. In one case, male crew members harassed female crew members by pulling such pranks as locking the restroom door at the work site and disabling their vehicles.[56] "But for" the harassed victims being women and unwanted by this particular male work crew, the harassment they experienced would not have happened. This, then, became a "but for their sex" situation.

Sexual harassment became the focus of national media attention in 1992 when Anita Hill accused Supreme Court Justice nominee, Clarence Thomas, of sexually harassing her.

In a politically charged, media-magnified hearing, Anita Hill brought forward for the U.S. Senate's consideration her allegation that Clarence Thomas sexually harassed her ten years earlier while he was chairman of the Federal EEOC and she was an attorney on his staff.

Millions of Americans watched days of testimony as they learned first-hand how difficult and complex the issue of sexual harassment in the workplace could be. The burden placed on a woman who alleges sexual harassment to *prove* that it happened in the absence of any third-part witness was no heavier than the burden placed on a man accused of sexual harassment to prove a negative—that something did not happen.

Credibility of the accused and accuser and character witnesses for both became the deciding factors. In that regard, Ms. Hill lost credibility in many viewers' eyes and certainly the Senate's, when she explained why she had failed ten years prior to bring charges of sexual harassment against her boss. The Senate Committee could not accept her contention that she did not want to hurt her career, that she felt somehow dependant upon Thomas's favorable opinion.

The "He said–She said," "He lied–She lied," debates continued. But Clarence Thomas is a U.S. Supreme Court Justice, and Ms. Hill has returned to teaching at an Oklahoma law school. Corporate response to the Thomas–Hill hearings was mixed. Some companies that had already had programs relevant to sexual harassment renewed publicity on them.

U.S. West, a Colorado-based company, already had formal procedures for addressing sexual harassment complaints and individuals within each department to help. After the hearings, reminders were sent out so victims could still feel comfortable participating in the process.

E. I. Dupont de Nemours & Co. instituted a sexual harassment prevention program called "A Matter of Respect." Not concerned only with compliance, the program uses interactive group training sessions and a confidential phone line service to enable employees to deal with each other in a respectful way. By ensuring confidential assistance, sexual harassment incidents can be diffused in an early stage and behavior changed without losing any employees.

Smaller companies like *Air Products & Chemicals Inc.,* in Allentown, Pennsylvania, and *Ceradyne Inc.,* a Costa Mesa, California, company are reissuing their sexual harassment policies and retraining employees about those policies. The shock and seriousness of the Hill–Thomas confrontation awakened corporate America to the dangers of belittling or ignoring sexual harassment charges.

Figure 12-3 details some steps employers can take to avoid sexual harassment in the workplace.

Comparable Worth

Comparable worth
More than equal pay for equal work; means that jobs should be valued for purpose of compensation on the comparable worth of the job to the organization.

Another right achieved by women in the workplace, only as a result of legislative action, is an equal day's pay for an equal day's work. Unfortunately, while the Equal Pay Act forbids sex discrimination in wage scales, it is applicable only for the same job classifications. Some question the effectiveness of the Act in actually closing the gap between men and women's wages. In 1963, when the Equal Pay Act was enacted, women received 60 cents for each dollar earned by a man. In 1993, that gap had only narrowed by 10 cents, women earned 70 cents in comparison to a man earning $1.00. The failure of the Act has been attributed to three reasons:

- EEOC is not aggressive in enforcing the Act.
- Salary information is not readily available in the private sector so women can't lobby for increases.
- Women tend to change jobs when faced with discriminatory pay practices.[57]

Because the Equal Pay Act does not go far enough, women have pushed for recognition of the comparable worth concept. *Comparable worth* means that jobs should be valued for purposes of pay scales, not on the identical but on the comparable skills, training, responsibility, and efforts needed to perform the job.

---

1. Establish a specific sexual harassment policy that defines and condemns the behavior.
2. Establish a grievance procedure that does not require an immediate supervisor as the first step.
3. Train supervisors about what sexual harassment is in the workplace.
4. Establish the atmosphere necessary so employees who feel harassed can feel free to complain.
5. Establish an investigation procedure that provides, to the extent possible, confidentiality.
6. Appoint an EEO (Equal Employment Opportunity) team to investigate allegations of sexual harassment in the workplace. Women have to be a part of the team to help understand the "reasonable woman" theory.
7. Try to discover any latent incidents or circumstances of sexual harassment that have gone unreported.

Source: Adapted from Jonathan A. Segal, "Seven Ways to Reduce Harassment Claims," *HRMagazine,* June 1992, pp. 84–86. Reprinted with the permission of *HRMagazine,* published by the Society for Human Resource Management, Alexandria, VA.

FIGURE 12-3
Employers' Policies and Practices to Reduce Sexual Harassment Claims

A basic component of such comparison is the job evaluation or job description. Job evaluations are used by employers to describe the duties and skills needed by someone to perform a particular job. Often times wage scales are based upon these evaluations.

A fair and unbiased job evaluation system which measures jobs according to their value and worth to the organization should result in pay equity. The most often recommended system is a point-factor job evaluation system which rates the job on the basis of objective criteria. For example, if experience is a value to the job, the different number years of experience are assigned different values or points. The number or types of employees supervised can be quantified, as well as the education requirements for the job.[58]

The State of Washington in 1986, used such a point system and dramatically increased the wage scales of jobs historically held by women. Under their system a secretarial position that used shorthand skills was awarded 197 points and a jail guard's position 190 points; a teacher's aide 176 points and a truck driver 97 points.[59]

Pay equity will not result from even *valid* job evaluations if the pricing of the jobs comes from the marketplace. The historic, social, and economic factors that caused female-dominated job classifications to land on the lower end of the pay scale, have not changed.[60] The pay scales must be determined within the organization by rewarding the relative importance of all of the jobs to the organization in relation only to each other.

Comparable worth will be an issue for women in the work force so long as the U.S. Dept of Labor reports that the average working woman earns three-fifths of what the average working man earns. The arguments for comparable worth pay scales in the workplace should not be confused with actual discrimination brought about by paying women less for the exact same job. Despite the Equal Pay Act, women professionals entering the job market from college with the same degree as a man can be started at a lower salary. This is a problem of sex discrimination, not comparable worth. Figure 12-4 presents some disturbing statistics. A woman who graduates from MIT can expect to earn 32 percent less than the man graduating next to her.

THE OTHER MINORITIES

Immigrants

In the earlier chapter on Cultural Diversity, it was noted that the United States will solve its problem of a shrinking work force base in the next decade just as it did in the last century, by an influx of immigrants. In the 1980s, 8.7 million people immigrated to the United States. This represented 39 percent of the total U.S. population growth.[61]

Today's immigrants come primarily from Asia and Latin America. By the year 2000 it is projected that Hispanics will account for 10 percent and Asian-Americans around 4 percent of the American work force. Together these people of color will outnumber by 2 percent African-Americans in the work force. But add them to the number of African-Americans in the work force and over one-quarter of the American work force will be people of color by the year 2000.

A fourth of the new immigrants coming into the United States are college graduates, while a third are high school dropouts. The immigrant work force in

Annual salary after graduation with MBA

By School

Men		Difference %	Women
$77,539	MIT	32.5	$58,500
67,397	Virginia	24.1	54,306
62,785	UCLA	22.8	51,147
65,009	Columbia	18.6	54,817
46,521	Rochester	15.2	40,367
80,412	Stanford	7.3	74,925
57,393	Dartmouth	5.0	54,643
54,058	Michigan	4.6	51,702
54,322	Berkeley	2.6	52,934
53,762	Cornell	–1.2	54,433

By Industry

Men		Difference %	Women
$50,441	Info Systems	29.5	$38,950
58,434	Management	13.6	51,445
72,704	Consulting	9.0	66,731
53,134	Marketing	6.5	49,902
56,664	Finance	3.3	54,840

Source: Monica Roman, "Women, Beware: An MBA Doesn't Mean Equal Pay," *Business Week,* October 29, 1990, p. 57. By permission of Business Week © 1990.

FIGURE 12-4

The Pay Gap between Men and Women

that aspect is like the American work force—split between the highly skilled and well-educated and those with minimal skills and little education. U.S. business is taking advantage of both groups.

For the skilled immigrant, the United States is seen as a place of opportunity. Subramonian Shankar was a successful computer expert in India before immigrating to the United States in 1980. In the United States he formed the American Megatrends, Inc., which in 1991 boasted of $70 million in sales. "I couldn't have done this in India," says Shankar.[62] The "OB in Practice" on page 410, Immigrants in Silicon Valley, is another example of U.S. opportunities taken by immigrants.

Many U.S. Industries—communications, computers, pharmaceuticals, research, and development—have found an advantage to teaming with those from other cultures. A chief executive at DuPont Merck Pharmaceutical Company, Joseph A. Mollica, found that people from different backgrounds bring a richness to outlook that means problems and solutions can be seen from a slightly different point of view.[63]

As immigrants gravitate to American's urban centers, some cities have seen a rebirth in older sections and suburbs where immigrants start businesses, buy homes, and pay taxes. In Dallas, Texas, Hispanics revitalized a decaying neighborhood near Jefferson Boulevard that had been a dying inner-city business district.

At the other end of the immigrant scale, however, unskilled workers face problems similar to, but perhaps even more severe than the unskilled American worker. These workers fill the low-paid jobs that make our modern service economy operate—hotel, restaurant, domestic, and child care workers. A downturn in the economy puts these laborers out of work. Most of these jobs have no health benefits, no retirement program, and no educational opportunities. Many immigrants don't qualify for or will not take welfare benefits. Although, a recent vote in California to deny welfare benefits to *illegal* immigrants, points to a trend

OB in Practice — Immigrants in Silicon Valley

A third of the engineering work force in Silicon Valley are Asians. Winston H. Chen, a Taiwanese immigrant bought half interest in a circuit board assembler company in 1979 when it was on its way down and turned it into a $181 million success story by 1992. CEO Andrew S. Grove of Intel Corporation, a major U.S. manufacturer of microchips, immigrated from Hungary in 1956. His corporation's latest microprocessor was created under the management of an East Indian native. A Frenchman, Philippe Kahn, founded Borland International Incorporated, a major software company.

The influence of immigrants on the workings of the high tech companies in Silicon Valley is significant. But their ability to move up the corporate ladder is still limited by language barriers and prejudice. Several Valley companies routinely send their managers to "managing diversity" courses and offer immigrants classes in American idioms and business culture. These high-tech companies are finding the cultural diversity and the entrepreneurial drive of the new immigrants a significant advantage for their future success.

Source: Adapted from Robert D. Hof, "High Tech's Huddled Masses: Making a Mark in Silicon Valley," *Business Week*, July 13, 1992, p. 120.

---

seen in California of an increased dependency on the welfare system from unskilled aliens.[64]

Unskilled immigrants compete with unskilled Americans for these low-paying jobs. Such competition threatens some African-Americans and causes racial tension in urban America. The reports of destruction to Asian businesses in Los Angeles in May of 1992 following the "Rodney King" court decision alerted many people to the resentment brewing among the disfranchised of that city.

A recent survey by Louis Harris and Associates, Inc., published in *Business Week* magazine reports that 73 percent of the African-Americans surveyed thought business more likely to hire immigrants than African-Americans. Nonetheless, African-Americans were still more positive than whites about the impact of immigration on the United States.[65]

The challenge facing U.S. business is to allow these first and second generation immigrants to full participation in the workplace. Some companies recognize the unique needs of foreign-born workers in designing their diversity programs. AT&T encouraged its Hispanic workers to form a Hispanic employee network. This network allowed this particular group of employees to decide what issues they faced and to approach top management in a professional, problem-solving manner. An Avon Asian networking group used Avon Asian Day to share cultural aspects of diverse Asian cultures—Chinese, Japanese, Korean, Filipino—to break down cultural stereotypes in the organization. Such cultural understanding leads to acceptance, so that Asian-American workers become more valuable contributors to the organization.[66]

Older Workers

Older workers present both unique problems and possibilities to a diverse workplace.

The Age Discrimination in Employment Act (ADEA) gives workers over *40 years of age* protections against job discrimination. When we discuss age in the workplace as presenting a particular challenge, however, we want to begin with a fifty-year-old person. From fifty-years-old and older we can distinguish as many as six groups of older persons who by their circumstances present particular problems and opportunities in the work force.

1. *Workers 50–62 years old* are the first distinct group of "older workers." He or she may have plateaued in his or her job or feel threatened that his or her job is not secure. They may want to move up, develop new skills, and earn more money. They value health care insurance benefits and their pension credits, so they are interested in maintaining a full-time job that includes full benefits. If they have not been on a promotion track, they probably cannot expect any more moves up.

2. *A displaced worker aged 62 years and younger* usually has recent work experience but is not on a pension or receiving social security benefits. He or she has a very strong economic need to work full time and receive full benefits but may be told his or her skills are obsolete. They are capable of doing many jobs but are not likely to be hired.

3. *Retirees age 62 and younger* may have pensions and some health coverage but are not yet receiving social security. They may have been encouraged to retire early or were simply eager to leave their last employment. These retirees would like to get back into the workplace. The workplace put structure in their lives and gave them a sense of belonging. They are more flexible when it comes to full- or part-time work, and their requirements as to benefits.

4. *Retirees aged 62–69* who are receiving social security have less incentive to go back to work because they jeopardize their social security benefits. In addition, they may believe they are no longer capable of competing in the job market. Their health conditions may make only part-time work possible for them.

5. *Retirees age 70 or older* who are on social security have concerns and problems similar to those above 60—only more so. Certainly, their health condition or their responsibilities to a spouse may mean they are only interested in part-time work and perhaps, working at home.[67]

6. *Women in all of the age groups* discussed above are seen also as a particular subgroup with particular problems. For too many of them, their work history has been in lower paying jobs and with industries less likely to offer pension benefits. Older women will rely more heavily on Social Security. Forty percent of the "older workers" (fifty five years plus) are women and they work in traditionally female jobs—clerical, service, and retail sales.[68]

The categories above demonstrate, that "older workers," which is the term we will use, are diverse among themselves and cannot be stereotyped. Nonetheless, we will make some generalizations about why older workers present a problem and an opportunity in the current workplace.

Older workers want to work out of necessity. Approximately one-fifth of the older population in the United States in 1985 were poor or near poor.[69] Women make up a significant portion of this population. As noted above, women may have entered the job market at a later age and have no earned pension benefits. Older workers need to work, too, for their own self-respect.

Studies that compared "baby boomers" to those born prior to WWII tell us something of the older workers in the work force today. Many started and stayed with one employer. They accepted a strict top-down organization where, they believed, everyone had an opportunity to climb the corporate ladder. They expected a "fair day's pay for a fair day's work" and accepted seniority as a legitimate way to increase compensation. More often than not, they defined themselves by the work they did.[70] So after leaving the work force, many retirees found, in addition to their money needs, they needed to work to retain or regain a sense of value in their lives.

A nonprofit organization in Boston, ABLE (Ability Based on Long Experience) tries to match retirees who desire to reenter the job market to jobs that will value their unique skills and experiences. Bob Howard, having retired as a chief engineer with Exxon Shipping Corp., was placed by ABLE with a bank trust department at the age of seventy-five. ABLE wants employers to understand that the most accomplished older workers, who have retired from top level positions, are those likely to want to escape the boredom of retirement. These older workers, however, aren't trying to recreate their last work experience. They are often more willing to give up position and authority for flexibility and job satisfaction. These older workers can be affordable resources for smaller businesses. ABLE's goal for placement is about 300 candidates per year.[71]

Hiring older workers is seen by some employers as a solution to the growing concern over a lack of qualified entry level employees. The projections for the year 2000 have, for some industries, already become a reality. In a study done by the Society for Human Resource Management in 1988, over half of the 700 companies surveyed were already reporting acute shortages of qualified applicants in low-skilled, low-paying jobs, such as waiters, cashiers, tellers, as well as better-paying higher-skilled jobs, such as nurses and secretaries.[72]

Industry is finding that the younger work force lacks fundamental job skills as a result of their poorer educational performance.[73] While business is recognizing its need to partnership with the education community in order to reverse these trends, results from these activities will not happen overnight.[74] In the meantime, the older worker supplies business with a proven product.

Finally, older workers should be sought by America's businesses as an entrance into the older customer consumer market. The older consumer is big business, and by the year 2005 when the last of the baby-boomers turn forty-something, it will be even bigger.

The American Health Care Association, which serves over 10,000 nursing homes and long-term care facilities, notes the serious staff shortages facing their federation members. Paul R. Willing, their executive vice president, sees older workers as a valuable labor pool. "Older workers make wonderful nurse assistants because they are dependable, compassionate, and they bring a special understanding to their jobs, which improves the quality of life enjoyed by elderly and disabled residents in the nursing facilities," he said.[75]

Companies that wish to recruit older workers will have to make an effort. Catherine Fyock, author of *America's Workforce is Coming of Age,* has some helpful suggestions on how to do that in the "Profile" opposite.

The most serious barrier to the productive use of the older workers in today's workplace stems from stereotyping and the prejudice displayed against them. Some typical misconceptions of older people based on stereotyping and prejudice are explored below.

1. *Older workers are less productive than other workers.* We have been taught to believe that workers loose productivity as they get older. A number of current studies debunk this myth by demonstrating that the quality and

Catherine D. Fyock
SPHR President, Innovative
Management Concept
PUTTING EXPERIENCE TO WORK

The work force is aging, and today's businesses, if they are to remain productive and efficient, will begin to examine the issue of increased employment of older workers, by either attracting more of these workers, keeping them within the corporation in full-time positions, or by working with them to find alternate solutions that make sense within the corporation.

With corporate America recognizing the need to remain productive in a global economy, keeping the aging work force productive and effective is a top priority. Several retailers have already developed some excellent strategies to respond to needs of the aging work force, and the staffing problems plaguing many businesses.

- Walt Disney World Company in Lake Buena Vista, Florida, employs older workers in about 9 percent of its positions throughout the organization.
- Hardee's Food Systems, Inc., headquartered in Rocky Mount, North Carolina, Kentucky Fried Chicken, based in Louisville, Kentucky, and other quick-service restaurants are turning to the older worker as one means to meet the labor shortages caused by the baby bust.
- Builders Emporium, headquartered in Irvine, California, finds that older workers not only understand customer service issues better than younger workers, but they also come from a do-it-yourself generation that makes their employment a natural fit.
- Joseph Horn Department Store in Pittsburgh, Pennsylvania, where unemployment is high, still prefers older workers, and 32 percent of its hourly employees are older workers.
- Wal-Mart Stores, Inc., based in Arkansas, employs older workers, because they are an important part of the company's future growth.

In order to successfully organize and implement a plan to employ and manage an aging work force effectively, businesses need to begin making strategy plans now to address these issues. What should companies do to encourage the employment of older workers?

1. Get Educated. The needs and concerns of the aging work force are different from the needs and concerns of yesterday's work force. Strategies to recruit and select, train, compensate, manage, and retire older workers are different for this new labor market segment. Companies need to look for ways to stay updated on aging issues that will affect the management of these workers.
2. Analyze Local, Regional, and National Resources. Many employers do not realize that there are myriad outside resources to provide information, guidance, and counseling on older worker issues.
3. Gain Total Management Support. The effectiveness of many corporate programs can be measured immediately by the degree of involvement, commitment, and support by top management. The initiative to respond to the needs of an aging work force demands high-level involvement.
4. Eliminate Barriers to the Employment of Older Workers. There are a great many barriers, internal and external, that prohibit employment of older workers within the corporate environment. Internal barriers include age discrimination or the more subtle ageism, inflexible work options, and outdated job designs, personnel policies, and procedures. External barriers are perceptions that the organization does not want to employ older workers, or recruitment messages that do not reach the older adult.

5. Implement Methods to Attract and Retain Older Workers. The increased and effective employment of an aging work force doesn't just happen. It comes about from careful planning that incorporates an understanding of the desires of older adults.

6. Train Supervisors for Managing A Changing and Aging Work Force. Managers today are largely unprepared for the challenges of supervising a diverse older work force. They need additional training.

7. Keep Communication Lines Open. Listening and responding to employee issues remains one of the most important steps a company can take in increasing productivity and morale.

Today's businesses must seek methods to make the continued employment of its aging work force a meaningful, productive, and positive one. Today's work force is indeed coming of age. Smart business leaders will begin to initiate strategies to make the effective employment of older workers a solution to many of the changes taking place in the work force today.

This article is excerpted from Catherine D. Fyock, *America's Work Force Is Coming of Age: What Every Business Needs to Know to Recruit, Train, Manage, and Retrain an Aging Work Force,* Lexington Books, July 1990.

Catherine D. Fyock, SPHR, is president of Innovative Management Concepts, a management consulting firm specializing in creative strategies for meeting the needs of a diverse work force, P.O. Box 905, Prospect, KY 40059.

quantity of the work done by individuals may as often improve by age as decrease by age.[76] In addition, the added dimension of age when dealing with an older customer base can improve the performance of the older worker. Organizations have found older workers exert a stabilizing force on the operation when working alongside younger workers. Fast food companies, such as Kentucky Fried Chicken, hire retirees as part-time managers. "Older workers provide a stabilizing effect and bring a good work ethic with them," says Don Doyle, former KFC, Inc. President. This informal mentoring situation that results from the pairing of older workers and teenagers improves overall productivity.[77]

2. *Older workers are hard to retrain, cost more to retrain, and do not stay at the job long enough to justify the investment.* Companies that value diversity learn how to approach the training of older workers. A redesigned training program does not have to cost more. Companies are finding that retraining older employees is, in fact, cost-effective and helps stabilize the work force. Bank of America was faced with the elimination of 1,500 jobs because of downsizing. Through controlling attrition and hiring, no one was laid off. Several thousand employees, many older workers, were retrained to fill other jobs with the bank. The bank believes it benefited by retaining its long-term employees because they help retain the long-time customers.[78] The older worker stays on the job longer than many of their younger counterparts whose career path is tied to greener pastures.[79] Job turnover is high in all age groups and higher among workers twenty-five to thirty-four years of age than workers over fifty years.

3. *Older workers lack the motivation of other workers to work hard, because they aren't on a career path; they would rather be retired, or they don't need the money.* As discussed earlier, 20 percent of the older population live below or near the poverty line. Older workers do need to be employed. In addi-

Older workers give McDonald's a "new" face.

tion, older workers are motivated to work by a need to feel productive and useful. Many older workers enter into a second career with every expectation to succeed and progress within the organization.

The myths and realities about older workers are summarized in Fig. 12-5. There are, however, some realities about older workers that have to be recognized by organizations.

The myth is that older workers . . .	The reality is that older workers . . .
are viewed negatively by customers	are viewed positively by customers
are slow, unproductive workers	are as productive as their younger counterparts
won't be with the company long	remain on the job longer than younger workers
don't want to advance	want to learn and grow
are inflexible and resistant to change	are willing to change and adapt
don't need to work	may need the money
are absent from work because of illness	have fewer incidence of absence and tardiness
are difficult to work with	are adept in interpersonal relationships
are expensive to train	repay the training investment quickly
incur higher insurance costs	may cost no more to insure
are not interested in work	are motivated to work
are more accident-prone	have fewer on-the-job accidents
won't work because of Social Security benefits	may need additional income, or want to work
are not as adept intellectually	are intellectually adept
lack experience	have a wealth of life experiences

Source: Catherine Fyock, *America's Work Force Is Coming of Age*, Lexington, Mass., Lexington Books, 1990, p. 42.

FIGURE 12-5
Older Workers: Myths and Realities

1. Older workers who are on social security or receiving pension benefits may jeopardize those benefits if they return to work.
2. Compensation and benefits issues have to be considered when hiring older workers.
3. Older workers who return to the job market will have to be retrained.
4. The workplace, and not the older worker, will have to change if older workers are going to be attracted and retrained.
5. Older workers are protected by law from discrimination in the workplace.

People with Disabilities

The primary lesson of valuing cultural diversity is that we need to change the workplace to better utilize the talents and contributions of those diverse employees entering the work force. People with disabilities can best exemplify that necessary change. What may be intangible in the way of workplace changes necessary to accommodate women, people of color, the aged, or immigrants becomes quite real and tangible when the workplace needs to change to accommodate wheelchairs, hearing impairments, and blindness.

WHO ARE PEOPLE WITH DISABILITIES? As discussed earlier, one of the primary dimensions by which we establish our core identities are our own physical abilities or qualities. Many of these abilities/qualities are inborn. Ignoring the other primary dimensions for a moment (of gender, race, ethnic, age, or sexual orientation) think about your own height, weight, looks, hair, upper body strength, dexterity, agility (both mental and physical), eyesight, hearing, your ability to retain information, and your ability to communicate that information to others. Now look around you. There are probably students around you who differ from you on all of the above attributes. Who may be what you consider the ideal height or weight; better looking; nicer hair; more capable, either physically or mentally; or perhaps, not as capable as you, not able to retain or regurgitate information quite as well as you, or may not be as pleasing to look at or as pleasant to be around.

Differences are all around us and have always been part of the workplace as well as society. Recognition and accommodation of personal differences happens daily and to a large extent, automatically. But at some point differences are judged to be more acute than the workplace is, or has been, willing to handle.

Judgments were made about the capability of a person because he or she used a wheelchair, didn't have twenty-twenty vision, or was hearing impaired. For many people with disabilities these judgments were made without an opportunity to demonstrate their own personal capabilities.

Employers can no longer afford to dismiss an entire group of potential employees on the basis of perceived nonability. "Workforce 2000" predicts that the workplace will go begging for qualified applicants by the turn of the century. In addition, with the passage of the Americans with Disabilities Act, people with disabilities have legal protection from discrimination. Through a review of the provisions of the ADA, you can see the kind of corporate culture change necessary to value these diverse employees.

Americans with Disabilities Act

The U.S. Department of Health and Human Services estimates the number of people in the United States with one or more disabilities to be at forty-three million people. A 1986 Lou Harris poll found that 66 percent, or slightly over twenty-eight million, of them were unemployed. The poll also found that two-thirds or over eighteen million of the people with disabilities in the United States who are unemployed want to work.[80]

The *Americans with Disabilities Act* was passed into law in July, 1990, to ensure that those eighteen million-plus Americans are given an equal opportunity to work. In addition, for the forty-three million disabled, the law bars discrimination in both the public and private sector in areas of public services, such as bus and rail transportation; public accommodations, such as restaurants and hotels; and in telecommunications. For businesses trying to attract the "diverse customer," compliance with these portions of the law is just good business. Following is a study of the major ADA provisions affecting employment.

Americans with Disabilities Act (ADA) The law says that the disabled must be given an equal opportunity to work, and it bars discrimination in the public and private sectors in the areas of public service, public accommodations, and telecommunications.

EMPLOYERS AFFECTED   All public employers and private employers of more than fifteen employees are subject to the ADA employment provisions.

The ADA prohibits discrimination against qualified individuals with disabilities in regard to all activities affecting employment, including hiring, promotions, and benefits.

WHO IS DISABLED UNDER ADA?   A person is considered disabled under the ADA if he or she has a physical or mental impairment limiting substantially one or more of the major life activities of the person.

Major life activities include such functions as caring for one's self, performing manual tasks, walking, seeing, hearing, speaking, breathing, learning, or working.

Every disabled person, however, is not covered by the ADA. Only qualified individuals can gain protection against discrimination. A "qualified individual" is one who can carry out the *essential functions* of the job, with or without *reasonable accommodation.*

It is important to note that a person with a disability may not be qualified for every job in the marketplace. It is still a question of matching the person with the right qualifications to the job. ADA puts the burden on the employer to make such matches without prejudice.

For the McDonald's Corporation, that means concentrating on what skills a job applicant has or can develop rather than on what skills the applicant does not have. In their McJobs program, McDonald's recruits, trains, and retrains people with disabilities across the corporate job scale.[81]

ESSENTIAL FUNCTIONS   As stated earlier, a person with a disability is protected under the ADA only if he or she can perform the essential functions of the job, with or without reasonable accommodation. Employers have an opportunity under ADA to review the job descriptions they are using and reassess their accuracy.

The Act provides guidance on what will prove that a particular function is essential to the job. These things are:

1. Employer's judgment as to what functions are essential. The ADA says that it will not dictate to an employer what job the person hired is needed to fill. That's for the employer to decide.

2. Written job descriptions. While written job descriptions are not required under the ADA, most people advising how to comply with it strongly suggest written job descriptions.

3. Amount of time spent on the job performing the function. If the majority portion of an employee's time will be spent on the road, having an

impairment that prohibits driving would disqualify one from consideration. But, if the driving was a very minor portion of the job, reasonable accommodation might be made.

4. Consequences of not requiring the incumbent to perform the function. Again, it is critical in the determination of the essential functions of the job to identify the consequences of that task not being done.

5. Terms of a collective bargaining agreement. Many collective bargaining agreements have established the respective duties of the union members. Their duties are reflected by their job classification and pay rates. Most unions consider it a violation of their collective bargaining agreement to switch job duties between employees with different job classifications. A history of strict union-driven job duties can be determinative as to the essential requirements of the job.

6. Work experience of past or current incumbents in the job or similar jobs. Often, if formal job descriptions do not exist, a narrative from a job incumbent or former incumbent can give a very detailed report of what the job entails.

Written job descriptions being done to comply with ADA will need to include the traditional knowledge, skill, and abilities needed for the particular job but only reflecting the minimum requirements. For many Human Resource professionals, this revision means tailoring job descriptions for selection decisions rather than for compensation purposes.[82]

For companies currently not using job descriptions, the requirements of ADA make it advisable to begin doing so. Usually, the incumbent in a particular job or a job category can describe those essential job duties she or he performs. A supervisor should provide input into the job description, as well. Figure 12-6 provides an outline of a job description that can be used to be in compliance with ADA.

Figure 12-6
Outline for Job
Description Development

Job Title: This is a description of the job title or classification.

Definition: This section should contain a brief description of the position, the level and/or type of supervision received by the employee, an identification of who the employee is responsible to, and the type and/or level of independent judgment used by the employee when performing tasks.

Equipment/Job Location: This section should describe the type of equipment used by the employee, the location and environment in which the job is usually undertaken, and any special environmental conditions of physical requirements the employee may encounter.

Essential Functions of the Job: This section should identify "essential functions" of the job—basic duties for which the job was created that cannot normally be transferred to another position without disruption in the flow or process of work.

Additional Examples of Work Performed: Here you may want to list the duties that are not "essential functions" but are typically undertaken or expected of the employee.

Required Knowledge and Abilities: List the basic abilities and knowledge the employee will need to adequately perform the job. These may be both specific and broad-based requirements. They should definitely be job-related.

Qualifications: List the basic or minimum qualifications every employee in this position must have to be considered for employment.

Source: *Complying with the Americans with Disabilities Act of 1990,* Washington, D.C., National League of Cities, 1991, p. D–1.

REASONABLE ACCOMMODATION   If a person can perform the essential functions of a job without the need of any accommodation, the employer is bound by the ADA not to discriminate against that person because of his or her disability.

If accommodation is needed, then ADA requires such reasonable accommodation that does not impose an undue hardship on the employer. An accommodation is a change in a work process or the work environment which enables a person with disabilities to do the job.

Nordstrom, a Seattle-based retailer, spent $20.69 to accommodate a job candidate. Melissa Kurtz has a rare disease that has limited her height to three feet and restricted her reach and movement. She had her own electric wheelchair and with Nordstrom purchased the $20 "reacher" to pick up items on the floor and the $0.69 back scratcher to extend her reach on her desk. She became a valuable employee.[83]

Any architectural changes to the workplace that could be readily achieved with little or no difficulty or expense, would be, by definition, a reasonable accommodation to make for a qualified individual with a disability otherwise qualified for employment. Many employers worry about the expense of such changes. A Honeywell Corporation survey found that in cases where accommodation was needed, the average cost was less than $50.[84] A study done by the Job Accommodation Network provided the following cost estimates:

31 percent of accommodations are no cost

19 percent of accommodations are between $1 to $50

19 percent of accommodations are between $50 to $500

19 percent of accommodations are between $500 to $1,000

11 percent of accommodations are between $1,000 to $5,000

less than 1 percent of accommodations are over $5,000[85]

Accommodating a disabled employee by providing keyboard supports,[86] voice amplifiers, TV screens that enlarge type can usually be done for less than $1,000. What employers may discover is that the investment is returned in multiples by the efficient and effective work of the employee. Blue Cross/Blue Shield of Ohio renovated its building over four years ago and renovated all of it with workers with disabilities in mind. Wide halls, adjustable furniture, elevators with braille buttons and sound signaling each floor, and accessible restrooms means that a qualified person with disabilities is a welcome employee. Ed Hartzell says, "We have . . . always made a point of recruiting the most qualified person . . . If that person happens to use a wheelchair, that's just his or her mode of conveyance."[87]

UNDUE HARDSHIP   If the accommodation necessary to remove barriers to employment is seen as presenting an undue hardship on the employer, it will not be required. The action necessary must require significant difficulty or expense.

Sexual Orientation and Affection

Valuing diversity is more than equal employment opportunity and affirmative action or being in compliance with antidiscrimination laws. It is recognizing and utilizing all of the talents of all the people who make up the work force. It is appreciating the differences among employees and using those differences to enhance the workplace.

Gay men and lesbians comprise one group of employees for whom being included in many diversity programs is their only avenue to nondiscrimination.

Sexual orientation Gay men and lesbians are a group of employees who are discriminated against and are not protected by federal legislation.

Unlike women, people of color, older workers, and people with disabilities, gay men and lesbians are not covered by any comprehensive federal legislation that protects them from job discrimination based upon their sexual orientation and affection.

The Civil Rights Movement spawned the Women's Movement, made activists of older Americans (American Association of Retired People), and gave people with disabilities a chance to exert their rights. In that same way, the Civil Rights Movement gave the gay and lesbian community a voice. Originally centered in the large urban settings of New York and San Francisco, gay men and lesbians demanded the equal right to step forward and be regarded with tolerance and to receive the protection of antidiscrimination laws.

In the early 1980s, the crisis of the AIDS epidemic brought the issue of homosexuality to the attention of the American people in an alarmingly new way. The spread of AIDS among homosexuals in large urban areas caused many to view AIDS as a homosexual disease. Fear of the AIDS disease and ignorance as to how it is transmitted caused increased discrimination for gay men and lesbians in the workplace. The response from that portion of the gay community that had long advocated equal protection was predictable. They became advocates of a more aggressive national policy to combat AIDS with significant research moneys and humane and affordable health care for people living with AIDS. In addition, they increased their advocacy for federal, state, and local legislation that would put equal protection for people regardless of their sexual orientation/affection into Civil Rights laws.

What was not predictable was that the AIDS epidemic brought many members of the gay community who previously had not publicly advocated any legislation "out of the closet." The AIDS epidemic that could give and did give for some, a reason to continue to hide their sexual orientation, freed others. *Fortune* magazine interviewed over 100 gay people for an article about gays in corporate America, and found that a majority were doing volunteer AIDS-related charity work. For many, this step signaled their refusal to shroud their lives with secrecy any longer.

Activism for protective legislation has not been overwhelmingly successful. In a 1989 study conducted for the National Gay and Lesbian Task Force, only one state, Wisconsin, had passed comprehensive, across the board protection for gays and lesbians against discrimination in public employment, public accommodations, private employment, education, real estate, housing, credit, and union practices. Only one county in the entire United States had afforded gays and lesbians all of those same protections—Howard County, Maryland. Thirteen U.S. cities have passed protections in all of the areas listed above: Washington D.C., five cities in California, two each in New York and Massachusetts, and one each in the states of Minnesota, Pennsylvania, and Michigan.

Figure 12-7 gives a breakdown of the numbers of cities, counties, and states that have enacted protection in at least one of the areas listed above.

Gay men and lesbians have some of the same problems in the workplace as women, people of color, older workers, and people with disabilities.

Women tried to assimilate into the corporate culture. The gay and lesbian corporate employees have acted similarly.

James Woods, in a Ph.D. dissertation, studied the coping strategies of more than 100 gay men in corporate life. The group ranged in age from twenty-one to sixty-eight and cut across the job stratum, from beginner to senior management. Woods identified three main types of coping: those who fabricate a heterosexual identity; those who are known to be gay; and those who avoid the

Protected Area	States	Counties	Cities
Public Employment	13	15	61
Public Accommodations	1	1	37
Private Employment	1	3	41
Education	1	1	24
Housing/Real Estate	1	4	37
Credit	1	3	36
Union Practices	1	2	30
Hate Crimes*	4	0	2

*Bias bills addressing antigay violence and/or intimidation.

Source: Partially adapted from Arthur S. Leonard, "Gay and Lesbian Rights Protections in the U.S.," National Gay and Lesbian Task Force, 1989.

FIGURE 12-7

Numbers of Jurisdictions with Laws Concerning Discrimination on the Basis of Sexual Orientation

issue.[88] The last type doesn't lie about it, but just doesn't expose one's sexual orientation for fear of repercussions.

As discussed in detail earlier in the chapter, women and people of color reach a glass ceiling within organizations because of their gender and race. Gay and lesbian executives fear that the same glass ceiling exists for them. In 1987, 66 percent of major-company CEOs surveyed by *The Wall Street Journal* said they would be reluctant to put homosexuals on management committees, one key way for advancement in most corporations.[89]

A Bank of America vice president, Ted Liebst, left the bank in 1988, because he could not imagine himself being promoted to senior management. He felt the bank would find his homosexuality a failing. "If we (the Bank) can pick from 1,000 people, why pick one who, by someone's standards, is less than perfect?" he asks.[90]

Older workers and people with disabilities are especially interested in health care coverage.

For gay men and lesbians, health care coverage for their life partners is often a high priority when benefits are discussed.

CONCLUSIONS AND APPLICATIONS

- Women and people of color have not been given the same opportunities in the workplace to advance up the corporate ladder. Access to top management, companywide experience, advanced training, and gender neutral, and race-blind performance standards are necessary if women and people of color are to have equal opportunity to compete for top management positions.

- Studies have identified certain success factors that contribute to the advancement of women into top management. A mentor is essential. To attract a mentor, women have to demonstrate an ability to do the job, potential is not enough. Women have to have a burning desire to achieve, a willingness to take risks, and an ability to manage subordinates while being tough, decisive, and demanding.

- Women have suffered in the workplace because they have been perceived as lacking adequate leadership skills. However, women have been judged on a traditional male leadership model—competitive, authoritative, and highly objective. A more cooperative, collaborative, and intuitive leadership style typical of a female leader can be just as effective. Corporations heading for a new "team building" management model will be more willing to accept alternate leadership models from its top management.

- Sexual harassment can take two forms: *quid pro quo,* when a threat or promise is made in exchange for a sexual favor; and a *hostile work environment,* when repetitive offensive conduct of a sexual nature victimizes a person in the workplace. To avoid incidents of sexual harassment, companies need to have a clear policy that outlaws such behavior.

- African-Americans face many of the same barriers as women in corporate America. Companies that want to help African-Americans break through the glass ceiling will need to reexamine their understanding of Equal Employment Opportunity, ensure their performance appraisal programs are color blind, allow for appointment of African-Americans to line positions, and improve their recruitment practices.

- Women of color shoulder a double burden as they are exposed to both racism and sexism in the workplace. Innovative companies recognize women of color as a distinct group and design development programs just for their benefit.

- Immigrants will become almost 15 percent of the work force by the year 2000. Integrating them into the workforce will require considerable flexibility. The wealth of talent and the richness of a different cultural perspective will be an asset to corporations that learn to value the diversity.

- The primary reason older workers work is financial. For many, Social Security and/or pensions cannot keep them out of the poor or nearly poor category of Americans. Many older workers also need the self-respect and sense of value that being part of the work force gives them. Myths that older workers are less productive, impossible to retrain, or not motivated have kept companies from utilizing the older work force. Companies are finding, however, that older workers can bring needed skills, stability, and a wealth of experience into the workplace.

- People with disabilities are those people who are limited in one or more major life activity such as caring for oneself, performing manual tasks, walking, seeing, hearing, speaking, breathing, or learning. Over eighteen million unemployed people with disabilities want to work. Matching capable people with disabilities to jobs they can perform will add a tremendous boost to the shrinking American work force pool.

- People who have been discriminated against because of their sexual orientation/affection are the only diverse group we are studying that does not enjoy the protection of federal law. Many local jurisdictions and company employment policies extend job protection to gay men and women. An activist gay men and lesbian movement begun in the 1970s is becoming more vocal in the decade following the discovery of the AIDS epidemic. Gays in corporate America are demanding the same kinds of support and acceptance as other diversity groups.

REVIEW QUESTIONS

1. Review the success and failure factors present when women succeed or fail on their climb up the corporate ladder. How many of each were evidenced in Ms. Greene's appointment as President of South Central Bell Company? Explain.

2. Why is the "command and control" style of leadership preferable to the "interactive" style of leadership?

3. What is *comparable worth* and why is it not mandated by the Equal Pay Act?

4. Why is the concept of the "Mommy Track" threatening to some women?

5. How can a company insure an equal opportunity for a person with a disability to be hired?

6. What progress has been made for African-Americans in the work force since the Civil Rights Act of 1964?

7. Identify the common traits exhibited by companies with bad records for promoting African-Americans. Also identify the common barriers to such promotion.

8. Why have older workers been underutilized in the workplace? Why does that need to change?

9. Why are more gay men and lesbian employee support groups being formed in major U.S. corporations?

DISCUSSION QUESTIONS

1. Women of color face both racism and sexism in the workplace. While both burden them, which do you think they can more easily confront and eliminate? Why?

2. "Charisma" is often an attribute of someone we consider a leader. John F. Kennedy, Martin Luther King, Jr., and Ronald Reagan are examples. Name a woman who has charisma. Is it the same type of charisma as the men listed? If not, why not?

3. African-Americans seem to have a worse record than women of breaking through the glass ceiling to management positions. Discuss the reasons why that might be so.

4. African-Americans do not seem to resent the influx of immigrants into the United States as much as whites do. Why do you think that is so?

5. Because of the projections of *Workforce 2000,* it would seem that members of the diversity groups would be in competition for the best jobs in the job market. Explain how you think diversity training helps bring these groups together.

6. Discuss some workplace changes that can make the corporate culture more accepting of older workers.

7. Do you agree or disagree that sexual orientation is a valid classification for antidiscrimination laws and policies? Why or why not?

CASE STUDY

Diverse Needs

Lisa has recently been promoted to a vice president's level as Director for Employee Benefits and Compensation for the Enlightened Corporation.

Enlightened Corp. has union employees and a diversified work force. It has over the years, recruited talented women (like Lisa) and African-Americans for management positions. It has carved out a number of part-time positions that are filled by people with disabilities found for the corporation through the local state rehabilitation center. Its retirees often are back to work for the corporation as consultants or temporaries when vacations or leaves cause employee shortages.

Not long after Lisa moved into her new office, she had this conversation with a new vice president, David, who heads up the Marketing Department.

DAVID: Well, has the ceiling caved in on you yet?

LISA: No, I don't think so. What do you mean?

DAVID: You know. The new benefits plan.

LISA: What new benefits plan?

DAVID: Gosh, I thought your taking the director's job was the signal that Enlightened Corp. was finally going to revamp its benefits program. Everybody's been saying for months that this year, before the Health Plan comes up for renewal, something has to be done.

LISA: I haven't really had time to evaluate things yet. Is the CEO interested in changes?

DAVID: I don't know. I'm not sure anyone's said anything to him.

LISA: Well, what kind of changes are people looking for?

DAVID: Well, that pretty much depends upon whom you're talking to. The guys in the production side don't want anything to change, unless they get more money or some job security. The sales reps think the pension plan needs sweetening. I know a couple of secretaries in my department who think they should get money instead of health coverage, because their husbands already cover them. I, personally, would like some flexibility to take some time off without feeling guilty.

LISA: Do you mean people want a complete overhaul of employee benefits—insurance coverage, leave time, pensions, death, and disability plans?

DAVID: Well, in a word . . . yes. I don't think we've taken a serious look at our benefits plans in ten years. I think the employees we have today want and need different benefits than they used to. Don't you?

CASE STUDY QUESTIONS

1. What should Lisa do to determine whether or not the Enlightened Corporation's benefits plans need to be overhauled?

2. If Lisa is to overhaul the benefits plans, what groups, interests, concerns, and problems should she be prepared to tackle?

3. Draw up a survey Lisa could use to make sure all employees had a chance to express an opinion on all aspects of Enlightened Corporation's benefits plans.

EXPERIENTIAL EXERCISE 1

Redesign a Company's Benefit Plan

Purpose

To gain experience in designing a work environment that can be flexible enough for the changing work force, but keep the company competitive.

Task 1

Your professor will distribute sample employee handbooks from different companies that describe their work schedules, insurance benefits, paid leave times, pension plans, and other employee benefit issues. List the basic policies and benefits offered by the companies.

Task 2

Create alternate policies and benefits that might be useful to the corporation in its efforts to hire and keep a diverse work force. Explain how each new policy is useful and why.

EXPERIENTIAL EXERCISE 2

Architectural Audit

Purpose

To gain personal knowledge of the architectural barriers facing many people with disabilities every day.

Task

Use the following checklist to survey a building on your campus or any other public building. Determine what changes, if any, would be mandated by the ADA as readily achievable.

Architectural Barriers Checklist

Building Access	Yes	No
Are 96"-wide parking spaces designated with a 60" access aisle?	_____	_____
Are accessible parking spaces near the main building entrance?	_____	_____
Is there a "drop off" zone at building entrance?	_____	_____
Is the gradient from parking to building entrance 1:12 or less?	_____	_____
Is the entrance doorway at least 32" wide?	_____	_____
Is door handle easy to grasp?	_____	_____
Is door easy to open (less than 8 lbs.)?	_____	_____
Are other than revolving doors available?	_____	_____

Building Corridors	Yes	No
Is path of travel free of obstruction and wide enough for a wheelchair?	_____	_____
Is floor surface hard and not slippery?	_____	_____
Do obstacles (phones, fountains) protrude more than 4"?	_____	_____
Are elevator controls low enough (48") to be reached from a wheelchair?	_____	_____
Are elevator markings in Braille?	_____	_____
Does elevator provide audible signals for the blind?	_____	_____
Does elevator interior provide a turning area of 51" for a wheelchair?	_____	_____

Restrooms	Yes	No
Are restrooms near building entrance and/or personnel office?	_____	_____
Do doors have lever handles?	_____	_____
Are all doors at least 32" wide?	_____	_____
Is restroom large enough for wheelchair turnaround (51" minimum)?	_____	_____
Are grab bars provided in toilet stalls?	_____	_____

Are sinks at least 30" high with room for a wheelchair to roll under?   _____   _____

Are sink handles easily reached and used?

Are soap dispensers, towels, et cetera, no more than 48" from floor?   _____   _____

Are exposed hot water pipes located under sinks wrapped in insulation to avoid injury to those individuals in wheelchairs?   _____   _____

Buildings that Serve the General Public	**Yes**	**No**
Are doors at least 32" wide?	_____	_____
Is the door easy to open?	_____	_____
Is the threshold no more than 1/2" high?	_____	_____
Is the path of travel between desk, tables, et cetera, wide enough for wheelchairs?	_____	_____
Do you have a counter that is too high to serve individuals in wheelchairs?	_____	_____

Take It to the Net   **You can find this chapter's World Wide Web exercise at:** http://www.prenhall.com/carrell

CHAPTER 13

Communication Processes

CHAPTER OBJECTIVES

1. To understand the communication process.
2. To describe the communication styles of written communication, verbal communication, and nonverbal communication.
3. To understand the various factors that influence communication.
4. To recognize formal and informal channels of organizational communication.
5. To describe the nature of downward, upward, and horizontal communication.
6. To explain communication channels within work groups and individual communication roles in organizations.
7. To understand how individual and organizational barriers affect the communication process.
8. To describe the individual and organizational factors that can be used to improve interpersonal and organizational communication.

Mike Walsh (deceased), Former CEO of Tenneco Corporation

Mike Walsh was an outsider brought in to revive Tenneco, an ailing conglomerate in gas pipelines, tractors, and other businesses. While Walsh was new to Tenneco, he was experienced in effective internal communications. Prior to becoming CEO of Tenneco, Walsh had been CEO of Union Pacific. At Union Pacific, Walsh had transformed the company into being more profitable and competitive by meeting with employees at all levels of the organization, including union heads. He asked everyone the same question: "If you were CEO of this company, what would you do?" Before long, Walsh kept hearing the same answers—Union Pacific was too bureaucratic, it didn't respond quickly to markets, and certain top managers were taking too

long to make decisions. He then knew where to direct his energies. Walsh states, "the people inside your new company know a lot more than you think they do."

Things were different, however, at Tenneco. Walsh learned that the Case agricultural–equipment subsidiary was about to report losses of $400 million larger than the board of directors or Wall Street expected. People in the corporate office did not openly talk with each other or the divisions. A lot of politics existed. People reported not the facts but what they thought

their superiors wanted to hear. It was difficult to get people to talk about what had to be done.

Walsh identified the key players at Tenneco, brought them into a room, closed the door, and announced, "We are facing a crisis. There is no way we can announce the losses from the Case division without announcing a serious action plan. We have seventy-two hours." Working together, Walsh and his key players developed a $2 billion restructuring program that included asset sales, a dividend cut, an equity infusion, downsizing the corporate staff by one-third, and a return to respectable profitability within a year. In implementing the proposed restructuring plan, Walsh not only listened to employee concerns, complaints, and suggestions, but explained Tenneco's new strategy.

Walsh indicated that the actions required for an outsider to turn around an ailing company involved reconceptualizing the business, energizing the enormous latent talents of the organization, and motivating employees to take action. Walsh stated that effective communication is a key factor in energizing and motivating employees.

Walsh's efforts at internal communications at Tenneco paid off. Within two years, operating profit had improved by $1.1 billion and the stock price increased by 25 percent. Unfortunately, Walsh developed a brain tumor. He communicated his health condition to his employees and to Tenneco's Board of Directors, received chemotherapy treatments and continued his hectic pace as CEO. Within a year, Walsh died of the brain tumor. To the end, he continued to function as CEO and communicating with his employees.[1]

Interpersonal and Organizational Communication

In this chapter we examine two types of communication—interpersonal and organizational. *Interpersonal communication* is communication between two individuals while *organizational communication* occurs among several individuals or groups. Studies indicate that managers spend nearly forty-eight minutes of every hour (80 percent) in communication with others.[2] *Communication* is a key factor in how successfully management and employees manage their relationships while accomplishing work unit and organizational objectives.[3]

The "OB In Practice" opposite describes how a General Motors division used a communication system to improve employee productivity and morale.

Purpose of Interpersonal Communication

Interpersonal communication allows individuals to exchange information and share meaning. The purpose of such communication allows an individual to: (1) Express his or her feelings and emotions to others; (2) Receive or exchange information regarding events or activities of concern; (3) Influence the opinions, attitudes, and behaviors of others; and (4) Use formal communication channels to reinforce the organization's structure.[4]

The Interpersonal Communication Process

Have you ever received directions that appear to be clear but you still got lost following them? Have you ever heard someone say, "But that's not what I

Interpersonal communication Communication between two individuals to exchange information and share meaning.

Organizational communication occurs among several individuals or groups.

Communication A key factor in how successfully management and employees manage their relationships, while accomplishing work unit and organizational objectives.

Using a Communication System to Improve Employee Productivity and Morale

anagement of General Motors' Saginaw Division sensed that poor communications existed between management and labor causing a lack of trust. An employee survey confirmed these suspicions and indicated that the lack of communication was affecting both employee productivity and morale. A communication system was designed that included a weekly newsletter that addressed items of local interest; another publication was mailed monthly to employees' homes and to the Saginaw community; focused publications dealing with how-to issues such as reducing costs, improving quality, staying competitive, improving communication, and improving union–management relationships were sent to targeted groups. A quarterly video presentation containing face-to-face interviews involving managers, customers, employees, suppliers, and union officials was present as well. The face-to-face interviews provided a forum in which a variety of business interests were openly discussed. Four years after the communication system was implemented, a follow-up employee survey revealed that the level of trust had increased significantly: more than 80 percent of the employees indicated they now believed management and were pleased with management's variety of mechanisms in getting information to employees.

While it is difficult to link bottom-line performance to any single program, the Saginaw Division's financial performance improved during the first seven years that the communication program was in effect. For example, annual operating costs decreased by 5 percent, sales per employee doubled, on-time deliveries improved 100 percent, and the savings generated by employee suggestions increased from $864 per employee to $5,748. Interestingly, the communication plan developed at the Saginaw Division is now used in all General Motors divisions.

Source: Adapted from P. J. McKeand, "GM Division Builds a Classic System to Share Internal Information," *Public Relations Journal,* November 1990, pp. 24–41.

---

meant"? Communication is a complex process that involves a sender and a receiver as illustrated in Fig. 13-1.

The sender is anyone who wishes to convey an idea to, seek information from, or express a thought or emotion to others. The receiver is the individual to whom the message is sent. The message is the idea that is being sent to the receiver. The sender encodes an idea by selecting symbols to compose the message. These symbols may be words, numbers, pictures, sounds, or physical gestures and movements. The message is sent through a communication channel, the carrier, which can be a telephone call, a formal report, or a face-to-face meeting.

The receiver decodes the symbols, to interpret the meaning of the message. The meaning that the receiver attaches to the symbols may be the same as or different from the meaning intended by the sender. If the meanings are different, then a misunderstanding is likely to occur. Encoding and decoding are potential sources for communication errors, because attitudes, background, and knowledge can act as filters and create noise when symbols are translated to provide meaning. Noise is any disturbance in the communication process that interferes with or distorts communication.

<figure>
FIGURE 13-1
The Communication
Process

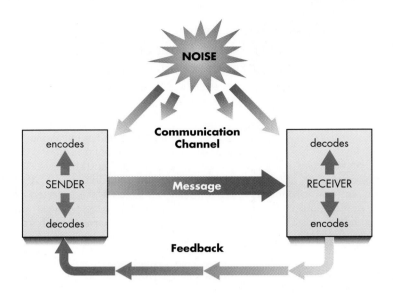
</figure>

**Feedback This occurs
when a receiver
responds to a sender's
communication with a
return message that
enables the sender to
determine whether or
not the receiver has
interpreted the mes-
sage correctly.**

Finally, *feedback* occurs when the receiver responds to the sender's communication with a return message. Communication is one-way without feedback;
with feedback, it is two-way. Feedback is an important aspect of communication, because it enables the sender to determine whether or not the receiver has
interpreted the message correctly.[5]

In essence, the communication process involves *who* (the sender) *says what*
(the message) *in what way* (the communication channel) *to whom* (the receiver)
with what effect (feedback).

Interpersonal Communication Styles

As described in Fig. 13-2, the three primary styles of interpersonal communication in organizations are written, verbal, and nonverbal. In many situations,
these styles are combined.

**Written communication
Letters, office memos,
reports, instructional
manuals, operating
policies, forms, E-mail,
and the like.**

Organizations produce many kinds of *written communications,* including letters, office memos, reports, instruction manuals, operating policies, and forms.
All of these items are designed to make communication more efficient and information more accessible. Although it takes longer to encode a written message,
more precise language can be used in written communication. For example, a
sentence in a labor agreement can be rewritten until everyone involved knows
its exact meaning. Consider the situation in which an employee receives a written message that he or she has been late for work, and if the practice continues

FIGURE 13-2
Interpersonal
Communication Styles in
Organizations

Style	Types
Written Communication	Letters, office memos, reports, instruction manuals, operating policies, forms, E-mail
Verbal Communication	Formal and informal conversations
Nonverbal Communication	Human behaviors: facial expressions, body language Physical elements: building design, office furnishings, space

then the employee will be fired. The written material also provides documentary evidence that the employee received a fair warning.

Verbal communication is the most prevalent form of communication in an organization. It occurs everywhere—in meetings, in presentations, in informal conversations, and in the process of performing work. Verbal communication is powerful, because it includes not only the speaker's words but also changes in tone, volume, pitch and speed. Verbal messages are generally efficient in handling the day-to-day problems that occur in an organizational setting. Verbal communication is likely to be quite accurate because messages can be clarified through ongoing dialogue.[6]

Nonverbal communications are the messages that are transmitted through human behavior rather than through words. Although nonverbal communication may be an unconscious process, it represents a large portion of the messages we send and receive.[7] Most supervisors and managers are shocked when they learn that major parts of a receiver's understanding through communication derives from nonverbal messages: facial expression, tone of voice, mannerisms, posture, and dress.

Nonverbal communications, such as body language, convey thoughts and feelings with greater force than the most carefully selected words do. When verbal and nonverbal messages are contradictory, the receiver may become confused and usually will give more weight to the behavioral actions than to the verbal messages.[8] For example, while your conscious mind may be formulating a message such as "Congratulations on your performance," your body language may be signaling your true feelings by avoiding eye contact, frowning, or showing an expression of disbelief.

Physical elements, such as buildings, office furniture, and space can also convey messages. For example, a large office with expensive draperies, plush carpeting, and elegant furniture reminds people that they are in the CEO's office while a small metal desk located on the plant floor accurately communicates the organizational rank of a front-line supervisor. Office arrangements convey status, power, and prestige.[9] The "OB in Practice" on page 434 describes several forms of nonverbal communication.

Managers need to pay close attention to nonverbal behavior when communicating. They must learn to coordinate their verbal messages with their nonverbal behavior and to be sensitive to what their subordinates, superiors, and peers are saying nonverbally. It is easy to underestimate the impact that nonverbal communication has on the perception of others. These messages can have powerful effects and can undermine verbal or written messages with which they disagree. Nonverbal communication can also lend credibility to verbal or written messages if there is obvious agreement. As illustrated in the "OB In Practice" on page 435, nonverbal behavior varies in different countries.

Verbal communication Formal and informal conversation—the most prevalent form of communication in an organization.

Nonverbal communication is transmitted through human behavior: facial expressions, body language; physical elements such as building design, office furnishing, and space.

FACTORS THAT INFLUENCE INTERPERSONAL COMMUNICATION

The process of interpersonal communication can be influenced by several factors. These factors, which are discussed in the following section, include: perception, listening, social influences, information richness, proxemics, spatial arrangements, and electronic communications.

Forms of Nonverbal Communication

- *Dress.* Communicating values and expectations through clothing and other dimensions of physical appearance.
- *Paralinguistics.* A form of language in which meaning is conveyed through variations in speech qualities, such as loudness, pitch, rate, and number of hesitations.
- *Kinesics.* The use of gestures, facial expressions, eye movements, and body postures in communicating emotions.
- *Haptics.* The use of touch in communicating, as in a handshake, a pat on the back, or an arm around the shoulder.
- *Chronemics.* Communicating status through the use of time; for example, making people wait or allowing some people to go ahead of others.
- *Iconics.* The use of physical objects or office designs to communicate status such as the display of trophies or diplomas.

Source: Adapted from A. Mehrabian, *Silent Messages,* Belmont, CA, Wadsworth, 1971; Mary Ellen Guffey, *Business Communication,* Belmont, CA, Wadsworth, 1994; F. Williams, *The New Communications,* Belmont, CA, Wadsworth, 1989.

Perception

Perception The meaning given to a message by both the sender and the receiver.

From the perspective of communication, *perception* is the meaning given to a message by both the sender and the receiver. An individual's perception is influenced by the objects that are seen, the way in which these objects are organized in the individual's memory, and the meaning attached to the objects. For example, a clenched fist raised in the air by a football player can be interpreted as an angry threat against the opposition or as an expression of team solidarity and accomplishment. If a manager is seen as influential in the company, everything that he or she says may be interpreted as being important even when it is not.[10] Perception is also discussed in Chap. 4.

A common form of perception is stereotyping, in which a widely held generalization is assigned to a group of people solely on the basis of a certain category, such as race, occupation, or age. For example, an interviewer who *expects* a female job applicant to put her family ahead of her career is likely to *see* that characteristic in all female applicants, regardless of whether the applicants feel that way or not. It is important for managers to understand that perceptual differences are natural and that they can distort messages and create noise that interfere with communications. Each individual interprets messages in a personal way, because everyone has a distinct personality and perceptual style. Managers should be aware that words mean different things to different people.

Listening

Rather than just giving orders, managers in the 1990s will need to be able to listen to both employees and customers. In the model of the communication process shown in Fig. 13-1, the receiver must listen to grasp facts and feelings accurately and to interpret the genuine meaning of the message. Of the 80 percent of the

OB in Practice

Nonverbal Communications in Different Countries

Nonverbal behaviors have different meanings in different countries. For example, the following five common behaviors are interpreted differently in different countries or geographical areas.

Standing close to a person while talking:

- In South America and Europe it is the normal distance used in conversations.
- In the United States it is viewed as an intrusion and the speaker is considered to be pushy.

Withholding eye contact:

- In the United States it indicates deception or shyness.
- In Japan it indicates a deference to authority.
- In Libya it is a compliment to a woman.

Displaying the palm of the hand:

- In Greece it is an insult.
- In the United States it is a form of greeting such as a handshake.

Crossing legs when seated:

- In Arab countries it is an insult to show the soles of the feet.
- In the United States it is done for comfort.

Joining the index finger and thumb to make an "O":

- In South America it is an obscene gesture.
- In the United States it means "okay."
- In Tunisia it means "I'll kill you."
- In Japan it means money.
- In Mediterranean countries it means "the pits" or "zero."

Source: Adapted from C. Barnum and N. Wolniansky, "Taking Cues from Body Language," *Management Review* 78, 1989, pp. 3–8; E. T. Hall, *The Silent Language,* New York, Doubleday, 1959; D. L. Nelson and J. C. Quick, *Organizational Behavior,* St. Paul, MN, West, 1994.

---

time that a manager spends communicating, nearly 50 percent is allocated to listening to others. Yet studies indicate that forty-eight hours after listening to a ten-minute message, the average listener can only recall 25 percent of it.[11]

Listening requires attention, energy, and skill. A good listener finds areas of interest, is flexible, works hard at listening, and mentally summarizes, weighs, and anticipates what the speaker will say. Figure 13-3 presents several guidelines for effective listening. Management author and lecturer, Tom Peters, states that managers can become good listeners by listening for ideas, asking dumb questions, breaking down barriers by participating with employees in casual get-togethers, taking notes, and providing feedback.[12]

As described earlier, management at General Motors' Saginaw Division listened to employee complaints regarding a lack of communication between man-

Listening In the communication process, the receiver must grasp facts and feelings accurately and interpret the genuine meaning of the message.

FIGURE 13-3
Guidelines for Effective
Listening

- Listen for content, not delivery. Don't be distracted by the speaker's unique speaking style.
- Use thought speed to mentally review the speaker's points. The average person speaks at a rate of 100–200 words per minute; the average listener can process at least 400 words per minute.
- Stop talking. You can't listen if you are talking.
- Show interest. Look and act interested. Listen to understand rather than to oppose.
- Remove distractions. Will it be quieter if the door is closed? Don't tap, doodle, or shuffle papers.
- Be flexible in your views. Try to understand the other person's point of view.
- Don't argue or criticize. Arguments and criticisms put people on the defensive and may cause them to "clam up" or become angry. Even if you win the argument, you lose.
- Ask questions. This is encouraging to a talker and shows that you are listening. Questions help to develop points further.

Source: Daniel F. Jennings, *Effective Supervision: Frontline Management for the 90s,* St. Paul, MN, West, 1993, p. 176. Reprinted by permission; Copyright © 1993 by West Publishing Company. All rights reserved.

agement and labor. Hewlett-Packard (H-P) learned by listening to its customers that they have different objectives when it comes to purchasing computers. Some buyers are looking for low price and high performance. Others are interested in support and want H-P to "walk" them through the whole computer installation and train their employees. And yet other customers want a solid company that promises to stay with them for the long haul. H-P identifies these issues early, so that they can be addressed in a sales proposal. The "Profile" opposite describes how top management at Sara Lee Corporation listens to employee concerns.

Social Influences

Social influences Status barriers between employees on different organizational levels have an impact on the communication process.

Communication within an organization can be affected by *social influences*. Status barriers between employees on different organizational levels may have an impact on the communication process described in Fig. 13-1 because the prevailing norms and roles may dictate who initiates which kinds of messages, who speaks to whom, and how one responds. Also, strong attributions are made regarding the type of clothes that are worn by individuals. For example, the "dress for success" phenomenon implies that the type of tie, scarf, shoes, or suit that is worn may make us a success.[13]

Information Richness

Information richness A quality of information that determines the effectiveness of communication.

Information is an important aspect of the communication process, because information feeds decision making about such things as technology, innovation, and structure and is the lifeline to supplies and customers. The quality of information, called *information richness,* determines the effectiveness of communication, because rich information facilitates understanding better than information that lacks richness. As illustrated in Fig. 13-4, four types of communication media are presented that differ with respect to feedback and the number of channels and cues each uses during a communication episode. These media types include face-to-face communication, telephone, addressed documents (letters, memos), and unaddressed documents (fliers, bulletins, general reports).

Face-to-face discussion provides immediate feedback and is the richest information medium because of the channels and cues of voice, eye contact, posture, blush, and body language. Telephone conversations lack the element of "being

Profile

Renee Rodriguez
Administrator Creative Services
LISTENING AT SARA LEE CORPORATION

Sara Lee Corporation is a 110,000 employee global corporation that ranks number four among U.S. consumer–products marketers and is expanding into Latin American and Pacific Rim countries. Sara Lee markets a variety of bakery products, Hanes and L'eggs hosiery, Playtex intimate apparel, and Coach leather goods.

I began working as a secretary in corporate affairs at Sara Lee and wrote some articles for Sara Lee's corporate newsletter. Later, while continuing to work for Sara Lee, I enrolled at Northwestern University to study newswriting, copyediting, and computer skills. After graduating from college, I was named administrator of creative services that was a newly created position. My responsibilities include being the editor of *News Updates,* the company newsletter, and coeditor of *Leeway,* the company's management magazine, and manager of "Time Out," a program of informal meetings between employees and top management. During these meetings management not only talks to employees about what is happening at Sara Lee but they also listen to employee concerns. This listening is an important part of the open communication that exists at Sara Lee.

Source: Adapted from Mary Ellen Guffey, "Career Track Profile at Sara Lee," *Business Communication,* Belmont, CA, Wadsworth, 1994, pp. 4–5.

there" and provide only the cue of voice inflection. Addressed documents, while personalized, convey only the cues written on paper and are slow to provide feedback. Unaddressed documents are the lowest in richness, are not focused on a single receiver, use limited information cues, and do not permit feedback.[14]

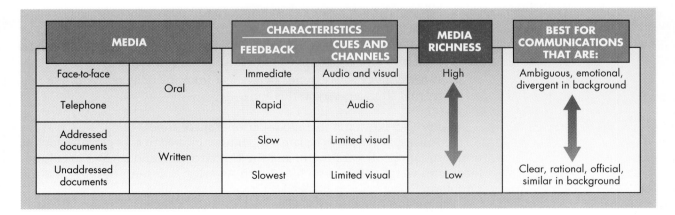

Figure 13-4 Hierarchy of Media Richness and Application for Managerial Applications

Source: Adapted from Richard L. Daft and Robert H. Lengel, "Information Richness: A New Approach to Managerial Information Processing and Organization Design," in Barry Staw and Larry L. Cummings, eds., *Research in Organizational Behavior,* vol. 6, Greenwich, CT, JAI Press, 1984, pp. 191–233. Reprinted from R. Daft and R. Steers, *Organizations: A Micro/Macro Approach,* Glenview, IL, Scott, Foresman, 1986, p. 532.

Research studies indicate that media selection is based on the message that managers wish to communicate. For example, if the message has a great potential for misunderstanding or is ambiguous, then a rich channel with immediate feedback enables managers to exchange information and ideas rapidly until a common understanding is reached.[15] As an example, if a chief executive officer is attempting to develop a press release with other company officials regarding a plant explosion that has killed and injured employees, then a rich information exchange is needed. The group will meet face-to-face, consider ideas, and provide rapid feedback to resolve disagreement and convey the correct information.[16]

On the other hand, when the message is clear, well defined, and everyone involved has similar backgrounds and understanding about an issue, then managers prefer written memos.[17] As an example, information regarding last month's cost figures would probably be transmitted through memos.[18]

Research also indicates that managers utilize multiple media to develop a more complete understanding of organizational issues.[19] Senior managers may become isolated from lower-level employees if they rely solely on written communications, because written reports do not provide the richness concerning possible problems that employees encounter or their attitudes. Managers such as Mike Walsh of Tenneco leave their office and talk face-to-face with employees.

Proxemics

Proxemics The study of the individual's perception about the use of physical space.

Proxemics is the study of an individual's perception about the use of physical space. Anthropologist Edward Hall states that proxemics serves an important purpose in communication because people tend to stand at a predictable distance from each other in accordance with specific roles they occupy.[20] According to Hall, the following four personal space zones exist.[21]

1. *Intimate space zone* extends outward from the body to about two feet. In this zone, we must have an intimate relationship with the other person or be socially domineering.
2. *Personal distance zone* extends from two feet outward to four feet. Friends interact within this distance.
3. *Social distance zone* extends from four feet to twelve feet. Most business associates and acquaintances interact within this zone.
4. *Public distance zone* extends twelve feet from the body outward. We prefer that strangers stay in this zone.

Figure 13-5 illustrates these four personal space zones.

Personal space tends to be larger in cultures located in cool climates such as northern Europe, Great Britain, and the United States, and smaller in cultures located in warm climates such as South America, Southern Europe, and the Caribbean.[22]

The notion of territory is also related to the concept of personal space. Although individuals carry their own personal space with them, territory is assigned to a specific physical location. Several analogies have been developed between human behavior in organizational settings and animal behavior in terms of territory.[23] For example, more dominant animals have larger territories than do less dominant animals, and lesser animals do not visit the territories of dominant animals. Also, when a lesser animal approaches the territory of a dominant animal or the animal itself, it shows signs of nervousness and submission.

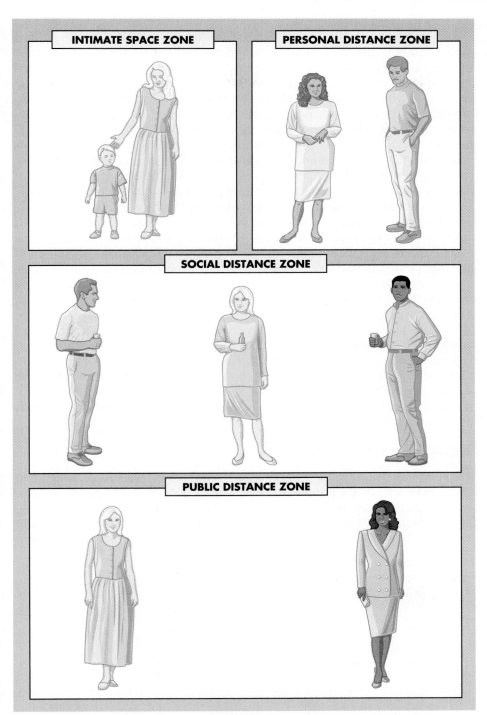

FIGURE 13-5
Hall's Four Personal
Space Zones

Within an organizational setting, higher status employees have larger offices than do lower status employees; supervisors intrude on the work space of employees while employees do not intrude on a supervisor's work space; and if an employee wishes to enter a supervisor's office, he or she will usually stand at the doorway and ask, "Are you busy?"[24]

Spatial Arrangements

Spatial arrangements
The arrangement of desks and chairs affects the nature of interpersonal communication.

Studies indicate that the arrangement of desks and chairs affects the nature of interpersonal communication.[25] Figure 13-6 illustrates how seating arrangements can affect the dynamics of communication. For example, Arrangement "A," in which the two parties are seated side-by-side and facing the same direction, encourages cooperation. Arrangement "B," in which the two parties are positioned directly across from each other, promotes competition. Arrangement "C," in which the parties are at right angles to each other, facilitates direct and open communication. Arrangement "D" can be used when attendees are disrupting a meeting held around a conference table. The person holding the meeting can place the disrupters on each side of himself or herself to stifle the disruption.

Architectural arrangements such as open-space offices can create psychological barriers to communication. An open-space office is characterized by an absence of the interior walls and partitions that more conventional designs use to define work areas. In an open-space office, all personnel from clerks to managers are located in one large open space. The purpose of an open-space office is to increase communication, improve work efficiency, and lower operating costs. Studies indicate that the intended purpose of open-air offices has not been realized, because the open offices can force people into too much interaction, and people have needs for privacy and personal space.[26] Organizations that have moved away from open to private offices or installed partitions report improved communication and greater job satisfaction.[27]

On the other hand, other types of arrangements channel the flow of people who are moving about to a certain area. This area can be a water fountain, reception area, or bank of elevators and can create opportunities for spontaneous interaction and communication.[28]

Electronic Communications

Electronic communications New technologies create new symbols and message-transmission methods that increase the speed of organizational communication.

New communication technologies such as electronic mail systems (E-mail), voice mail, teleconferencing, computerized report preparation, videotaping, car phones, and fax machines are being used in the workplace at an astonishing rate. (We discuss the future of *electronic communications* in Chap. 5.) These technologies create new symbols and message-transmission methods that increase the speed

FIGURE 13-6
How Seating
Arrangements Affect
the Dynamics of
Communication

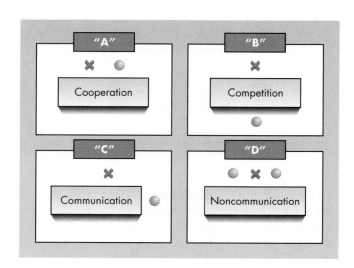

of organizational communication, and user attitudes have generally been favorable. However, these technologies do have important influences on individual behavior.[29] For example, dehumanizing effects occur when interpersonal skills such as tact and graciousness tend to diminish, and managers become more blunt. Also, the new technologies make it difficult to access the emotional aspect of messages because cues such as facial expressions, eye contact, touching, or gesturing are not available.[30]

Electronic communication also tends to change group interaction. One study reports that participation is equalized while reaching consensus takes longer.[31] However, new software programs such as *Lotus Notes Software for Groups* make it easier for groups to work together. In fact, Price Waterhouse, the large accounting firm, put together a proposal in four days and won a multimillion-dollar consulting contract by using Lotus's Notes Software for Groups. A major competitor had been working on its own bid for weeks.[32]

Because of the sheer volume of information that is available with the new technologies, the potential problem of information overload is particularly great. Managers tend to find a loss of privacy because they are more accessible to superiors, subordinates, and coworkers via telecommunications. Interactions are no longer confined to the normal work day.[33] In essence, problems resulting from electronic communications include information overload, the dehumanizing effects of electronic equipment, a disruption of the normal ways of accomplishing communication (the sender interacts with a machine, not a person), and an increased responsibility on managers. One must remember, however, that there is no one best way to design an effective communication environment. In today's high-tech world, tradeoffs are involved. Using impersonal machines creates an even greater need for social contacts, both formal and informal, that is so important to effective organizational communication.[34]

The "OB In Practice" on page 443 describes how a traveling executive using six pounds of electronic equipment works longer but more flexible hours.

ORGANIZATIONAL COMMUNICATION

What happens when organizational structure is imposed on the patterns of interpersonal communications? What happens to communication when individuals are placed into groups? In the following section we answer these questions by examining formal and informal communication channels, work group communication channels, and individual communication roles in organizations.

Formal Communication Channels

Every organization has a formal communication system through which "official" messages move from senders to receivers. These channels may be downward, upward, or horizontal as depicted in Fig. 13-7.

DOWNWARD COMMUNICATION CHANNELS   Certainly, effective *downward communication* from superior to subordinate is crucial to an organization's success. Plans, policies, and procedures originating at upper management levels must be communicated accurately to lower levels of the organization to ensure effective performance. Overall, the purpose of downward communication is to increase the subordinate's understanding of the organization and his or her job. Basic types of downward communication are described in Fig. 13-8.

Downward communication Downward communications from superior to subordinate to increase the subordinate's information about the organization relating to his or her job.

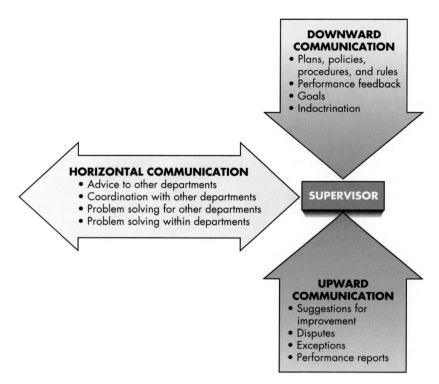

Although supervisors may consider their communication with subordinates to be informational, employees view other types of messages as important tools in developing a relationship with the boss. For example, subordinates may care about the extent to which the supervisor provides career advice, how well the supervisor listens to their suggestions and comments, and even how often the supervisor discusses family and other interests not related to work.

Downward communication may occur in a number of different forms. The most direct method involves face-to-face interaction, but written instructions and evaluations are commonly used to reach a wider audience or to provide a permanent record of the message. Many organizations use periodicals (known as house organs), employee manuals, public address systems, bulletin boards, and electronic technologies to communicate downward.

Research indicates that supervisors do not communicate with their employees as well as they believe they do. A dramatic reduction in information content

Figure 13-8

Types of Downward
Communication
in Organizations

Type	Example
1. Job instructions	Specific task directives.
2. Job rationale	Information designed to produce an understanding of the task and its relationship to other organizational tasks.
3. Procedures and practices	Information about the organization.
4. Feedback	To the subordinate about his or her performance.
5. Goal statements	Information designed to create a sense of purpose for the subordinate.

Source: Adapted from Charles D. Pringle, Daniel F. Jennings, and Justin G. Longenecker, *Managing Organizations: Functions and Behaviors,* Columbus, OH, Merrill, 1988.

Harriet Donnelly, 37, is an AT&T managing director of consumer products. Harriet travels the world promoting the company's interactive network services and products. Following is an interview between Donnelly and Alison Sprout, a *Fortune* reporter.

What's your typical day like?

Monday mornings I usually leave at 5:30 for the airport from my home in New Jersey. I'll be traveling to my second office in California or to Japan or Europe. Once I arrive, I'm often in meetings all day and don't get back to my hotel room until nine or ten at night.

How much equipment do you bring with you?

I bring my NCR Safari 3170 notebook computer, a Skyword alphanumeric pager, and an AT&T cellular phone. That's only six pounds of equipment, and it lets me work anywhere. The notebook has a built-in fax modem and AT&T Mail software, which helps manage my E-mail. I usually don't carry my two pound portable printer. When I need hard copy, I make a local phone call and fax myself the document at the hotel.

What about software?

I've tried lots, but I carry only what I need to be productive: DOS and Windows; Lotus Organizer, which has my schedule and address book; Lotus Ami Pro, for word processing; and Harvard Graphics for Windows, for presentations. I picked Ami Pro because I needed a word processor that could be used for presentations, memos, letters, newsletters, and still meet the old sales rules of KISS—keep it simple, stupid. Organizer is easy to use and doesn't include a lot of features I'll never need. I dislike reading manuals, so my software must be intuitive as well as meet my computing needs. Oh, and I've added Adobe Type Manager so I have a wide selection of fonts for presentations.

When does all your gear come in handy?

I call my voice mail three or four times a day for messages, but I do most of my communicating at night. The first thing I do when I get back to my hotel is pick up the phone and return any messages I can using voice mail. Next, I plug my computer into the phone and download an average of eight to ten E-mail messages. I answer them right away, which takes about an hour. I also get messages on my pager, which might be someone's phone number or a short text message. It works great for people who need to reach me but don't have E-mail, but, of course, I can't answer them without making a phone call.

Does this system ever break down?

Well, today I wrote a number of messages to E-mail from my hotel room in New Orleans. When I tried to plug the phone line into my Safari, the phone started buzzing. The hotel phone system wasn't PC compatible. Like many hotels, this one had an executive area with special lines that work with computers, but, of course, business hours were over and it was closed.

Traveling abroad presents additional phone problems. In Japan the dial tones are different, and American modems don't recognize them. That's easy to remedy by adding the appropriate line to the modem script in your computer—if you know how. I had to learn. In Europe, each country has different phone jacks. Once, in Germany, I couldn't hook up my modem because I didn't have the right adapter, and I couldn't get my E-mail. I was lost. I got more sleep on that trip but didn't feel very good about it.

Is carrying this equipment a better way to work?

Definitely. I'm not constrained by waiting for the major business centers to open or by having to be in my office. If I'm on a flight, I'll use that time to put together a presentation. You can get hooked on working this way. It takes away the nine-to-five restrictions that many people are still limited by. The bad part is that I work more hours, but I feel very productive.

Source: Alison Sprout, "Saving Time Around the Clock," *Fortune*, December 27, 1993, p. 157.

occurs as messages are transmitted from higher to lower organizational levels. Surveys involving nearly 48,000 employees indicate that less than 50 percent of them rate downward communication favorably in their organizations.[35] The reasons for this and for other organizational communication problems are discussed later in this chapter.

Upward communication Information from subordinates for improvements, disputes, and performance reports.

UPWARD COMMUNICATION CHANNELS *Upward communication* involves suggestions for improvement, disputes, exceptions, and performance reports. Without these forms of information, upper-level management cannot accurately monitor organizational performance and make decisions about future programs and activities. Performance reports—the most basic form of upward communication—can be troublesome because the subordinate occupies a position of dependency with respect to the superior. In essence, the subordinate's future depends on the supervisor's judgment. Whether or not the subordinate is to advance, earn pay increases, or receive choice assignments is the decision of the superior.

Because the supervisor's opinion is important, subordinates sometimes attempt to control the factors that influence their superior's judgment. The subordinate may wish to transmit a message and also to favorably influence the superior. The favorable message may be achieved by altering some aspect of the communication. As the communication travels upward through several management levels, it may paint an increasingly rosy picture that departs further and further from reality. For instance, studies indicate that subordinates do not share information about their own mistakes with their superiors.[36]

Research does indicate that subordinates may be more open and honest with supervisors who are strongly relationship-oriented. Openness of communication is improved when the subordinate trusts his or her supervisor. Research also indicates that subordinates often experience greater job satisfaction, less turnover, and better performance when they perceive that their supervisors welcome upward communication. The willingness of subordinates to pass information to their superiors can play an important role in increasing the quality of supervisory and managerial decision making, in improving subordinate attitudes and behaviors, and in enhancing overall organizational performance.

Horizontal communication The lateral or diagonal exchange of messages among coworkers or peers.

HORIZONTAL COMMUNICATION CHANNELS *Horizontal communication* is the lateral or diagonal exchange of messages among coworkers or peers. Figure 13-9 describes four categories of horizontal communication. The purpose of horizontal communication is to inform, request support, and coordinate activities. Horizontal flows of communication also reduce the strain on vertical (upward and downward) communication channels. For example, a supervisor in the credit department may communicate directly with an accounting department supervisor without first going through their common superior, the vice president of finance (unless it is necessary for the superior to be involved). This short-circuiting of

Activity	Example
Advice to other departments	Individuals in one department provide advice to other departments. A shipping department supervisor advises an inventory control supervisor about incoming material shortages: "Clark, we have not received all the material ordered for the Xerox project."
Coordination with other departments	Messages between departments facilitate the accomplishment of joint projects. The manufacturing, marketing, and engineering departments arrange a meeting to discuss the specifications of a new product: "Mary, please contact engineering and manufacturing to discuss the specifications of model ST-11."
Problem solving for other departments	One department helps another department to develop solutions to a problem. Engineering works with production to increase production efficiency: "Let's talk with the production supervisor about the problem with line slowdowns."
Problem solving within departments	Members of the same department send messages concerning the accomplishment of tasks: "Harry, can you show me how to fill out this travel-expense form?"

Source: Daniel F. Jennings, *Effective Supervision: Frontline Management for the 90s,* St. Paul, MN, West, 1993. Reprinted by permission; Copyright © 1993 by West Publishing Company. All rights reserved.

FIGURE 13-9
Categories of Horizontal Communication in Organizations

the chain of command avoids some of the problems involved in vertical communication, such as distortion and slowness.

Many organizations build in horizontal communications by creating task forces or committees composed of employees from different departments and areas of specialization. The "Profile" on page 446 describes how John Alex Floyd, Jr., editor of *Southern Living,* institutes frequent meetings among department heads to keep everyone informed and involved on a horizontal basis.[37]

Informal Communication Channels

Much of the communication within organizations is transmitted through an informal communication system known as the grapevine. The grapevine is a person-to-person communication network based on a normal rather than an abnormal set of relationships. Employees at all levels of the organization are linked to the grapevine. Informal communication occurs naturally wherever individuals come together in either work or social settings. This spontaneous communication can help to satisfy the social needs of many individuals.

The grapevine is often more informative than the formal communication system. For example, official channels may report that the organization's president has resigned "for personal reasons"; the grapevine supplements this pronouncement by reporting the inside details of the resignation. In addition, messages can be transmitted more rapidly through the grapevine than through formal communication channels. The grapevine tends to be more active during periods of change; it is often a service at such times, because the information it provides can help employees make sense of the uncertain situation.[38]

Although the impression may exist that only false rumors circulate through the grapevine, most of the information, surprisingly, is work-related and fairly accurate. Nearly 90 percent of all grapevine communication is related to busi-

Profile

John Alex Floyd, Jr.
Editor

KEEPING EVERYONE INFORMED AND INVOLVED AT SOUTHERN LIVING

Southern Living has five major editorial departments: Travel, Gardens, Homes, Foods, and Features. Not only must each of these individual sections deliver outstanding articles and photography each month, but together, they must form a cohesive magazine that's timely, informative, creative, and entertaining. That magazine must offer the highest possible quality to readers and advertisers alike. Producing it requires the combined talents and the cooperative efforts of writers, photographers, artists, the copy desk, and the production staff—and that's just on the editorial side. We also work closely with our colleagues in advertising and circulation. Needless to say, communication is the key. No single person could make *Southern Living* come together. It's a team effort. Everyone has to be informed and involved.

FIGURE 13-10

Configurations of Grapevine Communication Channels

Source: Keith Davis and John W. Newstrom, *Human Behavior at Work: Organizational Behavior,* 7th ed., New York, McGraw-Hill, 1985. Reprinted with permission of The McGraw-Hill Companies.

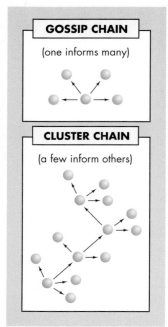

ness topics rather than personal gossip, and about 75 percent of the details are accurate.[39]

The accuracy of the grapevine may be due to the configuration of its communication channels. Usually, the grapevine is visualized as a long chain: A tells B, who passes it on to C, and so on, until it eventually reaches Z. Research, however, indicates that only a few individuals are responsible for the grapevine's success. Figure 13-10 illustrates two types of grapevines: the gossip chain and the cluster chain. A single individual informs many other individuals in the gossip chain; a few individuals each inform several others in the cluster chain.

From a supervisor's perspective, the grapevine can be helpful. Unless supervisors multiply their own communication efforts many times, it is difficult for them to channel all information through the official, formal communication system. Much of the supervisor's information about work assignments and company policies is picked up from other employees. The grapevine can supply supervisors with information about subordinates and their work experiences, which can increase the supervisor's understanding and effectiveness.

On occasion, the grapevine does produce false information. If a supervisor discovers that an unfounded rumor is circulating among subordinates, then the supervisor may simply call the employees together and discuss the matter with them. Whether or not subordinates accept the true facts depends on the supervisor's reputation for accuracy and candor in previous communications.

Communication Channels within Work Groups

Communication is an important aspect of building teamwork within work groups. (Work group behaviors are examined in Chap. 11.) Research indicates that the pattern of communication that a group uses to solve task problems affects the group's performance and the satisfaction of its members.

Three common work-group networks are illustrated in Fig. 13-11 and defined here. In the wheel network, each member can communicate only with the individual in the center, who, in turn, may communicate with any of the members. The circle network allows each individual to communicate with two other individuals—those on either side of her or him. Any member of the all-channel network can communicate with any other member. Fig. 13-12 indicates the effects that communication networks have on group performance and member satisfaction.

Because the research on work-group communication networks has been conducted in the laboratory (an artificial setting), the degree to which these findings can be extended to an organizational context is debatable. In the laboratory setting, each group is considered to be an independent system. Work groups within organizations are not independent: They are connected to other work groups, to supervisors, to incentive systems, and to the grapevine. However, some of these laboratory findings have been replicated in studies of actual organizations. Groups have dealt effectively with nonroutine or complex tasks by using decentralized communication patterns that involve extensive peer contacts in a form similar to the all-channel network described in Fig. 13-11. Groups have dealt effectively with more routine tasks by using a centralized communication pattern much like the wheel.[40]

Individual Communication Roles in Organizations

Individuals perform a variety of roles within the communication process. Four of these roles, as depicted in Fig. 13-13, are the gatekeeper, the liaison, the opinion leader, and the cosmopolitan.[41] Following is a discussion of these four roles.

The *gatekeeper* is an employee who has the ability to control the substance and/or the timing of information that is given to a decision maker. Examples include secretaries who screen which mail, visitors, or telephone calls are allowed to reach their bosses. Gatekeepers are essential to an organization because they prevent information overload from reducing the effectiveness of their bosses. The role of the chief of staff to the President of the United States is also that of a gatekeeper. The chief of staff shields the President from the multitude of people who ask for favors, seek his advice, or who want to influence him. This gatekeeper makes important decisions regarding who has access to the President. Gatekeepers themselves have a great deal of power because of their control over access to people in positions of power and authority.[42]

The *liaison* serves as a communications link between two or more groups or departments. Liaisons are not members of either group, but serve as a bridge

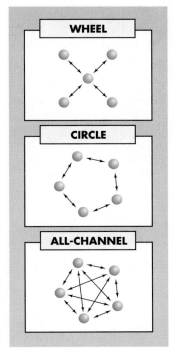

FIGURE 13-11
Work-group Networks

Gatekeeper **An employee that has the ability to control the substance and/or the timing of information that is given to the decision maker.**

Liaison **Serves as a communication link between two or more groups or departments that need to exchange information.**

FIGURE 13-12
Effects of Communication Networks on Group Performance and Member Satisfaction

---

- Simple problems are solved most rapidly by the wheel network. Information is channeled to the individual in the center, who then combines the information to solve the problem.
- Complex problems can be solved by the all-channel and circle networks, because these problems require considerable two-way communication: answering questions, confirming facts, and seeking additional information.
- Members have a higher satisfaction with their tasks in the circle and all-channel networks. However, the individual occupying the central position in the wheel has a much higher satisfaction than that of the peripheral members. Evidently, members in the circle and all-channel networks as well as the central figure in the wheel feel greater freedom and independence in their positions; the wheel's peripheral members feel that their behavior is controlled by the central member.
- The central individual in the wheel invariably emerges as the group leader; no leader appears consistently in the circle or all-channel networks. The leader in the wheel network has greater access to information and the opportunity to coordinate the activities of the other members. This leader, however, often suffers from information overload—particularly in complex problem situations.

Source: Adapted from Charles D. Pringle, Daniel F. Jennings, and Justin G. Longenecker, *Managing Organizations: Functions and Behaviors*, Columbus, OH, Merrill, 1988.

FIGURE 13-13

Individual
Communication Roles
in Organizations

Source: Everett M. Rogers and
Rekha Agarwala-Rogers,
Communication in Organizations,
New York, The Free Press, 1976,
p. 133. Reprinted with the
permission of The Free Press, a
division of Simon & Schuster.
Copyright © 1976 by The Free
Press.

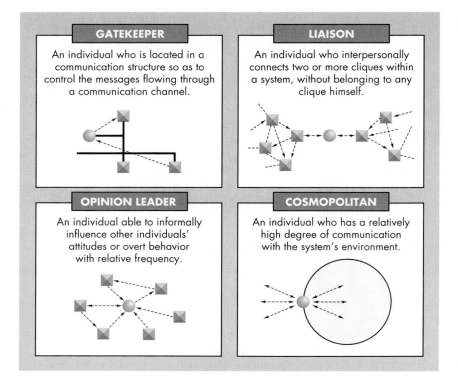

GATEKEEPER

An individual who is located in a
communication structure so as to
control the messages flowing through
a communication channel.

LIAISON

An individual who interpersonally
connects two or more cliques within
a system, without belonging to any
clique himself.

OPINION LEADER

An individual able to informally
influence other individuals'
attitudes or overt behavior
with relative frequency.

COSMOPOLITAN

An individual who has a relatively
high degree of communication
with the system's environment.

Opinion leader An individual who has the
ability to influence the
attitudes and behav-
iors of others in the
organization.

Cosmopolitan An
employee that has
interaction and com-
munication with the
organization's external
environment.

between groups that need to exchange information. Liaisons can either expe-
dite information flow or be a bottleneck in communication channels.[43] Organizations using liaisons to link departments tend to be more effective than those
that do not.[44]

The *opinion leader* has the ability to informally influence the attitudes or
behaviors of others in the organization. The opinion leader has special access to
the organization's informal communication channels (the grapevine) and has a
greater than average ability to communicate with others in the organization and
to influence them. An ex-supervisor who was respected by both management
and employees may still have informal ties to both that enable him or her to
shape organizational policies.[45]

The *cosmopolitan* has interaction and communication with the organization's external environment. Cosmopolitans have contacts with people outside
the organization who have special knowledge needed by the firm. Studies suggest that cosmopolitans are concentrated at the very top and very bottom of
organizations. At the top, cosmopolitans develop their contacts through their
travels and memberships in a variety of external organizations. At the bottom,
contact is made through an employee's work with customers and suppliers.[46]
Cosmopolitans can be a problem to an organization because they develop many
contacts outside the organization and many times decide to set up shop on their
own. Organizations tend not to try to restrict cosmopolitans from leaving the
organization but give them their freedom in return for service. For example,
some firms that downsize establish consulting arrangements with cosmopolitans. This allows the organization to reduce its overhead expense while retaining the services of people knowledgeable about its affairs.[47]

In summary, each of these four roles plays an important part in facilitating
organizational communication. The gatekeeper prevents information overload

by filtering and screening information, the liaison connects the various groups or cliques in the organization, the opinion leader facilitates informal decision making, and the cosmopolitan relates the organization to its external environment by providing an exchange of ideas and information.

BARRIERS TO COMMUNICATION

Perfect communication would accurately transmit an idea from one mind to another. Unfortunately, this transmission is often imperfect. Referring to Fig. 13-1, we can see the problem: The sender believes that the receiver understands the entire message as it was sent, and the receiver thinks that he or she understood the message as it was transmitted by the sender. Both may proceed on the assumption that perfect communication has occurred but be operating on incorrect premises.

Barriers to communication can be within the individual or from the organization. Earlier, we discussed how perception and listening affect communication. In Fig. 13-14 we list some remaining individual and organizational barriers to communication, although there are overlapping areas. A discussion of these barriers follows.

Individual Barriers to Communication

Some remaining individual barriers to communication include conflicting frame of reference, semantics, value judgments, and communication skills.

CONFLICTING FRAME OF REFERENCE   Individuals can interpret the same communication differently, depending on their previous experiences. This important factor breaks down the "commonness" in communications. Again referring to Fig. 13-1 when the sender's and receiver's encoding and decoding processes are not alike, communication tends to break down. In other words, the receiver's experience may cause him or her to interpret the message symbols in a different way than the sender interprets them. For example, departmental supervisors will view a problem of inefficiency in a manufacturing operation from their frame of reference and experience, which may result in different interpretations than those of, say, the engineering staff.

SEMANTICS   Organizations, departments, and members of similar work groups often devise their own language, or jargon, to facilitate communication among members of the same unit. Although such specialized language may increase the accuracy and understanding of communications among the individuals of a particular group, jargon is often a Source of dismay to outsiders. Individuals use jargon so often that they forget that clients or individuals who work in other units or occupations may not understand the special terminology.

Individual Barriers	Organizational Barriers
Conflicting frame of reference	Information overload
Semantics	Structural arrangements
Value judgments	Status differences
Communication skills	Task specialization
Cultural diversity	Filtering
	Timeliness

FIGURE 13-14
Barriers to
Communication

VALUE JUDGMENTS Value judgments are made by the receiver in every communication situation and are based on the receiver's evaluation of the sender or on previous experiences with the communicator. For example, a supervisor may intend to commend subordinates by telling them that their work is satisfactory. The subordinates may take offense at such a commendation, however, because they believe their work is superior, not merely satisfactory. Also, a cohesive work group may make negative value judgments regarding the actions of a particular supervisor or of management in general.

COMMUNICATION SKILLS Communication skills vary from individual to individual. Some variations in skill level stem from basic personality differences; others result from education and training. Articulate, persuasive, and confident individuals communicate more effectively than others do. Some individuals are naturally better listeners than others, or have trained themselves to be. People who are under considerable stress or are preoccupied with personal problems may be unable to listen attentively.

CULTURAL DIVERSITY Managers must understand that different cultural backgrounds between senders and receivers can cause breakdowns in the communication process. This includes communication between persons of different geographical or ethnic groupings from within one country as well as between different national cultures. Ethnocentrism, the tendency to consider one's culture and its values as being superior to others, is a common problem in cross-cultural communications.

Organizational Barriers to Communication

Some remaining organizational barriers to communication include overload, structural arrangements, status differences, task specialization, filtering, and timeliness.

INFORMATION OVERLOAD At times, a communication system may become defective as a result of information overload, which occurs when supervisors become deluged with information. The flow of information increases significantly when major changes occur in the corporate environment. In one study, supervisory communication skills decreased during information overload and overloaded individuals tended not to perform as well on the job as supervisors who reported they had insufficient information to accomplish the job properly. Over the past decade, technology and downsizing have combined to turn today's office into a quagmire of information. Secretaries and executive assistants used to serve as human information filters but downsizing has eliminated them. Many managers no longer have secretaries or executive assistants. Managers are finding it harder to keep up. They have to learn about other parts of the organization, even as the pact of knowledge accumulation within their own field is accelerating. In addition, they need to be able to think strategically and know what is going on with the rest of their industry. Managers find it harder than ever to deal with the Infobog, a pervasive, invasive information infrastructure that has become part of their lives.[48] The "OB In Practice" opposite describes the significance of the Infobog.

STRUCTURAL ARRANGEMENTS The more levels there are in the organization and the farther the receiver is from the sender, the harder it is to communicate a message effectively. A potential for distortion exists when a message is transmitted through a series of individuals at different management levels in the orga-

OB in Practice

The Infobog, by the Numbers

Change, since 1983, in number of computers in U.S. offices: +25,000,000[a]

Percentage change in tons, since 1983, of annual shipments of U.S. office paper: +51 percent[b]

Weeks of time lost each year, per U.S. executive, retrieving misplaced information: 6 weeks[c]

Hourly wage paid to Internet information guides: $100[d]

Change, since 1987, in number of U.S. E-mail addresses: +26,250,000[e]

Percentage of American adults who write and mail a letter during a given week: 28 percent[f]

Phone solicitations made by U.S. telemarketers each day: 18,000,000[g]

Percentage of Americans who have refused to participate in a telephone research poll: 31 percent[h]

Messages left on voice mailboxes last year: 11,900,000,000[i]

Percentage of Americans who say they don't have enough time to do all they want: 51 percent[j]

Percentage of Americans who watch two or more hours of TV in a given day: 45 percent[k]

Change, since 1987, in number of fax machines in U.S. offices and homes: +10,000,000[l]

Percentage change, since 1987, in population of Manhattan bike messengers: −63 percent[m]

Change, since 1987, in number of secretaries in the United States: −521,000[n]

Change, since 1987, in annual sales of over-the-counter pain relievers: +$500,000,000[o]

Source: [a]Dataquest. [b]American Forest & Paper Assn. [c]Accountemps. [d]Brian Johnson. [e]EMMS. [f,k]Times Mirror Center for the People and the Press. [g]U.S. House Committee on Appropriations. [h]Walker Research. [i]Eastern Management Group. [j]Gallup Poll. [l]Electronic Industries Assn. [m]The Courier Times. [n]Bureau of Labor Statistics. [o]Klein & Co.

nization. Parts of the message may be ignored, reinterpreted, omitted, or misunderstood. To minimize this problem, top-level managers increasingly use videotapes that deliver the same message to employees at various locations. Figure 13-15 describes how structural arrangements can distort organizational communication.

The "Profile" on page 453 describes how communicating in a computer network affects organizational structure.

Status Differences are expressed by titles, office furnishings, office location, clothing styles, and privileges, such as a company car or country-club membership. These status symbols can prevent or distort communication if they are perceived as threats by individuals who are lower in the organizational hierarchy. In many instances, to utilize their time efficiently, supervisors do not make themselves accessible to employees, thereby widening the communication gap.

Task Specialization can create communication barriers in at least two ways. One involves departmental needs and objectives; the other pertains to professionals within the organization. Communication problems regarding depart-

FIGURE 13-15
Structural Arrangements
and Communication
Distortion

During the Vietnam War, the 1st Air Calvary Division Commander issued the following order to a brigade commander: "On no occasion must hamlets be burned down."

The brigade commander radioed a battalion commander: "Do not burn down any hamlets unless you are absolutely convinced that the Viet Cong are in them."

The battalion commander radioed a company commander at the scene of a hamlet: "If you think there are any Viet Cong in the hamlet, burn it down."

The company commander ordered his troops: "Burn down that damn hamlet."

Source: Adapted from Charles D. Pringle, Daniel F. Jennings, and Justin G. Longenecker, *Managing Organizations: Functions and Behaviors,* Columbus, OH, Merrill, 1988, p. 418.

mental needs and goals occur, because each department perceives situations from its own perspective. For example, the production department is concerned with production efficiency and may not understand the marketing department's need to quickly get the product to the customer.

Professionals in one field often have difficulty communicating with individuals in other fields, because each group has its own jargon. An engineering supervisor and a purchasing department supervisor, for example, might have difficulty communicating successfully. Also, some individuals use the language of specialization to purposely obscure what is going on in an attempt to make themselves indispensable.

Filtering is the manipulation of information so that the receiver will perceive it as favorable. When information is passed to upper-level managers, it is condensed and synthesized by subordinates so that these managers will not experience information overload. The personal interests and perceptions of the individuals doing the synthesizing result in filtering. Filtering occurs because merit evaluations, promotions, and pay raises are generally granted based on information received by way of the upward communication channel.

Timeliness is a major factor in effective communication. It is important that messages be timed so that they receive the necessary attention. In some instances, memos to employees requesting specific actions give unrealistically short deadlines. Other situations include providing detailed instructions too far in advance. Performance failure can occur because of the lengthy time interval between task instruction and task performance.[49]

IMPROVEMENTS IN INTERPERSONAL AND ORGANIZATIONAL COMMUNICATION

All kinds of effective communication are needed for an organization's success. Managers who are sensitive and responsive in their communications with employees tend to have trusting and loyal relationships with their employees. In working to improve their communication skills, managers can foster an environment in which open communication thrives. Within an atmosphere of open communication managers become better informed, which benefits the decision-making process. In this section we examine a variety of individual and organizational factors that can improve the communication process.

Individual Factors

Individual factors that can improve interpersonal communication include active listening, providing feedback, and leveling.

Susan Falzon
Management Consultant
Athens, New York

COMMUNICATING IN A COMPUTER NETWORK AFFECTS ORGANIZATIONAL STRUCTURE

In 1993, at CSC Index, we conducted a study of computer networks in more than seventy-five companies. Following are some of our findings:

When work is carried out through networks, an organization's structure changes whether you want it to or not. I can't find a single case where it doesn't happen.

There were networks before there were computers: old-boy networks; the skein of contacts that led you to your job; the tangled macramé of connections and back channels in a company's "informal organization," which gets things done and fills out the paperwork later. Important as they are, these networks are unofficial.

What's new is the deliberately networked organization, made possible because it has become cheap enough to put a computer on every desk. A technological network supercharges social networks; no longer adjuncts of the hierarchy, they can supplant it—becoming the means by which the company does business. More and more, the operations companies conduct on-line are critical ones—trading at brokerage houses, stock management at Wal-Mart, and design and development of new aircraft at Boeing.

ACTIVE LISTENING   In an earlier section of this chapter we discussed how listening can influence interpersonal communication. Listening habits can be used to improve communication. The skill of active listening is an ability to help the source of a message say what he or she really means. When a listener restates the speaker's remarks and reflects on them, then a message is conveyed that the listener is interested in the speaker as a person, and that what is being said is important.[50]

PROVIDING FEEDBACK   Two-way communication improves the communication process. By using feedback, the sender can determine whether a message has been received. To be successful, feedback must be accepted and then used constructively. Feedback that is poorly given can cause resentment, alienation, and can be threatening.[51]

LEVELING   Leveling occurs when a manager or supervisor describes the specific, observed performance or behavior with an employee. Most people do not like confrontation. However, experienced managers—even those who prefer to avoid conflict—say that it is better to level with an employee when problems are developing than to wait.[52] Figure 13-16 describes guidelines that managers and supervisors can follow when leveling with employees.

Organizational Factors

Organizational factors that can improve the communication process include reducing noise; encouraging informal communication; balancing information load and information–processing capabilities; and managerial activities that improve organizational communication.

REDUCING NOISE   A significant barrier to effective organizational communication is noise. The rumor grapevine is a common form of noise. Although the grapevine tends to transmit information faster than do official channels, the

FIGURE 13-16
Guidelines for Leveling

1. Describe the specific behavior or performance that concerns you.
2. Explain its negative impact on performance or behavior.
3. Send "I" messages whenever possible instead of "you" messages.
4. Do not discuss what you think the employee's attitude may be.
5. Do not generalize or suggest causes of the poor performance or unacceptable behavior.
6. Do not make judgmental statements.
7. Speak in a calm, unemotional voice.

Source: Adapted from John M. Ivancevich and Michael T. Matteson, *Organizational Behavior and Management*, 2d ed., Homewood, IL, BPI/Irwin, 1990; J. Dreyfus, "Get Ready for the New Workforce," *Fortune*, April 23, 1990, pp. 165–81; Daniel F. Jennings, *Effective Supervision: Frontline Management for the 90s*, St. Paul, MN, West, 1993.

FIGURE 13-17

Guidelines for Improving Organizational Communication

- Develop trust. It is not automatically given and must be earned.
- Communicate openly. Actively share information and feelings.
- Be specific. Words mean different things to different people.
- Supply background information. Employees need to understand the reasons for change.
- Be honest with all employees.
- Talk to an employee as one adult to another.
- Always solicit employee ideas, suggestions, and reactions.
- Follow through. A major complaint against supervisors: We've all heard "Let me check it out, and I'll get back to you," while nothing happens.
- Avoid sarcastic remarks. Wise cracks that put people down, such as "I am glad to see you finally made it in on time" will be met with hostility. Supervisors tend to think that these remarks are harmless: "My employees know I was kidding. We have a great relationship and joke all the time." Supervisors do not connect their sarcasm to high turnover, low productivity, high absenteeism, and low morale.
- Remove roadblocks, irritants, and frustrations. Recognize that a supervisor's job is to remove these items, not to put them there.

Source: Adapted from *Ten Commandments of Good Communications*, New York, American Management Association, 1955; Len Sandler, "Rules for Management Communication," *Personnel Journal*, September 1988, pp. 40–44; Daniel F. Jennings, *Effective Supervision: Frontline Management for the 90s*, St. Paul, MN, West, 1993, pp. 188–190

grapevine can distort information. Managers can reduce this distortion by using the grapevine as an additional channel to disseminate information and by monitoring it constantly for accuracy.

ENCOURAGING INFORMAL COMMUNICATION Organizations can encourage internal communication by allowing information to be communicated when needed. Work areas and meeting rooms should be designed to encourage frequent, unscheduled, and unstructured communication. Informal communication can foster mutual trust and minimize the effects of status differences.[53]

BALANCING INFORMATION LOAD AND INFORMATION-PROCESSING CAPABILITIES Organizations need to realize that their communication system can generate more information than managers and decision makers can handle. These systems must be compatible with one another and fulfill the needs of the organization. For example, it is useless to produce sophisticated statistical reports that managers have no time to read.[54]

MANAGERIAL ACTIVITIES THAT IMPROVE ORGANIZATIONAL COMMUNICATION   Managers and supervisors can increase the effectiveness of organizational communication by following the suggestions presented in Fig. 13-17.

Admittedly, a supervisor or manager may find it difficult to identify with the personal values and career orientations of subordinates and more technically oriented individuals. However, the more that supervisors and managers understand the receiver's role in the communication process, the more likely they will be able to communicate appropriately and effectively.

CONCLUSIONS AND APPLICATIONS

- Managers spend nearly 80 percent of their time communicating. Thus, it is critical that they develop effective communication methods and be able to identify, analyze, and correct communication problems.

- Communication is the process by which the sender encodes an idea into a message that is sent through a channel and decoded by a receiver. Feedback occurs when the receiver responds to the sender with a return message.

- Three primary styles of communicating in organizations are written, verbal, and nonverbal communication. A major part of a receiver's understanding through communication derives from nonverbal messages: facial expressions, tone of voice, mannerisms, posture, and dress. Supervisors need to coordinate their verbal messages with their nonverbal behavior.

- Interpersonal communication is affected by perception, listening skills, social influences, information richness, proxemics, spatial arrangements, and electronic communications.

- Formal communication channels within an organization include communications in downward, upward, and horizontal directions. Especially in formal communication, the grapevine is often more informative than the formal communication system.

- Research indicates that the pattern of communication that a group uses to solve task problems affects the group's performance and the satisfaction of its members.

- Individual communication roles in an organization include gatekeeper, liaison, opinion leader, and cosmopolitan. The gatekeeper prevents information overload by filtering and screening information, the liaison connects the various groups or cliques in the organization, the opinion leader facilitates informal decision making, and the cosmopolitan relates the organization to its external environment by providing an exchange of ideas and information.

- Barriers to communication can be within the individual or from the organization. Individual barriers include a conflicting frame of reference, semantics, value judgments, communication skills, and cultural diversity. Organizational barriers include information overload, structural arrangements, status differences, task specialization, filtering, and timeliness.

- Communication barriers can be overcome by individual and organizational factors. Individual factors include active listening, providing feedback, and leveling. Organizational factors include reducing noise, encouraging informal communication, balancing information load and information–processing capabilities, and managerial activities that improve communication.

- Managerial activities that improve communication are: developing trust; communicating openly; being specific; supplying background information; being honest; talking to the employee as an adult; soliciting employee ideas, suggestions, and reactions; following through; avoiding sarcastic remarks; and removing roadblocks, irritants, and frustrations.

REVIEW QUESTIONS

1. Describe the elements of the communication process. Give an example of each element.
2. How can an individual become a more effective listener?
3. Describe how each of the following can influence interpersonal communication:
   Perception
   Listening
   Social influences
   Information richness
   Proxemics
   Spatial arrangements
   Electronic communications
4. Discuss the importance of nonverbal communication.
5. What are the purposes of downward communication? Upward communication? Horizontal communication?

6. Should the grapevine be eliminated? Why or why not? How can managers control information that is processed through the grapevine?
7. Is the wheel network appropriate for solving complex, nonroutine problems? Why or why not?
8. Explain the major barriers to communication.
9. How can a manager eliminate the major barriers to communication?
10. Describe the following individual communication roles:
    Gatekeeper Opinion leader
    Liaison Cosmopolitan
11. Explain the types of communication problems that new communication technologies will be likely to solve. How will these new technologies affect individual and group behavior?
12. Why are face-to-face discussions the richest information medium?

DISCUSSION QUESTIONS

1. Does the seating arrangement in your classroom foster or hinder communication? Discuss.
2. Using Figure 13-1 as a guide, describe a communication episode that you have observed. Who was the sender? The receiver? Was the communication effective? Why?
3. Analyze the communication skills of a person for whom you work (an instructor can be a possible choice). Is he or she an effective communicator? Explain. What could this person do to improve his or her communication with others?

4. Who is the best communicator you know? Why do you consider that person to be a good communicator?
5. Describe a situation in which you were involved with a gatekeeper. Did you feel frustrated? Explain.
6. Visit the office of an influential business leader in your community. Identify any nonverbal messages present in this person's office. How did they affect your communication with the business person?

CASE STUDY

Austin Systems

John Davis has recently joined Austin Systems as a production manager. Austin, a division of a large telecommunications company, manufactures facsimile (fax) machine systems and has experienced production problems, including an increased amount of individual employee errors. John previously had worked as a production supervisor for a competitor of Austin and has been hired to increase productivity at Austin. John's first assignment was to spend one week at corporate headquarters being exposed to the parent company's procedures, policies, and operating practices. During this first week, John learned that Austin Systems would hold its annual picnic at a local park the following weekend. John arranged his schedule to attend.

At the picnic, John learned that most of the employees and their families were there. Ken Ryan, the Personnel Manager, approached John and handed him a beer. The following conversation occurred:

KEN: Hey John, got a minute?

JOHN: Sure. What's up?

KEN: Well, I was talking with one of your production operators that I know pretty well. You know, an off-the-record chat about the company.

JOHN: Yeah?

KEN: He told me that the company's management style is the mushroom style: Keep them in the dark and feed 'em a lot of manure. He said that nobody knew you were hired until you showed up at the plant yesterday. We heard that the guard didn't even know who you were.

JOHN: Yeah, I guess that's so.

KEN: The operator said that he has been doing his job for ten years and has never received any feedback about his performance. He's seen other operators make serious mistakes and no one ever makes any attempts to correct these mistakes.

JOHN: I'm not totally sure. You know that I've been employed with Austin for a week that was spent at headquarters.

KEN: Yeah, I know that, but listen to this. Tom Kerr, the new head of industrial engineering, has not talked to or even been introduced to anybody in the paper-machine area, and Tom has been on the job for six weeks.

JOHN: Ken, how widespread do you think this feeling is about the mushroom style of management?

KEN: I don't know, John, but I think you ought to find out if you want this place to produce.

CASE STUDY QUESTIONS

1. Comment on the communication episode between Ken and John. Why does Ken discuss his concerns at the picnic rather than at the plant during business hours?
2. What does this communication episode tell you about Austin Systems?
3. Do any communication barriers exist?
4. What steps should John take?

EXPERIENTIAL EXERCISE 1

Listening Self-Inventory

Instructions

Go through the following questions, checking yes or no next to each question. Mark it as truthfully as you can in the light of your behavior in the last few meetings or gatherings you attended.

		Yes	No
1.	I frequently attempt to listen to several conversations at the same time.	_____	_____
2.	I like people to give me only the facts and then let me make my own interpretation.	_____	_____
3.	I sometimes pretend to pay attention to people.	_____	_____
4.	I consider myself a good judge of nonverbal communications.	_____	_____
5.	I usually know what another person is going to say before he or she says it.	_____	_____
6.	I usually end conversations that don't interest me by diverting my attention from the speaker.	_____	_____
7.	I frequently nod, frown, or whatever to let the speaker know how I feel about what he or she is saying.	_____	_____
8.	I usually respond immediately when someone has finished talking.	_____	_____
9.	I evaluate what is being said while it is being said.	_____	_____
10.	I usually formulate a response while the other person is still talking.	_____	_____
11.	The speaker's "delivery" style frequently keeps me from listening to content.	_____	_____
12.	I usually ask people to clarify what they have said rather than guess at the meaning.	_____	_____
13.	I make a concerted effort to understand other people's points of view.	_____	_____
14.	I frequently hear what I expect to hear rather than what is said.	_____	_____
15.	Most people feel that I have understood their point of view when we disagree.	_____	_____

The correct answers according to communication theory are as follows: No for questions 1, 2, 3, 5, 6, 7, 8, 9, 10, 11, 14; Yes for questions 4, 12, 13, 15. If you missed only one or two questions, you strongly approve of your own listening habits and you are on the right track to becoming an effective listener in your role as manager. If you missed three or four questions, you have uncovered some doubts about your listening effectiveness and your knowledge of how to listen has some gaps. If you missed five or more questions, you probably are not satisfied with the way you listen, and your friends and coworkers may not feel you are a good listener either. Work on improving your active listening skills.

Source: Ethel C. Glenn and Elliot A. Pood, "Listening Self-Inventory," *Supervisory Management*, January 1989, pp. 12–15. Used with permission. Reprinted by permission of publisher; © 1989 American Management Association, New York. All rights reserved.

EXPERIENTIAL EXERCISE 2

Nervous Behavior and Communication

Instructions

Your instructor will divide the class into groups of five.

Assignment

1. Students in each group will describe their behavior when they are nervous and answer the following questions: Does their nervousness show up in their voice? Can they tell when someone else is nervous? How? Does nervousness affect communication? How?

2. Each group will share the information developed in part one with the entire class.

3. What similarities did you notice? Differences?

Take It to the Net **You can find this chapter's World Wide Web exercise at:** http://www.prenhall.com/carrell

CHAPTER 14

Leadership

CHAPTER OBJECTIVES

1. To understand what is leadership.
2. To explain the different sources of leadership power.
3. To identify the different models of leadership.
4. To describe the attributes of the charismatic leader.
5. To know different methods of developing leadership skills.
6. To understand how successful leaders need to create a shared vision.
7. To explain the process of mentoring.
8. To identify the basic "Do's & Don'ts" of leadership.
9. To understand the goals of executive retreats.
10. To describe key attributes of effective leadership.

GE's Innovative Leader–Jack Welch

Jack Welch is Chairman and CEO of the General Electric Corporation, a manufacturer of products ranging from light bulbs to locomotives. Welch has transformed GE from the traditional, top-down management style to one of a horizontal structure with an environment in which everyone feels free to think for themselves, put forth new ideas, and participate in running GE.

Jack Welch is an entrepreneur. He is also the leader of his company. It may sound as though Welch is running a rather small company. That is far from accurate!

John F. "Jack" Welch, Jr., is Chairman and CEO of a company that had $3.8 billion sales growth last year. Gross sales were $58.4 billion and the company has 298,000 employees who were paid $23 billion last year.

Welch is highly respected in the world of big business. In the ten years he's been at his company's helm, he has gained a reputation as a hard-nosed manager who demands superior performance, an innovator who feels as comfortable totally revamping his company's management structure as he does buying or selling billions of dollars of its assets. As a leader, his oft-stated credo is, "there is no second place."

The company is General Electric and its product mix ranges from 65-cent light bulbs to $400,000 locomotives to billion-dollar power plants.

And now, Jack Welch wants to run GE as a . . . small business.

GE, in the view of many, wrote the canons of modern management—the same practices that Welch is currently mounting a radical assault upon. He believes that twenty-first-century managers will find it necessary to forgo their old powers for new duties . . .

primarily arranged around helping coworkers think for themselves, creating an environment where everyone in the organization is involved in developing and putting forth freely their ideas for performance, product, or how to run the company.

Harvard business school professor, Len Schlesinger, one of the two dozen academics and consultants Welch has hired to coach employees through the change says, "This is one of the biggest planned efforts to alter people's behavior since the Cultural Revolution."

Welch and his lieutenants have created new management techniques called Work-Out, Best Practices, and Process Mapping. Combined, they become a strategy that is designed to sustain rapid growth in productivity. Innocuous sounding, perhaps, but the strategy has risks. No big company has yet proved that so-called "soft techniques" deliver results over a long period. But entrepreneur Welch is willing to bet his sterling reputation on the potential results of his initiatives. He has committed the resources and set implementation systems. In the best traditions of a leader, he has challenged the entire organization of his immense company, to join the revolution.

These days, leader Welch spends most of his time helping his coworkers explicitly reject many of the old management principles that were virtually invented at GE. He admits that it will take a decade before the new management culture is as ingrained as the one it is to replace. Although hierarchical lines will blur, and the company will become a more horizontal structure, product managers and the principal of accountability will always be the core of the team effort.

Ten years from now entrepreneur/leader/manager Welch will be sixty-five and will have run GE for twenty years. He hopes to leave behind "a company that's able to change at least as fast as the world is changing," and whose managers "will be the people who are comfortable facilitating, greasing, finding ways to make it all seamless, who (are) not controllers and directors."[1]

What Is Leadership?

Leadership—the very word brings to mind names like George Washington, Thomas Jefferson, Abraham Lincoln, and in recent times, Colin Powell, Nelson Mandela, Lee Iacocca, and Newt Gingrich. But what exactly is leadership? Are successful leaders only those who achieve national recognition? Are managers also leaders? Can leaders be developed, or is leadership a trait one must inherit from his or her parents? All of these issues and others will be discussed in this chapter. First, however, we want you to expand your thinking about what is leadership and who are leaders. While there are probably hundreds of accurate definitions of leadership, the one by Vance Packard is a pointed, succinct definition:[2]

Leadership The ability to get others to want to do something that you are convinced should be done, and to follow direction.

Leadership appears to be the art of getting others to want to do something that you are convinced should be done.

There are several key words in this definition that should be noted. The first is "art"—leadership clearly is not an exact science, a set of skills, or attributes. Organizations spend millions of training dollars giving their managers skills to become more successful leaders. Yet there is a certain characteristic of leadership that is an art, and thus is difficult to measure or develop in people. A second key in this definition is the phrase "others"—leaders can only be successful if they can, through whatever means such as their position, power, charisma, et cetera, convince others to follow a course of action. A third key in the definition is "want"—not order, direct, or force—but want. Leaders are able to convince others to internally desire to achieve an objective: such as meet a deadline, win a ballgame, or simply work harder. If a leader only relies on external force—such as a manager giving direct orders, will their employees contribute their best efforts in the long-run? The final key in the definition is "should be done." Leaders clearly communicate the organization's goals and objectives, both long-run and immediate. For example, a bank manager might set customer service as a top long-run objective, and on a daily basis open up new teller lines according to demand.

Who are the leaders of an organization? They are people who decide what are the goals and objectives of an organization or group and then direct the activities needed to achieve these goals. They are people who, by their own behavior, beliefs, and words affect the actions of others. In our society leaders are not only presidents, corporate executives, and owners, they are also team captains, teachers, civic activists, and parents—everyone who inspires and directs others in work, leisure, religious, political, or other activities.

In today's organizations leaders must be able to motivate and bring together members of a different type of work force—one which is increasingly diverse, less loyal to the organization, has been downsized, and often disenfranchised. Today's leaders, thus, must lead a work force at a time when confidence in leaders is low.[3]

Dr. Martin L. King "had a dream" of what needed to be done and convinced others that they also wanted the dream fulfilled.

Managers and Leaders

Are all managers by virtue of their positions leaders? Are all leaders managers? While many leaders are managers, and many managers are leaders, there are important differences. *Managers* are people who develop budgets and plans, organize personnel by reporting structures, and execute by monitoring results against the plan. Leaders, however, establish direction by developing a vision of the future and strategies to achieve the vision. Leaders communicate their vision and strategy to employees and execute by inspiring people to overcome technical, bureaucratic, and personnel hurdles.[4] Most of all, people cannot be managed—they must be led. In today's workplace this is more valid than it was only a few years ago. The workplace of the 1990s is rapidly changing and needs managers who can successfully lead their employees. Exactly what is changing?[5]

Managers People who develop budgets and plans, organize personnel by reporting structure, and execute by monitoring results against the plan.

- The work force is more diverse (50 percent female, 43 percent minority, 20 percent foreign) and thus has more diverse needs.
- The work force is older (average age of forty).
- Illiteracy is an expanding problem (18 percent of adults).
- Entry-level job seekers are diminishing in number and demanding jobs with more flexibility and challenge.
- Job design alternatives have placed about half the work force on "nontraditional" schedules such as permanent part-time, flextime, and job-sharing.
- Organizations are "downsizing" and reducing the number of management layers, and thus increasing managers' span of control.

OB in Practice

Corporate CEOs in the White House?

James K. Glassman, editor of *Roll Call,* a Washington, D.C. newspaper, believes that the United States needs genuine leadership in the Presidency. He predicts that corporations today provide excellent training for White House hopefuls, because the day-to-day managerial side of the job (as opposed to the political side) is receiving a great deal of scrutiny—and, in that area, corporate CEOs are often very capable leaders.

Glassman also believes today's CEOs are more willing and financially capable of running for public office than in past years. Finally, Glassman goes out on a limb and selects four current corporate CEOs who would make the best presidents:

- *Bill Gates, Microsoft, 34.* Multibillionaire, both technical and marketing genius. Attractive to the thirtysomething generation and older baby boomers. Problem: no political experience; needs long apprenticeship. Career strategy: Retire from Microsoft within two years. Get directly involved in politics at nitty-gritty fund-raising level for congressional race. Shoot for an appointment as Commerce Secretary, then run for senator from Washington State. Take first shot at presidency at age forty-eight in the year 2004.

- *David Maxwell, Fannie Mae, 60.* Smart, politically savvy, successful in business and government, very presidential in demeanor. Former Pennsylvania Insurance Commissioner and budget secretary, also HUD general counsel. Potential problem: Age—he'll have to move quickly. Career strategy: Pick up foreign experience with a significant ambassadorship (Court of St. James would be appropriate). Reestablish Pennsylvania base with run for governor. Run for president in 2004.

- *John Reed, Citicorp, 51.* The manager as nonlinear, eclectic thinker. Could portray himself as a Jerry Brown who can also manage a $227.7 billion corporation. Great international experience. Potential problem: Not exactly a man of the people. Career strategy: Get named Treasury Secretary in the second term, leave to run for senator from New York after Pat Moynihan retires. Run for president in the year 2000.

- *Jim Robinson, American Express, 54.* Best qualified to be president among current CEOs. Good at public relations; strong international experience; actively involved in real political issues such as Canada–U.S. free trade; hobnobs with both the Business Council crowd and nuts-and-bolts politicos. Potential problem: Self-absorbed personality may make him poor campaigner, though egotism hasn't hurt any of the current 100 senators. Career strategy: Though Treasury or State are obvious places for Robinson, I suggest he go for broke. Shoot for second spot on either ticket by 2004.

Source: James K. Glassman, "Hail to the Chief Executive," *Business Month,* vol. 136, September 1990, pp. 12–14. Reprinted with permission, *Inc.* magazine, September 1990. Copyright © 1990 by Goldhirsh Group, Inc., 38 Commercial Wharf, Boston, MA 02110.

- More work is accomplished by teams of employees or even whole departments. The emphasis is on internal cooperation and quality, not competition and quantity.

To be successful under these conditions more managers are moving away from a style of "managing" to a style of "leadership." This style of leadership requires the approaches found in Fig. 14-1. What does this leadership style entail? First, a

From a style of MANAGING others	To a style of LEADING others
Directing others	Guiding/developing
Competing	Collaborating
Using hierarchy	Using network
Consistency/sameness	Diversity/flexibility
"Slow" decision making requiring permission	"Fast" decision making using judgment
Risk-Averse	Risk taking
Individual contributor	Team player
Being managed	Self-management
People as expense	People as asset

Source: Adapted from Dana Gains Robinson, "The 1990s: From Managing to Leading," *Supervisory Management,* June 1989, p. 7. Used by permission.

FIGURE 14-1
Leadership Transition Model

manager's primary role will be to coach and develop people, not simply give orders. Second, managers need to provide autonomy to employees so they become self-managed. Third, managers should participate in and encourage teamwork where reasonable. Fourth, managers should encourage fast decision making by those employees closest to the situation. Fifth, managers should encourage innovation and risk taking to meet the ever-changing challenges facing organizations. Finally, managers must treat employees as assets, not expenses, and they will need to invest more time and resources in the training and development of their human resources.[6]

Management, while most important, is about practices and procedures needed to cope with complexity. Leadership, also important, but different, is about coping with change. John Kotter of Harvard University emphasizes that the need to shift from "managing" to "leading" means that today's organizations don't just need effective leadership from the CEO but from "hundreds of individuals both above and below the plant manager level." It is easy for organizations today to be overmanaged and underled, because many of today's managers were trained to keep things on time and under budget. Leaders today, however, realize the rapid changes in technology, international competition, the financial markets, and the diversity of the work force require a manager who is also a leader—who can develop a vision of how to compete with these changes, a strategy to implement the vision, and the ability to communicate and inspire others to participate in that strategy.[7] An excellent example of a leader who is moving from managing to leading is Jack Welch of General Electric.

However, this demand for more leaders does not mean that good managers are not also needed or that being a leader is better than being a manager.[8] Organizations, without question, need both good leaders and good managers. Leaders need many good managers who demonstrate dynamic followership if they are to achieve any level of success.

Followership

A person marching down Main Street oddly dressed and waving a stick might be arrested for improper behavior. However the same person in front of a band—the drum major—is a parade leader. Leaders by definition have followers. When Jack Welch began holding "town meetings" with the employees of General Electric, his behavior might have been questioned. However, he quickly developed a large number of General Electric followers who believed in his values and visions for the company—and helped make him a successful leader.[9]

Followers Those who believe in and implement the values and visions for the organization set forth by the leader.

While organizations might attribute the responsibility for success or failure to their leaders, that leaves out the other half of the equation—the *follower*. Organizations require far more good followers than leaders to achieve success. Followers are the implementers of the visions of leaders.[10] In past decades the need for good followers was not always recognized. In fact a common altruism was "always be a leader never a follower." It was thought that leaders do one thing, followers another. Thus the contribution of dynamic followers was often devalued. Followers were passive individuals who simply imitated their leaders and blindly accepted their direction. Like many other aspects, this characteristic of organizational behavior has changed dramatically. In fact, today many successful leaders, including Dick Peck, General Manager of Wyoming Lower Valley Power & Light, believes leaders should serve followers instead of followers serving leaders.[11] And, due to the increased use of teams and horizontal organizational structures most leaders must also be followers and be able to successfully move back and forth between the two roles.[12] It is, in fact, common for a person in a leadership position within one unit of an organization to serve as a member of project teams, task forces, and committees that require them to be successful followers.

What are the characteristics of successful followers? A three-year study of over 10,000 employees, and other research, identified five important traits associated with successful followership:[13]

- *Cooperation.* The ability to work together with others, often in small groups, through good communication skills while displaying empathy for the needs and objectives expressed by others. Followers must be able to move away from viewing situations as "win-lose." They should not view another worker as "winning" at the expense of others. Instead they must view a situation in light of what is best for the overall organization. Such decisions should be viewed as "win-win" situations by everyone and not evaluated according to how they affect individuals or departments.

- *Flexibility.* Adapting to the rapid pace of change is a critical leadership skill. Being flexible in order to accept and implement needed changes is a critical skill for followers. They must successfully implement the change strategies developed by leaders and teams. Changing budgets, customer expectations, regulations and relationships with other organizations are only some of the elements that require greater and constant flexibility.

- *Integrity.* Leaders and followers should consistently communicate and practice their values and ethical standards. The measure of their own integrity is the degree of consistency between what they say and their actions. At Lower Valley Power & Light, for example, the focus is on customer service. Thus, the level of consistency between what an employee says is his or her quality of service, and the level reported by his or her customers through letters and surveys is how their integrity is measured. Also in addition, an important aspect of their integrity is their honesty and directness when working with other employees. People must be able to count on each other to deliver work as promised to achieve a high level of integrity.

- *Initiative.* Taking the initiative to do the things that need to be done to achieve the goals of the organization is important for followers. For followers to consistently take initiatives they need a high-trust environment that is supportive and doesn't punish them if every activity does not end exactly as planned. Organizations that use self-managed teams or horizontal structures require an even greater degree of initiative by followers, since there are fewer middle-level managers to direct their actions.

- *Problem solving.* Followers are able to increase productivity when they solve problems and develop cost-efficient work methods. In today's leaner management times, this often requires that followers recognize problems, design and evaluate alternative solutions, and choose and implement the one that is best for the organization without referring the problem to or receiving direction from others.

Leadership and followership are related in several important ways: (1) Leaders cannot be successful without followers that implement their vision; (2) Leaders, themselves, must be successful followers in various roles within the organization; (3) Leaders must recognize the need for followers to exhibit the traits discussed previously and reward them accordingly; and (4) Leaders must provide an organizational climate that supports and serves followers rather than one in which followers serve leaders.

Sources of Leadership Influence

In most organizations there are many leaders—people in positions of authority, people whom others seek out when they have technical problems, people who have the support of others on internal political issues, et cetera. All are leaders because they can influence the thoughts and behaviors of others. This gives them *leadership power* within the organization. This power may originate from one (or more) of five basic sources:[14]

- *Legitimate Power.* Perhaps the most common source of power is that given by the organization itself. Thus, positions that are allocated formal power of authority by the organization have *legitimate power.* Managerial and supervisory positions usually receive legitimate power from the organizations and accept the power of the individual occupying such a position.

- *Reward Power.* When an individual has the ability to grant rewards to others they have a source of power. This *reward power* may be due to the leader's position in the organization, such as a supervisor giving a merit pay raise or a more desirable work schedule. However, praise received from a highly respected senior colleague can be a valued reward as well—thus giving the colleague an informal source of power and ability to influence others who desire their recognition.

- *Coercive Power.* Some leaders have the authority to punish others by not granting a desired scheduled vacation, pay raise, or promotion recommendation. Other leaders are not directly in a position to decide such punishments, but have the ability to convince the person in the position of authority to use such coercive power. Employees, for example, may quickly learn "who the boss listens to" and thus try to keep in favor of those who possess *coercive power.*

- *Expert Power.* Some leaders become known to be experts within technical areas, or are known to be effective in getting things accomplished. This ability or knowledge gives them *expert power,* because others will seek their assistance or advice.

- *Referent Power.* A leader whose personality enables him or her to affect the behavior of others may be said to possess *referent power.* This personality characteristic may be charm, attraction, wit, or charisma.

How can an individual develop one of these bases of leadership power? The most common, direct method is to be appointed to a position of authority in an organization that has legitimate power. However, to achieve that first position of legitimate authority often requires a person to develop another basis of power. The most likely source is expert power. People who develop expert knowledge or skill in a particular field can continually build that knowledge base and are often then given the opportunity to occupy a position of legitimate power within the organization. Steps that can build such a power base are (see Figure 14-2):[15]

1. Develop a reputation as an expert in a certain aspect of the organization.
2. Spend more time in critical relationships (supervisor, key clients, etc.) instead of social relationships.
3. Develop a network of resource people who can provide career assistance.
4. Develop an arsenal of effective communication skills—including presentation methods, humor, and public speaking—and learn to use them according to the situation.
5. Determine methods to utilize developed expertise and skills to achieve organizational goals, not personal goals.

Thus, a person who develops expert knowledge or skill in a field, continually builds on that knowledge base, concentrates time where that knowledge can be utilized to achieve organizational goals, and develops a network of contacts. He or she utilizes effective communication skills utilized to convince others and to ultimately achieve organizational goals to achieve leadership power.[16]

A good example of a person who successfully utilized the above steps is a San Francisco area bank president. During his first years with the bank, as a young management trainee, he noticed that few people at the bank had any detailed knowledge of building design and office layout. Since he had worked briefly in a commercial interior design firm, he had some interest in the field and considered it a hobby. He decided this expertise could be valuable to the rapidly-expanding bank and thus on his own time completed additional courses in the field to expand his expertise.

He then found out who was responsible for coordinating the design and layout of new and remodeled branches. Although he had not been requested to do so, he offered this person his assistance. He then visited a new branch, carefully studied it, and asked a friend from his old firm to review it. After completing the review, he forwarded a list of suggestions for future branch designs to several people in the bank and asked to personally discuss the suggestions with them. One

FIGURE 14-2

Steps to Building a Leadership Base

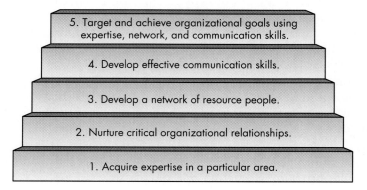

5. Target and achieve organizational goals using expertise, network, and communication skills.

4. Develop effective communication skills.

3. Develop a network of resource people.

2. Nurture critical organizational relationships.

1. Acquire expertise in a particular area.

vice president liked his initiative, as well as some of the suggestions, and arranged for the young trainee to be included in on the next design committee. The trainee quickly realized that he now was included in top-level planning discussions. He felt somewhat uncomfortable with his verbal communication skills, so he asked to enroll in and then completed a management training program in oral presentation techniques. After only three years, the young manager was appointed vice president (a new position in charge of branch designs and layout) and, after seven years was appointed senior vice president largely due to his record of enhancing the appearance and operating efficiency of over fifty branches.

LEADERSHIP MODELS

The study of leadership has been the center of management research by business executives, academicians, and political figures for several decades. Literally thousands of books and articles have been written on leadership, as well as an entire journal—*Leadership Quarterly*. And, what are the conclusions reached in these massive volumes of literature? Some would suggest that... "Leadership is like the Abominable Snowman, whose footprints are everywhere, but who is nowhere to be seen." While there is certainly some truth in that suggestion, it is also true that the volumes of leadership study and research have generally at least produced models of (1) leader traits, (2) leader behaviors, (3) situational factors, and (4) participative leadership.[17]

Leadership Traits

Some theorists believe that the primary factors in leadership effectiveness are the leader's personal characteristics or traits. In other words, these theorists explain leadership ability in terms of inherent characteristics or qualities that people possess to different degrees. Effective leaders have been hypothesized to be intelligent, tall, self-confident, and so on.[18] From such a perspective, leadership exists primarily in the personal characteristics of the leader.

What leadership traits are expected from followers? Perhaps this is the most important question concerning leadership traits. The answer is surprisingly clear when several research studies of over 7,500 employees are reviewed (see Fig. 14-3).[19]

When asked, "What values (personal traits or characteristics) do you look for and admire in your supervisors?" employees provided four traits in over 50 percent of their responses: (1) honest (87 percent); (2) Competent (74 percent); (3) Forward-looking (67 percent); and (4) Inspiring (61 percent). While fifteen other traits received support, none was listed by more than 50 percent of the employees. The twenty results are not surprising; if leaders expect others to follow, they must have a vision of the future, and through their own behavior and ability, inspire others to follow them.[20] In addition, their honest, ethical behaviors, which employees rated as the most important characteristic becomes the role model for all members of the organization. Employees, therefore, logically expect that their own ethical behaviors will be instrumental in achieving recognition and rewards from leaders.[21]

CHARISMA   A trait many people identify as important to leaders in society is charisma. The term charisma brings to mind names like Presidents John F.

FIGURE 14-3
Traits of Superior Leaders

Ranking	Characteristic	Percent Selected
1	Honest	88
2	Forward-looking	75
3	Inspiring	68
4	Competent	63
5	Fair-minded	49
6	Supportive	41
7	Broad-minded	40
8	Intelligent	40
9	Courageous	35
10	Dependable	32
11	Straightforward	29
12	Cooperative	28
13	Imaginative	28
14	Caring	23
15	Determined	17
16	Ambitious	13
17	Loyal	13
18	Mature	13
19	Self-controlled	11
20	Independent	5

Source: James M. Kouzes and Barry Z. Posner, *The Leadership Challenge: How to KEEP Getting Extraordinary Things Done in Organizations,* San Francisco, CA, Jossey-Bass, 1995, p. 21.

Kennedy or Ronald Reagan, film stars Cary Grant and Katherine Hepburn, or sports figures such as Orel Hershiser, Michael Jordan, and Nancy Lopez. The successful charismatic leader in organizations, however, is often not the great speech maker or quick wit. The charismatic leader in an organization is one who brings about changes in individuals' values, goals, needs, and aspirations. This leader achieves success through three components—envisioning, energizing, and enabling. This leader is able to *envision* the future of the organization in a method that excites people and provides a vehicle—a common goal around which they can feel successful by participating in the achievement of that goal. The charismatic leader must describe a vision in clear and precise terms—often specific goals and objectives—which people accept as challenging but attainable. The leader not only sets high expectations for others, but also leads by example. Thus, the leader does not ask of others what he or she does not exhibit in his or her own behavior. Through his or her own personal excitement and energy, the charismatic leader is able to motivate others to want to succeed and to celebrate an individual's contribution or the organization's achievement of organizational goals and objectives.

The charismatic leader also strives to *enable* others to achieve their goals through listening and understanding their feelings and problems. They support programs that meet the needs of their employees: such as flextime, child care, and employee assistance with personal problems. They support individuals and express confidence in their ability to perform effectively. Through these three basic behaviors, the charismatic leader provides a focal point for the energies, hopes, and aspirations for everyone in the organization. They also serve as role models whose behaviors, actions, and personal energy demonstrate the behaviors expected of others.[22] (See Fig. 14-4.)

A good example of the charismatic leader who utilized these three components of leadership in business is Thomas J. Watson, Jr., the former Chief Executive Officer of IBM, who inherited a company that manufactured manual tabulating machines (hence the company name, International Business Machines)

Figure 14-4
Three Attributes of the
Charismatic Leader

ENVISION
- developing and communicating a shared vision
- setting high expectations
- leading by example

MOTIVATE
- demonstrating personal enthusiasm
- demonstrating personal confidence
- celebrating achievements

ENABLING
- expressing personal support
- empathizing with others
- expressing confidence in others

Source: Adapted from David A. Nadler and Michael L. Tushman, "Beyond the Charismatic Leader: Leadership and Change," *California Management Review*, vol. 32, no. 2, Winter 1990, p. 82. Copyright 1990 by The Regents of the University of California. Reprinted from the California Management Review, vol. 32, no. 32. By permission of The Regents.

and provided the leadership to develop the world's largest computer manufacturer. Watson followed his father, Thomas Watson, Sr., who ran the company as a personal fiefdom, perhaps in the image of his idol (Italy's Benito Mussolini). Watson, Jr., achieved the impossible—he followed a legend and, as his son, succeeded in developing into an even greater legend. As Watson, Jr., tells his own story in his autobiography, *Father Son & Co.: My Life at IBM and Beyond,* through early failures with an autocratic style of leadership, Watson developed into a charismatic leader by nurturing the human side of IBM, its employees. He transformed the workplace climate from one of fear and suspicion to one of security and enthusiasm. He listened to employee complaints and personally followed through with resolutions, guaranteed job security, employee ownership, and regarded IBM's employees as its greatest assets. He also led by example and gained the respect of his employees.[23]

Charismatic organizational leaders usually have a high degree of style and skill. They are able to exert influence over others, even those not directly under their position, through the sheer force of personality. They have the power to offer a vision and to define its meaning to the organization whose members give it their commitment.[24]

It is possible, however, for charisma to cloak incompetence. Employee ratings of their supervisor indicate that six or seven out of ten believe their supervisors have significant administrative shortcomings. A primary method by which these somewhat incompetent supervisors stay in their job is their personal charisma. These individuals may be called "high likability floaters," because they are extremely loyal to the organization, are generally pleasant to work with, are congenial, cordial, and sometimes charming. They never complain or argue and thus steadily float up the organizational ladders. Along the way, they seldom initiate substantial improvements, for fear of failure, and they seldom take stands on important issues or express their point of view. Even though they achieve little, they are difficult to terminate because they have no enemies; in fact, many friends will be angry if they are fired.[25] Eventually, floaters may be fired by organizations with effective performance appraisal systems. Others, however, continue to float around, often changing jobs just fast enough to avoid detection. Is there a floater in your organization? (See Fig. 14-5.)

Gender Differences Research has shown that, in the past, men in organizations emerged as leaders more often than women. This phenomenon has been attributed to barriers both internal (self-confidence) and external (societal) to individuals. However, more recent research indicates that some of the barriers that prevented women from emerging as leaders may be disappearing. In the past research overwhelmingly associated masculine characteristics with leader

FIGURE 14-5
The "Charismatic Floater"

Source: Adapted from Robert Hogan, Robert Raskin, and Dan Fazzini, "How Charisma Cloaks Incompetence," *Personnel Journal,* vol. 69, May 1990, pp. 73–76.

- loyal
- charming
- quick wit
- never argues
- floats up the organizational ladder

emergence, but recent studies have found both masculine and feminine characteristics are commonly possessed by organizational leaders.[26] In addition, men and women managers generally select the same set of skills that are needed by male and female managers to be successful, another change from the past when different skill sets were identified. However, recent research also suggests that some typical stereotypes are still perceived by employees: Women managers cannot manage their emotions and tend to fall apart under pressure, respond impulsively, lack commitment, and don't understand team play. At the same time, though, employees perceive women as stronger in customer relations skills: such as, showing concern for others, listening carefully, being responsive to meeting the needs of others, and supporting others. Overall, males harbor more stereotypes about women managers than females do about men managers.[27] While gender differences in leader characteristics as perceived by employees apparently are declining, they still persist.

Contingency Model of Leadership

One of the most intuitive leadership models is based on Fred Fiedler's Contingency Theory. The model is based on the premise that the most effective leadership style depends upon the particular situation, and thus leaders must accurately determine the significant factors of the situation and adopt a style that can be effective. Leaders unable or unwilling to change their style of leadership must, therefore, find a position with the factors that match their style. Situations are classified in terms of their "favorableness" for the leader; that is, the degree to which the situation permits the leader to influence the behavior of group members.

SITUATIONAL FACTORS   The following three factors define any situation:

- *Leader-member relations*—the most important factor in a situation is the relationship between the leader and the group members. The trust and confidence members place in their leader depend, to a large extent, upon the leader's expert and reference power, as discussed previously in this chapter.
- *Task structure*—the degree to which the requirements of the subordinates' tasks are clearly specified.
- *Leader position power*—the extent of the leader's legitimate, reward, and coercive powers.

The most favorable situation combines close leader–member relations, well-defined tasks, and strong formal position power. Various combinations of these factors yield eight possible leadership situations, which range from highly favorable to highly unfavorable, as shown in Fig. 14-6.

Fiedler classifies leadership styles into task-oriented and relationship-oriented categories, and these two styles of leadership are considered to be opposite ends of a single continuum. Leadership style, according to Fiedler, reflects an individual's underlying need structure, which consistently motivates his or her behavior in various leadership situations. Consequently, one's leadership style depends upon one's personality and for many is not easily changed. Leadership style is measured by the leader's responses to a test instrument called the least-preferred coworker scale. This short questionnaire requires the leader to think of the person at work with whom he or she can work least well and to describe that person along such dimensions as the following:

$$\text{pleasant} \underset{8 \quad 7 \quad 6 \quad 5 \quad 4 \quad 3 \quad 2}{\rule{5cm}{0.4pt}} \text{unpleasant}$$

$$\text{supportive} \underset{8 \quad 7 \quad 6 \quad 5 \quad 4 \quad 3 \quad 2}{\rule{5cm}{0.4pt}} \text{hostile}$$

Individuals who describe their least-preferred coworker in relatively favorable terms (that is, pleasant, supportive, and so on) are relationship-oriented leaders. Task-oriented leaders, those who obtain major satisfaction from completing the task successfully, give their least-preferred coworker a relatively unfavorable description.[28]

COMBINING LEADERSHIP STYLE AND THE SITUATION   Fiedler's findings, based on over three decades of research, are summarized in Fig. 14-7. Task-oriented leaders are more effective (in terms of group performance) in the "most favorable" and "least favorable" situations. Relationship-oriented leaders perform best in "mixed situations"—those that are moderately favorable or unfavorable.

In other words, Fiedler's results indicate that task-oriented leaders are likely to have high-performing groups when the leader has either a great deal of influ-

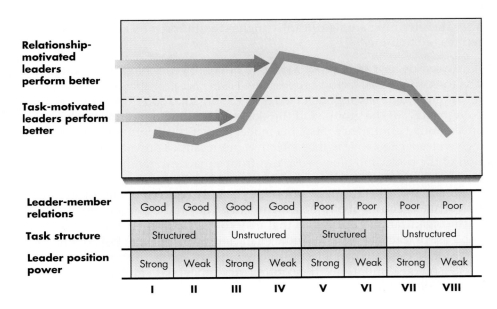

Relationship-motivated leaders perform better

Task-motivated leaders perform better

Leader-member relations	Good	Good	Good	Good	Poor	Poor	Poor	Poor
Task structure	Structured		Unstructured		Structured		Unstructured	
Leader position power	Strong	Weak	Strong	Weak	Strong	Weak	Strong	Weak
	I	II	III	IV	V	VI	VII	VIII

FIGURE 14-6

How the Style of Effective Leadership Varies with the Situation

Source: Reprinted by permission of the *Harvard Business Review*. An exhibit from "How the Style of Effective Leadership Varies with the Situation" from "Engineer the Job to Fit the Manager" by Fred E. Fiedler, September–October 1965. Copyright © 1965 by the President and Fellows of Harvard College; all rights reserved.

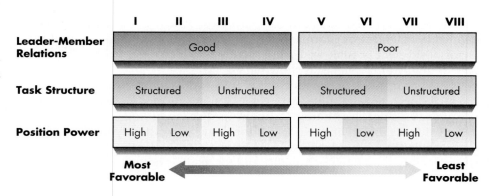

ence (columns I, II, and III) or very little influence (octants VII and VIII). In these situations, a leader concentrates primarily on the task required. In situations (octants IV, V, and VI) in which the leader has only moderate influence, a leader who focuses on interpersonal relationships is more likely to have a high-performance group.[29]

LEADERSHIP TRAINING   These conclusions influence Fiedler's recommendations concerning leadership training. If a leader's style depends on personality, then changing a leader's style would require a personality change. Fiedler contends it is more feasible to alter the situation to fit the leader's style.

This may be accomplished through a self-administered, programmed technique that requires the leader to complete the least-preferred coworker scale and determine his or her leadership style. Then the leader is shown how to diagnose a situation and change or modify the situation to match the leader's style.[30]

These changes in situational control might involve requests by the leader to be given routine assignments or to be given the less structured and unusual tasks; the leader might attempt to develop a closer, more supportive relationship with subordinates or to maintain more formal and distant relations; the leader might try to be "one of the gang" or emphasize rank and prerogatives.

Fiedler believes that the Leader Match program is cost-effective, because it requires no instructor time and only four to six hours of the trainee's time. Initial results indicate that the performance ratings of leaders two to six months after their training are significantly higher than those of leaders who did not receive the training.[31]

ASSESSMENT OF THE CONTINGENCY MODEL   The contingency model has weaknesses. The three situational factors proposed by Fiedler are probably only a partial listing of important factors. Such factors as the organization's reward system, the cohesiveness of the group, and the skill and training of group members may affect group performance. Also, the model predicts the conditions under which a given leadership style will be effective, but it fails to provide a clear explanation of the leadership process. Finally, from a practical standpoint, altering situational factors to match a leader's style may be difficult.[32]

Leadership effectiveness cannot be the only concern of administrators as they make decisions about job assignments. They must consider other aspects of the organization's operations that may conflict with their attempts to make good use of leadership talent. Some characteristics of the job, task, or organization simply may not be subject to change, at least in the short run.

Despite its limitations, the contingency model has emphasized the situational nature of leadership and helped us realize that almost anyone can succeed, or fail, as a leader. Leadership involves more than a person's traits or behavior. Contemporary leadership theories must consider not only the leader but also the leader's subordinates and the task to be accomplished.

Path-Goal Theory of Leadership

The path-goal model of leadership posits that leaders motivate people successfully by communicating how desired goals such as merit pay raises, promotions, recognition, et cetera, can be achieved if people achieve higher performance standards (paths). A leader can successfully utilize any of the following leadership styles:

- *Directive leadership*—lets subordinates know what is expected of them and how the task should be accomplished.
- *Supportive leadership*—shows concern for the needs of subordinates, makes the work more pleasant, and is friendly and approachable.
- *Participative leadership*—consults with subordinates and takes their suggestions into consideration when making decisions.
- *Achievement-oriented leadership*—emphasizes excellence in performance and displays confidence that subordinates will assume responsibility and accomplish challenging goals.

The most effective style is the one that has the greatest impact on the subordinates' performance and satisfaction.[33] The leader then can motivate employees by: (1) increasing the rewards when goals are accomplished; (2) clarifying the paths (work methods) that can be used to accomplish the goals; (3) reducing roadblocks and pitfalls that might impede someone from achieving a goal; and (4) increasing the number of opportunities for employees to strive for rewards.

Organizational research indicates all of the methods may improve employee motivation, performance, and reward attainment. However, research also indicates that in any one situation a number of variables may modify the effectiveness of a leader's behavior. Such moderating variables include job level, need for independence, task structure, professional orientation, and job involvement. Employees in lower-level jobs, those with a low need for independence and those in highly structured jobs are, for example, more likely to respond positively to a strong path-goal leadership style.[34]

The major situational variables to be considered are: (1) the subordinates' personal characteristics, and (2) the environmental pressures and demands with which subordinates must cope to accomplish work goals and attain satisfaction. Both variables must be taken into account by the leader in determining the most appropriate leadership style. Similar to the Contingency Model, the Path-Goal Theory emphasizes the utilization of different leadership styles depending on the situation. The Path-Goal Theory, however, allows more than one style to be engaged at any one time.

The path-goal general premise—that a leader should clearly communicate the desired behavior of employees (paths) and tie organizational rewards (goals)—is widely utilized today in "pay-for-performance" models.

Many employers today are utilizing a performance-based pay system. The purpose of an incentive or *performance-based system* is to relate employees' pay directly to their performance. The assumption is that employees are likely to be more highly motivated, and thus increase their productivity, if they perceive that there is a direct relationship between their level of performance (as individuals or as an organization) and the rewards that are received. Incentive pay-systems may provide employees with an additional base compensation, if their productivity exceeds a certain standard.

The use of performance-based systems has seen a resurgence. After critics had convinced many managers that such systems could not be accurate or motivational, many employers at least have found that Frederick Taylor may have been right all along. Five surveys of over 4,700 companies show that after switching from time-based to performance-based pay systems, organizations reported average productivity increases of 29 to 63 percent.[35] IBM, for example, was able to increase labor productivity in typewriter manufacturing by nearly 200 percent over a ten-year period. The reason cited was the use of two policies: (1) pay for productivity, only for productivity, and (2) promote for productivity, only for productivity.[36]

Performance-based systems are not new, however. At Andersen Corporation of Bayport, Minnesota, the nation's largest manufacturer of windows, profit-sharing has been a tradition since 1914. The Andersen program contains three basic points: (1) produce the best quality products; (2) hire the best people; and (3) pay the top wages in the industry.[37]

In general, performance-based systems can be divided into two categories: individual-based incentives systems, which provide a pay incentive to each worker based on his or her own level of productivity, and organizationwide incentive systems, such as profit sharing, which base their rewards on total organizational performance.

Participative Leadership

The leadership model that has experienced a great deal of interest in recent years is that of employee participation. A leader who allows employees to participate in decision making about their own jobs or other aspects of the organization may be called a *democratic leader*. A leader who usually retains all authority and decision making may be called an *autocratic leader*. In practice, few employees

Employee profit sharing has been a tradition at Andersen Corporation, Bayport, Minnesota, since 1914.

like to work for autocratic leaders, and few leaders claim to be autocratic. A person's style of leadership is usually not entirely autocratic or democratic. The extent to which one's style is more democratic, or participative, depends on certain factors such as the confidentiality of the issue, the amount of time a leader has to make a decision, and the extent to which others have the skills and relevant knowledge that would enable them to contribute to the decision-making process. One critical factor that should affect which style a leader utilizes is the organization's environment—as measured by the need for new work methods, ideas, and customer relations. Research indicates that when leaders empathize with employees and adopt a participatory style, the organization is more likely to benefit from innovative ideas and methods.[38] Since today's employees are increasingly better educated and more interested in participative leadership, leaders in many organizations are adopting a more participative style than their counterparts utilized twenty years ago.

The participative model requires leaders to share their leadership authority with others rather than making decisions alone. Leaders with substantial egos are not likely to have a participatory style. They may find it difficult to relinquish a portion of their authority, because they perceive it to be a reduction in their importance. Participative leadership may provide a number of benefits to the organization and to employees. Employees often find that participation in decision making can add meaning to their work and enhance their sense of accomplishment. Furthermore, employees who are active participants in departmental decision making probably develop faster than those who simply follow orders. Decisions arrived at jointly are more likely to be accepted and implemented by those who have participated in making the decisions.

These benefits are summarized in the three principles upon which the widely known Participative Management Program at Motorola is founded:[39]

- Every worker knows his or her job better than anyone else.
- People can and will accept the responsibility for managing their own work if that responsibility is given to them in the proper way.
- Intelligence, perspective, and creativity exist among people at all levels of the organization.

In practice, participative leadership generally follows one of two styles: (1) The leader involves other employees in the decision-making process but retains the authority to take independent action when necessary; and (2) The leader allows the employees to form autonomous teams or work-groups that are given a few specific objectives and allowed to determine their own leaders and make their own decisions.

In the first style, the leader generally follows a four-step process: ask, listen, act, and provide feedback.[40]

1. **Ask their opinion, delegate authority**

   One of the greatest compliments one may bestow upon employees is to ask their opinion and delegate to them the authority to make decisions about their work. This will build their professional self-esteem and make them feel a part of the problem-solving process. They will then be more likely to support the company's objectives. Methods for soliciting employee input include ad hoc committees, department meetings, suggestion systems, and voluntary employee-advisory committees.

2. Listen to them and build consensus

The leader must be an effective listener. He or she must learn to gain an understanding of not only the employee's ideas but also the employee's feelings about the issue. When asking a question, managers should take the time to listen, without interruption. They should never invite employee input if they have already made a decision on the issue, and are only trying to "sell" their decision. Allow the employees themselves, through discussion and consensus, to make decisions whenever possible.

3. Involve everyone

To truly be committed to the participative process, one must demonstrate to employees that their decision-making ability is trusted. Allow them autonomy. This doesn't mean leaders are obligated to use all ideas. But a timely, factual explanation of why a suggestion was not adopted should be provided. In circumstances where an employee's idea is used, in its entirety or in part, it is important to give proper credit or recognition to the employee(s) involved.

4. Provide feedback and demonstrate interest

Where leaders spend their time sends a clear message to employees as to what is important. Don't "micro-manage" (review every employee action and decision)—let employees make day-to-day decisions. If managers delay providing employees feedback on the success of a project they are saying the project is not important. A simple, clear, periodic method of feedback is essential to the success of the project and future employee motivation.

The most effective method of utilizing the four-step process of participative leadership is to simply practice it every day in all situations, not just when employees ask for the opportunity to participate. (See Fig. 14-8.) The effects can be tremendous.[41] For example, Worthington Industries and Chaparral Steel produce high quality steel products, but have no quality inspectors! The explanation is provided by Chaparral's Gordon Forward: "At Chaparral the Average Employee":[42]

- handles all quality control decisions
- performs all maintenance on machines
- records their own hours
- handles all housekeeping (no janitors)
- performs budget preparation
- recruits, hires, and runs the assessment center for new peers

FIGURE 14-8
Four Steps to
Participative Leadership,
with the Leader Retaining
Final Authority

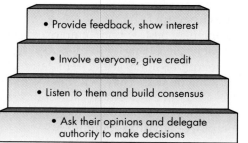

- Provide feedback, show interest
- Involve everyone, give credit
- Listen to them and build consensus
- Ask their opinions and delegate authority to make decisions

The second common form of participative leadership is the formation of self-led teams of employees as discussed in Chapter 11. The leader delegates almost all authority and responsibility to a team of employees, and usually serves as their coach, advisor, or administrator, depending on what type of organizational support the team requires to work effectively. The self-managed teams are usually small groups (eight to fifteen) of coworkers who share tasks and responsibilities for a well-defined portion of the organization. They are usually accountable to their external leaders for measures of performance such as quality of service or product, on-time delivery, quantity of output, and cost control. Usually they are allowed to select their own internal leaders, or operate with no appointed leader and make decision by consensus. Another common method of team leadership is shared leadership with defined duties and responsibilities, which may be rotated. At one Virginia manufacturing plant, for example, team leadership assignments included:[43]

- *Moderator:* conducts team meetings.
- *Schedule coordinator:* relays schedule requirements from production meetings and makes work assignments.
- *Recorder:* Keeps minutes, attendance records, and overtime and vacation schedules.
- *Goal tracker:* measures and posts performance results.
- *Training coordinator:* schedules training activities to upgrade group process skills and the use of multiple skills.
- *Cheerleader:* Schedules celebration events and prompts recognition from managers.

The external leader who, in the organizational chain of command, is responsible for the team, must be able to make the transition from boss to coach and relinquish a great deal of authority and responsibility. Some are not able to make the change easily, or at all; others respond more like the recently converted supervisors in a North Carolina factory:[44]

> "You know, I've been in that position for seventeen years, and most of the employees have worked for me there for almost that long. But now my relationship with them has entirely changed."

How did he feel about it?

> "I really feel good, because now I can work on the long-range planning and problem solving, areas in which I can make the best contribution. Now I'm not bothered every five minutes by forty someone wanting me to sign something. I just refuse to make the decisions when they know the right answers already. Some of them are uncomfortable about that, but they're learning, and together we are doing much better."

DEVELOPING LEADERSHIP SKILLS

Leadership was once thought to be an exclusive domain for top executives and "the country club set." Today, however, organizations realize the critical importance of developing leadership abilities among all levels of employees. Executives, managers, supervisors, technicians, and hourly workers can all learn to share the vision for the future of the organization and develop one for themselves and their position. They can all successfully accept new responsibilities, take risks, build consensus and trust among peers, and implement quality management programs. While not everyone has the potential to become a Lee Iacocca, everyone *does* possess some degree of innate leadership abilities that can be expanded through development.[45]

Skill Building

There are in general two schools of thought on leadership training and development. One stresses "awareness training," the other "skill building." Skill building is the focus of most in-house programs and usually concentrates on giving basic leadership skills to people who have been recently promoted from technical positions. Thus, important skills that organizational leaders must utilize on a daily basis—writing memos, reports, briefs, et cetera; calling and directing meetings; formal presentations to clients, boards of directors, peers, et cetera; planning work and scheduling people; motivating people; decision making; and budgeting. Because these people were successful in their previous nonleadership position, it may be falsely assumed they have these basic leadership skills. These are skills, however, which generally can be developed, to an extent, in most people. Thus, skill building leadership training, together with practice, can achieve a high rate of success.

Awareness Training

IDS Financial Services in Minneapolis instituted an awareness training leadership development program that contained components similar to other programs. The training focused on educating managers by giving them the current leadership vocabulary and methods that they should then apply on the job when they saw relevant opportunities. The program's impact, according to Tim Costello, manager of organization development at IDS: Probably the only new leaders produced were the managers who taught the classes. A two-year follow-up survey did, however, indicate that the participants found the information valuable. A more successful awareness program in the Leadership Development Program (LDP) includes only successful managers with ten to twenty years of leadership experience and the basic skills acquired through experience. The LDP helps participants pinpoint their leadership strengths and weaknesses on several dimensions and enables them, through self-awareness, to self-determine behavioral changes that will make them more effective leaders. Most central awareness programs include a questionnaire that is completed by peers and subordinates. The evaluation of this feedback enables leaders to learn how their behavior affects others and then to determine how they might change their behavior to become more effective in their positions.[46]

An increasingly popular extension (or alternative) to awareness-training is experiential learning—a physical approach to leadership and team-building that presumes people can learn more together in an unfamiliar environment trying to achieve totally new goals, than they can sitting through a series of lectures and discussions. One of the most popular of these programs is Outward Bound. (See Chapter 11.) In this and similar programs, participants trade their three-piece suits and shorts and T-shirts and embark on one or several days of canoeing, climbing, and all sorts of somewhat risky outdoor activities. The purpose of the retreat is to increase the participants' ability to accept risk and change and through leadership and teamwork develop methods of achieving new goals and objectives. Do these retreats really work? Several former participants claim substantial results:[47]

- *Intel Corporation.* Organization development manager Susan Studd and a highly skeptical group of engineers attended Seattle's Sports Mind:

> "On the "electric fence" you were supposed to pass people between two closely spaced ropes without touching either one. We jumped into it too quickly and messed it up. That is exactly what we'd been doing in the marketplace when we introduced a new product. It was a valuable lesson in communication."

- *Tupperware Worldwide.* Division heads from twenty-six countries were trained at Utah's Marcomm Associates. Tupperware President Allan Nagle concluded:

> "They did a great job of dramatizing the fact that change is constant in our business. Outside, they'd give us a challenge; we'd figure it out; and then they'd change the rules. Inside, every time we left the meeting room, they'd change the configuration. It got to be quite frustrating, but that's very much what our business is like. People still refer back to that experience."

- *Visa U.S.A.* Corporate-training manager Lillian Maremont utilized Proaction Associates in San Francisco:

> "The traditional role-playing and feedback sessions that I used to design don't even come close to what we accomplished with this program," she says. In one exercise, participants built a bridge out of two-by-fours. One group took a lot of time planning, and when they got on the bridge, it collapsed. On a second try they weren't listening to one another, and the bridge collapsed again. Then time ran out. "It's just like the mindset in the workplace," Maremont says. "Even when something is obviously wrong, people are not willing to look at things in a different way. It was a very powerful lesson, and I don't think our relationships will ever be the same as a result."

It is difficult to develop a cost/benefit analysis for executive retreats, or for almost any leadership training. Obviously, some programs and trainers are more effective than others. The benefits are long-term at best and cannot be directly measured. Critics contend they are simply the latest fad replacing EST, sensitivity–training, and other training methods of the past. They have grown in popularity and content for some reason and may evolve into yet another type of leadership training in the future.

Mentoring

A *mentor* is an experienced leader who provides guidance and support to a new manager or professional, and facilitates his or her personal development.[48] Mentoring is often used with young employees who have high career aspirations. Their mentors are usually ten to twenty years older and are considered successful leaders within the organization. Mentorships may be formally established by the organization as part of an employee's orientation or career development program, or they may form informally between two willing participants. Formal mentor programs are increasing in popularity and usually receive top management support and participation. Typically, a program emphasizes the development of realistic expectations by the protege, scheduled meetings between the mentor and protege, and stated topics to be discussed.[49]

Mentor **An experienced leader who provides guidance and support to a new employee and facilitates his or her personal development.**

The roles taken on by mentors not only vary from organization to organization, but may also vary from mentor to mentor within the same organization. Some of the roles a mentor may take on include: guide, teaching, adviser, friend, tutor, catalyst, coach, consultant, role model, and advocate. A prospective mentor will find some of these roles attractive and others unattractive. It is unlikely—and unnecessary—that a mentor play every role; mentors should chose those they feel comfortable with and those that emphasize their strengths.[50]

The possible benefits of mentoring to both the employee and protege include the following:[51]

1. The mentor may advance the career of the protege by nomination for promotion or sponsorship of membership.
2. The mentor may provide the protege visibility in the organization or profession through joint efforts.
3. The mentor may protect the protege from controversial situations and provide coaching by suggesting work strategies.
4. The mentor may provide counseling about work and personal problems.
5. Better job performance and longer service with the organization from proteges who develop more skills and self-confidence.

While women as well as men can benefit from mentoring, there are relatively few female mentors in many organizations; there are still few women in top-level positions. Unfortunately, the development of cross-gender mentorships has been inhibited by a number of factors. Substantial evidence suggests that a glass ceiling in an organization prohibits women from moving higher up in the organizational ladder—thus fewer women are able to serve as mentors to other women in the organization. Several effective, proven techniques for breaking the glass ceiling are outlined in Chapter 12.

LEADERSHIP DO'S AND DON'TS

Successful leaders can be found at all levels in every organization. Their strengths and weaknesses vary greatly, as do their methods of motivating others, making decisions, and communicating ideas. There are thousands of articles, surveys, and books on leadership written by successful leaders, scholars, and academics. In general they provide a consensus of what are the basic do's and don'ts of successful leaders. These key behaviors are summarized in Figure 14-10 and discussed below:

DO Create a Shared Vision

Perhaps the most important aspect of successful leadership, and the one that most differentiates it from managing, is the creation and maintenance of the future and the means to reach the goals and promises it holds. This aspect of leadership is the central bond or "big picture" that should be shared by each member of the organization and serves as a guidepost in his or her daily work activities. The successful leader creates an environment in which everyone wants to grow and achieve the goal of the organization as explained in the "Profile" of Sheryl Barbich.

Henry M. Boetlinger, former Director of Corporate Planning at AT&T summarized this key behavior very well: "To manage is to lead, and to lead others requires that one enlist the emotions of others to share a vision as their own.[52]

Profile

Sheryl L. Barbich
Barbich Associates, Management
Consulting
Bakersfield, California

ARTICULATING A VISION

Effective leadership is the most critical element in the success formula of any organization in today's increasingly voluntary society. Individuals have more options now than they have ever had, with respect to how and where they commit their time and energy. This voluntary component of the work force demands a leader, as opposed to a mere manager, in order for an organization to effectively accomplish its goals.

What leads an individual to make a commitment? The individual must see and understand the benefit to themselves of making that commitment.

What is the role of a leader in obtaining the commitment of an individual? It is the role of the leader to create an environment in which individuals can grow toward achieving their potential *while* accomplishing the goals of the organization.

What skills must you develop to be an effective leader? First, foremost, and pervasive throughout, you must have the ability to *communicate* clearly, concisely, and energetically. That communication skill is essential to success in integrating the goals of the individual with the goals of the organization.

What steps must be taken to insure that the goals of the organization and the goals of the individual are both effectively met?

- *Step One: Create a vision* of what the organization can be in the future if everyone works toward the same future. The act of leadership can be fundamentally seen as the act of articulating a vision and then acting in pursuit of that vision.
- *Step Two: Secure consensus* by active discussion of the vision by those involved. Solicit input as to how the vision can be better. Participation leads to commitment.
- *Step Three: Move from the vision* to specific goals, strategies, and tactics of how the vision is to be obtained. Identify each person's role.
- *Step Four: Develop teamwork* to maximize the efficiency of all of the players. A team, moving in the same direction, can achieve more than the sum of its individuals.
- *Step Five: Evaluate performance* to monitor progress toward accomplishment of the organizational goals and to provide coaching and counseling to individuals as to how they can improve their performance.
- *Step Six: Share praise and recognition.*

The leader, by integrating the goals of the individual and the goals of the organization, helps both achieve their potential. The leader provides their greatest service in this . . . in helping others reach toward their potential.

Life is more than just reaching our goals. As individuals and as a group, we need to reach our potential. Nothing else is good enough.

Perhaps this is why success is defined as a journey, not a destination.

The war in the Persian Gulf provided a shining, broadly shared example of this leadership. Immediately following the invasion of Kuwait by Iraq, President Bush forged a historical world alliance that shared the vision of a united force of the United Nations, the United States, and several other countries that would demand the immediate withdrawal of Iraq, restoration of the government of Kuwait, and reparations from Iraq to Kuwait for all damages. It was the acceptance of this vision, as articulated by specific goals, that enabled President Bush to secure and maintain the world alliance despite many attempts by Iraq to break it. The alliance held through the usual bickering in the U.S. Congress, the economic blockade against Iraq, and the Gulf War.[53] Why was this example of leadership so unusual? Countries, like people in organizations, members of Congress, and even family members, have separate agendas—their own interests, their view of what is right, their priority of what needs to be accomplished. Thus, to unite people behind one shared vision is very difficult. It requires persuasion, creativity, good, sound ideas, and—*leadership*. Peter Krieft of Boston College calls this skill "metaphysical sanity." "To be a leader you have to lead people to a goal worth having—something that's really good and really there."[54]

A similar example of leadership vision was developed by Liza Foley, the owner of Canton Industrial Corporation of Canton, Illinois. In 1984 an old International Harvester facility was closed and 2,500 people were laid off. Foley, who was with International Harvester, saw a plant closing and damaging the community of 14,000 people who wanted to work, and undervalued assets, but she had: "a very clear sense of purpose and vision of where I wanted to go . . . I wanted to make Canton, Illinois the mailbox capital of the world." It was not an easy task; Canton became the first publicly held female-owned and operated manufacturing facility in the United States.[55]

One effective means by which a leader can communicate his or her vision is by developing a mission/vision statement. While corporate mission statements have been in use for many years, recently not-for-profit organizations such as hospitals, governmental agencies, and universities have developed mission statements. Departments and units within an organization can also develop their own mission statement that supports that of the entire organization. The purpose of the mission statement is to clarify and publicize the purpose and philosophy of the organization or department. By reading it, employees should understand their common purpose and the overall direction of the organization or department. A mission statement is usually less than one page in length and answers the following:[56]

- What is our primary business (products or services)?
- Who are our customers?
- What technologies are used in the development of our products or services?
- Why do our customers determine our long-term survival?
- What image do we want to project to people outside?
- How do we want to be viewed by our employees?

In its *1994 Annual Report,* General Motors Corporation offers a vision statement that provides more information than most statements (Fig. 14-9). GM provides not only its vision to be the world leader in transportation products and services, but also the overall objectives, strategies employed, and how the vision directly affects four groups of people: stockholders, customers, employees, and the general public.

DO Be Enthusiastic

When the leader walks in the door each morning, or sits down to chair a meeting, or starts an address before a group of employees, they set the tone for the

FIGURE 14-9

General Motors Vision
Statement

Source: *1994 Annual Report,*
General Motors Corporation.

VISION:

Our vision is for GM to be the world leader in trnsportation products
and services, committed to total customer enthusiasm through people,
teamwork, technology, and continuous improvement. To achieve our
vision, we must generate customer enthusiasm in the marketplace that
translates into leadership in sales, earnings, and returns on investment
and assets.

OBJECTIVES:

• Global leadership in every segment in which we compete
• Leading financial performance throughout the business cycle

FUNDAMENTAL STRATEGIES:

• Globalization through aggressive pursuit of new market
  opportunities worldwide, resource leveraging, and development of
  an international team
• Concerted focus on the needs of current and new customers
  worldwide with emphasis on quality and innovation
• Rapid transition from "mass" to "lean" and "flexible" manufacturing

ADDING TO STOCKHOLDER VALUE	BUILDING CUSTOMER ENTHUSIASM	COMMITMENT TO EMPLOYEES	IN THE PUBLIC INTEREST
• Earnings	• Dedication	• Safety	• Environment
• Efficiency	• Value	• Diversity	• Safety
• Productivity	• Safety	• Caring	• GM Foundation
• Globalization	• Quality	• Communication	• Volunteerism
	• Service		
	• Technology		

day, meeting, or audience. The enthusiastic leader gives people a motivation
that cannot be replaced by pay raises, deadlines, or plush offices. Enthusiasm
does not replace sound decisions or careful planning, but it can greatly enhance
the ability of the leader to motivate others.

Perry Pascarella, Executive Editor of *Industry Week* believes that enthusiastic
leaders "share their excitement—excitement not about what they have accomplished, but what they want to do next." For example, Jan Carlzon, President of
SAS Airlines turned around the troubled company by designing a new customer
service program and personally presenting it to employees all across Sweden,
Denmark, and Norway. There is risk involved in being an enthusiastic leader—
if Carlzon's new program had not been accepted by the employees or simply
failed to attract customers, his personal reputation would have suffered. Another
example of the enthusiastic leader taking a risk is Lee Iacocca. By deciding to
feature himself in Chrysler Corporation's advertising, he took an enormous risk—
but few people would argue that his personal enthusiasm for the company and
its products did not substantially assist Chrysler's recovery.

At Hewlett-Packard enthusiasm is a corporate objective:[57]

Enthusiasm should exist at all levels. People in important management positions should not only be enthusiastic themselves, they should be selected for their ability to engender enthusiasm among their associates. There can be no place, especially among the people charged with management responsibility, for half-hearted interest or half-hearted effort.

DO Lead by Example

Leaders, like all people, have values that cause them to take certain actions, make certain decisions, and follow certain dreams. Values, however, are intangible. Employees can only learn, and follow, the values of a leader through their actions or behaviors. The old saying: "Do as I say, not as I do" simply doesn't work. A leader who walks through a "hard hat only" area without a hard hat cannot expect others to take the safety rule seriously. It obviously shows that the leader does not value the observance of safety rules—thus others probably will not observe them. Parents, who are perhaps the most important leaders in our society, often find leading by example difficult. In one leadership training session a highly successful real estate developer, and mother, confessed: "When I get home after a hard day I crave Oreo cookies. However, I firmly deny my children any snacks before dinner, so I hide in the closet and eat Oreos, but on several occasions they have caught me. Since I'm an adult, I think I have a right to eat what I want." Do you agree with this mother?

Jack Telnack, head of Ford Motor Company's Design Center provided a lesson in leading by example. He wanted to shift more attention to the Design Center, which had just won two "Car of the Year Awards" to the truck division. To demonstrate his seriousness, Telnack, who could drive any Ford product, started driving a Bronco truck to the office.[58]

DO Ask Why—Challenge the Status Quo/Taking Initiative

Successful leaders are not shy about challenging the status quo. Change is a way of life in all organizations. Rapidly changing technology, employee needs, government regulations, consumer tastes, and international competition cause every organization to change almost all aspects of operations—products and services, job responsibilities, production, and delivery systems. Successful change, however, always begins by challenging the status quo, and change almost always requires leadership. Leaders realize that they are the "change agents" of an organization. Others look to them to recognize the need for change and initiate it. To accomplish this successfully they act as internal entrepreneurs.

In fact, "taking initiative" and challenging "how we have always done things" may be the most important characteristic of the successful leader according to Robert Kelley and Janet Caplan of the AT&T Bell Laboratories. The Bell Laboratories have long been recognized as one of America's most prestigious OB research centers. From 1986 to 1993 Kelley and Caplan compared average professional employees with those who became leaders through their work. The common skill shared by those who became leaders was that of taking the initiative to challenge the status quo and initiate changes that improved performance. In general these leaders accepted responsibility beyond their job descriptions, volunteered for additional activities, and promoted new ideas.[59]

DO Celebrate Accomplishments

Leaders take the time to say "thanks for a job well done!" When a significant goal is reached, the audit is finished on time, new sales figures show record levels, or the rush season has ended; these accomplishments need to be observed, and those who helped achieve them feel appreciated. Common examples are the office potluck lunch or party, dinners out with spouses with guests invited, an extra all-expenses-paid vacation to Hawaii for the top performer, or even the traditional company picnic. Celebrations also take written form such as a letter from the president thanking each person involved, a notice posted on the employee bulletin board, announcement of a promotion in the local newspaper, or a column highlighting the success in the employee newsletter. A leader who plans and participates in a celebration conveys to others three important principles:[60]

1. The achievements they value.
2. Public recognition is important.
3. They care enough to be personally involved.

DON'T Micromanage

Delegate as much authority and responsibility to people as their job and experience permits. Leaders who must review every decision and manage every detail of the jobs performed by those who work for them are managing under a microscope, or "micromanaging." What employee wants to be micromanaged—very few. Employees who are creative and enjoy their work prefer autonomy. When people micromanage, they build layers of bureaucracy and create a climate of suspicion and distrust. It lowers morale and productivity and almost eliminates creativity. The micromanager usually becomes a bottleneck in the flow of communication and decision making. In one office, for example, the department manager went on an extended vacation. Employees ignored the old bureaucracy and made decisions on their own. The "natural order" of the organization emerged. The result was higher productivity and morale—the office simply ran better when the manager was gone. The CEO soon realized the organization was better off without the manager.[61]

DON'T Ignore Problems

Some problems can be left alone: bickering or jealousy among certain employees, a certain process that just doesn't work, high turnover in a department, et cetera. At least some people believe they can be left alone. Successful leaders, however, do not ignore problems. While resolving problems is often unpleas-

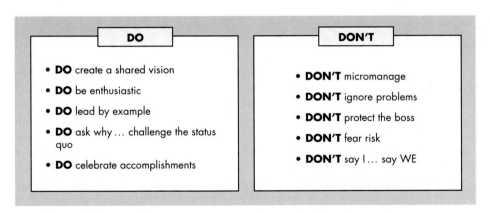

FIGURE 14-10
Leadership Do's and Don'ts

ant and time-consuming, it is an inherent component of leadership as the "Profile" on Jerry Stanners, CEO of Freymiller Trucking Company (the nation's largest independent trucking company) explains. Once they recognize the problem exists the following steps can be followed to resolve the problem:

1. *Investigate.* Why does the problem exist and why hasn't it been solved through normal operations.

2. *Seek input.* Determine who are the most knowledgeable people to resolve the problem and ask for their assistance.

3. *Evaluate alternatives.* Determine the pros and cons of each suggested method of resolution.

4. *Seek consensus.* Meet with the appropriate people and seek a consensus on which resolution technique should be followed.

5. *Implement and evaluate.* Take the chosen course of action and objectively evaluate its success. Share the evaluation with those involved.

An excellent example of this key leadership practice is Thomas Watson, Sr., former CEO of IBM. In the mid-1960s IBM was at a crossroads; its place in the computer industry was uncertain. A key project was the revolutionary System/360 that ran into constant delays and lost valuable time. Watson had appointed his brother, Dick Watson, in charge of the research and development of the System/360. The constant delays, however, caused Thomas Watson to move his brother to an insignificant staff position and end his hopes of succeeding Tom as CEO. In his autobiography, Tom Watson recalls the System/360 as "the greatest triumph of my business career . . . but whenever I look back on it, I think about the brother I injured."[62]

DON'T Protect the Boss

Sometimes leaders can't solve problems because overzealous assistants (themselves leaders) want to "protect the boss" from hearing bad news. Motivated out of simple ignorance, fear of reprisal, or a genuine desire to keep the boss happy, this type of assistant can, in fact, become a great obstacle to a leader's effectiveness. Since they often control the material and people the leader will see, they control the leader to an extent. Warren Bennis, former President of the University of Cincinnati, has written that he "was blessed with a staff of dedicated, honest, and intelligent men and women, with whom I had to endlessly struggle for the whole truth . . . they would say things like: "Well, I didn't want to bother you," or "I didn't want to burden you," or "I didn't want to argue with you." Successful leaders must prevent this "protecting the boss" by surrounding themselves with people who can recognize the truth and convey it to them whether they want to hear it or not.[63] They must be able to, as the old saying goes, "separate the bearer from the bad news"—a reference to ancient Roman times when couriers who delivered bad news (in sealed envelopes) were often beheaded by angry monarchs.

DON'T Fear Risk

The rapidly changing world requires new ideas, methods, and risks. Leaders encourage people to experiment and take risks that they view as a natural part of change, and they accept failures as a part of the process. Bill Gore, founder of W. L. Gore & Associates, views constant risk-taking and experimentation as

Profile

Jerry K. Stanners
President & Chief Executive Officer
Freymiller Trucking Inc.
Bakersfield, California

KEY ATTRIBUTES OF EFFECTIVE LEADERSHIP

For the past twenty-two years, I have been President and/or Chief Executive Officer for various companies engaged in the manufacture of extruded polyethylene film, rubber gaskets, polyethylene pen barrels, extruded swimming pool hose, distilled spirits and wine including grape concentrates, a daily metropolitan newspaper, and a national trucking company. Some of these companies were divisions of Fortune 200 corporations, others were family owned and one was publicly owned and traded on the NASDAQ market.

As a result of this diversification, people continue to ask me, "How do you manage a company where you do not have an extensive background either in the product line or the industry." The answer is really quite simple—leadership, and surround yourself with a capable and strong management team and compensate them accordingly!

Let me focus briefly on what I consider the key attributes of effective leadership:

- *The ability to communicate with people at all levels of the organization is critical.* My career path has taken me to a number of companies with round-the-clock operations. I made that extra effort to frequently spend time with the second and third shift managers and employees. Some of the best ideas have come from those employees on the "firing line" and in the "trenches."

- *The ability to effectively deal with problem/opportunity situations.* Every workday presents a myriad of problems and opportunities. I cannot recall a problem that was presented to me by a customer, employee, or board member that could not be resolved by our management team. My theory has always been, "If you have a problem or a concern, do not keep it to yourself as it will probably not be resolved; but if you share that problem with me, I guarantee you that we can find a solution."

    Create an environment where employees feel comfortable in sharing problems and ideas with you. This is not an easy task and requires considerable time and effort on your behalf, but the results are well worth the investment.

- *Fairness and integrity* with employees and coworkers is absolutely essential in an organization. I have always had an open-door policy for employees, and while it has been used, I can honestly say that in twenty-two years no one has abused this policy. When communicating with employees on sensitive and difficult issues, you must be honest and straightforward with them even when the final response is not always favorable to them.

- *Be a "coach" and continue building your team.* My participating in high school and college athletics in both individual and team sports has been responsible for my success in building and managing successful companies. If we spend as much time and energy with our employees as we do pouring over our balance sheets, we would discover a significant improvement in the net worth of our company. It is interesting that our most valuable asset is not reflected on our balance sheet—people!!

For those of you involved in managing companies, you might wish to reflect upon the story of the sea captain who said:

It is not important to recount the number of storms encountered at sea but ask yourself, did you bring the ship safely to port?

FIGURE 14-11
Taking Risks—Only
"Above the Waterline"

Source: Tom Peters, *Thriving On Chaos,* New York, Harper & Row, 1987, p. 322. Copyright © 1987 by Excel, a California Limited Partnership. Reprinted by permission of Alfred A. Knopf, Inc.

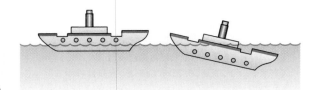

required—to simply survive in today's world. How far will Gore allow risk-taking? The answer is only "above the waterline" (see Fig. 14-11). If you want to drill holes below the waterline you need to check with your supervisor. Thus, anything that didn't threaten the existence of the organization was permitted (drilling holes below the waterline will sink the ship).[64]

DON'T Say I . . . Say WE

Successful leaders quickly learn that "I" can accomplish very little, but "WE" can accomplish a great deal. Employees quickly notice when a leader claims, "I" won the award, broke the sales record, finished the project, solved the problem, et cetera, especially if they were part of the effort. Leaders need to share the recognition and realize that the sharing helps motivate those involved to achieve the next goal.

CONCLUSIONS AND APPLICATIONS

- Leadership requires creating shared visions of future objectives, determining how they can be obtained, and convincing others to join the effort to succeed. Management and leadership are related but different. Management requires the development and implementation of policies and procedures, while leadership requires one to recognize the need for change to survive in today's world.

- Leaders secure their influence within an organization or group from different sources. A person trying to obtain leadership power often begins by developing a basis of expertise, seeking out critical relationships, developing a network of resource persons, establishing effective communication skills, while achieving organizational goals.

- The study of effective leaders has produced four primary models or theories of leadership. All of these models are supported by research findings and intuitive thinking. None, however, can be accepted as absolute models of effective leadership.

- The abilities required of effective leaders are not inborn; rather, abilities can to a great extent be developed in most employees. The training and development of leadership skills within employees is generally approached through "skill building" and "awareness training." In recent years, executive or employee retreats, such as Outward Bound have been utilized by many organizations to build leadership and teamwork among key employees.

- Mentoring, formal or informal, can be utilized by newer employees to enhance their leadership development and career opportunities. Mentors can provide their proteges counseling about work problems, skill development, and sponsorship of membership in important, work-related organizations.

- Successful leaders exist in all organizations, regardless of size or nature. While they differ in their "style of leadership," in general, they do create a vision of the future that is followed by others; they are usually enthusiastic; they lead by example; they challenge the status quo; and they take time to celebrate accomplishments. They usually do not micromanage the work of others; ignore organizational problems; encourage subordinates to protect them from bad news; fear risk; or take the credit for others' efforts.

REVIEW QUESTIONS

1. What is a succinct definition of leadership?
2. How can a supervisor move away from a style of "managing" to a style of "leading"?
3. Describe the sources of leadership influence (or power) within an organization. How can a person, who is not in a position of authority, build a base of influence?
4. What are the advantages to using a path-goal compensation system (pay-for-performance)?
5. Why should leaders allow other employees to be involved in decision making?
6. How can a leader assist autonomous work groups?
7. How can an organization develop people into successful leaders?
8. What are some effective methods by which a person can "lead by example"?
9. How can a leader create a shared vision and communicate it to everyone in the organization?
10. What methods can a leader utilize to successfully avoid "micromanaging"?

DISCUSSION QUESTIONS

1. Is it necessary for all managers in an organization to also be effective leaders? Should an organization provide leadership training for all managers?
2. Exactly what is charisma? How important is it for a leader to possess charisma? How important is it for a leader to have good written and oral communication skills? motivational skills? decision-making ability?
3. When should a leader be autocratic in making a decision? When should a leader be participative in decision making?
4. Why should an organization consider establishing formal mentors for new employees? What should they be asked to do?
5. Is the executive retreat merely a new fad in leadership training? What are the potential advantages and disadvantages?
6. Describe an example of how a leader you know "avoided a problem" and thus created a worse situation.
7. Describe how a leader you know was able to achieve success through creating a vision and then motivating others to follow. Was that person enthusiastic?

CASE STUDY

The Hospital President

Henry Stone has been the President of St. Jude Hospital in Springfield, Illinois, for the past three years. Before that he was the Chief Financial Officer at another hospital in St. Louis for eleven years. Henry is extremely well liked by the members of the hospital board of directors, the medical community, and his employees. He is also considered to be a fair and effective administrator. Three months ago Henry hired Burt Denning as his first Chief of Staff. He believed that having twelve staff directors reporting to him was too large a span of control. Now Denning chairs the staff meeting each Monday morning instead of Henry. Denning is also responsible for resolving any interdepartmental problems that arise and determines which problems, communications, and people have access to Henry.

Henry has been able to devote a much greater portion of his time to the external medical community and to corporate gift-giving efforts, which was exactly what the directors intended when the Chief of Staff position was approved. Henry has also been able to reduce his average workweek from eighty hours to sixty hours.

In the hallway this afternoon the following conversation occurred between Henry, Tina Hatcher, Director of Operations, and Nancy Lee, Director of Nursing:

HENRY: How is everything?

TINA: (pause) You really want to know?

HENRY: Of course, why, you sound like there is a problem.

TINA: Well, there is. First of all, we never have access to you anymore . . .

NANCY: And second, we don't like your new style of leadership.

HENRY: Style of leadership? . . . What do you mean by that?

TINA: We used to be able to share our problems with you, either in staff meetings or we could walk in your office. Now you're never at the staff meetings, and we can't get in to see you in your office.

HENRY: Well, you knew things would change when Burt came. He should resolve problems in the staff meetings just as I did. Doesn't he?

NANCY: Yes, but it's entirely different with Burt.

HENRY: What's different?

NANCY: You approach things differently—you let the group decide how to handle things if it meets with your approval. Burt, well, he just hears both sides and then makes a decision.

HENRY: Well, everyone has his own style of chairing a meeting.

TINA: I just don't like knowing that you are not making these decisions, and we can't get to you if we disagree with Burt.

HENRY: You know my door is always open.

TINA: But now you're gone most of the time, and when you are here, you're too busy with other things.

HENRY: But that was the purpose of hiring Burt, to free me to do other things. If you really need to see me, you can make an appointment.

TINA: Make an appointment! You know things around here can't wait; this is a hospital!

HENRY: I can't do everything—some things just have to be delegated.

TINA: Aren't you sorry you asked how things are?

HENRY: Well, I am sorry to hear you two feel this way; you are two of my best directors.

As Henry walked away he began feeling troubled about the conversation. Yet, overall, things were going well at the hospital; he liked Burt; and he did not want to go back to the way things were.

CASE STUDY QUESTIONS

1. What style of leadership is Henry using?
2. Has his leadership effectiveness been impaired?
3. Are Tina and Nancy being reasonable in their complaints?
4. What, if anything, should Henry do now?

EXPERIENTIAL EXERCISE 1

The Best Style of Leadership?

The following are ten situations encountered every week by many people in leadership positions. Assume as the leader you have the authority to choose one of four basic "styles of leadership" in handling the situation: (1) autocratic—decides alone, entirely without input from others; (2) semiautocratic—asks for input from those whose advice has been helpful in the past, but makes the decision alone; (3) democratic/participative—in a group meeting asks for others to analyze the situation with you and through consensus, reach a decision; (4) team—the leader turns over the situation for an autonomous team to analyze and resolve without pressure or any input from the leader.

Task

Your instructor will organize the class in teams. For each situation each group should indicate the style of leadership that you believe should be followed and then provide a brief explanation of your decision:

Situation 1:
   In the morning, deliveries of four dozen boxes of finished goods (retail value about $6,000) are returned, because the purchasing store believed they were defective. This is the largest quality problem your firm has had this year.

Situation 2:
   Next month is the fiftieth anniversary of your firm. In the suggestion box someone has dropped you a note asking if there will be any recognition of the event. Nothing is currently planned.

Situation 3:
   As you walk into the accounting office you see a crowd of employees around the coffeemaker. As you approach, you hear obscenities shouted by two of your employees who are in a heated argument.

Situation 4:
   The research and development (R&D) department has completed an eighty page report. It recommends the firm manufacture a new product that has been developed in response to customers' suggestions. You are interested, but cautious—R&D is always suggesting new products.

Situation 5:
   Last month your marketing director (who reports directly to you) retired. The human resource department has reduced a list of forty-nine applicants to four finalists. The finalists have already been tested, interviewed by the HR specialists, and their backgrounds have been thoroughly checked.

Situation 6:

The audit completed by your outside accounting firm lists seven managerial suggestions in the opinion. While not an unusual number, they must be addressed.

Situation 7:

The board of directors has decided the company should develop a mission statement and general policies and procedures (for board approval) to be published and distributed to each employee.

Situation 8:

As chair of the board of the local Junior Achievement, you realize that for the local chapter to survive it must raise the funds needed to purchase a permanent facility. There are eight other board members of JA, but none have extensive fund-raising experience. You are dedicated to JA but feel that you are already overcommitted with civic responsibilities.

Situation 9:

At a staff meeting two months ago, it was agreed to require the human resource director to develop a "Wellness Program" for all employees. At the last two staff meetings, it had been repeatedly stressed that all employees should be encouraged—but no one was required to participate. The program will contain four parts: (1) a smoking cessation program; (2) free weight and fitness counseling; (3) semiannual free, on-site blood pressure and cholesterol checks; and (4) free membership at the fitness center across the street. Like most of your staff, you are slightly overweight and don't exercise on a regular basis. You have no idea what your blood pressure and cholesterol checks will show. Like all other employees you must decide in which program activities you will participate.

Situation 10:

At the last staff meeting you recognized a department head whose suggestion has saved the company over $40,000 in transportation costs over the past three months. The person also received a $5,000 bonus for the suggestion. Today, someone from another department provides you strong evidence that, in fact, a new employee working for the head initiated the suggestion.

Situation	Style (Autocratic; Semiautocratic; Democratic/Participative; Team)	Explanation
Number 1 Defective goods		
Number 2 Fiftieth anniversary		
Number 3 Employee argument		
Number 4 R&D new product		
Number 5 Marketing director		
Number 6 Accounting audit		
Number 7 Mission statement		

Number 8
Junior achievement

Number 9
Wellness program

Number 10
Employee suggestion

EXPERIENTIAL EXERCISE 2

Influencing Others

Leaders can have a significant impact on the careers and lives of other people. Virtually everyone has been affected directly or indirectly by a supervisor, teacher, parent, coach, pastor, community activist, or the words of a prominent national figure. Thousands of young people in the 1960s joined the Peace Corps, inspired by President Kennedy's words: "Ask not what your country can do for you, but what you can do for your country." Almost everyone had someone they trusted or admired give them advice that forever changed their lives.

Task

This exercise has two parts. In Part A you must recall the names of three people who, as leaders, had a significant impact on your life, and briefly describe what they said or did that caused that impact. The person could have been a former supervisor, coach, friend, community leader, or family member.

Part A

Name	Relationship	Event
1.		
2.		
3.		

For Part B, now that you have had time to think about how others have impacted your life, it is time to repay them by taking the time to impact the life of someone else by giving informal recognition, praise, career advice, et cetera, to someone you know will appreciate it. After you have done it, record their name and the event below.

Part B

Name	Relationship	Event
1.		
2.		
3.		

 Take It to the Net **You can find this chapter's World Wide Web exercise at:** http://www.prenhall.com/carrell

CHAPTER 15

Conflict Resolution

CHAPTER OBJECTIVES

1. To understand the role *power* plays in the workplace and in conflict in the workplace.
2. To define the type of power and how such power is acquired and used in the workplace.
3. To study the elements of a conflict in the workplace and to understand how to reduce conflict.
4. To learn conflict behavior techniques that are most typically encountered in the workplace and know how to respond to them.
5. To examine elements of negotiating and how to design principled negotiation sessions.
6. To review various types of third party intervention techniques available in the workplace.
7. To explore how we communicate both verbally and nonverbally and what role communication plays in conflict.
8. To see how employee discipline might be handled in a nontraditional way to avoid conflicts.

Henri Mangeot, Mediator

For over forty years, the Louisville Labor–Management Committee has provided support, expertise, and direct services to community businesses, both management and workers, on workplace issues. The Labor–Management Committee is a locally created body formed to promote harmonious labor–management relations in the public and private sector. When requested, the Committee can provide an unbiased environment for a union election; provide arbitrators when disputes go unresolved; mediate contract disputes; and provide mediation in grievance procedures.

Henri Mangeot, Executive Director since 1976, personifies "mediator" for many who have used the Committee's services. Mangeot, whose 40 plus years as an attorney include stints as Assistant Attorney General for the Commonwealth of Kentucky and State Secretary of Justice, consistently preaches the value of mediation in resolving labor-management conflicts in the workplace. "To the extent that parties settle or otherwise resolve grievances through mediation rather than using arbitration, there are substantial savings of both time and money." Mediation requires a willingness on both parties to communicate and to compromise, Mangeot says. A mediator's role is to focus the willing parties toward workable solutions.

Mangeot has a gift for finding a middle ground according to one union representative familiar with his services. "This guy really listens . . . He hears the feelings. And he's able to take what he hears and put it into a workable solution for you," says Paul Schweitzer, former union president.

As the workplace changes and organized labor's influence within many businesses diminishes, the work and role of the Labor–Management Committee will also change. Mangeot sees an increased role for the Committee as a forum for discussion of common problems between the manager and the workers outside of a "dispute" situation. With the growth of employee involvement programs, such as TQM (total quality management) and JIT (just-in-time) techniques, the burden increases on both labor and management to share decision making. "It can be a shock to labor representatives to sit around a table with management talking about common problems, rather than a grievance or a contract. There has to be a learning process on both sides."

Mangeot, himself, enters into each new challenge offered him through the Labor–Management Committee, as an opportunity for growth and learning. "One would not last very long in this business if it ever became repetitive. Fortunately, there is no end of puzzles to be worked and problems to be solved. Nevertheless, the real thrill comes when parties demonstrate they have acquired the skills to solve a problem in their mutual best interests without third party intervention. That is the kind of growth we work toward continuously," Mangeot said.

Sources: Adapted from George H. Yater, "Henri Mangeot on Teamwork Between Labor and Business," *Louisville,* May 1982, pp. 72–75; Joe Ward, "Trusted Labor Mediator Has a Knack for Problem Solving," *Louisville Courier Journal,* June 22, 1987.

About Conflict

Henri Mangeot's talents are most often used when the two parties have failed to reach agreement because of a major "conflict." In this chapter we will examine how conflicts in the workplace arise, how workers react to such conflicts, and how an organization can make conflict work to improve, rather than impede, the mission of the organization. In doing this we will examine power and what role the exercise of power plays in creating or resolving conflicts. We will talk about *communication* and techniques for eliminating unnecessary conflicts that stem from misunderstandings. And finally, we will examine conflict resolution strategies such as *negotiations* and *third-party interventions.*

POWER

Conflict Arises in the workplace when two interdependent parties perceive that they have incompatible goals and scarce resources, and there is an interference from each other on achieving these goals or gaining the resources.

Power A struggle within a conflict either over the object of the conflict or over besting the opposing party.

Central to an understanding of *conflict* is an understanding of what part *power* plays in conflict. Within each conflict is a struggle for power, either over the object of the conflict or simply over besting the opposing party. We will revisit the sources of power, examine how imbalances of power influence conflict, and show how one seeks to balance power through conflict.

It is important in understanding conflicts and conflict resolution to reduce *power* to its smallest part. Most individuals within an organization will not engage in a direct power struggle with the boss, although they may watch such a struggle from the sidelines. They may not think, therefore, that they are part of any conflict. Nonetheless, each *exchange* in the workplace is an exercise of some element of power. That exercise of power is the source of conflict in the workplace. Many such conflicts are but a momentary pause before the work day goes on. However, some of those everyday occurrences can escalate into full blown "conflicts," or can be masking some fundamental disagreements between parties that must be resolved. Understanding power is necessary to a resolution of that conflict.

Power as Currency

To understand power for purposes of conflict resolution, you can think of it as a thing or a commodity—like money. One may possess money or currency, but the value of that currency is determined primarily by whether anyone wants the currency you are holding.

In the workplace *sources of power*—that is, the types of currencies people have, can be classified as *expertise, resource control, interpersonal linkages,* and *communication skills.*

- *Expertise currency* stems from a person's special skill or knowledge. Because of that skill or knowledge, people seek the person out for assistance or information. All professionals, doctors, lawyers, and accountants develop specialized expertise and are valued and rewarded for that expertise when it is needed. In today's workplace computer experts own a great deal of *expertise currency.*

- *Resource currency* stems from being in a position of authority. It includes the formal power to direct the work of individuals within an organization, and controlling resources so that rewards as well as punishments are theirs to distribute. Managers most often exert this kind of power by virtue of their *position* as manager.

- *Interpersonal linkage currency* stems from access to or control of sources of important information. An executive secretary often exercises considerable power in an organization by screening a boss's calls or in directing his or her correspondence. A person serving in a liaison role between two departments gains power from that role within both departments.

- *Communication skills currency* stems from an ability to persuade, to lead, or to form bonds with others. A person who has considerable interpersonal power or *charisma* can communicate caring and warmth, is looked at as an example and as a role model.

Sources of power Types of currencies people have classified as: expertise, resource control, interpersonal linkages, and communication skills.

Expertise currency Specialized skills or knowledge that are valued and rewarded when needed.

Resource currency The formal power to direct the work of individuals within an organization, and the ability to control resources to distribute rewards or punishments.

Interpersonal linkage currency stems from access to or control of sources of important information.

Communication skills currency stems from an ability to persuade, lead, or form bonds with others.

One's own use of power may contain one or more of these currencies. Most often if there is a concentration of power currency in one area exclusively, it actually limits one's powers. One who develops an interpersonal linkage with the boss may fail to develop any expertise. If the boss is no longer there, the power of that relationship evaporates. Likewise, if an expertise currency is developed but no communication skill exists, the person may lack the power to exert the expertise. Someone who has power because of resource control can neglect the interpersonal linkages and find the ability to reward or punish has been eroded. The person has become isolated and is no longer a part of the team.

The most effective power base is gained by developing a combination of the four currencies above and knowing how and when to use each one. A typical midlevel manager has resource power in relationship to his or her subordinates and expertise power in relationship to his or her superiors. If successful, he or she probably has interpersonal linkages with her peers and, at times, she exerts power over any number of groups through her communication skills.

Acquiring Power

Just as there are a number of power currencies within an organization, there are a number of ways to acquire power. Power currencies can be accumulated as a result of *job performance*. A person can develop an expertise or acquire information by just doing his or her job. In order to become valuable *currency*, however, the job activities need to be extraordinary, visible and relevant to the organization's needs.[1] Extraordinary job performance is necessary for the expertise to be developed, so that one is perceived as better than the next person. As discussed in an earlier chapter on women in the workplace, their inability to rise in the ranks of management stems partly from their nonvisibility. As competently as they performed their job, no one was aware of it.[2] Therefore, to develop power currency, your job performance must be *visible*. Finally, the *relevance* of the job performance to the organization's need is critical. When the organization's existence is threatened by lawsuits, for example, a lawyer gains power within the organization.

Power can also be attained through *relationships* with others. Being "mentored" by a person in a position of power adds to an individual's power—both through the access to important information (interpersonal linkages) but also because of the *message* such a relationship sends (communication skills).

Building coalitions through cooperation with others in the organization and networking builds both interpersonal linkage currency and communicative skill currency.[3]

Authority and Power

While *resource control currency* is often the result of a position within the organization that has the prerequisite authority attached to it to direct the use of resources, an individual in this position may not, in fact, have that authority. If a manager cannot actually reward or punish his subordinates, then that person is less powerful than originally perceived to be. One may have authority without power, power and authority, or power without the authority.

RELATIONAL POWER   All power stems from a relationship—one has power because another gives it to him or her. Having individual power sufficient to exercise some influence and control in one's life is an essential human need. Psychologists believe that from birth, a child's self-image is influenced by his or her ability to get a response from his or her environment. Children whose cries are answered in a positive way by a caregiver grow up confident in their ability to influence their surroundings. A child who is ignored or punished when crying later has difficulties in relationships because he or she has a poor self-image and feels worthless as a person.

Because power is relational, it can change in each situation. Power doesn't reside in the person but in the relationship of the person to the situation. What creates the reality of power within each situation? Need or dependency. If the currency you hold—expertise, resources, relationships, or charisma—is needed by the other, then a dependency is created. The degree of the dependency is in direct relationship to the need or scarcity of the currency you hold, and/or its availability or nonavailability elsewhere. Figure 15-1 briefly summarizes the sources of power in an organization.

ORGANIZATIONAL POLITICS   The exercise of power within an organization is often described as *office politics*. Again, this term comes with a connotation of some-

Office politics The exercise of power within an organization to acquire and shift power and influence among individuals, groups, departments, and divisions.

FIGURE 15-1
Sources of Power

Sources	Which can be acquired from
Expertise	Education; job performance; high visibility
Position	Job
Connection	Whom you know
Personal characteristics	Communication skills

thing unsavory. But the exercise of power within an organization is necessary and natural. If power is the ability to influence the outcome of events, then individuals within an organization are hired to exert influence over the organization's activities.

Because all parties in the organization serve some need of the organization (or else why are they there?), everyone in the organization shares some power to influence the outcome; that is, accomplish the goals of the organization. The shares of power, however, are not equal nor static. The efforts to acquire and shift power and influence among individuals, groups, departments, divisions, or even among groups within any of these larger groups, results in office politics.

The power acquisition/struggle can be focused on improving the organization's ability to reach its goals, or can merely be reflective of an individuals's ambitions. Researchers have found that the individual's investment and commitment to the organization determines which kind of politics is played. Companies that get employees to invest themselves into the organization benefit from the power politics being played.[4]

CULTURAL DIVERSITY, POWER, AND CONFLICT   Women and people of color often have considerable difficulty in acquiring or using power in the workplace. As seen in the earlier chapters on diversity, the ability of women and people of color to break through the glass ceiling to top management has been a real frustration.

Unfortunately, for many women and people of color acquiring or using power currencies at any management level is difficult. Even if they occupy a position that by its rank in the organization gives them resource currency, they may be challenged because of their gender or color. Expertise currency can be difficult to acquire if the woman or the person of color is not given an opportunity to move from place to place within an organization to prove competency. Through aggressive mentor programs some organizations are creating the opportunity for women and people of color to acquire interpersonal linkage currency. Some experts urge women and people of color to develop more power currency in the area of communication skill currency. The changing workplace in the United States will need employees with insight, sensitivity, and better listening skills.[5]

This woman manager has to use listening skills to represent her company with an irate customer.

CONFLICT

Defining Conflict

What is conflict? Conflict can be as simple as a disagreement between friends as to what movie to see, or as complex as a world war. Conflict arises when at least two *interdependent* parties perceive that they have *incompatible* goals and scarce resources and there is *interference* from each other on achieving these goals or using those resources. Two individuals in an organization who are both seeking the same promotion may be on a collision course. They can recognize the conflict and deal with it, or try to avoid it. The nature of conflict can be misunderstood.

- *Conflict is not abnormal and harmony normal.* Just as the only constant is change, harmony and conflict are intrinsic to any relationship. One wise woman advised her daughter-in-law in the earliest days of her marriage that marriage is "ebb and flow." Indeed all relationships are in constant flux between harmony and conflict.
- *Disagreements are not the same things as conflicts.* If disagreements are the same as conflicts, then if the parties were communicating properly, the disagreement would disappear. Conflicts, however, can still exist even if communication is perfect.
- *Personality clashes do not cause conflicts.* Again, by blaming the individuals involved for causing a conflict, the conflict as a real issue is ignored.
- *It is not true that conflict should be avoided or reduced, but never escalated.* A conflict might be resolved by stopping it, but unless the conflict is managed, the basic cause of the conflict might still exist. It may be useful to allow the conflict to completely surface in order to address it properly.
- *Love and aggression are not opposite forces.* Aggression is part of a healthy ego. It allows for self-definition and allows one to distinguish one's self separate from any other. Love and respect provide the keys to an aggression that is nondestructive.
- *Anger is not the most common emotion associated with conflict.* Actually fear and a feeling of loss are the most common emotions associated with a conflict. The destruction of the interdependence of the two parties leaves an emptiness.

Returning to our definition of conflict, let us examine the necessary elements in any conflict. Again, conflict arises when at least two interdependent parties perceive they have incompatible goals and/or scarce resources.

A perceived struggle. For purposes of this study of conflict, it is necessary that the parties to the conflict perceive that a conflict exists. Perception of the conflict need not be overt. In the workplace, conflict may be exhibited by avoidance and subtle behavior.

Interdependence. The parties to a conflict must share some dependence upon each other. If there is no relationship between the parties, there can be no conflict.

Incompatible goals. People will most often conflict over goals that are or seem to be incompatible. Communication may resolve the conflict by clarifying the goals as being compatible. But often incompatible goals do exist. For example, employees might want the same promotion; or two factions of a labor union might want two different benefits packages at the bargaining table.

Scarce resources. A resource can be physical, economic, or social. The scarcity of a resource can be real or perceived. Either way a conflict exists over competition for the resource. In most interpersonal conflicts, however, regardless of the content that is the object of the conflict, the conflict may be over a perceived scarcity of power or self-esteem. That is, the resource that is in short supply in the conflict is each individual's power or self-esteem.

Interference. Finally, to have a conflict the parties must be seen as interfering with each other's reaching their goals or using their limited resources. That interference can only take place if the parties are somehow interdependent.

A schematic representation of the nature of a conflict as it is defined in this chapter is seen in Fig. 15-2.

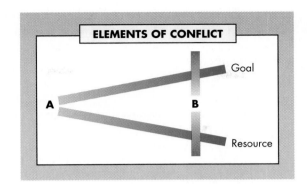

Figure 15-2
Elements of Conflict

Understanding Conflict

Common images of conflict as reflected in people's language can go a long way in helping one understand the nature of conflict. Certainly the most common image of conflict is conflict as war. "He shot down my arguments." "I fell back to fight another day." "I blew them away with my presentation."

Conflict can be viewed as a trial. "State your case." "I'll be the judge of that!" Or as an uncontrollable mess: "Don't open that can of worms."

Conflict may be compared to a game, "He made an end run;" "She's not playing by the rules."

All of these descriptions lead one to understand conflict as a win-lose situation.

A more collaborative view of conflict is reflected in references to conflict as a bargaining table. "Sit down at the table." Or as a dance, "We danced around the issues for a while." Or even as a balancing act, "He's walking a tightrope."

Conflict has also been described as a tide, which ebbs and flows with predictability. These images of conflict tend to imply that conflict can be managed in a win-win manner.

These views of conflict can be seen in Fig. 15-3.

Destructive Conflict   When conflict is engaged as a win-lose encounter, the conflict is, in itself, destructive. Even the winner in such a battle loses because the relationship between the parties has been destroyed.

Productive Conflict   Taking a win-win approach to resolving conflicts results in a strengthening of a relationship.[6] Productive conflicts must have cooperation between the parties and a positive personal commitment. This type of conflict resolution results in mutual feelings of power and self-esteem. Some organizations value the ability to handle conflict constructively as discussed in the "OB in Practice" on page 505.

Conflict Behavior

Human beings react to a threat being made against them in one of two ways—fight or flight. A choice is made to stand one's ground and fight or to take flight and run.

A person reacting to conflict has the same two choices—to engage in the conflict or to avoid the conflict.[7]

Avoiding conflict does not resolve the conflict. It can, in fact, escalate the conflict by allowing the conflict to grow and become more critical. At times, however, *avoidance* can be productive for a relationship if the conflict is of little importance and its avoidance at a particular time will, in fact, resolve the conflict by having it evaporate.

FIGURE 15-3
Images of Conflict

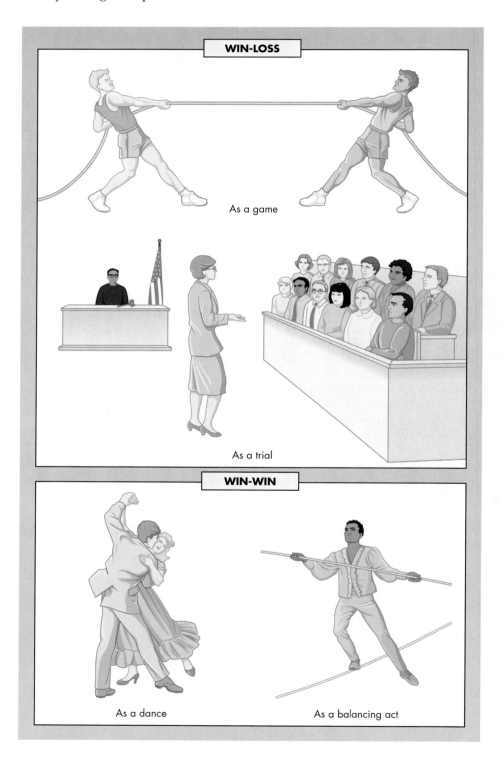

WIN-LOSS

As a game

As a trial

WIN-WIN

As a dance

As a balancing act

OB in Practice

Constructive Conflict

Richard Pascale is hailed as a new voice in organizational management for the ideas he advocates in *Managing on the Edge: How the Smartest Companies Use Conflict to Stay Ahead* (published by Simon and Schuster, 1990).

The central thesis of his book is that *adaptive* organizations build a great deal of *contention.* That these disagreements are ways of spurring people to reexamine assumptions. Successful organizations handle this energy constructively.

He believes companies follow a pattern of "fit, split, contend, and transcend" if they wish to handle contention constructively. A company "fits" well if it has a lot of congruence or alignment within the organization. However, if it fits too well, he suggests "splits." That is, splitting the organization into departments or teams to avoid having a huge monolith. The smaller units have a feeling of ownership and commitment that isn't equalled on a large scale.

However, the paradox of a "fit" and "split" is that the larger vision of the whole organization might be obscured by the goals of the smaller units in the organization. Pascale sees this as where the *contention* arises. And in his mind, the contention is a symptom of a healthy organization.

A manager who can allow the contention to be constructive has "transcended" for the fourth part of the description of the process. Pascale acknowledges that many managers do not have the skills necessary to *transcend,* but believes they can learn.

Source: Adapted from Tom Brown, "Richard Pascale: The 'Christopher Columbus' of Management?" *Industry Week,* January 7, 1991, pp. 12–20.

A response akin to avoidance is to be *accommodating.* In being accommodating, a person urges the other party to calm down, to wait, and put off the conflict to a different time. There is a hope that if the conflict is delayed it can be avoided. Again, this response might be helpful if the parties are so emotionally involved with the conflict as to be uncontrollable: But an accommodating style will never produce a solution to the underlying cause for the conflict.

Engaging conflict can be done in two ways—either in a competitive or a cooperative mode.

Competitive engagement focuses on a win-lose situation. Self-interest, that is, achieving one's goals at the other's expense, is the primary motivation. The tactics employed are to pressure the other person into changing his or her position. There is no attempt to modify or change your own position.

Collaborating in the solution to a conflict means that both parties are working toward a win-win solution. There is recognition of the interdependence of the parties and of the need to recognize and respond to the interests of both. This style has been described as both parties sitting on the same side of the table each confronting the problem on the other side.

Finally, *compromising* is a type of collaborating where both sides still sit across the table from one another and deal in a give-take manner. Both sides agree to give up some of their interests in return for achieving some of their goals. This format is most often the one employed in labor negotiations. And while an agreement is reached, there is often second guessing on whether the agreement was fair, or the best one could get. In Fig. 15-4 the five styles of conflict behavior are portrayed.

Competitive sports demand a win-lose scenario.

FIGURE 15-4
Five Styles of Conflict
Behavior

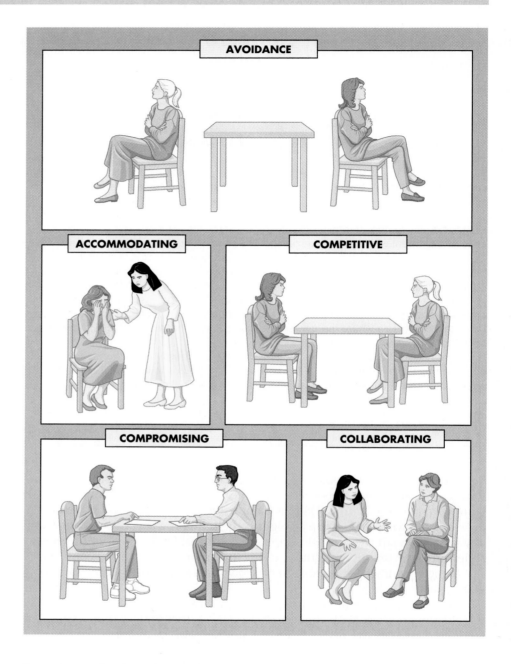

RECOGNIZING CONFLICT BEHAVIORS   While any individual's personality might lend itself to one of the above conflict behaviors, it is often the relationships or the nature of the conflict that will determine which behavior in yourself and in the other party may provide an avenue to redirect the conflict behavior toward a successful resolution.

Avoidance tactics can include any number of responses that seek to totally avoid the conflict or delay the discussion through accommodation. Following are some statements of a couple who disagree on the gifts given by the wife's parents to their children.

- Statements that deny the existence of a conflict: "That's not a problem."

- Statements that deny the existence of the substance of a conflict: "We don't see my parents enough to talk about whether they spoil their grandchildren."
- Statements that simply evade the conflict: "I cannot imagine there being any problem like that."
- Statements that change the subject before a full discussion is heard: "Fine, now about next week . . ."
- Statements that terminate the discussion unilaterally: "I'm not going to discuss this with you."
- Statements that are not denials of the conflict nor evasive replies or topic shifts but merely noncommittal statements: "You know, all in all, the kids behave very well."
- Statements that apply abstract principles or generalizations to the situation. "All children are spoiled by their grandparents."
- Statements that delay the discussion to some unstated time in the future: "Let's get through this visit and we can talk about it later, after they're gone."
- Statements that hope to kid someone out of their conflict. "If you're lucky my parents will give the kids that VCR you've been wanting, and we can't afford. Now that would be spoiling them!"

Competitive tactics rely upon exerting power over the other person. In the example below, two law partners have a number of issues facing the continuation of their relationship. Their approach to this conflict is competitive.

- Statements that directly criticize the personal characteristics or behavior of the other person: "You don't know what you're doing half the time."
- Statements in response that reject the criticism and displays mutual contempt through threats or demands: "You need to buckle down and get some work done. If you can't pull your weight, you're out of here."
- Statements that belittle the other with sarcasm or teasing: "By the way, I read your brief in the LaDonna's case and thought it was pretty good. You are representing the plaintiffs in that aren't you?" (When the partner really represents the defendant.)
- Statements that project feelings or motivations on the other party which that party does not acknowledge: "You're not pulling your share of the work just so I'll pick it up and get you out of trouble."
- Statements that deny or minimize personal responsibility for conflict: "This is your doing, not mine."

Compromising and collaborative tactics seek to reach a resolution through persuasion and inducing both parties to cooperate. The emphasis is on a "we" approach. The following are some typical collaborative or compromising statements where the two parties disagree about a workplace decision to reassign a person.

- Statements that describe the conflict in a nonevaluative way: "Yesterday I criticized your reassignment of Tom from our unit."
- Statements that disclose thoughts, feelings, and motivation about the conflict that the other party could not observe: "Tom's performance in the unit has been a concern of mine for some time."

- Statements that qualify and limit the nature of the conflict: " The unit's performance is certainly the main concern."
- Statements that seek disclosure in a nonhostile way. "When you say Tom's performance in the unit has been a concern, what do you mean?"
- Statements that solicit criticism of oneself in a nonhostile way. "Do you think I've missed something as it relates to Tom's performance?"
- Statements that display support, acceptance, positive regard for the other person, and the shared interests and goals: "I know your only concern is for the good of the unit and how to improve its performance."
- Statements that express a willingness to change, show flexibility, or consider mutually derived solutions. "I'm willing to see how we might improve the unit's performance with or without Tom's help."
- Statements that show mutual acceptance of responsibility for the conflict. "I'm sorry. We should have addressed these concerns together before they got out of hand."

None of the above behaviors are exclusive to particular individuals or conflict situations. Anyone might employ any of the techniques depending upon the circumstances. Indeed, any conflict may begin in one behavioral style and move through the others. The parties may begin by one party seeking to avoid the discussion but then changing to a competitive tactic, as they engage in the conflict. It may progress to a cooperative stage with a successful resolution being achieved.

Situational variables that influence the type of behavior exhibited are:

- nature of the conflict (resources, power, dependency of the parties);
- previous success in using a particular style;
- nature of the parties (family, intimates, supervisors, peers or subordinates).[8]

In addition, the conflict behavior by one party is obviously influenced by the response received. It is the interaction of the parties that determines the conflict dynamics. As seen in the dialogues in Fig. 15-5, if avoidance is matched by accommodation, then the conflict is avoided. But if avoidance is met by competition, the conflict can escalate. And if avoidance is met with a collaborative style, the conflict may be resolved. In each example, the discussion starts the same way, but the answer determines the course of the disagreement.

Reducing the Elements of Conflict

INTERDEPENDENCY   One approach to resolving the conflict is to focus the two parties first on the interdependency of the parties. If there was no relationship between the parties, there can be no conflict. The parties must recognize that part of each conflict includes not only the "what" of the conflict, but the "who" of the conflict—who the parties are and what relationship they have. It must be part of the resolution of the conflict to preserve that relationship, or the conflict becomes destructive.

BALANCING POWER   If the power balance between the two interdependent parties is unequal, then the parties seek to find a way to balance the power. This can happen in a number of ways.

First, the high power party to a conflict can refrain from exercising that power, thereby giving the lower powered party more power. Second, lower pow-

Figure 15-5
Conflict Dynamics

Husband confronts wife about her parents giving their children expensive gifts.

Avoidance—Accommodation

w: "I don't want to talk about this."

h: "Alright, maybe we'll talk about it later."

Avoidance—Competitive

w: "I don't want to talk about this."

h: "You never want to talk about anything."

w: "That's not true. You're the one avoiding problems."

h: "Look, if you're not going to discuss this rationally, I don't want to hear from you about it later."

w: "Don't blame me for this."

Avoidance—Collaborative

w: "I don't want to talk about this."

h: "I know you're upset with me, and I can understand why."

w: "There's no problem here. Just drop it."

h: "Does it bother you when I criticize your parents' attitude toward the kids?"

w: "Yes, of course it does.

h: "Why do you think they bring them so much?"

w: It makes them happy to give the things. After all they don't get to see them very often."

h: "Well, that's true. And certainly they're not to blame for that. Our career choices have caused us to move so far away. I just don't want the kids to misunderstand their love of their grandparents isn't dependent upon gifts."

w: "I think we could find a way to let the children know, without changing my parents, don't you?"

ered parties can be empowered either by the higher power party or by forming alliances or coalitions with other lower powered parties and evening the scales. Finally, both parties can *transcend* the basic relationship by placing the resolution of the conflict apart to be dealt with by both parties under some agreed-upon rules.

INCOMPATIBLE GOALS   There are two types of goals within every conflict—content goals and relationship goals. A content goal is the substance of the dispute such as a raise, or a promotion. The relationship goal is how the parties intend to relate to each other. For example, do they wish to be equals or does one want to have mastery over the other. Often times the parties are not aware that there are two goals within the conflict.

The parties might resolve the content goal without ever addressing the relationship goal. If this happens, the conflict continues, albeit in subtler ways.

Goals may also change or be more fully understood as the conflict progresses. The parties may have a *prospective goal* that is, the goal they identify at the start of a conflict. Often a clear communication of such a goal can lead to positive conflict—a win-win situation.[9] The following are some techniques used to clarify goals prospectively.

- Separate long-term goals from short-term goals. Short-term goals can be specific and accomplished thereby creating the necessary relationship for long-term goal achievement.

- Make the goals specific so that accomplishing the goals can be demonstrated. "I'll try and do better" should be changed to "I will report to work on time each day."

- Put the goals in the present and future tense. Don't present goals as a rehash of the past, "We cannot lose as much money as we did last year." The goals should be a positive endeavor, "Let's make this year a financial success."

There are also transactive goals within each conflict. *Transactive* goals are those that either arise or become apparent during the conflict, not before or after. Adaptability is crucial to successfully resolving transactive goals. The parties must be able to change their expected result during the conflict.

Finally, *retrospective* goals are present in most conflict situations. People continue to try and make sense of their conflict after it is over—either as a way to justify their decisions or as a learning process on how to resolve issues in the future. If, for example, a person whose encounter with his or her supervisor did not result in a raise but did give the employee a sense of how the supervisor values or does not value the employee, the goals of clarifying the relationship may become, in retrospect, the point of the conflict.

CLARIFYING GOALS   A key element to productive conflict is clarification of goals.

- Without an expressed goal, solutions go unrecognized.
- Clear goals can be understood and, therefore, shared with the parties to a conflict.
- Clear goals can be more easily altered than vague goals.
- Clear goals are more often reached than vague goals.

SET COLLABORATIVE GOALS   Another process used for productive conflict is to set collaborative goals, that is, to balance concern for self with concern for the other. A high concern for self coupled with a high concern for the other demands a creative solution to goals attainment. In other words, a win-win situation.

A successful conflict management will result in a wise agreement, one that is fair and durable, because it takes the interest of both sides into account. It has both solved the content dispute and enhanced the relationship of the parties.[10]

HOW TO RESOLVE CONFLICTS

Before you can decide the best avenue for resolving your conflict, you must be able to assess the conflict. By approaching a conflict situation with a systematic process you can remove your own prejudices from the assessment.

Assess the Conflict

The first step is to diagnose the problem. Start by focusing on the critical issues of the conflict and the factors that have led up to it. In doing this, identify all of the parties to the conflict. Not only the obvious parties, but any others who are likely to care or be affected by the conflict. Finally, determine if the source of the conflict is in "a failure to communicate," that is, in some type of misinformation; or is it incompatible goals; or a struggle over mastery in the relationship, a pure power struggle.[11]

Next, assess how the parties relate to each other in a conflict situation. As the parties are in some relationship, they may have developed some patterns for interaction during conflicts. Review the tactics of avoidance, accommodation, cooperation, and competition. Once these tactics have been recognized, you will need to assess which behavioral response would be most productive in constructively resolving the conflict. Those behaviors that lead to destructive resolution of a conflict should be eliminated.

You will have to be the one who will decide which tactic to use to resolve the conflict. That is because you are the only person you can control in a conflict situation. Trying to change the other party will not work. You can only adjust their behavior by making them react to your behavior pattern. As we learned earlier, if you avoid or accommodate the conflict is not engaged, but not necessarily resolved either. If you compete, it can be unending. If you cooperate, you may leave your opponent no option but to join you in resolving the problem. Changing the way one deals with conflict starts with changing oneself.

ANGER   Anger is a part of every conflict whether such anger is expressed or not, known or not. Anger is a human reaction to fear; one feels fear when threatened; and a conflict stems from a threat of some sort from someone who is interfering with a goal achievement or competing for scarce resources.

A person can learn to express anger responsibly, that is, express the anger verbally; separate clearly the acknowledgment of anger from venting anger; agree that the anger will not be physically expressed through an attack of any kind; and agree to go behind the anger to find and correct the cause. A good technique for responding to someone else's anger is seen in Figure 15-6.

ACTIVE LISTENING   Engaging in a true dialogue can resolve conflicts. True dialogue occurs when both parties speak and hear, and when both the words and the feelings behind the words are communicated and understood. The parties explore, by appropriate inquiry, what each is saying and feeling about the conflict. The dialogue is aimed at changing their attitudes about the conflict and about each other. Active listening is explored in greater detail in the section on communication.

SELF-RESTRAINT   Refusing to engage in destructive conflict resolution often takes self-control and self-restraint. As we saw in an earlier example, the behavioral response one makes to a conflict determines the path the conflict will take. If you are to stay with a cooperative response in spite of the other party, you must develop self-control.

COOPERATION   Joining together with your opponent to attack the problem is a learned technique. You must see the other person as a partner capable of joining with you—even if only in this one instance.

Some specific techniques to employ when confronting a conflict are:

- Fractionalize the conflict by reducing a large conflict into smaller parts and work on each part separately.
- Contain the conflict. Limit discussion to the present problem, not the past; refrain from assessing the conflict as the "fault" of one party; describe the problem in objective terms. If the conflict has been fractionalized, solve one part at a time.

---

1. Treat them like VIPs! Be courteous and polite.
2. Let them tell it from the top. Listen without interrupting.
3. After they finish, say you know how they feel! Tell them you see their point.
4. Ask what they want *you* to do about the problem.
5. Don't make promises you can't keep! Get the facts first.

Source: Adapted from James Van Fleet, *Lifetime Conversation Guide*, Prentice-Hall, Inc., 1991.

FIGURE 15-6
How to Handle Angry People

- Allow for griping. Let the gripes decide the agenda for problem solving. Then cooperate on solving that problem.

Negotiating

The most common means used to resolve a conflict is negotiation, although the term negotiation can mean different things to different people. To return to conflict behaviors, negotiation can be either a competitive or a collaborative behavior.

Competitive or distributive negotiations assume a win-lose strategy. The goals of each party are incompatible with the other's, or the resource they both cover is limited. In distributive bargaining, each party has a bargaining range as seen in Fig. 15-7 from which he or she will not deviate, and a resistance point above which he or she will not go. Each party's own bargaining range is kept secret from the other, while each tries to discover as much information about the other party's position as he or she can.

The bargaining position of each party starts high; concessions are made slowly and with many complaints; information is withheld; arguing is forceful; and the parties have to be willing to wait each other out.

The success of distributive bargaining is dependent upon the abilities of the parties to manipulate the process. Concessions need to be made by each side, but winning is making the fewest concessions. So the winning party has to convince the other party to make the biggest concessions.

Distributive bargaining encourages confrontation and does nothing to preserve the relationship. The need for secrecy breeds mistrust and frustrates communications. An alternative to distributive bargaining is collaborative negotiations. Focusing energies on the common interests of the parties as well as their diverse interests, collaborative bargaining seeks to establish a win-win scenario for negotiations. The goal of these negotiations is not to compromise the parties' interests but to satisfy the interests of both parties. In collaborative bargaining the parties recognize their interdependence and value common interests. A mutually agreed-upon solution that is fair to both parties will further the relationship. Limited resources can be distributed jointly, thereby solving both parties' self-interests.

PRINCIPLED NEGOTIATIONS A process called principled negotiations was developed by the Harvard Negotiations Project and published in a book titled *Getting to Yes*. The essential element of the process is to be "hard on the merits, soft on

FIGURE 15-7

Distributive Bargaining Negotiation; Employee Seeking Pay Raise

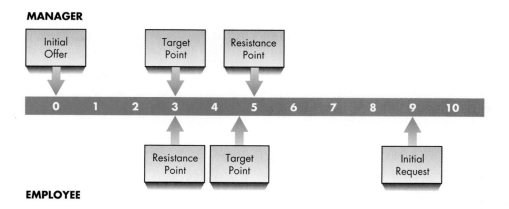

MANAGER

Initial Offer — Target Point — Resistance Point

0 1 2 3 4 5 6 7 8 9 10

Resistance Point — Target Point — Initial Request

EMPLOYEE

Most union contract negotiations follow the distributive bargaining model.

the people." The goal is to decide the issues presented at the negotiating table on their merits rather than through the traditional haggling process that focuses on what each side says it will or will not do. Substituting principle negotiations for the traditional pressure bargaining will theoretically result in a wiser agreement through a more efficient process that improves the relationship of the parties.

The key element in principled negotiations is to separate the people from the problem. This insures a focus on interests, not positions; it generates a variety of possible options before a decision on a given position is made; and it insists that the result of the bargaining be based upon some objective standard.

People. Under the principle negotiation model, the first objective is to separate the people from the problem. This is accomplished by accepting the human element involved in negotiations. An understanding of the attitudes and perceptions of the parties is vital, along with the realization that it is perceptions, not reality, that is important. Neither party can convince the other of the legitimacy of its position without understanding the other party's perception of that position. Therefore, the first task of a negotiator is to understand the other party's perception. It is best to discuss these perceptions openly and to understand their importance to both of the parties. For example, during hard economic times, a union's noneconomic demands for job security may be more important to the union than management perceives, and if management accurately understands that importance, it should be easier to reach a mutually satisfactory agreement.

Perceptions can be changed. Consistent with the old adage, "actions speak louder than words," behavior inconsistent with the other party's perception can help change that perception. Unions expect management to approach the bargaining table determined to maintain the status quo. Thus, if management were to present original proposals to improve employee performance and so give an employee more job satisfaction, the union's perception of management might change.[12]

Once a party's attitude is understood, but cannot be changed, a proposal framed in terms that are consistent with the attitude can lead to agreement. The compromises involved in negotiation often mean a loss to one party or the other. To enable the party not to perceive such a compromise as a loss may successfully separate the person from the problem.

Emotions affect the collective bargaining process. Both parties come to the negotiating process with personal feelings. There may be a strong negative feeling generated by a historically bad labor climate, or a strong positive feeling of power may prevail. Emotions must be recognized, and the parties must be allowed to express their pent-up frustrations. Releasing steam may defuse an otherwise explosive situation.

Finally, negotiating parties must learn to communicate. Too often they are not really trying to converse but are simply going through the motions. To communicate effectively, a party must first actively listen and acknowledge what is being said. If necessary, a party should repeat in its own words what the other party has said to insure understanding. When speaking, a party should remember the goal is to persuade. Dialogue should be simple, with each side expressing its own position, followed by silence that allows the parties to digest what was said.

People can also be prevented from becoming a problem by building working relationships before negotiations begin. A not-so-subtle tactic is mixing the seating of the two teams at a negotiating session. This increases the possibility that the parties will attack the problem rather than each other.

Interests. Attacking the problem is the second objective of principled bargaining. The parties are to focus on interests not positions. Generally, parties come to the negotiating table with a laundry list of demands. Since a party has invested time, energy, and thought in that list, there is a strong tendency to defend it no matter how absurd it may be.

In principled negotiations, the parties are to develop an understanding of their real desires, concerns, and interests rather than to simply list demands. The achievement of those interests is left for future resolution. Both sides have multiple interests, and if those interests can be identified without the parties hardening into a particular position, conflict is eliminated.

Options. Once interests are identified, the third objective is for both parties to seek as many options as possible in solving the conflicting interests.[13] More often than not, the interests of both parties can be satisfied in numerous ways. If creative thinking is applied, interests can overlap, allowing both parties to reach a successful compromise.

In order to seek numerous options, both parties must be willing to accept the existence of more than one right answer. In seeking new solutions, the parties must separate the acts of inventing and judging options. A proposal does not have to make a hard-and-fast position.

Options must be broadened. The belief that one party's gain will always result in the other party's loss often prevents successful bargaining. Therefore, options must be presented so both parties are allowed some advantage. When possible, identify interests that the parties share. For example, underlying every relationship between employer and employee is a shared interest in the health of the employer's industry; this fundamental interest must be present at the negotiating table. A creative negotiator will find ways to identify and explore shared interests, even as conflicting interests are negotiated.[14]

Objective criteria. The fourth objective in principled negotiating is to have the validity of each party's proposals judged by objective criteria. For example, the parties could agree to ask for expert advice when discussing technological changes that might affect workers' jobs. Working together to understand the expert's advice can more easily lead to agreement. This enables either party to criticize the other party's proposal or to defend its own without destroying the relationship. It puts the parties in side-by-side negotiations against an objective third party, the criterion, instead of in a head-to-head confrontation. Agreement becomes easier when the basis of the agreement is mutually agreed criteria.

Obviously, principled negotiation has its negative aspects. Realistically, parties in a negotiation do not often have equal bargaining power and so the temptation to engage in pressure bargaining may be strong. A party can try to keep the negotiations in a principled negotiations model by refusing to participate in pressure bargaining. Real communication is possible if the parties focus on the issues and resist reacting to attacks. Attacks on a position can be treated as an attack on the problem; the counterattack can then be limited to reasoned questions or criticisms on the issue involved.[15]

CULTIVATING SKILLED NEGOTIATORS   The success of a negotiation can be aided or impeded by the qualifications of the negotiators involved. In a 1976 study of successful negotiators, researchers were able to identify behaviors that can make the difference in a negotiation between success or failure. The negotiators were observed during the negotiations and identified as successful if they were rated *effective* by *both* sides; if they had a track record of significant successes, that is, where the parties agreed; and if they had a low incidence of failures, that is, where the parties could not reach agreement.

Skilled negotiators and *average* negotiators spent about the same time prior to the negotiations planning for the sessions. However, the skilled negotiator considered a *wider range of outcomes or options* than the average negotiator, averaging five ideas to their 2.5 ideas. In addition, the skilled negotiator anticipated three times as many *common ground areas* as did the average negotiator and twice as many *long-term* considerations. The average negotiators planned their goals for the negotiations around a fixed point, where the skilled negotiators had upper and lower limits for a range of possible settlement points. Finally, the average negotiators planned to cover issues sequentially in a predetermined order; whereas, the skilled negotiators allowed issues to be separated and dealt with independently to promote both flexibility and an atmosphere of agreement.

During negotiations, techniques of skilled and average negotiators also differed. Skilled negotiators used *irritating* phrases like "generous offer" less often than average negotiators. In the area of counterproposals, skilled negotiators did not immediately offer a counterproposal as often as an average negotiator did. The immediate counterproposal might indicate that the party didn't take the proposal offered seriously enough if a counteroffer was so quickly delivered.

The skilled negotiators did not attempt to list all the reasons why their arguments were better than their opponents. Often they averaged less than two reasons while the average negotiators averaged three reasons per idea. By focusing on the key or best reason for their argument, the skilled negotiators did a much better job of communicating the needs of their side to the negotiations. After the negotiations, differences also surfaced between the skilled and the average negotiator. Two-thirds of the skilled negotiators reviewed the negotiations afterwards to see what they could learn. While under half of the average negotiators bothered.[16]

Third-Party Interventions

Often times a conflict cannot be resolved by the two parties to the conflict acting alone. Many conflicts require the intervention of a third party who has no vested interest in the conflict. Such intervention can be formal or informal. Regardless, the goal will be the same: assist in resolving the conflict.

Third-party interven-tion A person with no vested interest in a conflict who assists in resolving the conflict.

The *third-party intervention,* formal or informal, follows a recognized pattern: an identification of the intervention used, a decision to intervene, an agreement on the role of the intervener, an assessment of the conflict, the utilization of actual intervention tactics, and an assessment of the intervention.

Identification. It is, obviously, more effective if the parties to conflict have mutually agreed to a third-party intervention. Often, however, a third party intervention is a result of *one* party's action—filing a lawsuit, requesting a mediator; or a result of a built-in mechanism to resolve disputes—an arbitration or grievance procedure.

Intervention is crucial if the relationship is stuck; no productive change is occurring; and one or both of the parties are feeling dissatisfied. It is also indicated when one party feels wronged and feels powerless in the relationship to effect changes. Repetitive, destructive conflict cycles will also indicate that third party intervention is necessary.

Decision. In formal intervention situations like arbitration, the selection of the right third party is very important. The framework for the conflict resolution must be carefully examined.

Negotiate Role. It is very important at this stage for the intervener to clearly define the role to be undertaken. The third-party intervener must remember that the conflict is not his or her conflict and he or she can choose not to be involved. If this is not the case, then the third-party intervener is not a disinterested party and can be of no assistance. Formal interveners are generally able to take this very neutral position. Informal interveners, like a person helping out two friends in a dispute, may not be so removed and will have to take care in intervening. It is important for the intervener to remember that he or she is entering into an ongoing relationship, and to appreciate that after the intervention, the relationship has to continue. If the third-party intervener only succeeds in uniting the two parties against himself or herself, the conflict will not be resolved.

Conflict Assessment. A third party intervener will need to gather significant information to assess the nature of the conflict. A conflict mapping guide might be used to help parties understand a dispute. Briefly stated, the map includes a short description of the dispute and a conflict history describing the origins of the dispute as well as the relationship of the parties. The mapping continues with a discussion of the setting in which the conflict takes place and includes all of the interested parties. Often, there are secondary and minor parties affected by the conflict whose interests should be noted. The nature of the issues in the conflict should be mapped to distinguish between fact-based disagreements (what is), value-based disagreements (what should be), and interest-based disagreements (who will get what).

The intervener needs to know the dynamics of the conflict—how the parties got from an issue of disagreement to an inability to resolve the conflict. Both parties and sometimes outside parties to the dispute have solutions to the conflict to suggest. In mapping the conflict, the intervener should gather all those solutions. Finally, the intervener should identify the resources available and made visible in the mapping process to limit or resolve the conflict, like common interests, a history of conflict resolution using a particular method, or other interested parties whose interest became controlling.[17]

Another approach at assessing a conflict was developed as a series of questions to solicit information about the conflict. These questions focus the parties on the *goals* of the conflict, the relative *power* of the parties, the *tactics and styles* being used by the parties to the conflict, and the *solutions* already tried by the parties.

Designing. A third party intervention can range from the totally informal—a parent resolving the dispute between two children, to the formal—litigation. Unless a formal intervention is dictated by the situation, the intervener has to decide which type of intervention is suited to the problem and the people. The types include: consultation, meditation, facilitation, or team building.

Tactics. Central to any technique employed by a third-party intervener is his or her ability to *communicate.* The intervener must be understanding, open, sensitive, engage in active listening, and have persuasive ability. The parties to the conflict must feel free to express their positions openly and not think they are being judged. If the intervener is trusted, then suggested solutions will have credibility with both parties.

An intervener will need to control the process of the conflict. The conflict that needs an intervener has been progressing in a nonproductive manner. The intervener decides meeting times and agendas, and guides the communicating behavior by balancing the power between the parties, reframing the issues, and fractionalizing the conflict into manageable parts.

Exit. At the conclusion of the successful intervention, the intervener should exit from the system and return at a later date for assessment. The truly successful intervener will have facilitated not just the resolution of a particular conflict but set up a mechanism for the parties to continue to resolve conflicts without the third party.

One company, Houston-based engineering firm, Brown & Root, Inc., decided in 1993 to implement an internal dispute resolution program that gives employees the option of selecting from four resolution techniques in lieu of filing a lawsuit. Brown & Root's program allows employees to choose one or all of four options: open-door policy, conference, mediation, or arbitration. Its open-door policy allows employees to take problems to any level of management. In addition, the company offered a hot line where employees could call and get advice on their problems, including legal advice paid for by the company as an employee benefit. A conference gives the employee a chance to sit down with someone in the dispute resolution program to discuss the problem and the appropriate process to use to solve the problem. Mediation is a nonbinding meeting utilizing an expert mediator to open the lines of communication between the parties. Finally, arbitration with a member of the American Arbitration Association, is an option that involves a binding hearing process without a jury.[18]

TYPES OF INTERVENTION

Adjudication. Court process is the most formal way of resolving disputes between two parties. It is certainly the most contentious way, because it begins by the act of one party to the dispute initiating this solution. There are advantages and disadvantages to adjudication as a conflict resolution method.

Advantages can be seen in the availability of a court process:

1. Balancing power between the parties
2. Providing rules for fairness through evidence requirements
3. Providing trained advocates for those less able to present their side
4. Providing a backup to other conflict resolutions systems, such as arbitration, giving the parties a sense of confidence in the fairness of the system

Disadvantages can be seen in the availability of a court process:

Some conflicts can only be resolved in the courtroom.

1. Being overutilized and overburdened causing delays and expense
2. Taking the decision out of the hands of the parties to the dispute and into either the hands of the judge and jury to decide or the lawyers to negotiate
3. Being based on a win-lose scenario, the conflict escalates during litigation and becomes more difficult to settle

Arbitration **The process used when both parties empower a third party to decide the outcome of a dispute.**

Arbitration. Arbitration is the process used when both parties empower a third party to decide the outcome of the dispute. This process is more likely to result in mutually agreeable decisions because of the mutual decision to use arbitration. However, if arbitration is built into a system, like a management-labor contract, the individual arbitration may not be as satisfying to the parties.

Positive aspects of arbitration include:

1. Since the parties agreed to use this method they will probably appreciate the results.
2. The process will keep the parties from engaging in other actions or impasse tactics.
3. The arbitrator is probably trained in the content area of the dispute—like labor arbitrators—and can give reasonable suggestions for resolving the dispute.
4. The process is more accessible than court processes.
5. The process can be used for a number of disputes like contract disagreements, landlord-tenant disputes, and domestic disagreements.

Arbitration is limited, however, in that:

1. It tends to resolve just the content dispute and contributes nothing to the relationship of the parties.
2. It reinforces that the parties cannot solve their own disputes.
3. It also reinforces a win-lose mentality between the parties.

Mediation. It is the simplest explanation mediation used to help the parties to the dispute change their positions so that they can resolve the dispute. The mediator is to facilitate the parties reaching agreement.

There are three obvious advantages to mediation:

1. Because mediation involves the parties to the dispute in deciding the resolution, the parties are more likely to carry out the solutions. Mediation also recognizes that the parties have a relationship that must continue into the future.
2. Because the parties to the conflict work toward a solution together, there is a higher probability that the solutions will be integrative and creative.
3. Mediation is a flexible process adaptable to many conflicts.[19]

A mediation follows the following pattern: decide the agenda, exchange information, negotiate a solution, and reach agreement. There are certain assumptions that should be made if mediation is to be successful:

- conflict is both inevitable and resolvable
- few situations are hopeless
- conformity is not required
- there is some commonality between the parties and some piece of truth on both sides
- the actions of one party affect the other
- present problems are the ones to solve
- there is no "right" answer
- the process used to resolve the issue is of prime importance[20]

There are, of course, downsides to mediation. These include:

1. If the dispute between the parties has escalated so far that the ability to trust the other side is destroyed, a mediation will not work.
2. Too much involvement or too little involvement between the parties might mean that the investment necessary for the mediation to work will not be made.
3. The conflict itself might not warrant the type of commitment required for mediation.

The attorney in the "Profile" on page 520 gives some pointers on how to use arbitration and mediation in conflict situation.

Consultation. Included in this last category of third party intervention techniques is the intervener who trains the parties in alternative ways to relate in the workplace so that conflicts are avoided. This includes consultants to train in team building, peer-mediation, manager-mediators and dual-advocate mediation.

Some examples of what is being used in the workplace to avoid or quickly identify and resolve conflict follows. Guidelines as contained in the "OB in Practice" on page 521 are applicable to any of the techniques discussed.

Common sense rules. Researchers at a conflict resolution center at George Mason University in Virginia devised a "prenegotiation workshop" concept. During this Prenegotiation phase, the parties to the dispute were required to explore the values of their opposing party in the dispute. These values were distinctively

Profile

Kevin Winstead
Labor Attorney
MEDIATION AND ARBITRATION

The use of mediation and arbitration services is becoming more common in today's business world. These forms of resolving conflicts or differences are commonly used in certain contracts, such as labor agreements, securities agreements, and many other commercial settings. Mediation and arbitration are often relatively quick and inexpensive methods for solving disagreements, especially when compared to the high cost and delays associated with litigation in the courts.

Mediation will produce the best results if you go into it with a willingness to resolve the conflict and with an understanding that you may need to compromise. This does not mean that you have to give in on every issue or let the other party have everything they want. However, an unwillingness to bend even a little will usually result in the issue remaining unresolved, and a lot of time and money being wasted on the mediation process. Patience and preparation also help the process be more successful. You should be knowledgeable about the issues being mediated, the facts involved, and just how much you are willing to compromise. Patience is useful because the mediation process usually does not go quickly, taking anywhere from a few hours (for relatively minor disputes) to days or weeks (for more major disputes).

The things that will make a mediation successful are also useful in an arbitration setting. A very thorough understanding of the facts and issues involved is especially important, since the arbitrator's decision will be based on them. The arbitrator will usually have no knowledge of the specifics of your matter before the arbitration meeting; it may help sway the arbitrator to your side if you can show that you know the facts and issues and if you are able to present your side of the matter in a clear and persuasive manner. You should also be honest and forthright with the arbitrator; if you are caught being less than truthful, then you should expect to lose the arbitration and not to be believed by the arbitrator in any future arbitrations.

Arbitrations usually take the form of a hearing, so you may need to have witnesses ready to testify and be prepared to show the arbitrator why he or she should decide in your favor. Arbitration is often a more formal process than mediation, although it is generally much less formal than a court proceeding. If possible, you should receive some training or at least observe some arbitration hearings, before you try to do one yourself.

Most parties agree to let the arbitrator's decision be binding on them, meaning that it is legally enforceable. Some arbitrator's decisions are nonbinding; while not necessarily legally enforceable, they should be given deference by the parties involved, since a court (if the matter were taken there) might well reach the same decision.

different from the interests of their opponent. It was found that such prenegotiation workshops facilitated more settlements. In addition the parties were more satisfied with the settlements, more willing to compromise and cooperate, and had a better opinion of their opponents.[21]

"Just-in-time" intervention.[22] There are a couple of intervention techniques that are a result of *just-in-time* management. Just in time (JIT) management functions with a team concept. Teams of employees, for example, who are manufacturing a product work together with their supplier to deliver the parts to them just in time for them to use the parts for the assembly of the finished product. Physical team work is essential to the ability of a manufacturer to produce with a JIT process.

Just-in-time intervention Teams of employees work together with a team concept.

OB in Practice

Attributes of an Effective Conflict Resolution Process

1. *Clarifies Interests*

   - by encouraging the parties to explore the interests underlying their respective bargaining positions.
   - by facilitating the exploration of common and nonconflicting interests.
   - by communicating each party's interests to the other without unduly exposing anyone to extortion on the basis of such interests.

2. *Builds a Good Working Relationship*

   - by enabling the parties to deal effectively with their differences in the dispute.
   - by fostering the type of relationship the parties would have wanted to have but for the present dispute.
   - by making it easier for the parties to deal with each other next time.

3. *Generates Good Options*

   - by spurring the parties to brainstorm many options before evaluating them and choosing among them.
   - by encouraging the parties to devise ways to create value for mutual gain.

4. *Is Perceived as Legitimate*

   - by not being seen to cause the parties to forfeit legal or other rights disproportionately (i.e., the process shouldn't be seen as itself tilting the balance of power).
   - by not being perceived as contrary to the public interests.
   - by instilling in the parties a sense that the solutions it produces will be fair and equitable.

5. *Is Cognizant of the Parties' Procedural Alternatives*

   - by allowing both sides to develop realistic assessments of their own and the other side's procedural and substantive alternatives.
   - by being more attractive to the parties along whatever side is most important to them (e.g., costs, time, degree of disclosure, nature of outcomes, and quality of compliance).

6. *Improves Communication*

   - by encouraging the questioning and testing of underlying assumptions.
   - by facilitating the understanding and discussion of partisan perceptions.
   - by establishing effective two-way communication between decision makers.

7. *Leads to Wise Commitments*

   - by enabling the parties to devise commitments that are realistic, operational, and compliance-prone.
   - by positioning the parties with efficient recourse to litigation in the event they fail to reach agreement or in the event of non-compliance.

Source: Danny Ertel, "How to Design a Conflict Management Procedure That Fits Your Dispute," *Sloan Management Review,* Summer 1991, pp. 29–42. Reprinted by permission of publisher. Copyright © 1991 by Sloan Management Review Association. All rights reserved.

Borrowing from this process, a consultant can teach *consensus decision making* techniques to teams of employees. The potential problem or conflict is presented to the groups, and it must reach consensus. It can only do so if they work together.

Sometimes facilitators are necessary to help the parties reach consensus. Facilitators guide the discussion, equalize the power balances, and increase the possible communication of the parties.

Peer–mediation, manager–mediator, and dual–advocacy mediation. Some consultants facilitate workplace changes in conflict resolution by preparing employees to take on the role of mediator. Nonmanagement employees are trained by some employers to be asked to mediate disputes in other departments or areas of the organization.[23] The employer is often able to match the mediator to the disputants in age, race, sex, level of the company, et cetera, which can facilitate the mediation.

Employers have also used dual–advocacy mediation. In these instances, a mediator is assigned to both parties to the dispute. The mediator is, in a sense, an advocate of the party they represent. At the same time, the mediator is objective enough to understand the other position and can perhaps facilitate agreement. Los Alamos National Laboratory in New Mexico employed this method of mediation very successfully.[24]

Some employers train managers in mediation techniques. The training involves developing a mediation mindset, learning "active listening" techniques, recognizing the dynamics of group consensus building, using win-win negotiating skills, and allowing for perception biases. Equipped with these mediation skills, managers can recognize potential conflict situations and eliminate them more quickly.[25]

In Fig. 15-8, showing a continuum from high involvement to low involvement by a third party intervener, you can compare intervention techniques. The two parties to a conflict must be willing to involve an outside party to the degree indicated, or the intervention is useless.

Communication

NONVERBAL   From the moment two people come in contact with each other they are communicating. Before the first word is spoken, messages have been sent and received. Unfortunately, very few people think about those unspoken messages and, therefore, may not evaluate them properly.

The image one presents will have an impact upon the reception one gets from another. In the workplace, for example, a professional image is cultivated and expected. As we saw in earlier chapters, a woman had to find a way to appear in the workplace dressed appropriately for the job, but not inappropriately for her sex.

Nonverbal communication also includes body language. In U.S. culture it is a sign of honesty to look someone in the eye when talking to them. It's a sign of being closed-minded to sit back with your arms folded during a discussion. Such external manifestations of internal thoughts can send more powerful messages than the spoken word.[26]

As seen in earlier chapters, stereotyping and prejudice can cause communication problems. Prejudging the person one sees because of his or her age, sex, race, physical disability, or sexual orientation can lead to poor communication. If one party assumes certain negative things about the other only because of his or her physical appearance, he or she may then evaluate any future messages from that person in that light.

Training employees in conflict resolution gives them the skills to diffuse or eliminate potential conflict early on.

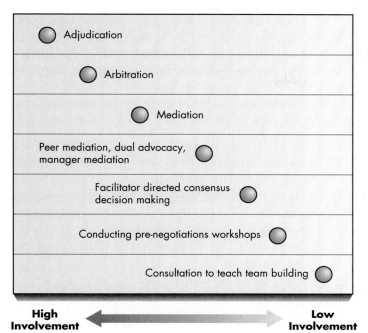

FIGURE 15-8
Involvement Continuum
for Third-party
Interveners

An equally inaccurate perception is giving someone a *halo*. That is, because of having a *favorable* impression of someone for one reason, the continued perception of that person is positive no matter what they do.

Some guidelines to use when trying to be accurate in your perceptions follow:

1. Knowing yourself makes it easier to see others accurately.
2. Your own characteristics affect your ability to perceive other's characteristics.
3. If you accept yourself, you are more likely to see favorable characteristics in others.
4. Accuracy in perceiving others is not a stand-alone skill. It depends on how sensitive you are to others' feelings.[27]

As discussed in an earlier chapter, the cultural context of some types of nonverbal communication must be understood. Eye contact, bowing, waving one's hand, or turning one's back may all mean different things in different cultures. If one is going to communicate effectively, the cultural context will need to be explored.

VERBAL Verbal communication, oddly enough, actually begins with listening. A child learns to speak by listening to others speak. It is interesting that a child's education is focused on speaking, reading, and writing and very seldom on listening. Listening means different things to different people:

- *Hearing* is the physiological process by which sound waves are received by the ear and transferred to the brain.
- *Information gathering* is listening for the facts, it involves no evaluation of what is heard.
- *Defensive listening* is hearing with an assumption that what you hear is a threat.

- *Offensive listening* is hoping to turn what you hear against your opponent.
- *Polite listening* is really just waiting for the other person to finish so you can start talking to the other party.
- *Active listening* requires understanding, empathy, and active involvement.

Techniques used to teach someone to listen actively are very beneficial in improving communication. Some do's and don'ts for active listening follow.

- Do grasp what the person is saying from his or her point of view. Listen for the content of the message (the "what") as well as the feeling or attitude of the party (the "why").
- Do test your understanding of the whole message you've received by restating what the other person has said and get agreement that it is actually the message—both in content and feeling.
- Don't try to change the other person's way of looking at whatever you are discussing.
- Don't pass judgment on what the other person is saying—either critical or favorable judgment. For active listening only comprehension is required, not agreement or disagreement.

TIME AND SPACE   We communicate in the workplace by other symbols or signals. How we deal with time is one way. Being on time in our culture signals competency and respect. Management being late for an appointment or a negotiating session with a union, for example, can communicate an unwillingness to reach agreement. In cultures with a cyclical vision of time, being on time does not mean as much.

The location and size of one's office often communicates the importance of the person to the organization. Also, having a private office as opposed to sharing space can be seen as a symbol of success. In companies that are changing the way they organize the workplace, from a pyramid to an inverted pyramid, walls for private offices are coming down. Shared spaces by all employees—managers and line workers—are sending a powerful message of participatory management.

Employee Discipline

TRADITIONAL DISCIPLINE   The most common source of conflict in the workplace is the conflict present between a manager and an employee who has violated some workplace rule or policy. The typical, time-honored approach to employee discipline as described below is certainly the most common approach still in the workplace.

1. *Give employees prior notice.* The employee should know the rules and the penalty for violating the rules.
2. *Make the rules reasonable.* The rules or regulations should have a relationship to the efficient and safe operation of the organization.
3. *Investigate the violation.* The facts as to what the employee did and why should be thoroughly explored.
4. *Treat the employee fairly.* The discipline should be administered in a fair and nondiscriminatory manner. The punishment should fit the crime not the criminal.[28]

NONTRADITIONAL DISCIPLINE   Enlightened managers, however, have employed some of the conflict resolutions techniques listed above and redesigned employee discipline in the workplace.

Following the approach laid out above, these managers add a twist of their own.[29]

1. *Give employees prior notice.* Employees should not only learn the rules, they should help write the rules.

2. *Make the rules reasonable.* If they have invested themselves in formulating the rules, employees are more likely to understand the reasons behind the rules, and the rules will relate to workplace needs.

3. *Investigate the violation.* Managers should keep up with an employee's performance. This will cause any problems to be detected early, and with appropriate feedback, the problems will correct themselves. It will also make it easier to investigate a particular problem because the relationship between the manager and employee is well established.

4. *Treat the employee fairly.* Even if this means imposing discipline, it should be done. Many companies operating in a team environment will let the team discipline one of their own members. After all, it is the team who is harmed by the employee's rule infraction.[30]

As you can see in Fig. 15-9, when you put employees into an active role in the workplace, even the disciplining of employees changes.

INCORRECT DISCIPLINE   Managers increase conflict in the workplace by choosing the wrong kinds of discipline. Some of the mistakes managers make include the following:

- *Punitive discipline.* Punitive discipline, sometimes referred to as *negative discipline,* is discipline through fear. Punitive discipline often involves threats, harassment, intimidation, and browbeating. Widespread in the industries of the early twentieth century, punitive discipline is little used today, largely because of union protection and greater acceptance of human–relations techniques.

- *Negative feedback.* Some managers give employees feedback only when unsatisfactory performance occurs and fail to provide positive reinforcement when performance improves or when a job is done well. Feedback should be both positive and negative, depending on the employee's level of performance.

- *Late intervention.* Perhaps best labeled *procrastination discipline,* this form of discipline takes place when managers allow a problem to drag on until it reaches a serious level. The problem may begin as a minor one, but inattention to the situation allows the unsatisfactory performance to become habitual and thus difficult to change.

Traditional	Nontraditional
1. Give notice of rules.	1. Employee teams develop rules
2. Make the rules reasonable.	2. Rules are reasonable to employees because they helped to write them.
3. Investigate the violation.	3. Document employees' performance.
4. Treat the employee fairly.	4. Let the team members discipline their own.

FIGURE 15-9
Employee Discipline

- *Inadequate definition.* During counseling to rectify a performance problem, a manager may tell an employee that he or she is "uncooperative," "disloyal," or not a "team player." Coaching a performance problem in such vague and ambiguous terms only serves to confuse and frustrate the employee.

- *Labeling employees, not behavior.* Unsatisfactory performance may result in an employee's being labeled lazy, shiftless, or a goof-off by the manager. Such labeling has two major problems. First, the employee may carry the label over to other jobs and work units, and the label may serve as a self-fulfilling prophecy. Second, such descriptions focus on the employee and not on the act of unsatisfactory performance that must be addressed.

- *Misplaced responsibility.* Managers often have to realize that they themselves sometimes contribute to the performance problems of their employees. When the entire responsibility for changing behavior falls on the employee and improvement does not occur, the manager applies further disciplinary action. But without a change in supervisory behavior, a change in employee behavior is unlikely.

Positive Discipline

Discipline that corrects employee behavior through support, respect, and people-oriented leadership is known as *positive discipline*. Positive discipline relies on management's desire to truly rehabilitate an employee with a performance problem, and an employee's willingness to accept personal responsibility for that problem. Positive discipline involves the following elements:

1. *Clarify who administers the discipline.* While ideally an immediate supervisor should be the appropriate party administering discipline, in large organizations managers often rely on a centralized human resources department for such decisions. Centralization contributes to a more uniform application of discipline but also removes control over employee performance from a manager responsible for that performance. To reconcile these two issues, control and uniformity, many organizations allow an immediate supervisor to impose the first layer of discipline—a warning or reprimand—and allow the human resources department to impose more severe forms of discipline—suspensions and dismissals.

2. *Define work expectations and communicate rules and regulations.* Unless an employer defines good performance, an employee cannot be held responsible for *bad* performance. Likewise, the rules for conduct in the workplace should be communicated to the employees. The clearer the statement, the easier it is for employees to meet the employer's expectations.

3. *Collect performance information.* Get your facts straight before initiating discipline. Concrete, indisputable examples of unsatisfactory performance should be presented to the employee. An employee is more likely to improve behavior if the employer can demonstrate what *behavior* is the problem. Vague accusations of being uncooperative or insubordinate may lead an employee into believing all that is involved is a clash of personalities between the employee and the supervisor.

4. *Use progressive discipline and corrective counseling.* Positive discipline should include a progressive effort to correct behavior by imposing the least

OB in Practice

The Hot Stove Rule

One effective way to approach the disciplinary process is to follow what is popularly known as the hot-stove rule, which suggests that applying discipline is much like touching a hot stove:

- The burn is *immediate;* the cause is clear-cut.
- The person had a *warning* knowing that the stove was hot; the person should have known what would happen if it was touched.
- The burn is *consistent;* all who touch the stove are burned every time it is touched.
- The burn is *impersonal;* the stove will burn anyone, regardless of whom he or she is.

Like touching a hot stove, the application of discipline should also be immediate, with warning, consistent, and impersonal. These guidelines are consistent with the positive approach to discipline. Supervisors who follow these guidelines should experience less tension and anxiety when applying discipline and should learn to view discipline as a supervisory responsibility rather than as a personal dilemma.

Source: Michael R. Carrell, Norbert F. Elbert, and Robert D. Hatfield, *Human Resource Management,* 5th ed., Englewood Cliffs, NJ, Prentice-Hall, 1995, pp. 702–711.

---

oppressive penalty commensurate with the offense and increasing the penalty with each repetitive unsatisfactory act. Penalties alone, however, may not resolve the problem. The final step of positive discipline is corrective counseling. Through corrective counseling, a supervisor identifies the problem but places the burden upon the employee to come up with the solution. For example, if the employee's problem is tardiness, the supervisor may require the employee in corrective counseling to arrive at a solution. It is far more likely that the employee will adhere to the solution he offers than the one imposed upon him.[31]

CONCLUSIONS AND APPLICATIONS

- Power, the use of power, or the lack of power is at the center of any conflict. In the workplace, balancing power can lead to resolving conflict in a positive manner.
- The types of power in the workplace stem from gaining knowledge or an expertise in a certain field: from personal contacts, from developing communication skills, and from the position one holds in the organization. The most effective power base is one that uses all four types of power appropriately.
- Conflict in the workplace arises when at least two interdependent parties perceive that they have incompatible goals and scarce resources, and there is interference from each other on achieving these goals or gaining the resources.

- Conflict is not an abnormal happening caused by a failure to communicate or personality clashes. It is a normal result of human interaction which, when handled properly, can be the source of growth and the finding of creative solutions to real problems.

- Five typical reactions to conflict in the workplace are: avoidance, accommodation, competition, compromise, and collaboration. Avoidance and accommodation are used to avoid or deescalate the conflict. Neither resolves the conflict. Competition, compromise, and collaboration are used to engage the conflict and, if possible, resolve it. Of the five ways to react to conflict, collaboration is the most effective way to resolve conflict constructively.

- When trying to resolve conflict, it is helpful to reduce the elements of the conflict by recognizing the *interdependency* of the parties, balancing any unequal power between the parties, and recognizing there can be more than one goal of the conflict. The parties should examine both the relational and content goals of the conflict to find common ground. They can clarify goals; separate long-term from short-term goals; fractionalize the content goals and resolve smaller parts of the conflict; and set collaborative goals.

- To resolve conflicts you must be able to accurately *assess* the conflict; *control* your emotions, *engage* in active listening, and *cooperate* with the other party, even if the other party does not seem to want to cooperate.

- Negotiation is often used to resolve conflict. *Competitive negotiation* is what most people think of when they use the term negotiation. This is when the two parties *barter* across a table, in a give and take manner to end the conflict with a win-lose scenario. *Collaborative negotiations* are designed to separate the parties from the issues and join the parties in finding mutually satisfactory resolution of those issues in a win-win scenario.

- Third-party intervention techniques used to resolve conflicts include litigation and arbitration, in which the third party decides the issues in conflict; mediation by outside parties or by fellow employees, in which the parties resolve the conflict with the help of a third party; and new work techniques, in which employees apply the skills necessary to resolve conflict on their own.

- Communication involves more than verbal communication. Active listening is an essential element for good communication. Understanding the cultural or generational context of speech and body language is also necessary for good communication.

- One common source of conflict in the workplace stems from disciplining employees. Techniques for empowering employees to involve them in the decisions of the organization can lessen the need for employee discipline. Consistent, fair, and clear enforcement of rules in the workplace can go a long way to reduce conflict.

REVIEW QUESTIONS

1. What are the types of power in the workplace and how are they acquired?

2. Define conflict and describe each element of a conflict.

3. Compare destructive and productive conflict and give examples of both.
4. Describe the five styles of conflict behavior.
5. How can you reduce the elements of a conflict?
6. Explain the two approaches to negotiations and how each works.
7. What are the various types of third-party interventions in conflict resolution?
8. List the various ways people communicate.
9. What approach to employee discipline might lessen the incidents of conflict over the disciplining?

DISCUSSION QUESTIONS

1. Discuss how developing and using the different types of power can be done without causing conflict.
2. Review the examples of metaphors used to describe conflict. Discuss which image you use most often and why? Can you learn to rethink those images?
3. Experiment with your response to a conflict situation to see if you can direct your partner toward a particular conflict style.
4. What are all of the various types of goals possible within one conflict? Describe each.
5. What steps can you take to begin to resolve a conflict? How will you know what method to use?
6. Describe the processes known as distributive negotiation and principled negotiations, adjudication, arbitration, and mediation. Compare and contrast these methods of conflict resolution and determine which is most effective and why.
7. Describe active listening and the advantages of such communication.
8. Compare traditional and nontraditional approaches to employee discipline.

CASE STUDY

Mid-America Banking, Inc.

Mid-America Banking and Trust, Inc., has a main branch in a racially mixed urban area with a number of poor, elderly customers on fixed income. It has six branch offices in the suburbs surrounding the urban area. The suburbs are, by and large, segregated areas peopled by the following ethnic and racial groups: three suburbs are upper and middle class white, Anglo-Saxon, Protestant; one suburb is well-to-do African-American; one suburb is Latino of mixed economic levels; and one suburb is poor, Asian-American.

The Mid-America's employees used to be mostly white men and women, with the men having the most seniority. Over the last ten years, however, the company has made a real effort to hire a culturally diverse work force and to promote employees to reflect a more representative management staff.

A number of white, male managers have been passed over for promotion as branch managers of the suburban branches that are now managed by a Latino woman, an Asian-American man, and an African-American man.

The Bank auditors have found a discrepancy in the records of the branch bank managed by the Asian-American man. When questioned about the discrepancy by his superior, the manager apologized and quit on the spot. His resignation sent shock waves throughout the organization. Some employees and customers believed he was fired; others believed he quit because he had taken the money.

The morale of the employees at his branch was already low when the head office sent a new branch manager, a white male, who previously had been an assistant branch manager in an all-white suburb branch. The employees of this branch asked for a face-to-face meeting with the Bank's CEO.

You are Mid-America's Personnel Director and are called by the Bank CEO and asked for advice on how to handle this problem.

1. Using the process outlined in this chapter, how would you advise your CEO to proceed?
2. If you are tapped as a third-party intervener, which technique or techniques could you use in this situation?
3. How could a communication problem contribute to the conflict presented in this case? What might have prevented that communication problem?

EXPERIENTIAL EXERCISE 1

Conflict Resolution

Purpose

To gain experience in analyzing a conflict to ascertain the best resolution technique to use and to gain experience in using a conflict resolution technique.

Task

Step 1: Divide the class into five groups. Each group will be assigned one of the following conflict resolution techniques: distributive negotiations, principled negotiations, adjudication/arbitration, mediation, and consultation.

Step 2: Assign the following roles within each group:

- negotiator, judge, mediator, or consultant
- Party A: with great power
- Party B: with little power

Step 3: Using the fact situation below, do two things:

1. As a group, detail the analysis, thought process, factual issues, et cetera, that you must have used for your group to reach the conclusion that your assigned conflict resolution technique is the right one to use. You may create any facts you need, but you are bound by these same facts in resolving the conflict.
2. Assume your respective roles and use the conflict resolution technique assigned to resolve the conflict.

Fact Situation

A family-owned business has about twenty managers and supervisors and about 250 union employees. It has always had a good relationship with its employees. Because of a business decision made by the owner to drop one of the six items it manufactures, approximately one-sixth of the employee positions must be cut out. The contract has never addressed layoffs, because it had never happened at this company before. The owners want to resolve the issue quickly by laying off the employees they pick. The union wants to have a say in who is laid off. Tempers are starting to rise. The conflict needs to be resolved.

EXPERIENTIAL EXERCISE 2

Your Conflict Style

Purpose

To discover how different relationships and fact situations will cause you to use different conflict behavior styles.

Task

Step 1: Imagine that you have been discovered in the act of doing something the other person considers wrong in one of these five cases:

1. By your life partner in your home.
2. By your boss in the office.
3. By a police officer on the highway.
4. By your coworker at a seminar.
5. By your child in a store.

Step 2: Pick at least two fact situations and develop a conflict scenario in which you respond to the question, "What do you think you are doing?" using each of these response styles: avoidance, accommodating, contentions, compromising, and collaborative.

Step 3: Using the same fact situations, now imagine you are the other party. Start the dialogues using each of the conflict behavior styles. Assume you are met with a contentious response in each case.

Step 4: Analyze what you have learned about controlling a conflict situation.

 Take It to the Net   **You can find this chapter's World Wide Web exercise at:**
http://www.prenhall.com/carrell

CHAPTER 16

Organizational Structure and Design

CHAPTER OBJECTIVES

1. To understand what organization structure is.
2. To explain the differences between mechanistic and organic structures.
3. To describe the characteristics of a bureaucracy.
4. To explain the relationship among organizational strategy, structure, and effectiveness.
5. To realize the importance of departmentation, unit coordination, and lateral coordination.
6. To explain how improvements in information technology can increase a manager's span of control and also serve as a coordinating mechanism.
7. To understand what organization design is.
8. To explain organizational effectiveness.
9. To define a matrix organization design and summarize its advantages and disadvantages.
10. To discuss contemporary approaches to organization design.
11. To understand what a horizontal corporation is.
12. To describe the concept of a boundaryless organization.

Ralph Larsen, CEO, Johnson & Johnson, Inc.

Marvin Woodall likes to keep his distance from the Tower. The independent-minded president of a small startup unit of Johnson & Johnson (J&J) prefers to run his 130-person staff from a low-slung building in rustic Warren, New Jersey, nearly an hour's drive from his parent company's gleaming 15-story headquarters in New Brunswick. If Woodall wants to develop a new marketing campaign or fly to Europe to check on operations, he does not think twice. "I don't ask permission—I just go," drawls the fifty-four-year-old Texan. "I'm almost never distracted by J&J management."

Most top managers would resent being called distractions, but at Johnson & Johnson, the presidents of its 166 separate companies are not just encouraged to act independently—they are expected to. These presidents may travel at will, decide who will work for them, what products they will produce, and which customers they will sell to.

As early as the 1930s, J&J's top man-

agement pushed the idea of decentralization. Believing that smaller, self-governing units were more manageable, quicker to react to their markets, and more accountable, the son of J&J's cofounder encouraged business units to operate independently. The J&J approach "provides a sense of ownership and responsibility that you simply cannot get any other way," states Chief Executive Ralph Larsen.

After fifty years, J&J has become a model of how to make decentralization work. However, the system is not static. J&J's management has had to fine-tune its approach over the years to achieve a balance between an entrepreneurial spirit and organization structure.

Larsen reports that J&J is now in the midst of one such adjustment: sharing more services among units, reducing redundancies, and smoothing customer relations. One of Larsen's concerns is overhead. J&J's autonomously operated divisions can lead to duplication in certain functions. In fact, J&J's overhead is 41 percent of sales as compared with 30 percent and 28 percent for two rivals, Merck and Bristol-Myers Squibb, respectively. As a result, Larsen is relentlessly attacking duplication. Despite this situation, J&J's earnings increased 15 percent to $1.5 billion on a sales rise of 11 percent to $12 billion.

Although companies such as IBM, PepsiCo, and DuPont are adopting J&J's approach to decentralization, the J&J concept has risks. In this free-wheeling culture, company presidents who stumble often find themselves swept aside. Chances for advancement can be hard to come by, especially in a smaller operating unit, because many individual companies want to hire only from within. Then there's the issue of supervision: Operating companies sometimes make costly and embarrassing mistakes that could have been avoided with more home–office guidance.

Decentralization can be troublesome in sales. Dozens of J&J representatives call on customers such as Wal-Mart or Kmart. Big retailers, however, want to simplify their dealings with manufacturers by reducing the number of contacts.

Decentralization "is not an end unto itself," indicates Larsen as he works toward having the 166 companies share more functions, but "we will never give up the principle of decentralization." It is little wonder that Larsen wants to stick with decentralization. Since 1980, J&J's yearly profit gains have averaged over 19 percent, while annual sales have risen by more than 10 percent in five of those years.[1]

WHAT IS ORGANIZATIONAL STRUCTURE?

J&J's chief executive, Ralph Larsen, is concerned about organizing his company. Larsen wants to achieve a balance between an entrepreneurial spirit and organization structure. Larsen is concentrating on reducing J&J's overhead expenses while still utilizing a decentralized organization structure.

In this chapter we describe both the formal and informal aspects of organization structure, discuss the advantages and disadvantages of organization charts, and identify the structural elements of work specialization, centralization and decentralization, formalization, and complexity. Next, we discuss aspects of an organization's vertical structure: responsibility and authority, chain of command, the scalar principle, span of management control, and line-staff relationships. Finally, we examine methods of coordination: departmentation, differentiation and integration, unit coordination mechanisms, lateral coordination mechanisms, and information technology.

Organization structure results from an organizing process in which an organization's resources are allocated and deployed to achieve strategic objectives. Organizing involves: assigning the organization's division of labor into specific jobs and departments, creating formal lines of authority, and developing mechanisms to coordinate diverse organization tasks.

The organizing process results in an organization structure which defines how tasks are defined and resources deployed. Organization structure is defined as:[2]

1. The formal tasks that are assigned to individuals and departments.
2. Formal reporting relationships including the number of hierarchical levels, managers' span of control, decision responsibilities, and lines of authority.
3. Systems to effectively coordinate employees both within and across departments.

In essence, organization structure is the manner in which an organization divides its labor into specific tasks and achieves coordination among these tasks.[3] Two types of structures exist in an organization: formal and informal. A formal structure consists of the processes and systems which are designed by management to achieve organizational objectives. An informal organization structure consists of a variety of arrangements that are usually neither planned nor written, but which tend to emerge over time. These include patterns of communication, power, and influence which often characterize how an organization may actually function.[4] For example, a secretary may have tremendous informal power because she has access to the boss. This secretary will develop followers who attempt to gain access to the boss through her. Also, when an individual knows more than anyone else about how to use a computer software package such as "Lotus 1-2-3," then this individual has tremendous power to influence others in the organization, although he or she may not be granted any formal authority. Even though an individual may report to a manager, they may not recognize the manager's authority and may go to someone else for needed opinions or technical information.

An organization's informal structure originates from informal groups that develop relationships on the basis of friendships or common interests. An informal group may form while individuals are at work or when they get together away from work. Participating on a bowling team or a softball team are examples of an informal group formed away from work. Informal work groups often provide important and accurate information to those individuals in the informal communication network. The informal structure helps to satisfy the social needs of individuals and can often provide a sense of self-esteem. Positive benefits occur when the work group's cohesiveness assists a manager in keeping a group working towards its objectives. Negative benefits develop from informal groups that are extremely cohesive but do not share the organization's objectives. Also, informal groups may resist change. Managers should be aware that an organization has an informal structure that may be very powerful. Managers must learn to manage informal groups. Chapter 11 provides insights into how informal groups may be effectively managed.

Organization structure
The formal process that allocates and deploys the organization's resources to achieve strategic objectives.

The "OB in Practice" opposite describes how an organization has become more innovative by utilizing its informal structure.

In this chapter, we concentrate on the formal aspects of organization structure. An organization's formal structure can be described by an organization chart, which indicates the allocation of tasks and responsibilities to individuals and departments within the organization, designates formal reporting relationships, defines the number of levels in the organizational hierarchy, and groups individuals together into departments. Figure 16-1 illustrates an organization chart for the commercial packaging division of Southwest Paperboard, Inc., a producer of specialty packaging materials.

Managers have debated the advantages and disadvantages of using organization charts for years. A major advantage is that the chart shows employees how various pieces of the organization fit together and how their own tasks relate to the whole operation. Employees know who reports to whom and what to do

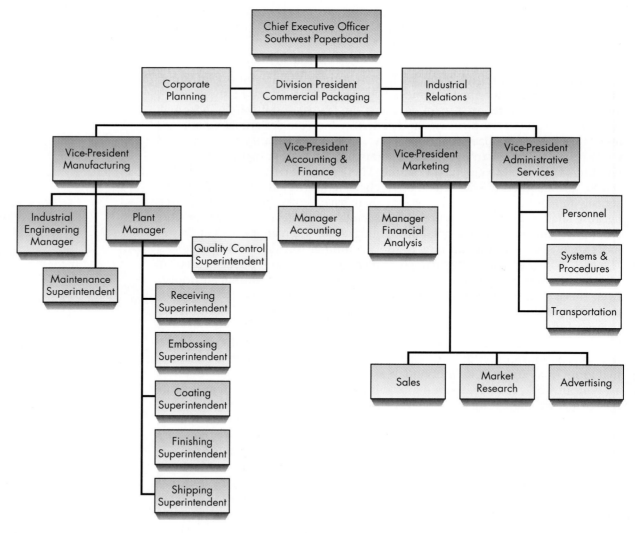

FIGURE 16-1 Organization Chart for Commercial Packaging Division of Southwest Paperboard, Inc.

OB in Practice

Reaping Benefits from an Informal Structure

Despite a history of fast growth and annual revenues of nearly $2 billion, Becton Dickinson's CEO, Raymond Gilmartin, began exploring ways to effectively use its informal structure. While the company still maintains traditional functions such as marketing, sales, and manufacturing—employees are being encouraged to take the initiative and form teams to innovate and go after business in new ways. Gilmartin states, "We wanted to create a hierarchy of ideas in which employees would say—this is the right thing to do here—instead of we are going to do this because I am the boss."

Rather than directing strategy from the top, Gilmartin presents a very broad vision and then allows his employees to:

- Develop proprietary ideas
- Beat the competition to market with these ideas
- Formulate business strategies for their own divisions

In 1990, Becton Dickinson developed a new instrument called the Bactec 860, designed to process blood samples. A team leader was assigned and immediately put together a project team of engineers, marketers, manufacturers, and suppliers. While the group eventually launched the Bactec 860 some 25 percent faster than its previous best efforts, Gilmartin wasn't satisfied.

There was still too much time-wasting debate between marketing and engineering over product specifications. Marketing argued that Bactec 860 needed more features to please the customer, while engineering countered that the features would be too costly and take too long to design. Further inquiry led management to the nub of the problem: Because the team leader reported to the head of engineering, he didn't have sufficient clout to resolve the conflict between the two sides. Today the company makes sure all its team leaders have access to a division head, which gives them the authority to settle disputes between different functions.

What's to keep an informal system from veering off in the wrong direction? Gilmartin believes something as simple as "focus on the customer" can do the job.

When people move from one team to another, they and their companies have to think about careers and pay in new ways. It's likely that tomorrow's workers and managers, instead of slowly climbing the ladder, will make more lateral moves, picking up expertise in different functions like marketing or manufacturing. For those who do well on teams, Becton Dickinson is trying out so-called lateral promotions, rotating, say, a financial person into a marketing or manufacturing job. In one division last year, the company rotated ten managers out of fifty. These people got a raise and change of title, just as they would with a regular promotion, but they weren't necessarily put in charge of any more people.

Source: Adapted from Brian Dumaine, "The Bureaucracy Busters," *Fortune,* June 17, 1991, pp. 36–50.

with a particular problem. The chart also helps managers to detect potential gaps in productivity or duplication of tasks.

A serious disadvantage of the organization chart is that it does not and cannot describe everything about an organization's structure. For example, the chart does not indicate informal channels of communication or show who has the most informal responsibility and authority. Employees may infer that the status of power of a particular manager or executive is based on the distance of that individual's box from the CEO's box. Organization charts can also become out-dated very quickly. In fact, many organizations are changing their organization charts because of ever-changing constellations of teams and projects.[5] For exam-ple, the Eastman Chemical Company, a division of Eastman Kodak, which has spun off as a separate company in January 1994, refers to their organization chart as the "pizza chart," because it looks like a pizza with a lot of pepperoni sitting on it. The president is the pepperoni in the center. Other pepperoni are cross-functional teams responsible for managing a business, a geographic area, a func-tion, or a "core competence" in a specific technology or area, such as innova-tion. The spaces around them are where collaborative interaction is supposed to occur. Some companies, such as NovaCare, the largest provider of rehabilitation care in the United States, have flipped their pyramidal organizations upside down. When highly dispersed nodes of service operations or customer contact must ineract with other directly and frequently, another form described as a "spider's web" because of the lightness yet completness of its interconnection structures is used. Arthur Andersen is an excellent example of a company that uses the spider's web. Management scholars have also devised certain types of organization charts. For example, Charles Handy has designed an organization chart as a shamrock image. Its three leaves symbolize the joining forces of core employees, external contractors, and part-time staffers. James Brian Quinn thought up the starburst to reflect the company that splits off units like shoot-ing stars. D. Quinn Mills suggests that organizations should form loosely related "clusters" or teams to carry out specific tasks.[6] Figure 16-2 illustrates these new forms of organization charts.

Efficiency or Flexibility: Mechanistic vs. Organic Structures

Generally, organization structures differ from one another along a dimension ranging from mechanistic to organic.[7]

Mechanistic structure
A system that stresses rules, policies, and procedures; techniques for making decisions are specified, and well-documented control systems are emphasized.

Organic structure
Procedures are minimal and work tasks are broad and interdependent.

As indicated in Fig. 16-3, a *mechanistic structure* stresses rules, policies, and procedures; techniques for making decisions are specified; and well-documented control systems are emphasized. The mechanistic structure results in a man-agement emphasis on the routine for efficiency. Wholly mechanistic structures are machinelike and much the same as Weber's bureaucratic organization form, described later in this chapter.

In the *organic structure,* procedures are minimal and are not formalized. Work tasks are broad and interdependent. and are continually modified and redefined by means of mutual adjustment. Communication involves information and advice and is both horizontal and vertical. Control is enhanced by the adoption of professional routines, standards, and procedures. Organic structures are more like living organisms, because they are innovative and can adapt to changing conditions. Because of their flexibility, organic structures lack the stability that allows more mechanistic structures to efficiently perform routine work.

An organization's structure may fit at any point along the mechanistic-organic dimension. The more mechanistic the structure, the more efficient but less flexible it will be. The more organic the structure, the more flexible but less efficient it will be.

Many U.S. auto firms, facing stiff competition from the Japanese, have changed from mechanistic structures to become more innovative, flexible, and participative. Ford, GM, and Chrysler have eliminated unnecessary rules and procedures, reduced centralized staffs, and developed small autonomous work teams.[8]

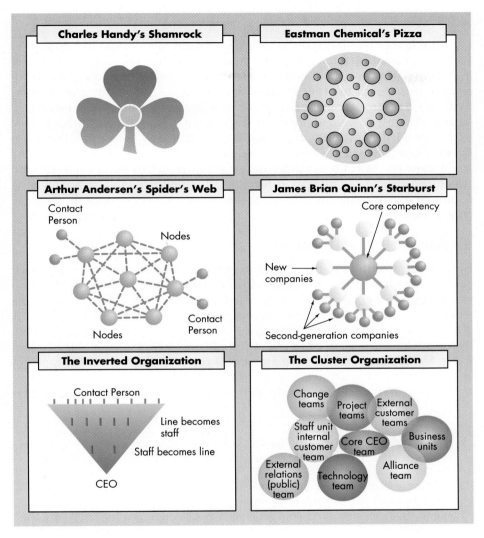

FIGURE 16-2

New Forms of
Organizational Charts

Source: Adapted from James
Brian Quinn, *Intelligent
Enterprise*, New York, The Free
Press, 1992; Quinn Mills,
Rebirth of the Corporation, New
York, John Wiley, 1991; Charles
Handy, *The Age of Paradox,*
Boston, Harvard Business
School Press, 1994.

FIGURE 16-3 Mechanistic vs. Organic Structures

Item	Mechanistic	Organic
Hierarchy of control	Centralized	Decentralized
Rules and procedures; Division of labor	Specific roles are prescribed for each employee. Tasks are highly specialized and remain rigidly defined unless changed by top management	Generalized roles are accepted. Tasks are interdependent and are continually adjusted and refined through interaction.
Coordination and control	Communication is primarily vertical, between superior and subordinate. Control, authority, and communication are hierarchical.	Communication is both vertical and horizontal, depending on where needed information resides. Control, authority, and communication are a network.
Managerial techniques	Instructions and decisions issued by superiors. Requests for decisions come from subordinates.	Instructions and advice take the form of information along all levels.

Source: Adapted from Tom Burns and G. M. Stalker, *The Management of Innovation,* London, Tavistock Publications, 1961, pp. 119–122.

Bureaucracy

Bureaucracy A system within an organization based on division of labor, hierarchical control, promotion by merit, and administration by rule.

The term *bureaucracy* has taken on a negative meaning in today's organization and is associated with red tape, rigid rules and procedures, sluggishness, and inefficiency. However, Max Weber, a German sociologist, considered a bureaucracy to be superior to other forms of designs because of its division of labor, hierarchical control, promotion by merit with careers for employees, and administration by rule. Weber argued that large organizations would thrive if they relied upon legal authority, logic, and order.[9] Figure 16-4 describes the seven essential characteristics of Weber's bureaucracy.

Weber was correct in his prediction that organizations using a bureaucratic structure, or some variation of its form, would dominate modern society. The dominant organizations have been bureaucracies.[10] However, most modern day bureaucracies have a number of dysfunctions that are described in Fig. 16-5.

Matching Strategy and Structure

James Bryan Quinn of Dartmouth College has defined strategy as "the pattern or plan that integrates an organization's major goals, policies, and action sequences into a cohesive whole."[11] A well-conceived strategy addresses three areas of concern: distinctive competence, scope, and resource deployment.[12] A distinctive competence is something the organization does exceptionally well. Nucor is acknowledged to be the most cost-efficient steel producer in the United States. Nucor's distinctive competence in low-cost steel making is the company's unique capacity to promote efficiency-seeking at all levels within the company.[13] The scope of a strategy specifies the range of markets in which an organization

Figure 16-4

Characteristics of Weber's Ideal Bureaucracy

---

1. *Rules and Procedures.* A system of rules and procedures defines the duties of employees and is strictly enforced so that the actions of all members of the organization are controlled and predictable.

2. *Division of labor.* Tasks are clearly divided among employees who have the competence and authority to carry them out.

3. *Hierarchy of authority.* Each position reports to a position one level higher in the hierarchy. This creates a chain of command (which later was called a *scalar chain*) in which each member of the organization is supervised by a single higher-ranking individual except the top position, which usually reports to a board of directors or the owners.

4. *Technical competence.* The selection and promotion of organization members are based on technical competence and training. This dictum ensures that individuals are qualified to do their jobs and enhances predictability and control. Favoritism, nepotism, and friendship are specifically excluded from the process of selection and promotion.

5. *Separation of ownership.* Employees, especially managers, should not share in the ownership of the organization. This ensures that employees will make decisions in the best interests of the organization rather than for their own interests.

6. *Rights and property of the position.* The rights and control over property associated with an office or position belong to the organization, not to the person who holds the office. This also prevents the use of a position for personal ends.

7. *Documentation.* All administrative decisions, rules, and actions are detailed in writing to provide a continuous record of the organization's activities.

Source: Adapted from Max Weber, *The Theory of Social and Economic Organizations,* trans. by A. M. Henderson and Talcott Parsons, New York, Oxford University Press, 1947; James M. Higgins, *The Management Challenge,* New York, Macmillan, 1991, pp. 42–43; Richard L. Daft, *Organization Theory and Design,* 4th ed., St. Paul, MN, West Publishing, 1991, pp. 156–157.

FIGURE 16-5 Characteristics of Weber's Ideal Bureaucracy and Some Associated Dysfunctions

Characteristics of Weber's ideal bureaucracy	Associated dysfunctions identified by critics
Labor is specialized so each person has clear authority and responsibility.	Overspecialization stimulates a divergence of interests that lead to conflict.
Offices and positions are arranged in a hierarchy of authority.	A very formal hierarchy creates inflexibility in following "official" channels.
Members are selected and promoted on the basis of technical competence.	Bureaucracies become political systems serving an elite corps of managers.
Members have administrative careers and work on a fixed salary.	Conformity to the organization's ways can be detrimental to one's mental health.
Members are subject to rules and control that are strict and impersonal and are applied universally.	Rules become ends in themselves: Rules can only specify minimum requirements.

Source: John R. Schermerhorn, Jr., James G. Hunt, Richard N. Osborn, *Managing Organization Behavior,* 5th ed., New York, John Wiley & Sons, 1994, p. 707. Copyright © 1994. Reprinted by permission of John Wiley & Sons, Inc.

will compete. Hershey has restricted its scope to the confectionery business while its major competitor, M&M/Mars, had adopted a broader scope by competing in the pet-food business and the electronics industry, among others.[14]

The resource deployment component of strategy involves the decision of how a firm will distribute its resources across the areas in which it competes. Raytheon has used profits from its large defense-contracting businesses to support growth in its publishing (D. C. Heath) and appliance (Amana and Speed Queen) businesses. Raytheon could have chosen to reinvest these profits in its defense business but chose, instead, a different deployment.[15]

In a classic study of seventy large American corporations, Alfred Chandler concluded that changes in an organization's external environment require modifications in its strategies for dealing with the environment. These strategic changes in turn necessitate modifications in organizational structure, so that it is consistent with the revised strategy. In essence, Chandler states that changes in an organization's strategy without structural adjustment leads to economic inefficiency. According to Chandler, structure follows strategy.[16] Chandler provides an example by using Henry Ford's venture into farm tractors during the 1930s. In an attempt to find substitutes for the declining automobile market of the 1930s, Ford's engineers designed and built an inexpensive tractor that had the potential for competing with existing tractors on the market. Although the design was appropriate and the quality was high, Ford attempted to sell the tractors through his car dealerships. These dealers were principally located in cities and were inexperienced in farm needs. The new tractor failed commercially until Ford designed a new structure (a marketing structure that focused on tractors) that was consistent with its strategy.[17] Additional research has modified Chandler's "structure follows strategy" concept because the structure of an organization may affect the strategy-making process via the centralization or decentralization of decision making and the formalization of rules and procedures.[18] In summary, from a strategy–structure match, research reveals that the fit between strategy and structure affects performance.[19]

Work Specialization

A key aspect of organization structure is *work specialization,* sometimes called division of labor, which is the degree to which organization tasks are subdivided into separate jobs. Managers divide the total task of the organization into specific

Work specialization
Division of labor in which organization tasks are subdivided into separate jobs.

jobs having specified activities. The activities define what the person performing a particular job is to do and to get done. Work specialization in Fig. 16-1 is illustrated by the separation of manufacturing tasks into industrial engineering, maintenance, quality control, receiving, embossing, coating, finishing, and shipping. Employees within each department perform only the tasks relevant to their specialized function.

The principal reason why organizations were created was to obtain the economic advantage of dividing work into specialized jobs. As societies become more and more industrialized, products are mass produced. Mass production depends on the ability to obtain the economic benefits of specialized labor, and organizations are the most effective means for obtaining specialized labor. Specialization yields economic benefits as a result of the following:

1. Production is efficient because employees perform small, well-defined tasks.
2. Employees can acquire expertise in their tasks.
3. Employees with the appropriate ability and attitude can be selected to perform the required tasks.

Organization, however, can overdo work specialization by designing tasks in which employees do only a single, small, boring job. If employees become alienated and bored, the organization can enlarge and enrich the tasks.

Differentiation and Integration

Another aspect of organization structure is differentiation and integration. Differentiation is the way in which work is divided into tasks and integration refers to how these tasks are coordinated.[20] Following is an expanded discussion of these two concepts.

Differentiation is the process by which organization designers divide the overall task to be accomplished into subtasks and assign them to various work units or individuals within the organization. Differentiation enables organization designers to divide a total complex task into more specialized tasks that can be performed more efficiently.

Differentiation The way in which work is divided into tasks and subtasks and assigned to work units or individuals within an organization.

Two types of differentiation occurs in organizations: horizontal and vertical. Horizontal differentiation refers to how the work is divided into tasks. For example, as we discussed in the introduction, Johnson & Johnson is horizontally differentiated into 166 separate divisions.

Vertical differentiation refers to the division of work by level of authority. The work is divided on the basis of the authority that each work unit or person has over each other unit or person in the organization. Before its 1990 reorganization, British Petroleum (BP) had eleven layers of management between its chief executive officer and first-line supervisors. Because this vertical differentiation had turned into a rigid, sluggish bureaucracy, BP's chief executive, Robert Horton, reduced the number of management levels from eleven to six.[21]

Integration Refers to how tasks and activities are integrated into a coordinated whole.

Integration. At the same time that organization designers are differentiating the organization, they must also integrate the various activities and tasks into a coordinated whole. Research indicates that organizations perform better when their levels of differentiation and integration match the level of environmental uncertainty. Organizations that performed well in uncertain environments had high levels of both differentiation and integration, while those performing well in less uncertain environments had lower levels of differentiation and integration.[22] Later in this chapter we describe the coordinating mechanisms that organization designers use to integrate an organization's tasks and activities.

Centralization and Decentralization

In a *centralized* organization, authority is not widely delegated. Virtually all decisions are made by the organization's top managers.

In a *decentralized* organization, authority is widely delegated to subordinates. Decentralization is an approach that requires managers to decide what and when to delegate, to carefully select and train personnel, and to develop adequate controls. Research studies indicate that a decentralized organization is better able to adapt to the demands of a changing environment.[23] However, these findings may change because information systems can now provide more information regarding the external environment to top managers allowing them to respond faster.

The "Profile" on page 544 describes how the Manville Corporation shifted from a centralized organizational structure to that of a decentralized structure.

Management's decision to centralize or decentralize is affected by a number of factors that are described in Fig. 16-6.

The advantages of decentralization include improved efficiency, flexibility, initiative, and management development.[26] Following is a brief discussion of these advantages.

Centralization An organization where authority is not widely delegated.

Decentralization An organization where authority is widely delegated to subordinates.

- *Cost of Decisions.* As a general rule, the more costly a decision is to the organization, the more likely it is that top management will make it.
- *Organizational Culture.* Organizational culture can be described as the norms, values, and beliefs that characterize an organization. An organization's culture plays a large part in determining whether authority is centralized. Decentralization is an important part of J&J's culture. According to J&J's chief executive, Ralph Larsen, "We may question a company president's strategy, but in the end it is this individual who is running the business and calling the shots."[24] The prevailing culture at J&J is that company presidents get to make decisions regarding their businesses.
- *Competent Manager.* An adequate supply of competent managers is an absolute necessity for decentralization. Organizations that utilize a decentralized structure believe that practical experience is the best approach for developing managerial potential. Managers are permitted to make mistakes involving small costs.
- *Environmental Conditions.* A number of external environmental conditions impact on an organization. These environmental conditions affect the degree of centralization within a firm. For example, local managers have to abide by policies regarding the health, safety, and employment opportunities for employees that are administered by governmental agencies. In some situations labor unions may exert a centralizing influence on an organization. If the union represents large numbers of employees in different locations, then labor negotiations will not be decentralized.
- *Company Policies.* Company policies are rules or guidelines that express the limits within which action should occur. These rules often take the form of contingent decisions for resolving conflicts among specific objectives. An example is: "Don't exceed two months' inventory in any item without corporate approval." Managers who value a consistent approach favor centralization of authority.
- *Control.* Both centralized and decentralized structures have control mechanisms to determine whether actual events are meeting expectations.[25]

Source: Adapted from David Nadler and Michael Tushman, *Organizational Design*, Glenview, IL, Scott, Foresman, 1988, pp. 192–202; Henry Mintzberg, "The Structuring of Organizations," in Henry Mintzberg and James Brian Quinn, eds., *The Strategy Process*, 2nd ed., Englewood Cliffs, NJ, Prentice-Hall, 1991, pp. 339–341; Don Hellrigel and John W. Slocum, Jr., *Management*, 6th ed., Reading, MA, Addison-Wesley, 1992, pp. 343–344.

FIGURE 16-6

Factors Affecting Centralization and Decentralization

Profile

W. Thomas Stephens
Chairman, President, and Chief Executive Officer
DECENTRALIZING MANVILLE

Earlier, our strategy at Manville was to evolve from a bureaucratic, highly centralized organization with an internal focus on our operations to one that is organized around customer needs with decisions made at the lowest possible level. Manville now has two highly focused businesses that are making operating decisions at lower and more appropriate levels in their organization. These two new businesses are Riverwood International and Schuller International. Riverwood is organized into three business segments: Coated Board System, Containerboard, and U.S. Timberlands/Wood Products. The Coated Board System segment includes the production of coated board at paperboard mills in the United States and Europe; converting facilities in the United States, Australia, and Europe; and worldwide packaging machinery operations related to the production and sale of beverage and folding cartons. The Containerboard segment includes timberlands and associated containerboard mills and corrugated box plants in Brazil as well as kraft paper, linerboard, and corrugating medium production at two U.S. mills. The U.S. Timberlands/Wood Products segment includes timberlands and operations engaged in the supply of pulpwood to the U.S. mill operations, and the manufacture of lumber and plywood.

Schuller International (Schuler) is one of the world's largest fiberglass manufacturers. Schuller produces and markets insulation products for buildings and equipment, high-efficiency air filtration media, commercial roofing systems, and textile glass used as reinforcements in buildings and industrial applications, and employs approximately 7,000 people and operates thirty-five manufacturing facilities in the United States, Canada, and Germany.

In essence, Manville Corporation is now a holding company with two principal subsidiaries: Riverwood International and Schuller International.

Efficiency is improved, because red tape and bottlenecks are reduced by decentralization. Also, if lower-level managers can make on-the-spot decisions, less time is lost in getting approvals up the line.

Flexibility is improved, because managers who can make decisions have the ability to cope with changing conditions and to adjust for unexpected circumstances.

Initiative is improved, because it is very challenging and motivating for managers to make decisions regarding problems and solutions in their own departments.

Management Development is improved, because the best management development training is to encourage managers at lower levels to manage their own departments.

The disadvantages of decentralization consist of reduced organizational control, increased duplication, failure to utilize centralized expertise, and problems with managerial competency.[27]

Following is a brief discussion of these disadvantages.

Organizational Control is reduced when managers have great latitude in making decisions. Coordinating overall activities becomes more difficult.

Duplication is increased if all department managers are autonomous. Several offices may be keeping identical records on customers, shipments, inventory, and so on. Increased duplication has been a problem for J&J, as we noted in the opening scenario of this chapter.

Managerial Competency is strained because additional decision making by lower-level managers makes it difficult to produce competent managers at all levels.

As more firms eliminate layers of managers, more and more decisions are being delegated downward in the organization. Lower-level employees are becoming increasingly more involved in organizational decision making. For example, in a Corning, Inc., plant that switched from manufacturing glass products to producing automobile pollution-control parts, the number of management levels has been reduced from five to two. There is now just one layer of management between the hourly employees and the divisional vice president–plant manager. Hourly employees now handle many of the jobs previously performed by front-line supervisors, such as scheduling overtime and vacations. Supervisors, in turn, now perform the jobs of middle managers, such as handling customer complaints, developing production schedules, and implementing cost-reduction programs.[28]

Formalization

Formalization is the extent to which the expectations concerning job activities are standardized and explicit. An organization with a highly formalized organization structure is one in which rules and procedures are available to prescribe what each individual should be doing. Such organizations have written standard operating procedures, specified directives, and explicit policies.

Formalization can also vary depending on a particular job or organization function. For example, professional positions tend to have a greater amount of freedom of activity than less skilled, more routine positions such as assembly line jobs. People in accounting or production departments have more standard procedures and methods for work accomplishment than members of marketing, human resource, or research and development departments.[29]

Formalization The extent to which the expectations concerning job activities are standardized and explicit.

Complexity

Complexity results from dividing the tasks of the organization and in creating departments. Specifically, complexity refers to the number of distinctly different job titles, or occupational groupings, and the number of distinctly different departments, or units. Organizations with a great many different kinds and types of jobs and departments tend to create more complicated managerial and organizational problems dealing with communication, coordination, and control needs than do those organizations with fewer jobs and departments.[30]

Complexity results from dividing the tasks of the organization and in creating departments.

Interrelationships

Despite a number of studies, the interrelationships among the preceding dimensions are not entirely clear. No particular type of relationship is best. Managers must select the organization structure that matches the firm's situation.[31]

METHODS OF COORDINATION

Top managers have to find a way to integrate the departments of an organization so as to produce desired results. Although the formal chain of command provides a means for supervision, more is needed. Systems are needed to process information and to enable communication among people in different departments. Managers use a variety of coordinating mechanisms to mesh a variety of task activities and to facilitate the flow of information between departments.[32]

Departmentation

Departmentation The grouping of jobs according to some common bases for the purposes of planning, coordination, and control.

Departmentation is the grouping of jobs according to some common, rational basis, for the purposes of planning, coordination, and control. Departmentation begins when work units are grouped into departments to form the organization. A variety of departmentation configurations exist and are discussed in a later section, "Patterns of Organization Design."

Unit Coordination

Unit coordination Work units are coordinated by working together to achieve desired results.

An important aspect of organization structure is how work unit tasks are coordinated to achieve desired results. By working together, members of the organization can accomplish outcomes that are unattainable if the members worked alone. Three unit coordinating mechanisms are mutual adjustment, direct supervision, and standardization.[33] These mechanisms that help to mesh task activities together are the glue that holds an organization together.[34]

Mutual adjustment achieves coordination by the process of informal communication.[35] Engineers who are discussing how to rearrange the layout of a work area are coordinating by the means of mutual adjustment.

Direct supervision occurs when one person coordinates by giving orders to others.[36] A maintenance superintendent is using direct supervision when he orders maintenance employees to stop working on the rearrangement of a work area and to repair a broken conveyor that caused an assembly line to stop.

Standardization is used to coordinate work activities by providing employees with standards and procedures to guide the performance of their tasks.[37] Four types of standardization exist: standardization of work processes, output, skills, and norms.

1. *Work Process Standardization* is the development of procedures to be followed, as in the case of an automobile assembly line. When a car comes down the assembly line, worker "A" bolts on the right frame assembly, and worker "B" bolts on the left assembly. These workers require minimal supervision and do not have to interact.[38] Rules and regulations can also be used to standardize work processes.

2. *Output Standardization* is the use of performance goals or output targets. In output standardization, concern shifts from how the work is done to insuring that the work meets certain economic or physical standards. For example, a division manager is instructed to achieve a sales growth of 15 percent so that the corporation can meet its sales objectives or when a machinist is told to drill holes in a certain place on a valve so that they will fit the bolts being inserted and welded by someone else.

3. *Skill Standardization* involves standardizing the worker rather than the work or the output. The worker is taught a set of skills that are subsequently applied to the work. Coordination occurs because the workers have learned what to expect from each other. For example, when a surgeon and an anesthetist meet in the operating room to remove an appendix, they both know what to expect from each other because of their standard training.

4. *Norm Standardization* occurs when workers share a common set of beliefs and can achieve coordination because of these beliefs. For example, the

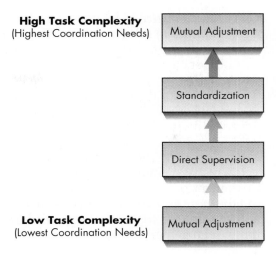

High Task Complexity
(Highest Coordination Needs)

Mutual Adjustment

Standardization

Direct Supervision

Low Task Complexity
(Lowest Coordination Needs)

Mutual Adjustment

FIGURE 16-7
A Continuum
of Coordinating
Mechanisms,
Coordination Needs,
and Task Complexity

top management at Xerox introduced a "Leadership-through-Quality" program telling Xerox employees that customer satisfaction was the firm's top priority. Xerox employees who believe that customer satisfaction is an important priority work in ways to achieve the satisfaction of customers.

As organizational tasks become complex, coordination tends to shift from mutual adjustment to direct supervision, to standardization, and then back to mutual adjustment. Interestingly, although mutual adjustment is used in the simplest of situations, it is also used in the most complex, because it is the only means that can be relied upon under difficult circumstances. However, no organization relies on a single one of these mechanisms—all are typically found in most developed organizations.[39] Figure 16-7 illustrates how the coordinating mechanisms of mutual adjustment, direct supervision, and standardization form a continuum with respect to task complexity.

Studies also indicate that differences in coordination occur from the way in which work tasks are divided. Upper management, as an example, uses mutual adjustment as a coordinating mechanism. In areas with routine tasks, such as lower parts of the organization's hierarchy, coordination is achieved by direct supervision or work process standardization, or output standardization. Work units staffed with professionals such as the legal department, market research, engineering, or research and development rely upon combinations of skill standardization and mutual adjustment.[40]

Lateral Coordination

In the preceding section, we described how work units can be coordinated. Another aspect of organizing is that departments also require coordination. The reason for this need is that although a department interacts with a number of other departments in the organization, the pattern and volume of these interactions are not uniform. A manufacturing department, for example, may interact with sales, personnel, engineering, accounting, legal, research, and other departments. Many of these interactions are direct contacts, as in the case when manufacturing personnel confer with peers in other departments.

Lateral coordination To function effectively, an organization must use horizontal forms of communication and horizontal cooperation.

To function effectively, therefore, organizations must use horizontal forms of communication and decision making. *Lateral coordination* involves the use of various mechanisms to improve information flow and horizontal cooperation.

Collaboration among departments takes various forms. These linking mechanisms are not always drawn on the organization chart but are a part of the organization's design. The following alternative forms of collaboration can improve horizontal coordination and information flow. Each form enables people to exchange information.[41]

DIRECT CONTACT   The simplest approach involves direct contact between managers who have a mutual problem. Suppose, for example, that managers in two departments prepare tentative, routine maintenance schedules that would overload the number of specialized maintenance personnel. Instead of referring such problems upward to a higher-level manager for resolution, the managers can simply get together and work out a solution.

LIAISON ROLE   In some organizations, the volume of interdepartmental contacts is so great that a liaison role is created to facilitate coordination. A computer department may assign a liaison to work with other departments that use its services. A liaison is located in one department, such as engineering, but has the responsibility for communicating and coordinating with other departments, such as the manufacturing department.

TASK FORCE   Direct contact and liaison roles usually link only two departments. When several departments are involved in accomplishing a specific requirement, a task force or team of representatives selected from the various departments can facilitate coordination. A task force is a temporary committee composed of representatives from each department that is affected by a problem. Each member of the committee represents the interest of one department and carries information from the meeting back to that department.

Task forces are common in firms that manufacture consumer products. For example, when Kellogg decides to create a new breakfast cereal, it brings together people with expertise in product design, food research, marketing, manufacturing, finance, and other relevant functions to formulate the product, design its package, determine its market, compute its manufacturing costs, and project its profits. Once the problems have been worked out of the product, and it is ready to be mass-produced, the task force disbands, and the cereal is integrated into the permanent organization structure.[42] In essence, task forces are temporary groups that are established to solve coordination problems across several departments. When an adequate integration is achieved, the task force is disbanded.

INTEGRATORS   Integrators are people in a full-time position created to coordinate the activities of several departments. An unusual feature of integrators is that the person is not a member of one of the departments being coordinated. In essence, an integrating position is a full-time problem-solving job. The person filling the position must be unbiased, have the ability to communicate with both departments, and rely heavily on expert power.[43] Florida Power and Light used permanent integrators coordinated design changes and developed innovative construction techniques.[44] Product managers in a matrix design are also integrators.

PROJECT TEAMS   As Fig. 16-8 shows, project teams provide the strongest horizontal linking mechanism.[45] Teams are permanent task forces and often involve

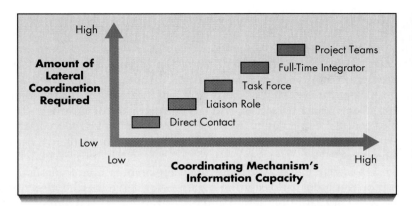

Figure 16-8

Relative Strength of
Lateral Coordinating
Mechanisms

Source: Adapted from Richard
L. Daft, *Organization Theory and
Design*, 4th ed., St. Paul, MN,
West Publishing, 1992, p. 188.
Reprinted by permission.
Copyright © 1992 by West
Publishing Company. All rights
reserved.

a full-time integrator. Project teams are used when organizations are involved
in large-scale projects requiring extensive coordination among several departments for several years. General Motors created sixty-six product development
teams to design and build the Buick Regal that has been praised as a well-
designed, well-built automobile.[46]

A project team that provides lateral coordination is not the same as a *work
team* that is a recent innovation in the use of groups in organizations. A work
team is a small group of employees responsible for a set of tasks previously performed by individual members of the organization and is primarily responsible
for managing itself.

Information Technology

From a broad perspective, *information technology*, which is also discussed in Chap.
5, has been defined as the generation, aggregation, storage, modification, and
speedy transmission of information made possible by the advent of computers
and related devices. In the past, however, information systems have not possessed the sophistication and simplicity needed by senior managers.[47] Recently,
advances in computer technology allow executives to interact with the organization's information system to retrieve, manipulate, and display data needed for
specific decisions.[48] Also, collaborative work systems have been developed to
facilitate group decision making.[49]

Many organization designers have used these improvements in information
technology to increase the management span of control, thus requiring fewer
managers. Supervisory and middle management personnel can be reduced because
electronic monitoring and feedback replaces routine supervision. Also, some
advanced technology systems can now conduct analyses previously performed
by middle managers. As a coordinating mechanism, information technology can
be viewed as providing managers with a span of communication.[50] Many examples exist, however, in which information technology systems were poorly implemented.[51] The issue of implementing change is discussed in Chap. 18.

Information technology
**The generation, aggre-
gation, storage, modifi-
cation, and speedy
transmission of infor-
mation made possible
by computers and
related devices.**

What Is Organizational Design?

The overall configuration of structural components described earlier in this chapter into a single, unified organizational system is known as organizational design.
In essence, the earlier discussed structural components are similar to pieces of a
jigsaw puzzle. These components can be arranged in a number of ways to cre-

ate a wide variety of organization designs. There are few definite rules for designing an organization. Every firm's organization design is the result of many decisions and historical circumstances. Even firms within the same environment can create different organization designs. For example, Coca-Cola and Pepsi-Cola are fierce competitors in the soft-drink market, yet these two firms have different organization designs. Coca-Cola has relatively specialized jobs, uses functional departmentalization, and has narrow spans of control and a relatively tall and centralized hierarchy. By contrast, Pepsico has less specialization, uses product departmentalization, and has wide spans of control and a flat decentralized hierarchy.[52]

As we describe how managers develop an organization design, we begin with a process model for designing organizations. We then discuss the relationship between organization design and organizational effectiveness. Next, we discuss the impact that the contingency factors of environment, technology, size, organizational age, and power relationships have on organizational design. Following this discussion, we describe a number of basic structural patterns. Finally, we conclude with a discussion of contemporary approaches to organization design. We now begin by examining a process model for designing organizations.

A Process Model for Organizational Design

As illustrated in Fig. 16-9, the manager's choice for organization structure is affected by: the contextual factors of environment, technology, and size; the goals of the organization; and the manager's personality, value system, and experience. Later, we also discuss how an organization's age and certain power relationships affect an organization's design. An organization's effectiveness depends on its strategy–structure fit.

Organizational Effectiveness

Organizational effectiveness is not the same thing as organizational productivity, because the latter does not take into account whether a firm is producing

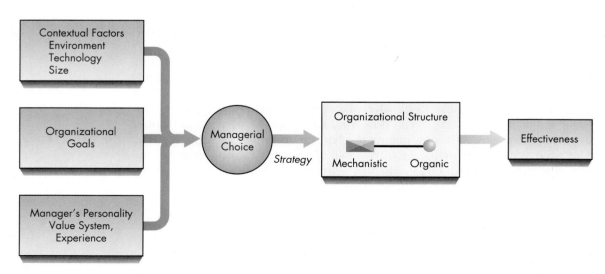

FIGURE 16-9 A Process Model for Organization Design

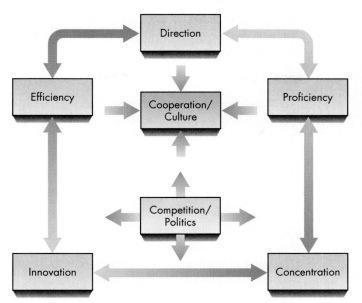

Figure 16-10
Seven Forces Required
for Organizational
Effectiveness
Source: Adapted from Henry
Mintzberg, "The Effective
Organization: Forces and
Forms," *Sloan Management
Review,* Winter 1991, pp. 54–67.

the right goods or services.[53] A modern company producing more buggy whips than ever before is certainly productive, but is also ineffective, because not many people need buggy whips in today's society.[54] Effectiveness is not efficiency. *Organizational efficiency* is usually measured as the ratio of outputs produced per unit of input consumed.[55] Efficiency has been defined as "doing things right" while effectiveness has been defined as "doing the right thing."[56] Henry Mintzberg has suggested that, to be effective, an organization must manage the interplay of seven basic forces. These seven forces are depicted in Fig. 16-10.

Organizational efficiency Measured as the ratio of outputs produced per unit of input consumed.

Following is a description of Mintzberg's seven forces required for organizational effectiveness. The first force, direction, is the organization's sense of vision and mission. The second force, efficiency, is the need to minimize costs. The third force, proficiency, is carrying out tasks with a high level of knowledge and skill. The fourth force, innovation, is the organization's need to develop new products and services. The fifth force, concentration, is focusing organizational efforts on particular markets. The sixth force, cooperation/culture, is the result of common cultural values and reflects the need for harmony and cooperation among a diverse set of people. The seventh force, competition/politics, occurs because competition can cause politics and a splitting apart of individuals and departments because of the need for individual success and recognition.[57]

An organization cannot maximize all of these needs simultaneously. By understanding these seven forces, managers can design the right structure to achieve their objectives. This is a continual management process, because a specific organization design may work for a period of time and then be revised to achieve a new round of effectiveness.[58]

PATTERNS OF ORGANIZATION DESIGN

As we have noted, managers have some discretion in choosing an appropriate structure for their organization. In this section we describe a variety of structural patterns including the functional pattern, three divisional patterns (product, process, and geographical), the strategic business unit (SBU) pattern, and the matrix pattern.[59] We also discuss the network pattern, a new structure gaining some acceptance.

Functional Pattern

In a functional pattern, people are grouped on the basis of the task they perform, such as sales and marketing, engineering, manufacturing, human resources, accounting and finance, and research and development. Figure 16-11 depicts a typical functional pattern.

The advantages of a functional pattern include the following:

- Promotes specialization because individuals who perform the same tasks are grouped together.
- Provides for the development of an in-depth functional expertise.
- Minimizes the need for elaborate control systems and increases flexibility, because individuals performing the same task can monitor one another to ensure that tasks are being performed effectively.

Disadvantages of a functional pattern are:

- Functional rivalry and conflict may develop.
- Career development is minimized, because individuals can only move up the career ladder within their functional area.
- Profit-making responsibility is forced to the top.
- Strategy implementation may be hindered, because it becomes increasingly difficult to communicate across functions.
- Functions develop different time and goal orientations. Manufacturing may be concerned with achieving short-run results such as reducing costs while research and development may have a long-run perspective such as developing new products.
- A functional mindset may develop that tends to attach more importance to what is best for the function rather than what is best for the organization.
- Each function may develop a different view regarding the strategic issues facing the organization, making it difficult to develop and implement a unified strategy.

Single-business firms tend to use a functional pattern, because key activities revolve around specialized functions. Universities also use a functional pattern

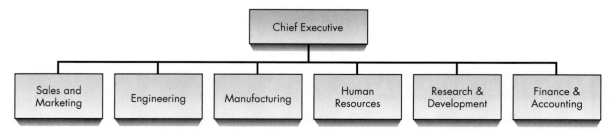

FIGURE 16-11 Functional Pattern of Organizational Design

including academic affairs, athletics, student services, alumni relations, accounting, and maintenance.

Divisional Pattern

As an organization diversifies, it becomes difficult to manage different products and services in different markets. A manufacturing manager's job becomes complex if he or she has to manage say, fifty different plants producing twenty different products (each with a different technology) in eight different industries.[60] The divisional pattern allows organizations to grow and diversify while overcoming control problems. In the divisional pattern, each distinct product line or business unit is placed in a self-contained division with support functions.

The advantages of a divisional pattern are:

- Functional coordination within the target market is improved.
- Control of local situations lies with the respective general manager.
- New businesses and products/services can be added easily.
- Career opportunities are available for promotion to higher-level managerial positions.
- Sales and profit responsibility is delegated to the respective general manager.

The disadvantages of a divisional pattern include:

- Divisional rivalries and conflicts may develop.
- Difficult to maintain consistent, companywide practices.
- Adds another layer of management.
- Duplication of staff services at headquarters and at division levels creates cost-disadvantages.

Three types of divisional patterns have been used: divisional pattern by product, process, and geographical area. Following is a description of these three divisional patterns.

In a *divisional product or geographical pattern,* activities are grouped by either product lines or geographical location. Figure 16-12 presents a divisional product pattern for an appliance company together with a divisional geographical pattern for a retailing company. In the appliance company, products are grouped in terms of their being washers and dryers, electric ranges, and refrigerators. Geographical regions are the Western Region, Central Region, and Eastern Region. The same range of products is manufactured in each region.

Examples of organizations using a divisional product pattern are Unisys, Maytag, Procter & Gamble, and DuPont, while Neiman-Marcus, Pfizer, Kelly Services, and the Internal Revenue Service use the divisional geographical pattern.

A *divisional pattern by process* is similar to a functional structure, because activities are organized by activities. A key difference between a divisional pattern by process design and a functional pattern design is that functional managers are not responsible for sales or profits, while divisional process managers are evaluated on these criteria. An example of a divisional pattern by process is a manufacturing business organized into four divisions: foundry and castings; milling and grinding; machining; and painting and finishing. All operations relating to these specific processes would be grouped under their respective division. Each process (division) is responsible for generating sales and profits.

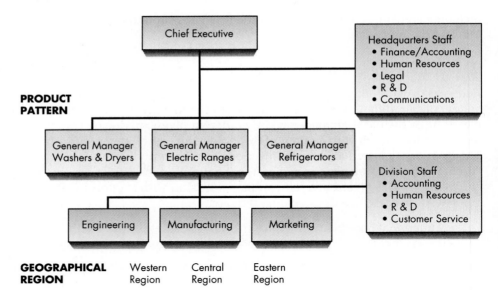

Figure 16-12
Product or Geographical
Pattern of Organization
Design

Strategic Business Unit (SBU) Pattern

When a company has hundreds of different divisions as does General Electric, top management finds it almost impossible to retain control over the organization. The SBU pattern groups similar divisions into strategic business units and delegates authority and responsibility for each unit to a senior executive who reports directly to the chief executive officer. General Electric, a pioneer in the concept of SBUs, grouped 190 divisions into forty-three SBUs and then aggregated them further into six sectors.[61] An example of an SBU pattern is shown in Fig. 16-13.

The advantages of an SBU pattern are:

- Provides a strategic approach to organize business units of a widely diversified company.
- Facilitates strategy implementation by improving coordination between similar divisions and channeling accountability to distinct business units.
- Allows each SBU to operate around its own set of key activities.
- Frees CEO to focus on corporate strategy.
- Places profit accountability on SBU managers.
- Career opportunities are available for promotion to higher-level managerial positions.

The disadvantages of an SBU pattern include:

- Adds another layer of management.
- SBUs may be myopic in developing their future direction.
- May lead to excessive rivalry between SBUs for corporate resources.
- Creates additional overhead expenses because of the duplication of staff services at headquarters and at the SBU level.
- May make the role of the SBU general managers ambiguous.
- Corporate management may lose touch with business unit situations, end up surprised, and not know how to correct the problem.

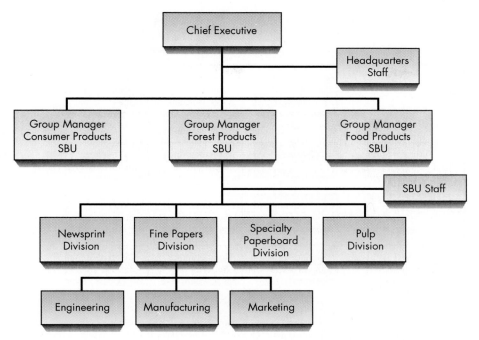

FIGURE 16-13
SBU Pattern of
Organization

- Corporate management may become heavily dependent on SBU managers.

Examples of organizations using an SBU pattern include General Electric, Union Carbide, Walt Disney, and GenCorp.

Matrix Pattern

Although functional and divisional patterns of organizational design depend primarily on vertical flows of authority and communication, matrix patterns depend on both a vertical and a horizontal flow of authority and communication. In the usual matrix design, activities on the vertical axis are grouped by function, so that tasks can be differentiated into functions such as engineering, finance, manufacturing, and marketing. Superimposed on this vertical grid is a horizontal grid based on a differentiation by-product or project.[62] Organizations tend to use the matrix pattern, shown in Fig. 16-14, when in-depth skills are needed in functional departments (manufacturing, engineering) together with a desire for a flexible response to changing environmental conditions.

The matrix pattern of organization design was first developed by high-technology firms in the aerospace and electronics industries. These companies were developing radically new products in competitive and uncertain environments. Also, the time required for product development was a critical factor. Existing functional and product patterns of organization design did not allow the necessary task interactions required to meet the new product requirements.[63] In essence, these companies needed an organization structure that would match the new strategy.

In a matrix structure, subordinates have a continuing assignment of reporting to two bosses: one boss is their functional manager (engineering, manufacturing), and the other boss is a product or project manager. A matrix organization does not adhere to the unity-of-command principle discussed in Chap. 13.

FIGURE 16-14
Matrix Pattern of
Organization Design

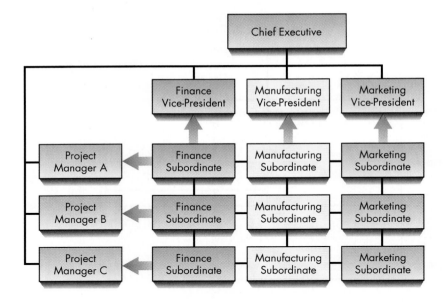

Instead, the use of two bosses and shared authority creates a new organization culture.

As projects move through different phases, different functional specialists are required. For example, the first phase may require research and development specialists, while engineering, marketing, and manufacturing specialists can be used at the second phase to prepare cost and marketing projections. As the demand for the type of specialist changes, employees can be moved to other projects that need their services. As a result, a matrix pattern can make maximum use of employee skills as existing projects are completed and newer ones emerge.[64] Examples of organizations using a matrix pattern are TRW, Texas Instruments, Boeing, and Bechtel.

The advantages of the matrix pattern are:

- Requires a minimum of direct hierarchical control.
- Creates an atmosphere in which project team members can learn from one another.
- Makes maximum use of employee skills.
- Creates checks and balances among competing viewpoints.
- Encourages consensus-building, conflict resolution, cooperation, and coordination of related activities.
- Frees the CEO to concentrate on corporate strategy.

The disadvantages of a matrix pattern include:

- Difficult to manage—care must be taken to avoid conflicts between functions and projects over resources.
- Power struggles may develop among managers.
- Project managers may take the dominate role over time.
- Difficult to move quickly, because clearance has to be obtained from many people.

- Disproportionate amounts of time may be spent on communications because of the shared authority.

After considering the preceding advantages, a matrix pattern should only be implemented unless a firm's strategy requires it. In dynamic and changing environments, the benefits of the matrix in terms of flexibility and innovation may well exceed the extra costs of using it. However, there is no real advantage to be gained by using a more complex and expensive structure than is necessary.[65]

Networking—A New Pattern?

A network pattern, shown in Fig. 16-15, is a form of disaggregation, in which one company contracts out certain functions (production, marketing, accounting, distribution) to other companies. The contracting company acts as a small central headquarters and communicates what actions are to be taken by the various functions. A network is different from a joint venture. In a joint venture, two or more companies collaborate on a new enterprise. A network involves securing specialized services from other companies to perform a particular function. In essence, the firms that use a network pattern are industrial companies without industrial production. As U.S. firms increasingly export their production component to third-world countries because of the high costs of penetrating world markets, network patterns are predicted to become more common and influential in the global business community.

The "OB in Practice" on page 558 describes how a company, Galoob Toys, has implemented a network pattern of organization design.

The advantages of a network pattern are:

- Less capital is needed.
- Overhead expenses are less.
- Low-cost labor can be employed.
- Outside technology can be easily used.
- Increased flexibility and innovativeness.

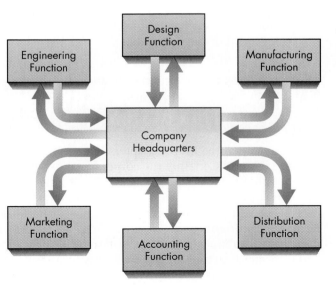

Figure 16-15

Network Pattern of Organization Design

OB in Practice

Network Organization Design: Farming Out Functions

The network pattern of organization design involves securing specialized services from other companies to perform a particular function, with the contracting company acting as a small central headquarters. For example, Galoob Toys had sales of $58 million with only 115 employees. Galoob employees never touch a product and do not even collect the money. A visit to central headquarters reveals that Galoob is held together with phones, fax machines, and other electronic technology. Independent engineers and designers develop the toys sold by Galoob. Manufacturing and packaging are performed by firms in Hong Kong and shipped to commissioned manufacturers' representatives, who market the toys. Accounts receivable are sold to a financial services company, which establishes credit policies, bills customers, and collects payment.

Source: Adapted from John Wilson and Judith Dobrzynski, "And Now The Post–Industrial Corporation," *Business Week*, March 3, 1989, pp. 64–71.

The disadvantages of a network pattern include:

- Coordination and control can be major obstacles.
- Vulnerable to competition from firms providing the functional task.

Such firms as publishers, garment makers, and construction companies have used the network pattern of organization design for many years. Small, start-up firms often organize as networks as a way of gaining flexibility and controlling costs. The network pattern is spreading to more and more industries as telecommunication breakthroughs continue to ease coordination between suppliers and customers around the world.

Despite this increased use of the network design pattern, scholars are uncertain about the extent to which networks will grow. Some predict that the network structure will be broadly adopted and will become a major organizational innovation. Others argue that networks constitute a transition stage and will not be the wave of the future.[66]

CONTEMPORARY APPROACHES TO ORGANIZATION DESIGN

As we have discussed in this chapter, managers can adopt a large number of organization designs. Certainly the corporate landscape is shifting fast: Competition is increasingly global; technology is developing quickly; and the work force is changing profoundly. The manager's task is to examine the organization within its specific situation and then to design a form of organization that meets its needs. A dominant theme of current design strategy is for managers to think more broadly about the organization in terms of how work, people, and formal and informal structures fit together. Organizations that empower their employees must ensure that performance appraisals and reward systems are integrated into the organization's design to provide feedback regarding employee efforts. Contemporary organization design must also be capable of handling new advances in information technology and to reflect a strong concern for people. Also, organizations must stay in touch with their customers. However, managers should remember that organization design principles are tools, and are neither good nor bad in themselves. They can be used properly or improperly.[67]

THE HORIZONTAL CORPORATION

Mere downsizing does little to change the fundamental way that work gets done in a corporation. In fact, simply downsizing did not produce the dramatic rises in productivity that many companies hoped for. Gaining quantum leaps in performance requires rethinking the way work gets done. To accomplish this, a different pattern of organizational design is required—the horizontal corporation. Already such companies as American Telephone & Telegraph, DuPont, General Electric, Ryder Systems, and Allied-Signal are moving toward the idea. The horizontal corporation eliminates both hierarchy and functional boundaries. In its purest state, the horizontal corporation might.have a skeleton group of senior executives at the top in such traditional support functions as finance and human resources. However, virtually everyone else in the organization would work together in multidisciplinary teams that perform core processes, such as product development, or sales generation. The upshot: The organization might have only three or four layers of management between the chairman and the staffers in a given process. If the concept takes hold, almost every aspect of corporate life will be profoundly altered. Companies would organize around processes— developing new products for example—instead of around narrow tasks, such as forecasting market demand for a given new product. Self-managing teams would become the building blocks of the new organization. Performance objectives would be linked to customer satisfaction rather than profitability or shareholder value. And staffers would be rewarded not just for individual performance but for the development of their skills and for team performance.

For most companies, the idea amounts to a major cultural transformation. Don't rush to write the obituary for functional management, however. No companies have completely eliminated functional specialization. And even advocates of the new model don't envision the end of managers who are experts in manufacturing, finance, and the like. "It's only the rarest of organizations that would choose to be purely vertical or horizontal," says consultant Douglas Smith. "Most organizations will be hybrids."

Still, the horizontal corporation is an idea that's gaining currency and one that will increasingly demand people who think more broadly and thrive on change, who manage process instead of people, and who cherish teamwork as never before.

In the days when business was more predictable and stable, companies organized themselves in vertical structures to take advantage of specialized experts. The benefits are obvious: Everyone has a place, and everyone understands his or her task. The critical decision-making power resides at the top. But while gaining clarity and stability, such organizations make it difficult for anyone to understand the task of the company as a whole, and how to relate his or her work to it. The result: Collaboration among different departments was often a triumph over formal organization charts.

Heightened global competition and the ever increasing speed of techno-logical change have since altered the rules of the game and have forced corpo-rate planners to seek new solutions. "We were reluctant to leave the command-and-control structure, because it had worked so well," says Philip Engel, president of CNA Corp., the Chicago-based insurance company that is refashioning its organization. "But it no longer fit the realities." This is not the first time orga-nizational theorists have tried to come up with a workable alternative to the ver-tical structure that has dominated business for a century or more.

Managers are quickly discovering, however, that eliminating the neatly arranged boxes on an organization chart in favor of a more horizontal structure can often be a complex and painful ordeal. Indeed, simply defining the processes of a given corporation may prove to be a mind-boggling and time-consuming exercise. Consider AT&T. Initially, the company's Network Services Division, which has 16,000 employees, tallied up some 130 processes before it narrowed them down to thirteen core ones.

After that comes the challenge of persuading people to cast off their old mar-keting, finance, or manufacturing hats and think more broadly. "This is the hard-est damn thing to do," says Terry M. Ennis, who heads up a group to help DuPont's businesses organize long horizontal lines. "It's very unsettling and threatening for people. You find line and function managers who have been honored and rewarded for what they've done for decades. You're in a white-water zone when you change."

Some management gurus, noting the fervor with which corporate chieftains embrace fads, express caution. "The idea draws together a number of fashion-able trends and packages them in an interesting way," says Henry Mintzberg, a management professor at McGill University. "But the danger is that an idea like this can generate too much enthusiasm. It's not for everyone." Mintzberg notes that there is no one solution to every organization's problems. Indeed, stream-lined vertical structures may suit some mass-production industries better than horizontal ones. Already, consultants say, some companies are rushing to orga-nize around processes without linking them to the corporation's key goals.[68]

THE BOUNDARYLESS ORGANIZATION

Research findings indicate that an organization's structure may constrain its strategy and thereby limit organizational effectiveness and performance.[69] Jack Welch, CEO of General Electric, became concerned that employee behavioral patterns are highly conditioned by boundaries between levels, functions, and other constructs. These boundaries, according to Welch, separate people, tasks, processes, and places and that ideas, information, decisions, talent, rewards, and action should be able to permeate boundaries. In 1990, Welch began using the term *boundaryless organization* as GE began initiating strategies to alter its bound-aries.[70] Askenas and his colleagues indicate that managers must deal with four enduring and intractable organizational boundaries before a change program can be successfully implemented. These four boundaries are:[71]

- *Vertical Boundaries* between hierarchical levels and ranks of people.
- *Horizontal Boundaries* between functions and disciplines.
- *External Boundaries* between customers, suppliers, and regulators.
- *Geographical Boundaries* between nations, cultures, and markets.

The transformation to a boundaryless organization can be accomplished by top managers who exercise a leadership for change and who identify the priorities for change.[72]

CONCLUSIONS AND APPLICATIONS

- Organization structure is the result of an organizing process that allocates and deploys the organization's resources to achieve strategic objectives.

- Organization structures differ from one another along a dimension ranging from mechanistic to organic. The mechanistic design is machinelike and results in a management emphasis on efficiency. Organic designs are more like living organisms because they are innovative and can adapt to changing situations. Organic designs, because of their flexibility, lack the stability to efficiently perform routine work.

- Weber's bureaucracy describes an idealized form of design based on rational guidelines and procedures.

- A well-conceived organizational strategy addresses the three areas of distinctive competence, scope, and resource deployment. Early studies indicated that structural changes followed a change in strategy. Later studies, however, revealed that an organization's structure may hinder the ability to make changes in strategy.

- The fundamental characteristics of organization structure include work specialization, differentiation and integration, centralization and decentralization, formalization, and complexity.

- Organizations grow and evolve over time. As they pass through the four life stages of birth, growth, midlife, and maturity, different organization design patterns will be chosen.

- Departmentation is the grouping of jobs for the purposes of planning, coordination, and control. A variety of departmentation patterns exist.

- Work unit tasks can be coordinated by mutual adjustment, direct supervision, and standardization.

- Lateral relationships are necessary to achieve interdepartmental coordination without overloading the chain of command. They take such forms as direct contact, liaison roles, task forces, integrators, and project teams.

- Design patterns that an organization can adopt include the functional and divisional forms. Each pattern has advantages and disadvantages associated with it. The strategic business (SBU) pattern, matrix pattern, and the networking pattern are specialized forms of organization design. Each has a specialized use.

- Contemporary approaches to organization design are contingency oriented: how work, people, and structures fit together; information technology; empowerment; belief that people are an important asset; reward systems; and the need to keep in touch with customers.

- The horizontal corporation model is an organization design model in which the company is organized around three to five core processes with specific performance goals. Teams are the main building blocks with each team having a common purpose and measurable performance goals.

REVIEW QUESTIONS

1. Explain the following: Work specialization, differentiation, integration, centralization, decentralization, formalization, and complexity.
2. Why is departmentation considered to be a form of coordination?
3. Compare and contrast unit coordination and lateral coordination.
4. What role does information technology play in the organizing process?
5. Describe the differences between a formal and informal organization structure.
6. Describe the contemporary approach to organization design.
7. What are the differences between a mechanistic and an organic structure?
8. Give some examples of organizations using a mediating, long-linked, and intensive technology.
9. Define organization design.
10. Describe the process model for organization design.

11. Describe the characteristics of Weber's ideal bureaucracy.
12. What is the relationship between strategy and structure?
13. How can a manager develop an effective organization design?
14. With respect to organization design, what is a contingency factor?
15. What are the contingency factors that affect organization design?
16. Describe the different perspectives that Woodward, Thompson, and Perrow used in describing technology.
17. The five organization design patterns of functional, divisional, SBU, matrix, and networking were described in this chapter. What are the advantages and disadvantages of each design pattern?
18. Explain the concept of a horizontal corporation.

DISCUSSION QUESTIONS

1. If you were the senior partner of a legal firm, what form of unit coordination would be appropriate for your firm? Why?
2. Describe the difference between formal and informal structure within organizations. How does the informal structure alter the authority of the formal structure?
3. What is the purpose of organization structure?
4. Discuss the difference between a project team and a task force with respect to lateral coordination.
5. Discuss the value of information technology on organization structure.
6. In an organization using a matrix organization design, in which position would you rather be: a functional department manager, a project manager, or a highly trained specialist? Explain why.
7. Discuss why the *ideal* bureaucracy is no longer considered to be the ideal form of organization design.

8. How can the manager of an organization tell whether his or her organization is in a stable environment? A dynamic environment?
9. Explain when management would use a matrix structure.
10. Describe how contingency factors affect an organization's design.
11. Which contingency factor might have the most significant impact on McDonald's organization design? Why?
12. What organization design contingency factors do you believe will be most important in the year 2000?
13. To what extent is the horizontal corporation model a fad?
14. How realistic are the new forms of organization charts described in Fig. 16-2?

CASE STUDY

Delta Service Company

Henry Allen, President of Delta Service Company, has become concerned about the profitability of his company. Allen has just talked with his partners and is worried about what happened during the meeting. Driving home, Allen recalls how he started the business.

Henry Allen was an assistant football coach for one of the state's football powers and was active in many civic organizations. Several years ago, the owner of a janitorial-supply firm had problems with the turnover of salespeople and approached Allen about becoming sales manager. After a series of meetings, Allen determined that if he left coaching for business, he wanted to be the boss and decided to puchase the firm. He immediately provided quicker deliveries, better service, and good advice to his customers about tough cleaning jobs. The business grew rapidly, although Allen's prices were higher than his competitors'.

Allen hired Earl Christopher, a former coaching buddy, as sales manager of existing products and also hired a janitorial products field representative, Bob Warren, from the state's largest janitorial supply firm. Delta Services began bidding on janitorial supply contracts offered by schools, governmental agencies, and large companies. Allen discovered that these large organizations were more interested in price than in service and quality, and adjusted accordingly. Allen was successful in obtaining several contracts but found that they were vulnerable to price competition from other suppliers. One of the largest volume items specified for bids was liquid detergent. Allen learned that the manufacturer's markup on liquid detergent was very high. Warren mentioned that he knew where to purchase the equipment and chemicals needed to manufacture a liquid detergent. Allen worked out a financial arrangement whereby Warren could become part owner of Delta Services. Allen and Warren purchased equipment to manufacture liquid detergent and moved their company to a much larger and expensive warehouse.

Shortly after the move to the new warehouse, Christopher advised Allen that he had been offered a head coaching job in another city but would stay with Delta Services provided increased opportunities were available to him. Warren didn't want to lose Christopher and began to consider ways to accomodate him. Delta Services did not offer swimming pool chemicals or certain other specialty chemicals. Again, Allen worked out a financial deal in which Christopher would have part ownership of Delta Services with the responsiblity of developing sales from swimming pool chemicals and specialty chemicals as well as continuing to perform his present duties.

Allen became concerned that not all of the space in the new warehouse location was being occupied. He approached Mack Burgess, who sold various types of packaging materials (tape cartons, labels, so forth), about buying into the company. Soon, Delta Services' warehouse was filled with packaging materials. Burgess had determined that prompt deliveries would allow Delta Services to increase its market share of packaging materials.

Burgess later mentioned to Warren that many of his customers had difficulty obtaining wooded shipping pallets. Burgess and Warren suggested to Allen that Delta Services offer wooden pallets. Charles Strong, who owned a small pallet-building operation that was experiencing working-capital problems, was offered the opportunity to buy into Delta Services. Strong quickly accepted. A larger building was rented for the pallet operation, and more equipment was purchased.

Several months after Strong invested in Delta Services, Allen became concerned. Overhead had greatly increased. Their detergent was not selling well despite a sizable investment in equipment, chemicals, and plastic bottles. The pallet business did not seem to be going anywhere. Inventories for Christopher's line of products had increased significantly. The sales literature had so many different kinds of cleaning and packaging products listed that customers seemed more confused than interested. Also, in some instances, sales were lost because items weren't available.

At the meeting, Warren, Burgess, Strong, and Christopher strongly stated that Delta Services should begin selling office furniture and carpeting. Their argument was that many of their existing customers would purchase these items and that no inventory would be carried beyond sample books. Delta Services' buying power would be useful in offering these services. Allen became nervous during and after the meeting.

CASE STUDY QUESTIONS

1. From an organization design perspective, what is the immediate threat to Delta Services?
2. What type of organization design would you recommend for Delta Services at the present time? Explain.
3. What other problems may be affecting Delta Services?

EXPERIENTIAL EXERCISE 1

Unit Coordinating Mechanisms

In this exercise, consider a machine shop that constructs a variety of complex valves requiring a combination of drilling, grinding, boring, and finishing operations. The physical specification of each valve determines how the actual work is to be performed.

1. What would production be like if mutual adjustment were used as the coordinating mechanism? Could many valves be produced in a day?
2. What form of unit coordinating mechanism would you recommend? Why? (Mutual adjustment may or may not be the correct unit coordinating mechanism.)

EXPERIENTIAL EXERCISE 2

Determining an Organization's Structural Characteristics

The purpose of this exercise is to determine the characteristics of an organization's structure.

Procedures

1. Select a local organization with between 25 and 200 employees. Don't select a part of your college or university. (The same organization may be used for the exercise from Chap. 14.) Make sure that top management has given

approval for this project and is aware when the interviews will be conducted. You may want to check with your professor before contacting the company.

2. Interview two employees of the company (one must be a top-level position), asking the following questions:

   A. What are the number of levels in the hierarchy?

   B. What is the typical span of control at each level in the organization?

   C. What is the degree of formalization (to what extent are rules and procedures written down in job descriptions, policy and procedures manuals, and memos)?

   D. How is the work coordinated (mutual adjustment, direct supervision, or standardization)? Is more than one type of these coordinating mechanisms used? Explain.

   E. Does the organization have departments? How many? What type of lateral coordinating mechanisms are used to facilitate communication between the departments? (Direct contact, task forces, liaison roles, integrators, or project teams?) Is more than one type of these coordinating mechanisms used? Explain.

3. Be sure to ask the preceding questions in a way that the management and employee will understand. They may not be familiar with some of the terminology used in this chapter.

4. Prepare a written report describing the structural and coordinating characteristics listed in this exercise. You may want to send a copy of the report to the organization's top manager that you interviewed.

Follow-Up Questions

(Do not include these questions in the report provided to the cooperating organization.)

1. How difficult was it to obtain information about the organization's structural and coordinating characteristics? What aspects were the most difficult? Why?

2. Were there differences in the responses of the employee and the manager you interviewed? What could have caused these differences?

3. If you were the top manager of the organization you analyzed, would you structure it the same way? Why or why not? If not, how would you structure it differently? Would you use the same coordinating mechanisms? Why or why not? If not, what coordinating mechanisms would you use?

Take It to the Net   **You can find this chapter's World Wide Web exercise at:**
http://www.prenhall.com/carrell

CHAPTER 17

Organizational Culture

Stride Rite Corporation

Stride Rite Corporation has been a leader in the shoe industry for over fifty years. Its name is a recognized leader in high-quality children's shoes. Two other company brands—Keds and Sperry Top-Siders are also recognized leaders in the U.S. footwear industry. While much of the industry has suffered financial losses in recent years, Stride Rite has posted rising sales and return on equity. As an employer, Stride Rite has an international reputation for initiating one of the nation's first corporate community child-care centers in 1971, a progressive family leave policy, public service scholarships, smoke-free offices, and a day-care center for children and elderly citizens. At the top of the Stride Rite organization is the builder of its "progressive" corporate culture—its chairman, Arnold Hiatt, who discussed his beliefs in an interview with *Harvard Business Review*:[1]

QUESTION: Stride Rite has often been recognized for workplace innovation; how do you react to such recognition?

ARNOLD HIATT: Our strength lies in building on classics (products), and on knowing who we are. That is how we've succeeded as a company. And that same quality lies behind the social policies we've introduced over the years. They are conservative in the best sense of the 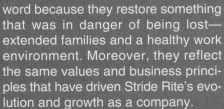 word because they restore something that was in danger of being lost—extended families and a healthy work environment. Moreover, they reflect the same values and business principles that have driven Stride Rite's evolution and growth as a company.

When Senator Ted Kennedy visited the day-care center in Cambridge, one woman told him she came all the way from Taunton to work at Stride Rite. Kennedy was astonished: "But that's two hours up and two hours back each day." The woman responded, "but it's worth it because my child gets quality care and opportunities I couldn't otherwise provide." It (the story) demonstrates why we have been able to attract capable, loyal employees in a region where good workers are often in short supply.

QUESTION: What was the thinking behind the family leave policy?

ARNOLD HIATT: A mother or father who wants to take time off to care for a newborn should have a job to come back to. It just made sense.

QUESTION: Policies like that are one reason for Stride Rite's reputation as a good employer. What do you think makes a company a good place to work?

ARNOLD HIATT: Two things. First, respect for people and conditions that reflect that respect. You just treat people the way you want to be treated. Second, the opportunity for everyone to contribute, to know that what you do can make a difference. That's where real commitment comes from, for senior managers and hourly employees alike. . .

Over time we introduced an employee stock purchase plan so that everyone could buy stock at a discount. We also developed incentive plans. Enlarging the circle of people who care is simple, common sense. That is far more motivating than cafeteria benefit plans or company ball games or even a good paycheck.

QUESTION: Why is the selling environment (in the stores) so important?

ARNOLD HIATT: What brings parents back to Stride Rite as their children grow is their experience at the point of sale. If customers are going to be committed to Stride Rite, we have to earn their commitment. We can't do that with magazine or television spots. We can only do it in the store by measuring the child's foot carefully, but making sure

we have the right size, the right width, the right product in stock, and by disciplining ourselves not to make a sale if the child's old shoe still fits.

QUESTION: Stride Rite takes a very responsible attitude toward its employees in the United States. Can that kind of corporate responsibility be exported?

ARNOLD HIATT: It's arrogant to think you can make a difference in another country's culture. But it's equally arrogant to imagine you can't find responsible business people everywhere . . . Before meeting the president of a Thailand company, I toured the factory. We walked by a door with a sign over it and were told it said "library" in Thai. I opened the door, and the room was filled with workers bent over books. I knew I was about to meet an unusual man. Mr. Narong, the president, was wary of us, because he had built a factory to supply another U.S. shoe company. When the business fell he had to lay off a great many workers. One young woman committed suicide. That experience shook him deeply. I proposed a partnership. . . . Today, the factory employs 1,200 people and produces 20,000 pairs of Keds each day. It is the nicest manufacturing facility I have ever seen, with landscaped gardens and pools and little windmills to circulate air through the plant.

Arnold Hiatt's brief discussion of Stride Rite should give you a general idea of the company's culture—its policies, values, and practices that define its essence. Several of Hiatt's phrases and words—"building on classics," "extended families," "a healthy work environment," "respect for people," "the opportunity for everyone to contribute," "enlarging the circle of people who care,"—gives one a general idea of the workplace atmosphere or organizational culture at Stride Rite. The concept of organizational culture and its implications for organizations are the topic of this chapter.

ORGANIZATIONAL CULTURE DEFINED

Each organization has its own personality, just like each individual has his or her own personality. Many different attributes or characteristics of organizations determine their personality or culture. These characteristics directly and indirectly, as part of the total culture, affect the attractiveness of the organization as a place to work, and therefore affect the productivity and morale of the people in the organization. *Organizational culture* can be more precisely defined as:[2]

Organizational culture
The underlying values, beliefs, and principles that form the foundation of an organization.

> the underlying values, beliefs, and principles that serve as a foundation for an organization's management system as well as the set of management practices and behaviors that both exemplify and reinforce those basic principles

or

> a set of key characteristics that describe the essence of an organization

The critical characteristics that define an organization's culture have been identified as:[3]

1. *Values.* The dominant values espoused by an organization. The importance of all employees sharing the same values is expressed by a partner of Arthur Andersen in Fig. 17-1.
2. The *philosophy* that guides an organization's policies towards its employees and customers.
3. *Norms* of behavior that evolve in working groups.
4. *Politics.* The rules of the game for getting along in the organization.
5. The *climate* of work which is conveyed by the physical layout and the way people interact.
6. *Behaviors* of people when they interact such as the language and demeanor: the social interaction.

To understand organizational behavior we must learn and understand these key characteristics of the organization's culture. They are unique to each organization just as personality traits are unique to each individual. The cultural characteristics of an organization affect and direct the behavior of the organization, just as an individual's personality characteristics affect and direct his or her behavior.

Now, for just a moment, think back briefly to the interview with Stride Rite's Arnold Hiatt. Can you choose one or two adjectives to describe Stride Rite in terms of each (or most) of the above characteristics? If you combine the six in a meaningful way, you might be able to broadly describe Stride Rite's organizational culture.

No matter whom I work with throughout our organization, we all share a culture that stresses the same values. This enables us to give our clients quality service that is consistent everywhere in the world.

Anonymous Partner
Arthur Andersen, Paris, France

Source: The Arthur Andersen Organization, 1992 Annual Report. © 1993 Arthur Andersen. All Rights Reserved. Used with permission.

FIGURE 17-1
The Importance of Culture and Values in the Arthur Andersen Organization

The above cultural characteristics are largely internal to the organization. External factors can exert influence on an organization's culture, and the most influential factor may be the industry within which the organization functions. Industries generally exert influences that provide parameters to organizational cultures. Therefore, organizations within the same industry often have similar characteristics. A general model of this process developed by George C. Gordon is presented in Fig. 17-2. It illustrates that organizations operate within an industry that generally has developed certain assumptions and operating procedures regarding customers, competitors, and society (including government). From these basic assumptions and practices certain beliefs and values develop regarding operations, customers, competition, et cetera. Management then develops strategies, structures, and processes needed to survive, and these greatly affect the culture of the organization.[4]

It is important to point out that culture at the national level and culture at the organizational level—corporate culture, are two very different phenomena. The use of the common term for both is unfortunate and confusing. National cultures differ primarily in the fundamental values held by a majority of their members. These largely invisible values are acquired in early childhood. Organizational cultures are more superficial phenomena that exist in the policies, practices, and norms of the organization. These practices are acquired with the socialization of new members, mostly young adults. National cultures change very slowly, whereas organizational cultures may be consciously changed in only a few years. Multinational corporations such as IBM, DuPont, and Coca-Cola have learned to utilize employees of different national cultures without trying to change their national cultures. What keeps their multinational units together is their organizational culture based on common practices.[5]

Symbols

A symbol generally refers to an object or event that conveys a certain meaning to others. In society certain symbols such as our country's flag, a crucifix, and the voting booth convey certain beliefs and ideals to almost everyone. Within many homes families have developed internal symbols such as the living room reclining chair, a prized trophy on the mantel, or a wedding gown handed down from generation to generation.

Organizations often develop their own internal and external symbols. Corporate logos—the Disney mouse ears, the script-written "Ford," the Coca-Cola sign, and the golden arches: All instantly convey similar thoughts to millions of people. Not all organizations have such easily recognized logos or other external symbols, but most have developed internal symbols that can tell someone a great deal about the culture that exists. Reserved parking spaces, the executive dining room, restricted restrooms, and company cars, for example, all convey a certain culture—one of two classes of employees—the privileged and the common workers. This culture and its symbols do not exist in all organizations, and some like General Motors are trying to change (see "OB in Practice") their culture of separateness. Other types of internal symbols are behaviors or actions, especially by the organizational leaders, which convey a certain culture. A company president who eats lunch in the cafeteria, drives and parks his or her personal car with everyone else, manages by walking around (MBWA), and not only listens but follows up on employee complaints and suggestions sets an example and becomes a symbol of equity that can have a strong influence on the organization's culture.

OB in Practice

GM Overhauls Corporate Culture

On January 1, 1993, the GM executive dining room on the fourteenth floor of its world headquarters, perhaps the ultimate company symbol of privilege and success, was closed. The executive dining room had survived wars, recessions, and even H. Ross Perot, but not the sweeping culture change of a new president—John F. Smith, Jr. In the past, the "big shooters went to the fourteenth floor, and the little people went somewhere else," explained Executive Vice President, William E. Hoglund. The closing was a "tiny step toward . . . a new GM."

Other symbolic actions—such as no neckties on Fridays and no free lunches from parts suppliers were combined with a new philosophy and new policies. Engineers, for example, were no longer required to get approvals for expenditures, and the number of management staffers who reviewed other people—the "checkers, and those who check the checkers"—was reduced from 13,000 to 2,000 people. Saturn, the most successful GM division, began sharing its secrets with other divisions, and putting their executives through outdoor training and team-building exercises.

GM President Smith told market analysts that the goal of the symbolic changes and new employee philosophy was to "change GM's traditional culture" and was his greatest challenge. Hoglund added, "We'll be less arrogant. We will respect the customer. We'll love our people. And we'll have good quality." The cultural revolution was given a 1997 target date for completion.

Source: Joseph B. White, "GM Is Overhauling Corporate Culture in an Effort to Regain Competitiveness," *The Wall Street Journal,* January 13, 1993, A1, p. 3. Reprinted by permission of *The Wall Street Journal,* © 1993 Dow Jones & Company, Inc. All rights reserved worldwide.

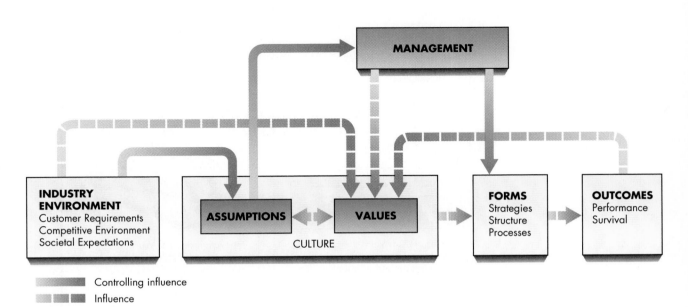

FIGURE 17-2 A Model of Industry-driven Culture Formation

Source: George C. Gordon, "Industry Determinants of Organizational Culture," *Academy of Management Review,* vol. 16, no. 2, 1991, p. 400. Used by permission.

Types of Cultures

Emory University researcher Jeffrey Sonnenfeld, after studying the cultures of a number of organizations, concluded that four "types" of cultures exist in organizations. Some organizations may have one dominant type of culture, some may contain several types located in different departments or locations, and still others may be in a state of transition from one type to another due to a change in leadership, increased competition, new technology, et cetera. The four types are called: academy; fortress; clubs; and baseball team. Perhaps the most important issue to arise from this categorization of cultures is: Does one culture best describe (see Fig. 17-3) a place where you would like to work and could be productive? Sonnenfeld's research concluded that each of the four cultures tends to attract different people. All types may be found within successful organizations. But all types of individuals and personalities would not "fit in" each type

FIGURE 17-3

Four Types of
Organizational Cultures

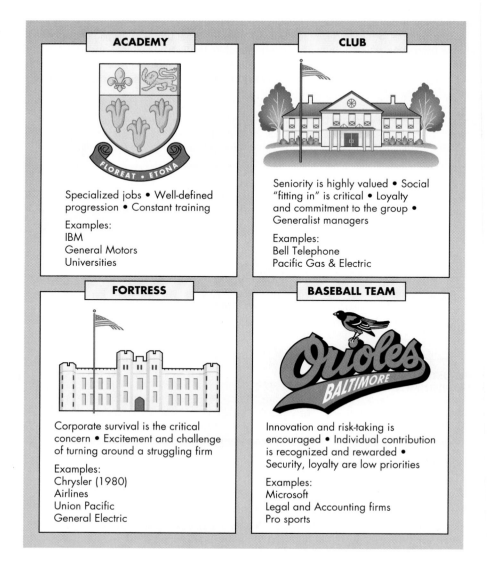

ACADEMY

Specialized jobs • Well-defined progression • Constant training

Examples:
IBM
General Motors
Universities

CLUB

Seniority is highly valued • Social "fitting in" is critical • Loyalty and commitment to the group • Generalist managers

Examples:
Bell Telephone
Pacific Gas & Electric

FORTRESS

Corporate survival is the critical concern • Excitement and challenge of turning around a struggling firm

Examples:
Chrysler (1980)
Airlines
Union Pacific
General Electric

BASEBALL TEAM

Innovation and risk-taking is encouraged • Individual contribution is recognized and rewarded • Security, loyalty are low priorities

Examples:
Microsoft
Legal and Accounting firms
Pro sports

of culture. Thus a person who achieves only mediocre success, or even fails, in one type of culture might thrive in another. For example, a person who values security and a career of planned job advances might best succeed in an "academy" culture. The risk-taker who likes to challenge the status quo and thrives on individual recognition would most likely find success in the "baseball team" culture.[6]

Subcultures

In small organizations culture may be a uniform force, "the rudder" that guides the organization. In larger, complex organizations, however, in addition to the broad, organizational-wide culture, which "guides the boat," there often exists a "collection of oars" paddled by employees and groups who have conflicting perceptions, goals, and values: For example, the salesperson, who makes promises the delivery department cannot possibly honor. These *subcultures* are often based on job function, operating units, key individuals, or even social interests, and may or may not interfere with the company's overall mission.[7] *Subcultures* can generally be defined as:

> groups of individuals with a unique set of values, beliefs, and principles that operates within a larger organization.

Organizational leaders need to recognize the existence and motivation of subcultures if they hope to affect the overall organizational culture. The most common subcultures are based on department, unit, function, social network, or managerial level (see Fig. 17-4). Members of these groups may develop a unique group subculture because they share similar values, expectations, and work environment. The subculture provides an identity to their members. New group members wanting to be accepted by the group, usually learn and adopt the norms and values of the group, even if it does not match their own.[8]

Subculture Groups of individuals with unique sets of values, beliefs, principles, and goals that operate within a large organization.

---

1. **Functional** subcultures develop around occupation. There may be a subculture of the accounting positions, for example, which promotes behaviors that focus on precision and value-quantitative assessment.
2. **Operating unit** subcultures tend to exist in diversified businesses. In this situation, the same company can contain many different industry cultures. The non-regulated side of telephone companies, for example, may become involved in such diverse businesses as publishing, information processing, real estate, and credit, creating the possibility of considerable cultural dissonance.
3. **Hierarchical** subcultures can develop at any level of the organization's management. For example, midlevel managers can manifest an exclusionary quality because stars attract stars. Patrick Vann, assistant professor of management and organizational behavior at the University of Colorado, in Boulder, explains, "These people know that they're on the way up, and in that sense, they're driven toward each other." High-level managers, on the other hand, may exude a sanctimonious or moralistic attitude.
4. **Social** subcultures may develop within organizations around social activities, such as company softball games. Unlike functional subcultures, social subcultures often include individuals from all the levels of the organization, making them the most difficult to identify. Informal but effective communication networks also can develop within social subcultures.

Source: Shari Caudron, "Subculture Strife Hinders Productivity," *Personnel Journal*, December 1992, pp. 60–64. Used by permission.

FIGURE 17-4

Sources of Subcultures

The most important question of a subculture is whether or not its values and norms are consistent with the mission of the organization. The potential for divergence from the organization's mission is great—particularly as organizations get larger and more bureaucratic. Certain types of institutions that are often large, bureaucratic, and do not experience substantial competition, can be particularly susceptible to breeding subcultures that suboptimize the organization's effectiveness: universities, hospitals, governmental units, and utility companies may fall into this category.

UNION CARBIDE AND UOP, INC.   Subcultures often clash within organizations—finance and research, marketing and distribution, "old guard" and "new guard," et cetera. The merger of two formerly separate cultures may cause such a problem. An excellent example occurred in 1987 when UOP, Inc., in Des Plaines, Illinois, was joined with Union Carbide. The UOP work force increased from 1,800 employees to 3,500 employees, and two very different organizational cultures collided. Union Carbide employees were accustomed to a "club" culture (see Fig. 17-3) with a highly structured style of operation that relied heavily on policy and procedure. UOP employees, however, were accustomed to a "baseball team" culture that encouraged innovation and risk-taking, and relied little on structure and policy. The two cultures quickly clashed and exchanges resulted, such as "at Union Carbide we do it this way" or "we never do that." To successfully unite the subcultures and employees, management launched a Total Quality Management training program. The key focus, according to Leo Schultz, a senior accountant at UOP, was communication: "We discovered that the main problem had been a lack of communication between employees . . . No one had any idea what other groups were up to, so they all assumed that their way was the best way." To resolve this clash of cultures and communication problems, the newly merged management of UOP developed a new mission statement that specified the responsibilities of each employee group. Then the groups were encouraged, but not required, to form self-managed work teams that could identify and resolve their problems in line with their new mission. These efforts, according to Schultz, enabled the company to resolve the "us versus them" subculture disputes.[9]

Perhaps the most publicized clash between two cultures occurred when General Motors purchased EDS financial services. EDS founder and chair H. Ross Perot (the 1992 independent presidential candidate) joined the board of GM. Perot's "baseball team" culture and GM's "academy" culture clashed and caused many to begin to doubt GM's leadership as national headlines carried the disputes (see "OB in Practice").

Cultural Change

When major factors external to an organization change, a new strategy may be required to meet the change. Organizational leaders then often respond by attempting to change the culture of an organization to meet the new demands. Implementing a Total Quality Management (TQM) program to better meet customer needs might be an example of such a change. Research and practice indicate two different models of culture change exist. The first model suggests that organizations emulate an "ideal company" and try to adopt its culture and follow its example. The second model suggests that the organization strive to better align its existing culture and strategy with its external environment. Thus instead of trying to copy an ideal culture develop a strategy which successfully

OB in Practice

A Clash of Cultures— GM and Ross Perot

Mergers between two organizations often seem easier to accomplish on paper than in reality. Reality often reveals that the cultures of the organizations and the personalities of their top executives fail to mesh as easily as corporate assets. In no case has this situation been more dramatically illustrated than in the 1984 merger of Electronic Data Systems (EDS) into General Motors.

The merger brought together two disparate cultures. Bureaucratic, tradition-bound, "by-the-book" GM found itself attempting to absorb a far smaller firm, best characterized as possessing a "can do, anything is possible," entrepreneurial spirit.

A cultural clash was inevitable. Dallas-based EDS, a nonunion firm, had an extremely stringent hiring and selection process followed by a grueling trial and training period that could last as long as two years. Those who survived displayed unusually high morale and a devotion for doing whatever was required to accomplish the task.

GM's white-collar workers, accustomed to automatic pay raises and cost-of-living adjustments, felt threatened by the EDS practice of rewarding only job performance. GM employees were taken aback by the hard-driving competitiveness of the EDS workers with their unquestioning adherence to rigid dress and personal grooming codes. As reported in *The Wall Street Journal,* "In some ways, EDS merging with GM is like a Green Beret outfit joining up with the Social Security Administration."

Frustrated by GM's slowness to change, top-level executives at EDS—particularly its founder and chairman, H. Ross Perot—began to criticize GM publicly. Finally, GM's management and board had enough. Perot was about to publicly chastise the GM board for considering paying end-of-the-year bonuses to senior management following a $338.5 million operating loss in the preceding quarter and a decision to lay off 29,000 workers. To forestall that criticism, the board voted unanimously to pay Perot about $700 million to leave EDS, and an additional $50 million to buy out three other EDS executives. As part of the agreement, Perot faced a fine of up to $7.5 billion if he continued to criticize GM in public.

H. Ross Perot, the 1992 Independent presidential candidate, exhibited a "challenge the status quo" entrepreneurial spirit which clashed with General Motors' "by-the-book" style when he joined GM's board of directors. To end Perot's public criticisms, GM paid Perot $700 million to leave.

Source: C. Pringle, D. Jennings, J. Longenecker, *Managing Organizations: Functions and Behaviors,* Columbus, OH, Merrill Pub. Co., 1988, p. 310. Used by permission. And based on Laurie P. Cohen and Charles F. McCoy, "Perot's Singular Style Raises Issues of How He'll Fit at GM," *The Wall Street Journal,* July 2, 1984 (source of quotation); Damon Darlin and Melinda Grenier Guiles, "Some GM People Feel Auto Firm, Not EDS, Was the One Acquired," *The Wall Street Journal,* December 19, 1984; "How Ross Perot's Shock Troops Ran into Flack at GM," *Business Week,* February 11, 1985, pp. 118–22; "GM Boots Perot" and "Perot to Smith: GM Must Change," *Newsweek,* December 15, 1986, pp. 56–62; and "GM Hasn't Bought Much Peace" and "The Risks of Running EDS without Perot," *Business Week,* December 15, 1986, pp. 24–27.

meets the external change. Organizations have successfully and unsuccessfully attempted to utilize both change models.[10]

Many organizational leaders have strived to change the culture of their organization using one of these two models. A fundamental change in an organization's culture often involves new slogans, symbols, and values. However, these are only part of a change that most efforts are designed to alter. The very essence of most change efforts in the organization is its culture. These substantial change efforts are often a response to increased competition that forces an organization to improve quality, increase productivity, and adopt a greater customer orientation. What are the keys to a successful culture change? According to DuPont

CEO Edgar Woolard—the change must originate at the bottom, and the CEO must guide it. Woolard explains: "Employees have been underestimated. You have to start with the premise that people at all levels want to contribute and make the business a success." The CEO, according to Woolard, must provide the direction of the change to make sure it's coherent. A cultural change is a change in the ways people think and behave in performing their everyday tasks.[11]

Successful cultural changes have been documented in several organizations including Ford Motor Company, General Electric (see Chap. 14), Union Pacific, IBM, Disney, and DuPont. While no recipe for change can guarantee success, seven keys to a successful change are commonly identified (Fig. 17-5):[12]

1. *Understand your old culture.* Organizations often utilize job satisfaction surveys to find out what employees like and dislike about the organization and their jobs. They can also use surveys to help determine what are the attributes of the current culture. However, the usual process of having employees complete the surveys and wait for management to take action should be avoided. Employees should be empowered to analyze the results and design plans to change their subcultures, but with the support of management. This mutual responsibility is critical to significant change. At British Petroleum Exploration (BP), for example, satisfaction and productivity survey results were discussed in joint work teams—management sessions in which plans for change were formulated.[13]

2. *Encourage innovative employees.* Change of any kind usually results in resistance and a desire to maintain the status quo by many employees and subcultures. Those few (usually a minority) who are willing to buck the old and try to build a new culture require special support from the organization's leadership. Florida Power & Light (FP&L), for example, had an entrenched culture of bureaucracy and poor customer service. In efforts to change its culture to one of top customer service, management at FP&L gave all employees the freedom to initiate changes. The meter readers in Boca Raton, for example, asked to form a team to study the problem of dog bites—the leading cause of on-the-job injuries. Under the old culture the idea would have been rejected outright—according to Wayne Runette, Vice President at FP&L. But the new management encouraged such innovation, a team was formed, and hand-held computers that beep when a dangerous address is approached (they are primarily used to record power usage) reduced bites and thus absenteeism and injuries went down and morale up.[14]

3. *Promote the best subculture.* Determine which subcultures are supportive of the desired change and overall mission and recognize, support, and identify them as models for the other subcultures. Then work to change those that continue to be counter-productive. How can well-established subcultures be changed? Some will quickly follow the new "models" you

FIGURE 17-5
Keys to Cultural Change

1. Understand your old culture.	5. Don't rely on a new vision.
2. Encourage innovative employees.	6. Expect five to ten years.
3. Promote the best subcultures.	7. Live the culture you want.
4. Don't confront culture directly.	

Source: Brian Dumaine, "Creating a New Company Culture," *Fortune*, vol. 127, January 15, 1990, pp. 127–131. Copyright © 1990 Time Inc. All rights reserved.

have established. Others may be very difficult to change. A few steps that can be followed to change subcultures include:[15]

First step: Determine the basic values and beliefs—how do things get done; what are the priorities? This can be done through interviews with key personnel, surveys, and by asking members of other work groups. Attending meetings of a group can reveal a great deal about its culture.

Second step: Acknowledge the unique contributions of the group that do support the organization's mission. This validates the positive contributions of the team and helps focus on those that require changing.

Third step: Translate the mission of the organization into specific behaviors and goals for each team—then identify what current actions need to be changed and why.

Fourth step: Communicate between subcultures in order that each understands the contributions of others—and how all are supporting the mission of the organization.

DuPont's CEO Edgar Woolard brought the vision of greater customer service to life with DuPont's "Adopt a Customer" program in which blue-collars directly visit a customer once a month to learn his or her needs and problems and provide direct service.

4. *Don't confront culture directly.* Strive to eliminate from peoples' vocabularies "killer phrases" such as: "It won't work here;" "We tried that years ago;" and "They won't let us" by responding in a forceful but pleasant tone; "then we can learn from that mistake in this effort;" or "things are different now—we have the authority to implement ideas." An important part of this key is to convince people that taking risks and being innovative will be supportive, and that failure will not result in punishment, but in fact provides valuable information. Not taking risks or changing is, in fact, failure.[16]

5. *Don't rely on a new vision.* Without question, as we discuss in Chap. 14, the leadership of an organization must create a shared vision that provides direction. And that vision should be reduced to writing in the form of a mission statement. However, relying on a well-stated mission without the proper encouragement and support for changes in behavior would invite failure.

    DuPont's CEO Edgar Woolard, for example, stresses the customer orientation mission with the philosophy, "nothing is worthwhile unless it touches the customers." To demonstrate his support of this philosophy DuPont initiated an "Adopt a Customer" program in which blue-collar workers visit customers once a month to learn their needs and problems, and provide hands-on service direct from the factory floor. The customers appreciate the direct service, and the workers better understand the customer's point of view.[17]

6. *Expect five to ten years.* Significant cultural change on an organizationwide basis requires an evolution, not a revolution. Five to ten years for such programs to gain acceptance, prove themselves, and truly change the culture is an average length of time.

7. *Live the culture you want.* Motivating speeches and well-written policies and mission statements are still only words. People believe actions and behaviors: If the behaviors of management conflict with the culture being preached, then little change can be expected. Instead, the change will be perceived to be only the "latest management fad."

    For example, management at Tandem, the California-based computer company, believed it fostered a caring, supportive culture for its employees. When a manager told CEO Jimmy Trezbig he wanted to fire someone, Trezbig instructed him to find out why the person's performance had fallen. The manager discovered the employee had suffered severe family problems, gave him another chance, and the employee returned to his previous form. The second chance set a signal to other employees that management was serious about maintaining a caring culture. Also, as we discussed earlier, symbols such as executive parking spaces, corporate jets, fat expense accounts, et cetera, send out powerful signals as to the culture management supports.[18]

When is an organizational cultural change likely to occur? During poor economic times? Under new management? After the CEO has returned from a management seminar? An interesting and thorough study of the relationship between the characteristics of Fortune 500 top management teams and strategic change produced surprising results. The study found that firms most likely to experience change had top management people who were: (1) relatively young (compared to other companies); (2) had relatively less experience with the organization; (3) had relatively greater experience with a management team; (4) had higher educational levels; (5) had academic training in the sciences; and (6) had educational diversity within the management team.[19] Thus, if a board of directors, owners, or CEO are interested in initiating substantial change in culture and strategy, they should consider appointing a team that is relatively young with short organizational tenure, but has experience working as a team, with diversity of management experience to initiate the change.

An excellent example of such a culture change team was formed at Nordstrom, Inc., the Seattle-based retailer that prospered during the 1980s under the leadership of three grandsons of the founder of the company. The three co-presidents were all young and had worked together for years before they led the remarkable growth and customer-oriented culture change. Then in 1992 faced by a horrendous industry slump and drop in sales and stock price, the three appointed a new team of four co-presidents—Raymond Johnson (age fifty, former personnel executive), Darrel Hume (forty-four, former sales manager), Galen Jefferson (forty-two, former mail-order and women's fashion executive), and John Whitacre (thirty-nine, former shoe department executive). Thus, the new Nordstrom team also followed, in general, the culture change model just discussed. What makes Nordstrom's unique, however, is that these two teams were not only empowered to change the culture at Nordstroms—but to manage the organizations as well! The key to this unusual situation is Nordstrom's highly decentralized structure and corporate culture that focuses on big commissions for salespeople, promotion from within, and loyal employees who decertified their union when it sued Nordstrom over an overtime wage issue.[20]

Obstacles to culture change are many including employee fear of the unknown, preference for maintaining the status quo, and anxiety over learning new methods, processes, and skills. The greatest threat, according to Warren Wilhelm, head of organizational and management development for Amoco Corporation, is subversion. Successful subversion is likely to occur, warns Wilhelm, if:[21]

- Employees perceive the CEO is uncommitted or unclear about the new mission or strategy.
- Company veterans treat the required change as a short-term management program that will pass, and they can "ride it out."
- Management continues to reward undesired behavior that does not lead to new objectives.

- Customers, suppliers, or employees perceive that the organization is losing its determination to change, which will most likely occur one to three years after the initiation.

One or more of these subversive factors can thwart a culture change program, and thus must be constantly monitored.

MISSION STATEMENTS

The essence of an organization can be found in its goals, values, and methods of operating. Such goals, cultural norms, and values largely direct organizational behavior. The organization often adopts a system of rules, policies, and operating procedures that provide the framework for expected personal behaviors that will follow the goals and norms of the organization. Cultural framework gives direction and mobilizes behavior within the organization. This potential relationship between an organization's success and its culture received significant national attention from the book, *In Search of Excellence,* New York, Harper & Row, 1982, by Thomas J. Peters and Robert H. Waterman. The authors linked the creative, positive cultures of Disney, IBM, and others to their cultures that encourage risk-taking and change to meet the demands of a rapidly changing external environment. Almost overnight organizational leaders across America began to question the culture of their own organization and its impact on success.

To provide focus to this direction many organizations develop and follow *mission statements* or corporate constitutions. The words, "We the people of these United States. . . ." provided a new direction, set of values, basic principles, and a vision to our nation over two hundred years ago. The U.S. Constitution provided a cornerstone for the growth and development of this country. Corporate constitutions or mission statements may also shape the culture, character, and quality of organizations in a similar manner. In recent years there has been a renewed interest by organizations to revise or develop initial mission statements. The root cause of this interest has been a sense of loss of purpose or direction suffered during a time of increased global competition, rapid technological change, and a changing domestic work force. For example, the executive vice president of a mining company in an address to middle management stated:[22]

Mission statement
A brief outline of the direction, values, basic principles, and vision that guide an organization.

> Some mines are going to close. Ours are not going to be among them.
> Our statement of mission, vision, and philosophy are the foundation
> on which we will build our future.

Organizations have been able, in some cases, to focus planning and provide real direction and commitment throughout the organization with a mission statement serving as the road map. Several successful firms in various industries have cited their mission statement as providing the visioning process needed to support their leadership and strategic development: MCI (telecommunications), Merck (pharmaceuticals), 3M (manufacturing), Motorola (electronics), Boeing (aircraft), and Hewlett-Packard (advanced technology) are excellent examples.[23]

Mission statements can provide such "road maps," because they can be used by an organization to meet a variety of needs. Generally a mission statement:[24]

- Expresses the organization's *reason for existence*—its mission. This focuses on what the organization does and doesn't do. The statement thus forms the foundation for future strategic and operational planning.

FIGURE 17-6
Common Elements of
Mission Statements

- *Tradition:* Respect for the past, for people who fashioned the present enterprise, for the products and services on which its reputation has been built, and for the values and principles that have been its foundation.
- *People:* Recognition that people are the organization's most important asset and that it is only through people that all things are accomplished.
- *Quality:* Commitment to continuous improvement, a belief that quality is both a mark of accomplishment and a symbol of dedication.
- *Principles:* Convictions about organizational governance that express the importance of learning, participation, autonomy, innovation, teamwork, equity, and justice.
- *Human values:* Respect for such personal values as integrity, dignity, respect, and competence.
- *The future:* A statement of vision, of direction, a conviction that we must be architects of our future and shapers of our destinies.

Source: Delmar L. Landen and Gayle A. Landen, "Corporate Constitutions Help Define Companies' Character, Culture, and Quality," *Employment Relations Today,* vol. 18, Summer 1991, p. 207. Used by permission.

- Articulates *fundamental values* of the organization—thus imposing on management the responsibility of developing and enforcing policies, procedures, and reward structures to support those values.
- Serves as the ultimate *litmus test,* or point of reference, against which all strategic and critical decisions are judged.
- Expresses the organization's *commitment to customers, shareholders, employees, and the community.* It is the organization's promise to all critical groups that it will function in a moral and ethical manner.
- Provides a *vision of the future* and continuity from the past.
- Gains a *commitment from employees* by clearly communicating the nature and concept of the organization's business.

Mission statements vary from organization to organization. They have no prescribed length, content, or list of specifics. However, they generally focus on six features of the organization: its tradition, people, commitment to quality, principles, human values, and its future (see Fig. 17-6).[25] The mission statements from three very different organizations in Fig. 17-7 all contain these features—in some cases one or two words is all that is needed to express the position of the organization.

The three statements vary greatly in length and focus. Quaker's focus is clearly, and solely, on increasing return to shareholders—to the extent that each brand is independently measured against that mission. Other features such as quality, principles of operation, and human values that are emphasized in the statement of the Pocono Produce Company, are absent in the Quaker statement. The Pocono Produce Company of Stroudsburg, Pennsylvania, is an independent, family-owned food-service distributor. The company president, Edward K. Driebe, and the entire management team spent many hours developing the mission statement and communicating it to all employees. The Pocono statement follows a format utilized in many statements—an opening umbrella statement that identifies the basic nature of the organization and the business in which it is engaged. And, which is often the case in other statements, the opening line is followed by a "to fulfill this goal the company is committed to" sentence which is then followed by a series of specific statements. The family values emphasized in the Pocono statement are somewhat common in statements of family-owned businesses, some of

FIGURE 17-7 Three Mission Statements

HONDA

HONDA MOTOR CO., LTD.
COMPANY PRINCIPLE

"Maintaining an international viewpoint, we are dedicated to supplying products of the highest efficiency yet at a reasonable price for worldwide customer satisfaction."

HONDA MOTOR CO., LTD.
MANAGEMENT POLICY

• Proceed always with ambition and youthfulness.
• Respect sound theory, develop fresh ideas, and make the most effective use of time.
• Enjoy your work and always brighten your working atmosphere.
• Strive constantly for a harmonious flow of work.
• Be ever mindful of the value of research and endeavor.

HONDA OF AMERICA MFG., INC.
OPERATING PRIORITIES

In all areas of manufacturing operations, Honda of America Manufacturing, Inc. observes the following priorities:

1. Safety   **2.** Quality   **3.** Production

HONDA OF AMERICA MFG., INC.
OPERATING PRINCIPLES

Quality in All Jobs   *Reliable Products*
Learn, think, analyze, evaluate, and improve   On time, with excellence and consistency

Better Communication
Listen, ask, and speak up

SLOGAN

"With increased associate involvement, we improve quality, reduce cost and secure our future."

POCONO PRODUCE COMPANY

A Mission statement:

Pocono Produce Company is a broad line, customer-oriented food-service distributor. Our goal is to be recognized as the best food-service distribution company in the Northeastern United States.

To fulfill this goal, Pocono Produce Company is committed to these values of the Driebe Family:

• That integrity is the foundation of our business, with excellent service and consistent quality as our cornerstones.
• That the needs of the customer will be identified and satisfied.
• That people are our most important resource. All people are to be treated with dignity and fairness—customers, employees, suppliers, competitors, friends and neighbors.
• That we have the best people who strive for excellence in achievement. We encourage the growth of each individual to reach his or her personal goals and professional potential.
• That our company atmosphere is supportive, informal, and friendly as well as goal oriented and demanding.
• That our physical plant, equipment, and vehicles will be safe, clean, and maintained to best serve our customers and our employees.
• That we stress the entrepreneurial spirit and encourage new ideas and innovation.
• That sound growth is essential to success. Therefore, we will be both aggressive and prudent, resulting in a return of equity that will provide sufficient earnings to support that growth.
• That we will be good corporate citizens, working to make our community a better place in which to live.

QUAKER OATS

Our Mission:

Our mission is to maximize value for our shareholders over the long term. This challenges us to employ our two key assets—our portfolio of brands and our people—to maximize their value creation potential. These two assets are vitally linked. Management is empowered to oversee the investment in and the maintenance of our brands. Its specific challenge is to maximize each brand's growth and profit contribution potential—to create economic value.

Source: Annual Reports of Honda of America Mfg., Inc. and Quaker; and permission of The Pocono Produce Company.

At Quaker Oats Company the mission is the maximum growth and profitability of each brand.

which will even include the intention of maintaining family ownership. The Honda Motor Co. statement reflects an emphasis on an "international viewpoint" that one might expect. However, the specific policies of "ambition and youthfulness," "enjoy your work, and "always brighten your working atmosphere," "develop fresh ideas," and "increased associate (employee) involvement" certainly provide some insight into Honda's organizational culture.

Mission statements have become an integral part of many organizations. Almost everyone has one, or more. They can, however, cause problems. If a mission statement includes something the organization does not practice in its daily business, then its credibility with its customers, stockholders, and own employees can be seriously jeopardized. Other problems can occur if the statement is merely window dressing. For example, a human resource executive had admired the wording of the mission statement of a company with which she did business. A copy of the statement was hanging on the lobby wall, and one day she asked a long-time employee of the company for a copy. "What?" he responded. "You know . . . it's on the wall as you walk in . . . " She finally had to take him to the lobby—and watched him read the statement for the first time. Needless to say her faith in the management of the company and its ability to provide quality service and maintain customer satisfaction was shaken.[26] To help avoid such a problem and ensure the successful development and implementation of a new mission statement, the following steps can be followed:[27]

Step 1: Management thoroughly discusses the *core values of the organization,* drafts are shared with employees until a final revision is agreed upon.

Step 2: In a series of meetings the *final statement is presented and discussed* with all employees in small groups.

Step 3: A second series of meetings is held for the purpose of determining exactly how the *statement can affect individual jobs and decisions.*

Step 4: *Periodic review and revision,* usually annually ensures that the statement remains current in the minds and actions of people. It becomes part of the new employee orientation program.

CULTURE RELATED PROBLEMS

The culture of an organization can have sizeable effects on the behavior of individuals, groups, and the organization as a whole. Not only can a person's work environment cause significant personal problems—such as stress, plateauing, or chemical dependency, which we will explore in this section, but the environment can provide assistance in alleviating work-related or other problems through employee empowerment, wellness programs, child/elder care, and other techniques that will be discussed in the following section.

Stress

Work-related stress is considered to be a rising concern in many organizations. The possible causes include: increased domestic and foreign competition that has led to a substantial number of downsizing, layoff, and merger activities; rapidly changing technology; tension among diverse groups of employees, and increased demands for higher quality and service. Organizational managers are interested in maintaining a lower level of job stress for good reasons—high levels of stress can result in low productivity, increased absenteeism and turnover,

The Family Business Needs a Mission Statement

The founder of a specialty-meat products manufacturing firm, his wife, and his four children spent sixteen long hours hammering out a mission statement. Was it worth the time and effort? The owner says, yes— "Energies once devoted to sibling rivalry are now put to better use. We now have a common understanding of the commitment we must have to the business. And we know what each of us can expect in return."

Some tough issues that can arise in the discussions of family-owned missions include: succession planning, often the most difficult; retirement programs; compensation; titles; and voting rights among family members.

Source: John L. Ward and Laurel S. Sorenson, "A Family Needs a Mission Statement," *Nation's Business*, October 1987, pp. 45-47. Reprinted by permission. Copyright 1987, U.S. Chamber of Commerce.

and an assortment of other employee problems including alcoholism, drug abuse, hypertension, and a host of cardiovascular problems. Since the topic of work-related stress was covered in Chap. 5, we will not discuss it in detail here. It is important to note, however, that an organization's culture can be a major contribution to stress. If carefully implemented, however, a cultural change program can lower employee stress levels.[28]

The Plateaued Employee

The symptoms of job stress are similar to those of a related phenomenon—the plateaued employee. An employee perceives they have plateaued when they have reached their highest level within the organization, and possibly their career. They realize there will be no more promotions, totally new challenges, or opportunities to grow in experience. For the individual who feels plateaued the problem then becomes a major feature of the organization's culture—and a significant barrier to their morale, initiative, and productivity. Managers, professionals, and employees in small or flat organizations are most likely to experience a plateau effect, but all employees are susceptible to the problem.

The symptoms of plateauing include work habits such as incomplete assignments, missed deadlines, procrastination, and increased tardiness and absenteeism. Changes in personality such as irritability, distrust of others, hypersensitivity to criticism are also common. Supervisors may not recognize these symptoms easily because the plateaued employee is usually an "average, reliable worker" who has been with the organization for many years and has achieved high levels of productivity in the past. And, most supervisors are busy dealing with the worst and best performers—not the average, steady workers. There are, however, three common types of plateauing, and an employee may experience one or more of them:[29]

1. *Structural plateauing*. The lack of any higher levels within the organization to which an employee could reasonably hope to be promoted. The downsizing and flattening of many organizational structures in recent years has increased the likelihood of this problem occurring. The baby

boom generation has reached this level in many organizations, and thus further increased the competition for fewer promotions.

2. *Content plateauing.* When an employee has completely mastered his or her job, and thus it no longer provides a challenge. Entry-level, technical, and professional employees who do not enter management are likely to experience this problem within three to five years.

3. *Life plateauing.* People who perceive they have experienced all of life's adventures—marriage, child-rearing, travel, owning their own home, job success, and thus become bored with life. This feeling often goes hand in hand with either of the other types of plateauing.

Like burnout, if plateauing is a problem that is not addressed, it can become a dominant factor in the culture of the organization and one that significantly impacts on an employee's morale and productivity. What can supervisors and co-workers do to alleviate the problems of a plateaued employee? First, of course, is to recognize the symptoms and provide counseling. Fortunately, there are realistic and proven means of addressing the problem of plateauing. The supervisor, human resource director, or counselor first needs to reassure the employee by letting him or her know there are people in the organization who care about him or her and realize that plateauing is a normal phase of career development experienced by many people. Then the employee needs to be convinced that promotion is not the only means of reaching new heights, achieving recognition, or being given new challenges. They should not be given false hopes of a promotion. However, they can often be offered other job changes such as: (1) reassignment to a new office or location—the same job in new surroundings working with new people is usually quite stimulating; (2) a lateral transfer to a new job in which their knowledge of the organization and experience in other departments can be beneficial, yet they are still taking on a new job; (3) redesigning their current job to add new tasks and delegate some that have become routine and boring;[30] and (4) the formation of self-directed work teams.

As explained in the profile of Jennifer Synhorst (Chap. 11), organizations that have few layers of management and thus few promotion opportunities may be able to offer employees significant new job opportunities through the creation of self-managed teams. Team members usually expand both the number of tasks performed and the number of managerial functions in which they participate. Perhaps the most important aspect of assisting the plateaued employee is letting them know someone is concerned about them; their problem is not unusual; and there are possible solutions. With the likelihood of increased downsizing, mergers, and the flattening of organizations, together with the changing demographics of the work force, the proportion of people who can expect promotion every few years is small—and thus the probability of employees experiencing plateauing is increasing.

Employee Layoffs

It is likely that no single feature can be more disruptive to an organization's culture than the event of an employee layoff. Even unsubstantiated rumors of a layoff during hard economic times can be devastating to employee morale and create high levels of stress. Layoffs were once a blue-collar problem, but increased competition mergers, corporate downsizing, and recession have left no organization immune from layoffs.

International Business Machines (IBM), for example, was once considered one of the most secure employers in the world thanks to continued growth and a widely-publicized "no-layoff" policy. Then the recession of the early 1990s forced IBM to lay off over 25,000 employees from an already trimmed work force that had already shrunk from 400,000 in 1985 to 300,000 in 1992. With the announced layoff, IBM Chairman John Akers noted that the company had to abandon one of its most cherished corporate principles—its no layoff policy.[31]

Organizational policies and programs that address employee layoff concerns generally fall into two areas—layoff avoidance strategy, and assistance to employees in cases of layoff. Layoff avoidance is an objective of most organizations; few, if any, managers deliberately overstaff to necessitate layoffs. The extent that an organization establishes a policy to avoid layoffs may have a great influence of the sense of security experienced by its employees, and thus its culture. While *layoff avoidance policies* can vary, and as IBM's experience proves, no guarantee is certain; they often take one of three forms:

The continued shrinkage of management positions, downsizing of organizations, and increased competition for middle and upper level jobs may increase the number of people who feel they have reached a plateau in their career.

1. *No-layoff policy.* A written guarantee that it is the policy of the organization to not lay off employees during hard economic times provides the greatest security to employees. The existence of such a policy means that during an economic downturn other methods of reducing costs—such as reducing dividend payments, employee bonuses, capital improvements, hiring freezes, et cetera, will be utilized. No-layoff policies often appear in an organization's mission statement or employee handbook.

    The commitment to its no layoff policy was a difficult and expensive decision at Federal Express when the decision was made to drop its ZAP mail service. Over 1,300 people became idle—yet not one was laid off. Why? Chairman Frederick Smith (see his "Profile: Creating an Empowered Environment" on page 590) believes that Federal Express's commitment to no layoffs is the very base of its people philosophy—and critical to a productive organizational culture.

2. *"Share-the-pain" plan.* Some organizations are able and willing to avoid layoffs by reducing the hours worked by all employees—thus everyone "shares-the-pain" and works fewer hours earning less pay—but avoiding layoffs. The Nucor Corporation, for example, one of the nation's largest steel producers has successfully avoided layoffs for over twenty-five years (see the opening of Chap. 10) by reducing the number of days employees are scheduled to work to four, three, and even two per week during hard economic times. All management and other staff personnel share the pain and work fewer days for reduced wages on the same schedule as the steelworkers. The rest of the steel industry has permanently laid off over 350,000 workers in the past twenty-five years, while Nucor has never laid off a single worker.

3. *Early retirement plans.* Offering early retirement plans with enhanced pension payments is an avoidance method successfully utilized by larger organizations with funded pension plans. If a substantial portion of the eligible work force chooses the early retirement window, the savings created by the vacant positions (or positions filled by less costly employees) can help avoid layoffs. Such programs, however, must be entirely voluntary to comply with the Age Discrimination Act, thus the number of employees who choose the option is unpredictable—making the cost savings estimate uncertain.

The second general layoff policy is the providing of *out-placement assistance* services to employees when layoffs do occur, which can substantially lessen their emotional and financial problems. Such a program also provides an important morale boost to remaining employees who must witness the struggles of their laid-off co-workers and consider that they may suffer the same fate. Providing substantial assistance to laid-off employees, reflects a genuine concern for them and can become a major factor in the organization's culture. For example, when the Ford Motor Company closed its Milpitas, California, plant, it offered extensive out-placement services to laid-off employees. In cooperation with the United Auto Workers (UAW), Ford assessed the training needs of over 2,000 hourly workers, used idle portions of the plant to teach remedial English and math, and offered vocational exploration classes that encouraged employees to learn new skills, such as auto upholstery and forklift operations.[32]

Chemical Dependency

The culture of an organization can be substantially altered if the use of illegal drugs becomes commonplace and employees believe they are not being provided a safe work environment. How serious are the problems potentially created by an employee using illegal drugs? According to an American Medical Association study, substance abusers compared to nonabusers have:[33]

- Medical claims that are three times higher.
- Workers compensation claims that are five times higher.
- Four times the number of accidents.
- Absenteeism rates that are 2.5 times higher.
- Productivity rates that are one-third lower.

EMPLOYEE DRUG TESTING   Today organizations are less likely to question the need for a drug-testing policy and instead are asking what key policy and legal issues should be considered when developing a comprehensive policy.

According to an American Management Association survey of more than 1,000 companies, 48 percent test employees for drug use. The survey found that drug-testing programs generally fall into two areas: the preemployment testing of job applicants and postemployment testing of current employees.[34]

APPLICANT TESTING   Employers may require any applicant to submit to a drug-screening test, unless limited by a state law. Employers, in a statement of policy, can express their desire to hire only qualified applicants. Since drug use may adversely affect job performance, they can choose to hire only applicants who pass a drug-screening test.

This practice was generally upheld by a U.S. Supreme Court decision in *New York City Transit Authority vs. Baeger.*[35] The court rules that the safety and efficiency of the public transportation system constituted a valid business necessity and was a justifiable reason to require drug testing of bus driver applicants.

The need for drug screening for all job candidates may increase in the future due to several factors:

- Increased concern by employees who want the assurance of a safe work environment.
- Reluctance of previous employers to report suspected or known drug use by former employees for fear of litigation.
- Employer liability for the negligent hiring of employees.

TESTING OF CURRENT EMPLOYEES   The testing of current employees raises more difficult policy issues, as well as the need to keep up to date with court decisions. Employers usually test employees according to one of three policies.

- *Random testing.* All employees are tested at random, periodic intervals, or randomly selected employees are tested on predetermined dates.
- *Probable cause.* An employee is only tested when his or her behavior causes a reasonable suspicion on the part of supervisors.
- *After accidents.* All employees involved are tested after any accident or major incident.

Of the three policies the use of random testing has raised the strongest criticisms in relation to employees' right of privacy. Executive Order no. 12564 (1988) provided that random drug testing would be initiated in those federal agencies where the employee's duties involved public safety or law enforcement. Private-sector employees not involved in public safety should probably not be randomly tested due to their court-upheld right to privacy. Instead, there should be a reasonable basis for probable cause before an employee is tested. For example, a computer programmer for Southern Pacific Transportation Co. was awarded $485,000 after she was fired for refusing to take a random urinalysis. Her case relied on the general right-of-privacy provisions of the California constitution, which would be similar to those found in many states.[36] In general, a random-testing policy has the greatest chance of being upheld by a court or arbitrator, if it is related to public safety.

PROBABLE CAUSE   A policy of testing employees for drug usage only when there is probable cause will be more readily accepted by employees. Probable-cause testing has also received support from the courts and from arbitrators, if the test is given based on a reasonable suspicion of drug use. A supervisor's reasonable suspicion of drug use based on an employee's absenteeism, erratic behavior, poor work performance, and the like, can generally be accepted as reason to test.

CULTURE ENHANCEMENT PROGRAMS

The culture of an organization may be directly enhanced through the successful implementation of programs that directly affect the attractiveness of the work environment. In this section we will discuss some of the more successful programs including employee empowerment, child and elder care programs, wellness programs, and programs that encourage fun at work. All of these policies and programs have been shown to positively affect the total work environment as well as the culture of organizations.

Employee Empowerment

Creating a successful culture begins with empowering the employees, according to Frederick Smith, Chairman and President of Federal Express Corporation, the world's largest cargo airline. Why is empowerment critical to a successful culture? Smith says that empowered employees identify problems and fix them, they do what it takes to keep customers happy—and they don't have time for turf battles.[37] Exactly what is empowerment? A generally accepted definition is:[38]

Power refers to control or authority. The prefix *em* means "to put on to." *Empowering* is passing on authority and responsibility to employees who then experience a sense of ownership and control over their jobs. They feel more responsible and thus show more initiative, get more accomplished, and enjoy their jobs more.

Employee empowerment To give nonmanagement employees the freedom to make decisions about their work without direct supervision.

The central concept of *employee empowerment* is to give nonmanagement employees the freedom to make decisions about their work without any supervision or approval. A written policy at Honeywell, for example, states that "decision making should be delegated to the lowest appropriate level." Thus managers are encouraged to empower employees—within the word "appropriate." Empowerment generally results in employees:[39]

- Believing they are an essential part of the organization and can implement their ideas to improve it.
- Knowing they can initiate changes and take risks without fear of reprisal.
- Feeling they are trusted with responsibility.
- Believing they are respected for their judgment and actions.

Empowerment is not only decentralizing decision making, it involves a basic corporate philosophy that employees are trusted to perform their jobs, make decisions they believe are necessary, accept the challenge to initiate changes, and take risks, and expect to be rewarded according to their performance. Exactly how does an organization create an empowered environment? To understand how this rather simple concept starts with a corporate philosophy and incorporate several organizational practices, first read the Frederick W. Smith "Profile: Creating an Empowered Environment," and then carefully follow the seven steps utilized by Federal Express in Fig. 17-8.

Empowerment may provide employees a great deal of latitude in decision making within broad guidelines—termed flexible empowerment, or employees may be given latitude to make decisions within specified limits. For example, management of the Hilton Hotel at Walt Disney World Village implemented a structured empowerment program that empowered employees to decide how to handle guest problems within certain limits. A sample of guidelines for employee actions appears in Fig. 17-9.[40]

In contrast to the structured empowerment program of the Hilton Hotel, the Ritz-Carlton Hotel Company utilizes the flexible empowerment model and provides employees with these guidelines: "Any employee who receives a guest

FIGURE 17-8
How to Create an
Empowered Environment

Lessons from Federal Express

Step 1 Develop a corporate philosophy that fosters respect for human dignity, ingenuity, and potential.

Step 2 Create a job-secure environment where people are not afraid to take risks and fail.

Step 3 Create communication systems that provide opportunity for employee input.

Step 4 Incorporate pay-for-performance programs that reward productivity at all levels.

Step 5 Give awards and recognition for individual and team quality efforts.

Step 6 Promote career opportunities and encourage promotion from within.

Step 7 Redesign jobs to increase employee power.

Source: Frederick W. Smith, "Empowering Employees," *Small Business Reports*, January 1991, p. 16. Used by permission.

FIGURE 17-9 Structured Empowerment Guidelines of the Hilton Hotel at Walt Disney World

Front Office Staff Guidelines

Guest complaints or problems	*Actions front-desk clerk is authorized to take*
1. A guest announces during checkout that he or she experienced a room-related problem (e.g., no hot water, bad television reception, room was too noisy, lack of heat)	Offer an upgrade for next visit or adjust current bill by as much as $100. Make logbook notation.
2. At checkout, a guest complains about something unrelated to his or her room as follows:	Adjust guest's current bill as indicated and make a logbook notation
• The service in the cafe or dining room	$50, and advise supervisor
• The guest did not receive some item that he or she requested (extra towels, soap, blankets, etc.)	$50, and advise supervisor
• The maintenance department was slow to respond to some complaint	$50, and advise supervisor
• Luggage or parcels were delivered late	$50, and advise supervisor
• Mail or messages were not received	$100, and advise supervisor
3. A guest is charged an incorrect rate	The supervisor should make the room adjustment.
4. Guest experiences a problem with the room key or lock	Offer an upgrade for next visit, or adjust current bill by as much as $100. Make a logbook notation.
5. Guest reports that a complaint was passed from department to department	Offer an upgrade for next visit, or adjust current bill by as much as $100. Advise the supervisor.
6. Guest insists that he or she did not incur any minibar charges.	Make the adjustment.
7. Guest disputes phone charges	Make the adjustment.
8. Guest complains about a rude or insensitive employee	Refer problem to the assistant manager

These sample guidelines for how a structured–empowerment program can be implemented by the front-office staff were developed by the management and employees of the Hilton Hotel at Walt Disney World Village.

Source: Robert A. Brymer, "Employee Empowerment," *The Cornell Hotel and Restaurant Administration Quarterly,* May 1991, p. 60. Reprinted by permission of Elsevier Science Inc. Copyright 1991 by Cornell University.

complaint "owns" the complaint. Instant guest satisfaction will be ensured by all. . . The employee must either take necessary steps to correct the complaint, if possible, or notify the proper staff members as soon as possible regarding the nature of the complaint to ensure that the complaint is resolved."[41]

Family-Work Issues

Despite the incredibly grim job market of the 1990s, a *Wall Street Journal* survey of job-hunting MBAs found that a progressive "work and family" program was a top concern when considering possible employees. Ten years earlier the MBA candidates did not list *family-work* policies as even a mild consideration. Today, however, flexible hours, family leave, limited travel, and relocation are prime issues for many employees. Employees as well as recent graduates believe it's okay to be concerned about family issues, to inquire about employer policies, and even to accept a lower-paying position because the organization touts a culture that supports a balanced lifestyle.[42]

The need for a family-friendly workplace is a major challenge for organizations due to a declining pool of skilled entrants, the increase of working mothers in the labor force, and employees who, like the MBA graduates just mentioned, place a high value on family-friendly culture. Major programs in this area include flextime, parental leave—programs that allow new parents time off

Profile

Frederick W. Smith
Chairman and President
Federal Express Corporation

CREATING AN EMPOWERED ENVIRONMENT

I am convinced that we don't motivate anybody to do anything. I believe our job as managers is to provide a workplace in which highly motivated people stay that way. Essentially, then, the challenge lies in creating a workplace in which people can be the best they can be.

Our experience at Federal Express is that goals that grow out of a corporate philosophy—and management systems and programs that are consistent with it—provide the basis for what we might call a "power environment." I'm convinced that quality circles, quality action teams, or any other isolated attempts to elicit employee power will be useless in the absence of such an environment.

We at Federal Express have worked from the beginning to create a workplace that fosters respect for human dignity, ingenuity, and potential. It all revolves around a simple philosophy: People, Service, Profit. That statement drives every action of every manager in our company. We believe that when people are treated with dignity and respect, they will carry that message throughout their daily work experience and directly to our customers. Profit is a natural by-product.

At the base of our people philosophy is a commitment to no layoffs—that we've observed, even in the face of our decision to discontinue our ZAP mail service several years ago. More than 1,300 people were affected by that decision, yet no jobs were lost. From what I have seen, a job-secure environment stimulates risk-taking and innovation. People are not afraid to fail.

We've learned that you've got to let people make a mistake or two once in a while. Well-intentioned efforts that don't work out are just as important as successes. And, if you hang the people who try to do something that doesn't quite work, you'll get people who don't do anything.

Source: Frederick W. Smith, "Empowering Employees," *Small Business Reports*, January 1991, pp. 15-18. Used by permission.

---

work to bond with their children; elder-care programs that assist employees in providing for their elderly relations; and, of course, child care assistance.

Child-Care Programs

Employer-provided child care in the United States is not a new phenomenon. Some programs were started in the 1850s, and the textile industry that employed mostly women, sponsored child-care centers from the early to mid-1890s.[43] However, it was World War II, which forced an unprecedented number of American women into the labor force, that caused over 2,800 day care centers to be opened. But when the war ended, most women returned home, and the centers closed.[44]

By 1985, more than half of all women with a child under age six were working, and the number of employer-sponsored child-care programs continues to grow to meet the demand. Employers find it increasingly difficult to resist the pressure to implement child-care programs, particularly as more women move into executive and managerial roles, and can influence the decision-making process.[45] What are the best employers for working mothers? See Fig. 17-10.

Today, employers are providing child care assistance to their employees through a wide variety of programs that offer different levels of service and varying costs:[46]

FIGURE 17-10
Top Ten Companies
for Working Mothers

Apple Computer, Cupertino, CA	IBM, Armonk, NY
Beth Israel Hospital, Boston, MA	Merck, Rahway, NJ
DuPont, Wilmington, DE	Morrison & Foerster, San Francisco, CA
Fel-Pro, Skokie, IL	SAS Institute, Cary, NC
Hoffmann-La Roche, Nutley, NJ	Syntex, Palo Alto, CA

Criteria: Salary; advancement opportunity; child care; benefits package, including maternity leave, parental leave, and adoption aid; flexible schedules; part-time work; job sharing; and support for the elderly.

Source: Adapted from *Working Mother,* October 1989.

1. *On-site programs.* Large employers, particularly in the health care industry, can offer to build a facility on the premises or nearby, which allows employees to bring their children to work and visit them during lunch. On-site programs, due to costs, are usually offered by larger employers. The employer and employee, however, generally share the expense.

2. *Flexible benefits.* Employers will provide, as one flexible benefit option, money to employees to reimburse (voucher systems) existing child-care programs. Employees who do not need child care can spend their dollars on other benefits. This flexible benefit approach is the fastest-growing approach to child care.

3. *Resource and referral centers.* For referral needs the organization contracts with a firm that maintains information on child-care facilities and assists employees in finding suitable service. The employer can also provide resource information to employees (see "OB In Practice" on the next page). This can be a low-cost approach.

4. *Consortium of employers.* Several organizations located together (in an industrial park or shopping center) pool their resources to purchase and manage a child-care center for their employees. The advantages are similar to those of an on-site facility.

5. *Public–private partnership.* Cities and counties have taken a wide variety of approaches to the provision of child care, but usually require private-sector involvement. San Francisco, for example, requires office-building and hotel developers either to provide facilities for their employees or contribute to a city fund. Louisville, KY has provided one-time construction funds to build centers that then must charge parents fees to cover all operating expenses.

6. *Pretax assistance.* Section 125 and 129 of the Internal Revenue Code allows employers to provide employees to pay for child-care assistance with pretax dollars—thus saving the employee up to 40 percent of their costs. This low-cost program has rapidly grown in popularity.

Why don't all employers offer at least one of the above programs? Cost is the answer one might expect. However, a national survey by the U.S. Department of Health and Human Services found that in 95 percent of the child-care programs the benefits outweigh the costs. One employer, Union Bank, an employer of 1,200 people in Monterey, California, with 170 branches, documented that finding:[47]

- *Start-up costs.* Included were $430,000 in an on-site building and fixed assets to be recovered in five years; and $105,000 first-year operating sub-

Lunchtime Is a Good Time to Discuss Work-and-Family Issues

Weyerhaeuser Co., with the help of Working Solutions, Inc., a Portland, Oregon-based dependent-care consulting company, has implemented a popular, brown-bag lunch lecture series as a part of a resource and referral service. The lecture series gives employees practical information on how to deal with child-care issues.

"Working Solutions gave us an extensive list of topics to choose from, and the steering committee decides which are the most appropriate at any given time," says Kim Johnson, a paralegal for Federal Way, Washington-based Weyerhaeuser. "Experts come in from the community to discuss topics relating to everything from dealing with a new infant to teen drug abuse."

Here are some of the topics that have come up at Weyerhaeuser's brown-bag child-care seminars:

Selecting a day care or preschool
Nutrition for infants and toddlers
Adjusting to being a new parent
Communicating with teenagers
Coping with behavior problems at school
Toys that teach
Stepparenting
Positive discipline
From diapers to toilet training
Helping a child through a divorce

Source: Jennifer Haupt, "Employee Action Prompts Management to Respond to Work-and-Family Needs," *Personnel Journal,* February 1993, p. 101. Used by permission.

---

sidy. Direct savings included at least $138,000 due to reduced absenteeism and turnover per year for a pay back period of less than four years.

- *Employee morale.* Before and after surveys indicated reduced tardiness and maternal leave time.

- *Effective recruitment.* 61 percent of job applicants cited the on-site center as a reason for accepting the job.

- *Supervisor support.* Supervisors reported that their own morale and that of their employees had increased due to the center, and the morale was high to begin with.

Small business owners may be particularly concerned about what they believe to be the high costs of child-care assistance programs. Yet over half of the female labor force is employed by small businesses—about twenty-six million women. Thus a national nonprofit research and public education organization, the Child Care Action Campaign (CCAC) points out that small organizations are critical to meeting the needs of working women. The CCAC has noted several model child-care assistance programs offered by small businesses:[48]

- *Bryne Electrical Specialists, Inc., Rockford, Michigan (110 employees)*
  In 1988 the owners realized their own daughter had difficulty finding quality child care near their company. In addition, ten employees

were expecting babies! Thus they decided to use an empty space for an on-site center. The Wee Folk Child Care-Center operates independently of Bryne Electrical and can serve up to 130 children. Bryne employees, however, receive a 30 percent discount at the facility. The building and start-up costs was $228,000. After two years the annual operating costs were $20,000, and a break-even year was within reach. Management saw employee morale increase, because parents believe it is important to have their children near by. Absenteeism and tardiness decreased after the center opened. The Bryne family-friendly culture also offers six weeks paid parental leave, flextime, and pretax payments.

- *G. T. Water Products, Inc., Moorpark, California (31 employees)*

     George Tash, the owner of G. T. Water Products, a manufacturer of plumbing supplies, saw rising problems with local private and public schools, and the effects they were having on his employees. Thus he established a state-licensed Montessori School on his company's premises. The school is available only to the children of G. T. Water Products employees, ages five to fifteen, at no cost to their parents. The school costs about $140,000 to operate each year and only requires $2,000 start-up expenses. Mr. Tash believes the school is critical to his company retaining good employees.

- *Mascoma Savings Bank, Lebanon, Maryland (90 employees)*

     CEO Bill Malaz and Personnel Director Sally McEwen knew Mascoma had a serious turnover problem. They also realized that the lack of accessible, affordable child care was the primary cause (80 percent of the work force is female). Thus to fight the problem the bank joined the Child Care Project—a consortium of twenty-five businesses. The project conducts on-site workshops on child-care issues for the businesses and locates suitable care for parents. The annual fee for the project is $350. The bank has seen a reduction in its turnover and credits the project that has successfully located suitable child care for all those requesting it.

- *Joseph Alfandre & Company, Inc., Rockville, Maryland (55 employees)*

     The owner of Alfandre, a real estate development company, decided to help the employees who needed child care by providing a subsidy to those who have children in a licensed facility or in their own home. The subsidy is the lesser of $60 per week or 50 percent of an employee's total child-care cost. The company also offers an eight-week maternity leave, three days of sick leave to care for children, and up to three months of unpaid parental leave.

Employer child-care programs are highly valued by working parents and can increase their loyalty and morale.

Thus, even the smallest employers can provide employees some form of child-care assistance. And more each year are finding that employee demands and the ability, at least, to break even on other child-care approaches are prompting them to offer a program.

The U.S. Department of Labor estimates that women and minorities will fill 80 percent of the twenty-one million new jobs that will be created by the year 2000. Many employers, however, have been slow to realize that this new work force will demand family care benefits—primarily maternity/paternity leave and day care. "They have been reluctant to venture into this area because family care changes the whole atmosphere at work—forever," claims Dana Friedman, senior research fellow at the Work and Family Life Center of the Department of Labor. Working women do not want to be forced to choose between a career and raising a family. They want and should be able to choose both, says Friedman. The new breed of fathers also want to help raise their children without fear of losing their jobs.[49]

Elder-Care Programs

While child care is the primary family-care issue today, elder Americans represent the fastest growing segment of the population. Thus elder care is the growing family-care issue of the future. The National Council on Aging estimates that one of four employees has some responsibility for the care of an elderly relative. And of those care-giving employees, 26 percent either quit or change to part-time work due to their increased problems. Another 28 percent consider quitting.[50] Research by large employers including IBM, Merck, and Corning Glass shows that those care-giving employees who remain at work experience work-related problems similar to employees with children including: higher turnover, higher absenteeism, greater stress, higher tardiness, greater personal telephone usage, and lower productivity.[51]

While the employee problems associated with elder care are similar to those associated with child care, it is estimated that only five percent of the employers offering child-care assistance programs offer similar elder-care assistance. Most elder-care programs, as described in Figure 17-11, are very similar to child-care programs—resource and referral services, dependent-care pretax spending accounts, and financial support for off-site facilities. The major differences are virtually no on-site care facilities for the elderly, and the increased counseling needed by elder caregivers who require help in managing the emotional and psychological consequences of caring for aging relatives. The U.S. population continues to grow older and more employees are providing both child care and elder care—they are the "sandwich generation." Organizations with family-friendly cultures can provide responsive programs to employees that assist them in meeting the time, financial, and stress demands of caring for family members.

A good example is the pioneering elder-care project announced by IBM in 1990. The company provided $3 million for a new IBM Elder-Care Project Development Fund. The program provides assistance to employees with elder-care responsibilities. Services include respite-care development, recruitment and training of in-home health and social service workers, and support programs. Why should IBM enter the elder-care field? According to IBM representative Jim Smith,

FIGURE 17-11
Elder-care Programs

A survey conducted by Hewitt Associates found that out of 1,006 large employers, 36 percent (362) offered elder-care benefits to their employees. The types of benefits available, as reported by these companies, are shown below:*

1. Offer resource and referral services	28%
• Use in-house resources	4%
• Use in-house referrals	1%
• Contract with referral services	20%
• Combine in-house resources with contracted referral services	3%
2. Offer counseling	11%
3. Offer dependent-care spending accounts	87%
4. Offer long-term care insurance	5%
5. Support elder-care programs in other ways, such as through providing financial support to outside agencies and facilities	3%

*Some employers offer more than one type of elder-care benefit.

Source: Jeff L. Lefkovich, "Business Responds to Elder-care Needs," *HRMagazine,* June 1992, p. 104. Reprinted with the permission of *HRMagazine,* published by the Society for Human Resource Management, Alexandria, VA.

the program represents IBM's continuing response to the changing social environment that affects the employees.[52]

Wellness Programs

Many employers have determined that developing a positive cultural environment requires efforts to help employees stay healthy, reduce stress, and provide the early detection of serious health problems.

In general these programs, which vary greatly in cost and services included are called *wellness programs*. The establishment of such programs by organizations can be considered as a clear signal of the value placed on employees' well-being and an employer's philosophy of treating them as valuable assets—important characteristics of an organization's culture.

Wellness program
An effort to help employees stay healthy, reduce stress, and provide the early detection of serious health problems.

While the term wellness program is used loosely to describe almost any health-care effort, the Health Insurance Association of America defines *wellness* as a "freely chosen life-style aimed at achieving and maintaining an individual's good health.[53] From management's perspective, employees are an organization's greatest asset, and their state of health affects their contribution to the company in such measurable ways as absenteeism, productivity, fatigue-caused accidents, alertness and creativity, and health-care claims and insurance premiums. At the same time, employees indicate a great interest in wellness programs by their high degree of participation. Reasons may include: (1) the presumption that it is a quality program because it is company sponsored; (2) the perception that it is a fringe benefit and thus should be taken advantage of; and (3) the recognition that it is a convenient way to take care of health concerns.[54]

A U.S. Department of Health and Human Services survey confirmed that wellness programs of some nature are offered by a majority of American employers. Although such programs were once perceived to be a fad or a frivolous employee benefit, about 66 percent of U.S. employers with at least fifty employees offer at least one wellness activity each year. What is the reason for the substantial growth rate in such programs? Employers report that they are an unqualified success. Employees who participate are more likely to have lower health-care costs and generally are healthier. The most common wellness activities offered by employers include:[55]

- smoking cessation (36 percent)
- health-risk appraisals (30 percent)
- back care (29 percent)
- stress management (27 percent)
- exercise/physical fitness (22 percent)
- off-the-job accident prevention (20 percent)
- nutrition education (17 percent)
- blood-pressure checks (17 percent)
- weight control (15 percent)

One successful corporate wellness program was established by the Mesa Petroleum Company. Their programs averaged $173 per participant in medical costs compared to $343 for nonparticipants.[56] General Motors's employee assistance program cut medical benefit payments by 60 percent after one year.[57] The Campbell Soup Company's colon-rectal cancer detection program recorded savings of $245,000 in medical payments.[58] And Burlington Industries reported that absen-

The Coors Company wellness program saves an estimated $6.15 for each one dollar of cost due to reduced medical costs, workers' compensation, reduced sick leave, fewer stress claims, and higher productivity.

teeism decreased from 400 days to nineteen days annually due to its "healthy back" program.[59]

The ability of a wellness program to provide quantifiable savings over several years may be doubted by some people. Adolph Coors Company in Golden, Colorado, however, has developed a wellness program that saves $1.9 million annually in documented savings. Coors estimates that for each dollar spent on their program, the company saves $6.15 in reduced medical costs, reduced sick leaves, reduced workers' compensation stress claims, and increased productivity.[60]

The Coors facility offers aerobics, strength training, cardiovascular equipment, and an indoor running track. The program is far more than just a facility, however; employees and their spouses can participate in health-risk assessments, nutritional counseling, stress management, smoking-cessation programs, on-site mammography and blood pressure screening, family counseling, and pre- and postnatal education. The goal of the Coors program is behavioral change—to help employees recognize their health problems and then change their life-style to achieve a healthier mind and body. The Coors Model to Achieve Behavioral Change includes:[61]

1. *Awareness.* The health-hazard appraisal (HHA) gives each employee and spouse personal information about their potential for premature death or disease.

2. *Education.* The HHA counselor describes the variety of on-site fitness activities as well as programs that can help change employees' behavior. Education is also achieved through brochures, luncheon lectures, and elevator posters, such as the early warning signs of a heart attack.

3. *Incentives.* The company provides the financial incentive of refunding the cost of a program, if participants achieve and maintain their personal goals. The programs are held on site.

4. *Programs.* A range of programs is offered and employees are given a choice of one that interests them and meets their needs. In addition, the company cafeteria provides low-calorie and low-fat food choices.

5. *Self-action.* Programs are made available to all employees and their dependents, since they are included in all medical benefits. On-site and off-site exercise facilities are also made available and participants are encouraged to continue a personal exercise program. It is believed that for the program to succeed in the long-run, employees must take responsibility for their health.

6. *Follow-up and support.* Follow-up information, such as direct-mail reminders of blood-pressure screening and mammograms are provided. Periodic follow-up classes are also conducted.

SMALL EMPLOYER PROGRAMS   Wellness programs can also be successfully implemented by small employers with limited budgets. Sunseeds, Inc., for example, implemented a basic program for its 200 employees at a total cost of only $2,000, less than the average cost of one hospital stay.[62] In fact, many of the major benefits of a full-scale program, such as the one at Coors, can be achieved in a scaled-down program. A number of effective wellness program activities can be established at a minimum cost, such as awareness brochures and pamphlets on the following subjects: smoking; weight loss; stress awareness; nutrition; on-site annual cholesterol and blood-pressure checks by an outside agency; lunchtime walking programs; subsidized fees for smoking-cessation and weight-loss programs; and the removal of cigarette- and candy-vending machines by replacing them with other healthful alternatives.[63]

Fun at Work

An increasing number of owners and managers are recognizing that an organizational culture that encourages humor and fun in the workplace can be an effective means of reducing stress and anxiety. Employees who are allowed and even encouraged to have a little fun at work generally report higher job satisfaction, creativity, and productivity. Some of the direct benefits include: (1) increased camaraderie and teamwork due to a more relaxed work environment; (2) employees more readily accept new ideas; (3) reduction in sick days (50 percent reduction in nine months at Digital Equipment Corp.); (4) reduced boredom; and (5) higher morale. A few corporate examples of humor and fun in the workplace include:[64]

- *Kodak* in Rochester, New York added a "humor room" for its 20,000 employees to utilize while on break at lunch or after work. The room includes: (1) a resource library of joke books, videos, and cartoons; (2) a group meeting area for a relaxed atmosphere for brainstorming or other creative group activities; (3) a "toy store" of gadgets and games; and (4) a high-tech area with computers loaded with creative problem-solving and speech writing software.

- *Price Waterhouse* the international accounting firm includes humor programs in its annual tax education seminar to provide stress-reducing breaks.

- *Sun Microsystems Laboratories, Inc.* targets a person in management to be the target of an elaborate April Fool's hoax. Past Aprils found a life-size replica of the vice-president's office constructed in the bottom of a shark tank at the San Francisco Steinhart Aquarium, and the CEO's office turned into a one-hole golf course!

• *Ben & Jerry's Ice Cream* of Waterbury, Connecticut, provides "joy grants" to employees who suggest creative ideas for adding fun to the workplace—like a hot chocolate machine for the office and an Elvis Day roller skating party.

What are some other examples of adding fun to the workplace? Here are a few:[65]

1. *Bulletin board.* Install a bulletin board near the coffee pot and encourage people to post their best jokes with prizes going to monthly winners.

2. *Theme days.* On specific holidays employees can dress according to a theme and have a pot-luck lunch. Award best costume certificates at the lunch.

3. *Fun committee.* Establish a volunteer fun committee to plan programs; provide a small annual budget.

4. *Company roast.* As an alternative to the traditional holiday dinner, have a company roast with those roasted selected by employees.

5. *Baby picture contest.* On the bulletin board or in the employee newsletter conduct a "name this baby" contest with a prize to the winner.

6. *Calling cards.* Print "You Made My Day: Thank You!" cards and make them available for employees to pass on to others who add fun to their day.

7. *Birthday celebrations.* Allow small working groups to take their members to lunch on their birthdays.

8. *Celebrate achievements.* When goals such as completing a project on time are achieved, throw an afternoon party and say "thank-you" to all who helped.

9. *Recognize personal achievements.* Include articles in employee newsletters or send special memos recognizing an employee's child who is the star of the high school team, an employee who finishes a triathlon, or an employee's fifth wedding anniversary.

10. *Encourage humor.* Managers can encourage humor by creating a relaxed atmosphere. Practical jokes, "goofing off," or inappropriate cartoons, however, are not needed nor should they be tolerated.

Developing an environment that allows and encourages fun at work may depend on three elements: people's personal intentions, a relaxed organizational culture, and the behavior of top management. The communications from top management are most critical. Gary Rogers, chief executive officer of Dreyer's Grand Ice Cream, has three company goals: quality, profits, and having fun. Rogers reminds us that "everyone only goes around the track once in life, and if you don't enjoy the trip, it's pretty pathetic.[66]

CONCLUSIONS AND APPLICATIONS

• Stride Rite Corporation has built a successful organizational culture through policies, values, and practices that generally reflect a strong respect for employees and treating them "the way you want to be treated." Chairman Hiatt believes that culture generates a high level of commitment from employees, which is the key to Stride Rite's success.

- The cultural framework of an organization that gives it real direction, mobilizes behavior, and affects major decisions throughout the organization is often found in its mission statement. Mission statements thus play a key role in shaping the culture, character, and quality of an organization.

- Within organizations at least four major types of cultures—academy, club, fortress, and baseball team—have been identified. More than one type may successfully work in the same organization. However, not all types of individuals and personalities can work successfully in each type of culture. Since most cultures are slow to change, individuals should carefully consider their "fit" with a new group or culture before joining it.

- Larger organizations often have a broad-based organizational culture that provides general direction, and in addition, there may exist many subcultures that may or may not be working in harmony with the overall culture. Subcultures may develop around functional or operating units of the organization, levels of management, or social groups. Ensuring that subcultures do not suboptimize the organization's effectiveness is a difficult and major challenge to its leadership.

- Cultures and their subcultures can be transformed through cultural change efforts. Several major companies such as Ford, General Electric, Union Pacific, Disney, and DuPont have documented their successful cultural change program. Seven elements common to most of these change efforts have been identified.

- An organization's culture can have a dramatic effect on the personal and work lives of its employees. Work-related stress, plateauing, and chemical dependency problems are major employee problems that may be successfully addressed through organizational programs.

- Work-related stress is a major and rising concern in many organizations. Possible causes include rapidly changing technology, organizational downsizing and layoffs, difficult managers, increased demands for higher quality and service, and greater tension among diverse groups of employees. Higher employee stress often leads to costly organizational problems including worker compensation claims, absenteeism and turnover, lower productivity, and chemical dependency. Policies and programs designed to control stress center on organizational and personal strategies that rely on a positive work climate.

- The culture of an organization can often be enhanced through policy changes or programs that increase the attractiveness of the workplace. Empowering employees in their jobs has been viewed by many to be a key to creating a positive, productive culture. Empowerment involves decentralized decision making, a secure environment that encourages risk-taking, and greater trust in employee judgment and actions.

- Employees also value a culture that has progressive family/work policies such as: child and elder care, family leave, flexible hours, and limited travel and relocation. Child/elder-care assistance can be provided through a wide variety of programs with levels of service and costs that may be affordable to even small employers.

- Wellness programs can help reduce employee stress, prevent health problems, and provide early detection of serious health concerns. Successful wellness programs have reduced related costs including workers' compensation claims, sick leave, direct medical payments, and medical insurance claims. In addition, employees may experience positive behavioral changes including decreased fatigue and enhanced mental alertness.

REVIEW QUESTIONS

1. What are the key characteristics that define an organization's culture?

2. In 1993 General Motors began an effort to change its culture. What was the focus of this change? From a review of current sources of information would you conclude that GM achieved its cultural change?

3. Why are mission statements often described as "road maps" that guide an organization?

4. The research of Jeffrey Sonnenfeld has identified four major "types" of organizational cultures—what are they and which one do you believe best describes the type that exists within your college or place of employment?

5. Many small and large organizations have experienced a successful cultural change. Describe in detail the keys necessary to such a change.

6. How does job plateauing differ from job stress? How can a manager help an employee they suspect feels plateaued? Why should they intervene?

7. Describe three common layoff avoidance policies. What are the comparative advantages of each?

8. What are common job-related behavioral problems of substance abusers?

9. What is generally meant by the term "employee empowerment"? Why has it been supported by organizations and employees?

10. Why are many employers providing some form of child-care assistance to their employees? What are the major types of programs offered?

11. What activities are generally included in a wellness program? Are such programs cost-effective?

DISCUSSION QUESTIONS

1. Stride Rite Chairman Arnold Hiatt in the chapter opening gave an inside perspective of the company's culture. Which actions, programs, or policies described by Hiatt could be adopted by most other organizations wanting a positive culture?

2. List at least five internal symbols from an organization you are familiar with, and describe the message each conveys to the employees.

3. What steps can an organization take to ensure that its mission statement provides real direction in its day-to-day operations?

4. Describe a dysfunctional subculture that you have directly observed or experienced. How might the leadership of the organization transform it into a productive subculture?

5. With the increased use of horizontal organizations, downsizing, mergers, and employee empowerment, employees are more likely to "plateau" at least once during their careers. What should organizations do to alleviate the problems of a plateaued employee?

6. Should an organization guarantee its employees "no layoffs"? Why? How does such a policy benefit the organization?

7. Discuss under what circumstances an organization should utilize each of the following drug-testing policies: random, probable cause, applicant.

8. Frederick Smith, Chairman and President of Federal Express Corporation, has stated his belief that creating a successful culture begins with employee empowerment. Do you agree? Why? Under what circumstances might empowerment not be advisable?

9. Family-work issues are increasingly important to many employees. How should an organization decide which programs should be offered to its employees? What about fairness to employees without families?

10. Is it *really* appropriate for a manager to encourage humor and fun in the workplace? What "fun" activities do you think are harmless but would actually lift the morale of people?

CASE STUDY

San Mateo Valley State University

A t San Mateo Valley State University, there about 6,000 students, two dozen build-ings, and about five hundred faculty and staff. SMVSU is one campus in a large state system. The mission statement adopted by the university is short but quite accurate:

> The primary mission of San Mateo Valley State University is to provide the highest quality educational programs to the diverse people of our service region. This teaching mission focuses on undergraduate programs especially in the liberal studies (teacher certification) and general arts and sciences areas. Basic, applied, and instructional research and service to our region are also priorities of the university.

To the casual observer SMVSU is a small, quite regional university that is usu-ally given a positive, but not glowing appraisal by the local community. The best of the local college-bound high school graduates generally attend college somewhere out of town, and those needing remedial work attend the local community college that has an equally good academic reputation.

The university is currently at a crossroads. Senior members of the faculty, some of which are the "founding fathers" of the university control most of the important campus committee positions, and thus have a significant influence on the president and other campus administrators. The senior faculty are generally good teachers who have engaged in little to no research in recent years. They have devoted a great per-centage of their time to faculty governance—serving on the Faculty Senate and its committees, related state-wide committees, attending professional seminars, et cetera. In the early years of the university this unusually high level of service was needed as new programs were initially developed and organized. The continued need, however, given the university has matured, has been seriously questioned. They have, over sev-eral years, developed a climate in which service on these committees, seniority, social acceptance, and following their informal advice has dictated which young faculty will receive tenure and promotion. The university faculty is unionized, and the collective bargaining agreement includes no merit pay but annual pay increases until one reaches the top pay step. Thus, a large percentage of the senior faculty are all paid the exact same salary, and junior faculty realize that the tenure and promotion decisions are the only critical personnel decisions they will encounter in their careers.

In recent years due to a 42 percent enrollment growth a substantial number of new faculty have been hired. They generally are more active in scholarly research and community service activities, and have resisted to a great extent the insistence of senior faculty that they spend more time on university committees and other inter-nal service. The "new breed" of faculty have also developed an excellent teaching reputation among the students. In several cases this has led to the junior, nontenured faculty being given heavier teaching loads and being assigned to teach the more dif-ficult courses. Combined with their greater productivity in research and service, the junior faculty have openly met with the president to protest the general lack of pro-ductivity, commitment to quality teaching, and the recent veiled threats (of tenure denial) that have been made by some senior faculty. The president recognizes the validity of their concerns and openly discussed them at a Faculty Senate meeting. At that meeting several senior faculty responded that they "built this place" and "the junior faculty don't appreciate the importance of committee work." Finally, one of the founding faculty said to the president, "We had similar complaints from the last president and look what happened to him!" The previous president after given a vote of no confidence by the faculty was removed by the regents.

The president of SMVSU has only this month learned that four of the brightest junior faculty have accepted positions at other universities next year. She realizes that the university needs a cultural change if it is going to prosper. Yet, she also realizes the senior faculty are strongly opposed to the type of change that is needed, and unfortunately it will be at least ten years before most of them retire.

CASE STUDY QUESTIONS

1. Which type of organizational culture exists at SMVSU (of the four discussed in the chapter)?
2. Is the mission statement really accurate? Why or why not?
3. Can the president change the culture of SMVSU? If so, how, and in what direction?
4. Do you agree more with the general position of the senior faculty or the junior faculty? Why?

EXPERIENTIAL EXERCISE 1

Your Personal Mission Statement

Purpose

A mission statement is probably the single most important document an organization develops. It establishes clear guidance for significant decisions and sets the organizational culture by expressing its values and principles.

A personal mission statement can provide similar benefits to an individual. It can help a person focus their energies on their goals, and keep them from investing time and resources in activities that are inconsistent with those goals. A personal mission statement can help one communicate their values and work philosophy to others with whom they come in contact—colleagues, co-workers, clients, supervisors, et cetera. A clear position on ethical, environmental, and family issues as well as quality of service, personal guarantees, and the like, can help avoid difficult situations or misunderstandings. In addition, it can help one create a professional image. Many professionals even post their personal statements in their offices or have them printed on the backs of their business cards.

Task

Seclude yourself for a minimum of two hours someplace where you cannot be interrupted. Then write down your answers to the following questions. You may modify the answers to fit your personal circumstances. Do not let anyone else influence your answers. Next ask someone other than a close friend or family member to act as a "facilitator" or "devil's advocate" by asking you to defend or explain your answers until they are clear and concise. Finally, draft your personal statement based on the answers to the questions. Not all answers will necessarily be utilized in the final statement. Set the first draft aside for at least forty-eight hours to "simmer" and then make your final changes. Utilize your personal mission statement as a point of reference when you are faced with important choices or decisions. Remember it's a living document and thus should be reviewed and changed periodically, perhaps annually on your birthday or New Year's Eve.

Questions

Answering the following questions will help you develop your mission statement.

- What is my personal business or profession?
- What business or profession would I like to be in? What do I really enjoy?
- What business or profession should I be in?
- What is my real purpose in business and in life?
- What are or should be my principal business functions and roles, present and future?
- What is unique or distinctive about what I can bring to my business or profession?
- Who are or should be my principal customers, clients, or users?
- What are the principal market segments, present and future, in which I am most effective?
- What is different about my personal business position from what it was three to five years ago?
- What is likely to be different about my personal business position three to five years in the future?
- What are my principal economic concerns?
- What are or should be my principal sources of income?
- What philosophical issues, personal values, and priorities are important to my professional future?
- What special considerations do I have in regard to the following? (a board of directors or other outside groups; employers; partners or associates; staff; customers, clients, or users; vendors or suppliers; professional colleagues; professional associations; family; church or community; myself; others)

Source: Adapted from George L. Morrisey, "Your Personal Mission Statement: A Foundation for Your Future," *Training and Development Journal,* November, 1992, pp. 71-74, and George L. Morrisey, *Creating Your Future: Personal Strategic Planning for Professionals,* San Francisco, CA, Berrett-Koehler Publishing Co., 1992.

EXPERIENTIAL EXERCISE 2

Describing an Organization's Culture

Purpose

To learn about the critical characteristics that define an organization's culture. Edgar Schein identified the following six organizational characteristics that were discussed earlier in this chapter. By evaluating these factors for an organization you should be able to develop a reasonably accurate description of its culture.

Task

Step 1: Interview three employees who work for the same organization, but not in the same department or unit. Ask each to briefly describe each of the six organizational characteristics as they exist in their organization. Summarize their comments in the table below.

Step 2: Based on what you have learned from your interviews write a one paragraph description of the organization's culture in the table below.

Step 3: In a second visit with the three employees ask them to read your culture description. Ask them if they feel that it is fairly accurate, if not ask that they suggest changes and revise your description.

Step 4: Your instructor may want you to share the final description with the class, and explain how it was developed.

Critical Organizational Culture Characteristics

1. Values _____

2. Philosophy_____

3. Norms _____

4. Climate _____

5. Politics _____

6. Social behaviors of employees _____

Initial Description of the Culture of the Organization

_____

_____

_____

_____

_____

_____

_____

Revised Description of the Culture of the Organization

_____

_____

_____

_____

_____

_____

_____

**Take It
to the Net**

You can find this chapter's World Wide Web exercise at:
http://www.prenhall.com/carrell

CHAPTER 18

Organizational Change and Development

CHAPTER OBJECTIVES

1. To understand what organizational change is and how to diagnose and predict organizational change.
2. To explain the differences between external and internal forces.
3. To describe the characteristics of change agents.
4. To define resistance to change at both the individual and organizational level.
5. To know the three processes of organizational change.
6. To describe organizational creativity and the process of creative thinking.
7. To explain organizational downsizing and business reengineering.
8. To understand what organizational development (OD) is and the ethical dilemmas associated with OD.
9. To describe problems involved in initiating OD and the four OD interventions.

John Akers, Former CEO at IBM

At one time, IBM was one of the largest and most profitable business enterprises on earth. However, IBM was hobbled by a bureaucracy that was bloated, slow-moving, and over-centralized. Its executives appeared to have a disdain for ideas and managers from anywhere else. In a mature industry, IBM had a hard time keeping up with innovative competitors that have made some of its products look like dinosaurs, and it had lost touch with its customers. During 1992, former CEO John Akers announced that IBM was retreating from all that the company had believed in: The future of mainframe computing was clouded; R&D spending was being reduced; and Layoffs of 25,000 employees were being announced. The layoffs were a particular torment for IBM who in the past had claimed that employee dismissals were intolerable.

Could this happen to IBM? Unfortunately, IBM was no longer something special. It was just another very big company in very deep trouble. In fact, IBM reported a net loss of $5 billion in 1992 with sales of $64.5 billion.[1] Interestingly, IBM's top management in 1984 reported that by 1990, revenues would reach $100 billion and returns on shareholders' equity would continue to exceed 20 percent. From a peak stock market value of $106 billion in 1987, IBM lost $76 bil-

lion in 1992. Akers announced several strategies to change IBM. These included: pushing power downward into what was for decades the consummate top-down company, breaking the company into thirteen divisions with increased autonomy, expanding service business, and making the company more responsive to customer needs. However, IBM's sheer vastness made it difficult to change its culture in a hurry. For example, IBM was four times the size of Digital, the number two computer maker, and ten times larger than Apple.[2] Unfortunately, Akers was unable to implement his proposed strategies. In late January 1993, Akers agreed to resign as IBM's CEO—a humiliating turnaround from his repeated insistence that he would lead IBM's struggle for years to come. Akers's top lieutenants were also forced aside. President Jack Kuehler was moved to vice chairman while Chief Financial Officer Frank Metz retired early.[3]

What Is Organizational Change?

It was a tough job to try to take a company that did everything as effectively and as well as IBM did as a unified, centralized, somewhat bureaucratic organization and try to take it toward where the world was going, stated Akers, following his forced resignation.[4]

In this chapter we describe environmental and internal forces involved in *organizational change,* identify change agents, discuss forces for change and how change is resisted, and describe several processes by which organizations can be changed. We will also explain individual creativity. Next, we describe how to diagnose and predict organizational change and then go on to examine organizational downsizing and business reengineering. Finally, we discuss the nature of organizational development (OD) including the ethics of OD and approaches for OD interventions.

Organizational change Environmental and internal forces are involved to change an organization that includes pressures or opportunities that arise outside the firm or may be composed of internal forces.

A number of basic forces, individually or in combination, can lead to significant changes within an organization. One broad set of forces consists of external or environmental forces that are pressures or opportunities that arise outside the firm. Another set is composed of internal forces. Figure 18-1 illustrates many of the major external and internal forces for change that affect contemporary organizations.

External Forces

External forces Forces that originate in the external environment cause a need for organization change.

In Chap. 16 we discussed the external environment of an organization. Forces can originate in the external environment causing the need for organizational change. A stagnant organization in a dynamic environment may well lose touch with its market and subsequently wither and die. As an example, General Motors failed to recognize environmental changes occurring in the auto industry during the late 1970s and through the 1980s. The same problem can be stated with respect to IBM. Environment changes that occurred in the computer industry during the 1980s were not recognized by IBM.

Internal Forces

Internal forces Internal activities and decisions create internal forces for change.

Internal activities and decisions create internal forces for change. Labor problems such as strikes, high grievance rates, or the threat of unionization often

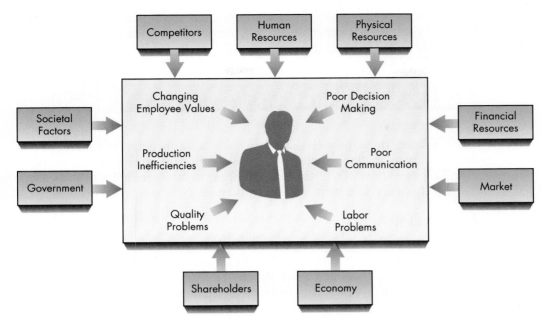

FIGURE 18-1 Internal and External Forces for Change

cause management to modify its personnel policies. High turnover among employees or excessive absenteeism can also cause management to reassess its operations. For example, "people pressures" may result in changes in job design, organizational structure, wage rates, hiring policies, management styles, and so on. Quality problems and production inefficiencies can also create internal pressures for change. General Motors' senior management became frustrated by a poor internal efficiency and designed the Saturn manufacturing plant to solve this internal need. In essence, demands by employees, labor unions, quality problems, and production inefficiencies can all generate a force to which management must respond with change.

Change Agents

A change agent is an individual or group who takes responsibility for overseeing the change process. Such an individual or group may be from outside the organization. External *change agents* are specialists who are familiar with organizational behavior, organizational development, and industrial psychology concepts. These specialists may be university professors or full-time employees of a consulting firm. Advantages of using an external change agent is that the change process can be managed in an unbiased manner. A disadvantage is that the external change agent is unlikely to know as much about the focal organization's culture, politics, and policies as someone from inside the organization.

In some instances, the change agent may already be employed by the focal organization. Internal change agents have the advantage of having insights into the day-to-day details of how the organization actually operates. However, the disadvantages of an internal change agent are that objectivity may be less than that of an external change agent, and internal change agents may have less training than external consultants.[5]

Change Agent is an individual or group who takes responsibility for coercing the change process.

Choosing between external and internal change agents involves tradeoffs between professional expertise and objectivity on the one hand, and insider familiarity and insight on the other.[6]

FORCES FOR CHANGE

Because organizational change is such a broad concept, it is difficult to predict what type of change will be the most significant during the 1990s. However, four areas in which change forces appear to be powerful include the labor force, technology, competition, and world politics.

The Labor Force

In 1985, women made up 43 percent of the labor force as illustrated by Fig. 18-2. By the year 2000, women will make up nearly half the labor force.

From 1985 to 2000, changes in the composition of the labor force have been projected. Fig. 18-3 presents the estimated percent growth in the labor force from 1985 to 2000.

These labor force changes will create more demand for child-care facilities, parental leave, and other arrangements to assist women in balancing both family and career responsibilities. Managers, both male and female, will be affected by a continuing conflict between family and job obligations faced by many women.[7]

Minorities will also be attracted to the work force in larger numbers as illustrated in Figs. 18-2 and 18-3. The Civil Rights Act of 1964, together with other laws, prohibits employers from discrimination on the basis of race, creed, color, religion, sex, or national origin in their employment practices. By the year 2000, projections indicate that one out of every four workers will be nonwhite compared to one out of every five workers at the end of the 1980s. Demographic assumptions indicate that the principal minority groups—African-Americans, Hispanics, and Asians—will comprise 12 percent, 10 percent, and 4 percent, respectively, of the labor force by the year 2000. Minorities will also present challenges

FIGURE 18-2

1985 Labor Force Composition

Source: Hudson Institute, 1990.

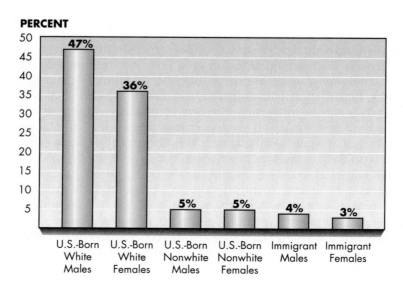

PERCENT

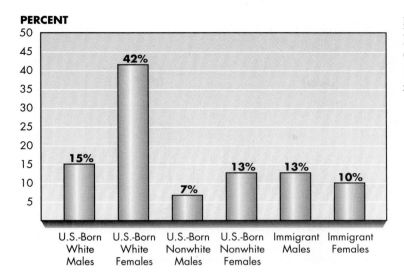

Figure 18-3
Estimated Percent
Growth in Labor Force:
1985-2000
Source: Hudson Institute, 1990.

to the organization. For example, firms will be required to provide transportation for minorities living in inner cities but working for firms in outlying locations. Training will become more important as the organization increases the skill level of the newly employable minorities. The corporate culture of many organizations may need to be changed to accept the influx of these new employees.[8]

The increased number of minorities can also create certain additional job tensions for managers. For example, minorities will tend to occupy most of the lower paying and lower skill level jobs. Employers will tend to implement preferential employment policies for minorities. White males will tend to file charges of reverse discrimination. Given these scenarios, managers will have to strive to be fair in managing diverse groups of employees through nondiscriminatory and progressive policies and actions. The "OB in Practice" on page 613 describes how Exxon's Baytown, Texas, chemical plant manages diversity.

Age categories of the labor force will also change. As the population of the United States becomes older, so will the labor force. For example, in 1990 about 20 percent of the labor force was between sixteen and twenty-four years of age, 30 percent between the ages of twenty-five and thirty-four, and 40 percent between the ages of thirty-five to fifty-four. These age groups will comprise 16 percent, 23 percent, and 51 percent, respectively, of the labor force in the year 2000.[9] Figure 18-4 illustrates these changes in age categories.

Differences in age groups may hurt a company's effectiveness. Individuals who were born between 1951 and 1962, boomers, are now moving into significant managerial positions. A younger group, Generation X as the new crop has taken to calling themselves, aged eighteen to twenty-nine, is being alienated by a culture dominated by the boomers. The Xers, or busters, complain that the boomers seemed to get the best of everything, from careers to free love, while today's young people get AIDS and jobs flipping hamburgers. Boomers are critical of busters saying that they are not loyal or committed to work, and do not respect authority. Unlike workaholic boomers, detractors state that busters refuse to go the extra mile to do things right, casually change jobs, and want time to play. These clashing workplace values and the sour economic scene has created lasting tensions with which managers will have to deal. Faced with working for boomer bosses they find oppressive, many busters have abandoned corporate America, retreating into slackerdom or striking out on their own as entrepre-

FIGURE 18-4

Percent of Labor Force by
Age Categories

Source: Hudson Institute, 1990.

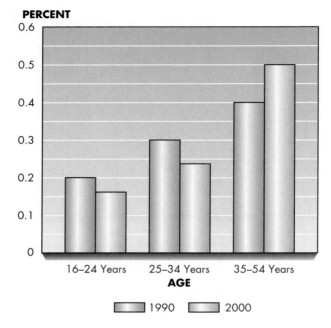

PERCENT

Age categories chart: 16–24 Years (1990: 0.2, 2000: ~0.16); 25–34 Years (1990: 0.3, 2000: ~0.24); 35–54 Years (1990: 0.4, 2000: 0.5)

AGE

1990   2000

neurs. The challenge for managers is to figure out ways to capture the busters' enthusiasm to enliven existing companies.[10] The "Profile" on page 615 describes what Generation Xers want in the workplace.

Managers also face the interesting challenge of managing employees that have a wide variety of skills. Today, much of the labor force is well educated. For example. in 1990, 25 percent of the labor force were college graduates and 85 percent of new entrants to the labor force had at least a high school education. Some management researchers have stated that problems with an "overeducated" labor force may develop. This may occur because more and more college-trained employees will compete for jobs that do not require a college education to perform. Yet other statistics indicate that the actual skill level of new workers entering the labor force from 1985 to 2000 varies considerably from the skill levels needed for new jobs created from 1985 to 2000. Figure 18-5 compares the skills required to the skills available in new jobs created between 1985 and 2000. Most of the new jobs created from 1985 to 2000 will require a skill level of Level 3 or greater with the majority of new jobs requiring a Level 4.[11]

One chief executive has noted that while many individuals entering the labor force have considerable formal education, these educated individuals lack specific skills or talents to perform in a manufacturing or service firm environment. Another chief executive stated that many employees are unable to operate modern equipment without additional company-provided education.[12] Certainly, organizations will attempt to provide training opportunities for these individuals who have limited special skills but have the motivation to work. It was Nobel Laureate Theodore Schultz who first equated skills and knowledge with human capital and argued that investments in education and training were crucial to a nation's productivity and growth.[13] Furthermore, studies have confirmed that corporations that spend the most on employee development and training are typically the most competitive ones in every developed country in the world.[14]

Early in 1994, one out of every four employee of U.S. firms was a member of the contingency work force: part-timers, free-lancers, subcontractors, and

OB in Practice

Managing Diversity

Exxon Chemical Co.'s 2,000-employee plant in Baytown, Texas, has attracted national attention for its pioneering efforts to turn work force diversity into an asset rather than a liability. Although heterogeneous work teams often underperform homogeneous teams, Exxon's objective is to make a heterogeneous work force perform as a homogeneous work team. Following are the five major components of the Baytown diversity effort:

1. *Awareness and understanding.* An employee group encourages employees to seek out and understand the differences in the 23 people around them and to think about behavior through cultural lenses through an extensive cultural awareness training program. For example, consider the different approaches between a typical North American businessman traveling to South America to do business with a typical South American businessman. The North American comes from a culture that believes time is scarce and that relationships are mostly personal and only tangentially related to business. The South American believes that relationships are crucial to business and that time is plentiful. The North American wants to fly in, do the deal, and fly back out—all on a tight schedule. The typical South American wants to spend some time building the relationship that will be the basis for future business. So at lunch the North American pulls out a sheaf of papers, and the South American pulls out pictures of his children. Both are pursuing the same transaction and both of them are wondering why the other is not doing the right thing.

   It may not be necessary to train everyone, but Exxon insists that those who will be leading the change efforts receive the cultural awareness training. About 70 percent of the Baytown employees have received their training.

2. *Provide support for people undergoing change.* Typically people who have undergone awareness training develop new attitudes toward others. Although they have changed, the workplace and others may still be the same. It is important to recognize this issue and to have plans in advance on how to deal with it. Otherwise, the training just brings everyone's cultural feelings to the surface and then rubs them raw against the same old organizational behavior. Exxon creates single-culture support groups and provides facilitators to ensure that employees focus on positive solutions and not on gripes.

3. *Make diversity real in the workplace.* This means adopting changes in policies and practices. Exxon has very clear policies that ensure that the best-qualified person is fairly selected for new job openings, but practices did not exist about the things that led to a person becoming the best qualified. Now, when an employee applies for a new job, he or she is kept informed about the status of the selection process and must receive an explanation if he or she fails to advance at any stage of the process. The employee can now ask: "If I am not ready for this job, how and when are you going to help me get ready?"

4. *Demonstrate that management is serious.* Cultural awareness and understanding is not very important in an environment in which anyone can be intentionally mistreated by another person. Management should anticipate that someone will test the cultural awareness programs and should decide in advance on how it will respond to violations. Employees should know with certainty what consequences to expect.

5. *Celebrate shared successes.* Exxon's Baytown management believes that as people become more focused on what to do next, they can get so wrapped up in what is left to do that they lose sight of what has been accomplished. Man-

agement must intervene and recognize accomplishments. Special events have been staged to salute employees who are nominated by their peers as having made special contributions to the management of diversity.

Source: Adapted from John H. Sheridan, "Dividends from Diversity," *Industry Week*, September 10, 1994, pp. 23-26.

---

independent professionals who are hired by companies to cope with unexpected or temporary challenges. By the year 2000, fully half of all working Americans—some 60 million people—will have joined the contingency work force. Contingency employees typically lead far riskier and more uncertain lives than do permanent employees and often are paid less and almost never receive benefits.[15] More organizations will create a two-tier labor system consisting of a small core of permanent employees supplemented by a continually expanding and shrinking pool of contingent workers.[16]

Technology

As indicated in Chap. 16, technology is the knowledge, techniques, and equipment that an organization uses to transform unprocessed resources (inputs) into finished goods or services (outputs). Technological changes are important to an

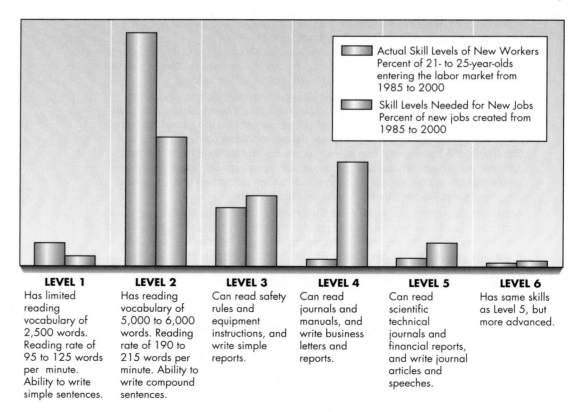

LEVEL 1	**LEVEL 2**	**LEVEL 3**	**LEVEL 4**	**LEVEL 5**	**LEVEL 6**
Has limited reading vocabulary of 2,500 words. Reading rate of 95 to 125 words per minute. Ability to write simple sentences.	Has reading vocabulary of 5,000 to 6,000 words. Reading rate of 190 to 215 words per minute. Ability to write compound sentences.	Can read safety rules and equipment instructions, and write simple reports.	Can read journals and manuals, and write business letters and reports.	Can read scientific technical journals and financial reports, and write journal articles and speeches.	Has same skills as Level 5, but more advanced.

Legend:
- **Actual Skill Levels of New Workers** Percent of 21- to 25-year-olds entering the labor market from 1985 to 2000
- **Skill Levels Needed for New Jobs** Percent of new jobs created from 1985 to 2000

FIGURE 18-5 Skills Required vs. Skills Available: 1985-2000

Source: "Where the Jobs Are Is Where the Skills Aren't," *Business Week*, September 19, 1988, pp. 104-108. Reprinted by special permission, copyright © 1995 by The McGraw-Hill Companies.

Profile

Maury Hanigan
President, Hanigan Consulting Group, New York City

GENERATION X

Hanigan Consulting Group has advised a number of firms on recruiting strategies. Following are Maury Hanigan's comments regarding what Generation Xers want in their jobs and careers.

Baby boomers wanted security and predictability in their jobs. They wanted a solid career path and were willing to play the game to get promotions. The Generation Xers, the age group born after the baby boom ended in 1962, don't believe that job security exists and are vitally interested in the skills they will develop in a job. Before Generation X people will take a job, they must be convinced that the job will be intellectually challenging and stimulating.

Generation X college graduates collectively see large corporations as lagging behind in technology. They feel the hot designs and uses of technology are taking place inside small garages.

Generation Xers aren't willing to take a job and pay their dues before getting ahead. They want a reasonably consistent quality of life throughout their careers. They realize that in modem flat organizations, there's little opportunity for them to become senior managers, so they are unwilling to lead a dreadful life now, in the hopes of a more privileged life down the road.

Reasonable quality of life means a balance between work and personal lives, having interesting content in their work, and enough money to live comfortably. These people watched their parents work obsessively only to end up downsized on the sidewalk. Generation X is saying, "No thank you. That's not the life-style that makes sense to me."

On the job, younger employees see lots of work generated for political rather than productive reasons, and they view that as a waste of time. There are so many baby boomers who have fought for visibility their entire careers that they automatically do a lot of things to get the attention of senior management. That kind of nonwork doesn't satisfy the younger generation. They want their managers to brief them on the issues that face the department and give them the opportunity to have input into the solution. They know they don't have the experience base to make those decisions, but they have brain power and want to be respected for it.

Source: Adapted from Brian Moskal, "Generation X Is Saying 'No, Thank You!'" *Industry Week*, October 3, 1994, p. 19.

---

organization because changes in technology affect the nature of work. For example, the Carrier Corporation has built a factory of the future in Arkadelphia, Arkansas, to manufacture compressors for air conditioners. Using flexible manufacturing concepts, the streamlined plant is spotless, quiet, and highly automated. Women work beside men in every area and can handle every job. No one has to lift anything heavier than twelve pounds. Flexibility is crucial, both among employees and the design of the plant. The entire plant can be reconfigured within several weeks. Employees learn blueprint reading, math such as fractions and metric calculations, statistical process-control methods, some computer skills, and solving problems involved in dealing with fellow employees. Employees perform multiple tasks and become involved in fixing machines when the machines break down and provide input into the hiring of new employees and promotion of others.

The quality of air conditioning compressors is critical to Carrier's success, because compressors account for as much as 50 percent of an air conditioner's production cost. Faulty compressors can quickly increase warranty costs. Carrier's new manufacturing plant has yielded significant improvements in quality and reduced costs.[17] As we discussed in Chap. 16, individuals performing narrow, specialized, and routine jobs are being replaced by teams whose members actively participate in team decisions and who can perform multiple tasks.

The "OB in Practice" opposite describes how General Motors, under the leadership of Jack Smith, has produced a remarkable earnings swing.

Competition

While organizations have always faced the pressure of change arising from competitive forces, the nature of competition is changing. The world is becoming a global economy in which competition will occur from industrialized countries, such as Japan and Germany, as well as from the booming businesses of developing countries. Products and services will be offered by small, innovative firms that can quickly adapt to environmental changes. One argument is that successful organizations will be those with a flexible and responsible work force that can rapidly adapt to a changing environment. Organizations that try to compete in the 1990s have to find a way to engage the mind of every single employee.[18]

World Politics

The new reality of global competition generates a vicious economic trap for worldwide prosperity: a permanent condition of overcapacity in production that insures destructive economic consequences. Simply put, the world's existing structure of manufacturing facilities, constantly being expanded on cheap labor and new technologies, can now produce far more goods than the world's consumers can possibly absorb. The auto industry is an example. Auto factories, worldwide, have the capacity to produce forty-five million cars annually for a market that, in the best years, will buy no more than thirty-five million cars. In essence, there are too many cars chasing too few drivers. The economic consequences are obvious. Someone has to close their auto factory and stop producing. Two effects, the instability of capital investment and the depression of wages, combine to guarantee that global demand can never catch up with global supply. New consumers for the world's output, to be sure, emerge with new development, but other existing consumers are lost, as their jobs are lost or their wages decline in real terms. So long as the process is allowed to run its course, the flight will continue downhill—too many factories making too many goods for a marketplace where too many families lack the wherewithal to buy them.

The way out of this economic trap is a grand political strategy for growth that focuses on workers and wages worldwide. The global economy can proceed to develop, without the destructive qualities, if an economic order of accelerated global growth is designed to generate rising incomes for ordinary citizens and thus, greater consumer capacity for what the world is able to produce. A strategy that fosters higher wage levels would gradually unwind the condition of enormous overcapacity, while it also reduces the desperate edge of capital flight.

This approach would require, of course, a great reversal in the conservative economic doctrines that now dominate most governments in the industrial world. It would also require convincing guarantees to the citizens of impoverished nations who long for jobs—guarantees that they will not be shut out of the rising prosperity. The economic policies for accomplishing such a strategy

GM Makes $11 Billion Recovery

Jack Smith, who became CEO of General Motors in April 1992, is engineering the biggest turnaround in American corporate history. In just 2$^1/_2$ years, he has driven GM's core car and truck businesses back from the brink of financial collapse, overhauled its essential operations, and steered it on down the road not just toward recovery but toward global preeminence. Smith led GM's North American car and truck operations from a $10.7 billion loss (before interest and taxes) in 1991 to a $362 million profit in 1993—an $1 1 billion swing. Companywide, the results were almost as impressive. After losing $4.5 billion in 1991 and a spectacular $23.5 billion in 1992, GM earned $2.5 billion in 1993. Already Smith's feats rank him with the legendary Alfred Sloan, Jr., a former GM CEO who took over GM in 1920 when it was close to bankruptcy and Henry Ford ruled the world. When Sloan retired in 1956, GM had become the largest automobile company on earth.

Source: Adapted from Joann Lublin, "GM's Remarkable Recovery," *The Wall Street Journal,* October 1, 1994, pg. B1; Alex Taylor III, "GM's $11 Billion Turnaround," *Fortune,* October 17, 1994, pp. 54-74.

---

are plausible enough. What is not plausible at this moment in history is the politics.[19] However, the passage of the North American Free Trade Agreement (NAFTA), together with trade agreements involving Asian and European countries, is a step toward reversing conservative economic doctrines.

RESISTANCE TO CHANGE

Change is not always resisted. Few of us would refuse a gift of a million dollars even though accepting it would likely lead to significant changes in our lifestyle. However, change is often not viewed in a positive sense—either because the benefits of the proposed change are unclear or because organizational members perceive that the benefits of the change are outweighed by its costs. People in organizations like the status quo. When management begins to change things, the good old days look better and better. Resistance to change may develop from the individual, the organization, or from both.

Individual Sources of Resistance

Researchers have identified seven reasons for individual resistance to change: fear of the unknown, self-interest, habit, personality conflicts, differing perceptions, general mistrust, and social disruptions.[20]

FEAR OF THE UNKNOWN Perhaps the greatest cause of an individual's resistance to change is fear of the unknown, or uncertainty. In the face of change, individuals may think that their job security is threatened, or have concerns about their ability to meet new job requirements. Also some individuals simply dislike ambiguity.

SELF-INTEREST   Individuals may believe that they will lose power, status, or influence during change.

HABIT   Individuals prefer the old way of doing things. Change requires new ways of performing tasks. Having to learn these new ways makes the job more difficult.

PERSONALITY CONFLICTS   Not getting along with others in the organization may limit an individual's ability to accept change.

DIFFERING PERCEPTIONS   In some instances, individuals may differ with respect to how change may affect them. Change may be viewed as being good for some organizational members and bad for others.

GENERAL MISTRUST   While individuals may understand the arguments for change, they may not trust the motives of those advocating the change.

SOCIAL DISRUPTIONS   Individuals may fear that change will disrupt existing traditions. Also, an individual who agrees to a change may be ridiculed by others who resist the change.

Organizational Sources of Resistance

Seven major organizational sources of resistance have been identified by researchers: structural inertia, bureaucratic inertia, group norms, a resistant organizational culture, threatened power, threatened expertise, and threatened resource allocations.[21] Not every change situation and not every organization displays all seven of the preceding sources.[22]

STRUCTURAL INERTIA   As indicated in Chap. 16, an organization's structure may be designed to maintain stability. Such a structure provides a resistance to change.

BUREAUCRATIC INERTIA   Some organizations use inflexible, bureaucratic rules, and rigid, standardized procedures to manage employee behavior. These rules and procedures make it difficult for employees to be innovative, flexible, and adaptive.

GROUP NORMS   Group norms are the shared standards that help to guide member behavior and to make it understandable. These group norms may prevent individual attempts for change.

A RESISTANT ORGANIZATIONAL CULTURE   Some organizations have cultures that stress stability and tradition. Change advocates in such cultures are viewed as being misguided.

THREATENED POWER   Organizational change often threatens an individual's power relationship with others. Certain managers may resist change because they fear the loss of their power base.

THREATENED EXPERTISE   Individuals and groups within organizations develop certain specialized expertise. A change may threaten this expertise causing a resistance to the change.[23]

THREATENED RESOURCE ALLOCATIONS   Individuals and groups may believe that change will threaten future resource allocations.

Resistance to change may indicate a legitimate concern that the change is not good for the organization and that the proposed change should be reexamined. Resistance to change can be managed through communicating and educating employees more effectively and involving them in the change process. The following section describes how organizational change can be managed.

THE PROCESS OF ORGANIZATIONAL CHANGE

By observing external trends and internal needs and patterns, change can be managed. Figure 18-6 includes a model describing the process of organizational change. The following four events illustrate the change sequence: (1) External and internal forces for change exist; (2) Organizational managers monitor these forces and become aware of the need for change; (3) This perceived need creates the development and initiation of a change, which (4) is then implemented. The extent to which these change activities are handled depends on the organization and its managers' styles.[24] The "Profile" on page 620 describes how the former manager of a $7.3 billion in sales subsidiary of AT&T managed change.

Researchers have identified three process models of organizational change: Lewin's three-step model, the planned change model, and the action research model. Organizational change can also be initiated through individual creativity, idea champions, corporation innovation, and new-venture teams.

Lewin's Three-Step Model

According to Kurt Lewin, a social scientist, planned organizational change can occur by changing the behavior and attitudes of organizational members. As illustrated in Fig. 18-7, these changes occur from the three distinct steps of unfreezing, change, and refreezing.[25]

Unfreezing, the first step, involves a diagnosis by an organizational development (OD) specialist who gathers and analyzes data through personal interviews,

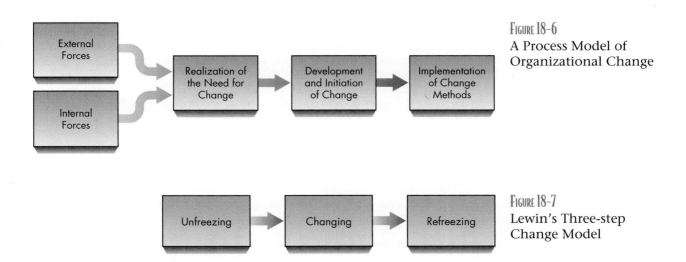

FIGURE 18-6
A Process Model of Organizational Change

FIGURE 18-7
Lewin's Three-step Change Model

Profile

Jerre Stead
Executive-In-Residence
University of Iowa

HOW TO MANAGE CHANGE

Five times Jerre Stead has led a business transformation—in two divisions of Honeywell; at Square D, the industrial control products-maker taken over by France's Groupe Schneider in 1991; at AT&T's Global Business Communications Systems (GBCS); and at AT&T's Global Information Solutions (GIS)—and each time it has been different, he says.

Ask business people why change is hard, and sooner or later, usually sooner, you'll hear the "culture." Changing corporate culture, that's murder. It will rise up and smite you. Ask Jerre Stead, and you'll hear: "culture is overused. What's really involved is a basic change in the things you do as a company." Early in his tenure at Square D, Stead trashed two fat books of policies and replaced them with just eleven important ones—covering for example, rules for capital spending. He did the same at GIS. Says Stead, "Those rules, aimed at 1 percent of employees, handcuff the other 99 percent. Nobody can do all that stuff in the book, so people end up following just one unofficial objective: Keep the boss happy. Get rid of the rules, and they can focus on keeping customers happy."

Rather than rule books, Stead relied on results and rewards. Compared with transactional leadership, the job of leading transformation was intensely interpersonal, according to Stead. "It's not like Moses going up the mountain and hearing God talk and getting a vision. It's us *as a people.* If you fall into the Moses trap, you won't get the change."

After leaving Square D, Stead had 18 offers to run corporations and chose AT&T because of the excitement of the computing and communications industry. He was named president and CEO of GBCS. At the time, GBCS was losing over $800 million a year. The mere $30 million generated outside the United States by GBCS was a major concern for Stead because of his background in building global markets. In three years, under Stead's leadership, GBCS had increased its international revenues to $350 million and earnings to a profitable $200 million. While reviving GBCS, Stead was elected chairman and CEO of NCR Corporation, an AT&T acquisition. NCR had lost $600 million in net income in 1992 and 1993. In a historic move, Stead renamed the NCR acquisition Global Information Solutions (GIS) and created 350 cross-functional, customer-focused teams that were assigned to provide service, sales, and engineering support to customers. In 1994, under Stead's direction, GIS earned a net profit of $160 million. While Stead was revamping GIS, AT&T purchased a California start-up, Terradata, and merged it into GBCS. The merging of the two businesses created tremendous employee anxiety which Stead responded to by launching an aggressive communications campaign. He set up a letter-writing forum called "Ask Jerre" and held live, quarterly, satellite sessions in which employees from all over the world could call and ask him anything during the broadcast.

When Stead's three-and-half-year contract ended with AT&T, he became chairman and CEO of Legent, a software concern. After serving in this position for five months, Stead negotiated the sale of Legent to Computer Associates that earned him $15 million in stock options. His lucrative departure from Legent means that Stead can do what he always intended to do in retirement: support education and business. Stead serves on six corporate boards, and on select academic boards at the University of Iowa, his alma mater, Northwestern, and Georgetown. As Executive-In-Residence at the University of Iowa, Stead addresses undergraduate and MBA students on a number of business topics and believes that he makes a contribution to students by helping them understand what really occurs in the corporate world.

Source: Adapted from Sally Clasen, "Executive-In-Residence: Jerre Stead," *Business at Iowa,* published by the College of Business Administration, University of Iowa, Fall 1995, pp. 12-15;

John Keller, "AT&T Computer Chief Resigns to Head Legent," *The Wall Street Journal*, January 5, 1995, pg. B1; Thomas A. Stewart, "Managing Change: How to Lead a Corporate Revolution," *Fortune*, November 28, 1994, pp. 48-61.

questionnaires, and observations at meetings. Participants are then made aware of the problem and must be willing to change.

Changing, the second step, occurs when a plan or program is implemented to alter existing activities or relationship. Change efforts can range from minor to major programs. Learning new skills through a training program or installing new equipment are examples of minor changes, because few organizational members are involved. Radically restructuring the organization is a major change because many organizational members are involved.

Refreezing, the third step, makes the change that occurred in step two become permanent. During refreezing, new behaviors, attitudes, and values are acquired and integrated into the everyday procedures of the organization.

The Planned Change Model

In the planned change model, top management has recognized the need for change, initiates a problem-solving process to design the change, and then implements and evaluates the change.[26] The planned change model expands Lewin's three-step model into seven steps as illustrated in Fig. 18-8.

From a planned change perspective, the steps of scouting and entry allows the change agent to explore a particular problem and then develop a mutual contract including mutual expectations with a client organization. Diagnosis identifies specific improvement goals, while planning allows the change agent to identify action steps and ways to cope with resistance to change. In the action step, the change agent directs implementation of the plan of action. Organizational members, working with the change agent, have determined what specific changes to make and how to implement these changes. During the stabilization and evaluation step, the change agent and management of the client organization evaluate the accomplishments of the action steps. The planned change process returns to the diagnosis step if further action is required. If further action is not required, then the change process moves to the termination step. The termination step ends the change agent–client organization relationship. If an external change agent is involved, then he or she will train organizational members to maintain the change and will then move on to another assignment. This assignment may be with a new organization or a new project with the existing client organization. If an internal change agent is involved, he or she will also train organizational members to maintain the change and will then be assigned new duties.

Action Research Model

While the planned change model generally uses standard techniques that have been used before, the action research model allows original, innovative procedures to be developed and assessed. In the action research model, data is collected on an organization, fed back to organizational members for action planning, results are evaluated by collecting and reflecting on more data after a certain action has been taken. Action research is a data-based and collaborative approach for problem solving and allows the change agent the opportunity of evaluating

FIGURE 18-8
A Comparison of the
Planned Change Model
with Lewin's Three-step
Model

Source: Edgar F. Huse,
*Organization Development and
Change,* 2nd ed, St. Paul, MN,
West Publishing, 1980, p. 87.
Reprinted by permission;
Copyright © 1980 by West
Publishing Company. All rights
reserved.

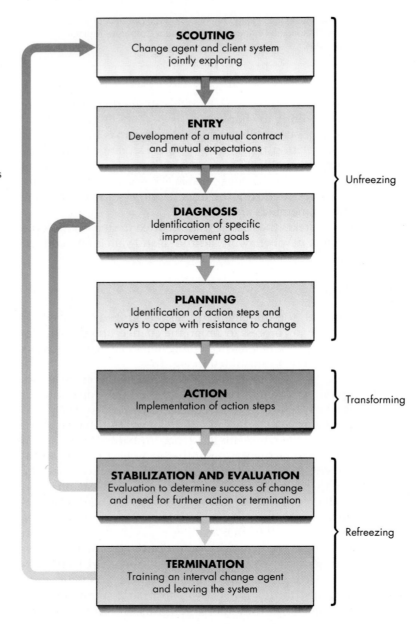

the effects of change on an organization.[27] Figure 18-9 illustrates the action research model.

The "OB in Practice" on page 625 illustrates the importance of people skills during an organizational change.

Creativity **The development of novel solutions to perceived problems.**

Individual Creativity

Another aspect of organization change is creative thinking by individuals. Creativity is defined as the development of novel solutions to perceived problems.[28] Creative individuals develop ideas that can be adopted by their organizations. For example, Ted Turner transformed a small Atlanta TV station, WTCG, into CNN by "delivering news on demand." Ross Perot avoided offering solutions to

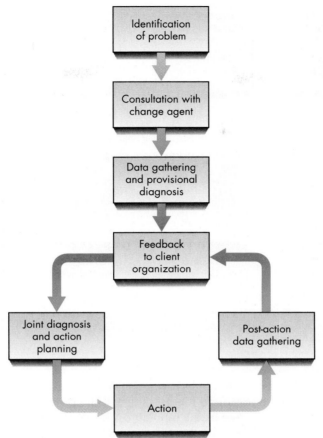

Figure 18-9

Action Research Model

Source: John A. Wagner and John R. Hollenbeck, *Management of Organization Behavior,* Englewood Cliffs, NJ, Prentice-Hall, 1992, p. 520. Used with permission.

problems and instead worked directly with his customers on developing nitty-gritty practical solutions to their practical problems. Other individuals noted for their creativity include George de Mestral, who created Velcro after noticing the tiny hooks on cockleburs caught on his wool socks, and Edwin Land who invented the Polaroid camera.[29]

A variety of models have been developed to describe the creative process used by individuals. For example, after reviewing many of the personality and environmental factors that determine individual creativity, T. M. Amabile placed them into a sequence of problem-solving steps. As illustrated in Fig. 18-10, Amabile argues that the creative process involves five stages.

At Stage 1, task presentation, a person can have a burning desire to discover something, be intrinsically motivated to learn about an issue, or simply find him- or herself in a situation in which someone demands that a difficult problem be solved. If the presented problem is motivating enough to capture the individual's attention, it leads to Stage 2, preparation. In the preparation stage, the individual builds up or activates information that is relevant to the problem including any tricks, shortcuts, or algorithms that might be useful for the task. After knowledge is activated, Stage 3, idea generation, occurs. In the idea generation stage, approaches to the problem are attempted using the individual's repertoire of previous experiences, insights, and fears. At Stage 4, idea validation, each potential solution is eventually tested against the problem. If the goal is attained or if no reasonable progress is made on the problem, the process is

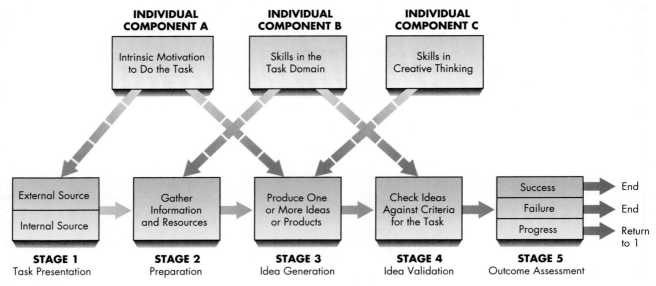

FIGURE 18-10 Amabile's Model of Creative Thinking

Source: Adapted from T. M. Amabile, "The Social Psychology of Creativity: A Componential Conceptualization," *Journal of Personality and Social Psychology* 45, 1983, p. 371. Copyright © 1983 by the American Psychological Association. Adapted with permission.

ended. For outcomes that are between these extremes, the individual is then seen as returning to the first stage of the problem.

As indicated in the top half of Fig. 18-10, three sets of components are identified that are contributors to creative performance. The first component, an intrinsic motivation to do the task, may provide the initial stimulus for a problem. Amabile notes that intrinsic motivation is better suited for creative endeavors than extrinsic motivation because intrinsic motivation is more conducive for (a) processing divergent information, (b) seeing the nonobvious sides of an issue, and (c) exploring alternative solution paths. This first creative component influences Stage 1 and Stage 3 of Amabile's model depicted in Fig. 18-10.

The second component, skills in the task domain, includes knowledge of the problem area, technical skills, and talents that provide the necessary background to solve the problem. As indicated in Fig. 18-10, the second creative component influences Stages 2 and 4.

The third component, creative thinking, includes the ability to (a) make random associations between ideas, (b) see divergent uses for a single idea, (c) access one's subconscious, (d) visualize potential solutions, (e) generate a number of diverse alternatives, and (f) hold back critical evaluation until the full range of possibilities is explored.[30]

A different approach in explaining individual creativity has been presented by D. T. Campbell. More than thirty years ago, Campbell argued against the notion that creativity is a mysterious process performed by a gifted or brilliant mind. Campbell argued that creativity is largely the product of sweaty trial and error, and that individuals must work long and hard to generate multiple solutions to different problems. The key to creativity, according to Campbell, is to persevere and use a diverse set of alternatives.[31]

Studies indicate that creativity can be designed into organizations by:[32]

OB in Practice
Fired Sunbeam CEO Lacked People Skills

To Wall Street, Paul Kazarian was a hard-driving and demanding leader who rescued Sunbeam-Oster from bankruptcy and made it profitable again. To Professor Steven Fenster of the Harvard Business School who authored a case study of Sunbeam-Oster's turnaround, Kazarian was a "genius" with "incredible" business acumen. However, to many of his employees, Kazarian was an overbearing boss whose frequent harangues and erratic, autocratic behavior made their lives miserable. Executives of Sunbeam-Oster state that Kazarian fired employees on a whim, made lewd suggestions to women, and every other word he used was the "F" word.

Six of Kazarian's top lieutenants pledged themselves to a "blood pact" to oust Kazarian following an eighteen-hour meeting in which they were berated and called "scum." One senior executive described the meeting as being similar to a fraternity hazing. The executives were called in one-by-one and berated by Kazarian with everything being taken down in notes. Later, the six executives agreed to contact Sunbeam-Oster's board of directors and provided "dozens" of examples in writing of Kazarian's behavior. Later, thirty other top executives joined the first six, and the three dozen informed the board that all of them would resign if Kazarian was not ousted. Within weeks, the board concluded that the hostility was serious enough to make Kazarian no longer able to effectively lead the company. The board voted Kazarian out as CEO.

Kazarian and a group of investors spent $205 million to buy out Sunbeam-Oster's creditors and recapitalize the company. Within three years, the investment had recouped $160 million and owned sixty-eight million shares of stock with a market value of $1.1 million. While Sunbeam-Oster had been a hodgepodge of businesses, as CEO Kazarian sold off the losers and restructured the remaining appliance division. In three years, Kazarian turned a $40 million loss into a $47 million profit with a cumulative profit of $190 million.

Stockholder reaction to Kazarian's dismissal was muted, because Kazarian left Sunbeam-Oster in excellent shape. Kazarian defended his actions as necessary. "You don't change a company in bankruptcy without making a few waves," he stated. "I wasn't there to be a polite manager. I was there to create value for the shareholders. Did you know that twenty of the thirty-fix managers who complained about my behavior are millionaires because of stock options?"

Source: Adapted from Geoffrey Smith, "How to Lose Friends and Influence No One," *Business Week,* January 25, 1993, pp. 42-43; Ron Suskind and Suzanne Alexander, "Fired Sunbeam Chief Harangued and Hazed Employees, They Say," *The Wall Street Journal,* January 14, 1993, Al, A8.

- Having open channels of communication.
- Allowing contact with outside sources.
- Assigning nonspecialists to teams.
- Allowing eccentricity.
- Having a decentralized organization with loosely defined positions, and loose control.
- Allowing mistakes to be made.
- Providing employees the freedom to choose and pursue problems.
- Allocating resources to creative personnel and projects without an immediate payoff.

- Rewarding and encouraging creative ideas.
- Absolving employees of peripheral responsibilities.

The characteristics of creative organizations correspond to those of individuals as illustrated in Fig. 18-11.

How To Diagnose and Predict Organizational Change

Management consultant Larry Greiner has developed a model of organizational growth and change as depicted in Fig. 18-12.

By studying typical patterns of organizational change as indicated in Figure 18-12, managers can diagnose and predict the need for organizational change. Following is a discussion of Greiner's five stages of growth with an explanation of the crisis that occurs within each stage.[33]

PHASE 1: CREATIVITY At the birth of an organization, the emphasis is on creating a product or service and surviving in the marketplace. The organization is informal and nonbureaucratic. Founders are entrepreneurial and spend their time on production and marketing. Microsoft was in the creativity stage when their original software programs were written and marketed. A *crisis of leadership* occurs when the organization starts to grow and the creative, technically oriented owners have to deal with management issues. However, the owners may prefer, instead, to continue to be involved with making or selling the product. A strong manager is needed who can introduce management techniques, or the organization may flounder. When Apple Computer began to grow rapidly, neither Steven Jobs nor Stephen Wozniak, the original owners, were interested or qualified in implementing needed management techniques. Instead, A. C. Markkula was hired as a general manager.

PHASE 2: DIRECTION After a strong leader is acquired, clear goals and direction are established and a functional organizational design pattern is introduced.

FIGURE 18-11

Characteristics of Creative People and Organizations

Source: Richard L. Daft, *Management,* 2nd ed., Chicago, Dryden Press, 1991, p. 310. Copyright © 1991 by The Dryden Press, reproduced by permission of the publisher.

The Creative Individual	The Creative Organization or Department
1. Conceptual fluency Openmindedness	1. Open channels of communication Contact with outside sources Overlapping territories Suggestion systems, brainstorming, nominal group techniques
2. Originality	2. Assigns nonspecialists to problems Allows eccentricity Uses teams
3. Less authoritarian Independent	3. Decentralized; loosely defined positions; loose control Mistakes okay Risk-taking norms
4. Playfulness Undisciplined exploration Curiosity	4. Allows freedom to choose and pursue problems Not run as a tight ship; playful culture Freedom to discuss ideas; long time horizon
5. Persistent Committed Highly focused	5. Resources allocated to creative personnel and projects without immediate payoff Reward system encourages innovation Absolved of peripheral responsibilities

GROWTH PHASES

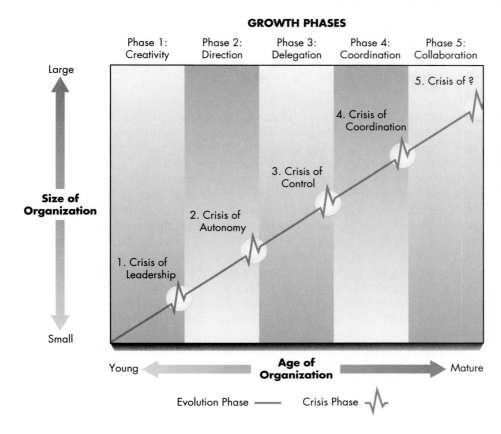

FIGURE 18-12

Greiner's Model of Organizational Growth and Change

Source: Adapted from L. E. Greiner, "Evolution and Revolution as Organizations Grow," *Harvard Business Review* 50, July-August 1972, pp. 55-64. Reprinted by permission of *Harvard Business Review*. Copyright © 1972 by the President and Fellows of Harvard College; all rights reserved.

Budgets and work standards are introduced and formal, impersonal communication begins. A *crisis of autonomy* develops because lower-level employees are restricted by the strong, top-down leadership. The crisis of autonomy develops, because top managers who are successful from their strong leadership want to give up responsibility. Mechanisms need to be found to coordinate and control departments without direct supervision from top management.

PHASE 3: DELEGATION   The organization becomes decentralized. Profit centers are created in which managers are given the leeway to act and are held accountable for results. Communication from the top becomes less frequent. A *crisis of control* develops, because top managers believe that they have lost control of the organization.

PHASE 4: COORDINATION   Top managers, in an attempt to seize control, emphasize coordination. Staff personnel, wielding greater power, are added. Formal organizationwide planning is introduced. Product groups or other decentralized units are formed to improve coordination. Incentive systems based on profits may be implemented to ensure that managers work toward what is best for the company. A *crisis of coordination* occurs when the proliferation of systems and programs begins to strangle middle managers. The organization seems bureaucratized with too much red tape. Innovation may be restricted.

PHASE 5: COLLABORATION   New people are oriented, and flexible systems are introduced. Formal systems are simplified, headquarters staff is reduced, and teams are used to solve problems. Risk taking and innovation are encouraged.

Greiner's model suggests that the need for change is constant—the solution to one set of problems creates another set of problems.

Organizational Downsizing

Organizational downsizing (OD) A phrase for a variety of approaches that organizations use to reduce the number of people they employ—usually due to the need to contain or reduce costs.

Downsizing is a catchall phrase for a variety of approaches that organizations use to reduce the number of people they employ. Downsizing has occurred on a massive scale in U.S. organizations. For example, 3.4 million jobs were eliminated from Fortune 500 companies during the 1980s and another 1.5 million were eliminated during the first three years of the 1990s.[34]

Organizations downsize by (1) making changes in their structure such as shutting down some operations, combining operating units, or selling off business units; (2) keeping the original structure intact but eliminating individual positions through layoffs, reductions in management staffs, and early retirement programs; or (3) changing employment practices including the institution of a hiring freeze or shifting employees to part-time work schedules.[35]

Studies indicate that the "single most important reason" for downsizing is the need to contain or reduce costs.[36] Thus it appears that the trend in downsizing has been motivated more by financial considerations rather than by strategic considerations and that the motives for downsizing are reactive rather than proactive.

Certainly, there is waste to be eliminated from many organizations and it is important for firms to "rightsize" or "rebalance" their work force in line with new technologies and the job mix. However, studies rarely describe downsizing as productive or regenerative.[37] On the contrary, downsizing is usually described as painful, wrenching, and bloody. Despite the pain experienced by organizations and their people, many downsizings fail to achieve desired results.[38] For example, one study of senior managers surveyed in 275 major corporations reported that cost-cutting programs and downsizing approaches had not achieved their objectives.[39] In another study involving 1,005 corporations, most responding senior managers reported their downsizing efforts had "missed the mark" because people had been cut without reducing workloads.[40]

More often than not, one round of downsizing merely leads to another. Two-thirds of corporations that thin their ranks one year follow up with another purge. the next year. This continuing downsizing is a form of corporate anorexia—firms can get thin, but it is no way to get healthy.[41]

The consequences of downsizing tend to be undesirable for most organizations. First, downsizing tends to have a negative impact on the morale of the remaining employees, because they have to find ways to do the work performed by former employees.[42] Remaining employees also indicate increased stress as discussed in Chap. 5. A second unfavorable consequence of downsizing is the human toll that is extracted. Laid-off employees experience a depression about future prospects as their unemployment continues. Anxiety and despair grow, while self-confidence wanes. Evidence indicates that family conflict, substance abuse, and suicide rates for laid-off workers is thirty times the national average.[43] Research also indicates that workers who have lost their jobs are more apt to be afflicted by high blood pressure, high cholesterol counts, high incidence of ulcers, and increased number of respiratory diseases.[44]

A third consequence of downsizing is the financial impact on the communities of laid-off employees. Downsizing has a double-barreled impact on communities in which jobs are lost: Unemployment first reduces tax revenues and then increases the need for additional public expenditures. A downsizing or plant closing is devastating in communities that rely on one industry or a primary employer.[45] The potential for community suffering received national attention in 1992 when General Motors considered the closing of an automobile assembly plant in either Ypsilanti, Michigan or Arlington, Texas.[46]

The real impact of how corporations manage downsizing will be measured as the United States returns to a period of growth, and another set of demands are placed on organizations. Which companies will have a dedicated, loyal, and well-trained work force? Which companies will have efficient structures and efficient approaches to getting tasks accomplished? Which will have learned from past downsizings to anticipate and respond to continuing needs to restructure and resize the business?[47] Those organizations that innovate in the management of organizational behavior will be better positioned for the changes ahead. The "OB in Practice" on page 630 describes a dangerous situation that may occur when a firm downsizes.

Business Reengineering

Most companies today—no matter what business they are in, how technologically sophisticated their product or service, or what their national origin—can trace their work styles and organizational roots back to the prototypical pin factory that economist Adam Smith described in *The Wealth of Nations,* published in 1776. Smith's principle of the division of labor embodied his observation that some number of specialized workers, each performing a single step in the manufacture of a pin, could make far more pins in a day than the same number of generalists, each engaged in making whole pins.[48]

Today's airlines, steel mills, accounting firms, and computer chip makers have all been built around Smith's central idea—the division or specialization of labor and the consequent fragmentation of work. The larger the organization, the more specialized is the work, and the more separate steps into which the work is fragmented. This rule applies not only to manufacturing jobs; insurance companies, for instance, typically assign separate clerks to process each line of a standardized form. They then pass the form to another clerk, who processes the next line. These workers never complete a job; they just perform piecemeal tasks.

The reality that organizations have to confront is that the old ways of doing business simply don't work anymore. In today's environment, nothing is constant or predictable—not market growth, customer demand, product life cycles, the rate of technological change, or the nature of competition. The overall process of producing or delivering a good or service inevitably has become increasingly complicated, and managing such processes has become more difficult. Business reengineering is the radical redesign of business processes to achieve major gains in cost, service, or time. The process of reengineering begins by asking "if we could start from scratch, how would we do this?" After receiving responses, the result is "then do it that way and throw away everything else."[49] In essence, the chief tool of reengineering is a clean sheet of paper. Most change efforts start with what exists and fix it up. Reengineering, according to its adherents, is not downsizing nor is it a program for bottom-up continuous improvement. Instead, reengineers start from the future and work backward, as if unconstrained by existing methods, people or departments.[50] The "OB in Practice" on page 631 provides a description of how IBM and Ford have utilized reengineering.

Michael Hammer, a former professor at MIT who now owns a consulting business, is the chief prophet of reengineering. Through speeches and writings,

Business reengineering
The radical redesign of business processes to achieve major gains in cost, service, or time.

The Effects of Downsizing: Becoming 'Lean and Mean' or 'Anorexic'?

Diet metaphors abound in corporate America. Businesses that have downsized are supposed to have trimmed the fat and become lean. However management consultant Craig Schneier argues that many firms who have "lost weight," so to speak, may be experiencing corporate anorexia. A shrinking company becomes anorexic when it gets so hooked on controlling expenses, closing plants, and eliminating jobs that it neglects the fact that a company should seek to grow, not fade away. James Stanford, president of Petro-Canada states that firms "can't shrink to greatness." Thomas Davenport, a management professor at the University of Texas who has studied the effects of downsizing on a number of firms, states that after nearly a decade of frantic cost-cutting, the effects of downsizing is beginning to take a toll on many companies. Some of these effects are: decimated sales staffs turn in lousy numbers, overburdened survivors go through the motions of working, new-product ideas languish, risk-taking dwindles because the culture of cost-cutting emphasizes the certainties of cutting cost over the uncertainties and expense of trying something new. On a more subtle level, excessive cost cutting tends to strengthen the authority of financial and accounting departments which see it as their mandate to control expenses rather than monitor opportunities and investments.

Francis Gouillart, senior vice president of Gemini Consulting, states that downsizing "is like a heat-seeking missile, it goes where the biggest costs are." Sales departments and customer-service departments are often fat targets for downsizing indicates Gouillart. When these two departments are whittled down a death spiral results because there is less time to sell products and less time to service existing customers. Gouillart suggests that the United States economy may ultimately be at risk and notes that during the past decade big United States firms have grown through acquisitions. The internal annual growth over the past decade has ranged from zero to two percent for large firms in the United States.

However, a new wave of change may be hitting big corporations. Dwight Gertz of Mercer Consulting states that the "biggest driver of shareholder value is profitable growth." Many executives, according to Gertz, have concluded that slashing costs can take a company only so far and that growth may be the paramount goal.

Source: Adapted from Francis Gouillart and James Kelly, *Transforming the Organization*, New York, McGraw Hill, 1995; Bernard Wysocki, " 'Lean and Frail,' Some Companies Cut Costs Too Far, Suffer 'Corporate Anorexia,' " *The Wall Street Journal*, July 5, 1995, p. A1.

Hammer does not perform reengineering projects himself but, instead, prepares the way for consultants and companies that do. A book, *Reengineering the Corporation,* written with management consultant James Champy, spent eight weeks on the *New York Times* bestseller list. Most major consulting firms such as Ernst & Young, McKinsey, Boston Consulting Group, Gemini Consulting, Andersen Consulting, Digital Equipment, and Symmetrix have added reengineering to their repertoire. Firms such as Union Carbide, GTE, AT&T, Ford, Eastman Kodak, Hallmark, Taco Bell, Mutual Benefit Life, and Bell Atlantic that have implemented reengineering programs have reported extraordinary gains in speed, productivity, and profitability. However, one study indicates that between 50 percent and 70 percent of reengineering efforts fail to achieve the goals set for them.[51]

OB in Practice

Reengineering at IBM and Ford Motor Company

Although IBM experienced a net loss in 1992 as described in the beginning of this chapter, IBM's Credit Operations is extremely profitable. Before reengineering, IBM's Credit Operations functioned as follows. When an IBM salesperson called in with a request for financing, he or she reached one of 14 people sitting around a conference table in Old Greenwich, Connecticut. The person taking the call logged the request for a deal on a piece of paper. That was the first of five steps—involving credit checkers, pricers who determined what interest rate to charge, and others—that bounced the request from department to department and took anywhere from six days to two weeks. From the sales rep's point of view this turnaround was too long, since it gave the customer six days to find another source of financing, be seduced by another computer vendor, or simply call the whole deal off. So the rep would call—and call and call—to ask, "Where is my deal, and when are you going to get it out?" Naturally, no one had a clue, since the request was lost somewhere in the chain.

One day two senior managers at IBM Credit had a brainstorm. They took a financing request and walked it themselves through all five steps, asking personnel in each office to put aside whatever they were doing and to process this request as they normally would, only without the delay of having it sit in a pile on someone's desk. They learned from their experiments that performing the actual work took in total only *90 minutes.* The remaining six or more days were consumed by handing the form off from one department to the next.

In the end, IBM Credit replaced its specialists—the credit checkers, pricers, and so on—with generalists. Now instead of sending an application from office to office, one person, called a deal structurer, processes the entire application from beginning to end. No handoffs.

How could one generalist replace four specialists? The old process design was, in fact, founded on a deeply held (but deeply hidden) assumption: that every bid request was unique and difficult to process, thereby requiring the intervention of four highly trained specialists. In fact, this assumption was false; most requests were simple and straightforward. The old process had been overdesigned to handle the most difficult applications management could imagine. When IBM Credit's senior managers closely examined the work the specialists did, they found that most of it was little more than clerical: finding a credit rating in a database, plugging numbers into a standard model, pulling boilerplate clauses from a file. These tasks fall well within the capability of a single individual when he or she is supported by an easy-to-use computer system that provides access to all the data and tools specialists would use. In really tough situations, the new deal structurer can get help from a small pool of real specialists—experts in credit checking, pricing, and so forth.

The performance improvement achieved by the redesign is extraordinary. IBM Credit slashed its six-*day* turnaround to four *hours.* It did so without an increase in head count—in fact, it has achieved a small work force reduction. At the same time, the number of deals that it handles has increased 100-fold. Not 100 percent, but *100 times.*

Ford Motor Company, like many other U.S. firms, was searching for ways to cut overhead and administrative costs. One of the places where Ford believed it could reduce costs was in its accounts payable department, the organization that paid the bills submitted by Ford's suppliers. At that time, Ford's North American accounts payable department employed 500 people. By using computers to automate some processes, Ford thought it could cut head count by 20 percent. Pretty good, thought Ford's executives—until they visited Mazda.

The Ford managers noted that the admittedly smaller company took care of its accounts payable chores with only *five* people. The contrast—Ford's 500 people to

Mazda's five—was too great to attribute just to the smaller company's size, esprit de corps, company songs, or morning calisthenics.

To match Mazda's efficiency, Ford realized that it would have to rethink the entire process in which the accounts payable department took part. The decision marked a critical shift in perspective for Ford because companies can reengineer only business processes, not the administrative organizations that have evolved to accomplish them. "Accounts payable" cannot be reengineered, because it is not a process. It is a department, an organizational artifact of a particular process design. But what the people in accounts payable *do* can be reengineered.

Source: Adapted from "The Promise of Reengineering," *Fortune*, May 3, 1993, pp. 94-97.

Michael Hammer states that reengineering is a major change that can yield big results, while requiring significant investments in training and information technology. According to Hammer, layoffs result and to succeed at reengineering a CEO needs to be "a visionary, a motivator, and a leg breaker."[52] However, reengineering is developing into an intriguing paradox. For example, many theorists are touting reengineering as the latest salvation for competitive advantage, while recent benchmarking data indicates 70 percent of reengineering efforts fail to produce their desired results.[53] The "OB in Practice" on page 635 describes how reengineering failed at Greyhound Lines, Inc.

Not only should reengineering be great for the performance of individual companies but virtually all economists agree that reengineering ultimately should bring about faster economic growth, greater international competitiveness, higher real wages, and improved living standards. But there is bad news associated with reengineering. For example, the University of Wisconsin's Business Competitiveness Center estimates that reengineering initiatives will wipe out 25 million jobs.[54] An important problem involves the dislocation of all those people whose current jobs win disappear. Absorbing displaced workers can be a serious problem in the short term and a very real tragedy for many families.

As stated earlier, with 70 percent of reengineering efforts failing, implementation is an important aspect. Figure 18-13 describes a variety of implementation problems that have occurred from a number of reengineering efforts.[55]

However, the problems depicted in Fig. 18-13 are really symptoms. A major contributing factor to the high failure rate of reengineering initiatives is that reengineers do not understand how each of the three layers (and the nine dimensions) portrayed in Fig. 18-14 are interrelated. For example, many reengineering efforts are focused only on the first layer with a neglect of the other two (Fig. 18-15 describes the three layers presented in Fig. 18-14). Such a focus is doomed for failure. Taking into account the dimensions of rewards/sanctions, measurement systems, management practices and techniques, individual beliefs, political power, and organizational culture separates those organizations who are serious about creating breakthrough change from those that are limited to changing a single function.

The best candidates for reengineering are organizations that face shifts in the nature of competition. For example, firms in financial services in which deregulated banks, brokerage houses, and insurance companies that compete for the same investment dollar are prime candidates. Firms in the telecommunication field such as local and long distance phone companies, cable television providers, and computer makers in which regulatory and technological entry

- Overrelying on technology as a solution
- Addressing the needs of a functional unit instead of seeking radical or breakthrough change in a business process
- Investing in technology that results in small, incremental improvements
- Concentrating on streamlining internal business processes and excluding a renewed strategic vision
- Limiting reengineering to a single function and excluding critical activities external to the area
- Changing processes but not employee behavior
- Radical structural change requires commitment, empowerment, ownership, and reculturalization
- Reengineering process gets bogged down and participants lose interest
- A knee jerk tendency for securities analysts and investors to applaud anything resembling "reengineering" causing top management to use technologies without questioning its feasibility or whether it is needed
- Poor communication
- Inadequate training
- Lack of commitment from top management
- Lack of understanding of the process to be reengineering
- Turf battles
- Powerful culture that resists change

Source: Daniel F. Jennings, "Reengineering the Credit Function: Shooting in the Dark?" *Journal of Finance and Credit Management* 1, 1995, pp. 18-26.

FIGURE 18-13

Implementation Problems Occurring from Reengineering Efforts

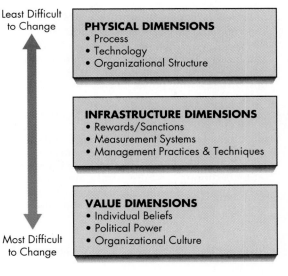

FIGURE 18-14

Dimensions of Reengineering

Source: Adapted from Dorine C. Andrews and Susan K. Stalick, *Business Reengineering: The Survival Guide,* PTR Prentice Hall, Englewood Cliffs, NJ, 1994; Gerald Burke and Joe Peppard, "Business Process Design: New Directions," *Business Change and Reengineering,* vol. 2, no. 1, 1994, pp. 36-50; Richard J. Schonberger, "Human Resource Management: Lessons from a Decade of TQM and Reengineering," *California Management Review,* vol. 36, no. 4, 1994, pp. 109-123; W. E. Deming, *Out of Crisis,* MIT Center for Advanced Engineering, Cambridge, MA, 1986.

barriers have fallen precipitously are also prime candidates for reengineering.[56] The "Profile" on page 636 describes a reengineering effort at an insurance company, Aetna Life and Casualty.

THE NATURE OF ORGANIZATIONAL DEVELOPMENT

Organizational Development (OD) is a special form of planned organizational change in which behavioral science knowledge is applied to help individuals and groups

Organization development (OD) is a special form of planned organizational change in which behavioral science knowledge is applied to help individuals and groups within organizations to work more efficiently together.

FIGURE 18-15

A Description of the Nine Dimensions of Reengineering

Layer One—Physical Dimensions

Process defines what, when, and how work is performed. Processes produce the products and services of the business. Processes are grouped into work flows; information flows, and time flows to indicate their interdependencies. Some processes are developed by design, while others emerge informally to meet real or perceived organizational needs.

Technology is the information, networking, automated communication, and computer systems used to support the process. Included are data, applications, platforms, which facilitate communication with just about anyone in any location at any time.

Organization structure is the framework in which the organization defines how tasks are divided, resources are deployed, and how activities are coordinated. Another aspect of organizational structure pertains to the hierarchical level at which decisions are made. Centralization means that decision authority is located near the top of the organization. With decentralization, decision authority is pushed downward to lower organizational levels.

Layer Two—Infrastructure Dimensions

Rewards/Sanctions are used to control behavior. Rewards may be formal or informal, financial or based on recognition. Rewards/sanctions can be important reinforcers of new behaviors required in reengineering initiatives.

Management Systems are the control and feedback systems that provide information on process performance.

Management Practices & Techniques are the activities used by management to supervise, develop, and support people who perform the business processes.

Layer Three—Value Dimensions

Individual Beliefs are the attitudes, perceptions, and mental models that individuals apply to themselves, those with whom they work, and the work itself

Political Power originates from formal authority or personal aspects. The former is acquired through the position held in the organization, while the latter through expertise, knowledge, or connections. If reengineering the physical dimensions of Layer One upsets the existing power balance, then resistance will be fierce. With the threat of a loss of power, responses may be either confrontational or subversive.

Organizational Culture is the set of key values, beliefs, understandings and norms that members of an organization share. The fundamental underlying values that characterize an organization's culture can be understood through the visible manifestations of symbols, stories, heroes, slogans, and ceremonies. A cultural change pertains to the organization as a whole, such as when Union Pacific Railroad changed its basic mindset by becoming less bureaucratic and focusing employees on customer service and quality through teamwork and employee participation. Training is the most frequently used tool for changing an organization's mindset.

within organizations to work more effectively together. A central figure in most types of OD activities is the change agent who provides the technical or professional leadership necessary to improve the functioning of the organization. Typically, this change agent is referred to as an OD expert or OD consultant and must inspire confidence in his or her ability to diagnose organizational problems as well as have a knowledge of behavioral science methodology.

The Ethics of OD

In the course of an OD program, certain ethical dilemmas may arise. These dilemmas concern the actions of the OD practitioner and the voluntary participation of the participants.

ACTIONS OF THE **OD PRACTITIONER** The OD practitioner or consultant should not use a technique that the client does not want to use or one that the consultant

OB in Practice

How Reengineering Failed at Greyhound Lines, Inc.

After Greyhound Lines emerged from Chapter 11 bankruptcy in October 1991, Frank Schmieder, chief executive officer, and J. Michael Doyle, chief financial officer, hammered together a reorganization plan that called for massive cuts in employees, routes, and the bus fleet. All this cutting, combined with an announced plan to computerize everything from passenger reservations to fleet scheduling, won so much approval on Wall Street that Greyhound's newly issued stock increased from $4 a share to $13.50 within a month after the company emerged from Chapter 11. But the cutbacks quickly hurt customer service, and ridership began to slip in 1992. However, Schmieder's and Doyle's cost cutting efforts led to a 1992 year-end profit of $11 million on revenues of $682 million, Greyhound's first profitable year since 1989—and analysts remained bullish on Greyhound stock.

During 1992, Greyhound paid $2.3 million in consulting fees to improve investor relations, executive searches, and a program to improve communications among junior managers. Also, during 1992, Schmieder moved Greyhound's headquarters from a spartan high-rise near its bus terminal into a sleek, new building near an attractive mall at a cost of $1.6 million. Schmieder's salary was increased 57 percent to $526,000 and Doyle's nearly 65 percent to $264,000. Meanwhile in the field, old-line regional executives were terminated, and bus terminals were staffed with customer-service associates who were paid $6 an hour whether they swept the floor or sold tickets, with little chance for a raise.

In early 1993, Greyhound promoted a $90 million stock offering largely on the promise of a computer reservation system called "Trips" that would be launched nationwide in time for the 1993 summer travel season. The original software for Trips was developed by an outside company, and the system began operating in April 1993. As ridership increased during the summer season, Trips crashed and became a flop. Publicly, Greyhound did not say a word, and in an era when most investors, analysts, and journalists travel by plane, only Greyhound's blue-collar passengers were aware of the mass confusion that reigned in Greyhound terminals. In late 1993, before announcing to analysts that ridership had declined 12 percent, Schmieder and Doyle exercised their stock options and sold a lot of Greyhound stock. The two men made hundreds of thousands of dollars profit.

By mid-1994, Greyhound's revenues had declined 13 percent with a net loss of $61.4 million. Schmieder and Doyle resigned and were later indicted in federal court for providing inaccurate and misleading information regarding Trips.

As a new Greyhound chief executive officer tries to make Trips operational and works with its lenders amid missed debt payments, bus and reservation scheduling problems, and disgruntled employees, one bondholder grumbled that Schmieder and Doyle had "reengineered Greyhound into Hell."

Source: Adapted from Robert Tomsho, "How Greyhound Lines Reengineered Itself Right into a Deep Hole," *The Wall Street Journal*, October 20, 1994, pp. A1, A4.

---

is not skilled in using. OD practitioners should not attempt to create programs that create a dependency on the consultant rather than developing a program in which the client organization can achieve its own continuous improvement. OD practitioners should not conduct activities in situations in which the participants do not have full knowledge about what is occurring. Also, the OD practitioner should not use data in such a way as to manipulate the client's system to the consultant's advantage or to the advantage of one individual or group within the system.[57]

Profile

Ronald Compton
Chairman of the Board
REENGINEERING AT AETNA LIFE AND CASUALTY

In the 1980s Aetna was guilty of plugging in more and more number-crunching individuals and trading up to every new gizmo out of Silicon Valley. However, problems existed in issuing insurance policies. In 1993, Aetna had twenty-two business centers, with a staff of 3,000. It took about fifteen days to get a basic policy out of the office, in part because sixty different employees had to handle the application. Now, the operation has been pared down to 700 employees in four centers—and customers get their policies within five days. How did Aetna accomplish this? By having a single representative using a personal computer tied into a network. Now, this one individual can perform all of the necessary steps to immediately process an application such as calling into an actuarial database, for example. When all of the information is gathered, the policy is passed along the network to headquarters in Hartford, where it is printed and mailed within a day.

This technology has also given Aetna's sales force more autonomy. The old hierarchy of supervisors and agents has been replaced by work teams of about seventeen people.

The new system for issuing policies will save Aetna $40 million and improve productivity by 25 percent. Reengineering helped us solve that modern business dilemma —how to do more with less, and do it better.

Source: Adapted from John Carey, "The Technology Payoff," *Business Week,* June 14,1993, pp. 56-68.

VOLUNTARY PARTICIPATION Participants are usually asked to reveal their personal frustrations; Why they may have difficulty with one another or with their supervisor. Do employees have the right to refuse to answer such questions? Do employees have the right to refuse to participate in an OD program? In essence, employees are under pressure to participate or to be labeled as "uncooperative." Management professor Stephen Robbins states that at the extreme, management could avoid all OD activities associated with the loss of employee rights, but then planned change would never occur. The challenge for management is to properly balance employee rights against improvements in the effectiveness of the organization.[58]

Problems Involved in Initiating OD

The problems involved in initiating an OD program are resistance to change. Both individual and organizational sources of resistance to change are described in an earlier section of this chapter.

OD INTERVENTIONS

The activities that are initiated to facilitate a planned OD change are called OD interventions and are undertaken to improve the effectiveness of individuals and groups within organizations. Usually, more than one intervention is used as the OD program increases in size with the identification of problems to be resolved. OD interventions involve the application of basic concepts from the field of organizational behavior and can be categorized as people, task-technology, structure, and culture approaches.

People Approach

OD activities involving the people approach consist of five interventions: team building, survey feedback, sensitivity training, quality of work life, and process consultation.[59]

TEAM BUILDING   This approach attempts to get members of a work group to diagnose how they work together, and to plan how this "working together" can be improved. Team building begins when members of a group admit that they have a problem and gather data to provide insight into it. The identified problems may come from attitude surveys, sensitivity training sessions, or production reports. The gathered data are then shared with the group members to develop a list of desired change goals together with plans for implementing these changes.

If the problems are solved, the process is completed and the team may stop meeting. If not, the process as described in Fig. 18-16 should be restarted. A change agent usually is needed at first but becomes increasingly less necessary as the group develops into a team. Some companies send their executives on team building exercises that involve such activities as a white-water rafting trip in swirling mountain rivers, mountain climbing expeditions, and dog sled trips.[60] The rationale for putting people in physically challenging conditions is that learning to overcome these obstacles will teach team members how to work together cooperatively. However, the value of the exercises is realized only when the principles of team work learned during the training are applied back on the job.[61]

SURVEY FEEDBACK   This technique involves three steps that are illustrated in Fig. 18-17. In the first step, a survey provides management with information from participants regarding their attitudes on such topics as job satisfaction, leadership styles, communication effectiveness, or the organization's culture. The second step involves analyzing and aggregating the data by group or department to ensure anonymity for individual respondents. Also, in this second step, a summary of the results are prepared and shared with employees during a group feedback meeting. In the third and final step, the group examines its process for making decisions, communicating, and accomplishing work, usually with the assistance of an OD consultant. Such discussions become more effective when they are carefully documented; specific implementation plans are made; and someone is placed in charge of the implementation.[62] In some situations managers fail to hold feedback and action planning meetings. When any of the three steps of the survey-feedback technique are omitted or compromised, it becomes less useful.

The survey-feedback technique is a widely used organizational development intervention. This technique is efficient because it allows a considerable amount of information to be gathered quickly, is flexible, and can be tailored to a variety of organizational problems.[63] However, the survey-feedback technique is no better than the quality of the survey questionnaire. Things that really matter to employees must be measured.

SENSITIVITY TRAINING   A method developed in the 1940s and sometimes called T-groups or encounter groups, sensitivity training is a technique in which people (usually eight to twelve) are brought together for a series of two to three hour sessions. An expert trainer, referred to as the facilitator, guides the group at all times. However, the facilitator does not take an active role in the group's discussion but serves as a guide. The objective of the sessions is to have open, honest communication in which personal insights may be gained. To achieve this

FIGURE 18-16
The Team Building
Process

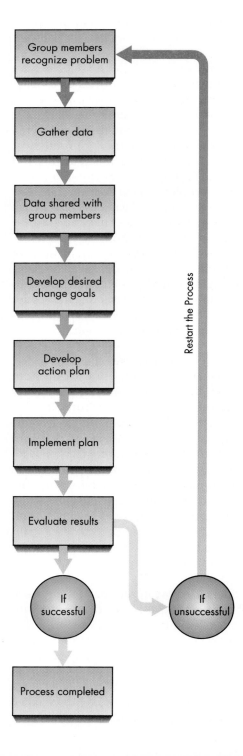

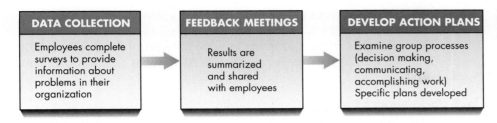

FIGURE 18-17
Survey-feedback Process

objective, members are expected to focus on behavior and on giving feedback about their perceptions of one another. Getting to the point in which social learning occurs is sometimes difficult, and the reactions of group members may get out of hand. For example, the group may severely criticize one particular member by turning on him or her without reaching a positive reconciliation at the end of the session. Some members may become uncomfortable, because the group does not have an agenda. At times, one member may attempt to become the group leader to fill the leadership vacuum created by the facilitator's refusal to control discussion or behavior. Also, some groups may have a difficult time in engaging in open and frank discussions, especially if the people work together. Freer discussions usually occur in groups in which the members do not know one another.[64]

The effectiveness of sensitivity training is difficult to assess. People will not always be able to transfer the interpersonal skills they have learned in sensitivity sessions when they leave the artificial training atmosphere and return to their jobs.[65]

QUALITY OF WORK LIFE (QWL)   Some organizations are interested in providing a work environment conducive to the satisfaction of individual needs. Also, some top managers believe that improving life at work is a means to improve productivity. As a result, organizations have QWL programs that focus on such issues as conflict resolution and reduction, employee satisfaction, and employee participation. QWL is not a set of specific techniques but encompasses job redesign (job enlargement and job enrichment), employment involvement in decision making, and the redesign of pay systems.[66] QWL may also involve the creation of quality circles that are discussed in Chap. 19.

Although QWL programs can be useful, several potential pitfalls must be avoided. First, both management and labor must cooperate in designing the program. Neither side should view the program as an opportunity to gain an advantage over the other. Second, the agreed to action plans must be fully implemented. All parties have the responsibility to follow through on their part of the plan.[67]

PROCESS CONSULTATION   In this intervention, an OD consultant works with a manager to help him or her understand the human processes such as leadership, communication, cooperation, and conflict that occur within an organizational setting and then how to manage them. The consultant does not solve the manager's problem but acts, instead, as a coach to help diagnose what improvement is needed. For example, top management was concerned because the subordinates of a bright, high-achieving, results-oriented vice president of manufacturing were complaining of her lack of sensitivity to the extent that the manufacturing vice president's effectiveness was being undermined. A process consultant learned that the manufacturing vice president had feelings of frustration when certain objectives were not met that caused her to act negatively and harshly to individuals who were not responsible for the objectives. The consultant assisted in developing a program to solve the frustration problems making the manufacturing vice president more effective in her dealings with subordinates.[68]

Task–Technology Approach

The task–technology intervention approach relies on changing the actual jobs of people and the technology used to perform these jobs. A change in the tasks that people perform is almost always accompanied by a change in technology— a modification in the way in which tasks are performed. The OD professional uses job redesign techniques that include job rotation, enlargement, enrichment, work teams, and coordinating mechanisms. Technology interventions emphasize improving equipment, facilities, methods, and work flows.

Structural Approach

OD interventions involving a structural approach concentrate on making an organization more organic as illustrated in Chap. 16. The structural intervention approach also includes examining the best "fit" between the organization's structure, technology, and environment as also suggested in Chap. 16.

A popular structural intervention used by OD consultants is to decentralize decision making. As indicated in Chap. 5, by pushing authority downward, power is equalized. Decentralization also provides lower-level employees with greater control over their work.

The Culture Approach

Proposed organizational changes may make it necessary for a firm's employees to adopt a culture of norms and values that favor flexibility, creativity, and innovation. Culture OD interventions are useful when broad-based cultural change is the goal. The notion of organizational culture is discussed in Chap. 17.

OD interventions differ from one another in the types of organizational behavior that is to be changed, and the depth of change they are intended to stimulate. All OD efforts should conclude with an evaluation of the program's effectiveness, regardless of which OD intervention was used.[69]

CONCLUSIONS AND APPLICATIONS

- External forces, the components of an organization's general environment, as well as internal forces, internal activities, and decisions create pressures for organizational change.
- A change agent is an individual who takes responsibility for overseeing the change process. Such an agent may be from outside the organization or, in some instances, be already employed by the organization.
- Four powerful forces for change include the labor force, technology, competition, and world politics.
- Eight reasons for individual resistance to change are: fear of the unknown, self-interest, habit, personality, conflicts, differing perceptions, general mistrust, and social disruptions.

- Seven major organizational sources of resistance to change are: structural inertia, bureaucratic inertia, group norms, a resistant organizational culture, threatened power, and threatened expertise, and threatened resource allocations.

- Resistance to change may indicate a legitimate concern that the change is not good for the organization, and that the proposed change should be reexamined. Resistance to change can be managed through communicating and educating employees more effectively and involving them in the change process.

- Planned organizational change involves the steps involved in preparing an organization for change. Lewin described organizational change in terms of unfreezing, change, and refreezing. In the planned change model, which is an expression of Lewin's approach, top management has recognized the need for change, initiates a problem-solving process to design the change, and then implements and evaluates the change. While the planned change model generally uses standard techniques that have been used before, the action research model allows original, innovative procedures to be developed and assessed. Other techniques for initiating change include designing the organization for creativity, encouraging idea champions, and establishing corporate innovation and new venture teams.

- Organizational development (OD) is a special form of planned organizational change in which behavioral science knowledge is applied to help individuals and groups within organizations to work more effectively together. Ethical aspects of OD require that the OD facilitator works with his or her client in such a way that the facilitator does not act beyond the boundaries of his or her expertise, allows informed choices on the part of all participants, and avoids creating unnecessary dependencies. In an OD program, management should properly balance employee rights against improvements in the effectiveness of the organization.

- OD interventions are undertaken to improve the effectiveness of individuals and groups within organizations. Usually, more than one intervention is used as the OD program increases in size with the identification of problems to be resolved. OD intervention approaches can be categorized as people, task-technology, structure, and culture approaches. All OD interventions involve the application of basic concepts from the field of organization behavior.

- T. M. Amabile suggests that the creative process involves five stages: task presentation, preparation, idea generation, idea validation, and outcome assessment. However, D. T. Campbell argues that creativity is not a mysterious process performed by a gifted or brilliant mind but is largely the product of sweaty trial and error with individuals having to work long and hard to generate multiple solutions to different problems.

- Organizations change over time, evolving through the four phases of creativity: direction, delegation, coordination, and collaboration. Each phase results in a crisis that must be resolved.

- Organizational downsizing is an approach that organizations use to reduce the number of people they employ.

- Business reengineering is the radical redesign of business processes to achieve major gains in cost, service, or time. However, 70 percent of all reengineering efforts are said to have failed.

REVIEW QUESTIONS

1. Describe the external and internal forces that create pressures for organizational change.
2. What is an external change agent? What is an internal change agent?
3. What are four areas in which change forces appear to be powerful?
4. Why do individuals resist change?
5. Why do organizations resist change?
6. Describe the three process models of organization change: Lewin's three-step model, the planned change model, and the action research model.
7. Explain the ethical considerations that consultants should be aware of when they facilitate OD efforts.

8. What is OD? Describe the approaches used in OD interventions.
9. Explain the five stages of Amabile's model of creative thinking.
10. Describe Campbell's concept of creativity.
11. Explain how organizations downsize.
12. Describe business reengineering.
13. What paradoxes are associated with reengineering?
14. Explain the reasons for failure of most reengineering efforts.

DISCUSSION QUESTIONS

1. How does organization development differ from organization change?
2. What are advantages and disadvantages of using an external change agent rather than an internal change agent?
3. Can positive change persist after the organization development program has ended?
4. Describe the internal and external forces for change that affect organizations. Which force do you think is the major cause of organizational change? Why?
5. How does the action research model of organization change differ from that of the planned change model?
6. Compare and contrast the team-building and survey-feedback techniques used in organizational development.
7. Why are some individuals creative and others not?
8. How can individual creativity affect organization change?

9. Can creativity be designed into an organization? Explain.
10. How is corporate innovation related to organizational change?
11. What skills are required for a consultant to initiate an organization development intervention?
12. Why is decentralizing decision making a popular OD intervention technique?
13. Have you ever worked for an organization that used a planned approach to change? Explain.
14. For an organization in which you have worked, can you identify a crisis described in Figure 18-12 that affected it? How was the crisis resolved?
15. Which has been the most successful—organizational downsizing or business reengineering? Explain.
16. What implementation issues are related to reengineering?
17. Compare and contrast reengineering with Lewin's Organizational Change Model.

CASE STUDY

PAPCO

Excerpt of a confidential memo from the vice president of Industrial Relations to the executive vice president:

Our converting division supervisors have to be motivated in some manner or be replaced. By refusing to participate in our management by objectives program, serious management control problems are developing.

A Troubling Acquisition

Serious problems were developing in an acquisition made by a Fortune 500 forest products firm. The firm had acquired a privately owned paper products company, Papco.*

Before the acquisition, corporate management of Papco utilized a business strategy where its two paper mills produced the maximum amount possible of commodity grades of paper and paperboard, and then had their converting plants sell these grades as commodity paper boxes and paper bags. The strategy of the converting plants was that of a volume producer. Marketing efforts were geared toward service and obtaining orders regardless of selling price. The emphasis in manufacturing was toward quality and meeting delivery dates. The four converting plants of Papco had operated at a loss for a number of years. Papco's top management believed that the primary mission of the converting group was to "move the product." The paper mill division of Papco transferred paper products to the converting group at a price established by the president of Papco. In some years, this transfer price was lower than market value but always above the variable cost of the paper mill (sometimes just barely). As long as the net contribution margin of paper products (transfer price of paper products from paper mill to converting plants less the cost of operating) was positive, profit objectives of Papco were considered to have been achieved.

Over time, the profitability of Papco had deteriorated to a point below the industry average. The converting division was viewed as a price-cutter and an ineffective competitor by other paper product firms. Eventually, Papco was acquired by a more aggressive and more profitable forest products company and became a division of the acquiring firm. As a division, Papco maintained its original name, but the existing top manager was replaced with an executive recruited from another paper company. Several executives from the acquiring firm were also transferred to the new Papco division to assume various responsibilities.

The new managers of the Papco Division developed a profit improvement program that called for a shift in business strategy and management philosophy. A key element in the revised business strategy was to transfer paper products from Papco's two paper mills located in the South to their four converting division plants at market prices, and to have specific profitability objectives for the four plants. One of the converting plants was located in the South, one in the Northeast, and two in the Midwest. Each plant was decentralized and had modem, state-of-the-art manufacturing equipment. All of the plant managers and their staff in the four converting plants had been employed by the original Papco Company and were retained by the new division managers. Total sales for the four plants were $250 million and total employment was 525 at acquisition.

The new management team developed a management by objectives program in an attempt to control costs at the four converting plants. The following three central points were developed to control these efforts toward cost.

1. *Responsibility.* Cost centers based on either a particular machine or workplace were assigned to the first line supervisors who were responsible for the work performed within cost centers. Each supervisor was held accountable for controlling the costs incurred in his or her own cost center. An accounting system was developed to collect, categorize, and present for analysis the actual expenses incurred; and standard allowances were applied to the tasks accomplished to determine a standard cost for each center.

   A cost center monthly report included: (a) actual expenses incurred in operating the cost center, (b) units produced, and (c) standard cost allowances.

2. *Objectives.* Actual expenses incurred in each cost center for a specific time period were reviewed by the supervisor responsible for the cost center. Cost

*The name of the acquired firm has been disguised.

objectives, developed by the supervisor and the plant manager, became the goal toward which the supervisor worked.

3. *Measured Progress.* Each month, the cost center report was compared against the cost center objective or goal. At monthly meetings, expenses were analyzed to determine the corrective action to be taken should expenses exceed the cost center goal.

Approximately one year after the installation of the preceding three central points of the management by objectives program, plant managers in the four converting plants reported that they were experiencing tremendous difficulty in maintaining the program. Supervisors were complaining that: (a) They had practiced the techniques of quality improvement and meeting delivery dates but were not skilled in cost reduction efforts; (b) the standard allowances were incorrect, and they did not understand the accounting system; (c) The accounting reports were not accurate and contained reporting errors; (d) The pressure of their existing duties prevented them from analyzing their cost center reports; (e) The base pay and annual raises were currently inadequate for the new expectations of expense control. Key supervisors had resigned to accept better paying positions with competitors. Others threatened to follow suit.

What had once been a division with supervisors of long years of service who prided themselves on quality and service was now a division with supervisors who were rejecting a key element of Papco's new strategy. In an internal confidential memorandum the corporate vice president of Industrial Relations advised the new division manager of Papco that either the converting division supervisors had to be motivated in some manner or be replaced. The industrial relations manager reported that by refusing to participate in the management by objectives program, serious management control problems were developing.

After reviewing the memo from the vice president of Industrial Relations, the executive vice president suggested that an OD program be initiated to resolve Papco's problems and that an external change agent be hired to facilitate the program.

CASE STUDY QUESTIONS

1. Is OD an effective approach to use in this situation? Explain.
2. If an OD program is to be initiated, what type of program would be best for Papco's situation?

EXPERIENTIAL EXERCISE 1

How Creative Are You?

After each statement, indicate with a letter the degree or extent with which you agree or disagree with it:

A = Strongly agree
B = Agree
C = In between or don't know
D = Disagree
E = Strongly disagree

Mark your answers as accurately and frankly as possible. Try not to second guess how a creative person might respond to each statement.

1. I always work with a great deal of certainty that I'm following the correct procedures forsolving a particular problem. _____

2. It would be a waste of time for me to ask questions if I had no hope of obtaining answers. _____

3. I feel that a logical step-by-step method is best for solving problems. _____

4. I occasionally voice opinions in groups that seem to turn some people off. _____

5. I spend a great deal of time thinking about what others think of me. _____

6. I feel that I may have a special contribution to give to the world. _____

7. It is more important for me to do what I believe to be right than to try to win the approval of others. _____

8. People who seem unsure and uncertain about things lose my respect. _____

9. I am able to stick with difficult problems over extended periods of time. _____

10. On occasion I get overly enthusiastic about things. _____

11. I often get my best ideas when doing nothing in particular. _____

12. I rely on intuitive hunches and the feeling of "rightness" or "wrongness" when moving toward the solution of a problem. _____

13. When problem solving, I work faster analyzing the problem and slower when synthesizing the information I've gathered. _____

14. I like hobbies that involve collecting things. _____

15. Daydreaming has provided the impetus for many of my more important projects. _____

16. If I had to choose from two occupations other than the one I now have, I would rather be a physician than an explorer. _____

17. I can get along more easily with people if they belong to about the same social and business class as myself. _____

18. I have a high degree of aesthetic sensitivity. _____

19. Intuitive hunches are unreliable guides in problem solving. _____

20. I am much more interested in coming up with new ideas than I am in trying to sell them to others. _____

21. I tend to avoid situations in which I might feel inferior. _____

22. In evaluating information, the source of it is more important to me than the content. _____

23. I like people who follow the rule "business before pleasure." _____

24. One's own self-respect is much more important than the respect of others. _____

25. I feel that people who strive for perfection are unwise. _____

26. I like work in which I must influence others. _____

27. It is important for me to have a place for everything and everything in its place. _____

28. People who are willing to entertain "crackpot" ideas are impractical. _____

29. I rather enjoy fooling around with new ideas, even if there is no practical payoff. _____

30. When a certain approach to a problem doesn't work, I can quickly reorient my thinking. _____

31. I don't like to ask questions that show ignorance. _____

32. I am able to more easily change my interests to pursue a job or career than change a job to pursue my interests. _____

33. Inability to solve a problem is frequently due to asking the wrong questions. _____

34. I can frequently anticipate the solution to my problems. _____

35. It is a waste of time to analyze one's failures. _____

36. Only fuzzy thinkers resort to metaphors and analogies. _____

37. At times I have so enjoyed the ingenuity of a crook that I hoped he or she would go scot-free. _____

38. I frequently begin work on a problem that I can only dimly sense and not yet express. _____

39. I frequently tend to forget things such as names of people, streets, highways, small towns, et cetera. _____

40. I feel that hard work is the basic factor in success. _____

41. To be regarded as a good team member is important to me. _____

42. I know how to keep my inner impulses in check. _____

43. I am a thoroughly dependable and responsible person. _____

44. I resent things being uncertain and unpredictable. _____

45. I prefer to work with others in a team effort rather than solo. _____

46. The trouble with many people is that they take things too seriously. _____

47. I am frequently haunted by my problems and cannot let go of them. _____

48. I can easily give up immediate gain or comfort to reach the goals I have set. _____

49. If I were a college professor, I would rather teach factual courses than those involving theory. _____

50. I'm attracted to the mystery of life. _____

Scoring Instructions. To compute your percentage score, circle and add up the values assigned to each item.

	Strongly Agree A	Agree B	In-between or Don't Know C	Disagree D	Strongly Disagree E
1.	−2	−1	0	+1	+2
2.	−2	−1	0	+1	+2
3.	−2	−1	0	+1	+2
4.	+2	+1	0	−1	−2
5.	−2	−1	0	+1	+2
6.	+2	+1	0	−1	−2
7.	+2	+1	0	−1	−2
8.	−2	−1	0	+1	+2
9.	+2	+1	0	−1	−2
10.	+2	+1	0	−1	−2
11.	+2	+1	0	−1	−2
12.	+2	+1	0	−1	−2
13.	−2	−1	0	+1	+2
14.	−2	−1	0	+1	+2
15.	+2	+1	0	−1	−2
16.	−2	−1	0	+1	+2
17.	−2	−1	0	+1	+2

18.	+2	+1	0	−1	−2
19.	−2	−1	0	+1	+2
20.	+2	+1	0	−1	−2
21.	−2	−1	0	+1	+2
22.	−2	−1	0	+1	+2
23.	−2	−1	0	+1	+2
24.	+2	+1	0	−1	−2
25.	−2	−1	0	+1	+1
26.	−2	−1	0	+1	+2
27.	−2	−1	0	+1	+2
28.	−2	−1	0	+1	+2
29.	+2	+1	0	−1	−2
30.	+2	+1	0	−1	−2
31.	−2	−1	0	+1	+2
32.	−2	−1	0	+1	+2
33.	+2	+1	0	−1	−2
34.	+2	+1	0	−1	−2
35.	−2	−1	0	+1	+2
36.	−2	−1	0	+1	+2
37.	+2	+1	0	−1	−2
38.	+2	+1	0	−1	−2
39.	+2	+1	0	−1	−2
40.	+2	+1	0	−1	−2
41.	−2	−1	0	+1	+2
42.	−2	−1	0	+1	+2
43.	−2	−1	0	+1	+2
44.	−2	−1	0	+1	+2
45.	−2	−1	0	+1	+2
46.	+2	+1	0	−1	−2
47.	+2	+1	0	−1	−2
48.	+2	+1	0	−1	−2
49.	−2	−1	0	+1	+2
50.	+2	+1	0	−1	−2

80 to 100	*Very creative*		*20 to 39*	*Below average*
60 to 79	*Above average*		*−100 to 19*	*Noncreative*
40 to 59	*Average*			

Source: Developed by Eugene Randsepp and reprinted from *Personnel Journal*, Costa Mesa, California. All rights reserved.

EXPERIENTIAL EXERCISE 2

Understanding the Complexities of Change

In this exercise, your instructor will divide the class into five groups of approximately equal size. Each group will be assigned one of the following changes:

1. A change from the semester system to the quarter system (or the opposite, depending on the school's current system).
2. A requirement that all work—homework, examinations, term papers, problem sets—be done on a computer.
3. A requirement that all students live on campus.

4. A requirement that all students have reading, writing, and speaking fluency in at least three languages, including English and Japanese, to graduate.

5. A requirement that all students room with someone in the same major.

First, decide what individuals and groups must be involved in the change process. Next, decide how the change will be implemented using Lewin's process of organization change (Fig. 18-8) as a framework. Consider how to deal with resistance to change. Decide whether a change agent (internal or external) should be used. Develop a realistic timetable for full implementation of the change.

After all of the groups have developed plans, they will present them to the class.

Follow-Up Questions

1. How similar were the implementation steps for each change?
2. Were the plans for managing resistance to change realistic?
3. Do you think any of the changes could be successfully implemented at your school? Why or why not?
4. Do you believe a technique other than Lewin's model would be more applicable in implementing the changes?

Source: Adapted from Gregory Moorhead and Ricky W. Griffin, *Organizational Behavior,* 3rd ed., Dallas, Houghton Mifflin, 1992. Used with permission.

Take It
to the Net

You can find this chapter's World Wide Web exercise at:
http://www.prenhall.com/carrell

CHAPTER 19

Quality and Innovation Within Organizations

CHAPTER OBJECTIVES

1. To understand what quality is and the historical perspectives of quality.
2. To explain how concepts from organizational behavior are related to the management of quality.
3. To know different philosophies regarding quality implementation.
4. To describe quality circles and quality in service organizations.
5. To explain how organizations may be selected for the Malcolm Baldrige National Quality Award.
6. To identify the characteristics of a total quality management (TQM) program.
7. To understand TQM implementation problems.
8. To explain the managerial implications of implementing a TQM program.
9. To describe the different types of innovation.
10. To explain the factors affecting the adoption of an innovation.

John Wallace, Former CEO of Wallace Company

John Wallace is the former chief executive officer of a family-owned, Houston-based supplier of pipes, valves, and fittings to the chemical, refining, and petrochemical industries. From 1984 until he stepped down in 1991, Mr. Wallace restrategized and restructured the organization into one of the most admired companies for its excellence in quality and service. So effective was the transformation that, in 1990, the Wallace Company was the only small business in the United States to win the prestigious Malcolm Baldrige National Quality Award along with such corporate titans as IBM and Federal Express.

As the oil crisis of the mid-1980s devastated the economy of the Gulf Coast area, Wallace Company revenues plummeted over 30 percent, and market share plunged as customers went bankrupt almost daily. A crucial external trigger for strategic change came in 1985 when Hoechst Celanese Chemical Company, a major Wallace customer, approached its main suppliers with the announcement that it was planning to restrict the number of its suppliers. Celanese asked the Wallace Company and others to enter into a partnership that stressed quick quality requirements on delivery and invoice accuracy or lose the business. According to CEO John Wallace, "In our case, embracing quality as a way of doing business literally meant our survival."[1]

In 1989, the Wallace Company decided to redesign their quality program using the Malcolm Baldrige Quality Award criteria as guidelines for new strategic planning and implementation. The purpose was not to win the award, but to employ the criteria as a tool that would allow the company to set it apart from its competitors. More importantly, it acted as a motivational force, where employees could get quick and tangible results of their strategy implementations.

To help target the areas of growth, Wallace developed a set of Quality Strategic Objectives (QSOs): leadership, information and analysis, strategic quality planning, human resource utilization and development, on-the-job training, employee reinforcement, suggestion system, internal audit, internal and external benchmarking, and customer satisfaction.[2] The QSOs served as the basis for team structure, and 100 task forces and specialty teams were created. Because Wallace employed a small force of 280, most employees were part of different teams and committees.

Using such concepts as decentralization, delegation, team consensus, and empowerment, the Wallace Company achieved the following accomplishments.[3]

- Received a 97.97 quality rating by Monsanto—the highest score ever attained by a vendor.
- Achieved 98 percent on-time delivery performance with partnering customers (92 to 96 percent with most other customers) compared to the industry average of 75 percent.
- Sales escalated by 69 percent during the 1985 to 1990 period, while inventory increased by a slight 5 percent.
- Market share shot up from 10.4 percent in 1987 to more than 18 percent in 1990.
- Sales per employee reached 25 percent above the average for high performing firms in the industry.
- Employees could answer customer inquiries within sixty minutes.

- Inventory turnover improved by 175 percent (a level 25 percent above industry average).
- Profit-to-sales ratio improved nearly 13 percent.
- Absenteeism was halved in three years.
- Employee turnover was reduced nearly 60 percent.

Unfortunately, reality crashed hard at the Wallace Company after the Baldrige Award victory celebration ended. In 1992, the Wallace Company suddenly began operating in Chapter 11 bankruptcy.

Analysts indicate that: (1) Wallace employees were preaching the gospel of quality programs rather than running the business; (2) Overhead expenses had significantly increased; and (3) Wallace's largest creditor, the Maryland National Bank, was in financial trouble and could no longer hold Wallace's note. A new lender had to be found.

Despite these problems, analysts predict an excellent and profitable outlook for the Wallace Company. The continued emphasis on quality has kept large customers like Celanese and Dow Chemical loyal.[4] On October 31, 1991, John Wallace resigned as CEO, but remained as chairman of the board. Some claim that John Wallace was a great leader, while others blame him for the firm's misfortunes. However, there is no question that without converting his small, family-owned business into a textbook example of a company totally committed to quality, the Wallace Company would not be alive today. He did away with the fear and barriers that existed between senior management and lower-level employees, and fostered honesty, trust, communication, and an open-door policy that permeated throughout the entire company.[5]

WHAT IS QUALITY?

Before we attempt to define quality, it is important to explain our rationale in writing this chapter. Effective quality depends on good planning, communication, organization, motivation, and control involving many levels of management and employees. Because all of these groups must function together as a team, participative approaches to problem solving are important methods for improving quality and productivity. The culture of an organization and types of reward systems used also affect how employees and management resolve quality and productivity issues. Certainly, many of the concepts (discussed later in this chapter) of organization behavior are related to the effective management of quality.

Following our discussion defining quality, we examine historical perspectives of quality and how organization behavior concepts are related to the management of quality. Next, we describe quality programs with an emphasis on quality implementation philosophies, quality circles, and the Malcolm Baldrige National Quality Award. Following these topics, we discuss Total Quality Management (TQM) characteristics, TQM implementation strategies, and problems associated with the implementation of TQM. Finally, we conclude the chapter by examining the different types of innovation and explaining how innovations are adopted. Now we focus on defining quality.

Quality is a relative term that means different things to different people at different times. For example, the quality of a product or service may refer to its reliability of performance, its durability, its timeliness, its appearance, its purity, its individuality, or some combination of these factors. In some instances, the term quality is used when the more appropriate term grade should be used. As an example, the Lincoln Town Car is a higher grade automobile than a Ford Escort. While both may be high-quality cars, built to give trouble-free performance and to conform to customer expectations appropriate for their market niches and price ranges, the Lincoln has more features, space, and comfort.

David Garvin of Harvard University has identified five perspectives of quality that are described in Fig. 19-1.[6]

From the perspective of a firm, the meaning of quality depends on one's position in the organization. For example, designers, customers, manufacturers,

Quality An offering that meets or exceeds customer requirements. The quality of a product or service refers to its reliability of performance, its durability, its timeliness, its appearance, and its purity.

---

1. *Innate Superiority.* A perspective in which quality cannot be precisely measured but can be universally recognized as excellent. Examples are German automobiles and Swiss banks.

2. *Degree of an Attribute.* This perspective defines quality in terms of some particular attribute or characteristic of the product or service. The color and clarity of the picture on a television set is an example.

3. *User Satisfaction.* In this perspective, the user's satisfaction is the basis for quality. A vigorous workout at a health club is an example.

4. *Conformance to Specifications.* This quality perspective evaluates quality in terms of how well the product or service is produced and delivered based on the specifications set by designers. McDonald's restaurants are frequently inspected by headquarters to verify that they "meet specifications."

5. *Value Delivered.* This perspective defines quality in terms of what is delivered relative to its price, and explains why there is such a range of successful restaurants.

Source: Adapted from David A. Garvin, "Competing on the Eight Dimensions of Quality," *Harvard Business Review* 65, November–December 1987, pp. 101–109.

FIGURE 19-1
Perspectives of Quality

FIGURE 19-2

Production–distribution
Cycle

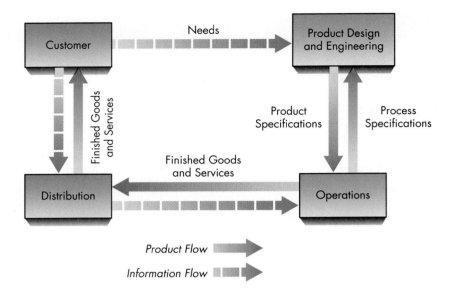

Goods are produced to meet a customer's needs. These needs are related to product performance, reliability, length of serviceable life, and price. The firm's marketing department assesses the customer's needs. A product meeting customer needs, in terms of both performance and price, can be described as having "quality." The "user satisfaction" perspective of quality described in Fig. 19-1 applies to this situation.

The manufacturer must translate customer requirements into detailed product and process specifications. Such functions as research and development, product design, and engineering are involved in this phase. Product specifications consist of attributes such as size, finish, dimensions, tolerances, materials, operational characteristics, and safety features. Process specifications focus on the types of equipment, tools, and facilities used in production. Product designers must balance product performance and cost. This phase illustrates the "value delivered" perspective of quality depicted in Fig. 19-1. Customers generally will buy the quality that they can afford.

Unfortunately, certain problems develop as firms attempt to implement the model described in Fig. 19-2. For example, customer needs can be misinterpreted as illustrated in Fig. 19-3.

Quality can be affected in a variety of ways during manufacturing operations. Production employees can make mistakes; machine settings can fall out of adjustment; materials can be defective. Variations will occur in product output even under the most controlled situations. The manufacturer's responsibility is to guarantee that design specifications are adhered to during production, and that the final product performs as intended.

The distribution of the product from the plant to the customer completes the product manufacturing cycle. Customers may have needs for various services such as installation, user information, and special training. These services are part of the product and cannot be ignored in the quality of a product.[7]

and distributors all have certain perceptions regarding quality. These perceptions are illustrated in Fig. 19-2 that describes the production–distribution cycle for a manufactured good.

FIGURE 19-3
Misinterpreting
Customer Needs

Historical Perspectives of Quality

Providing customers with quality products has been an important task of production operations throughout history. Egyptian wall paintings from 1450 B.C. provide evidence of measurement and inspection activity. In the late 1700s, Eli Whitney contributed the idea of interchangeable parts that created improvements in dependability, reliability, serviceability, and productive efficiency.[8]

The early pioneers of scientific management, including Frederick W. Taylor and Lillian Gilbreath, perfected work-study techniques, so that jobs could be decomposed into individual work tasks. Inspection tasks were separated from production tasks, and separate quality control departments were established in production operations.[9]

In the early 1900s an inspection department was created in the Western Electric Company to support the Bell operating companies.

(Western Electric manufactured telephones, switching equipment, and other items for the Bell Telephone System.) Quality control techniques were applied to the design, manufacturing, and installation functions of both Western Electric and the other Bell companies. Later, in the 1920s, employees of Western Electric's inspection department were transferred to Bell Telephone Laboratories. These employees were assigned the task of developing new theories and methods of inspection to improve and maintain quality. Members of this group included:

- Walter Shewart, developer of control charts
- Harold Dodge, sampling techniques
- George Edwards, economic analysis techniques for quality problem solving

Employees of the quality control department of Bell Laboratories coined the term "quality assurance" and laid the foundation for modern quality management programs.[10]

During the Second World War, the U.S. military imposed strict standards on suppliers. Because the military could not inspect every item, statistical sampling procedures were used. Sampling tables labeled "MILSTD" for "military standard" were developed and are still widely used today. These sampling techniques, later described as statistical quality control, became widely known and adopted by other industries.[11]

During the 1950s, two American consultants, Joseph Juran and W. Edwards Deming, introduced statistical quality control techniques to the Japanese during Japan's rebuilding period.[12] Figure 19-4 depicts a number of modern-day educators, authors, and consultants who have made significant contributions to the development of quality improvement programs.

Since 1970, the emphasis on quality has shifted from a technical approach centered around quality control personnel to a managerial philosophy that relates to every employee.[13]

Relationship of Organization Behavior Concepts to the Management of Quality

Management system of quality It is concerned with organizational behavior concepts: decision making, individual and group behaviors, motivation, leadership, organizational design, organizational culture, conflict resolutions, and organizational change.

Most practicing managers and quality control scholars state that, today, a comprehensive strategy for quality that integrates people, technology, information, and management is needed to meet global competition. Armand Fiegenbaum, who developed the concept of total quality control (TQC), suggested that a total quality system contains two related parts: the management system and the technical system.[14] The *management system* is concerned with organization behavior concepts described in this text: decision making, individual and group behaviors, motivation, leadership, organizational design, organizational culture, conflict resolution, and organizational change. Top management must understand how these organization behavior concepts are related to the management of the quality function, as well as being aware of customer needs and the financial constraints of the firm. Organization behavior concepts are important, because quality is now viewed as the responsibility of everyone in the organization from hourly employees to the chief executive officer.

The technical system involves assuring quality and reliability in engineering design, planning of manufacturing processes, and controlling raw materials as well as other inventory items. Statistical tools are employed in each of these areas for identifying quality problems. How the management and technical systems are integrated involves creativity.

- *W. Edwards Deming,* a statistician and consultant while a professor at New York University, was invited by the Japanese government to assist its industries in improving quality and productivity. Dr. Deming was so successful in his quality improvements that in 1951 the Japanese established the Deming Prize for innovation in quality management. This prize is awarded annually to a company that has distinguished itself in quality management programs. During the 1980s, U.S. companies flocked to Deming for his assistance in establishing quality improvement programs in their factories. Deming died in 1993 at age eighty-nine.

- *Joseph M. Juran* also played an important role in teaching the Japanese how to improve their product quality. Juran was also contacted later by U.S. corporations to assist in their quality improvement programs.

- *Phillip B. Crosby* contended that any level of defects is too high and that firms should put programs into place that will move them continuously toward the goal of *zero defects.* Crosby stated that the cost of poor quality is so understated that unlimited amounts can be profitably spent on improving quality.

- *Armand V. Feigenbaum* developed the concept of *total quality control* (TQC) and states that the responsibility for quality must rest with the individuals who do the work. In TQC, product quality is more important than production rates, and employees are given the authority to stop production whenever quality problems occur.

- *Kaoru Ishikawa* is credited with the concept of *quality circles* and also suggested the use of *fishbone diagrams* that are used to trace back customer complaints about quality problems to the responsible production operations.

- *Genichi Taguchi* has worked with large U.S. companies such as IBM and Ford to assist them in developing improved statistical control of their production processes. Taguchi states that constant adjustment of production machines to achieve consistent product quality is not effective and that, instead, products should be designed so that they are robust enough to function satisfactorily in spite of production line variations.

Source: Adapted from Norman Gaither, *Production and Operations Management,* 5th ed., New York, Dryden, 1992, pp. 638–639. Used with permission.

*For an expanded discussion of these contributors, see Howard S. Gitlow and Shelly J. Gitlow, *The Deming Guide to Quality and Competition Position,* Englewood Cliffs, NJ, Prentice-Hall, 1987; Joseph M. Juran, *Quality Control Handbook,* New York, McGraw-Hill, 1974; Armand V. Fiegenbaum, *Total Quality Control: Engineering and Management,* 3rd ed., New York, McGraw-Hill, 1983; Kaoru Ishikawa, *Guide to Quality Control,* Tokyo, Asian Productivity Organization, 1972; Phillip G. Crosby, *Quality Is Free,* New York, McGraw-Hill, 1979.

The process of creativity that involves developing original and imaginative views of situations is described in Chap. 3.

The "OB in Practice" on page 658 describes how Xerox has used total employee involvement in implementing a quality improvement program.

QUALITY PROGRAMS

The way in which quality programs are implemented is a matter of philosophy. In this section we discuss the philosophies of W. Edwards Deming, Joseph Juran, and Phillip Crosby.

Quality Implementation Philosophies[15]

Several different philosophies exist on how to best design and implement a quality improvement program. Because companies tend to be distinct, it is difficult to successfully apply any particular quality philosophy. While any of the philoso-

Quality implementation
Different philosophies
exist on how to best
design and implement
a quality improvement
program.

OB in Practice

Total Employee Involvement

The Xerox Corporation, winner of the 1989 Baldrige Award, produces more than 250 types of document-processing equipment. Attaining total quality at Xerox had been the top priority for David Kearns, its CEO from 1982 to 1990. Kearns introduced a "Leadership-through-Quality" process, telling Xerox employees that customer satisfaction was the top priority and that the culture of the company would be changed. Managers were trained with their own work groups. Emphasis was placed on identifying quality shortfalls and the problems that caused them, determining root causes, developing solutions, and implementing them. The work groups were taught interpersonal skills, a six-step problem-solving process, and a nine-step quality improvement process. The role of first-line supervisors was changed from that of the traditional, dictatorial foreman to that of a supervisor, functioning primarily as a coach and expediter. Employee involvement teams were given considerable empowerment. For example, manufacturing employees have the authority to stop an assembly line when problems are identified. According to Kearns, there is no magic formula for a successful quality program. The key is involvement. The entire management team, from top to bottom, must have a real commitment to employee involvement.

Source: Adapted from David T. Kearns, "Leadership Through Quality," *Academy of Management Executive* 3, 1990, pp. 86–89.

phies can be effective, it is best for a firm's management to understand the nature and differences among the philosophies, and then develop a quality management program that is tailored to the individual organization. Research indicates that successful programs use a composite approach, understanding, and drawing from the different philosophies. Successful programs involve all the levels of the organization in the selection, implementation, and commitment to a philosophy that becomes a central part of the corporate culture.[16]

Deming's Philosophy focuses on improving the conformance of products and services to specifications by reducing uncertainty and variability in the design and manufacturing processes. Deming advocates a never-ending cycle of product design, manufacture, testing, and sales, followed by market surveys, then redesign, and so forth. Deming claims that higher quality leads to higher productivity that leads to a long-term competitive position. Deming stresses that top management has the overriding responsibility for quality improvement.

Deming advocates that *all* employees be familiar with a variety of statistical techniques.[17] Two sources have been identified by Deming as approaches for improving processes. The first focuses on eliminating common causes" of quality problems that may be inherent in the production system, such as poorly designed products, inadequate training programs, and poor working conditions. The second approach considers the elimination of "special causes" that can be related to a specific individual, machine, or batch of materials.

Deming recommends that management and production employees, rather than quality professionals, be responsible for quality improvement. All employees are urged to study the organization and to suggest ways to improve it. Employees are not only to do the work but also to help improve the system. The core of Deming's recommendations consists of a 14-point program that is described in Fig. 19-5.

Deming's 14-point program has forced radical changes in many U.S. firms as well as major cultural upheavals. Unfortunately, a number of American companies have failed in successfully implementing Deming's program, because they failed to (1) rethink numerical goals and quotas, (2) change their incentive programs, (3) alter supplier relationships, (4) cultivate an intolerance for defective materials and products, and (5) undertake significant new training programs.[18]

Juran's Philosophy states that in order to achieve product quality, a "spiral" of activities must take place. These include market research, product development, inspection and testing, and sales followed by customer feedback that initiates the cycle all over again. A central theme of Juran is that senior managers must play an active and enthusiastic leadership role because of the interdependence of the preceding activities. Juran's approach focuses on three processes: (1) quality control and the control sequence; (2) quality improvement and the breakthrough sequence; and (3) quality planning and the annual quality program. The control sequence phase is designed to combat occasional quality problems (similar to Deming's special causes); the breakthrough sequence combats chronic problems (Deming's common causes); and the annual quality program institutionalizes managerial control and review over the quality management process. Juran advocates training for all employees in the use of statistical tools for quality improvement, cost reduction, data collection, and analysis. Project improvement is stressed by Juran. For example, at any point in time, hundreds of quality improvement projects should be underway within the firm. Juran also advocates developing a strategic plan for quality improvement. This strategic process should determine both short-term and long-term goals, establish prior-

---

Deming tells managers that they must accomplish the following:
1. Create consistency and continuity of purpose.
2. Refuse to allow commonly accepted levels of delay for mistakes, defective material, defective workmanship.
3. Eliminate the need for and dependence upon mass inspection.
4. Reduce the number of suppliers. Buy on statistical evidence, not price.
5. Search continually for problems in the system and seek ways to improve it.
6. Institute modern methods of training, using statistics.
7. Focus supervision on helping people to do a better job. Provide the tools and techniques for people to have pride of workmanship.
8. Eliminate fear. Encourage two-way communications.
9. Break down barriers between departments. Encourage problem solving through teamwork.
10. Eliminate the use of numerical goals, slogans, and posters for the work force.
11. Use statistical methods for continuing improvement of quality and productivity and eliminate all standards prescribing numerical quotas.
12. Remove barriers to pride of workmanship.
13. Institute a vigorous program of education and training to keep people abreast of new developments in materials, methods, and technologies.
14. Clearly define management's permanent commitment to quality and productivity.

Source: Myron Tribus, "Deming's Way," *Mechanical Engineering*, January 1988, pp. 26-30. Copyright ASME International.

FIGURE 19-5
Deming's 14-point Program

ities, compare results with previous plans, and integrate the strategic quality plan with other company strategic objectives.

Crosby's Philosophy places more emphasis on management and organizational processes (organization behavior concepts) than on the use of statistical techniques advocated by Deming and Juran.

Crosby, author of two popular books on quality improvement, estimates that the cost of quality ranges as high as 40 percent of sales with an average of 25 percent. Crosby and other experts believe that the cost of quality should only be 2.5 percent of sales.[19] Needless to say, obtaining this lower level of defects will yield substantial cost savings. Crosby stresses the basic elements of determination, education, and implementation. By determination, Crosby explains that top management must be serious about and committed to quality improvement. Education involves an understanding that quality is a conformance to requirements together with a knowledge of the production process. Implementation techniques must be practiced by all employees with the objective of discovering and eliminating all opportunities for error. The use of statistical tools is recommended by Crosby during the implementation phase.

Crosby also states that firms should move toward the goal of zero defects. He claims that most individuals accept zero defects as a standard in their personal lives and need only to be taught that zero defects is a reasonable and essential standard for their work lives. Crosby's consulting firm is widely regarded as the largest teaching and consulting firm in the quality area.

The "Profile" opposite describes how an emphasis on quality halted the decline of Xerox.

Quality Circles

Quality circles (originally called quality control circles) were first introduced in Japan by Kaoru Ishikawa during the 1960s. Some ten years later, Deming and Juran brought the idea of quality circles to the United States. Interestingly, it took another five years for the idea of quality circles to blossom in the United States.[20] Figure 19-6 describes how quality control circles operate in most firms.

FIGURE 19-6

How Quality Control Circles Operate

Source: Adapted from Norman Gaither, *Production and Operations Management,* 5th ed., New York, Dryden Press, 1992, p. 643; Jack R. Meredith, *Management of Operations,* 4th ed., New York, John Wiley, 1992, p. 331; James B. Dilworth, *Operations Management,* New York, McGraw-Hill, 1992, p. 619.

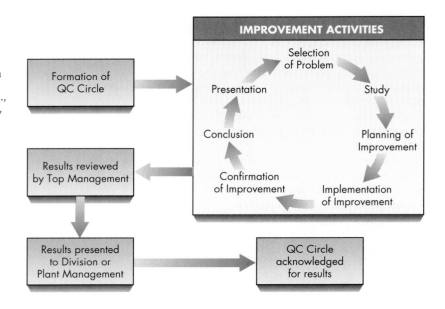

Profile

David T. Kearns
CEO of Xerox from 1982 to 1990

HOW AN EMPHASIS ON QUALITY
HALTED THE DECLINE OF XEROX

When I became CEO of Xerox in 1982, I learned that the company was literally facing extinction because Xerox's Japanese competition could sell copiers for what it cost us to *make* them. We adopted a quality improvement program at Xerox that we called "Leadership Through Quality." This renewed emphasis on quality allowed Xerox to slash its manufacturing costs by nearly 50 percent, double production, and cut the product development cycle by a full year. By 1990, Xerox was again the producer of the highest quality office products in the world and had gained back market share from the Japanese.

The solution that halted the decline of Xerox and richly renewed it with a new vision was quality. By now, that magic word is on the minds of just about every corporate executive—or at least it ought to be. But for all that has been written and spoken about quality, more companies than not seem baffled about exactly what it is and why they should be thinking about it.

We have a very simple view of quality. We believe that the world is made up of customers and suppliers. The customer comes to the supplier with a set of requirements and expectations. The supplier provides customers with what we call an offering.

People commonly think that customers buy a physical product. They buy a CD player or a popcorn maker. They really don't. They buy a total experience—the nomenclature, the software, the instruction booklet, and so forth that come with the popcorn maker. When that total offering satisfies the requirements and expectations of customers, then you have a happy situation. You have achieved quality. If any part of the offering is wanting, then discontent results. You don't have quality.

The need to pursue quality is obvious. In the past, there often were monopolies and oligopolies, which didn't provide many offerings for customers to choose from. But that all changed with the entrance of new suppliers, most notably the Japanese. They came in and provided competitive offerings that meshed better with the requirements and expectations of customers. And so they captured a great deal of business.

As a result of this, customer expectations have been raised to new levels and fresh requirements have been established. Back in the 1960s and early 1970s, Americans bought cars that on average had twenty-three defects in them. In those days, car owners would keep a pad and pencil handy in the glove compartment to write down the defects that they spotted. Then they would take their lists to the car dealer and try to get the defects fixed, sometimes succeeding. None of this seemed to bother us all that much. We didn't know then that we really wanted to have cars with fewer defects, not to mention no defects at all. Then one day we were able to buy a Datsun, and there was nothing to write down on the pad. Expectations were radically changed. Cars with twenty-three defects were now for losers.

As customers discover that they have choices, quality becomes a core competitive issue. Eventually, quality becomes a matter of survival, as it did at Xerox.

According to this perspective, the only reason to engage in quality is if you believe there is a marketplace—in other words, customers who have choices among different suppliers. If you believe your industry is on the brink of having new entrants—like consumer banking—you could be the one to change the rules yourself.

By our definition of quality—an offering that meets or exceeds customer requirements—what is quality one year is not necessarily quality the next year. It's not a constant. And so suppliers can be drivers of quality. Quality management, therefore, boils down to developing and operating work processes that are capable of consistently designing, producing, and delivering high-quality offerings.

What, then, is total quality management? This is the business process itself. It is not something that you lay on top of what you do. It is what you do. It is creating and implementing an architecture of organization that motivates, supports, and enables quality management in all the activities of the enterprise.

To help distinguish what we're talking about, we've identified six core concepts of quality, and they're worth listing.

1. The customer/supplier model. This has been derived from the work of W. Edwards Deming. Early on, he had the notion that the world was composed of customer/supplier chains, and quality was created all along the chain. It used to be that one only looked for quality at the final output point. You fixed things there and tried to meet customer requirements. This was the U.S. approach to quality, and it was a brutally expensive way to accomplish it.

2. Process control and capability. This means you need to look at all the steps in the work process to ensure quality. This requires the use of quantitative tools like statistical process control. This was something we didn't focus on enough in the beginning at Xerox, and it was one of our worst mistakes.

3. Management by fact. You need to collect plenty of data from the chains if you're going to manage effectively. You can't do it through guesswork.

4. Problem solving. You have to take that data you collected and use it to identify problems and come up with solutions.

5. The cost of quality. To figure out what quality costs you, you need to look at several elements. If you wait and inspect things once they're done and then try to fix problems, you incur a number of expenses. You are building things you can't use, called scrap, fixing things later on in the marketplace, called warranty costs, and making customers unhappy who don't return to buy from you, called lost opportunity. One of the major lumber companies finds that customers paw through two-by-fours at lumberyards to pick out ones they like. Rejected strips get returned and scrapped. The lumber company says there is no such thing as a perfect two-by-four, but there is one that meets customer requirements. If the company could make it right the first time, it wouldn't have to throw all that product out. All of this is very expensive, though tough to quantify. The number, however, is huge. Essentially, the cost of quality is the cost of conformance plus the cost of nonconformance. Phil Crosby reckons that the cost is 20 percent of the revenues of a manufacturing company. Some say the Japanese cost is a mere 3 percent.

6. Teamwork and involvement. The notion here is moving from the idea of quality as a bunch of engineers sitting on the side to getting everyone involved. Employees want to work hard and are interested in the future of the institution. It's management's job to create the appropriate environment to allow them to work well.

When you reflect on quality, it is also important to take note of what quality is not. It is not "everything"—the single answer to all your woes. There are any number of quality zealots around who think no matter what the problem, quality is the answer. Don't believe it.

It is not a substitute for "KKD"—a Japanese expression that translates into knowledge, experience, and guts. Tony Kobayashi of Fuji Xerox says that to run a company you need TQC and KKD. Without the KKD, you can't get the TQC.

Nor is quality a substitute for good strategic decision making. Managers get paid to make decisions, and while quality will help them it won't guarantee that they make the right decisions.

By no means is quality a replacement for an effective organizational design.

And, finally, quality is not a substitute for selecting the right people. The wrong people can do much better with quality than without it, but you're unquestionably better off with the right people.

Once you've got a good feel for what quality is and what it isn't, you're a long way toward determining whether you need it and what it can do for you. We're strong believers in quality, but we're also strong believers in your understanding what it is.

Source: Adapted from David T. Kearns and David A. Nadler, *Prophets in the Dark: How Xerox Reinvented Itself and Beat Back the Japanese*, New York, HarperCollins, 1992.

The basic concept behind *quality circles* is that employees best know the problems in production, because they face them every day. However, nearly all of these problems are beyond the individual employee's control, thus requiring a larger group to address them. In many instances, a particular quality circle cannot solve a problem from within the group itself and must contact another group. Quality circles are composed of natural work groups and range from a few employees to over a dozen—the average number is nine. In some firms, quality circles are not limited to production employees but include clerical, staff, and even managers and supervisors themselves. A trained facilitator, a supervisor or even a coworker, usually leads the quality circle. Members of the quality circle spend a couple of hours a week, usually on company time, analyzing and discussing their problems and brainstorming over solutions to them. Then they work on implementing the solutions on the job. Membership in quality circles is voluntary, and there are no direct cash incentives. Members indicate their principal reasons for belonging to quality controls are personal satisfaction for solving problems and recognition given at meetings.[21]

The "Profile" on page 664 describes how employees of L-S Electro-Galvanizing working together as quality teams have not only improved quality but have generated savings in an amount equal to 27.5 percent of L-SE's net income.

Although quality circles have been implemented by many firms, research studies indicate that a potential for failure exists. Figure 19-7 describes the reasons why some quality circles fail.

Even if the reasons for failure described in Fig. 19-7 can be avoided, other pitfalls may prevent the successful implementation of a quality circle. These include: friction developing within the group, running out of ideas, failing to reach savings goals for projects, pressuring management to provide financial rewards for improvements suggested by the group, developing burnout, and employee cynicism. This cynicism develops because the firm has not done a

Quality circles are composed of natural work groups of employees that come together to analyze and discuss problems, led by a trained facilitator or coworker, with hopes of solving the problems.

- Inadequate funding provided by top management.
- An insufficient number of volunteers.
- Members may not be able to learn problem-solving or group-process skills.
- Members may fail to reach agreement regarding which problem to address.
- Poor solutions may be developed.
- Middle managers, supervisors, or staff personnel may not cooperate.
- Ideas may be poorly presented.
- Proposals may be rejected, because implementation costs are prohibitive.
- Top management may be slow in implementing solutions.
- Supervisors or facilitators selected to lead the group may have received inadequate training in human relations, or group dynamics and meetings become a waste of time.
- Top management may fail to adequately implement solutions.

Source: Adapted from James R. Evans and William M. Lindsay, *The Management and Control of Quality*, St. Paul, MN, West Publishing, 1989, pp. 130–132; Edward E. Lawler and Susan A. Mohran, "Quality Circles after the Fad," *Harvard Business Review* 63, January–February 1985, pp. 65–71; Wayne S. Ricker and Shaun J. Sullivan, "Can the Effectiveness of QC Circles Be Measured?" *The Quality Circles Journal* 4, 1981, pp. 29–34.

FIGURE 19-7
Why Quality Circles Fail

Quality Team Members
L-S Electro-Galvanizing
USING EMPLOYEE TEAMS TO IMPROVE QUALITY AND PRODUCTIVITY

At L-S Electro-Galvanizing, rank-and-file employees switch shifts without telling their bosses. They keep track of their overtime. They do the scheduling. They do the hiring.

It may sound like a worker's dream. In reality, it's one specialty steel company's approach to enhancing quality by giving its sixty-five unionized plant workers an unusual degree of authority.

Before steel can be turned into fenders, hoods, and other car parts, it must first be electrogalvanized to prevent corrosion. That requires feeding rolls of steel into an 885-foot-long machine that essentially coats the steel with the right mix of zinc and other chemicals before rerolling it and spitting it out. Unfortunately, even barely discernible blemishes result in customers sending back bad steel, and the company shipping them new rolls to keep them satisfied.

So far, L-SE's employees-in-charge approach has worked. It has cut the costs from customer complaints—about everything from surface dimples to traces of rust to packaging problems—from $8 a ton in 1989 to $1.09 a ton last year. That translated into savings of about $2.2 million last year—an amount equal to 27.5 percent of L-SE's net income.

The key: A team of thirteen L-SE workers, all members of the company's integrated-process-control committee, whose work has permeated the entire company. The team, which developed the quality system used by L-SE since 1989, has won the RIT/USA TODAY Quality Cup in the small-business category (fewer than 500 employees). While teamwork is in vogue these days, L-SE takes it a step further than most. "The (line) employees really are running the company," says Don Vernon, general manager of the eighty-five-employee venture of LTV Steel and Sumitomo Steel of Japan. Vernon states that his Japanese owners "are freaked out. They can't believe I give employees this much responsibility."

As team-driven as L-SE is, the company sometimes still forgets. Recently, management added a procedure to the galvanizing process at the request of a customer and didn't consult employees. The result: botched steel and angry employees, who think they could've helped had the company stuck to the team approach. But such instances are rare.

Source: James Kim, "Employees Call Shots," *USA TODAY*, April 10, 1992, p. 4B. Copyright 1992, USA TODAY. Reprinted with permission.

---

good job selling the benefits of quality circles and explaining why they are necessary. Consequently, employees may see quality circles as a management ploy to reduce overtime, to increase productivity, to reduce the number of employees, or to eliminate the union.[22]

Quality in Service Organizations

Quality in service organizations Quality programs are implemented by organizations that provide services for individuals, businesses, and government establishments.

Most of our discussion regarding quality programs has focused on firms in the manufacturing sector. However, quality programs have also been implemented by organizations in the service sector. Service organizations have been described as those organizations primarily engaged in providing a variety of services for individuals, business, and government establishments. Included are real estate firms; financial services; retailers; public utilities; hotels and other lodging places; firms providing personal, business, repair, health care, amusement services, as well as professional services; and educational institutions.[23] The service sector is at least as capital intensive as the manufacturing sector, and many service industries have a high technology impact. The service sector has become an important part of American society and its growth is well documented. For example, approximately 75 percent of employment in the United States is engaged in service activities and nearly 74 percent of the gross national product stems from the service sector.[24]

The characteristics of services are different from physical goods in several respects as described in Fig. 19-8.

Research studies indicate that measuring the quality of services is difficult. In many instances, customers set their own standards, comparing the service they receive with the service they wished to receive. Also, the perceived quality of some services is affected by the surroundings. For example, cleanliness of facilities, convenient parking, pleasant decor, soft music, comfortable furniture, and friendly servers can determine the perceived quality of services more than the actual quality.[25]

Two approaches have been used in improving the quality of services. One is to methodically train the employees in standard procedures and to use equipment that reinforces this training. As an example, at McDonald's Hamburger University, managers and employees are intensively trained in McDonald's system for food preparation and delivery. Training is intensive, with continuous follow-up checkups. Rewards are given for continuing to pay attention to quality. McDonald's equipment is designed to reinforce the quality process that has been taught to employees, and to discourage sloppy habits that lead to lesser quality.[26] The second approach used to improve service quality is the process of total quality management that is described in a following section of this chapter. As service firms are started, many innovative and creative opportunities exist for implementing quality programs.

Malcolm Baldrige National Quality Award

Global competitors have placed considerable pressure on the product and service quality of U.S. firms. One aspect that has created a desire for improved product and service quality is the *Malcolm Baldrige National Quality Award,* sometimes referred to as the Baldrige Award. This award was established in 1987 and named for a former Secretary of Commerce. The purpose of the award is to recognize U.S. firms that attain preeminent quality leadership and to encourage other U.S.

Malcolm Baldrige National Quality Award Criteria established in 1987—the purpose of the award is to recognize U.S. firms that attain preeminent quality leadership and to encourage other U.S. companies to improve their quality programs.

---

1. *Services are more intangible.* Services are described in abstract ways by such expressions as experience, trust, feeling, and security, while a physical good is both tangible and visible.
2. *Service firms cannot inventory their products and must produce on demand.*
3. *Services are activities or a series of activities rather than a thing.*
4. *Customers do not normally participate in the production process of a physical good but are involved in the production of services.*
5. *Services cannot be subjected to the same type of "final inspection" before reaching the customer as can physical goods.* Services are produced and consumed simultaneously.

Source: Adapted from Valarie A. Zeithaml, A. Parasuraman, and Leonard L. Berry, *Delivering Quality Service: Balancing Customer Perceptions and Expectations,* New York, The Free Press, 1990, pp. 102–104; Carol A. King, "Service Quality Assurance Is Different," *Quality Progress* 18, 1985, pp. 14–18; Robert Normann, *Service Management,* New York, John Wiley, 1984, pp. 61–64.

FIGURE 19-8
Differences between Services and Physical Goods

companies to improve their quality programs. To be eligible for the award, a firm must be incorporated, located in the United States, and submit a seventy-five-page package. A panel of examiners reviews and evaluates the applications. High-scoring applications receive on-site examinations from the panel of examiners. Participants report that completing the application process forces a company to examine its product and service quality and determine how things can be changed for improvement. Fig. 19-9 outlines seven major categories included in the Baldrige Award along with the general guidelines for the type of information that should be submitted regarding that category. The maximum points that can be awarded in each category are also indicated. The total number of points in the Baldrige Award is 1,000.

FIGURE 19-9

Examination Categories of the Malcolm Baldrige National Quality Award

1.0 Leadership (100 Points)

Describe the senior executives' leadership, personal involvement, and visibility in developing and maintaining an environment for quality excellence. (30)

Describe the company's quality values, how they are projected in a consistent manner, and how adoption of the values throughout the company is assessed and reinforced. (20)

Describe how the company integrates its quality values into day-to-day management of all units. (30)

Describe how the company extends its quality and integrates its responsibilities to the public for health, safety, environmental protection, and ethical business practice into quality policies and practices leadership to the external community. (20)

2.0 Information and Analysis (60 Points)

Describe the company's database that is used for planning, management, and evaluation of quality as well as how data and information reliability, timeliness, and access are ensured. (35)

Describe how data and information are analyzed to support the company's key quality leadership objectives in a timely manner. (25)

3.0 Strategic Quality Planning (90 Points)

Describe the company's strategic quality planning process for short-term (1 to 2 years) and longer-term (3 to 5 years) quality leadership and customer satisfaction. (40)

Describe the company's approach to selecting quality-related competitive comparisons and world-class bench-marks to support strategic quality planning. (25)

Summarize the company's principal quality priorities and plans for the short term and for the longer term. (25)

4.0 Human Resource Management (150 Points)

Describe how the company's human resource plans support its quality leadership objectives; summarize principal short-term and longer-term priorities. (30)

Describe the means available for all employees to contribute effectively to the company's quality objectives; summarize trends in involvement. (40)

Describe how the company decides what type of education and training is needed, what is received by employees, and how the company utilizes the knowledge and skills acquired. (40)

Describe how the company's recognition and performance measurement processes support quality improvement; summarize trends in recognition. (20)

Describe how the company safeguards the health and safety of employees, ensures comfort and physical protection, and maintains a supportive work environment; summarize trends in employee well-being and morale. (20)

5.0 Quality Assurance of Products and Services (150 Points)

Describe how new or improved products and services are designed and introduced to meet or exceed customer requirements and how processes are designed to deliver according to the requirements. (30)

Describe how the processes which produce the products and services are controlled and how the company ensures that products and services meet design plans or specifications. (25)

Describe how products and services are continuously improved through optimization and improvement of processes. (25)

Describe how the company assesses the quality of products, processes, services, and quality practices. (15)

Describe documentation and other modes of knowlege preservation and transfer to support quality assurance, and improvement. (10)

Describe how the quality of support services and business processes is ensured, assessed, and improved. (25)

Describe how the quality of materials, components, and services furnished by other businesses is ensured, assessed, and improved. (20)

6.0 Quality Results (150 Points)

Summarize trends in quality improvement based upon key product and service quality measures derived from customer needs and expectations. (50)

Compare the company's current quality levels with industry averages, industry leaders, and world leaders, based upon the key product and service quality measures reported above. (35)

Summarize trends in quality improvement, based upon key measures of business processes, operations, and support services. (35)

Summarize trends in improvement in the quality of supplies and services furnished by other companies, based upon key measures of product and service quality. (30)

7.0 Customer Satisfaction (300 Points)

Describe how the company determines current and future customer expectations. (50)

Describe how the company provides effective management of its relationships with customers and how it ensures continuous improvement of customer relationship management. (30)

Describe the company's standards governing direct contact between employees and customers and how these standards are set and modified. (20)

Describe the company's commitment to customers in its explicit and implicit promises concerning its products and services. (20)

Describe how the company handles complaints, resolves them, and uses complaint information for quality improvement and prevention of recurrence of problems. (30)

Describe the company's methods for determining customer satisfaction, how this information is used in quality improvement, and how methods for determining customer satisfaction are improved. (50)

Briefly summarize trends in the company's customer satisfaction and in indicators of adverse customer response. (50)

Compare the company's customer satisfaction results and recognition with those of competitors that provide similar products and services. (50)

Source: "1991 Application Guidelines—Malcolm Baldrige National Quality Award," Gaithersburg, MD, National Institute of Standards and Technology, 1991.

FIGURE 19-9
Continued

Up to two awards may be issued annually for three types of firms: large manufacturers, large service firms, and small businesses. Winners of the Baldrige Award include IBM, Federal Express, Westinghouse Electric, Milliken, Xerox, and the Cadillac Division of General Motors. Out of 150 small business firms that have applied for the Baldrige Award, only three have been selected to receive the award. Winners receive a medal in a crystal case, plenty of publicity, and the right to advertise that they have won the award. Losers receive a feedback report telling them where their quality programs are lacking and how they can be improved.[27] Fig. 19-10 presents a framework illustrating how the seven major categories of the Baldrige Award interact to form a quality system yielding the goals of customer satisfaction, customer satisfaction relative to competitors, and market share.

The "Profile" on page 669 describes a new quality award that recognizes teams.

TOTAL QUALITY MANAGEMENT (TQM)

TQM is a management philosophy and strategy in which an organizational effort is utilized to continuously improve processes, dynamics, customer sensitivity,

Total Quality Management (TQM) A management philosophy and strategy in which an organizational effort is utilized to continually improve processes, dynamics, customer sensitivity, and output quality.

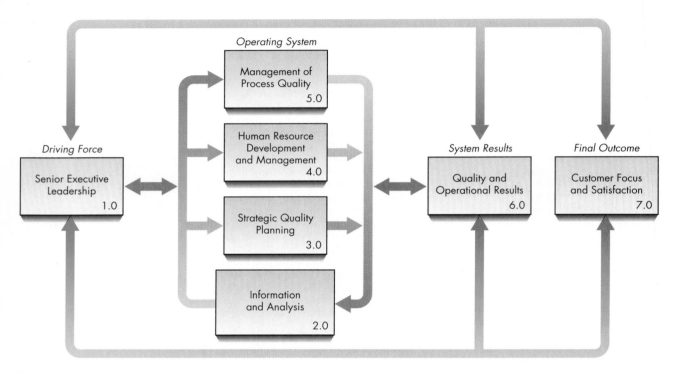

FIGURE 19-10 Interaction of the Baldrige Award Categories to Form a Quality System

and output quality. Increases in competitiveness and productivity occur as an organization's culture is changed through employee empowerment. Using a cost-effective system to deliver products or services, increased market share and reduced costs are achieved.[28] TQM programs have been implemented in a variety of manufacturing and service sector firms as well as in state and federal government agencies.[29] Interestingly, TQM began to blossom in the United States at about the same time as the Baldrige Award. Many managers indicate that TQM provides a framework for improving an organization in each of the seven Baldrige Award categories.[30]

In today's dynamic business environment, many organizations face the necessity to change. TQM is an effective vehicle for managing organizational change, because the entire organization's way of thinking and doing things is examined. Because TQM relies heavily on the effective management of human resources to change the organization's culture, structure, strategies, and reward systems, human resource professionals are positioned to play an important role in developing and implementing a TQM program.[31]

Characteristics of a TQM Program

As discussed earlier, a variety of approaches have been used to develop programs to improve product or service quality. Studies indicate that there is wide agreement on the essential characteristics, or factors, that are needed in developing a TQM program. Proponents of TQM argue that these factors apply to all organizations: those in manufacturing and service sectors, nonprofit organizations, academic institutions, and government agencies.[32] Following is a discussion of these characteristics:[33]

Profile

Richard Rosett
Dean of the College of Business and Director of the Quality Cup Program
Rochester Institute of Technology
Rochester, New York

NEW AWARD RECOGNIZES TEAMS

It is increasingly obvious that the worldwide quality movement is no passing fad. It is a powerful, fundamental change in the way organizations are managed. Because of it, patterns of international trade are shifting dramatically. Corporate giants that failed to make the change have been brought to the brink of disaster while new giants have risen to challenge them. U.S. industry, struggling to succeed against increasingly tough competition at home and abroad, asked business and engineering colleges to help them adapt to the change. Few colleges answered the call. In 1990, the Rochester Institute of Technology College of Business established itself as a leader among U.S. business schools by responding with Quality Management Education. QME committed the college to full integration of the concepts of Total Quality into its curriculum, the adoption of Total Quality as its own operating principle, and the education of Total Quality to the teaching process, itself.

In partnership with *USA Today,* the RIT College of Business created the Quality Cup Team Competition to recognize and promote Total Quality in U.S. business, industry, government, and not-for-profit organizations. The award honors teams that achieve outstanding results through the practical application of quality principles. Our greatest hope for the Quality Cup is that among the readers of *USA Today,* there are some who read about accomplishments of Quality Cup winners and say to themselves, "I have people working for me who could do things like that, if only I were to help them learn how to do them and then let them."

In the five years since launching the Quality Cup, our college has built a data base of fifteen hundred nominations containing unique and invaluable data. These detail the successful application of Total Quality to a wide range of problems. At the heavy industry end of the spectrum, a team of five hard hats reduced the rejection rate of steel shipped to Detroit from 5 percent to 2 percent and saved 7,800 steel workers' jobs. At the other end, a team of doctors and nurses at a military hospital were able, at reduced cost, to eliminate almost all disturbing and disruptive discontinuities of care for pediatric cancer patients. Cases like these are a rich source of material for use in courses and research by our faculty.

---

1. *Top Management Leadership.* While quality improvement programs can begin anywhere within an organization, top management leadership is required if TQM is to endure in the firm. The chief executive officer and his or her senior management team must be obsessed with the goal of customer satisfaction. These leaders must also act as role models and send signals that TQM is important for the organization's success.

2. *An Intense Focus on Customer Satisfaction.* The essence of TQM is that the firm be customer driven. TQM's definition of "customer" includes internal as well as external customers. An employee in the shipping department may be the internal "customer" of an employee who completes assembly of a product, for example, just as the person who buys that product is the customer of everyone in the company.

3. *Accurate Measurement.* Using readily available statistical techniques to analyze critical variables in a firm's operations, problems can be traced to their roots and eliminated.

4. *Continuous Improvement of Products and Services.* TQM is not a static concept. By eliminating chronic problems, TQM opens the way for a wave of never-ending innovation.

5. *Benchmarking.* The practice of comparing the performance and practice of a firm with those of industry leaders is benchmarking. This technique has been helpful to top managers in developing TQM programs. Benchmarking provides a means for "keeping score," as the gap is closed between the firm's actual state and its desired state.

6. *New Work Relationships.* A central aspect of TQM is empowerment, through which management gives employees wide latitude in how they go about achieving the company's goals.

7. *A Supportive Culture.* Firms must develop two sets of values in order for TQM to be effective. One set of values is the development of a hard analytical approach that focuses on product and service improvements and ways to improve customer satisfaction. The other value set involves a behavioral approach focusing on human resource improvement. This behavioral approach consists of many of the organization behavior concepts discussed in this text and mentioned at the beginning of this chapter. Studies indicate that developing behavioral values is the more critical task in developing TQM and the more difficult to achieve.[34] TQM is effective when every member of an organization understands the objectives and is empowered to assume additional responsibilities in solving quality related problems. As illustrated in Fig. 19-11, the preceding characteristics for developing TQM can be combined to describe a continuous model of TQM.

TQM Implementation Strategies

The five step procedure described in Fig. 19-12 is a summary of a variety of TQM implementation strategies.[35]

Following is a description of these five implementation steps.

1. *Determining What Quality Is.* While a definition for quality in TQM is meeting or exceeding customer expectations, organizations should express quality in terms of a specific goal. For example, Motorola defines its qual-

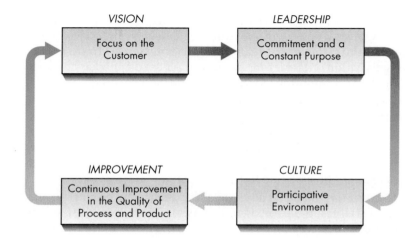

FIGURE 19-11

A Continuous Model of TQM

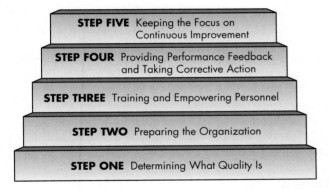

STEP FIVE Keeping the Focus on Continuous Improvement

STEP FOUR Providing Performance Feedback and Taking Corrective Action

STEP THREE Training and Empowering Personnel

STEP TWO Preparing the Organization

STEP ONE Determining What Quality Is

Figure 19-12   TQM Implementation Strategies

Source: Adapted from Charles N. Weaver, *Total Quality Management: A Step-by-Step Guide to Implementation,* Milwaukee, WI, ASQC Quality Press, 1991, pp. 48-54; Kim Cameron, "In What Ways Do Organizations Implement Total Quality Management," *Academy of Management Best Paper Proceedings,* Las Vegas, NV, August 1992; James A. F. Stoner, "What Happens When Organizations Implement Total Quality Management?" *Academy of Management Best Paper Proceedings,* Las Vegas, NV, August 1992.

ity goal as "six sigma." This means that Motorola managers and employees believe they can meet customers' expectations with only 3.4 defects per million opportunities or have production that is 99.99996 defect free. As a comparison, American Airlines has achieved a 3.5 sigma performance in their baggage handling operations.[36]

2. *Preparing the Organization.* Top management's strategy for implementing TQM must be communicated throughout the organization. Ideas that are communicated involve: (a) getting everyone in the organization to realize that quality is not the exclusive domain of the quality control department, but that everyone in the entire organization is responsible for quality, (b) determining how prepared individuals are to accept TQM, (c) identifying key people who can help communicate and sell TQM ideas to others and then motivate these people to accomplish TQM goals.

3. *Training and Empowering Personnel.* Usually, two types of training are provided to employees in a TQM program. One is statistical training used to measure performance, identify problem areas, and eliminate the causes. The second is problem-solving training designed to address issues that are best handled with a nonquantitative approach. These types of problem-solving techniques are discussed in Chap. 3.

   Regarding the empowerment of employees, new work relationships reflecting trust and teamwork need to be developed.

4. *Providing Performance Feedback and Taking Corrective Action.* Performance feedback systems must be installed on every aspect of the product or service generation process. From suppliers to final customers, feedback on quality must be continuously received and acted upon. It is common for firms using TQM to specify that their suppliers install TQM as a means of qualifying for orders. In many instances a firm using TQM will actually audit and help organize the quality systems used by suppliers.[37]

   Because the focus of TQM is on satisfying the customer, substantial customer feedback systems must be installed to permit the customer ease in reporting both good and bad quality. For example, General Electric has an "800" telephone number that is used to collect information on the problems customers are having. Many service firms, such as hotels and restaurants, place customer comment cards near places of service deliverance allowing customers to comment on various aspects of the service quality.[38]

5. *Keeping the Focus on Continuous Improvement.* As stated earlier, TQM is not a static concept. In some situations, management believes that no further changes are needed.[39] This step ensures that everyone in the organization continues to work toward eliminating problems.

TQM Implementation Problems

Although TQM concepts offer a new and enlightened approach for improving product and service quality, research studies indicate that implementation problems have hindered the effectiveness of many TQM programs. For example, in a study involving 950 major manufacturing and service sector firms that were using TQM, thirty-five percent of the respondents reported serious implementation problems.[40] Furthermore, in another study that surveyed division managers and vice presidents from seventy of the Fortune 500 industrial and service firms that were using TQM, thirty-six (51 percent) of the responding managers indicated serious implementation problems.[41] Following is a listing of factors that have hindered the implementation of TQM programs. These factors were developed from the participants included in the two preceding studies.

- *Communication*
    Problems included a lack of good communication.
    More top-down versus bottom-up communication.
    Concepts not explained to hourly employees.
    Lack of delegation to hourly employees.
    Customer satisfaction never explained.

- *Speed of Implementation*
    Proceeding too fast
        Attempted installation of TQM programs in all areas of the company at once.
        Aspects of the program could not be successfully coordinated or consistently applied because of rapid implementation.
    Proceeding too slow
        Takes forever to schedule and conduct training sessions.
        Top management indicates the lack of sense of urgency.

- *Structural Problems*
    Organization not structured to facilitate the TQM process.
    Engineering tries to dominate the organization.
    Manufacturing tries to dominate the organization.

- *Planning*
    Lack of good planning and philosophy.
    Crisis management style (reactive versus proactive) used.

- *Attitudes*
    Certain divisions are protective of their turf.
    Other division managers are not committed to TQM.
    Middle managers and supervisors do not support TQM.

"Good-old-boy" networks hinder the TQM process.
Competitiveness between departments and divisions drives out cooperation.

- *Rewards*

  Lack of emphasis on personal incentives.
  Employees have asked, "What's in it for me?"

- *Training*

  Employees and supervisors at lower levels are not properly trained.
  Overemphasis on statistical/quantitative methods and not enough on
  process dimensions of work activities.

Implications for Managers

Managers may be allocating too little time in preparing their organizations to
utilize TQM concepts. Reports on the successful implementation of TQM programs indicate that the implementation process often takes from four to six
years, and that this period is often fraught with struggles and setbacks.[42]

For a TQM program to be successfully implemented, top management must
understand the need for a program, the tools required for implementation, and
the specific barriers to success. Top managers should realize that the introduction of a TQM program is a major organizational undertaking and requires
a period of attitudinal changes, if it is to become an integral part of organizational functioning and culture. Effective training is an important aspect of
effectively implementing TQM. Members of the organization should receive
an accurate picture of the demands and limitations inherent within TQM approaches.[43]

Total quality management may well have a positive impact on U.S. firms
and institutions in the future. However, this possibility can be changed because
of the implementation methods that are used in TQM efforts. Scholars and practitioners of organization behavior have a role to play in the TQM movement,
because the knowledge of organization behavior concepts is so critical to the initiation, implementation, and success of TQM. The "OB in Practice" on page 674
describes implementation problems associated with TQM.

WHAT IS INNOVATION?

As discussed in Chap. 18, two major challenges that face organizations are how
to successfully adapt to change and how to implement change in an environment that is not conducive to our well-being and effectiveness. The study of
innovation offers approaches and strategies to meet the challenge of how to
bring about change in work environments.

Innovation is defined as the adoption of an idea or behavior that is new to
the adopting organization. Innovation does not occur when a new idea is generated, but rather when that new idea is put into use. An innovation is not considered in use when the decision for its adoption is made, but rather when its
actual utilization by organizational members has begun. Organizations adopt
innovations in order to maintain or enhance their performance. An innovation
cannot influence performance until it has been actually used.[44] Innovation is
also defined in terms of its newness to the adopting organization rather than
the first use ever in an organization.[45] Innovation is also considered in the con-

**Innovation The
adoption of an idea or
behavior that is new
to the adopting
organization.**

OB in Practice

Implementation Problems Associated with TQM Programs

In a $2 million study sponsored by the American Quality Foundation, Ernest & Young surveyed 584 companies in the United States, Canada, Germany, and Japan to determine the results of TQM programs. The study involved firms in automobile manufacturing, computer manufacturing, hospitals, and banking and revealed that many U.S. companies are failing in their attempts to achieve superior product quality through TQM. Some of the reported implementation problems are:

- Rather than focusing on a small number of decisive changes, most programs are too vague and unspecific. At Johnson & Johnson, at first its TQM was based on *doing things right the first time.* Then, after disappointing results, it focused on three explicit goals: boosting customer satisfaction, reducing product introduction time, and cutting costs. Then it told its 166 operating divisions to apply TQM in a way that made sense to them. Broad training programs were replaced by classes on narrow topics. Now Johnson & Johnson is doing fewer things better.

- Many try to do too many things at once. Most firms cannot implement 9,000 new practices simultaneously.

- Not enough employees are involved in idea–suggestion programs. Computer companies involve 12 percent and automakers, which rates the highest in this area, involved only 28 percent.

- Customers are not involved in identifying and designing new products. Customers were involved in 19 percent of banks and 26 percent of hospitals, which was the highest rated.

- Quality performance measures such as defect rates and customer satisfaction were not used to determine pay for senior managers.

- Japanese, German, and Canadian companies rate much better than U.S. companies in involving employees and customers in TQM. For example, 73 percent of computer makers in Japan and 60 percent in Germany involve customers, and 78 percent of Japanese automakers have successful employee suggestion programs.

- TQM programs are isolated from day-to-day operations and treated as something special. TQM tends to be seen as off to itself with 10,000 activities that are apart from all other operations.

Most successful programs target their TQM programs more tightly at specific projects or tactics. Additionally, they include strong personal involvement by senior executives, company-wide awareness of strategic plans and goals, and an emphasis on simplifying processes.

Most of the 584 companies in the study projected a more positive picture of the future of TQM. Most companies projected vast improvements in their quality practices in three years. But Mr. Hammond of the American Quality Foundation says that this will only get U.S. companies to the levels that companies in competing countries have already attained. "They're so far ahead of us that quality is no longer a competitive issue, now we've got to get into it to survive."

Source: Adapted from "Quality Programs Show Shoddy Results," *The Wall Street Journal,* May 14, 1992, B1; "Total Quality Is Termed Only Partial Success," *The Wall Street Journal,* October 1, 1992.

text of organizational change. As an organization's environment changes, the organization must adapt to the new conditions. All innovation is change in organizational terms, but not all change is innovation. For example, changing the work day schedule in a factory during the summer because of the heat does not constitute innovation. Neither would change involving routine actions (the laying-off of hotel staff in the winter when bookings fall) be considered as innovation. Also, certain organizational changes occur as routine responses to changes in external or internal environmental conditions, such as hiring new employees on the retirement of others, or promotions based strictly on length of service. Such changes would not be considered as innovation.[46]

Rosenfeld and Servo argue that creativity and innovation are *not* synonymous. Creativity refers to the generation of novel ideas while innovation is the adoption and use of ideas.[47] According to Rosenfeld and Servo:[48]

> Creativity is the starting point for any innovation: in many cases, a solitary process, conjuring up the image of an eccentric scientist buried under mounds of paper. Innovation is the hard work that follows idea conceptions and usually involves the labor of many people with varied, yet complementary skills. The challenge is to transform creative ideas into tangible products or processes that will improve customer services, cut costs and/or generate new earnings for an organization.

Rosenfeld and Servo state that the following equation describes the relationship between creativity and innovation.[49]

Innovation = Conception (creativity) + Invention + Exploitation.

In this context, "conception" refers to an idea that is novel with respect to some frame of reference (individual, departmental, organizational, or all accumulated knowledge); the word "invention" applies to any novel idea that is transformed into reality; and the word "exploitation" refers to the profitability resulting from the invention.[50]

In this section we examine the types of innovation, factors that affect the adoption of an innovation; as well as how to facilitate innovation within an organizational setting.

Types of Innovation

Several typologies of innovation appear in literature.[51] For example, one typology focuses on high-risk versus low-risk innovations while another considers radical versus incremental innovation.[52] For this section, we have selected Fabiborz Damanpour's model of technological, administrative, and ancillary innovation because it describes the differences in the nature of innovation.[53]

Technological innovations are those innovations that bring change to organizations by introducing changes in technology, such as a tool, technique, physical equipment, or system by which employees or the organization extend their capabilities. Technological innovations occur as a result of the use of a new tool, technique, device, or system. They produce changes in products or services, or in the way that those products are produced or services rendered. Examples of technological innovations for libraries include: computer-based circulation control systems, computer output microfilm catalog, video tape and video cassette devices, and automated purchasing systems.[54]

Administrative innovations change an organization's structure or its administrative processes. Examples include the structuring of tasks as described in the horizontal corporation's organizational design pattern illustrated in Chap. 16, job rotation, flextime, and zero-based budgeting.[55]

Ancillary innovations are contingent upon the joint efforts of an organization and some of its clients. This contrasts to technological and administrative innovations that are internal innovations and are most closely under the control of an organization's management. The successful adoption of an ancillary innovation depends on factors, such as customer participation, that are outside of the organization's boundary, and are not fully controllable by the organization's management. Examples include career development programs, adult continuing education programs, and community service programs of a library.[56]

Factors Affecting the Adoption of Innovations

Factors at various levels: individual, group, organizational, and environmental have been reported to influence the adoption of innovations.

Research on individual level factors on the adoption of innovations has focused on individual motivation, situational influences, individual differences, and the role of individuals. The likelihood of an individual introducing an innovation while in a work role is a function of the following four general factors.[57]

- The individual's perception about the need for change to occur in the work role.
- The individual's perception that change can be successfully implemented in the work role.
- The individual's perception that a positive outcome will result from the introduction of change.
- The individual's ability to generate new and useful ideas. This ability may include an awareness of an already existing procedure, process, or object that can be brought into the specific work setting or it may include knowledge that is sufficient to create a procedure, process, or object in those cases in which no appropriate alternative exists.

Individual differences that are associated with innovation are: the desire for autonomy, a high tolerance of ambiguity, a high degree of social independence, and a propensity for risk-taking.[58]

Situational influences that tend to be associated with innovation are: the freedom of choice on how to spend one's time, the need for participative and collaborative leadership styles, feedback and recognition from supervisors, and an organic organizational structure or a matrix organizational design pattern that provides the individual with the freedom to be innovative.[59]

Some researchers have noted that innovative individuals have a tendency toward being creative and have used Amabile's psychological model of creativity to describe how innovations are adopted at an individual level (Amabile's model is discussed more fully in Chap. 18). Although many researchers agree that innovative individuals tend to be creative, those researchers argue that there is a difference between creativity and innovation. As noted earlier, creativity is the development of an idea while innovation is the commercial adoption of an idea.[60]

Interestingly, Goldsmith argued that adaption is "doing things better" while innovation is "doing things differently."[61] Kirton has developed an instrument to measure people's position along an adaption–innovation dimension and suggests that the difference between adaptors and innovators is one of style, not level of creativity and that both adaptors and innovators may be equally creative.[62]

Groups play an important role in the innovation process within organizations. An innovation may be invented by an R&D team, adopted by a management group, and then implemented by a work group. Ideas that are new to the group may be *emergent* (developed entirely by the group), *imported* (adopted and/or adapted by the group from established practices elsewhere), or *imposed* (imposed upon the group by senior management).

Factors affecting group level innovation include:

1. A collaborative leadership style.
2. A high level of discretion involving supportive consultations with supervisors (freedom of choice of how to spend one's time has not been found to facilitate group innovations).
3. Group cohesiveness (cohesiveness facilitates innovation because it increases feelings of self-actualization and psychological safety).
4. Group longevity (research indicates that innovation is facilitated more in relatively short-lived groups).
5. Group composition (groups with members from different occupational fields or functions are more innovative than those having similar backgrounds).
6. The presence of individuals who will play a devil's advocate role (this role is discussed in Chap. 5).
7. The structure of the group (organic groups that have an integrative, team-based approach to tasks, blurred boundaries of authority and influence, and a professional commitment tend to facilitate innovation).

Although group cohesiveness has been found to positively facilitate innovation, a major inhibitor of innovation is groupthink (a phenomenon discussed in Chap. 5).[63]

A wide range of *organizational factors* have been studied as possible antecedents of innovation and include size, structure, resources, knowledge of innovation, age, strategy, and culture. The "OB in Practice" on page 678 describes what top management at Hewlett-Packard has done to create and maintain innovation.

Research findings regarding the relationship between *organizational size* and innovation have been mixed. Kimberly and Evanisko reported that the larger the hospital, the more innovations were adopted.[64] Utterback concluded in his review of innovation in one industry that firm size did not influence the speed of adoption of innovations.[65] In studying firm size and how it relates to innovative activity, a number of researchers have investigated the "Schumpeterian hypothesis." This hypothesis is based on Schumpeter's argument that economic growth occurs through a process of "creative destruction" where the old industrial structure—its process, or its organization—is continually changed by "new" innovative industrial activity. According to Schumpeter, large firm size is essential to the success of such innovative activity. Larger firms can provide economies of scale in production and innovation that make available sufficient resources necessary for successful completion of this process.[66]

Mansfield and his associates investigated firm size and innovation using the measures of inputs (R&D money and personnel) and outputs (number of patents) and reported that no significant evidence existed to indicate that R&D intensity, relative to firm size, increased beyond medium-sized firms and that "inven-

OB in Practice

Innovation at Hewlett-Packard

Lewis Platt, Chairman and CEO of Hewlett-Packard, describes what top management at H-P has done to create and maintain innovation.

- Top management must anticipate. Whatever made you successful in the past will not in the future.
- The fear of complacency should keep top managers awake at night.
- Senior management's role is *not* to tell business units what opportunity to take. Instead, our role is to create the environment that encourages business managers to take risks and create new growth opportunities. A strong sense of entrepreneurship must be cultivated in our business managers. In other words, vision at H-P isn't a straitjacket that constrains our managers, but rather a view of the many opportunities ahead.
- Senior management must create an environment in which technological developments are aligned with customer needs.
- Senior management must realize that strategic alliances are critical. It is impossible for a firm to do everything themselves.

Source: Adapted from John Sheridan, "Lew Platt: Creating a Culture for Innovation," *Industry Week,* December 16, 1994, pp. 26–30.

---

tive output" did not match measured input.[67] Two overviews of research regarding firm size and innovation have been reported. One overview surveyed these studies and concluded that the statistical evidence supporting Schumpeter's hypothesis is, in general, "wanting."[68] The other overview suggested that the most favorable industrial environment for rapid technological innovation would be to have a majority of medium-sized firms bounded on one side by a "horde" of small technology-oriented firms "bubbling over with bright new ideas" and on the other by a few larger companies with the resources to undertake "exceptionally ambitious" developments.[69]

Structural variables have received the most attention of any in the organizational innovation literature. Three which are frequently examined are centralization, formalization, and complexity. Centralization refers to the extent to which decision making is concentrated with the organization's top management. Complexity is the amount of occupational specialization and task differentiation in the organization. Research findings indicate that high centralization inhibits initiation of innovation, because it restricts channels of communication;[70] formalization inhibits innovation, because rules and procedures prohibit employees from seeking new sources of information;[71] and complexity is positively related to innovation initiation because a diversity in occupational backgrounds can facilitate an awareness or knowledge of innovations.[72]

The availability of *slack resources* have been examined with respect to innovation. Slack resources are the degree to which uncommitted resources are available to the organization. Rogers argues that slack resources are positively related to innovation.[73] However, an interesting argument states that there is an inverse link between slack resources and innovative activities. This view suggests that low-slack organizations intensify their activities as a form of corrective action, and that high-slack firms become complacent and engage in minimal innovative activities—success breeds failure.[74] When resources are in the form of "sunk costs," there is a negative relationship between resources in innovation because managers have the mindset "too much invested to quit."[75]

From the perspective *knowledge of innovation,* Tushman argues that the key personnel of some organizations have the attributes of professionalism and cosmopolitanism that enables them to identify potentially useful innovations in the environment.[76]

Research findings regarding the relationship between *organizational age* and innovativeness is mixed. Kimberly and Evanisko reported that older hospitals adopt innovations quicker than do younger hospitals as a way of insuring their status in the community. However, two research studies argue that there is a negative relationship between organizational age and innovativeness.[77]

Although *strategy* is an important determinant of the level and type of innovation, researchers consistently report that there is no one ideal strategy for innovation.[78]

Presently, *organizational culture* is an area of speculation in the innovation literature. Empirical studies are almost nonexistent.[79] Conceptually, Kanter argues that the "shared meanings" aspect of organizational culture may either facilitate or inhibit innovation.[80] Morgan argues that innovative activities may necessitate a change in the organization's culture.[81]

Environmental factors also have been found to be the antecedents of organizational innovation. Researchers report that competition is a prime source of innovation,[82] and that a high degree of environmental turbulence stimulates innovation by making managers more aware of "cues" to innovate.[83]

How to Facilitate Innovation in Organizational Settings

The facilitation of innovations within an organizational setting can be accomplished through the use of idea champions and new venture teams.

IDEA CHAMPIONS   While ideas may be generated, they must also be accepted and then implemented within the organization. The role of an idea champion is to carry new ideas forward for acceptance and implementation. The idea champion sees the need of an innovative idea and champions a productive change within the organization.[84] Because new ideas are often rejected by management, personal energy and effort are required to successfully promote a new idea. Researchers indicate that successfully championing an idea requires a number of roles depicted in Fig. 19-13.

A single person may play two or more of these roles but most innovations involve different people, each adopting one role. The *inventor* develops the new idea and understands its value but does not have the ability or the interest to promote it for acceptance within the organization. The *champion* believes in the idea, examines the realities of organizational costs and benefits, obtains political and financial support, and overcomes obstacles. The *sponsor* is a high-level manager who approves the idea, provides protection, and removes organizational barriers. The *critic* acts as a devil's advocate for the champion's enthusiasm by looking for shortcomings and defining criteria that the idea must pass. The critic prevents people in the other roles from adopting a bad idea.[85]

FIGURE 19-13
The Roles of Idea
Champions

INVENTOR
- Develops the new idea and understands its value.
- Does not have the ability or interest to promote the idea for acceptance within the organization.

CHAMPION
- Believes in the idea.
- Examines the realities of organizational costs and benefits.
- Obtains political and financial support.
- Overcomes obstacles.

SPONSOR
- High-level manager who approves the idea.
- Provides protection and removes organizational barriers.

CRITIC
- Acts as devil's advocate.
- Looks for shortcomings.
- Defines criteria that the idea must pass.

Source: Adapted from R. A. Burgelman and L. R. Sayles, *Inside Corporate Innovation,* New York, Free Press, 1986; R. R. Nelson and S. G. Winter, *An Evolutionary Theory of Economic Change,* Cambridge, MA, Harvard University Press, 1982; A. H. Van de Ven, H. L. Angle, and Mabel S. Poole, *Research in the Management of Innovation,* Cambridge, MA, Ballinger/Harper & Row, 1989.

NEW VENTURE TEAMS   A new venture team is a unit that is separate from the rest of the organization and is responsible for developing and initiating a major innovation.[86] These teams are typically small, loosely structured and organic—similar to the characteristics of a creative organization described in Fig. 19-10. In the new venture team concept, employees no longer report through the normal organizational structure, but become a separate department as illustrated in Fig. 19-14. In large firms, a new venture team frees employees from the constraints of the large corporation.

Some firms use a variation of venture teams, called skunkworks, in which small, informal, and sometimes unauthorized groups of employees create innovations. If the venture is successful, group members are rewarded and encouraged to manage the new business.[87] The "OB in Practice" opposite describes how Reynolds Metals used innovative activities to outmaneuver steelmakers.

FIGURE 19-14
Organization Structure
with a New Venture
Team

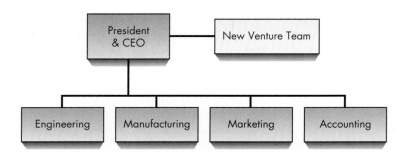

Agility and Innovation Help Reynolds Metals Outmaneuver Steelmakers

From foil to beverage cans to truck trailers to automobiles—Reynolds Metals, as well as other aluminum producers, now produce products that were once dominated by Bethlehem and other steel producers. Reynolds pioneered many aluminum products: grain bins, windows, boat hulls, appliance parts, semitrailers, and automobile frames.

Bethlehem, bureaucratic and slow-moving, lost control of its costs as it clung to old practices. Bethlehem Steel inflated its prices, scoffed at marketing, and resisted change. Even today, Bethlehem has difficulty in taking decisive action. Reynolds, however, encouraged risk-taking, pushed marketing hard, ignored national boundaries, and slashed costs to keep its prices competitive. Today, Reynolds's agility, innovation moves, and aggressiveness dominate its culture.

While many foreign steelmakers were installing more efficient procedures to manufacture steel, Bethlehem waited twenty years to install these new methods. Reynolds, however, built state-of-the-art plants that reduced costs by 23 percent. Bethlehem also never viewed overseas markets as a place to make and sell fabricated products while Reynolds now gets 40 percent of its profit from abroad.

Reynolds's vice chairman Yale Brandt states that Reynolds had to change and be more innovative in order to compete against the steel producers. For example, when Reynolds considered entering the beverage can market, steel makers had a natural edge, because steel was cheaper than aluminum. Bethlehem, the market leader, produced a three-piece steel can that required soldering. Reynolds developed a new can-making technique that stretches the aluminum to make an inexpensive two-piece can. The process is five times faster than the three-piece process, and Reynolds, by using stronger, thinner alloys, uses 40 percent less metal per can. Also, unlike steel, the U.S. aluminum industry has held foreign competitors at bay by keeping itself more efficient.

Source: Adapted from Dana Afilbank, "David vs. Goliath: How Reynolds Outmaneuvered Giant Bethlehem," *The Wall Street Journal*, July 1, 1992, Al, A6.

CONCLUSIONS AND APPLICATIONS

- The meaning of quality depends on an individual's position in the organization. Product designers, customers, manufacturers, and distributors all have certain perceptions regarding quality. Goods and services are produced to satisfy customers' needs. However, these needs must be translated into detailed product processes, and service specifications.

- Providing customers with quality products has been an important task for firms throughout history. The earlier pioneers of scientific management separated inspection tasks from production tasks. Quality control departments were established to monitor quality. The emphasis on quality has shifted from a technical approach centered around quality control personnel to a managerial philosophy that quality is the responsibility of everyone in the organization.

- Top management must have a knowledge and understanding of how the organizational behavior concepts of decision making, motivation, leadership, organizational design, organizational culture, conflict resolution, and organizational change are related to quality management.

- Several different philosophies exist on how to best design and implement quality improvement programs. Successful programs use a composite approach, understanding and drawing from the different philosophies. The successful programs involve all levels of the organization in selecting, implementing, and committing to a philosophy that becomes a central part of the organization's culture.

- Quality circles were first introduced in Japan and later implemented in the United States. The basic concept behind quality circles is that employees know best the problems in production, because they face them every day. Quality circles are composed of natural work groups and range from a few employees to over a dozen with an average of nine employees. Membership is voluntary and there are no direct cash incentives paid for the improvements developed by the group. A trained facilitator usually leads the quality circle. Quality circles fail because of friction developing within the group, running out of ideas, failing to reach savings goals for projects, pressuring management to provide financial rewards for improvements suggested by the group, developing burnout and employee cynicism.

- Quality programs have also been implemented in service sector firms. Measuring the quality of services is difficult because of the nature of a service. Two approaches have been used in improving the quality of services. The first involves the use of standard procedures and equipment. Training is intensive with continuous follow-up checks. The second approach involves creating an atmosphere that seeks and fulfills customer preferences.

- The purpose of the Malcolm Baldrige National Quality Award is a means for the Department of Commerce to recognize U.S. firms that attain preeminent quality leadership and to encourage other U.S. companies to improve their quality program. The Baldrige Award involves seven categories pertaining to the management of quality.

- Total Quality Management (TQM) is a managerial philosophy used to continuously improve processes, dynamics, customer sensitivity, and output quality. Increases in competitiveness and productivity occur as an organization's culture is changed through employee empowerment. Many organizations have utilized TQM programs for organizational change and as a framework for improving an organization in each of the seven Baldrige Award categories. TQM programs have been successfully implemented in both manufacturing and service firms. Because TQM relies heavily on the effective management of human resources to change the organization's culture, structure, strategies, and reward systems, human resource professionals are positioned to play an important role in developing and implementing a TQM program. Although TQM concepts offer a new and enlightened approach for improving product and service quality, research studies indicate that implementation problems have hindered the effectiveness of many TQM programs.

- Innovation is the adoption of an idea or behavior that is new to the adopting organization. Innovation does not occur when a new idea is generated, but when the idea is put into use.

- Creativity and innovation are not synonymous. Creativity refers to the generation of novel ideas, while innovation is the adoption and use of ideas.
- Technological innovations are those that introduce change in technology (tools, techniques, physical equipment, or systems). Administrative innovations change an organization's structure or its administrative processes. Ancillary innovations are the joint efforts of an organization and its clients.
- Individual, group, organizational level, and environmental factors affect the adoption of innovations.
- Idea champions and new venture teams are used to facilitate innovation in organizational settings.

REVIEW QUESTIONS

1. How is quality defined?
2. Describe how quality programs have evolved over time.
3. How are concepts from organization behavior related to the management of quality?
4. Describe the different philosophies advocated by Deming, Juran, and Crosby. How are they alike? How are they different?
5. What is the purpose of quality circles? How do they work?
6. How does the management of quality in service organizations differ from manufacturing firms?
7. What is the purpose of the Malcolm Baldrige National Quality Award? Name five categories used to select firms for the award. Name three recent winners.
8. Define total quality management (TQM). How does TQM differ from earlier quality assurance programs?
9. Explain the five steps used in implementing a TQM program.
10. Describe the factors that have hindered the implementation of TQM programs.
11. What is innovation?
12. Explain the difference between creativity and innovation.
13. Describe technological, administrative, and ancillary innovations.
14. Discuss how individual, group, organizational, and environmental factors affect innovation.
15. How do idea champions and new venture teams help facilitate innovations in organizational settings?

DISCUSSION QUESTIONS

1. Describe the five perspectives of quality identified by David Garvin. How are these perspectives related to Fig. 19-1?
2. Identify the synergies between total quality management (TQM) and concepts from organization behavior. Are there any conflicts?
3. Discuss the various definitions of quality used in this chapter. Can a single definition suffice? Explain.
4. In this chapter, "internal" and "external" customers were described. Explain this description and relate it to total quality management.
5. What factors, if any, make the management of quality more difficult in service sector firms than in manufacturing sector firms? What approaches have been developed to mitigate the effects of these differences?
6. Explain how total quality management can be an effective vehicle for managing organizational change.
7. Proponents of total quality management (TQM) programs argue that the seven factors needed to develop a TQM program apply to all organizations. Agree or disagree? Why?
8. The statement has been made that firms must develop two sets of values in order for total quality management to be effective. Identify these two values and explain which is the more difficult to achieve?
9. Studies indicate that the successful implementation of TQM programs have required a period of time. What is the length of this time period? What are the managerial implications for this length of time?

10. Explain the role that organization behavior scholars and practitioners can play in assisting implementation of a total quality management program.

11. All innovation is change in organizational terms but not all change is innovation. Explain.

12. Which type of innovation—technological, administrative, or ancillary—would be the most difficult to adopt? Why?

CASE STUDY

Total Quality Management at Spectrum Control

Spectrum Inc., headquartered in Erie, PA, was founded in 1968 by Thomas L. Venable, Glen L. Warnshuis, and John R. Lane, three engineers who had met at Erie Technological Products, Inc. In sixteen years, the company grew from a $300,000 start-up housed in an old hardware store to a solid, $22-million public company. Today, Spectrum has four manufacturing plants and some 1,500 customers, including the likes of IBM Corp. and Hewlett-Packard Co. For the past three years, it has reported after-tax returns of about 10 percent of sales.

In the early days, quality wasn't an issue. Venable, and Warnshuis designed and built Spectrum's sophisticated filters, while Lane marketed them. "There wasn't any point in making them wrong," Venable says with a chuckle. But, as the company began to prosper and grow, that kind of hands-on responsibility fell by the wayside.

Like most manufacturers—and like businesses—Spectrum began to operate on the philosophy of acceptable-quality levels, or AQLs. The company regularly checked a sample of the product, then shipped the whole batch, so long as the number of bad units fell within accepted limits. If there were too many bad ones, the lot was rejected, or subjected to 100 percent inspection, an expensive process.

Then, slowly Spectrum's marketplace began to change. A Japanese company, Murata Manufacturing Co., purchased Erie Technological Products (now Murata Erie North America Inc.), with which Spectrum competed, and raised the specter of Japanese-style quality. Several of Spectrum's customers began to make noises about quality as well. "About two or three years ago," says Venable, "Hewlett-Packard said that they were going to switch to the idea of 'zero defects'—no defects in any inbound materials." Soon IBM was joining the chorus—and implying, Venable remembers, that a business hoping to remain an IBM supplier better begin thinking seriously about quality.

Venable and other Spectrum managers began to assay likely strategies for attacking the newly discovered issue. They took a look at some Japanese quality techniques. . . . They bought forty copies of *Quality Is Free* by management consultant Phillip Crosby, a book that IBM had been pushing, and passed them out. They also bought and studied some videotapes featuring W. Edwards Deming, the dean emeritus of statistical control of quality.

Essentially, Crosby suggests that precise requirements be set for every business task, and that those standards be met each and every time. If problems occur, in either performance or product, permanent solutions must be found as soon as possible; temporary fixes won't do.

Crosby's evangelical approach paid off in at least one major way: It destroyed the shibboleth of AQLs. "I think the principal benefit," Venable says, "was that it convinced us that, given a structure, it was possible to work toward zero defects, toward error-free performance."

Venable's plan was to use Crosby's razzmatazz and routines to get things moving, then rely increasingly on Deming's techniques to control the process—modifying both, whenever it seemed necessary, with approaches of Spectrum's own design.

Some of the changes came easily, such as paying closer attention to customers' schedules. In the past, the company had often shipped its components too early, and the customers simply shipped them back. The cost of such errors, says Venable, was significant, particularly in the case of overseas deliveries—"$150 to $200 for transshipping, and $300 for paperwork." At the other end of the pipeline, Spectrum installed new order-entry checking systems, "so we've seen a tremendous improvement in our error rate there."

For the most part, though, the improvements came slowly. "Easy?" snorts one worker in the Electromagnetic Division. "It was like giving up smoking and drinking, plus going on a diet—all at the same time." Changing the habits and attitudes of Spectrum's workers was hard enough. But a thoroughgoing approach to quality involved the company's vendors and customers as well.

There was, for example, the matter of the bushings—small, threaded items used to connect glass-sealed filters to other devices. The bushings were manufactured by three screw-machine suppliers, inspected by Spectrum, sent to a plating vendor, and, once plated, inspected again. At that late date in the process, some 50 percent were rejected.

"After you'd gone through QES classes," says Electromagnetic Division unit manager David Weunski, "you were supposed to go back to your unit and think of things that had been giving you problems over the years. . . . This one, of course, leaped out at me."

The solution, however, did not. Only after endless hours of brainstorming and conferences with suppliers did Weunski hit on a strategy. During the initial inspection, he realized, Spectrum employed gauges that indicated only when the bushings exceeded the correct dimensions of the finished product; not until later, after another layer of metal had been added in plating, did other problems show up. So Weunski ordered $7,000 worth of new gauges, one set to measure the raw bushing and another to measure the plated one, and donated duplicate sets of gauges to his vendors. "Before," he says, "we would probably have put the burden of buying the gauges on them. Now, the attitude is much more cooperative." And the early results, he adds, are dramatic. "When all of the gauges are in place, we could be talking about a *doubling* of productivity."

Then there was the matter of Department Number Nine at the Electromagnetic Division, which produces, among other things, shielded windows. These windows—artfully crafted panels of dark, curved glass that are fastened to the front of a computer screen—absorb the six or seven watts of radiated energy produced by some computer terminals, and thus prevent anyone from "reading" the screen's information at a distance. But they are inordinately difficult to manufacture. Composed of layers of glass, wire screening, and laminating materials, they tend to delaminate when exposed to temperature extremes. "At worst, rejects were running as high as 15 percent," says unit manager Cy Ley.

Although Number Nine already had been wrestling with the issue, Spectrum's quality initiative pushed it to take some radical steps, such as changing vendors. For instance, Homalite Inc., of Wilmington, Del., had once provided the parts for the plastic laminate, but had lost the contract to another supplier; then, when quality became a top concern, it got it back. "Basically," says Homalite general manager Rod J. Field, "we lost them on price, but won them back with quality. They sent a four- or five-man team down to review what we were doing here—and then we were back in business."

Department Number Nine supervisors have also become aggressively receptive to suggestions from line personnel. "No one is really an expert except the person who's out there building that window," Ley concedes. "One of their suggestions actually increased our productivity by something like 50 percent."

The net effect: a scant .08 percent reject rate on the newest line of windows. "Because of the dramatic improvement," observes Venable, "we were actually able to reduce our pricing on this product line."

Overall, there a few people, processes, or products that haven't in some way been affected by Spectrum's quality crusade. There is now a vendor-selection committee, for example, and the number of active vendors has been trimmed by 8 percent. The company is also more demanding of customers. When it felt that one client's specifications for a filter used in the B-1 bomber were unattainable, it said so, and lost the work, but promptly got it back when the competitor that got the job discovered (and proved) that the unit couldn't be built as designed. Not even the company's outside directors have escaped the reeducation process: Venable recently asked several of them to attend Crosby's Quality College.

Tom Venable, for his part, is happy with the results, despite the difficulties. "In our first quarter of Quality Response Process operation," says Venable, "we're seen a 75 percent reduction in sales returns and allowances; if you annualize that, you're looking at savings of something like $767,000." Even more telling is Spectrum's profit-sharing balance. Believing that employees should have a fiscal, as well as a psychological, incentive to get involved in the program, Venable earmarked about half of the saving realized for the company's profit-sharing plan. Last year, management had put $150,000 into the program, but, high on quality, had budgeted $525,000 this year. Now, observed Venable, "We have the feeling that it's going to be quite a bit higher—more like $1 million-plus."

CASE STUDY QUESTIONS

1. Why did Spectrum undertake a total quality management (TQM) program?
2. Describe the major elements of Spectrum's TQM program. Are these elements similar to those described in Fig. 19-12?
3. Explain the role that employee training and education played in Spectrum's TQM program. How important is employee training and education in TQM?
4. What major benefits has Spectrum derived from its TQM program?

Source: Craig R. Waters, "Quality Begins at Home," *Inc.* magazine, August 1985, pp. 68–71. Adapted with permission, *Inc.* magazine, August 1985. Copyright 1985 by Goldhirsh Group, Inc., 38 Commercial Wharf, Boston, MA 02110.

EXPERIENTIAL EXERCISE 1

Evaluating Quality Perspectives

Task

The first phase of this exercise involves an individual evaluation of quality perspectives. Later, your instructor will organize the class into groups. Each group is first to reach an agreement regarding the evaluation and then select a spokesperson to present and explain the group's conclusions to the class.

Exercise

The five perspectives of quality described in Fig. 19-1 are listed opposite. Visit a fast-food outlet such as Wendy's, Burger King, or McDonald's, and rate each of these perspectives as either strong, average, or weak. Explain the rationale for your rating.

Business Evaluated: _____

Quality Perspectives	Rating (strong, average, weak)	Reason for the rating
Innate superiority		
Degree of an attribute		
User satisfaction		
Conformance to specifications		
Value delivered		

EXPERIENTIAL EXERCISE 2

Counting the Defects

Visual inspections are an important part of many quality assurance programs. However, research indicates that in conducting such activities, inspectors may not know what to look for, or not have the physical or psychological makeup required for the job. The following exercise involves a visual activity. Your instructor has the correct answer.

Exercise

During the Second World War, soldiers used to bet a new recruit $50 that he could not count all the e's on the back of a pack of a certain brand of cigarettes in one reading. The following is an approximate rendition of what the back of the 1940s package stated. Try it yourself for about 15 seconds.

Source: Jack R. Meredith, *The Management of Operations: A Conceptual Emphasis,* 4th ed., New York, John Wiley & Sons, 1992, p. 610. Copyright © 1992 John Wiley & Sons. Reprinted by permission of John Wiley & Sons.

"Don't look for coupons or premiums in this pack. The cost of the tobaccos blended in **HORSE** cigarettes prohibits the use of them."

Take It to the Net You can find this chapter's World Wide Web exercise at:
http://www.prenhall.com/carrell

ENDNOTES

CHAPTER 1

1 James R. Houghton, "Leadership's Challenge: The New Agenda for the 90s," *Conference Executive Summary* (September/October 1992), 8–9.

2 Thomas J. Peters and Robert Waterman, *In Search of Excellence* (New York: Alfred Knopf, 1989).

3 Mark R. Goldston, *The Turnaround Prescription* (New York: The Free Press, 1992).

4 James M. Kouzes and Barry Z. Posner, *The Leadership Challenge* (San Francisco: Jossey-Bass, 1987).

5 Richard S. Wellins, William C. Byham, Jeanne M. Wilson, *Empowered Teams* (San Francisco: Jossey-Bass, 1991).

6 Frederick W. Taylor, *Scientific Management* (New York: Harper Brothers, 1947), 45–46.

7 Elton Mayo and F. J. Roethlisberger, *Management and the Worker* (Cambridge, MA: Harvard University Press, 1939) and for an alternative view of the Hawthorne research see H. M. Parsons, "What Happened at Hawthorne?" *Science* (March 8, 1974), 922–32.

8 Joseph B. White, "GM is Overhauling Corporate Culture in an Effort to Regain Competitiveness, *Wall Street Journal* (January 13, 1993), A1, A3.

9 Lloyd Dobyns, "Ed Deming Wants Big Changes and He Wants Them Fast," *The Smithsonian* 21, no. 5 (August 1990), 74–82.

10 Henri Fayol, *Industrial and General Administration* (Paris: Dunod, 1916).

11 The Hudson Institute, *Workforce 2,000: Work and Workers for the 21st Century* (Washington, D.C.: U.S. Department of Labor, 1987).

12 "Diversity Training Becomes Business as Usual," *The Long Beach Press-Telegram* (November 8, 1992), 61.

13 Diane Filipouski, "How Federal Express Excels at Service," *Personnel Journal* (February 1992), 40–46.

14 Cari M. Dominquey, "The Glass Ceiling and Workforce 2,000," *Labor Law Journal* (1991), 715–17.

15 Patricia A. Galagan, "Beyond Hierarchy: The Search for High Performance," *Teaching & Development* (August 1992), 21–25.

16 Thomas A. Stewart, "GE Keeps Those Ideas Coming," *Fortune* (August 12, 1991), 41–49.

CHAPTER 2

1 I. I. Mitroff and S. A. Mohrman, "The Slack Is Gone: How the United States Lost Its Competitive Edge in the World Economy," *Academy of Management Executive* 2, 1987, 66–70.

2 Jeffrey Pfeffer, "The Theory-Practice Gap: Myth or Reality?" *Academy of Management Executive* 2, 1987, 31–33.

3 John B. Kervin, *Methods for Business Research* (New York: HarperCollins, 1992).

4 David A. Nadler, "Managing Organizational Change: An Integrative Perspective," *Journal of Applied Behavioral Science* 17, 1981, 191–211.

5 David A. Nadler, Marc S. Gerstein, and Robert B. Shaw, *Organizational Architecture: Designs for Changing Organizations* (San Francisco: Jossey-Bass, 1992).

6 David T. Kearns and David A. Nadler, *Prophets In the Dark: How Xerox Reinvented Itself and Beat Back the Japanese* (New York: Harper-Collins, 1992).

7 Harold S. Roberts, *Roberts' Dictionary of Industrial Relations,* revised ed. (Washington, DC: Bureau of National Affairs, 1971).

8 Daniel A. Wren, *The Evolution of Management Thought,* 4th ed. (New York: Wiley, 1992).

9 Elton Mayo, *The Human Problems of Industrial Civilization* (New York: Macmillan, 1933). Fritz J. Roethlisberger and William J. Dickson, *Management and the Worker: An Account of a Research Program Conducted by the Western Electric Company, Hawthorne Works, Chicago* (Cambridge, MA: Harvard University Press, 1939). H. M. Parsons, "What Caused the Hawthorne Effect? A Scientific Detective Story," *Administration and Society* 10, 1978, 259–83.

10 Ibid.

11 Alex Carey, "The Hawthorne Studies: A Radical Criticism," *American Sociological Review* 33, 1967, 403–16. R. H. Ranke and J. D. Kaul, "The Hawthorne Experiments: First Statistical Interpretation," *American Sociological Review* 43, 1978, 623–43. A. J. M. Stykes, "Economic Interests and the Hawthorne Researchers," *Human Relations* 19, 1965, 253–63. D. A. Whitsett, "Hawthorne, Topeka, and the Issue of Science Versus Advocacy in Organizational Behavior," *Academy of Management Review* 10, 1985, 21–30.

12 P. H. Lawrence, "Historical Development of Organizational Behavior," in J. W. Lorsch (ed.) *Handbook of Organizational Behavior* (Englewood Cliffs, NJ: Prentice-Hall, 1987), 1–9.

13 This definition of whistle-blowing was developed from J. P. Near and M. P. Miceli, "Organizational Dissidence: The Case of Whistle-Blowing," *Journal of Business Ethics* 4, 1985, 1–16.

14 Andy Paszor, "Marietta, GE Agree to Settle Federal Lawsuit," *Wall Street Journal* (December 27, 1994), A5.

15 This comment of retaliation against federal whistle-blowers was obtained from M. P. Miceli and J. P. Near, *Blowing the Whistle* (Lexington, MA: Lexington Books, 1992).

16 Kervin, *Methods for Business Research.*

17 Ibid.

18 Ibid.

19 For an expanded discussion of causality see D. T. Campbell and J. C. Stanley, *Experimental and Quasi-Experimental Designs for Research* (Chicago: Rand McNally, 1963).

20 Kervin, *Methods for Business Research.*

21 For a classic discussion on the use of significance tests see Denton E. Morrison and Ramon E. Henkel, *The Significance Test Controversy* (Chicago: Aldine, 1970).

22 R. Yin and K. Heald, "Using the Case Study Method to Analyze Policy Studies," *Administrative Science Quarterly* 20, 1975, 378–81.

23 Jerry Ross and Barry Staw, "Organizational Escalation and Exit: Lessons from the Shoreham Nuclear Power Plant," *Academy of Management Journal* 36, 1993, 701–32.

24 Fred N. Kerlinger, *Foundations of Behavioral Research,* 3d ed. (New York: Holt, Rinehart, and Winston, 1987).

25 M. P. Miceli and J. P. Near, "Relationships Among Value Congruence, Perceived Victimization, and Retaliation Against Whistle-Blowers," *Journal of Management* 20, 1994, 773–94.

26 Edwin Locke, *Generalizing from Laboratory to Field Settings* (Lexington, MA: Lexington Books, 1986). Karl E. Weick, "Laboratory Experimentation with Organizations," in J. G. March (ed.) *Handbook of Organizations* (Skokie, IL: Rand McNally, 1965).

27 P. Christopher Earley, "Self or Group? Cultural Effects of Training on Self-Efficacy and Performance," *Administrative Science Quarterly* 39, 1994, 89–117.

28 Eugene Stone, *Research Methods in Organizational Behavior* (Santa Monica, CA: Goodyear Publishing, 1978).

29 Judith M. Collins and Paul M. Muchinsky, "An Assessment of the Construct Validity of Three Job Evaluation Methods: A Field Experiment," *Academy of Management Journal* 36, 1993, 895–904.

30 G. V. Glass, G. McGaw, and F. J. Smith, *Meta-Analysis in Social Research* (Beverly Hills, CA: Sage Publications, 1981).

31 Anne M. O'Leary-Kelly, Joseph J. Martocchio, and Dwight D. Frink, "A Review of the Influence of Group Goals on Group Performance," *Academy of Management Journal* 37, 1994, 1285–1301.

32 E. J. Webb, D. T. Campbell, R. D. Schwartz, and L. Sechrest, *Unobtrusive Measures: Non-Reactive Research in the Social Sciences,* 2d ed. (Chicago: Rand McNally, 1966).

33 E. J. Webb and K. E. Weick, "Unobtrusive Measures in Organizational Theory: A Reminder," *Administrative Science Quarterly* 24, 1979, 650–59.

34 C. G. Hempel and P. Oppenheim, "Problems of the Concept and General Law," in A. Donato and S. Morgenbesse (eds.) *Philosophy of Science* (Cleveland, OH: Meridan Publishing, 1960).

35 Kerlinger, *Foundations of Behavioral Research,* 3d ed.

36 P. H. Mirvis and S. E. Seashore, "Being Ethical in Organizational Research," *American Psychologist* 34, 1979, 776–80. M. A. Von Glinow, "Ethical Issues in Organizational Behavior," *Academy of Management Newsletter,* March 1985, 1–3.

37 Fred Luthans, "The Contingency Theory of Management: A Path Out of the Jungle," *Business Horizons* 16, 1973, 62–72. James Thompson, *Organizations in Action* (New York: McGraw-Hill, 1967).

38 Richard L. Daft, *Management,* 2d ed. (Chicago: Dryden Press, 1991).

39 This question was adapted from Robert P. Vecchio, *Organizational Behavior,* 3d ed. (New York: Dryden Press, 1995).

CHAPTER 3

1 Randi L. Sims and K. Galen Kroeck, "The Influence of Ethical Fit on Employee Satisfaction, Commitment and Turnover," *Journal of Business Ethics* 13, no. 12 (December, 1994), 939–47.

2 Bruce Hager, "What's Behind Business' Sudden Fervor for Ethics?" *Business Week* (September 23, 1991), 65.

3 David Vogel, "Business Ethics: New Perspectives on Old Problems," *California Management Review* (Summer 1991), 101–17.

4 Lisa H. Newton and Maureen M. Ford (eds.) *Taking Sides: Clashing*

Views on Controversial Issues in Business Ethics and Society, 2d ed. (Guilford, CT: Duskin Publishing Group, Inc., 1992), xiv.

5 David Vogel, "It's Not Nice to Fool Business Ethicists," *Business and Society Review* (Summer 1991), no. 78, 23–32.

6 Roger Scruton, *A Dictionary of Political Thought* (New York: Hill and Wang, 1982), 289.

7 Ibid, 156.

8 Shaun F. O'Malley, "Getting Down to the Business of Business Ethics," *Proceedings of the 1991 Emerson Electric Center for Business Ethics Conference* (St. Louis, MO, St. Louis University, April 1991), 13–22.

9 Milton Rokeach, *The Nature of Human Values* (New York: Free Press, 1973).

10 Joseph L. Badaracco, Jr., "Business Ethics: Four Spheres of Executive Responsibility," *California Management Review* 24, no. 3 (Spring 1992), 64–79.

11 LaRue Tone Hosmer, "Managerial Responsibilities on the Micro Level." *Business Horizons* (July-August 1991) 49–55 and see John W. Collins, "Is Business Ethics an Oxymoron?" *Business Horizons* 37, no. 5 (September-October 1994), 1–8.

12 Thomas M. Jones, "Ethical Decision Making by Individuals in Organizations: An Issue-Contingent Model," *Academy of Management Review* 16 (April 1991), 366–89.

13 Ronald R. Sims, "The Institutionalization of Organizational Ethics," *Journal of Business Ethics* 10 (1991), 493–506.

14 Robert Allan Cooke, "Danger Signs of Unethical Behavior: How to Determine If Your Firm Is at Ethical Risk," *Journal of Business Ethics* 10 (1991), 249–53 and Robert Half (ed.) "Managing Your Career, 'How Can I Determine if a Firm is Ethical?'" *Management Accounting* (July 1991), 13.

15 Joseph R. DesJardins and John J. McCall, *Contemporary Issues in Business Ethics,* 2d ed. (Belmont, CA: Wadsworth Publishing Co., 1990), 305.

16 Richard Evans, "Business Ethics and Changes in Society," *Journal of Business Ethics* 10 (1991), 871–76. See also, Newton and Ford, *Taking Sides,* xx.

17 DesJardins and McCall, *Contemporary Issues in Business Ethics,* 2d ed., 305.

18 Simcha B. Werner, "The Movement for Reforming American Business Ethics: A Twenty Year Perspective," *Journal of Business Ethics* 11 (January 1992), 61–70.

19 Vogel, "Business Ethics: New Perspectives in Old Problems," 105.

20 Werner, "The Movement for Reforming American Business Ethics: A Twenty Year Perspective," 61.

21 *Hilton Business Ethics Week,* Loyola Marymount University (Spring 1992).

22 Robert A. Giacalone and D. Neil Ashworth, "From Lip Service to Community Service," *Business and Society Review,* 66 (Summer 1988), 31–33.

23 Ronald R. Sims, "The Institutionalization of Organizational Ethics," *Journal of Business Ethics* 10 (1991), 493–506.

24 Steven R. Reinemund, "Today's Ethics and Tomorrow's Work Place," *Business Forum* 17, no. 2 (Spring 1992), 6–9.

25 Denis Collins and Laura V. Page, "Teaching Business Ethics: A Practical Guide and Case Studies," *Small Business Forum* (Spring 1992), 63–80.

26 Marvin T. Brown, *Working Ethics, Strategies for Decision Making and Organizational Responsibility* (San Francisco, CA: Jossey-Bass, 1991).

27 Kim Macalister, "The X Generation," *HR Magazine* 39, no. 5 (May 1994), 66–71.

28 Lawrence J. Bradford and Claire Raines, *Twenty Something: Managing and Motivating Today's New Work Force* (New York: Master Media Ltd., 1992), 18.

29 David A. Kolb, Irwin M. Rubin, Joyce S. Osland (eds.) *The Organizational Behavior Reader* (Englewood Cliffs, NJ: Prentice-Hall, 1991), 11.

30 Macalister, "The X Generation," 66–71.

31 Bradford and Raines, *Twenty Something: Managing and Motivating Today's New Work Force,* 6.

32 "Work Ethic Top Job Skill," *CPA Journal* 64, no. 9 (September 1994), 9–10.

33 F. B. Guen and Eric Hatch, "Involvement and Commitment in the Workplace: A New Ethic Evolving," *SAM Advanced Management Journal* (Autumn 1990), 8–12.

34 Shirley Richard, "Give the Boomers What They Want," *Fortnightly* 132, no. 13 (July 1, 1994), 11–14.

35 Jon Meacham, "The Truth About Twenty-Somethings," *The Washington Monthly* 27, no. 1 and 2 (January/February 1995), 21.

CHAPTER 4

1 Audrey Choi, "Lopez Faces New Inquiry in Germany," *Wall Street Journal* (November 9, 1993), A10.

2 Paul Ingrassia, "April Fool's Day Comes Early at GM, But It's No Joke," *Wall Street Journal* (March 16, 1993), A1, A6. Kathleen Kerwin and Zachary Schiller, "GM Braces For Life after Lopez," *Business Week* (March 29, 1993), 28.

3 Paul Ingrassia and Douglas Lavin, "Lopez Reverses Plan to Quit GM for Volkswagen," *Wall Street Journal* (March 15, 1993), A3.

4 Milton Rokeach, *The Nature of Human Values* (New York: Free Press, 1973).

5 Shalom H. Schartz and Wolfgang Bilsky, "Toward A Theory of the Universal Content and Structure of Values: Extension and Cross-Cultural Replications," *Journal of Personality and Social Psychology* 49 (1980), 878–91.

6 Milton Rokeach and Sandra J. Ball-Rokeach, "Stability and Change in American Value Priorities, 1968–1981," *American Psychologist* (May 1989), 775–84.

7 Gordon Allport, Philip E. Vernon, and Gardner Lindzey, *Study of Values* (Boston: Houghton Mifflin, 1931).

8 R. Tagiuri, "Purchasing Executive: General Manager or Specialist?" *Journal of Purchasing* (August 1967), 16–21.

9 Rokeach, *The Nature of Human Values.*

10 Lawrence Kohlberg, *The Philosophy of Moral Development* 1 (New York: Harper and Row, 1981).

11 James C. Gibbs and Kenneth F. Widaman, *Social Intelligence: Measuring the Development of Sociomoral Reflection* (Englewood Cliffs, NJ: Prentice-Hall, 1982), 215. C. I. Malinowski and C. P. Smith, "Moral Reasoning and Moral Conduct: An Investigation Prompted by Kohlberg's Theory," *Journal of Personality and Social Psychology* 49 (1985), 1016–27. W. Y. Penn and B. D. Collier, "Current Research in Moral Development as a Decision Support System," *Journal of Business Ethics,* 4 (1985), 131–36.

12 C. Gilligan, *In a Different Voice: Psychological Theory and Women's Development* (Cambridge, MA: Harvard University Press, 1982).

13 Bruce M. Meglino, Elizabeth C. Ravlin, and Cheryl L. Adkins, "Value Congruence and Satisfaction with a Leader: An Examination of the Role of Interaction," *Working Paper* (University of South Carolina, 1990).

14 Martin Fishbein and Icek Ajzen, *Attitude Intention and Behavior: An Introduction to Theory and Research* (Reading, MA: Addison-Wesley, 1975).

15 J. Cooper and R. T. Croyle, "Attitude and Attitude Change," *Annual Review of Psychology* 35 (1984), 395–426.

16 Ibid.

17 Leon Festinger, *A Theory of Cognitive Dissonance* (Palo Alto, CA: Stanford University Press, 1957).

18 Gregory Moorhead and Ricky W. Griffin, *Organizational Behavior,* 3d ed. (Boston: Houghton Mifflin, 1992).

19 Gerald Salancik and Jeffrey Pfeffer, "A Social Information Processing Approach to Job Attitudes and Task Design," *Administrative Science Quarterly* 23 (1978), 224–53.

20 Lawrence Pervin, "Personality," in Mark Rosenzweig and Lyman Porter (eds.) *Annual Review of Psychology* 36 (1985), 83–114.

21 John Leon, "Exploring the Traits of Twins," *Time* (January 12, 1987), 61–63.

22 Sigmund Freud, "Psychopathology of Everyday Life," in J. Strachey (ed.) *The Complete Psychological Works of Sigmund Freud* (London: Hogarth Press, 1960).

23 Erik Erikson, *Childhood and Society,* 2d ed., (New York: Norton, 1963).

24 Jean Piaget, "The General Problems of the Psychological Development of the Child," in J. M. Tanner and B. Inhelder (eds.) *Discussions on Child Development* (New York: International Universities Press, 1960), 3–27.

25 Gordon Allport, *Pattern and Growth in Personality* (New York: Holt, 1961).

26 Raymond Cattell, *The Scientific Analysis of Personality* (Chicago: Aldine, 1965).

27 Philip G. Zimbardo, *Psychology and Life* (Glenview, IL: Scott, Foresman, 1985).

28 Gordon Allport and Henry Odbert, "Trait Names: A Psychological Study," *Psychological Monographs* 47 (1936), 208–11.

29 Carl Rogers, *On Personal Power: Inner Strength and Its Revolutionary Impact* (New York: Delacorte, 1977). Abraham Maslow, "A Theory of Human Motivation," *Psychological Review* (July 1943), 370–96.

30 Chris Argyris, *Personality and Organization: The Conflict Between the System and the Individual* (New York: Harper & Row, 1957).

31 Ibid.

32 Julian B. Rotter, "Generalized Expectancies for Internal versus External Control of Reinforcement," *Psychological Monographs* 80 (1966), 1–28.

33 Paul Spector, "Behavior in Organizations as a Function of Employees' Locus of Control," *Psychological¹ Bulletin* 91 (1982), 482–97.

34 T. W. Adorno, E. Frenkel-Brunswik, D. J. Levinson, and R. N. Sanford, *The Authoritarian Personality* (New York: Harper & Row, 1950). "Who Becomes An Authoritarian?" *Psychology Today* (March 1989), 66–70.

35 Niccolo Machiavelli, *The Prince*, trans. by George Bull (Middlesex: Penguin, 1961). Richard Christie and Florence L. Geis, *Studies in Machiavellianism* (New York: Academic Press, 1970).

36 Florence L. Geis and T. H. Moon, "Machiavellianism and Deception," *Journal of Personality and Social Psychology* 40 (1981), 766–75.

37 Joel Brockner, *Self-Esteem at Work* (New York: Lexington Books, 1988).

38 Ibid.

39 Rebecca Ellis and Susan Taylor, "Role of Self-Esteem within the Job Search Process," *Journal of Applied Psychology* 68 (1983), 632–40. Phyllis Tharenou and Phillip Harker, "Moderating Influences of Self-Esteem on Relationships Between Job Complexity, Performance, and Satisfaction," *Journal of Applied Psychology* 69 (1984), 623–32.

40 Joel Brockner and J. Guare, "Improving the Performance of Low Self-Esteem Individuals: An Attributional Approach," *Academy of Management Journal* 36 (1983), 642–56.

41 Meyer Friedman and Ray Rosenman, *Type A Behavior and Your Heart* (New York: Knopf, 1974).

42 J. R. Edwards and A. J. Baglioni, Jr., "Relationships Between Type A Behavior Pattern and Mental and Physical Symptoms: A Comparison of Global and Component Measures," *Journal of Applied Psychology* 75 (1991), 276–90. Redford Williams, Jr., *The Trusting Heart* (New York: Times Books, 1989).

43 Robert A. Baron, "Personality and Organizational Conflict: Effects of the Type A Behavior Pattern and Self-Monitoring," *Organizational Behavior and Human Decision Processes* 44 (1989), 281–97. Walter Keichell II, "Attack of the Obsessive Manager," *Fortune* (February 16, 1987), 127–28.

44 Isabel B. Myers and Katherine Briggs, *Myers-Briggs Type Indicators* (Princeton, NJ: Educational Testing Service, 1962).

45 Brian H. Kleiner, "The Interrelationship of Jungian Modes of Mental Functioning with Organizational Factors: Implications for Management Development," *Human Relations* 36 (1983), 997–1012.

46 Don Hellriegel, John W. Slocum, Jr., and Richard W. Woodman, *Organizational Behavior*, 5th ed. (St. Paul, MN: West Publishing, 1989).

47 Thomas More, "Personality Tests Are Back," *Fortune* (March 30, 1987), 71–82.

48 A. L. Edwards, *The Measurement of Personality Traits by Scales and Inventories* (New York: Holt, Rinehart, & Winston, 1970).

49 J. C. Nunnally, *Psychometric Theory* (New York: McGraw-Hill, 1978).

50 Walter Mischel, *Personality and Assessment* (New York: John Wiley, 1968).

51 J. Masling, "The Influence of Personal and Situational Variables in Projective Testing," *Psychological Bulletin* 57 (1960), 65–85.

52 R. M. Guion and R. F. Gottier, "Validity of Personality Measures in Personnel Selection," *Personnel Psychology* 18 (1965), 46–51.

53 "Can You Pass the Job Test?" *Newsweek* (May 5, 1986), 46–51.

54 P. F. Secord, C. W. Backman, and D. R. Slavitt, *Understanding Social Life: An Introduction to Social Psychology* (New York: McGraw-Hill, 1976).

55 S. S. Zelkind and T. W. Costello, "Perceptions: Some Recent Research and Implications for Administration," *Administrative Science Quarterly* 7 (1962), 218–35.

56 Robert Rosenthal and Leonore Jacobsen, *Pygmalion in the Classroom: Teacher Expectation and Pupils' Intellectual Development* (New York: Holt, Rinehart, & Winston, 1968).

57 Dov Eden, *Pygmalion in Management: Productivity as a Self-Fulfilling Prophecy* (Lexington, MA: Lexington Books, 1990).

58 A. G. Greenwald, "The Totalitarian Ego: Fabrication and Revision of Personal History," *American Psychologist* 35 (1980), 603–18.

59 This example was adapted from Gary Johns, *Organization Behavior*, 3d ed. (New York: HarperCollins, 1992).

60 J. Bartunek, "Why Did You Do That? Attribution Theory in Organizations," *Business Horizons* 24 (1981), 66–71.

61 M. J. Martinko and W. L. Gardner, "The Leader-Member Attribution Process," *Academy of Management Review* 12 (1987), 235–49.

62 Ibid.

63 Lawrence Pervin, "Personality," *Annual Review of Psychology* 36 (1985), 83–114.

CHAPTER 5

1 Ani Hadjian, "Andy Grove," "How Intel Makes Spending Pay Off," *Fortune* (February 22, 1992), 56–61. Janice Castro, "When the Chips Are Down," *Time* (December 26, 1994), 126. Alan Goldstein, "IBM Halts Pentium Sales," *Dallas Morning News* (December 13, 1994), A1, A10.

1A Wendy Bounds, "Intel Moves to Soothe Customers," *Wall Street Journal* (December 26, 1994), A1, A4.

2 "Ross Perot's Crusade," *Business Week* (October 6, 1986), 61.

3 Charles D. Pringle, Daniel F. Jennings, and Justin G. Longenecker, *Management Organizations: Functions and Behaviors* (Columbus, OH: Merrill Publishing, 1988). Herbert A. Simon, *The New Science of Management Decision* (Englewood Cliffs, NJ: Prentice-Hall, 1960).

4 Philip L. Junsaker and Johanna S. Junsaker, "Decision Styles—In Theory, In Practice," *Organizational Dynamics* 10 (1981), 23–36.

5 Wickham Skinner and W. Earl Sasser, "Managers with Impact: Versatile and Inconsistent," *Harvard Business Review* 55 (November-December, 1977), 140–48.

6 Bernard M. Bass, *Organizational Decision Making* (Homewood, IL: Irwin, 1983).

7 H. A. Linstone, *Multiple Perspectives for Decision Making* (New York: North-Holland, 1984).

8 Trish Hall, "For a Company Chief, When There's a Whim There's Often a Way," *Wall Street Journal* (October 4, 1990).

9 Arthur A. Thompson, Jr. and A. J. Strickland, III, *Strategy Formulation and Implementation*, 5th ed. (Homewood, IL: BPI-Irwin, 1993).

10 For an expanded discussion of environmental scanning, see Daniel F. Jennings and James R. Lumpkin, "Insights Between Environmental Scanning Activities and Porter's Generic Strategies: An Empirical Analysis," *Journal of Management* 18 (1993), 791–803.

11 Richard M. Cyert and James G. March, *A Behavioral Theory of the Firm* (Englewood Cliffs, NJ: Prentice-Hall, 1963).

12 Weston H. Agor, *Intuition in Organizations* (Newbury Park, CA: Cage, 1989). Carl Jung, *Psychological Types*, trans. by H. Godwin Baynes (New York: Harcourt, Brace, 1924).

13 Weston H. Agor, "How Executives Use Their Intuition to Make Important Decisions," *Business Horizons* 29 (1986), 49–53.

14 Herbert A. Simon, *Administrative Behavior*, 3d ed. (New York: Free Press, 1976).

15 Ibid.

16 This observation was developed from Stephen P. Robbins, *Management*, 4th ed. (Englewood Cliffs, NJ: Prentice-Hall, 1993).

17 Barry M. Staw, "Escalation of Commitment to a Course of Action," *Academy of Management Review* 6 (1981), 577–81.

18 Jerry Ross and Barry M. Staw, "Expo 86: An Escalation Prototype," *Administrative Sciences Quarterly* 31 (1986), 274–97.

19 "Whoops: How It Happened," *Dun's Business* (October 1993), 48–57.

20 Bass, *Organizational Decision Making*.

21 C. E. Lindblom, "The Science of Muddling Through," *Public Administration Review* 19 (1959), 78–88.

22 Marilyn Anderson, "Pillsbury—Just Drifting Along," *Business Week* (June 15, 1988), 62–64.

23 Henry Mintzberg, Duru Raisinghani, and Andre Theoret, "The Structure of Unstructured Decision Processes," *Administrative Science Quarterly* 21 (1976), 246–75. James B. Quinn, "Strategic Change: Logical Incrementalism," *Sloan Management Review* 20 (1978), 7–21.

24 Keith R. Hammons, "How a $4 Razor Ends Up Costing $300 Million," *Business Week* (January 29, 1990), 62–63.

25 Bass, *Organizational Decision Making*.

26 Linda K. Trevino, "Ethical Decision Making in Organizations: A Person-Situation Interactional Model," *Academy of Management Review* 11 (1986), 601–17.

27 E. F. Harrison, *The Managerial Decision-Making Process*, 3d ed. (Boston: Houghton Mifflin, 1987).

28 George P. Huber, *Managerial Decision Making* (Glenview, IL: Scott, Foresman, 1980).

29 G. DeSanctis and B. Galupe, "Group Decision Support Systems: A New Frontier," *Data Base* 9 (1991), 6–12.

30 Ibid.

31 George P. Huber, "A Theory of the Effects of Advanced Information Technologies on Organizational Design, Intelligence, and Decision Making," *Academy of Management Review* 15 (1990), 47–71.

32 Guisseppi A. Forgionne, "OR/MS and Decision Technology in the 1990s," *OR/MS Today* (June 1990), 18–24.

33 Alan J. Rowe and James D. Boulgarides, *Managerial Decision Making* (New York: Macmillan, 1992).

34 Peter D. Moore, "Networks That Mimic Thinking," *McKinsey Quarterly* (September 1993), 5–12.

35 Richard D. Arvey, "Indicators of Job Satisfaction," *Journal of Applied Psychology* 73 (1988), 434–46.

36 John D. Cook, Sue J. Hepworth, Toby D. Wall, and Peter B. Warr, *The Experience of Work: A Compendium and Review of 249 Measures and Their Use* (London: Academic Press, 1981).

37 Frederick Herzberg, *Work and the Nature of Man* (Cleveland: World Publishing, 1966).

38 P. D. Machungaws, P. D. and N. Schmitt, "Work Motivation in a Developing Country," *Journal of Applied Psychology* 68 (1983), 31–42.

39 E. A. Locke, "Job Satisfaction," in M. Gruenberg and T. Wall (eds.), *Social Psychology and Organizational Behavior* (London: Wiley, 1984).

40 D. B. McFarlin and R. W. Rice, "The Role of Facet Importance as a Moderator in Job Satisfaction Processes," *Journal of Organizational Behavior* 13 (1992), 41–54.

41 Gregory Moorhead and R. W. Griffin, *Organizational Behavior: Managing People and Organizations*, 3d ed. (Dallas: Houghton Mifflin, 1992).

42 C. N. Weaver, "Job Satisfaction in the United States in the 1970s," *Journal of Applied Psychology* 65 (1980), 364–67.

43 D. M. Eichar, E. M. Brady, and R. H. Fortinsky, "The Job Satisfaction of Older Workers," *Journal of Organizational Behavior* 12 (1991), 609–20.

44 A. G. Bedian, G. R. Ferris, and K. M. Kacmar, "Age, Tenure, and Job Satisfaction: A Tale of Two Perspectives," *Journal of Vocational Behavior* 40 (1992), 33–48.

45 S. L. Lambert, "The Combined Effect of Job and Family Characteristics on the Job Satisfaction, Job Involvement, and Intrinsic Motivation of Men and Women Workers," *Journal of Organizational Behavior* 12 (1991), 341–63.

46 H. S. Becker, "Notes on the Concept of Commitment," *American Journal of Sociology* 66 (1960), 32–40. J. P. Meyer, N. J. Allen, and I. R. Gellatly, "Affective and Continuance Commitment to Organizations: Evaluation of Measures and Analysis of Concurrent and Time-Lagged Relations," *Journal of Applied Psychology* 75 (1990), 710–20.

47 L. W. Porter, R. M. Steers, R. T. Mowday, and P. V. Boulian, "Organizational Commitment, Job Satisfaction, and Turnover Among Psychiatric Technicians," *Journal of Applied Psychology* 59 (1974), 603–9. R. T. Mowday, L. W. Porter, and R. M. Steers, *Employee-Organizational Linkages: The Psychology of Commitment* (New York: Academic Press, 1982).

48 R. M. Steers, "Antecedents and Outcomes of Organizational Commitments," *Administrative Science Quarterly* 22 (1977), 46–56. L. M. Shore and H. J. Martin, "Job Satisfaction and Organizational Commitment in Relation to Work Performance and Turnover Intentions," *Human Relations* 42 (1989), 625–38.

49 Arnon E. Reichers, "A Review and Reconceptualization of Organizational Commitment," *Academy of Management Review* 10 (1985), 463–76.

50 Michael J. Davidson and Charles L. Cooper, "A Model of Occupational Stress," *Journal of Occupational Stress* 23 (1981), 564–74.

51 C. Hymowitz, "Which Corporate Culture Fits You?" *Wall Street Journal* (July 17, 1989), B1.

52 J. M. Ivancevich and M. T. Matteson, *Stress at Work* (Glenview, IL: Scott, Foresman, 1980), 5–9.

53 Jeffrey R. Edwards, "A Cybernetic Theory of Stress, Coping, and Well-Being in Organization," *Academy of Management Review* 17 (1992), 238–74.

54 Chris Roush, Ann Therese Palmer, and Lori Bongiorno, "Work and Family," *Business Week* (June 28, 1993), 80–88.

55 Stephan J. Motowidlo, John S. Packard, and Michael R. Manning, "Occupational Stress: Its Causes and Consequences for Job Performance," *Journal of Applied Psychology* 71 (1986), 618–29.

56 Robert I. Sutton and Anat Rafaeli, "Characteristics of Work Stations as Potential Occupational Stressor," *Academy of Management Journal* 30 (1987), 260–76.

57 W. H. Hendrix, N. K. Ovalle, and R. G. Troxler, "Behavioral and Physiological Consequences of Stress and Its Antecedent Factors," *Journal of Applied Psychology* 70 (1985), 654–59.

58 Robert P. Vecchio, *Organizational Behavior*, 2d ed. (Chicago: Dryden Press, 1991).

59 S. E. Jackson and R. S. Schuler, "A Meta-Analysis and Conceptual Critique of Research on Role Ambiguity and Role Conflict in Work Settings," *Organizational Behavior and Human Decision Processes* 36 (1987), 16–78.

60 Vecchio, *Organizational Behavior*, 2d ed.

61 Jennifer J. Laabs, "Job Stress," *Personnel Journal* (April 1992), 39–46.

62 M. J. McCartly, "Stressed Employees Look for Relief in Workers' Compensation Claims," *Wall Street Journal* (April 7, 1988), B1, B27.

63 Hans Selye, *The Stress of Life* (New York: McGraw-Hill, 1956). R. M. Yerkes and J. D. Dodson, "The Relation of Strength of Stimulus to Rapidity and Habit-Formation," *Journal of Comparative Neurology and Psychology* 18 (1980), 459–82.

64 J. D. Quick, R. S. Horn, and J. C. Quick, "Health Consequences of Stress," *Journal of Organizational Behavior Management* 8 (1986), 19–36.

65 Thomas L. Brown, "Are You Living in 'Quiet Desperation'?" *Industry Week* (March 16, 1992), 17.

66 Harry Levinson, "When Executives Burn Out," *Harvard Business Review* 68 (1990), 69.

67 Leonard Moss, *Managing Stress* (Reading, MA: Addison-Wesley, 1981).

68 S. E. Jackson, R. L. Schwab, and R. S. Schuler, "Toward an Understanding of the Burnout Phenomenon," *Journal of Applied Psychology* 71 (1986), 630–40.

69 Hugh F. Stallworth, "Realistic Goals Help Avoid Burnout," *HR Magazine* (June 1990), 82–85.

70 Ibid.

71 Ellen Galinsky, "A National Study on the Changing Workforce—1993," (New York: Families at Work Institute, 1993).

72 Michael R. Carrell, Frank E. Kuzmits, and Norbert Elbert, *Personnel: Human Resource Management*, 4th ed. (New York: Macmillan, 1992).

CHAPTER 6

1 Abraham Maslow, "A Theory of Human Motivation," *Psychological Review* 50 (1943), 370–96.

2 C. P. Alderfer, *Existence, Relatedness and Growth* (New York: Free Press, 1972), 77.

3 Clayton P. Alderfer and R. A. Guzzo, "Life Experiences and Adults' Enduring Strength of Desires in Organizations," *Administrative Science Quarterly* 24 (1979), 347–61.

4 David C. McClelland, *The Achieving Society* (New York: Van Nostrand Reinhold, 1961).

5 David C. McClelland, "To Know Why Men Do What They Do," *Psychology Today* (January 1971), 35–38.

6 David C. McClelland and R. E. Boyatzis, "Leadership Motive Pattern and Long-Term Success in Management," *Journal of Applied Psychology* 67 (1982), 744–51.

7 Frederick Herzberg et al., *The Motivation to Work* (New York: John Wiley, 1959), 59–83.

8 Frederick Herzberg, "One More Time: How Do You Motivate Employees?" *Harvard Business Review* (September/October, 1987), and Ebrahim A. Maidani, "Comparative Study of Herzberg's Two-Factory Theory of Job Satisfaction Among Public and Private Sectors," *Public Personnel Management* 20, no. 4 (Winter 1991), 441–48.

9 N. J. Alder and J. L. Graham, "Cross-Cultural Interaction: The International Comparison Fallay," *Journal of International Business Studies* (Fall 1989), 515–37.

10 Douglas M. McGregor, *The Human Side of Enterprise* (New York: McGraw-Hill, 1960), 33–35.

11 Ibid, 81.

12 William G. Ouchi, *Theory Z* (Reading, MA: Addison-Wesley, 1981), 1–7.

13 Gary P. Latham and Edwin A. Locke, "Self-Regulation Through Goal Setting," *Organizational Behavior and Human Performance* 50 (1991), 212–47.

14 Edwin A. Locke and G. P. Latham, *Goal Setting: A Motivational Technique that Works* (Englewood Cliffs, NJ: Prentice-Hall, 1984).

15 Edwin A. Locke and G. P. Latham, *A Theory of Goal Setting and Task Performance* (Englewood Cliffs, NJ: Prentice-Hall, 1990).

16 M. E. Tubbs and S. E. Ekeberg, "The Role of Intentions in Work Motivation: Implications for Goal Setting Theory and Research," *Academy of Management Review* 16 (1991), 180–99.

17 M. C. Kernan and R. G. Lord, "Effects of Valence, Expectancies and Goal Performance Discrepancies in Simple and Multiple Goal Environments," *Journal of Applied Psychology* 75 (1990), 194–203.

18 P. C. Early, G. B. Northcraft, C. Lee, and T. R. Litucky, "The Impact of Process and Outcome Feedback on the Relation of Goal Setting to Task Performance," *Academy of Management Journal* 33 (1990), 87–105.

19 E. L. Thorndike, *Animal Intelligence* (New York: Macmillan, 1911), 77.

20 B. F. Skinner, *The Technology of Teaching* (New York: Appleton-Century-Crofts, 1968), 77.

21 Victor Vroom, *Work and Motivation* (New York: John Wiley and Sons, 1964).

22 M. S. Singer, B. G. Stacey, and C. Lange, "The Relative Utility of Expectancy—Value Theory and Social Cognitive Theory in Predicting Psychology Student Course Goals and Career Aspirations," *Journal of Social Behavior and Personality* 8, no. 4 (1993), 703–14.

23 John E. Mathieu, Scott I. Tannenbaum, and Eduardo Salas, "Influences of Individual and Situational Characteristics on Measures of Training Effectiveness," *Academy of Management Journal* 35, no. 4 (1992), 828–47.

24 Catherine S. Clark, Gregory H. Dobbinis, and Robert T. Ladd, "Exploratory Field Study of Training Motivation," *Group and Organization Management* 18, no. 3 (September 1993), 292–307.

25 J. Stacy Adams, "Toward an Understanding of Inequity," *Journal of Abnormal Psychology* 67 (1963), 422–36.

26 Michael R. Carrell and John E. Dittrich, "Equity Theory: The Recent Literature, Methodological Considerations, and New Directions," *Academy of Management Review* 3, no. 2 (April 1978), 202–10.

27 R. C. Huseman, J. D. Hatfield, and E. W. Miles, "A New Perspective on Equity Theory: The Equity Sensitivity Construct," *Academy of Management Review* 12, no. 2 (June 1987), 222–34.

28 Douglas M. Cowherd and David I. Levine, "Product Quality and Pay Equity Between Lower-level Employees and Top Management: An Investigation of Distributive Justice Theory," *Administrative Science Quarterly* 37 (1992), 302–320.

29 Ron Wolf, "Apple Workers Send Harsh 'Dear John' Notes," *San Jose Mercury News* (February 7, 1990), 6A.

30 Cowherd and Levine, "Product Quality and Pay Equity Between Lower-level Employees and Top Management: An Investigation of Distributive Justice Theory," 302.

31 Carrell and Dittrich, "Equity Theory: The Recent Literature, Methodological Considerations, and New Directions," 202–10.

32 Edwin A. Locke, "The Motivation Sequence, the Motivation Hub, and the Motivation Core," *Organizational Behavior and Human Decision Processes* 50 (1991), 288–99.

CHAPTER 7

1 Leonard A. Schlesinger and James L. Heskett, "The Service-Driven Service Company," *Harvard Business Review* (September-October 1991), 77–81.

2 Ibid.

3 Peggy Stuart, "Fresh Ideas Energize Reward Programs," *Personnel Journal* (January 1992), 102–3.

4 Catherine M. Meek, "Everyone Needs Attention," *Small Business Reports* (December 1991), 11–14.

5 J. Kenneth Matejka and Richard J. Demsing, "Managing Employee Rewards," *Administrative Management* (June 1986), 22–24.

6 Ibid.

7 Meek, "Everyone Needs Attention," 11–14.

8 Stuart, "Fresh Ideas Energize Reward Programs," 102–3.

9 Philip C. Grant, "How to Make a Program Work," *Personnel Journal* (January 1992), 103.

10 David G. Carnevale and Brett S. Sharp, "The Old Employee Suggestion Box," *Review of Public Personnel Administration* (Spring 1993), 82–92.

11 Michael E. Trunko, "Open to Suggestions," *HR Magazine* (February 1993), 85–89.

12 J. French-Parker, "Employee Ideas Show Profit," *The Sunday Oklahoman* (June 21, 1992), 4.

13 Trunko, "Open to Suggestions," 86.

14 Carnevale and Sharp, "The Old Employee Suggestion Box," 87–91.

15 Trunko, "Open to Suggestions," 89.

16 Mark McConkie, "A Clarification of the Goal-Setting and Appraisal Processes in MBO," *Academy of Management Review*, no. 1 (1979), 29–40.

17 Ralph Stoyer, "How I Learned to Let My Workers Lead," *Harvard Business Review* (November-December 1990), 66–83.

18 Ibid.

19 C. R. Walker and R. H. Guest, *The Man on the Assembly Line* (Cambridge, MA: Harvard University Press, 1952).

20 M. D. Kilbridge, "Reduced Costs through Enlargement: A Case," *Journal of Business* (October 1969), 357–62.

21 J. R. Hackman and G. R. Oldham, *Work Design* (Reading, MA: Addison-Wesley Publishing, 1980). See also "You See the Package from Beginning to End," *Business Week* (May 16, 1983), 103, and R. H. Waterman, *The Renewal Factor* (New York: Bantam Books, 1987), 4.

22 F. K. Plous, Jr., "Redesigning Work," *Personnel Administrator* 32, no. 5 (March 1987), 99.

23 Charlene Marmer Soloman, "24-Hour Employee," *Personnel Journal* (August 1991), 56–63.

24 "Flexible Work Schedules," *Small Business Report* (October 1978), 24–25.

25 Ibid.

26 James Fraze, "Preparing for a Different Future," *Resource* 7, no. 1 (January 1988), 1, 10.

27 Richard Upton, "The 'Home Office' and the New Homeworkers," *Personnel Management* 21 (September 1984), 39–43.

28 Toby Kahn, "Vermont Home Knitters," *People Weekly* 21 (March 19, 1984), 64.

29 Upton, "The 'Home Office' and the New Homeworkers," 39–43.

30 Randall B. Dunham and Jon L. Pierce, "Attitudes Toward Work Schedules: Construct Definition, Instrument Development, and Validation," *Academy of Management Journal* 29, no. 1 (March 1987), 170–82.

31 Matthew P. Gonring, "Communication Makes Employee Involvement Work," *Public Relations Journal* (November 1991), 40.

32 Ibid.

33 Richard Feldman and Michael Betzold, *End of the Line: Autoworkers and the American Dream* (New York: Weidenfeld & Nicolson Publishers, 1988), 17–21.

34 Gonring, "Communication Makes Employee Involvement Work," 38.

35 Donna Brown, "Why Participative Management Won't Work Here," *Management Review* (June 1992), 42–46.

36 C. Rosen and M. Quarrey, "How Well Is Employee Ownership Working?" *Harvard Business Review* 65, no. 5 (1987), 126–32.

37 Aaron A. Buchko, "Employee Ownership, Attitudes, and Turnovers: An Empirical Assessment," *Human Relations* 45, no. 7 (1992), 711–33.

38 Judith K. Thompson, "Promotion of Employee Ownership Through Public Policy: The British Example," *Journal of Economic Issues* 27, no. 3 (September 1993), 825–47.

39 K. Klein, "Employee Stock Ownership and Employee Attitudes: A Test of Three Models," *Journal of Applied Psychology* 72 (1987), 319–32.

40 Aaron A. Buchko, "The Effects of Employee Ownership on Employee Attitudes? An Integrated Causal Model and Path Analysis," *Journal of Management Studies* 30, no. 4 (July 1993), 633–57.

41 Aaron A. Buchko, "Effects of Employee Ownership on Employee Attitudes," *Work and Occupation* 19, no. 1 (February 1992), 59–79.

42 Jeffrey A. Bradt, "Pay for Impact," *Personnel Journal* (May 1991), 76–77.

43 C. F. Vough, *Productivity: A Practice Program for Improving Efficiency* (New York: AMACOM, 1979), 2.

44 Leonard R. Burgess, *Wages and Salary Administration* (Columbus, OH: Merrill Publishing, 1984), 242.

45 Tom Peters, *Thriving on Chaos* (New York: Harper & Row, 1987), 403–4.

46 Terry Stambaugh, "An Incentive Pay Success Story," *Personnel Journal* (April 1992), 48–54.

47 "Pay Day: Typical Ford Worker Gets $1,200 for Profit-Sharing," *The Courier Journal* (March 13, 1986), B8. "Auto Workers Will Feel Pinch of Lower or No Profits," *The Bakersfield Californian* (February 20, 1990), 87.

CHAPTER 8

1 C. Fred Bergsten, "The World Economy After the Cold War," *California Management Review* 34, no. 2 (Winter 1992), 55.

2 Arvind Parkhe, "U.S. National Security Export Controls Implications for Global Competitiveness of U.S. High Tech Firms," *Strategic Management Journal* 12 (1992), 47–66.

3 Bergsten, "The World Economy After the Cold War," 52.

4 Wayne F. Cascio and Manuel G. Serapino, Jr., "Human Resources Systems in an International Alliance: The Undoing of a Done Deal?" *Organizational Dynamics* (February 21, 1991), 63–74.

5 S. M. Jameel Hason, "Human Resource Management in a New Era of Globalism," *Business Forum* (Winter 1992), 56–59.

6 Charles R. Morris, *The Coming Global Boom* (New York: Bantam Books, 1990), 10–54.

7 Cascio and Serapino, "Human Resources Systems in an International Alliance: The Undoing of a Done Deal?"

8 Robert B. Reich, *The Work of Nations* (New York: Random House, 1991), 70.

9 Paul Kennedy, *Preparing for the Twenty-First Century* (New York: Random House, 1993), 47–81.

10 Carla Rapoport and Justin Martin, "Retailers Go Global," *Fortune* 131, no. 3 (February 20, 1995), 102–8.

11 Anthony P. Carnevale, *America and the New Economy* (Washington, D.C.: Government Printing Office, 1990).

12 Reich, *The Work of Nations*, 84.

13 Neil Gross, "This Is What the U.S. Must Do to Stay Competitive," *Business Week* (December 1991), 92–96.

14 William B. Johnston, "Global Work Force 2000: The New World Labor Market," *Harvard Business Review* (March-April 1991), 115–27.

15 Michel M. Robert, "Attack Competitors by Changing the Game Rules," *The Journal of Business Strategy* (September-October 1991), 53–56.

16 Carnevale, *America and the New Economy*.

17 Faneuil Adams, Jr., "Developing an International Workforce," *Columbia Journal of World Business* (Twentieth Anniversary Issue).

18 Geert Hofstede, *Culture's Consequences: International Differences in Work-Related Values* (Beverly Hills, CA: Sage, 1984) and Geert Hofstede and Michael H. Bond, "The Confucius Connection: From Cultural Roots to Economic Growth," *Organizational Dynamics* 16 (1988), 4–21.

19 Geert Hofstede, "Motivation, Leadership and Organizations: Do American Theories Apply Abroad?" *Organizational Dynamics* 8 (Summer 1980), 42–63.

20 Michael Kublin and Robert Brady, "International Business Negotiating," *NBDC Report*, no. 145 (December 1992), 1–4.

21 C. Barnum and N. Wolniansky, "Taking Cues from Body Language," *Management Review* (June 1989), 59–60.

22 Rosabeth Moss Kanter, "Transcending Business Boundaries: 12,000 World Managers View Change," *Harvard Business Review* (May-June 1991), 151–64.

23 Vern Terpstra and Kenneth David, *The Cultural Environment of International Business* (Cincinnati, OH: South-Western Publishing Co., 1991), 72–103.

24 Kanter, "Transcending Business Boundaries: 12,000 World Managers View Change," 151.

25 Charlene Marmer Solomon, "How Does Your Global Talent Measure Up?" *Personnel Journal* 73, no. 10 (October 1994), 96–108.

26 Patricia A. Galagan, "Execs Go Global, Literally," *Training and Development Journal* (June 1990), 58.

27 Avivah Wittenberg-Cox, "Delivering Global Leaders," *International Management* 40 (February 1991), 52.

28 Shari Caudron, "Training Helps United Go Global," *Personnel Journal* (February 1992), 103–5.

29 Natalia Wolniansky, "International Training for Global Leadership," *Management Review* 70 (May 1990), 27.

30 Mel Mandell, "A Matter of Degree," *World Trade* 7, no. 8 (September 1994), 80–84.

31 Shari Caudron, "Surviving Cross-Cultural Shock," *Industry Week* (July 6, 1992), 35–38.

32 Philip R. Harris and Robert T. Moran, *Managing Cultural Differences* (Houston, TX: Gulf Publishing Company, 1991), 224.

33 Stephanie Overman, "Shaping the Global Workplace," *Personnel Administrator* (October 1989), 41–44, 101. See also Charlene Marmer Solomon, "Global Operations Demand that HR Rethink Diversity," *Personnel Journal* 73, no. 7 (July, 1994), 40–50.

34 Kathryn Welds, "The Return Trip," HR Magazine (June 1991), 113–14. See also Peter Dolan, "Occupational Hazards: Culture Shock and Repatriation," *Pennsylvania CPA Journal* 65, no. 2 (April 1994), 20.

35 Kennedy, *Preparing for the Twenty-First Century*, 137–62.

36 Carla Rapoport, "Why Japan Keeps On Winning," *Fortune* (July 15, 1991), 76–85.

37 Michael M. Robert, "Attack Competitors by Changing the Rules," *The Journal of Business Strategy* (September-October 1991), 53–56.

38 Rapoport, "Why Japan Keeps On Winning," 80.

39 Kennedy, *Preparing for the Twenty-First Century*, 137–62.

40 James L. Cerruti and Joseph Holtzman, "Business Strategy in the New European Landscape, *The Journal of Business Strategy* (November-December 1990), 18–23.

41 Kennedy, *Preparing for the Twenty-First Century*, 255–89.

42 "North America Free Trade Agreement," *HR Magazine* (December 1991), 85.

43 Anthony DePalma, "Savvy Mexicans Are Using NAFTA to Make Deals in U.S.," *Louisville Courier-Journal* (March 20, 1994), 6E, and Allen R. Myerson, "Record Trade Reported Between U.S., Mexico Since Trade Agreement," *Louisville Courier-Journal* (June 6, 1994), 3A.

44 "Year After NAFTA, U.S. Looks Like Winner," *Louisville Courier-Journal* (November 26, 1994), 14B.

45 Martin Crutsinger, "Senate Gives Trade Pact Final Approval," *Louisville Courier-Journal* (December 2, 1994), 1A.

CHAPTER 9

1 Ralph K. Andrist (ed.), *The American Heritage History of the Confident Years* (New York: American Heritage Publishing Co., Inc., 1970), 306.

2 Alistair Cooke, *America* (New York: Alfred A. Knopf, 1973), 273–88.

3 Beverly Geber, "Managing Diversity," *Training* 27, (July 1990), 23–30.

4 Sami M. Abbasi and Kenneth W. Hollman, "Managing Cultural Diversity: The Challenge of the 90s," *Records Management Quarterly* (July 1991), 24–32.

5 Wayne E. Barlow, "Act to Accommodate the Disabled," *Personnel Journal* (November 1991), 119.

6 George K. Kronenberger, "Out of the Closet," *Personnel Journal* (June 1991), 40–44.

7 Linda Thornburg, "What's Wrong with Workforce 2000," *HR Magazine* (August 1991), 38.

8 Marilyn Loden and Judy B. Rosener, Ph.D., *Workforce America! Managing Employee Diversity as a Vital Resource* (Homewood, IL: Business One Irwin, 1991), 29.

9 Lennie Copeland, "Learning to Manage a Multicultural Workforce," *Training* (May 1988), 49.

10 Floyd Dickens, Jr. and Jacqueline Dickens, *The Black Manager* (AMACOM, 1991), 96–97.

11 Ann M. Morrison and Mary Ann Von Glinow, "Women and Minorities in Management," *American Psychologist* 45, no. 20 (February 1990), 200–8.

12 Morrison and Carol Hymowitz, "One Firm's Bid to Keep Blacks, Women," Marketplace Section, *Wall Street Journal*, 201.

13 Charlene Marmer Solomon, "Are White Males Being Left Out?" *Personnel Journal* (November 1991): 88–94.

14 Copeland, "Learning to Manage a Multicultural Workforce," 49–56.

15 Jerry Beilinson, "Workforce 2000: Already Here?" *Personnel* (October 1990), 3.

16 David Ream, "Employment Outreach: A Quality Approach to Workforce Diversity," *Public Management* (June 1992), 18–20.

17 Steve Weinstein, "Reaching Out To Minorities," *Progressive Grocer* (May 1991).

18 Beilinson, "Workforce 2000: Already Here?" 4.

19 Catherine D. Fyock, A.E.P., *America's Work Force is Coming of Age* (Lexington, MA: D.C. Heath and Co., 1990), 18.

20 Laura M. Litvan, "Casting a Wider Employment Net," *Nation's Business* 82, no. 12 (December 1994), 49–51.

21 Norman Hill, "Forging a Partnership Between Blacks and Unions," *Monthly Labor Review* 100, no. 8 (August 1987), 38–39.

22 "Forging Change for a New Generation of Families, Workers and, Unions," (New York: The Coalition of Labor Union Women, March 1974).

23 Norma M. Riccucci, "A Typology for Union Discrimination: A Public Sector Perspective," *Public Personnel Management* 17, no. 1 (Spring 1988), 41–51.

24 C. Gopal Pati and Guy Stubblefield, "The Disabled Are Able to Work," *Personnel Journal* (December 1990), 30–34.

25 Loden and Rosener, *Workforce America! Managing Employee Diversity as a Vital Resource*, 12.

26 Taylor Cox and Stacy Blake, "Managing Cultural Diversity: Implications for Organizational Competitiveness," *Academy of Management Executive* 5, no. 3, (August 1991), 53.

27 Beilinson, "Workforce 2000: Already Here?" 3–4.

28 Cox and Blake, "Managing Cultural Diversity: Implications for Organizational Competitiveness," 49.

29 Shari Caudron, "U.S. West Finds Strength in Diversity," *Personnel Journal* (March 1992), 40–44.

30 Cox and Blake, "Managing Cultural Diversity: Implications for Organizational Competitiveness," 51.

31 Charlene Marmer Solomon, "24-Hour Employees," *Personnel Journal* (August 1991), 61–62.

32 Cox and Blake, "Managing Cultural Diversity: Implications for Organizational Competitiveness," 45–56.

33 Lawrence M. Baztos, "Landing Successful Diversity Initiatives," *HR Magazine* (March 1992), 91–94.

34 Linda Mack Ross, "How to Have an Effective Diversity Effort," *Training & Development* 48, no. 6 (June 1994), 13–17.

35 Geber, "Managing Diversity," 26.

36 Stephanie Overman, "Managing the Diverse Work Force," *HR Magazine* (April 1991), 32–36.

37 *Training and Development Journal* (March 1991), 39–44.

38 Jim Kennedy and Anna Everest, "Put Diversity in Context," *Personnel Journal* (September 1991), 50–54.

39 Phillip R. Harris and Robert T. Moran, *Managing Cultural Differences*, 3d ed., (Houston: Gulf Publishing Co., 1991), 206–11.

40 Kennedy and Everest, "Put Diversity in Context," 53.

41 Sondra Threderman, Ph.D., "Managing the Foreign-born Work Force," *Manage* (October 1988), 26–29.

CHAPTER 10

1 John Bartlett, *Bartlett's Familiar Quotations* (Boston: Little, Brown & Company, 1980), 615.

2 Gerald R. Salavik and Jeffrey Pfeffer, "Who Gets Power and How They Hold Onto It: A Strategic Contingency Model of Power" *Organizational Dynamics* (Winter, 1977).

3 Rosabeth Moss Kanter, *Men and Women of the Corporation* (Harper Books, 1977), 174.

4 D. Kipnis, *The Powerholders* (Chicago: University Press, 1976).

5 Rollo May, *Power & Innocence: A Search for the Sources of Violence* (New York: Dell Publishing Co., Inc. 1972).

6 J. P. Folger & M. S. Poole, *Working through Conflict: A Communications Perspective* (Glenview, IL: Scott, Foresman, 1984).

7 Jeffrey Pfeffer, *Managing With Power, Politics & Influence in Organizations* (Boston, MA: Howard Business School Press, 1992), 83.

8 Robert A. Caro, *The Power Broker: Robert Moses and the Fall of New York* (New York: Random House, 1974).

9 David Mechanic, "Sources of Power of Lower Participants in Complex Organizations," *Administrative Science Quarterly* 7 (1962), 348–64.

10 Joseph Weber, "Letting Go Is Hard to Do," *Business Week* (October 22, 1993), 218.

11 Jack Welch, "The Art of Thinking Small," *Business Week* (October 22, 1993), 212–16.

12 Judy Quinn, "What a Work-Out!" *Performance* (November 1994), 58–63.

13 Lawrence R. Rothstein, "The Empowerment Effort That Came Undone," *Harvard Business Review* 73, no. 1 (January 1995), 20–31.

14 Patricia Smith, "Beacon's New Light," *Boston Globe* (March 24, 1993), 1.

15 Gerald R. Salancik and Jeffrey Pfeffer, "The Bases and Use of Power in Organizational Decision Making: The Case of a University," *Administrative Science Quarterly* 19 (1974), 453–73.

16 C. R. Hinings, et al., "Structural Conditions of Intraorganizational Power," *Administrative Science Quarterly* 19 (1974), 22–44.

17 Ronald Henkoff, "Smartest and Dumbest Managerial Moves," *Fortune* 131, no. 1 (January 16, 1995), 84–97.

18 Daniel J. Brass, "Being in the Right Place: A Structural Analysis of Individual Influence in an Organization," *Administrative Science Quarterly* 29 (December 1984), 518–39.

19 Jeffrey Gandy and Victor V. Murray, "The Experience of Workplace Politics," *Academy of Management Journal* 23, no. 2 (1980), 237–51.

20 K. Michele Koemar and Gerald R. Ferris, "Politics at Work: Sharpening the Focus of Political Behavior in Organizations," *Business Horizons* 36, no. 4 (July, 1993), 70–74.

21 David Krackbardt, "Assessing the Political Landscape: Structure, Cognition and Power in Organizations," *Administrative Science Quarterly* 35 (June 1990), 342–69.

22 James Bennet, "Outsider Smooths Chrysler's Ride," *The New York Times* (May 16, 1994), D1 and "Can Detroit Repeat its Record Year?" *U.S. News & World Report* 118, no. 6 (February 13, 1995), 19.

23 Ronald W. Clement, "Culture, Leadership, and Power: The Keys to Organizational Change," *Business Horizons* 37, no. 1 (January 1994), 33–39.

24 Robert W. Allen, et al., "Organizational Politics: Tactics and Characteristics of Its Actors" *California Management Review* 22, no. 1 (Fall 1979), 80.

25 David Vogel, "Business Ethics, New Perspectives on Old Problems," *California Management Review* (Summer 1991), 101–17.

26 Richard Burke, "Beech-Nut: Risking Responsibility and Professional Ethics for Profits," *Contemporary Issues in Business Ethics*, 2d ed., Joseph R. Des Jardins & John J. McCall (eds.) (Belmont: CA: 1990), 305–7.

27 Gandy & Murray, "The Experience of Workplace Politics," pp. 237–51

CHAPTER 11

1 Clare Ansberry, "Nucor Steel's Shen Is Marred by Deaths of Workers at Plants," *Wall Street Journal* (May 10, 1991), A1, A20.

2 F. Kenneth Iverson, Speech at the University of Nebraska at Omaha (Omaha, Nebraska, October 7, 1992).

3 Marvin E. Shaw, *Group Dynamics: The Psychology of Small Group Behavior*, 2d ed. (New York: McGraw-Hill, 1976).

4 "The Queen of Team," *Executive Female* (August 1991), 34, 40.

5 Jennifer M. George, "Extrinsic and Intrinsic Origins of Perceived Social Loafing in Organizations," *Academy of Management Journal* 35, no. 1 (1992), 191–202.

6 Ibid.

7 Michael R. Carrell and Christina Heavrin, *Collective Bargaining and Labor Relations*, 4th ed. (Englewood Cliffs, New Jersey: Prentice Hall, 1993), 37–44.

8 Robert L. Shook, *Turnaround: The New Ford Motor Company* (New York: Prentice-Hall, 1990).

9 Tracy E. Benson, "Pat Biedan Stumbles Onto the Right Path," *Industry Week* (April 15, 1991), 66–68.

10 See Chapter 19 for an expanded discussion of TQM.

11 L. K. Michaelsen, W. E. Watson, and R. H. Black, "A Realistic Test of Individual Versus Group Consensus Decision Making," *Journal of Applied Psychology* 74 (1989), 834–39.

12 Jerald Greenberg and Robert A. Baron, *Behavior in Organizations*, 4th ed. (Boston: Allyn and Bacon, 1993).

13 Michaelsen, Watson, and Black, "A Realistic Test of Individual Versus Group Consensus Decision Making."

14 T. J. Bouchard, Jr., J. Barsaloux, and G. Drauden, "Brainstorming Procedure, Group Size, and Sex as Determinants of the Problem-Solving Effectiveness of Groups and Individuals," *Journal of Applied Psychology* 59 (1974), 135–38.

15 R. P. Gallupe, L. M. Bastianutti, and W. H. Cooper, "Unblocking Brainstorms," *Journal of Applied Psychology* 76 (1991), 137–42.

16 Irving L. Janis, *Groupthink: Psychological Studies of Policy Decisions and Fiascoes*, 2d ed. (Boston: Houghton-Mifflin, 1982).

17 "It Was My Idea—Dropping His Didn't Know Defense, Reagan Takes Credit," *Newsweek* (May 25, 1987), 16–19.

18 Glen W. Hyte, "Groupthink Reconsidered," *Academy of Management Review* 14, no. 1 (1989), 40–56.

19 J. A. F. Stoner, "Risky and Cautious Shifts in Group Decisions: The Influence of Widely Held Values," *Journal of Experimental Social Psychology* 4 (1968), 442–59.

20 D. G. Meyers and H. Lamm, "The Group Polarization Phenomenon," *Psychological Bulletin* 83 (1976), 602–27.

21 G. R. Goethals and M. P. Zanna, "The Role of Social Comparison in Choice of Shifts," *Journal of Personality and Social Psychology* 37 (1979), 1469–76.

22 A. Vinokur and E. Burnstein, "Effects of Partially Shared Persuasive Arguments on Group-Induced Shifts: A Problem-Solving Approach," *Journal of Personality and Social Psychology* 29 (1974), 305–15.

23 Audre Pelberg, A. H. Van de Ven, and D. H. Gustafson, *Group Techniques for Problem Planning: A Guide to Nominal and Delphi Processes* (Glenview, IL: Scott, Foresman, 1975).

24 A. B. Van Gandy, *Creative Problem Solving: A Guide for Trainers and Managers* (New York: Quorum Books, 1987).

25 R. E. Willis, "A Simulation of Multiple Selection using Nominal Group Procedures," *Management Science* 25 (1979), 171–81.

26 R. Brent Gallupe, et al., "Electronic Brainstorming and Group Size," *Academy of Management Journal* 35, no. 2 (1992), 360–69.

27 Ibid.

28 S. Dillingham, "Topeka Revisited," *Human Resource Executive* 4, no. 5 (May 1990), 55–58.

29 R. Wellins, W. Byham, J. Wilson, *Empowered Teams* (San Francisco: Jossey-Bass, 1991), 6–10.

30 Ibid.

31 J. Connie, G. Gersick, "Marking Time: Predictable Transitions in Task Groups," *Academy of Management Journal* 31, no. 2 (1989), 274–309.

32 Ken Murphy, "Venture Teams Help Companies Create New Products," *Personnel Journal* (March 1992), 60–67.

33 Kun B. Clark and Steven C. Wheelwright, "Organizing and Leading 'Heavyweight' Development Teams," *California Management Review* 34, no. 3 (Spring 1992), 9–28.

34 Ken Murphy, "Venture Teams Help Companies Create New Products," *Personnel Journal* (March 1992), 60–67.

35 "An NCR Team That Could," *Industry Week* (June 17, 1991), 48–50.

36 D. Keith Denton, "Multiskilled Teams Replace Old Work Systems," *HR Magazine* (September 1992), 48–50.

37 Clark and Wheelwright, "Organizing and Leading 'Heavyweight' Development Teams," 14–16.

38 Richard Wellins and Jill George, "The Key to Self-Directed Teams," *Training and Development Journal* 45 (April 1991), 26–29.

39 Stephanie Overman, "Teamwork Boosts Quality at Wallace," *HR Magazine* (May 1991), 30–34.

40 Ibid.

41 Frank Shipper and Charles C. Manz, "Employee Self-Management Without Formally Designed Teams: An Alternative Road to Empowerment," *Organizational Dynamics* 20 (Winter 1992), 48–61.

42 Wellins and George, "The Key to Self-Directed Teams," 27.

43 Wellins, Byham, and Wilson, *Empowered Teams*, 3–5.

44 Clay Carr, "Managing Self-Managed Workers," *Training and Development Journal* 45 (September 1991), 36–42.

45 Shipper and Manz, 48.

46 Wellins, Byham, and Wilson, *Empowered Teams*, 10–13.

47 Wellins and George, "The Key to Self-Directed Teams," 28.

48 Jana Schilder, "Work Teams Boost Productivity," *Personnel Journal* (February 1992), 67–71.

49 Ibid.

50 Wellins, Byham, and Wilson, *Empowered Teams*, 13–15.

51 Schilder, "Work Teams Boost Productivity," 68.

52 Ibid., 70.

53 Jennifer M. George, "Extrinsic and Intrinsic Origins of Perceived Social Loafing in Organizations," *Academy of Management Journal* 35, no. 1 (1992), 191–202.

54 J. L. Cordery, W. S. Mueller, L. M. Smith, "Attitudinal and Behavioral Effects of Autonomous Group Working: A Longitudinal Field Study," *Academy of Management Journal* 34, no. 2 (1992), 464–76.

55 Dawn Gunsch, "Why Teams Aren't Always More Productive," *Personnel Journal* (February 1993), 16.

56 Phil Weis, "Achieving Zero-Defect Service Through Self-Directed Teams," *Journal of Systems Management* 43 (January 1992), 26–36.

57 Bruce W. Tuchman, "Developmental Sequence in Small Groups," *Psychological Bulletin* 63, no. 6 (1965), 384–99. Also see Garry D. Coleman and Eileen M. Van Aken, "Applying Small Group Behavior Dynamics to Improve Action-Team Performance," *Employment Relations Today* 18 (Autumn 1991), 343–53.

58 Ibid.

59 Briance Mascarenkas, "Strategic Group Dynamics," *Academy of Management Journal* 32, no. 2 (1989), 333–52.

60 Wellins and George, "The Key to Self-Directed Teams," 28–30.

61 Wellins, Byham, and Wilson, *Empowered Teams*, 163–68.

62 Judy Huret, "Paying for Team Results," *HR Magazine* (May 1991), 39–41.

63 Ibid.

64 Amy Harman, "Teamwork: Chrysler Builds a Concept as Well as a Car," *The Los Angeles Times* (February 26, 1992), D1, D3.

65 Stefan Aguren et al., *Volvo Kalmar Revisited: Ten Years of Experience* (Stockholm: Volvo, 1985).

66 Michael R. Carrell, Frank E. Kazmits, and Norbert Elbert, *Personnel: Human Resource Management*, 4th ed. (New York: Macmillan, 1992), 106–7, and *Business Week* (August 28, 1989), 92–93.

67 Ibid.

68 Robert L. Shook, *Turnaround: The New Ford Motor Company* (New York: Prentice-Hall, 1990), 139–63.

69 Ibid.

70 Ibid.

71 Chuck Casentino, John Allen, and Richard Wellins, "Choosing the Right People," *HR Magazine* 35, no. 3 (March 1990), 66–70.

72 Amy Harman, "Teamwork: Chrysler Builds a Concept as Well as a Car," *The Los Angeles Times* (February 26, 1992), D1, D3.

73 Ibid.

CHAPTER 12

1 James E. Ellis, "The Black Middle Class," *Business Week* (March 14, 1988), 62–70.

2 "The Affirmative Action Pipeline," *HR Magazine* 36, no. 6 (June 1991), 59.

3 "The 50 Best Places for Blacks to Work," *Black Enterprise* (February 1989), 73–91.

4 Ellis Cose, "Rage of the Privileged," *Newsweek* (November 15, 1993), 56–63.

5 Ibid., 74. See also, Mack Gracian, "Fueling the Growth of Black Companies," *Black Enterprise* 25, no. 4 (November 1994), 158–64.

6 "A Report on the Glass Ceiling Initiative," U.S. Department of Labor, Lynn Martin, Secretary, 1991.

7 Jeffery Greenhaus, Sarjob Parasuramon, and Wayne Wormley, "Effects of Race on Organizational Experience, Job Performance Evaluations, and Career Outcomes," *Academy of Management Journal* 33, no. 1 (1990), 64–86.

8 Public Law 102–166, 102d Congress, 105 *STAT* 1081, 42 USC 2000e.

9 Yolanda T. Moses, "Black Women in Academe," *Association of American Colleges*, August 1989.

10 Diane Feldman, "Women of Color Build a Rainbow of Opportunity," *Management Review* 70 (August 21, 1989), 18.

11 Marlene G. Fine, Fern L. Johnson, and M. Sallyanne Ryan, "Cultural Diversity in the Workplace," *Public Personnel Management* 19, no. 3 (Fall 1990), 305–19.

12 Ann M. Morrison, Randall P. White, Elen Van Velsor, & the Center for Creative Leadership, *Breaking the Glass Ceiling: Can Women Reach the Top of America's Largest Corporation?* (Reading, MA: Addison-Wesley, 1987), 53, 69.

13 Judy B. Rosener, "Ways Women Lead," *Harvard Business Review* (November/December 1990).

14 Judy B. Rosener, "The Valued Ways Men and Women Lead," *HR Magazine* 36, no. 6 (June 1991), 147–49.

15 Jonathan Segal, "Women on the Verge . . . of Equality," *HR Magazine* 36, no. 6 (June 1991), 117–23.

16 Liz Roman Gallese, "Why Women Aren't Making It to the Top," *Across the Board* (April 1991), 18.

17 Sharon Nelton, "Men, Women, and Leadership," *Nation's Business* 70 (May 1991), 17.

18 Edward Kazemek, "Interactive Leadership Gaining Sway in the 1990s," *Healthcare Financial Management* 45, 16.

19 Felice N. Schwartz, "Management Women and the New Facts of Life," *Harvard Business Review* (1989).

20 Linda Thornburg, "Working Toward Change," *HR Magazine* (June 1991), 52–55.

21 Deborah L. Jacobs, "Back from the Winning Track," *The New York Times* (October 9, 1994), D1.

22 Tamar Lewin, "Men Whose Wives Work Earn Less, Studies Show," *The New York Times* (October 12, 1994), A1.

23 J. I. A. Rowney and A. R. Cahoon, "Individual and Organizational Characteristics of Women in Managerial Leadership," *Journal of Business Ethics* 9 (1990), 293–316.

24 Gene Deloux, "Is Your Maternity Policy Ready for the 90s?" *HR Magazine* 35, no. 11 (November 1990), 57–59.

25 Susan G. Butruille, "Corporate Caretaking," *Training and Development Journal* (April 1990), 51.

26 Margaret Regan, "Beware the Work/Family Culture Shock," *Personnel Journal* 73, no. 1 (January 1994), 35–36.

27 Charlene Marmer Solomon, "24–Hour Employees," *Personnel Journal* (August 1991), 56–63.

28 Linda T. Thomas and Daniel C. Ganster, "Impact of Family-Supportive Work Variables or Work-Family Conflict and Strain: A Control Perspective," *Journal of Applied Psychology* 80, no. 1 (February 1995), 6–15.

29 Cari M. Dominquey, "The Glass Ceiling and Workforce 2000," *Labor Law Journal* (1991), 715–17.

30 Morrison, White, and Van Velsor, *Breaking the Glass Ceiling: Can Women Reach the Top of America's Largest Corporation?* 17–18.

31 Rosebeth Moss Kanter, *Men and Women of the Corporation* (New York: Basic Books, 1977), 238–40.

32 Butruille, "Corporate Caretaking," 55.

33 Ibid.

34 "The Move to the Top," *HR Magazine* 36, no. 6 (June 1991), 58. Also see, Rose Mary Wentling, "Breaking Down Barriers to Women's Success," *HR Magazine* 40, no. 5 (May, 1995), 79–85.

35 Ibid.

36 Michelle Neely Martinez, "The High Potential Women," *HR Magazine* 36, no. 6 (June 1991), 50.

37 "The Move to the Top," 57.

38 Mark Landler, "Through the Glass Ceiling," *Business Week* (June 8, 1991), 78.

39 Janice La Rouche and Regina Ryan, *Strategies for Women at Work* (New York: Avon Books, 1984), 175.

40 Martinez, "The High Potential Women," 49.

41 Ibid.

42 Laura Zinn, "She Had To Be An Owner," *Business Week* (June 8, 1992), 81.

43 Paula Eubanks, "Key Players Must Help Shatter the Glass Ceiling, Say Experts," *Hospitals* (October 5, 1991), 17–22.

44 Fine, Johnson, and Ryan, "Cultural Diversity in the Workplace," 313.

45 Morrison, White, and Van Velsor, *Breaking the Glass Ceiling: Can Women Reach the Top of America's Largest Corporation?* 57.

46 Kanter, *Men and Women of the Corporation,* 232; Morrison, White, and Van Velsor, *Breaking the Glass Ceiling: Can Women Reach the Top of America's Largest Corporation?* 24–53.

47 Martinez, "The High Potential Women," 49.

48 Morrison, White, and Van Velsor, *Breaking the Glass Ceiling: Can Women Reach the Top of America's Largest Corporation?* 53.

49 Ibid., 145.

50 Stephanie Overman, "In Search of Women Achievers," *HR Magazine* 36, no. 6 (June 1991), 60.

51 "The Move to the Top," 56.

52 Martinez, "The High Potential Women," 46–51.

53 *Corne v. Bausch & Lomb, Inc.,* 390 F. Supp. 161 (D. Ariz. 1975).

54 Ellen Wagner, *Sexual Harassment in the Workplace* (New York: AMA-COM, Creative Solutions, Inc. 1992), 18.

55 29 CFR s/s 1604.11(a) (1985).

56 *Hall v. Guss Construction Co.,* 46 FEP Cases 573 (8th Cir. 1988).

57 Joan E. Rigdon, "Three Decades after the Equal Pay Act, Women's Wages Remain Far from Parity," *Wall Street Journal* (June 9, 1993), B1, B3.

58 George Meng, "All the Parts of Comparable Worth," *Personnel Journal* (November 1990), 101. See also Richard Schol and Elizabeth Cooper, "The Use of Job Evaluation to Eliminate Gender Based Pay Differentials," *Public Personnel Management* 60.20, no. 1 (Spring 1991).

59 *HR Focus,* "Diverse Workforce, Comparable Worth Has Its Price," *Personnel* (September 1990), 3–4.

60 Jennifer M. Quinn, "Visibility and Value: The Role of Job Evaluation in Assuring Equal Pay for Women," *Law & Policy in International Business* 25, no. 4 (Summer, 1994), 1403–44.

61 Michael J. Mandel and Christopher Farrell, "The Immigrants," *Business Week* (July 13, 1992), 114–22.

62 Ibid., 116.

63 Ibid., 117.

64 James Aley, "Immigrants and Welfare," *Fortune* 130, no. 11 (November 28, 1994), 27.

65 Christopher Power, "America's Welcome Mat Is Wearing Thin," *Business Week,* July 13, 1993, 119.

66 Charlene Marmer Solomon, "Networks Empower Employees," *Personnel Journal* (October 1991), 51–54.

67 Joan L. Kelly, "What Went Wrong, Employers Must Recognize That Older People Want to Work," *Personnel Journal* (January 1990), 44–47.

68 Catherine D. Fyock, A.E.P., *America's Work Force Is Coming of Age* (Lexington, MA: D.C. Heath and Co., 1990), 45.

69 "A Profile of Older Americans," *American Association of Retired Persons* (Washington, D.C., 1986), 10.

70 Richard Chanick, "Career Growth for Baby Boomers," *Personnel Journal* (January 1992), 40–44.

71 Paul Spiers, "Hiring Experience, Restoring Dignity," *Nation's Business* (April 1990), 38.

72 Fyock, *America's Work Force Is Coming of Age,* 10.

73 Sami M. Abbasi and Kenneth W. Hollman, "Managing Cultural Diversity: The Challenge of the '90s," *Records Management Quarterly* (July 1991), 26.

74 William Dunn, "Survival by the Numbers," *Nation's Business* (August 1991), 14–21.

75 Joan Szabo, "The Earnings Test Has Failed," *Nation's Business* (May 1991), 43.

76 Fyock, *America's Work Force Is Coming of Age,* 33.

77 David V. Lewis, "Make Way for the Older Worker," *HR Magazine* (May, 1990), 75–77.

78 Ibid., 76.

79 Abbasi and Hollman, "Managing Cultural Diversity: The Challenge of the '90s," 28–30.

80 Adrienne Ward, "No More Excuses," *Advertising Age* 62 (November 25, 1991), 18.

81 Jennifer J. Laabs, "The Golden Arches Provide Golden Opportunities," *Personnel Journal* (July 1991), 52–57.

82 Matt Chalker, "Tooling Up for ADA," *HR Magazine* (December 1991), 61–65.

83 Gary Robins, "Employment of the Disabled," *Stores* (November 1991), 71–75.

84 C. Gopal Pati and Guy Stubblefield, "The Disabled Are Able to Work," *Personnel Journal* (December 1990), 30–34.

85 Michelle Neely Martinez, "Creative Ways to Employ People with Disabilities," *HR Magazine* 35, no. 11 (November 1990), 101.

86 John A. Adam, "Technology Combats Disabilities," *IEEE Spectrum* 31, no. 10 (October 1994), 24–26. Tara Mettzer and Samantha Stainburn, "Willing & Enabled," *Government Executive* 27, no. 1 (January 1995), 32–35. C. Gopal Pati and Elaine K. Bailey, "Empowering People with Disabilities," *Organizational Dynamics* 23, no. 3 (Winter 1995), 52–69.

87 Lura K. Romei, "No Handicap to Hiring," *Modern Office Technology* (September 1991), 87, 89, 90.

88 Thomas A. Stewart, "Gay in Corporate America," *Fortune* (December 16, 1991), 42–56, 45.

89 Ibid., 45.

90 Ibid., 46.

CHAPTER 13

1 Briane Dumaine, "What's So Hot about Outsiders?" *Fortune* (November 20, 1993), 63–67.

2 Henry Mintzberg, *The Nature of Managerial Work* (New York: Harper and Row, 1973). Courtland Bovee and John Thill, *Business Communication Today* (New York: Random House, 1986).

3 Fred Luthans and Janet Larsen, "How Managers Really Communicate," *Human Relations* 39 (1986), 161–78.

4 Adapted from Richard M. Steers and J. Stewart Black, *Organizational Behavior,* 5th ed. (New York: HarperCollins, 1994).

5 Everett Rogers and Rekha Agarwala-Rogers, *Communication in Organizations* (New York: Free Press, 1976).

6 D. Tannen, *That's Not What I Mean! How Conversations Style Makes or Breaks Your Relations with Others* (New York: Morrow, 1986).

7 William Seiler, E. Scott Baudhuin, and L. David Shuelke, *Communication in Business and Professional Organizations* (Reading, MA: Addison-Wesley, 1982).

8 I. Thomas Sheppard, "Silent Signals," *Supervisory Management* (March 1986), 31–33.

9 Albert Mehrabian, *Silent Messages* (Belmont, CA: Wadsworth, 1987).

10 These examples were developed from Don Hellriegel and John W. Slocum, Jr., *Management,* 5th ed. (Reading, MA: Addison-Wesley, 1989) and from Steers and Black, *Organizational Behavior,* 5th ed.

11 R. C. Huseman, J. Lahiff, and J. D. Hatfield, *Business Communications: Strategies and Skills,* 2d ed. (Hinsdale, IL: Dryden, 1985).

12 Tom Peters, "Learning to Listen," *Hyatt Magazines* 3 (1988), 16–21.

13 E. T. Hall, *The Silent Language* (New York: Doubleday, 1959).

14 Richard L. Daft and Robert H. Lengel, "Organizational Information Requirements, Media Richness, and Structural Design," *Management Science* 32 (1986), 554–72.

15 Robert H. Lengel and Richard L. Daft, "The Selection of Communication Media as an Executive Skill," *Academy of Management Executive* 2 (1988), 225–32.

16 This example was developed from Richard L. Daft, *Management,* 3d ed. (Chicago: Dryden Press, 1992).

17 Lengel and Daft, "The Selection of Communication Media as an Executive Skill."

18 This example was developed from Daft, *Management,* 3d ed.

19 Richard L. Daft, *Organization Theory and Design,* 4th ed. (St. Paul, MN: West, 1992).

20 E. T. Hall, "Proxemics," in A. M. Katz and V. T. Katz (eds.), *Foundations of Nonverbal Communication* (Carbondale, IL: Southern Illinois University Press, 1983).

21 E. T. Hall, "A System for the Notation of Proxemic Behavior," *American Anthropologist* 5 (1963), 1003–26.

22 R. T. Barker and C. G. Pearce, "The Importance of Proxemics at Work," *Supervisory Management* 35 (1990), 10–11.

23 R. Ardrey, *The Territorial Imperative* (New York: Atheneum, 1966).

24 These examples were developed from Ardrey, *The Territorial Imperative* and Robert P. Vecchio, *Organizational Behavior,* 2d ed. (Hinsdale, IL: Dryden Press, 1991).

25 O. W. Baskin and C. E. Aronoff, *Interpersonal Communication in Organizations* (Glenview, IL: Scott, Foresman, 1980).

26 M. D. Zalesny and R. V. Farace: "Traditional Versus Open Offices: A Com-

parison of Sociotechnical, Social Relations, and Symbolic Meaning Perspectives," *Academy of Management Journal* 30 (1987), 240–59.

27 G. R. Oldham, "Effects of Change in Workplace Partitions and Spatial Density on Employee Reactions: A Quasi-Experiment," *Journal of Applied Psychology* 73 (1988), 253–60.

28 F. Williams, *The New Communications* (Belmont, CA: Wadsworth, 1989).

29 L. D. Ritchie, "Another Turn of the Information Revolution," *Communication Research* 18 (1991), 412–27.

30 S. Kiesler, "Technology and the Development of Creative Environments," in Y. Ijiri and R. L. Kuhn (eds.), *New Directions in Creative and Innovative Management* (Cambridge, MA: Ballinger, 1988).

31 R. C. Huseman and E. W. Miles, "Organizational Communication in the Information Age: Implications of Computer-Based Systems," *Journal of Management* 14 (1988), 181–204.

32 David Kirkpatrick, "Groupware Goes Boom," *Fortune* (December 27, 1993), 99–106.

33 Don Tapscott, "Where Is the Electronic Workplace Going?" *Datamation* (August 1990), 13–38.

34 This insight was developed from Jerald Greenberg and Robert A. Baron, *Behavior in Organizations*, 4th ed. (Boston: Allyn and Bacon, 1993).

35 Walter Kiechel III, "No Word from on High," *Fortune* (January 6, 1986), 125.

36 Allen D. Frank, "Trends in Communication: Who Talks to Whom?" *Personnel* 62 (December 1985), 41–44.

37 Gary E. McCalla, "Life at Southern Living," *Southern Living* (January 1991), 4.

38 Keith Davis and John W. Newstrom, *Human Behavior at Work: Organizational Behavior*, 8th ed. (New York: McGraw-Hill, 1989).

39 Donald B. Simmons, "The Nature of the Organizational Grapevine," *Supervisory Management* (November 1985), 39–42.

40 Charles D. Pringle, Daniel F. Jennings, and Justin G. Longenecker, *Managing Organizations: Functions and Behaviors* (Columbus, OH: Merrill, 1988).

41 Rogers and Agarwala-Rogers, *Communication in Organizations*.

42 Andrew Pettigrew, "Information Control as a Power Resource," *Sociology*, 6 (1972), 187–204.

43 Rogers and Agarwala-Rogers, *Communication in Organizations*.

44 Paul H. Lawrence and Jay W. Lorsch, *Organization and Environment: Managing Differences and Integration* (Homewood, IL: Irwin, 1969).

45 Rogers and Agarwala-Rogers, *Communication in Organizations*.

46 Ibid.

47 Helen Bond, "How We Will Work In The Year 2000," *Dallas Morning News* (September 5, 1993), J1, J11.

48 Charles A. O'Reilly, III, "Individuals and Information Overload in Organizations: Is More Necessarily Better?" *Academy of Management Journal* 23 (1980), 684–95. Rick Tetzeli, "Surviving Information Overload," *Fortune* (July 11, 1994), 44–59.

49 Steers and Black, *Organizational Behavior*, 5th ed.

50 Carl R. Rogers and Richard E. Farson, "Active Listening" (Chicago: Industrial Relations Center of the University of Chicago, 1986).

51 B. J. Reilly and J. A. DiAngelo, Jr. "Communications: A Cultural System of Meaning and Value," *Human Relations* 43 (1990), 129–40.

52 Daniel F. Jennings, *Effective Supervision: Frontline Management for the 90s* (St. Paul, MN: West, 1993).

53 Mary E. Guffey, *Business Communication* (Belmont, CA: Wadsworth, 1994).

54 O'Reilly, III, "Individuals and Information Overload in Organizations: Is More Necessarily Better?"

CHAPTER 14

1 Adapted by David Parker, Management Consultant, Bakersfield, California, from: Thomas A. Stewart, "GE Keeps The Ideas Coming," *Fortune* (August 12, 1991), 40–49.

2 James M. Kouzes and Barry Z. Posner, *The Leadership Challenge* (San Francisco: Jossey-Bass, 1987), 1.

3 Genevieve Capowski, "Where Are the Leaders of Tomorrow?" *Management Review* 83, no. 3 (March 1994), 10–18.

4 John Kotter, *A Force for Change: How Leadership Differs from Management* (Free Press, 1990), and John P. Kotter, "What Leaders Really Do," *Harvard Business Review* 68 (May/June, 1990), 103–11.

5 Dana Gains Robinson, "The 1990s: From Managing to Leading," *Supervisory Management* (June 1989), 5–10.

6 Ibid.

7 Kotter, *A Force for Change: How Leadership Differs from Management*, 7.

8 Capowski, "Where are the Leaders of Tomorrow?" 13.

9 David Fagiano, "Designating a Leader," *Management Review* 83, no. 3 (March 1994), 4.

10 Patricia Buhler, "The Flip Side of Leadership: Cultivating Followers," *Supervision* (March 1993), 17–20.

11 David S. Alcorn, "Dynamic Followership: Empowerment at Work," *Management Quarterly* 33, no. 1 (Spring 1992), 9–13.

12 Buhler, "The Flip Side of Leadership: Cultivating Followers," 18–19.

13 Alcorn, "Dynamic Followership: Empowerment at Work," 11–13.

14 J. R. French and B. Raven, "The Bases of Social Power," in *Group Dynamics*, D. Cartwright and A. F. Zanders (eds.) (Evanston, IL: Row, Peterson, 1960), 607–23.

15 Bernard Keys and Tomas Case, "How to Become an Influential Manager," *The Executive* 4 (November 1990), 38–51.

16 Ibid.

17 Gary Yukl, "Managerial Leadership: A Review of Theory and Research," *Journal of Management* 15, no. 2 (1989), 251–89.

18 Gregory H. Dobbins and Stephanie J. Platz, "Sex Differences in Leadership: How Real Are They?" *Academy of Management Review* 11 (January 1986), 118–27.

19 James Kouzes and Barry Z. Posner, "The Credibility Factor: What Followers Expect from Their Leaders," *Business Credit* (July/August 1990), 24–28.

20 Ibid.

21 Ronald B. Morgan, "Self and Coworker Perceptions of Ethics and Their Relationships to Leadership and Salary," *Academy of Management Journal* 36, no. 1 (1993), 200–14.

22 David A. Nadler and Michael L. Tushman, "Beyond the Charismatic Leader: Leadership and Organizational Change," *California Management Review* 32 (Winter 1990), 77–97.

23 Thomas J. Watson, Jr., *Father Son & Co.: My Life at IBM and Beyond* (1990) and Richard Blow, "True Confessions," *Business Month* 136 (August 1990), 54–56.

24 Heather Hopfl, "The Making of the Corporate Acolyte: Some Thoughts on Charismatic Leadership and the Reality of Organizational Commitment," *Journal of Management Studies* 29, no. 1 (January 1992), 23–33.

25 Robert Hogan, Robert Raskin, and Dan Fazzini, "How Charisma Cloaks Incompetence," *Personnel Journal* 69 (Mary 1990), 73–76.

26 Russell L. Kent and Sherry Moss, "Effects of Sex and Gender Role on Leader Emergence," *Academy of Management Journal* 37, no. 5 (1994), 1335–46.

27 Jane Baack, Norma Carr-Ruffino, and Monique Pelletier, "Making It to the Top: Specific Leadership Skills," *Women in Management Review* 8, no. 2 (1993), 17–23.

28 Chester A. Schriesheim, Brendan D. Bannister, and William H. Money, "Psychometric Properties of the LPC Scale: An Extension of Rice's Review," *Academy of Management Review* 4 (April 1979), 287–90. and Robert W. Rice, "Reliability and Validity of the LPC Scale: A Reply," *Academy of Management Review* 4 (April 1979), 291–94.

29 Lawrence H. Peters, Darrell D. Hartke, and John T. Pohlmann, "Fiedler's Contingency Theory of Leadership: An Application of the Meta-Analysis Procedures of Schmidt and Hunter," *Psychological Bulletin* 97 (March 1985), 274–85.

30 Albert Leister, Donald Borden, and Fred E. Fiedler, "Validation of Contingency Model Leadership Training: Leader Match," *Academy of Management Journal* 20 (September 1977), 466.

31 See Jago, "Leadership," 323, and Fred E. Fiedler and Linda Mahar, "The Effectiveness of Contingency Model Training: A Review of the Validation of Leader Match," *Personnel Psychology* 32 (Spring 1979), 45–62.

32 Chester A. Schriesheim, James M. Tolliver, and Orlando C. Behling, "Leadership Theory: Some Implications for Managers," *MSU Business Topics* 26 (Summer 1978), 38.

33 Robert J. House and Terence R. Mitchell, "Path-Goal Theory of Leadership," *Journal of Contemporary Business* 3 (Autumn 1974), 81–97.

34 J. C. Wofford and Laurie Z. Liska, "Path-Goal Theories of Leadership: A Meta-Analysis," *Journal of Management* 19, no. 4 (1993), 857–76.

35 C. F. Vough, *Productivity: A Practice Program for Improving Efficiency* (New York: AMACOM, 1979), 2.

36 Leonard A. Burgess, *Wages and Salary Administration* (Columbus, OH: Merrill, 1984), 242.

37 Tom Peters, *Thriving on Chaos* (New York: Harper & Row, 1987), 403–4.

38 Julio J. Rotemberg and Garth Salener, "Leadership Style and Incentives," *Management Science* 39, no. 11 (November 1993), 1299–1318.

39 William J. Weisz, "Employee Involvement: How It Works at Motorola," *Personnel* 62 (February 1985), 29.

40 Michael E. Hackett, "A Worm's Eye View of Leadership," *Supervision Management* (September 1990), 8–9.

[41] Ibid.

[42] Ibid.

[43] Harlan R. Jessup, "New Roles in Team Leadership," *Training and Development Journal* (November 1990), 79–83.

[44] Ibid.

[45] Chris Lee, "Can Leadership Be Taught?" *Training* 26 (July 1989), 19–26.

[46] Ibid.

[47] Alex Prud'Homme, "Lets Get Physical," *Business Month* (March 1990), 60–65.

[48] K. E. Kram, *Mentoring at Work: Developmental Relationships in Organizational Life* (Glenview, IL: Scott, Foresman, 1985).

[49] E. Lean, "Cross-Gender Mentoring—Downright Upright and Good for Productivity," *Training and Development Journal*, 37, no. 5 (May 1983), 60–65.

[50] Beverly J. Bernstein and Beverly L. Kaye, "Teacher, Tutor, Colleague, Coach," *Personnel Journal* (November 1986), 44–51.

[51] Michael R. Carrell, Norbert Elbert, and Robert Hatfield, *Human Resource Management*, 5th ed. (Englewood Cliffs, NJ: Prentice-Hall, 1995), 90.

[52] Kouzes and Posner, "The Credibility Factor: What Followers Expect from Their Leaders," 79.

[53] "Why Nobody Can Lead America," *Fortune* (January 14, 1991), 44–45.

[54] Ibid.

[55] Kouzes and Posner, "The Credibility Factor: What Followers Expect from Their Leaders," 91–92.

[56] Jon A. Pierce, "The Company Mission as a Strategic Tool," *Sloan Management Review* (Spring 1982), 18–24.

[57] Myron Glassman and R. Bruce McAfee, "Enthusiasm: The Missing Link in Leadership," *SAM Advanced Management Journal* (Summer 1990), 4–6.

[58] Kouzes and Posner, "The Credibility Factor: What Followers Expect from Their Leaders," 200.

[59] James Braham, "Star Engineers Grab the Initiative," *Machine Design* (October 24, 1994), 79–84.

[60] Kouzes and Posner, "The Credibility Factor: What Followers Expect from Their Leaders," 260.

[61] David C. Geary, "Are You a Leader or a Manager," *Public Relations Journal* (August 1990), 16.

[62] Richard Blow, "True Confessions," *Business Month* (August 1990), 54–56.

[63] Warren Bennis, "Canceling the Doppelganger Effect," *Training & Development Journal* (December 1990), 36–37.

[64] Peters, *Thriving on Chaos*, 322.

CHAPTER 15

[1] Rosebeth Moss Kanter, *Men and Women of the Corporation* (New York: Basic Books, 1977), 176–81.

[2] Beth Milwid, *Working with Men* (Hillsboro, Oregon: Beyond Words Publishing, Inc., 1990), 127–78.

[3] "The Move to the Top," *HR Magazine* (June 1991), 56–58.

[4] June Firth, "A Proactive Approach to Conflict Resolution," *Supervisory Management* (November 1991), 3–4.

[5] Floyd Dickens, Jr. and Jacqueline B. Dickens, *The Black Manager Making It in the Corporate World*, revised ed. (New York: AMACOM, 1991), 361–66.

[6] Richard Tanner Pascale, "The Renewal Factor: Constructive Contention," *Planning Review* (July/August 1990), 4.

[7] Arthur Sondak, "What's Your Conflict Barometer?" *Supervisory Management* (May 1990), 1–2.

[8] Joyce Hocker and William Wilmont, *Interpersonal Conflict*, 3d ed. (Dubuque, IA: William C. Brown, 1991), 128–29.

[9] David Stiebel, "They Won't Cooperate? Reach Agreement Anyway!" *Personnel Management* (July 1991), 13–15.

[10] Sybil Evans, "Conflict Can Be Positive," *HR Magazine* (May 1992), 49–51.

[11] Nancy G. Neslund, "Why Teach Conflict Resolution in Business Schools? *American Business Law Journal* 26 (1988), 557–73.

[12] Rajiv P. Dant and Patrick L. Schul, "Conflict Resolution Processes in Contractual Channels of Distribution," *Journal of Marketing* 56 (January 1992), 38–54.

[13] Katra P. Sycara, "Problem Restructuring in Negotiations," *Management Science* 27, no. 10 (October 1991), 1248–68.

[14] Marshall Scott Poole, Michael Holmes, and Gerardine De Sanctis, "Conflict Management in a Computer-Supported Meeting Environment," *Management Science* 37, no. 8 (August 1991), 926–53.

[15] Michael R. Carrell and Christina Heavrin, *Collective Bargaining and Labor Relations*, 3d ed. (New York: Macmillan, 1991), 140–42.

[16] Phillip R. Harris and Robert T. Moran, "Skills of Successful Negotia-

tors," *Managing Cultural Differences* (Houston, TX: Gulf Publishing Company, 1991), 64–67.

[17] Hocker and Wilmont, *Interpersonal Conflict*, 3d ed., 170–73.

[18] Jennifer J. Laabs, "Brown & Root's Dispute Resolution Program Heads Off Employee Conflicts," *Personnel Journal* 73, no. 12 (December 1994), 69.

[19] Peter J. Berman, "Resolving Business Disputes Through Mediation and Arbitration," *CPA Journal* 64, no. 11 (November 1994), 74–77 and Seymour W. Miller, "Mediation—An Alternate Dispute Resolution Methodology Whose Time Has Come," *CPA Journal* 64, no. 7 (July 1994), 54–55.

[20] Rebecca A. Thacker, Mark Stein, and Samuel Bresler, "Mediation Keeps Complaints Out of Court," *HR Magazine* 39, no. 5 (May 1994), 72–75.

[21] Marilee S. Niehoff, "Common Sense Rules," *Public Relations Journal* (February 1988), 19–20.

[22] Lee M. Finkel, "'Just-in-time' Principles Can Strengthen Dispute Resolution Processes," *Employment Relations Today* (Summer 1991), 167–73.

[23] Ibid., 170.

[24] Deanne G. Phillips, Jerry A. Coke, and Amy E. Anderson, "A Surefire Resolution to Workplace Conflicts," *Personnel Journal* 71, no. 5 (May 1992), 111–14.

[25] Lee M. Finkel and Harry Kaminsky, "Teaching Managers to Mediate Win-Win Solutions," *Employee Relations Today* 18, no. 1 (Spring 1991).

[26] Philip R. Harris and Robert T. Moran, *Managing Cultural Differences*, 3d ed. (Houston, TX: Gulf Publishing Company, 1991), 42–44.

[27] Sheldon S. Zalkind and Timothy W. Costello, "Perception: Implications for Administration," *Administrative Science Quarterly* VII (September 1962), 218–35.

[28] Aaron R. Pulhamus, "Conflict Handling—A Common Sense Approach to Appraising Supervisory Performance," *Public Personnel Management* 20, no. 4 (Winter 1991), 485–92.

[29] Mark R. Tavernier and Brian H. Kleiner, "A Different Way to Discipline," *Management World* (July-August 1988), 24–25.

[30] Walter Kiechel, III, "How to Discipline in the Modern Age," *Fortune* (May 1990), 179–80.

[31] Michael R. Carrell, Norbert Elbert, and Robert Hatfield, *Human Resource Management*, 5th ed. (Englewood Cliffs, NJ: Prentice-Hall, 1995), 702–11.

CHAPTER 16

[1] Joseph Weber, "A Big Company That Works," *Business Week* (May 4, 1992), 124–32.

[2] John Child, *Organization: A Guide to Problems and Practice*, 2d ed. (London: Harper & Row, 1984), 137–39. Henry Mintzberg, *The Structuring of Organizations* (Englewood Cliffs, NJ: Prentice-Hall, 1979), 62–68.

[3] Mintzberg, *The Structuring of Organizations*.

[4] David A. Nadler, "Managing Organizational Change: An Integrative Perspective," *The Journal of Applied Behavioral Science* 17 (1981), 191–211.

[5] Brian Dumaine, "The Bureaucracy Busters," *Fortune* (June 17, 1991), 36–50.

[6] James Brian Quinn, *Intelligent Enterprise* (New York: The Free Press, 1992). D. Quinn Mills, Rebirth of the Corporation (New York: John Wiley, 1991). Charles Handy, *The Age of Paradox* (Boston: Harvard Business School Press, 1994).

[7] Tom Burns and G. M. Stalker, *The Management of Innovation* (London: Tavistock Publications, 1961), 119–22.

[8] John Hoerr, "The Profit from Teamwork," *Business Week* (July 10, 1989), 58–59.

[9] Max Weber, *The Theory of Social and Economic Organization*, trans. by A. M. Henderson and Talcott Parsons (New York: Oxford University Press, 1947).

[10] Robert Quinn, *Beyond Rational Management* (New York: Jossey-Bass, 1988), 49.

[11] James B. Quinn, *Strategies for Change: Logical Incrementalism* (Homewood, IL: Irwin, 1980), 22.

[12] Jay Barnet and Ricky Griffin, "The Management of Organizations: Strategy, Structure, Behavior." (Boston: Houghton Mifflin, 1992).

[13] Chris Burritt, "Foreign Steel Doesn't Scare Nucor's CEO," *The Atlanta Journal* (August 24, 1986), 1M, 5M.

[14] Catherine Bond, "Chocolate Wars: Sweet Stakes," *Marketing* (May 5, 1988), 17–20.

[15] Harlan Byrne, "Raytheon Co.: In Diversifying Years Ago—We Did the Right Thing," *Barron's* (April 2, 1990), 61–62.

16 Alfred D. Chandler, Jr., *Strategy and Structure* (Cambridge, MA: MIT Press, 1962).

17 Ibid.

18 David J. Hall and Maurice A. Saias, "Strategy Follows Structure," *Strategic Management Journal* 1 (1980), 149–63.

19 Richard Rumelt, "Diversification Strategy and Performance," *Strategic Management Journal* 3 (1982), 359–69.

20 Billy J. Hodge and William P. Anthony, *Organization Theory: A Strategic Approach,* 4th ed. (Boston: Allyn and Bacon, 1991), 298–300.

21 Peter Nulty, "Batman Shakes BP to Bedrock," *Fortune* (November 19, 1990), 155–62.

22 Paul R. Lawrence and Jay W. Lorsh, *Organizations and Environment* (Homewood, IL: Irwin, 1969), 59–62.

23 For a general review of organizational environments, see John W. Meyer and W. Richard Scott, *Organizational Environments* (Beverly Hills, CA: Sage, 1983).

24 Weber, "A Big Company That Works," 130.

25 Vijay Govindarajan, "A Contingency Approach to Strategy Implementation at the Business Unit Level: Integrating Administrative Mechanisms with Strategy," *Academy of Management Journal* 31 (1988), 256–57.

26 James M. Higgins, *The Management Challenge* (New York: Macmillan, 1991), 256–57.

27 Ibid.

28 Thomas A. Stewart, "When Firms Slash Middle Management, Those Spared Often Bear a Heavy Load," *Fortune* (August 28, 1991), 42–52.

29 For an expanded discussion of formalization, see Peter H. Grinyear and Masoud Yasai-Ardekani, "Dimensions of Organization Structure: a Critical Replication," *Academy of Management Journal* 23 (1980), 405–21.

30 Henry Mintzberg, *Management: Inside Our Strange World of Organizations* (New York: Free Press, 1989), 238–43.

31 Henry Mintzberg, "The Structuring of Organizations," in Henry Mintzberg and James Brian Quinn (eds.), *The Strategy Process,* 2d ed. (Englewood Cliffs, NJ: Prentice-Hall, 1991), 330–31.

32 Jerald Hage, *Theories of Organizations* (New York: John Wiley, 1980).

33 Henry Mintzberg, *Structure in Fives: Designing Effective Organizations* (Englewood Cliffs, NJ: Prentice-Hall, 1985), 47–49.

34 Mintzberg, "The Structuring of Organizations," in Mintzberg and Quinn's *The Strategy Process,* 2d ed, 334.

35 Ibid., 332–33.

36 Ibid., 333–34.

37 Ibid., 334.

38 This example was adapted from Gary Johns, *Organization Behavior: Understanding Life at Work,* 3d ed. (New York: HarperCollins, 1992), 546.

39 Mintzberg, *Structure in Fives: Designing Effective Organizations,* 62.

40 Richard H. Hall, "Intraorganizational Structure Variation: Application of the Bureaucratic Model," *Administrative Science Quarterly* 7 (1962), 295–308.

41 Portions of this section were adapted from Daniel F. Jennings, *Effective Supervision* (St. Paul, MN: West Publishing, 1993), 68–74.

42 "Developing New Products at Kellogg," *Business Week* (September 23, 1991), 56–61.

43 Paul R. Lawrence and Jay W. Lorsch, "New Managerial Job: The Integrator," *Harvard Business Review* 43 (November-December, 1967), 142–51.

44 Ron Winslow, "Utility Cuts Red Tape, Builds Nuclear Plant Almost on Schedule," *Wall Street Journal* (February 22, 1984), 1, 18.

45 Richard L. Daft, *Organization Theory and Design,* 4th ed. (St. Paul, MN: West Publishing, 1992), 186.

46 Dale D. Buss and Doron P. Levin, "GM Readies New Line Aimed at Regaining Mid-Size Auto Sales," *Wall Street Journal* (May 1, 1987), 1, 12.

47 Lynda M. Applegate, James I. Cash, Jr., and D. Quinn Mills, "Information Technology and Tomorrow's Management," *Harvard Business Review* 69 (March-April, 1993), 48–53.

48 Jeremy Main, "At Last, Software CEOs Can Use," *Fortune* (March 13, 1989), 77–81.

49 George P. Huber, "A Theory of the Effects of Advanced Information Technologies on Organizational Design, Intelligence, and Decision Making," *Academy of Management Review* 15 (1990), 47–71.

50 Ibid.

51 John W. Medcof, "The Effect and Extent of Use of Information Technology and Job of the User upon Task Characteristics," *Human Relations* 42 (1989), 23–41.

52 Jay B. Barney and Ricky W. Griffin, *The Management of Organizations: Strategy, Structure, Behavior* (Boston: Houghton Mifflin, 1992), 346–47. Francis J. Aguilar, "Coca-Cola Versus Pepsi-Cola and the Soft Drink Industry" in *General Managers In Action: Policies and Strategies,* 2d ed. (New York: Oxford University Press, 1992), 282–305.

53 Jeffrey Pfeffer and Gerald R. Salancik, *The External Control of Organizations* (New York: Harper and Row, 1978), 36.

54 This example was developed by John A. Wagner III and John R. Hollenbeck, *Management of Organizational Behavior* (Englewood Cliffs, NJ: Prentice-Hall, 1992), 595.

55 Raymond F. Zammuto, "A Comparison of Multiple Constituency Models of Organizational Effectiveness," *Academy of Management Review* 9 (1984), 606–15.

56 Peter Drucker, *The Effective Executive* (New York: Harper and Row, 1967), 1–3.

57 Henry Mintzberg, "The Effective Organization: Forces and Forms," *Sloan Management Review* (Winter, 1991), 54–67.

58 Danny Miller, "Organizational Configuration: Cohesion, Change, and Prediction," *Human Relations* 43 (1990), 771–89.

59 Material for this section was developed from Fred David, *Strategic Management,* 3d ed. (New York: Macmillan, 1989), 261–64. Arthur A. Thompson, Jr. and A. J. Strickland, III, *Strategic Management: Concepts and Cases,* 6th ed. (Homewood, IL: Irwin, 1992), 223–32. Charles W. L. Hill and Gareth R. Jones, *Strategic Management: An Integrated Approach,* 2d ed. (Boston: Houghton Mifflin, 1992), 319–34.

60 This example was developed from Thompson and Strickland, *Strategic Management: Concepts and Cases,* 6th ed., 226.

61 Aguilar, "General Electric," in *General Managers In Action: Policies and Strategies,* 2d ed., 410–12.

62 Jay R. Galbraith, "Matrix Organization Designs: How to Combine Functional and Project Forms," *Business Horizons* 14 (1971), 29–40.

63 For an expanded discussion of the matrix pattern of organization design see Stanley M. Davis and Paul R. Lawrence, *Matrix* (Reading, MA: Addison-Wesley, 1977).

64 Hill and Jones, "Strategic Management: An Integrated Approach," 2d ed., 333–34.

65 Erik W. Larson and David H. Gobel, "Matrix Management: Contradictions and Insights," *California Management Review* 29 (1987), 126–38.

66 James L. Bowditch and Anthony F. Buono, *A Primer on Organizational Behavior,* 2d ed. (New York: John Wiley & Sons, 1990), 236–37. Charles D. Pringle, Daniel F. Jennings, and Justin G. Longenecker, *Managing Organizations: Functions and Behaviors* (Columbus, OH: Merrill Publishing, 1988), 197–98. Raymond E. Miles and Charles C. Snow, "Organizations: New Concepts for New Forms," *California Management Review* 28 (1986), 62–73.

67 Peter Drucker, *Management: Tasks, Responsibilities, Practices* (New York: Harper & Row, 1974), 601–2.

68 John A. Byrne, "The Horizontal Corporation," *Business Week* (December 20, 1993), 76–81.

69 D. J. Hall and M. A. Saias, "Strategy Follows Structure," *Strategic Management Journal* 1 (1980), 149–63. D. F. Jennings and S. L. Seaman, "High and Low Levels of Organizational Adaptation: An Empirical Analysis of Strategy, Structure, and Performance," *Strategic Management Journal* 15 (1994), 459–75.

70 R. Ashkenas, "Beyond the Fads: How Managers Drive Change with Results," in C. E. Schneier (ed.), *Managing Cultural and Strategic Change* (New York: Human Resource Planning Society, 1995).

71 R. Ashkenas, D. Ulrich, T. Jick, and S. Kerr, *The Boundaryless Organization: Breaking the Chains of Organizational Structure* (San Francisco: Jossey-Bass, 1995).

72 Ibid.

CHAPTER 17

1 Nan Stone, "Building Corporate Character: An Interview with Stride Rite Chairman Arnold Hiatt," *Harvard Business Review* 70, no. 1 (March-April 1992), 95–104.

2 Daniel R. Denison, *Corporate Culture and Organizational Effectiveness* (New York: Wiley, 1990), 2.

3 Edgar H. Schein, *Organizational Culture and Leadership* (San Francisco: Jossey-Bass, 1985), 6.

4 George G. Gordon, "Industry Determinants of Organizational Culture," *Academy of Management Review* 16, no. 2 (1991), 396–415.

5 Geert Hofstede, "Culture Constraints in Management Theories," *Academy of Management Executive* 7, no. 1 (1993), 81–94.

6 Shari Caudron, "Subculture Strife Hinders Productivity," *Personnel Journal* (December 1992), 60–64.

7 Ibid.

8 Ibid.

9 Brian Dumaine, "Creating a New Company Culture," *Fortune* 121 (January 15, 1990), 127–31.

10 Alan L. Wilkins and W. Gibb Dyer, Jr., "Toward Culturally Sensitive Theories of Culture Change," *Academy of Management Review* 13, no. 4 (1988), 522–33.

11 Ibid.

12 Tom Standing, Jerry Martin, and Milan Moranes, "Attitude Surveys: A Catalyst for Cultural Change," *Management* (December 1991), 17–18.

13 Dumaine, "Creating a New Company Culture," 128.

14 Caudron, "Subculture Strife Hinders Productivity," 61.

15 Michael Bice, "Corporate Culture Must Foster Innovation," *Hospitals* (November 20, 1990), 58.

16 Dumaine, "Creating a New Company Culture," 127–30.

17 Ibid.

18 Margarethe Wiersema and Karen A. Bantel, "Top Management Team Demography and Corporate Strategic Change," *Academy of Management Journal* 35, no. 1 (1992), 91–121.

19 "Nordstroms' Gang of Four," *Business Week* (June 15, 1992), 122–23.

20 M. J. McCarthy, "Stressed Employees Look for Relief in Workers' Compensation Claims," *Wall Street Journal* (April 7, 1988), 27.

21 Warren Wilhelm, "Changing Corporate Culture—or Corporate Behavior? How to Change Your Company," *Academy of Management Executive* 6, no. 4 (1992), 72–77.

22 Delmar L. Landen and Gayle A. Landen, "Corporate Constitutions Help Define Companies' Character, Culture, and Quality," *Employment Relations Today* 18 (Summer 1991), 203–11.

23 Jerome H. Want, "Managing Change in a Turbulent Business Climate," *Management Review* 79 (November 1993), 38–41.

24 Landen and Landen, "Corporate Constitutions Help Define Companies' Character, Culture, and Quality," 207 and George L. Morrisey, "Who Needs a Mission Statement? You do," *Training and Development Journal* (March 1988), 50–52.

25 Landen and Landen, "Corporate Constitutions Help Define Companies' Character, Culture, and Quality," 207.

26 Laura Nash, "Mission Statements—Mirrors and Windows," *Harvard Business Review* (March-April 1988), 155.

27 Joyce Anderson, "Mission Statements and Corporate Culture," *Personnel Journal* (October 1987), 120–22.

28 McCarthy, "Stressed Employees Look for Relief in Workers' Compensation Claims," 27.

29 Alan Schiska, "Revitalizing the Plateaued Employee on Your Staff," *Supervisory Management* (September 1991), 1–2.

30 Ibid.

31 Laurence Hooper and Michael Miller, "IBM Shares Fall 11 Percent as Firm Announces Layoffs and Says Dividends May Be Cut," *Wall Street Journal* (December 12, 1992), A3.

32 "A Ford Plant Closing May Prove a Model of Labor-Management Cooperation," *Wall Street Journal* (October 11, 1983), 1.

33 Doreen Mangan, "An Rx for Drug Abuse," *Small Business Reports* (May 1992), 28–38.

34 Michael R. Carrell and Christina Heavrin, "Before You Drug Test . . ." *HR Magazine* 35, no. 4 (April 1990), 61–62.

35 *New York City Transit Authority v. Beazer*, 440 U.S. 568, 99 S. Ct. 1355, 59 L. Ed. 2d 598 (1979).

36 Katie Hafner and Susan Garland, "Testing for Drug Use: Handle with Care," *Business Week* (March 28, 1988), 65.

37 Frederick W. Smith, "Empowering Employees," *Small Business Reports* (January 1991), 15.

38 R. S. Wellins, W. C. Byham, and J. M. Wilson, *Empowered Teams* (San Francisco, Jossey-Bass, 1991), 22.

39 Edward Betof and Frederic Harwood, "The Power of Empowerment," *Training and Development* (September 1992), 29–34.

40 Robert A. Brymer, "Employee Empowerment: A Guest-Driven Leadership Strategy," *The Cornell H. R. A. Quarterly* (May 1991), 58–68.

41 Ibid.

42 Sue Shellenbarger, "MBAs Hope to Keep Jobs in Their Place," *Wall Street Journal* (January 19, 1993), B1.

43 Sandra E. La Marre and Kate Thompson, "Industry-Sponsored Day Care," *Personnel Administrator* 29, no. 2 (February 1984), 53–65.

44 Thomas I. Miller, "The Effects of Employer Sponsored Child Care on Employee Absenteeism, Turnover, Productivity, Recruitment on Job Satisfaction," *Personnel Psychology* 37, no. 2 (Summer 1984), 277–87.

45 Donald J. Peterson and Douglass Marsengil, "Childcare Programs Benefit Employers, Too," *Personnel* 65, no. 5 (May 1988), 58.

46 "Take Care of Kids and Employees Take Better Care of You," *ABA Banking Journal* (September 1989), 26–28; and Peterson and Marsengil, "Childcare Programs Benefit Employers, Too," 58–62.

47 C. Ransom, P. Aschbacker, and S. Burud, "The Returns in the Child-Care Investment," *Personnel Administrator* 10 (October 1989), 54–58.

48 Caroline Eichman and Barbara Reisman, "How Small Employers are Benefiting from Offering Child-Care Assistance," *Employment Relations Today* 19, no. 1 (Spring 1992), 51–62.

49 James Fraze, "Preparing for a Different Future," *Resource* 7, no. 1 (January 1988), 1, 10.

50 Jeff Lefkovich, "Business Responds to Elder-Care Needs," *HR Magazine* (June 1992), 103–6.

51 "Home Is Where the Heart Is," *Time* (October 3, 1988), 46–53.

52 Anne Ritter, "Dependent Care Proves Profitable," *Personnel* 67, no. 3 (March 190), 12–16.

53 *Your Guide to Wellness at the Worksite* (Washington, DC: Health Insurance Association of America, 1983), 3.

54 Steven Hartman and Janet Cozzetto, "Wellness in the Workplace," *Personnel Administrator* 29 (August 1984), 108–9.

55 Lynn E. Densford, "Wellness Programs Show Healthy Returns," *Employee Benefit News* 1, no. 8 (November-December 1987), 17–19.

56 "Reduced Costs Increased Worker Production Are Rationale for Tax-Favored Corporate Fitness Plans," *Employee Benefit Plan Review* 37 (November 1983), 21.

57 Charles A. Berry, *An Approach to Good Health for Employees and Reduced Health-Care Costs for Industry* (Washington, DC: Health Insurance Association of America, 1981), 9.

58 Jane Daniel, "An Offer Your Doctor Can't Refuse," *American Health* (November-December 1982), 82.

59 *Your Guide to Wellness at the Worksite*, 15.

60 "Cost-Benefit Analysis of the Coors' Wellness Program," *University of Oregon Graduate School of Management* (December 1988).

61 Shari Caudron, "The Wellness Payoff," *Personnel Journal* 69, no. 7 (July 1990), 55–60.

62 Michael Rozek, "A Decrease in Employee Sick Days Is Only One Bonus from Sunseeds' Wellness Program. Morale at the Company Also Has Increased Considerably," *Personnel Journal* 69, no. 7 (July 1990), 60–62.

63 Dennis Thompson, "Wellness Programs Work for Small Employers, Too," *Personnel* 3 (March 1990), 26–28.

64 David J. Abramis, "Fun at Work," *Personnel Administrator* 11 (November 1989), 60–63 and "Building Fun in Your Organization," *Personnel Administrator* 10 (October 1989), 68–72.

65 Unpublished manuscripts by Patrick Arnold, Cher Ami Calderwood, Molly Hansen, Michele Marotta, and Staci Wilkins (Bakersfield, CA, 1990).

66 Shari Caudron, *The Wellness Payoff*, 65–66.

CHAPTER 18

1 Laurence Hooper, "IBM Loses $5 Billion in 1992," *Wall Street Journal* (January 20, 1993), A3.

2 Adapted from Carol J. Loomis, "King John Wears An Uneasy Crown," *Fortune* (January 11, 1993), 44–48. David Kirkpatrick, "Breaking Up IBM," *Fortune* (July 27, 1992), 44–58.

3 Michael Miller and Laurence Hooper, "Akers Quits at IBM Under Heavy Pressure: Dividend is Slashed," *Wall Street Journal* (January 27, 1993), A1.

4 Michael Miller, "IBM Panel Searching for Next CEO," *Wall Street Journal* (January 28, 1993), A3.

5 Material from this section developed from Edgar F. Huse and Thomas G. Cummings, *Organization Development and Change*, 4th ed. (St. Paul, MN: West Publishing, 1989). Manuel London, *Change Agents* (San Francisco: Jossey-Bass, 1989).

6 John A. Wagner and John R. Hollenbeck, *Management of Organizational Behavior* (Englewood Cliffs, NJ: Prentice-Hall, 1992).

7 Elizabeth Ehrlich and Susan Garland, "For American Business, A New World of Workers," *Business Week* (September 19, 1990), 112–16.

8 Ibid.

9 "Workforce 2000," (Indianapolis, IN: Hudson Institute, 1990).

10 Suneel Ratan, "Why Busters Hate Boomers," *Fortune* (October 4, 1993), 55–70.

11 Terence Pare, "Why Some Do It the Wrong Way," *Fortune* (May 21, 1990), 75–76.

12 Ibid.

13 Theodore W. Schultz, "Reflections on Investments in Man," *Journal of Political Economy* 70 (1962), 1–20.

14 Michael Porter, *The Competitive Advantage of Nations* (New York, Free Press, 1990).

15 Jaclyn Fierman, "The Contingency Work Force," *Fortune* (January 24, 1994), 30–36.

16 Charles Handy, *The Age of Paradox* (New York: HarperCollins, 1994).

17 Erle Norton, "Factories of the Future," *Wall Street Journal* (January 13, 1993), A1–A2.

18 Noel Tichy and Stratford Sherman, *Control Your Destiny or Someone Else Will* (New York: Doubleday, 1993).

19 William Greider, *Who Will Tell the People?* (New York: Simon and Schuster, 1992).

20 David Nadler, "Concepts for the Management of Change," in J. Richard Hackman, Edward E. Lawler, and Lyman Porter (eds.), *Perspectives on Behavior in Organizations,* 2d ed. (New York: McGraw-Hill, 1983), 550–62. Joseph Stanislao and Bettie Stanislao, "Dealing With Resistance to Change," *Business Horizons* 26 (1983), 74–78.

21 Daniel Katz and Robert Kahn, *The Social Psychology of Organizations,* 2d ed. (New York: Wiley, 1978), 36–68. Paul R. Lawrence, "How to Deal with Resistance to Change," in G. W. Dalton, P. R. Lawrence, and L. E. Greiner (eds.), *Organizational Change and Development* (Homewood, IL: Irwin-Dorsey, 1970), 181–97. Rino J. Patty, "Organizational Resistance to Change: The View from Below," *Social Service Review* 48 (1974), 371–72.

22 Gregory Moorhead and Ricky Griffin, *Organizational Behavior: Managing People and Organizations,* 3rd ed. (Boston: Houghton Mifflin, 1992), 663.

23 Andrew M. Pettigrew, "Information Control as a Power Resource," *Sociology* 6 (1972), 187–204.

24 Daniel F. Jennings, *Effective Supervision: Frontline Management for the '90s* (St. Paul, MN: West Publishing, 1993), 305–7.

25 Kurt Lewin, *Field Theory in Social Science* (New York: Harper & Row, 1951).

26 Michael Beer, *Organization Change and Development: A Systems View* (Santa Monica, CA: Goodyear Publishing, 1980), 78. R. Lippit, J. Watson, and B. Westley, *The Dynamics of Planned Change* (New York: Harcourt, Brace, and World, 1958), 129–44.

27 Peter Clark, *Action Research and Organization Change* (New York: Harper & Row, 1972).

28 Timothy M. Amabile, "A Model of Creativity and Innovation in Organizations," *Research in Organizational Behavior* 10 (1988), 123–67.

29 These examples were developed from Tom Peters, *Liberation Management* (New York: Alfred Knopf, 1992).

30 Gordon Vessels, "The Creative Process: An Open-Systems Conceptualization," *Journal of Creative Behavior* 16 (1982), 185–96.

31 T. M. Amabile, "The Social Psychology of Creativity: A Componential Conceptualization," *Journal of Personality and Social Psychology* 45 (1983), 357–76. B. M. Staw, "An Evolutionary Approach to Creativity and Innovation," in M. A. West and J. L. Farr (eds.), *Innovation and Creativity At Work* (West Sussex, England: John Wiley, 1992).

32 D. T. Campbell, "Blind Variation and Selective Retention in Creative Thought as in Other Knowledge Processes," *Psychological Review* 67 (1960), 380–400.

33 Adapted from Richard L. Daft, *Management,* 2d ed. (Chicago: Dryden Press, 1991), 310.

34 Humphrey Taylor, Robert Leitman, and Ron Bass, *Laborforce 2000 Study* (New York: Louis Harris and Associates, 1993).

35 Mitchell L. Marks, "Restructuring and Downsizing," in Philip M. Mirvis (ed.), *Building the Competitive Work Force* (New York: John Wiley, 1993).

36 T. Kochan and M. Useem, *Transforming Organizations* (New York: Oxford University Press, 1992).

37 Marks, "Restructuring and Downsizing."

38 R. L. Bunning, "The Dynamics of Downsizing," *Personnel Journal* (September 1990), 69–75.

39 Alex Fischer, "Morale Crisis," *Fortune* (November 18, 1992), 70–80.

40 Ibid.

41 Ronald Henkoff, "Getting Beyond Downsizing," *Fortune* (January 10, 1994), 58–64.

42 Marks, "Restructurng and Downsizing."

43 Ibid.

44 Towers Perrin, *Workforce 2000 Today: A Bottom Line Concern* (New York: Towers Perrin, 1992).

45 American Management Association, *Responsible Reductions in Force: An AMA Research Report on Downsizings and Outplacement* (New York: AMA Briefings and Surveys, 1990).

46 Marilyn Jensk, "Closing a Plant: The Saga of Two Cities," *Wall Street Journal* (March 11, 1992), B1, B9.

47 These questions were adapted from Marks, "Restructuring and Downsizing."

48 Adam Smith, *An Inquiry Into the Nature and Causes of the Wealth of Nations* (London: Longsman, 1776). Republished by Modern Library, 1937.

49 Michael Hammer and James Champy, *Reengineering the Corporation: A Manifesto for Business Revolution* (New York: HarperCollins, 1993).

50 Ibid.

51 "The Promise of Reengineering," *Fortune* (May 3, 1993), 94–97.

52 Thomas A. Stewart, "Reengineering: The Hot New Managing Tool," *Fortune* (August 23, 1993), 41–48.

53 Terence T. Burton, "How Successful Is Your Reengineering Effort?" *APICS* (July 1994), 76–81. Al Ehrbar, "Reengineering Gives Firms New Efficiency, Workers the Pink Slip," *Wall Street Journal* (March 16, 1993), A1, A11. Thomas A. Stewart, "Reengineering: The Hot New Managing Tool," *Fortune* (August 23, 1993), 41–48. The 70 percent failure rate of reengineering projects has also been confirmed by both Andersen Consulting, Dallas, Texas office (December 1994) and the American Productivity and Quality Center, Houston, Texas office (December 1994).

54 Ehrbar, "Reengineering Gives Firms New Efficiency, Workers the Pink Slip." "Strategies for Business Competitiveness," Third Annual Bradley Lecture (1993). Center for Business Competitiveness, University of Wisconsin.

55 Daniel F. Jennings, "Reengineering the Credit Function: Shooting in the Dark?" *Journal of Finance and Credit Management* 1 (1995), 18–26.

56 Stewart, "Reengineering: The Hot New Managing Tool."

57 L. E. Greiner, "Evolution and Revolution as Organizations Grow," *Harvard Business Review* 50 (July-August 1972), 55–64.

58 Huse and Cummings, *Organizational Development and Change,* 4th ed.

59 Stephen P. Robbins, *Organizational Behavior: Concepts, Controversies, and Applications,* 5th ed. (Englewood Cliffs, NJ: Prentice-Hall, 1991).

60 J. S. McClenahen, "Not Fun in the Sun," *Industry Week* (October 15, 1990), 22–24.

61 L. Fisher, "The Latest Word on Teamwork? 'Mush,'" *New York Times* (January 12, 1992), B16.

62 E. Abrahamson, "Managerial Fads and Fashions: The Diffusion and Rejection of Innovations," *Academy of Management Review* 16 (1991), 586–612.

63 J. L. Franklin, "Improving the Effectiveness of Survey Feedback," *Personnel* (May-June, 1978), 11–17.

64 Wendell L. French and Cecil H. Bell, Jr., *Organization Development,* 4th ed. (Englewood Cliffs, NJ: Prentice-Hall, 1990).

65 J. I. Porras and P. O. Berg, "The Impact of Organization Development," *Academy of Management Review* 4 (1978), 249–66.

66 R. W. Griffin, "Consequences of Quality Circles in an Industrial Setting: A Longitudinal Assessment," *Academy of Management Journal* 31 (1988), 338–58.

67 G. W. Meyer and R. G. Scott, "Quality Circles: Panacea or Pandora's Box?" *Organizational Dynamics* (May 1985), 34–50.

68 Diane Jennings, "How Consultants Make Managers Successful," *Dallas Morning News* (December 16, 1994), A1, A8.

69 French and Bell, *Organization Development,* 4th ed.

CHAPTER 19

1 Patricia A. Galagan, "How Wallace Changed Its Mind," *Training and Development* (June 1991), 23–28.

2 Louis Kraar, "Twenty-Five Who Help the U.S. Win," *Fortune* (Spring/Summer 1991), 40–45.

3 Don Nichols, "The Company That Quality Built," *Management Review* (August 1991), 34–38.

4 Steve Zurier, "Wallace Co's on the Mend," *Industrial Distribution* (January 15, 1992), 13–15.

5 Sara M. Freedman and Robert C. Hill, "Managing the Quality Process: Lessons from a Baldrige Aware Winner. A Conversation with John W. Wallace, CEO of the Wallace Company," *Academy of Management Executives* 4 (1992), 76–88.

6 David A. Garvin, "Competing on the Eight Dimensions of Quality," *Harvard Business Review* 65 (November-December 1987), 101–9.

[7] Material for this section was adapted from James R. Evans and William M. Lindsay, *The Management and Control of Quality* (St. Paul, MN: West Publishing 1989), 6–10.

[8] Delmer C. Dague, "Quality-Historical Perspective" in Delmer C. Dague, (ed.), *Quality Control in Manufacturing* (Warrendale, PA: Society of Automobile Engineers, 1981), 7–12.

[9] Ibid.

[10] Malcolm D. Fagan, *A History of Engineering and Science in the Bell System: The Early Years (1875–1935)* (New York: Bell Telephone Laboratories, 1974), 112–18.

[11] Elwood S. Buffa, *Meeting the Competitive Challenge* (Homewood, IL: Richard Irvin, 1984), 16–19.

[12] Wickham Skinner, "The Productivity Paradox," *Harvard Business Review* 64 (July-August 1986), 55–59.

[13] Norman Gaither, *Production and Operations Management*, 5th ed. (New York: Dryden Press, 1992), 633–34.

[14] Armand V. Feigenbaum, *Total Quality Control: Engineering and Management*, 3rd ed. (New York: McGraw-Hill, 1983), 12–32.

[15] This section has been adapted from Charles H. Fine and David H. Bridge, "Managing Quality Improvement," in M. Sepehri (ed.), *Quest for Quality: Managing the Total System* (Norcross, GA: Institute of Industrial Engineers, 1987), 66–74.

[16] Ray Wachniak, "World Class Quality: An American Response to the Challenge," in M. Sepehri, (ed.), *Quest for Quality: Managing the Total System*, 102–16.

[17] The statistical techniques include histograms, control charts, scatter diagrams, pareto analysis, and Ishikawa diagrams. These statistical techniques are more fully discussed by Eugene L. Grant and Ronald S. Levenworth, *Statistical Quality Control*, 6th ed. (New York: McGraw-Hill, 1988).

[18] W. Edwards Deming, *Out of Crisis* (Cambridge, MA: MIT Press, 1986), 102–5.

[19] Crosby's two books are: Phillip Crosby, *Quality Is Free* (New York: McGraw-Hill, 1979) and Phillip Crosby, *Quality Without Tears* (New York: McGraw-Hill, 1989). Crosby's argument regarding the cost of quality is supported by others. For an expanded discussion see J. William Semich, "The Costs of Quality," *Purchasing* 81 (November 5, 1987), 61–63 and David A. Garvin, *Managing Quality: The Strategic and Competitive Edge* (New York: Free Press, 1988), 181–84.

[20] For an expanded discussion of how quality circles were developed in Japan and later implemented in the United States, see J. M. Juran, "The QC Circle Phenomenon," *Industrial Quality Control* (January 1967), 329–36. T. H. Berry, *Managing The Total Quality Transformation* (New York: McGraw-Hill, 1991), 42–51.

[21] Robert Handfield, "Quality Management in Japan versus the United States," *Production and Inventory Management* (Second Quarter) (1988), 63–70.

[22] Edward E. Lawler and Susan A. Mohrman, "Quality Circles after the Fad," *Harvard Business Review* 63 (January-February, 1985), 65–71.

[23] "Standard Industrial Classification," *United States Statistical Abstract* (Washington, DC: US Government Printing Office, 1991), 57–63.

[24] Christian Gronroos, *Service Management And Marketing* (Lexington, MA: Lexington Books, 1990), 27–31.

[25] Ibid.

[26] Stephen S. Roach, "Services Under Siege: The Restructuring Imperative," *Harvard Business Review* 69 (September-October, 1991), 82–91.

[27] *Malcolm Baldrige National Quality Award* (Washington, DC: US Department of Commerce, 1991).

[28] E. Nick Maddox, Walter J. Wheatley, and Carrie Manuel, "Practical Dilemmas In Total Quality Management Programs: A Managerial Development Training Focus," *Academy of Management Best Papers Proceedings*, Las Vegas, NV (August 1992), 437–38.

[29] J. Talley, *Total Quality Management* (Milwaukee, WI: ASQC Quality Press, 1991), 109.

[30] Harry L. Gilmore, "Continuous Incremental Improvement: An Operations Strategy for Higher Quality, Lower Costs, and Global Competitiveness," *Advanced Management Journal* 55 (1990), 21–25.

[31] Fred Luthans, "Quality Is an HR Function," *Personnel* (May 1990), 72–73.

[32] John M. Dorris, "Organizational Transformation," *Advanced Management Journal* 55 (1990), 13–18. Talley, *Total Quality Management*.

[33] The characteristics of TQM were developed from Talley, *Total Quality Management*. J. M. Juran and A. Blanton Godfrey, *Total Quality Management: Magic Words or Hard Work* (New York: U.S. Chamber of Commerce, 1991). Michael Barrier, "TQM: Total Quality Management," *Nation's Business* (May 1992), 22–32.

[34] James W. Dean, "Challenges and Benefits of TQ Effectiveness Research," *Academy of Management Best Papers Proceedings*, Las Vegas, NV (August 1992).

[35] TQM implementation strategies were developed from Charles N. Weaver, *Total Quality Management: A Step-by-Step Guide to Implementation* (Milwaukee, WI: ASQC Quality Press, 1991), 48–54. Kim Cameron, "In What Ways Do Organizations Implement Total Quality Management," *Academy of Management Best Papers Proceedings*, Las Vegas, NV (August 1992). James A. F. Stoner, "What Happens When Organizations Implement Total Quality Management?" *Academy of Management Best Papers Proceedings*, Las Vegas, NV (August 1992).

[36] Bartholomew M. Cook, "In Search of Six Sigma: 99.9997 Defect-free," *Industry Week* (October 1, 1990), 60–64.

[37] John Dreyfuss, "Shaping Up Your Suppliers," *Fortune* (April 10, 1989), 116–24.

[38] Gerald De Souza, "Now Service Businesses Must Manage Quality," *The Journal of Business Strategy* (May-June 1989), 21–25.

[39] Stoner, "What Happens When Organizations Implement Total Quality Management?"

[40] Cameron, "In What Ways Do Organizations Implement Total Quality Management?"

[41] Daniel F. Jennings, "Implementation Issues Affecting TQM: Views From Managers Themselves," Baylor University Working Paper (1992).

[42] Alexander B. Badiru, "A Systems Approach to Total Quality Management," *Industrial Engineering* 22 (1990), 33–36.

[43] James G. Johnson, "Successful TQM Is a Question of Leadership," *Journal of Quality and Participation* (June 1990), 16–20.

[44] F. Damanpour and W. M. Evan. "Organizational Innovation and Performance: The Problem of Organizational Lag," *Administrative Science Quarterly* 29 (1984), 392–409.

[45] R. L. Daft and S. W. Becker, *The Innovative Organization* (New York: Elsevier, 1978).

[46] These examples were developed from M. A. West and J. L. Farr, "Innovation at Work," in M. A. West and J. L. Farr (eds.), *Innovation and Creativity At Work* (West Sussex, England: John Wiley & Sons, 1992).

[47] Robert Rosenfeld, and Jenny Servo, "Making Ideas Connect," *The Futurist* (August 1984), 21–26.

[48] Ibid., 23.

[49] Ibid., 24.

[50] Ibid., 25.

[51] For an expanded discussion of typologies of innovation see A. H. Van de Ven, H. L. Angle, and M. S. Poole, *Research on the Management of Innovation* (New York: Harper and Row, 1989).

[52] A risk typology of innovation is described by A. D. Kaluzny, J. E. Veney, and J. T. Gentry, "Innovation of Health Services: A Comparative Study of Hospitals and Health Departments," *Health and Society* 52 (1974), 51–82. A radical versus incremental typology of innovation is described by R. D. Dewar and J. E. Dutton, "The Adoption of Radical and Incremental Innovations: An Empirical Analysis," *Management Science* 32 (1986), 1422–33.

[53] F. Damanpour, "The Adoption of Technological, Administrative, and Ancillary Innovations: Impact of Organizational Factors," *Journal of Management* 13 (1987), 675–88.

[54] Ibid.

[55] Ibid.

[56] Ibid.

[57] J. L. Farr and C. M. Ford, "Individual Innovation," in M. A. West and J. L. Farr (eds.), *Innovation and Creativity At Work* (West Sussex, England: John Wiley & Sons, 1992).

[58] Ibid.

[59] Ibid.

[60] G. W. Downs, Jr. and L. B. Mohr, "Conceptual Issues in the Study of Innovation," *Administrative Science Quarterly* 21 (1978), 700–14.

[61] R. E. Goldsmith, "Personality Characteristics: Association with Adaptation and Innovation," *Journal of Psychology* 117 (1984), 159–65.

[62] M. J. Kirton, "Adaptors and Innovators: A Description and Measure," *Journal of Applied Psychology* 6 (1976), 622–29.

[63] T. M. Amabile, "A Model of Creativity and Innovation in Organizations," in B. Staw and L. L. Cummings (eds.), *Research in Organizational Behavior* 10 (Greenwich, CT: JAI Press, 1981, 123–67. C.J.C. Gersick, "Time and Transition in Work Teams: Toward A New Model of Group Development," *Academy of Management Journal* 31 (1988), 9–41. H. Nystrom, *Creativity and Innovation* (New York: Wiley, 1979).

64 J. R. Kimberly and M. J. Evanisko, "Organizational Innovation: The Influence of Individual Organizational, and Contextual Factors on Hospital Adoption of Technological and Administrative Innovations," *Academy of Management Journal* 24 (1981), 689–713.

65 J. M. Utterback, "Innovation in Industry and the Diffusion of Technology," *Science* 183 (1975), 620–26.

66 J. A. Schumpeter, *Capitalism, Socialism, and Democracy,* 3d ed. (New York: Harper and Bros., 1950).

67 E. Mansfield, et al., *The Production and Application of New Industrial Technology* (New York: Norton, 1977).

68 M. I. Kamien and N. L. Schwartz, "Market Structure and Innovation: A Survey," *Journal of Economic Literature* 13 (1975), 1–37. A. N. Link, "Firm Size and Efficient Entrepreneurial Activity: A Reformulation of the Schumpeter Hypothesis," *Journal of Political Economy* 88 (1980), 771–83.

69 F. M. Scherer, *Industrial Market Structure and Economic Performance* 2nd ed. (Chicago: Rand McNally, 1972).

70 E. M. Rogers, *Diffusion of Innovation,* 3d ed. (New York: The Free Press, 1983).

71 Ibid.

72 Ibid.

73 Ibid.

74 M. L. Tushman and E. Romanelli, "Organization Evolution: A Metamorphosis Model of Convergence and Reorientation," in B. M. Staw and L. L. Cumings (eds.), *Research in Organizational Behavior* 7 (Greenwich, CT: JAI Press, 1985), 171–232.

75 A. I. Teger, *Too Much Invested to Quit* (New York: Pergamon, 1980).

76 M. L. Tushman, "Special Boundary Roles in the Innovation Process," *Administrative Science Quarterly* 22 (1977), 587–605.

77 Kimberly and Evanisko, "Organizational Innovation: The Influence of Individual Organizational, and Contextual Factors on Hospital Adoption of Technological and Administrative Innovations." M. Aiken and R. Alford, "Community Structure and Innovation: The Case for Urban Renewal," *American Sociological Review* 35 (1970), 650–65. J. L. Pierce and A. Delbecq, "Organizational Structure, Individual Attitude, and Innovation," *Academy of Management Review* 2 (1977), 27–33.

78 R. E. Miles and C. C. Snow, *Organizational Strategy, Structure, and Process* (New York: McGraw-Hill, 1978).

79 R. Foster, *Innovation: The Attacker's Advantage* (New York: Macmillan, 1986).

80 R. M. Kanter, *The Change Masters* (New York: Simon and Schuster, 1983).

81 G. Morgan, *Images of Organizations* (Beverly Hills, CA: Sage, 1986).

82 L. J. Bourgeois, "Strategic Management and Determinism," *Academy of Management Review* 9 (1984), 586–96. R. L. Daft, "A Dual-Core Model of Organizational Innovation," *Academy of Management Journal* 21 (1978), 193–210.

83 D. Miller and P. H. Friesen, "Innovation In Conservative and Entrepreneurial Firms: Two Models of Strategic Momentum," *Strategic Management Journal* 3 (1982), 1–25.

84 Robert A. Burgelman and Leonard R. Sayles, *Inside Corporate Innovation* (New York: Free Press, 1986).

85 Andrew H. Van de Ven, Harold L. Angle, and Mabel S. Poole, *Research in the Management of Innovation* (Cambridge, MA: Ballinger/Harper & Row, 1989).

86 Christopher K. Bart, "New Venture Units: Use Them Wisely to Manage Innovation," *Sloan Management Review* (1988), 35–43.

87 Daniel F. Jennings, *Multiple Perspectives of Entrepreneurship: Theory, Readings, and Cases* (Cincinnati, OH: South-Western Publishing, 1994).

PHOTO CREDITS

INDEX